The Horizon Reader

The Horizon Reader

HARRY BRENT

Baruch College, The City University of New York

WILLIAM LUTZ

Rutgers University—Camden

ST. MARTIN'S PRESS, New York

Senior editor: Mark Gallaher
Development editor: Joyce Hinnefeld
Development associate: Kristin Bowen
Production supervisor: Alan Fischer
Text design: Gene Crofts
Cover design: Judy Forster
Cover art: *Inverary Pier, Loch Fyne: Morning,* c. 1840–50, Joseph Mallard William
    Turner. 36 × 48 inches. Reproduced by courtesy of the Yale Center for British
    Art, Paul Mellon Collection.

Library of Congress Catalog Card Number: 90-63558

For information, write:

St. Martin's Press, Inc.
175 Fifth Avenue
New York, NY 10010

ISBN: 0-312-04199-3

ACKNOWLEDGMENTS

Edward Abbey, "Blood Sport." From *One Life at a Time, Please* by Edward Abbey.
    Copyright © 1978, 1983, 1984, 1985, 1986, 1988 by Edward Abbey. Reprinted by
    permission of Henry Holt and Company, Inc.
Joel Achenbach, "Fake Up, America!" Reprinted with permission from *Mother Jones*
    Magazine, © 1988, Foundation for Natural Progress.
Michael J. Arlen, "Life and Death in the Global Village." Reprinted by permission of
    Donadio & Ashworth, Inc. Copyright © 1968 by Michael Arlen; first appeared in
    The New Yorker.

*Acknowledgments and copyrights are continued at the back of the book on pages 1278–
1285, which constitute an extension of the copyright page.*

 The text of this book has been printed on recycled paper.

for Robert M. Gorell

PREFACE

When we started editing the *Horizon Reader*, we began by listing the most interesting essays and short stories that we had come across during the last few years. We then added to that list those short works of fiction and nonfiction that have proved themselves in composition courses over time. Our aim was, and is, to create a book wide in scope, one that will allow instructors to teach pieces of writing that are familiar *and* to address issues that are central to contemporary thought. Because the readings also demonstrate how ideas can be conveyed clearly, logically, and powerfully, they serve as strong models for students entering the world of academic discourse. Our hope is that the book will supplement your own teaching strategies to broaden your students' intellectual horizons and to help them become better thinkers and writers.

We have tested nearly all of this material in our own classes to learn how our students were likely to react to it. We have kept only those essays and short stories that provoked lively discussion and led to thoughtful writing. The final table of contents, the one you have here, is thus a result not only of our editorial preferences, but of our teaching experiences as well. Our students, who come from a variety of cultural backgrounds, helped to write this book. Their reactions have shown us that the selections here can stimulate critical thinking and lead to better writing.

Many of the selections in this book (such as Ryszard Kapuściński's "The Snow in Ghana," Michelle Cliff's "A Journey into Speech," and Francis Fukuyama's "The End of History?") are by writers not previously included in leading anthologies. Some of these writers are relatively new to their craft. Others have been in print for some time but may not have been recognized widely or may have written about subjects once thought to be on the margins of general interest. We have used all of these "new" selections in our own writing courses and have found that they connect well with the personal worlds of our students. We have also included many essays and stories with which instructors are likely to be familiar and which have traditionally found a place in college writing classes—selections such as Virginia Woolf's "Professions for Women," Henry David Thoreau's "On the Duty of Civil Disobedience," and George Orwell's "Politics and the English Language." This juxtaposition of the familiar and the new should create fertile ground for class discussion and writing assignments.

In general, we have designed the *Horizon Reader* to challenge students, to raise questions that will take them beyond the limits of a simple, unquestioning view of their lives and the world in which they live. This aim is reflected in the organization of the readings into twelve thematic sections that move from issues of personal identity, to issues of cultural and national concern, to those of global importance.

We begin with the close and familiar ground of "Family and Friendship" in Section 1 and move on to more complex issues of identity and the self in Section 2, "Becoming a Person." Section 3, "A World of Cultures," steps beyond the personal to provide a range of views into some of the varied cultures of the world. Sections 4 and 5, "American Society: The Legacy" and "American Society: The Present," explore some of the myths and realities of *American* culture, past and present. And building on the issues raised in Sections 3, 4, and 5, Section 6, "Culture and Tradition," raises the question of just what culture *is* and asks, within that broader question, what we think makes up the "culture" of the United States today.

With Section 7, "The Politics of Language," which presents striking examples of the power of words and images to shape our perceptions, we move toward issues that span cultures and nations. Following in Sections 8 and 9, "The Pleasures of Art, Reading, and Music" and "Sports: *Mens Sana in Corpore Sano*," are considerations of some of the pursuits that give our lives meaning. Section 10, "War," provides an enlightening overview of both the legendary glory and the very real horror of war. The final sections—Section 11, "Science, Technology, and Society," and Section 12, "The Idea of Progress"—ask what technological advancement and the whole notion of progress truly mean for our world today, and what they will mean for its future. The twelve sections need not be read sequentially, and sections can be skipped or rearranged according to individual interests. But we hope our arrangement can provide a meaningful framework for discussing and writing about stimulating and challenging issues, from the individual to the global.

We would like to acknowledge the help we have had in the production of this book. We owe our first thanks to Mark Gallaher, English editor of St. Martin's Press, who undertook the project with us in the beginning, who guided us through the difficult task of developing the book's theoretical underpinning, and who helped us hammer out several draft versions of the manuscript. We owe special thanks to Joyce Hinnefeld, development editor at St. Martin's, for carefully coordinating the manuscript's development, for going beyond the call of duty in searching out several selections for inclusion here, and for helping to devise questions for the *Instructor's Guide.* Special thanks are owed to Catherine Klusek, who provided much of the material in the sections on art and science. We would also like to thank Kristin Bowen, development associate at St. Martin's, who served as project editor, overseeing the book's production, and Amy Horowitz, editorial assistant for development, who coordinated reviews and contributed greatly to the selection of terms for footnoting.

In the course of editing this text, we tested our material not only with our own students, but also with a number of colleagues throughout the country who were gracious enough to lend us their thoughts on our work. These include Poonam Arora, University of Michigan, Dearborn; Lynne Beene, University of New Mexico; Patricia Connors, Memphis State University; Janet Constantinides, University of Wyoming; Robert Johnson, Mesa State College; Rodney Keller, Ricks College; Gary Olson, University of South Florida; Thomas Recchio, University of Connecticut; Phil Sipiora, University of South Florida; Barbara Sloan, Santa Fe Community College; John M. Thompson, United States Naval Academy; John Trimbur, Worcester Polytechnic Institute; William Woods, Wichita State University; and Linda Woodson, University of Texas, San Antonio.

Thanks also go to Louise Klusek and Denise Gess for editorial suggestions. Without all of these people, this book would not exist in its present form.

HARRY BRENT
WILLIAM LUTZ

CONTENTS

THREE

A World of Cultures   193

SIX
Culture and Tradition   561

S E V E N
The Politics of Language   685

E I G H T
The Pleasures of Art, Reading, and Music   787

INTRODUCTION

In editing the *Horizon Reader,* we have brought together a wide range of interesting pieces of nonfiction and fiction on a variety of contemporary and historical topics. As the title of the book suggests, our aim is to provide you with opportunities for extending your intellectual horizons. To that end, the selections in this book look at the world from a variety of traditional and nontraditional perspectives.

Your aim in reading this book should be to think critically, to challenge explicit lines of argument as well as unstated assumptions in what others have written, so that you can become a better thinker, and writer, yourself. Your instructor will no doubt ask you to react to these readings in class discussion and in your own writing. When forming your reactions, try to get "behind" what an author is saying. Test what he or she says against your own experience and against what you have read elsewhere. We have not included any material here with the intent of teaching you to think in one particular way or another. We are both scholars of the works of George Orwell; as such, we know only too well how pressures for "correct thinking" can limit dialogue. We therefore strongly urge you, as a reader of this book, not only to learn from the material you read, but to challenge the contentions in that material. Respect for an author's intellectual or social accomplishments should not lead you to confer infallibility upon everything that author has said. Challenge the writers in this book, especially the ones with whom you automatically tend to agree. You may find that the questions you ask will support and extend an author's argument. You may find the opposite.

While you can begin using this book at almost any point, we have arranged the selections in an order that moves from personal experience to the more general concerns of society and culture. Thus, the first section is set on the familiar ground of family and friends, with special emphasis given to relationships between mothers and daughters and between fathers and sons, in a variety of different cultural contexts. This section also explores the nature of other relationships, both within and outside the family.

In Section 2, the theme is again personal growth, but this time the focus is on those complex issues, many of them ethical, that individuals face as they move through life. Why do we get angry at other people? Is it ever all right to tell lies? Why do we envy our friends? When does envy become jealousy? When does jealousy become hatred? How can hatred be transformed into mass hysteria? These and other challenging questions, including the significance of gender in society, are addressed in this section.

The selections in Section 3 contain insights from differing cultural perspectives, including Native American, Asian, and African. In addition, this section includes a number of essays which examine the impact of American ideas, habits, and tastes upon the traditions of people in places as far away from the United States as Nepal. Here are some starting points for evaluating the positive and negative aspects of the worldwide influence of American culture.

Sections 4 and 5 deal with America's past and present. Authors ranging from Thomas Jefferson to Martin Luther King, Jr., from Frederick Douglass to Gloria Steinem, deal with such topics as Native Americans' perceptions of European civilization, the development of the idea of liberty in the United States, and the extension of that liberty to women and minorities. Other writers focus on the problems of the physically disabled, the homeless, and people with AIDS. Broader subjects include the relationship between government involvement and personal privacy, the real nature of education, and the shrinking of the world through instantaneous communication. Where has America been? Where is it likely to go? These are the kinds of questions suggested by the readings in Sections 4 and 5.

Section 6 examines the intellectual and cultural contexts that have given birth to those ideas that govern our lives—ideas derived from European traditions and from traditions outside Europe as well. This section also addresses the widening of college curricula to include varieties of non-Western traditions. The readings in this section implicitly ask questions about how we determine what is valuable in any cultural tradition. Can cultural traditions combine to form a new culture? What are the roots of what we believe?

Section 7 is about language, the means by which we shape ideas. Writers show how language helps us to discover new worlds of thought, and also how it can be used to mislead. This section also includes a number of essays that analyze the significance of language in the contexts of race and gender.

Section 8 addresses some of the finer pursuits of life: art, reading, and music. Writers ask how we determine whether a work of art has enduring value, or any value at all. How can we say that one painting, one book, or one musical composition is really *better* than another? Is there any such thing as "higher" culture?

The subtitle of Section 9, "*Mens Sana in Corpore Sano,*" echoes the Roman injunction that a sound mind deserves a sound body in which to reside. While many of the selections here celebrate particular sports, they all ask explicit or implicit questions that go to the heart of sports in general: Why do we want to compete with others? What benefits come from competing with ourselves? Why do we like to watch other people compete? Some selections, such as Joyce Carol Oates's essay on boxing, view various athletic pursuits from unexpected angles.

War (and by implication, peace) is the subject of Section 10. Wars often begin unexpectedly, and they often radically change the lives of those who fight in them. Wars also shape the societies touched by them, sometimes profoundly, sometimes subtly—topics explored here by several writers from ancient times through our own century. Some of the readers of this book may well be veterans of recent conflicts and may want to use their experiences to extend the points of discussion raised in this unit.

In many ways, science and technology, the topics addressed in Section 11, are the defining aspects of the present world. In one way or another our lives are continually reshaped, for better or worse, by what science and technology produce. Connections between scientific theory and society are at the heart of this section. But some of the essays here address practical concerns that have emerged as a result of scientific or technological "advances." Before your next airplane trip, for example, be sure to read the essay by Captain X, an airline pilot.

Section 12, the concluding section of the book, addresses the idea of progress. It is an unspoken premise of almost everything we do that life will continue to become better for us and for those who come after us. But more and more this assumption is coming to be questioned. Can we say with Francis Fukuyama that the fundamental problems of history have been solved? Can we take for granted that what Shakespeare called "the better angels of our nature" will guide humanity to a "brave new world"? Or will human beings always have to contend with those dark forces outside us and within us that have led to plague and massacre? Is progress—in material comfort, in social equality, in ethics, and in other spheres of life—nothing more than an illusion? To bring this book full circle, can we say that there are possibilities for progress in our personal worlds, in our relationships, in the way we see other peoples and cultures, in the ways in which we define our ethical selves?

In all its sections, this book recognizes a cultural diversity in both authors and subject matter, while at the same time emphasizing the traditional cultural contributions of such writers as Plato, Machiavelli, Thomas Jefferson, and John Stuart Mill, among others. We have included such a wide range of people and points of view because they are interesting and worthy of discussion. Not only do we believe that in a free society voices from all quarters have a right to be heard, we also believe that critical thinking and good writing originate in appreciating diverse points of view.

We hope this is a provocative book, provocative in the sense that it questions many assumptions about the social, political, and cultural dimensions of our society. We hope that your reading of the selections here will suggest no easy answers, but will invite you to ask fundamental questions. We agree with the thirteenth century philosopher Siger of Brabant, who said, "Question everything." The future of our world is too valuable to expect anything less of us.

ONE

Family and Friendship

Happy families are all alike; every unhappy family is unhappy in its own way.

Leo Tolstoy

Friendship is a disinterested commerce between equals.

Oliver Goldsmith

For each of us, our world revolves to a great extent around those closest to us. The relationships we build and maintain with our families and friends are often the most important in our lives. Yet these are the relationships that are often the most complex and most difficult.

So important are our families and friends that we often take them for granted, assuming that they will always be there; we simply cannot imagine life without them. It is only when we lose a friend or a family member, when our sense of loss seems overwhelming, that we realize how intimately we are tied to others. The essays and short stories in this section touch on some of the experiences that arise from the ties of family life and from the close relationships we develop with friends.

Families are very complicated organizations. Each one is different, and probably no family accurately reflects its inner workings to any outsider. Only the members of a family truly recognize its workings, and sometimes even family members have trouble understanding how their family works.

Many of the writers included in this section began their examination of family relationships by concentrating on the complicated role played by fathers and mothers. The selection by Mark Mathabane, for example, focuses on the relations of fathers and sons, and the interaction of fathers with the family; those by Grace Paley, Alice Walker, Cynthia Ozick, and Maxine Hong Kingston focus on mothers and daughters, and the interaction of mothers with the family.

Other writers look at how children gain independence from family ties. The stories by Joyce Carol Oates and Susan Minot deal with young people attempting to form relationships outside their families. Each story explores not just how we form friendships, but also how forming friendships helps us break away from our families. No one can teach us how to make this break. Yet we must do so if we are to find our own identities. This time of separating, which usually occurs when we are teenagers, is one of the most difficult times in

6

our lives. While we do need our families, we also need independence and individual identities. Forming friendships with people outside our families is an important way to gain both.

Five of the selections in this section are fictional. As you read these short stories, ask yourself if the same subject could have been covered as effectively in expository writing. What does telling a story about family or friendship allow writers to do that they could not do if they were writing an essay on the same subject? And in those selections that are not fictional, ask how the selection might have been different if it had been written as a story.

The subject of family and friendships is far too complicated to be covered completely in the selections in this section. Yet these essays and stories should prompt you to think more seriously about the subject than you may have before. While you may want to use your own experiences in discussing these selections, it is not necessary that you do so. You may simply want to consider your own idea of what a family is and how it should function, or what a friend is and what roles friends play in your life. You may also want to discuss the essential difference between family and friends: you choose your friends, you do not choose your family. Finally, you may want to direct some of your writing along the same lines as those chosen by the writers in this section, exploring the joys and the tensions of family life and friendships.

PHYLLIS ROSE

Mothers and Fathers

Phyllis Rose (1942–   ) is the author of *Woman of Letters: A Life of Virginia Woolf* (1978), *Parallel Lives: Five Victorian Marriages* (1983), and *Jazz Cleopatra: Josephine Baker in Her Time* (1989). Her book reviews have appeared in the *New York Times Book Review, Atlantic, The Nation*, and other publications. The following selection first appeared in the *New York Times.*

My mother has always said: "The daughters come back to you eventually. When the sons go they're gone." She has other favorite sayings—"A father's not a mother," "The beginning is the half of all things," and "De gustibus non disputandum est,"[1] which she translated as "That's what makes horse races"—all of which have become increasingly meaningful to me with time. Recently I told her that she was right in a fight we had twenty-seven years ago about which language I should study in high school. This came up because I had just had the same discussion with my son and took the side my mother took then (French). She laughed when I told her that she was right twenty-seven years ago. There have been more and more nice moments like that with my mother as we both grow older.

She is seventy-five, ash blond, blue-eyed, a beauty. When my father died three years ago she suddenly developed glaucoma and lost a lot of her vision. She says she literally "cried her eyes out." She can read only very slowly, with the help of a video enhancer supplied by the Lighthouse for the Blind. Nevertheless, her lipstick is always perfect. She doesn't use a mirror. She raises her hand to her lips and applies it. When I praise her for this, she says, "By now I should know where my mouth is."

She doesn't walk alone at night and during the day rarely gets beyond the area she can reach on foot, between 50th and 60th streets, First Avenue and Fifth. She loves to transgress those boundaries, so when I come in from Connecticut I usually pick her up in my car and drive her to distant parts of Manhattan: the Lower East Side, the Seaport, TriBeCa, SoHo, the Village. One of our favorite things to

---

[1] "There is no accounting for taste." (ED.)

do together is to have Sunday brunch at a restaurant on West Broadway near Houston Street. We go there especially for the pecan pancakes and the scrambled eggs with salmon and dill.

One day this winter we went there for Sunday brunch. It was a particularly cold day and I was suffering from a pulled muscle in my neck. I walked with one shoulder higher than the other. My mother walked slowly and with a slight stoop. But as soon as we entered the door, the restaurant buoyed us up. We were patrons, to be pampered. We had a reservation. We could share in the general atmosphere of youth, energy, chic, competence, success. The waiters were stylishly dressed with an accent of the 1940's. This was SoHo.

One young man, wearing a plaid shirt and pinch-pleated trousers, showed us to a table in a bright front section overlooking the sidewalk. This was excellent for my mother, who often finds restaurants too dark and carries a spelunker's light to read menus by. But we didn't need a menu; we ordered pecan pancakes and scrambled eggs with salmon and dill. When they arrived we split them and I began with the eggs. "Eat the pancakes first," my mother said. I didn't ask why. She's my mother. She has to tell me how to do things.

Three beautiful women dressed in black who were eating lunch at a table nearby finished eating, cleared their table and moved it aside. From the corner they took a cello, a violin and a flute, removed their covers and positioned themselves to play. They started with Schubert and went on to a medley of Strauss waltzes. My spirits soared. I looked at my mother to see if she was listening to the music. She was. I could see she was as ravished by it as I was, and for the same reason. Without exchanging a word both of us moved simultaneously thirty years backward in our minds and to another place.

"Palm Beach," I said.

My mother nodded. "Hoops, crinolines, strapless dresses with net skirts, white fox stoles. Each of us took three suitcases. Those days are gone forever."

In the 1950's my father, in his proud and powerful middle age, took my mother, my brother, my sister and me to Palm Beach for two weeks every winter until just after New Year's Day. We stayed at a hotel called the Whitehall; its core was originally the mansion of Henry F. Flagler, the railroad man and Florida pioneer. The lobby had floors of inlaid marble and variegated marble pillars.

The Whitehall dining room was a gigantic sunken area that, family legend said, was Mr. Flagler's indoor swimming pool. Whether it was or not didn't matter then, doesn't now. It was a magical place. The families as they came in for dinner and took their usual places were brilliantly dressed: fathers in the light-colored raw silk jackets appropriate for the South; mothers in strapless dresses with wide skirts supported by hoops and crinolines; children, after a day on the beach and the tennis courts, scraped, peeling, but burnished for dinner. Nothing was casual. The hotel hairdresser was heavily booked. Elaborate sets and comb-outs several times a week were not unusual. Jewelry was not left in the vault at home. The room sparkled. There was general splendor, the result of all that effort and the discipline of dressing for dinner. And at the center of the room a quintet in black formal clothes played music throughout the four-course meal. Every night, usually during the clear consommé, they played a medley of Strauss waltzes.

My mother and I are tied together because we share the same memories. My brother and sister share them, too. We are a family because the Whitehall, a certain dude ranch in the Great Smokies, the layout of our house on Central Avenue and other recondite geographies exist in our minds and no others. We move in the same mental spaces. In some of our dreams we wander the same streets, trying to get back to the same house. One form of loneliness is to have a memory and no one to share it with. If, in twenty years, I want to reminisce about Sunday brunch in a certain SoHo restaurant I may have nobody to reminisce with. That will be lonely.

   Often I feel I do not do enough for my mother. When I read *King Lear* I realize that I'd be flattering myself to identify with Cordelia. I have the awful suspicion that I am much more like Regan or Goneril—from Lear's point of view monsters of ingratitude; from their own just two women taking their turn at the top, enjoying their middle-aged supremacy. When these guilty thoughts afflict me a folk tale comes to mind.

There once was a bird with three young to carry across a river. She put the first on her back and, halfway across, asked, "Will you care for me in my old age as I have cared for you?" "Yes, Mama," said the first bird, and the mother dumped him in the river, calling him a liar. Second bird, same result. "Will you care for me in my old age as I have cared for you?" "Yes." "Liar." But the third bird, asked if he would care for his mother in her old age as she had cared for him, answered: "I can't promise that. I can only promise to care for my own children as you have cared for me."

It's a truthful response and it satisfied the mother bird, a philosophic spirit if ever there was one. But when I imagine my son saying
the same thing to me—"I can only promise to care for my own
children as you have cared for me"—I don't seem to find much
comfort in it.

MARK MATHABANE

My Father's Tribal Rule

Mark Mathabane (1960–) was born in South Africa under the
discriminatory system of apartheid. He recounts his early experiences in *Kaffir Boy* (1986), from which the following selection is
taken. In *Kaffir Boy in America* (1989), he writes about his experience of life as a tennis player in the United States. In his second
book, he notes that "the word *Kaffir* is of Arabic origin. It means
'infidel.' In South Africa, it is used pejoratively by whites to refer
to blacks. It is the equivalent of the term 'nigger.' "

One night our dingy shack, which had been leaning precipitously on
the edge of a *donga*,[1] collapsed. Luckily no one was hurt, but we
were forced to move to another one, similiary built. This new shack,
like the old one, had two rooms and measured something like fifteen
by fifteen feet, and overlooked the same unlit, unpaved, potholed
street. It had an interior flaked with old whitewash, a leaky ceiling
of rusted zinc propped up by a thin wall of crumbling adobe bricks,
two tiny windows made of cardboard and pieces of glass, a creaky,
termite-eaten door too low for a person of average height to pass
through without bending double, and a floor made of patches of
cement and earth. It was similar to the dozen or so shacks strewn
irregularly, like lumps on a leper, upon the cracked greenless piece
of ground named yard number thirty-five.

In this new shack my brother, George, was weaned. It was amusing to witness my mother do it. The first day she began the process
she secretly smeared her breasts with red pepper and then invited

---

[1] gully or ravine (ED.)

my brother to suckle. Unsuspecting, George energetically attacked my mother's breast only to let go of it instantly and start hollering because of the hot pepper. This continued throughout the day whenever he wanted to suckle. Finally, after a few days, he began to dread the sight of my mother's breast, and each time she teased him with it he would turn his face. He was now weaned. My father bought a small white chicken, my mother brewed beer, a few relatives were invited, and a small celebration was held to mark George's passage from infancy to childhood. He was almost two years old. He now had to sleep with Florah and me in the kitchen.

Soon after George was weaned my father began teaching him, as he had been teaching me, tribal ways of life. My father belonged to a loosely knit group of black families in the neighbourhood to whom tribal traditions were a way of life, and who sought to bring up their offspring according to its laws. He believed that feeding us a steady diet of tribal beliefs, values and rituals was one way of ensuring our normal growth, so that in the event of our returning to the tribal reserve, something he insistently believed would happen soon, we would blend in perfectly. This diet he administered religiously, seemingly bent on moulding George and me in his image. At first I had tried to resist the diet, but my father's severe looks frightened me.

A short, gaunt figure, with a smooth, tight, black-as-coal skin, large prominent jaws, thin, uneven lips whose sole function seemed to be the production of sneers, a broad nose with slightly flaring nostrils, small, bloodshot eyes which never cried, small, close-set ears, and a wide, prominent forehead—such were my father's fearsome features.

Born and bred in a tribal reserve and nearly twice my mother's age, my father existed under the illusion, formed as much by a strange innate pride as by a blindness to everything but his own will, that someday all white people would disappear from South Africa, and black people would revert to their old ways of living. To prepare for this eventuality, he ruled the house strictly according to tribal law, tolerating no deviance, particularly from his children. At the same time that he was force-feeding us tribalism we were learning other ways of life, modern ways, from mingling with children whose parents had shed their tribal cloth and embraced Western culture.

My father's tribal rule had as its fulcrum the constant performing of rituals spanning the range of day-to-day living. There were rituals to protect the house from evildoers, to ward off starvation, to prevent us from becoming sick, to safeguard his job, to keep the police away, to bring us good luck, to make him earn more money and many others which my young mind could not understand. Somehow they did not make sense to me; they simply awed, confused and embarrassed me, and the only reason I participated in them night after night was because my father made certain that I did, by using, among other things, the whip, and the threat of the retributive powers of my ancestral spirits, whose favour the rituals were designed to curry. Along with the rituals, there were also tribal laws governing manners.

One day I intentionally broke one of these laws: I talked while eating.

"That's never done in my house," my father screamed at me as he rose from the table where he had been sitting alone, presiding over our meal. I was eating *pap 'n vleis*[2] out of the same bowl with George and Florah. We were sitting on the floor, about the brazier, and my mother was in the bedroom doing something.

"You don't have two mouths to afford you such luxury!" he fumed, advancing threateningly toward me, a cold sneer on his thin-lipped, cankerous mouth. He seemed ten feet tall.

Terrified, I deserted the *pap 'n vleis* and fled to Mother.

"Bring him back here, woman!" my father called through the door as he unbuckled his rawhide belt. "He needs to be taught how to eat properly."

I began bawling, sensing I was about to be whipped.

My mother led me into the kitchen and pleaded for me. "He won't do it again. He's only a child, and you know how forgetful children are." At this point George and Florah stopped eating and watched with petrified eyes. "Don't give me that," snarled my father. "He's old enough to remember how to eat properly." He tore me away from my mother and lashed me. She tried to intervene, but my father shoved her aside and promised her the same. I never finished my meal; sobbing, I slunk off to bed, my limbs afire with pain where the rawhide had raised welts. The next day, as I nursed my wounds, while my father was at work, I told my mother that I hated him and promised her I would kill him when I grew up.

"Don't say that!" my mother reprimanded me.

"I will," I said stoutly, "if he won't leave me alone."

"He's your father, you know."

"He's not my father."

"Shut that bad mouth of yours!" My mother threatened to smack me.

---

[2] meat porridge (ED.)

"Why does he beat me, then?" I protested. "Other fathers don't beat their children." My friends always boasted that their fathers never laid a hand on them.

"He's trying to discipline you. He wants you to grow up to be like him."

"What! Me! Never!" I shook with indignation. "I'm never going to be like him! Why should I?"

"Well, in the tribes sons grow up to be like their fathers."

"But we're not living in the tribes."

"But we're still of the tribes."

"I'm not," I said. Trying to focus the conversation on rituals, my nemesis, I said, after a thoughtful pause, "Is that why Papa insists that we do rituals?"

"Yes."

"But other people don't."

"Everybody does rituals, Mr. Mathabane," my mother said. "You just don't notice it because they do theirs differently. Even white people do rituals."

"Why do people do rituals, Mama?"

"People do rituals because they were born in the tribes. And in the tribes rituals are done every day. They are a way of life."

"But we don't live in the tribes," I countered. "Papa should stop doing rituals."

My mother laughed. "Well, it's not as simple as that. Your father grew up in the tribes, as you know. He didn't come to the city until he was quite old. It's hard to stop doing things when you're old. I, too, do rituals because I was raised in the tribes. Their meaning, child, will become clear as you grow up. Have patience."

But I had no patience with rituals, and I continued hating them.

Participation in my father's rituals sometimes led to the most appalling scenes, which invariably made me the laughingstock of my friends, who thought that my father, in his ritual garb, was the most hilarious thing they had ever seen since natives in Tarzan movies. Whenever they laughed at me I would feel embarrassed and would cry. I began seeking ways of distancing myself from my father's rituals. I found one: I decided I would no longer, in the presence of my friends, speak Venda, my father's tribal language. I began speaking Zulu, Sotho and Tsonga, the languages of my friends. It worked. I was no longer an object of mockery. My masquerade continued until my father got wind of it.

"My boy," he began. "Who is ruler of this house?"

"You are, Papa," I said with a trembling voice.

"Whose son are you?"

"Yours and Mama's."

"Whose?"

"Yours."

"That's better. Now tell me, which language do I speak?"

"Venda."

"Which does your mama speak?"

"Venda."

"Which should you speak?"

"Venda."

"Then why do I hear you're speaking other tongues; are you a prophet?" Before I could reply he grabbed me and lashed me thoroughly. Afterward he threatened to cut out my tongue if he ever again heard I wasn't speaking Venda. As further punishment, he increased the number of rituals I had to participate in. I hated him more for it.

GRACE PALEY

Mother

Grace Paley (1922–   ) is a writer whose works include *The Little Disturbances of Man* (1959), *Enormous Changes at the Last Minute* (1974), and *Later the Same Day* (1985), in which the following selection appears. Paley's writing reflects her skill in catching the nuances of American urban speech and portraying the unique characters of New York City. A Guggenheim fellow and a member of the faculty at Sarah Lawrence College, Paley has also published a volume of poetry, *Leaning Forward* (1985).

One day I was listening to the AM radio. I heard a song: "Oh, I Long to See My Mother in the Doorway." By God! I said, I understand that song. I have often longed to see my mother in the doorway. As a matter of fact, she did stand frequently in various doorways looking at me. She stood one day, just so, at the front door, the darkness of the hallway behind her. It was New Year's Day. She said sadly, If you come home at 4 A.M. when you're seventeen, what time will you come home when you're twenty? She asked this question without humor or meanness. She had begun her worried preparations for death. She would not be present, she thought, when I was twenty. So she wondered.

Another time she stood in the doorway of my room. I had just issued a political manifesto attacking the family's position on the Soviet Union. She said, Go to sleep for godsakes, you damn fool, you and your Communist ideas. We saw them already, Papa and me, in 1905. We guessed it all.

At the door of the kitchen she said, You never finish your lunch. You run around senselessly. What will become of you?

Then she died.

Naturally for the rest of my life I longed to see her, not only in doorways, in a great number of places—in the dining room with my aunts, at the window looking up and down the block, in the country garden among zinnias and marigolds, in the living room with my father.

They sat in comfortable leather chairs. They were listening to Mozart. They looked at one another amazed. It seemed to them that they'd just come over on the boat. They'd just learned the first English words. It seemed to them that he had just proudly handed in a 100 percent correct exam to the American anatomy professor. It seemed as though she'd just quit the shop for the kitchen.

I wish I could see her in the doorway of the living room.

She stood there a minute. Then she sat beside him. They owned an expensive record player. They were listening to Bach. She said to him, Talk to me a little. We don't talk so much anymore.

I'm tired, he said. Can't you see? I saw maybe thirty people today. All sick, all talk talk talk. Listen to the music, he said. I believe you once had perfect pitch. I'm tired, he said.

Then she died.

ALICE WALKER

In Search of Our Mothers' Gardens

Alice Walker (1944–   ), whose parents were sharecroppers, was born in Georgia and was active in the civil rights movement. Her short stories, poems, essays and novels, including the Pulitzer

Prize winning *The Color Purple* (1982), focus on the experience of
black women. Other works include the novels *The Third Life of
Grange Copeland* (1970) and *The Temple of My Familiar* (1989)
and the essay collection *In Search of Our Mothers' Gardens* (1983),
from which the following selection is taken.

I described her own nature and temperament. Told how they needed a larger
life for their expression. I pointed out that in lieu of proper channels, her
emotions had overflowed into paths that dissipated them. I talked, beautifully
I thought, about an art that would be born, an art that would open the way
for women the likes of her. I asked her to hope, and build up an inner life
against the coming of that day. . . . I sang, with a strange quiver in my voice,
a promise song.

Jean Toomer, "Avey," Cane

The poet speaking to a prostitute who falls asleep while he's talking—

When the poet Jean Toomer walked through the South in the early
twenties, he discovered a curious thing: black women whose spirituality was so intense, so deep, so *unconscious,* that they were themselves unaware of the richness they held. They stumbled blindly
through their lives: creatures so abused and mutilated in body, so
dimmed and confused by pain, that they considered themselves unworthy even of hope. In the selfless abstractions their bodies became
to the men who used them, they became more than "sexual objects,"
more even than mere women: they became "Saints." Instead of being
perceived as whole persons, their bodies became shrines: what was
thought to be their minds became temples suitable for worship. These
crazy Saints stared out at the world, wildly, like lunatics—or quietly,
like suicides; and the "God" that was in their gaze was as mute as a
great stone.

Who were these Saints? These crazy, loony, pitiful women?

Some of them, without a doubt, were our mothers and grandmothers.

In the still heat of the post-Reconstruction South, this is how
they seemed to Jean Toomer: exquisite butterflies trapped in an evil
honey, toiling away their lives in an era, a century, that did not
acknowledge them, except as "the *mule* of the world." They dreamed
dreams that no one knew—not even themselves, in any coherent
fashion—and saw visions no one could understand. They wandered
or sat about the countryside crooning lullabies to ghosts, and drawing
the mother of Christ in charcoal on courthouse walls.

They forced their minds to desert their bodies and their striving spirits sought to rise, like frail whirlwinds from the hard red clay. And when those frail whirlwinds fell, in scattered particles, upon the ground, no one mourned. Instead, men lit candles to celebrate the emptiness that remained, as people do who enter a beautiful but vacant space to resurrect a God.

Our mothers and grandmothers, some of them: moving to music not yet written. And they waited.

They waited for a day when the unknown thing that was in them would be made known; but guessed, somehow in their darkness, that on the day of their revelation they would be long dead. Therefore to Toomer they walked, and even ran, in slow motion. For they were going nowhere immediate, and the future was not yet within their grasp. And men took our mothers and grandmothers, "but got no pleasure from it." So complex was their passion and their calm.

To Toomer, they lay vacant and fallow as autumn fields, with harvest time never in sight: and he saw them enter loveless marriages, without joy; and become prostitutes, without resistance; and become mothers of children, without fulfillment.

For these grandmothers and mothers of ours were not Saints, but Artists, driven to a numb and bleeding madness by the springs of creativity in them for which there was no release. They were Creators, who lived lives of spiritual waste, because they were so rich in spirituality—which is the basis of Art—that the strain of enduring their unused and unwanted talent drove them insane. Throwing away this spirituality was their pathetic attempt to lighten the soul to a weight their work-worn, sexually abused bodies could bear.

What did it mean for a black woman to be an artist in our grandmothers' time? In our great-grandmothers' day? It is a question with an answer cruel enough to stop the blood.

Did you have a genius of a great-great-grandmother who died under some ignorant and depraved white overseer's lash? Or was she required to bake biscuits for a lazy backwater tramp, when she cried out in her soul to paint watercolors of sunsets, or the rain falling on the green and peaceful pasturelands? Or was her body broken and forced to bear children (who were more often than not sold away from her)—eight, ten, fifteen, twenty children—when her one joy was the thought of modeling heroic figures of rebellion, in stone or clay?

How was the creativity of the black woman kept alive, year after year and century after century, when for most of the years black people have been in America, it was a punishable crime for a black person to read or write? And the freedom to paint, to sculpt, to expand the mind with action did not exist. Consider, if you can bear to imagine it, what might have been the result if singing, too, had been forbidden by law. Listen to the voices of Bessie Smith, Billie Holiday, Nina Simone, Roberta Flack, and Aretha Franklin, among others, and imagine those voices muzzled for life. Then you may begin to comprehend the lives of our "crazy," "Sainted" mothers and grandmothers. The agony of the lives of women who might have been Poets, Novelists, Essayists, and Short-Story Writers (over a period of centuries), who died with their real gifts stifled within them.

And, if this were the end of the story, we would have cause to cry out in my paraphrase of Okot p'Bitek's[1] great poem:

> O, my clanswomen
> Let us all cry together!
> Come,
> Let us mourn the death of our mother,
> The death of a Queen
> The ash that was produced
> By a great fire!
> O, this homestead is utterly dead
> Close the gates
> With *lacari* thorns,
> For our mother,
> The creator of the Stool is lost!
> And all the young women
> Have perished in the wilderness!

But this is not the end of the story, for all the young women— our mothers and grandmothers, *ourselves*—have not perished in the wilderness. And if we ask ourselves why, and search for and find the answer, we will know beyond all efforts to erase it from our minds, just exactly who, and of what, we black American women are.

One example, perhaps the most pathetic, most misunderstood one, can provide a backdrop for our mothers' work: Phillis Wheatley, a slave in the 1700s.

Virginia Woolf, in her book *A Room of One's Own,* wrote that in order for a woman to write fiction she must have two things, certainly: a room of her own (with key and lock) and enough money to support herself.

---

[1] Okot p'Bitek (1931–   ) is an African writer who compiled and translated folk songs. (ED.)

What then are we to make of Phillis Wheatley, a slave, who owned not even herself? This sickly, frail black girl who required a servant of her own at times—her health was so precarious—and who, had she been white, would have been easily considered the intellectual superior of all the women and most of the men in the society of her day.

Virginia Woolf wrote further, speaking of course not of our Phillis, that "any woman born with a great gift in the sixteenth century" [insert "eighteenth century," insert "black woman," insert "born or made a slave"] would certainly have gone crazed, shot herself, or ended her days in some lonely cottage outside the village, half witch, half wizard [insert "Saint"], feared and mocked at. For it needs little skill and psychology to be sure that a highly gifted girl who had tried to use her gift for poetry would have been so thwarted and hindered by contrary instincts [add "chains, guns, the lash, the ownership of one's body by someone else, submission to an alien religion"], that she must have lost her health and sanity to a certainty."

The key words, as they relate to Phillis, are "contrary instincts." For when we read the poetry of Phillis Wheatley—as when we read the novels of Nella Larsen or the oddly false-sounding autobiography of that freest of all black women writers, Zora Hurston—evidence of "contrary instincts" is everywhere. Her loyalties were completely divided, as was, without question, her mind.

But how could this be otherwise? Captured at seven, a slave of wealthy, doting whites who instilled in her the "savagery" of the Africa they "rescued" her from . . . one wonders if she was even able to remember her homeland as she had known it, or as it really was.

Yet, because she did try to use her gift for poetry in a world that made her a slave, she was "so thwarted and hindered by . . . contrary instincts, that she . . . lost her health. . . ." In the last years of her brief life, burdened not only with the need to express her gift but also with a penniless, friendless "freedom" and several small children for whom she was forced to do strenuous work to feed, she lost her health, certainly. Suffering from malnutrition and neglect and who knows what mental agonies, Phillis Wheatley died.

So torn by "contrary instincts" was black, kidnapped, enslaved Phillis that her description of "the Goddess"—as she poetically called the Liberty she did not have—is ironically, cruelly humorous. And, in fact, has held Phillis up to ridicule for more than a century. It is usually read prior to hanging Phillis's memory as that of a fool. She wrote:

> The Goddess comes, she moves divinely fair,
> Olive and laurel binds her *golden* hair.
> Wherever shines this native of the skies,
> Unnumber'd charms and recent graces rise. [My italics]

It is obvious that Phillis, the slave, combed the "Goddess's" hair every morning; prior, perhaps, to bringing in the milk, or fixing her mistress's lunch. She took her imagery from the one thing she saw elevated above all others.

With the benefit of hindsight we ask, "How could she?"

But at last, Phillis, we understand. No more snickering when your stiff, struggling, ambivalent lines are forced on us. We know now that you were not an idiot or a traitor; only a sickly little black girl, snatched from your home and country and made a slave; a woman who still struggled to sing the song that was your gift, although in a land of barbarians who praised you for your bewildered tongue. It is not so much what you sang, as that you kept alive, in so many of our ancestors, *the notion of song.*

Black women are called, in the folklore that so aptly identifies one's status in society, "the *mule* of the world," because we have been handed the burdens that everyone else—*everyone* else—refused to carry. We have also been called "Matriarchs," "Superwomen," and "Mean and Evil Bitches." Not to mention "Castraters" and "Sapphire's Mama." When we have pleaded for understanding, our character has been distorted; when we have asked for simple caring, we have been handed empty inspirational appellations, then stuck in the farthest corner. When we have asked for love, we have been given children. In short, even our plainer gifts, our labors of fidelity and love, have been knocked down our throats. To be an artist and a black woman, even today, lowers our status in many respects, rather than raises it: and yet, artists we will be.

Therefore we must fearlessly pull out of ourselves and look at and identify with our lives the living creativity some of our great-grandmothers were not allowed to know. I stress *some* of them because it is well known that the majority of our great-grandmothers knew, even without "knowing" it, the reality of their spirituality, even if they didn't recognize it beyond what happened in the singing at church—and they never had any intention of giving it up.

How they did it—those millions of black women who were not Phillis

Wheatley, or Lucy Terry or Frances Harper or Zora Hurston or Nella Larsen or Bessie Smith; or Elizabeth Catlett, or Katherine Dunham,[2] either—brings me to the title of this essay, "In Search of Our Mothers' Gardens," which is a personal account that is yet shared, in its theme and its meaning, by all of us. I found, while thinking about the far-reaching world of the creative black woman, that often the truest answer to a question that really matters can be found very close.

In the late 1920s my mother ran away from home to marry my father. Marriage, if not running away, was expected of seventeen-year-old girls. By the time she was twenty, she had two children and was pregnant with a third. Five children later, I was born. And this is how I came to know my mother: she seemed a large, soft, loving-eyed woman who was rarely impatient in our home. Her quick, violent temper was on view only a few times a year, when she battled with the white landlord who had the misfortune to suggest to her that her children did not need to go to school.

She made all the clothes we wore, even my brothers' overalls. She made all the towels and sheets we used. She spent the summers canning vegetables and fruits. She spent the winter evenings making quilts enough to cover all our beds.

During the "working" day, she labored beside—not behind—my father in the fields. Her day began before sunup, and did not end until late at night. There was never a moment for her to sit down, undisturbed, to unravel her own private thoughts, never a time free from interruption—by work or the noisy inquiries of her many children. And yet, it is to my mother—and all our mothers who were not famous—that I went in search of the secret of what has fed that muzzled and often mutilated, but vibrant, creative spirit that the black woman has inherited, and that pops out in wild and unlikely places to this day.

---

[2] *Lucy Terry* (1730–1821) was an early black American poet. *Frances Harper* (1825–1911) was a popular black author and social reformer who worked on the Underground Railroad. *Zora Neale Hurston* (1901–1960) was a black writer and anthropologist whose works include the novel *Their Eyes Were Watching God* and *Mules and Men*, a study of folk customs in her native Florida. *Nella Larsen* (1891–1964) a black American novelist associated with the Harlem Renaissance, wrote *Quicksand* and *Passing*. *Bessie Smith* (1894–1937) was a black entertainer and blues singer. *Elizabeth Catlett* (1911–   ), a sculptor and painter, was involved in the civil rights movement. *Katherine Dunham* (1912–   ) is a black dancer and choreographer who staged adaptations of African dances. (ED.)

But when, you will ask, did my overworked mother have time to know or care about feeding the creative spirit?

The answer is so simple that many of us have spent years discovering it. We have constantly looked high, when we should have looked high—and low.

For example: in the Smithsonian Institution in Washington, D.C., there hangs a quilt unlike any other in the world. In fanciful, inspired, and yet simple and identifiable figures, it portrays the story of the Crucifixion. It is considered rare, beyond price. Though it follows no known pattern of quilt-making, and though it is made of bits and pieces of worthless rags, it is obviously the work of a person of powerful imagination and deep spiritual feeling. Below this quilt I saw a note that says it was made by "an anonymous Black woman in Alabama, a hundred years ago."

If we could locate this "anonymous" black woman from Alabama, she would turn out to be one of our grandmothers—an artist who left her mark in the only materials she could afford, and in the only medium her position in society allowed her to use.

As Virginia Woolf wrote further, in *A Room of One's Own*:

> Yet genius of a sort must have existed among women as it must have existed among the working class. [Change this to "slaves" and "the wives and daughters of sharecroppers."] Now and again an Emily Brontë or a Robert Burns [change this to "a Zora Hurston or a Richard Wright"] blazes out and proves its presence. But certainly it never got itself on to paper. When, however, one reads of a witch being ducked, of a woman possessed by devils [or "Sainthood"], of a wise woman selling herbs [our root workers], or even a very remarkable man who had a mother, then I think we are on the track of a lost novelist, a suppressed poet, of some mute and inglorious Jane Austen. . . . Indeed, I would venture to guess that Anon, who wrote so many poems without signing them, was often a woman.

And so our mothers and grandmothers have, more often than not anonymously, handed on the creative spark, the seed of the flower they themselves never hoped to see: or like a sealed letter they could not plainly read.

And so it is, certainly, with my own mother. Unlike "Ma" Rainey's songs,[3] which retained their creator's name even while blasting forth from Bessie Smith's mouth, no song or poem will bear my mother's

---

[3] Gertrude "Ma" Rainey (1886–1939) was a black American singer who introduced blues music to the general public. (ED.)

name. Yet so many of the stories that I write, that we all write, are my mother's stories. Only recently did I fully realize this: that through years of listening to my mother's stories of her life, I have absorbed not only the stories themselves, but something of the manner in which she spoke, something of the urgency that involves the knowledge that her stories—like her life—must be recorded. It is probably for this reason that so much of what I have written is about characters whose counterparts in real life are so much older than I am.

But the telling of these stories, which came from my mother's lips as naturally as breathing, was not the only way my mother showed herself as an artist. For stories, too, were subject to being distracted, to dying without conclusion. Dinners must be started, and cotton must be gathered before the big rains. The artist that was and is my mother showed itself to me only after many years. This is what I finally noticed:

Like Mem, a character in *The Third Life of Grange Copeland*,[4] my mother adorned with flowers whatever shabby house we were forced to live in. And not just your typical straggly country stand of zinnias, either. She planted ambitious gardens—and still does—with over fifty different varieties of plants that bloom profusely from early March until late November. Before she left home for the fields, she watered her flowers, chopped up the grass, and laid out new beds. When she returned from the fields she might divide clumps of bulbs, dig a cold pit, uproot and replant roses, or prune branches from her taller bushes or trees—until night came and it was too dark to see.

Whatever she planted grew as if by magic, and her fame as a grower of flowers spread over three counties. Because of her creativity with her flowers, even my memories of poverty are seen through a screen of blooms—sunflowers, petunias, roses, dahlias, forsythia, spirea, delphiniums, verbena . . . and on and on.

And I remember people coming to my mother's yard to be given cuttings from her flowers; I hear again the praise showered on her because whatever rocky soil she landed on, she turned into a garden. A garden so brilliant with colors, so original in its design, so magnificent with life and creativity, that to this day people drive by our house in Georgia—perfect strangers and imperfect strangers—and ask to stand or walk among my mother's art.

I notice that it is only when my mother is working in her flowers that she is radiant, almost to the point of being invisible—except as

---

[4] a novel by Walker, published in 1977 (ED.)

Creator: hand and eye. She is involved in work her soul must have. Ordering the universe in the image of her personal conception of Beauty.

Her face, as she prepares the Art that is her gift, is a legacy of respect she leaves to me, for all that illuminates and cherishes life. She has handed down respect for the possibilities—and the will to grasp them.

For her, so hindered and intruded upon in so many ways, being an artist has still been a daily part of her life. This ability to hold on, even in very simple ways, is work black women have done for a very long time.

This poem is not enough, but it is something, for the woman who literally covered the holes in our walls with sunflowers:

> They were women then
> My mama's generation
> Husky of voice—Stout of
> Step
> With fists as well as
> Hands
> How they battered down
> Doors
> And ironed
> Starched white
> Shirts
> How they led
> Armies
> Headragged Generals
> Across mined
> Fields
> Booby-trapped
> Kitchens
> To discover books
> Desks
> A place for us
> How they knew what we
> *Must* know
> Without knowing a page
> Of it
> Themselves

Guided by my heritage of a love of beauty and a respect for strength—in search of my mother's garden, I found my own.

And perhaps in Africa over two hundred years ago, there was just such a mother, perhaps she painted vivid and daring decorations in oranges and yellows and greens on the walls of her hut; perhaps she sang—in a voice like Roberta Flack's—*sweetly* over the compounds of her village; perhaps she wove the most stunning mats or told the most ingenious stories of all the village storytellers. Perhaps she was herself a poet—though only her daughter's name is signed to the poems that we know.

Perhaps Phillis Wheatley's mother was also an artist.

Perhaps in more than Phillis Wheatley's biological life is her mother's signature made clear.

CYNTHIA OZICK

On Excellence

Cynthia Ozick (1928–   ), who writes fiction, poetry, and criticism, was born in the Bronx, New York. Her books include the novels *Trust* (1966), *The Messiah of Stockholm* (1987), and *The Shawl* (1989); the story collection *The Pagan Rabbi and Other Stories* (1971); and the essay collections *Art and Ardor* (1983) and *Metaphor and Memory* (1989). The following essay originally appeared in *Ms.* magazine.

In my Depression childhood, whenever I had a new dress, my cousin Sarah would get suspicious. The nicer the dress was, and especially the more expensive it looked, the more suspicious she would get. Finally she would lift the hem and check the seams. This was to see if the dress had been bought or if my mother had sewed it. Sarah could always tell. My mother's sewing had elegant outsides, but there was something catch-as-catch-can about the insides. Sarah's sewing, by contrast, was as impeccably finished inside as out; not one stray thread dangled.

My uncle Jake built meticulous grandfather clocks out of rosewood; he was a perfectionist, and sent to England for the clockworks. My mother built serviceable radiator covers and a serviceable cabinet, with hinged doors, for the pantry. She built a pair of bookcases for the living room. Once, after I was grown and in a house of my own, she fixed the sewer pipe. She painted ceilings, and also landscapes; she reupholstered chairs. One summer she planted a whole yard of tall corn. She thought herself capable of doing anything, and did everything she imagined. But nothing was perfect. There was always some clear flaw, never visible head-on. You had to look underneath where the seams were. The corn thrived, though not in rows. The stalks elbowed one another like gossips in a dense little village.

"Miss Brrrroooobaker," my mother used to mock, rolling her Russian *r*s, whenever I crossed a *t* she had left uncrossed, or corrected a word she had misspelled, or became impatient with a *v* that had tangled itself up in a *w* in her speech. ("Vvventriloquist," I would say. "Vvventriloquist," she would obediently repeat. And the next time it would come out "wiolinist.") Miss Brubaker was my high school English teacher, and my mother invoked her name as an emblem of raging finical obsession. "Miss Brrrroooobaker," my mother's voice hoots at me down the years, as I go on casting and recasting sentences in a tiny handwriting on monomaniacally uniform paper. The loops of my mother's handwriting—it was the Palmer Method—were as big as hoops, spilling generous splashy ebullience. She could pull off, at five minutes' notice, a satisfying dinner for 10 concocted out of nothing more than originality and panache. But the napkin would be folded a little off-center, and the spoon might be on the wrong side of the knife. She was an optimist who ignored trifles; for her, God was not in the details but in the intent. And all these culinary and agricultural efflorescences were extracurricular, accomplished in the crevices and niches of a 14-hour business day. When she scribbled out her family memoirs, in heaps of dog-eared notebooks, or on the backs of old bills, or on the margins of last year's calendar, I would resist typing them; in the speed of the chase she often omitted words like "the," "and," "will." The same flashing and bountiful hand fashioned and fired ceramic pots, and painted brilliant autumn views and vases of imaginary flowers and ferns, and decorated ordinary Woolworth platters with lavish enameled gardens. But bits of the painted petals would chip away.

Lavish: my mother was as lavish as nature. She woke early and saturated the hours with work and inventiveness, and read late into the night. She was all profusion, abundance, fabrication. Angry at her children, she would run after us whirling the cord of the electric iron, like a lasso or a whip; but she never caught us. When, in the seventh grade, I was afraid of failing the Music Appreciation final exam because I could not tell the difference between "To a Wild Rose" and "Barcarolle," she got the idea of sending me to school with a gauze sling rigged up on my writing arm, and an explanatory note that was purest fiction. But the sling kept slipping off. My mother gave advice like mad—she boiled over with so much passion for the predicaments of strangers that they turned into permanent cronies. She told intimate stories about people I had never heard of.

Despite the gargantuan Palmer loops (or possibly because of them), I have always known that my mother's was a life of—intricately abashing word!—excellence: insofar as excellence means ripe generosity. She burgeoned, she proliferated; she was endlessly leafy and flowering. She wore red hats, and called herself a gypsy. In her girlhood she marched with the suffragettes and for Margaret Sanger[1] and called herself a Red. She made me laugh, she was so varied: like a tree on which lemons, pomegranates, and prickly pears absurdly all hang together. She had the comedy of prodigality.

My own way is a thousand times more confined. I am a pinched perfectionist, the ultimate fruition of Miss Brubaker; I attend to crabbed minutiae and am self-trammeled through taking pains. I am a kind of human snail, locked in and condemned by my own nature. The ancients believed that the moist track left by the snail as it crept was the snail's own essence, depleting its body little by little; the farther the snail toiled, the smaller it became, until it finally rubbed itself out. That is how perfectionists are. Say to us Excellence, and we will show you how we use up our substance and wear ourselves away, while making scarcely any progress at all. The fact that I am an exacting perfectionist in a narrow strait only, and nowhere else, is hardly to the point, since nothing matters to me so much as a comely and mascular sentence. It is my narrow strait, this snail's road: the track of the sentence I am writing now; and when I have eked out the wet substance, ink or blood, that is its mark, I will begin the next sentence. Only in reading out sentences am I perfectionist; but then there is nothing else I know how to do, or take much interest in. I miter every pair of abutting sentences as scrupulously as Uncle Jake fitted one strip of rosewood against another. My mother's worldly and bountiful hand has escaped me. The sentence I am writing is my cabin and my shell, compact, self-sufficient. It is the burnished horizon—a merciless planet where flawlessness is the single standard, where even the inmost seams, however hidden from a laxer eye, must meet perfection. Here "excellence" is not strewn casually from a tipped cornucopia, here disorder does not account for charm, here trifles rule like tyrants.

I measure my life in sentences, and my sentences are superior to

---

[1] Margaret Sanger (1883–1966) was an early promoter of birth control in the United States. (ED.)

my mother's, pressed out, line by line, like the lustrous ooze on the underside of the snail, the snail's secret open seam, its wound, leaking attar. My mother was too mettlesome to feel the force of a comma. She scorned minutiae. She measured her life according to what poured from the horn of plenty, which was her ample, cascading, elastic, susceptible, inexact heart. My narrower heart rides between the tiny horns of the snail, dwindling as it goes.

And out of this thinnest thread, this ink-wet line of words, must rise a visionary fog, a mist, a smoke, forging cities, histories, sorrows, quagmires, entanglements, lives of sinners, even the life of my furnace-hearted mother: so much wilderness, waywardness, plentitude on the head of the precise and impeccable snail, between the horns.

MAXINE HONG KINGSTON

No Name Woman

Maxine Hong Kingston (1940–   ) is a California-born author. Her autobiographical works, *The Woman Warrior: Memoirs of a Girlhood Among Ghosts* (1976) and *China Men* (1980), reveal the life experiences of a first-generation Chinese American. She has recently published a novel, *Tripmaster Monkey: His Fake Book* (1989). The following selection is excerpted from *The Woman Warrior.*

"You must not tell anyone," my mother said, "what I am about to tell you. In China your father had a sister who killed herself. She jumped into the family well. We say that your father has all brothers because it is as if she had never been born.

"In 1924 just a few days after our village celebrated seventeen hurry-up weddings—to make sure that every young man who went 'out on the road' would responsibly come home—your father and his brothers and your grandfather and his brothers and your aunt's new husband sailed for America, the Gold Mountain. It was your grandfather's last trip. Those lucky enough to get contracts waved good-bye from the decks. They fed and guarded the stowaways and helped them off in Cuba, New York, Bali, Hawaii. 'We'll meet in California next year,' they said. All of them sent money home.

"I remember looking at your aunt one day when she and I were dressing; I had not noticed before that she had such a protruding melon of a stomach. But I did not think, 'She's pregnant,' until she began to look like other pregnant women, her shirt pulling and the white tops of her black pants showing. She could not have been pregnant, you see, because her husband had been gone for years. No one said anything. We did not discuss it. In early summer she was ready to have the child, long after the time when it could have been possible.

"The village had also been counting. On the night the baby was to be born the villagers raided our house. Some were crying. Like a great saw, teeth strung with lights, files of people walked zigzag across our land, tearing the rice. Their lanterns doubled in the disturbed black water, which drained away through the broken bunds. As the villagers closed in, we could see that some of them, probably men and women we knew well, wore white masks. The people with long hair hung it over their faces. Women with short hair made it stand up on end. Some had tied white bands around their foreheads, arms, and legs.

"At first they threw mud and rocks at the house. Then they threw eggs and began slaughtering our stock. We could hear the animals scream their deaths—the roosters, the pigs, a last great roar from the ox. Familiar wild heads flared in our night windows; the villagers encircled us. Some of the faces stopped to peer at us, their eyes rushing like searchlights. The hands flattened against the panes, framed heads, and left red prints.

"The villagers broke in the front and the back doors at the same time, even though we had not locked the doors against them. Their knives dripped with the blood of our animals. They smeared blood on the doors and walls. One woman swung a chicken, whose throat she had slit, splattering blood in red arcs about her. We stood together in the middle of our house, in the family hall with the pictures and tables of the ancestors around us, and looked straight ahead.

"At that time the house had only two wings. When the men came back, we would build two more to enclose our courtyard and a third one to begin a second courtyard. The villagers pushed through both wings, even your grandparents' rooms, to find your aunt's, which was also mine until the men returned. From this room a new wing for one of the younger families would grow. They ripped up her clothes and shoes and broke her combs, grinding them underfoot. They tore her work from the loom. They scattered the cooking fire and rolled the new weaving in it. We could hear them in the kitchen breaking our bowls and banging the pots. They overturned the great waist-high earthenware jugs; duck eggs, pickled fruits, vegetables burst out and mixed in acrid torrents. The old woman from the next field swept a broom through the air and loosed the spirits-of-the-broom over our heads. 'Pig.' 'Ghost.' 'Pig,' they sobbed and scolded while they ruined our house.

"When they left, they took sugar and oranges to bless themselves. They cut pieces from the dead animals. Some of them took bowls that were not broken and clothes that were not torn. Afterward we swept up the rice and sewed it back up into sacks. But the smells from the spilled preserves lasted. Your aunt gave birth in the pigsty that night. The next morning when I went up for the water, I found her and the baby plugging up the family well.

"Don't let your father know that I told you. He denies her. Now that you have started to menstruate, what happened to her could happen to you. Don't humiliate us. You wouldn't like to be forgotten as if you had never been born. The villagers are watchful."

Whenever she had to warn us about life, my mother told stories that ran like this one, a story to grow up on. She tested our strength to establish realities. Those in the emigrant generations who could not reassert brute survival died young and far from home. Those of us in the first American generations have had to figure out how the invisible world the emigrants built around our childhoods fit in solid America.

The emigrants confused the gods by diverting their curses, misleading them with crooked streets and false names. They must try to confuse their offspring as well, who, I suppose, threaten them in similar ways—always trying to get things straight, always trying to name the unspeakable. The Chinese I know hide their names; sojourners take new names when their lives change and guard their real names with silence.

Chinese-Americans, when you try to understand what things in you are Chinese, how do you separate what is peculiar to childhood, to poverty, insanities, one family, your mother who marked your growing with stories, from what is Chinese? What is Chinese tradition and what is the movies?

If I want to learn what clothes my aunt wore, whether flashy or ordinary, I would have to begin, "Remember Father's drowned-in-the-well sister?" I cannot ask that. My mother has told me once and for all the useful parts. She will add nothing unless powered by Necessity, a riverbank that guides her life. She plants vegetable gardens rather than lawns; she carries the odd-shaped tomatoes home from the fields and eats food left for the gods.

Whenever we did frivolous things, we used up energy; we flew high kites. We children came up off the ground over the melting cones our parents brought home from work and the American movie on New Year's Day—*Oh, You Beautiful Doll* with Betty Grable one year, and *She Wore a Yellow Ribbon* with John Wayne another year. After the one carnival ride each, we paid in guilt; our tired father counted his change on the dark walk home.

Adultery is extravagance. Could people who hatch their own chicks and eat the embryos and the heads for delicacies and boil the feet in vinegar for party food, leaving only the gravel, eating even the gizzard lining—could such people engender a prodigal aunt? To be a woman, to have a daughter in starvation time was a waste enough. My aunt could not have been the lone romantic who gave up everything for sex. Women in the old China did not choose. Some man had commanded her to lie with him and be his secret evil. I wonder whether he masked himself when he joined the raid on her family.

Perhaps she encountered him in the fields or on the mountain where the daughters-in-law collected fuel. Or perhaps he first noticed her in the marketplace. He was not a stranger because the village housed no strangers. She had to have dealings with him other than sex. Perhaps he worked an adjoining field, or he sold her the cloth for the dress she sewed and wore. His demand must have surprised, then terrified her. She obeyed him; she always did as she was told.

When the family found a young man in the next village to be her husband, she stood tractably beside the best rooster, his proxy, and promised before they met that she would be his forever. She was lucky that he was her age and she would be the first wife, an advantage secure now. The night she first saw him, he had sex with her. Then he left for America. She had almost forgotten what he looked like. When she tried to envision him, she only saw the black and white face in the group photograph the men had had taken before leaving.

The other man was not, after all, much different from her husband. They both gave orders: she followed. "If you tell your family, I'll beat you. I'll kill you. Be here again next week." No one talked sex, ever. And she might have separated the rapes from the rest of living if only she did not have to buy her oil from him or gather wood in the same forest. I want her fear to have lasted just as long as rape lasted so that the fear could have been contained. Not drawn-out fear. But women at sex hazarded birth and hence lifetimes. The fear did not stop but permeated everywhere. She told the man, "I think I'm pregnant." He organized the raid against her.

On nights when my mother and father talked about their life back home, sometimes they mentioned an "outcast table" whose business they still seemed to be settling, their voices tight. In a commensal tradition, where food is precious, the powerful older people made wrongdoers eat alone. Instead of letting them start separate new lives like the Japanese, who could become samurais and geishas, the Chinese family, faces averted but eyes glowering sideways, hung on to the offenders and fed them leftovers. My aunt must have lived in the same house as my parents and eaten at an outcast table. My mother spoke about the raid as if she had seen it, when she and my aunt, a daughter-in-law to a different household, should not have been living together at all. Daughters-in-law lived with their husband's parents, not their own; a synonym for marriage in Chinese is "taking a daughter-in-law." Her husband's parents could have sold her, mortgaged her, stoned her. But they had sent her back to her own mother and father, a mysterious act hinting at disgraces not told me. Perhaps they had thrown her out to deflect the avengers.

She was the only daughter; her four brothers went with her father, husband, and uncles "out on the road" and for some years became western men. When the goods were divided among the family, three of the brothers took land, and the youngest, my father, chose an education. After my grandparents gave their daughter away to her husband's family, they had dispensed all the adventure and all the property. They expected her alone to keep the traditional ways, which her brothers, now among the barbarians, could fumble without detection. The heavy, deep-rooted women were to maintain the past against the flood, safe for returning. But the rare urge west had fixed upon our family, and so my aunt crossed boundaries not delineated in space.

The work of preservation demands that the feelings playing about in one's guts not be turned into action. Just watch their passing like cherry blossoms. But perhaps my aunt, my forerunner, caught in a slow life, let dreams grow and fade and after some months or years went toward what persisted. Fear at the enormities of the forbidden kept her desires delicate, wire and bone. She looked at a man because she liked the way the hair was tucked behind his ears, or she liked the questionmark line of a long torso curving at the shoulder and straight at the hip. For warm eyes or a soft voice or a slow walk— that's all—a few hairs, a line, a brightness, a sound, a pace, she gave up family. She offered us up for a charm that vanished with tiredness, a pigtail that didn't toss when the wind died. Why, the wrong lighting could erase the dearest thing about him.

It could very well have been, however, that my aunt did not take subtle enjoyment of her friend, but, a wild woman, kept rollicking company. Imagining her free with sex doesn't fit, though. I don't know any women like that, or men either. Unless I see her life branching into mine, she gives me no ancestral help.

To sustain her being in love, she often worked at herself in the mirror, guessing at the colors and shapes that would interest him, changing them frequently in order to hit on the right combination. She wanted him to look back.

On a farm near the sea, a woman who tended her appearance reaped a reputation for eccentricity. All the married women blunt-cut their hair in flaps about their ears or pulled it back in tight buns. No nonsense. Neither style blew easily into heart-catching tangles. And at their weddings they displayed themselves in their long hair for the last time. "It brushed the backs of my knees," my mother tells me. "It was braided, and even so, it brushed the backs of my knees."

At the mirror my aunt combed individuality into her bob. A bun could have been contrived to escape into black streamers blowing in the wind or in quiet wisps about her face, but only the older women in our picture album wear buns. She brushed her hair back from her forehead, tucking the flaps behind her ears. She looped a piece of thread, knotted into a circle between her index fingers and thumbs, and ran the double strand across her forehead. When she closed her fingers as if she were making a pair of shadow geese bite, the string twisted together catching the little hairs. Then she pulled the thread away from her skin, ripping the hairs out neatly, her eyes watering from the needles of pain. Opening her fingers, she cleaned the thread, then rolled it along her hairline and the tops of her eyebrows. My mother did the same to me and my sisters and herself. I used to believe that the expression "caught by the short hairs" meant a captive held with a depilatory string. It especially hurt at the temples, but my mother said we were lucky we didn't have to have our feet bound when we were seven. Sisters used to sit on their beds and cry together, she said, as their mothers or their slave removed the bandages for a few minutes each night and let the blood gush back into their veins. I hope that the man my aunt loved appreciated a smooth brow, that he wasn't just a tits-and-ass man.

Once my aunt found a freckle on her chin, at a spot that the almanac said predestined her for unhappiness. She dug it out with a hot needle and washed the wound with peroxide.

More attention to her looks than these pullings of hairs and pickings at spots would have caused gossip among the villagers. They owned work clothes and good clothes, and they wore good clothes for feasting the new seasons. But since a woman combing her hair hexes beginnings, my aunt rarely found an occasion to look her best. Women looked like great sea snails—the corded wood, babies, and laundry they carried were the whorls on their backs. The Chinese did not admire a bent back; goddesses and warriors stood straight. Still there must have been a marvelous freeing of beauty when a worker laid down her burden and stretched and arched.

Such commonplace loveliness, however, was not enough for my aunt. She dreamed of a lover for the fifteen days of New Year's, the time for families to exchange visits, money, and food. She plied her secret comb. And sure enough she cursed the year, the family, the village, and herself.

Even as her hair lured her imminent lover, many other men looked at her. Uncles, cousins, nephews, brothers would have looked, too, had they been home between journeys. Perhaps they had already been restraining their curiosity, and they left, fearful that their glances, like a field of nesting birds, might be startled and caught. Poverty hurt, and that was their first reason for leaving. But another, final reason for leaving the crowded house was the never-said.

She may have been unusually beloved, the precious only daughter, spoiled and mirror-gazing because of the affection the family lavished on her. When her husband left, they welcomed the chance to take her back from the in-laws; she could live like the little daughter for just a while longer. There are stories that my grandfather was different from other people, "crazy ever since the little Jap bayoneted him in the head." He used to put his naked penis on the dinner table, laughing. And one day he brought home a baby girl, wrapped up inside his brown western-style greatcoat. He had traded one of his sons, probably my father, the youngest, for her. My grandmother made him trade back. When he finally got a daughter of his own, he doted on her. They must have all loved her, except perhaps my father, the only brother who never went back to China, having once been traded for a girl.

Brothers and sisters, newly men and women, had to efface their sexual color and present plain miens. Disturbing hair and eyes, a smile like no other, threatened the ideal of five generations living under one roof. To focus blurs, people shouted face to face and yelled from room to room. The immigrants I know have loud voices, un-modulated to American tones even after years away from the village where they called their friendships out across the fields. I have not been able to stop my mother's screams in public libraries or over telephones. Walking erect (knees straight, toes pointed forward, not pigeon-toed, which is Chinese-feminine) and speaking in an inaudible voice, I have tried to turn myself American-feminine. Chinese communication was loud, public. Only sick people had to whisper. But at the dinner table, where the family members came nearest one another, no one could talk, not the outcasts nor any eaters. Every word that falls from the mouth is a coin lost. Silently they gave and accepted food with both hands. A preoccupied child who took his bowl with one hand got a sideways glare. A complete moment of total attention is due everyone alike. Children and lovers have no singularity here, but my aunt used a secret voice, a separate attentiveness.

She kept the man's name to herself throughout her labor and dying; she did not accuse him that he be punished with her. To save her inseminator's name she gave silent birth.

He may have been somebody in her own household, but intercourse with a man outside the family would have been no less abhorrent. All the village were kinsmen, and the titles shouted in loud country voices never let kinship be forgotten. Any man within visiting distance would have been neutralized as a lover—"brother," "younger brother," "older brother"—115 relationship titles. Parents researched birth charts probably not so much to assure good fortune as to circumvent incest in a population that has but one hundred surnames. Everybody has eight million relatives. How useless then sexual mannerisms, how dangerous.

As if it came from an atavism deeper than fear, I used to add "brother" silently to boys' names. It hexed the boys, who would or would not ask me to dance, and made them less scary and as familiar and deserving of benevolence as girls.

But, of course, I hexed myself also—no dates. I should have stood up, both arms waving, and shouted out across libraries, "Hey, you! Love me back." I had no idea, though, how to make attraction selective, how to control its direction and magnitude. If I made myself American-pretty so that the five or six Chinese boys in the class fell in love with me, everyone else—the Caucasian, Negro, and Japanese boys—would too. Sisterliness, dignified and honorable, made much more sense.

Attraction eludes control so stubbornly that whole societies designed to organize relationships among people cannot keep order, not even when they bind people to one another from childhood and raise them together. Among the very poor and the wealthy, brothers married their adopted sisters, like doves. Our family allowed some romance, paying adult brides' prices and providing dowries so that their sons and daughters could marry strangers. Marriage promises to turn strangers into friendly relatives—a nation of siblings.

In the village structure, spirits shimmered among the live creatures, balanced and held in equilibrium by time and land. But one human being flaring up into violence could open up a black hole, a maelstrom that pulled in the sky. The frightened villagers, who depended on one another to maintain the real, went to my aunt to show her a personal, physical representation of the break she made in the "roundness." Misallying couples snapped off the future, which was to be embodied in true offspring. The villagers punished her for acting as if she could have a private life, secret and apart from them.

If my aunt had betrayed the family at a time of large grain yields and peace, when many boys were born, and wings were being built on many houses, perhaps she might have escaped such severe punishment. But the men—hungry, greedy, tired of planting in dry soil, cuckolded—had been forced to leave the village in order to send food-money home. There were ghost plagues, bandit plagues, wars with the Japanese, floods. My Chinese brother and sister had died of an unknown sickness. Adultery, perhaps only a mistake during good times, became a crime when the village needed food.

The round moon cakes and round doorways, the round tables of graduated size that fit one roundness inside another, round windows and rice bowls—these talismans had lost their power to warn this family of the law: a family must be whole, faithfully keeping the descent line by having sons to feed the old and the dead who in turn look after the family. The villagers came to show my aunt and lover-in-hiding a broken house. The villagers were speeding up the circling of events because she was too shortsighted to see that her infidelity had already harmed the village, that waves of consequences would return unpredictably, sometimes in disguise, as now, to hurt her. This roundness had to be made coin-sized so that she would see its circumference: punish her at the birth of her baby. Awaken her to the inexorable. People who refused fatalism because they could invent small resources insisted on culpability. Deny accidents and wrest fault from the stars.

After the villagers left, their lanterns now scattering in various directions toward home, the family broke their silence and cursed her. "Aiaa, we're going to die. Death is coming. Death is coming. Look what you've done. You've killed us. Ghost! Dead Ghost! Ghost! You've never been born." She ran out into the fields, far enough from the house so that she could no longer hear their voices, and pressed herself against the earth, her own land no more. When she felt the birth coming, she thought that she had been hurt. Her body seized together. "They've hurt me too much," she thought. "This is gall, and it will kill me." With forehead and knees against the earth, her body convulsed and then relaxed. She turned on her back, lay on the ground. The black well of sky and stars went out and out forever; her body and her complexity seemed to disappear. She was one of the stars, a bright dot in blackness, without home, without a companion, in eternal cold and silence. An agoraphobia rose in her, speeding higher and higher, bigger and bigger; she would not be able to contain it; there would be no end to fear.

Flayed, unprotected against space, she felt pain return, focusing her body. This pain chilled her—a cold, steady kind of surface pain. Inside, spasmodically, the other pain, the pain of the child, heated her. For hours she lay on the ground, alternately body and space. Sometimes a vision of normal comfort obliterated reality: she saw the family in the evening gambling at the dinner table, the young people massaging their elders' backs. She saw them congratulating one another, high joy on the mornings the rice shoots came up. When these pictures burst, the stars drew yet further apart. Black space opened.

She got to her feet to fight better and remembered that old-fashioned women gave birth in their pigsties to fool the jealous, paindealing gods, who do not snatch piglets. Before the next spasms could stop her, she ran to the pigsty, each step a rushing out into emptiness. She climbed over the fence and knelt in the dirt. It was good to have a fence enclosing her, a tribal person alone.

Laboring, this woman who had carried her child as a foreign growth that sickened her every day, expelled it at last. She reached down to touch the hot, wet, moving mass, surely smaller than anything human, and could feel that it was human after all—fingers, toes, nails, nose. She pulled it up on her belly, and it lay curled there, butt in the air, feet precisely tucked one under the other. She opened her loose shirt and buttoned the child inside. After resting, it squirmed and thrashed and she pushed it up to her breast. It turned its head this way and that until it found her nipple. There, it made little snuffling noises. She clenched her teeth at its preciousness, lovely as a young calf, a piglet, a little dog.

She may have gone to the pigsty as a last act of responsibility: she would protect this child as she had protected its father. It would look after her soul, leaving supplies on her grave. But how would this tiny child without family find her grave when there would be no marker for her anywhere, neither in the earth nor the family hall? No one would give her a family hall name. She had taken the child with her into the wastes. At its birth the two of them had felt the same raw pain of separation, a wound that only the family pressing tight could close. A child with no descent line would not soften her life but only trail after her, ghostlike, begging her to give it purpose. At dawn the villagers on their way to the fields would stand around the fence and look.

Full of milk, the little ghost slept. When it awoke, she hardened her breasts against the milk that crying loosens. Toward morning she picked up the baby and walked to the well.

Carrying the baby to the well shows loving. Otherwise abandon it. Turn its face into the mud. Mothers who love their children take them along. It was probably a girl; there is some hope of forgiveness for boys.

"Don't tell anyone you had an aunt. Your father does not want to hear her name. She has never been born." I have believed that sex was unspeakable and words so strong and fathers so frail that "aunt" would do my father mysterious harm. I have thought that my family, having settled among immigrants who had also been their neighbors in the ancestral land, needed to clean their name, and a wrong word would incite the kinspeople even here. But there is more to this silence: they want me to participate in her punishment. And I have.

In the twenty years since I heard this story I have not asked for details nor said my aunt's name; I do not know it. People who comfort the dead can also chase after them to hurt them further—a reverse ancestor worship. The real punishment was not the raid swiftly inflicted by the villagers, but the family's deliberately forgetting her. Her betrayal so maddened them, they saw to it that she would suffer forever, even after death. Always hungry, always needing, she would have to beg food from other ghosts, snatch and steal it from those whose living descendants give them gifts. She would have to fight the ghosts massed at crossroads for the buns a few thoughtful citizens leave to decoy her away from village and home so that the ancestral spirits could feast unharassed. At peace, they could act like gods, not ghosts, their descent lines providing them with paper suits and dresses, spirit money, paper houses, paper automobiles, chicken, meat, and rice into eternity—essences delivered up in smoke and flames, steam and incense rising from each rice bowl. In an attempt to make the Chinese care for people outside the family, Chairman Mao encourages us now to give our paper replicas to the spirits of outstanding soldiers and workers, no matter whose ancestors they may be. My aunt remains forever hungry. Goods are not distributed evenly among the dead.

My aunt haunts me—her ghost drawn to me because now, after fifty years of neglect, I alone devote pages of paper to her, though not origamied into houses and clothes. I do not think she always means me well. I am telling on her, and she was a spite suicide, drowning herself in the drinking water. The Chinese are always very frightened of the drowned one, whose weeping ghost, wet hair hanging and skin bloated, waits silently by the water to pull down a substitute.

STEVE TESICH

Focusing on Friends

Steve Tesich (1943–) was born in Yugoslavia and came to the United States as a teenager. A playwright, as well as the author of essays and fiction, he composed the Oscar-winning screenplay for the movie *Breaking Away*. His plays include *Passing Game* (1978), *Division Street* (1980), and *Speed of Darkness,* which opened on Broadway in March of 1991. The following selection first appeared in the *New York Times Magazine*.

When I think of people who were my good friends, I see them all, as I do everything else from my life, in cinematic terms. The camera work is entirely different for men and women.

I remember all the women in almost extreme close-ups. The settings are different—apartments, restaurants—but they're all interiors, as if I had never spent a single minute with a single woman outside. They're looking right at me, these women in these extreme close-ups; the lighting is exquisite, worthy of a Fellini or Fosse film,[1]

---

[1] *Federico Fellini* is an Italian filmmaker who is famous for films such as *La Dolce Vita*

and their lips are moving. They're telling me something important or reacting to something even more important that I've told them. It's the kind of movie where you tell people to keep quiet when they chew their popcorn too loudly.

The boys and men who were my friends are in an entirely different movie. No close-ups here. No exquisite lighting. The camera work is rather shaky but the background is moving. We're going somewhere, on foot, on bicycles, in cars. The ritual of motion, or action, makes up for the inconsequential nature of the dialogue. It's a much sloppier film, this film that is not really a film but a memory of real friends: Slobo, Louie, Sam. Male friends. I've loved all three of them. I assumed they knew this, but I never told them.

Quite the contrary is true in my female films. In close-up after close-up, I am telling every woman who I ever loved that I love her, and then lingering on yet another close-up of her face for a reaction. There is a perfectly appropriate musical score playing while I wait. And if I wait long enough, I get an answer. I am loved. I am not loved. Language clears up the suspense. The emotion is nailed down.

Therein lies the difference, I think, between my friendships with men and with women. I can tell women I love them. Not only can I tell them, I am compulsive about it. I can hardly wait to tell them. But I can't tell the men. I just can't. And they can't tell me. Emotions are never nailed down. They run wild, and I and my male friends chase after them, on foot, on bicycles, in cars, keeping the quarry in sight but never catching up.

My first friend was Slobo. I was still living in Yugoslavia at the time, and not far from my house there was an old German truck left abandoned after the war. It had no wheels. No windshield. No doors. But the steering wheel was intact. Slobo and I flew to America in that truck. It was our airplane. Even now, I remember the background moving as we took off down the street, across Europe, across the Atlantic. We were inseparable: The best of friends. Naturally, not one word concerning the nature of our feelings for one another was ever exchanged. It was all done in actions.

The inevitable would happen at least once a day. As we were flying over the Atlantic, there came, out of nowhere, that wonderful moment: engine failure! "We'll have to bail out," I shouted. "A-a-a-a-a!" Slobo made the sound of a failing engine. Then he would turn and look me in the eye: "I can't swim," he'd say. "Fear not." I put

---

(1960). *Bob Fosse,* an American choreographer and stage and screen director, is most remembered for the musical, *Cabaret* (1972). (ED.)

my hand on his shoulder. "I'll drag you to shore." And, with that, both of us would tumble out of the truck onto the dusty street. I swam through the dust. Slobo drowned in the dust, coughing, gagging. "Sharks!" he cried. But I always saved him. The next day the ritual would be repeated, only then it would be my turn to say "I can't swim," and Slobo would save me. We saved each other from certain death over a hundred times, until finally a day came when I really left for America with my mother and sister. Slobo and I stood at the train station. We were there to say goodbye, but, since we weren't that good at saying things and since he couldn't save me, he just cried until the train started to move.

The best friend I had in high school was Louie. It now seems to me that I was totally monogamous when it came to male friends. I would have several girl friends but only one real male friend. Louie was it at that time. We were both athletes, and one day we decided to "run till we drop." We just wanted to know what it was like. Skinny Louie set the pace as we ran around our high-school track. Lap after lap. Four laps to a mile. Mile after mile we ran. I had the reputation as being a big-time jock. Louie didn't. But this was Louie's day. There was a bounce in his step and, when he turned back to look at me, his eyes were gleaming with the thrill of it all. I finally dropped. Louie still looked fresh; he seemed capable, on that day, of running forever. But we were the best of friends, and so he stopped. "That's it," he lied. "I couldn't go another step farther." It was an act of love. Naturally, I said nothing.

Louie got killed in Vietnam. Several weeks after his funeral, I went to his mother's house, and, because she was a woman, I tried to tell her how much I had loved her son. It was not a good scene. Although I was telling the truth, my words sounded like lies. It was all very painful and embarrassing. I kept thinking how sorry I was that I had never told Louie himself.

Sam is my best friend now, and has been for many years. A few years ago, we were swimming at a beach in East Hampton. The Atlantic! The very Atlantic I had flown over in my German truck with Slobo. We had swum out pretty far from the shore when both of us simultaneously thought we spotted a shark. Water is not only a good conductor of electricity but of panic as well. We began splashing like madmen toward shore. Suddenly, at the height of my panic, I realized how much I loved my friend, what an irreplaceable friend he was, and, although I was the fastest swimmer, I fell back to protect him. Naturally, the shark in the end proved to be imaginary. But not my feelings for my friend. For several days after that I wanted to share my discovery with him, to tell him how much I loved him. Fortunately, I didn't.

I say fortunately because on reflection, there seems to be sufficient evidence to indicate that, if anybody was cheated and shortchanged by me, it was the women, the girls, the very recipients of my uncensored emotions. Yes, I could hardly wait to tell them I loved them. I did love them. But once I told them, something stopped. The emotion was nailed down, but, with it, the enthusiasm and the energy to prove it was nailed down, too. I can remember my voice saying to almost all of them, at one time or another: "I told you I love you. What else do you want?" I can now recoil at the impatient hostility of that voice but I can't deny it was mine.

The tyranny of self-censorship forced me, in my relations with male friends, to seek alternatives to language. And just because I could never be sure they understood exactly how I felt about them, I was forced to look for ways to prove it. That is, I now think, how it should be. It is time to make adjustments. It is time to pull back the camera, free the women I know, and myself, from those merciless close-ups and have the background move.

DONALD BARTHELME

The Author

Donald Barthelme (1931–1989) was born in Philadelphia, raised in Texas, and is widely considered to be one of the most innovative writers of contemporary fiction. Best known for his short stories, his collections include *Come Back, Dr. Caligari* (1964), *Unspeakable Practices, Unnatural Acts* (1968), and *Forty Stories* (1987). His novels include *Snow White* (1967) and *The King* (1990). The following selection first appeared in the *New Yorker*.

My deranged mother has written another book. This one is called "The Bough" and is even worse than the others. I refer not to its quality—it exhibits the usual "coruscating wit" and "penetrating social observation"—but to the extent to which it utilizes, as a kind of mulch pile, the lives of her children.

This one, as I say, is even worse than the others (two American

Book Award nominations and a Literary Guild alternate). My poor brother Sampson, who appears as "Rafe," is found, in the first chapter, performing a laparoscopy[1] upon a patient who had been under the impression she was paying for quite another procedure. My brother is a very busy and popular doctor, and a hiatus in his office staffing was responsible for this understandable if lamentable mixup. What the book does not say is that the laparoscopy disclosed a fair amount of endometriosis which was then dealt with in a highly skilled and professional manner, thus averting considerable patient disgruntlement. Mother never puts anything good about any of us into her books.

"Rafe"'s relations with "Molly" (read Callie, Sam's wife) are, as you might imagine, not spared. Some time ago Sam and Callie had a little disagreement about his conduct during the Miami OB-GYN meeting when he was missing for some hours during a presentation on ultrasound and she learned that he had been out drinking with a bunch of heavily armed survivalists who liked to shoot up life-size plywood cutouts of Gorbachev with their (more or less illegal) Ingram M-11s which they can fire one-handed with a can of Stroh's in the other. Girl survivalists were also present. O.K., so my brother Sam is a gun nut. Why tell everybody in the world? Intervention is what surgeons are all about. How my mother gleans these details is beyond me, as none of us has spoken to her since 1974, when "Fumed Oak" was published.

My mother's treatment of my sister Virginia—"Alabama" in the book (Mother's masks are clear glass)—is flatly vicious. Virginia has had some tough times of late, what with the accident and the fallout from the accident. In "The Bough" "Alabama" has a blood-alcohol reading of .18% immediately after the crash, and that happens to be the right number, as many of Virginia's friends have recognized. What is truly reprehensible is the (painfully accurate) analysis of my sister's character. Virginia did her dissertation on Emerson: so does "Alabama." That certain passages in "Alabama" 's dissertation offer striking parallels to recent work by Joel Porte (Harvard University Press) and Eric Cheyfitz (Johns Hopkins University Press) is announced for the first time in "Bough;" I had not thought Mother that much of a scholar. The line in the book "They shouldn't let me go into a bar without training wheels on" is pure Virginia.

---

[1] An operation in which a tube-like optical instrument is inserted, giving the physician a view into the body. (ED.)

My other brother, Denis (the "good brother" in the book), has asked his lawyers to look into the legal aspects. They have told him that suing one's mother is an awkward business at best and the appearance of filial impiety more or less cancels, for jurors, any merit such a suit might possess. They also pointed out, very reasonably, that the public nature of such an action, involving a well-known author, would tend to call attention to some of the very things we are not anxious to emphasize: for example, Denis's practice of purchasing U.S. Army morphine Syrettes from disaffected Medical Corps master sergeants and the ingenious places he finds to hide them in the office (hollowed-out cigars, his computer's surge suppressor) and the consequences of this for his brokerage business, all finely detailed in "The Bough." I must say I have never read a more telling account of the *jouissance*[2] produced by high-grade morphine. What busy little bee brought her this news?

"The Bough" is No. 9 this week on the Los Angeles *Times* list. Thus does Stamford provide titillation for Santa Barbara, by way of Mother's bee-loud glade in Old Lyme. Somehow she uncovered the specifics of my "theft" of several inconsequential medicine bundles (cloth, painted wood, feathers) from the Native American Institute, where I am the former curator-at-large. I say "theft" because I wish to be as hard on myself as possible in this matter; others might call it "creative deaccessioning," and the Ghost Dance material (drum charts, dance notation) received in exchange, which the board would never have realized the value of, will be my monument. Yes, the finder's fee charged to the transaction was quite substantial, in the high six figures, as Mother does not fail to note, but Willie Leaping Deer and I earned every penny of it. No one who fully understands the Ghost Dance, whose object was to render the participants impervious to the encroachments of the white man (rifle bullets included), would have hesitated for a moment. "Mark" has a ridiculous affair with a Dakota shaman of ambiguous sex, and none of that is true except the trance scene; furthermore, the chanting on that occasion involved no intoxicants save "Pinafore," which I was teaching Wokodah and which he greatly enjoyed.

It is not that we, my mother's children, lead or claim to lead exemplary lives. But couldn't she widen her horizons just a bit?

"Mother, why do you do this to us?" I asked her recently.

---

[2] jollity, enjoyment (ED.)

Mother is handsome still, and bears a carefully cultivated resemblance to Virginia Woolf.

"What?" she said. "Do what?"

I was holding up a copy of "The Bough." "This," I said, more or
less pointing it at her.

"But you're *mine*," she said.

JOYCE CAROL OATES

Where Are You Going,
Where Have You Been?

Joyce Carol Oates (1938–   ) is an American novelist, poet, essayist, short story writer, dramatist, and critic. Her novels include
them (1969), *American Appetites* (1989), *I Lock the Door upon
Myself* (1990), *Because It Is Bitter, and Because It Is My Heart*
(1990), and *The Rise of Life on Earth* (1991). Her short story collections include *Where Are You Going, Where Have You Been?:
Stories of Young America* (1974) and *Raven's Wing* (1986). The
characters in Oates's fiction often inhabit a world filled with violence and mental illness. She has also published nonfiction works,
including the book *On Boxing* (1987). The following selection
appears in the short story collection *The Wheel of Love* (1970).

To Bob Dylan

Her name was Connie. She was fifteen and had a quick nervous
giggling habit of craning her neck to glance into mirrors or checking
other people's faces to make sure her own was all right. Her mother,
who noticed everything and knew everything and who hadn't much
reason any longer to look at her own face, always scolded Connie
about it. "Stop gawking at yourself, who are you? You think you're
so pretty?" she would say. Connie would raise her eyebrows at these
familiar complaints and look right through her mother, into a shadowy vision of herself as she was right at that moment: she knew she
was pretty and that was everything. Her mother had been pretty once

too, if you could believe those old snapshots in the album, but now her looks were gone and that was why she was always after Connie.

"Why don't you keep your room clean like your sister? How've you got your hair fixed—what the hell stinks? Hair spray? You don't see your sister using that junk."

Her sister June was twenty-four and still lived at home. She was a secretary in the high school Connie attended, and if that wasn't bad enough—with her in the same building—she was so plain and chunky and steady that Connie had to hear her praised all the time by her mother and her mother's sisters. June did this, June did that, she saved money and helped clean the house and cooked and Connie couldn't do a thing, her mind was all filled with trashy daydreams. Their father was away at work most of the time and when he came home he wanted supper and he read the newspaper at supper and after supper he went to bed. He didn't bother talking much to them, but around his bent head Connie's mother kept picking at her until Connie wished her mother were dead and she herself were dead and it were all over. "She makes me want to throw up sometimes," she complained to her friends. She had a high, breathless, amused voice which made everything she said sound a little forced, whether it was sincere or not.

There was one good thing: June went places with girlfriends of hers, girls who were just as plain and steady as she, and so when Connie wanted to do that her mother had no objections. The father of Connie's best girlfriend drove the girls the three miles to town and left them off at a shopping plaza, so that they could walk through the stores or go to a movie, and when he came to pick them up again at eleven he never bothered to ask what they had done.

They must have been familiar sights, walking around that shopping plaza in their shorts and flat ballerina slippers that always scuffed the sidewalk, with charm bracelets jingling on their thin wrists; they would lean together to whisper and laugh secretly if someone passed by who amused or interested them. Connie had long dark blond hair that drew anyone's eye to it, and she wore part of it pulled up on her head and puffed out and the rest of it she let fall down her back. She wore a pullover jersey blouse that looked one way when she was at home and another way when she was away from home. Everything about her had two sides to it, one for home and one for anywhere that was not home: her walk that could be childlike and bobbing, or languid enough to make anyone think she was hearing music in her head, her mouth which was pale and smirking most of the time, but bright and pink on these evenings out, her laugh which was cynical and drawling at home—"Ha, ha, very funny"—but high-pitched and nervous anywhere else, like the jingling of the charms on her bracelet.

Sometimes they did go shopping or to a movie, but sometimes they went across the highway, ducking fast across the busy road, to a drive-in restaurant where older kids hung out. The restaurant was shaped like a big bottle, though squatter than a real bottle, and on its cap was a revolving figure of a grinning boy who held a hamburger aloft. One night in midsummer they ran across, breathless with daring, and right away someone leaned out a car window and invited them over, but it was just a boy from high school they didn't like. It made them feel good to be able to ignore him. They went up through the maze of parked and cruising cars to the bright-lit, fly-infested restaurant, their faces pleased and expectant as if they were entering a sacred building that loomed out of the night to give them what haven and what blessing they yearned for. They sat at the counter and crossed their legs at the ankles, their thin shoulders rigid with excitement, and listened to the music that made everything so good: the music was always in the background like music at a church service, it was something to depend upon.

A boy named Eddie came in to talk with them. He sat backward on his stool, turning himself jerkily around in semicircles and then stopping and turning again, and after a while he asked Connie if she would like something to eat. She said she did and so she tapped her friend's arm on her way out—her friend pulled her face up into a brave droll look—and Connie said she would meet her at eleven, across the way. "I just hate to leave her like that," Connie said earnestly, but the boy said that she wouldn't be alone for long. So they went out to his car and on the way Connie couldn't help but let her eyes wander over the windshields and faces all around her, her face gleaming with a joy that had nothing to do with Eddie or even this place; it might have been the music. She drew her shoulders up and sucked in her breath with the pure pleasure of being alive, and just at that moment she happened to glance at a face just a few feet from hers. It was a boy with shaggy black hair, in a convertible jalopy painted gold. He stared at her and then his lips widened into a grin. Connie slit her eyes at him and turned away, but she couldn't help glancing back and there he was still watching her. He wagged a finger and laughed and said, "Gonna get you, baby," and Connie turned away again without Eddie noticing anything.

She spent three hours with him, at the restaurant where they ate

hamburgers and drank Cokes in wax cups that were always sweating, and then down an alley a mile or so away, and when he left her off at five to eleven only the movie house was still open at the plaza. Her girlfriend was there, talking with a boy. When Connie came up the two girls smiled at each other and Connie said, "How was the movie?" and the girl said, "*You* should know." They rode off with the girl's father, sleepy and pleased, and Connie couldn't help but look at the darkened shopping plaza with its big empty parking lot and its signs that were faded and ghostly now, and over at the drive-in restaurant where cars were still circling tirelessly. She couldn't hear the music at this distance.

Next morning June asked her how the movie was and Connie said, "So-so."

She and that girl and occasionally another girl went out several times a week that way, and the rest of the time Connie spent around the house—it was summer vacation—getting in her mother's way and thinking, dreaming, about the boys she met. But all the boys fell back and dissolved into a single face that was not even a face, but an idea, a feeling, mixed up with the urgent insistent pounding of the music and the humid night air of July. Connie's mother kept dragging her back to the daylight by finding things for her to do or saying, suddenly, "What's this about the Pettinger girl?"

And Connie would say nervously, "Oh, her. That dope." She always drew thick clear lines between herself and such girls, and her mother was simple and kindly enough to believe her. Her mother was so simple, Connie thought, that it was maybe cruel to fool her so much. Her mother went scuffling around the house in old bedroom slippers and complained over the telephone to one sister about the other, then the other called up and the two of them complained about the third one. If June's name was mentioned her mother's tone was approving, and if Connie's name was mentioned it was disapproving. This did not really mean she disliked Connie and actually Connie thought that her mother preferred her to June because she was prettier, but the two of them kept up a pretense of exasperation, a sense that they were tugging and struggling over something of little value to either of them. Sometimes, over coffee, they were almost friends, but something would come up—some vexation that was like a fly buzzing suddenly around their heads—and their faces went hard with contempt.

One Sunday Connie got up at eleven—none of them bothered with church—and washed her hair so that it could dry all day long, in the sun. Her parents and sister were going to a barbecue at an

aunt's house and Connie said no, she wasn't interested, rolling her
eyes to let her mother know just what she thought of it. "Stay home
alone then," her mother said sharply. Connie sat out back in a lawn
chair and watched them drive away, her father quiet and bald,
hunched around so that he could back the car out, her mother with
a look that was still angry and not at all softened through the
windshield, and in the back seat poor old June all dressed up as if
she didn't know what a barbecue was, with all the running yelling
kids and the flies. Connie sat with her eyes closed in the sun,
dreaming and dazed with the warmth about her as if this were a kind
of love, the caresses of love, and her mind slipped over onto thoughts
of the boy she had been with the night before and how nice he had
been, how sweet it always was, not the way someone like June would
suppose but sweet, gentle, the way it was in movies and promised
in songs; and when she opened her eyes she hardly knew where she
was, the back yard ran off into weeds and a fence line of trees and
behind it the sky was perfectly blue and still. The asbestos "ranch
house" that was now three years old startled her—it looked small.
She shook her head as if to get awake.

It was too hot. She went inside the house and turned on the radio
to drown out the quiet. She sat on the edge of her bed, barefoot, and
listened for an hour and a half to a program called XYZ Sunday
Jamboree, record after record of hard, fast, shrieking songs she sang
along with, interspersed by exclamations from "Bobby King": "An'
look here you girls at Napoleon's—Son and Charley want you to pay
real close attention to this song coming up!"

And Connie paid close attention herself, bathed in a glow of slow-
pulsed joy that seemed to rise mysteriously out of the music itself
and lay languidly about the airless little room, breathed in and
breathed out with each gentle rise and fall of her chest.

After a while she heard a car coming up the drive. She sat up at
once, startled, because it couldn't be her father so soon. The gravel
kept crunching all the way in from the road—the driveway was
long—and Connie ran to the window. It was a car she didn't know.
It was an open jalopy, painted a bright gold that caught the sunlight
opaquely. Her heart began to pound and her fingers snatched at her
hair, checking it, and she whispered "Christ, Christ," wondering how
bad she looked. The car came to a stop at the side door and the horn
sounded four short taps as if this were a signal Connie knew.

She went into the kitchen and approached the door slowly, then
hung out the screen door, her bare toes curling down off the step.
There were two boys in the car and now she recognized the driver:

he had shaggy, shabby black hair that looked crazy as a wig and he was grinning at her.

"I ain't late, am I?" he said.

"Who the hell do you think you are?" Connie said.

"Toldja I'd be out, didn't I?"

"I don't even know who you are."

She spoke sullenly, careful to show no interest or pleasure, and he spoke in a fast bright monotone. Connie looked past him to the other boy, taking her time. He had fair brown hair, with a lock that fell onto his forehead. His sideburns gave him a fierce, embarrassed look, but so far he hadn't even bothered to glance at her. Both boys wore sunglasses. The driver's glasses were metallic and mirrored everything in miniature.

"You wanta come for a ride?" he said.

Connie smirked and let her hair fall loose over one shoulder.

"Don'tcha like my car? New paint job," he said. "Hey."

"What?"

"You're cute."

She pretended to fidget, chasing flies away from the door.

"Don'tcha believe me, or what?" he said.

"Look, I don't even know who you are," Connie said in disgust.

"Hey, Ellie's got a radio, see. Mine's broke down." He lifted his friend's arm and showed her the little transistor the boy was holding, and now Connie began to hear the music. It was the same program that was playing inside the house.

"Bobby King?" she said.

"I listen to him all the time. I think he's great."

"He's kind of great," Connie said reluctantly.

"Listen, that guy's *great*. He knows where the action is."

Connie blushed a little, because the glasses made it impossible for her to see just what this boy was looking at. She couldn't decide if she liked him or if he was just a jerk, and so she dawdled in the doorway and wouldn't come down or go back inside. She said, "What's all that stuff painted on your car?"

"Can'tcha read it?" He opened the door very carefully, as if he was afraid it might fall off. He slid out just as carefully, planting his feet firmly on the ground, the tiny metallic world in his glasses showing down like gelatine hardening and in the midst of it Connie's bright green blouse. "This here is my name, to begin with," he said. ARNOLD FRIEND was written in tarlike black letters on the side, with a drawing of a round grinning face that reminded Connie of a pumpkin, except it wore sunglasses. "I wanta introduce myself, I'm

Arnold Friend and that's my real name and I'm gonna be your friend, honey, and inside the car's Ellie Oscar, he's kinda shy." Ellie brought his transistor radio up to his shoulder and balanced it there. "Now these numbers are a secret code, honey," Arnold Friend explained. He read off the numbers 33, 19, 17 and raised his eyebrows at her to see what she thought of that, but she didn't think much of it. The left rear fender had been smashed and around it was written, on the gleaming gold background: DONE BY CRAZY WOMAN DRIVER. Connie had to laugh at that. Arnold Friend was pleased at her laughter and looked up at her. "Around the other side's a lot more—you wanta come and see them?"

"No."

"Why not?"

"Why should I?"

"Don'tcha wanta see what's on the car? Don'tcha wanta go for a ride?"

"I don't know."

"Why not?"

"I got things to do."

"Like what?"

"Things."

He laughed as if she had said something funny. He slapped his thighs. He was standing in a strange way, leaning back against the car as if he were balancing himself. He wasn't tall, only an inch or so taller than she would be if she came down to him. Connie liked the way he was dressed, which was the way all of them dressed: tight faded jeans stuffed into black, scuffed boots, a belt that pulled his waist in and showed how lean he was, and a white pullover shirt that was a little soiled and showed the hard small muscles of his arms and shoulders. He looked as if he probably did hard work, lifting and carrying things. Even his neck looked muscular. And his face was a familiar face, somehow: the jaw and chin and cheeks slightly darkened, because he hadn't shaved for a day or two, and the nose long and hawklike, sniffing as if she were a treat he was going to gobble up and it was all a joke.

"Connie, you ain't telling the truth. This is your day set aside for a ride with me and you know it," he said, still laughing. The way he straightened and recovered from his fit of laughing showed that it had been all fake.

"How do you know what my name is?" she said suspiciously.

"It's Connie."

"Maybe and maybe not."

"I know my Connie," he said, wagging his finger. Now she remembered him even better, back at the restaurant, and her cheeks warmed at the thought of how she sucked in her breath just at the moment she passed him—how she must have looked at him. And he had remembered her. "Ellie and I come out here especially for you," he said. "Ellie can sit in back. How about it?"

"Where?"

"Where what?"

"Where're we going?"

He looked at her. He took off the sunglasses and she saw how pale the skin around his eyes was, like holes that were not in shadow but instead in light. His eyes were like chips of broken glass that catch the light in an amiable way. He smiled. It was as if the idea of going for a ride somewhere, to some place, was a new idea to him.

"Just for a ride, Connie sweetheart."

"I never said my name was Connie," she said.

"But I know what it is. I know your name and all about you, lots of things," Arnold Friend said. He had not moved yet but stood still leaning back against the side of his jalopy. "I took a special interest in you, such a pretty girl, and found out all about you like I know your parents and sister are gone somewheres and I know where and how long they're going to be gone, and I know who you were with last night, and your best girlfriend's name is Betty. Right?"

He spoke in a simple lilting voice, exactly as if he were reciting the words to a song. His smile assured her that everything was fine. In the car Ellie turned up the volume on his radio and did not bother to look around at them.

"Ellie can sit in the back seat," Arnold Friend said. He indicated his friend with a casual jerk to his chin, as if Ellie did not count and she should not bother with him.

"How'd you find out all that stuff?" Connie said.

"Listen: Betty Schultz and Tony Fitch and Jimmy Pettinger and Nancy Pettinger," he said, in a chant. "Raymond Stanley and Bob Hutter—"

"Do you know all those kids?"

"I know everybody."

"Look, you're kidding. You're not from around here."

"Sure."

"But—how come we never saw you before?"

"Sure you saw me before," he said. He looked down at his boots, as if he were a little offended. "You just don't remember."

"I guess I'd remember you," Connie said.

"Yeah?" He looked up at this, beaming. He was pleased. He began to mark time with the music from Ellie's radio, tapping his fists lightly together. Connie looked away from his smile to the car, which was painted so bright it almost hurt her eyes to look at it. She looked at that name, ARNOLD FRIEND. And up at the front fender was an expression that was familiar—MAN THE FLYING SAUCERS. It was an expression kids had used the year before, but didn't use this year. She looked at it for a while as if the words meant something to her that she did not yet know.

"What're you thinking about? Huh?" Arnold Friend demanded. "Not worried about your hair blowing around in the car, are you?"

"No."

"Think I maybe can't drive good?"

"How do I know?"

"You're a hard girl to handle. How come?" he said. "Don't you know I'm your friend? Didn't you see me put my sign in the air when you walked by?"

"What sign?"

"My sign." And he drew an X in the air, leaning out toward her. They were maybe ten feet apart. After his hand fell back to his side the X was still in the air, almost visible. Connie let the screen door close and stood perfectly still inside it, listening to the music from her radio and the boy's blend together. She stared at Arnold Friend. He stood there so stiffly relaxed, pretending to be relaxed, with one hand idly on the door handle as if he were keeping himself up that way and had no intention of ever moving again. She recognized most things about him, the tight jeans that showed his thighs and buttocks and the greasy leather boots and the tight shirt, and even that slippery friendly smile of his, that sleepy dreamy smile that all the boys used to get across ideas they didn't want to put into words. She recognized all this and also the singsong way he talked, slightly mocking, kidding, but serious and a little melancholy, and she recognized the way he tapped one fist against the other in homage of the perpetual music behind him. But all these things did not come together.

She said suddenly, "Hey, how old are you?"

His smile faded. She could see then that he wasn't a kid, he was much older—thirty, maybe more. At this knowledge her heart began to pound faster.

"That's a crazy thing to ask. Can'tcha see I'm your own age?"

"Like hell you are."

"Or maybe a coupla years older, I'm eighteen."

"Eighteen?" she said doubtfully.

He grinned to reassure her and lines appeared at the corners of his mouth. His teeth were big and white. He grinned so broadly his eyes became slits and she saw how thick the lashes were, thick and black as if painted with a black tarlike material. Then he seemed to become embarrassed, abruptly, and looked over his shoulder at Ellie. "*Him,* he's crazy," he said. "Ain't he a riot, he's a nut, a real character." Ellie was still listening to the music. His sunglasses told nothing about what he was thinking. He wore a bright orange shirt unbuttoned halfway to show his chest, which was a pale, bluish chest and not muscular like Arnold Friend's. His shirt collar was turned up all around and the very tips of the collar pointed out past his chin as if they were protecting him. He was pressing the transistor radio up against his ear and sat there in a kind of daze, right in the sun.

"He's kinda strange," Connie said.

"Hey, she says you're kinda strange! Kinda strange!" Arnold Friend cried. He pounded on the car to get Ellie's attention. Ellie turned for the first time and Connie saw with shock that he wasn't a kid either—he had a fair, hairless face, cheeks reddened slightly as if the veins grew too close to the surface of his skin, the face of a forty-year-old baby. Connie felt a wave of dizziness rise in her at this sight and she stared at him as if waiting for something to change the shock of the moment, make it all right again. Ellie's lips kept shaping words, mumbling along with the words blasting in his ear.

"Maybe you two better go away," Connie said faintly.

"What? How come?" Arnold Friend cried. "We come out here to take you for a ride. It's Sunday." He had the voice of the man on the radio now. It was the same voice, Connie thought. "Don'tcha know it's Sunday all day and honey, no matter who you were with last night today you're with Arnold Friend and don't you forget it!— Maybe you better step out here," he said, and this last was in a different voice. It was a little flatter, as if the heat was finally getting to him.

"No. I got things to do."

"Hey."

"You two better leave."

"We ain't leaving until you come with us."

"Like hell I am—"

"Connie, don't fool around with me. I mean, I mean, don't fool *around,*" he said, shaking his head. He laughed incredulously. He placed his sunglasses on top of his head, carefully, as if he were indeed wearing a wig, and brought the stems down behind his ears. Connie stared at him, another wave of dizziness and fear rising in her so that for a moment he wasn't even in focus but was just a blur, standing there against his gold car, and she had the idea that he had driven up the driveway all right but had come from nowhere before that and belonged nowhere and that everything about him and even about the music that was so familiar to her was only half real.

"If my father comes and sees you—"

"He ain't coming. He's at a barbecue."

"How do you know that?"

"Aunt Tillie's. Right now they're—uh—they're drinking. Sitting around," he said vaguely, squinting as if he were staring all the way to town and over to Aunt Tillie's back yard. Then the vision seemed to get clear and he nodded energetically. "Yeah. Sitting around. There's your sister in a blue dress, huh? And high heels, the poor sad bitch—nothing like you, sweetheart! And your mother's helping some fat woman with the corn, they're cleaning the corn—husking the corn—"

"What fat woman?" Connie cried.

"How do I know what fat woman, I don't know every goddam fat woman in the world!" Arnold laughed.

"Oh, that's Mrs. Hornby . . . Who invited her?" Connie said. She felt a little light-headed. Her breath was coming quickly.

"She's too fat. I don't like them fat. I like them the way you are, honey," he said, smiling sleepily at her. They stared at each other for a while, through the screen door. He said softly, "Now what you're going to do is this: you're going to come out that door. You're going to sit up front with me and Ellie's going to sit in the back, the hell with Ellie, right? This isn't Ellie's date. You're my date. I'm your lover, honey."

"What? You're crazy—"

"Yes, I'm your lover. You don't know what that is, but you will," he said. "I know that too. I know all about you. But look: it's real nice and you couldn't ask for nobody better than me, or more polite. I always keep my word. I'll tell you how it is, I'm always nice at first, the first time. I'll hold you so tight you won't think you have to try to get away or pretend anything because you'll know you can't. And I'll come inside you where it's all secret and you'll give in to me and you'll love me—"

"Shut up! You're crazy!" Connie said. She backed away from the door. She put her hands against her ears as if she'd heard something terrible, something not meant for her. "People don't talk like that, you're crazy," she muttered. Her heart was almost too big now for her chest and its pumping made sweat break out all over her. She looked out to see Arnold Friend pause and then take a step toward the porch lurching. He almost fell. But, like a clever drunken man, he managed to catch his balance. He wobbled in his high boots and grabbed hold of one of the porch posts.

"Honey?" he said. "You still listening?"

"Get the hell out of here!"

"Be nice, honey. Listen."

"I'm going to call the police—"

He wobbled again and out of the side of his mouth came a fast spat curse, an aside not meant for her to hear. But even this "Christ!" sounded forced. Then he began to smile again. She watched his smile come, awkward as if he were smiling from inside a mask. His whole face was a mask, she thought wildly, tanned down onto his throat but then running out as if he had plastered makeup on his face but had forgotten about his throat.

"Honey—? Listen, here's how it is. I always tell the truth and I promise you this: I ain't coming in that house after you."

"You better not! I'm going to call the police if you—if you don't—"

"Honey," he said, talking right through her voice, "honey, I'm not coming in there but you are coming out here. You know why?"

She was panting. The kitchen looked like a place she had never seen before, some room she had run inside but which wasn't good enough, wasn't going to help her. The kitchen window had never had a curtain, after three years, and there were dishes in the sink for her to do—probably—and if you ran your hand across the table you'd probably feel something sticky there.

"You listening, honey? Hey?"

"—going to call the police—"

"Soon as you touch the phone I don't need to keep my promise and can come inside. You won't want that."

She rushed forward and tried to lock the door. Her fingers were shaking. "But why lock it," Arnold Friendly said gently, talking right into her face. "It's just a screen door. It's just nothing." One of his boots was at a strange angle, as if his foot wasn't in it. It pointed out to the left, bent at the ankle. "I mean, anybody can break through a screen door and glass and wood and iron or anything else if he needs to, anybody at all and specially Arnold Friend. If the place got lit up with a fire honey you'd come runnin' out into my arms, right into my arms an' safe at home—like you knew I was your lover and'd stopped fooling around. I don't mind a nice shy girl but I don't like no fooling around." Part of those words were spoken with a slight

rhythmic lilt, and Connie somehow recognized them—the echo of a
song from last year, about a girl rushing into her boyfriend's arms
and coming home again—

Connie stood barefoot on the linoleum floor, staring at him.
"What do you want?" she whispered.

"I want you," he said.

"What?"

"Seen you that night and thought, that's the one, yes sir. I never
needed to look any more."

"But my father's coming back. He's coming to get me. I had to
wash my hair first—" She spoke in a dry, rapid voice, hardly raising
it for him to hear.

"No, your Daddy is not coming and yes, you had to wash your
hair and you washed it for me. It's nice and shining and all for me,
I thank you, sweetheart," he said, with a mock bow, but again he
almost lost his balance. He had to bend and adjust his boots. Evidently his feet did not go all the way down; the boots must have
been stuffed with something so that he would seem taller. Connie
stared out at him and behind him Ellie in the car, who seemed to be
looking off toward Connie's right into nothing. This Ellie said, pulling
the words out of the air one after another as if he were just discovering them, "You want me to pull out the phone?"

"Shut your mouth and keep it shut," Arnold Friend said, his face
red from bending over or maybe from embarrassment because Connie
had seen his boots. "This ain't none of your business."

"What—what are you doing? What do you want?" Connie said.
"If I call the police they'll get you, they'll arrest you—"

"Promise was not to come in unless you touch that phone, and
I'll keep that promise," he said. He resumed his erect position and
tried to force his shoulders back. He sounded like a hero in a movie,
declaring something important. He spoke too loudly and it was as if
he were speaking to someone behind Connie. "I ain't made plans for
coming in that house where I don't belong but just for you to come
out to me, the way you should. Don't you know who I am?"

"You're crazy," she whispered. She backed away from the door
but did not want to go into another part of the house, as if this
would give him permission to come through the door. "What do
you . . . You're crazy, you . . ."

"Huh? What're you saying, honey?"

Her eyes darted everywhere in the kitchen. She could not remember what it was, this room.

"This is how it is, honey: you come out and we'll drive away, have a nice ride. But if you don't come out we're gonna wait till your people come home and then they're all going to get it."

"You want that telephone pulled out?" Ellie said. He held the radio away from his ear and grimaced, as if without the radio the air was too much for him.

"I toldja shut up, Ellie," Arnold Friend said, "you're deaf, get a hearing aid, right? Fix yourself up. This little girl's no trouble and's gonna be nice to me, so Ellie keep to yourself, this ain't your date—right? Don't hem in on me. Don't hog. Don't crush. Don't bird dog. Don't trail me," he said in a rapid meaningless voice, as if he were running through all the expressions he'd learned but was no longer sure which one of them was in style, then rushing on to new ones, making them up with his eyes closed, "Don't crawl under my fence, don't squeeze in my chipmunk hole, don't sniff my glue, suck my popsicle, keep your own greasy fingers on yourself!" He shaded his eyes and peered in at Connie, who was backed against the kitchen table. "Don't mind him honey he's just a creep. He's a dope. Right? I'm the boy for you and like I said you come out here nice like a lady and give me your hand, and nobody else gets hurt, I mean, your nice old bald-headed daddy and your mummy and your sister in her high heels. Because listen: why bring them in this?"

"Leave me alone," Connie whispered.

"Hey, you know that old woman down the road, the one with the chickens and stuff—you know her?"

"She's dead!"

"Dead? What? You know her?" Arnold Friend said.

"She's dead—"

"Don't you like her?"

"She's dead—she's—she isn't here any more—"

"But don't you like her, I mean, you got something against her? Some grudge or something?" Then his voice dipped as if he were conscious of a rudeness. He touched the sunglasses perched on top of his head as if to make sure they were still there. "Now you be a good girl."

"What are you going to do?"

"Just two things, or maybe three," Arnold Friend said. "But I promise it won't last long and you'll like me the way you get to like people you're close to. You will. It's all over for you here, so come on out. You don't want your people in any trouble, do you?"

She turned and bumped against a chair or something, hurting her leg, but she ran into the back room and picked up the telephone. Something roared in her ear, a tiny roaring, and she was so sick with fear that she could do nothing but listen to it—the telephone was clammy and very heavy and her fingers groped down to the dial but were too weak to touch it. She began to scream into the phone, into the roaring. She cried out, she cried for her mother, she felt her breath start jerking back and forth in her lungs as if it were something Arnold Friend were stabbing her with again and again with no tenderness. A noisy sorrowful wailing rose all about her and she was locked inside it the way she was locked inside this house.

After a while she could hear again. She was sitting on the floor with her wet back against the wall.

Arnold Friend was saying from the door, "That's a good girl. Put the phone back."

She kicked the phone away from her.

"No, honey. Pick it up. Put it back right."

She picked it up and put it back. The dial tone stopped.

"That's a good girl. Now you come outside."

She was hollow with what had been fear, but what was now just an emptiness. All that screaming had blasted it out of her. She sat, one leg cramped under her, and deep inside her brain was something like a pinpoint of light that kept going and would not let her relax. She thought, I'm not going to see my mother again. She thought, I'm not going to sleep in my bed again. Her bright green blouse was all wet.

Arnold Friend said, in a gentle-loud voice that was like a stage voice, "The place where you came from ain't there any more, and where you had in mind to go is canceled out. This place you are now—inside your daddy's house—is nothing but a cardboard box I can knock down any time. You know that and always did know it. You hear me?"

She thought, I have got to think. I have to know what to do.

"We'll go out to a nice field, out in the country here where it smells so nice and it's sunny," Arnold Friend said. "I'll have my arms tight around you so you won't need to try to get away and I'll show you what love is like, what it does. The hell with this house! It looks solid all right," he said. He ran a fingernail down the screen and the noise did not make Connie shiver, as it would have the day before. "Now put your hand on your heart, honey. Feel that? That feels solid too, but we know better, be nice to me, be sweet like you can because what else is there for a girl like you but to be sweet and pretty and give in?—and get away before her people come back?"

She felt her pounding heart. Her hand seemed to enclose it. She thought for the first time in her life that it was nothing that was hers, that belonged to her, but just a pounding, living thing inside this body that wasn't really hers either.

"You don't want them to get hurt," Arnold Friend went on. "Now get up, honey. Get up all by yourself."

She stood.

"Now turn this way. That's right. Come over here to me—Ellie, put that away, didn't I tell you? You dope. You miserable creepy dope," Arnold Friend said. His words were not angry but only part of an incantation. The incantation was kindly. "Now come out through the kitchen to me honey, and let's see a smile, try it, you're a brave sweet little girl and now they're eating corn and hot dogs cooked to bursting over an outdoor fire, and they don't know one thing about you and never did and honey you're better than them because not a one of them would have done this for you."

Connie felt the linoleum under her feet; it was cool. She brushed her hair back out of her eyes. Arnold Friend let go of the post tentatively and opened his arms for her, his elbows pointing in toward each other and his wrists limp, to show that this was an embarrassed embrace and a little mocking, he didn't want to make her self-conscious.

She put out her hand against the screen. She watched herself push the door slowly open as if she were safe back somewhere in the other doorway, watching this body and this head of long hair moving out into the sunlight where Arnold Friend waited.

"My sweet little blue-eyed girl," he said, in a half-sung sigh that had nothing to do with her brown eyes but was taken up just the same by the vast sunlit reaches of the land behind him and on all sides of him, so much land that Connie had never seen before and did not recognize except to know that she was going to it.

SUSAN MINOT

Lust

Susan Minot (1956–   ), a native of suburban Boston, is a writer of short fiction. Her first book, *Monkeys* (1986), is a collection of interconnected stories that explore the relationships within an upper-middle-class New England family with seven children. The

following story is from her collection *Lust and Other Stories*
(1989).

Leo was from a long time ago, the first one I ever saw nude. In the
spring before the Hellmans filled their pool, we'd go down there in
the deep end, with baby oil, and like that. I met him the first month
away at boarding school. He had a halo from the campus light behind
him. I flipped.

Roger was fast. In his illegal car, we drove to the reservoir, the
radio blaring, talking fast, fast, fast. He was always going for my
zipper. He got kicked out sophomore year.

By the time the band got around to playing "Wild Horses," I had
tasted Bruce's tongue. We were clicking in the shadows on the other
side of the amplifier, out of Mrs. Donovan's line of vision. It tasted
like salt, with my neck bent back, because we had been dancing so
hard before.

Tim's line: "I'd like to see you in a bathing suit." I knew it was
his line when he said the exact same thing to Annie Hines.

You'd go on walks to get off campus. It was raining like hell, my
sweater as sopped as a wet sheep. Tim pinned me to a tree, the
woods light brown and dark brown, a white house half-hidden with
the lights already on. The water was as loud as a crowd hissing. He
made certain comments about my forehead, about my cheeks.

We started off sitting at one end of the couch and then our feet
were squished against the armrest and then he went over to turn off
the TV and came back after he had taken off his shirt and then we
slid onto the floor and he got up again to close the door, then came
back to me, a body waiting on the rug.

You'd try to wipe off the table or to do the dishes and Willie
would untuck your shirt and get his hands up under in front, standing behind you, making puffy noises in your ear.

He likes it when I wash my hair. He covers his face with it and
if I start to say something, he goes, "Shush."

For a long time, I had Philip on the brain. The less they noticed you, the more you got them on the brain.

My parents had no idea. Parents never really know what's going on, especially when you're away at school most of the time. If she met them, my mother might say, "Oliver seems nice" or "I like that one" without much of an opinion. If she didn't like them, "He's a funny fellow, isn't he?" or "Johnny's perfectly nice but a drink of water." My father was too shy to talk to them at all, unless they played sports and he'd ask them about that.

The sand was almost cold underneath because the sun was long gone. Eben piled a mound over my feet, patting around my ankles, the ghostly surf rumbling behind him in the dark. He was the first person I ever knew who died, later that summer, in a car crash. I thought about it for a long time.

"Come here," he says on the porch.
I go over to the hammock and he takes my wrist with two fingers.
"What?"
He kisses my palm then directs my hand to his fly.

Songs went with whichever boy it was. "Sugar Magnolia" was Tim, with the line "Rolling in the rushes/down by the riverside." With "Darkness Darkness," I'd picture Philip with his long hair. Hearing "Under my Thumb" there'd be the smell of Jamie's suede jacket.

We hid in the listening rooms during study hall. With a record cover over the door's window, the teacher on duty couldn't look in. I came out flushed and heady and back at the dorm was surprised how red my lips were in the mirror.

One weekend at Simon's brother's, we stayed inside all day with the shades down, in bed, then went out to Store 24 to get some ice cream. He stood at the magazine rack and read through *MAD* while I got butterscotch sauce, craving something sweet.

I could do some things well. Some things I was good at, like math or painting or even sports, but the second a boy put his arm around me, I forget about wanting to do anything else, which felt like a relief at first until it became like sinking into a muck.

It was different for a girl.

When we were little, the brothers next door tied up our ankles.
They held the door of the goat house and wouldn't let us out till we
showed them our underpants. Then they'd forget about being after
us and when we played whiffle ball, I'd be just as good as them.

Then it got to be different. Just because you have on a short skirt,
they yell from the cars, slowing down for a while and if you don't
look, they screech off and call you a bitch.

"What's the matter with me?" they say, point-blank.
Or else, "Why won't you go out with me? I'm not asking you to
get married," about to get mad.
Or it'd be, trying to be reasonable, in a regular voice, "Listen, I
just want to have a good time."
So I'd go because I couldn't think of something to say back that
wouldn't be obvious, and if you go out with them, you sort of have
to do something.

I sat between Mack and Eddie in the front seat of the pickup.
They were having a fight about something. I've a feeling about me.

Certain nights you'd feel a certain surrender, maybe if you'd had
wine. The surrender would be forgetting yourself and you'd put your
nose to his neck and feel like a squirrel, safe, at rest, in a restful
dream. But then you'd start to slip from that and the dark would
come in and there'd be a cave. You make out the dim shape of the
windows and feel yourself become a cave, filled absolutely with air,
or with a sadness that wouldn't stop.

Teenage years. You know just what you're doing and don't see
the things that start to get in the way.

Lots of boys, but never two at the same time. One was plenty to
keep you in a state. You'd start to see a boy and something would
rush over you like a fast storm cloud and you couldn't possibly think
of anyone else. Boys took it differently. Their eyes perked up at any
little number that walked by. You'd act like you weren't noticing.

The joke was that the school doctor gave out the pill like aspirin.
He didn't ask you anything. I was fifteen. We had a picture of him

in assembly, holding up an IUD shaped like a T. Most girls were on the pill, if anything, because they couldn't handle a diaphragm. I kept the dial in my top drawer like my mother and thought of her each time I tipped out the yellow tablets in the morning before chapel.

If they were too shy, I'd be more so. Andrew was nervous. We stayed up with his family album, sharing a pack of Old Golds. Before it got light, we turned on the TV. A man was explaining how to plant seedlings. His mouth jerked to the side in a tic. Andrew thought it was a riot and kept imitating him. I laughed to be polite. When we finally dozed off, he dared to put his arm around me but that was it.

You wait till they come to you. With half fright, half swagger, they stand one step down. They dare to touch the button on your coat then lose their nerve and quickly drop their hand so you—you'd do anything for them. You touch their cheek.

The girls sit around in the common room and talk about boys, smoking their heads off.

"What are you complaining about?" says Jill to me when we talk about problems.

"Yeah," says Giddy. "You always have a boyfriend."

I look at them and think, As if.

I thought the worst thing anyone could call you was a cock-teaser. So, if you flirted, you had to be prepared to go through with it. Sleeping with someone was perfectly normal once you had done it. You didn't really worry about it. But there were other problems. The problems had to do with something else entirely.

Mack was during the hottest summer ever recorded. We were renting a house on an island with all sorts of other people. No one slept during the heat wave, walking around the house with nothing on which we were used to because of the nude beach. In the living room, Eddie lay on top of a coffee table to cool off. Mack and I, with the bedroom door open for air, sweated and sweated all night.

"I can't take this," he said at 3 A.M. "I'm going for a swim." He and some guys down the hall went to the beach. The heat put me on edge. I sat on a cracked chest by the open window and smoked and smoked till I felt even worse, waiting for something—I guess for him to get back.

One was on a camping trip in Colorado. We zipped our sleeping bags together, the coyotes' hysterical chatter far away. Other couples murmured in other tents. Paul was up before sunrise, starting a fire for breakfast. He wasn't much of a talker in the daytime. At night, his hand leafed about in the hair at my neck.

There'd be times when you overdid it. You'd get carried away. All the next day, you'd be in a total fog, delirious, absent-minded, crossing the street and nearly getting run over.

The more girls a boy has, the better. He has a bright look, having reaped fruits, blooming. He stalks around, sure-shouldered, and you have the feeling he's got more in him, a fatter heart, more stories to tell. For a girl, with each boy it's like a petal gets plucked each time.

Then you start to get tired. You begin to feel diluted, like watered-down stew.

Oliver came skiing with us. We lolled by the fire after everyone had gone to bed. Each creak you'd think was someone coming downstairs. The silver-loop bracelet he gave me had been a present from his girlfriend before.

On vacations, we went skiing, or you'd go south if someone invited you. Some people had apartments in New York that their families hardly ever used. Or summer houses, or older sisters. We always managed to find some place to go.

We made the plan at coffee hour. Simon snuck out and met me at Main Gate after lights-out. We crept to the chapel and spent the night in the balcony. He tasted like onions from a submarine sandwich.

The boys are one of two ways: either they can't sit still or they don't move. In front of the TV, they won't budge. On weekends they play touch football while we sit on the sidelines, picking blades of grass to chew on, and watch. We're always watching them run around. We shiver in the stands, knocking our boots together to keep our toes warm and they whizz across the ice, chopping their sticks around the puck. When they're in the rink, they refuse to look at you, only eyeing each other beneath low helmets. You cheer for them but they don't look up, even if it's a face-off when nothing's happening, even if they're doing drills before any game has started at all.

Dancing under the pink tent, he bent down and whispered in my ear. We slipped away to the lawn on the other side of the hedge. Much later, as he was leaving the buffet with two plates of eggs and sausage, I saw the grass stains on the knees of his white pants.

Tim's was shaped like a banana, with a graceful curve to it. They're all different. Willie's like a bunch of walnuts when nothing was happening, another's as thin as a thin hot dog. But it's like faces; you're never really surprised.

Still, you're not sure what to expect.

I look into his face and he looks back. I look into his eyes and they look back at mine. Then they look down at my mouth so I look at his mouth, then back to his eyes then, backing up, at his whole face. I think, Who? Who are you? His head tilts to one side.

I say, "Who are you?"

"What do you mean?"

"Nothing."

I look at his eyes again, deeper. Can't tell who he is, what he thinks.

"What?" he says. I look at his mouth.

"I'm just wondering," I say and go wandering across his face. Study the chin line. It's shaped like a persimmon.

"Who are you? What are you thinking?"

He says, "What the hell are you talking about?"

Then they get mad after when you say enough is enough. After, when it's easier to explain that you don't want to. You wouldn't dream of saying that maybe you weren't really ready to in the first place.

Gentle Eddie. We waded into the sea, the waves round and plowing in, buffalo-headed, slapping our thighs. I put my arms around his freckled shoulders and he held me up, buoyed by the water, and rocked me like a sea shell.

I had no idea whose party it was, the apartment jam-packed, stepping over people in the hallway. The room with the music was

practically empty, the bare floor, me in red shoes. This fellow slides
onto one knee and takes me around the waist and we rock to jazzy
tunes with my toes pointing heavenward, and waltz and spin and
dip to "Smoke Gets in Your Eyes" or "I'll Love You Just for Now."
He puts his head to my chest, runs a sweeping hand down my inside
thigh and we go loose-limbed and sultry and as smooth as silk and
I stamp my red heels and he takes me into a swoon. I never saw him
again after that but I thought, I could have loved that one.

You wonder how long you can keep it up. You begin to feel like
you're showing through, like a bathroom window that only lets in
grey light, the kind you can't see out of.

They keep coming around. Johnny drives up at Easter vacation
from Baltimore and I let him in the kitchen with everyone sound
asleep. He has friends waiting in the car.
"What are you crazy? It's pouring out there," I say.
"It's okay," he says. "They understand."
So he gets some long kisses from me, against the refrigerator,
before he goes because I hate those girls who push away a boy's face
as if she were made out of Ivory soap, as if she's that much greater
than he is.

The note on my cubby told me to see the headmaster. I had no
idea for what. He had received complaints about my amorous displays
on the town green. It was Willie that spring. The headmaster told
me he didn't care what I did but that Casey Academy had a reputation
to uphold in the town. He lowered his glasses on his nose. "We've
got twenty acres of woods on this campus," he said. "Smooch with
your boyfriend there."

Everybody'd get weekend permissions for different places then
we'd all go to someone's house whose parents were away. Usually
there'd be more boys than girls. We raided the liquor closet and
smoked pot at the kitchen table and you'd never know who would
end up where, or with whom. There were always disasters. Ceci got
bombed and cracked her head open on the bannister and needed
stitches. Then there was the time Wendel Blair walked through the
picture window at the Lowes' and got slashed to ribbons.

He scared me. In bed, I didn't dare look at him. I lay back with
my eyes closed, luxuriating because he knew all sorts of expert angles,

his hands never fumbling, going over my whole body, pressing the hair up and off the back of my head, giving an extra hip shove, as if to say *There*. I parted my eyes slightly, keeping the screen of my lashes low because it was too much to look at him, his mouth loose and pink and parted, his eyes looking through my forehead, or kneeling up, looking through my throat. I was ashamed but couldn't look him in the eye.

At boarding school, everyone gets depressed. We go in and see the housemother, Mrs. Gunther. She got married when she was eighteen. Mr. Gunther was her high-school sweetheart, the only boyfriend she ever had.

"And you knew you wanted to marry him right off?" we ask her. She smiles and says, "Yes."
"They always want something from you," says Jill, complaining about her boyfriend.
"Yeah," says Giddy. "You always feel like you have to deliver something."
"You do," says Mrs. Gunther. "Babies."

You wonder about things feeling a little off-kilter. You begin to feel like a piece of pounded veal.

After sex, you curl up like a shrimp, something deep inside you ruined, slammed in a place that sickens at slamming, and slowly you fill up with an overwhelming sadness, an elusive gaping worry. You don't try to explain it, filled with the knowledge that it's nothing after all, everything filling up finally and absolutely with death. After the briskness of loving, loving stops. And you roll over with death stretched out alongside you like a feather boa, or a snake, light as air, and you . . . you don't even ask for anything or try to say something to him because it's obviously your own damn fault. You haven't been able to—to what? To open your heart. You open your legs but can't, or don't dare anymore, to open your heart.

It starts this way:
You stare into their eyes. They flash like all the stars are out. They look at you seriously, their eyes at a low burn and their hands no matter what starting off shy and with such a gentle touch that the only thing you can do is take that tenderness and let yourself be

swept away. When, with one attentive finger they tuck the hair behind your ear, you—

You do everything they want.

Then comes after. After when they don't look at you. They scratch their balls, stare at the ceiling. Or if they do turn, their gaze is altogether changed. They are surprised. They turn casually to look at you, distracted, and get a mild distracted surprise. You're gone. Their black look tells you that the girl they were fucking is not there anymore. You seem to have disappeared.

ELIZABETH BOWEN

The Demon Lover

Elizabeth Bowen (1899–1973), an Irish writer admired for her exploration of women's minds in her novels and short stories, was a long-standing contributor to the British *Tatler* magazine. Bowen's works include *The Death of the Heart* (1938), *Collected Impressions* (1950), *Afterthought: Pieces about Writing* (1962), *A Day in the Dark and Other Stories* (1965), and *The Collected Stories of Elizabeth Bowen* (1946), from which the following selection is taken.

Towards the end of her day in London Mrs. Drover went round to her shut-up house to look for several things she wanted to take away. Some belonged to herself, some to her family, who were by now used to their country life. It was late August; it had been a steamy, showery day: at the moment the trees down the pavement glittered in an escape of humid yellow afternoon sun. Against the next batch of clouds, already piling up ink-dark, broken chimneys and parapets stood out. In her once familiar street, as in any unused channel, an unfamiliar queerness had silted up; a cat wove itself in and out of railings, but no human eye watched Mrs. Drover's return. Shifting some parcels under her arm, she slowly forced round her latchkey in an unwilling lock, then gave the door, which had warped, a push with her knee. Dead air came out to meet her as she went in.

The staircase window having been boarded up, no light came down into the hall. But one door, she could just see, stood ajar, so she went quickly through into the room and unshuttered the big window in there. Now the prosaic woman, looking about her, was more perplexed than she knew by everything that she saw, by traces of her long former habit of life—the yellow smoke-stain up the white marble mantlepiece, the ring left by a vase on the top of the escritoire; the bruise in the wallpaper where, on the door being thrown open widely, the china handle had always hit the wall. The piano, having gone away to be stored, had left what looked like claw-marks on its part of the parquet. Though not much dust had seeped in, each object wore a film of another kind; and, the only ventilation being the chimney, the whole drawing-room smelled of the cold hearth. Mrs. Drover put down her parcels on the escritoire and left the room to proceed upstairs; the things she wanted were in a bedroom chest.

She had been anxious to see how the house was—the part-time caretaker she shared with some neighbours was away this week on his holiday, known to be not yet back. At the best of times he did not look in often, and she was never sure that she trusted him. There were some cracks in the structure, left by the last bombing, on which she was anxious to keep an eye. Not that one could do anything—

A shaft of refracted daylight now lay across the hall. She stopped dead and stared at the hall table—on this lay a letter addressed to her.

She thought first—then the caretaker *must* be back. All the same, who, seeing the house shuttered, would have dropped a letter in at the box? It was not a circular, it was not a bill. And the post office redirected, to the address in the country, everything for her that came through the post. The caretaker (even if he *were* back) did not know she was due in London today—her call here had been planned to be a surprise—so his negligence in the matter of this letter, leaving it to wait in the dusk and the dust, annoyed her. Annoyed, she picked up the letter, which bore no stamp. But it cannot be important, or they would know . . . She took the letter rapidly upstairs with her, without a stop to look at the writing till she reached what had been her bedroom, where she let in light. The room looked over the garden and other gardens: the sun had gone in; as the clouds sharpened and lowered, the trees and rank lawns seemed already to smoke with dark. Her reluctance to look again at the letter came from the fact that she felt intruded upon—and by someone contemptuous of her ways. However, in the tenseness preceding the fall of rain she read it: it was a few lines.

> Dear Kathleen: You will not have forgotten that today is our anniversary, and the day we said. The years have gone by at once slowly and fast. In

view of the fact that nothing has changed, I shall rely upon you to keep your promise. I was sorry to see you leave London, but was satisfied that you would be back in time. You may expect me, therefore, at the hour arranged. Until then . . .   K.

Mrs. Drover looked for the date: it was today's. She dropped the letter on to the bedsprings, then picked it up to see the writing again—her lips, beneath the remains of lipstick, beginning to go white. She felt so much the change in her own face that she went to the mirror, polished a clear patch in it and looked at once urgently and stealthily in. She was confronted by a woman of forty-four, with eyes starting out under a hatbrim that had been rather carelessly pulled down. She had not put on any more powder since she left the shop where she ate her solitary tea. The pearls her husband had given her on their marriage hung loose round her now rather thinner throat, slipping in the V of the pink wool jumper her sister knitted last autumn as they sat round the fire. Mrs. Drover's most normal expression was one of controlled worry, but of assent. Since the birth of the third of her little boys, attended by a quite serious illness, she had had an intermittent muscular flicker to the left of her mouth, but in spite of this she could always sustain a manner that was at once energetic and calm.

Turning from her own face as precipitately as she had gone to meet it, she went to the chest where the things were, unlocked it, threw up the lid and knelt to search. But as rain began to come crashing down she could not keep from looking over her shoulder at the stripped bed on which the letter lay. Behind the blanket of rain the clock of the church that still stood struck six—with rapidly heightening apprehension she counted each of the slow strokes. "The hour arranged . . . My God," she said, "*what* hour? How should I . . . ? After twenty-five years . . ."

The young girl talking to the soldier in the garden had not ever completely seen his face. It was dark; they were saying goodbye under a tree. Now and then—for it felt, from not seeing him at this intense moment, as though she had never seen him at all—she verified his presence for these few moments longer by putting out a hand, which he each time pressed, without very much kindness, and painfully, on to one of the breast buttons of his uniform. That cut of the button on the palm of her hand was, principally, what she was to carry away. This was so near the end of a leave from France that she could only wish him already gone. It was August 1916. Being not kissed, being drawn away from and looked at intimidated

Kathleen till she imagined spectral glitters in the place of his eyes. Turning away and looking back up the lawn she saw, through branches of trees, the drawing-room window light: she caught a breath for the moment when she could go running back there into the safe arms of her mother and sister, and cry: "What shall I do, what shall I do? He has gone."

Hearing her catch her breath, her fiancé said, without feeling: "Cold?"

"You're going away such a long way."

"Not so far as you think."

"I don't understand?"

"You don't have to," he said. "You will. You know what we said."

"But that was—suppose you—I mean, suppose."

"I shall be with you," he said, "sooner or later. You won't forget that. You need do nothing but wait."

Only a little more than a minute later she was free to run up the silent lawn. Looking in through the window at her mother and sister, who did not for the moment perceive her, she already felt that unnatural promise drive down between her and the rest of all human kind. No other way of having given herself could have made her feel so apart, lost and foresworn. She could not have plighted a more sinister troth.

Kathleen behaved well when, some months later, her fiancé was reported missing, presumed killed. Her family not only supported her but were able to praise her courage without stint because they could not regret, as a husband for her, the man they knew almost nothing about. They hoped she would, in a year or two, console herself—and had it been only a question of consolation things might have gone much straighter ahead. But her trouble, behind just a little grief, was a complete dislocation from everything. She did not reject other lovers, for these failed to appear: for years she failed to attract men—and with the approach of her thirties she became natural enough to share her family's anxiousness on this score. She began to put herself out, to wonder; and at thirty-two she was very greatly relieved to find herself being courted by William Drover. She married him, and the two of them settled down in this quiet, arboreal part of Kensington: in this house the years piled up, her children were born and they all lived till they were driven out by the bombs of the next war. Her movements as Mrs. Drover were circumscribed, and she dismissed any idea that they were still watched.

As things were—dead or living the letter-writer sent her only a threat. Unable, for some minutes, to go on kneeling with her back exposed to the empty room, Mrs. Drover rose from the chest to sit on an upright chair whose back was firmly against the wall. The desuetude of her former bedroom, her married London home's whole air of being a cracked cup from which memory, with its reassuring power, had either evaporated or leaked away, made a crisis—and at just this crisis the letter-writer had, knowledgeably, struck. The hollowness of the house this evening cancelled years on years of voices, habits and steps. Through the shut windows she only heard rain fall on the roofs around. To rally herself, she said she was in a mood— and for two or three seconds shutting her eyes, told herself that she had imagined the letter. But she opened them—there it lay on the bed.

On the supernatural side of the letter's entrance she was not permitting her mind to dwell. Who, in London, knew she meant to call at the house today? Evidently, however, this had been known. The caretaker, *had* he come back, had had no cause to expect her: he would have taken the letter in his pocket, to forward it, at his own time, through the post. There was no other sign that the caretaker had been in—but, if not? Letters dropped in at doors of deserted houses do not fly or walk to tables in halls. They do not sit on the dust of empty tables with the air of certainty that they will be found. There is needed some human hand—but nobody but the caretaker had a key. Under circumstances she did not care to consider, a house can be entered without a key. It was possible that she was not alone now. She might be being waited for, downstairs. Waited for—until when? Until "the hour arranged". At least that was not six o'clock: six has struck.

She rose from the chair and went over and locked the door.

The thing was, to get out. To fly? No, not that: she had to catch her train. As a woman whose utter dependability was the keystone of her family life she was not willing to return to the country, to her husband, her little boys and her sister, without the objects she had come up to fetch. Resuming work at the chest she set about making up a number of parcels in a rapid, fumbling-decisive way. These, with her shopping parcels, would be too much to carry; these meant a taxi—at the thought of the taxi her heart went up and her normal breathing resumed. I will ring up the taxi now; the taxi cannot come too soon: I shall hear the taxi out there running its engine, till I walk calmly down to it through the hall. I'll ring up—But no: the telephone is cut off . . . She tugged at a knot she had tied wrong.

The idea of flight . . . He was never kind to me, not really. I don't remember him kind at all. Mother said he never considered me. He was set on me, that was what it was—not love. Not love, not meaning a person well. What did he do, to make me promise like that? I can't remember—But she found that she could.

She remembered with such dreadful acuteness that the twenty-five years since then dissolved like smoke and she instinctively looked for the weal left by the button on the palm of her hand. She remembered not only all that he said and did but the complete suspension of *her* existence during that August week. I was not myself—they all told me so at the time. She remembered—but with one white burning blank as where acid was dropped on a photograph: *under no conditions* could she remember his face.

So, wherever he may be waiting, I shall not know him. You have no time to run from a face you do not expect.

The thing was to get to the taxi before any clock struck what could be the hour. She would slip down the street and round the side of the square to where the square gave on the main road. She would return in the taxi, safe, to her own door, and bring the solid driver into the house with her to pick up the parcels from room to room. The idea of the taxi driver made her decisive, bold: she unlocked her door, went to the top of the staircase and listened down.

She heard nothing—but while she was hearing nothing the *passé* air of the staircase was disturbed by a draught that travelled up to her face. It emanated from the basement: down there a door or window was being opened by someone who chose this moment to leave the house.

The rain had stopped; the pavements steamily shone as Mrs. Drover let herself out by inches from her own front door into the empty street. The unoccupied houses opposite continued to meet her look with their damaged stare. Making towards the thoroughfare and the taxi, she tried not to keep looking behind. Indeed, the silence was so intense—one of those creeks of London silence exaggerated this summer by the damage of war—that no tread could have gained on hers unheard. Where her street debouched on the square where people went on living, she grew conscious of, and checked, her unnatural pace. Across the open end of the square two buses impassively passed each other: women, a perambulator, cyclists, a man wheeling a barrow signalized, once again, the ordinary flow of life. At the square's most populous corner should be—and was—the short taxi rank. This evening, only one taxi—but this, although it presented its blank rump, appeared already to be alertly waiting for her. Indeed, without looking round the driver started his engine as she panted up from behind and put her hand on the door. As she did so, the

clock struck seven. The taxi faced the main road: to make the trip
back to her house it would have to turn—she had settled back on
the seat and the taxi *had* turned before she, surprised by its knowing
movement, recollected that she had not "said where". She leaned
forward to scratch at the glass panel that divided the driver's head
from her own.

The driver braked to what was almost a stop, turned round and
slid the glass panel back: the jolt of this flung Mrs. Drover forward
till her face was almost into the glass. Through the aperture driver
and passenger, not six inches between them, remained for an eternity
eye to eye. Mrs. Drover's mouth hung open for some seconds before
she could issue her first scream. After that she continued to scream
freely and to beat with her gloved hands on the glass all round as
the taxi, accelerating without mercy, made off with her into the
hinterland of deserted streets.

JULIET MITCHELL

Kinship Systems

Juliet Mitchell (1940–   ), born in New Zealand, is a psychoanalyst
who has written many groundbreaking feminist articles and books.
Among her works are *Woman's Estate* (1971), *Psychoanalysis and
Feminism* (1974), and *Women: The Longest Revolution* (1984), from
which the following selection is taken.

In an essay entitled 'On the Sexual Theories of Children', Freud
wrote:

If we could divest ourselves of our corporeal existence and could view
the things of this earth with a fresh eye as purely thinking beings, from
another planet for instance, nothing perhaps would strike our attention
more forcibly than the fact of the existence of two sexes among human
beings, who, though so much alike in other respects, yet mark the
difference between them with such obvious external signs.[1]

---

[1] Freud, *Standard Edition*, IX, 1908, pp. 211–12.

Feminists are also struck by the numerous human insignia that divide the sexes and they are, I hope, looking at the matter with a fresh eye. Men and women are like each other and are distinct from other animate or inanimate forms, yet whatever constitutes the difference between men and women is socially insisted upon in human societies and always elaborated. It is this social stress on the difference between men and women that is the subject of feminism.

I would suggest that what is important is that feminism in initiating a system of thought, transforms the ideological notion that there is a biological opposition between the sexes which determines social life, and asserts instead that there is a contradiction in the social relations between men and women. This contradiction—which is never static, as a biological opposition would be—shifts, moves and is moved and is therefore one force among others that effects social change and the movement of human history itself.

If we proceed to look at a social relationship between the sexes we can see that this has certain implications for the way we consider the question of the oppression of women, which is, after all, what feminism is about. Even the most progressive thought (both without and within feminism) tends to view women either in isolation from the men of their society or only in relation to the women of other societies. At its crudest, this argument will take the form of a European pointing out that though it is true that women in, say, Italy have a raw deal, women in America enjoy all the wealth-earning power glories of the so-called matriarchy. Somewhat more sophisticated research will engage in the type of cross-cultural argument that shows that Arapesh men are gentler and more feminine than the stereotype of women within advanced capitalist societies. In other words, this type of research tries to show that as there are no absolutes and all values are relative, there is no universal oppression of women.

But as feminists, what we should be talking about is not relativism but a social relationship. What we are therefore concerned with has two aspects: first we are concerned with the particular relationship between men and women within a particular society; and second, we have to draw from that particular relationship any universal features of it that we can. The cross-cultural work that has to be done is to discover the relationship between Arapesh men and women, American men and women, and then to discover what is common not to the men on their own or to the women on their own, or to a man and a woman of different societies, but what is common to the relationship between men and women itself.

Every society makes some distinction between the sexes. This does not mean that every society makes the biological male into a social man, or a biological female into a social woman. Among the Mohave, an American Indian group, for instance, a male in his own behaviour and in the regard of others, can be a social female or vice versa. Nor does it mean that all societies have only two social sexes; among the Navaho there are three gender groups, masculine, feminine, and the nadle, an intersex person who may or may not have intersex physiological morphology. Thus, all societies make a distinction between at least two social sexes and a distinction, which, with all the many variations, can be described as a distinction between social men and social women. Some societies mark the difference in extreme ways, others only marginally, but the distinction has always been there.

Across the world, throughout history and, indeed, within prehistory, woman's situation has varied enormously, but relative to the man of her society, woman has always held a very particular place. Since the distinction between the sexes among human beings is a social one (whatever its coincidence with biology), and human beings distinguish themselves from other primates and animals in general by their organisation of society, we can expect the social distinction between the sexes to find expression in ways that are relevant to this organisation.

Reducing the background of my argument about the contradiction in the social relationship between men and women which forms the basic premise of feminism, to its simple essentials, we should argue that mankind transforms nature both by its labour and by its social organisation. It is not that other primates do not have skills or know the use of primitive tools, that animal groups have no systems of communication—clearly they do—but the learned accumulation of both the techniques of labour and the complexities of language is a characteristic peculiar to humans. Humans—male and female—form not groups, but societies.

If then, both labour and social organisation and with it, language, are human characteristics, we would expect to find that the universal social distinction between the sexes takes up its place within these terms. This, indeed, would seem to be the case.

The division of labour by sex is a universal feature of human society. Whatever the degree of overlap, whatever the weight of labour carried by either men or women, a distinction is made between the work predominantly done by men and that predominantly done by women. In this case, it is not a question of which group's labour provides the chief source of a society's subsistence—in some, woman's labour contributes virtually nothing, in others practically the whole—the question is rather what we find to be a constant characteristic of women's work as it relates to men's. Here it would seem that in all societies, relative to their men, women undertake more child care. The Nuer man of East Africa may nurture the young more than a man or even an upper-class woman in England, he may cuddle and care for, but a Nuer woman still does that bit more than he does. Even if we exclude her physiological ability to breastfeed, the Nuer woman's social role as nurse is more extensive than that of the man of her tribe.

In a short note written for *The American Anthropologist,* Judith Brown speculated that the contribution women make to the subsistence of their society was determined by the compatibility of the main subsistence activity with child care. She wrote:

> I would like to suggest that the degree to which women contribute to the subsistence of a particular society, can be predicted with considerable accuracy from a knowledge of the major subsistence activity. It is determined by the compatibility of this pursuit with the demands of child care . . . Nowhere in the world is the rearing of children primarily the responsibility of men, and only in a few societies are women exempted from participation in the subsistence activities. If the economic role of women is to be maximised, their responsibilities in child care must be reduced or the economic activity must be such that it can be carried out concurrently with child care.[2]

Since we are interested in human society, and the social relationship between the sexes, what has to concern us here in the physiological and biological arguments that are bound to be made, is that the females of all species of animals, including humans, give birth, and females of all primates can give primary nourishment to their young. However, what should interest us, in fact, are not the similarities between humans and animals, but the differences. And, in this case, the relevant physiological fact is that the human infant is born prematurely; it is less well-developed at birth, and hence more dependent. This in turn means a reduced capacity for instinctual behaviour and an increased capacity for learning. It is not that women do have a 'natural animal instinct' for mother love that matters in this context—they may or may not do so—but that the social organ-

---

[2] Judith K. Brown, 'A Note on the Division of Labour by Sex', The *American Anthropologist,* 72, 1970, p. 1075.

isation of mankind requires women to be the group that provides for the human animal becoming a social being at this primary level. Mother love is a social requisite even where it coincides with a natural urge.

The sexual division of labour with its characteristic of more child care for women would seem to be a significant element in the organisation of human society. It can be either oppressive or non-oppressive. The second universal feature that I want to isolate in the structures of social organisation is the taboo on incest. Just as the universal division of labour according to sex is a universal form with a very various content—in some societies men farm and in others, women— so the taboo on incest is a universal proscription with a very diverse expression—some societies forbid marriage between brothers and sisters, others desire precisely that union for their ruling groups. Again, we have to remember that we're talking about a general social system. The taboo on incest seems to us so natural precisely because it is a key point at which mankind organises its own animal nature into a social nature.

A human kinship system, which is a system within which the taboo on incest is contained, organises human behaviour in a symbolic manner: 'Human kinship is above all a symbolic organisation of behaviour, a cultural construct upon the biological individuals involved.' Kinship involves the socialisation of sexuality into prescribed patterns and the naming of the kinsfolk with whom one may or may not have sexual relations. In other words, it involves both social interchange and language. Whom you call 'mother' may not be your biological mother, but your naming her such tells you your place in a social relationship to her.

The kinship system, like the sexual division of labour, utilises and institutes a social distinction between social men and women. Going back to Freud's quotation, we note that the visitor from outer space was struck (if we looked around us at the literature on the subject we may think that he was indeed struck dumb) by the elaborate effort that the human species has made to distinguish between two sexes which otherwise are so alike. Indeed, we might be right in thinking that this very inordinate desire to thus socially distinguish is one of the marks of human society. Primates such as chimpanzees and baboons, are characterised by a natural biological division between the sexes. As mankind starts to master nature (and we must remember that it is always man's own nature as well as external nature that is bound up in this question of the control of nature, that it is a process that has not only gone on throughout prehistory and all recorded history but is still very much going on and will always go on), it would seem that a natural division between the sexes, such as the primates know, would gradually be overcome. Instead, we find that far from being overcome, it is forcefully redefined in social terms—no primates distinguish between the sexes as assiduously as humans do. In the gap between our hypothetical expectation of mankind's control of its own nature, and hence what we would expect to be a gradual social elimination of natural differences and what, in fact, we do, which is to reinforce sexual differences—lies the question to which we have to address ourselves.

The social behaviour of primates is one of reciprocity: feed and be fed, protect and be protected, produce survival and survive by reproduction. It would also seem that in their most residual elements, the two features of human life that distinguish it from the lives of other primates and, in addition to this, are also universal features of human society—the social divisions of labour by sex and the kinship system—are also reciprocal relationships. In fact, they could be defined as systems set up to ensure reciprocity. The anthropologist Claude Lévi-Strauss suggests that the sexual division of labour is an artificial device whereby the two sexes, who in their human ability to labour could be so alike, are yet kept distinct and hence, mutually dependent. In proposing this, Lévi-Strauss is extending the work of Marcel Mauss on the significance of the gift. Mauss defines the gift as the first form of social contract—if you give a gift it is expected that you will at some point be given something in return. According to Lévi-Strauss, what else is the kinship system but a complex giving of people to each other in the understanding that one day you will be given someone in return? At first sight, then, it would seem that human kinship and the sexual division of labour reinterpret at a social level the natural reciprocity of primate groups. But do they?

Reciprocal relations are dual relationships—give and take/take and give; but social relations cannot be dual relations because a dual relation is a closed system—a happy or vicious circle. Any social relationship must have as a minimum a third element and a fourth which gives meaning to the third: the gift and the significance of a gift. It is this meaning that transforms a piece of meat exchanged between primates to a shell necklace exchanged between humans— the one is reciprocal survival, the other symbolic of social relations. For two sounds to move from animal communication to become language, a third and fourth term must intervene: the space between the words and the meaning it thus gives to their relationship.

Because of this, it seems that, contrary to most anthropology that has been concerned with explaining the position of women, the key event that marks the humanisation of the primate is kinship and its attendant event language, and that the sexual division of labour is not causal but consequent upon this. In other words, where, for instance, Engels in *The Origin of the Family, Private Property and the State* argues that a natural division of labour becomes a social division of labour which becomes oppressive only with the accumulation of wealth and, hence, property, I think we should see that kinship and language already structure human beings into socially different places before you have any massive accumulation of wealth. Or, to put it schematically, instead of a theory that goes as follows: the natural division of labour among the primates becomes the social-sexual division among humans which becomes organised oppressively by kinship and then by class society, my suggestion goes as follows: the natural division of labour among primates is first transformed by human kinship and language which for its functioning sets up its social human division of labour by sexes. This may seem a pointless quibble—and after all, how can anyone tell whether the egg or chicken came first—but, in fact, it is not an argument about a chronological priority of events, but about the structural place of women's oppression.

Kinship organises sexuality in such a way that it prescribes social relations. To do this it exchanges people from one group to another and sometimes within a group. As a system it doesn't matter who is exchanged, and, doubtless, a complex anthropology of any given society would find within it that various categories of people are being exchanged. However, what we are looking for within kinship systems, just as it is what we are looking for in class society, is both what is the main social relationship and what is the principal system of organisation? It would seem that whatever other exchanges go on, women are always exchanged between men, thus though it may well be that there are some societies in which some women exchange some men, there are none in which women are not exchanged predominantly by men. Clearly the particular conditions of any kinship group's material base for survival will affect the form of kinship or the form of family organisation, that is to say whether it is agricultural, pastoral, or so on. Later, of course, the form of family will also be determined by class structures. But the other aspect of a material base will also be determinate; that base is the reproduction of human life. Mankind transforms external nature for the production of the needs of life and transforms its own nature, not for the reproduction of the species, but for the reproduction of society. In exchanging women, humans transform the primate ability to continue the species and give a social form to the reproduction of human society. In exchanging women in a way that ensures the reproduction of the society, the sexual division of labour that ties women to child care in a particular social manner is instituted.

Exactly at which point these conditions become oppressive of women is hard to determine. Engels' thesis would suggest that, while labour (as he sees it, the male-dominated sphere) was primitive, it had no more importance than the reproduction of people (the female-dominated sphere), and that hence the sexes occupied equilateral positions. But behind this analysis (and despite its intentions) there seems to me to be a biological determinism—that is to say, that because women give birth they got left behind when labour and production, which determine social change, leaped ahead. At the very least, the exchange of women (itself possibly a determinate system within the various exchanges of kinship) was a precondition for women's oppression. I think it may be more than a precondition. It made their productive labour dependent on their ascribed social functions as mothers, nurses and educators and those functions were already constituted in their 'future': they were subordinate functions.

The question of matrilineal or patrilineal societies—inheritance down the mother's line or down the father's line—is likewise a vexed one. Because of the role of the mother's brother, even where the line of descent is traced through women (matrilineality), women as re-producers are exchanged between men. But in that the exchange is only one exchange among many and in that the role of the mother's brother is only one aspect even of this situation—the husband will probably come to live in the wife's place of residence for instance, he may even be given some gift as recognition of his move of social and geographical location (the male equivalent of bride-price)—then the woman's situation is potentially less oppressive. No more than are class societies uniformly exploitative are kinship systems uniformly oppressive.

What I'm suggesting, however, is that we have a situation which is doubly determined. The internal movement of kinship systems is determined by the nature of the exchange of women. But the relationship *between* the kinship organisation and the economic mode of production of the larger society and the eventual subordination of kinship to class means that class determines the particular form of kinship. There is a contradiction *within* kinship between men and women whose determining moment is the exchange of women, and there is a contradiction *between* kinship systems and the mode of production.

I'm suggesting that the exchange of women always determines the nature of the kinship group from within, but this is not the same as saying that this particular exchange is always dominant. In matrilineal, matrilocal tribes it would not seem to be dominant and this would make the position of women very different from that within patrilineal societies.

The woman who is exchanged is the promise of the next generation—no one wants to receive or, therefore, give, an infertile woman. In the kinship system heterosexuality is assured as the dominant mode and in the exchange of women, women become confined not to the species, as is often argued, but to the social task of reproduction—to mankind's transformation and humanisation of its own nature.

At first sight, there is nothing in itself oppressive about this situation, nor, of course, is it an exclusive one—women do other things than get exchanged. But it is in the interlocking of this determinate aspect of kinship (which in most societies which are, after all, patrilineal ones, is also the dominant one) and the sexual division of labour that I think we have to start asking questions about women's oppression. If in her note in *The American Anthropologist* Judith Brown is correct and we can gauge the degree of women's contribution to the subsistence economy by the extent to which women's work is compatible with child care, then we can see that women's contribution to production is determined by their place in the system of the reproduction of human beings. As the level of production dominates over that of reproduction in society as a whole, we can see that women's ability to produce being dominated by their having to reproduce has very serious consequences. In other words, it is not only, as Engels claims, that as production gets more advanced, class societies come to dominate over kinship groups and women, who are bound to the kinship family, become oppressed. It would seem that in the pre-class intersection of the kinship exchange system and the sexual division of labour (the system which still continues), as the people whose ability to produce is determined by the demand to reproduce social human beings, women must hold a subordinate position to men whose ability to reproduce not themselves but the other material conditions of their society (such as the reproduction of capital), depends on the social demand for them to produce those material goods in the first place.

Thus it is not just a question of class society—the dominance of production over reproduction—coming to dominate over the organisation of the society by kinship (and thus men coming to dominate over women) but rather that within the very system of kinship and its implications for the division of labour the conditions of men's domination over women are instituted.

What implications does this have for feminism? I want to end not by answering this question—because it's too big a question—but by giving two illustrations that might help direct the way in which we should look for answers. The first illustration I've borrowed from an observation I heard an American anthropologist, Norma Diamond, make recently about the Chinese communes. On her visit to the Chinese communes, she noticed that despite egalitarian job possibilities, communal, domestic and child-care facilities and a political policy of sexual equality, women in the communes rarely held positions with as high a status attached to them as did the men. Being a feminist, and a good scholar, she asked two questions: 'Why not?' and 'What particular characteristics did the few women who had managed to get important positions have in common?' To cut a long story short, she found that as a result of the Chinese policy of not only eradicating faults in social practices but also of building on social strengths, many communes were based on old pre-liberation kinship groups. The evil practices, whereby the father of the family was absolute head often with rights of life and death over the rest of the family, whereby the older generation oppress the younger, whereby women were literally chattels without any rights at all, problems of inheritance, and so on, were all absolutely removed, and most of the social reforms that feminists in the west craved for were instituted. But the seemingly harmless residual organisation of kinship was retained. Communes often had old kin names, and the old kin groups had been patrilocal, that is to say, a woman moved to her husband's place of residence on marriage. This practice continued in the communes. Now the women who had high status positions were married women who had, for some reason, stayed in their original commune—their commune of origin. For example, they had married youths who had come out from the cities during the Cultural Revolution. Other women were either unmarried and therefore likely to leave their commune of origin or had come to the commune on marriage. In both cases, they had not the same positions of power—in one case because they were going to leave and in the other case because they had just arrived and had not the well-established influential ties. In other words, an apparently harmless means of social organisation, invisible unless one looked at it, had quite serious consequences for women.

The more frivolous illustration comes from our own type of society. It exemplifies how kinship still operates even if concealed beneath other complex ideologies and other forms of organisation. The daughter of the Queen of England married a commoner. Her father, who himself was not the king, gave her away to her husband, to whose place of residence she then removed. Princess Anne, as she herself said, is an 'old-fashioned' girl and she embellished the proceedings by promising to honour and obey her husband.

But even without the 'extras' of a patriarchal religious ceremony, the exchange of women and all its consequences still goes on in our society. It has, I think, important implications not only for women's subordination to men in the family but for the unequal sexual division at the place of work. Feminism needs to bring the unseen structures of kinship into the light of day.

T W O

Becoming a Person

He who desires but acts not, breeds pestilence.

William Blake

The sad truth is that most evil is done by people who never make up
their minds to be either good or evil.

Hannah Arendt

"To thine own self be true, and it must follow, as the night the day,
thou canst not then be false to any man." So says Polonius in
Shakespeare's *Hamlet.* The advice comes from a meddling fool, but
it is nonetheless true. How many times have you, in your dealings
with others, found it hard to be true to yourself? How many times
have you discovered that in being false to others you denied an
important part of yourself?

We all have such moments, points in time when we ask one of
life's most difficult questions: "Who am I?" Though the question can
never be answered with absolute certainty, it nonetheless bears examination and reexamination. One is reminded of the French writer
Albert Camus's ideas about Sisyphus, the character in Greek legend
who endlessly rolled his rock out of the pit only to have it fall back
on him each time he got it near the edge. Somehow, Camus thought,
the very rolling of that rock gave meaning to Sisyphus's existence.
So too, the repeated asking of the question "Who am I?" may help
us see life as a continual process of *becoming,* an ongoing search for
awareness of who we are.

Although we may never fully "know" ourselves, we can learn
much about our inner being by closely examining how we behave,
especially in those contexts where ethical choices must be made.
Several such contexts are discussed in this section. In her essay
"Uncivil Rights—The Cultural Rules of Anger," Carol Tavris explores
the reasons that lead us to utter words that we would sometimes
wish to take back. In "White Lies," Sissela Bok shows how seemingly
innocent manipulation of the truth "for good reasons" can lead to
habitual patterns of lying. Joseph H. Berke, in "So Will I Turn Her
Virtue into Pitch," examines the uncompromising hatred in the heart
of Shakespeare's malevolent character Iago, from the play *Othello.*

In these essays we can all see bits of ourselves. Almost all of us
will recognize that we have been tempted at times to allow our anger
at someone to deepen into irrational hatred. When this happens on

a larger, social level, the results can be catastrophic, as suggested in Eric Hoffer's essay, "The True Believer."

We can all see ourselves as well, and in a much more positive way, in Rollo May's "The Experience of Becoming a Person." Here the author asks, in essence, "In what ways are human beings different from animals?" May also helps distinguish between the self-assertion of a truly independent personality and the pathological rebelliousness of people who have never grown up emotionally. May's is perhaps the key essay in this section, for it suggests ways in which all human beings, despite the traumas and temptations of modern life, can meet their potential.

It is not only *man's* search for *himself*, but *woman's* search for *herself* that defines the journey of humanity. Several selections in this section are starting points for issues specific to women, among them Dorothy L. Sayers's "Are Women Human?" and Virginia Woolf's "Professions for Women." The final selection, the short story entitled "The Roundhouse," by Gayl Jones, may suggest to you some surprising possibilities for positive human interaction.

Keep a notebook or journal at hand as you read these essays. Jot down your honest responses, even if they are not "nice." You don't have to show what you have written to anyone, but you might be able to use your reactions later on, perhaps in writing assigned by your instructor. You might also find that, as a result of this exercise, you have come a little closer to knowing who you are.

CAROL TAVRIS

Uncivil Rights—The Cultural Rules of Anger

Carol Tavris (1944–   ) is a social psychologist who has written for *Psychology Today, Ms.,* and *Discover,* among other publications. She is the editor of *Everywoman's Emotional Well-Being: Heart and Mind, Body and Soul* (1986) and the author of *Anger: The Misunderstood Emotion* (1989), from which the following selection is taken.

The full potential of human fury cannot be reached until a friend of both parties tactfully intervenes.

> G. K. Chesterton[1]

The young wife leaves her house one afternoon to draw water from the local well. She saunters down the main street, chatting amiably with her neighbors, as her husband watches from their porch. On her return from the well, a stranger stops her and asks for a cup of water. She obliges, and in fact invites the man home for dinner. He accepts. The husband, wife, and guest spend a pleasant evening together, and eventually the husband puts the lamp out and retires to bed. The wife also retires to bed—with the guest. In the morning, the husband leaves early to bring back some breakfast for the household. Upon his return, he find his wife again making love with the visitor.

At what point in this sequence of events will the husband become angry or jealous? Is his anger inevitable? The answer, observes psychologist Ralph Hupka, depends on the tribe and culture he belongs to:

— A Pawnee Indian husband, a century ago, would, in fury, bewitch any man who dared to request a cup of water from his wife.

— An Ammassalik Eskimo husband who wants to be a proper host invites his guest to have sex with his wife; he signals his invitation by putting out the lamp. (The guest might feel angry if this

---

[1] G. K. Chesterton (1874–1936) was an English critic and author of poetry, essays, novels, and short stories, known particularly for his detective series, *Father Brown.* (ED.)

invitation were not extended.) An Ammassalik husband would be angry, however, if he found his wife having sex with a man in circumstances other than the lamp game, such as that morning encore, or without a mutual agreement to exchange mates.

— A middle-class husband belonging to most modern American tribes would tend to get angry with any guest who, however courteously, tried to seduce his wife, and with the wife who, however hospitably, slept with their guest.

— A husband who belonged to the polyandrous Toda tribe of southern India at the turn of the century would find the whole sequence of events perfectly normal; nothing to raise a fuss about. The Todas practiced *mokhthoditi,* a custom that allowed both spouses to take lovers. If a man wanted to make love to a married woman, he first got her permission and then the permission of her husband or husbands; a yearly fee was negotiated; and then the wife was free to visit her new lover and the lover free to visit the wife at her home. But a Toda husband and wife would undoubtedly be angry with any man who tried to establish an affair by sneaking around the husband's back (and not paying the proper fee).

People everywhere get angry, but they get angry in the service of their culture's rules. Sometimes those rules are explicit ("Thou shalt not covet thy neighbor's wife"); more often they are implicit, disguised in the countless daily actions performed because "That's the way we do things around here." These unstated rules are often not apparent until someone breaks them, and anger is the sign that someone has broken them. It announces that someone is not behaving as (you think) she or he *ought.* This "assertion of an ought" is, according to psychologist Joseph de Rivera, the one common and essential feature of anger in all its incarnations. "Whenever we are angry," he writes, "we somehow believe that we can influence the object of our anger. We assume that the other is responsible for his actions and ought to behave differently."

This "ought" quality suggests that a major role of anger is its policing function. Anger, with its power of forcefulness and its threat of retaliation, helps to regulate our everyday social relations: in family disputes, neighborly quarrels, business disagreements, wherever the official law is too cumbersome, inappropriate, or unavailable (which is most of the time). Psychologist James Averill observes that for most of Western history, it has been up to individuals to see to it that their rights were respected and justice seen to; in the absence of a formal judiciary, anger operates as a personal one.

Perhaps the best way to understand the policing power of anger is to step outside of our own complex environment, and observe the way anger works in small societies. Small societies are highly revealing, whether they are families, tribes, high-school marching bands, or the U.S. Congress. Members of such groups understand very well the importance of the rules that govern anger, because everyone has to get along with each other in the morning. Anger is society's servant, and you can see this in the day-to-day life of small tribes. They may seem exotic, but they are, close up, a mirror on ourselves.

THE JUDICIAL EMOTION

N!uhka, age seventeen, was furious. Her father had reminded her that she was getting on in years and that it was high time for her to marry. N!uhka, who was rebellious and vain, was uninterested in the eligible young men her father suggested, and at last, in the heat of argument, she cursed him aloud. He was shocked. *She* was shocked. So were all the neighbors and relations who had overheard her.

Now N!uhka was angry and also ashamed of her disrespectful outburst. She grabbed her blanket and stormed out of the camp to a lone tree some seventy yards away. There she sat, all day, covered in the blanket. This was not a trivial penance, since the temperature that day was 105 degrees Fahrenheit in the shade (without a blanket), but by the time she returned to camp her anger and embarrassment had subsided.

The !Kung hunter-gatherers of the Kalahari Desert are called "the harmless people" because of their renowned lack of aggression. This does not mean that they are free from the petty plagues of human life, such as jealousies, resentments, suspicions, and sulks. Teenagers disagree with their parents' wishes, relatives squabble about who owes what to whom, and husbands and wives bicker about marital matters. The difference is that the !Kung know that they must manage these emotions and dampen them down to tolerable levels, and that if they don't their very survival is endangered.

The !Kung are nomadic, foraging constantly for food, and their only insurance against hard times is each other. No individual can lay in a supply of frozen pizzas and beer in the event of famine and drought, and no individual could long survive on his or her own. Sharing is therefore the dominant value and obsession of their society. As one of their principal ethnographers, Elizabeth Marshall

Thomas, observed: "It has never happened that a Bushman [today they are called !Kung or !Kung-san] failed to share objects, food, or water with the other members of his band, for without very rigid co-operation Bushmen could not survive the famines and droughts that the Kalahari offers them." Under such conditions, any antisocial or angry outburst threatens the whole group; so it is to the !Kung interest to avoid direct physical confrontation or violence, and to be suspicious of individuals who cannot control their behavior or their tempers. "Their hold on life," says Thomas, "is too tenuous to permit quarreling among themselves."

The same structure of camp life that increases the chances of group solidarity and survival—lack of privacy, each hut close to the other huts, extended family nearby—also means that every flare-up and dispute is immediately available for public discussion and reso-lution. Such lack of privacy would be cause enough for anger in the West, where "It's none of your business" is an accepted refrain. Among the !Kung, everything is everyone's business. "Once a person attacks his victim he is like a fly that attacks an insect already caught in a spider's web," writes anthropologist Patricia Draper. "Immedi-ately both are caught. If the combatants forget the sticky web in the heat of their anger, the onlookers do not. Real anger frightens and sickens the !Kung, for it is so destructive of their web of relation-ships." Anyone who becomes angry will have the assistance ("inter-ference" to the West) of the entire tribe, if need be. Perhaps this is why, in nearly a year and a half of fieldwork, one anthropologist saw only four examples of overt discord and heard of only a few others. Another recorded only three serious disputes: one over possession of an animal that had been killed, another about a marital disagree-ment, and a third in which a mother raged at a curer who failed to attend her sick child.

Although the !Kung are not aggressive, they are expert at bick-ering and complaint. "The outsider wonders how the !Kung can stand to live with each other," says Patricia Draper. "In the early months of my own fieldwork I despaired of ever getting away from continual harassment." Some psychoanalytically inclined observers take this as evidence of the !Kung's "displaced" aggressive instinct, which, if not released physically (they say), takes this verbal outlet. But a closer look at the content of the bickering reveals two things about it: It has a distinct social purpose, and although it may seem to outsiders like a sign of anger it is really a ritual game, devoid of anger's heat.

After several months, Draper discovered that the key to !Kung bickering was its emphasis on dunning for food. What idle conversation about the weather and the economy is to Europeans, she noticed, reminders about food obligations were to the !Kung. In time she learned the "properly melodramatic disclaimers" that allowed her to join the game:

> You expect *me*, one lonely European, a stranger in this territory, living away from 'ny own kin, without even one spear or arrow or even a digging stick, and with no knowledge of the bush . . . you expect *me* to give *you* something to eat? You are a person whose hut is crammed full of good things to eat. Berries, billtong, sweet roots, stand shoulder high in your hut and you come to me saying you are hungry!

The !Kung visitor would be delighted with such a spirited reply (as would the inevitable onlookers), and once this exchange was completed, Draper and the !Kung could go on to talk about other things. But food-dunning jokes and complaints are important because they remind everyone of the responsibility to recirculate food and property. The have-nots press for their share; the haves are reminded that their fortune is only temporary.

I have found Draper's observations useful in understanding my own particular tribe, Eastern European Jews whose forebears came from the shtetls of Russia and Poland, and for whom ritual dunning has been a long tradition. Indeed, the rich curse repertoire of Yiddish makes the four-letter-word grunts of English a pale and gutless thing. As Barbara Myerhoff recorded in *Number Our Days*:

> *Jake*: In those days, everybody gave curses. You couldn't live without it. A woman there was on our street who could curse like Heifetz plays the violin. The things she would fix up for her enemies! 'May your teeth get mad and eat your head off.' 'May you inherit a hotel with one hundred rooms and be found dead in every one.' 'May you have ten sons and all your daughters-in-law hate you.' 'May all your teeth fall out but one, and that one has a cavity.' 'May your chickens lay eggs in your neighbor's house.' 'May the gypsies camp on your stomach and their bears do the *kazotskhi* in your liver.'
> *Basha*: This last one you are getting from Sholom Aleichem.
> *Jake*: And where do you think Sholom Aleichem learned it?

Today these curses are a fading talent (I think they require the original Yiddish), just as the ritual dunning is a mere shadow of its former self: "You don't call me any more"; "Write your Aunt Hannah a thank-you letter *today*"; "Do your fingers have leprosy that you can't pick up your socks?" But the curses and the dunning have their origin in survival needs as great as those for food in the African bush.

The repeated bickering reminded shtetl Jews of their social obligations to the family and the culture, emphasizing the importance of
staying in line and paying attention to the traditions that kept the
precarious group together. A visitor to such cultures is likely, as
Patricia Draper was among the !Kung, to feel under attack, at least
until he or she learns the rules and can play the game.

A BRIEF MADNESS

A culture's values and needs determine not only our everyday
angers but even when we may be allowed to "go crazy" with rage.
"Anger," wrote Horace some two thousand years ago, "is a brief
madness," succinctly noting the affinity between "mad" and "angry."
The match is psychological as well as linguistic, because in many
cultures (including our own) an enraged individual and an insane
one are both regarded as being out of control, unable to take responsibility for their actions. Yet other cultures, such as the Eskimo,
distinguish the two conditions: A person who is legitimately insane
cannot be expected to control himself, but one who is merely angry
can and must control himself. What distinguishes us from the Eskimo, aside from the weather? What role does the *belief* in the
similarity between rage and madness play?

— One evening, apparently out of the blue, a young Malay man
  armed himself with traditional weapons, the parang and the kris,
  and embarked on a killing spree. By the time his rampage was
  over, several hours later, he had accosted customers in three local
  coffeehouses and murdered five innocent men. His friends were
  surprised that the young man had "run amok"; he seemed so
  polite and well mannered.
— In San Francisco in 1979, a civil servant named Dan White
  resigned his seat on the city's Board of Supervisors. Shortly thereafter he changed his mind, but he was too late: Mayor George
  Moscone had decided to give the job to someone else. White took
  his snubnosed revolver, climbed in through the window of City
  Hall (so the metal detectors wouldn't reveal his gun), and pumped
  nine bullets into Moscone and supervisor Harvey Milk, who had
  been one of White's outspoken opponents (and who was a homo-
  sexual whom White disliked). In what the press played up as the
  "Twinkie defense," White's lawyers argued that his excessive
  consumption of junk food had caused his "diminished mental
  capacity," leaving him unable to premeditate anything, much less
  murder. The jury agreed. White was convicted of voluntary man-

slaughter and given a maximum sentence of seven years and eight months in jail. (Twenty months after his release, he committed suicide.)

— The Gururumba tribesman was behaving strangely. He had suddenly taken to looting his neighbors' huts, stealing food and objects, and one afternoon his kinsmen found him hiding behind a tree, shooting arrows at passersby. He was clearly suffering a mental aberration, the tribe agreed, which they diagnosed as "being a wild pig."

— In New York in 1980, Jean Harris shot and killed Herman Tarnower, her lover of fourteen years, in what the prosecution called a "jealous rage" and the defense a "tragic accident." Tarnower was found with four bullets in his body; Harris said she was trying to kill herself, not him. The jury did not believe her. She was convicted of intentional murder and given a minimum sentence of fifteen years in prison.

Running amok, being a wild pig, and temporary insanity are, within their respective tribes, legitimate signs of "a brief madness." These rages are, however, regarded as something other than psychosis, true mental illness, or other sorts of "long" madnesses, and they are often treated differently. Certainly some individuals who suffer organic abnormalities or psychoses that produce rage attacks can properly be diagnosed as insane; they do not, for one thing, revert to normalcy after a violent episode. And there are other individuals, such as the disturbed loners who have tried to assassinate or succeeded in assassinating our presidents and heroes, whose aggressive acts have little to do with anger and more to do with fantasies of power and fame. But most cases of "temporary insanity" caused apparently by rage, those heralded cases that capture the public eye, can be explained better in terms of their social causes than their organic ones, junk food to the contrary notwithstanding.

Start with "running amok," a phenomenon that originally referred to violent, often homicidal attacks among the indigenous peoples of the Malay Archipelago. Most people assume that the acts committed while a person is in such a state are unconscious, random, and without purpose. The *pengamok* (those who run amok) themselves think so, and so do their neighbors and relatives. But a closer look suggests otherwise. The frequency of this supposedly impulsive, uncontrollable act declined precipitately when the cultural response to it shifted from supportive tolerance to vicious punishment (at one point in Malay history, the *pengamok* were drawn and quartered).

Further, the objects of amok attacks are not random victims: Almost all of them are known to the amok and have been continuing sources of provocation. In one study that compared true *pengamok* to a control group of psychotics, the victims of the *pengamok* proved to be "rational" choices: a wife suspected of infidelity, a quarrelsome neighbor, an oppressive religion teacher. The Malay who killed the five customers of coffeehouses had carefully assured that his victims were Chinese: As his record showed, he had harbored anger at the Chinese who had killed some Malays several years before. The so-called psychotic symptoms of the *pengamok* vanish within a month or two of the episode, which is hardly the case for true psychotics.

Traditionally, the Malay are expected to be courteous and self-effacing, never to reprimand each other, and never to strive for success at the expense of another. Other cultures that have invaded the Malay Archipelago, such as the Chinese, have had rather more aggressive values, and therefore interpreted Malay behavior as signs of weakness and inferiority—which they promptly exploited. "Running amok," whether on an individual level or at a group level of rebellion, is a brilliant solution for Malay conflict: It allows the Malay to remain true to his cultural values while attacking the sources of his oppression and rage.

"Being a wild pig" is to the Gururumba what "running amok" is to the Malay. The Malay think that amok results from witchcraft or possession by evil spirits; the Gururumba think it comes from being bitten by a ghost. But wild pigs, like the *pengamok,* are not randomly distributed throughout the society. The only people who seem to get bitten, for example, are men between the ages of twenty-five and thirty-five, which is an especially stressful decade for the Gururumba male. He must abandon his youthful irresponsibility, take a wife, and assume a sudden burden of social obligations to the group. Success or failure at meeting these obligations will reflect not only on him, but on his clan.

Anthropologist P. L. Newman thinks that "being a wild pig" is a way of calling attention to the difficulties of shouldering these obligations. The victim of ghost bite, by his wild behavior, thereby announces to the tightly knit group that he wants to do something that his kinsmen might otherwise prohibit: change wives, move somewhere else, give up a particular responsibility. In the same way that a vociferous display of anger in our own culture finally convinces the recipient that the angry person *means* it, wild-pigdom convinces the Gururumba that the victim really is having a hard time and that something must be done. (Some Gururumba, consciously or not, put themselves in places where they are likely to be bitten by a ghost—a remote part of the forest or a gravesite.)

The Gururumba react with tolerance to a man who is being a wild pig. They are sympathetic to him, because they believe he is not responsible for his actions; they expect the seizure to run its course in a few days, like the flu. While the man is in this state they gently direct his "craziness": They leave food and little things for him to steal, and they don't let him hurt anyone seriously. The victim retreats to the forest for a few days on his own—not unlike our paid vacations—and if he returns still in a "wild" state, the tribesmen set up a ritual to cure him. They "capture" him and treat him as if he *were* a pig that had gone wild: They hold him over a smoking fire and rub him all over with pig fat. (This, the anthropologists assure us, is not as bad as it sounds.) A prominent person kills a real pig in the victim's name, and the victim is given a feast of pig meat and roots. Most important, however, are the reassessment and usually reduction of his obligations that occur after this ritual. That component of the procedure seems most likely to prevent remissions.

The Malay and Gururumba examples suggest that acceptable varieties of "temporary insanity" occur in cultures in which two equally powerful value systems conflict. In Western culture, a powerful taboo exists against intentional acts of violence, especially murder; yet the culture often counteracts that taboo with as great a passion for revenge, retribution, and defense of moral values. In America, when "an eye for an eye" meets "turn the other cheek"; when "thou shalt not kill" meets "thou shalt not commit adultery," temporary insanity is a temporary solution. This is a legal loophole in a Gordian knot: the law allows individuals to become angry enough to kill, but only if they kill in the service of society's dominant values, and only if they kill without premeditation or self-control—"in the heat of passion."

This is one reason, I think, that Dan White got off with such a light sentence for murdering two men and Jean Harris got a severe sentence for killing one. White and Harris both had had time, before their actions, to think about what they were doing. Both packed up their little guns at home and sought their victims. Both believed that they had been cruelly and unfairly treated by their victims. But Dan White's lawyers played on his "diminished mental capacity" to the hilt, bringing in plenty of psychiatrists to testify to his unstable mental condition. "The killing was done out of passion," the foreman of the jury later said, "given the stress he was under." Jean Harris's defense emphasized the "tragic accident" explanation, and called on no psychiatrists to exonerate her behavior or describe the stress she was under. The only person to describe her mental state was Harris herself, and that was her undoing; for the anger she expressed, even there on the witness stand, was cold and deliberate. She gave no evidence of having been enraged at Tarnower; angry with the "other woman," yes, but with the lover who left her, no. Had she done so, had she used the enormous sympathy usually extended to scorned lovers, had she argued that she had committed a crime of passion, I believe the outcome would have been different. But she did not. She took responsibility for her emotions. And so the jury had to find her guilty of her actions.

Although people frequently deplore the association between anger and violence in the United States, our customs and our laws (to say nothing of the easy availability of handguns) encourage the link. Why do we resist the idea that we can control our emotions, that feeling angry need not inevitably cause us to behave violently? Seneca the Stoic[2] had a good idea of the answer. We refuse to follow his philosophy of self-restraint, he suggested, "Because we are in love with our vices; we uphold them and prefer to make excuses for them rather than shake them off." And why do we make excuses for them? *Because they excuse us.*

In a timely update of Seneca's observation, James Averill notices that we do not abdicate responsibility for all of our emotions, just the negative ones. No one apologizes for being swept away by a tidal wave of kindness and donating five thousand dollars to a worthy cause. A bystander who intervenes to prevent an assault or mugging is unlikely to apologize for acting courageously. We want credit for our noble emotions and tolerance for our negative ones; and losing one's temper, "misplacing" it in a fleeting hour of insanity, is the apology that begs such tolerance. While anger serves our private uses, it also makes our social excuses.

MANNERS, EMOTIONS, AND THE AMERICAN WAY

The class was basic English for foreign students, and an Arab student, during a spoken exercise, was describing a tradition of his home country. Something he said embarrassed a Japanese student in

---

[2] Lucius Annaeus Seneca (4 B.C.–A.D. 65) was a Roman statesman, author, and philosopher whose tragedies reflected the conflict between reason and passion. (ED.)

the front row, who reacted the proper Japanese way: He smiled. The Arab saw the smile and demanded to know what was so funny about Arab customs. The Japanese, who was now publicly humiliated as well as embarrassed, could reply only with a smile and, to his misfortune, he giggled to mask his shame. The Arab, who now likewise felt shamed, furiously hit the Japanese student before the teacher could intervene. Shame and anger had erupted in a flash, as each student dutifully obeyed the rules of his culture. Neither could imagine, of course, that his rules might not be universal.

Because a major function of anger is to maintain the social order, through its moralizing implications of how people "should" behave, it is predictable that when two social orders collide they would generate angry sparks. It is easiest to see this when the colliding cultures are foreign to each other, but we have plenty of such collisions within our society as well. For some groups in America, anger is an effective way to get your way; for others it is the last resort. (Some groups have to learn assertiveness training to deal with others.) You may find your attitudes about anger, and the rules you learned to govern it, in conflict with those of different groups. Often it is this conflict about anger rules, not the rules per se, that can stir up trouble.

Each of us is tied to a group—a minitribe, if you will—by virtue of our sex, status, race, and ethnicity, and with countless unconscious reactions we reveal those ties as surely as Eliza Doolittle did when she opened her mouth. Anthropologist Edward T. Hall speaks of the "deep biases and built-in blinders" that every culture confers on its members. You can observe them at work every time you hear someone grumble, "I'll never understand women," or, "Why can't he just say what he feels?" or, "The (Japanese) (Mexicans) (Irish) (etc.) are utterly inscrutable."

Hall, who lives in New Mexico, has long observed the clash that occurs between groups when deeply felt rules about the "correct" management of anger are broken. The Spanish are sensitive to the slightest suggestion of criticism, Hall explains. "Confrontations are therefore to be avoided at all costs." The resulting misunderstandings between Spanish- and Anglo-Americans, he says, would be amusing if they weren't so often tragic.

When Anglo-Americans are angry, they tend to proceed in stages from small steps to larger ones. First, they hint around ("Mort, are you sure that fence is on *your* side of the property line?"). Then they talk to neighbors and friends of Mort. If they get no results, they may talk directly, and calmly, to Mort ("Mort, can we discuss our fence problem?"). Next they will express anger directly to Mort ("Dammit, that fence is on my property"). Eventually, if they are angry enough, they will take the matter to the courts. And as a last resort, they may resort to violence—and burn the fence down.

These steps, from smallest to largest, seem natural, logical, and inevitable. Actually, they are not only not natural, they are not even very common, worldwide. In many societies, such as in Latin cultures and in the Middle East, the first step is . . . to do nothing. Think about it. Brood. This brooding may go on for weeks, months, or even years (some cultures have long memories). The second step is . . . to burn the fence down. Now that matters are back to square one, participants are ready for direct discussions, negotiations, lawyers, and intermediaries. But notice, says Hall, that the act of force, which is the last step to Anglos, signaling the failure of negotiation, is the start of the conversation to Hispanics.

A culture's rules of anger are not arbitrary; they evolve along with its history and structure. The Japanese practice of emotional restraint, for example, dates back many centuries, when all aspects of demeanor were carefully regulated: facial expressions, breathing, manner of sitting and standing, style of walking. Not only were all emotions— anger, grief, pain, even great happiness—to be suppressed in the presence of one's superiors, but also regulations specified that a person submit to any order with a pleasant smile and a properly happy tone of voice. At the time of the Samurai knights, these rules had considerable survival value, because a Samurai could legally execute anyone who he thought was not respectful enough. (You may notice the similarity to American blacks and to women, who likewise had to be careful to control anger in the presence of the white man.)

Even today in Japan, an individual who feels very angry is likely to show it by excessive politeness and a neutral expression instead of by furious words and signs. A Japanese who shows anger the Western way is admitting that he has lost control, and therefore lost face; he is thus at the extreme end of a negotiation or debate. In other cultures, though, showing anger may simply mark the *beginning* of an exchange, perhaps to show that the negotiator is serious; a man may lose face if he does *not* show anger when it is appropriate and "manly" for him to do so.

Psychotherapy, of course, takes place within a culture and is deeply embedded in cultural rules. Arthur Kleinman, himself both an anthropologist and psychiatrist, tells of a psychiatrist in south-central China who was treating a patient who had become depressed and anxious ever since her demanding mother-in-law had moved in. "She is your family member. It is your responsibility to care for an old mother-in-law," the Chinese psychiatrist said. "You must contain your anger. You know the old adage: 'Be deaf and dumb! Swallow the seeds of the bitter melon! Don't speak out!' "

I am not recommending that Americans learn to "swallow the seeds of the bitter melon"; in our society, most of us would choke on them. Cultural practices cannot be imported from society to society like so many bits of cheese, because they are part of a larger pattern of rules and relationships. Indeed, that is the reason we cannot avoid the anger we feel when someone breaks the rules that we have learned are the only civilized rules to follow. But we might emulate the Arapesh, who criticize the provocateur; or the Eskimo, who settle in for a good round of verbal dueling; or Mbuti, who have a good laugh, understanding as they do the healing power of humor. We might also retrieve the old-fashioned standard of manners, which is, as small tribes teach us, an organized system of anger management. The conventions of the U.S. Senate, for example—the ornate language, the rules of debate—regulate anger over disagreements into acceptable channels. A senator does not call his or her opposition a stupid blithering moron, for instance. He says, "My distinguished colleague from the great state of Blitzhorn, an otherwise fine and noble individual, is, in this rare moment, erring in judgment." The elaborate language that seems so comically deceptive to the rest of us is what keeps political conversation going without bloodshed and mayhem.

Good manners melt resentment because they maintain respect between the two disagreeing parties. Indeed, one of the basic principles of parliamentary law is courtesy, "respect for the rights of individuals and for the assembly itself." You don't have to join Congress to feel the effect of this principle at work. Someone steps on your toe, you feel angry, the person apologizes, your anger vanishes. Your toe may still hurt, but your dignity is intact. (A friend tells me he loudly shushed a talkative man sitting behind him at the movies, and immediately felt bad that he had expressed himself so angrily. After the show, the man touched him on the shoulder. "You were quite right to tell me to keep quiet," he said, "I was rude." "I could have kissed him," said my friend.)

Without rules for controlling anger, it can slip into emotional anarchy, lasting far longer than its original purposes require. Observe how friends and family react to someone undergoing a bitter divorce: They extend sympathy and a willing ear to the enraged spouse for a while, but eventually they expect the person to "shape up" and "get on with it." What these friends and relatives are doing is imposing unofficial rules of anger management. The victim may grouse and mutter about the loss of sympathy, but actually the friends and relatives are doing what any decent tribe would do: keeping anger in bounds after it has done its job and making sure the victim stays in the social circle. Well-meaning friends and therapists who encourage a vengeful spouse to ventilate rage for years are doing neither the spouse nor the tribe a service.

People in all cultures, even the pacifistic !Kung and the Utku, do occasionally feel irritable and angry. But they do not *value* anger. They strive for a state of mind that philosopher Robert Solomon calls "equanimity under trying circumstances," the worldview of small societies that live in dangerous environments. "The Utku," says Solomon, "much more than any of us, are used to extreme hardship and discomfort. Their philosophy, therefore, is that such things must be tolerated, not flailed against. Captain Ahab and Sisyphus would have no role in their literature."

In this country, the philosophy of emotional expression regards self-restraint as hypocrisy. The cultures of the Far East do not have this conflict; a person is expected to control and subdue the emotions because it is the relationship, not the individual, that comes first. Here, where the reverse is true, some people express their emotions even at the expense of the relationship, and manners seem to be as rare as egrets. This analogy is not arbitrary, for the same ideology that gave us emotional ventilation is responsible for the scarcity of egrets: the imperial "I."

Consider the gentle, forgiving environment of Tahiti, where people learn that they have limited control over nature and over other people. They learn that if they try to change nature, she will swiftly destroy them, but if they relax and accept the bounty of nature— and the nature of people—they will be taken care of. Anthropologist Robert Levy calls this resulting world view among the Tahitians "passive optimism."

Such a philosophy would not have lasted long among the ancient Hebrews, whose God gave them "dominion over the fish of the sea, and over the fowl of the air, and over the cattle, and over all the earth, and over every creeping thing that creepeth upon the earth" (Genesis 1:26). And a good thing He did, too, because in the harsh deserts of the Middle East, adherents of a laissez-faire Tahitian religion would have met a swift demise. The Judeo-Christian philosophy, however, produces "active pessimists": people who assume that na-

ture and other people are to be conquered, indeed must be conquered, and that individual striving is essential to survival. But a
universe defined as the Tahitians see it is intrinsically less infuriating
than a universe in which almost everything is possible if the individual tries hard enough. The individualism of American life, to our
glory and despair, creates anger and encourages its release; for when
everything is possible, limitations are irksome. When the desires of
the self come first, the needs of others are annoying. When we think
we deserve it all, reaping only a portion can enrage.

SISSELA BOK

White Lies

Sissela Bok (1934–   ) is a Swedish-born philosopher who teaches
courses in medical ethics at Harvard Medical School and Brandeis
University. "White Lies" is from her acclaimed work, *Lying: Moral
Choice in Public and Private Life* (1978), in which she questions the
immorality of lying. Her other books include *Secrets: On the Ethics
of Concealment and Revelation* (1982), *A Strategy for Peace: Human
Values and the Threat of War* (1989), and *Alva Myrdal* (1991), a
biography of her mother.

Never have I lied in my own interest; but often I have lied through
shame in order to draw myself from embarrassment in indifferent matters
[. . .] when, having to sustain discussion, the slowness of my ideas and
the dryness of my conversation forced me to have recourse to fictions in
order to say something.

　　　　　　　　Jean Jacques Rousseau, Reveries of a Solitary[1]

When a man declares that he "has great pleasure in accepting" a vexa-
tious invitation or he is the "obedient servant" of one whom he regards as
an inferior, he uses phrases which were probably once deceptive. If they are

---

[1] Jean Jacques Rousseau (1712–1778) was a French philosopher who maintained, in
works such as *The Social Contract* and the *Confessions,* that the "general will" of
humanity is right and good. (ED.)

so no longer, Common Sense condemns as over-scrupulous the refusal to use them where it is customary to do so. But Common Sense seems doubtful and perplexed where the process of degradation is incomplete and there are still persons who may be deceived: as in the use of the reply that one is "not at home" to an inconvenient visitor from the country.

Henry Sidgwick, Methods of Ethics[2]

HARMLESS LYING

White lies are at the other end of the spectrum of deception from lies in a serious crisis. They are the most common and the most trivial forms that duplicity can take. The fact that they are so common provides their protective coloring. And their very triviality, when compared to more threatening lies, makes it seem unnecessary or even absurd to condemn them. Some consider *all* well-intentioned lies, however momentous, to be white; in this book, I shall adhere to the narrower usage: a white lie, in this sense, is a falsehood not meant to injure anyone, and of little moral import. I want to ask whether there *are* such lies; and if there are, whether their cumulative consequences are still without harm; and, finally, whether many lies are not defended as "white" which are in fact harmful in their own right.

Many small subterfuges may not even be intended to mislead. They are only "white lies" in the most marginal sense. Take, for example, the many social exchanges. "How nice to see you!" or "Cordially Yours." These and a thousand other polite expressions are so much taken for granted that if someone decided, in the name of total honesty, not to employ them, he might well give the impression of an indifference he did not possess. The justification for continuing to use such accepted formulations is that they deceive no one, except possibly those unfamiliar with the language.

A social practice more clearly deceptive is that of giving a false excuse so as not to hurt the feelings of someone making an invitation or request: to say one "can't" do what in reality one may not *want* to do. Once again, the false excuse may prevent unwarranted inferences of greater hostility to the undertaking than one may well feel. Merely to say that one can't do something, moreover, is not deceptive in the sense than an elaborately concocted story can be.

---

[2] Henry Sidgwick (1838–1900) was an English philosopher known particularly for his work in the field of ethics. (ED.)

Still other white lies are told in an effort to flatter, to throw a cheerful interpretation on depressing circumstances, or to show gratitude for unwanted gifts. In the eyes of many, such white lies do no harm, provide needed support and cheer, and help dispel gloom and boredom. They preserve the equilibrium and often the humaneness of social relationships, and are usually accepted as excusable so long as they do not become excessive. Many argue, moreover, that such deception is so helpful and at times so necessary that it must be tolerated as an exception to a general policy against lying. Thus Bacon[3] observed:

> Doth any man doubt, that if there were taken out of men's minds vain opinions, flattering hopes, false valuations, imaginations as one would, and the like, but it would leave the minds of a number of men poor shrunken things, full of melancholy and indisposition, and unpleasing to themselves?

Another kind of lie may actually be advocated as bringing a more substantial benefit, or avoiding a real harm, while seeming quite innocuous to those who tell the lies. Such are the placebos given for innumerable common ailments, and the pervasive use of inflated grades and recommendations for employment and promotion.

A large number of lies without such redeeming features are nevertheless often regarded as so trivial that they should be grouped with white lies. They are the lies told on the spur of the moment, for want of reflection, or to get out of a scrape, or even simply to pass the time. Such are the lies told to boast or exaggerate, or on the contrary to deprecate and understate;[4] the many lies told or repeated in gossip; Rousseau's lies told simply "in order to say something"; the embroidering on facts that seem too tedious in their own right; and the substitution of a quick lie for the lengthy explanations one might otherwise have to provide for something not worth spending time on.

Utilitarians[5] often cite white lies as the *kind* of deception where

---

[3] Francis Bacon (1561–1626) was an English philosopher and author. (ED.)

[4] Aristotle, in *Nicomachean Ethics* (pp. 239–45), contrasts these as "boasting" and "irony." He sees them as extremes between which the preferable mean of truthfulness is located.

[5] People who adhere to the ethical theory of utilitarianism, which maintains that the rightness or wrongness of an action depends on the effect it has on the quality of people's lives. (ED.)

their theory shows the benefits of common sense and clear thinking. A white lie, they hold, is trivial; it is either completely harmless, or so marginally harmful that the cost of detecting and evaluating the harm is much greater than the minute harm itself. In addition, the white lie can often actually be beneficial, thus further tipping the scales of utility. In a world with so many difficult problems, utilitarians might ask: Why take the time to weigh the minute pros and cons in telling someone that his tie is attractive when it is an abomination, or of saying to a guest that a broken vase was worthless? Why bother even to define such insignificant distortions or make mountains out of molehills by seeking to justify them?

Triviality surely does set limits to when moral inquiry is reasonable. But when we look more closely at practices such as placebo-giving, it becomes clear that all lies defended as "white" cannot be so easily dismissed. In the first place, the harmlessness of lies is notoriously disputable. What the liar perceives as harmless or even beneficial may not be so in the eyes of the deceived. Second, the failure to look at an entire practice rather than at their own isolated case often blinds liars to cumulative harm and expanding deceptive activities. Those who begin with white lies can come to resort to more frequent and more serious ones. Where some tell a few white lies, others may tell more. Because lines are so hard to draw, the indiscriminate use of such lies can lead to other deceptive practices. The aggregate harm from a large number of marginally harmful instances may, therefore, be highly undesirable in the end—for liars, those deceived, and honesty and trust more generally.

In the post-Watergate period, no one need regard a concern with the combined and long-term effects of deception as far-fetched. But even apart from political life, with its peculiar and engrossing temptations, lies tend to spread. Disagreeable facts come to be sugar-coated, and sad news softened or denied altogether. Many lie to children and to those who are ill about matters no longer peripheral but quite central, such as birth, adoption, divorce, and death. Deceptive propaganda and misleading advertising abound. All these lies are often dismissed on the same grounds of harmlessness and triviality used for white lies in general.

It is worth taking a closer look at practices where lies believed trivial are common. Triviality in an isolated lie can then be more clearly seen to differ markedly from the costs of an entire practice—both to individuals and to communities. One such practice is that of giving placebos.

LETTERS OF RECOMMENDATION

Another deceptive practice where not much may seem to be at stake yet which has high accumulated costs is that of the inflated recommendation. It seems a harmless enough practice, and often an act of loyalty, to give extra praise to a friend, a colleague, a student, a relative. In the harsh competition for employment and advancement, such a gesture is natural. It helps someone, while injuring no one in particular, and balances out similar gestures on the part of many others. Yet the practice obviously injures those who do not benefit from this kind of assistance; and it injures them in a haphazard and inequitable way. Two applicants for work, who are equally capable, may be quite differently rated through no fault of their own.

The existing practices also pose many problems for the individuals caught up in them. Take, for instance, a system where all recommendations given to students are customarily exaggerated— where, say, 60 percent of all graduates are classified as belonging to the top 10 percent. If a professor were to make the honest statement to an employer that a student is merely among the top 60 percent, he might severely injure that student's ability to find work, since the statement would not be taken at face value but would be wrongly interpreted to mean that his real standing was very near the bottom.

Or consider officer evaluation reports in the U.S. Army. Those who rate officers are asked to give them scores of "outstanding," "superior," "excellent," "effective," "marginal," and "inadequate." Raters know, however, that those who are ranked anything less than "outstanding" (say "superior" or "excellent") are then at a great disadvantage,[6] and become likely candidates for discharge. Here, superficial verbal harmlessness combines with the harsh realities of the competition for advancement and job retention to produce an inflated set of standards to which most feel bound to conform.

In such cases, honesty might victimize innocent persons. At the same time, using the evaluations in the accepted manner is still burdensome or irritating to many. And the blurring of the meaning of words in these circumstances can make it seem easier, perhaps even necessary, not to be straightforward in others.

It is difficult for raters to know what to do in such cases. Some

---

[6] Form DA 67-7, 1 January 1973, U.S. Army Officer Evaluation Report.

feel forced to say what they do not mean. Others adhere to a high standard of accuracy and thereby perhaps injure those who must have their recommendations.

To make choices on the basis of such inflated recommendations is equally difficult. This is especially true in large organizations, or at great distances, where those who receive the ratings never know who the raters are or by what standards they work.

The entire practice, then, is unjust for those rated and bewildering for those who give and make use of ratings. It also robs recommendations of whatever benefits they are intended to bring. No one can know what is meant by a particular rating. Such a practice is fraught with difficulties; the costs to deceivers and deceived alike are great.

For this reason, those who give ratings should make every effort to reduce the injustice and to come closer to the standard of accuracy which they would accept were it not for the inflated practice. But if one goes against such a practice, one does have the responsibility of indicating that one is doing so, in order to minimize the effect on those rated. To do so requires time, power, and consistency. A counselor at a school for highly sought-after students, for example, can make it clear to college recruiters that he means every word he uses in his recommendations of students. So can colleagues who know each other well, when they discuss job applicants. But many are caught up in practices where they are nearly anonymous, perhaps transient, and where they have no contact with those who ask them to make out ratings for students or staff members or military personnel. They are then quite powerless: while it may be demeaning to participate in the inflated practices, it is hard to resist them singlehandedly. In verbal inflation as with monetary inflation, more general measures are often necessary. It must, therefore, be more excusable for those individuals to cooperate with the general norm, who cannot establish a different verbal "currency" for what they say.

Institutions, on the other hand, do have more leverage. Some can seek to minimize the reliance on such reports altogether. Others can try to work at the verbal inflation itself. But it is very difficult to do so, especially for large organizations. The U.S. Army tried to scale down evaluations by publishing the evaluation report I have cited. It suggested mean scores for the different ranks, but few felt free to follow these means in individual cases, for fear of hurting the persons being rated. As a result, the suggested mean scores once again lost all value.

TRUTHFULNESS AT WHAT PRICE?

These examples show that one cannot dismiss lies merely by claiming that they don't matter. More often than not, they do matter, even where looked at in simple terms of harm and benefit. Any awareness of how lies spread must generate a real sensitivity to the fact that most lies believed to be "white" are unnecessary if not downright undesirable. Many are not as harmless as liars take them to be. And even those lies which would generally be accepted as harmless are not needed whenever their goals can be achieved through completely honest means. Why tell a flattering lie about someone's hat rather than a flattering truth about their flowers? Why tell a general white lie about a gift, a kind act, a newborn baby, rather than a more specific truthful statement? If the purpose is understood by both speaker and listener to be one of civility and support, the *full* truth in such cases is not called for.[7]

I would not wish to argue that all white lies should be ruled out. Individuals caught up in the practices of making inflated recommendations, for example, may have no other recourse. In a few cases, placebos may be the only reasonable alternative. And certain marginally deceptive social excuses and conventions are unavoidable if feelings are not to be needlessly injured.

But these are very few. And it is fallacious to argue that all white lies are right because a few are. As a result, those who undertake to tell white lies should look hard for alternatives. They should see even these lies as links in much wider practices and should know the ways in which these practices can spread. If they do, white lies, where truly harmless and a last resort—told, for instance, to avoid hurting someone's feelings—can be accepted as policy, but *only* under such limited circumstances.

Most of us doubtless come into more frequent contact with white lies than with any other form of deception. To the extent that we train ourselves to see their ramifications and succeed in eliminating them from our speech, the need to resort to them will diminish. If we can then make it clear to others that we stand in no need of white lies from *them,* many needless complications will have been avoided.

---

[7] If, on the other hand, one is asked for one's honest opinion, such partial answers no longer suffice. A flattering truth that conceals one's opinion is then as deceitful as a flattering lie. To avoid deception, one must then choose either to refuse to answer or to answer honestly.

A word of caution is needed here. To say that white lies should be kept at a minimum is *not* to endorse the telling of truths to all comers. Silence and discretion, respect for the privacy and for the feelings of others must naturally govern what is spoken. The gossip one conveys and the malicious reports one spreads may be true without therefore being excusable. And the truth told in such a way as to wound may be unforgivably cruel, as when a physician answers a young man asking if he has cancer with a curt Yes as he leaves the room. He may not have lied, but he has failed in every professional duty of respect and concern for his patient.

Once it has been established that lies should not be told, it still remains to be seen whether anything should be conveyed, and, if so, how this can best be done. The self-appointed removers of false beliefs from those for whom these beliefs may be all that sustains them can be as harmful as the most callous liars.

JOSEPH H. BERKE

"So Will I Turn Her Virtue into Pitch"

Joseph H. Berke (1939–) is an author and psychotherapist. A founding member of the Institute of Phenomenological Studies in 1966, his controversial writings include *Counter Culture: The Creation of an Alternative Society* (1969), *Mary Barnes: Two Accounts of a Journey through Madness* (1971), *The Cannabis Experience: An Interpretive Study of the Effects of Marijuana and Hashish* (1974), and *The Tyranny of Malice: Exploring the Dark Side of Character and Culture* (1988), from which the following selection is taken.

Envy is a state of exquisite tension, torment, and ill will provoked by an overwhelming sense of inferiority, impotence, and worthlessness. It begins in the eye of the beholder and is so painful to the mind that the envious person will go to almost any lengths to diminish, if not destroy, whatever or whoever may have aroused it.

The Russian writer Yuri Olesha has provided a superb description of the spiteful, spoiling essence of envy in his short novel *Envy,* written not long after the Russian revolution.[1] One of the central characters is Ivan Babichev, a self-hating layabout and elder brother of an ambitious people's commissar. Ivan loathes the revolution, fears the new technology, and longs for the old regime. For him life revolves around bitter obsessions, especially about his childhood when a girl upstaged him and love and attention seemed to pass him by. Consumed with self-pity, Ivan recalls a party at which he defamed and defiled "a little beauty" all dressed in pink and satin, who had the temerity to outsing, outdance, leap higher, and play better than anyone else.

> She was the queen of the ball. She had it all her way. Everyone admired her, everything radiated from her and was drawn in around her.
> I was thirteen, a high school student. I didn't have a chance, despite the fact that I was also used to admiration, to an enthusiastic following.
> I caught the girl in the corridor and gave her a going over: tore her ribbons, mussed her curls, scratched her charming features. At that moment I loved that girl more than life itself, worshipped her, and hated her with all my strength. Mussing up her pretty curls, I thought I would dishonor her, dispel her pinkness, her glow; I thought I would show everyone they were wrong.
> That is how I came to know envy. The terrible heartburn of envy. It is burdensome to envy! Envy catches you by the throat, squeezes your eyes from their sockets.[2]

Ivan loved that girl, not for herself, but because he wanted to be her. This couldn't be, so he ruined her ribbons and curls (beauty), disfigured her charming features (goodness), and dispelled her pinkness and glow (life). Here is an unusual man, not in the extent of his envy but in the outspoken awareness of his ill will. Ivan shares this quality with another outstanding personification of envy, Iago, the villain in Shakespeare's tragedy *Othello.*[3]

Othello is a successful general in the service of the Venetian state. Moreover, his conquests embrace love as well as war, for he has just eloped with Desdemona, the beautiful daughter of a Venetian senator. Iago is his ensign, recently passed over for promotion by another soldier who has become Othello's lieutenant. This is the ostensible

[1] Yuri Olesha, *Envy* (Garden City, N.Y.: Anchor Books, Doubleday & Co., 1967).

[2] Ibid., 78–79.

[3] William Shakespeare, *The Tragedy of Othello* (New York: Pocket Books, 1957).

reason for Iago's anger, but it is only a rationalization. Iago's villainy is part of his nature, and as the play develops we see that his ruthless destructiveness is directed not only to Othello, but to Desdemona and others as well.

Iago is a master of cunning and deceit. To Othello, to Desdemona, to his rivals, he appears honest and helpful. But to himself and the audience his intentions are clear. After Othello has declared his joy and contentment, Iago asides that although the general may be "well-tuned now," he will not find a right note once his own plans take shape.[4] Later he adds: "Knavery's plain face is never seen till used."[5]

The ensuing knavery is far worse than physical abuse or even murder. Iago attacks his victims from within. He is a psychic sadist who wreaks vengeance on Othello by destroying his peace of mind. Iago demonstrates a central feature of envious ill will: the determination to undermine happiness and replace contentment and calm with agitation and anger, doubt and despair.

Othello confirms this mental torture. Previously he had been certain in his love for Desdemona and trusted Iago. Now confusion reigns. One moment he thinks his wife is just and honest, the other not. One moment he sees a woman who is pure and white, the other one who is "begrimed and black." Poor Othello. He doesn't know where to turn or what to think. A once tranquil mind falls prey to an agony almost beyond endurance.

But Othello's pain does not satisfy Iago, whose envy also touches Desdemona. Slowly, insidiously, he ruins her reputation, as he puts it, by purveying pestilence and poisoning Othello's love.

> I'll pour this pestilence into his ear—
> That she repeals him for her body's lust;
> And by how much she strives to do him good,
> She shall undo her credit with the Moor.
> So will I turn her virtue into pitch,
> And out of her own goodness make the net
> That shall enmesh them all.[6]

---

[4] "O, you are well tuned now!
But I'll set down the pegs that make this music,
As honest as I am."
Ibid., act 2, scene 1, lines 231–34.

[5] Ibid., act 2, scene 1, line 340.

[6] Ibid., act 2, scene 3, lines 358–64.

Envy corrupts and corrodes "charming features" and love. It turns good into bad and makes life the rationale for death. To accomplish this, Iago employs a lethal mixture of slander and duplicity, a process of bad-mouthing and back-stabbing. And he makes his hatred all the more effective because he is able to convince Othello to look to him for advice and support, while turning him into a fool, "*an ass,*" who must kiss the ass of the very person who attacks his peace of mind and drives him mad.

According to compelling but incomplete legend, the eighteenth-century Viennese court composer Antonio Salieri used similar tactics to humiliate, impoverish, and ultimately murder Wolfgang Amadeus Mozart, who lived and worked in Vienna at the same time. This relationship has been dramatized by Peter Shaffer in his play *Amadeus.*

Shaffer's Salieri is a cultured and immensely ambitious man who achieves considerable renown during his lifetime. But in comparison with Mozart he is a musical mediocrity. And Salieri knows this. Overtly he tries to help Mozart and appears concerned about his career. But secretly Salieri plots to grind Mozart into the ground— to deter his students, to prevent his advancement, and to hinder the performance of his compositions.

Fate intervenes to help Salieri in his machinations. Mozart embarks on a new opera, *The Marriage of Figaro.* It is based on real people and real places instead of myths and folktales, as is the custom. The nobility becomes alarmed and raises a storm of objections, just as the court musicians vehemently oppose Mozart's use of the vernacular.[7] At Salieri's suggestion Count Rosenberg, director of the Imperial Opera, takes exception to a dance sequence and tries to have it deleted. Himself alarmed, Mozart begs Salieri to use his influence to invite the emperor to a rehearsal so he can present his case. Salieri agrees, intending to do no such thing. But entirely against the usual practice, the emperor does attend and takes Mozart's side. The dance remains. Believing that Salieri is responsible for his good luck, Mozart is grateful and decides Salieri is truly a friend. This allows Salieri to continue his dirty work and remain unsuspected.

Although ill and overwhelmed by debt, Mozart continues to compose. Meanwhile Salieri prospers and is regarded by the public as

---

[7] Vernacular is the language of the common people. In music it refers to "folk" as opposed to "legitimate" compositions. (ED.)

infinitely the superior composer, a success spoiled by his continuing obsession with Mozart's genius.

> I confess that I poisoned Mozart's reputation with the Emperor by constant slander.
> I confess that I pushed him deeper into poverty by the simplest means.[8]

Not satisfied, Salieri turns to arsenic, to destroy Mozart in body as well as mind. Again and again he comes to Mozart in disguise and in secret, leaving bottles of poisoned wine. Finally he appears, a dark messenger of death, and demands that Mozart rush a new commission, a requiem mass. But his victim protests. He can't do it. He is sick, has just shit himself, is covered in muck. And a bitter taste in his mouth makes him think he's been poisoned. So he demands a reprieve.

Suddenly Salieri casts off his mask and reveals himself. Mozart is incredulous. How could it be? Was it a joke? Was Salieri really behind everything that happened to him? "Why?" he asks. "Why?" Yet to understand, Mozart would have had to know about a pact Salieri had made with God at an early age, when he proposed to honor God with music in exchange for fame and fortune and, more important, inspiration.

The pact seemed to bear fruit. To all Vienna, indeed to all of Europe, Salieri was a prolific and respected composer, a musical giant. But, as befits the envious man, he did not measure his worth by intrinsic accomplishments. He only considered his work in comparison with another, Mozart. By that token he and his music were nothing.

Salieri sought a terrible revenge, like Ivan Babichev and like Iago. When aroused by envy, Ivan directed his ire against a pretty girl whose presence set his teeth on edge and made his lips tremble. In response he ripped her satins and bloodied her skin. He hated her beauty.

> I don't remember saying anything when I was beating her up, but I must have whispered: This is my revenge! Don't try to outdo me! Don't try to take what's mine by right.[9]

---

[8] Peter Shaffer, *Amadeus,* (London: Andre Deutsch, 1980), 94–95.

[9] Yuri Olesha, op. cit., 79.

Iago directed his fury against a Venetian soldier. He hated his power. Iago's vengeance was more subtle, if not more cruel. He drove Othello to a jealous frenzy, whereby he blew fond love, and his beloved, to hell.

> Arise, black vengeance, from the hollow cell!
> Yield up, O love, thy crown and hearted throne
> To tyrannous hate! . . .
> O, blood, blood, blood![10]

Salieri directed his rage against God and that embodiment of the divine spark, the creativity of Mozart. He could not accept "a giggling child" whose casual notes were finer than his finest efforts. He refused the privilege of perceiving the incomparable, while remaining aware of relative mediocrity. Therefore he denied his goodness, all goodness, and became an agent of evil, God's rival, the devil. He hated himself.

> I'll not accept it from you—Do you hear? . . . They say God is not mocked! . . . *Dio Ingiusto!*—You are the Enemy!—*Nemico Eterno!* What use, after all, is Man, if not to teach God his lessons?[11]

Envious revenge is fueled by arrogance and pride. It is based on imaginary hurts rather than actual injury. Although Mozart could be uncouth and derogatory, his bearing did not touch Salieri so much as his being. This was the grave offense. Similarly Iago and Ivan Babichev did not seek revenge for what had been done to them in fact. The girl was probably not even aware of Ivan's presence until he attacked her. And Othello treated Iago well, like a friend and confidant. Yet Ivan and Iago begrudged them their vitality and prowess, if not their very existence.

Begrudging is characteristic of envious people who take pleasure in depriving others of what they have or could have, without deriving any sort of advantage from this. Such people go to great lengths to inflict harm or unhappiness. In the summer of 1981 the London *Times* reported the sad story of two Greek spinster sisters, one aged eighty and the other aged eighty-five, who locked a third sister, aged seventy-five, in a stable for eight years as punishment for marrying

---

[10] William Shakespeare, op. cit., act 3, scene 3, lines 500–502 and 505.

[11] Peter Shaffer, op. cit., 67.

late in life and "making us look ridiculous."[12] These ladies were no more ridiculous than Salieri, who, after all, composed music that was widely enjoyed. But in their own minds they felt humiliated, no doubt, when they thought of their own wasted lives. They gained nothing from locking up their sister, except perhaps temporary relief from their own anguish.

The begrudging nature of envy helps to distinguish it from greed. Greed does not begrudge. The greedy person wants as much as he can get, and more, in order to overcome a frightening inner emptiness. He is concerned not with preventing others from having what they have, but with getting whatever is good and life-giving for himself. Security consists of a freedom from emptiness.

The envious person feels inferior rather than empty. He can't stand to see others full of life and goodness, because he is preoccupied with his own limitations and defects. So he aims to debunk and debase what others have. Security consists of an equality of emptiness.

Envy is graspingness for self. Greed is a graspingness for life. Both are never satisfied, because the envious person can always imagine someone else has more, or is worth more than he, while the greedy person can never imagine that he can get, or will have, enough.

But greed recognizes life. The greedy person admits that there is goodness in the world. I mean that he can acknowledge and value care, tenderness, nourishment, beauty, and love. That is why greed is not as shameful as envy, which denies all these things. For the envious person, love is delusion, life is death, and God is the devil.

Greed hoards, envy abhors. The greedy person wants to get more and more, and keep more and more, and will go to any lengths to do this. Greedy destructiveness is unintended but inevitable because of the ruthless, intemperate, gnashing, voracious manner of taking things in and keeping them. Since damaged goods do not relieve hunger, the greedy person may feel compelled to seek out and acquire more of what he has damaged—a vicious, circular, self-defeating process.

Envious destructiveness is deliberate. The envious person denies goodwill or love toward the object of his ire. What he wants is to remove the bilious anger and bitter vindictiveness from within him-

---

[12] *The Times*, London, 19 August 1981, 4.

self, to get rid of it and put it elsewhere. Since he blames what he envies for how he feels, he sets out to make it feel bad or appear bad. Any relief is temporary because the source of his torment is not in what he envies, but in himself.

This wish to force gratuitous hurt onto others is an important part of an envious, begrudging attack, typified by the case of a disgruntled Nigerian security guard who killed a visiting American banker out for a stroll in London. When caught, the man told police that he had long felt lonely and degraded, an outcast from society. One night while walking in a well-to-do area, he came across a large man who looked "rich and comfortable," someone who went to plenty of "posh places." All of a sudden he felt terribly cheated:

> I had to let off steam. I had to cut someone. . . . I stabbed him in the stomach with all the force and hatred that had been building up inside me.[13]

Crimes of theft and arson also illustrate the differences between greed and envy. The street thief and housebreaker want to empty you of what you have and get away as quickly as possible. They don't set out to do damage, which nevertheless may happen, by accident or out of frustration when they don't get what they expect. On the other hand, the arsonist who burns down a house does not wish to possess it or its contents. He wants to evacuate his own burning displeasure by discomforting the owner or by destroying the unique qualities of the house itself. Thus, a man who had set fire to eight cars in Bridgeport, Connecticut, explained: "I couldn't afford to own an automobile . . . and I didn't want anyone else to have one."[14]

On the larger social scene envy and greed seem to be predominant considerations affecting the style, if not policies, of many political figures. The envy-oriented politician tends to play on people's prejudices against the rich and privileged. He argues for a lower but more equal national per capita income and is against great disparities of wealth for whatever the reason.

The greed-oriented politician stresses rapid and unrestricted economic growth and development, no matter who or what gets hurt or

[13] Heather Mills, "Banker 'Killed because He Looked Rich,'" *The Daily Telegraph*, 7 January 1986, 3; and Heather Mills, "Life for Man Who Killed Rich Stranger," *The Daily Telegraph*, 14 January 1986, 3.

[14] *Time*, 3 November 1952.

ruined in the process. He favors high-profit policies often associated with free enterprise and capitalism. Not all capitalists are greedy, but "capitalist" has become synonymous with greed. Terms like "capitalist pig" or "imperialist running dog" convey the contempt and derision of the envious, just as "radical left" or "Trotskyite" are damnations that express the fear of people who want to hang on to their possessions.

Envy and greed rarely operate separately. My colleague, Dr. Nina Coltart, has suggested the term "grenvy" to denote the fusion of these two emotional forces and the simultaneous expression of them. In 1730 Dr. Patrick Delany, a friend of the satirist Jonathan Swift, wrote a telling verse that essentially describes the way Harpyes[15] and slugs embody grenvy:

> At highest worth dull malice reaches
> As slugs pollute the fairest peaches:
> Envy defames, as Harpyes vile
> Devour the fruit they first defile.

Devouring and defiling characterize grenvy and distinguish the grenvious act from a greedy or envious one. The grenvious impulse is more common than pure greed or envy. At least it acknowledges goodness before trying to ruin it. Envy itself admits no desire except to destroy.

The grenvious student, for example, combines stealing and spoiling. He yearns for the information and ideas his teachers possess, so much so that he will go to almost any lengths to get them. Yet as soon as this happens, he forgets what he has learned and debunks what he hasn't. Similarly, in therapy the grenvious patient is very demanding, for time, for interpretations, for help, while simultaneously mocking and distorting the therapist's thoughts.

Newspaper reports of the antics of housebreakers who don't just steal but leave places a wreck also refer to grenvy. A friend of mine owned a house in London that he was planning to sell. He had left it unoccupied but locked up after moving to another house. One Saturday he received a frantic call from a former neighbor who said that there was water pouring from the house onto the street. Hurrying to see what was the matter, my friend discovered that thieves had

---

[15] In Greek and Roman mythologies, monsters who served as ministers of the gods' vengeance. They were half woman, half bird. (ED.)

broken in, systematically ripped out the central heating pipes, and then taken anything else of value. But the intruders had not bothered to turn off the main water, so it was cascading throughout the house. Worse than that, they left piles of their excrement all over the house and had smeared it over walls and ceilings. During the course of their investigation, the police told the owners that the damage was probably the work of a gang of teenaged vandals. Professional thieves rarely disturb anything they don't take. But it is quite common for amateurs to break into a house and defile it.

This crime demonstrates two forms of spoiling. Greedy spoiling occurs when the person or place robbed is emptied, injured, or wrecked during the process of stealing. This spoiling is secondary to greed's ruthless, rapacious acquisitiveness. The plumbing damage indicated greedy spoiling, but the deliberate smearing of shit exemplified envious spoiling. By such extraneous damage, and by allowing water to flow all over the house, a pissing as well as shitting on things, the thieves expressed their contempt and hatred for the owner and for the house, too. It is this mixture of envy with greed that makes the grenvious impulse so damaging and difficult to alleviate.

Envy can hide behind greed as well as fuse with it. Many people accumulate things in order to numb an overweening sense of inferiority or worthlessness. In a materialistic society these "things" might be clothes or cars. In another culture they might be titles, privileges, or work points. However, if the flow of things slows or stops, then the same unhappy people tend to feel humiliated, unworthy, and full of hate toward a world that, in their experience, has robbed and cheated them of their rights and privileges. These grievances can quickly become an obsession, and their envious malice, previously held in check by the illusory fullness, may burst out against relatives, friends, neighbors, colleagues, or "the system" with annihilating accusations of selfishness, cruelty, and greed! Giving more may be palliative or not, because once envy is aroused people tend to rubbish whatever they get, while wanting more. Even good experiences may be trampled under the weight of ingratitude and discontent. Such envy surfaces in the child who "bites the hand that feeds him" and repays parental love with scorn while demanding more.

Love scorned is a central theme of jealousy. The jealous person wants to love and be loved, but he or she fears the loss of a beloved to another. If this happens, or even if there is a threat of it happening, jealous passions soon erupt. They aim to eliminate the unwelcome third party, the rival, so that the original relationship can continue. Alternatively the jealous person may be the outsider, an excluded third party full of desire who comes between two others so that a new loving relationship can begin.

Here love is the primary issue, not hate. However, jealous anger and hatred can be quite as cruel, malicious, and spiteful as envy. What differs is the focus—love lost; the direction of the anger— toward the rival; and the possibility of resolution—love regained and retained.

Jealousy is popularly associated with sexual jealousy, the subject of countless plays, films, and books. Jilly Cooper, who writes on racy topics for the London *Sunday Times,* has described her reaction when she thinks her husband is off with another woman:

> About once a year something triggers off a really bad attack of jealousy, and I turn from an insane irrational being into a raving maniac, all perspective blotted out. "He's late home from work," I reason. "He must be with another woman." Or he's early. "He must be feeling guilty about having a boozy lunch with her." And so on and on, lashing myself with misery. Once the octopus jealousy gets me in its stranglehold, it is almost impossible to wriggle free.[16]

Ms. Cooper highlights irrationality, infidelity, passion, and possessiveness. These issues arise from relationships, any relationship where two people are having fun with each other, whether sex or a "boozy lunch," to the exclusion of someone else. Jealousy is always group-oriented. It involves a threesome. In contrast, envy and greed are more primitive emotional states not concerned with relationships, as such, at all.

The irrational component of jealousy stems from the tendency of the jealous person to exaggerate loss when it has occurred or to imagine loss when it hasn't, as with Ms. Cooper's husband. However, in the latter circumstance, there is usually some kernel of truth, a missed meeting, a delayed dinner, which jealous fears can play on. Envy needs no basis in fact. Therefore, while conflict over love gives

---

[16] Jilly Cooper, in "Jilly Cooper vs. the Green-Eyed Monster," *The Sunday Times* 25 April 1971, 36.

rise to jealousy, envy itself gives rise to conflicts that destroy love, including jealous conflict!

Jealous possessiveness signals the wish to hold on to one's partner and never let her go. It is a further response to the threat of loss and can also serve as a warning or punishment. There is a very aggressive, as well as adoring, quality to it, as with wives who won't let their husbands out of their sight. Such aggressiveness may explain why some people are ashamed of their possessive wishes, then deny them and attribute them to their loved one. The wife who doesn't want her husband to spend a minute away from her may become a woman who constantly complains that her husband won't let her out of the flat or won't let her do anything on her own. Ms. Cooper is not like that, but she does attribute possessiveness to her own jealousy. She then experiences the jealousy as an octopus threatening to strangle her with its emotional ramifications, as opposed to her own wish to tie her husband so he can't have an affair. This possessiveness is quite different from greedy possessiveness, which treats people as if they were possessions. Ms. Cooper did not say that she had a collection of husbands or lovers. Some women do. This greedy accumulation of partners can also be a defense against anticipated infidelities.

Infidelity is the major issue for the jealous person who suspects that his loved one is having a close relationship with another. Suspicions of unfaithfulness indicate great insecurity, not only about relationships but about the individual's own attractiveness, lovability, or capacity for loving. This can lead to obsessive feelings of unworthiness and inferiority and murderous attacks on anyone who arouses them—the alleged third party for interfering and the loved person, too. The direct attack on one's partner is an expression of the vindictive rage stimulated by jealousy—revenge for lost love and hurt pride. Jealous revenge is the operational link between jealousy and envy because the jilted man or woman is hitting back for disloyalty and for being cast in an excluded and inferior position. The malicious aggression that is a feature of such retribution is a form of envious spoiling of the former partner's happiness and superior charms.

This link does not mean that jealousy and envy are identical. On the contrary, jealousy has a separate and distinct meaning and emotional flavoring. Unlike envy or greed, jealousy is not present at birth but only emerges after the infant is able to recognize his parents in their own right.

The distinction between the two terms can be traced back over two millennia. The ancient Greeks, who were keenly aware of envy, employed two terms, *phthonos* for envy and *zelos* for jealousy.[17] Demosthenes, the greatest of the Athenian orators, claimed that *phthonos* was the sign of a wicked nature in every way, and that the man who experienced envy was beyond pardon.[18] *Zelos,* jealousy, was considered much less bad and even connoted admiration.[19] These moral associations might be expected, as jealousy commands both love and hate, but envy is concerned only with hate.

In many countries the difference between envy and jealousy has been recognized in law. Crimes committed "with malice afore-thought" are punished in full, but "crimes of passion" are treated more leniently. Obviously loss of love and infidelity are extenuating circumstances! Still their remains considerable confusion about the two words. Jilly Cooper adds to this when she quips that people are invariably jealous of close friends or acquaintances. She herself would not mind if one of them won a Nobel Prize for chemistry or a gold medal for discus throwing. But should a chum marry a millionaire or win the pools, she would be very irritated. The worst is when people threaten her own interests:

> If one of them dyed her hair blonde and started pushing sex in a posh Sunday, I should be tempted to pop the odd bullet through her. . . . Alas, when one is in the grip of a grand passion all moral considerations go by the board. Beware, my dears, of jealousy. It is the green-eyed monster comes roaring out of the bedroom with a shotgun before you have time to leap out of bed and into the wardrobe.[20]

Although Ms. Cooper has correctly used jealousy to describe a furious response to her husband's alleged affairs, she incorrectly uses the word to convey outrage at her friends' good fortune, knowledge, or sexy characteristics. This outrage is envy. Qualities, characteristics, possessions (like a large bust, big lips, blond hair), attract envy. Jealousy would imply a state of active conflict and competition with a friend who was deploying her sexiness to entice Cooper's husband. Maybe this happened. She did not say so in the article.

---

[17] Peter Walcott, *Envy and the Greeks* (Warminster, England: Aris & Phillips Ltd., 1978), 2.

[18] Ibid., 69.

[19] Ibid., 3.

[20] Cooper, op. cit., 36.

Whatever the usage, Jilly Cooper gives a firm warning about jealousy. It is a "green-eyed monster" liable to shoot first and ask questions after. Her allusion is to the warning that Iago gave Othello about his dangerous state of mind:

> O, beware, my lord, of jealousy;
> It is the green-ey'd monster which doth mock
> The meat it feeds on.[21]

The warning is double-edged. It refers to Othello's jealousy and to Iago's envy, which makes a mockery of Othello by driving him berserk with doubt, despair, and rage.

But could it be that Iago was not really so bad, that he was afflicted with a "grand passion" for Desdemona and only wanted to get Othello out of the way so that he could have her for himself? After all, he did accuse Othello of having slept with his wife (an indication of what he may have wanted to do). And he did scheme with Roderigo, Desdemona's former suitor, to woo her back. Perhaps Roderigo represents Iago's alter ego, and the "green-eyed monster" is not Iago's envy but his jealousy.

I'm afraid this picture does not fit the facts. The Iago Shakespeare paints is devious and scheming, a man with no redeeming virtues, a paragon of vice. His sole interest in Desdemona is to hurt Othello; in fact, he aims to begrudge both of them happiness and life. And if Roderigo represents another aspect of himself, he isn't too benevolent toward it, for he also murders Roderigo, and his wife, Emilia, too.

For Iago, jealousy, inasmuch as there is any case for it, serves simply to camouflage overweening envy. This is not an uncommon function of jealousy, to act as a defense against envy. It is especially evident in people who suffer from pathological jealousy. Sigmund Freud called this "projected jealousy" and "delusional jealousy." It is also known as "morbid jealousy."[22]

Morbid jealousy manifests itself in men and women who develop a firm belief that their partners, and various named or unnamed third parties, want to rob them of everything: want to taunt, tantalize, outrage, strip them of self-respect and self-confidence, spoil their love, and leave them feeling full of doubt and despair. Upon closer

---

[21] William Shakespeare, op. cit., act 3, scene 3, lines 191–3.

[22] Sigmund Freud, "Some Neurotic Mechanisms in Jealousy, Paranoia and Homosexuality," in *Standard Edition of the Complete Psychological Works of Freud*, ed. J. Strachey (London: The Hogarth Press, 1968), vol. 18, 221–32.

examination, these thoughts are held by people with limited self-esteem and deeply ingrained feelings of inferiority. The accusations tend to be projections of what they want to do to others.

Did Othello suffer from morbid jealousy? Did he succumb to Iago's intrigues because he secretly harbored great enmity toward the woman he married? Shakespeare provides considerable evidence toward this view. Othello is a Moor, a soldier of fortune, a hustler, while Desdemona is the daughter of a Venetian senator, an aristocrat. And she is white, while he is black. I don't think these details are an accident. Shakespeare depicted the class and race conflicts of this time in order to mirror his society. Among the many reasons we continue to be fascinated by his plays is the conviction that this mirror also depicts the endless, envious, guilt-laden preoccupations of the future. Iago is no more, but no less, than another side of the modern man who cannot endure evil. Therefore he blackens others and makes them suffer instead.

Nowadays envy is just as prevalent as it was in Shakespeare's time, but people are less straightforward about it. The emotional meaning and motivation of the term tends to be clouded, if not actually reversed, by idiomatic usages and theoretical justifications. Chic phrases deploy envy in order to declare admiration, interest, desire, strong feeling, frustration, resentment, indignation, and identification (or the opposite) and have become part of common parlance:

> I envy you.
> You'll be envied for sitting in this seat.
> I so envy your new car.
> What an enviable position.
> I don't envy anyone with money these days.
> I don't envy him trying to write.

Admen advise that envy is not to be feared. On the contrary, it's a useful stimulant for "the folks back home."[23] And sociologists imply that envy, influenced by "uninhibited reference group choice," may

---

[23] I refer to an advertisement about the exclusive New York hotel, the Waldorf-Astoria: "If you've never been a Waldorf guest, you could unthinkingly believe it to be expensive. . . . The admiration (if not envy) of the folks at home is included in the room rate." *The New York Times*, 7 December 1961, 29.

have a salutary effect on social reform.[24] In September 1977 the Vickers Company placed a large cartoon advertisement in *The Sunday Times*. On one side of the page the reader sees a modern, open-plan office block filled with new furniture, new equipment, and smiling, cheerful people. On the other side there is an older brick building from which a multitude of clerks, secretaries, typists, and bosses peer out of rows of small, narrow windows, exclaiming, "Envy! Envy! Envy!" Some of these faces are overcome with despair, resentment, or rage, while others evince interest, admiration, and desire. The caption comments that the cartoonist wanted to convey the whole range of Vickers's products as well as the envy of those who have to make do without them.

This cartoon captures the multiple meanings ascribed to envy and demonstrates how envy can be used to sell products, if not a way of life, by preying on people's latent inferiority. The central image is two adjacent buildings and two adjacent groups of office workers. Their "social proximity" provides the context for the "invidious comparisons" that follow.[25] The advert assumes the workers are unhappy about their conditions of employment. It seeks to awaken them to the relative impoverishment of their labors and implies that they should feel deprived in relation to the get-ahead employees next door (even though they may previously have been content). The cartoonist seems to be aware of the theories of the sociologist W. G. Runciman, for whom envy signifies "relative deprivation." Runciman believes that "the poorest appear to be entitled to a greater magnitude of relative deprivation than the evidence shows them to feel."[26]

Feeling appropriately deprived, one man is green, sick to the stomach at the thought of what he is missing. Another is crying, and a third is in a state of near total despair. Nearby, however, his

---

[24] Helmut Schoeck points out that the sociologist W. G. Runciman demands "uninhibited reference group choice" in regard to all inequalities in order to maximize social justice. Schoeck, *Envy: A Theory of Social Behavior,* (Indianapolis: Liberty Fund, 1987), 209.

[25] Sometimes envy is mistaken for the context in which it occurs: social proximity or "invidious proximity," a term employed by the American historian David M. Potter in *People of Plenty: Economic Abundance and the American Character* (Chicago: University of Chicago Press, 1954), 102.

[26] Quoted by Schoeck, op. cit., 209. See W. G. Runciman, *Relative Deprivation and Social Justice: A Study of Attitudes to Social Inequality in Twentieth Century England* (London: Routledge & Kegan Paul, 1966).

colleague can be seen gnashing his teeth in rage and resentment, while another glowers with indignation. Down a floor someone else is so frustrated at the sight of the new equipment, he can't bear to look.

Resentment, indignation, and frustration are often used synonymously with envy. But they are not identical phenomena, rather reactions to actual injustice or deprivation—in other words, to an actual conflict of interest. Envy is rooted in imaginary conflict, although actual events can conceal or incite it. Vickers's products may also dispel resentment or indignation, but the grievances of a truly envious person do not disappear even when the alleged source of frustration is removed.

The ad does try to foster positive feelings. Vickers obviously hopes and expects that all their potential customers in old brick-fronted buildings will be charmed and delighted by what they see and anticipate using. It wants everyone to emulate the new working practices of the glass-walled, fully automated get-ahead company next door. Why call this envy? Admiration is an "antidote" for envy, not the expression of it. As Sören Kierkegaard[27] has pointed out, envy embraces unhappy self-assertion, while admiration equals happy self-surrender.

Similarly, emulation is quite different from an envious competitiveness, which is spiteful, self-seeking, and begrudging. The wish to be like someone is based on admiration, not ill will. I presume the Vickers Company wants its new customers to equal or surpass its old ones, not disparage, damage, or grind them to the ground. Yet this cartoon does incite envy, not by the overt use of the word, but by the covert message "You are not good or at least not as good as everyone else, unless you use our products."

Why don't people who are aroused by this message, and by the barrage of equivalent messages on TV, radio, newspapers, magazines, and billboards, immediately go on a rampage? Well, sometimes they do, collectively, as in a ghetto riot, or individually, in a seemingly unprovoked attack on a relative or friend. The government of Indonesia ended commercial television solely because the sight of unattainable goods unsettled the inhabitants of their outer islands.

Usually, however, envy lurks behind a facade of probable hurts or is fused with greed and jealousy, as we have seen. Most important,

---

[27] Sören Kierkegaard (1813–1855), a Danish religious philosopher, is regarded as a founder of existential philosophy. (ED.)

envy is continually opposed by gratitude, generosity, and compassion—all fundamental virtues that convey our love of life. Even Salieri was not totally motivated by malice. He admired Mozart and wanted to compose music like him so he could repay God for making him a famous man. Envy only got the upper hand when, in his view, this ambition was thwarted. Then he abandoned social duties and charitable pursuits and devoted himself to ruining Mozart's life.

Salieri, Iago, Ivan Babichev, all demonstrate the essential criteria of unrestrained envy. It is an intense, implacable, irrational, irreconcilable, spiteful passion solely concerned with spoiling, corrupting, defaming, and begrudging. No wonder it seems to operate in secret. It has always been considered one of the most deadly sins amply conveyed by the iconography of a satanic serpent and, more recently, by a bumper sticker seen on a car in Mexico: "Down with everyone going up!"[28]

ROLLO MAY

The Experience of Becoming a Person

Rollo May (1909–   ) is a well-known psychologist, famous for his role in the "self-actualization" movement of the fifties and sixties and his popularization of existential themes in psychotherapy. Some of his works include *The Meaning of Anxiety* (1950), *Man's Search for Himself* (1953), from which the following selection is taken, *Psychology and the Human Dilemma* (1967), *The Courage to Create* (1975), and *Freedom and Destiny* (1981).

I

This consciousness of self, this capacity to see one's self as though from the outside, is the distinctive characteristic of man. A friend of mine has a dog who waits at his studio door all morning

---

[28] The car sticker is mentioned in David Ward Tresemer, *Fear of Success* (New York: Plenum Press, 1977), 21.

and, when anybody comes to the door, he jumps up and barks, wanting to play. My friend holds that the dog is saying in his barking: "Here is a dog who has been waiting all morning for someone to come to play with him. Are you the one?" This is a nice sentiment, and all of us who like dogs enjoy projecting such cozy thoughts into their heads. But actually this is exactly what the dog cannot say. He can show that he wants to play and entice you into throwing his ball for him, but he cannot stand outside himself and see himself as a dog doing these things. He is not blessed with the consciousness of self.

Inasmuch as this means the dog is also free from neurotic anxiety and guilt feelings, which are the doubtful blessings of the human being, some people would prefer to say the dog is not cursed with the consciousness of self. Walt Whitman, echoing this thought, envies the animals:

> I think I could turn and live with animals. . . .
> They do not sweat and whine about their condition,
> They do not lie awake in the dark and weep for
>   their sins . . .

But actually man's consciousness of himself is the source of his highest qualities. It underlies his ability to distinguish between "I" and the world. It gives him the capacity to keep time, which is simply the ability to stand outside the present and to imagine oneself back in yesterday or ahead in the day after tomorrow. Thus human beings can learn from the past and plan for the future. And thus man is the historical mammal in that he can stand outside and look at his history; and thereby he can influence his own development as a person, and to a minor extent he can influence the march of history in his nation and society as a whole. The capacity for consciousness of self also underlies man's ability to use symbols, which is a way of disengaging something from what it is, such as the two sounds which make up the word "table" and agreeing that these sounds will stand for a whole class of things. Thus man can think in abstractions like "beauty," "reason," and "goodness."

This capacity for consciousness of ourselves gives us the ability to see ourselves as others see us and to have empathy with others. It underlies our remarkable capacity to transport ourselves into someone else's parlor where we will be in reality next week, and then in imagination to think and plan how we will act. And it enables us to imagine ourselves in someone else's place, and to ask how we would feel and what we would do if we were this other person. No matter how poorly we use or fail to use or even abuse these capacities, they are the rudiments of our ability to begin to love our neighbor, to have ethical sensitivity, to see truth, to create beauty, to devote ourselves to ideals, and to die for them if need be.

To fulfill these potentialities is to be a person. This is what is meant when it is stated in the Hebrew-Christian religious tradition that man is created in the image of God.

But these gifts come only at a high price, the price of anxiety and inward crises. The birth of the self is no simple and easy matter. For the child now faces the frightful prospect of being out on his own, alone, and without the full protection of the decisions of his parents. It is no wonder that when he begins to feel himself an identity in his own right, he may feel terribly powerless in comparison with the great and strong adults around him. In the midst of a struggle over her dependency on her mother, one person had this eloquent dream: "I was in a little boat tied to a big boat. We were going through the ocean and big waves came up, piling over the sides of my boat. I wondered whether it was still tied to the big boat."

The healthy child, who is loved and supported but not coddled by his parents, will proceed in his development despite this anxiety and the crises that face him. And there may be no particular external signs of trauma or special rebelliousness. But when his parents consciously or unconsciously exploit him for their own ends or pleasure, or hate or reject him, so that he cannot be sure of minimal support when he tries out his new independence, the child will cling to the parents and will use his capacity for independence only in the forms of negativity and stubbornness. If, when he first begins tentatively to say "No," his parents beat him down rather than love and encourage him, he thereafter will say "No" not as a form of true independent strength but as a mere rebellion.

Or if, as in the majority of cases in the present day, the parents themselves are anxious and bewildered in the tumultuous seas of the changing times, unsure of themselves and beset by self-doubts, their anxiety will carry over and lead the child to feel that he lives in a world in which it is dangerous to venture into becoming one's self.

This brief sketch is schematic, to be sure, and it is meant to give us as adults a kind of retrospective picture in the light of which we can better understand how one fails to achieve selfhood. Most of the data for these conflicts of childhood come from adults who are struggling, in dreams, memories or in present-day relations, to overcome what in their past lives originally blocked them in becoming fully born as persons. Almost every adult is, in greater or lesser degree, still struggling on the long journey to achieve selfhood on the basis of the patterns which were set in his early experiences in the family.

Nor do we for a moment overlook the fact that selfhood is always born in a social context. Genetically, Auden[1] is quite right:

> . . . for the ego is a dream
> Till a neighbor's need by
> name create it.

Or, as we put it above, the self is always born and grows in interpersonal relationships. But no "ego" moves on into responsible selfhood if it remains chiefly the reflection of the social context around it. In our particular world in which conformity is the great destroyer of selfhood—in our society in which fitting the "pattern" tends to be accepted as the norm, and being "well liked" is the alleged ticket to salvation—what needs to be emphasized is not only the admitted fact that we are to some extent created by each other but also our capacity to experience, and create, ourselves.

II

The consciousness of one's identity as a self certainly is not an intellectual idea. The French philosopher Descartes,[2] at the beginning of the modern period three centuries ago, crawled into his stove, according to legend, to meditate in solitude all one day trying to find the basic principle for human existence. He came out of his stove in the evening with the famous conclusion "I think, therefore I am." That is to say, I exist as a self because I am a thinking creature. But this is not enough. You and I never think of ourselves as an idea. We rather picture ourselves as doing something, like the psychologist writing his paper, and we then experience in imagination the feelings that we will have when we are in actuality doing that thing. That is to say, we experience ourselves as a thinking-intuiting-feeling and acting unity. The self is thus not merely the sum of the various "roles" one plays—it is the capacity by which one knows he plays these roles; it is the center from which one sees and is aware of these so-called different "sides" of himself.

---

[1] W. H. Auden (1907–1973), an English poet (ED.)

[2] René Descartes (1596–1650) was a French mathematician and philosopher. He has been called the father of modern philosophy. (ED.)

After these perhaps high-sounding phrases, let us remind ourselves that after all the experience of one's own identity, or becoming
a person, is the simplest experience in life even though at the same
time the most profound. As everyone knows, a little child will react
indignantly and strongly if you, in teasing, call him by the wrong
name. It is as though you take away his identity—a most precious
thing to him. In the Old Testament the phrase "I will blot out their
names"—to erase their identity and it will be as though they never
had existed—is a more powerful threat even than physical death.

Two little girl twins gave a vivid illustration of how important it
is for a child to be a person in her own right. The little girls were
good friends, a fact made especially possible because they complemented each other, one being extrovert and always in the center of
the crowd if people came to visit in the house, the other being
perfectly happy by herself to draw with her crayons and make up
little poems. The parents, as parents generally do with twins, had
dressed them alike when they went out walking. When they were
about three and a half, the little extrovert girl began to want always
to wear a different kind of dress from her sister. If she dressed after
her sister, she would even, if necessary, wear an older and less pretty
dress so that it would not be the same as the twin was wearing. Or
if the sister dressed after her before they went out, she would beg
her, sometimes weeping, not to put on the matching dress. For days
this puzzled the parents, since the child was not anxious in other
ways. Finally the parents, on a hunch, asked the little girl, "When
you two go out walking, do you like to have the people on the street
say, 'Look at these nice twins'?" Immediately the little girl exclaimed,
"No, I want them to say, 'Look at these two different people!'"

This spontaneous exclamation, obviously revealing something
very important to the little girl, cannot be explained by saying that
the child wanted attention; for she would have gotten more attention
if she had dressed as a twin. It shows, rather, her demand to be a
person in her own right, to have personal identity—a need which
was more important to her even than attention or prestige.

The little girl rightly stated the goal for every human being—to
become a person. Every organism has one and only one central need
in life, to fulfill its own potentialities. The acorn becomes an oak,
the puppy becomes a dog and makes the fond and loyal relations
with its human masters which befit the dog; and this is all that is
required of the oak tree and the dog. But the human being's task in
fulfilling his nature is much more difficult, for he must do it in self-
consciousness. That is, his development is never automatic but must

be to some extent chosen and affirmed by himself. "Among the works of man," John Stuart Mill[3] has written, "which human life is rightly employed in perfecting and in beautifying, the first importance surely is man himself. . . . Human nature is not a machine to be built after a model and set to do exactly the work prescribed for it, but a tree, which requires to grow and develop itself on all sides, according to the tendency of the inward forces which make it a living thing." In this charmingly expressed thought, John Stuart Mill has unfortunately omitted the most important "tendency of the inward forces" which make man a living thing, namely that man does not grow automatically like a tree, but fulfills his potentialities only as he in his own consciousness plans and chooses.

If any organism fails to fulfill its potentialities, it becomes sick, just as your legs would wither if you never walked. But the power of your legs is not all you would lose. The flowing of your blood, your heart action, your whole organism would be the weaker. And in the same way if man does not fulfill his potentialities as a person, he becomes to that extent constricted and ill. This is the essence of neurosis—the person's unused potentialities, blocked by hostile conditions in the environment (past or present) and by his own internalized conflicts, turn inward and cause morbidity. "Energy is Eternal Delight," said William Blake;[4] "he who desires but acts not, breeds pestilence."

Kafka was a master at the gruesome task of picturing people who do not use their potentialities and therefore lose their sense of being persons. The chief character in *The Trial* and in *The Castle* has no name—he is identified only by an initial, a mute symbol of one's lack of identity in one's right. In the staggering and frightful parable, *Metamorphosis,* Kafka illustrates what happens when the human being forfeits his powers. The hero of this story is a typical, empty modern young man, who lives a routine, vacuous life as a salesman, returning regularly to his middle-class home, eating the same menu of roast beef every Sunday while his father goes to sleep at the table. The young man's life was so empty, implies Kafka, that he woke up one morning no longer a human being but a cockroach. Because he

[3] John Stuart Mill (1806–1873) was an English politician and a leader of the Utilitarian movement. (ED.)

[4] William Blake (1757–1827) was an English poet, painter, engraver, and religious mystic. Blake's spirituality, as expressed in his writings and art works, took a highly symbolic and mythical form. (ED.)

had not fulfilled his status as a man, he forfeited his human potentialities. A cockroach, like lice and rats and vermin, lives off others'
leavings. It is a parasite, and in most people's minds a symbol for
what is unclean and repugnant. Could there be any more powerful
symbol of what happens when a human being relinquishes his nature
as a person?

But to the extent that we do fulfill our potentialities as persons,
we experience the profoundest joy to which the human being is heir.
When a little child is learning to walk up steps or lift a box, he will
try again and again, getting up when he falls down and starting over
again. And finally when he does succeed, he laughs with gratification,
his expression of joy in the use of his powers. But this is nothing in
comparison to the quiet joy when the adolescent can use his newly
emerged power for the first time to gain a friend, or the adult's joy
when he can love, plan and create. Joy is the affect which comes
when we use our powers. Joy, rather than happiness, is the goal of
life, for joy is the emotion which accompanies our fulfilling our
natures as human beings. It is based on the experience of one's
identity as a being of worth and dignity, who is able to affirm his
being, if need be, against all other beings and the whole inorganic
world. This power in its ideal form is shown in the life of a Socrates,[5]
who was so confident in himself and his values that he could take
his being condemned to death not as a defeat but as a greater
fulfillment than compromising his beliefs. But we do not wish to
imply such joy is only for the heroic and the outstanding; it is as
present qualitatively in anyone's act, no matter how inconspicuous,
which is done as an honest and responsible expression of his own
powers.

---

[5] Socrates (469–399 B.C.?), a teacher and philosopher in ancient Greece, made enemies
because of his unorthodox views. He was brought to trial for corrupting the youth of
Athens and for showing disrespect for religious traditions. (ED.)

DENISE GESS

Underground

Denise Gess (1952–) was born in Philadelphia, and has a B.A. in
psychology from LaSalle University and an M.A. in English from
Rutgers University. She is the author of the novels *Good Deeds*
(1984) and *Red Whiskey Blues* (1989). Gess has taught creative
writing at Temple University and Rutgers University, but now de-
votes her full time to writing.

My husband Daniel thought it was unwise, not to mention depressing, but I continued to read the obituaries every day anyway. Usually
I searched for a woman like myself in the section, someone thirty-
six who through some error had been saddled with bad ovaries and
a diseased uterus, who'd had to have it all removed prematurely, and
of course, had died prematurely too. Religiously, after Daniel left for
work in the morning, I would lift the paper from the kitchen table
and flip to the obituary section, my heart thumping with equal parts
of fecklessness and fear. I thoroughly read each entry: Bradford,
Thomas; Harkins, Sheila; Miller, Norma; Tegliano, Joseph, then shuddered with relief when the deceased were older than I, the victims
of strokes and heart attacks—or younger—the victims of accidents.
I had not yet found the phantom dead woman with whom I was in
collusion, the one who would rise up from the newsprint and carry
me into oblivion with her.

In another season I would have had too much to do, too little
time left over to coddle my fear of surgery, which hinged—not so
much on the idea of being cut—as it did the depth of the sleep. But
it was summer, a dense humid summer, and I wasn't teaching any
courses at the college. The children too were gone. Madeline was off
at dance camp in Vermont for a month and Michael, after much
pleading with us, was spending the summer at the shore in a rented
duplex with four other eighteen-year-old boys. My gynecologist had
remarked that I couldn't have planned a better time for surgery if I
tried. She pointed out that I would be able to recuperate nicely with
the kids gone. Perhaps if it had been a different kind of operation—
appendectomy or gall bladder—something not quite as *fundamental,*
I told her. "I miss them," I said. "I miss looking at the faces that are

the fruits of my long labors." She assured me the feelings were natural and complimented me on the eloquence of the sentiment.

On the other hand, my older sister Lolly scolded me, by telephone, at least every other day. She quoted whole passages from articles she hunted down in AMA journals about mental preparedness for surgery. She pointed out the moxie of numerous television personalities and actresses who'd undergone radical mastectomies, drug addictions and alcohol abuse. "It might not even hurt to think about healing crystals," she said.

"Would you clench an amethyst in your hand and mumble a chant?"

"No. Of course not," she said. "But I'm not as attached to my reproductive organs as you are. Obviously you *like* the rigors of PMS."

No, that wasn't it at all, but I didn't mind Lolly's reprimands or the lists of books she typed out on yellow legal pad paper and sent to me. Sometimes she added postscripts: "Think of it as liberation!" or "Reproduction's not what it's cracked up to be." It was a very Lolly-brand of commiseration: make light, make light, make light. That's why her idea of a pre-surgery dinner didn't at all surprise me. I was scheduled for Friday morning and would have to enter the hospital on Thursday to be pricked, cleansed and deprived of food and water. On a Monday morning Lolly called to invite me and Daniel to dinner on Wednesday night. Lolly loved an excuse to throw a dinner party. She especially liked theme dinners.

"Will we call this The Last Supper?" I asked.

Lolly exhaled a great breath of air on her end of the line.

"I'm cooking Chinese—from scratch," she said, "so think about it and ask Danny. Just call me within the next twenty-four hours before I buy the shrimp and the chicken and the cashews and—"

I told her we would be there even though the idea of a pre-surgery dinner struck me as a variation of fattening the cow before the slaughter.

It must have been the reality of the impending surgery closing in, but on Monday night and then again on Tuesday night I was startled awake by the same nightmare—a nocturnal vision of the inside of my body, my organs wrapped and tangled in a spidery web I was sure meant cancer.

"It's growing," I told Daniel. He brought me a cold glass of water and two aspirin, pressed them into my sweaty palm.

"Take these."

"I don't have a headache, Danny. I have cancer."

He sat down on the bed next to me. "You have cysts. Lots of

cysts and they're going to take them out so you don't get cancer."
He cupped my hand with his own, moved it to my lips. "Come on,
take the aspirin. It'll help you sleep."

I popped the aspirin in my mouth, drank the water down and
handed him the glass. When he returned from the bathroom, he slid
into bed beside me and pulled me close so my face rested against his
hairy chest. "I want you to promise me something, Viv."

"I already promised to love you for better or for worse, richer or
poorer. You want more?"

"Very funny." He sighed. "No more obituaries with your morning
coffee. Now promise."

"I promise," I said.

"Now kiss me." And I did.

"You taste like garlic," I told him.

"Your tomato sauce, Viv. So do you."

I kissed him again, mightily again this time, my tongue seeking
his, drawing life from him until the vision of the spidery web inside
disappeared.

We woke up late on Wednesday morning, hungover from our
lovemaking and the sudden stultifying heat that rolled in at daybreak,
so Danny decided to take the car instead of the train into Philadelphia. "I'll come back and pick you up to go to Lolly's," he said. But
it was silly, all that driving back and forth over the bridge when the
train station was only several blocks from the house. I told him I
would take the train instead and meet him at Lolly's at seven.

I believe I had every intention of keeping my promise to him,
but when I went down into the kitchen the morning paper was lying
on the table next to his half-filled coffee cup. I poured myself a glass
of juice, set the air-conditioner on high and settled in with the paper,
ignoring the earth-shaking events of the front page and rifling quickly
to what I had begun to think of fondly as My Section. I should have
realized before then that if you look for something long enough you
usually find it. The name Bova caught my attention immediately.
Anthony Bova, dead at the age of 36, of a heart attack, survived by
his wife and two children. Suddenly I could feel the heat of the early
morning pressing in on me, as if the sun had crashed through the
windows and stopped the flow of cold air through the house. My
throat was dry. I reread the obit. Until that moment I had not thought
of him, had pushed our relationship into the dark, unchecked corner
of memory that opens up uncalled, unwanted.

Anthony Bova came to my grammar school in the fourth grade. He
was fat and had a head of wild hair with cowlicks front and crown,

and strange hooded eyelids, puffy and pinkish around the rims that always made him appear sleepy. The second day of class he told Sister Mary Joseph not to call him Anthony, that he preferred Tony, and of course, the thin handsome boys jumped on the opening immediately. That same day at recess in the school yard they mimicked him. "Oh, Sister," Patrick Dukes said, "call me Tony. Call me Tubby." Then some of the other boys joined in and began calling him Tubby too, then Tubby Bubby—the name that stuck.

That year we had abandoned teasing Leslie Shultz about her skinny pigtails, or poking fun at John Loomis for his big ears because Anthony Bova with his oversized, lummoxy body and heavy Brooklyn accent was truly foreign. Like some secret uniformed society that had used up its sacrificial lambs we were restless, edgy and overflowing with mischief. Tension was high in the classroom from the start because Sister Mary Joseph had a reputation as the strictest nun in the school, and perhaps we feared she'd dispense some of her unprovoked wrath on one of us unless we could direct it toward one child, one child so obviously out of step with the group. Anthony was it.

He wasn't stupid, but he couldn't keep his mouth shut either. He had a terrible habit of screaming out an answer in class before Sister could even finish asking the question and the first time he corrected Sister's mistake in a word problem she'd written on the board, she was so flustered that the chalk she was holding broke in two between her clenched fingers. "I'll speak to you after school, Mr. Bova," she said. Everyone exchanged knowing glances, we grinned at his plight, even me. We thought he deserved it.

That same afternoon while I was waiting for Lolly by the back exit of the school, I saw Anthony Bova leave the building, his face stained with tears. He pushed his way out the door so quickly, he didn't even notice me hanging out there and as he stomped off I watched him pull two candy bars from his coat pockets. He tore into the wrappers and threw them on the sidewalk then stuffed the candy bars into his mouth till his cheeks puffed out like a squirrel storing nuts. I thought he was disgusting, to be so fat already and still eat like there was no tomorrow.

On the way home Lolly chattered as usual while I half-listened. Her friend Susan Menza was walking home with us that day and all they talked about were the boys they liked and whether or not they might just be the two prettiest girls in the seventh grade that year. They walked too slowly for me, so I moved ahead of them, past the new split level houses on down the hill of Bridge Street toward the heart of town where we lived, where the old frame Victorian houses stood like pastel-colored birthday cakes in a row on the block. I wanted to get to Ceil's, the corner store where we stopped to buy gum or juice.

We must have been about ten yards away from the store, Lolly and Susan were still gabbing behind me, when I saw Anthony Bova coming out of Ceil's carrying fistfuls of candy. I stopped suddenly and Lolly tripped on my heel and then smacked me for making her bang into me. "Why'd you do that?" she said, shoving me a little.

"I was looking at something."

Lolly, who needed glasses but refused to tell our parents because she was afraid it would ruin her looks, squinted hard.

"I don't see anything," she said. "Come on, Susie, let's go to Ceil's."

They started to walk away from me, then Lolly turned. "Hurry up, Vivian."

By then Anthony's back was to me and he was stalking away, unwrapping candy. For just a second there, he didn't seem as disgusting as he did in the school yard.

The following day as soon as our class entered the room, Sister Mary Joseph announced that she was changing everyone's seats. She kept glancing in my direction. While we cleaned out our desks and waited for our seat assignments, she sidled up beside me.

"Vivian, come into the cloakroom with me."

I held my books and pencil case close to my chest and followed her. Our cloakroom was a large sectioned off space at the back of the room with hooks on either side of the glazed brick walls for coats, and shelves above the hooks for lunch boxes. The cloakroom always smelled of damp wool and tuna fish, but it was a comforting room, muffled with coats from which voices could not carry.

"Vivian," she began in a stern but kind voice, "I have a job for you to do from now on."

"Yes, Sister."

"I'm going to seat you behind Mr. Bova," she said. "He talks out of turn quite a lot and he shouts his answers and we don't shout in Sister's class, do we, Vivian?"

"No, Sister, we don't."

She patted my arm. "Good girl. Well, because you know the rules and always follow them, you're going to be in charge of Anthony. Whenever he shouts or calls out of turn, you reach out in front of you and hit him on the shoulder."

A very faint smile crossed her lips.

"Hit him?"

"Yes, Vivian. You'll be teaching him, helping him to control himself. After just a little while you'll see you won't even need to do it. Anthony will finally learn his lesson."

She leaned a little bit closer to me and I recognized the smell of Jean Naté on her navy blue habit. Her voice was low and soft, pretty almost, the way she sounded when she was in church, teaching us Gregorian chant. She led me out of the cloakroom, down the aisle to my new seat, then she called out Anthony's name and instructed him to sit in front of me.

And that was how it began, my reign as Anthony Bova's personal torturer. The first time he shouted out in class I had no trouble delivering the blow, a half-fisted punch at the top of his arm. Sister nodded approvingly from the front of the class. He turned halfway in his seat and glared at me. I shrugged and whispered to him that it was my job now. "Sister said to hit you if you call out." He looked at me as if he hadn't understood me, as if I were speaking Latin to him.

I didn't think I'd need to hit him ever again, but as the month wore on, it seemed I had to hit him more and more. Sometimes I would hit him harder than other times, hoping that the force behind the blow would finally make him shut up, keep him out of trouble, but it only seemed to make matters worse. In the school yard he got into fist fights with the other boys. He continued to correct Sister in class, and I wanted her to do something, but she would only make that same faint smile and nod in my direction. Often she would keep him after school and if I happened to be waiting for Lolly, I would see him leave the building with those angry tears and candy, all kinds, in his hands. On one of those afternoons, after I watched him stalk off, and Lolly and I started our walk home, I asked her if a nun would ever make someone do something bad on purpose.

Lolly shook her head and laughed at me. "No. That's stupid. They're nuns, dummy. They're married to God."

I believed Lolly. She was very smart, always got A's, and seemed to know everything about the nuns. She'd already had Sister Mary Joseph and it was Lolly who explained to me that the nuns wore Jean Naté because it was only toilet water and not real perfume.

"Okay," I said. "That's all I wanted to know."

She nudged me with her school bag. "You're so queer," she said. Maybe she was right, maybe I was queer because sometimes, even though I was starving right after school, by dinnertime I couldn't eat.

I felt full, as if I'd eaten as much candy as I'd seen Anthony Bova eating every day.

The days rolled on, one after another with little change in our class until the event of one unseasonably warm day in February put an end to my job and my association with Anthony Bova. It might have been the warm, spring-like air wafting through the open windows that made him more unrestrained than usual, but Anthony seemed to have lost all control that day. I had to strike him so many times I lost count. "Please stop," I said to him once, "Sister's really getting mad." But it was no use.

After dismissal I waited for Lolly, but for some reason it was taking her longer than usual to come meet me. I thought she might have been at the front exit, gabbing with Susan Menza. As soon as I rounded the corner of the building I saw the crowd of kids, all grades, some laughing loudly, others with their hands covering their mouths as if they were sick. Out of the corner of my eye I saw Lolly running toward me, one of her knee socks sliding down her shin, her school bag banging against her hip. "Vivian, come on," she screamed, "somebody's having a fit. Somebody kicked a nun!" When she caught up to me she yanked my hand and pulled me after her back toward the throng of uniformed kids.

We got close enough to see the end of it, of Anthony being held by two nuns. He was kicking and screaming at them while everyone watched. Finally, exhausted, he collapsed to the ground. His books were strewn all over. Some of the nuns were clapping their hands, trying to call everyone to order and send us on our way home. Someone said to call his parents; I think it was Mother Superior. Sister Mary Joseph was wiping dusty footprints from the hem of her habit, muttering.

Lolly prodded me. "Come on," she said.

At first I couldn't move. Most of the other kids were already leaving. Lolly's arm went around my shoulder and she pulled me away before Anthony Bova could look up and see me.

That night, after dinner, I went straight to my room and lay on the bed recalling every punch, the feel of my knuckles against his fleshy arm. Sister Mary Joseph was respected in the school and the parish. No one would have believed me if I spoke out against her, not even my parents, who'd heard the story of that afternoon and thought that Anthony Bova must be crazy.

The next day, the seat in front of me was empty. Sister Mary Joseph carried on as if nothing out of the ordinary had occurred the day before. Anthony Bova transferred out of the school. Kids talked about Anthony and his "fit" for about a week and then it was forgotten, the way things are forgotten when you're in fourth grade, when you're nine years old and so unsure of everything you do, everything you see.

At thirty-six things change. Suddenly who you were twenty-seven years ago enlarges your regrets. Monsters float up out of the dust to remind you of your imperfections, whatever they may have been, continue to be. At 6:45 in the evening I was sitting on my front porch, still wearing my shorts and shirt from the morning. I hadn't even thought about getting dressed up to go to Lolly's. I pictured her in her new Euro style kitchen, in her renovated city brownstone, cabinets gleaming white, counter surfaces covered with the makings for cashew chicken, shrimp with snow peas and broccoli. My nieces and nephews, four of them, would be complaining about the late supper, snitching snacks from the refrigerator behind her back. She would have cool drinks, gin and tonics, maybe mint juleps, waiting for her husband Mark, for Danny and for me. There would be very thin, very long tapers glowing on the lacquered dining room table. Halfway through the meal she would present me with some silly gift for my post-op amusement, and then, when the evening was over, she would hug me at the door, tell me she'd see me when I opened . my eyes on Friday, she would be so sure I would open my eyes.

But despite the thoughts of her slaving away for my good luck dinner, I continued to sit on the porch, the wicker making its criss-cross pattern against the backs of my thighs. I could barely remember the day or what I'd done with it, except for the heat, the aftertaste of three scotches I'd downed one after the other at three, the disjointed phone conversation I'd had with my daughter who was impatient to get to her body movement class and couldn't begin to fathom, at sixteen, the weird circles in which time travelled, how it owed nothing to no one. I called my son too, but he'd already left for his job slinging hamburgers at some boardwalk cafe. Once or twice I considered walking to Oak Glenn, the town the newspaper said Tony Bova, an attorney, had lived in. I wanted to see his widow, his children. I wanted to explain myself to them.

At seven-fifteen I heard the phone ringing inside. Ten, twenty times but I made no move to answer it, even though I knew it was Danny calling, worried that something had happened to me. At seven-thirty when it pealed again I went into the shadowy house and stood listening to its insistent jangle until it stopped. The newspaper was where I'd left it that morning. I picked it up and studied the address, then without really thinking about what I was doing, I called information, got Bova's number and dialed. After a few rings a woman answered. Her voice was deep and tired.

"Is this Mrs. Bova?"

"Yes," she said. "Who's calling?"

I hesitated and the pause must have frightened her. "Yes?" she asked, her voice rising.

"Mrs. Bova, I knew your husband," I started.

"Who is this? Who are you?"

Perhaps she thought I was a mistress she had no knowledge of before that night, someone calling to stake a claim on her husband.

"Mrs. Bova, I just wanted to say that I'm sorry about Tony. I'm very, very sorry."

I began to cry and had to swallow hard to keep the tears back. I could hear mumbling in the background and when she asked again who it was, I couldn't answer.

"Is this some kind of a sick joke? Why won't you say who you are?"

My breath was caught in my throat. What could I tell her? That I hurt him, repeatedly and with little thought in the fourth grade? That his death seemed like an omen to me? That I believed his spirit would take its just revenge finally while I lie in an unnatural sleep on Friday?

Before I could say anything, she hung up. I left the phone off the hook, poured another scotch. Then I took my drink and the newspaper out to the backyard.

It was dusk when I heard the cars pulling up out front, the slamming of doors and the cacophony of familiar voices—Lolly's, Daniel's, Mark's, even my nieces's and nephews'. They were calling my name, turning on lights inside the house while I sat on my knees in the grass, mute. I'd read the obituary several times that evening as the light faded, creating different scenarios of Anthony Bova's life, but with each invented life I gave him, I still couldn't erase my silent culpability.

"Oh, for God's sake," I heard Lolly yell out the porch window, "there she is!" I turned then and pushed myself up, smacked the dirt from my hands, then reached down for the empty glass and the paper. They were all running toward me out the back door, all hollering and swearing at once. They'd been calling, they said. Had

I been hurt? they asked. Why was the line busy? The dinner was ruined. What the hell was I doing sitting in the yard?

Their angry, half-illuminated faces surrounded me, bright-eyed monkey faces on a jungle hot night, demanding an explanation. I took one step toward them, holding out the newspaper in the dark, open space between us.

"I have something to tell you . . ." I began.

MILAN KUNDERA

The Golden Apple of Eternal Desire

Milan Kundera (1929–   ) is a Czechoslovakian writer and political activist who has long fought against censorship in his native country. With the 1968 invasion of Czechoslovakia by the Soviet Union, he lost his job at the Prague Film Factory, his plays were no longer produced, and his books were banned. *Laughable Loves* (1974), from which the following selection is taken, is among his early published works and was one of only a few of his books published in Czechoslovakia. His other works include *The Book of Laughter and Forgetting* (1980), *The Joke* (1982), *The Unbearable Lightness of Being* (1984), and *Immortality* (1991).

. . . they do not know that they seek only the chase and not the quarry.
Blaise Pascal[1]

MARTIN

Martin is able to do something I'm incapable of. Stop any woman on any street. I must say that during the time I've known Martin I've greatly profited by this skill of his, for I like women not a whit less than he, but I wasn't granted his reckless audacity. On the other hand, through an error of Martin the so-called *arresting* of a woman itself sometimes became the goal of his virtuosity and he would very often stop at that. For this reason he used to say, not

---

[1] Blaise Pascal (1623–1662) was a French mathematician, physicist and religious philsopher and writer. (ED.)

without a certain bitterness, that he was like a forward, who unself-ishly passes certain balls to his teammate, who then shoots cheap goals and reaps cheap glory.

Last Monday afternoon after work I was waiting for him in a cafe on Vaclav Square, looking through a thick German book on ancient Etruscan culture. It had taken several months for the university library to negotiate its loan from Germany, and now that it had finally come just that day, I carried it off as if it were a relic, and I was actually quite pleased that Martin had kept me waiting for him, and that I could leaf through the book I'd long wanted at a cafe table.

Whenever I think about ancient cultures nostalgia seizes me. Perhaps this is nothing but envy of the sweet slowness of the history of that time: the era of ancient Egyptian culture lasted for several thousand years; the era of Greek antiquity for almost a thousand. In this respect, a single human life imitates the history of mankind; at first it is plunged into immobile slowness and only then gradually does it accelerate more and more. Just two months ago Martin had turned forty.

THE ADVENTURE BEGINS

It was he who disturbed my thoughtful mood. He appeared suddenly in the glass door of the cafe and headed for me, making expressive gestures and grimaces in the direction of a table at which a woman was sitting over a cup of coffee. Without taking his eyes off her, he sat down beside me and said, "What do you say about that?"

I felt humiliated; I'd actually been so engrossed in my thick volume that only now did I notice the girl; I had to admit that she was pretty. And at that moment the girl straightened up and called the man with the black bowtie, saying that she wished to pay.

"Pay too!" ordered Martin.

We thought that we would have to run after the girl, but luckily she was detained at the cloakroom. She had left a shopping bag there and the cloakroom attendant had to hunt for a while before placing it on the counter in front of the girl. As the girl gave the cloakroom attendant a couple of tenhaller pieces, Martin snatched the German book out of my hands.

"It will be better to put it in here," he said with daredevil non-chalance, and slipped the book carefully into the girl's bag. The girl looked surprised, but didn't know what she was supposed to say.

"It's uncomfortable to carry in one's hand," continued Martin,

and when the girl went to pick up the bag herself, he told me off for
not knowing how to behave.

The young woman was a nurse in a country hospital. She was in
Prague, she said, only for a look around and was hurrying off to the
bus terminal. The short distance to the streetcar stop was enough
for us to say everything essential and to agree that on Saturday we
would come to B. to visit this lovely young woman, who, as Martin
meaningfully pointed out, would certainly have some pretty colleague.

The streetcar arrived. I handed the young woman her bag, and
she began to take the book out of it, but Martin prevented her with
a grand gesture, saying we would come for it on Saturday, and that
she should read through it carefully in the meantime. The young
woman smiled in a bewildered fashion, the streetcar carried her away,
and we waved.

Nothing could be done; the book, which I'd been looking forward
to for so long, suddenly found itself in a faraway place; when you
came to think of it it was quite annoying; but nonetheless a certain
lunacy happily uplifted me on the wings it promptly provided. Martin
immediately began thinking about how to make an excuse for Saturday afternoon and night to his young wife (for this is how things
stand: at home he has a young wife; and what is worse, he loves her;
and what is still worse, he is afraid of her; and what is still far worse,
he is anxious about her).

A SUCCESSFUL REGISTRATION

For our excursion I borrowed a neat little Fiat and on Saturday
at two o'clock I drove up in front of Martin's apartment; Martin was
waiting for me and we set off. It was July and oppressively hot.

We wanted to get to B. as soon as possible, but when we saw, in
a village through which we were driving, two young men only in
swimming trunks and with eloquently wet hair, I stopped the car.
The lake was actually not far away, a few paces, a mere stone's throw.
I needed to be refreshed; Martin was also for swimming.

We changed into our swimming trunks and leaped into the water.
I dove into the water and swam quickly to the other side. Martin,
however, barely took a dip, washed himself off, and came out again.
When I'd had a good swim and returned to shore, I caught sight of
him in a state of intent absorption. On the shore a crowd of kids
was yelling, somewhere further off the local young people were
playing ball, but Martin was staring at the sturdy little figure of a

young girl, who was perhaps fifty feet away with her back toward us. Totally motionless, she was observing the water.

"Look," said Martin.

"I am looking."

"And what do you say?"

"What should I say?"

"You don't know what you should say about that?"

"We'll have to wait until she turns round," I suggested.

"Not at all. We don't have to wait until she turns round. What's showing from this side is quite enough for me."

"Okay. But we haven't time to spend with her."

"At least let's get her registered," said Martin, and turned to a little boy a short distance away who was putting on his swimming trunks: "Say, kid, d'you know the name of that girl over there?" and he pointed to the girl, who, apparently in some curious state of apathy, went on, standing in the same position.

"That one there?"

"Yeah, that one there."

"That one is not from here," said the little boy.

Martin turned to a little girl of about twelve, who was sunbathing close by:

"Say, kid, d'you know who that girl over there is, the one standing on the edge?"

The little girl obediently sat up. "That one there?"

"Yeah, that one."

"That's Manka . . ."

"Manka? Manka what?"

"Manka Panku . . . from Traplitse . . ."

And the girl still stood with her back to us looking at the water. Now she bent down for her swimming cap and when she straightened up again, putting it on her head as she did so, Martin was already at my side saying, "That's a certain Manka Panku from Traplitse. Now we can drive on."

He was completely calmed down and satisfied, and obviously no longer thinking of anything but the rest of the journey.

A LITTLE THEORY

That's what Martin calls *registration*. From his vast experience, he has come to the conclusion that it is not so difficult to *seduce* a girl—if in this area we have high quantitative pretensions—as it is always to *know* enough girls whom we have not yet seduced.

Therefore, he asserts that it is necessary always, no matter where, and at every opportunity, to compile a wide registration, i.e., to record in a notebook or in our memories, the names of women who have attracted us and whom we could contact sometime.

Making contact is a higher level of activity and means that we will get in touch with a particular woman, make her acquaintance, and gain access to her.

He who likes to look back boastfully will stress the names of the women he's made love to; but he who looks forward, toward the future, must above all see to it that he has plenty of *registered* and *contacted* women.

Above making contact there exists only one last level of activity, and I am happy to point out, in deference to Martin, that those who do not go after anything but this last level are wretched, primitive men, who remind me of village footballers, pressing forward thoughtlessly toward the rival goal and forgetting that a rash desire to shoot will not necessarily lead to this goal (or many further goals), but that a competent and fair game on the field will.

"Do you think that you'll go look her up in Traplitse sometime?" I asked Martin, when we were driving again.

"One can never know . . ." said Martin.

Then I said, "In any case the day is beginning propitiously for us."

GAME AND NECESSITY

We arrived at the hospital in B. in excellent spirits. It was about three-thirty. We called our nurse on the phone in the lobby. Before long she came down in her cap and white uniform; I noticed that she was blushing and I took this to be a good sign.

Martin began to talk right away and the girl informed us that she finished work at seven and that we should wait for her at that time in front of the hospital.

"Have you already arranged it with your girl friend?" asked Martin and the girl nodded:

"Yes, we'll both come."

"Fine," said Martin, "but we can't confront my colleague here with a fait accompli."

"O.K.," said the girl, "we can drop in on her; she is in the internal medicine ward."

As we walked slowly across the hospital courtyard I shyly said: "I wonder if you still have that thick book?"

The nurse nodded, saying that she did and in fact it was right here at the hospital. A weight fell from my heart and I insisted that we had to get it first.

Of course it seemed improper to Martin that I should openly give preference to a book over a woman about to be presented to me, but I just couldn't help it.

I confess that I had suffered greatly during those few days, having the book on Etruscan culture out of my sight. And it was only through great self-restraint that I had stoically put up with this, not wishing under any circumstances to spoil the Game, which has such value for me. Over the years I've learned to appreciate the Game and to subordinate to it all my personal interests and desires.

While I was having a touching reunion with my book, Martin continued his conversation with the pretty nurse, and got as far as getting her to promise that she would borrow a cabin by the nearby Hotersky Lake from a colleague for the evening. We were all perfectly happy. Finally we went across the hospital courtyard to a small green building, where the internal medicine ward was.

A nurse and a doctor were just walking toward us. The doctor was a funny-looking bean pole with protruding ears, which fascinated me all the more because at this moment our nurse elbowed me: I let out a short laugh. When they had passed us Martin turned to me: "So you're in luck, fella. You don't deserve such a gorgeous young woman."

I was ashamed to say that I had only looked at the bean pole, so I simulated approbation. After all, there wasn't any hypocrisy on my part. That is to say, I trust in Martin's taste more than in my own, because I believe that his taste is supported by a much greater *interest* than mine. I like objectivity and order in everything, even in love affairs, and consequently, I have more respect for the opinion of a connoisseur than for that of a dilettante.

Someone might consider it hypocritical for me to call myself a dilettante[2]—I a divorced man who is right now relating one of his (obviously in no way exceptional) affairs. But still I am a dilettante. It could be said that I am *playing* at something which Martin *lives*. Sometimes I have the feeling that the whole of my polygamous life is a consequence of nothing but my imitation of other men; although

---

[2] an amateur, or someone who dabbles in a certain field but never becomes an expert (ED.)

I am not denying that I take a liking to this imitation. But I cannot rid myself of the feeling that in this liking there remains, all the same, something entirely free, playful, and revocable, something that characterizes visits to art galleries or foreign countries, something not submitted to the unconditional imperative which I have suspected at the back of Martin's erotic life. It is precisely the presence of this unconditional imperative that has raised Martin in my eyes. His judgment about a woman seems to me to be that of Nature herself, Necessity herself speaking through his lips.

HOME SWEET HOME

When we found ourselves outside the hospital Martin pointed out that everything was going tremendously well for us, and then added: "Of course we'll have to hurry this evening. I want to be home by nine."

I was amazed: "By nine? That means we'll have to leave here at eight. But then we came here for no reason! I counted on having the whole night!"

"Why should you want to waste time!"

"But what sense is there in driving here for one hour? What can you do between seven and eight?"

"Everything. As you noticed I got hold of the cabin, so that everything will go swimmingly. It will depend only on you, you'll have to show that you're sufficiently determined."

"But why, I ask, must you be home at nine?"

"I promised Jirzhinka. She's used to playing a game of rummy before going to bed on Saturdays."

"Oh God . . ." I sighed.

"Yesterday again Jirzhinka had a bad time at the office, so I should give her this little bit of joy on Saturday, shouldn't I? You know, she's the best woman I've ever had. After all," he added, "you should be pleased anyway that you'll still have the whole night before you in Prague."

I understood that it was useless to object. Martin's misgivings about his wife's peace of mind could never be appeased, and his faith in the endless erotic possibilities of every hour or minute could never be shaken by anything.

"Come," said Martin, "there are still three hours till seven! We won't be idle!"

A DELUSION

We started on our way along the broad path of the local park, which served the inhabitants as a promenade. We inspected several pairs of girls who walked by us or were sitting on the benches, but we didn't like the look of them too well.

Martin, it must be admitted, accosted two of them, entered into conversation with them, and finally arranged a meeting with them, but I knew that he didn't mean it seriously. This was a so-called *practice contact,* which Martin performed from time to time in order to stay in practice.

Dissatisfied, we went out of the park into the streets, which yawned with small-town vacuity and boredom.

"Let's get something to drink, I'm thirsty," I said to Martin.

We found an establishment above which was the sign CAFE. We entered, but inside there was only self-service. It was a tiled room that gave off an air of coldness and hostility. We went over to the counter and bought ourselves watered-down lemonades from a sullen woman, and then carried them over to a table, which being moist with gravy, invited us to depart hastily.

"Don't worry about it," said Martin. "In our world ugliness has its positive function. No one feels like staying anywhere, people hurry on and thus arises the desirable pace of life. But we won't let ourselves be provoked by this. We can now talk about all sorts of things in the safety of this ugly place." He drank some lemonade and asked: "Have you contacted that medical student yet?"

"Naturally," I replied.

"And what's she like then? Describe to me exactly how she looks!"

I described the medical student to him. This was not very difficult for me to do, even though no medical student existed. Yes. Perhaps this puts me in a bad light, but it's like this: *I invented her.*

I give my word that I didn't do it maliciously, neither to show off in front of Martin nor because I wanted to lead him by the nose. I invented the medical student simply because I couldn't resist Martin's insistence.

Martin's claims about my activities were boundless. Martin was convinced that I met new women every day. He saw me as other than I am, and if I had truthfully told him that not only had I not possessed any new women for a week, but hadn't even come close, he would have taken me for a hypocrite.

For this reason, about a week earlier, I had been forced to dream up my registration of some medical student. Martin was satisfied and he urged me to contact her. And today he was checking up on my progress.

"And about what level is she on? Is she on the level . . ." He closed his eyes and in the darkness searched for a standard of measure: then he remembered a mutual friend: ". . . is she on Marketa's level?"

"She's far better," I said.

"Don't say . . . ," marveled Martin.

"She's on your Jirzhinka's level."

For Martin his own wife was the highest standard of measure. Martin was greatly pleased by my news and fell into a dreamlike state.

SUCCESSFULLY MAKING CONTACT

Then some girl in corduroy pants and a short jacket walked into the room. She went to the counter, waited for a soda, and took it away to drink. She approached a table adjoining ours, put the glass to her lips, and drank without sitting down.

Martin turned to her: "Miss," he said, "we're strangers here and we'd like to ask you a question."

The girl smiled. She was rather pretty.

"We are terribly hot and we don't know what we should do."

"Go and take a swim."

"That's just it. We don't know where to go swimming around here."

"There isn't any swimming here."

"How is that possible?"

"There's one swimming pool, but it's been empty for a month now."

"And what about the river?"

"It's being dredged."

"So where do you go swimming?"

"Only at Hotersky Lake, but it's at least five miles away."

"That's a small matter, we have a car, it would be very nice if you'd accompany us."

"As our guide," I said.

"Our guiding light," Martin corrected me.

"Our starlight," said I.

"Our North Star," said Martin.

"Our planet Venus," I said.

"You're simply our constellation and you should go with us," said Martin.

The girl was confused by our foolish banter and finally said that she would go, but that she had to take care of something first and then she'd pick up her bathing suit; she said that we should be waiting for her in exactly an hour at this same spot.

We were glad. We watched her as she walked away, cutely swinging her backside and tossing her black curls.

"You see," said Martin, "life is short. We must take advantage of every minute."

IN PRAISE OF FRIENDSHIP

We went once again into the park. Once again we examined several pairs of girls on the benches; it happened that many a young woman was good-looking, but it never happened that her companion was also good-looking.

"In this there is some special law," I said to Martin. "An ugly woman hopes to gain something from the luster of her pretty friend; a pretty woman, for her part, hopes that she will stand out more lustrously against the background of the ugly woman; and for us it follows from this that our friendship is subjected to continuous trials. And it is precisely this that I value, that we will never leave the choice to the random development of events, nor even to some mutual struggle; choice for us is always a matter of courtesy. We'd offer each other the prettier girl like two old-fashioned gentlemen who can never enter a room because neither wants to be the one who goes first."

"Yes," said Martin with emotion. "You're a great buddy. Come, let's go sit down for a while, my legs are aching."

And thus we sat comfortably with our faces turned up toward the face of the sun, and we let the world around us rush on unnoticed.

THE GIRL IN WHITE

All of a sudden Martin got up (moved evidently by some mysterious sense) and stared along a secluded path of the park. A girl in a white dress was coming our way. Already from afar, before it was possible to ascertain with complete confidence the proportions of her body or the features of her face, we saw that she possessed unmistakable, special, and very perceptible charm, that there was a certain purity or tenderness in her appearance.

When the girl was fairly close to us, we realized that she was quite young, something between a child and a young woman, and this at once threw us into a state of complete agitation. Martin shot up off the bench: "Miss, I am the director Forman, the film director; you must help us."

He gave her his hand and the young girl with an utterly astonished expression shook it.

Martin nodded in my direction and said: "This is my cameraman."

"Andricek," I offered my hand.

The girl nodded.

"We are in an awkward situation here. I am looking for outdoor locations for my film. Our assistant, who knows this area well, was supposed to meet us here, but he hasn't arrived so that right now we are wondering how to get about in this town and in the surrounding countryside. My friend Andricek here," joked Martin, "is always studying his fat German book but unfortunately it is not to be found in there."

The allusion to the book, which I had been deprived of for the whole week, somehow irritated me all of a sudden: "It's a pity that you don't take a greater interest in this book," I attacked my director. "If you prepared thoroughly and didn't leave the studying to your cameramen maybe your films wouldn't be so superficial and there wouldn't be so much nonsense in them . . . forgive me." I turned then to the girl with an apology. "Anyhow, we won't bother you with our quarrels about our work; our film is to be a historical film and will touch upon Etruscan culture in Bohemia . . ."

"Yes," the girl nodded.

"It's a rather interesting book—look." I handed the girl the book and she took it in her hands with a certain religious awe, and when she saw that I wanted her to, turned the pages lightly.

"The Phachek castle must surely not be far from here," I continued. "It was the center of the Bohemian Etruscans . . . but how can we get there?"

"It's only a little way," said the girl and beamed all over, because her secure knowledge of the road to Phachek gave her a little bit of firm ground in the somewhat obscure conversation that we were carrying on with her.

"Yes? Do you know the area around there?" asked Martin, feigning great relief.

"Sure I know it!" said the girl. "It's an hour away!"

"On foot?" asked Martin.

"Yes, on foot," said the girl.

"But luckily we have a car here," I said.

"Wouldn't you like to be our guide?" said Martin, but I didn't continue the customary ritual of witticisms, because I have a more precise sense of psychological judgment than Martin, and I felt that frivolous joking would be more inclined to harm us in this case and that our best weapon was absolute seriousness.

"We do not want, miss, to disturb you in any way," I said, "but if you would be so kind as to devote a short time to us and show us some of the places we're looking for, you would help us a great deal—and we would both be very grateful."

"But yes," the girl nodded again, "I am happy . . . but I . . ." Only now did we notice that she had a shopping bag in her hand and in it two heads of lettuce. "I must take Mom the lettuce, but it's only a little way away and I would come right back . . ."

"Of course you must take the lettuce to Mom on time and intact," I said. "We will be happy to wait here."

"Yes. It won't take more than ten minutes," said the girl and once again she nodded, and then she walked off quickly and anxiously.

"God!" said Martin and sat down.

"Isn't it great, eh?"

"I should say so. For this I'd be willing to sacrifice our two female barber surgeons."

THE TRAP OF EXCESSIVE FAITH

But ten minutes passed, a quarter of an hour, and the girl didn't come.

"Don't be afraid," Martin consoled me. "If anything is certain, then it's this, that she'll come. Our performance was completely plausible and the girl was in raptures."

I too was of this opinion, and so we went on waiting, with each moment becoming more and more eager for this childish young girl. In the meanwhile, also, the time appointed for our meeting with the girl in corduroy pants went by, but we were so set on our little girl in white that it didn't even occur to us to leave.

And time was passing.

"Listen, Martin, I think that she won't come now," I said at last.

"How do you explain it? After all, that girl believed in us as in God Himself."

"Yes," I said, "and in that lies our misfortune. That is to say she believed us only too well!"

"What? Perhaps you'd have wanted her not to believe us?"

"It would perhaps have been better like that. Too much faith is the worst ally." A thought took my fancy; I got really involved in it: "When you believe in something literally, through your faith you'll turn it into something absurd. One who is a genuine adherent, if you like, of some political outlook, never takes its *sophistries*[3] seriously, but only its practical aims, which are concealed beneath these sophistries. Political rhetoric and sophistries do not exist, after all, in order that they be believed; rather, they have to serve as *a common and agreed upon alibi.* Foolish people, who take them in earnest, sooner or later discover inconsistencies in them, begin to protest, and finish finally and infamously as heretics and apostates. No, too much faith never brings anything good—and not only to political or religious systems but even to our own system, the one we used to convince the girl."

"Somehow I'm not quite following you any more."

"It's quite simple: for the girl we were actually two serious and respectable gentlemen, and she, like a well-behaved child who offers her seat to an older person on a streetcar, wanted to please us."

"So why didn't she please us?"

"Because she believed us so completely. She gave Mom the lettuce and at once told her enthusiastically all about us: about the historical film, about the Etruscans in Bohemia, and Mom . . ."

"Yes, the rest is perfectly clear to me . . ." Martin interrupted me and got up from the bench.

THE BETRAYAL

The sun was already slowly going down over the roofs of the town. It was cooling off a bit and we felt sad. We went to the cafe just in case the girl in the corduroy pants was by some mistake still waiting for us. Of course she wasn't there. It was six-thirty. We walked down to the car, and feeling all of a sudden like two people who had been banished from a foreign city and its pleasures, we said to ourselves that nothing remained for us but to retire to the extra-territorial domain of our own car.

"Come on!" remonstrated Martin in the car. "Anyhow, don't look so gloomy! We don't have any reason for that! The most important thing is still before us!"

I wanted to object that we had no more than an hour for the

---

[3] clever, but perhaps deceptive or misleading, arguments (ED.)

most important thing, because of Jirzhinka and her rummy—but I chose to keep silent.

"Anyway," continued Martin, "it was a fruitful day; the registration of that girl from Traplitse, contact with the girl in the corduroy pants; after all, we have it all set up whenever we feel like it. We don't have to do anything but drive here again!"

I didn't object at all. Registration and contact had been excellently brought off. This was quite in order. But at this moment it occurred to me that for the last year, apart from countless registrations and contacts, Martin had not come by anything more worthwhile.

I looked at him. As always his eyes shone with a lustful glow. I felt at that moment that I liked Martin and that I also liked the banner under which he had been marching all his life: the banner of the eternal pursuit of women.

Time was passing and Martin said, "It's seven o'clock."

We drove to within about thirty feet of the hospital gates, so that in the rear-view mirror I could safely observe who was coming out.

I was still thinking about that banner. And also about the fact that in this pursuit of women from year to year it had become less a matter of women and much more a matter of the pursuit itself. Assuming that the pursuit is known to be *vain* in advance, it is possible to pursue any number of women and thus to make the pursuit *an absolute pursuit*. Yes: Martin had attained the state of being in absolute pursuit.

We waited five minutes. The girls didn't come.

It didn't put me out in the least. It was a matter of complete indifference to me whether they came or not. Even if they came, could we in a mere hour drive with them to the isolated cabin, become intimate with them, make love to them, and at eight o'clock say goodbye pleasantly and take off? No, at that moment when Martin limited our available time to ending on the stroke of eight, he had shifted the whole affair to the sphere of a self-deluding game.

Ten minutes went by. No one appeared at the gates.

Martin became indignant and almost yelled: "I'll give them five more minutes! I won't wait any longer!"

Martin hasn't been young for quite a while now, I speculated further. He truly loves his wife. As a matter of fact he has the most regular sort of marriage. This is a reality. And yet—above this reality (and simultaneously with it), Martin's youth continues, a restless, gay, and erring youth transformed into a mere game, a game that was no longer in any way up to crossing the line into real life and realizing itself as a fact. And because Martin is the knight obsessed by Necessity, he has transformed his love affairs into the harmlessness of a Game, *without knowing it;* so he continues to put his whole inflamed soul into them.

O.K., I said to myself. Martin is the captive of his self-deception, but what am I? What am I? Why do I assist him in this ridiculous game? Why do I, who know that all of this is a delusion, pretend along with him? Am I not then still more ridiculous than Martin? Why at this time should I behave as if an amorous adventure lay before me, when I know that at most a single aimless hour with unknown and indifferent girls awaits me?

At that moment in the mirror I caught sight of two young women at the hospital gates. Even from that distance they gave off a glow of powder and rouge. They were strikingly chic and their delay was obviously connected with their well made-up appearance. They looked around and headed toward our car.

"Martin, there's nothing to be done." I renounced the girls. "It's over a quarter of an hour. Let's go." And I put my foot on the gas.

REPENTANCE

We drove out of B. We passed the last little houses and drove into the countryside through fields and woods, toward whose treetops a large sun was sinking.

We were silent.

I thought about Judas Iscariot, about whom a brilliant author relates that he betrayed Jesus just because he *believed* in him infinitely: he couldn't wait for the miracle through which Jesus was to have shown all the Jews his divine power; so he handed Him over to His tormentors in order to provoke Him at last to action; he betrayed Him, because he longed to hasten His victory.

Oh God, I said to myself, I've betrayed Martin from far less noble motives; I betrayed him in fact just because I stopped believing in him (and in the divine power of his womanizing); I am a vile compound of Judas Iscariot and of the man whom they called Doubting Thomas. I felt that as a result of my wrongdoing my sympathy for Martin was growing and that his banner of the eternal chase (which was to be heard still fluttering above us) was reducing me to tears. I began to reproach myself for my overhasty action.

Shall I be in a position more easily to part with these gestures which signify youth for me? And will there remain for me perhaps something other than to *imitate* them and endeavor to find a small, safe place for this foolish activity within my otherwise sensible life?

What does it matter that it's all a futile game? What does it matter that I *know* it? Will I stop playing the game just because it is futile?

THE GOLDEN APPLE OF ETERNAL DESIRE

He was sitting beside me and little by little his indignation subsided.

"Listen," he said, "is that medical student really so high-class?"

"I'm telling you she's on Jirzhinka's level."

Martin put further questions to me. I had to describe the medical student to him once again.

Then he said: "Perhaps you could hand her over to me afterward, eh?"

I wanted to appear plausible. "That may be quite difficult. It would bother her that you're my buddy. She has firm principles . . ."

"She has firm principles . . . ," said Martin sadly, and it was plain that he was upset by this.

I didn't want to upset him.

"Unless I could pretend I don't know you," I said. "Perhaps you could pass yourself off as someone else."

"Fine! Perhaps as Forman, like today!"

"She doesn't give a damn about film directors. She prefers athletes."

"Why not?" said Martin, "it's all within the realm of possibility," and we spent some time involved in this discussion. From moment to moment the plan became clearer and after a while it dangled before us in the advancing twilight like a beautiful, ripe, shining apple.

Permit me to name this apple with a certain ceremoniousness The Golden Apple of Eternal Desire.

ERIC HOFFER

The True Believer

Eric Hoffer (1902–1983) was born in New York City but worked
as a migrant farmer, a gold miner in Nevada, and a longshoreman
in San Francisco. He is perhaps best known for his book *The True
Believer* (1951), a study of mass movements from which the following selection is taken. Other works include *The Temper of Our
Time* (1964), *Before the Sabbath* (1979), and *Truth Imagined*
(1983).

I

It is a truism that many who join a rising revolutionary movement are attracted by the prospect of sudden and spectacular change
in their conditions of life. A revolutionary movement is a conspicuous
instrument of change.

Not so obvious is the fact that religious and nationalist movements too can be vehicles of change. Some kind of widespread
enthusiasm or excitement is apparently needed for the realization of
vast and rapid change, and it does not seem to matter whether the
exhilaration is derived from an expectation of untold riches or is
generated by an active mass movement. In this country the spectacular changes since the Civil War were enacted in an atmosphere
charged with the enthusiasm born of fabulous opportunities for self-
advancement. Where self-advancement cannot, or is not allowed to,
serve as a driving force, other sources of enthusiasm have to be found
if momentous changes, such as the awakening and renovation of a
stagnant society or radical reforms in the character and pattern of
life of a community, are to be realized and perpetuated. Religious,
revolutionary and nationalist movements are such generating plants
of general enthusiasm.

In the past, religious movements were the conspicuous vehicles
of change. The conservatism of a religion—its orthodoxy—is the
inert coagulum of a once highly reactive sap. A rising religious
movement is all change and experiment—open to new views and
techniques from all quarters. Islam when it emerged was an organizing and modernizing medium. Christianity was a civilizing and modernizing influence among the savage tribes of Europe. The Crusades

and the Reformation both were crucial factors in shaking the Western world from the stagnation of the Middle Ages.

In modern times, the mass movements involved in the realization of vast and rapid change are revolutionary and nationalist—singly or in combination. Peter the Great[1] was probably the equal, in dedication, power and ruthlessness, of many of the most successful revolutionary or nationalist leaders. Yet he failed in his chief purpose, which was to turn Russia into a Western nation. And the reason he failed was that he did not infuse the Russian masses with some soul-stirring enthusiasm. He either did not think it necessary or did not know how to make of his purpose a holy cause. It is not strange that the Bolshevik revolutionaries who wiped out the last of the Czars and Romanovs should have a sense of kinship with Peter—a Czar and Romanov. For his purpose is now theirs, and they hope to succeed where he failed. The Bolshevik revolution may figure in history as much an attempt to modernize a sixth of the world's surface as an attempt to build a Communist economy.

The fact that both the French and the Russian revolutions turned into nationalist movements seems to indicate that in modern times nationalism is the most copious and durable source of mass enthusiasm, and that nationalist fervor must be tapped if the drastic changes projected and initiated by revolutionary enthusiasm are to be consummated. One wonders whether the difficulties encountered by the present Labor government in Britain are not partly due to the fact that the attempt to change the economy of the country and the way of life of 49,000,000 people has been initiated in an atmosphere singularly free from fervor, exaltation and wild hope. The revulsion from the ugly patterns developed by most contemporary mass movements has kept the civilized and decent leaders of the Labor party shy of revolutionary enthusiasm. The possibility still remains that events might force them to make use of some mild form of chauvinism so that in Britain too "the socialization of the nation [might have] as its natural corollary the nationalization of socialism."

The phenomenal modernization of Japan would probably not have been possible without the revivalist spirit of Japanese nationalism. It is perhaps also true that the rapid modernization of some European countries (Germany in particular) was facilitated to some

---

[1] Peter the Great (1672–1725) was a Tsar of Russia who reformed the government and the military and brought his country into closer contact with Western Europe. (ED.)

extent by the upsurge and thorough diffusion of nationalist fervor. Judged by present indications, the renascence of Asia will be brought about through the instrumentality of nationalist movements rather than by other mediums. It was the rise of a genuine nationalist movement which enabled Kemal Ataturk[2] to modernize Turkey almost overnight. In Egypt, untouched by a mass movement, modernization is slow and faltering, though its rulers, from the day of Mehmed Ali,[3] have welcomed Western ideas, and its contacts with the West have been many and intimate. Zionism is an instrument for the renovation of a backward country and the transformation of shopkeepers and brain workers into farmers, laborers and soldiers. Had Chiang Kai-shek[4] known how to set in motion a genuine mass movement, or at least sustain the nationalist enthusiasm kindled by the Japanese invasion, he might have been acting now as the renovator of China. Since he did not know how, he was easily shoved aside by the masters of the art of "religiofication"—the art of turning practical purposes into holy causes. It is not difficult to see why America and Britain (or any Western democracy) could not play a direct and leading role in arousing the Asiatic countries from their backwardness and stagnation: the democracies are neither inclined nor perhaps able to kindle a revivalist spirit in Asia's millions. The contribution of the Western democracies to the awakening of the East has been indirect and certainly unintended. They have kindled an enthusiasm of resentment against the West; and it is this anti-Western fervor which is at present rousing the Orient from its stagnation of centuries.

Though the desire for change is not infrequently a superficial motive, it is yet worth finding out whether a probing of this desire might not shed some light on the inner working of mass movements. We shall inquire therefore into the nature of the desire for change.

II

There is in us a tendency to locate the shaping forces of our existence outside ourselves. Success and failure are unavoidably related in our minds with the state of things around us. Hence it is

[2] Kemal Atatürk (1881–1938), a soldier, reformer, and statesman, was the founder and first president (from 1923 to 1930) of the Republic of Turkey. (ED.)

[3] Mehmed Ali (1805–1882) was a Viceroy of Egypt who led invasions of neighboring Arab countries and reorganized the government in Cairo. (ED.)

[4] Chiang Kai-shek (1887–1975) was a general who fled to Taiwan in 1949 after the Communists came to power in China. (ED.)

that people with a sense of fulfillment think it a good world and would like to conserve it as it is, while the frustrated favor radical change. The tendency to look for all causes outside ourselves persists even when it is clear that our state of being is the product of personal qualities such as ability, character, appearance, health and so on. "If anything ail a man," says Thoreau, "so that he does not perform his functions, if he have a pain in his bowels even . . . he forthwith sets about reforming—the world."

It is understandable that those who fail should incline to blame the world for their failure. The remarkable thing is that the successful, too, however much they pride themselves on their foresight, fortitude, thrift and other "sterling qualities," are at bottom convinced that their success is the result of a fortuitous combination of circumstances. The self-confidence of even the consistently successful is never absolute. They are never sure that they know all the ingredients which go into the making of their success. The outside world seems to them a precariously balanced mechanism, and so long as it ticks in their favor they are afraid to tinker with it. Thus the resistance to change and the ardent desire for it spring from the same conviction, and the one can be as vehement as the other.

III

Discontent by itself does not invariably create a desire for change. Other factors have to be present before discontent turns into disaffection. One of these is a sense of power.

Those who are awed by their surroundings do not think of change, no matter how miserable their condition. When our mode of life is so precarious as to make it patent that we cannot control the circumstances of our existence, we tend to stick to the proven and the familiar. We counteract a deep feeling of insecurity by making of our existence a fixed routine. We hereby acquire the illusion that we have tamed the unpredictable. Fisherfolk, nomads and farmers who have to contend with the willful elements, the creative worker who depends on inspiration, the savage awed by his surroundings— they all fear change. They face the world as they would an all-powerful jury. The abjectly poor, too, stand in awe of the world around them and are not hospitable to change. It is a dangerous life we live when hunger and cold are at our heels. There is thus a conservatism of the destitute as profound as the conservatism of the privileged, and the former is as much a factor in the perpetuation of a social order as the latter.

The men who rush into undertakings of vast change usually feel they are in possession of some irresistible power. The generation that made the French Revolution had an extravagant conception of the omnipotence of man's reason and the boundless range of his intelligence. Never, says de Tocqueville,[5] had humanity been prouder of itself nor had it ever so much faith in its own omnipotence. And joined with this exaggerated self-confidence was a universal thirst for change which came unbidden to every mind. Lenin and the Bolsheviks who plunged recklessly into the chaos of the creation of a new world had blind faith in the omnipotence of Marxist doctrine. The Nazis had nothing as potent as that doctrine, but they had faith in an infallible leader and also faith in a new technique. For it is doubtful whether National Socialism would have made such rapid progress if it had not been for the electrifying conviction that the new techniques of blitzkrieg and propaganda made Germany irresistible.

Even the sober desire for progress is sustained by faith—faith in the intrinsic goodness of human nature and in the omnipotence of science. It is a defiant and blasphemous faith, not unlike that held by the men who set out to build "a city and a tower, whose top may reach unto heaven" and who believed that "nothing will be restrained from them, which they have imagined to do."

IV

Offhand one would expect that the mere possession of power would automatically result in a cocky attitude toward the world and a receptivity to change. But it is not always so. The powerful can be as timid as the weak. What seems to count more than possession of instruments of power is faith in the future. Where power is not joined with faith in the future, it is used mainly to ward off the new and preserve the status quo. On the other hand, extravagant hope, even when not backed by actual power, is likely to generate a most reckless daring. For the hopeful can draw strength from the most ridiculous sources of power—a slogan, a word, a button. No faith is potent unless it is also faith in the future; unless it has a millennial component. So, too, an effective doctrine: as well as being a source of power, it must also claim to be a key to the book of the future.

[5] Alexis de Tocqueville (1805–1859) was a French politician and writer who reached prominence around the time of the French Revolution of 1848; his work *Democracy in America,* an analysis of the American government of the time, is considered a classic of political literature. (ED.)

Those who would transform a nation or the world cannot do so by breeding and captaining discontent or by demonstrating the reasonableness and desirability of the intended changes or by coercing people into a new way of life. They must know how to kindle and fan an extravagant hope. It matters not whether it be hope of a heavenly kingdom, of heaven on earth, of plunder and untold riches, of fabulous achievement or world dominion. If the Communists win Europe and a large part of the world, it will not be because they know how to stir up discontent or how to infect people with hatred, but because they know how to preach hope.

V

Thus the differences between the conservative and the radical seem to spring mainly from their attitude toward the future. Fear of the future causes us to lean against and cling to the present, while faith in the future renders us receptive to change. Both the rich and the poor, the strong and the weak, they who have achieved much or little can be afraid of the future. When the present seems so perfect that the most we can expect is its even continuation in the future, change can only mean deterioration. Hence men of outstanding achievement and those who live full, happy lives usually set their faces against drastic innovation. The conservatism of invalids and people past middle age stems, too, from fear of the future. They are on the lookout for signs of decay, and feel that any change is more likely to be for the worse than for the better. The abjectly poor also are without faith in the future. The future seems to them a booby trap buried on the road ahead. One must step gingerly. To change things is to ask for trouble.

As for the hopeful: it does not seem to make any difference who it is that is seized with a wild hope—whether it be an enthusiastic intellectual, a land-hungry farmer, a get-rich-quick speculator, a sober merchant or industrialist, a plain workingman or a noble lord— they all proceed recklessly with the present, wreck it if necessary, and create a new world. There can thus be revolutions by the privileged as well as by the underprivileged. The movement of enclosure[6] in sixteenth and seventeenth century England was a revolution by the rich. The woolen industry rose to high prosperity, and grazing

---

[6] The transference of land by nobles from use for farming to sheep grazing, and the consequent eviction of poor farm families. (ED.)

became more profitable than cropping. The landowners drove off their tenants, enclosed the commons and wrought profound changes in the social and economic texture of the country. "The lords and nobles were upsetting the social order, breaking down ancient law and custom, sometimes by means of violence, often by pressure and intimidation." Another English revolution by the rich occurred at the end of the eighteenth and the beginning of the nineteenth century. It was the Industrial Revolution. The breathtaking potentialities of mechanization set the minds of manufacturers and merchants on fire. They began a revolution "as extreme and radical as ever inflamed the minds of sectarians," and in a relatively short time these respectable, Godfearing citizens changed the face of England beyond recognition.

When hopes and dreams are loose in the streets, it is well for the timid to lock doors, shutter windows and lie low until the wrath has passed. For there is often a monstrous incongruity between the hopes, however noble and tender, and the action which follows them. It is as if ivied maidens and garlanded youths were to herald the four horsemen of the apocalypse.

VI

For men to plunge headlong into an undertaking of vast change, they must be intensely discontented yet not destitute, and they must have the feeling that by the possession of some potent doctrine, infallible leader or some new technique they have access to a source of irresistible power. They must also have an extravagant conception of the prospects and potentialities of the future. Finally, they must be wholly ignorant of the difficulties involved in their vast undertaking. Experience is a handicap. The men who started the French Revolution were wholly without political experience. The same is true of the Bolsheviks, Nazis and the revolutionaries in Asia. The experienced man of affairs is a latecomer. He enters the movement when it is already a going concern. It is perhaps the Englishman's political experience that keeps him shy of mass movements.

DOROTHY L. SAYERS

Are Women Human?

Dorothy L. Sayers (1893–1957) was born in Oxford, England, and is best known for her detective novels about Lord Peter Whimsey, which she wrote to support herself while she worked on poetry, plays, criticism, and essays, often on theological topics. Her nonfiction works include *The Mind of the Maker* (1941), *Creed and Chaos* (1947), and *Unpopular Opinions* (1947), the collection of essays in which the following selection appears.

When I was asked to come and speak to you, your Secretary made the suggestion that she thought I must be interested in the feminist movement. I replied—a little irritably, I am afraid—that I was not sure I wanted to "identify myself," as the phrase goes, with feminism, and that the time for "feminism," in the old-fashioned sense of the word, had gone past. In fact, I think I went so far as to say that, under present conditions, an aggressive feminism might do more harm than good. As a result I was, perhaps not unnaturally, invited to explain myself.

I do not know that it is very easy to explain, without offence or risk of misunderstanding, exactly what I do mean, but I will try.

The question of "sex-equality" is, like all questions affecting human relationships, delicate and complicated. It cannot be settled by loud slogans or hard-and-fast assertions like "a woman is as good as a man"—or "woman's place is the home"—or "women ought not to take men's jobs." The minute one makes such assertions, one finds one has to qualify them. "A woman is as good as a man" is as meaningless as to say, "A Kaffir[1] is as good as a Frenchman" or "a poet is as good as an engineer" or "an elephant is as good as a racehorse"—it means nothing whatever until you add: "at doing what?" In a religious sense, no doubt, the Kaffir is as valuable in the eyes of God as a Frenchman—but the average Kaffir is probably less skilled in literary criticism than the average Frenchman, and the average Frenchman less skilled than the average Kaffir in tracing the

---

[1] a member of the Bantu tribes, especially those of southern Africa (ED.)

spoor[2] of big game. There might be exceptions on either side: it is largely a matter of heredity and education. When we balance the poet against the engineer, we are faced with a fundamental difference of temperament—so that here our question is complicated by the enormous social problem whether poetry or engineering is "better" for the State, or for humanity in general. There may be people who would like a world that was all engineers or all poets—but most of us would like to have a certain number of each; though here again, we should all differ about the desirable proportion of engineering to poetry. The only proviso we should make is that people with dreaming and poetical temperaments should not entangle themselves in engines, and that mechanically-minded persons should not issue booklets of bad verse. When we come to the elephant and the racehorse, we come down to bedrock physical differences—the elephant would make a poor showing in the Derby, and the unbeaten Eclipse himself would be speedily eclipsed by an elephant when it came to hauling logs.

That is so obvious that it hardly seems worth saying. But it is the mark of all movements, however well-intentioned, that their pioneers tend, by much lashing of themselves into excitement, to lose sight of the obvious. In reaction against the age-old slogan, "woman is the weaker vessel," or the still more offensive, "woman is a divine creature," we have, I think, allowed ourselves to drift into asserting the "a woman is as good as a man," without always pausing to think what exactly we mean by that. What, I feel, we ought to mean is something so obvious that it is apt to escape attention altogether, viz: not that every woman is, in virtue of her sex, as strong, clever, artistic, level-headed, industrious, and so forth as any man that can be mentioned; but, that a woman is just as much an ordinary human being as a man, with the same individual preferences, and with just as much right to the tastes and preferences of an individual. What is repugnant to every human being is to be reckoned always as a member of a class and not as an individual person. A certain amount of classification is, of course, necessary for practical purposes: there is no harm in saying that women, as a class, have smaller bones than men, wear lighter clothing, have more hair on their heads and less on their faces, go more pertinaciously to church or the cinema, or have more patience with small and noisy babies. In the same way,

---

[2] the trail of a wild animal (ED.)

we may say that stout people of both sexes are commonly better-tempered than thin ones, or that university dons of both sexes are more pedantic in their speech than agricultural labourers, or that Communists of both sexes are more ferocious than Fascists—or the other way round. What is unreasonable and irritating is to assume that *all* one's tastes and preferences have to be conditioned by the class to which one belongs. That has been the very common error into which men have frequently fallen about women—and it is the error into which feminist women are, perhaps, a little inclined to fall into about themselves.

Take, for example, the very usual reproach that women nowadays always want to "copy what men do." In that reproach there is a great deal of truth and a great deal of sheer, unmitigated, and indeed quite wicked nonsense. There are a number of jobs and pleasures which men have in times past cornered for themselves. At one time, for instance, men had a monopoly of classical education. When the pioneers of university training for women demanded that women should be admitted to the universities, the cry went up at once: "Why should women want to know about Aristotle?" The answer is NOT that *all* women would be the better for knowing about Aristotle—still less, as Lord Tennyson seemed to think, that they would be more companionable wives for their husbands if they did know about Aristotle—but simply: "What women want as a class is irrelevant. *I* want to know about Aristotle. It is true that most women care nothing about him, and a great many male undergraduates turn pale and faint at the thought of him—but I, eccentric individual that I am, do want to know about Aristotle, and I submit that there is nothing in my shape or bodily functions which need prevent my knowing about him."

That battle was won, and rightly won, for women. But there is a sillier side to the university education of women. I have noticed lately, and with regret, a tendency on the part of the women's colleges to "copy the men" on the side of their failings and absurdities, and this is not so good. Because the constitution of the men's colleges is autocratic, old-fashioned, and in many respects inefficient, the women are rather inclined to try and cramp their own collegiate constitutions—which were mapped out on freer democratic lines—into the mediaeval mould of the men's—and that is unsound. It contributes nothing to the university and it loses what might have been a very good thing. The women students, too, have a foolish trick of imitating and outdoing the absurdities of male undergraduates. To climb in drunk after hours and get gated is silly and harmless if done out of pure high spirits; if it is done "because the men do it," it is worse than silly, because it is not spontaneous and not even amusing.

Let me give one simple illustration of the difference between the right and the wrong kind of feminism. Let us take this terrible business—so distressing to the minds of bishops—of the women who go about in trousers. We are asked: "Why do you want to go about in trousers? They are extremely unbecoming to most of you. You only do it to copy the men." To this we may very properly reply: "It is true that they are unbecoming. Even on men they are remarkably unattractive. But, as you men have discovered for yourselves, they are comfortable, they do not get in the way of one's activities like skirts and they protect the wearer from draughts about the ankles. As a human being, I like comfort, and dislike draughts. If the trousers do not attract you, so much the worse; for the moment I do not want to attract you. I want to enjoy myself as a human being, and why not? As for copying you, certainly you thought of trousers first and to that extent we must copy you. But we are not such abandoned copy-cats as to attach these useful garments to our bodies with braces. There we draw the line. These machines of leather and elastic are unnecessary and unsuited to the female form. They are, moreover, hideous beyond description. And as for indecency—of which you sometimes accuse the trousers—we at least can take our coats off without becoming the half-undressed bedroom spectacle that a man presents in his shirt and braces."

So that when we hear that women have once more laid hands upon something which was previously a man's sole privilege, I think we have to ask ourselves: is this trousers or is it braces? Is it something useful, convenient, and suitable to a human being as such? Or is it merely something unnecessary to us, ugly, and adopted merely for the sake of collaring the other fellow's property? These jobs and professions, now. It is ridiculous to take on a man's job just in order to be able to say that "a woman has done it—yah!" The only decent reason for tackling any job is that it is *your* job and *you* want to do it.

At this point, somebody is likely to say: "Yes, that is all very well. But it *is* the woman who is always trying to ape the man. She *is* the inferior being. You don't as a rule find the men trying to take the women's jobs away from them. They don't force their way into the household and turn women out of their rightful occupations."

Of course they do not. They have done it already.

Let us accept the idea that women should stick to their own

jobs—the jobs they did so well in the good old days before they started talking about votes and women's rights. Let us return to the Middle Ages and ask what we should get then in return for certain political and educational privileges which we should have to abandon.

It is a formidable list of jobs: the whole of the spinning industry, the whole of the dyeing industry, the whole of the weaving industry. The whole catering industry and—which would not please Lady Astor,[3] perhaps—the whole of the nation's brewing and distilling. All the preserving, pickling, and bottling industry, all the bacon-curing. And (since in those days a man was often absent from home for months together on war or business) a very large share in the management of landed estates. Here are the women's jobs—and what has become of them? They are all being handled by men. It is all very well to say that woman's place is the home—but modern civilisation has taken all these pleasant and profitable activities out of the home, where the women looked after them, and handed them over to big industry, to be directed and organised by men at the head of large factories. Even the dairy-maid in her simple bonnet has gone, to be replaced by a male mechanic in charge of a mechanical milking plant.

Now, it is very likely that men in big industries do these jobs better than the women did them at home. The fact remains that the home contains much less of interesting activity than it used to contain. What is more, the home has so shrunk to the size of a small flat that—even if we restrict woman's job to the bearing and rearing of families—there is no room for her to do even that. It is useless to urge the modern woman to have twelve children, like her grandmother. Where is she to put them when she has got them? And what modern man wants to be bothered with them? It is perfectly idiotic to take away women's traditional occupations and then complain because she looks for new ones. Every woman is a human being— one cannot repeat that too often—and a human being *must* have occupation, if he or she is not to become a nuisance to the world.

I am not complaining that the brewing and baking were taken over by the men. If they can brew and bake as well as women or better, then by all means let them do it. But they cannot have it both ways. If they are going to adopt the very sound principle that the job should be done by the person who does it best, then that rule

---

[3] Lady Nancy Astor (1879–1964), was the first woman to sit in the British Parliament's House of Commons and a passionate supporter of temperance. (ED.)

must be applied universally. If the women make better officeworkers than men, they must have the office work. If any individual woman is able to make a first-class lawyer, doctor, architect, or engineer, then she must be allowed to try her hand at it. Once lay down the rule that the job comes first and you throw that job open to every individual, man or woman, fat or thin, tall or short, ugly or beautiful, who is able to do that job better than the rest of the world.

Now, it is frequently asserted that, with women, the job does not come first. What (people cry) are women doing with this liberty of theirs? What woman really prefers a job to a home and family? Very few, I admit. It is unfortunate that they should so often have to make the choice. A man does not, as a rule, have to choose. He gets both. In fact, if he wants the home and family, he usually has to take the job as well, if he can get it. Nevertheless, there have been women, such as Queen Elizabeth and Florence Nightingale, who had the choice, and chose the job and made a success of it. And there have been and are many men who have sacrificed their careers for women—sometimes, like Antony or Parnell,[4] very disastrously. When it comes to a *choice,* then every man or woman has to choose as an individual human being, and, like a human being, take the consequences.

As human beings! I am always entertained—and also irritated— by the newsmongers who inform us, with a bright air of discovery, that they have questioned a number of female workers and been told by one and all that they are "sick of the office and would love to get out of it." In the name of God, what human being is *not,* from time to time, heartily sick of the office and would *not* love to get out of it? The time of female officeworkers is daily wasted in sympathising with disgruntled male colleagues who yearn to get out of the office. No human being likes work—not day in and day out. Work is notoriously a curse—and if women *liked* everlasting work they would not be human beings at all. *Being* human beings, they like work just as much and just as little as anybody else. They dislike perpetual washing and cooking just as much as perpetual typing and standing behind shop counters. Some of them prefer typing to scrubbing—

---

[4] *Marc Antony* (82 or 81–30 B.C.) was a Roman soldier and ruler who lost his power in the Senate and in Rome when he allied himself with Cleopatra and lost a naval battle to Augustus Caesar. *Charles Stewart Parnell* (1846–1891) was an Irish nationalist leader who lost the support of his parliamentary colleagues on proof of his adultery with the wife of a former supporter. (ED.)

but that does not mean that they are not, as human beings, entitled to damn and blast the typewriter when they feel that way. The number of men who daily damn and blast typewriters is incalculable; but that does not mean that they would be happier doing a little plain sewing. Nor would the women.

I have admitted that there are very few women who would put their job before every earthly consideration. I will go further and assert that there are very few men who would do it either. In fact, there is perhaps only one human being in a thousand who is passionately interested in his job for the job's sake. The difference is that if that one person in a thousand is a man, we say, simply, that he is passionately keen on his job; if she is a woman, we say she is a freak. It is extraordinarily entertaining to watch the historians of the past, for instance, entangling themselves in what they were pleased to call the "problem" of Queen Elizabeth. They invented the most complicated and astonishing reasons both for her success as a sovereign and for her tortuous matrimonial policy. She was the tool of Burleigh, she was the tool of Leicester, she was the fool of Essex;[5] she was diseased, she was deformed, she was a man in disguise. She was a mystery, and must have some extraordinary solution. Only recently has it occurred to a few enlightened people that the solution might be quite simple after all. She might be one of the rare people who were born into the right job and put that job first. Whereupon a whole series of riddles cleared themselves up by magic. She was in love with Leicester—why didn't she marry him? Well, for the very same reason that numberless kings have not married their lovers— because it would have thrown a spanner into the wheels of the State machine. Why was she so blood-thirsty and unfeminine as to sign the death-warrant of Mary Queen of Scots? For much the same reasons that induced King George V to say that if the House of Lords did not pass the Parliament Bill he would create enough new peers to force it through—because she was, in the measure of her time, a constitutional sovereign, and knew that there was a point beyond which a sovereign could not defy Parliament. Being a rare human being with her eye to the job, she did what was necessary; being an

---

[5] *William Cecil, 1st Baron of Burleigh* (1520–1598) was a principal adviser, diplomat, and politician during most of the reign of England's Queen Elizabeth I. *Robert Dudley, 1st Earl of Leicester* (1532–1588) was an English politician and a confidant and possible lover of Queen Elizabeth. *Walter Devereux, 2nd Earl of Essex* (1566–1601) was an English soldier who led an unsuccessful colonizing expedition to the Irish province of Ulster. He was later sentenced to death for treason. (ED.)

ordinary human being, she hesitated a good deal before embarking on unsavoury measures—but as to feminine mystery, there is no such thing about it, and nobody, had she been a man, would have thought either her statesmanship or her humanity in any way mysterious. Remarkable they were—but she was a very remarkable person. Among her most remarkable achievements was that of showing that sovereignty was one of the jobs for which the right kind of woman was particularly well fitted.

Which brings us back to this question of what jobs, if any, are women's jobs. Few people would go so far as to say that all women are well fitted for all men's jobs. When people do say this, it is particularly exasperating. It is stupid to insist that there are as many female musicians and mathematicians as male—the facts are otherwise, and the most we can ask is that if a Dame Ethel Smyth or a Mary Somerville[6] turns up, she shall be allowed to do her work without having aspersions cast either on her sex or her ability. What we ask is to be human individuals, however peculiar and unexpected. It is no good saying: "You are a little girl and therefore you ought to like dolls"; if the answer is, "But I don't," there is no more to be said. Few women happen to be natural born mechanics; but if there is one, it is useless to try and argue her into being something different. What we must *not* do is to argue that the occasional appearance of a female mechanical genius proves that all women would be mechanical geniuses if they were educated. They would not.

Where, I think, a great deal of confusion has arisen is in a failure to distinguish between special *knowledge* and special *ability*. There are certain questions on which what is called "the woman's point of view" is valuable, because they involve special *knowledge*. Women should be consulted about such things as housing and domestic architecture because, under present circumstances, they have still to wrestle a good deal with houses and kitchen sinks and can bring special knowledge to the problem. Similarly, some of them (though not all) know more about children than the majority of men, and their opinion, *as women,* is of value. In the same way, the opinion of colliers is of value about coal-mining, and the opinion of doctors is valuable about disease. But there are other questions—as for example, about literature or finance—on which the "woman's point of

---

[6] *Dame Ethel Smyth* (1858–1944) was an English composer, writer, and suffragist. *Mary Somerville* (1780–1872) was a Scottish writer on mathematics and physical science. (ED.)

view" has no value at all. In fact, it does not exist. No special knowledge is involved, and a woman's opinion on literature or finance is valuable only as the judgment of an individual. I am occasionally desired by congenital imbeciles and the editors of magazines to say something about the writing of detective fiction "from the woman's point of view." To such demands, one can only say, "Go away and don't be silly. You might as well ask what is the female angle on an equilateral triangle."

In the old days it used to be said that women were unsuited to sit in Parliament, because they "would not be able to think imperially." That, if it meant anything, meant that their views would be cramped and domestic—in short, "the woman's point of view." Now that they *are* in Parliament, people complain that they are a disappointment: they vote like other people with their party and have contributed nothing to speak of from "the woman's point of view"— except on a few purely domestic questions, and even then they are not all agreed. It looks as though somebody was trying to have things both ways at once. Even critics must remember that women are human beings and obliged to think and behave as such. I can imagine a "woman's point of view" about town-planning, or the education of children, or divorce, or the employment of female shop-assistants, for here they have some special knowledge. But what in thunder is the "woman's point of view" about the devaluation of the franc or the abolition of the Danzig Corridor?[7] Even where women have special knowledge, they may disagree among themselves like other specialists. Do doctors never quarrel or scientists disagree? Are women really *not human,* that they should be expected to toddle along all in a flock like sheep? I think that people should be allowed to drink as much wine and beer as they can afford and is good for them; Lady Astor thinks nobody should be allowed to drink anything of the sort. Where is the "woman's point of view"? Or is one or the other of us unsexed? If the unsexed one is myself, then I am unsexed in very good company. But I prefer to think that women are human and differ in opinion like other human beings. This does not mean that their opinions, as individual opinions, are valueless; on the contrary, the more able they are the more violently their opinions will be likely to differ. It only means that you cannot ask for "the

[7] The city of Danzig (Gdansk) was made Polish territory at the end of World War I and later became a principle reason for the Nazi invasion of Poland when Hitler demanded its return. (ED.)

woman's point of view," but only for the woman's special knowledge—and this, like all special knowledge, is valuable, though it is
no guarantee of agreement.

"What," men have asked distractedly from the beginning of time,
"what on earth do women want?" I do not know that women, *as*
women, want anything in particular, but as human beings they want,
my good men, exactly what you want yourselves: interesting occupation, reasonable freedom for their pleasures, and a sufficient emotional outlet. What form the occupation, the pleasures, and the
emotion may take, depends entirely upon the individual. You know
that this is so with yourselves—why will you not believe that it is so
with us. The late D. H. Lawrence, who certainly cannot be accused
of underrating the importance of sex and talked a good deal of
nonsense upon the subject, was yet occasionally visited with shattering glimpses of the obvious. He said in one of his *Assorted Articles:*

> "Man is willing to accept woman as an equal, as a man in skirts, as
> an angel, a devil, a baby-face, a machine, an instrument, a bosom, a
> womb, a pair of legs, a servant, an encyclopaedia, an ideal or an obscen
> ity; the one thing he won't accept her as is a human being, a real human
> being of the feminine sex."

"Accepted as a human being!"—yes; not as an inferior class and
not, I beg and pray all feminists, as a superior class—not, in fact, as
a class at all, except in a useful context. We are much too much
inclined in these days to divide people into permanent categories,
forgetting that a category only exists for its special purpose and must
be forgotten as soon as that purpose is served. There is a fundamental
difference between men and women, but it is not the only fundamental difference in the world. There is a sense in which my charwoman and I have more in common than either of us has with, say,
Mr. Bernard Shaw; on the other hand, in a discussion about art and
literature, Mr. Shaw and I should probably find we had more fundamental interests in common than either of us had with my charwoman. I grant that, even so, he and I should disagree ferociously
about the eating of meat—but that is not a difference between the
sexes—on that point, that late Mr. G. K. Chesterton[8] would have
sided with me against the representative of his own sex. Then there
are points on which I, and many of my own generation of both sexes,

---

[8] G. K. Chesterton (1874–1936) was an English critic and author of poetry, essays,
novels, and short stories. (ED.)

should find ourselves heartily in agreement; but on which the rising generation of young men and women would find us too incomprehensibly stupid for words. A difference of age is as fundamental as a difference of sex; and so is a difference of nationality. *All* categories, if they are insisted upon beyond the immediate purpose which they serve, breed class antagonism and disruption in the state, and that is why they are dangerous.

The other day, in the "Heart-to-Heart" column of one of our popular newspapers, there appeared a letter from a pathetic gentleman about a little disruption threatening his married state. He wrote:

> "I have been married eleven years and think a great deal of the wedding anniversary. I remind my wife a month in advance and plan to make the evening a success. But she does not share my keenness, and, if I did not remind her, would let the day go by without a thought of its significance. I thought a wedding anniversary meant a lot to a woman. Can you explain this indifference?"

Poor little married gentleman, nourished upon generalisations—and convinced that if his wife does not fit into the category of "a woman" there must be something wrong! Perhaps she resents being dumped into the same category as all the typical women of the comic stories. If so, she has my sympathy. "A" woman—not an individual person, disliking perhaps to be reminded of the remorseless flowing-by of the years and the advance of old age—but "a" woman, displaying the conventional sentimentalities attributed to her unfortunate and ridiculous sex.

A man once asked me—it is true that it was at the end of a very good dinner, and the compliment conveyed may have been due to that circumstance—how I managed in my books to write such natural conversation between men when they were by themselves. Was I, by any chance, a member of a large, mixed family with a lot of male friends? I replied that, on the contrary, I was an only child and had practically never seen or spoken to any men of my own age till I was about twenty-five. "Well," said the man, "I shouldn't have expected a woman [meaning me] to have been able to make it so convincing." I replied that I had coped with this difficult problem by making my men talk, as far as possible, like ordinary human beings. This aspect of the matter seemed to surprise the other speaker; he said no more, but took it away to chew it over. One of these days it may quite likely occur to him that women, as well as men, when left to themselves, talk very much like human beings also.

Indeed, it is my experience that both men and women are fundamentally human, and that there is very little mystery about either sex, except the exasperating mysteriousness of human beings in general. And though for certain purposes it may still be necessary, as it undoubtedly was in the immediate past, for women to band themselves together, as women, to secure recognition of their requirements as a sex, I am sure that the time has now come to insist more strongly on each woman's—and indeed each man's—requirements as an individual person. It used to be said that women had no *esprit de corps;*[9] we have proved that we have—do not let us run into the opposite error of insisting that there is an aggressively feminist "point of view" about everything. To oppose one class perpetually to another—young against old, manual labour against brain-worker, rich against poor, woman against man—is to split the foundations of the State; and if the cleavage runs too deep, there remains no remedy but force and dictatorship. If you wish to preserve a free democracy, you must base it—not on classes and categories, for this will land you in the totalitarian State, where no one may act or think except as the member of a category. You must base it upon the individual Tom, Dick, and Harry, on the individual Jack and Jill—in fact, upon you and me.

VIRGINIA WOOLF

Professions for Women

Virginia Woolf (1882–1941) was born in England into a social class in which women were rarely encouraged to pursue careers. Yet she became one of our most influential novelists and writers, known especially for her innovative narrative technique. Among her novels are *Mrs. Dalloway* (1925), *To the Lighthouse* (1927), and *The Waves* (1931). Woolf's essay collections include *A Room of One's Own* (1929), *The Common Reader* (1938), *Three Guineas* (1938), and *The Death of the Moth and Other Essays* (1942), from which the following selection is taken.

---

[9] camaraderie (ED.)

When your secretary invited me to come here, she told me that your Society is concerned with the employment of women and she suggested that I might tell you something about my own professional experiences. It is true I am a woman; it is true I am employed; but what professional experiences have I had? It is difficult to say. My profession is literature; and in that profession there are fewer experiences for women than in any other, with the exception of the stage—fewer, I mean, that are peculiar to women. For the road was cut many years ago—by Fanny Burney, by Aphra Behn, by Harriet Martineau, by Jane Austen, by George Eliot[1]—many famous women, and many more unknown and forgotten, have been before me, making the path smooth, and regulating my steps. Thus, when I came to write, there were very few material obstacles in my way. Writing was a reputable and harmless occupation. The family peace was not broken by the scratching of a pen. No demand was made upon the family purse. For ten and sixpence one can buy paper enough to write all the plays of Shakespeare—if one has a mind that way. Pianos and models, Paris, Vienna and Berlin, masters and mistresses, are not needed by a writer. The cheapness of writing paper is, of course, the reason why women have succeeded as writers before they have succeeded in the other professions.

But to tell you my story—it is a simple one. You have only got to figure to yourselves a girl in a bedroom with a pen in her hand. She had only to move that pen from left to right—from ten o'clock to one. Then it occurred to her to do what is simple and cheap enough after all—to slip a few of those pages into an envelope, fix a penny stamp in the corner, and drop the envelope into the red box at the corner. It was thus that I became a journalist; and my effort was rewarded on the first day of the following month—a very glorious day it was for me—by a letter from an editor containing a cheque for one pound ten shillings and sixpence. But to show you how little I deserve to be called a professional woman, how little I know of the

---

[1] *Fanny Burney* (1752–1840) was an English novelist and letter writer. She was the first English woman to write satirically about contemporary modes of conduct, in her novel *Evelina*. *Aphra Behn* (1640–1689), author of *Oroonoko*, was a dramatist, novelist, and poet. *Harriet Martineau* (1802–1876) was an English writer, economist, and social reformer who supported women's suffrage. *Jane Austen* (1775–1817), the well-known English novelist, is the author of *Emma* and *Pride and Prejudice*, among other works. *George Eliot* (1819–1880) is the pseudonym of Mary Ann Evans, famed English novelist and author of *The Mill on the Floss* and *Middlemarch*, among other works. (ED.)

struggles and difficulties of such lives, I have to admit that instead
of spending that sum upon bread and butter, rent, shoes and stock-
ings, or butcher's bills, I went out and bought a cat—a beautiful cat,
a Persian cat, which very soon involved me in bitter disputes with
my neighbours.

What could be easier than to write articles and to buy Persian
cats with the profits? But wait a moment. Articles have to be about
something. Mine, I seem to remember, was about a novel by a famous
man. And while I was writing this review, I discovered that if I were
going to review books I should need to do battle with a certain
phantom. And the phantom was a woman, and when I came to know
her better I called her after the heroine of a famous poem, The Angel
in the House. It was she who used to come between me and my
paper when I was writing reviews. It was she who bothered me and
wasted my time and so tormented me that at last I killed her. You
who come of a younger and happier generation may not have heard
of her—you may not know what I mean by the Angel in the House.
I will describe her as shortly as I can. She was intensely sympathetic.
She was immensely charming. She was utterly unselfish. She excelled
in the difficult arts of family life. She sacrificed herself daily. If there
was chicken, she took the leg; if there was a draught she sat in it—
in short she was so constituted that she never had a mind or a wish
of her own, but preferred to sympathize always with the minds and
wishes of others. Above all—I need not say it—she was pure. Her
purity was supposed to be her chief beauty—her blushes, her great
grace. In those days—the last of Queen Victoria—every house had
its Angel. And when I came to write I encountered her with the very
first words. The shadow of her wings fell on my page; I heard the
rustling of her skirts in the room. Directly, that is to say, I took my
pen in hand to review that novel by a famous man, she slipped
behind me and whispered: "My dear, you are a young woman. You
are writing about a book that has been written by a man. Be sympathetic; be tender; flatter; deceive; use all the arts and wiles of our
sex. Never let anybody guess that you have a mind of your own.
Above all, be pure." And she made as if to guide my pen. I now
record the one act for which I take some credit to myself, though
the credit rightly belongs to some excellent ancestors of mine who
left me a certain sum of money—shall we say five hundred pounds
a year?—so that it was not necessary for me to depend solely on
charm for my living. I turned upon her and caught her by the throat.
I did my best to kill her. My excuse, if I were to be had up in a court
of law, would be that I acted in self-defence. Had I not killed her

she would have killed me. She would have plucked the heart out of my writing. For, as I found, directly I put pen to paper, you cannot review even a novel without having a mind of your own, without expressing what you think to be the truth about human relations, morality, sex. And all these questions, according to the Angel in the House, cannot be dealt with freely and openly by women; they must charm, they must conciliate, they must—to put it bluntly—tell lies if they are to succeed. Thus, whenever I felt the shadow of her wing or the radiance of her halo upon my page, I took up the inkpot and flung it at her. She died hard. Her fictitious nature was of great assistance to her. It is far harder to kill a phantom than a reality. She was always creeping back when I thought I had despatched her. Though I flatter myself that I killed her in the end, the struggle was severe; it took much time that had better have been spent upon learning Greek grammar; or in roaming the world in search of adventures. But it was a real experience; it was an experience that was bound to befall all women writers at that time. Killing the Angel in the House was part of the occupation of a woman writer.

But to continue my story. The Angel was dead; what then remained? You may say that what remained was a simple and common object—a young woman in a bedroom with an inkpot. In other words, now that she had rid herself of falsehood, that young woman had only to be herself. Ah, but what is "herself"? I mean, what is a woman? I assure you, I do not know, I do not believe that you know. I do not believe that anybody can know until she has expressed herself in all the arts and professions open to human skill. That indeed is one of the reasons why I have come here—out of respect for you, who are in process of showing us by your experiments what a woman is, who are in process of providing us, by your failures and successes, with that extremely important piece of information.

But to continue the story of my professional experiences. I made one pound ten and six by my first review; and I bought a Persian cat with the proceeds. Then I grew ambitious. A Persian cat is all very well, I said; but a Persian cat is not enough. I must have a motor car. And it was thus that I became a novelist—for it is a very strange thing that people will give you a motor car if you will tell them a story. It is a still stranger thing that there is nothing so delightful in the world as telling stories. It is far pleasanter than writing reviews of famous novels. And yet, if I am to obey your secretary and tell you my professional experiences as a novelist, I must tell you about a very strange experience that befell me as a novelist. And to understand it you must try first to imagine a novelist's state of mind. I hope I am not giving away professional secrets if I say that a novelist's chief desire is to be as unconscious as possible. He has to induce in himself a state of perpetual lethargy. He wants life to proceed with the utmost quiet and regularity. He wants to see the same faces, to read the same books, to do the same things day after day, month after month, while he is writing, so that nothing may break the illusion in which he is living—so that nothing may disturb or disquiet the mysterious nosings about, feelings round, darts, dashes and sudden discoveries of that very shy and illusive spirit, the imagination. I suspect that this state is the same both for men and women. Be that as it may, I want you to imagine me writing a novel in a state of trance. I want you to figure to yourselves a girl sitting with a pen in her hand, which for minutes, and indeed for hours, she never dips into the inkpot. The image that comes to my mind when I think of this girl is the image of a fisherman lying sunk in dreams on the verge of a deep lake with a rod half out over the water. She was letting her imagination sweep unchecked round every rock and cranny of the world that lies submerged in the depths of our unconscious being. Now came the experience, the experience that I believe to be far commoner with women writers than with men. The line raced through the girl's fingers. Her imagination had rushed away. It had sought the pools, the depths, the dark places where the largest fish slumber. And then there was a smash. There was an explosion. There was foam and confusion. The imagination had dashed itself against something hard. The girl was roused from her dream. She was indeed in a state of the most acute and difficult distress. To speak without figure she had thought of something, something about the body, about the passions which it was unfitting for her as a woman to say. Men, her reason told her, would be shocked. The consciousness of what men will say of a woman who speaks the truth about her passions had roused her from her artist's state of unconsciousness. She could write no more. The trance was over. Her imagination could work no longer. This I believe to be a very common experience with women writers—they are impeded by the extreme conventionality of the other sex. For though men sensibly allow themselves great freedom in these respects, I doubt that they realize or can control the extreme severity with which they condemn such freedom in women.

These then were two very genuine experiences of my own. These were two of the adventures of my professional life. The first—killing the Angel in the House—I think I solved. She died. But the second, telling the truth about my own experiences as a body, I do not think

I solved. I doubt that any woman has solved it yet. The obstacles against her are still immensely powerful—and yet they are very difficult to define. Outwardly, what is simpler than to write books? Outwardly, what obstacles are there for a woman rather than for a man? Inwardly, I think, the case is very different; she has still many ghosts to fight, many prejudices to overcome. Indeed it will be a long time still, I think, before a woman can sit down to write a book without finding a phantom to be slain, a rock to be dashed against. And if this is so in literature, the freest of all professions for women, how is it in the new professions which you are now for the first time entering?

Those are the questions that I should like, had I time, to ask you. And indeed, if I have laid stress upon these professional experiences of mine, it is because I believe that they are, though in different forms, yours also. Even when the path is nominally open—when there is nothing to prevent a woman from being a doctor, a lawyer, a civil servant—there are many phantoms and obstacles, as I believe, looming in her way. To discuss and define them is I think of great value and importance; for thus only can the labour be shared, the difficulties be solved. But besides this, it is necessary also to discuss the ends and the aims for which we are fighting, for which we are doing battle with these formidable obstacles. Those aims cannot be taken for granted; they must be perpetually questioned and examined. The whole position, as I see it—here in this hall surrounded by women practising for the first time in history I know not how many different professions—is one of extraordinary interest and importance. You have won rooms of your own in the house hitherto exclusively owned by men. You are able, though not without great labour and effort, to pay the rent. You are earning your five hundred pounds a year. But this freedom is only a beginning; the room is your own, but it is still bare. It has to be furnished; it has to be decorated; it has to be shared. How are you going to furnish it, how are you going to decorate it? With whom are you going to share it, and upon what terms? These, I think are questions of the utmost importance and interest. For the first time in history you are able to ask them; for the first time you are able to decide for yourselves what the answers should be. Willingly would I stay and discuss those questions and answers—but not tonight. My time is up; and I must cease.

GAYL JONES

The Roundhouse

Gayl Jones (1949–   ) is a Kentucky-born author whose work is
known for its sexual explicitness and its portrayal of psychological
deprivation. The following selection appears in her short story
collection White Rat (1977); other books include the novels
Corregidora (1975) and Eva's Man (1976).

I didn't know what was wrong with him, even after I went to see
him. I'd heard at work that he was sick, and asked if he had anybody
to do for him. They said he had a room in Will Darcy's rooming
house. He didn't have a family, and nobody knew anything about
him, and there was no one to take care of him. I hadn't known him
long, just three weeks, and we'd never really said more than "Hi."
He was a quiet man. He was the kind you feel close to even though
you've said no more than "Hi."

I was working at the roundhouse in Garrett, Indiana. Garrett, not
Gary. Just after the war, the first one. The roundhouse was where
the trains came in. It was our job to polish the parts, and keep the
engines shining. I was hired during the war, when they were hiring
women. I'd been working a year there, and my kids were going to
school, when he came. He never said anything to anybody. He did
his work. He did more work than he had to, and he didn't talk to
anyone. He looked like a foreigner, reddish brown. Maybe he was a
Negro, maybe he was Puerto Rican or something or maybe mixed.
People said maybe he couldn't speak English. He never bothered
anybody, and nobody bothered him. He came to work and he left
work and he never talked. I don't even know if he stopped for lunch.

One day we'd been assigned to the same engine. He was there
before I was, polishing away. He looked up when I came. "Hi," I
said. He didn't smile. He looked back down. He wasn't being unfriendly. There are some people who just don't talk. I could tell he
knew English though. I don't know how but I could tell. He didn't
have the look of someone who didn't know the language.

We worked. At lunchtime I quit and started away but saw he was
still working. I started to ask, "Aren't you going to have lunch?" but
didn't. I thought maybe he wouldn't want me to.

I went and sat down on a bench, eating a sandwich. Some other people were there. Joe McDowell was there.

"Did he say anything to you?" he asked.

"He said 'Hi,'" I said.

"That's more than he said to me," McDowell said. "I worked with him a whole day. Funny thing, though. I didn't feel uncomfortable. Most people don't talk, you feel uncomfortable as hell. With him you don't."

"I know," I said. "It's nice."

"Nobody knows anything about him," McDowell said. "Henderson say's he's taken a room over at Darcy's place. That's not far from where you live. I've heard of people that don't talk much. He don't talk at all."

"He probably does when he has to," I said.

"Ask for a job or a room," McDowell said, not sarcastically.

"Anyway, he seems very nice," I said.

McDowell nodded. It was time to start working again. Four more hours. The kids would be home from school.

When five o'clock came, he stopped work, and left. He was practically the first to be gone. It was summer and he didn't need to grab a coat. He rolled down his shirt-sleeves. Neither Darcy's nor where I lived was far from the station, so we both walked home, about a fifteen or twenty minute walk, a half hour on bad days. He walked fast. I didn't try to catch up with him. When I got to the street, he was a block ahead of me. I saw him turn into the rooming house. I passed where he lived and walked a block more up the street.

The next day we walked home the same way, he walking rapidly ahead again. He seemed always in a hurry, even when he worked. He worked hard and fast. It was a wonder the men hadn't got together and told him to slow down, he made the others look bad, but people liked him, though he didn't talk much. As I said, he was walking ahead and turned in at his gate, but when I passed the rooming house this time, he had not gone in the door, but was standing there, his hand on the doorknob, his head turned looking at me. He didn't say anything and went inside. I walked on. I felt funny.

"I knew a switchman I worked with," McDowell was saying then he stopped and looked up.

I looked up. *He* was standing there, looking down at me.

"I want to walk you home," he said to me.

"O—kay," I said, bewildered. Then he walked away. McDowell looked at me and grinned.

When I got outside, he was waiting for me. It had been cooler this morning and he had a jacket slung over his shoulder. He looked down and smiled. We started walking.

"How are you?" I asked.

"Okay," he said.

We walked on.

"I didn't know you came this way," he said, the first time he'd said more than a word or two. "We could have walked together before."

Now I didn't say anything.

"You live a block away from me," he said. I wondered how he knew. "In a house."

"I have two kids," I said.

"You're married?" he asked, as if I might not be.

"I was."

"How do you mean?"

"He died."

"In the war?"

"No."

I was waiting for him to ask how, like most people had, but he didn't. He seemed to feel if I wanted him to know I'd tell him. I wanted him to know. "From alcohol," I said.

"Oh," he said. I guess I hadn't really expected an "I'm sorry" from him either. The platitudes. I guess he didn't do things that way.

Then we were at the boarding house. I was stopping for him to turn in, but he didn't. He took my elbow slightly.

"I'll see you some," he said.

He saw me home, and then went back. I went inside.

"Who's he?" Jean asked. "He's handsome." Jean was my daughter, thirteen, with her hairs in plaits.

"His name's . . . I don't know his name. He works where I work."

"I haven't seen him before."

"He hasn't walked me home before. Where's Ben?"

"He's in the kitchen."

Ben was my son. He was fourteen. He was light, almost white. Jean was brown. My grandmother had been white. It was hard explaining to people. It was better in Indiana.

"How was school?" I asked.

"The same."

"Much homework?"

"Yes."

Ben came in and said "Hi." I started supper.

"Mama's got a beau," I heard Jean tell Ben.

"I have not," I called. "He works at the roundhouse."

"He walked her home," Jean said, triumphantly. "He's good-looking," she added. "You'll have to check him out."

I didn't hear Ben say anything. I was thinking Ben might like him.

The next day I didn't see him at all, not even after work, and the day after he was not there. I had lunch with McDowell.

"He's probably gone," McDowell said.

"Gone?" I asked.

"You know how it is with them. Come to one town. Hold down a job for a while. Have to keep moving."

"You don't mean he's running from the law?"

"Don't have to be the law."

"What then?"

"Himself. Somebody. How should I know?"

"I didn't know his name," I said.

"James Buchanan Jones, named for the President. Henderson says he calls himself Jake. Wants the people that know him to."

Lunchtime was over. I went back to work.

The next day, McDowell came over to where I was working.

"Henderson says Jake's sick."

"What's wrong?"

"Don't know."

"Hasn't anybody been to see about him?"

"Don't think so. He didn't get close with people."

I frowned and put down the rag and started away. McDowell grabbed my arm.

"Where *you* going?" he asked.

"To see about him."

"The Man won't like it, stopping on the job."

"I don't care."

"You've got two kids."

"Tell him I got sick, Joe."

Joe shook his head slowly.

"It's an hour till lunch," he said.

"All right." I picked up the rag.

He started away.

"Thanks, Joe," I called. He nodded.

At lunchtime I went outside.

"What did the boss say when I didn't come back?" I asked McDowell, the first thing in the morning, before I even started.

"I told him you got sick," he said.

"Thank you."

"How is he?"

"Fever. Wouldn't let me call a doctor. I'm doing what I can. He didn't have any food."

"How are you going to work and take care of him and yourself and the kids?"

"I can manage," I said.

"If you need me you know where to reach me," he said.

"Sure, Joe," I said. I thanked him again. He tapped my arm and went to work. I thought I wouldn't know what to do without him. He had been awfully good to me and the kids.

That afternoon I stopped at the rooming house before going home. I had a bundle with me. A loaf of bread and some curtains. I put the bundle down and went over to him and placed my hand on his forehead. He hadn't been able to shave for about a week now.

"How do you feel?" I asked.

"Better, thanks to you," he said.

"You still have a fever," I said.

I went over to the bundle and started taking the curtains out.

"What are they for? I have curtains," he said.

"Your curtains are ugly," I said.

"They're not, if you don't look at them," he said.

"These you can look at," I said, and started putting the curtains up. The window was small and faced the street. There was only the bed in the room and a chest of drawers, a table and a chair.

"Now you won't be able to tell I'm a bachelor," he said.

"I can tell," I said.

I sat down in the chair.

"I've got to go home and fix supper," I said. "I'll be back a little later and bring you something over."

I started up to go but he took one of my hands in both his and said thank you. I smiled and went home.

I went back with some chicken soup. He didn't eat much.

"Your fever's going down. You couldn't tell by the way you eat, though."

"I never eat much. You have to learn not to."

"Joe McDowell says you're the kind of person that never stays in one place."

"I guess that's right," he said.

"Where are you from?" I asked.

He didn't answer. I didn't press him to.

"You have kids," he said. "What are they like?"

"They're nice," I said.

"You know you live with people a long time and then when somebody asks you what they're like you say they're nice. I guess that's all you can say really." He wasn't being sarcastic.

"I have their pictures," I said. I took out a billfold from my purse and opened it and showed him their pictures.

"The boy's half white," he said.

"Is there a crime against having white blood?" I asked. I was jumpy on that subject.

"The same crime as having black," he said.

"My grandmother," I said.

"You don't have to explain," he said.

"I know," I said.

"They say my mother was a gypsy," he said. "If she showed anybody my picture they would have asked, 'What makes the boy so brown?'"

"You didn't know her?"

"I didn't know her or my father," he said. "I grew up in homes."

"I'm sorry."

He grew angry suddenly. "Don't say you're sorry."

"Okay, Jake." I was hurt.

He touched my hand.

"Don't take it wrong," he said.

"Okay."

I stood up. "I'd better go."

"You're not angry?"

"No, no."

"Promise?"

"I promise."

The next day I saw McDowell for lunch.

"How's he doing?" he asked.

"The fever's almost gone," I said. "I think it's just overwork. He doesn't take care of himself. He doesn't eat."

"He needs a wife," Joe said.

I didn't say anything.

In a couple of days, Jake was well but didn't come back to work again. He had done what McDowell said people like that did.

"You miss him don't you?" McDowell said. "You knew what he'd do. Men like that . . ."

"Yeah, I know about men like that," I said.

He touched my arm, "I'm sorry," he said.

"Don't be," I said.

When the war was over and the men had come home, the roundhouse had kept some of us on, mostly those who didn't have husbands. Now they were laying some of us off again, or reducing our hours. My hours had been reduced, and what I was making now would hardly buy chicken feed, less more support two kids.

When somebody started paying my grocery bills and coal bills, the first person I thought of was McDowell.

"What are you doing?" I asked Joe. I explained. He said he wasn't doing anything. No, it couldn't be, I decided.

The mysterious bill payments went on for several months. I asked the store not to take any more money, but they said there was nothing they could do about it.

I was in the kitchen fixing supper when the doorbell rang. Jean went to answer it. She came back into the kitchen, smiling.

"Who is it?" I asked.

"Go see," she said.

I frowned and wiped my hands on my apron. I stopped in the doorway to the hall.

"Jake!" I exclaimed. I went over to him. "How are you?"

"Very well," he said. "You look well."

There was a bench in the hall.

"Let's sit down," I said.

He said he'd rather stand, and if things went well then we could sit down. I asked him what he was talking about.

He said he wanted to take care of me. He said I had taken care of him when he was sick, and now he was ready to take care of me.

I looked up at him. He wasn't smiling. He was waiting.

I sat down.

He sat down beside me.

THREE

A World of Cultures

Culture: The totality of socially transmitted behavior patterns, arts, belief, institutions and all other products of human work and thought characteristic of a community or population.

American Heritage Dictionary

Culture implies all that which gives the mind possession of its own powers.

Ralph Waldo Emerson

Do we live in one culture, or do we live in many? We speak of "American culture," but do Americans have a single unified culture in the same way that one might argue the French or the Masai do? Or is "American culture" really more a global culture, the end product of the multitude of different cultures that have entered this country through the great variety of peoples who have come to live here? Do you look upon what we might call the "American mosaic" as a feast, an opportunity to enjoy aspects of cultures new to you? Or do you see in cultural diversity a potential for disunity?

The selections in this section are largely reflective of cultural heritages that have not traditionally been in the American main-stream. Some are set in regions of the world from which recent immigrants have come to America; however, the first piece, by Native American Joseph H. Suina, ironically testifies to some of the cultural impositions that the first inhabitants of this country have had forced upon them.

As you read these selections, ask yourself what it would be like to live in the culture being discussed. If you do in fact have contact with that culture, ask yourself what elements in it are the most difficult to explain to outsiders. Several selections here, for instance, deal with Asian cultures that have traditionally placed emphasis on the importance of the family and the group rather than on the individual. For example, Scott Seligman's essay on his experiences in China, "Some Basic Cultural Differences," explores some of the difficulties a person from a Chinese background, educated to take direction from the group, encounters at work in non-group situations.

In a similar vein, Mark Salzman's piece, "Unsuitable Reading," excerpted from his book (later a film) *Iron and Silk,* explores the relativity of terms such as "decadent" and "pornographic" from one culture to another. Salzman suggests that behind their manifest cul-

194

tural "differences," Asians and Westerners may have more in common than they know. In Xiao Hong's "A Tale of Hulan River," on the other hand, we see that cultural differences can often be deep and enduring. On the lighter side of observing and (mis)understanding cultural differences stands Alan Booth's narrative "Buddha and the Floating Bridge of Heaven," taken from the account of his experience walking the entire length of Japan, north to south.

Pico Iyer's "Video Night in Kathmandu," another of the lighter and more humorous pieces in this section, details with sarcastic precision the perverse effects of American popular culture on societies whose traditions precede the European discovery of America by thousands of years. This essay reminds us that many people in the world see the United States in contradictory ways. In much the same vein, Nicholas Coleridge's "The Emperor's New Clothes" assesses the impact of Western clothing fashions around the world.

Some of the selections here address the hardship and oppression that for many of the world's people are a routine part of daily life. Wycliffe Kato's "An Escape from Kampala" demonstrates in chilling detail how dictators stamp out the smallest dissent through terror. Kato's account and several of the other pieces, notably P.J. O'Rourke's "A Ramble through Lebanon" and Ian Jack's "Unsteady People," implicitly raise questions about the developed world's attitudes toward people in developing countries.

Some of the selections toward the end of this section address the intersection of the cultures of European colonial powers with those of the peoples of Africa and Asia. George Orwell's classic "A Hanging" is concerned with the perceptual contradictions experienced by the author of *Nineteen Eighty-Four* when he worked for the British colonial administration in Burma. Equally rich in detail, but in a lighter vein, Ryszard Kapuscinski's "The Snow in Ghana" recounts an exchange between a European visitor and African tribal elders. The collision of cultures in southern Africa—a meeting that may well chart some of the possibilities for intercultural relations throughout the world—is explored by Vincent Crapanzano in "Growing Up White in South Africa" and by Bessie Head in "Looking for a Rain God."

Given the rapidly changing demographics of America generally, and of college campuses in particular, it should be relatively easy for you to meet people from cultural backgrounds different from your own. Use your campus as a gathering field for your research. Test some of the assumptions and insights in the selections that follow against the realities you and your fellow students have experienced. Glean particular examples from these experiences, and use those examples in your own writing to extend and question the observations of writers in the pages that follow.

JOSEPH H. SUINA

And Then I Went to School

Joseph H. Suina (1944–   ) teaches in the Department of Curriculum and Instruction in Multicultural Teacher Education at the University of New Mexico. Born and raised on the Cochiti Pueblo Reservation in New Mexico, Suina still lives there today. He recently served as an elected official in his tribe in a position dealing with ceremonial internal affairs, a position that he says "is not translatable into English." He is coauthor of the book *An Instructional Strategy* (1982). The following selection appears in the collection *Linguistic and Cultural Influences on Learning Mathematics* edited by Rodney Cocking and Jose Mestre (1988).

I lived with my grandmother from the ages of 5 through 9. It was the early 1950s when electricity had not yet invaded the homes of the Cochiti Indians. The village day school and health clinic were first to have it and to the unsuspecting Cochitis this was the approach of a new era in their uncomplicated lives.

Transportation was simple then. Two good horses and a sturdy wagon met most needs of a villager. Only five or six individuals possessed an automobile in the Pueblo of 300. A flatbed truck fixed with wooden rails and a canvas top made a regular Saturday trip to Santa Fe. It was always loaded beyond capacity with Cochitis taking their wares to town for a few staples. With an escort of a dozen barking dogs, the straining truck made a noisy exit, northbound from the village.

During those years, Grandmother and I lived beside the plaza in a one-room house. It consisted of a traditional fireplace, a makeshift cabinet for our few tin cups and dishes, and a wooden crate that held our two buckets of all-purpose water. At the far end of the room were two rolls of bedding we used as comfortable sitting "couches." Consisting of thick quilts, sheepskin, and assorted blankets, these bed rolls were undone each night. A wooden pole the length of one side of the room was suspended about 10 inches from the ceiling beams. A modest collection of colorful shawls, blankets, and sashes draped over the pole making this part of the room most interesting. In one corner was a bulky metal trunk for our ceremonial wear and few valuables. A dresser, which was traded for some of my grandmother's well-known pottery, held the few articles of clothing we owned and the "goody bag." Grandmother always had a flour sack filled with candy, store bought cookies, and Fig Newtons. These were saturated with a sharp odor of moth balls. Nevertheless, they made a fine snack with coffee before we turned in for the night. Tucked securely in my blankets, I listened to one of her stories or accounts of how it was when she was a little girl. These accounts seemed so old fashioned compared to the way we lived. Sometimes she softly sang a song from a ceremony. In this way I fell asleep each night.

Earlier in the evening we would make our way to a relative's house if someone had not already come to visit us. I would play with the children while the adults caught up on all the latest. Ten-cent comic books were finding their way into the Pueblo homes. For us children, these were the first link to the world beyond the Pueblo. We enjoyed looking at them and role playing as one of the heroes rounding up the villains. Everyone preferred being a cowboy rather than an Indian because cowboys were always victorious. Sometimes, stories were related to both children and adults. These get-togethers were highlighted by refreshments of coffee and sweet bread or fruit pies baked in the outdoor oven. Winter months would most likely include roasted pinon nuts or dried deer meat for all to share. These evening gatherings and sense of closeness diminished as the radios and televisions increased over the following years. It was never to be the same again.

The winter months are among my fondest recollections. A warm fire crackled and danced brightly in the fireplace and the aroma of delicious stew filled our one-room house. To me the house was just right. The thick adobe walls wrapped around the two of us protectingly during the long freezing nights. Grandmother's affection completed the warmth and security I will always remember.

Being the only child at Grandmother's, I had lots of attention and plenty of reasons to feel good about myself. As a pre-schooler, I already had the chores of chopping firewood and hauling in fresh water each day. After "heavy work," I would run to her and flex what I was certain were my gigantic biceps. Grandmother would state that at the rate I was going I would soon attain the status of a man like the adult males in the village. Her shower of praises made me feel like the Indian Superman of all times. At age 5, I suppose I was as close to that concept of myself as anyone.

In spite of her many years, grandmother was still active in the village ceremonial setting. She was a member of an important women's society and attended all the functions taking me along to many of them. I would wear one of my colorful shirts she handmade for just such occasions. Grandmother taught me the appropriate behavior at these events. Through modeling she taught me to pray properly. Barefooted, I would greet the sun each morning with a handful of cornmeal. At night I would look to the stars in wonderment and let a prayer slip through my lips. I learned to appreciate cooperation in nature and my fellowmen early in life. About food and material things, grandmother would say, "There is enough for everyone to share and it all comes from above, my child." I felt very much a part of the world and our way of life. I knew I had a place in it and I felt good about me.

At age 6, like the rest of the Cochiti 6-year-olds that year, I had to begin my schooling. It was a new and bewildering experience. One I will not forget. The strange surroundings, new concepts about time and expectations, and a foreign tongue were overwhelming to us beginners. It took some effort to return the second day and many times thereafter.

To begin with, unlike my grandmother, the teacher did not have pretty brown skin and a colorful dress. She was not plump and friendly. Her clothes were one color and drab. Her pale and skinny form made me worry that she was very ill. I thought that explained why she did not have time just for me and the disappointed looks and orders she seemed to always direct my way. I didn't think she was so smart because she couldn't understand my language. "Surely that was why we had to leave our 'Indian' at home." But then I did not feel so bright either. All I could say in her language was "yes teacher," "my name is Joseph Henry," and "when is lunch time." The teacher's odor took some getting used to also. In fact, many times it made me sick right before lunch. Later, I learned from the girls that this odor was something she wore called perfume.

The classroom too had its odd characteristics. It was terribly huge and smelled of medicine like the village clinic I feared so much. The walls and ceiling were artificial and uncaring. They were too far from me and I felt naked. The fluorescent light tubes were eerie and blinked suspiciously above me. This was quite a contrast to the fire and sunlight that my eyes were accustomed to. I thought maybe the lighting did not seem right because it was man-made, and it was not natural. Our confinement to rows of desks was another unnatural demand from our active little bodies. We had to sit at these hard things for what seemed like forever before relief (recess) came midway through the morning and afternoon. Running carefree in the village and fields was but a sweet memory of days gone by. We all went home for lunch because we lived within walking distance of the school. It took coaxing and sometimes bribing to get me to return and complete the remainder of the school day.

School was a painful experience during those early years. The English language and the new set of values caused me much anxiety and embarrassment. I could not comprehend everything that was happening but yet I could understand very well when I messed up or was not doing so well. The negative aspect was communicated too effectively and I became unsure of myself more and more. How I wished I could understand other things just as well in school.

The value conflict was not only in school performance but in other areas of my life as well. For example, many of us students had a problem with head lice due to "the lack of sanitary conditions in our homes." Consequently, we received a severe shampooing that was rough on both the scalp and the ego. Cleanliness was crucial and a washing of this type indicated to the class how filthy a home setting we came from. I recall that after one such treatment I was humiliated before my peers with a statement that I had "She'na" (lice) so tough that I must have been born with them. Needless to say, my Super Indian self-image was no longer intact.

My language, too, was questionable from the beginning of my school career. "Leave your Indian (language) at home" was like a trademark of school. Speaking it accidentally or otherwise was a sure reprimand in the form of a dirty look or a whack with a ruler. This punishment was for speaking the language of my people which meant so much to me. It was the language of my grandmother and I spoke it well. With it, I sang beautiful songs and prayed from my heart. At that young and tender age, comprehending why I had to part with it was most difficult for me. And yet at home I was encouraged to attend school so that I might have a better life in the future. I knew I had a good village life already but this was communicated less and less each day I was in school.

As the weeks turned to months, I learned English more and more. It would appear comprehension would be easier. It got easier to understand all right. I understood that everything I had and was a part of was not nearly as good as the white man's. School was determined to undo me in everything from my sheepskin bedding to the dances and ceremonies that I learned to believe in and cherish. One day I fell asleep in class after a sacred all-night ceremony. I was startled to awakening by a sharp jerk on my ear and informed coldly, "That ought to teach you not to attend 'those things' again." Later, all alone I cried. I could not understand why or what I was caught up in. I was receiving two very different messages, both intending to be for my welfare.

Life-style values were dictated in various ways. The Dick and Jane reading series in the primary grades presented me with pictures of a home with a pitched roof, straight walls, and sidewalks. I could not identify with these from my Pueblo world. However, it was clear I did not have these things and what I did have did not measure up. At night, long after grandmother went to sleep, I would lay awake staring at our crooked adobe walls casting uneven shadows from the light of the fireplace. The walls were no longer just right for me. My life was no longer just right. I was ashamed of being who I was and I wanted to change right then and there. Somehow it became so important to have straight walls, clean hair and teeth, and a spotted dog to chase after. I even became critical and hateful toward my bony fleabag of a dog. I loved the familiar and cozy surroundings of grandmother's house but now I imagined it could be a heck of a lot better if only I had a white man's house with a bed, a nice couch, and a clock. In school books, all the child characters ever did was run around chasing their dog or a kite. They were always happy. As for me, all I seemed to do at home was go back and forth with buckets of water and cut up sticks for a lousy fire. "Didn't the teacher say that drinking coffee would stunt my growth?" "Why couldn't I have nice tall glasses of milk so I could have strong bones and white teeth like those kids in the books?" "Did my grandmother really care about my well-being?"

I had to leave my beloved village of Cochiti for my education beyond Grade 6. I left to attend a Bureau of Indian Affairs boarding school 30 miles from home. Shined shoes and pressed shirt and pants were the order of the day. I managed to adjust to this just as I had to most of the things the school shoved at me or took away from me. Adjusting to leaving home and the village was tough indeed. It seemed the older I got, the further away I became from the ways I was so much a part of. Because my parents did not own an automobile, I saw them only once a month when they came up in the community truck. They never failed to come supplied with "eats" for me. I enjoyed the outdoor oven bread, dried meat, and tamales they usually brought. It took a while to get accustomed to the diet of the school. I longed for my grandmother and my younger brothers and sisters. I longed for my house. I longed to take part in a Buffalo Dance. I longed to be free.

I came home for the 4-day Thanksgiving break. At first, home did not feel right anymore. It was much too small and stuffy. The lack of running water and bathroom facilities were too inconvenient. Everything got dusty so quickly and hardly anyone spoke English. I did not realize I was beginning to take on the white man's ways, the ways that belittled my own. However, it did not take long to "get back with it." Once I established my relationships with family, relatives, and friends I knew I was where I came from and where I belonged.

Leaving for the boarding school the following Sunday evening was one of the saddest events in my entire life. Although I enjoyed myself immensely the last few days, I realized then that life would never be the same again. I could not turn back the time just as I could not do away with school and the ways of the white man. They were here to stay and would creep more and more into my life. The effort to make sense of both worlds together was painful and I had no choice but to do so. The schools, television, automobiles, and other white man's ways and values had chipped away at the simple cooperative life I grew up in. The people of Cochiti were changing. The winter evening gatherings, exchanging of stories, and even the performing of certain ceremonies were already only a memory that someone commented about now and then. Still the demands of both worlds were there. The white man's was flashy, less personal, but comfortable. The Indian was both attracted and pushed toward these new ways that he had little to say about. There was no choice left but to compete with the white man on his terms for survival. For that I knew I had to give up a part of my life.

Determined not to cry, I left for school that dreadfully lonely night. My right hand clutched tightly the mound of cornmeal grandmother placed there and my left hand brushed away a tear as I made my way back to school.

SCOTT SELIGMAN

Some Basic Cultural Differences

Scott Seligman (1952–) has worked as a trade representative to China. He is the coauthor of *Chinese at a Glance: A Phrase Book and Dictionary for Travelers* (1986) and the author of *Dealing with*

the Chinese: A Practical Guide to Business Etiquette in the People's
Republic of China (1989), from which the following selection is
taken.

INDIVIDUALISM VS. GROUP-CENTEREDNESS

The single most important and fundamental difference between Chinese and Occidental peoples is undoubtedly the role played
by the individual in the society. In the West, we place a strong
emphasis on personal achievement, creativity, and initiative. We
glory in our individual differences, nurture them, and value them as
the essential features that make us unique. Indeed, uniqueness is a
goal unto itself in the West; it's vitally important to us that we *not*
be exactly like other people.

Who in the West hasn't been admonished to be your own person,
or to look out for yourself because no one else can be counted on
to look out for you? Who has never been praised for standing up for
what you personally believe in, especially when the tide of opinion
is flowing in the opposite direction? Among Western peoples, the
premium is not on conformity; it is on individual expression and
rugged independence.

In China, on the other hand—and no matter which side of the
Taiwan strait—children are given an entirely different set of messages. Don't question the world around you or try to change it; accept
it. Submit willingly and unquestioningly to authority. Your importance as an individual is not nearly as great as that of the role you
play in a larger group.

That "larger group" may have appeared different in ancient China
from what it looks like today. In Imperial China it would have been
one's extended family—grandparents, father, mother, siblings, uncles, aunts, and cousins of all descriptions, all of whom might well
have lived together in the same compound. In modern-day China
the group might be one's nuclear family, one's class at school, one's
military unit, fellow members of a delegation, or one's *danwei* or
work unit (see below). The situation varies; the dynamics, however,
are much the same no matter what the group is.

Group process in China is not merely based on the authority of
the leaders; there is a real premium on consensus. Matters are often
debated at great length until agreement is reached on a course of
action. And once a decision has been made, individual group members are expected to embrace it and act on it. This is one reason you
will seldom hear a Chinese make an irreverent comment, or openly

express a view at odds with that of his or her unit. Toeing the mark is important, and it is enforced.

In essence, Chinese enter into a sort of compact with their groups; in exchange for obedience and loyalty, they can expect protection and support and be confident that their well-being will be a matter of concern to the group as a whole. Group membership requires that they subordinate their own wills to that of the whole and make decisions based on the best interests of the larger group, not personal selfishness. Chinese people must listen to those in authority and do as they say. And their actions, for good or ill, reflect not only on themselves but also on all of their compatriots.

Consider the fate of former Korean President Chun Doo Hwan, who in spring of 1988 was forced to resign the few government and party posts he had retained after he stepped down from the presidency. Chun's action was necessary not because he had personally done anything wrong, but rather because his *brother* was charged with embezzling money. "Although I exerted myself to the utmost to promote the welfare of the people during my presidential term," Chun was quoted as saying, "I failed to control my brother. It is because of my lack of virtue." He continued: "I feel very sorry for causing trouble to the people with various scandalous actions brought about by my brother's ineptitude."

Though this example comes from Korea—another Confucian society (see below)—rather than China, it might have taken place in Taipei nearly as easily as in Seoul. The principle is the same: you bear responsibility for the actions of members of your family—or your group. Chun's own words contain an apology for "causing trouble" even though it was clearly not he personally who was at fault.

It would be difficult to imagine a similar situation in the West. It would hardly have occurred to former U.S. president Jimmy Carter, for example, to resign because of any of his brother Billy's transgressions. On the other hand, the case should not be overstated. The ideal is one thing; actual practice is another. In truth, many Chinese cadres try desperately to remain in office even after members of their family are caught trading on their positions and engaging in very questionable activities.

For another example, take the case of Chinese tennis star Hu Na, who defected to the United States from the PRC in the early 1980s. The American government, in reaching a decision on whether to grant her political asylum, cited, among other things, the fact that Ms. Hu did not wish to return to the PRC. But the Chinese position was that the young woman's wishes were only one consideration, and a minor one at that; it was also important to take into account the interests and desires of her parents, her work unit, and the government of the society that had given her so much.

Telephone etiquette provides still another illustration of the preeminence of the group in Chinese society. You generally do not identify yourself personally when answering the telephone; what is deemed important is your work unit. The fact that common practice is to answer "I am the Ministry of Foreign Trade" rather than "I am Mr. Wang" speaks volumes about the relative importance of the individual and the group. So does the fact that it is units, and not individuals, that invite foreign guests, arrange activities for them, and sign contracts with them. None of this should be interpreted to mean that the Chinese do not possess unique personalities, however. They most certainly do. The distinction lies in the issue of when and under what circumstances it is permissible for people to express their individual differences.

Although Chinese people must be ever vigilant in fulfilling obligations to fellow group members, it's important to note that as a rule they feel no comparable responsibility toward outsiders. Courtesy and hospitality are frequently not forthcoming when Chinese deal with people with whom they have no connections. Indeed, they are capable of treating one another with indifference that can border on cruelty. The "us-them" dichotomy often surfaces in the work of the government in the form of intractable bureaucratic rivalries that impede progress and innovation. It has sometimes been pointed out that one of the Chinese culture's major failings is that its people just don't know how to treat outsiders. Ironically but luckily, foreigners are generally exempt from this kind of treatment, their very foreignness earning them favorable treatment as honored guests.

THE *DANWEI* OR "WORK UNIT"

It is the work unit or *danwei* that tends to wield the most power over an individual's life in China today. Employers in Taiwan and Hong Kong probably hold more sway over the lives of their employees than those in the West, but they do not have nearly as much influence as the *danwei* in the PRC. In China, the work unit has a say in just about any major decision in one's life, and in a great number of minor ones as well.

Chinese typically do not choose their work units the way an individual may shop for an employer in the capitalist economies of the West, except in the case of foreign joint ventures. Typically, once a young person has graduated from school, the local government's labor bureau will *fenpei* or assign him or her to a job in the community. This bureau's responsibility is to coordinate with all the other government units in the area to identify available jobs and establish relevant qualifications and then to attempt to match people with slots.

It is an impersonal and inefficient system. While it can sometimes be manipulated through the use of *guanxi* (see below), the system mostly manages to assign individuals to positions they do not want. Indeed, individual preferences are largely irrelevant to the process. To compound the problem, there has traditionally been almost no job mobility in the PRC—someone assigned to be a factory worker, for example, can for all practical purposes expect to work in the same unit for the rest of his or her working life, though promotions and job changes within the unit are possible.

Switching to another *danwei* is also difficult because it requires that both the old and new unit sign off on the transfer. Someone who is talented may thus find it relatively easy to get a job offer elsewhere, but next to impossible to persuade his or her work unit to grant a discharge. This system is becoming more liberal, however, and switching *danwei* is becoming more commonplace. Job swapping, accomplished through *guanxi* and even through advertising, is on the increase. But organizational change in China is always a painfully slow process.

The influence of a typical Chinese unit extends far beyond employees' working lives and well into their personal lives. Not only does the unit decide what job you do, how much you are paid, and when promotions come; it also may control where you live; how much space you are allocated; whether and when you may travel within China or to other countries, study abroad, or take a vacation. Through your work unit—and only through your work unit—you obtain coupons that permit you to purchase certain scarce commodities: at various times in the last twenty years pork, sugar, eggs, salt, grain, cooking oil, cotton cloth, gas, coal, bicycles, and wooden furniture have all been rationed in the PRC. The unit also controls your access to health care and child care, and pays you your pension after you retire.

Workers must also obtain permission from the unit before they may marry, a decision that has obvious implications for where they live, single people being assigned to dormitories with roommates.

Apartments, when available at all, are reserved for those who are married and need the additional space. The *danwei* also has a role in enforcing the one-child-per-couple policy. A good relationship with the decision makers in the unit can pave the way for many comforts and privileges; similarly, the unit can make your life a living hell if you buck the system, and it may discipline you if you break a rule.

The exception to most of these rules is the joint-venture unit. An enterprise that is a joint venture between a Chinese organization and a foreign company operates quite a bit differently from the typical Chinese unit. Here there is a great deal of mobility; jobs are advertised and filled by applicants in a more or less supply-and-demand fashion. Employers find it far easier to hire and fire staff. Subsidies have been reduced to bare bones and are generally limited to housing, medical care, and unemployment compensation. And there are far fewer intrusions into individuals' personal affairs. Though joint-venture employees constitute only a small fraction of China's workers today, the government has said that such enterprises are to be treated as models for future development of state-owned enterprises. Thus the tremendous social control exerted by the *danwei* is quite likely to diminish considerably in the future.

Though there is little direct insubordination in a Chinese work unit, this is not to say that there isn't a good deal of passive resistance on the part of the workers. When decisions come down from above, one is obligated to obey, but one doesn't have to like it. Since socialism traditionally offered workers nothing in the way of material incentives to perform, the work of people in the PRC has historically been uninspired and their performance lackluster. Raising productivity has thus become a key goal of the Chinese regime, and in recent years they have proven themselves willing to experiment with a system of material incentives that owes a good deal to capitalism.

The best example I know of the pervasive control exercised by the work unit is the story of a young American woman who went to Beijing to teach English at a small language institute. After she arrived in China, it became clear to her that the meager salary to which she had naïvely agreed before her arrival was going to be insufficient to meet her expenses. She complained to the school's authorities, who immediately convened a committee to look into the problem. The teacher was asked to appear before the committee and to submit to them a detailed listing of her monthly expenses. The matter was ostensibly resolved—to their satisfaction if not to hers—when the committee members offered her "helpful" suggestions as to ways in which she might economize to stretch the salary she was already receiving.

CONFUCIANISM

The position of the individual in Chinese society cannot be fully understood without a discussion of the teachings of the sage Confucius (551–479 B.C.) and his disciples, which has exerted a potent influence on Chinese culture through the centuries. Confucianism is actually more a system of ethics and morals than a religion per se, and it stresses the obligations of people to one another as a function of the relationship among them.

It would be hard to overstate the contribution of Confucius, who delineated the five important human relationships—those between ruler and subject, husband and wife, father and son, brother and brother, and friend and friend. He taught of a social order that emphasized duty, loyalty, filial piety, respect for age and seniority, and sincerity. Such traits remain valued among Chinese the world over even to this day, despite a brief period toward the end of the Cultural Revolution when Confucius's teachings were severely criticized on the mainland as feudalistic and counterrevolutionary.

Confucius's philosophy can be seen at work in myriad ways in China today. Deference to people in authority and to elders is an obvious one. Chinese are seldom guilty of outright insubordination and are taught to know their places in any given hierarchy. Characteristic Chinese unwillingness to depart from the straight and narrow path set by the leaders—as evidenced in the reluctance to offer an irreverent opinion discussed above—is also traceable to Confucius; to do otherwise would mean to fail in your duty and to be disloyal.

None of the above should be construed to mean that Chinese are not capable of sabotage, subversion, or revenge—their capacity for these things is as great as anyone's. It's just that expressing them directly or overtly would be un-Confucian. Passive resistance can be every bit as effective as the active kind, and it goes it one better in that it needn't involve any disturbance of the surface harmony.

China's bureaucracy probably owes as much to the Confucian heritage as it does to the Soviet Union, on which the government structure of the PRC is largely modeled. Far from the "classless" organization of communist mythology, it is in fact strictly hierarchical, with rank and its privileges defined extremely clearly. People relate to one another not as individuals, but rather according to their relative ranks. Decision making is strictly from the top down, and nothing much is accomplished without support from the higher echelons. Personal loyalty is highly valued, and it is common for high-ranking cadres to install cronies in important positions under their control.

Confucianism is an inherently conservative belief system. It suffers innovation rather badly, and does nothing whatever to encourage it. On the contrary; a hierarchical, vertical system of government where decisions of even minor import must be referred upward is no crucible for revolutionary change. No one is willing to stick his or her neck out, and so new ground is seldom broken, except by those at the very top. Characteristically, the Chinese bureaucracy is notorious for long delays and nearly imperceptible progress.

In Confucius's ideal society, each individual occupies his or her proper place—rank is critical and there is no real equality. In his writings, Confucius speaks frequently of the "superior man," who embodies a number of virtues, most of which are as highly valued among Chinese today as they have ever been. Traditionally, there are eight such virtues: *zhong* (loyalty); *xiao* (filial piety); *ren* (benevolence); *ai* (love); *xin* (trust); *yi* (justice); *he* (harmony), and *ping* (peace). The superior man embodies all of them in some measure.

The superior man is modest, even self-deprecating; he is moderate in habits, generous, and given to compromise and conciliation rather than direct confrontation. He has no need to parade his belongings or his accomplishments before others. He is driven by a well-developed sense of duty. He endeavors to make others comfortable, and is solicitous of guests. He never loses his temper, and remains poised no matter what the situation. A man of integrity, he overlooks deficiencies in others and demonstrates honesty and propriety in all of his dealings.

Confucius and all he stood for took a major drubbing in China during the tumultuous Cultural Revolution period from the mid-1960s to the mid-1970s, when his teachings were widely and vehemently criticized as bourgeois and counterrevolutionary. But more recently there has been a pronounced return to Confucian values. Even the government stepped in with a manufactured propaganda campaign that began in the early 1980s urging people to learn and follow the *wu jiang si mei* or the "five stresses and the four beauties." These are admonitions to stress culture, etiquette, hygiene, order, and morals and to strive for beauty in spirit, language, environment, and behavior.

MIANZI OR "FACE"

Another important cultural concept is that of *mianzi*, which is Chinese for "face." Interestingly, the Chinese term is the exact equivalent of the English word, no matter whether one means by it the area between one's forehead and one's chin, the surface of an object, or the less tangible commodity that is related to a person's dignity and prestige.

The Chinese are acutely sensitive to the regard in which they are held by others or the light in which they appear, and it is very important to be aware of the concept of *mianzi* if only to head off situations in which you cause someone to lose it. The consequences can be severe; at the very least you will cease to receive cooperation from the person; you are quite likely as well to open yourself up to some form of retaliation.

Face is a fragile commodity in China, and there are many ways in which one can cause someone to lose it. One sure way is to dress someone down or insult someone in front of his or her peers. Another is to treat someone as if his or her feelings do not matter, or to deliberately patronize someone. Failing to treat someone with proper respect is a real sin with the Chinese, and it almost always comes back to haunt you. For if you cause someone to lose face you will not only lose the respect of the person you have wronged; you will also lose that of others who are aware of your transgression.

The story of the Chinese minister who was insulted after being met at the airport by a deputy assistant secretary is an excellent case study in *mianzi*. The reason the Chinese were so furious at the treatment the minister received was that it appeared to them for all the world as if the U.S. government was delivering a deliberate slap in the face. Only after it was made clear that the offense had been inadvertent rather than deliberate could the Chinese forgive; forgetting was out of the question.

I can offer another, more personal "losing face" story. I once wrote a business letter to a Chinese minister in an attempt to set up a meeting with him for my boss, who was coming to China the following month. In the letter I mentioned that he would be visiting China at the personal invitation of a vice premier. In point of fact, although the vice premier had indeed suggested to my boss that he lead a delegation to China, the actual invitation had been issued by our host organization, which considered itself the official host and thus interpreted my letter as patronizing.

I was summoned in the very next day by the host unit and

summarily dressed down for my perceived offense. I explained that I had certainly not intended a slight and to this day believe that my hosts overreacted to the situation. But offense exists in the eye of the beholder and my intentions were seen as somewhat less important than my crime. The matter was not to end to their satisfaction until I wrote a formal retraction, which of course was a blow to my *own* prestige. The fact that *I* was caused to lose face in the process was of little concern because I was seen as responsible for the whole situation. Having delivered the first blow, I apparently had no right to expect any magnanimity in my host unit's posture toward me. And I got none.

The vehemence of my host unit's reaction surprised me, but it really just underscores how important face is to the Chinese. When you cause someone to lose it, you can just about count on retribution of one type or another. The Chinese do not usually show anger; to do so would fly in the face of the Confucian virtues. They do, however, get even. And while active confrontation would also be viewed as unacceptable behavior on the part of the superior man, passive aggression is always fair game. The Chinese, in fact, are masters of the art. It can take different forms, but often appears as "inability" to accomplish something they know you wish to get done, or failure to show up at an appointed time with an obviously fabricated excuse. All the while, however, etiquette will never be breached.

One of my favorite examples of "saving face" is a volleyball game in which I once participated at the Chinese Embassy in Washington. The Embassy team played volleyball nearly every day; it was their chief form of recreation and exercise. The American challengers, on the other hand, were a pick-up team that had never really practiced together and whose members varied tremendously in skill. From the beginning it was clear that this was not to be a serious match; it had been billed as more of a social occasion than anything else. But from the start the Chinese played to win, and win they did—the first game was, as I recall, a shutout.

The second game turned out to be quite the opposite. Without so much as a word being spoken among them, the Chinese team members suddenly started to miss shots they had had no trouble making during the previous game. In the end they tallied up a respectable score, but it was the Americans who won—or, as I quickly realized, had been *permitted* to win—the second game. Had it been a legitimate test of skill, the Chinese would no doubt have played mercilessly and the second game would have ended up very much like the first. But it was a social gathering and it would have been

unsociable in the extreme to cause guests to lose self-respect—face—
in such a situation. Far better to even out the score and let everyone
go away feeling like a winner.

The concept of "face" certainly exists in the West as well, but
perhaps not to the same degree as it does in the Orient. In the West
people tend to be more willing to forgive slights that cause them to
lose face. Friendly hazing is, after all, somewhat acceptable in the
West. Name-calling, playful dressing down, and sarcastic commentary may occur, but all is seen as good, clean fun. Such behavior,
however, seldom occurs among Asians, for whom face is always very
serious business.

The Chinese concept of face is also broader and better defined
than it is in the West. In English you can *lose* face and you can *save*
face; in Chinese, however, you can also *give* face. Giving face means
doing something to enhance someone else's reputation or prestige.
Complimenting a worker to his or her superior and publicly recognizing someone's contribution are good ways of giving face. Thanking
someone who has worked hard on a particular project, even someone
of very low rank, is also an excellent example of this. Such actions
carry a great deal of weight among Chinese when they come from
foreign guests.

My host organization once placed me in the seat of honor next
to its chairman during a reception held in Beijing. Though I was
flattered by the attention, I did not think much of it until a representative of that organization approached me for a favor a few months
later. To ensure my compliance, he was careful to remind me of how
much face the unit had accorded to me through that action.

GUANXI OR "CONNECTIONS"

It's often the case that you can't even get to first base in China
without *guanxi,* and you can do just about anything—even things
you probably ought not to do—when you have it. *Guanxi* literally
means "relationships," but "connections" is a far better translation
in this sense of the word. It has everything to do with who you know
and what these people are willing—or obligated—to do for you.

To the Chinese, *guanxi* is a sort of "tit-for-tat," "you-scratch-my-
back-I'll-scratch-yours" kind of arrangement. Someone with whom
you have *guanxi* can be counted on to do you favors, bend the rules,
and even break them sometimes on your behalf. It is a cultural
phenomenon common to Chinese all over the world, and by no
means the exclusive province of the PRC. In an economy of scarcity

such as that of China, however, the use of *guanxi* can gain you access to goods and services that are otherwise difficult or impossible to come by.

Guanxi is, of course, a reciprocal obligation. You are expected to behave in similar fashion and to deliver favors to those with whom you have *guanxi*. Most often the currency of *guanxi* is not cash. You might be asked to procure airplane or train tickets, admission to a movie or a play, or even a hospital. Or the request might be for foreign electronic equipment, hard-to-get foodstuffs such as fresh fish or fruit, or even an introduction to someone you know who has the bureaucratic power to do an important favor. It may, however, also be a loan of money. In its more advanced form, *guanxi* becomes *houmen*—literally, the "back door." "Going through the back door" is often the only real way to get some things accomplished in the PRC.

The Chinese tend to extrapolate from their own system and they generally expect foreigners to understand *guanxi* and behave according to its rules. A woman I knew in Beijing once explained to me that she had worked hard to develop *guanxi* within her work unit, and she had established a relationship with someone who had access to the chop—the official seal—of the unit. This person could be counted on to stamp her application to the Public Security Bureau for a passport. Luckily, a former colleague of her father's was well-placed at the Bureau and she was reasonably certain that her father's relationship with this man would guarantee that the application would be approved after it was submitted.

She lacked only *guanxi* at the U.S. Embassy, which would have to issue her a visa before she could leave China and travel to the U.S.—her fondest wish. That was where I was to come in; although she knew I was not a diplomat, she figured that as an American I was very likely to know someone at the Embassy I could pressure on her behalf. When I attempted to explain to her that the U.S. system didn't really work the same way and that I had no particular sway with the U.S. consular officers, it was like talking to a brick wall. I had a dreadfully difficult time convincing her that I wasn't simply shirking what she perceived as my responsibility as her friend and refusing to help.

This same woman once asked a colleague of mine who was leaving for a week in Hong Kong to make a purchase on her behalf. She asked for a Japanese cassette deck, which my associate generously agreed to bring back for her. This was no small favor, for it involved laundering some local Chinese currency and exchanging it for hard,

Hong Kong dollars, and it also involved evading Chinese Customs, which assessed excessive duties on such articles.

It turned out that the tape player wasn't even intended for her—it was really for a friend of hers. She was using her *guanxi* with my colleague to do a favor for a friend to whom she herself had an obligation. When the deed was done, my coworker and I were invited to a dinner hosted by the recipient of the cassette deck as a way of expressing her own appreciation. But since *her* parents' apartment was too small to accommodate all the people, the home of *another* friend was borrowed for the purpose. Again, *guanxi* at work.

RECIPROCITY

Closely related to the concept of *guanxi* is that of reciprocity. It is as applicable to interpersonal relationships as it is to business dealings, and what it means is that the economy of favors between two individuals or units is expected to remain in rough balance over a period of time. Reciprocity is the reason that Chinese people feel comfortable presuming on those with whom they have *guanxi*—if they have done a favor for a friend, they feel they are owed a favor in return.

A corollary to this is that you should proceed with extreme caution before putting a Chinese in a position in which he or she is totally unable to return a favor. Giving an extremely expensive gift can place the recipient in an uncomfortable situation. If there is no possibility of the person ever repaying the gift with something of approximately equal value, he or she will always be beholden to the giver.

Sometimes someone seeking a favor will approach even a relative stranger with a gift. Though it is seldom expressed overtly, the obvious implication is that accepting the gift means accepting an obligation to perform the favor. If you do not wish to be beholden to such a supplicant, you should decline the present.

The Chinese New Year—called Spring Festival on the mainland—is a common time chosen to settle accounts, and many gifts change hands at this time of the year. People visit friends, colleagues, bosses, and business associates bearing fruit, meat, and other presents that may be very expensive. Sometimes they are repaying specific favors done for them in the course of the previous year; other times it is more like positioning themselves for favors they may need to ask in the future.

Guanxi is not an inexhaustible commodity. A former colleague of mine once treated his organization's relationship with a Chinese official as if it were, and the strategy backfired badly. Because his company had once hosted the official's delegation trip to the United States, my friend constantly asked this person for favors. He was successful up to a point—the point, presumably, at which the Chinese official figured that the obligation had pretty much been repaid. After that, when the requests did not cease, the Chinese official became more remote and less and less available. The relationship ultimately deteriorated to the point that my friend's telephone calls to the unit were no longer returned.

PRIVACY

I count views of privacy as a basic cultural difference not because the Chinese would consider it a particularly important concept in their society, but because Westerners find it to be conspicuously absent. There is no direct translation in Chinese for the English word "privacy"; the notion simply doesn't exist in the same way among Chinese people.

Perhaps the difference is that the idea of being alone and unobserved never had much meaning in a land that has always been overpopulated and overcrowded, where a half-dozen people may live in one room, and where there has never been much mobility. Prying eyes are everywhere in China, aimed not only in the direction of foreigners, but also at the Chinese themselves. Neighbors are *encouraged* to know one another's business and people are generally very much aware of the comings and goings of those around them.

This can be seen as a form of social control, and indeed, it is; suspicious goings-on are noted and reported to the authorities. One of the many unfortunate consequences of the Cultural Revolution, during which people were encouraged to inform on one another if any bourgeois activities were suspected, is that many people in China harbor suspicion of other Chinese they do not know well. Only close friends may be completely trusted.

When foreigners encounter the issue of privacy, it is generally in their apartments or hotels, and then primarily in the Chinese-style hotels where service personnel are everywhere. Until recently it was standard practice in the PRC for hotel staff to enter guest rooms at will, often without knocking first. Many old Chinese hotels did not even have locks on guest room doors, and there was simply no awareness of the fact that a guest might be indisposed to entertaining visitors, or engaged in any sort of private activity. This is not so much of a problem in the joint-venture hotels, and in fact it is much less of an issue than before in Chinese-run hotels in the major cities catering to foreigners. Enough embarrassing incidents occurred that most Chinese service personnel have learned to knock before entering.

PRC guesthouses typically have a service desk on each floor that commands a view of all the guest rooms. The desk is strategically placed so that all guests and visitors must pass it on their way to the rooms, and it provides an excellent means of keeping tabs on the guests. Similarly, elevators in high-rise buildings in which diplomats and other long-term foreign residents reside are generally operated by service personnel. The fact that an occasional foreign male has been "busted" for inviting a local female into his room for ostensibly nefarious purposes supports the notion that these people are expected to spy on foreign guests and report any suspicious goings-on to the Public Security Bureau.

When Chinese need to be alone, they generally go outside for a walk. There is enough anonymity in the larger cities, especially after dusk, to allow people to be apart with their own thoughts. Where the real problem comes in is when couples wish some privacy to court or to make love. So few single people have access to private quarters that if they can't persuade a roommate to make him or herself scarce for a period of time, they, too, will take to the streets. Public parks in Beijing, Shanghai, Tianjin, Guangzhou, and indeed, in nearly any large city in China are jammed after dark with young couples locked in passionate embrace who literally have nowhere else to go. The irony is that it is only in the most public of situations that many Chinese are able to find privacy.

PICO IYER

Video Night in Kathmandu: Love Match

Pico Iyer (1957–   ) was born in England to Indian parents and studied at Oxford and Harvard Universities. A writer for *Time* magazine, Iyer has also published articles in the *Village Voice*, *Smithsonian*, *Partisan Review*, and the *Times Literary Supplement*. The following selection is from his book, *Video Night in Kathmandu: And Other Reports from the Not-So-Far-East* (1988), a report on amusing encounters between Eastern and Western cultures. He has recently published *The Lady and the Monk: A Season in Kyoto* (1991).

Wind in the west,
fallen leaves
gathering in the east.
> *Buson*

All tourist people are my bread and butter. So I need to help everything as I could. If I do not help them, they will never forgive me because I fully understand their love or sincerity. I don't have enough money, but I need to pay their gratitude at one day.

> *The credo of Maung-Maung, trishaw driver, chalked up on a blackboard inside his hut in Mandalay*

Rambo had conquered Asia. In China, a million people raced to see *First Blood* within ten days of its Beijing opening, and black marketeers were hawking tickets at seven times the official price. In India, five separate remakes of the American hit went instantly into production, one of them recasting the macho superman as a sari-clad woman. In Thailand, fifteen-foot cutouts of the avenging demon towered over the lobbies of some of the ten Bangkok cinemas in which the movie was playing, training their machine guns on all who passed. And in Indonesia, the Rambo Amusement Arcade was going great guns, while vendors along the streets offered posters of no one but the nation's three leading deities: President Suharto, Siva[1] and Stallone.

As I crisscrossed Asia in the fall of 1985, every cinema that I visited for ten straight weeks featured a Stallone extravaganza. In Chengdu, I heard John Rambo mumble his *First Blood* truisms in sullen, machine-gun Mandarin and saw the audience break into tut-tuts of headshaking admiration as our hero kerpowed seven cops in a single scene. In Jogjakarta, I went to *Rambo* on the same night as the *Ramayana*[2] (though the modern divinity was watched by hosts of young couples, stately ladies in sarongs and bright-eyed little scamps, many of whom had paid the equivalent of two months' salary for their seats, while, on the other side of town, the replaying of the

---

[1] an important Hindu god (ED.)

[2] the later of the two great Hindu epics (ED.)

ancient myth remained virtually unvisited). Just five days later, I took
an overnight bus across Java, and, soon enough, the video screen
next to the driver crackled into life and there—who else?—was the
Italian Stallion, reasserting his Dionysian beliefs against Apollo
Creed. As the final credits began to roll, my neighbor, a soldier just
returned from putting down rebels in the jungles of East Timor, sat
back with a satisfied sigh. "That," he pronounced aptly, "was very
fantastic."

Silencing soldiers, toppling systems, conquering millions and
making money fist over fist across the continent, Rambo was unri-
valed as the most powerful force in Asia that autumn. "No man, no
law, no woman can stop him," gasped the ads in the Bangkok papers.
"Everyone Is Applauding Screen's Most Invincible Hero," agreed one
of the three ads on a single page of India's respected *Statesman*. "The
Second Greatest U.S. Box Office Hit in History," roared the marquee
in faraway Sabah. "I think he's very beautiful," cooed a twenty-three-
year-old Chinese girl to a foreign reporter. "So vigorous and so
graceful. Is he married?"

Rambo had also, I knew, shattered box-office records everywhere
from Beirut to San Salvador. But there seemed a particular justice in
his capturing of Asian hearts and minds. For Rambo's great mission,
after all, was to reverse the course of history and, single-fisted, to
redress America's military losses in the theaters of Asia. And in a
way, of course, the movie's revisionism had done exactly that, succeeding where the American army had failed, and winning over an
entire continent. Some of the appeal of the blockhead-buster lay, no
doubt, in its presentation of a kung fu spectacular more professional
than the local efforts and more polished than the competing displays
of Norris and Bronson. Some might just have reflected the after-
tremors of its earthshaking reception in the States. But whatever the
cause of the drama's success, the effect was undeniable: millions of
Asians were taking as their role model an All-American mercenary.
When William Broyles returned to his old battlegrounds in Vietnam
in 1984, he found the locals jiving along to "Born in the U.S.A.,"
Bruce Springsteen's anthem for the disenfranchised Vietnam vet, and
greeting him with cries of "America Number One!" "America," concluded Broyles, "is going to be much more difficult to defeat in this
battle than we were in the others. Our clothes, our language, our
movies and our music—our way of life—are far more powerful than
our bombs."

The prospect of witnessing that low-intensity conflict was one of
the impulses that took me first to Asia. Over the course of two years,

I spent a total of seven months crisscrossing the continent on four separate trips, mostly in order to see its sights, but also in order to visit the front lines of this cultural campaign. I was interested to find out how America's pop-cultural imperialism spread through the world's most ancient civilizations. I wanted to see what kind of resistance had been put up against the Coca-Colonizing forces and what kind of counter-strategies were planned. And I hoped to discover which Americas got through to the other side of the world, and which got lost in translation.

This contest for cultural sovereignty was nothing new, of course. Colonel Sanders and General Motors had first set up base camps across the global village years ago, and America's Ambassador-at-Large throughout the world had long been the retired World War I flying ace Snoopy. Fifteen years before the first American troops showed up, Norman Lewis described families in Saigon listening respectfully to a local rendition of "When Irish Eyes Are Smiling." And fully a quarter century ago, Arthur Koestler had stated as a given that the world was moving toward "a uniform, mechanized, stereotyped culture," a mass culture that struck him as a form of mass suicide. The syllogism was old enough now to be almost an axiom: pop culture ruled the world, and America ruled pop culture. Thus America ruled the waves—or at the very least, the airwaves.

In recent years, however, the takeover had radically intensified and rapidly accelerated. For one thing, satellites were now beaming images of America across the globe faster than a speeding bullet; the explosion of video had sent history spinning like the wheels of an overturned bicycle. For another, as the world grew smaller and ever smaller, so too did its props: not only had distances in time and space been shrunk, but the latest weapons of cultural warfare—videos, cassettes and computer disks—were far more portable than the big screens and heavy instruments of a decade before. They could be smuggled through border checkpoints, under barbed-wire fences and into distant homes as easily, almost, as a whim. In the cultural campaign, the equivalent of germ warfare had replaced that of heavy-tank assaults.

Suddenly, then, America could be found uncensored in even the world's most closed societies, intact in even its most distant corners. Peasants in China or the Soviet Union could now employ images of swimming pools, shopping malls and the other star-spangled pleasures of the Affluent Society inside their own living rooms; remote villagers in rural Burma could now applaud Rambo's larger-than-life heroics only days after they hit the screens of Wisconsin; and the

Little House on the Prairie was now a part of the neighborhood in 108 countries around the world.

More important, the video revolution was bringing home the power of the Pax Americana with greater allure and immediacy than even the most cunning propaganda. Already, the ruling mullahs in Iran were fretting that their capital's newly formed clandestine Michael Jackson clubs could easily turn into revolutionary cells. And I once heard one of Washington's most senior foreign policy veterans privately maintain that the single issue that most exercised the Soviets was not the nuclear arms race, or the war of espionage, or Afghanistan or Nicaragua or Cuba, or even the rising confidence of China, but simply the resistless penetration of video.

In 1985, another influence was also carrying American dollars and dreams to every corner of the world with more force and more urgency than ever before: people. Tourists were the great foot soldiers of the new invasion; tourists, in a sense, were the terrorists of cultural expansionism, what Sartre once called "the cool invaders." Scarcely forty years ago, most of the world's secret places were known only to adventurers, soldiers, missionaries and a few enterprising traders; in recent years, however, the secrets were open, and so too was the world—anyone with a credit card could become a lay colonialist. Nepal, which had never seen a tourist until 1955, now welcomed 200,000 foreign visitors each year; China, which had rigidly closed its doors for decades, had 11,000 tourists a day clambering along the Great Wall by 1985. The road to Mandalay and even the road to Xanadu were crowded now with Westerners—men in search of women, dreamers in search of enlightenment, traders in search of riches. In 1985, many Asians considered the single great import from the West, after Rambo, to be AIDS.

Not all the incoming forces, of course, were American. Mick Jagger was as much the poet laureate of the modern world as Michael Jackson, and Sophie Marceau vied with Phoebe Cates as the poster queen of Southeast Asia. If Springsteen turned out to be my unexpected traveling companion across the continent, so too did the British group Dire Straits: their latest album greeted me in a tiny inn in Hiroshima, then blasted my eardrums from a car in Beijing, then wafted over me in the soft tropical night of a Balinese guesthouse, then serenaded me once more in the Kathmandu home of a local Lothario.[3] And the back roads of Asia were far more crowded with

---

[3] A man who seduces many women. Lothario is the name of the seducer in the play, *The Fair Penitent* (1703), by English dramatist Nicholas Rowe. (ED.)

Canadians and Germans and Australians than with Americans. But still, when it came to movies and TV, the United States remained the Great Communicator. And if pop culture was, in effect, just a shorthand for all that was young and modern and rich and free, it was also a virtual synonym for America.

Everywhere, in fact, dreams of pleasure and profit were stamped "Made in America." Cities from San Salvador to Singapore turned themselves into bright imitations of Californian, not Parisian or Liverpudlian, suburbs; Garfield, not Tintin, had become the alter ego of millions of Germans and Japanese; and it was not the yen or the Deutschemark that had become the universal currency, but the dollar, even—no, especially—in the Communist bloc. The hymn of the East Side, as well as the West, was still "I Want to Live in America."

This kind of influence was not by any means stronger or more pervasive in Asia than elsewhere in the developing world. Yet of all the fronts on which the battle was being waged, Asia seemed to be the fiercest and most complex. Asia, after all, had been the site of the world's most vexed and various colonial struggles, and Asia was also the theater for most of America's recent military confrontations. Asia was also increasingly mounting a formidable counterattack upon the long-unquestioned economic domination of the West, and Asia now included three out of four of all the world's souls. Asia, above all, seemed home to most of history's oldest and subtlest cultures. How, I wondered, would proud, traditionalist societies founded on a sense of family and community respond to the Fighting Machine's grunting individualism and back-to-basics primitivism? How would developing nations deal with refugees from affluence, voluntary dropouts from the Promised Land? And what would decorous Buddhists make of the crucifix-swinging Madonna?

Asia also appealed to me because it was unmatched in its heterogeneity; in China, Japan and India alone, the continent had three great traditions as deep as they were diverse. Texts read us as much as we do them, and in the different ways that different cultures responded to forces from the West, I hoped to see something of their different characters and priorities.

Rambo again proved illustrative. In China, the very showing of the film had advertised a new cultural openness to the West, even as the black-market chicanery it set off betrayed some of the less happy foreign influences streaming in through the open door; ideologically, the movie served both as political propaganda (confirming the Chinese in their belief that the Vietnamese were devious swine) and as a subject for earnest self-criticism, dialectically worked out in the letter columns of the *China Daily*. In India, the movie had been seized upon by the quick-witted moguls of the world's largest film industry and swiftly redesigned to fit the mythic contours of Indian formula fantasy; yet its heroic success had also set off bouts of typical Indian philosophizing—even a newspaper ad couched its come-on in a kind of marveling rumination: "No sex, no romance, no lady character, yet constantly patronized by Male and Female. The RAMBO syndrome."

In the Philippines, the movie had passed, like so much American cultural debris, into the very language and mythology of the country, blurring even further the country's always uncertain division between politics and show biz: onetime Defense Minister Juan Ponce Enrile was wont to represent himself, on posters and in threats, as a kind of homegrown Rambo. And in Vietnam, to complete the circle, this latest version of the war had, inevitably, become an instrument of propaganda: the Vietnamese accused Ronald Reagan of trying to "Ramboize" the youth of America, hardly mentioning the more unsettling fact that Rambo was "Reaganizing" the youth of all the world.

As I drifted out of the theater where I had seen *Rambo,* and into the warm Indonesian night, only one line from the movie really stayed with me. The hero's boss, Colonel Trautman, had been discussing the maverick naked ape with the heartless Washington bureaucrat Murdock. "What you choose to call hell," he had said of his explosive charge, "he calls home." However inadvertently, that sentence suggested many of the other ideas that first sent me East: that home has nothing to do with hearth, and everything to do with a state of mind; that one man's home may be his compatriot's exile; that home is, finally, not the physical place, but the role and the self we choose to occupy.

I went to Asia, not only to see Asia, but also to see America, from a different vantage point and with new eyes. I left one kind of home to find another: to discover what resided in me and where I resided most fully, and so to better appreciate—in both senses of the word— the home I had left. The point was made best by one great traveler who saw the world without ever leaving home, and, indeed, created a home that was a world within—Thoreau: "Our journeying is a great-circle sailing."

To travel across the globe simply to locate the facilities of the place one has quit would, of course, be an elaborate exercise in perversity. Only those who travel for business, and nothing more, would really wish to ask the questions addressed by Anne Tyler's Accidental Tourist: "What restaurants in Tokyo offered Sweet 'n

Low? Did Amsterdam have a McDonald's? Did Mexico City have a
Taco Bell? Did any place in Rome serve Chef Boyardee ravioli? Other
travelers hoped to discover distinctive local wines; Macon's readers
searched for pasteurized and homogenized milk." Pasteurized and
homogenized cultures are not what take us abroad. Yet, at the same
time, many a traveler knows that the Temple of the Golden Arches
and the Palace of the Burger King never seem so appealing as when
one is searching for a regular meal in the back streets of Kyoto. And
Father *Time* never seems so authoritative, or so agreeably familiar,
as when one is yearning for news in the mountains of Tibet.

If the great horror of traveling is that the foreign can come to
seem drearily familiar, the happy surprise of traveling is that the
familiar can come to seem wondrously exotic. Abroad, we are not
ourselves; and as the normal and the novel are transposed, the very
things that we might shun at home are touched with the glamour of
the exotic. I had never seen, or wished to see, a Burt Reynolds movie
until I found myself stuck in a miserable guesthouse in Bandar Sari
Begawan; I had never been to a Dunkin' Donuts parlor until I decided
to treat myself after a hard day's work in Bangkok. I enjoyed my first
ever Yorkie bar in Surabaya (and my second there too, a few minutes
later). And my first experience of the Emmy Awards came in the
darkened lobby of a run-down hotel in Singapore, where the ceremonies were annotated, with beery profanities, by a gang of tattooed
European and Australian sailors who broke off from their lusty commentary only when a French or Filipina trollop drifted barefoot
through the room and out into the monsoony night.

While I was in Asia, I made ritual pilgrimages to the Taj Mahal,
Pagan and Borobudur; I climbed live volcanoes in the dead of the
Javanese night and rode elephants through the jungles of Nepal. I
spent nights in an Indonesian hut, where my roommates consisted
of two pack rats, a lizard and a family-size cockroach, and other
nights in a Mogul palace on a lake, where I sat for hours on the
marbled roof, watching the silver of moon on water. In Bali, I witnessed a rare and sumptuous cremation, and in Kyoto, I saw the
unearthly Daimonji Festival, when all the town is lit with lanterns
to guide departed spirits home. None of this, however, is recorded
in the pages that follow, partly because all of it has gone on, and
will go on, one hopes, for centuries, and partly because such familiar
marvels may be better described by travelers more observant than
myself.

More than such postcard wonders, however, what interested me
were the brand-new kinds of exotica thrown up by our synthetic

age, the novel cultural hybrids peculiar to the tag end of the twentieth century. "Travel itself," observes Paul Fussell in *Abroad*, "even the most commonplace, is an implicit quest for anomaly," and the most remarkable anomalies in the global village today are surely those created by willy-nilly collisions and collusions between East and West: the local bands in socialist Burma that play note-perfect versions of the Doors' "L.A. Woman," in Burmese; the American tenpin bowling alley that is the latest nighttime hot spot in Beijing; the Baskin-Robbins imitation in Hiroshima that sells "vegetable" ice cream in such flavors as mugwort, soy milk, sweet potato and "marron"; or the bespectacled transvestite in Singapore who, when asked to name the best restaurant in a town justly celebrated for its unique combination of Chinese, Indian and Malaysian delicacies, answers, without a moment's hesitation, "Denny's."

I wanted also, while I was in Asia, to see how America was regarded and reconstituted abroad, to measure the country by the shadow it casts. Much of the world, inevitably, looks to its richest industrial nation for promiscuous images of power and affluence; abroad, as at home, the land of Chuck Bronson and Harold Robbins will always command a greater following than that of Emerson and Terrence Malick. Often, in fact, the America one sees around the globe seems as loud and crass and overweight as the caricatured American tourist. And just as celebrities pander to the images they foster, acting out our dreams of what they ought to be, so America often caters to the world's image of America, cranking out slick and inexpensive products made almost exclusively for foreign consumption—in Jogjakarta, the cinema that was not showing *Rambo* offered *The Earthling*, with Ricky Schroder and William Holden, and *Dead and Buried*, starring Melody Anderson and James Farentino.

Yet America also projects a more promising and more hopeful image around the world, as a culture of success stories and of the youthful excesses that may accompany them. Lee Iacocca's memoirs are devoured far more eagerly from Rio to Riyadh than those of Akio Morita or Giovanni Agnelli,[4] and George Washington is a folk hero in many Asian classrooms in a way that George III will never be. The most popular contemporary American writer in the very different markets of France and West Germany is Charles Bukowski, the disheveled boho laureate of booze and broads in low-life L.A. In the

---

[4] Akio Morita is the co-founder of Sony Corporation; Giovanni Agnelli is the founder of the Fiat Automobile Company. (ED.)

world's collective popular imagination, America the Beautiful stands next to America the Technicolor Dreamcoast.

This division in itself is hardly unique: every culture casts conflicting images before the world. We associate India with desperate poverty and maharajah opulence, Britain with punks and patricians. But in the case of America, subject of so many daydreams and ideals, so intensely felt and so eagerly pursued, the contradictions are even more pronounced: for not only is the country's political power enormous, but it is matched—and sometimes opposed—by its cultural influence. When Reagan speaks, the world listens; yet Springsteen is shouting the opposite message in the other ear. While Congress sends money to the contras, the global village tunes in to Jackson Browne.

And if the image of America is perplexingly double-edged, the responses it provokes in many parts of the globe are appropriately fork-tongued: with one breath, they shout, "Yankee Go Home," and with the next, "America Number One!" "In the Third World," writes Michael Howard, "anti-Americanism is almost a *lingua franca.*"[5] Yet in the Third World, a hunger for American culture is almost taken for granted, and "making it" often means nothing more than making it to the Land of the Free. The Communist guerrillas in the Philippines fight capitalism while wearing UCLA T-shirts. The Sandinista leaders in Nicaragua wage war against "U.S. Imperialism" while watching prime-time American TV on private satellite dishes. And many whites in South Africa cling to apartheid, yet cannot get enough of Bill Cosby, Eddie Murphy and Mr. T.

All these contradictions are further exacerbated by one simple but inevitable fact: the disproportion between America's formidable power around the globe and the much more modest presence of individual Americans abroad. "We think of the United States," writes Octavio Paz, on behalf of all Latin Americans, "simultaneously, and without contradiction, as Goliath, Polyphemus and Pantagruel."[6] Yet that daunting weight falls upon the shoulders of the small and decidedly unmythic traveler, tourist or expatriate. Around the world, S. J. Perelman noted, the American occupies "the curious dual role of skinflint and sucker, the usurer bent on exacting his pound of flesh and the hapless pigeon whose poke was a challenge to any

---

[5] one common language used by people of diverse cultures (ED.)

[6] *Goliath* is the biblical giant slain by David. *Polyphemus* is the most famous of the Cyclops in Greek mythology. *Pantagruel* is the son of the giant Gargantua in French humorist Rabelais' *Gargantua* (1532). (ED.)

smart grifter." The incongruity applies equally, of course, to the Russians abroad, as it did to the Englishman, the Chinese and all the other imperialists of the past. But in the case of America, at once so ubiquitous and so many-headed throughout the world, the schizophrenia seems especially charged. If Bruce Springsteen is not Reagan, still less is that backpacking social worker from Tacoma. Again and again in my travels, I had been asked, by Greeks, Nicaraguans and Moroccans, how the American government could be such a ruthless bully, while the American people seemed so friendly, good-natured and warm. I went to Asia in part to find out.

XIAO HONG

A Tale of Hulan River

Xiao Hong (1911–1942) was a Chinese novelist and short story writer whose work includes *The Field of Life and Death* (1935) and *Tales of Hulan River* (1942), from which the following selection is taken. Her writing focuses on the difficulties experienced by women in traditional Chinese society.

In addition to The Crossroads, there are two other streets, one called Road Two East and the other called Road Two West. Both streets run from north to south, probably for five or six *li*.[1] There is nothing much on these two streets worth noting—a few temples, several stands where flatcakes are sold, and a number of grain storehouses. . . .

As for Road Two West, not only is it without a fire mill, it has but one school, a Moslem school situated in the Temple of the City God. With this exception, it is precisely like Road Two East, dusty and barren. When carts and horses pass over these roads they raise up clouds of dust, and whenever it rains the roads are covered with a layer of mud. There is an added feature on Road Two East: a five-

Translated by Howard Goldblatt

[1] A measure equal to 654 yards or 598.02 meters.

or six-foot-deep quagmire. During dry periods the consistency of the mud inside is about that of gruel, but once it starts to rain the quagmire turns into a river. The people who live nearby suffer because of it: when they are splashed with its water, they come away covered with mud; and when the waters subside as the sun reappears in the clearing sky, hordes of mosquitos emerge and fly around their homes. The longer the sun shines, the more homogenized the quagmire becomes, as though someone were trying to refine something inside it. If more than a month goes by without any rain, that big quagmire becomes even more homogenized in makeup. All the water having evaporated, the mud has turned black and has become stickier than the gummy residue on a gruel pot, stickier even than paste. It takes on the appearance of a big melting vat, gummy black with an oily glisten to it, and even flies and mosquitos that swarm around stick to it as they land. . . .

One very rainy day a young child fell into the quagmire and was rescued by a bean-curd peddler. Once they got him out they discovered he was the son of the principal of the Agricultural School. A lively discussion ensued. Someone said that it happened because the Agricultural School was located in the Dragon King Temple, which angered the venerable Dragon King. He claimed it was the Dragon King who caused the heavy downpour in order to drown the child.

Someone disagreed with him completely, saying that the cause of the incident rested with the father, for during his highly animated lectures in the classroom he had once said that the venerable Dragon King was not responsible for any rainfall, and for that matter, did not even exist. "Knowing how furious that would make the venerable Dragon King, you can imagine how he would find some way to vent his anger! So he grabbed hold of the son as a means of gaining retribution."

Someone else said that the students at the school were so incorrigible that one had even climbed up onto the old Dragon King's head and capped him with a straw hat. "What are the times coming to when a child who isn't even dry behind the ears would dare to invite such tremendous calamities down upon himself? How could the old Dragon King not seek retribution? Mark my word, it's not finished yet; don't you get the idea that the venerable Dragon King is some kind of moron! Do you think he'd just let you off once you've provoked his anger? It's not like dealing with a ricksha boy or a vegetable peddler whom you can kick at will, then let him be on his way. This is the venerable Dragon King we're talking about!

Do you think that the venerable Dragon King is someone who can easily be pushed around?"

Then there was someone who said that the students at that school were truly undisciplined, and that with his own eyes he had once seen some of them in the main hall putting silkworms into the old Dragon King's hands. "Now just how do you think the old Dragon King could stand for something like that?"

Another person said that the schools were no good at all, and that anyone with children should on no account allow them to go to school, since they immediately lose respect for everyone and everything.

Someone remarked that he was going to the school to get his son and take him home—there would be no more school for him.

Someone else commented that the more the children study, the worse they become. "Take, for example, when their souls are frightened out of their bodies; the minute their mothers call for the souls to return, what do you think they say? They announce that this is nothing but superstition! Now what in the world do you think they'll be saying if they continue going to school?"

And so they talked, drifting further and further away from the original topic.

Before many days had passed, the big quagmire receded once again and pedestrians were soon passing along either side unimpeded. More days passed without any new rainfall, and the quagmire began to dry up, at which time carts and horses recommenced their crossings; then more overturned carts, more horses falling into it and thrashing around; again the ropes and levers appeared, again they were used to lift and drag the horses out. As the righted carts drove off, more followed: into the quagmire, and the lifting began anew.

How many carts and horses are extricated from this quagmire every year may never be known. But, you ask, does no one ever think of solving the problem by filling it in with dirt? No, not a single one.

An elderly member of the gentry once fell into the quagmire at high water. As soon as he crawled out he said: "This street is too narrow. When you have to pass by this water hazard there isn't even room to walk. Why don't the two families whose gardens are on either side take down their walls and open up some paths?"

As he was saying this, an old woman sitting in her garden on the other side of the wall chimed in with the comment that the walls could not be taken down, and that the best course of action would be to plant some trees; if a row of trees were planted alongside the wall, then when it rained the people could cross over by holding on to the trees.

Some advise taking down walls and some advise planting trees, but as for filling up the quagmire with dirt, there isn't a single person who advocates that.

Many pigs meet their end by drowning in this quagmire; dogs are suffocated in the mud, cats too; chickens and ducks often lose their lives there as well. This is because the quagmire is covered with a layer of husks; the animals are unaware that there is a trap lying below, and once they realize that fact it is already too late. Whether they come on foot or by air, the instant they alight on the husk-covered mire they cannot free themselves. If it happens in the daytime there is still a chance that someone passing by might save them, but once night falls they are doomed. They struggle all alone until they exhaust their strength, then begin to sink gradually into the mire. If, on the contrary, they continue to struggle, they might sink even faster. Some even die there without sinking below the surface, but that's the sort of thing that happens when the mud is gummier than usual.

What might happen then is that some cheap pork will suddenly appear in the marketplace, and everyone's thoughts turn to the quagmire. "Has another pig drowned in that quagmire?" they ask.

Once the word is out, those who are fast on their feet lose no time in running to their neighbors with the news: "Hurry over and get some cheap pork. Hurry, hurry, before it's all gone."

After it is bought and brought home, a closer look reveals that there seems to be something wrong with it. Why is the meat all dark and discolored? Maybe this pork is infected. But on second thought, how could it really be infected? No, it must have been a pig that drowned in the quagmire. So then family after family sautés, fries, steams, boils, and then eats this cheap pork. But though they eat it, they feel always that it doesn't have a fragrant enough aroma, and they fear that it might have been infected after all. But then they think: "Infected pork would be unpalatable, so this must be from a pig that drowned in the quagmire!"

Actually, only one or two pigs drown each year in the quagmire, perhaps three, and some years not a single one. How the residents manage to eat the meat of a drowned pig so often is hard to imagine, and I'm afraid only the Dragon King knows the answer.

Though the people who eat the meat say it is from a pig drowned in the quagmire, there are still those who get sick from it, and those unfortunates are ready with their opinions: "Even if the pork was from a drowned pig, it still shouldn't have been sold in the market-place; meat from animals that have died isn't fresh, and the revenue office isn't doing its job if it allows meat like this to be sold on the street in broad daylight!"

Those who do not become ill are of a different opinion: "That's what you say, but you're letting your suspicions get the best of you. If you'd just eat it and not give it another thought, everything would be all right. Look at the rest of us; we ate it too, so how come we're not sick?"

Now and then a child lacking in common sense will tell people that his mother wouldn't allow him to eat the pork since it was infected. No one likes this kind of child. Everyone gives him hard looks and accuses him of speaking nonsense.

For example, a child says that the pork is definitely infected—this he tells a neighbor right in front of his mother. There is little reaction from the neighbor who hears him say this, but the mother's face immediately turns beet-red. She reaches out and smacks him.

But he is a stubborn child, and he keeps saying: "The pork is infected!"

His mother, feeling terribly embarrassed, picks up a poker that is lying by the door and strikes him on the shoulder, sending him crying into the house. As he enters the room he sees his maternal grandmother sitting on the edge of the *kang*,[2] so he runs into her arms. "Grannie," he sobs, "wasn't that pork you ate infected? Mama just hit me."

Now this maternal grandmother wants to comfort the poor abused child, but just then she looks up to see the wet nurse of the Li family who shares the compound standing in the doorway looking at her. So she lifts up the back of the child's shirttail and begins spanking him loudly on the behind. "Whoever saw a child as small as you speaking such utter nonsense!" she exclaims. She continues spanking him until the wet nurse walks away with the Li's child in her arms. The spanked child is by then screaming and crying uncontrollably,

[2] Brick platform running along the side of a room and warmed by fire providing sitting and sleeping space.

so hard that no one can make heads or tails of his shouts of "infected pork this" and "infected pork that."

In all, this quagmire brings two benefits to the residents of the area: the first is that the overturned carts and horses and the drowned chickens and ducks always produce a lot of excitement, which keeps the inhabitants buzzing for some time and gives them something to while away the hours.

The second is in relation to the matter of pork. Were there no quagmire, how could they have their infected pork? Naturally, they might still eat it, but how are they to explain it away? If they simply admit they are eating infected pork, it would be too unsanitary for words, but with the presence of the quagmire their problem is solved: infected pork becomes the meat of drowned pigs, which means that when they buy the meat, not only is it economical, but there are no sanitation problems either.

ALAN BOOTH

Buddha and the Floating Bridge of Heaven

Alan Booth (1946–   ) is a graduate of Birmingham University; he is fluent in Japanese and has spent much of his time exploring Japan. He arrived in Japan in 1970 to study Noh drama and remained to live there. He recounts his journey by foot down the entire length of Japan in *The Roads to Sata* (1985), from which this selection is taken. He is also the author of *Japan: A Complete Guide* (1988).

On the curb of the main road out of Kanazawa a dozen or so mourners fresh from a funeral stood fidgeting in loose black suits around a hearse. The hearse was a long maroon-brown limousine on which a marvelous folly of black and gold lacquer had been constructed to resemble a portable shrine. The driver bowed solemnly to the mourners, who plucked bits of invisible fluff off their suits and then sprinkled pinches of salt over themselves before lapsing into a large two-story restaurant for lunch. They looked like an outing of tired crows, sitting at the long wooden table of the restaurant eating their pork cutlets in complete silence while the color television set in the corner blared an advertisement for a "new sexy" brassiere called Top Feel.

I had had enough of main roads and cities. The Cafe Terrace Love Love (the menu included Love Love Pudding) brought that home to me with a wallop, so straight after lunch I turned sharp across the railway tracks onto the old coast road that the Hokuriku Expressway had left puddingless and empty. It was a scorching hot day. The cement piles of the expressway shut the sea off like the bars of a prison, but between them I could glimpse it close and blue. The narrow streets of the one or two little villages I passed through on this flat coastal strip were silent and packed with solid black shadows, but the heat bounced wickedly off the open tar road. In the sky real crows flapped, rasping to each other, surveying the stubble in the fields that had been cut, while gray wisps of smoke trailed up from the pale fires burning autumn husks.

Far, far to the southwest, very faint through the haze, the bluish-pink peak of Mount Hakusan rode above the grayer smoke of a string of small factories. Some of the fields were still unharvested, flowing and golden in the hot wind from the sea, and the husk smoke skittered like kite streamers across them, while the factory smoke mounted in stolid verticals, as impervious to wind as to season.

The road turned into a path and the path into a narrow meandering track between paddies, so that I had to keep an eye on landmarks: the piles of the expressway, Hakusan, the tantalizing ocean. I stopped for a beer in a little restaurant near a small-town station that was as deserted as the shadowy villages. The man who owned the restaurant had been born in the north of Honshu and told me he had worked all over Japan, in department stores and factories, driving trucks, laundering overalls, saving up for fifteen years to build this tiny shop that can barely have earned him a bachelor's living.

"But it's near the sea and the fields and that's what counts. There's so much of this country I haven't seen, and—my goodness—here you are walking the length of it! I see no point in going abroad, myself. What's the use of swanking about Hawaii and Guam when you've seen no more of your own country than the place you were born and the inside of an office? If I had my life to live again, I'd spend a year of it in each of the forty-seven prefectures—getting to know them all, their people and their ways. It's too late now, and I've a business to run, but if I ever have kids I'll make sure they see at least as much of Japan as I have."

He made me a free cup of coffee "for the road," and when I left the restaurant and set off along the track that had turned once again into an avenue, the crows were still flapping noisily over the stubble, but the sparkle had gone from the afternoon sea.

That night I was the only guest in a ryokan where the screens, as I sat eating dinner, opened onto a perfect moonlit garden. The old woman who owned the ryokan, and who was dressed in an exquisite chrysanthemum kimono, had brought her budgerigar to watch me eat, and throughout the meal he ran backwards and forwards across my shoulders, staring in lunatic fascination at each piece of red fish I slipped into my mouth. His name was Piko, the old woman told me. And what was my name? Aran-san? Ah, Aran Deron? No? Well, never mind, I was just as handsome as Aran Deron. And was I French, too? And did all Frenchmen write such lovely Japanese as Aran-san had written in her register? Would Aran-san not like some sakè? And could she not fill Aran-san's rice bowl again? It was such a pleasure to have a friend to talk to, wasn't it, Piko-san? Piko-san was sure it was. And would Aran-san mind if Piko-san stayed to watch him drink? Piko-san loved to watch his friends do that.

The old woman knelt on the cushion next to me and poured my sakè, cup after cup of it, smiling and chatting till I grew drowsy. She spoke to the budgerigar and to me with exactly the same measured politeness, and in the end we both ran out of replies. A breeze sprang up and the old woman moved away to draw the screens across the moon. I shut my eyes for a second and opened them half an hour later, sprawled out on the tatami mats with my feet under the table, my thin summer kimono wide open at the front, revealing my thighs and chest and belly and penis. The old woman was kneeling, talking quietly to her budgerigar, glancing across at me from the other side of the room where she had gone, a long while ago, to close the screens.

Would Aran-san like any more sakè? She could heat it for him in a trice if he did. No? Ah, well then, perhaps, since he was tired, he would like her to leave him and let him go to sleep. Piko-san could help his old granny lay out the mattress for Aran-san, who was really much too weary to talk any more. What a nice talk we had, though, didn't we, Aran-san? How fast the time goes when you're with a friend.

I watched the old woman silently clear away the dinner plates

and lay my mattress out on the tatami, well away from the screens
so that no drafts would disturb me. I sat up and pulled the cotton
kimono around me while she knelt in the middle of the room and
carefully lit the green mosquito coil. The budgerigar sat on her
shoulder and watched, absorbed, as the blue ribbon of smoke swam
up toward the ceiling.

"Say goodnight to Aran-san."

"Goodnight, Piko-san," I said.

The old woman quietly turned out the light and, with her friend,
disappeared down the dark passage toward her kitchen.

The morning of September seventh, the seventy-first morning of my
walk, was another baking hot one, and these Ishikawa roads were
behaving oddly—continuing for several kilometers broad and tree-
lined between smart little ball-valve factories and neat green lawns,
then trailing off into thin rubble tracks, then suddenly broad and
surfaced again. There was absolutely no traffic. The little village of
Ataka, where I stopped to ask directions, seemed as empty as a ghost
town, and I had to rattle the doors of three shops before I found one
open. In the dark, dusty cool of the shop, a tall old man with white
hair and no teeth treated me to a lecture on village history, while a
fighter plane screamed low over the rooftops, circled tightly out to
sea, then screamed back round the same circuit like a toy plane on
a wire.

"That's the trouble," the old man said, growling up at the ceiling
from which small specks of dust were flaking down onto his bananas.

"The commercial jets we could put up with; there's only half a
dozen a day. But these blasted Self-Defense Force training flights—
take-offs and landings and what have you—can you wonder people
move away, and the ones that don't stay locked up indoors? In fine
weather it goes on from morning till night. It's enough to make you
pray for a storm."

Where was the airport, I asked, looking at my map.

"About three kilometers down the road. There was an airfield
there during the war. Then the Americans came and chewed it up
with bulldozers, and we were all allowed to farm the land. Everyone
grew plots of rice there, me included, and we got a couple of fair
harvests out of it. But as soon as this Self-Defense lark started, the
government—the *Japanese* government, mind you—came and took
the land away again with not so much as a please or thank you, so
today we've got cracked eardrums instead of suppers."

The old man gave me the directions I wanted to the site of the Ataka barrier gate. He also gave me a withering scowl.

"What on earth d'you want to go and see that for?"

"I'm interested in history."

He squinted down at the little cassette recorder that I carried in a pouch on my belt for making notes.

"You a writer, then?" he asked, perceptively (someone else had thought it was a digital brandy flask). Yes, I told him, I had written a few things.

"Well, just you remember this," he said, getting up off his stool for the conclusion of his lecture, so that he stood a good deal taller than I did: "A country is like a sheet of paper; it's got two sides. On one side there's a lot of fancy lettering—that's the side that gets flaunted about in public. But there's always a reverse side to a piece of paper—a side that might have ugly doodlings on it, or bits of graffiti, or goodness knows what. If you're going to write about a country, make good and sure you write about both sides."

With this admonition swimming in my head, I crossed the narrow Ataka River and clumped down through a grove of silent pine trees to the welcoming, one-sided sea.

> The dune at Ataka where the pine trees stand,
> amid which—
> How clear! This ancient barrier gate!

That poem was written in 1933, and the poet was, quite properly, exercising her fancy. There is no barrier gate, nor was there one then. In the eight hundred years since the shogun Yoritomo is supposed to have set up a barrier here, the sea has eaten a good half kilometer into the coast, and the gate, if it ever existed in physical form, is now a mass of barnacles. But the site is that of one of the best-known incidents in Japanese legend—an incident celebrated in the popular Kabuki play *Kanjincho* (The Subscription List). It is worth summarizing the plot of this play for the example it contains of the tension between duty *(giri)* and humanity *(ninjo)*, a tension that some maintain still forms the basis of much Japanese thought and behavior.

The shogun's younger brother, Yoshitsune, a victim of fraternal jealousy, fled the capital in 1187 and made for the far north. To prevent his escape, the shogun commanded the setting up of barrier gates in all the provinces. Yoshitsune was fortunate in having as a retainer a man of prodigious wit and strength called Benkei. (The relationship between Yoshitsune and Benkei is similar to that between their contemporaries Robin Hood and Little John, and, interestingly, legend has them meet in the same way—on a bridge where they fight each other to establish superiority. In the English story Little John wins but sees in his adversary a leader worth following. This would never do in Japan, where feudal propriety requires the lord to hold all the trump cards, so Yoshitsune gains the victory, turning Benkei's subservience into a nice uncomplicated norm.)

In order to pass the Ataka barrier, Benkei and the other retainers have disguised themselves as *yamabushi*, or "mountain priests," fierce Buddhist mendicants who went about armed with iron-tipped staves. Yoshitsune, at Benkei's suggestion, is inconspicuously dressed as their bearer and brings up the rear. But the guardian of the gate, a samurai called Togashi, has been forewarned of Benkei's ruse and has made up his mind to kill all *yamabushi* on sight, so when the fugitives approach the barrier, their plight is more serious than they realize.

Benkei confronts Togashi with the story that they are collecting donations for the restoration of a great temple and Togashi abruptly demands to see his list of subscribers. Benkei, of course, has no such list, but he calmly draws a blank scroll from his pack, holds it close to his face so that Togashi cannot read it, and brilliantly improvises the sort of elaborate formal preamble that such a document would require. Togashi's suspicions are aroused, however, and he sneaks a glimpse of the blank scroll, which plunges him straight into the *giri*-versus-*ninjo* dilemma. Benkei is lying, and Togashi's duty demands that he kill or take them all prisoner. But, as a man, he cannot help admiring the fearless way in which Benkei is conducting himself; so instead of ordering their arrest, he cross-examines Benkei on the garments, habits, and beliefs of *yamabushi*. Benkei, whose father was a priest and who has taken religious orders himself, answers all the questions faultlessly, displaying an astonishing knowledge of Buddhist arcana. Togashi is so overawed that he gives permission for the fugitives to march through the barrier, which they begin to do. But then the disguised Yoshitsune is pointed out to him, and the conflict between admiration and duty flares up once again. Togashi orders the bearer to halt.

Benkei now delivers his masterstroke. Pretending to be angry that the bearer's sluggish pace has caused them to be delayed again, he seizes a staff and beats Yoshitsune, threatening to kill him. Togashi is aghast. Raising a hand against one's lord is an unpardonable sin, and if the bearer really is Yoshitsune, then by all the codes of feudal behavior Benkei has no recourse but suicide. So moved is Togashi that he swiftly restrains Benkei and sends the whole party on its way.

As soon as Togashi is out of sight Benkei grovels apologetically before Yoshitsune, who nobly forgives him for saving his life and then priggishly recites the tale of his own woes, especially the persecution he has suffered at the hands of his brother, to whom he was completely loyal, thus rounding out the theme of fidelity and disgrace. Finally Togashi reappears and offers Benkei some sakè, which he consumes in massive doses out of the lid of a tub. He then performs a lively dance while the members of his party steal away, having "trodden on the tail of a tiger."

The Greeks wouldn't have seen a play in it at all. Shakespeare might have turned it into an entertaining episode (a bit like Gad's Hill probably), though his attention would no doubt have focused on Togashi, the complex man of divided loyalties, caught between the worlds of responsibility and moral courage. But for the Japanese dramatist and his audience, the real hero of the affair is Benkei, a figure of simpleminded devotion, taking his life into his hands for a lord who displays far less wit and invention than he does. His heroic stature is enhanced by the fact that he drinks like a fish and is uncommonly clever with words.

At the cash desk of the little Ataka museum the custodian yawned and drowsed, while an endless tape droned out the tale of the subscription list to the ears of a bronze Togashi and Benkei, who stood immortalized on a large plinth outside the shuttered "rest house." The noodle shops and restaurants were all closed, including the Tea Room Sydney. Plywood cutouts of the three Kabuki characters, with holes for sightseers to poke their faces through, had been set up in front of a big hooded camera; but there were no sightseers, no cameraman, no movement or sound whatever—only the endless drone of the tape and the soft wash of the patient sea that, eight hundred years into the future, will have found all these lovely new monuments to lavish barnacles on.

It began to rain as I was tramping through the nearby hot spring resort of Katayamazu, but none of the huge Western-style hotels (The Grand Hotel, The Kaga Plaza) looked inviting enough for me to want to spend the night in them. Nor did the flashy little boutiques, nor the neon strip joints, nor the Adult Shop Venus entice me on this stormy afternoon; though it was nice to think of Yoshitsune and his friends emerging from their perils at the Ataka barrier to find all these entertainments waiting for them: honey traps more sticky than the shogun could devise.

I trudged on into the city of Daishoji, where the woman who ran the ryokan I stayed at delivered opinions on the weather with the air of a professional meteorologist.

"It's not going to rain today," she promised as I left her looking up at the sky next morning. Parts of the streets had dried out in the night but the wind was still high and the clouds dark and ugly. Within five minutes of the woman's forecast great spots of rain had begun to come down again—first a drizzle, then a downpour—and this was to prove the most memorable rain of a long rainy summer.

In April the cherry blossoms open and fall; in June the steady rains come, coating the shoes in the shoe cupboard with white mold. In October the maples turn startling crimson; in the winter months, on the Japan Sea coast, the snow lies so deep that in the mountain villages people must burrow about like moles. Japan is a land of vivid seasons, glowing, cruel, blessed, or cursed. Autumn brings the fiery leaves and it also brings typhoons.

The worst typhoon of the year was Typhoon 9. The Americans christened it Babe, but in Japan it was called the Okinoerabu Typhoon after the small island, 350 kilometers south of the southernmost tip of Kyushu, where towards midnight on September ninth it caused the lowest atmospheric pressure ever recorded in the Japanese islands (907.3 millibars). The eye of Typhoon 9 never came closer than that to the mainland. It was spawned eight thousand kilometers away in the South Pacific and finally blew itself out in China after striking land near the mouth of the Yangtze River. But its claws had a ferocious reach. In Japan Typhoon 9 sparked fifty-seven landslides, killed one person and injured scores, closed four hundred roads, buried or blew down five thousand houses and flooded three thousand more. It dumped rain in torrents all over the country. In poor little Okinoerabu, at its height, an incredible 1.37 inches fell in the space of ten minutes, while the wind screeched through the treetops at more than 196 feet a second.

Here, as I crossed the prefectural boundary from Ishikawa into Fukui on the morning of the eighth, the wind loosened rooftiles, overturned bicycles, and spun plastic detergent containers in wild pink dances across the teeming roads. The rain ran down my face like little rivers, and in the streaming chill of it my bones ached. There was nowhere to shelter, nothing to do but to trudge on singing songs to myself that I could barely hear above the noise the wind made. In the rain and wind of Typhoon 9 I climbed the thirty-six kilometers of twisting mountain roads that lead to the great Zen temple of Eiheiji.

It was dark when I reached the gate of the temple and too late to stay there as a guest. The government lodging house was full, and the man at the desk looked stunned when I interrupted his careful explanation of how to get to the youth hostel and told him I would rather stay at a ryokan.

"Do you mean a *Japanese* ryokan . . . ?"

But there were no ryokans of any kind to be had that night. It was *shiizun ofu* (off season), the man explained, and they would all be either closed or reluctant to take anything short of a busload. In the end I found a room above one of the small souvenir shops that crowded the road to the temple gate, and collapsed gratefully onto the floor of it. Drenched, cold, and very tired, I hung my dripping clothes over an electric fire to dry them and lay down to sleep as soon as dinner was over. The wind still roared and the rain beat upon the windows of my room as though they were taiko drums. All night the claws of the typhoon ripped at the shuttered streets, at the six-hundred-year-old cedar trees, and at the carved wooden gates and thin paper screens of Eiheiji, the Temple of Eternal Peace.

By morning the claws had worn themselves blunt and a quieter, gentler rain was falling. In the gentler rain, as I strolled round Eiheiji, the roofs of the temple shone like old silver, and the green moss in the cluttered gardens looked preened and vibrant and freshly alive. Eiheiji is a vast, beautiful temple, its rooms and halls connected to each other by corridors and long flights of covered wooden steps. Black-robed monks with shaven heads and trainee monks in loose black jackets and trousers sauntered through the corridors and halls with little smirks on their scrubbed faces, ignoring the tourists who were being ushered about, shuffling and whispering; and as the rain still fell, the rustle of robes, the ring of curious fingers brushing a gong, the patter of slippered feet on the cold, smooth boards or the shush of silk *tabi* socks over soft straw matting—all rose and fell in volume like the gasps of air in a bamboo flute and left in their wake a greater silence than before.

The churches of Europe—the great ones—soar up in dizzying verticals at the sky. Eiheiji hugs the contours of the earth. When the sun strikes the stained-glass windows of a cathedral they explode in primary colors like a carousel. But the colors of Eiheiji are earth colors—the somber greens of the garden, the browns and grays of smooth polished wood and slate, the soft gold color of old tatami. The builders of the Christian churches of Europe—churches in which a religion of humility is preached—seem often boastful, often to be saying to us: "Now, look here, this is the House of God. It is here— *here*—not over the road with those dingy Presbyterians but here in *this* church that God dwells." The builders of Eiheiji were a lot less strident: "Oh, God dwells in our temple, if you like. But then, he dwells in everything else as well—in clods of earth, in the eyes of the blind, in the pebbles of the seashore as well as in our shrines."

> The landscape of the mountains,
> the sound of streams—
> all are the body and voice of Buddha.

Eiheiji was founded in the middle of the thirteenth century by the author of that poem, a priest named Dogen. Dogen had spent four of his most formative years in China, being trained in Zen at Mount T'ien-t'ung, and because the Chinese are a practical people, his revelations, when they came, were of a practical kind. Dogen did not look for spirits in the air or worship an arcane, invisible Buddha who moved only in mysterious ways. "The truth is everywhere," he insisted. "The truth is where we are. One small step separates earth from heaven."

Despite the comparative sobriety of its architecture, Zen often seems to inspire in its adherents a supercilious attitude to the rest of mankind; an attitude that delights in one-upmanship, in riddles, puzzles, and the power of extraordinary experience. But Dogen maintained that in order to grasp the meaning of existence it was not necessary for a person to be unusually clever or to spend his life doing remarkable things. Simply by "sitting still and doing nothing" a man could discover what there was to be learned about life. Prayer and ritual were important to Dogen, but not much more so than cooking or sweeping the yard. All functions of the body, including the most basic, became, in the temple he founded, limbs of Zen. The toilet in Eiheiji contains an altar to Ususama Myo-o (The Guardian of the Impure), and together with the bath and the meditation hall, it is one of the three places in the temple where speech is forbidden and where a particularly strict code of contemplative behavior is observed by everyone who enters. It was Dogen's intention to make of Zen not an abstract philosophy, but a practice. The advice he gave his meditating disciples was blunt, straightforward, and mind-wrenchingly practical:

> Think of not thinking.
> How do you think of not thinking?
> By not thinking.

The rain had stopped when I left Eiheiji and began the long descent of the mountain. Blue dragonflies danced over the grass by the roadside and parched brown grasshoppers with lemon-colored wings flitted with soft clicks from stalk to stalk. I imagined the dragonflies dancing around Dogen on his trips to and from the temple, and his seeing in them, as he saw in all things, an endlessly renewable shard of the Buddha.

Then, as I walked, I notice that several of the dragonflies had stopped dancing and were beating their wings against the dirt. I bent to look at them and I saw at once that all the dragonflies were dying. There was not a soul on the road and no sound but the clock of the lemon-winged grasshoppers. I watched the dragonflies for a while as they shook in this heat that had come after the typhoon. Then I stood up and walked down the mountain, across the highway and the shady river, and on into the meadows of Fukui.

That afternoon I felt more drained than at any other time on this four-month journey. It was not a depression exactly, nor one of the passing spells of frustration that I had grown so used to dealing with, but a deep emptiness not rooted in anything that I could readily explain or shrug away. I tramped on through the harvest wondering why it was I felt like this. Because the summer was ending? Because dragonflies die? Because I knew, as I had known for years, that I did not have the strength or the patience to sit for so much as an hour and think of not thinking?

The sun came out near the town of Sabae and shone on the trees, still green and wonderfully fresh from the rain. It shone on the brown faces of village women who smiled at me on their way home from the fields. It shone on the golden heads of rice that were waiting for the women to come and cut them. The holiness of living things can scoop a terrible hollow in a pilgrim's stomach. Blake[1] would have got along well with Dogen.

That night I had a dinner of barbequed liver in a little restaurant at the top of an iron fire escape. The owner and his wife were both Koreans, and when by eight o'clock it seemed likely that I was going to be their only customer, the owner—a jolly, big-boned man— decided to close up shop for the evening and we went out together to have a few beers.

Both the owner and his wife had been born in Japan—the children of Koreans brought over just before the war to work as forced labor in the naval yards and mines—but neither had been granted Japanese

---

[1] William Blake (1757–1827) was an English poet, painter, engraver, and religious mystic. Blake's spirituality, as expressed in his writings and art works, took a highly symbolic and mythical form. (ED.)

citizenship (their parents were "subjects," not "citizens"), although the wife no longer spoke a word of Korean and the owner had not spoken it for twenty-odd years. There are something like 670,000 Koreans living in Japan at present, the majority of whom were born here and know no other language or way of life. Yet most of these must renew their residence permits every three years and carry their alien registration cards about with them, or risk being sent "home" to a country they may never have seen.

The owner told me he didn't think he would have wanted Japanese nationality anyway. He appeared happy enough with his situation, though a bit sheepish about forgetting his parents' language. He had a daughter who had never learned Korean, and neither he nor his wife was capable of teaching her. At first he had wanted to send her to a Korean school, but the nearest was in Fukui city, two and a half hours away by train, so she attended an ordinary local school instead, where she was completely indistinguishable from any of her classmates—except for the card she carried in her bag, with its photograph and fingerprint.

Amanohashidate—the Floating Bridge of Heaven—is a narrow sandbar about three and a half kilometers long which stretches across the Bay of Miyazu, enclosing half of it like a lagoon. Just as Kenrokuen in Kanazawa is one of the Three Most Beautiful Landscape Gardens in Japan, so Amanohashidate is considered one of the Three Most Beautiful Scenic Places. The habit of counting and classifying things is deeply ingrained among the guardians of Japan's natural assets, as the explanatory English signboard at the southern end of Amanohashidate makes particularly clear. The main section of the sandbar, it records, is 2,425 meters long and has an area of 130,484 square meters. At its greatest width it is 149 meters across and at its slimmest 19. The "investigation" of 1934 revealed that there were 3,990 pine trees on it, while a second "investigation" in May 1950 showed that this number had risen to 4,522. Such investigations, then, not only content minor government officials but, on the evidence of these statistics, excite the pine trees too. The signboard also advises that the "distance necessary time on foot" from the small revolving bridge at the southern tip of the bar to Kasamatsu Park at the northern end is exactly sixty minutes, and so I set out jauntily along the sandy track that on this sunny September day was splattered with the shadows of the busily procreating pines.

Few people, it seems, walk the length of the sandbar. At Chionji temple, near the southern end, a group of tourists had just broken off their prayers at the urgent beck of several bullhorns and had rushed down the old temple steps and boarded a boat for a sightseeing cruise. That is certainly a better way of appreciating the sandbar as a whole than to walk along it, where only the details are viewable; but it was the details that I liked most.

Whether they are procreating or not, pine trees are nicely eccentric plants, and it is not an accident that the Japanese accord ancient ones the same veneration due hermits and saints. Nor is it only ancient pines that possess a touch of human idiosyncrasy. At the narrowest, least protected point of the sandbar, where the full force of the wind cuts across it from the open sea, the trees are fiercely, tortuously bent, as though a life spent resisting the siege of gales had driven them to permanent distraction. Walking, I had the leisure to see them as individual creatures rather than as globs of green lost in a larger landscape, and perhaps because of this I left the sandbar feeling not that it was heavenly at all, but that, as with Eiheiji, its proper element was the earth. Others have clearly felt the same:

> Ah, floating bridge!
> Why does the ferryman
> grow older?

asked the poet Hosokawa Yusai, disappointed perhaps that, on the Bridge of Heaven, men, like pine trees, shake and bend as they age.

By tradition, the finest view of Amanohashidate is obtained neither by walking along it nor by circling it in a boat, but by climbing the hill at the northern end and looking down at it from the height of Kasamatsu Park—the Park of the Umbrella Pine. Nor, as I discovered on traipsing up to the park, do you simply stand and look at it—that would be far too earthly. What you do is climb onto one of three stone benches, stand with your back to the Bay of Miyazu, and then bend down and look at the Bridge of Heaven from between your spread thighs. This remarkable method of viewing scenery is supposed to give you the impression that the Floating Bridge is actually floating; and it is worth wondering what the person who first made that discovery was up to at the time.

Anyway, the sight of group after group of Japanese tourists going through the motions of this obligatory ritual provided me with a solid hour's entertainment. I especially like the attempts of the girls wearing skirts to prevent the stiff sea breeze from revealing other heavenly things and the attempts of the middle-aged businessmen to keep both their dignity and their spectacles intact. Best of all I enjoyed the performance of one keen amateur photographer who, not content

with simply peering at the sandbar through his thighs, exposed about
half a roll of film through them too, which involved a dexterity that
one had to envy. (Questions about why he didn't take his photographs the right way up and stick them in his album upside down
are idle: he was having A Good Time.) He was also just about the
only viewer in an hour who looked at the heavenly bridge for more
than two or three seconds. Most got it over with as quickly as
possible, climbing down off the benches and resuming an upright
position with a great flood of relief on their faces. Some months
before, the Mona Lisa had been exhibited at a Tokyo gallery and had
attracted such throngs of art lovers that the time each was allowed
to spend in front of it had to be carefully rationed. The gallery owners
decided eventually that the optimum time for viewing the Mona Lisa
was seven seconds, and this was felt by most art lovers to be satisfactory. It is not surprising, then, that two or three seconds suffice
for the Bridge of Heaven. Mount Fuji generally rates five or six and
the Second Coming of Christ will merit ten.

Of course I couldn't end my visit to Kasamatsu Park without
testing tradition for myself, so when a break finally occurred in the
long stream of people, I marched to the middle bench, stepped up
onto it, bent down smartly, and looked at the sandbar through my
thighs. It did a jackknife, a triple somersault, and a belly flop, though
I am prepared to believe that its acrobatic talents owed as much to
the three bottles of beer I had drunk as to any bodily contortions.
(Later on I tried viewing the Umbrella Pine through my thighs, but
it was much less frisky and looked nothing like an umbrella.)

In the early evening, back on the road, the four black chimneys
of the Iwataki Power Station added their own thick clouds to the
September dusk that was creeping down. One by one the lights went
on in the ring of hotels round Miyazu Bay, quiet now, but soon to
pack in the droves who descend annually when the leaves turn.
Ahead of me, a mass of gray-blue shadows, lay the mountains of
western Honshu, which I must cross in a grueling two-week trek
before meeting the coast again at Hiroshima. The lights were coming
on in the city of Miyazu, too, and in the last few pleasure boats of
the afternoon as they made their rounds of the sandbar. Steeped in
its own shadows, with the clouds darkening above it, Amanohashidate lay now like some half-exhausted Nessie[2]—no heavenly bridge

---

[2] Nickname for the Loch Ness monster, a legendary sea creature that has been the
subject of numerous searches in Loch Ness, Scotland. (ED.)

at all, but an earth-bound prankster that came home each evening gratefully to roost.

MARK SALZMAN

Unsuitable Reading

Mark Salzman (1960–), born in Connecticut, is both a Sinologist and a master of Chinese martial arts. He holds a degree in Chinese language and literature from Yale University. The following essay is taken from *Iron and Silk* (1986), a memoir of his experience teaching English in China and the basis for the film of the same name (1990). His latest book is *The Laughing Sutra* (1991), a novel.

On October 1, China's National Day, the Provincial Foreign Affairs Bureau arranged a banquet for all the foreigners living and working in Hunan. Prior to the banquet our host, a high official within the Provincial Government, held a meeting at which he gave us a "brief review of current political, economic and social issues affecting the province." This brief review, translated a sentence at a time into English, turned out to be a very lengthy recitation of statistics, all showing remarkable growth, interspersed with firm declarations of purpose, goals for the year 2000 and conclusive evidence that these goals would be met. The official sat completely still as he delivered this speech, moving his lips only as much as he had to except at the end of paragraphs, when he pulled them open to smile, shaking his head from side to side so that the smile fell upon all members of the audience equally.

After two hours the translator showed signs of fatigue. Something about striving from victory to victory was translated as "And the broad collective masses, by means of the leadership of the Chinese Communist Party, and under the protection of the new Constitution approved during the Twelfth Party Congress, shall—shall strike from factory to factory in order to realize the goals of the Four Modernizations by the year 2000." By the third hour, the poor translator had become delirious, stumbling over nearly every sentence.

No one experienced fatigue more than the audience, however,

for of the fifty foreigners there, about ten spoke both English and
Chinese, whereas the rest, from Japan and Romania, understood
neither English nor Chinese.

In the room sat an almost equal number of Chinese, mostly
Foreign Affairs representatives, some local government bureaucrats
and translators from the institutions with foreign expert programs.
Watching them, I could understand why they do not appreciate the
Westerner's irritation with long, boring meetings. The Chinese have,
by necessity, increased their endurance manyfold by making listening
optional. During meetings they talk with one another, doze, get up
to stretch or walk around, and in general do not pretend to pay
attention. This does not seem to offend the speaker, who, in general,
does not pretend to be interested in what he or she is saying.

A Chinese man sitting next to me had been dozing quite freely
since the first hour of the speech. He opened his eyes during the
third hour to reach for his teacup, and noticed me looking at him.
He had extremely thick glasses, a bloated face and a few beads of
sweat on his forehead that he wiped at with a dirty handkerchief. He
stared at me with no expression on his face for a long time, then
suddenly asked me what I thought of the meeting. I said I thought
it was very boring, too long and repetitious. His face did not change
at all and he continued to stare at me. "That is because you are
listening," he said, and went back to sleep.

I happened to see this man again on several occasions, and each
time talked with him at greater length. Though extremely shy at first,
he eventually loosened up and spoke freely about his interests and
ambitions. In time I found him to be a very warm person, and despite
his stiff, expressionless manner, he had a sense of humor as well. No
matter how funny something was, however, he always told or heard
it with that deadpan face, wiping at his forehead and staring at me
from behind his colossal lenses.

Some time later he came to my house to talk about a project that
he wanted help with. He translated Western novels into Chinese in
his spare time and hoped one day to publish. The problem was that,
like most Chinese, he had no access to recent works—meaning nearly
everything published since 1930. He wondered if I could lend him
some contemporary American novels that might be suitable for translation. I said that he could borrow as many as he liked from my
bookcase, and that if he had anything specific in mind, I would try
to get it for him. He didn't seem to have anything specific in mind,
so I let him take a few books at random and asked that he return
them by the end of the year.

To my surprise he returned a few weeks later, having read all of them. He put them carefully back into the bookcase, exactly where they had been before, and stared at me. "How did you like them?" I asked. Without blinking he replied, "Thank you very much, but I'm afraid these books would be unsuitable for publication in China. They contain scenes and language that would be considered decadent, or even pornographic." I said that I was sorry to hear that, and tried to think of books I had that might be more suitable. I chose a few short story collections and told him to read through them. "Even though these aren't novels, they are examples of recent American literature, and since this is a high school English textbook, I doubt they contain much pornography." He thanked me again and left.

A month or so later he returned, and once again put the books very carefully back into the bookcase. He wiped his forehead and apologized for keeping the books so long. "I'm afraid that these stories are also unsuitable for publication in China. They have heroes who represent pessimism, alienation and individualism, all of which, as you know, are considered detrimental to the cause of Socialism. Do you have anything else?" I had to admit, with some irritation, that I could think of no books in my possession that would be considered beneficial to the cause of Socialism. "I understand," he said, and began to leave. Passing by the bookshelf he noticed a large book that had not been there before. It was *The World According to Garp*. He asked what it was about, and I laughed and said he should read it and find out. He took it down, put it in his bag and said he would.

Several months passed. One day I found him sitting stiffly on a chair in my room; Old Sheep had seen him waiting and put him in my room while I taught class. After saying hello he took the book from his bag and apologized for keeping it so long. "It contained many words not found in most dictionaries," he said, "and was long to begin with." I asked him what he thought of it, noticing that he was not putting it back in the bookcase as he usually did. He looked at it, seemed to think for a few moments, then stared at me. "This book," he began, "is very, very unsuitable." He paused, then went on. "In fact, in my whole life, I have never read or even imagined something so unsuitable." Here he stopped, still staring at me. He held the book up slightly and pointed at it with his chin. "May I keep it?"

NICHOLAS COLERIDGE

The Emperor's New Clothes

Nicholas Coleridge (1957–   ) is a British magazine editor and reporter whose book *The Fashion Conspiracy* (1989), from which the
following selection is taken, is based on hundreds of interviews in
more than fourteen countries and takes the reader through the
world of high fashion.

I became seriously intrigued by fashion entirely by accident. In January 1985 I flew to Madras to interview Tamil[1] terrorists for a
television programme. Between interviews I killed time in a steam
bath at the Holiday Inn hotel. Every evening the only other customer
was a corpulent Indian who sweated cardamon[2] through his enormous pores. On the third day he said suddenly, 'Are you acquainted
with Her Majesty the Queen's dressmaker By Appointment, Mr Hardy
Amies?'

I replied that I had not met Mr Amies, but that I passed his
premises in Savile Row every morning on my way into work.

'At one time,' replied the Indian, whose name was Mr Kumar, 'I
had the honour to be manufacturing in my factory accessories for
the Hardy Amies boutique. But lately,' he said, 'we are hitting the
big time and working for Liz Claiborne in New York. You know Liz
Claiborne?'

'Only by reputation.' I had recently read an article about her
American sportswear empire in *Fortune* magazine, which estimated
her annual turnover at $1.8 billion.

'Each day we are manufacturing one thousand garments for Liz
Claiborne,' said Mr Kumar. 'You would like to visit my factory? It is
not far.'

We took a motor rickshaw along the beach road and then headed
inland for a few miles to a suburb of Madras called Shenoynagar.
The buildings in this part of the city are mostly bamboo shacks,
punctuated by gimcrack garages and light-industrial factories. Even-

---

[1] a people of southern India and Sri Lanka (ED.)

[2] the seeds of an East Indian herb of the ginger family, used as a seasoning (ED.)

tually we arrived at an arcade of shops and Mr Kumar led me to a flight of concrete steps at the back. Upstairs was a large warehouse room, occupying most of the upper storey of the arcade, in which about eighty young girls were working. They sat in their saris at long, wooden trestles, twenty girls to each table, operating prehistoric industrial sewing machines. Through their nostrils were fine gold *mookuthi* (Tamil nose jewellery) and many had white vertical stripes painted on their foreheads.

Mr Kumar gazed contentedly around his factory, while loosening the buttons on his shirt that strained over his obese stomach.

'It is the busy time now,' he said. 'January to March are most busy because these garments must be available in the stores by September for winter collection.' We watched as a girl fed a length of pink and blue check material through her machine. She smiled bashfully when she saw us standing over her, and pulled her sari across her face. I asked Mr Kumar how old she was, and he translated my question into Tamil.

'Thirteen,' he replied. 'Or that is what she says. Maybe she is younger, but they are paid more at 13.'

Eight or nine months later, when I had all but forgotten my excursion to the Madras sweatshop, I happened to be in Manhattan one Sunday morning and was reading the *New York Times* when an advertisement for Macy's department store caught my eye. A teenage American girl with long blonde hair was smiling out of the page, wearing a familiar pink and blue check jumpsuit. The caption read, 'Herald the season with gifts and gladness from Macy's . . . something for little girls to celebrate in the terrific holiday collection from Liz Claiborne. In dusty pink and blueberry cotton. $43. Fifth Floor.'

The dusty pink and blueberry cotton outfit seemed to be the very garment I had seen in production in the Shenoynagar suburb of Madras.

The journey from 40-rupee outfit in a backstreet sweatshop to a full-page advertisement for a major department store is only one leg of the fashion conspiracy. What inspired this book on the fashion industry was the realisation that you can follow a piece of clothing— exactly like you might follow the course of a river—from the place where the cotton is grown to the moment that the customer finally disposes of it. On its way, however, the skirt or coat is subjected to the most extraordinary hype by designers, fashion editors, store buyers, publicists, shop assistants and the rest of the fashion circus.

In Nongkhai in northern Thailand, close to the Cambodian border, there is a community of Irish nuns called the Good Shepherd

Sisters. They came to Nongkhai in 1981 to set up self-sufficient communities in an area of Thailand prone to malnutrition. One project the Good Shepherd Sisters set up was a weaving co-operative, producing a local variety of fabric called *ky khit*.

Two years after the looms were established, the nuns were approached by Yohji Yamamoto, the introspective Japanese designer, who bought several thousand yards of dark, rough cotton for his summer collection. It was shipped from Thailand to Yamamoto's headquarters in Tokyo, where he designed a selection of jackets and trousers and sent them to his factories in the Japanese countryside for manufacture.

Yohji Yamamoto does not show his collections in Tokyo; he shows in Paris which is more convenient for foreign store buyers, so the sample clothes are flown from Japan to France for fashion week. After the catwalk show, watched by the world's press and buyers, the samples remain in Paris for two weeks for the stores to place orders, while the press file their excited first reactions to the new shapes to their newspapers.

In due course the samples are flown on to Yamamoto's press office in Manhattan. American magazines, having checked with the store buyers which pieces they are ordering, need to photograph them for their collections issues. A New York fashion editor has the brainwave of styling the pictures in the Seychelles, so the Japanese clothes are again packed into trunks and flown back across the Atlantic, to be photographed on a Swiss model by a German photographer.

Three months later, when the pictures are published, a jet-lagged Kuwaiti woman flicks through a copy of the new *Vogue* in her hotel bedroom. Her eye is caught by a pair of black copra trousers being modelled underneath a palm tree.

'Those I like,' she thinks, and directs her limousine driver to the designer store.

Back in Kuwait she wears the trousers to an all-girls tea party. Later they are delivered to the Meshal dry-cleaner on Sharq Jaber Mubarak Street. And there, since she never troubles to collect them, they remain, a modest addition to the hundreds of thousands of pounds' worth of unclaimed Arab designer cleaning.

This fashion network—from Thailand to Tokyo to Paris to New York to the Seychelles, then back to New York and ending up in the Gulf—is no longer especially unusual. There are, of course, variations. A garment might begin its life in a sweatshop in South Korea or Sri Lanka, and end up in a shopping mall in Houston, Texas or Bal Harbour, Florida. It might start at one of the giant Italian mills near Lake Como and end up on the bargain rail of a boutique in Singapore.

But the fashion conspiracy is not simply a conspiracy of expensive clothes being marked up around the world, it is a conspiracy of taste and compromise: the prerogative of the international fashion editors in determining how the world dresses, and how their objectivity can be undermined, the despotic vanity of the designers and the ruthlessness of the store buyers in distributing their immense 'open to buy' budget. Often the conspiracy is a conspiracy of silence. A magazine goes to great lengths to make bad clothes look good, because the designer is advertising heavily in its pages. Major designers exert extraordinary pressure on department stores for more prominent square-footage while simultaneously pirating ideas from smaller rivals. Department stores, in turn, condone espionage to add a particular label to their designer room.

But this was not a conspiracy that I could grasp all at once. Fashion is an infinitely larger and more complex world than it appears from outside. The decade from 1978 has been decisive for fashion, as important as the 1950s were for the motor industry and the 1970s for computers. Designers like Ralph Lauren, Calvin Klein and Giorgio Armani have created from nothing fashion empires on a scale and with a speed that seemed impossible in the mid-1970s. In less than ten years they have achieved annual turnovers of $1.3, $1.1 and $1 billion respectively, and furthermore have largely held on to the equity themselves. This has produced a compelling new factor in the world economy: designer money.

'What happened,' says Fred Hughes, president of the Andy Warhol Trust, 'is that the entire western world—the entire world—is clothes conscious. People are living longer and staying fashion conscious; it's just going to go on and on, getting bigger and bigger and richer and richer.'

Designer money, like the first wave of Arab money to leave the Gulf, has been directed at a few enormous, rather similar status symbols: *palazzos* around Milan and Lake Como, cattle ranches in Colorado, châteaux in Normandy, apartments overlooking Central Park, yachts, jets and eighteenth-century paintings. Unlike the Arabs', however, these status symbols have not been accumulated in secrecy. Designers can rarely resist being photographed at their *palazzo,* ranch or château or assuming the helm of their new yacht.

More significantly, designer money has transformed the social status of designers. Few fashion designers before the mid-seventies were regarded as even half-respectable. At the most basic level, fashion designers were not asked to dinner by their customers. If they were invited to a customer's wedding they were seated inconspicuously at the back. This is no longer so. The relentless growth of the designer empires, and their diversification into billion-dollar licensing arrangements, has upscaled them to the status of chief executive officers of multi-national corporations.

'We have become world businessmen,' the New York designer Oscar de la Renta told me. 'In the old days fashion designers— seamstresses really—made and sold only dresses; today we sell a lifestyle to the whole world. We have moved into more and more areas of influence, and this has made a huge difference to how we are perceived. It has made the career more socially acceptable. And I think that in the end all social structures come to depend on power and influence. And, of course, on the influence and power that money brings.'

As the fashion industry has become international, however, it also gives the impression of being smaller. The five fashion capitals— New York, Paris, Milan, London and Tokyo—each have the same designer shops. Chanel, Saint Laurent Rive Gauche, Giorgio Armani, Ralph Lauren, Calvin Klein . . . whichever city you happen to be in, there is the same collection for sale in identically designed boutiques with identical carrier bags. It is fashion colonialism. Important designers must have a presence in every fashion capital. The boutiques are their embassies, their press offices are intelligence-gathering agencies telexing bulletins of rumour and counter-rumour to headquarters. The speed with which this takes place is sometimes incredible. While I was researching this book I flew from London to Tokyo to interview designers. A couple of hours before my flight I was told a beguiling item of gossip about an American designer.

'I am only telling you,' said my informant, 'because you are leaving the country. This is totally confidential. It's just been telexed from New York, and nobody even knows the story there.'

I arrived in Tokyo exhausted, slept for four hours, then met a Japanese friend in the fashion business for breakfast.

'How discreet can you be?' she asked as soon as we sat down, 'We have received a cable from New York . . .'

It is normal in the fashion industry to have exactly the same conversation in Milan as in London, and in Tokyo as in New York. Because the fashion circus is constantly on the move—not just the designers, but the photographers, store buyers, fashion editors and models—it creates its own homogeneous society, at once international and profoundly xenophobic. A buyer for a New York store will fly 200,000 miles a year from fashion capital to fashion capital, inspecting collections, but she will eat at the same few fashion restaurants and discuss the same tiny cast of characters. At the Bagutta in Milan she talks about the Tokyo designer Issey Miyake; at the i piselli in Tokyo she broods darkly about Ralph Lauren's Madison Avenue store; at the Quai Voltaire in Paris she philosophises about the Italian ready-to-wear of Giorgio Armani, or the seriousness of Jasper Conran's winter coats in London. In London, sitting at her window table at Le Caprice, the buyer is terribly, terribly concerned about the long-term future of Givenchy.

The private language of fashion embraces the five capitals. In his essay on 'Linguistics and Anthropology' in *Structural Anthropology,* Claude Lévi-Strauss defines the relationship between language and culture. 'Among us [western developed man],' he writes, 'language is used in a rather reckless way—we talk all the time, we ask questions about many things. This is not at all a universal situation. There are cultures—and I am inclined to say most of the cultures of the world—which are rather thrifty in relation to language. They don't believe that language should be used indiscriminately, but only in specific frames of reference and somewhat sparingly.'

The fashion industry is the antithesis of Lévi-Strauss's thrifty culture. It uses language so indiscriminately that it has actually created a parallel vocabulary, in which everyday words take on specific fashion connotations, entirely misleading to the outsider. Basic (as in 'your basic wardrobe', 'your best basic') and essential ('the essential black leather skirt') are straightforward antitheses when hijacked by fashion writers. A black leather skirt is clearly not an 'essential' garment, any more than a fuchsia wool-and-cashmere Gianfranco Ferre shawl, costing $1,595, can reasonably be described as 'basic'. But language of fashion is not restricted to magazine copywriting. Because people in the fashion industry tend to be more visually than verbally literate, their conversation takes on an exaggerated cartoon quality. Places are described as 'fabulous' or 'a nightmare'; collections are 'brilliant' or 'hideous'; particular restaurants are 'to die for' or to be avoided.

The larger the fashion industry grows, the fewer the players that really count. In the developed world, fashion employs eleven million people. And yet, when you pare the cast of leading characters to the minimum, it reduces to sixty. Thirty of these are designers: eight in New York, nine in Paris, three in Tokyo, five or six in Milan and three, perhaps four, in London. The next twenty are the fifth columnists: five or six crucial fashion editors, a dozen buyers for stores and boutiques, a handful of backers and entrepreneurs who underwrote the boom. The final five are fashion legends like Paloma Picasso, Tina Chow and Loulou de la Falaise Klossowski, the French-

Tunisian columnist Hebe Dorsey (who has passed away since the initial publication of this work), and John Fairchild, chairman and editorial director of *Women's Wear Daily.*

It is scarcely surprising, with such a tiny nucleus of opinion-makers hurtling around the world, that the level of paranoia is so high. No industry induces insecurity on the scale of fashion. Of the 400 people I interviewed, only about fifty seemed altogether sane. The structure of the fashion year provokes paranoia. Designers become paranoid under the pressure of producing two, sometimes more, collections a year; store buyers become paranoid at buying millions of dollars' worth of clothes that might not sell; fashion editors over the age of 40 become paranoid and begin to fear for their jobs.

Rivalry in fashion is more intense than in apparently comparable industries, like the record or film business, for this reason: everything happens in direct competition. Twice a year *all* the new collections are shown within a few days of each other, and directly compared. 'Ungaro was fabulous this season,' trills the fashion editor, 'but Dior was a nightmare.' 'Christian Lacroix was to die for,' says the buyer, 'but Balmain was *hideous.*'

A film may be previewed with other films at a festival, but their premières and release dates are carefully spaced. Fashion collections are simultaneously shown to the store buyers, who are selecting what to purchase from a finite budget. Within two weeks of a collection, the designer has an accurate idea of the level of orders, and whether these will occupy the seamstresses and outworkers for the next three months.

The invention of licensing (the means by which designers rent their names to the manufacturers of ties and sardine cans) has heightened paranoia since it emphasises the chasm between the successful and the less successful. Pierre Cardin has 840 licences, ranging from scuba-diving suits to designer igloos, which produce an estimated annual personal income of $10 million. Yves Saint Laurent, already licensed up to his sun-glasses, is pledged to a massive escalation over the next three years, and is vying with Gianni Versace to be the first designer to gain a full listing on a stock market. The average fashion designer has one or two licences or perhaps none at all.

All the time, however, the prospect of attracting the first licensee becomes more remote. The designer billionaires in their Italian *palazzos* and French châteaux retain staff to administer their licensing deals and to solicit new ones, and with every new licence their celebrity is more firmly established. It is a conspiracy to perpetuate income from endorsement, which looks set to continue for the next fifty years.

'Even when men like Saint Laurent or Lagerfeld are gone, their labels will continue,' says a French fashion writer. 'The same in America too, with Bill Blass and Geoffrey Beene. Somebody else in their studio will continue the label. For the licenseeing it is imperative. Just like Dior and Chanel were kept going after Christian and Coco.'

But there are aspects of the fashion industry that reminded me not of the madhouse but of a Middle Eastern emirate. The sheikhs of fashion are remote, protected by their bodyguards inside walled palaces, while the populace speculate and whisper. In no other profession have I encountered so much conjecture and innuendo. This designer is about to go bankrupt; that designer has AIDS; this one is so jealous of that one that his name must never be mentioned in his presence. And yet nothing of this is ever written down. The biographies of fashion houses—hagiographies really—read like propaganda from Gulf tourist offices. The lives of designers are reduced to inventories of statistics: he won this many Coty Awards, that many Neiman-Marcus awards, he produced so many ready-to-wear garments in 1987. I cannot fully explain fashion journalists' reticence, unless they are genuinely afraid of causing offence and being banned from the next collection. Or unless it is the half-antagonistic, half-protective view of fashion that gradually overtakes you if you spend too much time in the circus.

When I began researching this book, I assumed that the fashion industry would be like 'The Emperor's New Clothes'—founded largely on hype. This is not true. The industry can be more dangerous and sinister than I had appreciated. While I was in South Korea investigating the sweated labour of Seoul, a letter from a sweatshop boss was posted underneath my hotel door warning me out of the city. Whenever I think of the typed rice-paper sheet with its cryptic advice to 'go from Seoul city' it presents a chilling perspective on the 'basic' fuchsia wool-and-cashmere $1,595 shawl from Gianfranco Ferre.

After I visited the Madras factory, long before I had the idea of writing about fashion, I had a drink with Mr Kumar back in the Holiday Inn hotel. Mr Kumar drank imported gin and ate greedy handfuls of peanuts.

'Does it worry you,' I asked him, 'employing young girls for so little money, and to work such long hours?'

Mr Kumar shifted his weight on the plastic stool, so that his stomach could rest comfortably on the bar.

'Let me tell you a story,' he said, 'from Indian mythology. It will help you to understand. The young prince Gautama, the Buddha, was riding his white steed across a ploughed field when he saw that the ground was covered with insects killed by the plough. This filled him with deep sorrow, so he alighted from his horse and pondered on the subjects of birth and destruction. And then, desiring to be alone, he went apart to sit underneath a rose-apple tree where he attained the first stage of contemplation.' Mr Kumar was so absorbed in his story that he did not notice that his enormous stomach was now resting in a pool of Kingfisher lager. 'Whereupon,' said Mr Kumar, 'the young prince saw standing before him an old holy man. "Who are you?" asked Prince Gautama. "I am a beggar," replied the old man, "wandering without family and without hope, accepting any fare, I live now for nothing but the highest good." Whereupon,' said Mr Kumar, 'he rose into the sky and disappeared, for he had been a god.'

Mr Kumar scooped up another large fistful of peanuts. 'You are getting the point of my story?' he asked.

'Not really, I'm afraid.'

'It is obvious,' said Mr Kumar. 'It is a story about India. The landlord or the employer—that is me—is the prince. The poor people are like the holy man, wandering without hope and accepting whatever is available. At the moment what is available is manufacturing sportswear for American stores. Before, it was something different. Next it will be something different again. But today, it is fashion that people are wanting, so we are making it for them.'

IAN JACK

Unsteady People

Ian Jack (1945–   ) is a Scottish journalist who has written for *Vanity Fair* and the British newspaper the *Sunday Times,* and is now an editor for the *Independent on Sunday.* In 1988 he won the British Press Reporter of the Year Award for his coverage of the killing of three Irish Republican Army terrorists in Gibraltar. He recently published a collection of his journalism, *Before the Oil Ran Out* (1987). The following selection first appeared in *Granta* magazine.

On 6 August last year a launch overturned in the River Ganges near Manihari Ghat, a remote ferry station in the Indian state of Bihar. Many people drowned, though precisely how many will never be known. The district magistrate estimated the number of dead at around 400, the launch-owner at fourteen. The first estimate was reached by subtraction: 529 tickets had been sold and only a hundred passengers had swum ashore. The second estimate came from the number of bodies the launch-owner said he had counted stretched out on the bank. But then the river was in flood; hundreds of bodies could have been swept far downstream; scores may still be entangled in the wreckage or buried in the silt. The launch-owner had good reason to lie.

It was, in its causes and consequences, an accident which typified the hazards of navigating the River Ganges. Monsoon rains had swollen the river and changed its hydrography, cutting new channels and raising new shoals. The launch was overcrowded. Licensed to carry 160, it seems to have set out with at least three times that number, nearly all of whom were fervent Hindu pilgrims travelling from their villages in north Bihar to a shrine which lies south of the river. Devotees of Lord Shiva, the destroyer, they wore saffron robes and carried pots of sacred Ganges water on their shoulders. Eyewitnesses said the launch left the north bank to the chanting of Shiva's name, the chorus 'bol bam' rising from the massed saffron on the upper deck; until, hardly a hundred metres from the shore, the chants turned into screams.

According to a survivor quoted in the Calcutta newspapers, what happened was this. As the launch moved off, its stern got stuck in the shallows near the bank. The skipper decided to redistribute his vessel's weight, to lighten the stern by weighing down the bow. He asked his passengers to move forward; the stern bobbed up and the launch surged forward, head down and listing badly, to run a few hundred feet into a submerged sandbank and capsize.

In Bihar a revengeful clamour arose which sought to identify the guilty and exact punishment. The Bihar government and its servants blamed the launch-owner and charged him with murder. The opposition blamed government corruption and the conduct of the police. According to Ajit Kumar Sarkar, a Marxist member of the Bihar

Legislative Assembly, the launch took six hours to sink, and many victims could have been saved had not the police beaten back agitated crowds of would-be rescuers on the shore. According to the police, corruption had made their job impossible; almost every Ganges ferry flouted safety legislation because the ferryowners organized 'gangs to protect their interest.' Bihar had a 'steamer mafia' whose profits had perverted the political administration. Chief among this mafia was Mr Bachcha Singh, the 'steamer tycoon of Bihar' and owner of the launch that had gone down at Manihari Ghat.

Some days after the accident another of Mr Singh's vessels approached the wreck, ostensibly with the task of dragging it off the sandbank and on to the shore. Watchers on the bank, however, saw something different. They saw the second vessel pressing down on the wreckage of the first. It seemed to them that the other ship had come to bury the launch and not to raise it, thus destroying the evidence and, in the words of the *Calcutta Telegraph,* 'obscuring the gravity of the tragedy.' In the face of public protest the second ship backed off.

Where, meanwhile, was the steamer tycoon, Mr Bachcha Singh? Nobody could say. The Chief Minister of Bihar promised 'stern action', charges of murder and negligence were registered in the courts and some of Mr Singh's property was seized. But the police said they could not find Singh himself. He was, in the English of official India, 'absconding' and so the courts declared him an 'absconder'.

Thereafter public interest evaporated with the monsoon rains. Manihari Ghat became just another Ganges launch disaster. The people who had died were poor. None had relatives influential enough to secure the lasting attention of the press or the government, both of which in any case were soon preoccupied with other problems.

What was the precise truth of the affair? Nobody could say. Truth in its least elevated and most humble sense, truth as detail, truth as times and numbers, truth arrived at by observation and deduction— this kind of truth left the scene early. Like Mr Singh, it absconded. Unlike Mr Singh, it did not reappear.

Six months later I met the steamer tycoon at his house in Patna, the state capital. To European eyes, the house looked like something a Nazi cineaste[1] might have built. It had the smooth curves of a pre-

---

[1] a motion picture enthusiast (ED.)

war suburban Odeon and a large tower with two large swastikas etched high up in the concrete; they were visible from my cycle rickshaw long before the mansion itself swung into view. Mr Singh had called it 'Swastika House'—the name was on the gate—but only because he was a devout Hindu and the swastika is an ancient Hindu symbol of good fortune.

Fortune had been good to Mr Singh. It was manifest in his living arrangements, the dozens of domestic servants, his house's fifty bedrooms and thirty bathrooms, the superior quality of his tipped cigarettes. All of this (and a good deal else—apartments in Calcutta, real estate in the USA) derived from Mr Singh's role as the Ganges' principal ferryman. But his person as opposed to his surroundings seemed untouched by wealth. He was a small old man with heart trouble who wore loose Indian clothes and tapped ash from his Gold Flake King Size into an old spittoon.

We sat on his terrace and drank tea from mugs. I wondered about the murder charge. What had happened to it?

Nothing, said Singh, the case would never come to court. Did I understand the caste system? In Bihar caste was the key to everything. The murder charge had been instigated by the then Chief Minister, who was a Brahmin. Singh belonged to the Rajput caste, and Rajputs were the Brahmins' greatest political rivals. The charge had been politically inspired.

And now?

'Now the Chief Minister is a Rajput. He is known to me. Case finish.'

He apologized for his English and called for his son, who, he said, would be more intelligible to me. This proved to be only partly true. The younger Singh was reading Business Administration at Princeton University, ferry profits having dispatched him to the United States when he was an infant, and his English crackled with the abrasive nouns of the new capitalism. 'Cash-burn . . . acquisition and diversification . . . buy-out.' It was strange to hear these words in Bihar, still governed by ancestry and feudal law, but they completely matched the younger Singh's appearance. In T-shirt, shorts and sneakers, he might have stepped out of a college tennis game. The sight of son next to father, crouched beside his spittoon, was a testament to the transforming power of money.

The father had recalled his son to Patna soon after what both referred to, opaquely, as 'the tragedy'. The son looked at his new surroundings with cold eyes. Corruption, poverty, ignorance, tradition—they ruled life here. It was sickening. Outside the family, nobody could be trusted. Did I know, for example, that after the tragedy peasants from adjacent villages had brought newly-dead relatives to the river, so that their bodies could be discreetly inserted among the launch's victims and compensation claimed?

I hadn't heard that, but maybe it was true; Bihar can sometimes be a desperate place. But what did he think had caused the accident?

'Panic and stupidity,' said the younger Singh. He thought for a moment. 'Basically these people weren't willing to make the smart move and analyse the situation.'

Of course these were ludicrous words; passengers packed on a tilting motor launch cannot be expected to plan their next five minutes like Wall Street commodity brokers. But the longer I travelled through Bihar, squashed on trains and river boats, the more I recognized the younger Singh's detachment as an indigenous sentiment rather than an American import.

Certain facts about Bihar were undeniable. The launchowners were greedy and their craft decrepit and dangerous; the police were corrupt and tended to enforce the law of the highest bidder—the younger Singh said himself that his family had put off police inquiries with a few thousand rupees; and covert supplies of money moved through the system at every level—an honest police-officer could have his orders countermanded by a corrupt district administrator, an honest district administrator could be transferred or demoted by a corrupt politician. To behave dutifully and honestly in this amoral environment involved great courage and sacrifice. It was no surprise that the safety of the travelling public, especially a public so lacking in clout, did not figure highly in the minds of their appointed guardians.

My fellow-travellers would talk quite frankly about all this—humbug is not a Bihari vice—but then they also echoed the younger Singh: people in Bihar, they would say, did not know how to behave. They were 'uneducated' and 'ignorant' and, most of all, 'backward'. The populations of western democracies hesitate—still—to describe their fellow-citizens so bluntly, at least in public. But Biharis have no such inhibitions. The ancient social pyramid of caste enables those at the top to look down at those below with a dispassionate prejudice, at an inferior form of human life.

'I'm afraid we are not a *steady* people,' an old man said to me one day, and I could see exactly what he meant. Often the unsteadiness was frightening. The resources of transportation are scarce all over India; there is a continual press and scramble for tickets and seats wherever you go. But young Biharis travel on the roofs of trains even when the compartments below are empty and rush listing ferries like a piratical horde. Even the old and lame press forward as though fleeing some imminent disaster.

Towards the end of my journey in Bihar I met another Singh, a relative of the steamer tycoon, who operated a couple of old steamboats just upriver from Manihari Ghat. In an interval between crossings he took me up on to the bridge of his ferry, which was berthed at the foot of a steep bank, glistening and slippery with unseasonal rain. At the top of the slope men with staves, Singh's employees, were restraining a crowd of waiting passengers. Then the steamer's whistle gave two hoots; the men with staves relented; and the crowd, with its bicycles and milk-churns, came rushing down the bank towards us, slithering and whooping.

Singh looked down at his customers as they milled across the gangplank and then laughed like a man in a zoo. 'Crazy people. What can you do with them?'

On 15 April this year ninety-five people were crushed to death on the terraces of a football stadium in Sheffield, northern England. Most of the dead came from Liverpool, and all of them were supporters of Liverpool football club, who that day were to play Nottingham Forest in the semi-final of English football's premier knockout competition, the Football Association Cup. The deaths came six minutes after the kick-off. The match was then abandoned.

I read about the disaster in Delhi on my way back to London. Newspaper reports speculated on the possible causes and recalled that the behaviour of Liverpool fans had prompted the crush which killed thirty-nine people at the European Cup Final in Brussels in 1985, all of them Italian supporters of the other finalists, Juventus of Turin. It seemed something similar had happened in Sheffield. Liverpool fans had swept into the ground and pressed their fellow-supporters forward until they were squashed against the barriers and fences which had been erected some years before to prevent unruly spectators rushing on to the pitch and interfering with the game.

All that winter in India I'd heard about death in Britain. Planes fell to earth and trains left the rails, and Mrs Thatcher's face appeared on Indian television talking of her sympathy and concern. There were shots of disintegrated fuselages, body bags, shattered railway coaches. Indian friends tutted at the carnage, and I recognized in their reaction the momentary interest—the shake of the head, the small ripple of fascination—that passes through a British living-room when news of some distant tragedy flits before it; say, of the last typhoon to strike Bengal.

Meanwhile, the India I saw reported every day on the news—orderly, calm, soporific—looked more and more like the country I came from—or at least as I had once thought of it. Accidents such as Manihari Ghat were certainly reported, but rarely filmed. We watched the prime minister greeting foreign delegations at the airport, men in good suits addressing seminars and shaking hands, women cutting tapes and accepting bouquets. Indian news, or what India's government-controlled television judged to be news, took place indoors in an atmosphere notably free of dust, flies and mess. There was a lot of cricket. The mess—grief and ripped metal under arc lights—came from abroad, imported by satellite and shiny film-cans—they were like luxury items, a new spice trade going the other way—which the makers of Indian bulletins slotted in between the hand-shaking and the seminars as if to prove that disaster could overtake the foreign rich as well as the native poor, and that it was not confined to terrorism in the Punjab or the chemical catastrophe at Bhopal.

There were two train crashes in the southern suburbs of London (forty dead); a Pan Am Jumbo which exploded over Lockerbie (270 dead); a Boeing forced to crash-land on a motorway (forty-seven dead). All of them had specific and identifiable causes—a bomb, signal failure, faulty engines—though the roots (what caused the cause?) led to a vaguer territory: under-investment in public utilities, 'international terrorism', the collapse of civic feeling under a political leader who has said she cannot grasp the idea of community. This kind of worry—the cause of the cause—had bobbed to the surface of British life like old wreckage ever since the Channel ferry *Herald of Free Enterprise* turned over at Zeebrugge in 1987, the first in a series of large accidents which has marked Britain out as a literally disastrous country. But from the distance of India, Sheffield looked different. It seemed to turn on the behaviour of a fervent crowd; there was, in that sense, something very Indian about it.

When my landlord in Delhi said he thought football in England must have assumed 'a religious dimension', it was difficult to resist the parallel: saffron pilgrims struggling to board their launch at Manihari Ghat, the mass of Liverpudlian red and white which surged into the stadium at Sheffield. And the parallels did not end there. In fact the nearer I got to home the closer they became.

Changing planes in Paris, I bought a newspaper and read about M. Jacques Georges, the French president of the European Football

Association. An interviewer on French radio had asked M. Georges if he thought Liverpool was peculiar in some way, given its football club's recent history of violent disaster. Well, said Georges, Liverpool certainly seemed to have 'a particularly aggressive mentality'. The crowd that had stormed into the ground at Sheffield had scorned all human feeling. 'I have the impression—I am distressed to use the expression—but it was like beasts who wanted to charge into an arena.'

The English are not a steady people. Today all Europe knows that. None the less M. George's words had scandalized England. At Heathrow the papers were full of him, even though he had said little more than the Sheffield police. According to Mr Paul Middup, chairman of the South Yorkshire Police Federation, there was 'mass drunkenness' among the 3,000 Liverpool supporters, who turned up at the turnstiles shortly before the kick-off: 'Some of them were uncontrollable. A great number of them had obviously been drinking heavily.' According to Mr Irvine Patrick, a Sheffield MP, the police had been 'hampered, harassed, punched, kicked and urinated on.'

But then the police themselves had behaved ineptly. Seeking to relieve the crush outside the stadium, they had opened a gate and sent an excited crowd—drunks, beasts or otherwise—into a section of the terracing which was already filled to capacity. And then, for some minutes at least, they had watched the crowd's desperate attempt to escape over the fences and mistaken it for hooliganism. They had hardly made a smart move and analysed the situation.

It would have all been familiar to any citizen of Bihar. An underclass which, in the view of the overclass, did not know how to behave. 'Drunks . . . beasts . . . uneducated . . . ignorant.' An antique and ill-designed public facility. A police force which made serious mistakes. Clamorous cross-currents of blame.

At home, I watched television. The disaster excited the medium. For several days it replayed the scene at Sheffield and then moved on to Liverpool, where the football ground was carpeted with wreaths. Funeral services were recorded, football players vowed that they might never play again and political leaders in Liverpool demanded the presence in their city of royalty—a prince, a duke—so that the scale of the 'national tragedy' might be acknowledged. When members of Liverpool's rival team turned up at a burial, the commentator spoke reverently of how the disaster had 'united football', as though the French and Germans in Flanders had stopped bombardment for a day to bury their dead. One football official said he hoped that ninety-five people had not 'died in vain.' Another said that they had 'died for football.'

Nobody in Bihar would have suggested that the dead of Manihari Ghat had made such a noble sacrifice. Nobody would have said: 'They died to expunge corruption, caste and poverty.' Whatever their other faults, Biharis are not a self-deluding people.

P. J. O'ROURKE

A Ramble through Lebanon

P. J. O'Rourke (1947–   ), who runs the Foreign Affairs Desk for *Rolling Stone* magazine, frequently writes as a satirical essayist. His work has appeared in the *New Republic, National Lampoon, Playboy, The American Spectator,* and other periodicals. O'Rourke is the author of the books *Bachelor's Home Companion* (1987), *Republican Party Reptile* (1987), *Holidays in Hell* (1988), from which the following selection is taken, *Modern Manners: An Etiquette Book for Rude People* (1989), and *Parliament of Whores: A Lone Humorist Attempts to Explain the Entire U.S. Government* (1991).

OCTOBER 1984

I visited Lebanon in the fall of '84, which turned out to be pretty much the last time an American could travel in that country with only a risk (rather than a certainty) of being kidnapped. I was just taking a vacation. Somehow I had convinced Vanity Fair *magazine to let me do a piece on the holiday pleasures of Beirut and its environs. What follows is, with a few parenthetical addenda, the article I wrote for* Vanity Fair, *an article that they—wisely, I think—decided was much too weird to publish.*

"Bassboat." "Bizport." "Passboot." "Pisspot." It's the one English word every Lebanese understands and no Lebanese can say. The first, deepest and most enduring impression from a visit to Lebanon is an endless series of faces, with gun barrels, poking through the car window and mispronouncing your travel documents.

Some of these faces belong to the Lebanese Army, some to the Christian Phalange, some to angry Shiites or blustering Druse or grumpy Syrian draftees or Scarsdale-looking Israeli reservists. And who knows what the rest of them belong to. Everybody with a gun has a checkpoint in Lebanon. And in Lebanon you'd be crazy not to have a gun. Though, I assure you, all the crazy people have guns, too.

You fumble for passes and credentials thinking, "Is this Progressive Socialist or Syrian Socialist National Party territory? Will the Amal militia kill me if I give them a Lebanese Army press card? And what's Arabic, anyway, for '*Me? American?* Don't make me laugh'?"

The gun barrels all have the bluing worn off the ends as though from being rubbed against people's noses. The interesting thing about staring down a gun barrel is how small the hole is where the bullet comes out, yet what a big difference it would make in your social schedule. Not that people shoot you very often, but the way they flip those weapons around and bang them on the pavement and poke them in the dirt and scratch their ears with the muzzle sights . . . Gun safety merit badges must go begging in the Lebanese Boy Scouts.

On the other hand, Lebanon is notably free of tour groups and Nikon-toting Japanese. The beaches, though shell-pocked and occasionally mined, are not crowded. Ruins of historical interest abound, in fact, block most streets. Hotel rooms are plentiful. No reservation is necessary at even the most popular restaurant (though it is advisable to ask around and find out if the place is likely to be bombed later). And what could be more unvarnished and authentic than a native culture armed to the teeth and bent on murder, pillage and rape?

One minor difficulty with travel to Lebanon is you can't. There's no such thing as a tourist visa. Unless you're a journalist, diplomat or arms salesman, they won't let you in. And if you believe that, you'll never understand the Orient. Type a letter saying you're an American economist studying stabilization of the Lebanese pound or something. (Sound currency is one thing all factions agree on. The Central Bank is the best guarded and least shelled building in Beirut.) I had a letter saying I was studying the tourism industry in Lebanon.

"The *tourism* industry?" said the pretty young woman at the Lebanese Consulate.

"Yes," I said.

"*Tourism?*"

I nodded.

She shrugged. "Well, be sure to go see my village of Beit Mery. It's very beautiful. If you make it."

Middle East Airlines is the principal carrier to Beirut. They fly from London, Paris, Frankfurt and Rome—sometimes. When the airport's being shelled, you can take a boat from Larnaca, Cyprus.

There are a number of Beirut hotels still operating. The best is the Commodore in West Beirut's El Hamra district. This is the headquarters for the international press corps. There are plenty of rooms available during lulls in the fighting. If combat is intense, telex Beirut 20595 for reservations. The Commodore's basement is an excellent bomb shelter. The staff is cheerful, efficient and will try to get you back if you're kidnapped.

There's a parrot in the bar at the Commodore that does an imitation of an in-coming howitzer shell and also whistles the Marseillaise. Only once in ten years of civil war has this bar been shot up by any of the pro-temperance Shiite militias. Even then the management was forewarned so only some Pepsi bottles and maybe a stray BBC stringer were damaged. Get a room away from the pool. It's harder to hit that side of the building with artillery. Rates are about fifty dollars per night. They'll convert your bar bill to laundry charges if you're on an expense account.

Beirut, at a glance, lacks charm. The garbage has not been picked up since 1975. The ocean is thick with raw sewage, and trash dots the surf. Do not drink the water. Leeches have been known to pop out the tap. Electricity is intermittent.

It is a noisy town. Most shops have portable gasoline generators set out on the sidewalk. The racket from these combines with incessant horn-honking, scattered gunfire, loud Arab music from pushcart cassette vendors, much yelling among the natives and occasional car bombs. Israeli jets also come in from the sea most afternoons, breaking the sound barrier on their way to targets in the Bekáa Valley. A dense brown haze from dump fires and car exhaust covers the city. Air pollution probably approaches a million parts per million. This, however, dulls the sense of smell.

There are taxis always available outside the Commodore. I asked one of the drivers, Najib, to show me the sights. I wanted to see the National Museum, the Great Mosque, the Place des Martyrs, the Bois de Pins, the Corniche and Hotel Row. Perhaps Najib misunderstood or maybe he had his own ideas about sight-seeing. He took me to the Green Line. The Green Line's four crossings were occupied by the Lebanese Army—the Moslem Sixth Brigade on one side, the Christian Fifth Brigade on the other. Though under unified command, their guns were pointed at each other. This probably augurs ill for political stability in the region.

The wise traveler will pack shirts or blouses with ample breast pockets. Reaching inside a jacket for your passport looks too much like going for the draw and puts armed men out of continence.

At the Port Crossing, on the street where all the best whorehouses were, the destruction is perfectly theatrical. Just enough remains of the old buildings to give an impression of erstwhile grandeur. Mortars, howitzers and rocket-propelled grenades have not left a superfluous brush stroke on the scrim. Turn the corner into the old marketplace, the Souk, however, and the set is a Hollywood back lot. Small arms and sniper fire have left perfectly detailed havoc. Every square inch is painstakingly bullet-nibbled. Rubble spills artfully out of doorways. Roofs and cornices have been deftly crenulated by explosion. Everything is ready for Ernest Borgnine, John Cassavetes and Lee Marvin in a remake of *The Dirty Dozen,* except the Lebanese can't figure out how to remove the land mines.

We went back and forth across the Green Line six times, then drove into Beirut's south suburbs. This area was once filled with apartment buildings housing the Moslem middle class. The buildings were destroyed by Israeli air strikes during the invasion of 1982. Modern construction techniques and modern war planes create a different kind of ruin. Balconies, windows and curtain walls disintegrate completely. Reinforced concrete floors fold like Venetian-blind slats and hang by their steel rebars from the buildings' utility cores. Or they land in a giant card-house tumble. Shiite squatter families are living in the triangles and trapezoids formed by the fallen slabs. There's a terrible lack of unreality to this part of the city.

Outside the areas controlled by the Lebanese Army the checkpoints are more numerous, less organized and manned by teenagers in jeans, T-shirts and Adidas running shoes. They carry Russian instead of U.S. weapons. Some belong to the Shiite Amal militia, others to the even more radical Hezbullah. All have strong feelings about America. Fortunately, they can't read. One even held my Arabic press credentials upside down, picture and all, and tipped his head like a parakeet to see if I matched my inverted photo. At the most dangerous-looking checkpoints, Najib said something that made the guards laugh and wave us through.

"Najib," I said, "what are you telling them?"

He said, "I tell them you travel for pleasure."

Finally, we got to a place where we could go no further. Down the street the Sunni Moslem Mourabitoun militia was having it out with the Shiite Amal militia—part of the long-standing Sunni/Shiite dispute about whether Muhammad's uncle Abbas or Muhammad's son-in-law Ali should have succeeded the Prophet and, also, about who gets the take from the south-side gambling joints.

West Beirut can also be toured on foot. You'll find the city is full of surprises—a sacking of the Saudi embassy because of long lines for visas to Mecca, for instance, or shelling of the lower town by an unidentified gunboat or car bombs several times a day. Renaults are the favored vehicles. Avoid double-parked Le Cars. Do not, however, expect the population to be moping around glassy-eyed. There's lots of jewelry and make-up and the silliest Italian designer jeans on earth. The streets are jammed. Everyone's very busy, though not exactly working. They're rushing from one place to another in order to sit around drinking hundreds of tiny cups of Turkish coffee and chat at the top of their lungs. The entire economy is fueled, as far as I could see, by everyone selling cartons of smuggled Marlboros to each other.

It turns out I didn't miss much on Najib's style of guided tour. The Bois de Pins, planted in the 1600s by Emir Fakhr ed Din to protect Beirut from encroaching sand dunes, had all its foliage blown off by Israeli jets and looks like a phone-pole farm. The Place des Martyrs, so-called because eleven nationalists were hanged there by the Turks in 1915, is right on the Green line and now all that much more aptly named. Most of the buildings on the Corniche have literally been face-lifted. The old American Embassy is here, in the same state as U.S. Middle East policy. The British Embassy down the street is completely draped in anti-bomb nets imported from Belfast. Hotel Row was ravaged at the beginning of the civil war in 1975. The high-rise Holiday Inn is a delight to the eye. Who, when traveling around the earth faced with endless Holiday Inns, has not fantasized blowing one to flinders? The National Museum is bricked up and surrounded with tanks—no nagging sense of cultural obligation to tour this historical treasure trove. I couldn't find the Great Mosque at all.

A surprising lot of Beirut stands, however. A building with a missing story here, a lot with a missing building there, shattered this next to untouched that—all the usual ironies of war except with great restaurants.

The Summerland Hotel, on the beach in the ruined south suburbs, has good hamburgers. The wealthy Moslems, including Shiites, go here. All Shiites are not stern zealots. Some have string bikinis. And, like an American ethnic group with origins nearby, they wear their jewelry in the pool. (It was at the Summerland where the Amal militia feted its American captives during the 1985 TWA hostage crisis.)

Downtown on the Corniche you can lunch at the St. Georges Hotel, once Beirut's best. The hotel building is now a burned shell, but the pool club is still open. You can go waterskiing here, even during the worst fighting.

I asked the bartender at the pool club, "Don't the waterskiers worry about sniper fire?"

"Oh, no, no, no," he said, "the snipers are mostly armed with automatic weapons—these are not very accurate."

Down the quay, pristine among the ruins, Chez Temporal serves excellent food. A short but careful walk through a heavily armed Druse neighborhood brings you to Le Grenier, once a jet-set mob scene, now a quiet hideaway with splendid native dishes. Next door there's first-rate Italian fare at Quo Vadis. Be sure to tip the man who insists, at gunpoint, on guarding your car.

Spaghetteria is a favorite with the foreign press. The Italian specials are good, and there's a spectacular view of military patrols and nighttime skirmishing along the beachfront. Sit near the window if you feel lucky.

Addresses are unnecessary. Taxi drivers know the way and when it's safe to go there. Service at all these establishments is good, more than good. You may find ten or a dozen waiters hovering at your side. If trouble breaks out, the management will have one or two employees escort you home. When ordering, avoid most native wines, particularly the whites. Mousar '75, however, is an excellent red. Do not let the waiters serve you Cypriot brandy after the meal. It's vile.

The Commodore also has restaurants. These are recommended during fighting. The Commodore always manages to get food delivered no matter what the situation outdoors.

Nightlife begins late in Beirut. Cocktail hour at the Commodore is eight P.M., when U.S. editors and network executives are safely at lunch (there's a seven-hour time difference). The Commodore is strictly neutral territory with only one rule. No guns at the bar. All sorts of raffish characters hang about, expatriates from Palestine, Libya and Iran, officers in mufti from both sides of the Lebanese Army, and combatants of other stripes. I overheard one black Vietnam veteran loudly describe to two British girls how he teaches orthodox Moslem women to fight with knives. And there are diplomats, spooks and dealers in gold, arms and other things. At least that's what they seem to be. No one exactly announces his occupation—except the journalists, of course.

I met one young lady from Atlanta who worked on a CNN camera crew. She was twenty-six, cute, slightly plump and looked like she should have been head of the Georgia State pep squad. I sat next to her at the Commodore bar and watched her drink twenty-five gin and tonics in a row. She never got drunk, never slurred a word, but along about G&T number twenty-two out came the stories about dismembered babies and dead bodies flying all over the place and the Red Cross picking up hands and feet and heads from bomb blasts and putting them all in a trash dumpster. "So I asked the Red Cross people," she said, in the same sweet Dixie accent, "like, what's this? Save 'em, collect 'em, trade 'em with your friends?"

Everyone in Beirut can hold his or her liquor. If you get queasy, Muhammad, the Commodore bartender, has a remedy rivaling Jeeves's in P.G. Wodehouse's novels. It will steady your stomach so you can drink more. You'll want to. No one in this part of the world is without a horror story, and, at the Commodore bar, you'll hear most of them.

Dinner, if anyone remembers to have it, is at ten or so. People go out in groups. It's not a good idea to be alone and blonde after dark. Kidnapping is the one great innovation of the Lebanese civil war. And a Reuters correspondent, Johnathan Wright, had disappeared thus on his way to the Bekáa Valley a few days before I arrived.

If nabbed, make as much noise as possible. Do not get in anyone's car. If forced in, attack the driver. At least this is what I'm told.

Be circumspect when driving at night. Other cars should be given a wide berth. Flick headlights off and on to indicate friendly approach. Turn on the dome light when arriving at checkpoints. Militiamen will fire a couple of bursts in your direction if they want you to slow down.

Clubs, such as the Backstreet near the Australian Embassy, keep going as late as you can stand it. There's some dancing, much drinking and, if you yell at the management, they'll keep the Arab music off the tape deck. Cocaine is available at about fifty dollars a gram and is no worse than what you get in New York.

Beirut nightlife is not elaborate, but it is amusing. When danger waits the tables and death is the busboy, it adds zest to the simple pleasures of life. There's poignant satisfaction in every puff of a cigarette or sip of a martini. The jokes are funnier, the drinks are stronger, the bonds of affection more powerfully felt than they'll ever be at Club Med.

East Beirut is said to also have good restaurants and nightclubs. But the visitor staying on the West side probably won't see them. No one likes to cross the Green Line at night. And, frankly, the East isn't popular with the West-side crowd. All the window glass is taped, and the storefronts are sandbagged over there. It gives the place a gloomy look. No one would think of doing this in the West. It would be an insult to the tradition of Oriental fatalism, and nobody would be able to see all the cartons of smuggled Marlboros stacked in the window. Anyway, the East-side Christians are too smug, too pseudo-French and haven't been shelled enough to turn them into party reptiles.

Travel to the North is less arduous. George Moll, the video editor at ABC-TV's Beirut bureau, and I went on a trip to the Bsherri Cedars. Traffic on the coast road north of the city is stalled by checkpoints. Amazing what a few guys standing around with guns can do to create gridlock. "I ♡ Lebanon" bumper stickers are popular with the motorists. "Kill them all—Let God sort them out" T-shirts are popular with the militias.

It's important to remember, when dealing with these militias, that the gunmen are mostly just kids and they're getting a big kick out of the whole thing. I suppose this is only natural when young people lack proper recreational facilities and well-supervised activities to keep them out of mischief. They need sympathy and understanding. Or a sixteen-inch shell from the battleship New Jersey.

I wanted to visit the gorge of the Nahr el Kelb, the River of the Dog, a strategic point on the Lebanese coast just north of Beirut where for more than three thousand years invading armies have carved stelae commemorating their passage. A tunnel for the coast highway now cuts through the gorge wall, and the carvings are reached via a ramp above the traffic. The cuneiform characters of Nebuchadnezzar II, the stela of the Pharaoh Ramses, the Assyrian bas reliefs, a Latin inscription from the Emperor Marcus Aurelius, Greek carvings from the Seleucid empire—they've all been completely effaced by air pollution.

Don't go to the famous Jeita Grottoes at the source of the Dog River, either. These have been turned into a military training base. Although what kind of military training goes on among a bunch of stalactites lit by colored spotlamps, I can't tell you.

A few miles north of Nahr el Kleb is the Casino de Liban on Juniye Bay. This was pre-war Lebanon's attempt at Monte Carlo and used to have elaborate floor shows featuring plump blondes who were out of work in Europe. You can still gamble there, though just being in this part of the world is a gamble enough for most people. The blondes are gone.

On up the coast road, twenty-four miles from Beirut, is Byblos. Since the Christians were run out of the Beirut airport, the Phalange has taken to landing planes on the highway here. Expect another traffic jam. Byblos was considered by the ancients to be the oldest city in the world. In fact, it has been an established metropolis for at least six thousand years. Main Street, however, looks most like the oldest part of Fort Lauderdale.

By the seaport, however, is an Arab fortification atop a Frankish castle constructed with chunks of Roman temples which had been built over a Phoenician town that was established on the foundations of a Neolithic village—quite a pile of historic vandalism.

The war has not touched Byblos except to keep anyone from coming here. We found one consumptive tour guide playing solitaire in a shack by the entrance to the ruins. He took us through the deserted remains spieling, with pauses only to cough, a litany of emperors, catastrophes and dimensions.

The Lebanese are chock-full of knowledge about their past. Those who *do* learn history apparently get to repeat it of their own free will. The whole business filled me with inchoate emotions and a desire for lunch.

The Byblos Fishing Club at the base of the Crusader seawall has wonderful food and no other customers. They don't speak English anymore so I went back to the kitchen and picked out what I wanted. Seafood got with dynamite fishing is very tender, it seems. On the wall of the Fishing Club are dusty photos of better days—Ray Milland, Ann-Margret, David Niven, Jean-Paul Belmondo. "Now *this*," said George, "is archaeology."

There's a very good hotel in Byblos, the Byblos-Sur-Mer, whose owner hadn't seen anyone in so long he bought us drinks when we stopped to use the pay phone.

You can proceed to Tripoli on the coast road, but shouldn't. The Arab Democratic Party, which supports Islamic unification, is having a big fight there with the Islamic Unification Party, which is in favor of Arab democracy. And the Syrians are shooting at both of them.

We turned east toward the mountains at the Syrian lines near Batrun. There's a medieval Arab castle here that's worth seeing. It sits in the middle of a cement plant.

Once into Syrian-controlled territory the checkpoint scrutiny becomes severe. Ahmed, our driver, began making long explanations to the glowering soldiers. He wouldn't quite confess what he was saying, but I have an idea it went something like: "I have the brother of an important American strongman here and the president of England's cousin. They are traveling in secret as journalists so they may see the justice and resolve of the great Syrian army in its struggle against Zionist oppressors everywhere. Soon they will return to their homeland and tell rich men there to drop a bomb on Tel Aviv."

The Syrian army has dozens of silly hats, mostly berets in yellow, orange and shocking pink, but also tiny pillbox chapeaux, peaked officer's caps with half a foot of gold braid up the front and lumpy Russian helmets three sizes too large. The paratroopers wear shiny gold jumpsuits, and crack commando units have skintight fatigues in a camouflage pattern of violet, peach, flesh tone and vermilion on a background of vivid purple. This must give excellent protective coloration in, say, a room full of Palm Beach divorcees in Lily Pulitzer dresses.

The rest of the scenery is also spectacular—Californian, but as though the Sierras had been moved down to Santa Barbara. The mountains of Lebanon rise ten thousand feet only twenty miles from the sea. You can ski in the morning and swim in the afternoon. Actually, of course, it's raining on the beach that time of year, and the skiing is mediocre at best. But it's the kind of thing that made for great Lebanese travel-brochure writing in the old days.

We drove to Bsherri on the lip of the dramatic Qadisha Valley, 650 feet deep and only a half-mile wide. This is the heartland of the Maronites, seventh century A.D. Christian schismatics who sought refuge among these dangerous hairpin turns lacking guard rails and speed limits.

Bsherri was the home of Kahlil Gibran and also where Danny Thomas's family comes from. Thus, the two great cultural figures of modern Lebanon, though in many ways opposites (Danny Thomas does not write poetry. Kahlil Gibran never did "spit-takes."), are linked. Or so I was told. I wouldn't spoil that piece of information with research.

We visited Gibran's house above the town. It's probably the world's only example of the California bungalow style carved out of living rock. Interesting but damp. The place is decorated with a hundred or so of Gibran's artworks. He was a dreadful painter—the gentle insouciance of Rodin and the technical abilities of Blake, all done in muddy earth tones. Gibran's coffin is bricked into the wall of his bedroom if that says anything about the man.

While we were asking directions in Bsherri, a young man named Antoine attached himself to us. He got us into the Gibran house, which was supposedly closed for repairs, then took us home for a Lebanese sit-around with his mother, aunts, sisters, cousins, etc. Hospitality is a must in the Middle East whether anyone wants to have it or not. Pomegranate juice is served, lots of cigarettes are smoked and tiny cups of coffee are drunk while everyone smiles and stares because you can't speak Arabic and they can't speak English, and Lebanese are the only people in the world who pronounce French worse than Americans.

Antoine's house was extraordinary. Like Gibran's it was carved into the side of a hill. The main room was windowless, floored with layers of Persian carpets and hung wall and ceiling with ornate cloths. There were stuffed falcons, brass things, photographs and religious statuettes all over the place and a dozen Mafia-Mediterranean-style dining room chairs. Antoine let us know he thought Kahlil Gibran's house was underdecorated. Antoine's mother told us that she'd lost five sons in the war so far, though that may have been the usual polite exaggeration of the Levantine.

Ahmed, though Moslem, was a great hit with Antoine's family. He brought them up-to-date on Beirut politics and then told Syrian checkpoint stories. Syrian checkpoint stories are the Polish jokes of Lebanon.

A Syrian soldier stops a Volkswagen Beetle and demands that the driver open the trunk. The driver begins to open the luggage compartment at the front of the car. "No!" says the Syrian, "I said the *trunk*."

"This *is* the trunk," says the driver.

"I am not a donkey," says the Syrian, pointing to the back of the car. "Open the trunk!" So the driver does as he's told, exposing the VW's engine. "Aha!" says the Syrian, "You have stolen a motor. Furthermore, you have just done it because it's still running."

Another of Ahmed's stories—and he swears this one is true—is about a checkpoint on a hill where the Syrian soldier wanted to inspect a car trunk. "I can't get out," said the driver, "I have no emergency brake, and I must keep my foot on the brake pedal or the car will roll away."

"Don't worry," said the Syrian, "I will sit in the car and hold the brake pedal." So they changed places. "Now open the trunk," said the Syrian. The driver opened it. "All right," yelled the Syrian from inside the car, "is there any contraband in there?"

What the Syrians are looking for in your trunk, by the way, is *Playboy* magazines. Be sure to carry some.

We sat and smoked more cigarettes. Lebanon is not the place to go if you're trying to give that up. Everyone over the age of six chain-smokes. Long-term health effects are not, these days, a major concern, and it's the worst sort of rudeness not to offer cigarettes at every turn. George fell in love with Carmen, Antoine's sister, a beauty of about fifteen. George could talk of nothing else for the rest of the trip but getting married and becoming Maronite. Maybe the feeling was mutual. Antoine took me aside later and asked me if George was a Christian. I assured him most blond, blue-eyed Americans over six feet tall are not Druse. He then nicked me, instead of George, for the two hundred Lebanese pounds it allegedly cost to get in the Gibran house.

We went on up into the mountains to the Cedars, one of only three small groves of these trees left. Once the country was forested with them, a hundred feet high at full growth and forty feet in circumference. It was from these the tall masts of the Phoenician galleys were made and the roof beams of Solomon's temple and so forth. The trees in the Bsherri grove look like they need flea collars, and the grounds are a mess.

We found a good hotel, the La Mairie, about ten miles west of Bsherri in Ehdene. Ehdene is notable for the country's best-looking martyr pictures. There are martyr pictures everywhere in Lebanon. The Phalangists put up photographs of the ox-faced Bashir Gemayel, who got elected president in '82 and blown to bits within the month. The Shiites plaster walls with the face of some dumpy Ayatollah who went MIA in Libya. The Druse have Kamal Jumblatt, who looked dead even before the hitmen ventilated his limo. Ehdene, however, is the headquarters of the Giants militia, led by the very photogenic Franjieh family. In 1978 the Phalangists attacked the Franjieh home and killed a handsome son, his pretty wife, and their little daughter too. If you have to look at pictures of dead people all day, they might as well be cute.

From Ehden, with light traffic and no mood swings at the checkpoints, it's only two hours back to Beirut.

The remaining great thing to see in Lebanon is Baalbek, site of three immense Roman temples, among the largest in the ancient world. Baalbek, however, is in the Bekáa Valley, where Israeli and Syrian forces are faced off and where Israel has been making periodic airstrikes on Syrian missile emplacements. Take sturdy and practical clothing.

Baalbek itself is controlled by an extremely radical pro-Khomeini Shiite group called Islamic Amal. The leader of Islamic Amal is Hussein Mussawi. He has close ties to Iran, and many people believe he personally ordered the suicide attacks on the American Embassy and the U.S. Marine base at Green Beach.

The Islamic Amal people are so far out there that they think *Syria* is a puppet of international Zionism. When I first arrived in Beirut, the Syrian army had Baalbek surrounded with tanks and was shelling downtown.

I went to Baalbek with ABC's chief Beirut correspondent, Charles Glass, and two drivers, one Syrian and one Lebanese Shiite. (Glass was later kidnapped by radical Shiites, possibly this same Islamic Amal; after two months in captivity, he made a harrowing escape.) The ride over the crest of the Lebanese range is breathtaking. The arid reaches of the Anti-Lebanese mountains rise in the distance. Below is the flat, green trough of the Bekáa, where Syrian and Israeli lines are lost in verdant splendor. The thin neck of the fertile crescent is spread out before you, cradle of the civilization that has made air strikes possible. It's overwhelming.

At the foot of the descent is the large Christian town of Zahle, a Phalange outpost surrounded by Moslems. The Syrians shell this sometimes, too. Zahle has a good hotel, the Kadri, and an arcade of outdoor restaurants built along a stream in the Wadi Arayesh, or "Valley of Vines."

The road north to Baalbek runs up the middle of the Bekáa. Marijuana fields stretch for miles on either side. This is the source of Lebanon's renowned hashish. Don't try to export any yourself, however. The airport customs officials won't search you when you arrive, but they're very thorough when you leave. Taking hashish out of the country without payoffs is one of the few crimes they still prosecute in Lebanon.

Bedouins from the Syrian desert camp beside the hemp fields. They're not very romantic up close. Their tents are made from old grain sacks, and everything around them stinks of goat.

The ruins of the Roman temples at the Baalbek are, words fail me, big. The amount of mashed thumbs and noses full of stone dust that went into chiseling these is too awesome to contemplate. The largest, the Temple of Jupiter, is 310 feet long, 175 feet wide, and was originally enclosed by fifty-four Corinthian pillars, each sixty-six feet high and seven and a half feet thick. Only six are left standing now. The temple complex was three centuries in building and never finished. The Christian Emperor Theodosius ordered the work stopped in hope of suppressing paganism and bringing a halt to a very lively-sounding cult of temple prostitution.

Once again we found a lonely tour guide who took us around, spouting names and numbers and pointing out things that are extra odd or large.

The ruins are policed by the Syrians, who are doing a better job

than the Israelis at Tyre. The captain in charge came up and introduced himself. His English consisted of "Hello." "Hello," he said and
shook hands. "Hello," he said and waved goodbye.

Outside the ruins, Baalbek is a tense and spooky place. All the
Christians, Sunnis and Druse have fled. Giant posters of Khomeini
are hanging everywhere. There are few women on the streets, and
they are carefully scarved and dressed down to the feet. The men
gave us hard looks and fingered their weapons. The streets were dirty
and grim. Syrian soldiers stayed bunched together. The tanks are still
dug in around the city. You cannot get a drink or listen to Western
music or dance or gamble, and you'd better not whistle the "Star
Spangled Banner."

The tour guide led us directly from the temples to a souvenir
store. There was something about risking my life to visit a pest hole
full of armed lunatics and then going shopping that appealed to me.
The store looked like it hadn't been visited since the Crusades, except
all the ancient artifacts were new, made this month and buried in
the yard for a week.

The nonsense you hear about bargaining in the Orient is, like
most nonsense about the Orient, perfectly true. I had not been in
the shop three seconds before the owner was quoting prices that
would do justice to a Pentagon parts supplier and flopping greasy,
ill-made rugs in every direction—like somebody house-training a
puppy with the Sunday *New York Times*. There's a charming banter
that goes with all this. I mean, I suppose there is. Some of the verbal
flourishes of the Levant are lost in a minimal English vocabulary.
"Good, huh? Real good, huh? Good rug! Very good!"

"He has a cousin in St. Louis," added the tour guide, helpfully.

It seemed I had to hold up both ends in this legendary duel of
wit in the Bazaar. "Tell him," I said to the guide, "his goods are of
the greatest magnificence and pleasure flows into my eyes at their
splendor. Yes, and I am astonished at the justice of his prices. And
yet I must abase myself into the dust at the humbleness of my means.
I, a poor traveler, come many miles over great distances . . ." And
so forth. Out came bogus Egyptian dog-head statues, phony Roman
coins, counterfeit Phoenician do-dads, and more and worse and
bigger rugs. After an hour and a half I felt I had to pay for my fun.
I settled on a small bronze "Babylonian" cow with some decidedly
un-Babylonian rasp marks on the casting. I bargained the shopkeeper
down from $200 to $30. Good work if the cow hadn't been worth
$0.

Charles Glass has spent years in the Middle East and was completely bored by this, however. He said we should go meet Hussein Mussawi.

Our Shiite driver was sent to negotiate. After the customary amount of temporizing and dawdle, Hussein consented to see us. We were taken to a shabby and partly destroyed section of town, where we were surrounded by nervous young gunmen. Though whether they were nervous about us or nervous that they might get a sudden invite to make like a human Fourth of July, I don't know. We were marched into a tiny and dirty office and told to sit down. We waited. Then we were marched to a larger office furnished Arab-style with couches around the sides of the room. Khomeini pictures abounded. We were served tea, and Charles and I, though not our Moslem drivers, were very thoroughly searched. Charles's tape recorder was taken apart with special care. Our guards were pleasant, but small talk did not seem the order of the day. We waited some more. Finally, another group of armed young men came and took us through a warren of narrow filthy alleys to a modest and well-protected house. We were put into a small study lined with Arabic books and decorated with more pictures of Khomeini. There were two young men who spoke English waiting for us. They asked in an affable way what was going on with U.S. foreign policy. "After all," said one, "this part of the world has a Moslem majority. Is your government crazy or what?"

Half an hour later Hussein came in and shook hands with everyone. He's a thin man of middle size, about forty-five. He was dressed in a sort of semi-military leisure suit and was very calm and dignified in his bearing but had, I swear it, a twinkle in his eye.

Hussein ordered a gunman to bring us coffee and cigarettes. The young man who spoke English less well acted as translator. "Were you responsible for the bombing of the Marine base?" asked Charles. I nearly lit my nose instead of the Marlboro. Hussein answered with equanimity, pointing out that any number of people, including the American Democratic Party, stood to benefit from the attack on the Marines.

"How long will this peace last in Lebanon?" asked Charles.

"This is not peace."

"When will there be peace?"

"When there is Islamic justice everywhere," came the answer.

"Everywhere?" asked Charles. "Will there be a place for Christians and Jews under Islamic justice?"

"Islam allows a place for everyone," said Hussein. The translator paused and added on his own, "Except, you know, Zionists and imperialists and other types."

"The Zionists will have to be driven out?"

"Yes."

"That may take a long time," said Charles.

Hussein fixed him with a smile. "Long for you. Short for us."

Hussein expounded upon the destiny of Islam and a believing man's place therein. The translator got himself tangled up with "Allah's great wishes . . . I mean, large would-be's . . . That is . . ."

"The will of God," I suggested.

Hussein turned to me and spoke in English. "Do you understand Arabic?"

"No," I said, "I just recognized the concept."

He said something to the translator, who said to me, "He wants to know if you believe in God."

I didn't think I should quibble. "Of course," I said. Hussein nodded. There was intensity in his look and no little human concern. He continued on subjects theological.

"To get back down to earth for a moment . . ." said Charles.

Hussein laughed. "Oh," said the translator, "all this is *very much* down to earth."

Charles continued to ask questions. I continued to ponder Hussein. He was practically the first Lebanese I'd met who didn't tell me he had a cousin in Oklahoma City. Although, as it turns out, his brother is a petroleum engineer who used to work in Dallas.

Charles asked Hussein about Johnathan Wright, the missing Reuters correspondent. "I hadn't heard about this," was the reply. "Also he wasn't headed this way."

Hussein told Charles he should study the Koran.

At length we took our leave. As we were being escorted back to our car I noticed a woman on a nearby roof wearing a chador and hanging out lacy black lingerie on the clothes line.

Less than a week after our visit, the U.S. embassy annex in East Beirut got blown up. I hope it wasn't anything we said.

The hotel at Baalbek is the Palmyra, built in the 1870s. It's a massive Ottoman structure furnished with antique carpets and heavy mahogany Victorian furniture. The leather-bound guest register bears the signatures of Louis Napoleon, the Duc D'Orleans, the Empress of Abyssinia and Kaiser Wilhelm II. There's an air of twilight and deliquescence to the place. Only the owner and a couple old servants are left. No room had been occupied for months, and only an occasional Syrian military officer comes to dinner.

Charles and I sat alone that night in the vast dining room. Pilgrims were still returning from Mecca, and celebratory gunshots sounded outside. "Happy fire" it's called. The electricity guttered in the bulbs and cast the long tables and tall ceiling into gloom. The forces of darkness and barbarism seemed to gather around. It was as though we were the last two white men in Asia. We sat up past midnight drinking the bottle of Arak a grizzled waiter had smuggled to us, talking politics and literature and citing apt quotations:

> Turning and turning in the widening gyre
> The falcon cannot hear the falconer;
> Things fall apart; the center cannot hold;
> Mere anarchy is loosed upon the world,
> The blood-dimmed tide is loosed, and . . .

. . . and you just can't find travel like this anymore.

WYCLIFFE KATO

An Escape from Kampala

Wycliffe Kato (1940–), a contributer to *Granta* magazine, held the position of director of civil aviation in Uganda. He lived in exile in Kenya until Idi Amin was overthrown in 1979. In 1989, he wrote *Escape from Idi Amin's Slaughterhouse,* which reinforced for the world some of the horrors that took place under the dictator's rule. The following selection originally appeared in *Granta* and was his first published work.

THE ARREST

I have a story. It's an escape story, and one I have been wanting to tell for ten years. The story is set in Uganda: the Uganda of President Idi Amin Dada.

I was a professional man, with years of experience in civil aviation. And I was, I suppose, quite successful. I had a farm in the country, a wife and eight children. I had a place to stay when I worked in the city, a car, even a driver. I was not the kind of man who should figure in the story I am about to tell. Except that I was living then in the Uganda of President Idi Amin Dada, where coming from the wrong tribe, or having a beautiful girlfriend, or driving a shiny car, or being too strict at the office, or asking a messenger boy to make you a cup of tea, was a potential death sentence. And I had been an unwitting character in something much worse: President Idi Amin Dada's greatest humiliation.

My story begins on Friday, 9 September 1977, when I was arrested.

But it really beings in the early morning hours of 4 July 1976, when Israeli commandos flew 2,000 miles from Tel Aviv to release the hostages held at Entebbe Airport in Uganda. I was at the time Assistant Director General of Civil Aviation for the East African Community, and was responsible for air traffic in Kenya, Tanzania and Uganda. Although I was working in Nairobi when the Air France jet was hijacked to Entebbe, I was in touch with the Ugandan authorities on an hourly basis. At the outset, I informed the Ugandan Air Force that it must not rule out the possibility of a rescue attempt. I was told not to worry: everything was under control; Amin was negotiating with the hijackers; the Big Man himself was at the steering wheel. A few nights later the Israelis arrived, and killed the Ugandan soldiers guarding Entebbe, killed the terrorists and rescued the hijackers. Amin was furious. He took his hands off the steering wheel and sent his thugs from the State Research Bureau to look for scapegoats. They found many. They also found my friends Rweigembe and Muhindo. Why, the State Research Bureau demanded, hadn't this pair of unarmed air traffic controllers been able to stop the Israeli attack? Muhindo's body was discovered the following week in Namanve Forest. There were nails driven through his forehead. Rweigembe was also found. There was of course no autopsy and therefore no death certificate; I had to inspect the body myself to confirm his death for the Nairobi company that had insured his life.

Shortly thereafter I was arrested as well, but I was cleared of all suspicion, and several months later I was promoted to Director of Civil Aviation. I suppose I was able to understand Amin's fury—the Israeli raid was a national humiliation—but I was also made uneasy by it. For even though I had already been arrested once, I often feared that the events at Entebbe would catch up with me. On Friday, 9 September 1977, I found out how.

I remember the morning as fine and sunny. I had spent the night in Kampala and was driven that morning to Entebbe, about twenty-five miles from the city, for a flight to Montreal. I was going there along with several others for an international meeting on civil aviation, and had secured a travel clearance through one of the ministers. It was a new procedure, getting clearance through a minister, and it

had only been introduced because the old system, under which all
foreign travel had to be authorized by Amin's Vice-President, proved
unworkable: the Vice-President couldn't read.

At the airport, all tickets had to be endorsed again, this time by
a State Research official, who sat at a counter some twenty yards
from the check-in. I was joined by Louis Kerujik, an undersecretary
at the Aviation Ministry, who would be travelling with me. The State
Research official was a woman. She looked as though she might be
Rwandese. Or perhaps she came from the western part of the country.
She was tall, with wide hips and shapely, attractive legs. She was
cheerful and had an engaging smile. I could not understand how she
could let herself work as an agent for Amin.

There was something that distressed her, however: our clearance
to leave Uganda, she said, did not seem to be entirely in order. She
asked us to step behind the counter, into the airport's State Research
office.

Inside was another woman, sitting behind a desk, operating a
radio. She was serious and fierce and said little. A young man came
in and asked my friend to follow him. That was the last time I ever
saw Mr Kerujik. I learned later that he was permitted to leave. He
made it to Montreal. I suspect he had been set free because he came
from Amin's home area of Arua. People from Amin's tribe rarely got
into trouble.

I was alone, facing the State Research woman. I was in that office
for over thirty minutes. State Research boys came in and out, laughing and joking. They were polite. But I was in a panic: I began to
fear that I was about to be arrested, and, although I had survived
arrest before, I also knew that an arrest usually ended in death. I
thought of running away and stood up. The woman reached for a
pistol. I sat down again. My panic increased. I had forgotten by then
about my flight or reaching Montreal. I thought of my family. There
was no phone on the farm; there was no way to reach my wife. There
was no one here waiting with me at the airport, except for Louis
Kerujik, and he had simply disappeared. Nobody would expect to
hear from me for six weeks. If I was arrested, I would not be missed
for perhaps two months. A lot can happen in two months.

The boys who worked for the State Research Bureau had quite a
reputation. They were usually fairly young—between the ages of
eighteen and twenty-five—and were accomplished kidnappers. Their
victims would be abducted, killed, the body disposed of, and only
then would ransom be demanded from the relatives. It was the boys

from the State Research Bureau who finally escorted me from the airport to the parking lot: 'There is something we would like to discuss with you.' There were six of them with me in the car. They were cheerful and talked constantly. '*Mzee*,' one asked, 'why are you so quiet? Are you scared?' They had pistols in their socks.

A few months before my brother-in-law had been taken by the State Research boys. I had searched through the corpses dumped in Namanve Forest for his body. A few of the corpses were fresh but most had rotted beyond recognition. Some had their wrists cut off. One had not, and my guide grabbed the arm and chopped off the hand: there was a watch on the wrist. He was pleased: it was rare to find a corpse with anything valuable. I had failed to find the body of my brother-in-law.

The State Research boys drove me towards the State House but went past the turn-off and on towards Kampala. We turned left up the Speke Road, past the Imperial Hotel and on to the junction at All Saints Cathedral. This is where Amin claimed that Archbishop Luwum had died in a car accident, together with Ministers Olyema and Oboth-Ofumbi. Whose hands had been on the steering wheel that time? We drove on and turned into an enclosure just past the cathedral, on the right-hand side. I tried to pray but I could not get past the first line of the Lord's Prayer: 'Our Father, who art in Heaven . . . Our Father, who art in Heaven.' I couldn't remember anything else. We had arrived at Nakasero. Nakasero was the head-quarters of the State Research Bureau. It was notorious. It was Amin's slaughterhouse.

I was searched, and taken to a room on the ground floor. I told myself that there had been some kind of mistake: my documents were, after all, in order, and it was only a few months since I had been promoted—by Amin himself. But then the guards reappeared and emptied my briefcase. I was then kneed in the stomach, and kicked in the ribs and the side of the head.

When they left I noticed that there was one other person in the room, an old woman, sitting on the floor in the corner. She had swollen eyes and a terrible face. We sat together for several hours. The day before, she said, she shared this room with a married couple. During the night soldiers appeared, one after another, and raped the wife. The husband sat where I was sitting now on an empty Pepsi-Cola crate. When the soldiers had finished with the wife, they re-moved the couple. She went on to tell me how people were tortured here and how they were killed. 'Be brave,' she said, 'pull yourself together. What you are about to see is worse than you ever imagined.'

She asked if I knew what Winston Churchill had called Uganda. He had called it the pearl of Africa. The next day, I was moved downstairs.

IN THE CELL

This is what the cell was like. It lay in a basement, at the bottom of two flights of concrete stairs. It was built from brick and painted white, but the paint was chipped and discoloured. The first thing I heard was a man screaming to Jesus to save him. The first thing I saw was a soldier kicking the same man in the head, and beating him with a rifle butt. But my first impression was the air: it was thick and hot, and there was an overpowering stench of stale sweat and human excrement.

At the bottom of the stairs was an open area. On the right was a long corridor closed off by an iron gate. This was called Cell One. There were about thirty prisoners in Cell One. There was no room to sit down and no ventilation. There was also no water. Some of the people in Cell One were handcuffed, some not; they were constantly begging cigarettes from guards; complaining of thirst. The men in this cell, I later learned, were coffee smugglers, pickpockets, thieves, rapists and murderers.

On the left was another cell, much less crowded, where all the prisoners were handcuffed. It was about forty or fifty feet wide and around thirty feet deep, with a pillar in the centre. There were three ventilators at the back, nine feet above the ground and about two feet across. The cell had once been used as a storage area, and in one corner there was a large pile of rubbish. There were crates and clothing and shoes. There were even two big film projectors, mounted on iron stands. The walls were chipped and stained. There was some graffiti, and, in the corners, mildew and moss. Near the gate, there was a steel dustbin, with excrement spilling down the side. The night before it had rained heavily and the rain had poured through the three ventilators, flooding the room. Everywhere in the water there was movement, and I realized that it was from rats. There were rats everywhere; I have no idea how many: maybe a hundred, maybe two hundred.

This was Cell Two. The guard handcuffed me and then removed my shoes. I was put inside.

There were only seven men in Cell Two, and they were waiting to die. They were uneasy at first, suspecting that I might be a spy. But it did not take them long to overcome their suspicions: they were desperate for news from outside the cell.

Fifteen others had been in the cell the day before, but they had been removed during the night. I was asked whether it was true that they had been executed. The guards had said so, but the soldiers were unreliable and like to play tricks. I told them that I didn't know. But when I was driven through Kampala, I told them, I had seen a gathering for a public firing squad. And, while sitting in the room with the old woman, I had overheard the sentries outside talk of an execution. They had mentioned a man by the name of Nsereko. He was meant to have been a magician, for he refused to die. In the end, thirty-six shots had been fired into his chest.

For some time, no one said anything. Nsereko, it appears, was not a man, but a boy. He had been with them in the cell the day before.

Cell Two was for political prisoners. Only those arrested on orders from Amin himself were locked up in Cell Two, and only three people could authorize a prisoner's release or his death. These were Amin and his henchmen Adrisi and the hated Englishman Bob Astles. If anyone from Cell Two was killed without Amin's orders, Amin was notified directly and a report prepared. There was some consolation in this: it protected the prisoners from any unforeseen accidents and some of the guards' more uncontrolled excesses.

Most of the prisoners in Cell Two were from the Ugandan Air Force, and had been involved in the recent attempt to assassinate Amin. They had planned to ambush his car near the cemetery on the road from Entebbe. Amin was hoping that they would confess under torture, so that he could try them publicly before executing them.

I learned all this from Pilot Officer Cadet Nicodemus Kasujja Majwala, from Bukolwa, Bulemezi County in Buganda. Kasujja was twenty-seven and a chatterbox. He spent facts like small change. He was a helicopter pilot, trained in the USSR. He was very boastful. He was, for instance, the best pilot in the Ugandan Air Force, even though he was merely a cadet. He was also the best fighter. He was also the strongest. He was also the most handsome. In fact there were few accomplishments at which he did not excel. After a bout of food-poisoning, everyone in the cell suffered diarrhoea; Kasujja, true to form, claimed the greatest volume, the least noise, the most inoffensive smell . . . But Kasujja was also clever. He had found a piece of metal in the rubbish heap and honed it to a sharp point on the concrete floor. With this he was able to release the locks of our handcuffs. He said this was a triumph for Soviet training, which, of course, was the best there is.

There was something else about Kasujja: his right leg was amputated at the knee. He told me what had happened. After the coup failed, he was shot in the leg while trying to escape. He was dragged before Amin. Kasujja agreed to betray his fellow-conspirators and proceeded to take Amin's men on a wild goose chase all over Kampala, pretending disbelief and consternation when no one was found. Meanwhile, many of his friends escaped.

'Go and cut off his leg,' Amin had ordered.

Kasujja introduced me to the others in the cell.

First, Major Patrick Kimumwe: he was slender, disciplined, and somehow succeeded in wearing a tweed jacket, despite the heat and the damp of the prison. He had been in the army twelve years and was only thirty-one, although he looked like an older man. He had an officer's habit of behaving with great seriousness, so that he would be feared and, being feared, respected.

There was Lieutenant Nambale: small, about twenty-four, with a very dark skin. He had trained as a jet pilot, as had his friend Lieutenant Silvester Mutumba, also in his early twenties.

The other three from the Air Force were not pilots but technicians. Warrant Officer II Christopher Ssekalo had a broad chest and a bad temper. Kasujja said he usually lost it when playing draughts. 'It's because I beat him,' said Kasujja. Warrant Officer I Eddie Ssendawula was short and light-skinned, about thirty-three.

Which left Warrant Officer II John Okech. He was the most impressive of the lot. He was tall and extremely fat, a barrel of a man. He wore a black shirt—although most of the buttons had popped off—and a pair of trousers that were too long and kept getting tangled in his feet. Kasujja described Okech as a gentle man, unless you got to the food before him. 'Then he is no longer so gentle. Okech likes to share everything out himself, to make sure he gets the biggest portions.' Okech roared with laughter: a happy fat man.

It seems strange to say it, but I felt encouraged by the men around me, hopeful. My arrest was most certainly a mistake. After all, these men had actually tried to kill President Idi Amin Dada. I had committed no such offence. I had been associated with the Entebbe disaster, that was all. Or else someone in my office had informed on me, wanting to get back at me for being the boss. Assassination? I wasn't in the same division as these men.

Major Kimumwe asked me why I had been imprisoned.

I told him that I wasn't sure. I wasn't a political prisoner. I wasn't even opposed to the government. I believed in justice and the rule of law, and I had no reason to doubt that I would be treated fairly.

On the whole, I had been treated fairly by the country, and had, in turn, obeyed its rules. My being here was an error. I would soon be released.

Kasujja whistled in disbelief.

Major Kimumwe pointed to the watch on his wrist. He said it had belonged to the boy who died the day before. He pointed to the chipped brick in the walls: they were from bullets. And after showing me the dried blood, he asked if I was, perhaps, out of my mind. Or just being naïve. 'Once you're in here, you don't get out alive,' he said.

I didn't entirely believe him.

Conversation at Nakasero Prison was always conducted in a whisper.

They spoke of women. What was the most important feature in a woman? Was it the breasts or the buttocks? Was it the legs? The lips?

They spoke of torture. They had suffered many different kinds. Whippings, electric shocks, dunkings, canes across the face. It was astonishing how much pain, for instance, could be administered by a simple cigarette lighter. They described what the pain was like when you were grabbed by the testicles and the testicles were twisted until you passed out.

They spoke of death. There were also many different ways to die at Nakasero. You could be strangled—that was quite common. You could be tortured or simply beaten until your brain bled. You could have your chest opened with a knife. Or you could be shot by firing squad. Everyone agreed that being shot by a firing squad was the best way to die.

> Germany is the right place where, when Hitler was the Prime Minister and supreme commander, he burnt over six million Jews. This is because Hitler and all German people knew that Israelis are not people who are working in the interest of the people of the world and that is why they burnt the Israelis alive with gas in the soil of Germany.
>
> *Telegram from Idi Amin Dada to Dr Kurt Waldheim,*
> *Secretary General of the United Nations.*
> *11 September 1972.*

But mainly they spoke about escaping. How was it possible? How could they manage it? Could they overwhelm a guard and shoot their way out using his gun? Too risky. Could they somehow make a key? Or a hack-saw? Too difficult. It sounded as though they'd had this conversation a hundred times. Escape was an obsession.

In the afternoon a guard brought food: one banana between eight and a repulsive-smelling stew which Okech said was made from the head of a cow. 'No meat at all,' he said, serving the stew round the cell. Ssekalo and Kasujja played draughts. Kasujja won, and boasted of his superior brain, his success at draughts being the obvious proof. Ssekalo was furious, and swept the board aside, sending pieces skittering around the cell. He said that Kasujja was an idiot. Kasujja hopped up and down.

That evening Ssendawula advanced an idea that I was surprised had not occurred to the others long before.

'Gentlemen, behold our saviour,' Ssendawula said and made a melodramatic gesture towards the ventilator. There was a metal screen in front of it. He said, 'We have been stupid not to think of this before. We take away the screen, then up through the ventilation shaft and into the yard.' The suggestion resulted in a tremendous excitement. It was a new idea. It was also an idea that everyone thought would work. There was no debate: they decided to escape that night. I was asked to come along: I declined.

'Why should I risk my life in an escape attempt? And what will you do once you get out? Borrow a car from one of the soldiers? Wait for a bus? I have been arrested before, and I was cleared of all charges. I will be cleared again. There is still a system of justice.'

Major Kimumwe looked at me and said nothing.

At nine o'clock the fluorescent light above our heads was turned off. That night, before we fell asleep, the guards removed three prisoners from Cell One.

I slept through the escape attempt, and in the morning when I woke my seven companions were already up. Major Kimumwe began by saying prayers. Nambale was in a tetchy mood. He said there had bloody well better be an afterlife. The attempt had been a failure.

They explained what happened. At around two in the morning, Kasujja had unlocked the handcuffs, and Ssekalo, the tallest, climbed on top of two wooden crates to attack the ventilator. He had worked on it for several minutes before reporting that the grille of gauze wire could not be moved: it would have to be cut. There were glass slats which would have to be broken. And all this was going to make a lot of noise. Okech then tried to remove the grille, but he also failed. Their escape was obviously going to require more preparation.

Even though they had failed, the mood the next morning was

one of optimism: at least there was the possibility of an escape; there was a strategy. They asked me again if I would join them, and again I declined.

Major Kimumwe reminded me of the three men who had been removed the night before. 'Where are they now?' he asked. 'What do you think has happened to them?' Major Kimumwe was right: they were still missing. 'How can we make you understand?' he said. 'No one has left this room alive. *No one*. Look at the blood. Look at the shoes. Where do you think they come from. Whose trousers do you think those are? You must think of escaping.'

I said nothing. My case was surely different from theirs. I said little all morning. I was thinking about my chances. I was praying.

Just before lunch, two State Research boys appeared at our cell gate. One was the leader of the group which had arrested me at the airport. He shouted, 'Where is the director of Civil Aviation?' Nobody said anything. 'Are you deaf, you fools?'

In 1952, I was told when I was going to die. I was told this in a dream. I was told also I will be the highest rank in the army in Uganda, I will be head of State and also when I have a lot of people criticizing me it's very good for me. I was also told that an attempt might be made on my life, and the people who made that attempt would be crushed completely. And it is true.

Idi Amin Dada, interviewed by David Frost
1 April 1973.

I thought of two possibilities: freedom and death. I said, 'Here I am, sir.'

A sheaf of papers was thrust through the bars: the travellers' cheques I had bought for my trip, more than 3,500 American dollars.

'Sign all of them,' he said. 'Make sure you use your usual signature.'

I signed the cheques. They left, but returned within minutes. 'Look!' said the State Research boy, screaming with fury. 'Your signature on the cheques is different from that in your passport. Sign again. And this time sign on the back of each cheque as well.'

I did as instructed and they went, this time for good.

'Don't worry,' said Kasujja, 'Now they've taken all that money, you might be released. You probably will be released. They've no serious case against you. I wish I were you.'

There was a silence. Then Nambale spoke, quietly. He said Kasujja was being extremely stupid, as usual. He said he was sorry, but the taking of the money could only hasten my death. 'Don't you see? They will feel too guilty to release you. In fact, now, having got your signature, there is no reason to keep you alive. It confirms what we've been saying all along. They don't expect any of us to come out of here alive.'

That night two things happened.

There was a commotion in Cell One. An old Kenyan had asked for a razor blade to commit suicide. The guard agreed, but said the old man was not to slit his wrists; if he wanted to kill himself, he must chew the blade and swallow. The old man did this. His moaning was long and terrible. When he was dead, an hour later, the guard came over to our cell and picked Ssendawula and Okech and me to carry away the body. We took the old Kenyan up the steps and were instructed to throw the corpse on the back of a truck. His face had no lips. His mouth was a mess of blood and shredded flesh.

Later that night, there was a terrible thumping. There was an insistent rasping sound, and more thumping. It seemed to come from the top of the stairs.

'Strangulation,' Major Kimumwe whispered in the dark, 'is probably the most popular method here for killing the prisoners.'

'Major Kimumwe,' I said, 'I am with you. We must escape.'

THE ESCAPE DREAM

Tuesday. Early in the morning the sentries came to check on us. They relieved their boredom by shouting abuse. They let us know we were at their mercy. They could make us eat our own shit, or theirs. They could torture us at will.

This no longer concerned us. We had our dream of escape: we would go out through the ventilator; we would cross the courtyard; and then, having crossed the courtyard, we would walk to safety. It would be simple, we said. We had searched through the rubbish and found a variety of nails, rusted spoons and other pieces of metal which could be used as tools. Ssekalo started in on the gauze. Progress was slow, terribly slow. It became obvious that we had underestimated the difficulty of the task. Ssekalo worked the entire morning to create a tiny hole in the gauze through which the glass could be seen. Then he widened the hole some more, and broke the glass.

The noise was a terrifying crack. We froze. Detection seemed certain. We awaited the arrival of the guards. And sure enough we heard boots coming down the concrete stairs. 'Let us pray,' said

Major Kimumwe and Okech at once, as though they'd rehearsed it.
We bowed our heads while Major Kimumwe said the Lord's Prayer
and waited for the guard to unlock the gate and come in. He didn't.
He turned round and went away.

Kasujja chose this moment to announce that Russian guns were
remarkably, *unbelievably,* silent, and had in fact been used by the
Israeli commandos in the raid at Entebbe. Everyone burst out laughing. 'You, Kasujja, are far too stupid to have been a pilot,' said
Nambale.

Wednesday. Ssekalo reported that there were steel bars behind the
glass.

'Bars?' said Major Kimumwe.

'Bars?' said Kasujja. 'We'll never be able to move them.'

Major Kimumwe said we shouldn't give up. If we could cut the
rest of the gauze, if we could get rid of the glass and make space to
lever at the bars, if we could do all this without being detected, and
if we could do it before we were hauled before a firing squad, then
there was a chance.

'Some chance,' said Kasujja.

Ssekalo pressed on. He cut through the gauze and now wrapped
each of the glass slats in a shirt he had found in the rubbish heap
before breaking it. The effect was like using a gun with a silencer.
With extreme care the fragments of glass were removed. The process
was agonizingly slow. But at last he was face to face with the iron
bars. He could not contain his excitement. So much energy had gone
into removing the gauze and the glass slats that it seemed our problems were over. They weren't. Ssekalo leaped up and found the bars
quite immovable. They were so close together that he could not even
squeeze his head through.

'It's hopeless,' he said.

Each of us wanted to see for himself. One by one we climbed up.
Kasujja boasted that he would pull the bars apart with his hands. He
failed. Even Soviet training could not help here.

Thursday. We were despondent. That morning, instead of his usual
prayers, Major Kimumwe said: 'I pray for the dead. I pray for the
dead because we are as good as dead. May our souls rest in peace.
God has given up on Uganda.'

Kasujja said, 'If only I had been trained in China. I would be a
magician. Then I would get our heads through those bars, no problem.' Even Nambale could not be bothered to tease him.

Okech started talking about food. When things weren't going well he always liked to talk about food. He said, 'I imagine such a feast. Goats will be slaughtered and roasted. There will be three goats. No, I think there will be *four* goats. And I will roast them myself. And eat them myself. There will also be beer, lots of beer.'

'Champagne,' said Nambale. 'What about champagne?'

'I think not,' said Okech. 'Beers all around.'

The escape dream was over.

It was Ssendawula who got it going again. He dragged the two film projectors from the rubbish heap. 'Look,' he said, pointing to the stand on which each projector was mounted. The stand was made of two diagonal metal pieces attached to metal struts. It looked heavy and strong. 'We can take this thing to pieces. Use the stand to bend the bars. What do you think?'

'And what do we use for tools?'

'There must be something,' Ssendawula said. 'We can think of something.'

We inspected the projectors. Ssendawula had a point. It might work. Kasujja giggled, saying: 'These projectors. Weren't they made in Russia?'

'I think so,' Ssendawula said.

Kasujja said, 'In that case, the Lord really has delivered us.'

We tightened our own security. We hung a shirt to hide the hole in the ventilator. We posted watch. Our code words for the guards were *masse* (Luganda for 'rat') and *panya* (Kiswahili for 'rat'), because there were so many rats in the cell. Kasujja stood at the gate. He was good at chasing people off. He would demand cigarettes or spout information about Soviet technology. Guards stalked off, hurling insults.

Using his fingers Ssendawula removed piece after piece of the projector, fashioning them together so he could dismantle the rest. It took him almost the entire day. Then we inserted the stand between the bars, deadening the noise by wrapping old shirts around the base.

'*Panya!*' Kasujja shouted, '*Panya!*' A guard was coming down the stairs. We pulled the stand away, hid it in the rubbish, and took up our positions, trying to be casual, playing draughts or leaning against the pillar.

'What are you saying?' said the guard.

Kasujja hopped up and down. 'My Lord,' he said, 'My Lord, there are so many rats here.'

'Good,' said the guard. 'I hope they will nibble your toes in your sleep.'

Friday; Saturday morning. For the next two days, the escape dream was definitely on again. We pushed the stand against the bars. And pushed again. Guards came. And went. And we pushed. We were tortured on several occasions. We were weak from hunger. For two days we were brought no food or water. The thirst made Kasujja and Nambale quarrel even more than usual. But one of the bars was beginning to bend, very slightly.

Saturday afternoon. The projector stand disintegrated. It fell to pieces in Okech's hands. Major Kimumwe cursed the day he had been born. God had forsaken us, he said. Was there any reason why we should continue praying to Him?

Saturday night. Several prisoners were taken from Cell One and shot. We were taken for torture. Ssekalo and Kasujja returned with swollen eyes and cheeks, and bruises all over. I was next up. The torture room was at the top of the building. It was about fourteen feet square and dimly lit. Three soldiers held whips. The interrogator sat at a small table. I was asked about the flight I was going to take abroad.
'Where were you going that day at the airport?'
'Montreal.'
'You were running away?'
'It was business.'
'Why were you running away?'
'I wasn't . . .'
It went on like this for thirty minutes or so. And then I was beaten.
Back in the cell we talked again about what it would be like to die, the various ways we might be killed. By now, we had heard someone being strangled on the top of stairs on five different occasions. The sound of someone being strangled is very disturbing. We all agreed that it was the worst possible death.
Except Okech. He said, 'I'd hate to starve.'
Kasujja said, 'None of you feels the same sorrow as me.'
'You are so stupid,' said Nambale.
'You don't understand,' said Kasujja. 'You have a child. The only child I'll ever have is unborn. My girlfriend is pregnant. Can you imagine leaving a pregnant girlfriend behind?'

Sunday. Kasujja said he wanted to make a saw. Nambale asked him if he was, really, normal. I helped Kasujja grind the saw from a piece of metal. Anything to keep the dream going. The saw took us two hours to make, and was useless. 'Another triumph for the Soviets,' said Nambale.

I suggested that we take the motor from the projector, rig it to the light socket with a piece of cable, and press the motor against the bars. It took us another two hours to get the motor out. We took the strip light out and hooked up the cable. The motor worked, and made a noise like the end of the world. That was the end of that plan.

Two more prisoners were taken from Cell One.

I suggested we dismantle the other projector and try to use that stand to lever the bars. Nobody liked the idea. I said we must do something. I said that this time we should proceed with caution, to make sure the stand did not break. Ssendawula went to work.

To keep up spirits I made everyone talk about the possible escape routes. What would we do once we were out of the cell? There were three possibilities. The shortest route was to turn right after coming out of the ventilator, then duck into the concrete drains which led towards the prison entrance and came out on the other side of the road. That sounded simple. It wasn't. There would certainly be poisonous snakes. The second possibility was to crawl around the back of the building, climb the fence and go out through the grounds of the French Embassy which lay next to the prison. But the problem was that the area was so well lit, detection was certain. Which left route number three: out across the fences that were immediately opposite our building and then through the neighbouring compound.

Kasujja thought the fences were electrified. He said, 'One of us will have to sacrifice himself. Whoever touches the fence first will be electrocuted. But at the same time the fuses will blow. This will let the rest of us out.'

Nambale said, 'Don't you know that you're at the mercy of the rest of us?'

And the rest of us joined in. We teased Kasujja. We said it would be impossible to take him with us. After all, he had only one leg. He'd delay us, he could be seen easily at a distance, we'd all be captured. Kasujja dropped to the floor. He proved his skill at disguise. He imitated a dog. He imitated a cat. He scampered around the cell to prove his agility. He leaped high to prove he could scale the fences.

'All right,' said Nambale. 'You can come along. So long as you don't mention the Soviet Union.'

That night we heard the shots of a firing squad. The two prisoners removed that morning had been killed.

Monday morning. We pushed at the bars.

Monday afternoon. We pushed at the bars. We also tried to dig them out with spoons and nails.

Tuesday morning. We pushed at the bars. We tried making another hack-saw. Like the first, it fell apart.

Tuesday afternoon. This afternoon it was Okech who pushed at the bars. And, finally, the incredible happened. They suddenly gave way.

'Do the rest of you see what I see?' said Okech.

He punched the air. At the gate Kasujja hopped up and down. And Major Kimumwe prayed. He thanked God for showing his power. He begged forgiveness for his lack of faith.

We worked the bars further and further apart until all our heads would go through. A memory from childhood told me that where the head would go the rest of the body could follow. We would leave that night. It would be Ssekalo first, then Nambale, Mutumba, Ssendawula, Okech, Kasujja, Major Kimumwe and myself.

Tuesday night. At one a.m. we were ready. We had taken off our handcuffs and opened up the hole. Ssekalo climbed on to the boxes and Okech lifted him up and pushed him into the ventilator. He moved his shoulders to and fro, working himself down the ventilator. He pushed his head through the bars. He wriggled and then cried out in pain. His shoulders were too wide. Major Kimumwe also tried, but without success. I'd been wrong about the idea of the shoulders always following the head through a hole.

'*Panya!*' screamed Kasujja. '*PANYA!*'

A soldier with a machine-gun was coming down the steps. We took down the projector stand and pushed it into the rubbish. We didn't have time to cover the hole in the ventilator. The soldier was at the gate, holding a ring of keys. He was coming in. Kasujja hopped like a frantic monkey. He pleaded for cigarettes. He roared facts about the firepower of Soviet helicopter gunships. The soldier had his key in the lock. If he came in, he was certain to discover the wrecked ventilator. There was a strong chance that we would be killed there and then: 'Shot trying to escape'—a report that Amin would certainly accept.

Kasujja rolled on the floor, crying in sudden and terrible agony, demanding medicine and a fresh bandage. He said he was dying. He ripped off the filthy rag wrapped round his leg, exposing the stump, and flexed his muscles, causing the wound to open and close like a fish sucking water. It was a repulsive sight.

'I'm not a doctor,' said the soldier, 'and if I were I wouldn't waste medicine on scum like you.' He locked the gate and removed the key.

'Yes, my Lord,' said Kasujja, beaming.

Wednesday. We spent the day widening the gap between the bars. We organized ourselves for the escape. That night we lifted Ssekalo once more. This time he was able to force himself through the bars, but only just. Which meant that Kasujja and Okech had no chance. We conferred—Ssekalo's legs still poking out of the wall—and agreed to delay the escape until we were sure that even Okech, the biggest, could get through. In the meanwhile Ssekalo had inched his way further along and was almost through, disappearing from our view. Okech grabbed his feet. Ssekalo kicked his hands away. Okech took one leg, Kasujja the other, and they tugged the wriggling Ssekalo back into the cell.

'Why shouldn't I go?' said Ssekalo.

'What about us, you selfish bugger?' said Kasujja.

There was a fierce argument. The thin ones didn't want to wait; they said we could be executed at any time. The fatties wanted to wait; they said no further attempt should be made until, as agreed, Okech could get out. The mediums (myself included) didn't know; we felt confused, wanting to be fair to everyone. We took a vote. The vote was five to three. We were to stay.

That night another prisoner from Cell One was strangled at the top of the stairs.

Thursday. It is difficult to describe the state we were in. It was almost hysterical. For some, an escape was not just a dream, but a real possibility, one that could be realized merely by slipping through a hole in the wall. But for all of us, death was an even greater possibility. We felt our time was running out. We believed that at any moment Amin would order us to be killed.

It was then that Major Kimumwe suggested an idea that I thought was preposterous. He wanted to confess. He wanted to be taken to Amin.

'If we confess now to the assassination attempt,' he said, 'it will buy us some safe time. Amin will not want to kill us straight away. The opportunity is too rich: he'll want a show trial. He'll want publicity. And only then will he want us executed.'

I am not superstitious. In my culture, however, there is a form of witchcraft: certain people are sometimes able to get what they want just by saying it. Moments after this idea had occurred to Major Kimumwe he was summoned, along with Ssekalo, Kasujja and Mutumba, to attend an interrogation by Major Faruk Minawa of the State Research Bureau.

Everything was happening far too quickly. I told Major Kimumwe to abandon his idea: he would be killed and then they would return to kill those of us remaining behind. But Major Kimumwe's idea had excited the others. As the four of them climbed the stairs out of the basement, I was convinced I would never see them again. I was convinced I was dead.

They were gone for the entire day. What happened next was related to me by Kasujja.

Minawa, to whom they were presented, was Amin's number one killer. He had terrible, glassy eyes and a vast belly. He never smiled except when a prisoner was being tortured. The tools of his trade included the following: hippo-hide whips, metal canes, electric cables, Zippo lighters, matches, knives, hammers, lighted cigarettes, broken Coca-Cola bottles and rope. Minawa took his job seriously, and often brought his children with him to work so they could watch him. He was so powerful, and so mad, that he would even order the torture of one of his own soldiers if he felt the man had been derelict in his duty of inflicting pain. Once he made me watch him torture a prisoner from Cell One. This prisoner was beaten horribly and suspended from the ceiling by his feet. 'Now,' said Minawa, 'he'll be able to admit he wanted to overthrow the Government.' Which, in due course, is what happened. The prisoner was killed that night.

Minawa's interrogations followed a pattern. A diesel generator was turned on in the next room so that French Embassy officials would not be disturbed. Prisoners were showered, so that Minawa would not be bothered by their stench. They were then brought in, lectured, invited to sign a confession, and tortured, sometimes by Minawa himself, often by the notorious Palestinian, 'Faizal of the Nile'.

On this occasion Major Kimumwe, Ssekalo, Kasujja and Mutumba entered Minawa's room, and were invited to sign a confession. This was the routine. What followed was not the routine: Major Kimumwe, Ssekalo, Kasujja and Mutumba agreed to the invitation. They felt that, yes, they should sign the confession. They went further: they invented other crimes.

'Minawa grew very excited,' Kasujja told me later. 'He even smiled. He promised to take us to see the President himself, and he was certain that a pardon would be arranged. Minawa chided us for being obstinate for so long. "Look at those scars on your poor bodies," he said, touching our skin gently. "Now you know how unnecessary this unpleasantness has been."'

Kasujja could read Minawa's thoughts. Minawa knew this would give Amin the chance to show the world's press that those killed by the Ugandan regime genuinely deserved to die; after all, they were self-confessed traitors. The arrangement could only reflect well on Minawa.

And then, Kasujja said, he couldn't resist. '*Effendi,*'[1] Kasujja said, 'my Lord, we are treated badly. May we have cigarettes?'

Major Faruk Minawa was appalled by the notion that anyone in his custody should be treated badly. He ordered cigarettes. He ordered that all food for Cell Two should in future be brought from the Standard Hotel.

In his confession, Major Kimumwe was asked to list the reasons for his being unhappy with the Amin government. Major Kimumwe obliged. The reasons included the following: the brain-drain of professionals; the promotion of individuals on a tribal basis instead of merit (leading to the dominance of the Kakwa and Lugbara tribes at the expense of efficiency); the acute shortage of salt, sugar, soap, cooking oil and other various essentials; the consequent black market and price inflation; the collapse of Uganda's currency; the universal disregard of the constitution and the established laws; and a regime of military brutality.

Kimumwe described the list as a modest one, one that would interest the Mighty One.

As it turned out, the four were summoned to appear before the Mighty One that very day. Each was given a new shirt and a new pair of trousers, though Kasujja was denied a walking stick. Perhaps they thought he would try to attack the President with it. Minawa escorted them into a waiting car and they were driven through the centre of Kampala, out towards Amin's villa at Cape Town. Minawa was pleased and proud. He gave the group a tour, pointing out the charms of the palace, the statues, the fruit-trees, the works of art. The palace swarmed with sentries. Patrol boats crossed the lake

---

[1] a title of respect, similar to *sir* or *mister* in English (ED.)

constantly, and in every corner there seemed to be a man with a pair of binoculars. It seemed that Amin was expecting another coup attempt. At one point Amin appeared, gestured to a beautiful home across the lake, noted that it was a danger to presidential security and said, 'Bomb it.' Then he went back inside.

The four waited for two-and-a-half hours. Amin was apparently haranguing lawyers and church leaders, organizing the resignation of Sheikh Mufti, leader of the Moslem Council, and his replacement by a member of Amin's own tribe.

Eventually they were shown into a small circular room. Amin was seated at the far end, surrounded by TV cameras, journalists and various henchmen. Minawa was there, so was a woman from the government newspaper *The Voice of Uganda*. Kasujja described how he was repelled by the grotesque bulk of the man he and the others had wanted to kill: and still wanted to kill. Amin weighed over 310 pounds.

Amin ordered the prisoners closer, so the cameramen could film them for the television news. He then spoke to them in Swahili and Luganda and sometimes in English.

He spoke to them about their crimes. He put on a terrifying show. His eyes bulged. He banged the arms of his chair with his fists. He made as if to grasp Major Kimumwe by the neck and throttle him. He pulled out a gun and wondered out loud if he should shoot him in the head. 'It was then,' Kasujja said, 'that we thought we had made an awful miscalculation about the President's wish for a show trial. We thought we would be shot on the spot.'

Amin thrust the pistol under Major Kimumwe's chin. He said, 'You are the one who organized and supervised the killing of all the Acholis and Langis[2] around Kampala. Why did you do this? Tell me now. Did you do this so the world would say, "Amin is a murderer"?'

This was the first Major Kimumwe had heard of the killings of the Acholis and Langis.

Amin pushed the gun closer and then turned to a journalist: 'Did you get that? This fellow wished to spoil my name. He wanted to take my good name. I knew I would get hold of him eventually. I fear no one, except God.'

---

[2] The Acholis, a group of people from northern Uganda and southern Sudan, joined the British colonial army, frequently fighting other African groups; they have been persecuted since 1971 in retaliation. The Langis are a people who inhabit the marshy lowlands of Uganda. (ED.)

The journalist glanced sideways to a colleague, a look which apparently convinced Major Kimumwe that his death was imminent. Amin continued, berating him first in English, then Swahili, then English once more. 'Fool!' he screamed. 'Idiot! Instead of commanding your forces as you should, you planned to kill me. You are obviously mad.'

Major Kimumwe started to speak, 'Your Excellency . . .' but Amin was in full swing, and had now turned on Mutumba, telling him that he must surely remember the time they went together to check the border, that time they put up such a good show against Nyerere.

Amin said, 'Mutumba. You were one of my favourites. I liked you because you were a revolutionary. Why do you think I promoted you so many times? I trusted you. I trusted you implicitly. What made you turn against me? What more did you want? Did you think these people would give you better things? You fool. You also are mad.'

Kasujja, who had been standing unaided on his one foot, now began to jerk convulsively. Amin switched his attention. He asked Kasujja to remember the time he had saved his life. The soldiers had wanted to kill Kasujja. He had merely ordered the removal of Kasujja's leg. This had been merciful. He could now, if he chose, order him a new one. Didn't Kasujja know how powerful he was? 'Stop fidgeting, man,' he barked.

Amin now turned to Ssekalo. He said, 'And you are one of those I personally recruited when Obote . . .'

Ssekalo interrupted. He started speaking to Amin. He spoke in a quiet voice. He said that Amin was a butcher. He said that Amin was a tribalist. He said, 'We had a very good plan. You would be dead now if it hadn't been for that Sergeant.' The Sergeant was Sergeant Dick, so called because of his fondness for the expression 'every Tom, Dick and Harry.' Sergeant Dick had known about the assassination plot and had betrayed those involved (for money, or a woman, or both) only hours before the planned ambush.

Nobody expected Ssekalo's outburst. And nobody expected the calm that characterized Amin's response: 'You'll face a firing squad and be killed by your own guns, the Chinese guns you imported from Tanzania to kill me and my ministers.'

Amin issued orders. They were to be taken back to prison via Nakasero market, where they would have the opportunity to admire the splendid range of goods now available in the Uganda of President Idi Amin Dada, and then via a bar in Bokassa Street which belonged to Sergeant-Major Peter Mulefu. They understood the point of visiting

Mulefu. Besides being a bar owner, Mulefu was also the chief executioner at Nakasero. He was a member of the Kakwa tribe. The Kakwa were superstitious. They feared the spirits of revenge. To fend off these spirits, the Kakwa killer followed the practice of eating the vital organs of his victims. Mulefu's method was to rip open the chests of those he killed with a bayonet, and eat the heart while it was still pumping.

The group was led to Mulefu's bar. 'He inspected each man carefully,' Kasujja told me, 'and then he reached out his hand and tapped Major Kimumwe gently on the chest. He actually tapped him on the chest.'

It is difficult to express the relief I felt when I saw the familiar face of Major Kimumwe coming down the stairs.

Thursday night. The story of Thursday night is the story of Warrant Officer John Okech.

Warrant Officer John Okech was both saviour and potential death warrant. He saved us at midnight, risking his life to divert the attention of a guard who came into the cell to inspect the shirt hanging in front of the ventilator. We thought we'd had it, but Okech positioned his bulk in front of the guard and refused to budge. The guard went away. And yet an hour later Okech was endangering us all because he delayed the escape.

Since the fluorescent light was put out at nine o'clock, we had worked relentlessly on bending the bars. Most of this work was done by Okech himself. His strength was enormous; so, too, was his desperation: he knew that, after the others had confessed, we had very little time left; he knew that tonight, Thursday night, was his— and our—last chance for escape. But, hours later, he still could not squeeze through.

There was an argument. The thin ones demanded that Okech be left behind. Ssekalo made a break for the bars and had to be restrained by Major Kimumwe. There was bad feeling, and it was growing worse. Nambale and Mutumba then joined with Ssekalo: they did not see why their lives should be endangered by Okech's weight.

It was Major Kimumwe who pointed out that it was precisely one hour ago that Okech's weight had saved all of us.

Mutumba said nothing.

'One more day,' Major Kimumwe said. 'We owe it to Okech. Without him the bars would never have been moved in the first place.'

Finally, Mutumba said: 'Tomorrow is the last day. I will not die here like a dumb animal. Tomorrow I'm going. Nobody will stop me.'

Okech said nothing.

Friday, 23 September 1977. We attacked the bars early, at about seven a.m. Work was progressing when I looked through one of the other ventilators and saw a pair of improbably dressed legs just outside. The legs were wrapped in pink trousers and tucked into shoes with platform heels. It must have been a State Research boy. He was standing right next to 'our' ventilator. We gently removed the stand, closed the hole and hung up a shirt. We waited. The fellow stood there, motionless. We were certain he must have heard our noise. He moved away, and we expected guards to burst in at any moment. We knelt and prayed. Major Kimumwe told us the story of Jesus and Peter and the cock crowing three times. No guard came. It seemed a miracle.

By eleven a.m. the bars had opened much more. Major Kimumwe was convinced that Okech would be able to get through. We measured the diameter of the hole with a piece of cable and compared it against Okech's chest. 'You'll be all right,' Major Kimumwe assured him.

That day we were brought lunch. The usual cattle-head stew. We tried to eat, but we were too excited. The rats had a feast. We talked in low voices. We played draughts. We longed for the night.

At one point, Okech posed the question that had so far gone unstated: 'Gentlemen,' he said, 'suppose I fail to go through. What happens then?'

Nobody replied.

'Gentlemen, what then?'

Nothing.

'I'm not convinced I will go through.'

'You will,' said Major Kimumwe.

'But suppose I don't.'

'I'm sure you will.'

'You think so?'

'Of course.'

It was clear that even Major Kimumwe was determined to go that night.

We discussed escape routes. Our ideas were vague. Ssendawula and I planned to travel together. Kasujja wanted to join us. We didn't think it was a good idea. He understood. He would make it on his own, he said.

At eight p.m. soldiers came down to the cell area. One was fat and bare-chested, wearing only a pair of shorts. He carried a rifle in one hand and held a machete in the other. He laughed and scraped the machete across the concrete floor. '*Hi itakula nyinyi leo,*' he repeated: 'This will cut you tonight.' He was crazed and had been smoking *bhang,* African cannabis. It was common for the soldiers to smoke *bhang* before an execution.

He led the soldiers back upstairs. We heard them assemble outside, as if on parade. Then cars began to arrive, including one with an engine that chugged like a train: it was the Austin Cambridge of Sergeant-Major Peter Mulefu, the Kakwa killer. This meant one thing: executions.

'We're going to die tonight,' I said.

Prisoners were taken from Cell One. There was the familiar wail for mercy. And then there were shots. We heard bodies being thrown on to the back of a lorry. I panicked. I said we should escape now, immediately, take our chances outside.

'Cool down,' said Major Kimumwe. 'Keep calm.'

More soldiers appeared. Galabuzi Mukasa was taken from Cell One. He was not a coffee smuggler or a rapist or a thief. He had written a play, one that Amin himself had seen and approved, but had later taken against because he was told it was a satire on his own character. So: Mukasa was to die. I wondered if I was next.

I said, 'We must get out.'

Then, unbelievably, the cars began to leave. First one, then another and, last of all, the noisy Austin Cambridge. The prison was silent. From outside we heard music from a distant night-club, the barking of dogs. At first no one dared say it. I felt ashamed for having panicked. We had been spared for another night.

But this was also, clearly, our chance. At one a.m. we sat in a circle and prayed. This would be the last time we prayed together. We prayed for courage and good luck. We asked God to bless our escape.

Okech said, 'Let us go in the name of Our Lord Jesus Christ.'

We removed our handcuffs. We were all rather solemn. We shook hands and hugged each other. We opened up the hole in the ventilator. The moon was bright, and we watched until clouds passed in front of it.

Okech was to be first. He turned and said, 'I'll see you on the outside.'

This was it: the moment of the escape. Okech climbed on the wooden crates and we pushed him into the hole, head first. But then he stopped. We pushed harder and harder. It was no good. He came down again.

Major Kimumwe smiled. He said we would have to push Okech through feet first. That way would work. We could twist his body round as we pushed.

We tried it, but this, too, did not work. We pulled Okech back out again.

'Now what?' he said.

Nambale said, 'What do you mean, "Now what?"? We're going.'

Okech was grim. 'Do that and I'll make sure you don't get very far. I'll make sure you get shot outside.'

Silence.

'So what do we do?' said Kasujja.

We tried again. We pushed Okech until we thought that his collarbone would crack and that he might suffocate. He was just too fat.

'Mr Okech . . .' I began to say.

'Don't say it,' Okech said. 'The rest of you are not going. We'll have to work tomorrow and remove one of the bars. They're loose enough.'

Ssekalo said he couldn't believe this was happening. Did he have to sacrifice his life for Okech? Mutumba buried his face in his hands. The others lay on their backs, and stared at the ceiling.

I knew what had to be done. I moved over to Okech. I slid an arm over his shoulder. I asked him to listen to me like a brother. I said he must stay.

Okech explained his position. He said he had been arrested only because his friend Ssendawula had refused to stop his car for the State Research boys one night after the assassination attempt. Now it was Ssendawula who wished to leave him to die, alone. Was that justice?

I knew that Okech was speaking the truth. If we left him alone in that cell he would die. But I told him he must be a good statesman. I told him he would be pardoned. His innocence was well-known. He needed only to invent a story which would dissociate him from the escape. He could say that he had been asleep. Or that unknown soldiers had stormed the cell and refused to take him along. He would be OK.

There was silence. Okech looked at me for a long time. He took a deep breath and shook his head. Silence. The sound of dogs barking.

He said, 'Very well.'

The relief we felt was overpowering.

Okech said, 'You may try your luck. You know I will not be pardoned. So please remember, I am going to die for you.'

Each of us embraced Okech. We told him we owed him our lives. Okech nodded, and said nothing.

It was nearly three a.m. when we lifted Ssekalo to the bars. He struggled and was through, giving the thumbs up to the rest of us below. Major Kimumwe was next, followed by Ssendawula, then me. It wasn't easy, even for a man of my medium build. I lifted myself off the floor by pulling on the bars. Nambale then lifted my body so it was level with the ventilator. I pushed my right arm through, and my head, and twisted on my side so that my shoulders were vertical, and received another push from below. With my chest already outside, and my hands on the ground, pulling my legs and hips through was easy. I signalled to Nambale, who followed. Mutumba was the last, helped through by Okech.

Okech watched through the bars. He asked me to give a message to his wife and children. He said, 'Good luck, gentlemen. Go well.' He was crying.

OUT

The night was cool, bright, silent except for the barking of dogs. For some reason I thought of my wife, and the night of our honeymoon. I thought I was as good as reunited with her. Then a burst of laughter came from the guardhouse, and booming voices. I realized how much we had concentrated our energies on getting out of the cell, and how little we had thought about what would happen afterwards. It was another story.

We had agreed, however, that there would be no talking, except in an emergency. We would follow the orders of Major Kimumwe as though we were on a military operation. He would communicate by hand signal. He motioned, and we began to crawl along the side of the cell block.

At the corner of the building we came to an area that was brightly lit. Ssekalo peered round, to see if all was clear. It was. There were no soldiers. We crossed quickly to a wall. This was about seven feet high, and we had to climb it to get up to the level where we could tackle the fences. We lifted Ssekalo, and he pulled up Major Kimumwe, who in turn helped Kasujja, and so on.

We moved along the first perimeter fence. The security lights were dazzling. We could be seen easily. So we went along and found a darker spot. Kasujja followed us with astonishing agility.

Now we faced a much bigger fence. We couldn't climb this one, and we also feared it was electrified. Major Kimumwe signalled us to stop. We waited while Ssekalo searched for a place to crawl through. It was some minutes before he returned to report that he had found a spot, but that it would mean going *over* the fence and into the compound of a neighbouring house. There were problems. The guardhouse was close by. And there were two large dogs in the compound. Kasujja suggested that two of us go on ahead, get through the fence and strangle the dogs. We argued. The plan wasn't practical. What about the noise? Wouldn't the guards be alerted?

A soldier came round the corner. We were silenced. We watched as he walked round the side of the building. He stopped, as though he'd seen the hole in the ventilator. We waited for him to raise the alarm. Instead he dropped his rifle on the ground and lit a cigarette. He smoked for a while, turned round and went back round the corner.

Major Kimumwe found a hollow in the ground at the bottom of the fence, probably there for drainage. It looked possible to crawl under. But someone would have to lift the fence. And this, of course, was the one we thought was electrified. Someone would have to try it. Major Kimumwe began to scan our faces just as Kasujja hopped forward and grasped the wire.

Kasujja turned, smiling.

We wriggled through. Now we were outside the second perimeter fence, but still in a corridor surrounded by a roll of wire. We thought there would be a way out to the east, through the French Embassy. This meant we had to go round the front of the building, where the guards were. We crawled slowly, heads down. Ssendawula followed Major Kimumwe, and I was third. We were now in front of the reception area at the front of the gaol, and about to walk into an area that was brilliantly lit. We had come the wrong way. There were scores of soldiers, some on a veranda, some in jeeps, and others at attention, holding rifles to their shoulders.

'We must go back,' whispered Major Kimumwe.

We worked our way back. It was slow work. I waited for bullets to smash into my body. The dogs in the compound of the house were barking constantly. Why had no guard been sent to check on them?

We were back in the dark, huddling together to decide on our next move. Then a light was switched on and we were exposed once more. A woman officer was in the toilet on the first floor, in front of a mirror, putting on lipstick. A moment later there was another light. In an adjoining room a male soldier was relieving himself. This went on for a long time. He must have been drinking a lot of beer. Kasujja giggled. I kicked him. The officer, satisfied with her appearance, turned away. We waited. The dogs were still barking. At last the soldier finished, and turned off the light.

Again, darkness.

We were retracing our steps when Nambale found a hole in the wire. It was as simple as that. Could it have been used by soldiers to smuggle in their girlfriends? I don't know. But within a few minutes we had passed through the wire, crossed from the shadow of one tree to another and then another, crawled through a gap beneath the side gate of the presidential lodge itself, and were on the road leading to All Saints Cathedral. Kasujja had picked up a stick and was walking fast. Stones on the road hurt my bare feet; I couldn't believe we were out. I waited for the noise of pursuing soldiers, and heard only the dogs. I felt light-headed.

UP COUNTRY

We split up at the crossroads by the cathedral. We hugged each other and wished each other luck. Then Kasujja was gone. And Major Kimumwe. And the rest. Ssendawula and I hurried across the well-lit junction.

Our plan was to cross the golf course and climb the hill on the other side. After that, I would turn right and walk until I hit the Jinja road heading east, while Ssendawula would head in the opposite direction, to a suburb where a friend lived. That was the plan. The plan didn't work out. We got lost as soon as we were on the golf course. Worse: we were up to our thighs in a marsh, falling repeatedly.

I don't know how much time we wasted. An hour? Perhaps more. When we extricated ourselves and moved on down a hill, we found that we were on a road, back where we had started. We had come in a circle.

Ssendawula and I agreed to part, and I went back on to the golf course, this time making sure I kept parallel to the road. My home was in south Kampala. I knew I couldn't go there; it was the first place that would be searched. I'd decided to make for Nairobi, 450 miles away, in Kenya.

I guessed the time to be about five a.m. when I heard the cars. I knew it must be the State Research boys. No one else dared drive in the city at that hour. I hurried on.

I was on the Jinja road, somewhere between Nakawa and Kyambago, when a white Peugeot came up behind me. I turned off the road and ran into the bush, running for my life, making sudden turns—right, left, right, right, left—hoping to throw them off my trail. I didn't think I had much chance.

I hid in a half-finished building. It was made of red brick but had no roof. Perhaps an Asian family had been building it and had then been forced to leave the country. Trees and grass as high as the walls of the house had grown inside. I went in through a window frame so as not to leave any marks around the door, and hid, deep in the grass. I tried to keep quiet. I tried not to think of the snakes that were probably all around me.

Some time later I heard a man's voice. He was asking a woman if she had seen anyone. I knew it must be a State Research boy. I held my breath and prayed, praying for myself, praying for my survival. The woman said she'd seen no one, and the boy went away.

I waited. I tried to make plans. Instead I found myself thinking of irrelevant things: cold beer, buttered toast, the time one of my children had chicken pox. I dozed. Hours must have passed, and there was a rainstorm. It left me soaked again but at least, I reasoned, it should have washed away most of my scent, making it more difficult if they came after me with dogs.

I heard a helicopter overhead. I burrowed deep into the grass. I didn't need a prize to guess that the helicopter was looking for us.

Later in the morning I heard gunshots. I was relieved because they were a long off. Then I was ashamed: it meant one of the others had probably been shot. I felt sure it must be Kasujja. He was the most vulnerable. Poor Kasujja. They'd got him. The Soviet training had not saved him after all. Kasujja: then I saw movement in the grass. It was what I feared: a snake. It was a mamba, very poisonous. I kept still, telling myself that snakes attacked only moving things, and then only because they are afraid, not because they are aggressive. Snakes are not violent animals. I hoped the mamba would remember this. It had seen me, raised its head, lowered it again, and then raised it once more, tongue flickering, as if preparing to strike. I don't know how long this went on. It seemed like hours. Then the mamba decided it didn't like the look of me, executed a sinuous turn, climbed a wall and was gone.

I decided I'd risk the State Research boys, after all.

I was hungry and thirsty. I found a row of houses and from a dustbin scavenged a sodden crust of bread and half-full bottle of beer. I made my way to an open air market. The crowd was good cover. I followed two old men, one carrying a sack of flour on his head. White powder leaked on to his shoulders. I was close enough to hear their conversation, about the day being the worst business of the year. It was a pleasure listening to their concerns.

I spotted a middle-aged woman carrying a rattling bunch of saucepans, and decided it was best to walk beside her, as if I was with her. We walked for some time along the road when I flagged down a car, an ancient Austin. The car was blue. The man was grey: grey hair, grey overalls and grey bushy eyebrows. He was about sixty.

'Won't your wife come too?' he asked.

I told him the woman wasn't my wife. He shrugged, and I closed the door.

He said, 'Where do you work?'

'The Ministry of Agriculture,' I said. The lie came from my mouth before I'd really thought about it.

'That's interesting,' he said. 'What do you do?'

'I've been showing some people round here the advantages of mixed farming.'

'Which crops?'

This man was full of questions.

'Corn and coffee,' I said. I was beginning to panic. 'And there was a lot of manure. That's why I don't smell so good.'

'And is that why you're barefoot?'

'W-e-l-l,' I said, my mind racing. 'My shoes were stolen. One of the workers on the farm.'

'I see.'

The conversation faltered. I was relieved. He stopped to buy sugar, bread and milk. I sat in the car. He was gone for five minutes. I didn't like the way he'd been asking all those questions, and thought about making a run for it, but that would arouse even more suspicions. When he returned I decided I would ask the questions.

'And what do you do?' I said.

'I work at Naguru, the State Security Prison. I'm a policeman.'

I looked at him, trying to show no surprise. Was he joking? Or playing a game? Perhaps he had guessed who I was, and was driving me to the nearest station. I thought about throwing myself from the car. I waited a few minutes, humming a tune, Frank Sinatra's 'My Way'. We were on a deserted stretch of the Kampala-Jinja road.

I said, as casually as I could, 'You can let me out now.'

He said, 'But there's nothing here.'

I said, 'You can't see it from the road. A path goes through the bush to a village. My uncle lives there.'

'Right over there?' He pointed.

'That's it. Right over there.'

'Will you be safe?'

'I'll be all right, thank you.'

'It looks wild. Perhaps I should come with you.'

'That's very kind. But I'll be all right.'

'I think I'd better come with you.'

The man was either stupid, stubborn or a terrible sadist. I said, 'Really, no. Thanks.'

He looked at me, assessing me. I thought he must know. I waited for him to say he was arresting me.

Instead, he said, 'Suit yourself.'

He dropped me at the side of the road. It was pitch-dark. I watched the red tail-lights of the Austin disappear. I was back in the bush. Now I was faced with the highway robbers and the wild animals. And the snakes, of course.

I walked for days. I slept at night in the bush. I ate little. I'd concocted a story for anyone I met. I'd been released from Mulago Hospital and had no money. I was walking to Jinja. The story worked. I used the story on two old women, who gave me a meal, and an old man, who gave me clothes.

My next problem was crossing the River Nile. There were two bridges, both swarming with soldiers. I waited for a day. The bridges were quiet much of the time, except in the morning and evenings when workers were coming on and off shift. I overheard two men talking about the escape. It had been on South African radio. Some of us had apparently reached Germany. One of the men mentioned the Israelis.

The Israelis? I wondered what they were talking about.

The next morning I chanced it. I went with the morning shift across one of the bridges. I kept my head down, expecting to hear shouts from the soldiers. They didn't come. I crossed the Kenya/Uganda border in the bush, avoiding the paths in case I ran into one of Amin's anti-smuggling patrols. I reached a big road around midday and calculated I was already well into Kenya. I'd made it. I felt that

God existed after all. I jumped for joy. I thought that must be the end of the story. It wasn't.

There were police road-blocks.

It seemed unlikely that they could be looking for me. But it was possible. And if it was possible, then I could be caught, judged an undesirable and repatriated. I invented a new story: I was an employee of the East African Community, working in the research institute near Busia, and had been on my way home when thieves robbed me of everything, including my identity card. I retreated into the bush, expressing all my thoughts in Swahili.

The nights were freezing. I dined on the usual dustbin leftovers and gashed my foot on a broken bottle on the side of the road. I came down with malaria. My temperature rocketed. I told myself this was ridiculous. I hadn't expected this. I had escaped from Nakasero, got out of Uganda and was now going to die from malaria by the side of the road in Kenya. In despair I went to a police station and told my story, trusting to luck that they wouldn't send me back to Uganda. They told me I was a drunkard, and chased me away.

I joined a group of night-watchmen. I slept by their fire. In the morning I felt better. I didn't have malaria after all, just a bout of fever. One of the men told me his friend was driving a lorry to Nairobi that day. I could have a lift. The lorry broke down.

But at least the driver gave me fifty shillings. I had to walk from Kericho. I walked through Nakuru, Naivasha and the Rift Valley and finally Limuru. The sun was setting when I reached the suburbs of Nairobi. I had some change remaining: I took a bus.

At 8:45 on the night of 30 October 1977 I knocked on the door of a friend's house in Nairobi. His children answered. They said daddy was in the shower. They wouldn't let me in. They thought I was a thief. Then I saw my friend, coming down the stairs, wearing a towel round the waist, and heard his wife shrieking with surprise. They embraced me, saying at first they'd thought I was a ghost. They'd heard I was dead.

I drank tea. I ate mountains of buttered toast. I had a bath, my first in two months, and slept. On a mattress.

IN NAIROBI

I remained in hiding. If Amin or his henchmen discovered I was alive my relatives in Uganda would certainly be killed. I remained in exile until Amin's fall, in 1979.

I learned what had happened to my friends. One got out across the southern part of Lake Victoria. Another crossed Lake Kioga in a canoe. Miraculously, they all made it, even Kasujja. I saw him in Nairobi. He teased me about the fact that Ssendawula and I had not allowed him to come with us. I felt ashamed. Kasujja just laughed, and demanded that I buy him lots of vodka, Russian vodka.

I learned also about John Okech. When the guards came down into the cell area, he told them the rest of us had escaped while he slept. The guards inspected the cell with disbelief. They knew they would be blamed and became terrified for their lives. They ran away, and even left Okech with a gun when he told them he wished to kill himself rather than undergo torture. Some time later another six guards appeared. Okech shot them all, threw the gun into the corridor alongside the bodies, put back on his handcuffs, and waited in the cell. Soon there were more guards.

'*Effendi*,' said Okech. 'Some soldiers, they were white, they came down in the middle of the night, opened the cell and took the others. They wouldn't take me. I wasn't on the list.'

'What nationality were they?' said one of the guards.

'I don't know, *effendi*.' said Okech. 'I think perhaps they were Israeli.'

Okech's story was reported to Amin. It seemed that the Israelis had humiliated him once more. He ordered the immediate arrest of Major Faruk Minawa. Okech was summoned, and told to repeat his story. Amin became suspicious, demanded more facts, picked at the flaws in Okech's story, ordered an inspection of Cell Two. When the wrecked ventilator was discovered it became obvious, even to Idi Amin Dada, that Okech had been telling complex lies.

John Okech was transferred to Makindye prison, and killed there after a month of torture.

This story is written in his memory.

RYSZARD KAPUŚCIŃSKI

The Snow in Ghana

Ryszard Kapuściński (1932–   ) is a Polish journalist who reports
on international events, especially those in Latin America, the
Middle East, and West Africa. Among his works are *Another Day
of Life* (1976), *The Emperor* (1978), about the fall of Emperor
Haile Selassie, and *Shah of Shahs* (1982). The following selection
first appeared in *Granta* magazine.

The fire stood between us and linked us together. A boy added wood
and the flames rose higher, illuminating our faces.
'What is the name of your country?'
'Poland.'
Poland was far away, beyond the Sahara, beyond the sea, to the
north and the east. The *Nana* repeated the name aloud. 'Is that how
it is pronounced?' he asked.
'That's the way,' I answered. 'That's correct.'
'They have snow there,' Kwesi said. Kwesi worked in town. Once,
at the cinema, there was a movie with snow: The children applauded
and cried merrily *'Anko! Anko!'* asking to see the snow again. The
white puffs fell and fell. Those are lucky countries, Kwesi said. They
do not need to grow cotton: the cotton falls from the sky. They call
it snow and walk on it and even throw it into the river.
We were stuck here by this fire by chance—three of us, my friend
Kofi from Accra, a driver and I. Night had already fallen when the
tyre blew—the third tyre, rotten luck. It happened on a side road,
in the bush, near the village of Mpango in Ghana. Too dark to fix
it. You have no idea how dark the night can be. You can stick out
your hand and not see it. They have nights like that. We walked into
the village.
The *Nana* received us. There is a *Nana* in every village, because
Nana means boss, head man, a sort of mayor but with more authority.
If you want to get married back home in your village, the mayor
cannot stop you, but the *Nana* can. He has a Council of Elders, who
meet and govern and ponder disputes. Once upon a time the *Nana*

Translated by William Brand.

was a god. But now there is the independent government in Accra. The government passes laws and the *Nana* has to execute them. A *Nana* who does not carry them out is acting like a feudal lord and must be got rid of. The government is trying to make all *Nana*s join the party.

The *Nana* from Mpango was skinny and bald, with thin Sudanese lips. My friend Kofi introduced us. He explained where I was from and that they were to treat me as a friend.

'I know him,' my friend Kofi said. 'He's an African.'

That is the highest compliment that can be paid a European. It opens every door for him.

The *Nana* smiled and we shook hands. You always greet a *Nana* by pressing his right hand between both of your own palms. This shows respect. He sat us down by the fire, where the elders had just been holding a meeting. The bonfire was in the middle of the village, and to the left and right, along the road, there were other fires. As many fires as huts. Perhaps twenty. We could see the fires and the figures of the women and the men and the silhouettes of the clay huts—they were all visible against a night so dark and deep that it felt heavy like a weight.

The bush had disappeared, even though the bush was everywhere. It began a hundred metres away, immobile, massive, a tightly packed, coarse thicket surrounding the village and us and the fire. The bush screamed and cried and crackled: it was alive; it smelled of wilted green; it was terrifying and tempting; you knew that you could touch it and be wounded and die, but tonight, this night, you couldn't even see it.

Poland.

They did not know of any such country.

The elders looked at me with uncertainty, possibly suspicion. I wanted to break their mistrust somehow. I did not know how and I was tired.

'Where are your colonies?' the *Nana* asked.

My eyes were drooping, but I became alert. People often asked that question. Kofi had asked it first, long ago, and my answer was a revelation to him. From then on he was always ready for the question with a little speech prepared, illustrating its absurdity.

Kofi answered: 'They don't have colonies, *Nana*. Not all white countries have colonies. Not all whites are colonialists. You have to understand that whites often colonize whites.'

The elders shuddered and smacked their lips. They were surprised. Once I would have been surprised that they were surprised. But not any more. I can't bear that language, that language of white, black and yellow. The language of race is disgusting.

Kofi explained: 'For a hundred years they taught us that the white is somebody greater, super, extra. They had their clubs, their swimming pools, their neighbourhoods. Their whores, their cars and their burbling language. We knew that England was the only country in the world, that God was English, that only the English travelled around the globe. We knew exactly as much as they wanted us to know. Now it's hard to change.'

Kofi and I stuck up for each other; we no longer spoke about the subject of skin, but here, among new faces, the subject had to come up.

One of the elders asked, 'Are all the women in your country white?'

'All of them.'

'Are they beautiful?'

'They're very beautiful,' I answered.

'Do you know what he told me, *Nana?*' Kofi interjected. 'That during their summer, the women take off their clothes and lie in the sun to get black skin. The ones that become dark are proud of it, and others admire them for being as tanned as blacks.'

Very good, Kofi, you got them. The elders' eyes lit up at the thought of those bodies darkening in the sun, because, you know how it is, boys are the same all over the world: they like that sort of thing. The elders rubbed their hands together, smiled; women's bodies in the sun; they snuggled up inside their loose *kente* robes that looked like Roman togas.

'My country has no colonies,' I said after a time, 'and there was a time when my country was a colony. I respect what you've suffered, but, we too, have suffered horrible things: there were streetcars, restaurants, districts *nur für Deutsch*. There were camps, war, executions. You don't know camps, war and executions. That was what we called fascism. It's the worst colonialism.'

They listened, frowning, and closed their eyes. Strange things had been said, which they needed time to take in.

'Tell me, what does a streetcar look like?'

The concrete is important. Perhaps there was not enough room. No, it had nothing to do with room; it was contempt. One person stepping on another. Not only Africa is a cursed land. Every land can be like it—Europe, America, any place. The world depends on people, needs to step on them.

'But *Nana*, we were free afterwards. We built cities and ran lights into the villages. Those who couldn't read were taught how to read.'

The *Nana* stood up and grasped my hand. The rest of the elders did the same. We had become friends, *przyjaciele, amigos.*

VINCENT CRAPANZANO

Growing Up White in South Africa

Vincent Crapanzano (1939–   ) is an anthropologist who contributes to a wide range of periodicals from *The International Journal of Middle Eastern Studies* to the *New Yorker*. His works include *The Hamadsha: A Study in Moroccan Ethnopsychiatry* (1973) and *Waiting: The Whites of South Africa* (1985), from which the following selection is taken.

Hennie, the third of three brothers and a sister, was born in 1924 in a small town in the northwestern Cape near the Namibian border. His great-grandfather on his father's side had trekked into the Orange Free State. He was a restless sort of man who, like so many of the Voortrekkers, never seemed satisfied with the land he was farming. "He kept moving on," Hennie explained. "Those Voortrekkers were nomads. They could never settle down. The grass was always greener on the other side. And it often was. Trekking ran in their blood, and I suppose it runs in mine too. I've never lived in any one place for very long. We're not like the people on Wyndal. They've been on the same farm for generations. They have a sense of family history. It's in their homes and on their land. I am the seventh generation born here but I don't know where my ancestors came from. I don't even know where my mother's father was born."

Hennie's grandfather left his father in the Free State and settled down with his two brothers in the northwestern Cape. They staked out a vast farm in an area that was so dry—it was a desert really— that they moved around it according to where the rains fell. "They would settle down with their sheep where it had rained until the springs ran dry and there was no more pasturage. Then they would move on. Some of those farms were over forty thousand morgen.[1] Ours wasn't that big. I don't know how big it was. I'm not sure anyone did. It wasn't big enough though. There was a long drought. It lasted seven years. It rained on the neighbors' farms but not on ours.

"My grandfather was a stubborn old bloke. He wouldn't sell, but his sons didn't much fancy sheep farming. They sold off the few sheep they had left. My grandfather had given them a few sheep when they were kids—that was the custom—and it was those sheep that they sold. I don't think that between them they got more than two hundred rand, but land was cheap in those days and they were able to buy fifteen morgen of completely undeveloped land right along the Orange River. My dad had a lot of faith in irrigation farming. They started clearing the land, stumping the great trees out. They had to level it, too. For the first two years they planted just enough to keep themselves going. It was difficult, and eventually my uncle got out of the venture and started a cartage business with an old ox wagon and some donkeys. They hadn't built the railway to the southwest yet, and there was a lot of work for him, but the business petered out. Then he moved to the South West to look for diamonds, but I don't think he ever saw one. He was starving to death when my dad finally bought him a little plot of land.

"We used to have two and a half, sometimes three, crops a year. We would underplant one crop with the next so that as we reaped one, the other was already growing. We wanted to make maximum use of the land. The soil was so rich we had to fertilize only once a year. We always had something to eat, even during the Depression. We weren't rich, but we were never really poor. My dad used to say he would never again farm more than a stone's throw from a river.

"After my dad married and had children, he sold the farm and bought another one, a smaller one, nearer town. It was about six morgen, but his kids could go to school by donkey cart. By the time I went to school, he had sold the second farm and bought an even smaller one, right in town. I used to walk to school. The farm was only about three morgen, but it could be even more intensively cultivated. The railway was in by then, and we used to ship fruit and vegetables up to the South West. It's very dry up there, and vegetables

---

[1] An old Dutch unit of land area equal to 2.116 acres. (ED.)

were so expensive that people began to write to my dad and ask him to send them ten bobs' worth a week. It wasn't long before the shops got hold of his name and started ordering through him. When I took over the farm, I stopped the small orders. It was easier that way. And then later a friend of mine and I started our own shop up there. We captured the market in no time."

Hennie remembers little of his childhood, and what memories he has seem flat to me, fragmented, and devoid of those resonances that make memories come alive. I was not surprised. Many of the Afrikaner men with whom I talked seemed unable to re-create the first years of their life in a vibrant fashion. I attributed this, without sufficient evidence, I suppose, to the presence of an authoritarian father who was never to be questioned.

"In the Afrikaans tradition you do what dad tells you," Hennie explained. "You don't question him. You want to be like him. There is a tremendous identification between father and son. The son puts on a show of masculinity. We have a special word for it in Afrikaans: *kragdadigheid,* 'power,' 'strength.' 'Potency,' I think, is the best translation. The son must show his potency, his *kragdadigheid,* before his father. He must show it, but he can't question his father's *kragdadigheid.* There's the rub."

Hennie laughed. "This all began in the early days, when people were living in a frontier situation. Once you started shaving, once you started growing a beard, you were considered a man. Now you could go with your dad on some of his hunting expeditions. You were allowed to ride with a rifle. The rifle was more or less a sign of manhood. And we have in our history, I believe, an example that has inspired more youth than anything else. That is the story of Dirkie Uys. He was only about twelve years old when his dad was mortally wounded by the Zulus. He stood over his dad until help finally arrived. Now, you see, that is *the* example for youth. The great thing was to prove your manhood, your *manlikheid.* And really it's a stupid sort of thing and carried to stupid extremes. 'If you can hold your liquor, then you're a man' sort of thing. If you're really a man, you don't need to prove it.

"Now, in many ways, my brothers and I were brought up differently. My dad never forced us into anything. If my brother wanted to go to university, that was all right. He never told him he had to become a minister. In the old Afrikaner tradition, the first clever son always became a minister. The next one became a lawyer or a teacher, and the third took over the farm. My dad never insisted that we go on with our schooling. I'll never forget, one day my eldest brother complained to my father that his teachers didn't know what they were talking about. My dad told him he didn't have to go back to school if he felt that way. Of course, he was back at school early the next morning. That was the way my dad was. He wasn't very strict, I suppose, given all the mischief my brothers got into. I was only given a hiding once. I can remember it, but I can't remember why. I think that my mother was more of the disciplinarian in our home.

"Of course, I was sort of catapulted into manhood when my dad died. I was only thirteen. My eldest brother was already up in the Transvaal in the mines, and my second brother was at varsity. I had to go to school and manage the farm by myself. My mother—she had always been rather ill—took to her bed after my father died. I hardly remember her during those years anywhere but in bed or, on summer evenings, on the stoep, staring out over the fields onto the river. That lasted two or three years.

"She was, in her way, a gutsy lady. She was over ninety when she died. She could talk to you on nearly any subject. The week before she died she took part in the talent contest they had in her old-age home. She had five books of poetry on her deathbed—she was already looking for a new poem to recite at the next do they were going to have at the home.

"During those years I was the man around the house. I just suddenly realized that I had extra responsibilities. I had to accept this. What else can you do? Your dad has died, and you just have to carry on. I don't think I thought about it very much. So, you see, in some ways, my dad's death protected me from having to prove my manhood. I didn't have to play rugby to prove that I was a man. That what rugby's all about, you know."

Hennie had no time for rugby. He insists that after his father's death he managed the farm by himself. His brothers were away; his mother was ill; his uncle was not much of a farmer. He rarely mentions any relatives when he talks about his life immediately after his father's death, though there were some cousins on his father's side and his mother's two brothers, who lived nearby. Nor does he mention the Coloured farm workers. Hennie prefers to remember himself alone.

I asked him who took care of him when he was a child.

"My sister Katrin did. We never had a nanny as such. There was a Coloured girl who stayed with us. My parents adopted her, and she grew up with the rest of us.

"There were Coloured people who lived on the plot next to us, and I played with their kids. Naturally, my first friends were Col-

oured. Children don't notice the color of their friends' skin. You only
become aware of it when you're told that you're big now and must
not play with Coloured girls anymore. I was about ten, I suppose,
when I became aware of the fact that people had different-color skin.
It didn't much matter. My parents were friendly with the *volk* who
lived around us. My mom used to visit them, and they would visit
us too. There was nothing odd about that! And yet somehow . . .
Well, I remember there was a European who had married a Coloured
woman. They didn't live too far from us. They had a lot of goats,
and the goats kept getting into our yard. I chased them back one
day and I told the European that my dad said he should be more
careful with his goats. I called him *outa*. You only call Coloureds
outa. He corrected me, and I said, 'But you're married to a Coloured
woman.' I had to depart in a hurry. That was my first awareness of
color, and I suppose that is why I always remember it. It is from
moments like this that you become aware of differences. You begin
to think about it. You begin to notice that there are certain people
who are different and live differently.

"It started with the first settlers. South Africa was never colonized
to the extent that Jamaica was for instance. For many years there
was a very small minority battling against tremendous odds to keep
their identity and way of life—in a world around them that was
terribly different. There are a lot of laws that we have today that got
started then in that struggle. If an African or a Coloured man raped
a white woman, he would be hanged. If a white man raped a Coloured
woman or an African, he probably wouldn't even have had to go to
court.

"In my younger days I was like a little rhino. I just went charging
through life, and what didn't suit me, I kind of brushed out of the
way. And if I didn't like you, I'd tell you in no uncertain terms. And
if you didn't grasp it, I'd hammer it into you. When my father and
his brother moved to town, they were only the sixth European family
up there. All the land belonged to the Coloureds, and they had to
buy it from them. My dad and his brother always used to say that
they had tamed that part of the world. They hammered those others
into submission. I suppose I shouldn't laugh, but that was the way
it was in those days.

"I've been wondering whether I should tell you this or not, but
as we're on the subject, I might as well. Everything about my family
wasn't always respectable and good. When my uncle came back to
farming, he grew a lot of watermelons. You get to know your watermelons. You've got to keep an eye on them to see which are ready

for picking. My uncle suddenly found that some of his melons were disappearing. So one night he sat up in the bushes to see who was helping himself to them. There was a tremendous storm that night, and in the lightning my uncle could see this bloke coming toward him and eventually recognized him. He was one of those very cheeky Coloureds who used to boast that no white man had ever hammered him. My uncle watched and waited and caught him red-handed. The bloke tried to make a run for it, but before he could get over the fence, my uncle had him down and was punching away at him. Then he started pulling out his hair—his eyebrows even, every bit of hair on his body. And when he ran out of hair, he pulled out his pocketknife and began stabbing him, just little stabs, on his inside thighs. The bloke couldn't walk for weeks.

"Now, I'm not telling you this with pride. But as a child, it made a tremendous impression on me. You see, here's a guy who boasted that no white man had ever hammered him, and then one of your own relatives—one you respect—puts him in his place. You want to imitate him. You don't even think about it. You do it automatically until something happens to make you really think about what you're doing. It just can't come from within. It's got to come from outside—from God. You need the courage to change.

"We've got to teach our children to question why they're doing the things they do. But when I was in school we just sat there like a lot of little birds with our mouths open, and the worms were stuck down. That was that. We never asked questions."

BESSIE HEAD

Looking for a Rain God

Bessie Head (1937–1986) was a South-African-born novelist, journalist, and educator who adopted Botswana as her home country. The following selection is from *The Collector of Treasures* (1977), a collection of village tales Head reworked, which like her other work is concerned with the theme of displacement. Her other books include *When Rain Clouds Gather* (1969), *A Question of Power* (1973), and *A Bewitched Crossroad: An African Saga* (1984).

It is lonely at the lands where the people go to plough. These lands are vast clearings in the bush, and the wild bush is lonely too. Nearly all the lands are within walking distance from the village. In some parts of the bush where the underground water is very near the surface, people made little rest camps for themselves and dug shallow wells to quench their thirst while on their journey to their own lands. They experienced all kinds of things once they left the village. They could rest at shady watering places full of lush, tangled trees with delicate pale-gold and purple wild flowers springing up between soft green moss and the children could hunt around for wild figs and any berries that might be in season. But from 1958, a seven-year drought fell upon the land and even the watering places began to look as dismal as the dry open thorn-bush country; the leaves of the trees curled up and withered; the moss became dry and hard and, under the shade of the tangled trees, the ground turned a powdery black and white, because there was no rain. People said rather humorously that if you tried to catch the rain in a cup it would only fill a teaspoon. Towards the beginning of the seventh year of drought, the summer had become an anguish to live through. The air was so dry and moisture-free that it burned the skin. No one knew what to do to escape the heat, and tragedy was in the air. At the beginning of that summer, a number of men just went out of their homes and hung themselves to death from trees. The majority of the people had lived off crops, but for two years past they had all returned from the lands with only their rolled-up skin blankets and cooking utensils. Only the charlatans, incanters, and witchdoctors made a pile of money during this time because people were always turning to them in desperation for little talismans and herbs to rub on the plough for the crops to grow and the rain to fall.

The rains were late that year. They came in early November, with a promise of good rain. It wasn't the full, steady downpour of the years of good rain, but thin, scanty, misty rain. It softened the earth and a rich growth of green things sprang up everywhere for the animals to eat. People were called to the village kgotla¹ to hear the proclamation of the beginning of the ploughing season; they stirred themselves and whole families began to move off to the lands to plough.

The family of the old man, Mokgobja, were among those who

¹ the village council and place for discussion (ED.)

left early for the lands. They had a donkey cart and piled everything onto it, Mokgobja—who was over seventy years old; two little girls, Neo and Boseyong; their mother Tiro and an unmarried sister, Nesta; and the father and supporter of the family, Ramadi, who drove the donkey cart. In the rush of the first hope of rain, the man, Ramadi, and the two women, cleared the land of thorn-bush and then hedged their vast ploughing area with this same thorn-bush to protect the future crop from the goats they had brought along for milk. They cleared out and deepened the old well with its pool of muddy water and still in this light, misty rain, Ramadi inspanned two oxen and turned the earth over with a hand plough.

The land was ready and ploughed, waiting for the crops. At night, the earth was alive with insects singing and rustling about in search of food. But suddenly, by mid-November, the rain fled away; the rain-clouds fled away and left the sky bare. The sun danced dizzily in the sky, with a strange cruelty. Each day the land was covered in a haze of mist as the sun sucked up the last drop of moisture out of the earth. The family sat down in despair, waiting and waiting. Their hopes had run so high; the goats had started producing milk, which they had eagerly poured on their porridge, now they ate plain porridge with no milk. It was impossible to plant the corn, maize, pumpkin and water-melon seeds in the dry earth. They sat the whole day in the shadow of the huts and even stopped thinking, for the rain had fled away. Only the children, Neo and Boseyong, were quite happy in their little girl world. They carried on with their game of making house like their mother and chattered to each other in light, soft tones. They made children from sticks around which they tied rags, and scolded them severely in an exact imitation of their own mother. Their voices could be heard scolding the day long: "You stupid thing, when I send you to draw water, why do you spill half of it out of the bucket!" "You stupid thing! Can't you mind the porridge-pot without letting the porridge burn!" And then they would beat the rag-dolls on their bottoms with severe expressions.

The adults paid no attention to this, they did not even hear the funny chatter; they sat waiting for rain; their nerves were stretched to breaking-point willing the rain to fall out of the sky. Nothing was important, beyond that. All their animals had been sold during the bad years to purchase food, and of all their herd only two goats were left. It was the women of the family who finally broke down under the strain of waiting for rain. It was really the two women who caused the death of the little girls. Each night they started a weird, high-pitched wailing that began on a low, mournful note and whipped up to a frenzy. Then they would stamp their feet and shout as though they had lost their heads. The men sat quiet and self-controlled; it was important for men to maintain their self-control at all times but their nerve was breaking too. They knew the women were haunted by the starvation of the coming year.

Finally, an ancient memory stirred in the old man, Mokgobja. When he was very young and the customs of the ancestors still ruled the land, he had been witness to a rain-making ceremony. And he came alive a little, struggling to recall the details which had been buried by years and years of prayer in a Christian church. As soon as the mists cleared a little, he began consulting in whispers with his youngest son, Ramadi. There was, he said, a certain rain god who accepted only the sacrifice of the bodies of children. Then the rain would fall; then the crops would grow, he said. He explained the ritual and as he talked, his memory became a conviction and he began to talk with unshakable authority. Ramadi's nerves were smashed by the nightly wailing of the women and soon the two men began whispering with the two women. The children continued their game: "You stupid thing! How could you have lost the money on the way to the shop! You must have been playing again!"

After it was all over and the bodies of the two little girls had been spread across the land, the rain did not fall. Instead, there was a deathly silence at night and the devouring heat of the sun by day. A terror, extreme and deep, overwhelmed the whole family. They packed, rolling up their skin blankets and pots, and fled back to the village.

People in the village soon noted the absence of the two little girls. They had died at the lands and were buried there, the family said. But people noted their ashen, terror-stricken faces and a murmur arose. What had killed the children, they wanted to know? And the family replied that they had just died. And people said amongst themselves that it was strange that the two deaths had occurred at the same time. And there was a feeling of great unease at the unnatural looks of the family. Soon the police came around. The family told them the same story of death and burial at the lands. They did not know what the children had died of. So the police asked to see the graves. At this, the mother of the children broke down and told everything.

Throughout that terrible summer the story of the children hung like a dark cloud of sorrow over the village, and the sorrow was not assuaged when the old man and Ramadi were sentenced to death for ritual murder. All they had on the statute books was that ritual murder was against the law and must be stamped out with the death penalty. The subtle story of strain and starvation and breakdown was inadmissable evidence at court; but all the people who lived off crops knew in their hearts that only a hair's breadth had saved them from sharing a fate similar to that of the Mokgobja family. They could have killed something to make the rain fall.

GEORGE ORWELL

A Hanging

George Orwell (1903–1950) was the pen name of Eric Blair, English journalist, essayist, novelist, and critic who was born in Bengal, India. His classic novels *Animal Farm* (1945) and *Nineteen Eighty-four* (1949) examine the roots of totalitarianism. His other important works include *Down and Out in Paris and London* (1933) and his account of his participation in the Spanish Civil War in *Homage to Catalonia* (1938). He is generally regarded as one of this century's leading commentators on literature and politics. He published articles, reviews, and several collections of essays, including *Shooting an Elephant* (1950) in which the following selection appears.

It was in Burma, a sodden morning of the rains. A sickly light, like yellow tinfoil, was slanting over the high walls into the jail yard. We were waiting outside the condemned cells, a row of sheds fronted with double bars, like small animal cages. Each cell measured about ten feet by ten and was quite bare within except for a plank bed and a pot for drinking water. In some of them brown silent men were squatting at the inner bars, with their blankets draped round them. These were the condemned men, due to be hanged within the next week or two.

One prisoner had been brought out of his cell. He was a Hindu, a puny wisp of a man, with a shaven head and vague liquid eyes. He had a thick, sprouting moustache, absurdly too big for his body, rather like the moustache of a comic man on the films. Six tall Indian warders were guarding him and getting him ready for the gallows. Two of them stood by with rifles and fixed bayonets, while the others

handcuffed him, passed a chain through his handcuffs and fixed it
to their belts, and lashed his arms tight to his sides. They crowded
very close about him, with their hands always on him in a careful,
caressing grip, as though all the while feeling him to make sure he
was there. It was like men handling a fish which is still alive and
may jump back into the water. But he stood quite unresisting, yielding his arms limply to the ropes, as though he hardly noticed what
was happening.

Eight o'clock struck and a bugle call, desolately thin in the wet
air, floated from the distant barracks. The superintendent of the jail,
who was standing apart from the rest of us, moodily prodding the
gravel with his stick, raised his head at the sound. He was an army
doctor, with a gray toothbrush moustache and a gruff voice. "For
God's sake hurry up, Francis," he said irritably. "The man ought to
have been dead by this time. Aren't you ready yet?"

Francis, the head jailer, a fat Dravidian[1] in a white drill suit and
gold spectacles, waved his black hand. "Yes sir, yes sir," he bubbled.
"All iss satisfactorily prepared. The hangman iss waiting. We shall
proceed."

"Well, quick march, then. The prisoners can't get their breakfast
till this job's over."

We set out for the gallows. Two warders marched on either side
of the prisoner, with their rifles at the slope; two others marched
close against him, gripping him by arm and shoulder, as though at
once pushing and supporting him. The rest of us, magistrates and
the like, followed behind. Suddenly, when we had gone ten yards,
the procession stopped short without any order or warning. A dreadful thing had happened—a dog, come goodness knows whence, had
appeared in the yard. It came bounding among us with a loud volley
of barks, and leapt round us wagging its whole body, wild with glee
at finding so many human beings together. It was a large woolly dog,
half Airedale, half pariah. For a moment it pranced round us, and
then, before anyone could stop it, it had made a dash for the prisoner
and, jumping up, tried to lick his face. Everyone stood aghast, too
taken aback even to grab at the dog.

"Who let that bloody brute in here?" said the superintendent
angrily. "Catch it, someone!"

A warder, detached from the escort, charged clumsily after the

---

[1] a group of people of intermixed races in southern India and Sri Lanka (ED.)

dog, but it danced and gamboled just out of his reach, taking every-thing as part of the game. A young Eurasian jailer picked up a handful of gravel and tried to stone the dog away, but it dodged the stones and came after us again. Its yaps echoed from the jail walls. The prisoner, in the grasp of the two warders, looked on incuriously, as though this was another formality of the hanging. It was several minutes before someone managed to catch the dog. Then we put my handkerchief through its collar and moved off once more, with the dog still straining and whimpering.

It was about forty yards to the gallows. I watched the bare brown back of the prisoner marching in front of me. He walked clumsily with his bound arms, but quite steadily, with that bobbing gait of the Indian who never straightens his knees. At each step his muscles slid neatly into place, the lock of hair on his scalp danced up and down, his feet printed themselves on the wet gravel. And once, in spite of the men who gripped him by each shoulder, he stepped slightly aside to avoid a puddle on the path.

It is curious, but till that moment I had never realized what it means to destroy a healthy, conscious man. When I saw the prisoner step aside to avoid the puddle I saw the mystery, the unspeakable wrongness, of cutting a life short when it is in full tide. This man was not dying, he was alive just as we are alive. All the organs of his body were working—bowels digesting food, skin renewing itself, nails growing, tissues forming—all toiling away in solemn foolery. His nails would still be growing when he stood on the drop, when he was falling through the air with a tenth of a second to live. His eyes saw the yellow gravel and the gray walls, and his brain still remembered, foresaw, reasoned—reasoned even about puddles. He and we were a party of men walking together, seeing, hearing, feeling, understanding the same world; and in two minutes, with a sudden snap, one of us would be gone—one mind less, one world less.

The gallows stood in a small yard, separate from the main grounds of the prison, and overgrown with tall prickly weeds. It was a brick erection like three sides of a shed, with planking on top, and above that two beams and a crossbar with the rope dangling. The hangman, a gray-haired convict in the white uniform of the prison, was waiting beside his machine. He greeted us with a servile crouch as we entered. At a word from Francis the two warders, gripping the prisoner more closely than ever, half led half pushed him to the gallows and helped him clumsily up the ladder. Then the hangman climbed up and fixed the rope round the prisoner's neck.

We stood waiting, five yards away. The warders had formed in a rough circle round the gallows. And then, when the noose was fixed, the prisoner began crying out to his god. It was a high, reiterated cry of "Ram! Ram! Ram! Ram!" not urgent and fearful like a prayer or cry for help, but steady, rhythmical, almost like the tolling of a bell. The dog answered the sound with a whine. The hangman, still standing on the gallows, produced a small cotton bag like a flour bag and drew it down over the prisoner's face. But the sound, muffled by the cloth, still persisted, over and over again: "Ram! Ram! Ram! Ram! Ram!"

The hangman climbed down and stood ready, holding the lever. Minutes seemed to pass. The steady, muffled crying from the prisoner went on and on, "Ram! Ram! Ram!" never faltering for an instant. The superintendent, his head on his chest, was slowly poking the ground with his stick; perhaps he was counting the cries, allowing the prisoner a fixed number—fifty, perhaps, or a hundred. Everyone had changed color. The Indians had gone gray like bad coffee, and one or two of the bayonets were wavering. We looked at the lashed, hooded man on the drop, and listened to his cries—each cry another second of life; the same thought was in all our minds: oh, kill him quickly, get it over, stop that abominable noise!

Suddenly the superintendent made up his mind. Throwing up his head he made a swift motion with his stick. "Chalo!" he shouted almost fiercely.

There was a clanking noise, and then dead silence. The prisoner had vanished, and the rope was twisting on itself. I let go of the dog, and it galloped immediately to the back of the gallows; but when it got there it stopped short, barked, and then retreated into a corner of the yard, where it stood among the weeds, looking timorously out at us. We went round the gallows to inspect the prisoner's body. He was dangling with his toes pointed straight downward, very slowly revolving, as dead as a stone.

The superintendent reached out with his stick and poked the bare brown body; it oscillated slightly. "*He's* all right," said the superintendent. He backed out from under the gallows, and blew out a deep breath. The moody look had gone out of his face quite suddenly. He glanced at his wrist watch. "Eight minutes past eight. Well, that's all for this morning, thank God."

The warders unfixed bayonets and marched away. The dog, sobered and conscious of having misbehaved itself, slipped after them. We walked out of the gallows yard, past the condemned cells with their waiting prisoners, into the big central yard of the prison. The convicts, under the command of warders armed with lathis,[2] were already receiving their breakfast. They squatted in long rows, each man holding a tin pannikin, while two warders with buckets marched round ladling out rice; it seemed quite a homely, jolly scene, after the hanging. An enormous relief had come upon us now that the job was done. One felt an impulse to sing, to break into a run, to snigger. All at once everyone began chattering gaily.

The Eurasian boy walking beside me nodded toward the way we had come, with a knowing smile: "Do you know, sir, our friend [he meant the dead man] when he heard his appeal had been dismissed, he pissed on the floor of his cell. From fright. Kindly take one of my cigarettes, sir. Do you not admire my new silver case, sir? From the boxwalah,[3] two rupees eight annas. Classy European style."

Several people laughed—at what, nobody seemed certain.

Francis was walking by the superintendent, talking garrulously: "Well, sir, all hass passed off with the utmost satisfactoriness. It was all finished—flick! like that. It iss not always so—oah, no! I have known cases where the doctor wass obliged to go beneath the gallows and pull the prissoner's legs to ensure decease. Most disagreeable!"

"Wriggling about, eh? That's bad," said the superintendent.

"Ach, sir, it iss worse when they become refractory! One man, I recall, clung to the bars of hiss cage when we went to take him out. You will scarcely credit, sir, that it took six warders to dislodge him, three pulling at each leg. We reasoned with him. 'My dear fellow,' we said, 'think of all the pain and trouble you are causing to us!' But no, he would not listen! Ach, he wass very troublesome!"

I found that I was laughing quite loudly. Everyone was laughing. Even the superintendent grinned in a tolerant way. "You'd better all come out and have a drink," he said quite genially. "I've got a bottle of whisky in the car. We could do with it."

We went through the big double gates of the prison into the road. "Pulling at his legs!" exclaimed a Burmese magistrate suddenly, and burst into a loud chuckling. We all began laughing again. At that moment Francis' anecdote seemed extraordinarily funny. We all had a drink together, native and European alike, quite amicably. The dead man was a hundred yards away.

---

[2] heavy sticks of ironbound bamboo (ED.)

[3] a peddler or merchant (ED.)

URSULA K. LE GUIN

Imaginary Countries

Ursula K. Le Guin (1929–   ) is a California-born writer who has
won both the Hugo and Nebula awards for her science fiction. Her
novels include *The Farthest Shore* (1972) and *The Dispossessed: An
Ambiguous Utopia* (1974). Her later works, such as *Orsinian Tales*
(1976), from which this selection is taken, speculate on utopian
themes in contexts drawn from classical mythology.

"We can't drive to the river on Sunday," the baron said, "because
we're leaving on Friday." The two little ones gazed at him across the
breakfast table. Zida said, "Marmalade, please," but Paul, a year older,
found in a remote, disused part of his memory a darker dining-room
from the windows of which one saw rain falling. "Back to the city?"
he asked. His father nodded. And at the nod the sunlit hill outside
these windows changed entirely, facing north now instead of south.
That day red and yellow ran through the woods like fire, grapes
swelled fat on the heavy vines, and the clear, fierce, fenced fields of
August stretched themselves out, patient and unboundaried, into the
haze of September. Next day Paul knew the moment he woke that
it was autumn, and Wednesday. "This is Wednesday," he told Zida,
"tomorrow's Thursday, and then Friday when we leave."

"I'm not going to," she replied with indifference, and went off to
the Little Woods to work on her unicorn trap. It was made of an
egg-crate and many little bits of cloth, with various kinds of bait.
She had been making it ever since they found the tracks, and Paul
doubted if she would catch even a squirrel in it. He, aware of time
and season, ran full speed to the High Cliff to finish the tunnel there
before they had to go back to the city.

Inside the house the baroness's voice dipped like a swallow down
the attic stairs. "O Rosa! Where is the blue trunk then?" And Rosa
not answering, she followed her voice, pursuing it and Rosa and the
lost trunk down stairs and ever farther hallways to a joyful reunion
at the cellar door. Then from his study the baron heard Tomas and
the trunk come grunting upward step by step, while Rosa and the
baroness began to empty the children's closets, carrying off little
loads of shirts and dresses like delicate, methodical thieves. "What
are you doing?" Zida asked sternly, having come back for a coat-

hanger in which the unicorn might entangle his hoof. "Packing," said the maid. "Not my things," Zida ordered, and departed. Rosa continued rifling her closet. In his study the baron read on undisturbed except by a sense of regret which rose perhaps from the sound of his wife's sweet, distant voice, perhaps from the quality of the sunlight falling across his desk from the uncurtained window.

In another room his older son Stanislas put a microscope, a tennis racket, and a box full of rocks with their labels coming unstuck into his suitcase, then gave it up. A notebook in his pocket, he went down the cool red halls and stairs, out the door into the vast and sudden sunlight of the yard. Josef, reading under the Four Elms, said, "Where are you off to? It's hot." There was no time for stopping and talking. "Back soon," Stanislas replied politely and went on, up the road in dust and sunlight, past the High Cliff where his half-brother Paul was digging. He stopped to survey the engineering. Roads metalled with white clay zigzagged over the cliff-face. The Citroen and the Rolls were parked near a bridge spanning an erosion-gully. A tunnel had been pierced and was in process of enlargement. "Good tunnel," Stanislas said. Radiant and filthy, the engineer replied, "It'll be ready to drive through this evening, you want to come to the ceremony?" Stanislas nodded, and went on. His road led up a long, high hillslope, but he soon turned from it and, leaping the ditch, entered his kingdom and the kingdom of the trees. Within a few steps all dust and bright light were gone. Leaves overhead and underfoot; an air like green water through which birds swam and the dark trunks rose lifting their burdens, their crowns, towards the other element, the sky. Stanislas went first to the Oak and stretched his arms out, straining to reach a quarter of the way around the trunk. His chest and cheek were pressed against the harsh, scored bark; the smell of it and its shelf-fungi and moss was in his nostrils and the darkness of it in his eyes. It was a bigger thing than he could ever hold. It was very old, and alive, and did not know that he was there. Smiling, he went on quietly, a notebook full of maps in his pocket, among the trees towards yet-uncharted regions of his land.

Josef Brone, who had spent the summer assisting his professor with documentation of the history of the Ten Provinces in the Early Middle Ages, sat uneasily reading in the shade of elms. Country wind blew across the pages, across his lips. He looked up from the Latin chronicle of a battle lost nine hundred years ago to the roofs of the house called Asgard. Square as a box, with a sediment of porches, sheds, and stables, and square to the compass, the house stood in its flat yard; after a while in all directions the fields rose up slowly, turning into hills, and behind them were higher hills, and behind them sky. It was like a white box in a blue and yellow bowl, and Josef, fresh from college and intent upon the Jesuit seminary he would enter in the fall, ready to read documents and make abstracts and copy references, had been embarrassed to find that the baron's family called the place after the home of the northern gods. But this no longer troubled him. So much had happened here that he had not expected, and so little seemed to have been finished. The history was years from completion. In three months he had never found out where Stanislas went, alone, up the road. They were leaving on Friday. Now or never. He got up and followed the boy. The road passed a ten-foot bank, halfway up to which clung the little boy Paul, digging in the dirt with his fingers, making a noise in his throat, rrrm, rrrrm. A couple of toy cars lay at the foot of the bank. Josef followed the road on up the hill and presently began expecting to reach the top, from which he would see where Stanislas had gone. A farm came into sight and went out of sight, the road climbed, a lark went up singing as if very near the sun; but there was no top. The only way to go downhill on this road was to turn around. He did so. As he neared the woods above Asgard a boy leapt out onto the road, quick as a hawk's shadow. Josef called his name, and they met in the white glare of dust. "Where have you been?" asked Josef, sweating.—"In the Great Woods," Stanislas answered, "that grove there." Behind him the trees gathered thick and dark. "Is it cool in there?" Josef asked wistfully. "What do you do in there?"—"Oh, I map trails. Just for the fun of it. It's bigger than it looks." Stanislas hesitated, then added, "You haven't been in it? You might like to see the Oak." Josef followed him over the ditch and through the close green air to the Oak. It was the biggest tree he had ever seen; he had not seen very many. "I suppose it's very old," he said, looking up puzzled at the reach of branches, galaxy after galaxy of green leaves without end. "Oh, a century or two or three or six," said the boy, "see if you can reach around it!" Josef spread out his arms and strained, trying vainly to keep his cheek off the rough bark. "It takes four men to reach around it," Stanislas said. "I call it Yggdrasil.[1] You know. Only of course Yggdrasil was an ash, not an oak. Want to see Loki's Grove?"[2] The road and the hot white sunlight were gone

---

[1] The great tree of the world which, according to Norse mythology, had branches and roots extending through all the universe. (ED.)

[2] Loki was the Norse giant or deity personifying evil. (ED.)

entirely. The young man followed his guide farther into the maze and game of names which was also a real forest: trees, still air, earth. Under tall grey alders above a dry streambed they discussed the tale of the death of Baldur,[3] and Stanislas pointed out to Josef the dark clots, high in the boughs of lesser oaks, of mistletoe. They left the woods and went down the road towards Asgard. Josef walked along stiffly in the dark suit he had bought for his last year at the University, in his pocket a book in a dead language. Sweat ran down his face, he felt very happy. Though he had no maps and was rather late arriving, at least he had walked once through the forest. They passed Paul still burrowing, ignoring the clang of the iron triangle down at the house, which signalled meals, fires, lost children, and other noteworthy events. "Come on, lunch!" Stanislas ordered. Paul slid down the bank and they proceeded, seven, fourteen and twenty-one, sedately to the house.

That afternoon Josef helped the professor pack books, two trunks full of books, a small library of medieval history. Josef liked to read books, not pack them. The professor had asked him, not Tomas, "Lend me a hand with the books, will you?" It was not the kind of work he had expected to do here. He sorted and lifted and stowed away load after load of resentment in insatiable iron trunks, while the professor worked with energy and interest, swaddling incunabula[4] like babies, handling each volume with affection and despatch. Kneeling with keys he said, "Thanks, Josef! That's that," and lowering the brass catchbars locked away their summer's work, done with, that's that. Josef had done so much here that he had not expected to do, and now nothing was left to do. Disconsolate, he wandered back to the shade of the elms; but the professor's wife, with whom he had not expected to fall in love, was sitting there. "I stole your chair," she said amiably, "sit on the grass." It was more dirt than grass, but they called it grass, and he obeyed. "Rosa and I are worn out," she said, "and I can't bear to think of tomorrow. It's the worst, the next-to-last day—linens and silver and turning dishes upside down and putting out mousetraps and there's always a doll lost and found after everybody's searched for hours under a pile of laundry—and then sweeping the house and locking it all up. And I hate every bit of it,

---

[3] Norse god of light and son of Odin, he was killed by a dart made of mistletoe, aimed at him by Loki. (ED.)

[4] books printed before 1501 (ED.)

I hate to close this house." Her voice was light and plaintive as a
bird's calling in the woods, careless whether anybody heard its plaintiveness, careless of its plaintiveness. "I hope you've liked it here,"
she said.

"Very much, baroness."

"I hope so. I know Severin has worked you very hard. And we're
so disorganized. We and the children and the visitors, we always
seem to scatter so, and only meet in passing. . . . I hope it hasn't
been distracting." It was true; all summer in tides and cycles the
house had been full or half full of visitors, friends of the children,
friends of the baroness, friends, colleagues and neighbors of the
baron, duckhunters who slept in the disused stable since the spare
bedrooms were full of Polish medieval historians, ladies with broods
of children the smallest of whom fell inevitably into the pond about
this time of the afternoon. No wonder it was so still, so autumnal
now: the rooms vacant, the pond smooth, the hills empty of dis-
persing laughter.

"I have enjoyed knowing the children," Josef said, "particularly
Stanislas." Then he went red as a beet, for Stanislas alone was not
her child. She smiled and said with timidity, "Stanislas is very nice.
And fourteen—fourteen is such a fearful age, when you find out so
fast what you're capable of being, but also what a toll the world
expects. . . . He handles it very gracefully. Paul and Zida now, when
they get that age they'll lump through it and be tiresome. But Stanislas
learned loss so young. . . . When will you enter the seminary?" she
asked, moving from the boy to him in one reach of thought. "Next
month," he answered looking down, and she asked, "Then you're
quite certain it's the life you want to lead?" After a pause and still
not looking at her face, though the white of her dress and the green
and gold of leaves above her filled his eyes, he said, "Why do you
ask, baroness?"

"Because the idea of celibacy terrifies me," she replied, and he
wanted to stretch out on the ground flecked with elm leaves like
thin oval coins of gold, and die.

"Sterility," she said, "you see, sterility is what I fear, I dread. It
is my enemy. I know we have other enemies, but I hate it most,
because it makes life less than death. And its allies are horrible:
hunger, sickness, deformation, and perversion, and ambition, and
the wish to be secure. What on earth are the children doing down
there?" Paul had asked Stanislas at lunch if they could play Ragnarok[5]

---

[5] the doom of the Norse gods, following the end of the world (ED.)

once more. Stanislas had consented, and so was now a Frost Giant storming with roars the ramparts of Asgard represented by a drainage ditch behind the pond. Odin[6] hurled lightning from the walls, and Thor[7]—"Stanislas!" called the mother rising slender and in white from her chair beside the young man, "don't let Zida use the hammer, please."

"I'm Thor, I'm Thor, I got to have a hammer!" Zida screamed. Stanislas intervened briefly, then made ready to storm the ramparts again, with Zida now at his side, on all fours. "She's Fenris the Wolf now," he called up to the mother, his voice ringing through the hot afternoon with the faintest edge of laughter. Grim and stern, one eye shut, Paul gripped his staff and faced the advancing armies of Hel and the Frozen Lands.

"I'm going to find some lemonade for everybody," the baroness said, and left Josef to sink at last face down on the earth, surrendering to the awful sweetness and anguish she had awakened in him, and would it ever sleep again? while down by the pond Odin strove with the icy army on the sunlit battlements of heaven.

Next day only the walls of the house were left standing. Inside it was only a litter of boxes and open drawers and hurrying people carrying things. Tomas and Zida escaped, he, being slow-witted amid turmoil and the only year-round occupant of Asgard, to clean up the yard out of harm's way, and she to the Little Woods all afternoon. At five Paul shrilled from his window, "The car! The car! It's coming!" An enormous black taxi built in 1923 groaned into the yard, feeling its way, its blind, protruding headlamps flashing in the western sun. Boxes, valises, the blue trunk and the two iron trunks were loaded into it by Tomas, Stanislas, Josef, and the taxi-driver from the village, under the agile and efficient supervision of Baron Severin Egideskar, holder of the Follen Chair of Medieval Studies at the University of Krasnoy. "And you'll get us back together with all this at the station tomorrow at eight—right?" The taxi-driver, who had done so each September for seven years, nodded. The taxi laden with the material impediments of seven people lumbered away, changing gears down the road in the weary, sunny stillness of late afternoon, in which the house stood intact once more room after empty room.

The baron now also escaped. Lighting a pipe he strolled slowly

---

[6] The supreme god of Germanic religion, as chief of the gods of Asgard, he established the laws that governed the universe. (ED.)

[7] Norse god of thunder and of war, Thor, the son of Odin, was armed with a magic hammer. (ED.)

but softly, like one escaping, past the pond and past Tomas's chick-encoops, along a fence overgrown with ripe wild grasses bowing their heavy, sunlit heads, down to the grove of weeping birch called the Little Woods. "Zida?" he said, pausing in the faint, hot shade shaken by the ceaseless trilling of crickets in the fields around the grove. No answer. In a cloud of blue pipesmoke he paused again beside an egg-crate decorated with many little bits of figured cloth and colored paper. On the mossy, much-trodden ground in front of it lay a wooden coat hanger. In one of the compartments of the crate was an eggshell painted gold, in another a bit of quartz, in another a breadcrust. Nearby, a small girl lay asleep with her shoes off, her rump higher than her head. The baron sat down on the moss near her, relit his pipe, and contemplated the egg-crate. Presently he tickled the soles of the child's feet. She snorted. When she began to wake, he took her onto his lap.

"What is that?"

"A trap for catching a unicorn." She brushed hair and leafmold off her face and arranged herself more comfortably on him.

"Caught any?"

"No."

"Seen any?"

"Paul and I found some tracks."

"Split-hoofed ones, eh?"

She nodded. Delicately through twilight in the baron's imagination walked their neighbor's young white pig, silver between birch trunks.

"Only young girls can catch them, they say," he murmured, and then they sat still for a long time.

"Time for dinner," he said. "All the tablecloths and knives and forks are packed. How shall we eat?"

"With our fingers!" She leapt up, sprang away. "Shoes," he ordered, and laboriously she fitted her small, cool, dirty feet into leather sandals, and then, shouting "Come on, papa!" was off. Quick and yet reluctant, seeming not to follow and yet never far behind her, he came on between the long vague shadows of the birch trees, along the fence, past the chickencoops and the shining pond, into captivity.

They all sat on the ground under the Four Elms. There was cold ham, pickles, cold fried eggplant with salt, hard bread and hard red wine. Elm leaves like thin coins stuck to the bread. The pure, void, windy sky of after-sunset reflected in the pond and in the wine. Stanislas and Paul had a wrestling match and dirt flew over the remains of the ham; the baroness and Rosa, lamenting, dusted the ham. The boys went off to run cars through the tunnel in High Cliff, and discuss what ruin the winter rains might cause. For it would rain. All the nine months they were gone from Asgard rain would beat on the roads and hills, and the tunnel would collapse. Stanislas lifted his head a moment thinking of the Oak in winter when he had never seen it, the roots of the tree that upheld the world drinking dark rain underground. Zida rode clear round the house twice on the shoulders of the unicorn, screaming loudly for pure joy, for eating outside on the ground with fingers, for the first star seen (only from the corner of the eye) over the high fields faint in twilight. Screaming louder with rage she was taken to bed by Rosa, and instantly fell asleep. One by one the stars came out, meeting the eye straight on. One by one the young people went to bed. Tomas with the last half-bottle sang long and hoarsely in the Dorian mode[8] in his room above the stable. Only the baron and his wife remained out in the autumn darkness under leaves and stars.

"I don't want to leave," she murmured.

"Nor I."

"Let's send the books and clothes on back to town, and stay here without them. . . ."

"Forever," he said: but they could not. In the observance of season lies order, which was their realm. They sat on for a while longer, close side by side as lovers of twenty; then rising he said, "Come along, it's late, Freya."[9] They went through darkness to the house, and entered.

In coats and hats, everyone ate bread and drank hot milk and coffee out on the porch in the brilliant early morning. "The car! It's coming!" Paul shouted, dropping his bread in the dirt. Grinding and changing gears, headlamps sightlessly flashing, the taxi came, it was there. Zida stared at it, the enemy within the walls, and began to cry. Faithful to the last to the lost cause of summer, she was carried into the taxi head first, screaming, "I won't go! I don't want to go!" Grinding and changing gears the taxi started. Stanislas's head stuck out of the right front window, the baroness's head out of the left rear, and Zida's red, desolate, and furious face was pressed against the oval back window, so that those three saw Tomas waving good-bye under the white walls of Asgard in the sunlight in the bowl of

[8] one of the eight scales used in medieval music (ED.)

[9] goddess of love, marriage, and fertility (ED.)

hills. Paul had no access to a window; but he was already thinking of the train. He saw, at the end of the smoke and the shining tracks, the light of candles in a high dark dining-room, the stare of a rockinghorse in an attic corner, leaves wet with rain overhead on the way to school, and a grey street shortened by a cold, foggy dusk through which shone, remote and festive, the first streetlight of December.

But all this happened a long time ago, nearly forty years ago; I do not know if it happens now, even in imaginary countries.

F O U R

American Society: The Legacy

The history of the world is none other than the progress of the consciousness of freedom.

Friedrich Hegel

The idea of the world's progress toward freedom is debated at some length in Section 12 of this book. But in considering the notion of progress we must also bear in mind that as a nation, a culture, and a society we are a product of our past. The central concern of this section is with our debt to our past: the inheritance we who live in the United States have received from those who were here before us. The past not only provides us with a measure of the present, but also with a sense of the legacy upon which we must build. While not all that we have received from the past is worth keeping, we must learn to build upon that which is most valuable, discard that which is of no use or even harmful, and nurture that which we can develop into something of value. It is a daunting task.

Jared Diamond and Alfred W. Crosby, Jr. recount how the vagaries of geography, which in turn affected plant and animal life, combined with other factors to affect the rise and spread of particular civilizations and nations, and the destruction of others. These authors contend that to a great extent our world today is the way it is as a result of geography—a more important factor, perhaps, than the actions of particular groups or individuals.

Still, the contributions of human beings play an important part in who we are today. The Declaration of Independence, the Constitution of the United States, and the Bill of Rights are all products of some of the most outstanding minds in recorded history. The effects of these documents reach far beyond the time and place in which they were written. Constitutions in dozens of other countries around the world have been based upon the United States Constitution. The important ideas and ideals of freedom, the worth of the individual, and strict limits on the power of the state have been incorporated not just into the formal structures of governments but into the minds of people all over the world.

Yet our past includes much that cries out for redress. The clarity of detail and the cry of pain in Frederick Douglass's narrative sear the mind and heart of the reader. In a country that prides itself on its legacy of freedom, there is also a history of slavery.

Both Chief Seattle and the women who wrote the Declaration of Sentiments and Resolutions from the Seneca Falls Convention remind us that other groups in our society did not, and do not yet, participate fully in the legacy of freedom of which we are so proud. Here too there is much to be done to fulfill the promise of freedom for all who live in our society, as well as to build a more complete legacy of freedom for future generations to cherish.

Often in the history of the United States, the government and the individual have come into conflict over matters of conscience. When such a conflict occurs, according to Henry David Thoreau, the individual has the right to commit civil disobedience. In his classic statement of this philosophy, Thoreau argues the rights of the individual over those of the government. Thoreau's ideas, too, are part of our legacy of freedom, a very important part.

The journey from the past to the present has been torturous, noble, ugly, bloody, heroic, and ultimately rewarding. It is a history of struggle, loss, discovery, and not a little progress. But as Frances FitzGerald points out in her essay, the richness of this history has been lost in a misguided attempt to make it appear pretty and inoffensive. This rewriting of history has glossed over the struggle of thousands of people of all races, cultures, and backgrounds to defend and extend the legacy of freedom.

You are probably familiar with some of the selections in this section, such as the Preamble to the Constitution, the Bill of Rights, the Declaration of Independence, and perhaps Thoreau's essay. Selections such as the statement from the Seneca Falls Convention, Chief Seattle's speech, and Clarence Darrow's speech, however, are probably new to you. As you read these latter selections, you might take notes recording your reactions. Your notes could then be used for a longer essay in which you explore how these readings affected your view of the history of the United States. You might also explore the similarities you find in Frances FitzGerald's and Jared Diamond's essays, for example. A more complicated topic to explore would be your idea of just what history is, and how you think history gets written.

JARED DIAMOND

The Accidental Conqueror

Jared Diamond (1937–   ) is a scientist and writer who studies the
birds of New Guinea and is a professor of physiology at the University of California Los Angeles School of Medicine. Diamond
writes on such diverse topics as smallpox, bird taxonomy, and language for a variety of publications including *Nature, Natural History,* and *Discover,* where he is a contributing editor and where
this selection first appeared.

Look around you in most locations in the United States and Australia
and most of the people you'll see will be of European ancestry. At
the same sites 500 years ago everyone without exception would have
been an American Indian or an aboriginal Australian. This is an
obvious feature of our daily life, and yet it poses a difficult question,
one with a far from obvious answer: Why is it that Europeans came
to replace most of the native population of North America and
Australia, instead of Indians or native Australians replacing the original population of Europe?

This question can be rephrased to ask, Why was the ancient rate
of technological development fastest in Eurasia, slower in the Americas (and in Africa south of the Sahara), and slowest in Australia? If
we look at the state of civilization in 1492—a highly significant year
for both Europeans and Native Americans—we find that Eurasian
peoples used iron tools, had writing and agriculture, and were on
the verge of industrialization. People in the Americas had agriculture
but no iron tools, only the Mayan and their neighbors had some
form of writing, and technology stood a few thousand years behind
that of Eurasia. Australians, meanwhile, lacked agriculture and writing altogether, and their stone tools were comparable to Eurasian
tools made more than 10,000 years earlier.

Nineteenth-century Europeans had a simple, racist explanation
for such inequality. They concluded that they themselves were inherently more intelligent than their New World counterparts; they
also concluded that they therefore had a manifest destiny to conquer,
displace, or kill these "inferior" peoples. The trouble with this answer
is not just that it was loathsome and arrogant but also that it was
completely wrong. Obviously people differ enormously in the knowl-

edge they acquire, depending on their circumstances as they grow up. But no convincing evidence of genetic differences in mental ability among peoples has ever been found—despite considerable effort.

Because of this history of racism, all questions regarding differences in the level of civilization among various peoples are rightly suspect. Nonetheless, the subject demands proper explanation. Technological differences among peoples have led to great tragedies in the past 500 years, and the legacies of colonialism and conquest still powerfully shape our world today. Until we can come up with a convincing alternative explanation for why those differences existed, the suspicion that racist genetic theories might be true will linger.

Yet we need not look so very far to find that alternative. Indeed, all we have to do is turn our attention from the people themselves to the land on which they lived, and we'll discover that the differences in the level of their respective civilizations arose not from genetics but from geography. Continents differed in the resources on which civilization depended—especially in the wild animal and plant species that proved useful for domestication. Continents also differed in the ease with which domesticated species could spread from one area to another. Even today we are painfully aware how distant geographic features, like the Strait of Hormuz or the Isthmus of Panama, can affect our lives. But geography has been molding human lives even more profoundly for hundreds of thousands of years.

As the biologist J.B.S. Haldane remarked, "Civilization is based, not only on men, but on plants and animals." Agriculture and herding made it possible to feed far more people per square mile of land than could live on the wild foods available in that same area. Storable food surpluses grown by some individuals permitted others to devote themselves to metallurgy, manufacturing, and writing. Domestic animals provided not only meat and milk to feed people but also wool and hides to clothe them and power to transport them and their goods. Animals also provided power to pull plows and carts and thus enabled people to increase agricultural productivity greatly over that previously attainable by human muscle power alone.

As a result, the world's human population rose from 10 million some 10,000 years ago, when we were all still hunter-gatherers, to its present count of more than 5 billion. Dense populations were a prerequisite to the rise of centralized states. Dense populations also promoted the evolution of infectious diseases, to which exposed populations evolved some resistance but other populations didn't. All these factors determined who colonized and conquered whom.

Europeans' conquest of America and Australia was due not to their better genes but to their worse germs (especially smallpox), more advanced technology (including weapons and ships), information storage through writing, and political organization—all stemming ultimately from continental differences in geography.

Let's start with the differences in domestic animals. By 4000 B.C. western Eurasia already had the "big five" domestic livestock that continue to dominate today: sheep, goats, pigs, cows, and horses. All provided food, power, and clothing. But the horse, in addition, was of incalculable military value, serving as the tank, the truck, and the jeep of warfare until the twentieth century. Why didn't Indians reap similar benefits by domesticating the corresponding native American mammal species: mountain sheep, mountain goats, peccaries, bison, and tapirs? Why didn't Indians mounted on tapirs, and native Australians mounted on kangaroos, invade and terrorize Eurasia?

The answer is simply that most animals don't take kindly to domestication. Even today people have managed to domesticate only a tiny fraction of the world's wild mammal species. Consider all the attempts that have failed. Innumerable species have reached the necessary first step of being kept captive as tame pets. In New Guinea villages you can routinely find tamed opossums and kangaroos, while in American Indian villages you can see tamed monkeys and weasels. Ancient Egyptians had tamed gazelles, antelopes, even hyenas and possibly giraffes. Romans were terrorized by the tamed African elephants with which Hannibal[1] crossed the Alps (not Asian elephants, the species seen in most circuses today).

But all these incipient efforts were flops. Since the domestication of horses about 4000 B.C. and reindeer a few thousand years later, no large European mammal has been added to our repertoire of successful domesticates. Our few species of domestic mammals were quickly winnowed from hundreds of others that had been tried and abandoned.

Why have efforts at domesticating most animal species proved futile? It turns out that a wild animal must possess a whole suite of unusual characteristics for domestication to succeed. First, in most cases the animal must be a social species living in herds. A herd's subordinate individuals are instinctively submissive toward dominant

---

[1] Hannibal (247–181 B.C.), a famous ancient general from Carthage, a city in what is now Tunisia, marched from Spain through France and the Alps to fight and lose to a Roman army. He is known for his use of elephants as pack animals. (ED.)

members of the herd, and they can transfer that behavior toward humans. Asian mouflon sheep (the ancestors of domestic sheep) have such submissive behavior, but North American bighorn sheep do not—a crucial difference that prevented their domestication by Indians. Among solitary territorial species, in fact, the only animals that have been domesticated are cats and ferrets.

Second, species such as gazelles and many deer and antelopes, which instantly take flight at signs of danger instead of standing their ground, prove too nervous to manage. Our failure to domesticate deer is especially striking, since there are few other wild animals with which humans have been so closely associated. Although deer have always been hunted and often tamed, only reindeer, among all the world's 41 deer species, have been successfully domesticated. Territorial behavior, flight reflexes, or both eliminated the other 40 species as candidates. Reindeer alone had the necessary tolerance of intruders and gregarious, nonterritorial behavior.

Finally, domestication requires that an animal can be bred in captivity. As zoos often discover to their dismay, captive animals may refuse to carry out a lengthy courtship and copulate under the watchful eyes of others. This problem has derailed persistent attempts to domesticate some potentially very valuable animals. For example, the finest wool in the world comes from vicuñas, a small camellike species native to the Andes. But neither the Incas nor modern ranchers have ever been able to domesticate them, and wool must still be obtained by capturing wild vicuñas. Royalty throughout history, from ancient Assyrian kings to nineteenth-century Indian maharajas, have tamed cheetahs for hunting. But every royal cheetah had to be captured from the wild, and not even zoos were able to breed them until 1960.

Collectively these reasons help explain why Eurasians succeeded in domesticating the big five but not other closely related species. American Indians did not domesticate bison, peccary, and mountain sheep and goats. The horse is especially interesting in illustrating what seemingly slight differences make one species prized, another useless. Horses belong to the order Perissodactyla, which consists of the hoofed mammals with an odd number of toes: horses, tapirs, and rhinoceroses. Of the 17 living species of Perissodactyla, all four tapirs and all five rhinos plus five of the eight wild horse species have never been domesticated. Africans or Indians mounted on rhinos or tapirs probably would have trampled any European invaders—but the animals never allowed that event to happen.

A sixth wild horse relative, the African wild ass, gave rise to domestic donkeys, which proved splendid as pack animals but useless as military chargers. The seventh wild horse relative, the onager of western Asia, may have been used to pull wagons for some centuries after 3000 B.C. But all accounts of the onager blast its disposition with words like "bad-tempered," "unapproachable," and "inherently intractable." The vicious beasts had to be kept muzzled to prevent them from biting their attendants. When domesticated horses reached the Middle East about 2300 B.C., onagers were finally kicked onto the scrap heap of failed domesticates.

Horses revolutionized warfare in a way that no other animal, not even elephants or camels, ever rivaled. At first, hitched to battle chariots, they became the unstoppable Sherman tanks of ancient war. After the invention of saddles and stirrups, they enabled Attila the Hun to devastate the Roman Empire, Genghis Khan to conquer an empire from the Adriatic to the Pacific coast of China, and military kingdoms to arise in West Africa. A few dozen horses helped Cortés and Pizarro, leading only a few hundred Spaniards each, to overthrow the two most populous and advanced New World states, the Aztec and Incan empires. Not until the futile Polish cavalry charges against Hitler's invading armies in September 1939 did the military importance of this most universally prized of all domestic animals finally come to an end, after 6,000 years.

Ironically, relatives of the horses that Cortés and Pizarro rode had formerly been native to the New World. Had those horses survived, Montezuma and Atahuallpa might have shattered the conquistadores with cavalry charges of their own. But, in a cruel twist of fate, the Americas' horses had become extinct long before that, along with 80 to 90 percent of the other large animal species of the Americas and Australia.

It happened around the time that the first human settlers—ancestors of modern Indians and native Australians—reached those continents. The Americas lost not only their horses but also other potentially domesticable species (after all, you never know until you try) like large camels, ground sloths, mammoths, and mastodons. Australia lost all its giant kangaroos, giant wombats, and rhinoceroslike diprotodonts. In fact Australia and North America ended up with no domesticable mammal species at all, unless Indian dogs were derived from North American wolves. South America was left with only the guinea pig (used for food), the alpaca (used for wool), and the llama (used as a pack animal but too small to carry a rider).

Consequently, domestic mammals made little contribution to the protein needs of native Australians and Americans. No native American or Australian mammal ever pulled a plow, cart, or war chariot, ever gave milk or bore a rider. The civilizations of the New World limped forward on human muscle power alone, while those of the Old World ran on the power of animal muscle, wind, and water.

Scientists still debate whether the prehistoric extinctions of most large American and Australian mammals were caused by climatic factors or by the first human settlers. Whichever was the case, the extinctions virtually ensured that, more than 10,000 years later, the descendants of those first settlers would be conquered by people from Eurasia and Africa, the continents that retained most of their large mammal species.

Do similar arguments apply to plants? Some parallels jump out immediately. As is true of animals, only a very few of all wild plant species have proved suitable for domestication. For example, plant species in which a single hermaphroditic individual can pollinate itself (like wheat) were domesticated earlier and more easily than cross-pollinating species (like rye). The reason is that self-pollinating varieties are easier to select and then maintain as true strains, since they're not continually mixing with their wild relatives. Oaks are another example. Although acorns were a major food source in prehistoric Europe and North America, no oak has ever been domesticated. For every domesticated plant that we still use today, many others were domesticated in the past and discarded. (What living American has eaten sumpweed, which Indians in the eastern United States domesticated for its seeds by 2000 B.C.?)

Such considerations certainly help explain the slow rate of technological development in Australia. That continent's relative poverty in wild plants appropriate for domestication undoubtedly contributed to the failure of aboriginal Australians to develop agriculture. But it's not so obvious why agriculture in the Americas lagged behind that in the Old World. After all, many plants now of worldwide importance were domesticated in the New World—potatoes, tomatoes, and squash, to name just a few. To find the solution to this puzzle, we need to take a close look at the New World's most important crop: corn.

Corn is a cereal—that is, a grass with edible starchy seeds, like barley kernels or wheat grains. Cereals still provide most of the calories consumed by the human race. While all civilizations have depended on them, different native cereals have been domesticated by different civilizations: wheat, barley, oats, and rye in the Near East and Europe; rice, foxtail millet, and broomcorn millet in China and southeast Asia; sorghum, pearl millet, and finger millet in sub-Saharan Africa; but only corn in the New World. Soon after Columbus's arrival, corn was brought back to Europe and spread around the globe, and it now covers more of the world's acreage than any other crop except wheat. Today corn is the most important crop in the United States. Why, then, didn't corn enable Indian civilizations to develop as fast as the Old World civilizations fed by wheat and other cereals?

Unfortunately, corn was a much bigger pain in the neck to develop, and it gave an inferior product. The Near East had more than a dozen wild grasses that were easy to domesticate and grow. Their large seeds, required by the highly seasonal climate (a very wet growing season, followed by an intense dry spell), made their value obvious to incipient farmers. They were easy to harvest en masse with a sickle, easy to grind, easy to prepare for cooking, and easy to sow. Another subtle advantage, first recognized by University of Wisconsin botanist Hugh Iltis, was that people didn't have to figure out for themselves that those wild grass seeds could be stored, since wild rodents in the Near East already made caches of up to 60 pounds of them.

The Old World grains were already productive in the wild. You can still harvest up to 700 pounds of grain per acre from wild wheat growing naturally on hillsides in the Near East. In a few weeks a family could harvest enough to feed itself for a year. Hence, even before wheat and barley were domesticated, there were villages in Palestine that had already developed sickles, mortars and pestles, and storage pits, and that were supporting themselves on wild grains.

Domestication of wheat and barley wasn't a conscious act. It wasn't the case that several hunter-gatherers sat down one day, mourned the extinction of big game animals, discussed which particular wheat plants were best, planted the seeds of those plants, and thereby became farmers the next year. Instead, the process we call domestication—the effecting of changes in wild plants under cultivation—was an unintended byproduct of people preferring some wild plants over others, and hence accidentally spreading the preferred seeds. In the case of wild cereals, people naturally preferred to harvest ones with big seeds, ones whose seeds were easy to remove from the seed coverings, and ones with firm, nonshattering stalks that held all the seeds together. It took only a few mutations, favored by this unconscious human selection, to produce the large-seeded, nonshattering cereal varieties that we refer to as domesticated.

Archeological evidence from ancient Near Eastern village sites shows that by 8000 B.C. wheat and barley were beginning to show these changes. The development of other domestic varieties and intentional sowing soon followed. Gradually the dependence on wild foods diminished. By 6000 B.C. crop cultivation had been integrated with animal herding into a complete food-production system. For better or worse, people were no longer hunter-gatherers but farmers and herders, en route to being civilized.

Now contrast these relatively straightforward Old World developments with the story in the New World. Mexico, the Andes, and the Amazon—where American farming began—lacked the Near East's type of highly seasonal climate, hence lacked large-seeded grasses that were already productive in the wild. Indians did start to domesticate three small-seeded wild grasses—maygrass, little barley, and a wild millet—but these were eventually displaced by corn. Yet the process was a tortuous one: the ancestor of corn was a Mexican wild grass called teosinte that, although it did have big seeds, in other respects hardly seemed promising at all.

Teosinte ears look so different from corn ears that teosinte's precise role in corn's ancestry has remained the subject of scientific argument until recently; even now some botanists remain unconvinced. No other crop underwent such drastic changes on domestication. Teosinte has only 6 to 12 kernels per ear, and they are inedible because they're enclosed in stone-hard cases. You can chew teosinte stalks like sugarcane, as Mexican farmers still do. But no one uses its seeds today, and probably no one did prehistorically either.

The key step that Itlis identified in teosinte's becoming useful sounds a bit drastic: the plant underwent a permanent sex change. In teosinte the side branches end in a tassel composed of male flowers; in corn they end in a female structure, the ear. Although that seems like a huge difference, it's really a simple hormonally controlled change that could have been started by a fungus, a virus, or a change in climate. Once some flowers on the tassel had changed sex to female, they would have produced edible naked grains likely to catch the attention of hungry hunter-gatherers. The tassel's central branch would then have been the beginning of a corn cob. Early Mexican sites have yielded remains of ears barely an inch long and much like the tiny ears of our "Tom Thumb" corn variety.

With that abrupt sex change, teosinte (alias corn) was now finally on the road to domestication. However, in contrast with Near Eastern cereals, thousands of years of development still lay ahead before high-yield corns capable of sustaining villages or cities resulted. Even then the final product was much harder for Indian farmers to manage than were the cereals of Old World farmers. Corn ears had to be harvested individually and by hand, rather than en masse with a sickle; the cobs had to be shucked; the kernels didn't fall off but had to be scraped or bitten off; and the seeds had to be planted individually, rather than scattered by the handful.

And the result was still poorer nutritionally than Old World cereals: lower protein content, deficiencies of important amino acids, and a deficiency of the vitamin niacin (a lack of which tends to cause the disease pellagra).[2] Alkali treatment of the grain was necessary to partially overcome these deficiencies.

In short, characteristics of the New World's staple food crop made its potential value much harder to discern in the wild plant, harder to develop by domestication, and harder to extract even after domestication. Much of the lag between New World and Old World civilization may have been due to the peculiarities of one plant.

In determining what suitable wild animal and plant species would be available for domestication, geography set the pace of Old and New World civilizations. But geography had another major role that deserves mention. Each civilization depended not only on its local domesticated food plants but also on others that arrived after having been domesticated elsewhere. The predominantly north-south axis of the New World made such diffusion of food plants difficult; the predominantly east-west axis of the Old World made it easy.

Today we take plant diffusion so much for granted that we seldom stop to think where our foods originated. A typical American meal might consist of chicken (of southeast Asian origin) with corn (from Mexico) or potatoes (from the southern Andes), seasoned with pepper (from India), accompanied by a piece of bread (from Near Eastern wheat) and butter (from Near Eastern cattle), and washed down by a cup of coffee (from Ethiopia). But this diffusion of valued plants and animals didn't begin just in modern times: it has been happening for thousands of years.

Plants and animals spread easily within a climate zone to which they're already adapted. To spread farther they have to develop new varieties with different tolerances. A glance at the map of the Old World shows how species could shift long distances without encountering a change of climate. Many of these shifts proved tremendously important in launching farming or herding in new areas or

---

[2] a disease marked by skin eruptions, gastrointestinal problems, and symptoms of nervous disorders (ED.)

enriching it in old areas. Species moved among China, India, the Near East, and Europe without ever leaving temperate latitudes. "America the Beautiful" may invoke our spacious skies, our amber waves of grain. But in reality the most spacious skies of the Northern Hemisphere were in the Old World, where amber waves of related grains came to stretch for 7,000 miles, from the English Channel to the China Sea.

The Romans were already growing wheat and barley from the Near East, peaches and citrus fruits from China, cucumbers and sesame from India, and hemp and onions from central Asia, along with oats and poppies originating locally in Europe. Horses spread from Russia to West Africa to transform the practice of warfare there, while goats and sheep spread down the highlands of East Africa to launch herding in southern Africa among the Hottentots,[3] who lacked locally domesticated animals of their own. African sorghum and cotton reached India by 2000 B.C., while bananas and yams from tropical southeast Asia crossed the Indian Ocean to enrich agriculture in tropical Africa.

In the New World, however, the temperate zone of North America is isolated from the temperate zone of the Andes and southern South America by thousands of miles of tropics, in which temperate-zone species can't survive. As a result, the llama, alpaca, and guinea pig of the Andes never spread in prehistoric times even as far north as Mexico, which remained without any domestic mammals to carry packs or to produce wool or meat. Likewise, potatoes failed to spread from the Andes to North America, while sunflowers never spread from North America to the Andes.

Many crops that were apparently shared prehistorically between North and South America actually occurred as different varieties or even species in the two continents, suggesting that they were domesticated independently in both areas. This seems true of cotton, lima beans, chili peppers, and tobacco. Corn did spread from Mexico to the rest of the Americas, but it evidently wasn't easy, perhaps because of the time it took to develop varieties suited to other latitudes. Not until A.D. 900—thousands of years after corn had emerged in Mexico—did it become a staple food in the Mississippi Valley.

If the Old and New Worlds had each been tilted, say, 90 or 60

---

[3] a people who live mainly in southwest Africa (ED.)

degrees away from their respective axes, the spread of crops and domestic animals would have been slower in the Old World and faster in the New World. The pace of civilization would have been correspondingly different. Who knows whether that difference would have sufficed to let Montezuma or Atahuallpa invade Europe, despite their lack of horses?

Continental differences in civilization, then, weren't an accident caused by a few individual geniuses. Nor were they the result of average differences in inventiveness among whole peoples. Instead, they were determined by geography, which sets ground rules for the biology of all plant and animal species, including our own. In the long run, and on a broad scale, where we live makes us who we are.

ALFRED W. CROSBY, JR.

Conquistador y Pestilencia

Alfred W. Crosby, Jr. (1931–) is a professor of history at the University of Texas, Austin. Crosby's writing frequently deals with international and health-oriented themes. His books include: *America, Russia, Hemp, and Napoleon: American Trade with Russia and the Baltic, 1783–1812* (1965), *The Columbian Exchange: Biological and Cultural Consequences of 1492* (1972), from which the following selection is taken, *Epidemic and Peace, 1918* (1976), and *Ecological Imperialism* (1986).

Why were the Europeans able to conquer America so easily? In our formal histories and in our legends, we always emphasize the ferocity and stubbornness of the resistance of the Aztec, Sioux, Apache, Tupinamba, Araucanian, and so on, but the really amazing thing about their resistance was its ineffectiveness. The Orientals held out against the Europeans much more successfully; they, of course, had the advantage of vast numbers and a technology much more advanced than that of the Indians. The Africans, however, were not "thousands of years ahead" of the Indians, except in possessing iron weapons, and yet the great mass of black Africans did not succumb to European conquest until the nineteenth century.

There are many explanations for the Europeans' success in America: the advantage of steel over stone, of cannon and firearms over bows and arrows and slings; the terrorizing effect of horses on foot soldiers who have never seen such beasts before; the lack of unity among the Indians, even within their empires; the prophecies in Indian mythology about the arrival of white gods. All these factors combined to deal to the Indian a shock such as only H. G. Wells's *War of the Worlds* can suggest to us. Each factor was undoubtedly worth many hundreds of soldiers to Cortés and Pizarro and other great Indian-killers.

For all of that, one might have at least expected the highly organized, militaristic societies of Mexico and the Andean highlands to survive the initial contact with the European societies. Thousands of Indian warriors, even if confused and frightened and wielding only obsidian-studded war clubs, should have been able to repel the first few hundred Spaniards to arrive. And what is the explanation for the fact that Indians were really only a little more successful in defending themselves and their lands after they learned that the invaders were not gods, after they obtained their own horses and guns and developed tactics to deal with the Europeans?

After the Spanish conquest an Indian of Yucatan wrote of his people in the happier days before the advent of the European:

> There was then no sickness; they had no aching bones; they had then no high fever; they had then no smallpox; they had then no burning chest; they had then no abdominal pain; they had then no consumption; they had then no headache. At that time the course of humanity was orderly. The foreigners made it otherwise when they arrived here.[1]

It would be easy to attribute this statement to the nostalgia that the conquered always feel for the time before the conqueror appeared, but the statement is probably in part true. During the millennia before the European brought together the compass and the three-masted vessel to revolutionize world history, men moved slowly, seldom over long distances and rarely across the great oceans. Men lived in the same continents where their great-grandfathers had lived and seldom caused violent and rapid changes in the delicate balance between themselves and their environments. Diseases tended to be endemic rather than epidemic. It is true that man did not achieve perfect accommodation with his microscopic parasites. Mutation, ecological changes, and migration brought the Black Death to Europe,

---

[1] *The Book of Chilam Balam of Chumayel,* trans. Ralph L. Roy, 83.

and few men lived to the proverbial age of three-score years and ten without knowing epidemic disease. Yet ecological stability did tend to create a crude kind of mutual toleration between human host and parasite. Most Europeans, for instance, survived measles and tuberculosis, and most West Africans survived yellow fever and malaria.

Migration of man and his maladies is the chief cause of epidemics. And when migration takes place, those creatures who have been longest in isolation suffer most, for their genetic material has been least tempered by the variety of world diseases. Among the major divisions of the species Homo sapiens, with the possible exception of the Australian aborigine, the American Indian probably had the dangerous privilege of longest isolation from the rest of mankind. Medical historians guess that few of the first rank killers among the diseases are native to the Americas.[2]

These killers came to the New World with the explorers and the conquistadors. The fatal diseases of the Old World killed more effectively in the New, and the comparatively benign diseases of the Old World turned killer in the New. There is little exaggeration in the statement of a German missionary in 1699 that "the Indians die so easily that the bare look and smell of a Spaniard causes them to give up the ghost."[3]

The most spectacular period of mortality among the American Indians occurred during the first hundred years of contact with the Europeans and Africans. Almost all the contemporary historians of the early settlements, from Bartolomé de las Casas to William Bradford of Plymouth Plantation, were awed by the ravages of epidemic disease among the native populations of America. In Mexico and Peru, where there were more Europeans and Africans—and, therefore, more contact with the Old World—and a more careful chronicle of events kept than in most other areas of America, the record shows something like fourteen epidemics in the former and perhaps as many as seventeen in the latter between 1520 and 1600.[4]

---

[2] P. M. Ashburn, *The Ranks of Death. A Medical History of the Conquest of America,* passim; Henry H. Scott, *A History of Tropical Medicine,* 1:128, 283; Sherburne F. Cook, "The Incidence and Significance of Disease among the Aztecs and Related Tribes," 321, 335; Jehan Vellard, "Causas Biológicas de la Desparición de los Indios Americanos," 77–93; Woodrow Borah, "America as Model: The Demographic Impact of European Expansion upon the Non-European World," 379–387.

[3] Quoted in E. Wagner Stern and Allen E. Stearn, *The Effect of Smallpox on the Destiny of the Amerindian,* 17.

[4] Charles Gibson, *The Aztecs under Spanish Rule,* 448–451; Henry F. Dobyns, "An Outline of Andean Epidemic History to 1720," 494.

The annals of the early Spanish empire are filled with complaints about the catastrophic decline in the number of native American subjects. When Antonio de Herrera wrote his multivolume history of that empire at the beginning of the seventeenth century, he noted as one of the main differences between the Old and New Worlds the extreme susceptibility of the natives of the latter to diseases, especially smallpox. Indian women, he wrote, were especially quick to succumb to it, but it rarely infected anyone of European birth. The Indians became so enraged by the invulnerability of the Spaniards to epidemic disease that they kneaded infected blood into their masters' bread and secreted corpses in their wells—to little effect.[5]

The victims of disease were probably greatest in number in the heavily populated highlands of New Spain (Mexico) and Peru, but, as a percentage of the resident population, were probably greatest in the hot, wet lowlands. By the 1580s disease, ably assisted by Spanish brutality, had killed off or driven away most of the peoples of the Antilles and the lowlands of New Spain, Peru, and the Caribbean littoral, "the habitation of which coasts is . . . so wasted and condemned, that of thirty parts of the people that inhabit it, there wants twenty-nine; and it is likely the rest of the Indians will in short time decay."[6]

It has often been suggested that the high mortality rates of these post-Columbian epidemics were due more to the brutal treatment of the Indians by the Europeans than to the Indians' lack of resistance to imported maladies. But the early chroniclers reported that the first epidemics following the arrival of Old World peoples in a given area of the New World were the worst, or at least among the worst. European exploitation had not yet had time to destroy the Indians' health.

The record shows that several generations of Indian contact with

[5] Antonio de Herrera y Tordesillas, *Historia General,* 2:35, Charles Gibson, *Spain in America,* 141–142.

[6] Joseph de Acosta, *The Natural and Moral History of the Indies,* 1:160. For specific references on depopulation see Antonio Vazquez de Espinosa, *Compendium and Description of the West Indies,* paragraphs 98, 102, 115, 271, 279, 334, 339, 695, 699, 934, 945, 1025, 1075, 1079, 1081, 1102, 1147, 1189, 1217, 1332, 1342, 1384, 1480, 1643, 1652, 1685, 1852, 1864, 1894, 1945, 1992, and 2050. An interesting comparison can be made between Spanish America and the Spanish Philippines. The aborigines of each suffered exploitation, but there were fewer epidemics and much less depopulation in the Philippines. Contact between these islands and the mainland of Asia had existed for many generations, and the Filipinos had acquired mainland immunities. See John L. Phelan, *The Hispanization of the Philippines,* 105–107; Emma H. Blair and James A. Robertson, eds., *Philippine Islands,* 12:311; 13:71; 30:309; 32:93–94; 34:292.

Europeans and Africans seemed to lead not to the total destruction of the Indians, but only to a sharp diminution of numbers, which was then followed by renewed population growth among the aborigines.[7] The relationships between these phenomena are too complex to be explained by any one theory. However, their sequence is perfectly compatible with the theory that the Indians had little or no resistance to many diseases brought from the Old World, and so first died in great numbers upon first contact with immigrants from Europe and Africa; and when those Indians with the weakest resistance to those maladies had died, interbreeding among the hardy survivors and, to some unmeasured extent, with the immigrants, led to the beginning of population recovery.

The record of early post-Columbian medical history of America was never kept carefully and much of it has been erased since, but it does seem to show a greater number of epidemics, characterized by a higher mortality rate, than was typical even in insalubrious Europe of that time. The very first was a pandemic which began in 1519 in the Greater Antilles and swept through Mexico, Central America, and—probably—Peru. It caused "in all likelihood the most severe single loss of aboriginal population that ever occurred," to quote one expert who has examined its history carefully.[8] It is the best documented of all of the first epidemics. We have no more than snatches of information on the others. Hans Staden, captive to the Tupinamba of Brazil in the early 1550s, was—ironically—saved from death by what may have been an epidemic. He convinced the local chief that the malady carrying off many of the Indians had been sent by the Christian God to punish them for their intention to eat Staden. In 1552 a respiratory disease killed many natives around Pernambucò. In the same decade epidemic broke out among the famished Frenchmen at Río de Janeiro, spread to the mission Indians there and killed eight hundred of them. In 1558 pleurisy and bloody flux spread along the coast from Río to Espírito Santo. In 1558 and 1560 smallpox arrived in Río de la Plata and swept off thousands of Indians, without touching a single Spaniard. Smallpox came to Brazil in 1562 and 1563 and carried off tens of thousands of Indians, but left the Portuguese unscathed. In some villages no one was left who

---

[7] Sherburne F. Cook and Woodrow Borah, *The Indian Population of Central Mexico, 1531–1610;* Sherburne F. Cook and Woodrow Borah, *The Aboriginal Population of Central Mexico on the Eve of the Spanish Conquest.*

[8] Dobyns, "Andean Epidemic History," 514.

was healthy enough to tend the sick, "not even someone who could go to the fountain for a gourdful of water."[9]

The English were as efficient disease carriers as the Latins. In 1585 Sir Frances Drake led a large expedition against Spain's overseas possessions. His men picked up some highly contagious fever— probably typhus—in the Cape Verde Islands and brought it along with them to the Caribbean and Florida. The malady spread to the Indians in the environs of St. Augustine and, "The wilde people . . . died verie fast and said amongst themselves, it was the Inglisshe God that made them die so faste."[10]

In 1587 the English founded a colony at Roanoke Island, a few hundred miles north of St. Augustine. The colonists' diagnoses of their immediate and fatal effect on many of the Indians was similar in medical philosophy to that expressed by the Florida Indians. Thomas Hariot wrote that there was no Indian village where hostility, open or hidden, had been shown,

> but that within a few dayes after our departure from everies such townes, that people began to die very fast, and many in short space; in some townes about twentie, in some fourtie, in some sixtie, & in one sixe score, which in trueth was very manie in respect to their numbers. . . . The disease also was so strange that they neither knew what it was, nor how to cure it; the like by report of the oldest men in the countrey never happened before, time out of mind.[11]

The natives of what is now the Atlantic coast of Canada had contact with Europeans—fishermen and fur traders—from very early in the sixteenth century, long before the English attempted coloni- zation at Roanoke or any other place in America. Depopulation was already apparent among their tribes by the time of French settlement. The Jesuit *Relations* contain a report dated 1616 from which the following paragraph is extracted. The Indians, it states,

> are astonished and often complain that, since the French mingle with and carry on trade with them, they are dying fast and the population is

---

[9] *Hans Staden, The True History of His Captivity,* trans. Malcolm Letts, 85–89; Alexander Marchant, *From Barter to Slavery: The Economic Relations of the Portuguese and Indians in the Settlement of Brazil, 1500–1580,* 116–117; Claude Lévi-Strauss, *A World on the Wane,* 87; Juan López de Velasco, *Geografia y Descripción Universidad de las Indias,* 552.

[10] David B. Quinn, ed., *The Roanoke Voyages,* 1:378.

[11] Ibid.

thinning out. For they assert that, before this association and intercourse, all their countries were very populous and they tell how one by one the different coasts, according as they have begun to traffic with us, have been more reduced by disease.[12]

These Indians looked south enviously to New England, where tribes were not diminishing. The turn of these Armouchiquois, as the Canadian Indians called them, came in the same year that the above report was written. In 1616 and 1617 a pestilence swept through New England, clearing the woods, in the words of Cotton Mather, "of those pernicious creatures, to make room for better growth." Whatever the sickness was, Europeans were immune to it. The handful of whites who passed the winter of 1616–1617 with the Indians of coastal Maine "lay in the cabins with those people that died, [but] not one of them ever felt their heads to ache, while they stayed there." The Massachusetts tribe was nearly completely exterminated, depopulating the area of Plymouth Bay at just about the same time that the Pilgrims were deciding to come to America. The same epidemic also swept the environs of Boston Bay. A European who lived in that area in 1622 wrote that the Indians had

> died on heapes, as they lay in their houses; and the living, that were able to shift for themselves, would runne away and let them dy, and let there Carkases ly above the ground without burial. . . . And the bones and skulls upon the severall places of their habitations made such a spectacle after my coming into those partes, that, as I travailed in the Forrest nere the Massachusetts, it seemed to me a new found Golgotha.[13]

There is no need to continue this lugubrious catalog. The records of every European people who have had prolonged contact with the native peoples of America are full of references to the devastating impact of Old World diseases. The Russians, the last to come, had the same experiences as the Spanish, Portuguese, English, and French; and thousands of Aleuts, Eskimos, and Tlingits were thrust into their graves by the maladies which the promyshlenniki[14]—as

---

[12] Quoted in Alfred G. Bailey, *The Conflict of European and Eastern Algonkian Cultures, 1504–1700: A Study in Canadian Civilization,* 13.

[13] Charles Francis Adams, *Three Episodes of Massachusetts History,* 1:1–12. [Golgotha was the place of Christ's crucifixion. (ED.)]

[14] industrialists (ED.)

innocent of intent as the conquistadors—brought to the New World with them.[15]

It would take a work of many volumes to give the full history of Old World diseases and New World peoples. We will limit ourselves to a detailed study of the first recorded American epidemic, an epidemic whose influence on the history of America is as unquestionable and as spectacular as that of the Black Death on the history of the Old World.

We know that the most deadly of the early epidemics in America were those of the eruptive fevers—smallpox, measles, typhus, and so on. The first to arrive and the deadliest, said contemporaries, was smallpox. Even today, however, smallpox is occasionally misdiagnosed as influenza, pneumonia, measles, scarlet fever, syphilis, or chicken pox.[16] Four hundred years ago such mistakes were even more common, and writers of the accounts upon which we must base our examination of the early history of smallpox in America did not have any special interest in accurate diagnosis. The early historians were much more likely to cast their eyes skyward and comment on the sinfulness that had called down such epidemics as obvious evidence of God's wrath than to describe in any detail the diseases involved. It should also be noted that conditions which facilitate the spread of one disease will usually encourage the spread of others, and that "very rarely is there a pure epidemic of a single malady." Pneumonia and pleurisy, for instance, often follow after smallpox, smothering those whom it has weakened.[17]

Furthermore, although the Spanish word *viruelas,* which appears again and again in the chronicles of the sixteenth century, is almost invariably translated as "smallpox," it specifically means not the disease but the pimpled, pustuled appearance which is the most obvious symptom of the disease. Thus the generation of the conquistadores may have used "viruelas" to refer to measles, chicken pox, or typhus. One must remember that people of the sixteenth century were not statistically minded, so their estimates of the num-

---

[15] Hubert Howe Bancroft, *History of Alaska, 1730–1885,* 350, 560–563.

[16] C. W. Dixon, *Smallpox,* 68.

[17] Franklin H. Top et al., *Communicable and Infectious Diseases,* 515; Hans Zinsser, *Rats, Lice and History,* 87–88.

bers killed by epidemic disease may be a more accurate measurement of their emotions than of the numbers who really died.

When the sixteenth-century Spaniard pointed and said "viruelas," what he meant and what he saw was usually smallpox. On occasion he was perfectly capable of distinguishing among diseases: for instance, he called the epidemic of 1531 in Central America *sarampión*—measles—and not viruelas.[18] We may proceed on the assumption that smallpox was the most important disease of the first pandemic in the recorded history of the Americas.

Smallpox has been so successfully controlled by vaccination and quarantine in the industrialized nations of the twentieth century that few North Americans or Europeans have ever seen it. But it is an old companion of humanity, and for most of the last millennium it was one of the commonest diseases in Europe. It was long thought, with reason, to be one of the most infectious maladies. Smallpox is usually communicated through the air by means of droplets or dust particles; its virus enters the new host through the respiratory tract. There are many cases of hospital visitors who have contracted the disease simply by breathing the air of a room in which someone lies ill with the disease.[19]

Because it is extremely communicable, before the eighteenth century it was usually thought of as a necessary evil of childhood, such as measles is today. Sometimes the only large group untouched by it was also that which had been relatively unexposed to it—the young. Yet even among Spanish children of the sixteenth century, smallpox was so common that Ruy Díaz de Isla, a medical writer, recorded that he had once seen a man of twenty years sick with the disease, "and he had never had it before."[20]

Where smallpox has been endemic, it has been a steady, dependable killer, taking every year from 3 to 10 percent of those who die. Where it has struck isolated groups, the death rate has been awesome. Analysis of figures for some twenty outbreaks shows that the case mortality among an unvaccinated population is about 30 percent. Presumably, in people who have had no contact whatever with smallpox, the disease will infect nearly every single individual it touches.

[18] Donald B. Cooper, *Epidemic Disease in Mexico City, 1761–1813*, 87–88; Raúl Porras Barrenechea, ed., *Cartas del Perú, 1524–1543*, 22, 24, 33, 46.

[19] Dixon, *Smallpox*, 171, 299–301.

[20] Ashburn, *Ranks of Death*, 86.

When in 1707 smallpox first appeared in Iceland, in two years 18,000 out of the island's 50,000 inhabitants died of it.[21]

The first people of the New World to meet the white and black races and their diseases were Arawaks of the Greater Antilles and the Bahamas. On the very first day of landfall in 1492 Columbus noted that they "are very unskilled with arms . . . [and] could all be subjected and made to do all that one wished."[22] These Arawaks lived long enough to provide the Spaniards with their first generation of slaves in America and Old World diseases with their first beachhead in the New World.

Oviedo, one of the earliest historians of the Americas, estimated that a million Indians lived on Santo Domingo when the Europeans arrived to plant their first permanent colony in the New World. "Of all those," Oviedo wrote, "and of all those born afterwards, there are not now believed to be at the present time in this year of 1548 five hundred persons, children and adults, who are natives and are the progeny or lineage of those first."[23]

The destruction of the Arawaks has been largely blamed on the Spanish cruelty, not only by the later Protestant historians of the "Black Legend" school but also by such contemporary Spanish writers as Oviedo and Bartolomé de Las Casas. Without doubt the early Spaniards brutally exploited the Indians. But it was obviously not in order to kill them off, for the early colonists had to deal with a chronic labor shortage and needed the Indians. Disease would seem to be a more logical explanation for the disappearance of the Arawaks, because they, like other Indians, had little immunity to Old World diseases. At the same time, one may concede that the effects of Spanish exploitation undoubtedly weakened their resistance to disease.

Yet it is interesting to note that there is no record of any massive smallpox epidemic among the Indians of the Antilles for a quarter of a century after the first voyage of Columbus. Indians apparently suffered a steady decline in numbers, which was probably due to extreme overwork, other diseases, and a general lack of will to live

---

[21] Dixon, *Smallpox,* 325; John Duffy, *Epidemics in Colonial America,* 20, 22; Stearn and Stearn, *Effect of Smallpox,* 14.

[22] Samuel Eliot Morison, *Admiral of the Ocean Sea, A Life of Christopher Columbus,* 1:304–305.

[23] Gonzalo Fernández Oviedo y Valdés, *Historia General y Natural de las Indias,* 2d ed., 1:66–67.

after their whole culture had been shattered by alien invasion.[24] How can the absence of smallpox be explained, if the American Indian was so susceptible and if ships carrying Europeans and Africans from the pestilential Old World were constantly arriving in Santo Domingo? The answer lies in the nature of the disease. It is a deadly malady, but it lasts only a brief time in each patient. After an incubation period of twelve days or so, the patient suffers from high fever and vomiting followed three or four days later by the characteristic skin eruptions. For those who do not die, these pustules dry up in a week or ten days and form scabs which soon fall off, leaving the disfiguring pocks that give the disease its name. The whole process takes a month or less, and after that time the patient is either dead or immune, at least for a period of years. Also there is no nonhuman carrier of smallpox, such as the flea of typhus or the mosquito of malaria; it must pass from man to man. Nor are there any long-term human carriers of smallpox, as, for instance, with typhoid and syphilis. It is not an over-simplification to say that one either has smallpox and can transmit it, or one has not and cannot transmit it.

Except for children, most Europeans and their slaves had had smallpox and were at least partially immune, and few but adults sailed from Europe and America in the first decades after discovery. The voyage was one of several weeks, so that, even if an immigrant or sailor contracted smallpox on the day of embarkation, he would most likely be dead or rid of its virus before he arrived in Santo Domingo. Moist heat and strong sunlight, characteristic of a tropical sea voyage, are particularly deadly to the smallpox virus. The lack of any rapid means of crossing the Atlantic in the sixteenth century delayed the delivery of the Old World's worst gift to the New.

It was delayed; that was all. An especially fast passage from Spain to the New World; the presence on a vessel of several nonimmune persons who could transmit the disease from one to the other until arrival in the Indies; the presence of smallpox scabs, in which the virus can live for weeks, accidentally packed into a bale of textiles— by any of these means smallpox could have been brought to Spanish America.[25]

In December 1518 or January 1519 a disease identified as small-

---

[24] Ibid.; *Colección de Documentos Inéditos Relativos al Descubrimiento, Conquista y Colonización de las Posesiones Españolas en América y Oceanía*, 1:428.

[25] S. P. Bedson et al., *Virus and Rickettsial Diseases*, 151–152, 157; Dixon, *Smallpox*, 174, 189, 296–297, 304, 359; Jacques M. May, ed., *Studies in Disease Ecology*, 1, 8.

pox appeared among the Indians of Santo Domingo, brought, said Las Casas, from Castile. It touched few Spaniards, and none of them died, but it devastated the Indians. The Spaniards reported that it killed one-third to one-half of the Indians. Las Casas, never one to understate the appalling, said that it left no more than one thousand alive "of that immensity of people that was on this island and which we have seen with our own eyes."[26]

Undoubtedly one must question these statistics, but they are not too far out of line with mortality rates in other smallpox epidemics, and with C. W. Dixon's judgment that populations untouched by smallpox for generations tend to resist the disease less successfully than those populations in at least occasional contact with it. Furthermore, Santo Domingo's epidemic was not an atypically pure epidemic. Smallpox seems to have been accompanied by respiratory ailments (*romadizo*), possibly measles, and other Indian-killers. Starvation probably also took a toll, because of the lack of hands to work the fields. Although no twentieth-century epidemiologist or demographer would find these sixteenth-century statistics completely satisfactory, they probably are crudely accurate.[27]

In a matter of days after smallpox appeared in Santo Domingo, it appeared in Puerto Rico. Before long, the Arawaks were dying a hideous and unfamiliar death throughout the islands of the Greater Antilles.[28] Crushed by a quarter-century of exploitation, they now performed their last function on earth: to act as a reserve of pestilence in the New World from which the conquistador drew invisible biological allies for his assault on the mainland.

Smallpox seems to have traveled quickly from the Antilles to Yucatán. Bishop Diego de Landa, the chief sixteenth-century Spanish informant on the people of Yucatán, recorded that sometime late in the second decade of that century "a pestilence seized them; characterized by great pustules, which rotted their bodies with a great stench, so that the limbs fell to pieces in four or five days." The *Book of Chilam Balam of Chumayel*, written in the Mayan language with

[26] *Colección de Documentos Inéditos*, 1:367, 369–370, 429; *Colección de Varios Documentos para la Historia de la Florida y Tierras Adyzacentes*, 1:44; Fray Bartolomé de Las Casas, *Obras Escogidas de Bartolomé de Las Casas*, 2:484.

[27] *Colección de Documentos Inéditos*, 1:368, 397–398, 428–429; Dixon, *Smallpox*, 317–318, 325.

[28] Pablo Alvarez Rubiano, *Pedrarias Dávila*, 608; *Colección de Varios Documentos para la Historia de la Florida*, 1:45.

European script after the Spanish settlement of Yucatán, also records that some time in the second decade "was when the eruption of pustules occurred. It was smallpox." It has been speculated that the malady came with Spaniards shipwrecked on the Yucatán coast in 1511 or with the soldiers and sailors of Hernández de Cordoba's expedition which coasted along Yucatán in 1517. Both these explanations seem unlikely, because smallpox had not appeared in the Greater Antilles, the likeliest source of any smallpox epidemic on the continent, until the end of 1518 or the beginning of 1519. Be that as it may, there is evidence that the Santo Domingan epidemic could have spread to the continent before Cortés's invasion of Mexico. Therefore, the epidemic raging there at that time may have come in two ways—north and west from Yucatán and directly from Cuba to central Mexico, brought by Cortés's troops.[29]

The melodrama of Cortés and the conquest of Mexico needs no retelling. After occupying Tenochtitlán and defeating the army of his rival, Narváez, he and his troops had to fight their way out of the city to sanctuary in Tlaxcala. Even as the Spanish withdrew, an ally more formidable than Tlaxcala appeared. Years later Francisco de Aguilar, a former follower of Cortés who had become a Dominican friar, recalled the terrible retreat of the *Noche Triste*. "When the Christians were exhausted from war, God saw fit to send the Indians smallpox, and there was a great pestilence in the city. . . ."[30]

With the men of Narváez had come a black man suffering from smallpox, "and he infected the household in Cempoala where he was quartered; and it spread from one Indian to another, and they, being so numerous and eating and sleeping together, quickly infected the whole country." The Mexicans had never seen smallpox before and did not have even the European's meager knowledge of how to deal with it. The old soldier-chronicler, Bernal Díaz del Castillo, called the Negro "a very black dose [for Mexico] for it was because of him that the whole country was stricken, with a great many deaths."[31]

[29] Diego de Landa, *Landa's Relación de las Cosas de Yucatán,* trans. Alfred M. Tozzer, 42; *Book of Chilam Balam,* 138.

[30] Patricia de Fuentes, ed. and trans., *The Conquistadors. First-Person Accounts of the Conquest of Mexico,* 159. For the argument that this was measles, not smallpox, see Horacio Figueroa Marroquin, *Enfermedades de los Conquistadores,* 49–67.

[31] Bernal Díaz del Castillo, *The Bernal Díaz Chronicles: The True Story of the Conquest of Mexico,* trans. Albert Idell, 250; Diego Durán, *The Aztecs: The History of the Indies in New Spain,* trans. Doris Heyden and Fernando Horcasitas, 323; Francisco López de

Probably, several diseases were at work. Shortly after the retreat from Tenochtitlán Bernal Díaz, immune to smallpox like most of the Spaniards, "was very sick with fever and was vomiting blood." The Aztec sources mention the racking cough of those who had smallpox, which suggests a respiratory complication such as pneumonia or a streptococcal infection, both common among smallpox victims. Great numbers of the Cakchiquel people of Guatemala were felled by a devastating epidemic in 1520 and 1521, having as its most prominent symptom fearsome nosebleeds. Whatever this disease was, it may have been present in central Mexico along with smallpox.[32]

The triumphant Aztecs had not expected the Spaniards to return after their expulsion from Tenochtitlán. The sixty days during which the epidemic lasted in the city, however, gave Cortés and his troops a desperately needed respite to reorganize and prepare a counterattack. When the epidemic subsided, the siege of the Aztec capital began. Had there been no epidemic, the Aztecs, their war-making potential unimpaired and their warriors fired with victory, could have pursued the Spaniards, and Cortés might have ended his life spread-eagled beneath the obsidian blade of a priest of Huitzilopochtli. Clearly the epidemic sapped the endurance of Tenochtitlán. As it was, the siege went on for seventy-five days, until the deaths within the city from combat, starvation, and disease—probably not smallpox now—numbered many thousands. When the city fell "the streets, squares, houses, and courts were filled with bodies, so that it was almost impossible to pass. Even Cortés was sick from the stench in his nostrils."[33]

Peru and the Andean highlands were also hit by an early epidemic, and if it was smallpox it most probably had to pass through the Isthmus of Panama, as did Francisco Pizarro himself. The documen-

Gómara, *Cortés, the Life of the Conqueror by His Secretary,* trans. Lesley Byrd Simpson, 204–205; Toribio Motolinía, *Motolinía's History of the Indians of New Spain,* trans. Elizabeth A. Foster, 38; Bernardino de Sahagún, *Florentine Codex: General History of the Things of New Spain,* trans. Arthur J. O. Anderson and Charles E. Dibble, 9:4.

[32] *Anales de Tlatelolco, Unos Anales Históricos de la Nación Mexicana y Códice de Tlatelolco,* 64. *The Annals of the Cakchiquels and Title of the Lords of Totonicapan,* trans. Adrian Recinos, Dionisio José Chonay and Delia Goetz, 115–116; Bedson, *Virus,* 155; Díaz del Castillo, *Chronicles,* 289; Miguel Léon-Portilla, ed., *The Broken Spears: The Aztec Account of the Conquest of Mexico,* 132; Top, *Diseases,* 515.

[33] Hernando Cortés, *Five Letters,* trans. J. Bayard Morris, 226; Díaz del Castillo, *Chronicles,* 405–406; López de Gómara, *Cortés,* 285, 293; León-Portilla, *Broken Spears,* 92; Sahagún, *Florentine Codex,* 13:81.

tation of the history of Panama in the first years after the conquest is not as extensive as that of Mexico or the Incan areas, because the Isthmus had fewer riches and no civilized indigenous population to learn European script from the friars and write its own history. We do know that in the first decades of the sixteenth century the same appalling mortality took place among the Indians in Central America as in the Antilles and Mexico. The recorded medical history of the Isthmus began in 1514 with the death, in one month, of seven hundred Darien[34] settlers, victims of hunger and an unidentified disease. Oviedo, who was in Panama at the time of greatest mortality, judged that upwards of two million Indians died there between 1514 and 1530, and Antonio de Herrera tells us that forty thousand died of disease in Panama City and Nombre de Dios alone in a twenty-eight-year period during the century. Others wrote of the depopulation of "four hundred leagues" of land that had "swarmed" with people when the Spanish first arrived.[35]

What killed the Indians? Contemporaries and many historians blame the carnage on Pedrarias Dávila, who executed Balboa and ruled Spain's first Central American settlements with such an iron hand that he was hated by all the chief chroniclers of the age. It can be effectively argued, however, that he was no more a berserk butcher of Indians than Pizarro, for the mortality among Indians of the Isthmus during his years of power is parallel to the high death rates among the Indians wherever the Spaniards went.[36] When charges against Pedrarias were investigated in 1527, his defenders maintained that the greatest Indian-killer had been an epidemic of smallpox. This testimony is hard to reject, for another document of 1527 mentions the necessity of importing aboriginal slaves into Panama City, Nata, and the port of Honduras, because smallpox had carried off all the Indians in those areas.[37]

The Spaniards could never do much to improve the state of public

---

[34] a province in Panama (ED.)

[35] Colección de Documentos Inéditos, 37:200; Oviedo, Historia General, 2d ed., 3:353. For corroboration see M. M. Alba C., Etnología y Población Historica, passim; Porras Barrenechea, Cartas del Perú, 24; López de Velasco, Geografía, 341; Relaciones Históricas y Geográficas de América Central, 216–218.

[36] Herrera, Historia General, 5:350; Relaciones Históricas y Geográficas, 200.

[37] Alvarez, Pedrarias Dávila, 608, 619, 621, 623; Colección de Documentos para la Historia de Costa Rica, 4:8.

health in Panama. In 1660 those who governed Panama City listed as resident killers and discomforters smallpox, measles, pneumonia, suppurating abscesses, typhus, fevers, diarrhea, catarrh, boils, and hives—and blamed them all on the importation of Peruvian wine![38] Of all the killers operating in early Panama, however, smallpox was undoubtedly the most deadly to the Indians.

If we attempt to describe the first coming of Old World disease to the areas south of Panama, we shall have to deal with ambiguity, equivocation, and simple guesswork, for eruptive fever, now operating from continental bases, apparently outstripped the Spaniards and sped south from the Isthmus into the Incan Empire before Pizarro's invasion. Long before the invasion, the Inca Huayna Capac was aware that the Spaniards—"monstrous marine animals, bearded men who moved upon the sea in large houses"—were pushing down the coast from Panama. Such is the communicability of smallpox and the other eruptive fevers that any Indian who received news of the Spaniards could also have easily received the infection of the European diseases. The biological defenseless Indians made vastly more efficient carriers of such pestilence than the Spaniards.[39]

Our evidence for the first post-Columbian epidemic in Incan lands is entirely hearsay, because the Incan people had no system of writing. Therefore, we must depend on secondary accounts by Spaniards and by Indians born after the conquest, accounts based on Indian memory and written down years and even decades after the epidemic of the 1520s. The few accounts we have of the great epidemic are associated with the death of Huayna Capac. He spent the last years of his life campaigning against the people of what is today

[38] Pascual de Andagoya, *Narrative of the Proceedings of Pedrarias Dávila,* trans. Clements R. Markham, 6; *Colección de Documentos Inéditos,* 17:219–222; Herrera, *Historia General,* 4:217; Scott, *Tropical Medicine,* 1:192, 288.

[39] Garcilaso de la Vega, *First Part of the Royal Commentaries of the Yncas,* trans. Clements R. Markham, 2:456–457. Fernando Montesinos, *Memorias Antiguas Historiales del Perú,* trans. Philip A. Means, 126. Pedro Sarmiento de Gamboa, *History of the Incas,* trans. Clements R. Markham, 187. It has been suggested that the source of the great epidemic in question was two men, Alonso de Molina and Ginés, left behind by Pizarro at Tumbez on the reconnaissance voyage of 1527. Pedro de Cieza de León, *The Incas of Pedro Cieza de León,* ed. Victor W. von Hagen, trans. Harriet de Onis, n. 51. If the epidemic was smallpox or measles, this explanation is unlikely, because these diseases are of short duration and have no carrier state. The expedition of which these men were members had had no contact with pestilential Panama for some time before it returned there from Tumbez. If these two men caught smallpox or measles, it must have been already present among the Indians.

northern Peru and Ecuador. There, in the province of Quito, he first
received news of an epidemic raging in his empire, and there he
himself was stricken. Huayna Capac and his captains died with shocking rapidity, "their faces being covered with scabs."

Of what did the Inca and his captains die? One of the most
generally reliable of our sources, Garcilaso de la Vega, describes
Huayna Capac's death as the result of "a trembling chill . . . , which
the Indians call *chucchu,* and a fever, called by the Indians *rupu.* . . ."
We dare not, four hundred years later, state unequivocally that the
disease was not one native to the Americas. Most accounts call it
smallpox, or suggest that it was either smallpox or measles. Smallpox
seems the best guess because the epidemic struck in that period when
the Spaniards, operating from bases where smallpox was killing multitudes, were first coasting along the shores of Incan lands.[40]

The impact of the smallpox pandemic on the Aztec and Incan
Empires is easy for the twentieth-century reader to underestimate.
We have so long been hypnotized by the daring of the conquistador
that we have overlooked the importance of his biological allies.
Because of the achievements of modern medical science we find it
hard to accept statements from the conquest period that the pandemic
killed one-third to one-half of the populations struck by it. Toribio
Motolinía claimed that in most provinces of Mexico "more than one
half of the population died; in others the proportion was little
less. . . . They died in heaps, like bedbugs."

The proportion may be exaggerated, but perhaps not as much as
we might think. The Mexicans had no natural resistance to the
disease at all. Other diseases were probably operating quietly and
efficiently behind the screen of smallpox. Add the factors of food
shortage and the lack of even minimal care for the sick. Motolinía
wrote, "Many others died of starvation, because as they were all taken
sick at once, they could not care for each other, nor was there anyone
to give them bread or anything else." We shall never be certain what

[40] Felipe Guamán Poma Ayala, *Nueva Corónica y Buen Govierno,* 85–86. Cieza de León,
Incas, 52, 253; Bernabé Cobo, *Obras,* 2:93. Garcilaso de la Vega, *Royal Commentaries,*
2:461; Martín de Murúa, *Historia General del Perú, Origen y Descendencia de los Incas,*
1:103–104; Clements R. Markham, ed. and trans., *Narratives of the Rites and Laws of
the Incas,* 110; Pedro Pizarro, *Relation of the Discovery and Conquest of the Kingdoms
of Peru,* trans. Philip A. Means, 1:196–198; Sarmiento de Gamboa, *History of the Incas,*
167–168; Miguel Cabello Valboa, *Miscelánea Antártica, una Historia del Perú Antiguo,*
393–394; Marcos Jiménez de la Espada, ed., *Relaciones Geograficas de Indias-Perú,*
2:267.

the death rate was, but from all evidence, it must have been immense. Sherburne F. Cook and Woodrow Borah estimate that, for one cause and another, the population of central Mexico dropped from about 25 million on the eve of conquest to 16.8 million a decade later. This estimate strengthens confidence in Motolinía's general veracity.[41]

South of Panama, in the empire of the Incas, our only means of estimating the mortality of the epidemic of the 1520s is by an educated guess. The population there was thick, and it provided a rich medium for the transmission and cultivation of communicable diseases. If the malady which struck in the 1520s was smallpox, as it seems to have been, then it must have taken many victims, for these Indians probably had no more knowledge of or immunity to smallpox than the Mexicans. Most of our sources tell us only that many died. Cieza de León gives a figure of 200,000, and Martín de Murúa, throwing up his hands, says, "infinite thousands."[42]

We are reduced to guesswork. Jehan Vellard, student of the effect of disease on the American Indian, states that the epidemics in Peru and Bolivia after the Spanish conquest killed fewer than those in Mexico and suggests the climatic conditions of the Andean highlands as the reason. But smallpox generally thrives under dry, cool conditions. Possibly historians have omitted an account of the first and, therefore, probably the worst post-Columbian epidemic in the Incan areas because it preceded the Spanish conquest.[43] A half century or so after the conquest, Indians in the vicinity of Lima maintained that the Spanish could not have conquered them if, a few years before Pizarro's invasion, respiratory disease had not "consumed the greater part of them."[44] Was this the great killer of the 1520s in the Incan Empire? Perhaps future archaeological discoveries will give us more definite information.

The pandemic not only killed great numbers in the Indian empires, but it also affected their power structures, striking down the leaders and disrupting the processes by which they were normally replaced. When Montezuma died, his nephew, Cuitláhuac, was

---

[41] Cook and Borah, *Aboriginal Population*, 4, 89; Motolinía, *History*, 38; Sahagún, *Florentine Codex*, 13:81.

[42] Ashburn, *Ranks of Death*, 20; Cieza de León, *Incas*, 52; Murúa, *Historia General*, 1:104; Pizarro, *Relation*, 1:196.

[43] Vellard, "Causas Biológicas," 85; Bedson, *Virus*, 157, 167; Dixon, *Smallpox*, 313.

[44] Reginaldo de Lizárrago, *Descripción Colonial por Fr. Reginaldo de Lizárrago*, 1:136.

elected lord of Mexico. It was he who directed the attacks on the Spaniards during the disastrous retreat from Tenochtitlán, attacks which nearly ended the story of Cortés and his soldiers. Then Cuitláhuac died of smallpox. Probably many others wielding decisive power in the ranks of the Aztecs and their allies died in the same period, breaking dozens of links in the chain of command. Bernal Díaz tells of an occasion not long after Tenochtitlán when the Indians did not attack "because between the Mexicans and the Texcocans there were differences and factions"[45] and, of equal importance, because they had been weakened by smallpox.

Outside Tenochtitlán the deaths due to smallpox among the Indian ruling classes permitted Cortés to cultivate the loyalty of several men in important positions and to promote his own supporters. Cortés wrote to Charles V about the city of Cholula: "The natives had asked me to go there, since many of their chief men had died of the smallpox, which rages in these lands as it does in the islands, and they wished me with their approval and consent to appoint other rulers in their place." Similar requests, quickly complied with, came from Tlaxcala, Chalco, and other cities. "Cortés had gained so much authority," the old soldier Bernal Díaz remembered, "that Indians came before him from distant lands, especially over matters of who would be chief or lord, as at the time smallpox had come to New Spain and many chiefs died."[46]

Similarly in Peru the epidemic of the 1520s was a stunning blow to the very nerve center of Incan society, throwing that society into a self-destructive convulsion. The government of the Incan Empire was an absolute autocracy with a demigod, the Child of the Sun, as its emperor. The loss of the emperor could do enormous damage to the whole society, as Pizarro proved by his capture of Atahualpa. Presumably the damage was greater if the Inca were much esteemed, as was Huayna Capac. When he died, said Cieza de León, the mourning "was such that the lamentation and shrieks rose to the skies, causing the birds to fall to the ground. The news traveled far and wide, and nowhere did it not evoke great sorrow." Pedro Pizarro, one of the first to record what the Indians told of the last days before the conquest, judged that had "this Huayna Capac been alive when

---

[45] Díaz del Castillo, *Chronicles,* 282, 301; López de Gómara, *Cortés,* 238–239.

[46] Cortés, *Five Letters,* 136; Díaz del Castillo, *Chronicles,* 289, 311.

we Spaniards entered this land, it would have been impossible for us to win it, for he was much beloved by all his vassals."[47]

Not only the Inca but many others in key positions in Incan society died in the epidemic. The general Mihcnaca Mayta and many other military leaders, the governors Apu Hilaquito and Auqui Tupac (uncle and brother to the Inca), the Inca's sister, Mama Coca, and many others of the royal family all perished of the disease. The deaths of these important persons must have robbed the empire of much resiliency. The most ominous loss of all was the Inca's son and heir Ninan Cuyoche.[48]

In an autocracy no problem is more dangerous or more chronic than that of succession. One crude but workable solution is to have the autocrat himself choose his successor. The Inca named one of his sons, Ninan Cuyoche, as next wearer of "the fringe" or crown, on the condition that the *calpa,* a ceremony of divination, show this to be an auspicious choice. The first *calpa* indicated that the gods did not favor Ninan Cuyoche, the second that Huascar was no better a candidate. The high nobles returned to the Inca for another choice, and found him dead. Suddenly a terrible gap had opened in Incan society: the autocrat had died, and there was no one to take his place. One of the nobles moved to close the gap. "Take care of the body," he said, "for I go to Tumipampa to give the fringe to Ninan Cuyoche." But it was too late. When he arrived at Tumipampa, he found that Ninan Cuyoche had also succumbed to the smallpox pestilence.[49]

Among the several varying accounts of the Inca's death the one just related best fits the thesis of this chapter. And while these accounts may differ on many points, they all agree that confusion over the succession followed the unexpected death of Huayna Capac. War broke out between Huascar and Atahualpa, a war which devastated the empire and prepared the way for a quick Spanish conquest. "Had the land not been divided between Huascar and Atahualpa," Pedro Pizarro wrote, "we would not have been able to enter

---

[47] Cieza de León, *Incas,* 53; Pizarro, *Relation,* 1:198–199.

[48] Ayala, *Nueva Corónica,* 86; Cobo, *Obras,* 2:93; Sarmiento de Gamboa, *History of the Incas,* 167–168; Valboa, *Miscelánea Antártica,* 393.

[49] Sarmiento de Gamboa, *History of the Incas,* 167–168, 197–199; for corroboration see Cieza de León, *Incas,* 253; Valboa, *Miscelánea Antártica,* 394.

or win the land unless we could gather a thousand Spaniards for the task, and at that time it was impossible to get together even five hundred Spaniards."[50]

The psychological effect of epidemic disease is enormous, especially of an unknown disfiguring disease which strikes swiftly. Within a few days smallpox can transform a healthy man into a pustuled, oozing horror, whom his closest relatives can barely recognize. The impact can be sensed in the following terse, stoic account, drawn from Indian testimony, of Tenochtitlán during the epidemic.

> It was [the month of] Tepeilhuitl when it began, and it spread over the people as great destruction. Some it quite covered [with pustules] on all parts—their faces, their heads, their breasts, etc. There was a great havoc. Very many died of it. They could not walk; they only lay in their resting places and beds. They could not move; they could not stir; they could not change position, nor lie on one side; nor face down, nor on their backs. And if they stirred, much did they cry out. Great was its [smallpox] destruction. Covered, mantled with pustules, very many people died of them.[51]

In some places in Mexico the mortality was so great that, as Motolinía recorded, the Indians found it impossible to bury the great number of dead. "They pulled down the houses over them in order to check the stench that rose from the dead bodies," he wrote, "so that their homes became their tombs." In Tenochtitlán the dead were cast into the water, "and there was a great, foul odor; the smell issued forth from the dead."[52]

For those who survived, the horror was only diminished, for smallpox is a disease which marks its victims for the rest of their lives. The Spanish recalled that the Indians who survived, having scratched themselves, "were left in such a condition that they frightened the others with the many deep pits on their faces, hand, and bodies." "And on some," an Indian said, "the pustules were widely separated; they suffered not greatly, neither did many [of them] die. Yet many people were marred by them on their faces; one's face or

[50] Pizarro, *Relation,* 1:199.

[51] Sahagún, *Florentine Codex,* 13:81.

[52] Motolinía, *History,* 38; Sahuagún, *Florentine Codex,* 9:4.

nose was pitted." Some lost their sight—a fairly common aftereffect of smallpox.[53]

The contrast between the Indians' extreme susceptibility to the new disease and the Spaniards' almost universal immunity, acquired in Spain and reinforced in pestilential Cuba, must have deeply impressed the native Americans. The Indians, of course, soon realized that there was little relationship between Cortés and Quetzalcoatl, and that the Spaniards had all the vices and weaknesses of ordinary men, but they must have kept a lingering suspicion that the Spaniards were some kind of supermen. Their steel swords and arquebuses, their marvelously agile galleys, and, above all, their horses could only be the tools and servants of supermen. And their invulnerability to smallpox—surely this was a shield of the gods themselves!

One can only imagine the psychological impact of smallpox on the Incans. It must have been less than in Mexico, because the disease and the Spaniards did not arrive simultaneously, but epidemic disease is terrifying under any circumstances and must have shaken the confidence of the Indians that they still enjoyed the esteem of their gods. Then came the long, ferocious civil war, confusing a people accustomed to the autocracy of the true Child of the Sun.[54] And then the final disaster, the coming of the Spaniards.

The Mayan peoples, probably the most sensitive and brilliant of all American aborigines, expressed more poignantly than any other Indians the overwhelming effect of epidemic. Some disease struck into Guatemala in 1520 and 1521, clearing the way for the invasion shortly thereafter by Pedro de Alvarado, one of Cortés's captains. It was apparently not smallpox, for the accounts do not mention pustules but emphasize nosebleeds, coughs, and illness of the bladder as the prominent symptoms. It may have been influenza;[55] whatever it was, the Cakchiquel Mayas, who kept a chronicle of the tragedy for their posterity, were helpless to deal with it. Their words speak for all the Indians touched by Old World disease in the sixteenth century:

---

[53] Sahagún, *Florentine Codex*, vol. 13:81, López de Gómara, *Cortés*, 204–205; Dixon, *Smallpox*, 94; A. J. Rhodes and C. E. van Rooyen, *Textbook of Virology*, 2d. ed., 319.

[54] The Inca Indians considered the sun god Inti their divine ancestor; thus, the Incan ruler was considered the Child of the Sun. (ED.)

[55] F. Webster McBryde, "Influenza in America during the Sixteenth Century," 296–297.

Great was the stench of the dead. After our fathers and grandfathers succumbed, half of the people fled to the fields. The dogs and vultures devoured the bodies. The mortality was terrible. Your grandfathers died, and with them died the son of the king and his brothers and kinsmen. So it was that we became orphans, oh, my sons! So we became when we were young. All of us were thus. We were born to die![56]

THOMAS JEFFERSON

Letter to James Madison

Thomas Jefferson (1743–1826), third president of the United States (1801–1809), drafted the Declaration of Independence and, as president, negotiated the Louisiana Purchase. Best known as a statesman who believed in equality and individual liberty, he was also an architect, lawyer, scientist, inventor, city planner, and the founder of the University of Virginia. *Notes on Virginia* (1785) is his only full-length book, but he was a prolific writer of letters, essays, political documents, and biographical and autobiographical sketches.

Paris, Dec. 20, 1787

Dear Sir

. . . I like much the general idea of framing a government which should go on of itself peaceably, without needing continual recurrence to the state legislatures. I like the organization of the government into Legislative, Judiciary and Executive. I like the power given the Legislature to levy taxes; and for that reason solely approve of the greater house being chosen by the people directly. For tho' I think a house chosen by them will be very illy qualified to legislate for the Union, for foreign nations &c. yet this evil does not weigh against the good of preserving inviolate the fundamental principle that the people are not to be taxed but by representatives chosen immediately by themselves. I am captivated by the compromise of

---

[56] *Annals of the Cakchiquels,* trans. Recinos, Chonay, Goetz, 116.

the opposite claims of the great and little states, of the latter to equal, and the former to proportional influence. I am much pleased too with the substitution of the method of voting by persons, instead of that of voting by states: and I like the negative given to the Executive with a third of either house, though I should have liked it better had the Judiciary been associated for that purpose, or invested with a similar and separate power. There are other good things of less moment. I will now add what I do not like. First the omission of a bill of rights providing clearly and without the aid of sophisms for freedom of religion, freedom of the press, protection against standing armies, restriction against monopolies, the eternal and unremitting force of the habeas corpus laws, and trials by jury in all matters of fact triable by the laws of the land and not by the law of Nations. To say, as Mr. Wilson does that a bill of rights was not necessary because all is reserved in the case of the general government which is not given, while in the particular ones all is given which is not reserved might do for the Audience to whom it was addressed, but is surely gratis dictum,[1] opposed by strong inferences from the body of the instrument, as well as from the omission of the clause of our present confederation which had declared that in express terms. It was a hard conclusion to say because there has been no uniformity among the states as to the cases triable by jury, because some have been so incautious as to abandon this mode of trial, therefore the more prudent states shall be reduced to the same level of calamity. It would have been much more just and wise to have concluded the other way that as most of the states had judiciously preserved this palladium, those who had wandered should be brought back to it, and to have established general right instead of general wrong. Let me add that a bill of rights is what the people are entitled to against every government on earth, general or particular, and what no just government should refuse, or rest on inference. The second feature I dislike, and greatly dislike, is the abandonment in every instance of the necessity of rotation in office, and most particularly in the case of the President. Experience concurs with reason in concluding that the first magistrate will always be re-elected if the constitution permits it. He is then an officer for life. This once observed it becomes of so much consequence to certain nations to have a friend or a foe at the head of our affairs that they will interfere with money and

[1] gratuitous (ED.)

with arms. A Galloman or an Angloman will be supported by the
nation he befriends. If once elected, and at a second or third election
outvoted by one or two votes, he will pretend false votes, foul play,
hold possession of the reins of government, be supported by the
states voting for him, especially if they are the central ones lying in
a compact body themselves and separating their opponents: and they
will be aided by one nation of Europe, while the majority are aided
by another. The election of a President of America some years hence
will be much more interesting to certain nations of Europe than ever
the election of a king of Poland was. Reflect on all the instances in
history ancient and modern, of elective monarchies, and say if they
do not give foundation for my fears, the Roman emperors, the popes,
while they were of any importance, the German emperors till they
became hereditary in practice, the kings of Poland, the Deys of the
Ottoman dependancies. It may be said that if elections are to be
attended with these disorders, the seldomer they are renewed the
better. But experience shews that the only way to prevent disorder
is to render them uninteresting by frequent changes. An incapacity
to be elected a second time would have been the only effectual
preventative. The power of removing him every fourth year by the
vote of the people is a power which will not be exercised. The king
of Poland is removeable every day by the Diet, yet he is never
removed.—Smaller objections are the Appeal in fact as well as law,
and the binding all persons Legislative, Executive and Judiciary by
oath to maintain that constitution. I do not pretend to decide what
would be the best method of procuring the establishment of the
manifold good things in this constitution, and of getting rid of the
bad. Whether by adopting it in hopes of future amendment, or, after
it has been duly weighed and canvassed by the people, after seeing
the parts they generally dislike, and those they generally approve, to
say to them 'We see now what you wish. Send together your deputies
again, let them frame a constitution for you omitting what you have
condemned, and establishing the powers you approve. Even these
will be a great addition to the energy of your government.'—At all
events I hope you will not be discouraged from other trials, if the
present one should fail of its full effect.—I have thus told you freely
what I like and dislike: merely as a matter of curiosity for I know
your own judgment has been formed on all these points after having
heard every thing which could be urged on them. I own I am not a
friend to a very energetic government. It is always oppressive. The
late rebellion in Massachusetts has given more alarm than I think it
should have done. Calculate that one rebellion in 13 states in the

course of 11 years, is but one for each state in a century and a half. No country should be so long without one. Nor will any degree of power in the hands of government prevent insurrections. France with all it's despotism, and two or three hundred thousand men always in arms has had three insurrections in the three years I have been here in every one of which greater numbers were engaged than in Massachusetts and a great deal more blood was spilt. In Turkey, which Montesquieu[2] supposes more despotic, insurrections are the events of every day. In England, where the hand of power is lighter than here, but heavier than with us they happen every half dozen years. Compare again the ferocious depredations of their insurgents with the order, the moderation and the almost self extinguishment of ours.—After all, it is my principle that the will of the Majority should always prevail. If they approve the proposed Convention in all it's parts, I shall concur in it chearfully, in hopes that they will amend it whenever they shall find it work wrong. I think our governments will remain virtuous for many centuries; as long as they are chiefly agricultural; and this will be as long as there shall be vacant lands in any part of America. When they get piled upon one another in large cities, as in Europe, they will become corrupt as in Europe. Above all things I hope the education of the common people will be attended to; convinced that on their good sense we may rely with the most security for the preservation of a due degree of liberty. I have tired you by this time with my disquisitions and will therefore only add assurances of the sincerity of those sentiments of esteem and attachment with which I am Dear Sir your affectionate friend & servant,

Th: Jefferson

P.S. The instability of our laws is really an immense evil. I think it would be well to provide in our constitutions that there shall always be a twelvemonth between the ingrossing a bill and passing it: that it should then be offered to it's passage without changing a word: and that if circumstances should be thought to require a speedier passage, it should take two thirds of both houses instead of a bare majority.

---

[2] Charles de Montesquieu (1689–1755) was a French political philosopher whose major work, *The Spirit of the Laws,* was an important contribution to the writing of constitutions around the world, including the Constitution of the United States. (ED.)

Preamble to the Constitution of the United States and the Bill of Rights

We the people of the United States, in order to form a more perfect union, establish justice, insure domestic tranquillity, provide for the common defense, promote the general welfare, and secure the blessings of liberty to ourselves and our posterity, do ordain and establish this Constitution for the United States of America.

AMENDMENTS

First Ten Amendments passed by Congress Sept. 25, 1789. Ratified by three-fourths of the States December 15, 1791.

AMENDMENT I

Congress shall make no law respecting an establishment of religion, or prohibiting the free exercise thereof; or abridging the freedom of speech, or of the press; or the right of the people peaceably to assemble, and to petition the government for a redress of grievances.

AMENDMENT II

A well regulated militia, being necessary to the security of a free State, the right of the people to keep and bear arms, shall not be infringed.

AMENDMENT III

No soldier shall, in time of peace be quartered in any house, without the consent of the owner, nor in time of war, but in a manner to be prescribed by law.

AMENDMENT IV

The right of the people to be secure in their persons, houses, papers, and effects, against unreasonable searches and seizures, shall not be violated, and no warrants shall issue, but upon probable cause, supported by oath or affirmation, and particularly describing the place to be searched, and the persons or things to be seized.

AMENDMENT V

No person shall be held to answer for a capital, or otherwise infamous crime, unless on a presentment or indictment of a grand jury, except in cases arising in the land or naval forces, or in the militia, when in actual service in time of war or public danger; nor shall any person be subject for the same offense to be twice put in jeopardy of life or limb; nor shall be compelled in any criminal case to be a witness against himself, nor be deprived of life, liberty, or property, without due process of law; nor shall private property be taken for public use without just compensation.

AMENDMENT VI

In all criminal prosecutions, the accused shall enjoy the right to a speedy and public trial, by an impartial jury of the State and district wherein the crime shall have been committed, which district shall have been previously ascertained by law, and to be informed of the nature and cause of the accusation; to be confronted with the witnesses against him; to have compulsory process for obtaining witnesses in his favor, and to have the assistance of counsel for his defense.

AMENDMENT VII

In suits at common law, where the value in controversy shall exceed twenty dollars, the right of trial by jury shall be preserved, and no fact tried by a jury shall be otherwise re-examined in any court of the United States, than according to the rules of the common law.

AMENDMENT VIII

Excessive bail shall not be required, nor excessive fines imposed, nor cruel and unusual punishments inflicted.

AMENDMENT IX

The enumeration in the Constitution of certain rights shall not be construed to deny or disparage others retained by the people.

AMENDMENT X

The powers not delegated to the United States by the Constitution, nor prohibited by it to the States, are reserved to the States
respectively, or to the people.

THOMAS JEFFERSON

The Declaration of Independence

Thomas Jefferson (1743–1826), the third president of the United
States (1801–1809), was a prolific writer of letters, essays, and
political documents. As head of the committee that prepared the
Declaration of Independence, Jefferson wrote and presented the
first draft to Congress. The final draft was adopted July 4, 1776.

When, in the course of human events, it becomes necessary for one
people to dissolve the political bands which have connected them
with another, and to assume, among the powers of the earth, the
separate and equal station to which the laws of nature and of nature's
God entitle them, a decent respect to the opinions of mankind requires that they should declare the causes which impel them to the
separation.

We hold these truths to be self-evident, that all men are created
equal; that they are endowed by their Creator with certain inalienable
rights; that among these, are life, liberty, and the pursuit of happiness.
That, to secure these rights, governments are instituted among men,
deriving their just powers from the consent of the governed; that,
whenever any form of government becomes destructive of these ends,
it is the right of the people to alter or to abolish it, and to institute
a new government, laying its foundation on such principles, and
organizing its powers in such form, as to them shall seem most likely
to effect their safety and happiness. Prudence, indeed, will dictate
that governments long established, should not be changed for light
and transient causes; and, accordingly, all experience hath shown,
that mankind are more disposed to suffer, while evils are sufferable,
than to right themselves by abolishing the forms to which they are
accustomed. But, when a long train of abuses and usurpations, pur-

suing invariably the same object, evinces a design to reduce them under absolute despotism, it is their right, it is their duty, to throw off such government and to provide new guards for their future security. Such has been the patient sufferance of these colonies, and such is now the necessity which constrains them to alter their former systems of government. The history of the present King of Great Britain is a history of repeated injuries and usurpations, all having, in direct object, the establishment of an absolute tyranny over these States. To prove this, let facts be submitted to a candid world:—

He has refused his assent to laws the most wholesome and necessary for the public good.

He has forbidden his governors to pass laws of immediate and pressing importance, unless suspended in their operation till his assent should be obtained; and, when so suspended, he has utterly neglected to attend to them.

He has refused to pass other laws for the accommodation of large districts of people, unless those people would relinquish the right of representation in the legislature: a right inestimable to them, and formidable to tyrants only.

He has called together legislative bodies at places unusual, uncomfortable, and distant from the depository of their public records, for the sole purpose of fatiguing them into compliance with his measures.

He has dissolved representative houses repeatedly for opposing, with manly firmness, his invasions on the rights of the people.

He has refused, for a long time after such dissolutions, to cause others to be elected; whereby the legislative powers, incapable of annihilation, have returned to the people at large for their exercise; the state remaining, in the meantime, exposed to all the danger of invasion from without, and convulsions within.

He has endeavored to prevent the population of these States; for that purpose, obstructing the laws of naturalization of foreigners, refusing to pass others to encourage their migration hither, and raising the conditions of new appropriations of lands.

He has obstructed the administration of justice, by refusing his assent to laws for establishing judiciary powers.

He has made judges dependent on his will alone, for the tenure of their offices, and the amount and payment of their salaries.

He has erected a multitude of new offices, and sent hither swarms of officers, to harass our people, and eat out their substance.

He has kept among us, in time of peace, standing armies, without the consent of our legislatures.

He has affected to render the military independent of, and superior to, the civil power.

He has combined, with others, to subject us to a jurisdiction foreign to our Constitution, and unacknowledged by our laws; giving his assent to their acts of pretended legislation:

For quartering large bodies of armed troops among us:

For protecting them by a mock trial, from punishment, for any murders which they should commit on the inhabitants of these States:

For cutting off our trade with all parts of the world:

For imposing taxes on us without our consent:

For depriving us, in many cases, of the benefit of trial by jury:

For transporting us beyond seas to be tried for pretended offenses:

For abolishing the free system of English laws in a neighboring province, establishing therein an arbitrary government, and enlarging its boundaries, so as to render it at once an example and fit instrument for introducing the same absolute rule into these colonies:

For taking away our charters, abolishing our most valuable laws, and altering, fundamentally, the powers of our governments:

For suspending our own legislatures, and declaring themselves invested with power to legislate for us in all cases whatsoever.

He has abdicated government here, by declaring us out of his protection, and waging war against us.

He has plundered our seas, ravaged our coasts, burnt our towns, and destroyed the lives of our people.

He is, at this time, transporting large armies of foreign mercenaries to complete the works of death, desolation, and tyranny, already begun, with circumstances of cruelty and perfidy scarcely paralleled in the most barbarous ages, and totally unworthy the head of a civilized nation.

He has constrained our fellow citizens, taken captive on the high seas, to bear arms against their country, to become the executioners of their friends, and brethren, or to fall themselves by their hands.

He has excited domestic insurrections amongst us, and has endeavored to bring on the inhabitants of our frontiers, the merciless Indian savages, whose known rule of warfare is an undistinguished destruction of all ages, sexes, and conditions.

In every stage of these oppressions, we have petitioned for redress, in the most humble terms; our repeated petitions have been answered only by repeated injury. A prince, whose character is thus marked by every act which may define a tyrant, is unfit to be the ruler of a free people.

Nor have we been wanting in attention to our British brethren.

We have warned them, from time to time, of attempts made by their legislature to extend an unwarrantable jurisdiction over us. We have reminded them of the circumstances of our emigration and settlement here. We have appealed to their native justice and magnanimity, and we have conjured them, by the ties of our common kindred, to disavow these usurpations, which would inevitably interrupt our connections and correspondence. They, too, have been deaf to the voice of justice and consanguinity. We must, therefore, acquiesce in the necessity which denounces our separation, and hold them, as we hold the rest of mankind, enemies in war, in peace, friends.

We, therefore, the representatives of the United States of America, in general Congress assembled, appealing to the Supreme Judge of the world for the rectitude of our intentions, do, in the name, and by the authority of the good people of these colonies, solemnly publish and declare, that these united colonies are, and of right ought to be, free and independent states: that they are absolved from all allegiance to the British Crown, and that all political connection between them and the state of Great Britain is, and ought to be, totally dissolved; and that, as free and independent states, they have full power to levy war, conclude peace, contract alliances, establish commerce, and to do all other acts and things which independent states may of right do. And, for the support of this declaration, with a firm reliance on the protection of Divine Providence, we mutually pledge to each other our lives, our fortunes, and our sacred honor.

SENECA FALLS CONVENTION

Declaration of Sentiments and Resolutions

The Seneca Falls Convention, held July 19–20, 1848, in Seneca Falls, New York, was the first assembly for women's rights in the United States. It was organized by abolitionists and suffragists Elizabeth Cady Stanton and Lucretia Coffin Mott. Stanton's Declaration of Sentiments and Resolutions, which was modelled after the Declaration of Independence, was debated, amended, and adopted by the convention and became the foundation of the women's movement in this country.

When, in the course of human events, it becomes necessary for one portion of the family of man to assume among the people of the earth a position different from that which they have hitherto occupied, but one to which the laws of nature and of nature's God entitle them, a decent respect to the opinions of mankind requires that they should declare the causes that impel them to such a course.

We hold these truths to be self-evident: that all men and women are created equal; that they are endowed by their Creator with certain inalienable rights; that among these are life, liberty, and the pursuit of happiness; that to secure these rights governments are instituted, deriving their just powers from the consent of the governed. Whenever any form of government becomes destructive of these ends, it is the right of those who suffer from it to refuse allegiance to it, and to insist upon the institution of a new government, laying its foundation on such principles, and organizing its powers in such form, as to them shall seem most likely to effect their safety and happiness. Prudence, indeed, will dictate that governments long established should not be changed for light and transient causes; and accordingly all experience hath shown that mankind are more disposed to suffer, while evils are sufferable, than to right themselves by abolishing the forms to which they were accustomed. But when a long train of abuses and usurpations, pursuing invariably the same object, evinces a design to reduce them under absolute despotism, it is their duty to throw off such government, and to provide new guards for their future security. Such has been the patient sufferance of the women under this government, and such is now the necessity which constrains them to demand the equal station to which they are entitled.

The history of mankind is a history of repeated injuries and usurpations on the part of man toward woman, having in direct object the establishment of an absolute tyranny over her. To prove this, let facts be submitted to a candid world.

He has never permitted her to exercise her inalienable right to the elective franchise.

He has compelled her to submit to laws, in the formation of which she had no voice.

He has withheld from her rights which are given to the most ignorant and degraded men—both natives and foreigners.

Having deprived her of this first right of a citizen, the elective franchise, thereby leaving her without representation in the halls of legislation, he has oppressed her on all sides.

He has made her, if married, in the eye of the law, civilly dead.

He has taken from her all right in property, even to the wages she earns.

He has made her, morally, an irresponsible being, as she can commit many crimes with impunity, provided they be done in the presence of her husband. In the covenant of marriage, she is compelled to promise obedience to her husband, he becoming to all intents and purposes, her master—the law giving him power to deprive her of her liberty, and to administer chastisement.

He has so framed the laws of divorce, as to what shall be the proper causes, and in case of separation, to whom the guardianship of the children shall be given, as to be wholly regardless of the happiness of women—the law, in all cases, going upon a false supposition of the supremacy of man, and giving all power into his hands.

After depriving her of all rights as a married woman, if single, and the owner of property, he has taxed her to support a government which recognizes her only when her property can be made profitable to it.

He has monopolized nearly all the profitable employments, and from those she is permitted to follow, she receives but a scanty remuneration. He closes against her all the avenues to wealth and distinction which he considers most honorable to himself. As a teacher of theology, medicine, or law, she is not known.

He has denied her the facilities for obtaining a thorough education, all colleges being closed against her.

He allows her in Church, as well as State, but a subordinate position, claiming Apostolic authority for her exclusion from the ministry, and, with some exceptions, from any public participation in the affairs of the Church.

He has created a false public sentiment by giving to the world a different code of morals for men and women, by which moral delinquencies which exclude women from society, are not only tolerated, but deemed of little account in man.

He has usurped the prerogative of Jehovah himself, claiming it as his right to assign for her a sphere of action, when that belongs to her conscience and to her God.

He has endeavored, in every way that he could, to destroy her confidence in her own powers, to lessen her self-respect, and to make her willing to lead a dependent and abject life.

Now, in view of this entire disfranchisement of one-half the people of this country, their social and religious degradation—in view of the unjust laws above mentioned, and because women do feel themselves aggrieved, oppressed, and fraudulently deprived of their most sacred rights, we insist that they have immediate admission to all the rights and privileges which belong to them as citizens of the United States.

In entering upon the great work before us, we anticipate no small amount of misconception, misrepresentation, and ridicule; but we shall use every instrumentality within our power to effect our object. We shall employ agents, circulate tracts, petition the State and National legislatures, and endeavor to enlist the pulpit and the press in our behalf. We hope this Convention will be followed by a series of Conventions embracing every part of the country.

[The following resolutions were discussed by Lucretia Mott, Thomas and Mary Ann McClintock, Amy Post, Catharine A. F. Stebbins, and others, and were adopted:]

WHEREAS, The great precept of nature is conceded to be, that "man shall pursue his own true and substantial happiness." Blackstone[1] in his Commentaries remarks, that this law of Nature being coeval with mankind, and dictated by God himself, is of course superior in obligation to any other. It is binding over all the globe, in all countries and at all times; no human laws are of any validity if contrary to this, and such of them as are valid, derive all their force, and all their validity, and all their authority, mediately and immediately, from this original; therefore,

Resolved, That such laws as conflict, in any way, with the true and substantial happiness of woman, are contrary to the great precept of nature and of no validity, for this is "superior in obligation to any other."

Resolved, That all laws which prevent woman from occupying such a station in society as her conscience shall dictate, or which place her in a position inferior to that of man, are contrary to the great precept of nature, and therefore of no force or authority.

Resolved, That woman is man's equal—was intended to be so by

[1] Sir William Blackstone (1723–1780) was an English jurist who wrote *Commentaries on the Laws of England,* a well-known description of the doctrines of English law. (ED.)

the Creator, and the highest good of the race demands that she should be recognized as such.

Resolved, That the women of this country ought to be enlightened in regard to the laws under which they live, that they may no longer publish their degradation by declaring themselves satisfied with their present position, nor their ignorance, by asserting that they have all the rights they want.

Resolved, That inasmuch as man, while claiming for himself intellectual superiority, does accord to woman moral superiority, it is pre-eminently his duty to encourage her to speak and teach, as she has an opportunity, in all religious assemblies.

Resolved, That the same amount of virtue, delicacy, and refinement of behavior that is required of woman in the social state, should also be required of man, and the same transgressions should be visited with equal severity on both man and woman.

Resolved, That the objection of indelicacy and impropriety, which is so often brought against woman when she addresses a public audience, comes with a very ill-grace from those who encourage, by their attendance, her appearance on the stage, in the concert, or in feats of the circus.

Resolved, That woman has too long rested satisfied in the circumscribed limits which corrupt customs and a perverted application of the Scriptures have marked out for her, and that it is time she should move in the enlarged sphere which her great Creator has assigned her.

Resolved, That it is the duty of the women of this country to secure to themselves their sacred right to the elective franchise.

Resolved, That the equality of human rights results necessarily from the fact of the identity of the race in capabilities and responsibilities.

Resolved, therefore, That, being invested by the Creator with the same capabilities, and the same consciousness of responsibility for their exercise, it is demonstrably the right and duty of woman, equally with man, to promote every righteous cause by every righteous means; and especially in regard to the great subjects of morals and religion, it is self-evidently her right to participate with her brother in teaching them, both in private and in public, by writing and by speaking, by any instrumentalities proper to be used, and in any assemblies proper to be held; and this being a self-evident truth growing out of the divinely implanted principles of human nature, any custom or authority adverse to it, whether modern or wearing the hoary sanction of antiquity, is to be regarded as a self-evident falsehood, and at war with mankind.

[At the last session Lucretia Mott offered and discussed the following resolution:]

Resolved, That the speedy success of our cause depends upon the zealous and untiring efforts of both men and women, for the overthrow of the monopoly of the pulpit, and for the securing to woman an equal participation with men in the various trades, professions, and commerce.

HENRY DAVID THOREAU

On the Duty of Civil Disobedience

Henry David Thoreau (1817–1862) was an essayist, poet, and natural historian now considered to be one of the greatest figures in nineteenth-century literature and history. Thoreau, who was born and lived most of his life in Concord, Massachusetts, is best known for his book *Walden: or, Life in the Woods* (1854). His other works include *A Week on the Concord and Merrimack Rivers* (1849), *The Maine Woods* (1864), *Cape Cod* (1865), and *A Yankee in Canada* (1866). In 1849, to protest slavery and the Mexican– American War, Thoreau refused to pay a poll tax. While in jail for this offense he wrote the following essay, "Civil Disobedience"; its message of passive resistance was later embraced by both Mahatma Ghandi and Martin Luther King, Jr.

I heartily accept the motto—"That government is best which governs least"; and I should like to see it acted up to more rapidly and systematically. Carried out, it finally amounts to this, which also I believe,—"That government is best which governs not at all"; and when men are prepared for it, that will be the kind of government which they will have. Government is at best but an expedient; but most governments are usually, and all governments are sometimes, inexpedient. The objections which have been brought against a standing army, and they are many and weighty, and deserve to prevail, may also at last be brought against a standing government. The standing army is only an arm of the standing government. The government itself, which is only the mode which the people have chosen to execute their will, is equally liable to be abused and perverted before the people can act through it. Witness the present Mexican war,[1] the work of comparatively a few individuals using the standing government as their tool; for, in the outset, the people would not have consented to this measure.

This American government—what is it but a tradition, though a recent one, endeavoring to transmit itself unimpaired to posterity, but each instant losing some of its integrity? It has not the vitality and force of a single living man; for a single man can bend it to his will. It is a sort of wooden gun to the people themselves. But it is not the less necessary for this; for the people must have some complicated machinery or other, and hear its din, to satisfy that idea of government which they have. Governments show us how successfully men can be imposed on, even impose on themselves, for their own advantage. It is excellent, we must all allow. Yet this government never of itself furthered any enterprise, but by the alacrity with which it got out of its way. *It* does not keep the country free. *It* does not settle the West. *It* does not educate. The character inherent in the American people has done all that has been accomplished; and it would have done somewhat more, if the government had not sometimes got in its way. For government is an expedient by which men would fain succeed in letting one another alone; and, as has been said, when it is most expedient, the governed are most let alone by it. Trade and commerce, if they were not made of India-rubber, would never manage to bounce over the obstacles which legislators are continually putting in their way; and, if one were to judge these men wholly by the effects of their actions and not partly by their intentions, they would deserve to be classed and punished with those mischievous persons who put obstructions on the railroads.

But, to speak practically and as a citizen, unlike those who call themselves no-government men, I ask for, not at once no government, but *at once* a better government. Let every man make known what kind of government would command his respect, and that will be one step toward obtaining it.

---

[1] The Mexican War was fought between Mexico and the United States from 1846 to 1848; though a number of factors were involved, the most immediate cause was the U.S. annexation of Texas in December of 1845. (ED.)

After all, the practical reason why, when the power is once in the hands of the people, a majority are permitted, and for a long period continue, to rule is not because they are most likely to be in the right, nor because this seems fairest to the minority, but because they are physically the strongest. But a government in which the majority rule in all cases cannot be based on justice, even as far as men understand it. Can there not be a government in which majorities do not virtually decide right and wrong, but conscience—in which majorities decide only those questions to which the rule of expediency is applicable? Must the citizen ever for a moment, or in the last degree, resign his conscience to the legislator? Why has every man a conscience, then? I think that we should be men first, and subjects afterward. It is not desirable to cultivate a respect for the law so much as for the right. The only obligation which I have a right to assume is to do at any time what I think right. It is truly enough said, that a corporation has no conscience; but a corporation of conscientious men is a corporation with a conscience. Law never made men a whit more just; and, by means of their respect for it, even the well-disposed are daily made the agents of injustice. A common and natural result of an undue respect for law is, that you may see a file of soldiers, colonel, captain, corporal, privates, powder-monkeys, and all, marching in admirable order over hill and dale to the war, against their will, ay, against their common sense and consciences, which makes it very steep marching indeed, and produces a palpitation of the heart. They have no doubt that it is a damnable business in which they are concerned; they are all peaceably inclined. Now, what are they? Men at all? or small movable forts and magazines, at the service of some unscrupulous man in power? Visit the Navy-Yard, and behold a marine, such a man as an American government can make, or such as it can make a man with its black arts—a mere shadow and reminiscence of humanity, a man laid out alive and standing, and already, as one may say, buried under arms with funeral accompaniments, though it may be,—

> Not a drum was heard, not a funeral note,
>   As his corpse to the rampart we hurried;
> Not a soldier discharged his farewell shot
>   O'er the grave where our hero we buried.[2]

The mass of men serve the state thus, not as men mainly, but as machines, with their bodies. They are the standing army, and the

---

[2] From "The Burial of Sir John Moore at Carunna" by Irish poet Charles Wolfe. (ED.)

militia, jailors, constables, posse comitatus, etc. In most cases there is no free exercise whatever of the judgment or of the moral sense; but they put themselves on a level with wood and earth and stones; and wooden men can perhaps be manufactured that will serve the purpose as well. Such command no more respect than men of straw or a lump of dirt. They have the same sort of worth only as horses and dogs. Yet such as these even are commonly esteemed good citizens. Others—as most legislators, politicians, lawyers, ministers, and officeholders—serve the state chiefly with their heads; and, as they rarely make any moral distinctions, they are as likely to serve the Devil, without intending it, as God. A very few, as heroes, patriots, martyrs, reformers in the great sense, and men, serve the state with their consciences also, and so necessarily resist it for the most part; and they are commonly treated as enemies by it. A wise man will only be useful as a man, and will not submit to be "clay," and "stop a hole to keep the wind away," but leave that office to his dust at least:—

> I am too high-born to be propertied,
> To be a secondary at control,
> Or useful serving-man and instrument
> To any sovereign state throughout the world.[3]

He who gives himself entirely to his fellow-men appears to them useless and selfish; but he who gives himself partially to them is pronounced a benefactor and philanthropist.

How does it become a man to behave toward this American government to-day? I answer, that he cannot without disgrace be associated with it. I cannot for an instant recognize that political organization as my government which is the slave's government also.

All men recognize the right of revolution; that is, the right to refuse allegiance to, and to resist, the government, when its tyranny or its inefficiency are great and unendurable. But almost all say that such is not the case now. But such was the case, they think, in the Revolution of '75. If one were to tell me that this was a bad government because it taxed certain foreign commodities brought to its ports, it is most probable that I should not make an ado about it, for I can do without them. All machines have their friction; and possibly this does enough good to counterbalance the evil. At any rate, it is a great evil to make a stir about it. But when the friction comes to have its machine and oppression and robbery are organized, I say,

---

[3] From Shakespeare's *King John*, Act V, Scene 2. (ED.)

let us not have such a machine any longer. In other words, when a sixth of the population of a nation which has undertaken to be the refuge of liberty are slaves, and a whole country is unjustly overrun and conquered by a foreign army, and subjected to military law, I think that it is not too soon for honest men to rebel and revolutionize. What makes this duty the more urgent is the fact that the country so overrun is not our own, but ours is the invading army. . . .

> A drab of state, a cloth-o'-silver slut,
> To have her train borne up, and her soul trail in the dirt[4]

Practically speaking, the opponents to a reform in Massachusetts are not a hundred thousand politicians at the South, but a hundred thousand merchants and farmers here, who are more interested in commerce and agriculture than they are in humanity, and are not prepared to do justice to the slave and to Mexico, *cost what it may*. I quarrel not with far-off foes, but with those who, near at home, coöperate with, and do the bidding of, those far away, and without whom the latter would be harmless. We are accustomed to say, that the mass of men are unprepared; but improvement is slow, because the few are not materially wiser or better than the many. It is not so important that many should be as good as you, as that there be some absolute goodness somewhere; for that will leaven the whole lump. There are thousands who are *in opinion* opposed to slavery and to the war, who yet in effect do nothing to put an end to them, who, esteeming themselves children of Washington and Franklin, sit down with their hands in their pockets, and say that they know not what to do, and do nothing; who even postpone the question of freedom to the question of free-trade, and quietly read the prices-current along with the latest advices from Mexico, after dinner, and, it may be, fall asleep over them both. What is the price-current of an honest man and patriot to-day? They hesitate, and they regret, and sometimes they petition; but they do nothing in earnest and with effect. They will wait, well disposed, for others to remedy the evil, that they may no longer have it to regret. At most, they give only a cheap vote, and a feeble countenance and God-speed, to the right, as it goes by them. There are nine hundred and ninety-nine patrons of virtue to one virtuous man. But it is easier to deal with the real possessor of a thing than with the temporary guardian of it.

---

[4] From *The Revenger's Tragedy* (1607) by English dramatist Cyril Tourneur. (ED.)

All voting is a sort of gaming, like checkers or backgammon, with a slight moral tinge to it, a playing with right and wrong, with moral questions; and betting naturally accompanies it. The character of the voters is not staked. I cast my vote, perchance, as I think right; but I am not vitally concerned that that right should prevail. I am willing to leave it to the majority. Its obligation, therefore, never exceeds that of expediency. Even voting *for the right* is *doing* nothing for it. It is only expressing to men feebly your desire that it should prevail. A wise man will not leave the right to the mercy of chance, nor wish it to prevail through the power of the majority. There is but little virtue in the action of masses of men. When the majority shall at length vote for the abolition of slavery, it will be because they are indifferent to slavery, or because there is but little slavery left to be abolished by their vote. *They* will then be the only slaves. Only *his* vote can hasten the abolition of slavery who asserts his own freedom by his vote.

I hear of a convention to be held at Baltimore, or elsewhere, for the selection of a candidate for the Presidency, made up chiefly of editors, and men who are politicians by profession; but I think, what is it to any independent, intelligent, and respectable man what decision they may come to? Shall we not have the advantage of his wisdom and honesty, nevertheless? Can we not count upon some independent votes? Are there not many individuals in the country who do not attend conventions? But no: I find that the respectable man, so called, has immediately drifted from his position, and despairs of his country, when his country has more reason to despair of him. He forthwith adopts one of the candidates thus selected as the only *available* one, thus proving that he is himself *available* for any purposes of the demagogue. His vote is of no more worth than that of any unprincipled foreigner or hireling native, who may have been bought. O for a man who is a *man,* and, as my neighbor says, has a bone in his back which you cannot pass your hand through! Our statistics are at fault: the population has been returned too large. How many *men* are there to a square thousand miles in this country? Hardly one. Does not America offer any inducement for men to settle here? The American has dwindled into an Odd Fellow,—one who may be known by the development of his organ of gregariousness, and a manifest lack of intellect and cheerful self-reliance; whose first and chief concern, on coming into the world, is to see that the Almshouses are in good repair; and, before yet he has lawfully donned the virile garb, to collect a fund for the support of the widows and orphans that may be; who, in short, ventures to live only by the aid

of the Mutual Insurance Company, which has promised to bury him
decently.

It is not a man's duty, as a matter of course, to devote himself to
the eradication of any, even the most enormous wrong; he may still
properly have other concerns to engage him; but it is his duty, at
least, to wash his hands of it, and, if he gives it no thought longer,
not to give it practically his support. If I devote myself to other
pursuits and contemplations, I must first see, at least, that I do not
pursue them sitting upon another man's shoulders. I must get off
him first, that he may pursue his contemplations too. See what gross
inconsistency is tolerated. I have heard some of my townsmen say,
"I should like to have them order me out to help put down an
insurrection of the slaves, or to march to Mexico;—see if I would
go"; and yet these very men have each, directly by their allegiance,
and so indirectly, at least, by their money, furnished a substitute.
The soldier is applauded who refuses to serve in an unjust war by
those who do not refuse to sustain the unjust government which
makes the war; is applauded by those whose own act and authority
he disregards and sets at naught; as if the state were penitent to that
degree that it hired one to scourge it while it sinned, but not to that
degree that it left off sinning for a moment. Thus, under the name
of Order and Civil Government, we are all made at last to pay homage
to and support our own meanness. After the first blush of sin comes
its indifference; and from immoral it becomes, as it were, unmoral,
and not quite unnecessary to that life which we have made.

The broadest and most prevalent error requires the most disinterested virtue to sustain it. The slight reproach to which the virtue
of patriotism is commonly liable, the noble are most likely to incur.
Those who, while they disapprove of the character and measures of
a government, yield to it their allegiance and support are undoubtedly
its most conscientious supporters, and so frequently the most serious
obstacles to reform. Some are petitioning the state to dissolve the
Union, to disregard the requisitions of the President. Why do they
not dissolve it themselves—the union between themselves and the
state,—and refuse to pay their quota into its treasury? Do not they
stand in the same relation to the state that the state does to the
Union? And have not the same reasons prevented the state from
resisting the Union which have prevented them from resisting the
state?

How can a man be satisfied to entertain an opinion merely, and
enjoy it? Is there any enjoyment in it, if his opinion is that he is
aggrieved? If you are cheated out of a single dollar by your neighbor,

you do not rest satisfied with knowing that you are cheated, or with saying that you are cheated, or even with petitioning him to pay you your due; but you take effectual steps at once to obtain the full amount, and see that you are never cheated again. Action from principle, the perception and the performance of right, changes things and relations; it is essentially revolutionary, and does not consist wholly with anything which was. It not only divides states and churches, it divides families; ay, it divides the *individual,* separating the diabolical in him from the divine.

Unjust laws exist; shall we be content to obey them, or shall we endeavor to amend them, and obey them until we have succeeded, or shall we transgress them at once? Men generally, under such a government as this, think that they ought to wait until they have persuaded the majority to alter them. They think that, if they should resist, the remedy would be worse than the evil. But it is the fault of the government itself that the remedy *is* worse than the evil. *It* makes it worse. Why is it not more apt to anticipate and provide for reform? Why does it not cherish its wise minority? Why does it cry and resist before it is hurt? Why does it not encourage its citizens to be on the alert to point out its faults, and *do* better than it would have them? Why does it always crucify Christ, and excommunicate Copernicus and Luther, and pronounce Washington and Franklin rebels?

One would think, that a deliberate and practical denial of its authority was the only offense never contemplated by government; else, why has it not assigned its definite, its suitable and proportionate penalty? If a man who has no property refuses but once to earn nine shillings for the state, he is put in prison for a period unlimited by any law that I know, and determined only by the discretion of those who placed him there; but if he should steal ninety times nine shillings from the state, he is soon permitted to go at large again.

If the injustice is part of the necessary friction of the machine of government, let it go, let it go: perchance it will wear smooth,— certainly the machine will wear out. If the injustice has a spring, or a pulley, or a rope, or a crank, exclusively for itself, then perhaps you may consider whether the remedy will not be worse than the evil; but if it is of such a nature that it requires you to be the agent of injustice to another, then, I say, break the law. Let your life be a counter friction to stop the machine. What I have to do is to see, at any rate, that I do not lend myself to the wrong which I condemn.

As for adopting the ways which the state has provided for remedying the evil, I know not of such ways. They take too much time, and a man's life will be gone. I have other affairs to attend to. I came

into this world, not chiefly to make this a good place to live in, but
to live in it, be it good or bad. A man has not everything to do, but
something; and because he cannot do *everything*, it is not necessary
that he should do *something* wrong. It is not my business to be
petitioning the Governor or the Legislature any more than it is theirs
to petition me; and if they should not hear my petition, what should
I do then? But in this case the state has provided no way: its very
Constitution is the evil. This may seem to be harsh and stubborn
and unconciliatory; but it is to treat with the utmost kindness and
consideration the only spirit that can appreciate or deserves it. So is
all change for the better, like birth and death, which convulse the
body.

I do not hesitate to say, that those who call themselves Abolitionists should at once effectually withdraw their support, both in
person and property, from the government of Massachusetts and not
wait till they constitute a majority of one, before they suffer the right
to prevail through them. I think that it is enough if they have God
on their side, without waiting for that other one. Moreover, any man
more right than his neighbors constitutes a majority of one already.

I meet this American government, or its representative, the state
government, directly, and face to face, once a year—no more—in the
person of its tax-gatherer; this is the only mode in which a man
situated as I am necessarily meets it; and it then says distinctly,
Recognize me; and the simplest, most effectual, and, in the present
posture of affairs, the indispensablest mode of treating with it on this
head, of expressing your little satisfaction with and love for it, is to
deny it then. My civil neighbor, the tax-gatherer, is the very man I
have to deal with,—for it is, after all, with men and not with parchment that I quarrel,—and he has voluntarily chosen to be an agent
of the government. How shall he ever know well what he is and does
as an officer of the government, or as a man, until he is obliged to
consider whether he shall treat me, his neighbor, for whom he has
respect, as a neighbor and well-disposed man, or as a maniac and
disturber of the peace, and see if he can get over this obstruction to
his neighborliness without a ruder and more impetuous thought or
speech corresponding with his action. I know this well, that if one
thousand, if one hundred, if ten men whom I could name,—if ten
honest men only,—ay, if *one* HONEST man, in this State of Massachusetts, *ceasing to hold slaves,* were actually to withdraw from this
copartnership, and be locked up in the county jail therefor, it would
be the abolition of slavery in America. For it matters not how small

the beginning may seem to be: what is once well done is done forever. But we love better to talk about it: that we say is our mission. Reform keeps many scores of newspapers in its service, but not one man. If my esteemed neighbor, the State's ambassador, who will devote his days to the settlement of the question of human rights in the Council Chamber, instead of being threatened with the prisons of Carolina, were to sit down the prisoner of Massachusetts, that State which is so anxious to foist the sin of slavery upon her sister,—though at present she can discover only an act of inhospitality to be the ground of a quarrel with her,—the Legislature would not wholly waive the subject the following winter.

Under a government which imprisons any unjustly, the true place for a just man is also a prison. The proper place to-day, the only place which Massachusetts has provided for her freer and less desponding spirits, is in her prisons, to be put out and locked out of the State by her own act, as they have already put themselves out by their principles. It is there that the fugitive slave, and the Mexican prisoner on parole, and the Indian come to plead the wrongs of his race should find them; on that separate, but more free and honorable ground, where the State places those who are not *with* her, but *against* her,—the only house in a slave State in which a free man can abide with honor. If any think that their influence would be lost there, and their voices no longer afflict the ear of the State, that they would not be as an enemy within its walls, they do not know by how much truth is stronger than error, nor how much more eloquently and effectively he can combat injustice who has experienced a little in his own person. Cast your whole vote, not a strip of paper merely, but your whole influence. A minority is powerless while it conforms to the majority; it is not even a minority then; but it is irresistible when it clogs by its whole weight. If the alternative is to keep all just men in prison, or give up war and slavery, the State will not hesitate which to choose. If a thousand men were not to pay their tax-bills this year, that would not be a violent and bloody measure, as it would be to pay them, and enable the State to commit violence and shed innocent blood. This is, in fact, the definition of a peaceable revolution, if any such is possible. If the tax-gatherer, or any other public officer, asks me, as one has done, "But what shall I do?" my answer is, "If you really wish to do anything, resign your office." When the subject has refused allegiance, and the officer has resigned his office, then the revolution is accomplished. But even suppose blood should flow. Is there not a sort of blood shed when the conscience is wounded? Through this wound a man's real manhood and immortality flow out, and he bleeds to an everlasting death. I see this blood flowing now.

I have contemplated the imprisonment of the offender, rather than the seizure of his goods,—though both will serve the same purpose—because they who assert the purest right, and consequently are most dangerous to a corrupt State, commonly have not spent much time in accumulating property. To such the State renders comparatively small service, and a slight tax is wont to appear exorbitant, particularly if they are obliged to earn it by special labor with their hands. If there were one who lived wholly without the use of money, the State itself would hesitate to demand it of him. But the rich man—not to make any invidious comparison—is always sold to the institution which makes him rich. Absolutely speaking, the more money, the less virtue; for money comes between a man and his objects, and obtains them for him; and it was certainly no great virtue to obtain it. It puts to rest many questions which he would otherwise be taxed to answer; while the only new question which it puts is the hard but superfluous one, how to spend it. Thus his moral ground is taken from under his feet. The opportunities of living are diminished in proportion as what are called the "means" are increased. The best thing a man can do for his culture when he is rich is to endeavor to carry out those schemes which he entertained when he was poor. Christ answered the Herodians according to their condition. "Show me the tribute-money," said he;—and one took a penny out of his pocket;—if you use money which has the image of Caesar on it and which he has made current and valuable, that is, *if you are men of the State,* and gladly enjoy the advantages of Caesar's government, then pay him back some of his own when he demands it. "Render therefore to Caesar that which is Caesar's, and to God those things which are God's,"—leaving them no wiser than before as to which; for they did not wish to know. . . .

I have paid no poll-tax for six years. I was put into a jail once on this account, for one night; and, as I stood considering the walls of solid stone, two or three feet thick, the door of wood and iron, a foot thick, and the iron grating which strained the light, I could not help being struck with the foolishness of that institution which treated me as if I were mere flesh and blood and bones, to be locked up. I wondered that it should have concluded at length that this was the best use it could put me to, and had never thought to avail itself of my services in some way. I saw that, if there was a wall of stone between me and my townsmen, there was a still more difficult one to climb or break through before they could get to be as free as I was. I did not for a moment feel confined, and the walls seemed a great waste of stone and mortar. I felt as if I alone of all my townsmen had paid my tax. They plainly did not know how to treat me, but behaved like persons who are underbred. In every threat and in every compliment there was a blunder; for they thought that my chief desire was to stand the other side of that stone wall. I could not but smile to see how industriously they locked the door on my meditations, which followed them out again without let or hindrance, and *they* were really all that was dangerous. As they could not reach me, they had resolved to punish my body; just as boys, if they cannot come at some person against whom they have a spite, will abuse his dog. I saw that the State was half-witted, that it was timid as a lone woman with her silver spoons, and that it did not know its friends from its foes, and I lost all my remaining respect for it, and pitied it.

Thus the State never intentionally confronts a man's sense, intellectual or moral, but only his body, his senses. It is not armed with superior wit or honesty, but with superior physical strength. I was not born to be forced. I will breathe after my own fashion. Let us see who is the strongest. What force has a multitude? They only can force me who obey a higher law than I. They force me to become like themselves. I do not hear of *men* being *forced* to live this way or that by masses of men. What sort of life were that to live? When I meet a government which says to me, "Your money or your life," why should I be in haste to give it my money? It may be in a great strait, and not know what to do: I cannot help that. It must help itself; do as I do. It is not worth the while to snivel about it. I am not responsible for the successful working of the machinery of society. I am not the son of the engineer. I perceive that, when an acorn and a chestnut fall side by side, the one does not remain inert to make way for the other, but both obey their own laws, and spring and grow and flourish as best they can, till one, perchance, overshadows and destroys the other. If a plant cannot live according to its nature, it dies; and so a man. . . .

When I came out of prison,—for some one interfered, and paid that tax,—I did not perceive that great changes had taken place on the common, such as he observed who sent in a youth and emerged a tottering and grayheaded man; and yet a change had to my eyes come over the scene,—the town, and State, and country,—greater than any that mere time could effect. I saw yet more distinctly the State in which I lived. I saw to what extent the people among whom I lived could be trusted as good neighbors and friends; that their friendship was for summer weather only; that they did not greatly propose to do right; that they were a distinct race from me by their prejudices and superstitions, as the Chinamen and Malays are; that in their sacrifices to humanity they ran no risks, not even to their property; that after all they were not so noble but they treated the thief as he had treated them, and hoped, by a certain outward observance and a few prayers, and by walking in a particular straight though useless path from time to time, to save their souls. This may be to judge my neighbors harshly; for I believe that many of them are not aware that they have such an institution as the jail in their village.

It was formerly the custom in our village, when a poor debtor came out of jail, for his acquaintances to salute him, looking through their fingers, which were crossed to represent the grating of a jail window. "How do ye do?" My neighbors did not thus salute me, but first looked at me, and then at one another, as if I had returned from a long journey. I was put into jail as I was going to the shoemaker's to get a shoe which was mended. When I was let out the next morning, I proceeded to finish my errand, and, having put on my mended shoe, joined a huckleberry party, who were impatient to put themselves under my conduct; and in half an hour,—for the horse was soon tackled,—was in the midst of a huckleberry field, on one of our highest hills, two miles off, and then the State was nowhere to be seen. . . .

I have never declined paying the highway tax, because I am as desirous of being a good neighbor as I am of being a bad subject; and as for supporting schools, I am doing my part to educate my fellow-countrymen now. It is for no particular item in the tax-bill that I refuse to pay it. I simply wish to refuse allegiance to the State, to withdraw and stand aloof from it effectually. I do not care to trace the course of my dollar, if I could, till it buys a man or a musket to shoot with,—the dollar is innocent,—but I am concerned to trace the effects of my allegiance. In fact, I quietly declare war with the State, after my fashion, though I will still make what use and get what advantage of her I can, as is usual in such cases.

If others pay the tax which is demanded of me, from a sympathy with the State, they do but what they have already done in their own case, or rather they abet injustice to a greater extent than the State requires. If they pay the tax from a mistaken interest in the individual taxed, to save his property, or prevent his going to jail, it is because they have not considered wisely how far they let their private feelings interfere with the public good.

This, then, is my position at present. But one cannot be too much on his guard in such a case, lest his action be biased by obstinacy or an undue regard for the opinions of men. Let him see that he does only what belongs to himself and to the hour.

*I think sometimes, Why, these people mean well, they are only ignorant; they would do better if they knew how: why give your neighbors this pain to treat you as they are not inclined to? But I think again. This is no reason why I should do as they do, or permit others to suffer much greater pain of a different kind. Again, I sometimes say to myself, When many millions of men, without heat, without ill will, without personal feeling of any kind, demand of you a few shillings only, without the possibility, such is their constitution, of retracting or altering their present demand, and without the possibility, on your side, of appeal to any other millions, why expose yourself to this overwhelming brute force? You do not resist cold and hunger, the winds and the waves, thus obstinately; you quietly submit to a thousand similar necessities. You do not put your head into the fire. But just in proportion as I regard this as not wholly a brute force, but partly a human force, and consider that I have relations to those millions as to many millions of men, and not of mere brute or inanimate things, I see that appeal is possible, first and instantaneously, from them to the Maker of them and, secondly, from them to themselves. But if I put my head deliberately into the fire, there is no appeal to fire or to the Maker of fire, and I have only myself to blame. If I could convince myself that I have any right to be satisfied with men as they are, and to treat them accordingly, and not according, in some respects, to my requisitions and expectations of what they and I ought to be, then, like a good Mussulman[5] and fatalist, I should endeavor to be satisfied with things as they are, and say it is the will of God. And, above all, there is the difference between resisting this and a purely brute or natural force, that I can resist this with some effect; but I cannot expect, like Orpheus,[6] to change the nature of the rocks and trees and beasts.

I do not wish to quarrel with any man or nation. I do not wish to split hairs, to make fine distinctions, or set myself up as better than my neighbors. I seek rather, I may say, even an excuse for

---

[5] Moslem (ED.)

[6] In Greek myth, Orpheus was a musician who played the lyre so sweetly that he charmed the animals and trees. (ED.)

conforming to the laws of the land. I am but too ready to conform
to them. Indeed, I have reason to suspect myself on this head; and
each year, as the tax-gatherer comes round, I find myself disposed
to review the acts and position of the general and State governments,
and the spirit of the people, to discover a pretext for conformity.

> We must affect our country as our parents,
> And if at any time we alienate
> Our love or industry from doing it honor,
> We must respect effects and teach the soul
> Matter of conscience and religion
> And not desire of rule or benefit.[7]

I believe that the State will soon be able to take all my work of this
sort out of my hands, and then I shall be no better a patriot than my
fellow-countrymen. Seen from a lower point of view, the Constitution, with all its faults, is very good; the law and the courts are very
respectable; even this State and this American government are, in
many respects, very admirable, and rare things, to be thankful for,
such as a great many have described them; but seen from a point of
view a little higher, they are what I have described them; seen from
a higher still, and the highest, who shall say what they are, or that
they are worth looking at or thinking of at all?

However, the government does not concern me much, and I shall
bestow the fewest possible thoughts on it. It is not many moments
that I live under a government, even in this world. If a man is
thought-free, fancy-free, imagination-free, that which *is not* never for
a long time appearing *to be* to him, unwise rulers or reformers cannot
fatally interrupt him.

I know that most men think differently from myself; but those
whose lives are by profession devoted to the study of these or kindred
subjects content me as little as any. Statesmen and legislators, standing so completely within the institution, never distinctly and nakedly
behold it. They speak of moving society, but have no resting-place
without it. They may be men of a certain experience and discrimination, and have no doubt invented ingenious and even useful systems, for which we sincerely thank them; but all their wit and
usefulness lie within certain not very wide limits. They are wont to
forget that the world is not governed by policy and expediency.

---

[7] From "The Battle of Alcazar" by English poet George Peele. (ED.)

Webster never goes behind government, and so cannot speak with authority about it. His words are wisdom to those legislators who contemplate no essential reform in the existing government; but for thinkers, and those who legislate for all time, he never once glances at the subject. I know of those whose serene and wise speculations on this theme would soon reveal the limits of his mind's range and hospitality. Yet, compared with the cheap professions of most re-formers, and the still cheaper wisdom and eloquence of politicians in general, his are almost the only sensible and valuable words, and we thank Heaven for him. Comparatively, he is always strong, orig-inal, and, above all, practical. Still, his quality is not wisdom, but prudence. The lawyer's truth is not Truth, but consistency or a consistent expediency. Truth is always in harmony with herself, and is not concerned chiefly to reveal the justice that may consist with wrong-doing. He well deserves to be called, as he has been called, the Defender of the Constitution. There are really no blows to be given by him but defensive ones. He is not a leader, but a follower. His leaders are the men of '87. "I have never made an effort" he says "and never propose to make an effort; I have never countenanced an effort, and never mean to countenance an effort, to disturb the arrangement as originally made, by which the various States came into the Union." Still thinking of the sanction which the Constitution gives to slavery, he says, "Because it was a part of the original compact,—let it stand." Notwithstanding his special acuteness and ability, he is unable to take a fact out of its merely political relations, and behold it as it lies absolutely to be disposed of by the intellect,— what, for instance, it behooves a man to do here in America to-day with regard to slavery,—but ventures, or is driven, to make some such desperate answer as the following while professing to speak absolutely, and as a private man,—from which what new and singular code of social duties might be inferred? "The manner," says he, "in which the governments of those States where slavery exists are to regulate it is for their own consideration, under their responsibility to their constituents, to the general laws of propriety, humanity, and justice, and to God. Associations formed elsewhere, springing from a feeling of humanity, or other cause, have nothing whatever to do with it. They have never received any encouragement from me, and they never will."

They who know of no purer sources of truth, who have traced up its stream no higher, stand, and wisely stand, by the Bible and the Constitution, and drink at it there with reverence and humility;

but they who behold where it comes trickling into this lake or that pool, gird up their loins once more, and continue their pilgrimage towards its fountainhead.

No man with a genius for legislation has appeared in America. They are rare in the history of the world. There are orators, politicians, and eloquent men, by the thousand; but the speaker has not yet opened his mouth to speak who is capable of settling the much-vexed questions of the day. We love eloquence for its own sake, and not for any truth which it may utter, or any heroism it may inspire. Our legislators have not yet learned the comparative value of free-trade and of freedom, of union, and of rectitude, to a nation. They have no genius or talent for comparatively humble questions of taxation and finance, commerce and manufactures and agriculture. If we were left solely to the wordy wit of legislators in Congress for our guidance, uncorrected by the seasonable experience and the effectual complaints of people, America would not long retain her rank among the nations. For eighteen hundred years, though perchance I have no right to say it, the New Testament has been written; yet where is the legislator who has wisdom and practical talent enough to avail himself of the light which it sheds on the science of legislation?

The authority of government, even such as I am willing to submit to,—for I will cheerfully obey those who know and can do better than I and in many things even those who neither know nor can do so well,—is still an impure one; to be strictly just, it must have the sanction and consent of the governed. It can have no pure right over my person and property but what I concede to it. The progress from an absolute to a limited monarchy, from a limited monarchy to a democracy, is a progress toward a true respect for the individual. Even the Chinese philosopher was wise enough to regard the individual as the basis of the empire. Is a democracy, such as we know it, the last improvement possible in government? Is it not possible to take a step further towards recognizing and organizing the rights of man? There will never be a really free and enlightened State until the State comes to recognize the individual as a higher and independent power, from which all its own power and authority are derived, and treats him accordingly. I please myself with imagining a State at last which can afford to be just to all men, and to treat the individual with respect as a neighbor; which even would not think it inconsistent with its own repose if a few were to live aloof from it, not meddling with it, nor embraced by it, who fulfilled all the duties of neighbors and fellow-men. A State which bore this kind of fruit, and suffered it to drop off as fast as it ripened, would prepare the way for a still more perfect and glorious State, which also I have imagined, but not yet anywhere seen.

FREDERICK DOUGLASS

Narrative of the Life of Frederick Douglass, an American Slave

Frederick Douglass (1817–1895) was an American slave who escaped to the North at the age of twenty-one, taught himself to read and write, and became one of the leading figures in the abolitionist movement. As an editor of the *North Star*, an abolitionist newspaper, he worked to bring about the issuing of the Emancipation Proclamation. The following selection is from his autobiography, which he revised and updated several times, publishing the first version in 1845 and the complete and final version, *The Life and Times of Frederick Douglass,* in 1881 and 1892.

CHAPTER I

I was born in Tuckahoe, near Hillsborough, and about twelve miles from Easton, in Talbot county, Maryland. I have no accurate knowledge of my age, never having seen any authentic record containing it. By far the larger part of the slaves know as little of their ages as horses know of theirs, and it is the wish of most masters within my knowledge to keep their slaves thus ignorant. I do not remember to have ever met a slave who could tell of his birthday. They seldom come nearer to it than planting-time, harvest-time, cherry-time, spring-time, or fall-time. A want of information concerning my own was a source of unhappiness to me even during childhood. The white children could tell their ages. I could not tell why I ought to be deprived of the same privilege. I was not allowed to make any inquiries of my master concerning it. He deemed all such inquiries on the part of a slave improper and impertinent, and evidence of a restless spirit. The nearest estimate I can give makes me now between twenty-seven and twenty-eight years of age. I come to this, from hearing my master say, some time during 1835, I was about seventeen years old.

My mother was named Harriet Bailey. She was the daughter of Isaac and Betsey Bailey, both colored, and quite dark. My mother was of a darker complexion than either my grandmother or grandfather.

My father was a white man. He was admitted to be such by all I ever heard speak of my parentage. The opinion was also whispered that my master was my father; but of the correctness of this opinion, I know nothing; the means of knowing was withheld from me. My mother and I were separated when I was but an infant—before I knew her as my mother. It is a common custom, in the part of Maryland from which I ran away, to part children from their mothers at a very early age. Frequently, before the child has reached its twelfth month, its mother is taken from it, and hired out on some farm a considerable distance off, and the child is placed under the care of an old woman, too old for field labor. For what this separation is done, I do not know, unless it be to hinder the development of the child's affection toward its mother, and to blunt and destroy the natural affection of the mother for the child. This is the inevitable result.

I never saw my mother, to know her as such, more than four or five times in my life; and each of these times was very short in duration, and at night. She was hired by a Mr. Stewart, who lived about twelve miles from my home. She made her journeys to see me in the night, travelling the whole distance on foot, after the performance of her day's work. She was a field hand, and a whipping is the penalty of not being in the field at sunrise, unless a slave has special permission from his or her master to the contrary—a permission which they seldom get, and one that gives to him that gives it the proud name of being a kind master. I do not recollect of ever seeing my mother by the light of day. She was with me in the night. She would lie down with me, and get me to sleep, but long before I waked she was gone. Very little communication ever took place between us. Death soon ended what little we could have while she lived, and with it her hardships and suffering. She died when I was about seven years old, on one of my master's farms near Lee's Mill. I was not allowed to be present during her illness, at her death, or burial. She was gone long before I knew any thing about it. Never having enjoyed, to any considerable extent, her soothing presence, her tender and watchful care, I received the tidings of her death with much the same emotions I should have probably felt at the death of a stranger.

Called thus suddenly away, she left me without the slightest intimation of who my father was. The whisper that my master was my father, may or may not be true; and, true or false, it is of but little consequence to my purpose whilst the fact remains, in all its glaring odiousness, that slaveholders have ordained, and by law established, that the children of slave women shall in all cases follow the condition of their mothers; and this is done too obviously to administer to their own lusts, and make a gratification of their wicked desires profitable as well as pleasurable; for by this cunning arrangement, the slaveholder, in cases not a few, sustains to his slaves the double relation of master and father.

I have had two masters. My first master's name was Anthony. I do not remember his first name. He was generally called Captain Anthony—a title which, I presume, he acquired by sailing a craft on the Chesapeake Bay. He was not considered a rich slaveholder. He owned two or three farms, and about thirty slaves. His farms and slaves were under the care of an overseer. The overseer's name was Plummer. Mr. Plummer was a miserable drunkard, a profane swearer, and a savage monster. He always went armed with a cowskin and a heavy cudgel. I have known him to cut and slash the women's heads so horribly, that even master would be enraged at his cruelty, and would threaten to whip him if he did not mind himself. Master, however, was not a humane slaveholder. It required extraordinary barbarity on the part of an overseer to affect him. He was a cruel man, hardened by a long life of slaveholding. He would at times seem to take great pleasure in whipping a slave. I have often been awakened at the dawn of day by the most heart-rending shrieks of an own aunt of mine, whom he used to tie up to a joist, and whip upon her naked back till she was literally covered with blood. No words, no tears, no prayers, from his gory victim, seemed to move his iron heart from its bloody purpose. The louder she screamed, the harder he whipped; and where the blood ran fastest, there he whipped longest. He would whip her to make her scream, and whip her to make her hush; and not until overcome by fatigue, would he cease to swing the blood-clotted cowskin. I remember the first time I ever witnessed this horrible exhibition. I was quite a child, but I well remember it. I never shall forget it whilst I remember any thing. It was the first of a long series of such outrages, of which I was doomed to be a witness and a participant. It struck me with awful force. It was the blood-stained gate, the entrance to the hell of slavery,

through which I was about to pass. It was a most terrible spectacle.
I wish I could commit to paper the feelings with which I beheld it.

CHAPTER VI

Very soon after I went to live with Mr. and Mrs. Auld, she
very kindly commenced to teach me the A, B, C. After I had learned
this, she assisted me in learning to spell words of three of four letters.
Just at this point of my progress, Mr. Auld found out what was going
on, and at once forbade Mrs. Auld to instruct me further, telling her,
among other things, that it was unlawful, as well as unsafe, to teach
a slave to read. To use his own words, further, he said, "If you give
a nigger an inch, he will take an ell. A nigger should know nothing
but to obey his master—to do as he is told to do. Learning would
spoil the best nigger in the world. Now," said he, "if you teach that
nigger (speaking of myself) how to read, there would be no keeping
him. It would forever unfit him to be a slave. He would at once
become unmanageable, and of no value to his master. As to himself,
it could do him no good, but a great deal of harm. It would make
him discontented and unhappy." These words sank deep into my
heart, stirred up sentiments within that lay slumbering, and called
into existence an entirely new train of thought. It was a new and
special revelation, explaining dark and mysterious things, with which
my youthful understanding had struggled, but struggled in vain. I
now understood what had been to me a most perplexing difficulty—
to wit, the white man's power to enslave the black man. It was a
grand achievement, and I prized it highly. From that moment,
I understood the pathway from slavery to freedom. It was just what I
wanted, and I got it at a time when I the least expected it. Whilst I
was saddened by the thought of losing the aid of my kind mistress,
I was gladdened by the invaluable instruction which, by the merest
accident, I had gained from my master. Though conscious of the
difficulty of learning without a teacher, I set out with high hope, and
a fixed purpose, at whatever cost of trouble, to learn how to read.
The very decided manner with which he spoke, and strove to impress
his wife with the evil consequences of giving me instruction, served
to convince me that he was deeply sensible of the truths he was
uttering. It gave me the best assurance that I might rely with the
utmost confidence on the results which, he said, would flow from
teaching me to read. What he most dreaded, that I most desired.
What he most loved, that I most hated. That which to him was a
great evil, to be carefully shunned, was to me a great good, to be

diligently sought; and the argument which he so warmly urged, against my learning to read, only served to inspire me with a desire and determination to learn. In learning to read, I owe almost as much to the bitter opposition of my master, as to the kindly aid of my mistress. I acknowledge the benefit of both.

CHAPTER VII

I lived in Master Hugh's family about seven years. During this time, I succeeded in learning to read and write. In accomplishing this, I was compelled to resort to various strategems. I had no regular teacher. My mistress, who had kindly commenced to instruct me, had, in compliance with the advice and direction of her husband, not only ceased to instruct, but had set her face against my being instructed by any one else. It is due, however, to my mistress to say of her, that she did not adopt this course of treatment immediately. She at first lacked the depravity indispensable to shutting me up in mental darkness. It was at least necessary for her to have some training in the exercise of irresponsible power, to make her equal to the task of treating me as though I were a brute.

My mistress was, as I have said, a kind and tender-hearted woman; and in the simplicity of her soul she commenced, when I first went to live with her, to treat me as she supposed one human being ought to treat another. In entering upon the duties of a slaveholder, she did not seem to perceive that I sustained to her the relation of a mere chattel, and that for her to treat me as a human being was not only wrong, but dangerously so. Slavery proved as injurious to her as it did to me. When I went there, she was a pious, warm, and tender-hearted woman. There was no sorrow or suffering for which she had not a tear. She had bread for the hungry, clothes for the naked, and comfort for every mourner that came within her reach. Slavery soon proved its ability to divest her of these heavenly qualities. Under its influence, the tender heart became stone, and the lamblike disposition gave way to one of tiger-like fierceness. The first step in her downward course was in her ceasing to instruct me. She now commenced to practise her husband's precepts. She finally became even more violent in her opposition than her husband himself. She was not satisfied with simply doing as well as he had commanded; she seemed anxious to do better. Nothing seemed to make her more angry than to see me with a newspaper. She seemed to think that here lay the danger. I have had her rush at me with a face made all up of fury, and snatch from me a newspaper, in a manner that fully revealed her apprehension. She was an apt woman; and a little experience soon demonstrated, to her satisfaction, that education and slavery were incompatible with each other.

From this time I was most narrowly watched. If I was in a separate room any considerable length of time, I was sure to be suspected of having a book, and was at once called to give an account of myself. All this, however, was too late. The first step had been taken. Mistress, in teaching me the alphabet, had given me the *inch,* and no precaution could prevent me from taking the *ell.*

The plan which I adopted, and the one by which I was most successful, was that of making friends of all the little white boys whom I met in the street. As many of these as I could, I converted into teachers. With their kindly aid, obtained at different times and in different places, I finally succeeded in learning to read. When I was sent on errands, I always took my book with me, and by going one part of my errand quickly, I found time to get a lesson before my return. I used also to carry bread with me, enough of which was always in the house, and to which I was always welcome; for I was much better off in this regard than many of the poor white children in our neighborhood. This bread I used to bestow upon the hungry little urchins, who, in return, would give me that more valuable bread of knowledge. I am strongly tempted to give the names of two or three of those little boys, as a testimonial of the gratitude and affection I bear them; but prudence forbids;—not that it would injure me, but it might embarrass them; for it is almost an unpardonable offence to teach slaves to read in this Christian country. It is enough to say of the dear little fellows, that they lived on Philpot Street, very near Durgin and Bailey's shipyard. I used to talk this matter of slavery over with them. I would sometimes say to them, I wished I could be as free as they would be when they got to be men. "You will be free as soon as you are twenty-one, *but I am a slave for life!* Have not I as good a right to be free as you have?" These words used to trouble them; they would express for me the liveliest sympathy, and console me with the hope that something would occur by which I might be free.

I was now about twelve years old, and the thought of being *a slave for life* began to bear heavily upon my heart. Just about this time, I got hold of a book entitled "The Columbian Orator." Every opportunity I got, I used to read this book. Among much of other interesting matter, I found in it a dialogue between a master and his slave. The slave was represented as having run away from his master three times. The dialogue represented the conversation which took place between them, when the slave was retaken the third time. In this dialogue, the whole argument in behalf of slavery was brought forward by the master, all of which was disposed of by the slave. The slave was made to say some very smart as well as impressive things in reply to his master—things which had the desired though unexpected effect; for the conversation resulted in the voluntary emancipation of the slave on the part of the master.

In the same book, I met with one of Sheridan's mighty speeches on and in behalf of Catholic emancipation. These were choice documents to me. I read them over and over again with unabated interest. They gave tongue to interesting thoughts of my own soul, which had frequently flashed through my mind, and died away for want of utterance. The moral which I gained from the dialogue was the power of truth over the conscience of even a slaveholder. What I got from Sheridan was a bold denunciation of slavery, and a powerful vindication of human rights. The reading of these documents enabled me to utter my thoughts, and to meet the arguments brought forward to sustain slavery; but while they relieved me of one difficulty, they brought on another even more painful than the one of which I was relieved. The more I read, the more I was led to abhor and detest my enslavers. I could regard them in no other light than a band of successful robbers, who had left their homes, and gone to Africa, and stolen us from our homes, and in a strange land reduced us to slavery. I loathed them as being the meanest as well as the most wicked of men. As I read and contemplated the subject, behold! that very discontentment which Master Hugh had predicted would follow my learning to read had already come, to torment and sting my soul to unutterable anguish. As I writhed under it, I would at times feel that learning to read had been a curse rather than a blessing. It had given me a view of my wretched condition, without the remedy. It opened my eyes to the horrible pit, but to no ladder upon which to get out. In moments of agony, I envied my fellow-slaves for their stupidity. I have often wished myself a beast. I preferred the condition of the meanest reptile to my own. Any thing, no matter what, to get rid of thinking! It was this everlasting thinking of my condition that tormented me. There was no getting rid of it. It was pressed upon me by every object within sight or hearing, animate or inanimate. The silver trump of freedom had roused my soul to eternal wakefulness. Freedom now appeared, to disappear no more forever. It was heard in every sound, and seen in every thing. It was ever present to torment me with a sense of my wretched condition. I saw nothing without seeing it, I heard nothing without hearing it, and felt nothing without feeling it. It looked from every star, it smiled in every calm, breathed in every wind, and moved in every storm.

I often found myself regretting my own existence, and wishing myself dead; and but for the hope of being free, I have no doubt but that I should have killed myself, or done something for which I should have been killed. While in this state of mind, I was eager to hear any one speak of slavery. I was a ready listener. Every little while, I could hear something about the abolitionists. It was some time before I found what the word meant. It was always used in such connections as to make it an interesting word to me. If a slave ran away and succeeded in getting clear, or if a slave killed his master, set fire to a barn, or did any thing very wrong in the mind of a slaveholder, it was spoken of as the fruit of *abolition*. Hearing the word in this connection very often, I set about learning what it meant. The dictionary afforded me little or no help. I found it was "the act of abolishing"; but then I did not know what was to be abolished. Here I was perplexed. I did not dare to ask any one about its meaning, for I was satisfied that it was something they wanted me to know very little about. After a patient waiting, I got one of our city papers, containing an account of the number of petitions from the north, praying for the abolition of slavery in the District of Columbia, and of the slave trade between the States. From this time I understood the words *abolition* and *abolitionist,* and always drew near when that word was spoken, expecting to hear something of importance to myself and fellow-slaves. The light broke in upon me by degrees. I went one day down on the wharf of Mr. Waters; and seeing two Irishmen unloading a scow of stone, I went, unasked, and helped them. When we had finished, one of them came to me and asked, "Are ye a slave for life?" I told him that I was. The good Irishman seemed to be deeply affected by the statement. He said to the other that it was a pity so fine a little fellow as myself should be a slave for life. He said it was a shame to hold me. They both advised me to run away to the north; that I should find friends there, and that I should be free. I pretended not to be interested in what they said, and treated them as if I did not understand them; for I feared they might be treacherous. White men have been known to encourage slaves to escape, and then, to get the reward, catch them and return them to their masters. I was afraid that these seemingly good men might use me so; but I nevertheless remembered their advice, and from that time I resolved to run away. I looked forward to a time at which it would be safe for me to escape. I was too young to think of doing so immediately; besides, I wished to learn how to write, as I might have occasion to write my own pass. I consoled myself with the hope that I should one day find a good chance. Meanwhile, I would learn to write.

The idea as to how I might learn to write was suggested to me by being in Durgin and Bailey's ship-yard, and frequently seeing the ship carpenters, after hewing, and getting a piece of timber ready for use, write on the timber the name of that part of the ship for which it was intended. When a piece of timber was intended for the larboard side, it would be marked thus—"L." When a piece was for the starboard side, it would be marked thus—"S." A piece for the larboard side forward, would be marked thus—"L. F." When a piece was for starboard side forward, it would be marked thus—"S. F." For larboard aft, it would be marked thus—"L. A." For starboard aft, it would be marked thus—"S. A." I soon learned the names of these letters, and for what they were intended when placed upon a piece of timber in the ship-yard. I immediately commenced copying them, and in a short time was able to make the four letters named. After that, I met with any boy who I knew could write, I would tell him I could write as well as he. The next word would be, "I don't believe you. Let me see you try it." I would then make the letters which I had been so fortunate as to learn, and ask him to beat that. In this way I got a good many lessons in writing, which it is quite possible I should never have gotten in any other way. During this time, my copy-book was the board fence, brick wall, and pavement; my pen and ink was a lump of chalk. With these, I learned mainly how to write. I then commenced and continued copying the Italics in Webster's Spelling Book, until I could make them all without looking on the book. By this time, my little Master Thomas had gone to school, and learned how to write, and had written over a number of copy-books. These had been brought home, and shown to some of our near neighbors, and then laid aside. My mistress used to go to class meeting at the Wilk Street meetinghouse every Monday afternoon, and leave me to take care of the house. When left thus, I used to spend this time writing in the spaces left in Master Thomas's copy-book, copying what he had written. I continued to do this until I could write a hand very similar to that of Master Thomas. Thus, after a long, tedious effort for years, I finally succeeded in learning how to write.

CHAPTER X

I left Master Thomas's house, and went to live with Mr. Covey, on the 1st of January, 1833. I was now, for the first time in my life, a field hand. In my new employment, I found myself even more awkward than a country boy appeared to be in a large city. I had been at my new home but one week before Mr. Covey gave me a severe whipping, cutting my back, causing the blood to run, and raising ridges on my flesh as large as my little finger. The details of this affair are as follows: Mr. Covey sent me, very early in the morning of one of our coldest days in the month of January, to the woods, to get a load of wood. He gave me a team of unbroken oxen. He told me which was the in-hand ox, and which the off-hand one. He then tied the end of a large rope around the horns of the in-hand ox, and gave me the other end of it, and told me, if the oxen started to run, that I must hold on upon the rope. I had never driven oxen before, and of course I was very awkward. I, however, succeeded in getting to the edge of the woods with little difficulty; but I had got a very few rods into the woods, when the oxen took fright, and started full tilt, carrying the cart against trees, and over stumps, in the most frightful manner. I expected every moment that my brains would be dashed out against the trees. After running thus for a considerable distance, they finally upset the cart, dashing it with great force against a tree, and threw themselves into a dense thicket. How I escaped death, I do not know. There I was, entirely alone, in a thick wood, in a place new to me. My cart was upset and shattered, my oxen were entangled among the young trees, and there was none to help me. After a long spell of effort, I succeeded in getting my cart righted, my oxen disentangled, and again yoked to the cart. I now proceeded with my team to the place where I had, the day before, been chopping wood, and loaded my cart pretty heavily, thinking in this way to tame my oxen. I then proceeded on my way home. I had now consumed one half of the day. I got out of the woods safely, and now felt out of danger. I stopped my oxen to open the woods gate; and just as I did so, before I could get hold of my ox-rope, the oxen again started, rushed through the gate, catching it between the wheel and the body of the cart, tearing it to pieces, and coming within a few inches of crushing me against the gate-post. Thus twice, in one short day, I escaped death by the merest chance. On my return, I told Mr. Covey what had happened, and how it happened. He ordered me to return to the woods again immediately. I did so, and he followed on after me. Just as I got into the woods, he came up and told me to stop my cart, and that he would teach me how to trifle away my time, and break gates. He then went to a large gum-tree, and with his axe cut three large switches, and, after trimming them up neatly with his pocket-knife, he ordered me to take off my clothes. I made him no answer, but stood with my clothes on. He repeated his order. I still made him no answer, nor did I move to strip myself. Upon this he rushed at me with the fierceness of a tiger, tore off my clothes, and lashed me till he had worn out his switches, cutting me so savagely as to leave the marks visible for a long time after. This whipping was the first of a number just like it, and for similar offenses.

I lived with Mr. Covey one year. During the first six months, of that year, scarce a week passed without his whipping me. I was seldom free from a sore back. My awkwardness was almost always his excuse for whipping me. We were worked fully up to the point of endurance. Long before day we were up, our horses fed, and by the first approach of day we were off to the field with our hoes and ploughing teams. Mr. Covey gave us enough to eat, but scarce time to eat it. We were often less than five minutes taking our meals. We were often in the field from the first approach of day till its last lingering ray had left us; and at saving-fodder time, midnight often caught us in the field binding blades.

If at any one time of my life more than another, I was made to drink the bitterest dregs of slavery, that time was during the first six months of my stay with Mr. Covey. We were worked in all weathers. It was never too hot or too cold; it could never rain, blow, hail, or snow, too hard for us to work in the field. Work, work, work, was scarcely more the order of the day than of the night. The longest days were too short for him, and the shortest nights too long for him. I was somewhat unmanageable when I first went there, but a few months of this discipline tamed me. Mr. Covey succeeded in breaking me. I was broken in body, soul, and spirit. My natural elasticity was crushed, my intellect languished, the disposition to read departed, the cheerful spark that lingered about my eye died; the dark night of slavery closed in upon me; and behold a man transformed into a brute!

Sunday was my only leisure time. I spent this in a sort of beast-like stupor, between sleep and wake, under some large tree. At times I would rise up, a flash of energetic freedom would dart through my soul, accompanied with a faint beam of hope, that flickered for a moment, and then vanished. I sank down again, mourning over my wretched condition. I was sometimes prompted to take my life, and that of Covey, but was prevented by a combination of hope and fear. My sufferings on this plantation seem now like a dream rather than a stern reality.

I have already intimated that my condition was much worse, during the first six months of my stay at Mr. Covey's, than in the last six. The circumstances leading to the change in Mr. Covey's course toward me form an epoch in my humble history. You have seen how a man was made a slave; you shall see how a slave was made a man. On one of the hottest days of the month of August 1833, Bill Smith, William Hughes, a slave named Eli, and myself, were engaged in fanning wheat. Hughes was clearing the fanned wheat from before the fan. Eli was turning. Smith was feeding, and I was carrying wheat to the fan. The work was simple, requiring strength rather than intellect; yet, to one entirely unused to such work, it came very hard. About three o'clock of that day, I broke down; my strength failed me; I was seized with a violent aching of the head, attended with extreme dizziness; I trembled in every limb. Finding what was coming, I nerved myself up, feeling it would never do to stop work. I stood as long as I could stagger to the hopper with grain. When I could stand no longer, I fell, and felt as if held down by an immense weight. The fan of course stopped; every one had his own work to do; and no one could do the work of the other, and have his own go on at the same time.

Mr. Covey was at the house, about one hundred yards from the treading-yard where we were fanning. On hearing the fan stop, he left immediately, and came to the spot where we were. He hastily inquired what the matter was. Bill answered that I was sick, and there was no one to bring wheat to the fan. I had by this time crawled away under the side of the post and rail-fence by which the yard was enclosed, hoping to find relief by getting out of the sun. He then asked where I was. He was told by one of the hands. He came to the spot, and, after looking at me awhile, asked me what was the matter. I told him as well as I could, for I scarce had strength to speak. He then gave me a savage kick in the side, and told me to get up. I tried to do so, but fell back in the attempt. He gave me another kick, and again told me to rise. I again tried, and succeeded in gaining my feet; but, stooping to get the tub with which I was feeding the fan, I again staggered and fell. While down in this situation, Mr. Covey took up the hickory slat with which Hughes had been striking off the half-bushel measure, and with it gave me a heavy blow upon the head, making a large wound, and the blood ran freely; and with this again told me to get up. I made no effort to comply, having now made up my mind to let him do his worst. In a short time after receiving this blow, my head grew better. Mr. Covey had now left me to my fate. At this moment I resolved, for the first time, to go to my master, enter a complaint, and ask his protection. In order to do this, I must that afternoon walk seven miles; and this, under the circumstances, was truly a severe undertaking. I was exceedingly feeble; made so as much by the kicks and blows which I received, as by the severe fit of sickness to which I had been subjected. I, however, watched my chance, while Covey was looking in an opposite direction, and started for St. Michael's. I succeeded in getting a considerable distance on my way to the woods, when Covey discovered me and called after me to come back, threatening what he would do if I did not come. I disregarded both his calls and his threats, and made my way to the woods as fast as my feeble state would allow; and thinking I might be overhauled by him if I kept the road, I walked through the woods, keeping far enough from the road to avoid detection, and near enough to prevent losing my way. I had not gone far before my little strength again failed me. I could go no farther. I fell down, and lay for a considerable time. The blood was yet oozing from the wound on my head. For a time I thought I should bleed to death; and think now that I should have done so, but that the blood so matted my hair as to stop the wound. After lying there about three quarters of an hour, I nerved myself up again, and started on my way, through bogs and briers, barefooted and bareheaded, tearing my feet sometimes at nearly every step; and after a journey of about seven miles, occupying some five hours to perform it, I arrived at master's store. I then presented an appearance enough to affect any but a heart of iron. From the crown of my head to my feet, I was covered with blood; my shirt was stiff with blood. My legs and feet were torn in sundry places with briers and thorns, and were also covered with blood. I suppose I looked like a man who had escaped a den of wild beasts, and barely escaped them. In this state I appeared before my master, humbly entreating him to interpose his authority for my protection. I told him all the circumstances as well as I could, and it seemed, as I spoke, at times to affect him. He would then walk the floor, and seek to justify Covey by saying he expected I deserved it. He asked me what I wanted. I told him, to let me get a new home; that as sure as I lived with Mr. Covey again, I should live with but to die with him; that Covey would surely kill me; he was in a fair way for it. Master Thomas ridiculed the idea that there was any danger of Mr. Covey's killing me, and said that he knew Mr. Covey; that he was a good man, and that he could not think of taking me from him; that, should he do so, he would lose the whole year's wages; that I belonged to Mr. Covey for one year, and that I must go back to him, come what might; and that I must not trouble him with any more stories, or that he would himself *get hold of me.* After threatening me thus, he gave me a very large dose of salts, telling me that I might

remain in St. Michael's that night, (it being quite late,) but that I
must be off back to Mr. Covey's early in the morning; and that if I
did not, he would *get hold of me,* which meant that he would whip
me. I remained all night, and, according to his orders, I started off
to Covey's in the morning, (Saturday morning,) wearied in body and
broken in spirit. I got no supper that night, or breakfast that morning.
I reached Covey's about nine o'clock; and just as I was getting over
the fence that divided Mrs. Kemp's fields from ours, out ran Covey
with his cowskin, to give me another whipping. Before he could
reach me, I succeeded in getting to the cornfield and as the corn was
very high, it afforded me the means of hiding. He seemed very angry,
and searched for me a long time. My behavior was altogether unaccountable. He finally gave up the chase, thinking, I suppose, that I
must come home for something to eat; he would give himself no
further trouble in looking for me. I spent that day mostly in the
woods, having the alternative before me,—to go home and be
whipped to death, or stay in the woods and be starved to death. That
night, I fell in with Sandy Jenkins, a slave with whom I was somewhat
acquainted. Sandy had a free wife who lived about four miles from
Mr. Covey's; and it being Saturday, he was on his way to see her. I
told him my circumstances, and he very kindly invited me to go
home with him. I went home with him, and talked this whole matter
over, and got his advice as to what course it was best for me to
pursue. I found Sandy an old adviser. He told me, with great sol-
emnity, I must go back to Covey; but that before I went, I must go
with him into another part of the woods, where there was a certain
root, which, if I would take some of it with me, carrying it *always
on my right side,* would render it impossible for Mr. Covey, or any
other white man, to whip me. He said he had carried it for years;
and since he had done so, he had never received a blow, and never
expected to while he carried it. I at first rejected the idea, that the
simple carrying of a root in my pocket would have any such effect
as he had said, and was not disposed to take it; but Sandy impressed
the necessity with much earnestness, telling me it could do no harm,
if it did no good. To please him, I at length took the root, and,
according to his direction, carried it upon my right side. This was
Sunday morning. I immediately started for home; and upon entering
the yard gate, out came Mr. Covey on his way to meeting. He spoke
to me very kindly, bade me drive the pigs from a lot near by, and
passed on towards the church. Now, this singular conduct of Mr.
Covey really made me begin to think that there was something in
the *root* which Sandy had given me; and had it been on any other

day than Sunday, I could have attributed the conduct to no other cause than the influence of that root; and as it was, I was half inclined to think the root to be something more than I at first had taken it to be. All went well till Monday morning. On this morning, the virtue of the *root* was fully tested. Long before daylight, I was called to go and rub, curry, and feed, the horses. I obeyed, and was glad to obey. But whilst thus engaged, whilst in the act of throwing down some blades from the loft, Mr. Covey entered the stable with a long rope; and just as I was half out of the loft, he caught hold of my legs, and was about tying me. As soon as I found what he was up to, I gave a sudden spring, and as I did so, he holding to my legs, I was brought sprawling on the stable floor. Mr. Covey seemed now to think he had me, and could do what he pleased; but at this moment—from whence came the spirit I don't know—I resolved to fight; and, suiting my action to the resolution, I seized Covey hard by the throat; and as I did so, I rose. He held on to me, and I to him. My resistance was so entirely unexpected, that Covey seemed taken all aback. He trembled like a leaf. This gave me assurance, and I held him uneasy, causing the blood to run where I touched him with the ends of my fingers. Mr. Covey soon called out to Hughes for help. Hughes came, and, while Covey held me, attempted to tie my right hand. While he was in the act of doing so, I watched my chance, and gave him a heavy kick close under the ribs. This kick fairly sickened Hughes, so that he left me in the hands of Mr. Covey. This kick had the effect of not only weakening Hughes, but Covey also. When he saw Hughes bending over with pain, his courage quailed. He asked me if I meant to persist in my resistance. I told him I did, come what might; that he had used me like a brute for six months, and that I was determined to be used so no longer. With that, he strove to drag me to a stick that was lying just out of the stable door. He meant to knock me down. But just as he was leaning over to get the stick, I seized him with both hands by his collar, and brought him by a sudden snatch to the ground. By this time, Bill came. Covey called upon him for assistance. Bill wanted to know what he could do. Covey said, "Take hold of him, take hold of him!" Bill said his master hired him out to work, and not to help to whip me; so he left Covey and myself to fight our own battle out. We were at it for nearly two hours. Covey at length let me go, puffing and blowing at a great rate, saying that if I had not resisted, he would not have whipped me half so much. The truth was, that he had not whipped me at all. I considered him as getting entirely the worst end of the bargain; for he had drawn no blood from me, but I had from him. The whole six months afterwards, that I spent with Mr. Covey, he never laid the weight of his finger upon me in anger. He would occasionally say, he didn't want to get hold of me again. "No," thought I, "you need not; for you will come off worse than you did before."

This battle with Mr. Covey was the turning-point in my career as a slave. It rekindled the few expiring embers of freedom, and revived within me a sense of my own manhood. It recalled the departed self-confidence, and inspired me again with a determination to be free. The gratification afforded by the triumph was a full compensation for whatever else might follow, even death itself. He only can understand the deep satisfaction which I experienced, who has himself repelled by force the bloody arm of slavery. I felt as I never felt before. It was a glorious resurrection, from the tomb of slavery, to the heaven of freedom. My long-crushed spirit rose, cowardice departed, bold defiance took its place; and I now resolved that, however long I might remain a slave in form, the day had passed forever when I could be a slave in fact. I did not hesitate to let it be known of me, that the white man who expected to succeed in whipping, must also succeed in killing me.

From this time I was never again what might be called fairly whipped, though I remained a slave four years afterwards. I had several fights, but was never whipped.

On the first of January, 1834, I left Mr. Covey, and went to live with Mr. William Freeland, who lived about three miles from St. Michael's. I soon found Mr. Freeland a very different man from Mr. Covey. Thought not rich, he was what would be called an educated southern gentleman. Mr. Covey, as I have shown, was a well-trained negro-breaker and slave-driver. The former (slaveholder though he was) seemed to possess some regard for honor, some reverence for justice, and some respect for humanity. The latter seemed totally insensible to all such sentiments. Mr. Freeland had many of the faults peculiar to slaveholders, such as being very passionate and fretful; but I must do him the justice to say, that he was exceedingly free from those degrading vices to which Mr. Covey was constantly addicted. The one was open and frank, and we always knew where to find him. The other was a most artful deceiver, and could be understood only by such as were skilful enough to detect his cunningly-devised frauds.

The year passed off smoothly. It seemed only about half as long as the year which preceded it. I went through it without receiving a single blow. I will give Mr. Freeland the credit of being the best master I ever had, *till I became my own master*. For the ease with which I passed the year, I was, however, somewhat indebted to the society of my fellow-slaves. They were noble souls; they not only possessed loving hearts, but brave ones. We were linked and inter-linked with each other. I loved them with a love stronger than any thing I have experienced since. It is sometimes said that we slaves do not love and confide in each other. In answer to this assertion, I can say, I never loved any or confided in any people more than my fellow-slaves, and especially those with whom I lived at Mr. Free-land's. I believe we would have died for each other. We never un-dertook to do any thing, of any importance, without a mutual con-sultation. We never moved separately. We were one; and as much so by our tempers and dispositions, as by the mutual hardships to which we were necessarily subjected by our condition as slaves.

At the close of the year 1834, Mr. Freeland again hired me of my master, for the year 1835. But, by this time, I began to want to live *upon free land* as well as *with Freeland;* and I was no longer content, therefore, to live with him or any other slave-holder. I began, with the commencement of the year, to prepare myself for a final struggle, which should decide my fate one way or the other. My tendency was upward. I was fast approaching manhood, and year after year had passed, and I was still a slave. These thoughts roused me—I must do something. I therefore resolved that 1835 should not pass without witnessing an attempt, on my part, to secure my liberty. But I was not willing to cherish this determination alone. My fellow-slaves were dear to me. I was anxious to have them participate with me in this, my life-giving determination. I therefore, though with great prudence, commenced early to ascertain their views and feelings in regard to their condition, and to imbue their minds with thoughts of freedom. I bent myself to devising ways and means for our escape, and mean-while strove, on all fitting occasions, to impress them with the gross fraud and inhumanity of slavery. I went first to Henry, next to John, then to the others. I found, in them all, warm hearts and noble spirits. They were ready to hear, and ready to act when a feasible plan should be proposed. This was what I wanted. I talked to them of our want of manhood, if we submitted to our enslavement without at least one noble effort to be free. We met often, and consulted frequently, and told our hopes and fears, recounted the difficulties, real and imagined, which we should be called on to meet. At times we were almost disposed to give up, and try to content ourselves with our wretched lot; at others, we were firm and unbending in our determination to go. Whenever we suggested any plan, there was shrinking—the odds were fearful. Our path was beset with the greatest obstacles; and if we succeeded in gaining the end of it, our right to be free was yet questionable—we were yet liable to be returned to bondage. We could see no spot, this side of the ocean, where we could be free. We knew nothing about Canada. Our knowledge of the north did not extend farther than New York; and to go there, and be forever harassed with the frightful liability of being returned to slavery—with the certainty of being treated tenfold worse than before—the thought was truly a horrible one, and one which it was not easy to overcome. The case sometimes stood thus: At every gate through which we were to pass, we saw a watchman—at every ferry a guard—on every bridge a sentinel—and in every wood a patrol. We were hemmed in upon every side. Here were the difficulties, real or imagined—the good to be sought, and the evil to be shunned. On the one hand, there stood slavery, a stern reality, glaring frightfully upon us—its robes already crimsoned with the blood of millions, and even now feasting itself greedily upon our own flesh. On the other hand, away back in the dim distance, under the flickering light of the north star, behind some craggy hill or snow-covered mountain, stood a doubtful freedom—half frozen—beckoning us to come and share its hospitality. This in itself was sometimes enough to stagger us; but when we permitted ourselves to survey the road, we were frequently appalled. Upon either side we saw grim death, assuming the most horrid shapes. Now it was starvation, causing us to eat our own flesh;—now we were contending with the waves, and were drowned;—now we were overtaken, and torn to pieces by the fangs of the terrible bloodhound. We were stung by scorpions, chased by wild beasts, bitten by snakes, and finally, after having nearly reached the desired spot,—after swimming rivers, encountering wild beasts, sleeping in the woods, suffering hunger and nakedness,—we were overtaken by our pursuers, and, in our resistance, we were shot dead upon the spot! I say, this picture sometimes appalled us, and made us

> "rather bear those ills we had,
> Than fly to others, that we knew not of."

In coming to a fixed determination to run away, we did more than Patrick Henry, when he resolved upon liberty or death. With us it was doubtful liberty at most, and almost certain death if we failed. For my part, I should prefer death to hopeless bondage.

Sandy, one of our number, gave up the notion, but still encouraged us. Our company then consisted of Henry Harris, John Harris, Henry Bailey, Charles Roberts, and myself. Henry Bailey was my uncle, and belonged to my master. Charles married my aunt: he belonged to my master's father-in-law, Mr. William Hamilton.

The plan we finally concluded upon was, to get a large canoe belonging to Mr. Hamilton, and upon the Saturday night previous to Easter holidays, paddle directly up the Chesapeake Bay. On our arrival at the head of the bay, a distance of seventy or eighty miles from where we lived, it was our purpose to turn our canoe adrift, and follow the guidance of the north star till we got beyond the limits of Maryland. Our reason for taking the water route was, that we were less liable to be suspected as runaways; we hoped to be regarded as fishermen; whereas, if we should take the land route, we should be subjected to interruptions of almost every kind. Any one having a white face, and being so disposed, could stop us, and subject us to examination.

The week before our intended start, I wrote several protections, one for each of us. As well as I can remember, they were in the following words, to wit:—

> "This is to certify that I, the undersigned, have given the bearer, my servant, full liberty to go to Baltimore, and spend the Easter holidays. Written with mine own hand, &c., 1835.
>
> "WILLIAM HAMILTON,
>
> "Near St. Michael's, in Talbot county, Maryland."

We were not going to Baltimore; but, in going up the bay, we went toward Baltimore, and these protections were only intended to protect us while on the bay.

As the time drew near for our departure, our anxiety became more and more intense. It was truly a matter of life and death with us. The strength of our determination was about to be fully tested. At this time, I was very active in explaining every difficulty, removing every doubt, dispelling every fear, and inspiring all with the firmness indispensable to success in our undertaking; assuring them that half was gained the instant we made the move; we had talked long enough; we were now ready to move; if not now, we never should be; and if we did not intend to move now, we had as well fold our arms, sit down, and acknowledge ourselves fit only to be slaves. This none of us were prepared to acknowledge. Every man stood firm; and at our last meeting, we pledged ourselves afresh, in the most solemn manner, that, at the time appointed, we would certainly start in pursuit of freedom. This was in the middle of the week, at the end of which we were to be off. We went, as usual, to our several fields of labor, but with bosoms highly agitated with thoughts of our truly hazardous undertaking. We tried to conceal our feelings as much as possible; and I think we succeeded very well.

After a painful waiting, the Saturday morning, whose night was to witness our departure, came. I hailed it with joy, bring what of sadness it might. Friday night was a sleepless one for me. I probably felt more anxious than the rest, because I was, by common consent, at the head of the whole affair. The responsibility of success or failure lay heavily upon me. The glory of the one, and the confusion of the other, were alike mine. The first two hours of that morning were such as I never experienced before, and hope never to again. Early in the morning, we went, as usual, to the field. We were spreading manure; and all at once, while thus engaged, I was overwhelmed with an indescribable feeling, in the fulness of which I turned to Sandy, who was near by, and said, "We are betrayed!" "Well," said he, "that thought has this moment struck me." We said no more. I was never more certain of any thing.

The horn was blown as usual, and we went up from the field to the house for breakfast. I went for the form more than for want of any thing to eat that morning. Just as I got to the house, in looking out at the lane gate, I saw four white men, with two colored men. The white men were on horseback, and the colored ones were walking behind, as if tied. I watched them a few moments till they got up to our lane gate. Here they halted, and tied the colored men to the gate-post. I was not yet certain as to what the matter was. In a few moments, in rode Mr. Hamilton, with a speed betokening great excitement. He came to the door, and inquired if Master William was in. He was told he was at the barn. Mr. Hamilton, without dismounting, rode up to the barn with extraordinary speed. In a few moments, he and Mr. Freeland returned to the house. By this time, the three constables rode up, and in great haste dismounted, tied their horses, and met Master William and Mr. Hamilton returning from the barn; and after talking awhile, they all walked up to the kitchen door. There was no one in the kitchen but myself and John. Henry and Sandy were up at the barn. Mr. Freeland put his head in at the door, and called me by name, saying, there were some gentlemen at the door who wished to see me. I stepped to the door, and inquired what they wanted. They at once seized me, and, without giving me any satisfaction, tied me—lashing my hands closely together. I insisted upon knowing what the matter was. They at length said, that they had learned I had been in a "scrape," and that I was to be examined before my master; and if their information proved false, I should not be hurt.

In a few moments, they succeeded in tying John. They then turned to Henry, who had by this time returned, and commanded him to cross his hands. "I won't!" said Henry, in a firm tone indicating his readiness to meet the consequences of his refusal. "Won't you?" said Tom Graham, the constable. "No, I won't!" said Henry, in a still stronger tone. With this, two of the constables pulled out their shining pistols, and swore, by their Creator, that they would make him cross his hands or kill him. Each cocked his pistol, and, with fingers on the trigger, walked up to Henry, saying, at the same time, if he did not cross his hands, they would blow his damned heart out. "Shoot me, shoot me!" said Henry; "you can't kill me but once. Shoot, shoot,—and be damned! *I won't be tied!*" This he said in a tone of loud defiance; and at the same time, with a motion as quick as lightning, he with one single stroke dashed the pistols from the hand of each constable. As he did this, all hands fell upon him, and after beating him some time, they finally overpowered him, and got him tied.

During the scuffle, I managed, I know not how, to get my pass out, and, without being discovered, put it into the fire. We were all now tied; and just as we were to leave for Easton jail, Betsy Freeland, mother of William Freeland, came to the door with her hands full of biscuits, and divided them between Henry and John. She then delivered herself of a speech, to the following effect:—addressing herself to me, she said, "*You devil! You yellow devil!* it was you that put it into the heads of Henry and John to run away. But for you, you long-legged mulatto devil! Henry nor John would never have thought of such a thing." I made no reply, and was immediately hurried off towards St. Michael's. Just a moment previous to the scuffle with Henry, Mr. Hamilton suggested the propriety of making a search for the protections which he had understood Frederick had written for himself and the rest. But, just at the moment he was about carrying his proposal into effect, his aid was needed in helping to tie Henry; and the excitement attending the scuffle caused them either to forget, or to deem it unsafe, under the circumstances, to search. So we were not yet convicted of the intention to run away.

When we got about half way to St. Michael's, while the constables having us in charge were looking ahead, Henry inquired of me what he should do with his pass. I told him to eat it with his biscuit, and own nothing; and we passed the word around, "*Own nothing*"; and "*Own nothing!*" said we all. Our confidence in each other was unshaken. We were resolved to succeed or fail together, after the calamity had befallen us as much as before. We were now prepared for any thing. We were to be dragged that morning fifteen miles behind horses, and then to be placed in the Easton jail. When we reached St. Michael's, we underwent a sort of examination. We all denied that we ever intended to run away. We did this more to bring out the evidence against us, than from any hope of getting clear of being sold; for, as I have said, we were ready for that. The fact was, we cared but little where we went, so we went together. Our greatest concern was about separation. We dreaded that more than any thing this side of death. We found the evidence against us to be the testimony of one person; our master would not tell who it was; but we came to a unanimous decision among ourselves as to who their informant was. We were sent off to the jail at Easton. When we got there, we were delivered up to the sheriff, Mr. Joseph Graham, and by him placed in jail. Henry, John, and myself, were placed in one room together—Charles, and Henry Bailey, in another. Their object in separating us was to hinder concert.

We had been in jail scarcely twenty minutes, when a swarm of slave traders, and agents for slave traders, flocked into jail to look at us, and to ascertain if we were for sale. Such a set of beings I never saw before! I felt myself surrounded by so many fiends from perdition. A band of pirates never looked more like their father, the devil. They laughed and grinned over us, saying, "Ah, my boys! we have got you, haven't we?" And after taunting us in various ways, they one by one went into an examination of us, with intent to ascertain our value. They would impudently ask us if we would not like to have them for our masters. We would make them no answer, and leave them to find out as best they could. Then they would curse and swear at us, telling us that they could take the devil out of us in a very little while, if we were only in their hands.

While in jail, we found ourselves in much more comfortable quarters than we expected when we went there. We did not get much to eat, nor that which was very good; but we had a good clean room, from the windows of which we could see what was going on in the street, which was very much better than though we had been placed in one of the dark, damp cells. Upon the whole, we got along very well, so far as the jail and its keeper were concerned. Immediately after the holidays were over, contrary to all our expectations, Mr. Hamilton and Mr. Freeland came up to Easton, and took Charles, the two Henrys, and John, out of jail, and carried them home, leaving me alone. I regarded this separation as a final one. It caused me more pain than any thing else in the whole transaction. I was ready for any thing rather than separation. I supposed that they had consulted together, and had decided that, as I was the whole cause of the intention of the others to run away, it was hard to make the innocent suffer with the guilty; and that they had, therefore, concluded to take the others home, and sell me, as a warning to the others that remained. It is due to the noble Henry to say, he seemed almost as reluctant at leaving the prison as at leaving home to come to the prison. But we knew we should, in all probability, be separated, if we were sold; and since he was in their hands, he concluded to go peaceably home.

I was now left to my fate. I was all alone, and within the walls of a stone prison. But a few days before, and I was full of hope. I expected to have been safe in a land of freedom; but now I was covered with gloom, sunk down to the utmost despair. I thought the possibility of freedom was gone. I was kept in this way about one week, at the end of which, Captain Auld, my master, to my surprise and utter astonishment, came up, and took me out, with the intention of sending me, with a gentleman of his acquaintance, into Alabama. But, from some cause or other, he did not send me to Alabama, but concluded to send me back to Baltimore, to live again with his brother Hugh, and to learn a trade.

Thus, after an absence of three years and one month, I was once more permitted to return to my old home at Baltimore. My master sent me away, because there existed against me a very great prejudice in the community, and he feared I might be killed.

In a few weeks after I went to Baltimore, Master Hugh hired me to Mr. William Gardner, an extensive ship-builder, on Fell's Point. I was put there to learn how to calk. It, however, proved a very unfavorable place for the accomplishment of this object. Mr. Gardner was engaged that spring in building two large man-of-war brigs, professedly for the Mexican government. The vessels were to be launched in the July of that year, and in failure thereof, Mr. Gardner was to lose a considerable sum; so that when I entered, all was hurry. There was no time to learn any thing. Every man had to do that which he knew how to do. In entering the shipyard, my orders from Mr. Gardner were, to do whatever the carpenters commanded me to do. This was placing me at the beck and call of about seventy-five men. I was to regard all these as master. Their word was to be my law. My situation was a most trying one. At times I needed a dozen pair of hands. I was called a dozen ways in the space of a single minute. Three or four voices would strike my ear at the same moment. It was—"Fred., come help me to cant this timber here."—"Fred., come carry this timber yonder."—"Fred., bring that roller

here."—"Fred., go get a fresh can of water."—"Fred., come help saw
off the end of this timber."—"Fred., go quick and get the crowbar."—
"Fred., hold on the end of this fall."—"Fred., go to the blacksmith's
shop, and get a new punch."—"Hurra, Fred.,! run and bring me a
cold chisel."—"I say, Fred., bear a hand, and get up a fire as quick
as lightning under that steam-box."—"Halloo, nigger! come, turn
this grindstone."—"Come, come! move, move! and bowse this timber
forward."—"I say, darky, blast your eyes, why don't you heat up
some pitch?"—"Halloo! halloo! halloo!" (Three voices at the same
time.) "Come here!—Go there!—Hold on where you are! Damn you,
if you move, I'll knock your brains out!"

This was my school for eight months; and I might have remained
there longer, but for a most horrid fight I had with four of the white
apprentices, in which my left eye was nearly knocked out, and I was
horribly mangled in other respects.

I went directly home, and told the story of my wrongs to Master
Hugh; and I am happy to say of him, irreligious as he was, his
conduct was heavenly, compared with that of his brother Thomas
under similar circumstances. He listened attentively to my narration
of the circumstances leading to the savage outrage, and gave many
proofs of his strong indignation at it. The heart of my once overkind
mistress was again melted into pity. My puffed-out eye and blood-
covered face moved her to tears. She took a chair by me, washed the
blood from my face, and, with a mother's tenderness, bound up my
head, covering the wounded eye with a lean piece of fresh beef. It
was almost compensation for my suffering to witness, once more, a
manifestation of kindness from this, my once affectionate old mistress. Master Hugh was very much enraged. He gave expression to
his feelings by pouring out curses upon the heads of those who did
the deed. As soon as I got a little the better of my bruises, he took
me with him to Esquire Watson's, on Bond Street, to see what could
be done about the matter. Mr. Watson inquired who saw the assault
committed. Master Hugh told him it was done in Mr. Gardner's ship-
yard, at midday, where there were a large company of men at work.
"As to that," he said, "the deed was done, and there was no question
as to who did it." His answer was, he could do nothing in the case,
unless some white man would come forward and testify. He could
issue no warrant on my word. If I had been killed in the presence of
a thousand colored people, their testimony combined would have
been insufficient to have arrested one of the murderers. Master Hugh,
for once, was compelled to say this state of things was too bad. Of
course, it was impossible to get any white man to volunteer his

testimony in my behalf, and against the white young men. Even those who may have sympathized with me were not prepared to do this. It required a degree of courage unknown to them to do so; for just at that time, the slightest manifestation of humanity toward a colored person was denounced as abolitionism, and that name subjected its bearer to frightful liabilities. The watchwords of the bloody-minded in that region, and in those days were, "Damn the abolitionists!" and "Damn the niggers!" There was nothing done, and probably nothing would have been done if I had been killed. Such was, and such remains, the state of things in the Christian city of Baltimore.

Master Hugh, finding he could get no redress, refused to let me go back again to Mr. Gardner. He kept me himself, and his wife dressed my wound till I was again restored to health. He then took me into the ship-yard of which he was foreman, in the employment of Mr. Walter Price. There I was immediately set to calking, and very soon learned the art of using my mallet and irons. In the course of one year from the time I left Mr. Gardner's, I was able to command the highest wages given to the most experienced calkers. I was now of some importance to my master. I was bringing him from six to seven dollars per week. I sometimes brought him nine dollars per week: my wages were a dollar and a half a day. After learning how to calk, I sought my own employment, made my own contracts, and collected the money which I earned. My pathway became much more smooth than before; my condition was now much more comfortable. When I could get no calking to do, I did nothing. During these leisure times, those old notions about freedom would steal over me again. When in Mr. Gardner's employment, I was kept in such a perpetual whirl of excitement, I could think of nothing, scarcely, but my life; and in thinking of my life, I almost forgot my liberty. I have observed this in my experience of slavery,—that whenever my condition was improved, instead of its increasing my contentment, it only increased my desire to be free, and set me to thinking of plans to gain my freedom. I have found that, to make a contented slave, it is necessary to make a thoughtless one. It is necessary to darken his moral and mental vision, and, as far as possible, to annihilate the power of reason. He must be able to detect no inconsistencies in slavery; he must be made to feel that slavery is right; and he can be brought to that only when he ceases to be a man.

I was now getting, as I have said, one dollar and fifty cents per day. I contracted for it; I earned it; it was paid to me; it was rightfully my own; yet, upon each returning Saturday night, I was compelled to deliver every cent of that money to Master Hugh. And why? Not

because he earned it,—not because he had any hand in earning it,—
not because I owed it to him,—nor because he possessed the slightest
shadow of a right to it; but solely because he had the power to
compel me to give it up. The right of the grim-visaged pirate upon
the high seas is exactly the same.

CHIEF SEATTLE

"We Know That the White Man Does Not Understand Our Ways"

Chief Seattle (1786–1866) was the leader of the Dewamish and
other Pacific Northwest tribes; the city of Seattle, Washington,
bears his name. In 1854, Chief Seattle reluctantly agreed to sell
tribal lands to the United States government and move to the
government-established reservations. His speech, translated and recorded by Dr. Henry Smith, is noteworthy for its description of
the cultural differences between the Dewamish and the mostly
European settlers.

Yonder sky that has wept tears of compassion upon my people for
centuries untold, and which to us appears changeless and eternal,
may change. Today is fair. Tomorrow may be overcast with clouds.
My words are like the stars that never change. Whatever Seattle says
the great chief at Washington can rely upon with as much certainty
as he can upon the return of the sun or the seasons. The White Chief
says that Big Chief at Washington sends us greetings of friendship
and goodwill. That is kind of him for we know he has little need of
our friendship in return. His people are many. They are like the grass
that covers vast prairies. My people are few. They resemble the
scattering trees of a storm-swept plain. The great, and—I presume—
good, White Chief sends us word that he wishes to buy our lands
but is willing to allow us enough to live comfortably. This indeed
appears just, even generous, for the Red Man no longer has rights

Translated by Henry A. Smith.

that he need respect, and the offer may be wise also, as we are no longer in need of an extensive country. . . . I will not dwell on, nor mourn over, our untimely decay, nor reproach our paleface brothers with hastening it, as we too may have been somewhat to blame.

Youth is impulsive. When our young men grow angry at some real or imaginary wrong, and disfigure their faces with black paint, it denotes that their hearts are black, and then they are often cruel and relentless, and our old men and old women are unable to restrain them. Thus it has ever been. Thus it was when the white men first began to push our forefathers westward. But let us hope that the hostilities between us may never return. We would have everything to lose and nothing to gain. Revenge by young men is considered gain, even at the cost of their own lives, but old men who stay at home in times of war, and mothers who have sons to lose, know better.

Our good father at Washington—for I presume he is now our father as well as yours, since King George has moved his boundaries further north—our great good father, I say, sends us word that if we do as he desires he will protect us. His brave warriors will be to us a bristling wall of strength, and his wonderful ships of war will fill our harbors so that our ancient enemies far to the northward—the Hydas and Tsimpsians[1]—will cease to frighten our women, children, and old men. Then in reality will he be our father and we his children. But can that ever be? Your God is not our God! Your God loves your people and hates mine. He folds his strong and protecting arms lovingly about the paleface and leads him by the hand as a father leads his infant son—but He has forsaken His red children—if they really are his. Our God, the Great Spirit, seems also to have forsaken us. Your God makes your people wax strong every day. Soon they will fill the land. Our people are ebbing away like a rapidly receding tide that will never return. The white man's God cannot love our people or He would protect them. They seem to be orphans who can look nowhere for help. How then can we be brothers? How can your God become our God and renew our prosperity and awaken in us dreams of returning greatness? If we have a common heavenly father He must be partial—for He came to his paleface children. We never saw Him. He gave you laws but He had no word for His red children whose teeming multitudes once filled this vast continent as stars fill

---

[1] People of the northern Pacific coast who lived near the Gulf of Alaska. (ED.)

the firmament. No; we are two distinct races with separate origins and separate destinies. There is little in common between us.

To us the ashes of our ancestors are sacred and their resting place is hallowed ground. You wander far from the graves of your ancestors and seemingly without regret. Your religion was written upon tables of stone by the iron finger of your God so that you could not forget. The Red Man could never comprehend nor remember it. Our religion is the traditions of our ancestors—the dreams of our old men, given them in solemn hours of night by the Great Spirit; and the visions of our sachems;[2] and it is written in the hearts of our people.

Your dead cease to love you and the land of their nativity as soon as they pass the portals of the tomb and wander way beyond the stars. They are soon forgotten and never return. Our dead never forget the beautiful world that gave them being.

Day and night cannot dwell together. The Red Man has ever fled the approach of the White Man, as the morning mist flees before the morning sun. However, your proposition seems fair and I think that my people will accept it and will retire to the reservation you offer them. Then we will dwell apart in peace, for the words of the Great White Chief seem to be the words of nature speaking to my people out of dense darkness.

It matters little where we pass the remnant of our days. They will not be many. A few more moons; a few more winters—and not one of the descendants of the mighty hosts that once moved over this broad land or lived in happy homes, protected by the Great Spirit, will remain to mourn over the graves of a people once more powerful and hopeful than yours. But why should I mourn at the untimely fate of my people? Tribe follows tribe, and nation follows nation, like the waves of the sea. It is the order of nature, and regret is useless. Your time of decay may be distant, but it will surely come, for even the White Man whose God walked and talked with him as friend with friend, cannot be exempt from the common destiny. We may be brothers after all. We will see.

We will ponder your proposition, and when we decide we will let you know. But should we accept it, I here and now make this condition that we will not be denied the privilege without molestation of visiting at any time the tombs of our ancestors, friends and children. Every part of this soil is sacred in the estimation of my people. Every hillside, every valley, every plain and grove, has been hallowed

---

[2] Chiefs of tribes or confederations among some North American Indians. (ED.)

by some sad or happy event in days long vanished. . . . The very dust upon which you now stand responds more lovingly to their footsteps than to yours, because it is rich with the blood of our ancestors and our bare feet are conscious of the sympathetic touch. . . . Even the little children who lived here and rejoiced here for a brief season will love these somber solitudes and at eventide they greet shadowy returning spirits. And when the last Red Man shall have perished, and the memory of my tribe shall have become a myth among the White Men, these shores will swarm with the invisible dead of my tribe, and when your children's children think themselves alone in the field, the store, the shop, upon the highway, or in the silence of the pathless woods, they will not be alone. . . . At night when the streets of your cities and villages are silent and you think them deserted, they will throng with the returning hosts that once filled and still love this beautiful land. The White Man will never be alone.

Let him be just and deal kindly with my people, for the dead are not powerless. Dead, did I say? There is no death, only a change of worlds.

CLARENCE DARROW

Address to the Prisoners in the Cook County Jail

Clarence Darrow (1857–1938) was an American defense lawyer and social reformer who was a vigorous foe of the death penalty. He received national recognition through his defense of John T. Scopes, a Tennessee teacher who broke state law by teaching Darwinian evolution. The story of the Scopes trial was later popularized in the play and film *Inherit the Wind.* Darrow's writings include *Crime: Its Cause and Treatment* (1922), *The Skeleton in the Closet* (1924), and *The Story of My Life* (1932). Darrow delivered the following speech to the prisoners in the Cook County, Illinois, penitentiary in 1902.

If I looked at jails and crimes and prisoners in the way the ordinary person does, I should not speak on this subject to you. The reason I talk to you on the question of crime, its cause and cure, is that I really do not in the least believe in crime. There is no such thing as a crime as the word is generally understood. I do not believe there is any sort of distinction between the real moral conditions of the people in and out of jail. One is just as good as the other. The people here can no more help being here than the people outside can avoid being outside. I do not believe that people are in jail because they deserve to be. They are in jail simply because they cannot avoid it on account of circumstances which are entirely beyond their control and for which they are in no way responsible.

I suppose a great many people on the outside would say I was doing you harm if they should hear what I say to you this afternoon, but you cannot be hurt a great deal anyway, so it will not matter. Good people outside would say that I was really teaching you things that were calculated to injure society, but it's worth while now and then to hear something different from what you ordinarily get from preachers and the like. These will tell you that you should be good and then you will get rich and be happy. Of course we know that people do not get rich by being good, and that is the reason why so many of you people try to get rich some other way, only you do not understand how to do it quite as well as the fellow outside.

There are people who think that everything in this world is an accident. But really there is no such thing as an accident. A great many folks admit that many of the people in jail ought to be there, and many who are outside ought to be in. I think none of them ought to be here. There ought to be no jails; and if it were not for the fact that people on the outside are so grasping and heartless in their dealings with the people on the inside, there would be no such institution as jails.

I do not want you to believe that I think all you people here are angels. I do not think that. You are people of all kinds, all of you doing the best you can—and that is evidently not very well. You are people of all kinds and conditions and under all circumstances. In one sense everybody is equally good and equally bad. We all do the best we can under the circumstances. But as to the exact things for which you are sent here, some of you are guilty and did the particular act because you needed the money. Some of you did it because you are in the habit of doing it, and some of you because you are born to it, and it comes to be as natural as it does, for instance, for me to be good.

Most of you probably have nothing against me, and most of you would treat me the same way as any other person would, probably better than some of the people on the outside would treat me, because you think I believe in you and they know I do not believe in them. While you would not have the least thing against me in the world, you might pick my pockets. I do not think all of you would, but I think some of you would. You would not have anything against me, but that's your profession, a few of you. Some of the rest of you, if my doors were unlocked, might come in if you saw anything you wanted—not out of any malice to me, but because that is your trade. There is no doubt there are quite a number of people in this jail who would pick my pockets. And still I know this—that when I get outside pretty nearly everybody picks my pocket. There may be some of you who would hold up a man on the street, if you did not happen to have something else to do, and needed the money; but when I want to light my house or my office the gas company holds me up. They charge me one dollar for something that is worth twenty-five cents. Still all these people are good people; they are pillars of society and support the churches, and they are respectable.

When I ride on the streetcars I am held up—I pay five cents for a ride that is worth two and a half cents, simply because a body of men have bribed the city council and the legislature, so that all the rest of us have to pay tribute to them.

If I do not want to fall into the clutches of the gas trust and choose to burn oil instead of gas, then good Mr. Rockefeller holds me up, and he uses a certain portion of his money to build universities and support churches which are engaged in telling us how to be good.

Some of you are here for obtaining property under false pretenses—yet I pick up a great Sunday paper and read the advertisements of a merchant prince—"Shirtwaists for 39 cents, marked down from $3.00."

When I read the advertisements in the paper I see they are all lies. When I want to get out and find a place to stand anywhere on the face of the earth, I find that it has all been taken up long ago before I came here, and before you came here, and somebody says, "Get off, swim into the lake, fly into the air; go anywhere, but get off." That is because these people have the police and they have the jails and the judges and the lawyers and the soldiers and all the rest of them to take care of the earth and drive everybody off that comes in their way.

A great many people will tell you that all this is true, but that it does not excuse you. These facts do not excuse some fellow who reaches into my pocket and takes out a five-dollar bill. The fact that the gas company bribes the members of the legislature from year to

year, and fixes the law, so that all you people are compelled to be
"fleeced" whenever you deal with them; the fact that the streetcar
companies and the gas companies have control of the streets; and
the fact that the landlords own all the earth—this, they say, has
nothing to do with you.

Let us see whether there is any connection between the crimes
of the respectable classes and your presence in the jail. Many of you
people are in jail because you have really committed burglary; many
of you, because you have stolen something. In the meaning of the
law, you have taken some other person's property. Some of you have
entered a store and carried off a pair of shoes because you did not
have the price. Possibly some of you have committed murder. I
cannot tell what all of you did. There are a great many people here
who have done some of these things who really do not know themselves why they did them. I think I know why you did them—every
one of you; you did these things because you were bound to do
them. It looked to you at the time as if you had a chance to do them
or not, as you saw fit; but still, after all, you had no choice. There
may be people here who had some money in their pockets and who
still went out and got some more money in a way society forbids.
Now, you may not yourselves see exactly why it was you did this
thing, but if you look at the question deeply enough and carefully
enough you will see that there were circumstances that drove you to
do exactly the thing which you did. You could not help it any more
than we outside can help taking the positions that we take. The
reformers who tell you to be good and you will be happy, and the
people on the outside who have property to protect—they think that
the only way to do it is by building jails and locking you up in cells
on weekdays and praying for you Sundays.

I think that all of this has nothing whatever to do with right conduct. I think it is very easily seen what has to do with right
conduct. Some so-called criminals—and I will use this word because
it is handy, it means nothing to me—I speak of the criminals who
get caught as distinguished from the criminals who catch them—
some of these so-called criminals are in jail for their first offenses,
but nine tenths of you are in jail because you did not have a good
lawyer and, of course, you did not have a good lawyer because you
did not have enough money to pay a good lawyer. There is no very
great danger of a rich man going to jail.

Some of you may be here for the first time. If we would open the
doors and let you out, and leave the laws as they are today, some of

you would be back tomorrow. This is about as good a place as you can get anyway. There are many people here who are so in the habit of coming that they would not know where else to go. There are people who are born with the tendency to break into jail every chance they get, and they cannot avoid it. You cannot figure out your life and see why it was, but still there is a reason for it; and if we were all wise and knew all the facts, we could figure it out.

In the first place, there are a good many more people who go to jail in the wintertime than in the summer. Why is this? Is it because people are more wicked in the winter? No, it is because the coal trust begins to get in its grip in the winter. A few gentlemen take possession of the coal, and unless the people will pay seven or eight dollars a ton for something that is worth three dollars, they will have to freeze. Then there is nothing to do but to break into jail, and so there are many more in jail in the winter than in summer. It costs more for gas in the winter because the nights are longer, and people go to jail to save gas bills. The jails are electric-lighted. You may not know it, but these economic laws are working all the time, whether we know it or do not know it.

There are more people who go to jail in hard times than in good times—few people, comparatively, go to jail except when they are hard up. They go to jail because they have no other place to go. They may not know why, but it is true all the same. People are not more wicked in hard times. That is not the reason. The fact is true all over the world that in hard times more people go to jail than in good times, and in winter more people go to jail than in summer. Of course it is pretty hard times for people who go to jail at any time. The people who go to jail are almost always poor people— people who have no other place to live, first and last. When times are hard, then you find large numbers of people who go to jail who would not otherwise be in jail.

Long ago, Mr. Buckle, who was a great philosopher and historian, collected facts, and he showed that the number of people who are arrested increased just as the price of food increased. When they put up the price of gas ten cents a thousand, I do not know who will go to jail, but I do know that a certain number of people will go. When the meat combine raises the price of beef, I do not know who is going to jail, but I know that a large number of people are bound to go. Whenever the Standard Oil Company raises the price of oil, I know that a certain number of girls who are seamstresses, and who work night after night long hours for somebody else, will be compelled to go out on the streets and ply another trade, and I know that Mr. Rockefeller and his associates are responsible and not the poor girls in the jails.

First and last, people are sent to jail because they are poor. Sometimes, as I say, you may not need money at the particular time, but you wish to have thrifty forehanded habits, and do not always wait until you are in absolute want. Some of you people are perhaps plying the trade, the profession, which is called burglary. No man in his right senses will go into a strange house in the dead of night and prowl around with a dark lantern through unfamiliar rooms and take chances of his life, if he has plenty of the good things of the world in his own home. You would not take any such chances as that. If a man had clothes in his clothespress and beefsteak in his pantry and money in the bank, he would not navigate around nights in houses where he knows nothing about the premises whatever. It always requires experience and education for this profession, and people who fit themselves for it are no more to blame than I am for being a lawyer. A man would not hold up another man on the street if he had plenty of money in his own pocket. He might do it if he had one dollar or two dollars, but he wouldn't if he had as much money as Mr. Rockefeller has. Mr. Rockefeller has a great deal better hold-up game than that.

The more that is taken from the poor by the rich, who have the chance to take it, the more poor people there are who are compelled to resort to these means for a livelihood. They may not understand it, they may not think so at once, but after all they are driven into that line of employment.

There is a bill before the legislature of this state to punish kid-naping children with death. We have wise members of the legislature. They know the gas trust when they see it and they always see it— they can furnish light enough to be seen; and this legislature thinks it is going to stop kidnaping children by making a law punishing kidnapers of children with death. I don't believe in kidnaping chil-dren, but the legislature is all wrong. Kidnaping children is not a crime, it is a profession. It has been developed with the times. It has been developed with our modern industrial conditions. There are many ways of making money—many new ways that our ancestors knew nothing about. Our ancestors knew nothing about a billion-dollar trust; and here comes some poor fellow who has no other trade and he discovers the profession of kidnaping children.

This crime is born, not because people are bad; people don't kidnap other people's children because they want the children or because they are devilish, but because they see a chance to get some money out of it. You cannot cure this crime by passing a law punishing by death kidnapers of children. There is one way to cure it. There is one way to cure all these offenses, and that is to give the people a chance to live. There is no other way, and there never was any other way since the world began; and the world is so blind and stupid that it will not see. If every man and woman and child in the world had a chance to make a decent, fair, honest living, there would be no jails and no lawyers and no courts. There might be some persons here or there with some peculiar formation of their brain, like Rockefeller, who would do these things simply to be doing them; but they would be very, very few, and those should be sent to a hospital and treated, and not sent to jail; and they would entirely disappear in the second generation, or at least in the third generation.

I am not talking pure theory. I will just give you two or three illustrations.

The English people once punished criminals by sending them away. They would load them on a ship and export them to Australia. England was owned by lords and nobles and rich people. They owned the whole earth over there, and the other people had to stay in the streets. They could not get a decent living. They used to take their criminals and send them to Australia—I mean the class of criminals who got caught. When these criminals got over there, and nobody else had come, they had the whole continent to run over, and so they could raise sheep and furnish their own meat, which is easier than stealing it. These criminals then became decent, respectable people because they had a chance to live. They did not commit any crimes. They were just like the English people who sent them there, only better. And in the second generation the descendants of those criminals were as good and respectable a class of people as there were on the face of the earth, and then they began building churches and jails themselves.

A portion of this country was settled in the same way, landing prisoners down on the southern coast; but when they got here and had a whole continent to run over and plenty of chances to make a living, they became respectable citizens, making their own living just like any other citizen in the world. But finally the descendants of the English aristocracy who sent the people over to Australia found out they were getting rich, and so they went over to get possession of the earth as they always do, and they organized land syndicates and got control of the land and ores, and then they had just as many criminals in Australia as they did in England. It was not because the world had grown bad; it was because the earth had been taken away from the people.

Some of you people have lived in the country. It's prettier than it is here. And if you have ever lived on a farm you understand that if you put a lot of cattle in a field, when the pasture is short they will jump over the fence; but put them in a good field where there is plenty of pasture, and they will be law-abiding cattle to the end of time. The human animal is just like the rest of the animals, only a little more so. The same thing that governs in the one governs in the other.

Everybody makes his living along the lines of least resistance. A wise man who comes into a country early sees a great undeveloped land. For instance, our rich men twenty-five years ago saw that Chicago was small and knew a lot of people would come here and settle, and they readily saw that if they had all the land around here it would be worth a good deal, so they grabbed the land. You cannot be a landlord because somebody has got it all. You must find some other calling. In England and Ireland and Scotland less than five per cent own all the land there is, and the people are bound to stay there on any kind of terms the landlords give. They must live the best they can, so they develop all these various professions—burglary, picking pockets, and the like.

Again, people find all sorts of ways of getting rich. These are diseases like everything else. You look at people getting rich, organizing trusts and making a million dollars, and somebody gets the disease and he starts out. He catches it just as a man catches the mumps or the measles; he is not to blame, it is in the air. You will find men speculating beyond their means, because the mania of money-getting is taking possession of them. It is simply a disease—nothing more, nothing less. You cannot avoid catching it; but the fellows who have control of the earth have the advantage of you. See what the law is: when these men get control of things, they make the laws. They do not make the laws to protect anybody; courts are not instruments of justice. When your case gets into court it will make little difference whether you are guilty or innocent, but it's better if you have a smart lawyer. And you cannot have a smart lawyer unless you have money. First and last it's a question of money. Those men who own the earth make the laws to protect what they have. They fix up a sort of fence or pen around what they have, and they fix the law so the fellow on the outside cannot get in. The laws are really organized for the protection of the men who rule the world.

They were never organized or enforced to do justice. We have no system for doing justice, not the slightest in the world.

Let me illustrate: Take the poorest person in this room. If the community had provided a system of doing justice, the poorest person in this room would have as good a lawyer as the richest, would he not? When you went into court you would have just as long a trial and just as fair a trial as the richest person in Chicago. Your case would not be tried in fifteen or twenty minutes, whereas it would take fifteen days to get through with a rich man's case.

Then if you were rich and were beaten, your case would be taken to the Appellate Court. A poor man cannot take his case to the Appellate Court; he has not the price. And then to the Supreme Court. And if he were beaten there he might perhaps go to the United States Supreme Court. And he might die of old age before he got into jail. If you are poor, it's a quick job. You are almost known to be guilty, else you would not be there. Why should anyone be in the criminal court if he were not guilty? He would not be there if he could be anywhere else. The officials have no time to look after all these cases. The people who are on the outside, who are running banks and building churches and making jails, they have no time to examine 600 or 700 prisoners each year to see whether they are guilty or innocent. If the courts were organized to promote justice the people would elect somebody to defend all these criminals, some-body as smart as the prosecutor—and give him as many detectives and as many assistants to help, and pay as much money to defend you as to prosecute you. We have a very able man for state's attorney, and he has many assistants, detectives, and policemen without end, and judges to hear the cases—everything handy.

Most all of our criminal code consists in offenses against property. People are sent to jail because they have committed a crime against property. It is of very little consequence whether one hundred people more or less go to jail who ought not to go—you must protect property, because in this world property is of more importance than anything else.

How is it done? These people who have property fix it so they can protect what they have. When somebody commits a crime it does not follow that he has done something that is morally wrong. The man on the outside who has committed no crime may have done something. For instance: to take all the coal in the United States and raise the price two dollars or three dollars when there is no need of it, and thus kill thousands of babies and send thousands of people to the poorhouse and tens of thousands to jail, as is done every year in the United States—this is a greater crime than all the people in our jails ever committed; but the law does not punish it. Why? Because the fellows who control the earth make the laws. If you and I had the making of the laws, the first thing we would do would be to punish the fellow who gets control of the earth. Nature put this coal in the ground for me as well as for them and nature made the prairies up here to raise wheat for me as well as for them, and then the great railroad companies came along and fenced it up.

Most all of the crimes for which we are punished are property crimes. There are a few personal crimes, like murder—but they are very few. The crimes committed are mostly those against property. If this punishment is right the criminals must have a lot of property. How much money is there in this crowd? And yet you are all here for crimes against property. The people up and down the Lake Shore have not committed crime; still they have so much property they don't know what to do with it. It is perfectly plain why these people have not committed crimes against property; they make the laws and therefore do not need to break them. And in order for you to get some property you are obliged to break the rules of the game. I don't know but what some of you may have had a very nice chance to get rich by carrying a hod for one dollar a day, twelve hours. Instead of taking that nice, easy profession, you are a burglar. If you had been given a chance to be a banker you would rather follow that. Some of you may have had a chance to work as a switchman on a railroad where you know, according to statistics, that you cannot live and keep all your limbs more than seven years, and you can get fifty dollars or seventy-five dollars a month for taking your lives in your hands; and instead of taking that lucrative position you chose to be a sneak thief, or something like that. Some of you made that sort of choice. I don't know which I would take if I was reduced to this choice. I have an easier choice.

I will guarantee to take from this jail, or any jail in the world, five hundred men who have been the worst criminals and lawbreakers who ever got into jail, and I will go down to our lowest streets and take five hundred of the most abandoned prostitutes, and go out somewhere where there is plenty of land, and will give them a chance to make a living, and they will be as good people as the average in the community.

There is one remedy for the sort of condition we see here. The world never finds it out, or when it does find it out it does not enforce it. You may pass a law punishing every person with death for burglary, and it will make no difference. Men will commit it just the same. In England there was a time when one hundred different offenses were punishable with death, and it made no difference. The English people strangely found out that so fast as they repealed the severe penalties and so fast as they did away with punishing men by death, crime decreased instead of increased; that the smaller the penalty the fewer the crimes.

Hanging men in our county jails does not prevent murder. It makes murderers.

And this has been the history of the world. It's easy to see how to do away with what we call crime. It is not so easy to do it. I will tell you how to do it. It can be done by giving the people a chance to live—by destroying special privileges. So long as big criminals can get the coal fields, so long as the big criminals have control of the city council and get the public streets for streetcars and gas rights—this is bound to send thousands of poor people to jail. So long as men are allowed to monopolize all the earth, and compel others to live on such terms as these men see fit to make, then you are bound to get into jail.

The only way in the world to abolish crime and criminals is to abolish the big ones and the little ones together. Make fair conditions of life. Give men a chance to live. Abolish the right of private ownership of land, abolish monopoly, make the world partners in production, partners in the good things of life. Nobody would steal if he could get something of his own some easier way. Nobody will commit burglary when he has a house full. No girl will go out on the streets when she has a comfortable place at home. The man who owns a sweatshop or a department store may not be to blame himself for the condition of his girls, but when he pays them five dollars, three dollars, and two dollars a week, I wonder where he thinks they will get the rest of the money to live. The only way to cure these conditions is by equality. There should be no jails. They do not accomplish what they pretend to accomplish. If you would wipe them out there would be no more criminals than now. They terrorize nobody. They are a blot upon any civilization, and a jail is an evidence of the lack of charity of the people on the outside who make the jails and fill them with the victims of their greed.

FRANCES FITZGERALD

Rewriting American History

Frances FitzGerald (1940–   ) is a writer and social historian who won the Pulitzer Prize in 1973 for Fire in the Lake: The Vietnamese and Americans in Vietnam. *The following selection is from* America Revised *(1980), a study of the influences on schoolbooks currently used in American education. She has also published* Cities on a Hill *(1986), which surveys contemporary cultures in the United States. FitzGerald is a frequent contributor to numerous publications, including the* New Yorker, *the* Atlantic, *the* Village Voice, *and* Vogue.

Those of us who grew up in the fifties believed in the permanence of our American-history textbooks. To us as children, those texts were the truth of things: they were American history. It was not just that we read them before we understood that not everything that is printed is the truth, or the whole truth. It was that they, much more than other books, had the demeanor and trappings of authority. They were weighty volumes. They spoke in measured cadences: imperturbable, humorless, and as distant as Chinese emperors. Our teachers treated them with respect, and we paid them abject homage by memorizing a chapter a week. But now the textbook histories have changed, some of them to such an extent that an adult would find them unrecognizable.

One current junior-high-school American history begins with a story about a Negro cowboy called George McJunkin. It appears that when McJunkin was riding down a lonely trail in New Mexico one cold spring morning in 1925 he discovered a mound containing bones and stone implements, which scientists later proved belonged to an Indian civilization ten thousand years old. The book goes on to say that scientists now believe there were people in the Americas at least twenty thousand years ago. It discusses the Aztec, Mayan, and Incan civilizations and the meaning of the word "culture" before introducing the European explorers.

Another history text—this one for the fifth grade—begins with the story of how Henry B. Gonzalez, who is a member of Congress from Texas, learned about his own nationality. When he was ten years old, his teacher told him he was an American because he was born in the United States. His grandmother, however, said, "The cat was born in the oven. Does that make him bread?" After reporting that Mr. Gonzalez eventually went to college and law school, the book explains that "the melting pot idea hasn't worked out as some thought it would," and that now "some people say that the people of the United States are more like a salad bowl than a melting pot."

Poor Columbus! He is a minor character now, a walk-on in the middle of American history. Even those books that have not replaced his picture with a Mayan temple or an Iroquois mask do not credit him with discovering America—even for the Europeans. The Vikings, they say, preceded him to the New World, and after that the Europeans, having lost or forgotten their maps, simply neglected to cross the ocean again for five hundred years. Columbus is far from being the only personage to have suffered from time and revision. Captain John Smith, Daniel Boone, and Wild Bill Hickok—the great self-promoters of American history—have all but disappeared, taking with them a good deal of the romance of the American frontier. General Custer has given way to Chief Crazy Horse; General Eisenhower no longer liberates Europe single-handed; and, indeed, most generals, even to Washington and Lee, have faded away, as old soldiers do, giving place to social reformers such as William Lloyd Garrison and Jacob Riis. A number of black Americans have risen to prominence: not only George Washington Carver but Frederick Douglass and Martin Luther King, Jr. W. E. B. Du Bois now invariably accompanies Booker T. Washington. In addition, there is a mystery man called Crispus Attucks, a fugitive slave about whom nothing seems to be known for certain except that he was a victim of the Boston Massacre and thus became one of the first casualties of the American Revolution. Thaddeus Stevens[1] has been reconstructed—his character changed, as it were, from black to white, from cruel and vindictive to persistent and sincere. As for Teddy Roosevelt, he now champions the issue of conservation instead of charging up San Juan Hill. No single President really stands out as a hero, but all Presidents—except certain unmentionables in the second half of the nineteenth century—seem to have done as well as could be expected, given difficult circumstances.

Of course, when one thinks about it, it is hardly surprising that modern scholarship and modern perspectives have found their way into children's books. Yet the changes remain shocking. Those who

---

[1] Thaddeus Stevens (1792–1868) was a congressman who led radical Republicans in developing a strict plan for Reconstruction after the Civil War. (ED.)

in the sixties complained of the bland optimism, the chauvinism, and the materialism of their old civics text did so in the belief that, for all their protests, the texts would never change. The thought must have had something reassuring about it, for that generation never noticed when its complaints began to take effect and the songs about radioactive rainfall and houses made of ticky-tacky began to appear in the textbooks. But this is what happened.

The history texts now hint at a certain level of unpleasantness in American history. Several books, for instance, tell the story of Ishi, the last "wild" Indian in the continental United States, who, captured in 1911 after the massacre of his tribe, spent the final four and a half years of his life in the University of California's museum of anthropology, in San Francisco. At least three books show the same stunning picture of the breaker boys, the child coal miners of Pennsylvania—ancient children with deformed bodies and blackened faces who stare stupidly out from the entrance to a mine. One book quotes a soldier on the use of torture in the American campaign to pacify the Philippines at the beginning of the century. A number of books say that during the American Revolution the patriots tarred and feathered those who did not support them, and drove many of the loyalists from the country. Almost all the present-day history books note that the United States interned Japanese-Americans in detention camps during the Second World War.

Ideologically speaking, the histories of the fifties were implacable, seamless. Inside their covers, America was perfect: the greatest nation in the world, and the embodiment of democracy, freedom, and technological progress. For them, the country never changed in any important way: its values and its political institutions remained constant from the time of the American Revolution. To my generation—the children of the fifties—these texts appeared permanent just because they were so self-contained. Their orthodoxy, it seemed, left no handholds for attack, no lodging for decay. Who, after all, would dispute the wonders of technology or the superiority of the English colonists over the Spanish? Who would find fault with the pastorale of the West or the Old South? Who would question the anti-Communist crusade? There was, it seemed, no point in comparing these visions with reality, since they were the public truth and were thus quite irrelevant to what existed and to what anyone privately believed. They were—or so it seemed—the permanent expression of mass culture in America.

But now the texts have changed, and with them the country that American children are growing up into. The society that was once uniform is now a patchwork of rich and poor, old and young, men and women, blacks, whites, Hispanics, and Indians. The system that ran so smoothly by means of the Constitution under the guidance of benevolent conductor Presidents is now a rattletrap affair. The past is no highway to the present; it is a collection of issues and events that do not fit together and that lead in no single direction. The word "progress" has been replaced by the word "change": children, the modern texts insist, should learn history so that they can adapt to the rapid changes taking place around them. History is proceeding in spite of us. The present, which was once portrayed in the con- cluding chapters as a peaceful haven of scientific advances and Pres- idential inaugurations, is now a tangle of problems: race problems, urban problems, foreign-policy problems, problems of pollution, pov- erty, energy depletion, youthful rebellion, assassination, and drugs. Some books illustrate these problems dramatically. One, for instance, contains a picture of a doll half buried in a mass of untreated sewage; the caption reads, "Are we in danger of being overwhelmed by the products of our society and wastage created by their production? Would you agree with this photographer's interpretation?" Two books show the same picture of an old black woman sitting in a straight chair in a dingy room, her hands folded in graceful resig- nation; the surrounding text discusses the problems faced by the urban poor and by the aged who depend on Social Security. Other books present current problems less starkly. One of the texts con- cludes sagely:

> Problems are part of life. Nations face them, just as people face them, and try to solve them. And today's Americans have one great advantage over past generations. Never before have Americans been so well equipped to solve their problems. They have today the means to conquer poverty, disease, and ignorance. The technetronic age has put that power into their hands.

Such passages have a familiar ring. Amid all the problems, the deus ex machina[2] of science still dodders around in the gloaming of pious hope.

Even more surprising than the emergence of problems is the discovery that the great unity of the texts has broken. Whereas in the fifties all texts represented the same political view, current texts follow no pattern of orthodoxy. Some books, for instance, portray

[2] God from a machine (ED.)

civil-rights legislation as a series of actions taken by a wise, paternal government; others convey some suggestion of the social upheaval involved and make mention of such people as Stokely Carmichael and Malcolm X. In some books, the Cold War has ended; in others, it continues, with Communism threatening the free nations of the earth.

The political diversity in the books is matched by a diversity of pedagogical approach. In addition to the traditional narrative histories, with their endless streams of facts, there are so-called "discovery," or "inquiry," texts, which deal with a limited number of specific issues in American history. These texts do not pretend to cover the past; they focus on particular topics, such as "stratification in Colonial society" or "slavery and the American Revolution," and illustrate them with documents from primary and secondary sources. The chapters in these books amount to something like case studies, in that they include testimony from people with different perspectives or conflicting views on a single subject. In addition, the chapters provide background information, explanatory notes, and a series of questions for the student. The questions are the heart of the matter, for when they are carefully selected they force students to think much as historians think: to define the point of view of the speaker, analyze the ideas presented, question the relationship between events, and so on. One text, for example, quotes Washington, Jefferson, and John Adams on the question of foreign alliances and then asks, "What did John Adams assume that the international situation would be after the American Revolution? What did Washington's attitude toward the French alliance seem to be? How do you account for his attitude?" Finally, it asks, "Should a nation adopt a policy toward alliances and cling to it consistently, or should it vary its policies toward other countries as circumstances change?" In these books, history is clearly not a list of agreed-upon facts or a sermon on politics but a babble of voices and a welter of events which must be ordered by the historian.

In matters of pedagogy, as in matters of politics, there are not two sharply differentiated categories of books; rather, there is a spectrum. Politically, the books run from moderate left to moderate right; pedagogically, they run from the traditional history sermons, through a middle ground of narrative texts with inquiry-style questions and of inquiry texts with long stretches of narrative, to the most rigorous of case-study books. What is common to the current texts—and makes all of them different from those of the fifties—is their engagement with the social sciences. In eighth-grade histories, the "concepts" of social sciences make fleeting appearances. But these "concepts" are the very foundation stones of various elementary-school social-studies series. The 1970 Harcourt Brace Jovanovich series, for example, boasts in its preface of "a horizontal base or ordering of conceptual schemes" to match its "vertical arm of behavioral themes." What this means is not entirely clear, but the books do proceed from easy questions to hard ones, such as—in the sixth-grade book—"How was interaction between merchants and citizens different in the Athenian and Spartan social systems?" Virtually all the American-history texts for older children include discussions of "role," "status," and "culture." Some of them stage debates between eminent social scientists in roped-off sections of the text; some include essays on economics or sociology; some contain pictures and short biographies of social scientists of both sexes and of diverse races. Many books seem to accord social scientists a higher status than American Presidents.

Quite as striking as these political and pedagogical alterations is the change in the physical appearance of the texts. The schoolbooks of the fifties showed some effort in the matter of design: they had maps, charts, cartoons, photographs, and an occasional four-color picture to break up the columns of print. But beside the current texts they look as naïve as Soviet fashion magazines. The print in the fifties books is heavy and far too black, the colors muddy. The photographs are conventional news shots—portraits of Presidents in three-quarters profile, posed "action" shots of soldiers. The other illustrations tend to be Socialist-realist-style drawings[3] (there are a lot of hefty farmers with hoes in the Colonial-period chapters) or incredibly vulgar made-for-children paintings of patriotic events. One painting shows Columbus standing in full court dress on a beach in the New World from a perspective that could have belonged only to the Arawaks.[4] By contrast, the current texts are paragons of sophisticated modern design. They look not like *People* or *Family Circle* but, rather, like *Architectural Digest* or *Vogue.* The amount of space given to illustrations is far greater than it was in the fifties; in fact, in certain "slow-learner" books the pictures far outweigh the text in importance. However, the illustrations have a much greater historical value.

---

[3] a style of art which originated in the Soviet Union and which glorified labor (ED.)

[4] At the time of the arrival of Columbus and the Spanish, the Arawaks inhabited the Carribean. (ED.)

Instead of made-up paintings or anachronistic sketches, there are cartoons, photographs, and paintings drawn from the periods being treated. The chapters on the Colonial period will show, for instance, a ship's carved prow, a Revere bowl, a Copley[5] painting—a whole gallery of Early Americana. The nineteenth century is illustrated with nineteenth-century cartoons and photographs—and the photographs are all of high artistic quality. As for the twentieth-century chapters, they are adorned with the contents of a modern-art museum.

The use of all this art and high-quality design contains some irony. The nineteenth-century photographs of child laborers or urban slum apartments are so beautiful that they transcend their subjects. To look at them, or at the Victor Gatto painting of the Triangle shirtwaist-factory fire, is to see not misery or ugliness but an art object. In the modern chapters, the contrast between style and content is just as great: the color photographs of junk yards or polluted rivers look as enticing as *Gourmet's* photographs of food. The book that is perhaps the most stark in its description of modern problems illustrates the horrors of nuclear testing with a pretty Ben Shahn picture of the Bikini explosion,[6] and the potential for global ecological disaster with a color photograph of the planet swirling its mantle of white clouds. Whereas in the nineteen-fifties the texts were childish in the sense that they were naïve and clumsy, they are now childish in the sense that they are polymorphous-perverse. American history is not dull any longer; it is a sensuous experience.

The surprise that adults feel in seeing the changes in history texts must come from the lingering hope that there is, somewhere out there, an objective truth. The hope is, of course, foolish. All of us children of the twentieth-century know, or should know, that there are no absolutes in human affairs, and thus there can be no such thing as perfect objectivity. We know that each historian in some degree creates the world anew and that all history is in some degree contemporary history. But beyond this knowledge there is still a hope for some reliable authority, for some fixed stars in the universe. We may know that journalists cannot be wholly unbiased and that "balance" is an imaginary point between two extremes, and yet we hope that Walter Cronkite will tell us the truth of things. In the

---

[5] John Singleton Copley (1738–1815), a painter, has been referred to as the greatest of the American old masters. (ED.)

[6] Bikini was the United States test site for 23 nuclear bomb explosions in the forties and fifties. Ben Shahn (1898–1969) was an American politically-oriented artist. (ED.)

same way, we hope that our history will not change—that we learned the truth of things as children. The texts, with their impersonal voices, encourage this hope, and therefore it is particularly disturbing to see how they change, and how fast.

Slippery history! Not every generation but every few years the content of American-history books for children changes appreciably. Schoolbooks are not, like trade books, written and left to their fate. To stay in step with the cycles of "adoption" in school districts across the country, the publishers revise most of their old texts or substitute new ones every three or four years. In the process of revision, they not only bring history up to date but make changes—often substantial changes—in the body of the work. History books for children are thus more contemporary than any other form of history. How should it be otherwise? Should students read histories written ten, fifteen, thirty years ago? In theory, the system is reasonable—except that each generation of children reads only one generation of schoolbooks. The transient history is those children's history forever—their particular version of America.

FIVE

American Society: The Present

I cannot and will not cut my conscience to fit this year's fashion.
Lillian Hellman (to the House Un-American Activities Committee)

I have a dream.
Martin Luther King, Jr.

The variety of issues that confront American society at the present moment is inexhaustible. In this section we have included writing that touches on some of the most compelling.

Gloria Steinem, in "What It Would Be Like if Women Win," charts some of the changes in sex roles already coming to pass in our society. As you read her essay, note her predictions one by one and ask yourself about the degree to which each has been achieved. Have such changes been desirable? What unforeseen difficulties have come with them? What implications do answers to these questions hold for the future?

Several of the essays in this section address racial issues. N. Scott Momaday, a Native American, writes in "The Way to Rainy Mountain" about some of the perennial problems of his people. Martin Luther King, Jr.'s "Letter from Birmingham Jail," a classic of the civil rights movement and of American history, makes the case for not backing down in the face of racism. In "Why I Left America," James Baldwin shows us how that same racism may be inextricably intertwined with other components of American life. In "On Being Black and Middle Class," Shelby Steele raises questions about the primacy of race and class in creating an individual's identity.

Each of the pieces in this section can be used as a starting point for writing. You can, of course, write personal reactions to one or more of them, but you can also use them to initiate research projects. If, for example, you begin with Russell Baker's "Big Brother Really Is Watching," you might want to check recent newspapers, magazines, and journals for articles about the intrusion of large organizations, including the government, into private life. If you have not already done so, you may want to read George Orwell's novel *Nineteen Eighty-Four* to learn what such intrusion might mean when carried to its logical conclusion. If you begin with Michael J. Arlen's "Life and Death in the Global Village," you might want to consult video archives, or pictures in newspapers of record (such as the *New York Times*) to try to discern differences between the substance of some of the great events of recent history and the pictographic record of those events. Your aim in this exercise might be to determine how newspaper pictures and TV images can distort the substance of history.

Some of the selections here are especially good starting points for developing your ability to argue a case. Do you agree or disagree with the thesis of Milton Friedman's essay, "The Social Responsibility of Business Is to Increase Its Profits"? Can you write an argument that further supports Friedman's case, or an argument that effectively demonstrates the shortcomings of that case?

The nature of argument itself is explored in Joel Achenbach's "Fake Up, America!" Achenbach addresses the ways in which "the technology of falsehood" may be leading us to see the issues of real life in much the same way as we see the artificially constructed issues of TV drama. Use this essay to question the spoken and unspoken premises of other arguments in this section, as well as your own ideas and those of your classmates.

Research need not confine itself to printed material or film. Using Nancy Mairs's "On Being a Cripple" as your starting point, you may want to interview people with physical handicaps to learn how they overcome the obstacles society leaves in their way. You might write an essay on the meaning of the two very different terms "differently abled" and "disabled," considering the different things these two terms imply about the people they are used to describe. Agencies and support groups for the homeless could provide you with avenues for interviews and other materials that you can use to react to Jonathan Kozol's essay, "The Homeless." Health organizations and community service groups may prove useful sources for responding to Randy Shilts's essay, "AIDS."

The final piece in this section, "Think about It," by Frank Conroy, provides material for reflection. In this selection, a college student, someone perhaps much like yourself, accidentally meets two of America's most famous jurists. He learns that they are just people, with faults and foibles much like anyone else. Yet they make decisions literally about life and death. They interpret the rules by which we live. Those rules, written and unwritten, are frequently questioned in our society, giving us all much to think and write about.

GLORIA STEINEM

What It Would Be Like if Women Win

Gloria Steinem (1934–   ), born in Toledo, Ohio, was one of the
founding editors of Ms. magazine. An influential spokesperson for
the women's movement, her books include the essay collection
Outrageous Acts and Everyday Rebellions (1983), and, with photographer George Barris, a biography of Marilyn Monroe entitled *Marilyn* (1986). The following selection first appeared in *Time* magazine in 1970.

Any change is fearful, especially one affecting both politics and sex
roles, so let me begin these utopian speculations with a fact. To break
the ice.

Women don't want to exchange places with men. Male chauvin-
ists, science-fiction writers and comedians may favor that idea for its
shock value, but psychologists say it is a fantasy based on ruling-
class ego and guilt. Men assume that women want to imitate them,
which is just what white people assumed about blacks. An assumption so strong that it may convince the second-class group of the
need to imitate, but for both women and blacks that stage has passed.
Guilt produces the question: What if they could treat us as we have
treated them?

That is not our goal. But we do want to change the economic
system to one more based on merit. In Women's Lib Utopia, there
will be free access to good jobs—and decent pay for the bad ones
women have been performing all along, including housework. Increased skilled labor might lead to a four-hour workday, and higher
wages would encourage further mechanization of repetitive jobs now
kept alive by cheap labor.

With women as half the country's elected representatives, and a
woman President once in a while, the country's *machismo* problems
would be greatly reduced. The old-fashioned idea that manhood
depends on violence and victory is, after all, an important part of
our troubles in the streets, and in Viet Nam. I'm not saying that
women leaders would eliminate violence. We are not more moral
than men; we are only uncorrupted by power so far. When we do

acquire power, we might turn out to have an equal impulse toward aggression. Even now, Margaret Mead believes that women fight less often but more fiercely than men, because women are not taught the rules of the war game and fight only when cornered. But for the next 50 years or so, women in politics will be very valuable by tempering the idea of manhood into something less aggressive and better suited to this crowded, post-atomic planet. Consumer protection and children's rights, for instance, might get more legislative attention.

Men will have to give up ruling-class privileges, but in return they will no longer be the only ones to support the family, get drafted, bear the strain of power and responsibility. Freud to the contrary, anatomy is not destiny, at least not for more than nine months at a time. In Israel women are drafted, and some have gone to war. In England, more men type and run switchboards. In India and Israel, a woman rules. In Sweden, both parents take care of the children. In this country, come Utopia, men and women won't reverse roles: they will be free to choose according to individual talents and preferences.

If role reform sounds sexually unsettling, think how it will change the sexual hypocrisy we have now. No more sex arranged on the barter system, with women pretending interest, and men never sure whether they are loved for themselves or for the security few women can get any other way. (Married or not, for sexual reasons or social ones, most women still find it second nature to Uncle-Tom.) No more men who are encouraged to spend a lifetime living with inferiors: with housekeepers, or dependent creatures who are still children. No more domineering wives, emasculating women, and "Jewish mothers," all of whom are simply human beings with all their normal ambition and drive confined to the home. No more unequal partnerships that eventually doom love and sex.

In order to produce that kind of confidence and individuality, child rearing will train according to talent. Little girls will no longer be surrounded by air-tight, self-fulfilling prophecies of natural passivity, lack of ambition and objectivity, inability to exercise power, and dexterity (so long as special aptitude for jobs requiring patience and dexterity is confined to poorly paid jobs: brain surgery is for males).

Schools and universities will help to break down traditional sex roles, even when parents will not. Half the teachers will be men, a rarity now at preschool and elementary levels: girls will not necessarily serve cookies or boys hoist up the flag. Athletic teams will be picked only by strength and skill. Sexually segregated courses like auto mechanics and home economics will be taken by boys and girls together. New courses in sexual politics will explore female subjugation as the model for political oppression, and women's history will be an academic staple, along with black history, at least until the white-male-oriented textbooks are integrated and rewritten.

As for the American child's classic problem—too much mother, too little father—that would be cured by an equalization of parental responsibility. Free nurseries, school lunches, family cafeterias built into every housing complex, service companies that will do household cleaning chores in a regular, businesslike way, and more responsibility by the entire community for the children: all these will make it possible for both mother and father to work, and to have equal leisure time with the children at home. For parents of very young children, however, a special job category, created by Government and unions, would allow such parents a shorter work day.

The revolution would not take away the option of being a housewife. A woman who prefers to be her husband's housekeeper and/or hostess would receive a percentage of his pay determined by the domestic relations courts. If divorced, she might be eligible for a pension fund, and for a job-training allowance. Or a divorce could be treated the same way that the dissolution of a business partnership is now.

If these proposals seem farfetched, consider Sweden, where most of them are already in effect. Sweden is not yet a working Women's Lib model; most of the role-reform programs began less than a decade ago, and are just beginning to take hold. But that country is so far ahead of us in recognizing the problem that Swedish statements on sex and equality sound like bulletins from the moon.

Our marriage laws, for instance, are so reactionary that Women's Lib groups want couples to take a compulsory written exam on the law, as for a driver's license, before going through with the wedding. A man has alimony and wifely debts to worry about, but a woman may lose so many of her civil rights that in the U.S. now, in important legal ways, she becomes a child again. In some states, she cannot sign credit agreements, use her maiden name, incorporate a business, or establish a legal residence of her own. Being a wife, according to most social and legal definitions, is still a 19th century thing.

Assuming, however, that these blatantly sexist laws are abolished or reformed, that job discrimination is forbidden, that parents share financial responsibility for each other and the children, and that sexual relationships become partnerships of equal adults (some pretty big assumptions), then marriage will probably go right on. Men and women are, after all, physically complementary. When society stops encouraging men to be exploiters and women to be parasites, they may turn out to be more complementary in emotion as well. Women's Lib is not trying to destroy the American family. A look at the statistics on divorce—plus the way in which old people are farmed out with strangers and young people flee the home—shows the destruction that has already been done. Liberated women are just trying to point out the disaster, and build compassionate and practical alternatives from the ruins.

What will exist is a variety of alternative life-styles. Since the population explosion dictates that childbearing be kept to a minimum, parents-and-children will be only one of many "families": couples, age groups, working groups, mixed communes, blood-related clans, class groups, creative groups. Single women will have the right to stay single without ridicule, without the attitudes now betrayed by "spinster" and "bachelor." Lesbians or homosexuals will no longer be denied legally binding marriages, complete with mutual-support agreements and inheritance rights. Paradoxically, the number of homosexuals may get smaller. With fewer overpossessive mothers and fewer fathers who hold up an impossibly cruel or perfectionist idea of manhood, boys will be less likely to be denied or reject their identity as males.

Changes that now seem small may get bigger:

Men's Lib. Men now suffer from more diseases due to stress, heart attacks, ulcers, a higher suicide rate, greater difficulty living alone, less adaptability to change and, in general, a shorter life span than women. There is some scientific evidence that what produces physical problems is not work itself, but the inability to choose which work, and how much. With women bearing half the financial responsibility, and with the idea of "masculine" jobs gone, men might well feel freer and live longer.

Religion. Protestant women are already becoming ordained ministers: radical nuns are carrying out liturgical functions that were once the exclusive property of priests: Jewish women are rewriting prayers—particularly those that Orthodox Jews recite every morning thanking God they are not female. In the future, the church will become an era of equal participation by women. This means, of course, that organized religion will have to give up one of its great historical weapons: sexual repression. In most structured faiths, from

Hinduism through Roman Catholicism, the status of women went down as the position of priests ascended. Male clergy implied, if they did not teach, that women were unclean, unworthy and sources of ungodly temptation, in order to remove them as rivals for the emotional forces of men. Full participation of women in ecclesiastical life might involve certain changes in theology, such as, for instance, a radical redefinition of sin.

Literary Problems. Revised sex roles will outdate more children's books than civil rights ever did. Only a few children had the problem of a *Little Black Sambo,* but most have the male-female stereotypes of "Dick and Jane." A boomlet of children's books about mothers who work has already begun, and liberated parents and editors are beginning to pressure for change in the textbook industry. Fiction writing will change more gradually, but romantic novels with wilting heroines and swashbuckling heroes will be reduced to historical value. Or perhaps to the sado-masochist trade. (*Marjorie Morningstar,* a romantic novel that took the '50s by storm, has already begun to seem as unreal as its '20s predecessor, *The Sheik.*) As for the literary plots that turn on forced marriages or horrific abortions, they will seem as dated as Prohibition stories. Free legal abortions and free birth control will force writers to give up pregnancy as the *deus ex machina.*

Manners and Fashion. Dress will be more androgynous, with class symbols becoming more important than sexual ones. Pro- or anti-Establishment styles may already be more vital than who is wearing them. Hardhats are just as likely to rough up antiwar girls as antiwar men in the street, and police understand that women are just as likely to be pushers or bombers. Dances haven't required that one partner lead the other for years, anyway. Chivalry will transfer itself to those who need it, or deserve respect: old people, admired people, anyone with an armload of packages. Women with normal work identities will be less likely to attach their whole sense of self to youth and appearance; thus there will be fewer nervous breakdowns when the first wrinkles appear. Lighting cigarettes and other treasured niceties will become gestures of mutual affection. "I like to be helped on with my coat," says one Women's Lib worker, "but not if it costs me $2,000 a year in salary."

For those with nostalgia for a simpler past, here is a word of comfort. Anthropologist Geoffrey Gorer studied the few peaceful human tribes and discovered one common characteristic: sex roles were not polarized. Differences of dress and occupation were at a minimum. Society, in other words, was not using sexual blackmail as a way of getting women to do cheap labor, or men to be aggressive.

Thus Women's Lib may achieve a more peaceful society on the way toward its other goals. That is why the Swedish government considers reform to bring about greater equality in the sex roles one of its most important concerns. As Prime Minister Olof Palme explained in a widely ignored speech delivered in Washington this spring: "It is *human beings* we shall emancipate. In Sweden today, if a politician should declare that the woman ought to have a different role from man's, he would be regarded as something from the Stone Age." In other words, the most radical goal of the movement is egalitarianism.

If Women's Lib wins, perhaps we all do.

N. SCOTT MOMADAY

The Way to Rainy Mountain

N. Scott Momaday (1934–   ), who is of Kiowa and Cherokee descent, was born in Oklahoma and grew up in New Mexico. Momaday writes fiction, poetry, and autobiography based on the myths, traditions, and history of the Kiowa; his first novel, *House Made of Dawn,* won a Pulitzer Prize in 1969. Other books include *The Way to Rainy Mountain* (1969), a collection of Kiowa folk tales; *The Gourd Dancer* (1976), a collection of poems; and *The Ancient Child* (1989), a novel.

A single knoll rises out of the plain in Oklahoma, north and west of the Wichita Range. For my people, the Kiowas, it is an old landmark, and they gave it the name Rainy Mountain. The hardest weather in the world is there. Winter brings blizzards, hot tornadic winds arise in the spring, and in summer the prairie is an anvil's edge. The grass turns brittle and brown, and it cracks beneath your feet. There are green belts along the rivers and creeks, linear groves of hickory and pecan, willow and witch hazel. At a distance in July or August the steaming foliage seems almost to writhe in fire. Great green-and-yellow grasshoppers are everywhere in the tall grass, popping up like corn to sting the flesh, and tortoises crawl about on the red earth, going nowhere in the plenty of time. Loneliness is an aspect of the land. All things in the plain are isolate; there is no confusion of objects in the eye, but *one* hill or *one* tree or *one* man. To look upon that landscape in the early morning, with the sun at your back, is to lose the sense of proportion. Your imagination comes to life, and this, you think, is where Creation was begun.

I returned to Rainy Mountain in July. My grandmother had died in the spring, and I wanted to be at her grave. She had lived to be very old and at last infirm. Her only living daughter was with her when she died, and I was told that in death her face was that of a child.

I like to think of her as a child. When she was born, the Kiowas were living that last great moment of their history. For more than a hundred years they had controlled the open range from the Smoky Hill River to the Red, from the headwaters of the Canadian to the fork of the Arkansas and Cimarron. In alliance with the Comanches, they had ruled the whole of the southern Plains. War was their sacred business, and they were among the finest horsemen the world has ever known. But warfare for the Kiowas was preeminently a matter of disposition rather than of survival, and they never understood the grim, unrelenting advance of the U.S. Cavalry. When at last, divided and ill-provisioned, they were driven onto the Staked Plains in the cold rains of autumn, they fell into panic. In Palo Duro Canyon they abandoned their crucial stores to pillage and had nothing then but their lives. In order to save themselves, they surrendered to the soldiers at Fort Sill and were imprisoned in the old stone corral that now stands as a military museum. My grandmother was spared the humiliation of those high gray walls by eight or ten years, but she must have known from birth the affliction of defeat, the dark brooding of old warriors.

Her name was Aho, and she belonged to the last culture to evolve in North America. Her forebears came down from the high country in western Montana nearly three centuries ago. They were a mountain people, a mysterious tribe of hunters whose language has never been positively classified in any major group. In the late seventeenth century they began a long migration to the south and east. It was a long journey toward the dawn, and it led to a golden age. Along the way the Kiowas were befriended by the Crows, who gave them the culture and religion of the Plains. They acquired horses, and their ancient nomadic spirit was suddenly free of the ground. They acquired Tai-me, the sacred Sun Dance doll, from that moment the object and symbol of their worship, and so shared in the divinity of the sun. Not least, they acquired the sense of destiny, therefore courage and pride. When they entered upon the southern Plains, they had been transformed. No longer were they slaves to the simple necessity of survival; they were a lordly and dangerous society of fighters and thieves, hunters and priests of the sun. According to their origin myth, they entered the world through a hollow log. From one point of view, their migration was the fruit of an old prophecy, for indeed they emerged from a sunless world.

Although my grandmother lived out her long life in the shadow of Rainy Mountain, the immense landscape of the continental interior lay like memory in her blood. She could tell of the Crows, whom she had never seen, and of the Black Hills, where she had never been. I wanted to see in reality what she had seen more perfectly in the mind's eye, and traveled fifteen hundred miles to begin my pilgrimage.

Yellowstone, it seemed to me, was the top of the world, a region of deep lakes and dark timber, canyons and waterfalls. But, beautiful as it is, one might have the sense of confinement there. The skyline in all directions is close at hand, the high wall of the woods and deep cleavages of shade. There is a perfect freedom in the mountains, but it belongs to the eagle and the elk, the badger and the bear. The Kiowas reckoned their stature by the distance they could see, and they were bent and blind in the wilderness.

Descending eastward, the highland meadows are a stairway to the plain. In July the inland slope of the Rockies is luxuriant with flax and buckwheat, stonecrop and larkspur. The earth unfolds and the limit of the land recedes. Clusters of trees and animals grazing far in the distance cause the vision to reach away and wonder to build upon the mind. The sun follows a longer course in the day, and the sky is immense beyond all comparison. The great billowing clouds that sail upon it are shadows that move upon the grain like water, dividing light. Farther down, in the land of the Crows and Blackfeet, the plain is yellow. Sweet clover takes hold of the hills and bends upon itself to cover and seal the soil. There the Kiowas paused on their way; they had come to the place where they must change their lives. The sun is at home on the plains. Precisely there does it have the certain character of a god. When the Kiowas came to the land of the Crows, they could see the dark lees of the hill at dawn across the Bighorn River, the profusion of light on the grain shelves, the oldest deity ranging after the solstices. Not yet would they veer southward to the caldron of the land that lay below; they must wean their blood from the northern winter and hold the mountains a while longer in their view. They bore Tai-me in procession to the east.

A dark mist lay over the Black Hills, and the land was like iron. At the top of a ridge I caught sight of Devil's Tower upthrust against the gray sky as if in the birth of time the core of the earth had broken through its crust and the motion of the world was begun. There are things in nature that engender an awful quiet in the heart of man; Devil's Tower is one of them. Two centuries ago, because they could not do otherwise, the Kiowas made a legend at the base of the rock. My grandmother said:

> "Eight children were there at play, seven sisters and their brother. Suddenly the boy was struck dumb; he trembled and began to run upon his hands and feet. His fingers became claws, and his body was covered with fur. Directly there was a bear where the boy had been. The sisters were terrified; they ran, and the bear after them. They came to the stump of a great tree, and the tree spoke to them. It bade them climb upon it and as they did so, it began to rise into the air. The bear came to kill them, but they were just beyond its reach. It reared against the tree and scored the bark all around with its claws. The seven sisters were borne into the sky, and they became the stars of the Big Dipper."

From that moment, and so long as the legend lives, the Kiowas have kinsmen in the night sky. Whatever they were in the mountains, they could be no more. However tenuous their well-being, however much they had suffered and would suffer again, they had found a way out of the wilderness.

My grandmother had a reverence for the sun, a holy regard that now is all but gone out of mankind. There was a wariness in her and an ancient awe. She was a Christian in her later years, but she had come a long way about, and she never forgot her birthright. As a child she had been to the Sun Dances; she had taken part in those annual rites, and by them she had learned the restoration of her people in the presence of Tai-me. She was about seven when the last Kiowa Sun Dance was held in 1887 on the Washita River above Rainy Mountain Creek. The buffalo were gone. In order to consummate the ancient sacrifice—to impale the head of a buffalo bull upon the medicine tree—a delegation of old men journeyed into Texas, there to beg and barter for an animal from the Goodnight herd. She was ten when the Kiowas came together for the last time as a living Sun Dance culture. They could find no buffalo; they had to hang an old hide from the sacred tree. Before the dance could begin, a company of soldiers rode out from Fort Sill under orders to disperse the tribe. Forbidden without cause the essential act of their faith, having seen the wild herds slaughtered and left to rot upon the ground, the Kiowas backed away forever from the medicine tree. That was July 20, 1890, at the great bend of the Washita. My grandmother was there. Without bitterness, and for as long as she lived, she bore a vision of deicide.

Now that I can have her only in memory, I see my grandmother in the several postures that were peculiar to her: standing at the wood stove on a winter morning and turning meat in a great iron skillet; sitting at the south window, bent above her beadwork, and afterwards, when her vision had failed, looking down for a long time into the fold of her hands; going out upon a cane, very slowly as she did when the weight of age came upon her; praying. I remember her most often at prayer. She made long, rambling prayers out of suffering and hope, having seen many things. I was never sure that I had the right to hear, so exclusive were they of all mere custom and company. The last time I saw her she prayed standing by the side of her bed at night, naked to the waist, the light of a kerosene lamp moving upon her dark skin. Her long, black hair, always drawn and braided in the day, lay upon her shoulders and against her breasts like a shawl. I do not speak Kiowa, and I never understood her prayers, but there was something inherently sad in the sound, some merest hesitation upon the syllables of sorrow. She began in a high and descending pitch, exhausting her breath to silence; then again and again—and always the same intensity of effort, of something that is, and is not, like urgency in the human voice. Transported so in the dancing light among the shadows of her room, she seemed beyond the reach of time. But that was illusion; I think I knew then that I should not see her again.

Houses are like sentinels in the plain, old keepers of the weather watch. There, in a very little while, wood takes on the appearance of great age. All colors wear soon away in the wind and rain, and then the wood is burned gray and the grain appears and the nails turn red with rust. The windowpanes are black and opaque; you imagine there is nothing within, and indeed there are many ghosts, bones given up to the land. They stand here and there against the sky, and you approach them for a longer time than you expect. They belong in the distance; it is their domain.

Once there was a lot of sound in my grandmother's house, a lot of coming and going, feasting and talk. The summers there were full of excitement and reunion. The Kiowas are a summer people; they abide the cold and keep to themselves; but when the season turns and the land becomes warm and vital, they cannot hold still; an old love of going returns upon them. The aged visitors who came to my grandmother's house when I was a child were made of lean and leather, and they bore themselves upright. They wore great black hats and bright ample shirts that shook in the wind. They rubbed fat upon their hair and wound their braids with strips of colored cloth. Some of them painted their faces and carried the scars of old and cherished enmities. They were an old council of warlords, come to remind and be reminded of who they were. Their wives and daughters served them well. The women might indulge themselves; gossip was at once the mark and compensation of their servitude. They made loud and elaborate talk among themselves, full of jest and gesture, fright and false alarm. They went abroad in fringed and flowered shawls, bright beadwork and German silver. They were at home in the kitchen, and they prepared meals that were banquets.

There were frequent prayer meetings, and great nocturnal feasts. When I was a child, I played with my cousins outside, where the lamplight fell upon the ground and the singing of the old people rose up around us and carried away into the darkness. There were a lot of good things to eat, a lot of laughter and surprise. And afterwards, when the quiet returned, I lay down with my grandmother and could hear the frogs away by the river and feel the motion of the air.

Now there is a funeral silence in the rooms, the endless wake of some final word. The walls have closed in upon my grandmother's house. When I returned to it in mourning, I saw for the first time in my life how small it was. It was late at night, and there was a white moon, nearly full. I sat for a long time on the stone steps by the kitchen door. From there I could see out across the land; I could see the long row of trees by the creek, the low light upon the rolling plains, and the stars of the Big Dipper. Once I looked at the moon and caught sight of a strange thing. A cricket had perched upon the handrail, only a few inches away from me. My line of vision was such that the creature filled the moon like a fossil. It had gone there, I thought, to live and die, for there of all places, was its small definition made whole and eternal. A warm wind rose up and purled like the longing within me.

The next morning I awoke at dawn and went out on the dirt road to Rainy Mountain. It was already hot, and the grasshoppers began to fill the air. Still, it was early in the morning, and the birds sang out of the shadows. The long yellow grass on the mountain shone in the bright light, and a scissortail hied above the land. There, where it ought to be, at the end of a long and legendary way, was my grandmother's grave. Here and there on the dark stones were ancestral names. Looking back once, I saw the mountain and came away.

MARTIN LUTHER KING, JR.

Letter from Birmingham Jail[1]

Martin Luther King, Jr. (1929–1968), a Baptist minister and Nobel Peace Prize–winning civil rights activist, was born in Atlanta, Georgia. Drawing on the teachings of Jesus in the New Testament and the passive resistance ideals of Mahatma Ghandi, King advocated nonviolent protest to effect social change. In 1963, Birmingham, Alabama, became the scene of a violent confrontation between blacks and whites. King wrote his "Letter from Birmingham Jail," which is included in his collection *Why We Can't Wait* (1964), while he was imprisoned for his nonviolent participation in those events. Later in 1963, in a march on Washington, D.C., in support of a civil rights bill, he gave his now famous "I Have a Dream" speech. King was assassinated in 1968 in Memphis, Tennessee, while helping to organize a strike by garbage collectors.

My Dear Fellow Clergymen:

While confined here in the Birmingham city jail, I came across your recent statement calling my present activities "unwise and untimely." Seldom do I pause to answer criticism of my work and ideas. If I sought to answer all the criticisms that cross my desk, my secretaries would have little time for anything other than such cor-

---

[1] This response to a published statement by eight fellow clergymen from Alabama (Bishop C. C. J. Carpenter, Bishop Joseph A. Durick, Rabbi Milton L. Grafman, Bishop Paul Hardin, Bishop Holan B. Harmon, the Reverend George M. Murray, the Reverend Edward V. Ramage and the Reverend Earl Stallings) was composed under somewhat constricting circumstances. Begun on the margins of the newspaper in which the statement appeared while I was in jail, the letter was continued on scraps of writing paper supplied by a friendly Negro trusty, and concluded on a pad my attorneys were eventually permitted to leave me. Although the text remains in substance unaltered, I have indulged in the author's prerogative of polishing it for publication.

respondence in the course of the day, and I would have no time for constructive work. But since I feel that you are men of genuine good will and that your criticisms are sincerely set forth, I want to try to answer your statement in what I hope will be patient and reasonable terms.

I think I should indicate why I am here in Birmingham, since you have been influenced by the view which argues against "outsiders coming in." I have the honor of serving as president of the Southern Christian Leadership Conference, an organization operating in every southern state, with headquarters in Atlanta, Georgia. We have some eighty-five affiliated organizations across the South, and one of them is the Alabama Christian Movement for Human Rights. Frequently we share staff, educational, and financial resources with our affiliates. Several months ago the affiliate here in Birmingham asked us to be on call to engage in a nonviolent direct-action program if such were deemed necessary. We readily consented, and when the hour came we lived up to our promise. So I, along with several members of my staff, am here because I was invited here. I am here because I have organizational ties here.

But more basically, I am in Birmingham because injustice is here. Just as the prophets of the eighth century B.C. left their villages and carried their "thus saith the Lord" far beyond the boundaries of their home towns, and just as the Apostle Paul left his village of Tarsus and carried the gospel of Jesus Christ to the far corners of the Greco-Roman world, so am I compelled to carry the gospel of freedom beyond my own home town. Like Paul, I must constantly respond to the Macedonian call for aid.

Moreover, I am cognizant of the interrelatedness of all communities and states. I cannot sit idly by in Atlanta and not be concerned about what happens in Birmingham. Injustice anywhere is a threat to justice everywhere. We are caught in an inescapable network of mutuality, tied in a single garment of destiny. Whatever affects one directly, affects all indirectly. Never again can we afford to live with the narrow, provincial "outside agitator" idea. Anyone who lives inside the United States can never be considered an outsider anywhere within its bounds.

You deplore the demonstrations taking place in Birmingham. But your statement, I am sorry to say, fails to express a similar concern for the conditions that brought about the demonstrations. I am sure that none of you would want to rest content with the superficial kind of social analysis that deals merely with effects and does not grapple with underlying causes. It is unfortunate that demonstrations are taking place in Birmingham, but it is even more unfortunate that the city's white power structure left the Negro community with no alternative.

In any nonviolent campaign there are four basic steps: collection of the facts to determine whether injustices exist; negotiation; self-purification; and direct action. We have gone through all these steps in Birmingham. There can be no gainsaying the fact that racial injustice engulfs this community. Birmingham is probably the most thoroughly segregated city in the United States. Its ugly record of brutality is widely known. Negroes have experienced grossly unjust treatment in the courts. There have been more unsolved bombings of Negro homes and churches in Birmingham than in any other city in the nation. These are the hard, brutal facts of the case. On the basis of these conditions, Negro leaders sought to negotiate with the city fathers. But the latter consistently refused to engage in good-faith negotiation.

Then, last September, came the opportunity to talk with leaders of Birmingham's economic community. In the course of the negotiations, certain promises were made by the merchants—for example, to remove the stores' humiliating racial signs. On the basis of these promises, the Reverend Fred Shuttlesworth and the leaders of the Alabama Christian Movement for Human Rights agreed to a moratorium on all demonstrations. As the weeks and months went by, we realized that we were the victims of a broken promise. A few signs, briefly removed, returned; the others remained.

As in so many past experiences, our hopes had been blasted, and the shadow of deep disappointment settled upon us. We had no alternative except to prepare for direct action, whereby we would present our very bodies as a means of laying our case before the conscience of the local and the national community. Mindful of the difficulties involved, we decided to undertake a process of self-purification. We began a series of workshops on nonviolence, and we repeatedly asked ourselves: "Are you able to accept blows without retaliating?" "Are you able to endure the ordeal of jail?" We decided to schedule our direct-action program for the Easter season, realizing that except for Christmas, this is the main shopping period of the year. Knowing that a strong economic-withdrawal program would be the by-product of direct action, we felt that this would be the best time to bring pressure to bear on the merchants for the needed change.

Then it occurred to us that Birmingham's mayoral election was coming up in March, and we speedily decided to postpone action until after election day. When we discovered that the Commissioner of Public Safety, Eugene "Bull" Connor,[2] had piled up enough votes to be in the run-off, we decided again to postpone action until the day after the run-off so that the demonstrations could not be used to cloud the issues. Like many others, we wanted to see Mr. Connor defeated, and to this end we endured postponement after postponement. Having aided in this community need, we felt that our direct-action program could be delayed no longer.

You may well ask, "Why direct action? Why sit-ins, marches, and so forth? Isn't negotiation a better path?" You are quite right in calling for negotiation. Indeed, this is the very purpose of direct action. Nonviolent direct action seeks to create such a crisis and foster such a tension that a community which has constantly refused to negotiate is forced to confront the issue. It seeks so to dramatize the issue that it can no longer be ignored. My citing the creation of tension as part of the work of the nonviolent-resister may sound rather shocking. But I must confess that I am not afraid of the word "tension." I have earnestly opposed violent tension, but there is a type of constructive, nonviolent tension which is necessary for growth. Just as Socrates felt that it was necessary to create a tension in the mind so that individuals could rise from the bondage of myths and half-truths to the unfettered realm of creative analysis and objective appraisal, so must we see the need for nonviolent gadflies to create the kind of tension in society that will help men rise from the dark depths of prejudice and racism to the majestic heights of understanding and brotherhood.

The purpose of our direct-action program is to create a situation so crisis-packed that it will inevitably open the door to negotiation. I therefore concur with you in your call for negotiation. Too long has our beloved Southland been bogged down in a tragic effort to live in monologue rather than dialogue.

One of the basic points in your statement is that the action that I and my associates have taken in Birmingham is untimely. Some have asked: "Why didn't you give the new city administration time to act?" The only answer that I can give to this query is that the new Birmingham administration must be prodded about as much as the outgoing one, before it will act. We are sadly mistaken if we feel that the election of Albert Boutwell as mayor will bring the millennium

---

[2] Police Chief Eugene "Bull" Connor of Birmingham, Alabama, became nationally known in 1963 for televised confrontations with civil rights activists. (ED.)

to Birmingham. While Mr. Boutwell is a much more gentle person than Mr. Connor, they are both segregationists, dedicated to maintenance of the status quo. I have hoped that Mr. Boutwell will be reasonable enough to see the futility of massive resistance to desegregation. But he will not see this without pressure from devotees of civil rights. My friends, I must say to you that we have not made a single gain in civil rights without determined legal and nonviolent pressure. Lamentably, it is an historical fact that privileged groups seldom give up their privileges voluntarily. Individuals may see the moral light and voluntarily give up their unjust posture; but, as Reinhold Niebuhr has reminded us, groups tend to be more immoral than individuals.

We know through painful experience that freedom is never voluntarily given by the oppressor; it must be demanded by the oppressed. Frankly, I have yet to engage in a direct-action campaign that was "well timed" in the view of those who have not suffered unduly from the disease of segregation. For years now I have heard the word "Wait!" It rings in the ear of every Negro with piercing familiarity. This "Wait" has almost always meant "Never." We must come to see, with one of our distinguished jurists, that "justice too long delayed is justice denied."

We have waited for more than 340 years for our constitutional and God-given rights. The nations of Asia and Africa are moving with jetlike speed toward gaining political independence, but we still creep at horse-and-buggy pace toward gaining a cup of coffee at a lunch counter. Perhaps it is easy for those who have never felt the stinging darts of segregation to say, "Wait." But when you have seen vicious mobs lynch your mothers and fathers at will and drown your sisters and brothers at whim; when you have seen hate-filled policemen curse, kick, and even kill your black brothers and sisters; when you see the vast majority of your twenty million Negro brothers smothering in an airtight cage of poverty in the midst of an affluent society; when you suddenly find your tongue twisted and your speech stammering as you seek to explain to your six-year-old daughter why she can't go to the public amusement park that has just been advertised on television, and see tears welling up in her eyes when she is told that Funtown is closed to colored children, and see ominous clouds of inferiority beginning to form in her little mental sky, and see her beginning to distort her personality by developing an unconscious bitterness toward white people; when you have to concoct an answer for a five-year-old son who is asking, "Daddy, why do white people treat colored people so mean?"; when you take a cross-country drive and find it necessary to sleep night after night in the uncomfortable corners of your automobile because no motel will accept you; when you are humiliated day in and day out by nagging signs reading "white" and "colored"; when your first name becomes "nigger," your middle name becomes "boy" (however old you are) and your last name becomes "John," and your wife and mother are never given the respected title "Mrs."; when you are harried by day and haunted by night by the fact that you are a Negro, living constantly at tiptoe stance, never quite knowing what to expect next, and are plagued with inner fears and outer resentments; when you are forever fighting a degenerating sense of "nobodiness"—then you will understand why we find it difficult to wait. There comes a time when the cup of endurance runs over, and men are no longer willing to be plunged into the abyss of despair. I hope, sirs, you can understand our legitimate and unavoidable impatience.

You express a great deal of anxiety over our willingness to break laws. This is certainly a legitimate concern. Since we so diligently urge people to obey the Supreme Court's decision of 1954 outlawing segregation in the public schools, at first glance it may seem rather paradoxical for us consciously to break laws. One may well ask: "How can you advocate breaking some laws and obeying others?" The answer lies in the fact that there are two types of laws: just and unjust. I would be the first to advocate obeying just laws. One has not only a legal but a moral responsibility to obey just laws. Conversely, one has a moral responsibility to disobey unjust laws. I would agree with St. Augustine that "an unjust law is no law at all."

Now, what is the difference between the two? How does one determine whether a law is just or unjust? A law is a man-made code that squares with the moral law or the law of God. An unjust law is a code that is out of harmony with the moral law. To put it in the terms of St. Thomas Aquinas: An unjust law is a human law that is not rooted in eternal law and natural law. Any law that uplifts human personality is just. Any law that degrades human personality is unjust. All segregation statutes are unjust because segregation distorts the soul and damages the personality. It gives the segregator a false sense of superiority and the segregated a false sense of inferiority. Segregation, to use the terminology of the Jewish philosopher Martin Buber, substitutes an "I-it" relationship for an "I-thou" relationship and ends up relegating persons to the status of things. Hence segregation is not only politically, economically, and sociologically unsound, it is morally wrong and sinful. Paul Tillich has said that sin is separation. Is not segregation an existential expression of man's tragic separation, his awful estrangement, his terrible sinfulness? Thus it is that I can urge men to obey the 1954 decision of the Supreme Court, for it is morally right; and I can urge them to disobey segregation ordinances, for they are morally wrong.

Let us consider a more concrete example of just and unjust laws. An unjust law is a code that a numerical or power majority group compels a minority group to obey but does not make binding on itself. This is *difference* made legal. By the same token, a just law is a code that a majority compels a minority to follow and that it is willing to follow itself. This is *sameness* made legal.

Let me give another explanation. A law is unjust if it is inflicted on a minority that, as a result of being denied the right to vote, had no part in enacting or devising the law. Who can say that the legislature of Alabama which set up that state's segregation laws was democratically elected? Throughout Alabama all sorts of devious methods are used to prevent Negroes from becoming registered voters, and there are some counties in which, even though Negroes constitute a majority of the population, not a single Negro is registered. Can any law enacted under such circumstances be considered democratically structured?

Sometimes a law is just on its face and unjust in its application. For instance, I have been arrested on a charge of parading without a permit. Now, there is nothing wrong in having an ordinance which requires a permit for a parade. But such an ordinance becomes unjust when it is used to maintain segregation and to deny citizens the First-Amendment privilege of peaceful assembly and protest.

I hope you are able to see the distinction I am trying to point out. In no sense do I advocate evading or defying the law, as would the rabid segregationist. That would lead to anarchy. One who breaks an unjust law must do so openly, lovingly, and with a willingness to accept the penalty. I submit that an individual who breaks a law that conscience tells him is unjust, and who willingly accepts the penalty of imprisonment in order to arouse the conscience of the community over its injustice, is in reality expressing the highest respect for law.

Of course, there is nothing new about this kind of civil disobedience. It was evidenced sublimely in the refusal of Shadrach, Meshach, and Abednego[3] to obey the laws of Nebuchadnezzar, on the

---

[3] According to the biblical story, Shadrach, Meschach, and Abednego were three companions of Daniel who remained unharmed in the fiery furnace of Nebuchadnezzar, a king of ancient Babylon. (ED.)

ground that a higher moral law was at stake. It was practiced superbly by the early Christians, who were willing to face hungry lions and the excruciating pain of chopping blocks rather than submit to certain unjust laws of the Roman empire. To a degree, academic freedom is a reality today because Socrates practiced civil disobedience.[4] In our own nation, the Boston Tea Party represented a massive act of civil disobedience.

We should never forget that everything Adolph Hitler did in Germany was "legal" and everything the Hungarian fighters[5] did in Hungary was "illegal." It was "illegal" to aid and comfort a Jew in Hitler's Germany. Even so, I am sure that, had I lived in Germany at the time, I would have aided and comforted my Jewish brothers. If today I lived in a Communist country where certain principles dear to the Christian faith are suppressed, I would openly advocate disobeying that country's antireligious laws.

I must make two honest confessions to you, my Christian and Jewish brothers. First, I must confess that over the past few years I have been gravely disappointed with the white moderate. I have almost reached the regrettable conclusion that the Negro's great stumbling block in his stride toward freedom is not the White Citizen's Counciler[6] or the Ku Klux Klanner, but the white moderate, who is more devoted to "order" than to justice; who prefers a negative peace which is the absence of tension to a positive peace which is the presence of justice; who constantly says, "I agree with you in the goal you seek, but I cannot agree with your methods of direct action"; who paternalistically believes he can set the timetable for another man's freedom; who lives by a mythical concept of time and who constantly advises the Negro to wait for a "more convenient season." Shallow understanding from people of good will is more frustrating than absolute misunderstanding from people of ill will. Lukewarm acceptance is much more bewildering than outright rejection.

I had hoped that the white moderate would understand that law and order exist for the purpose of establishing justice and that when

[4] Socrates (469–399 B.C.?), a teacher and philosopher in ancient Greece, made enemies because of his unorthodox views. He was brought to trial for corrupting the youth of Athens and for showing disrespect for religious traditions. (ED.)

[5] the anti-communists in a popular but unsuccessful revolution in 1956 (ED.)

[6] The White Citizen's Council was a league of Southern white business and civic leaders. They battled integration by threatening blacks with a loss of jobs and whites who supported the civil rights movement with a loss of business. (ED.)

they fail in this purpose they become the dangerously structured dams that block the flow of social progress. I had hoped that the white moderate would understand that the present tension in the South is a necessary phase of the transition from an obnoxious negative peace, in which the Negro passively accepted his unjust plight, to a substantive and positive peace, in which all men will respect the dignity and worth of human personality. Actually, we who engage in nonviolent direct action are not the creators of tension. We merely bring to the surface the hidden tension that is already alive. We bring it out in the open, where it can be seen and dealt with. Like a boil that can never be cured so long as it is covered up but must be opened with all its ugliness to the natural medicines of air and light, injustice must be exposed, with all the tension its exposure creates, to the light of human conscience and the air of national opinion, before it can be cured.

In your statement you assert that our actions, even though peaceful, must be condemned because they precipitate violence. But is this a logical assertion? Isn't this like condemning a robbed man because his possession of money precipitated the evil act of robbery? Isn't this like condemning Socrates because his unswerving commitment to truth and his philosophical inquiries precipitated the act by the misguided populace in which they made him drink hemlock? Isn't this like condemning Jesus because his unique God-consciousness and never-ceasing devotion to God's will precipitated the evil act of crucifixion? We must come to see that, as the federal courts have consistently affirmed, it is wrong to urge an individual to cease his efforts to gain his basic constitutional rights because the quest may precipitate violence. Society must protect the robbed and punish the robber.

I had hoped that the white moderate would reject the myth concerning time in relation to the struggle for freedom. I have just received a letter from a white brother in Texas. He writes: "All Christians know that the colored people will receive equal rights eventually, but it is possible that you are in too great a religious hurry. It has taken Christianity almost two thousand years to accomplish what it has. The teachings of Christ take time to come to earth." Such an attitude stems from a tragic misconception of time, from the strangely irrational notion that there is something in the very flow of time that will inevitably cure all ills. Actually, time itself is neutral; it can be used either destructively or constructively. More and more I feel that the people of ill will have used time much more effectively than have the people of good will. We will have to repent in this

generation not merely for the hateful words and actions of the bad
people, but for the appalling silence of the good people. Human
progress never rolls in on wheels of inevitability; it comes through
the tireless efforts of men willing to be co-workers with God, and
without this hard work, time itself becomes an ally of the forces of
social stagnation. We must use time creatively, in the knowledge that
the time is always ripe to do right. Now is the time to make real the
promise of democracy and transform our pending national elegy into
a creative psalm of brotherhood. Now is the time to lift our national
policy from the quicksand of racial injustice to the solid rock of
human dignity.

You speak of our activity in Birmingham as extreme. At first I
was rather disappointed that fellow clergymen would see my nonviolent efforts as those of an extremist. I began thinking about the
fact that I stand in the middle of two opposing forces in the Negro
community. One is a force of complacency, made up in part of
Negroes who, as a result of long years of oppression, are so drained
of self-respect and a sense of "somebodiness" that they have adjusted
to segregation; and in part of a few middle-class Negroes who, because of a degree of academic and economic security and because in
some ways they profit by segregation, have become insensitive to the
problems of the masses. The other force is one of bitterness and
hatred, and it comes perilously close to advocating violence. It is
expressed in the various black nationalist groups that are springing
up across the nation, the largest and best-known being Elijah
Muhammad's[7] Muslim movement. Nourished by the Negro's frustration over the continued existence of racial discrimination, this movement is made up of people who have lost faith in America, who have
absolutely repudiated Christianity, and who have concluded that the
white man is an incorrigible "devil."

I have tried to stand between these two forces, saying that we
need emulate neither the "do-nothingism" of the complacent nor the
hatred and despair of the black nationalist. For there is the more
excellent way of love and nonviolent protest. I am grateful to God
that, through the influence of the Negro church, the way of nonviolence became an integral part of our struggle.

If this philosophy had not emerged, by now many streets of the

---

[7] Elijah Muhammad (1897–1975) was the founder of the Black Muslims who advocated
separation of races and the formation of an all-black state. (ED.)

South would, I am convinced, be flowing with blood. And I am further convinced that if our white brothers dismiss as "rabble-rousers" and "outside agitators" those of us who employ nonviolent direct action, and if they refuse to support our nonviolent efforts, millions of Negroes will, out of frustration and despair, seek solace and security in black-nationalist ideologies—a development that would inevitably lead to a frightening racial nightmare.

Oppressed people cannot remain oppressed forever. The yearning for freedom eventually manifests itself, and that is what has happened to the American Negro. Something within has reminded him of his birthright of freedom, and something without has reminded him that it can be gained. Consciously or unconsciously, he has been caught up by the *Zeitgeist,*[8] and with his black brothers of Africa and his brown and yellow brothers of Asia, South America, and the Caribbean, the United States Negro is moving with a sense of great urgency toward the promised land of racial justice. If one recognizes this vital urge that has engulfed the Negro community, one should readily understand why public demonstrations are taking place. The Negro has many pent-up resentments and latent frustrations, and he must release them. So let him march; let him make prayer pilgrimages to the city hall; let him go on freedom rides—and try to understand why he must do so. If his repressed emotions are not released in nonviolent ways, they will seek expression through violence; this is not a threat but a fact of history. So I have not said to my people, "Get rid of your discontent." Rather, I have tried to say that this normal and healthy discontent can be channeled into the creative outlet of nonviolent direct action. And now this approach is being termed extremist.

But though I was initially disappointed at being categorized as an extremist, as I continued to think about the matter I gradually gained a measure of satisfaction from the label. Was not Jesus an extremist for love: "Love your enemies, bless them that curse you, do good to them that hate you, and pray for them which despitefully use you, and persecute you." Was not Amos an extremist for justice: "Let justice roll down like waters and righteousness like an ever-flowing stream." Was not Paul an extremist for the Christian gospel: "I bear in my body the marks of the Lord Jesus." Was not Martin

---

[8] the intellectual, moral, and cultural spirit of the times (ED.)

Luther an extremist: "Here I stand; I cannot do otherwise, so help
me God." And John Bunyan:[9] "I will stay in jail to the end of my
days before I make a butchery of my conscience." And Abraham
Lincoln: "This nation cannot survive half slave and half free." And
Thomas Jefferson: "We hold these truths to be self-evident, that all
men are created equal. . . ." So the question is not whether we will
be extremists, but what kind of extremists we will be. Will we be
extremists for hate or for love? Will we be extremists for the preservation of injustice or for the extension of justice? In that dramatic
scene on Calvary's hill three men were crucified. We must never
forget that all three were crucified for the same crime—the crime of
extremism. Two were extremists for immorality, and thus fell below
their environment. The other, Jesus Christ, was an extremist for love,
truth, and goodness, and thereby rose above his environment. Perhaps the South, the nation, and the world are in dire need of creative
extremists.

I had hoped that the white moderate would see this need. Perhaps
I was too optimistic; perhaps I expected too much. I suppose I should
have realized that few members of the oppressor race can understand
the deep groans and passionate yearnings of the oppressed race, and
still fewer have the vision to see that injustice must be rooted out
by strong, persistent, and determined action. I am thankful, however,
that some of our white brothers in the South have grasped the
meaning of this social revolution and committed themselves to it.
They are still all too few in quantity, but they are big in quality.
Some—such as Ralph McGill, Lillian Smith, Harry Golden, James
McBride Dabbs, Ann Braden, and Sarah Patton Boyle[10]—have written about our struggle in eloquent and prophetic terms. Others have
marched with us down nameless streets of the South. They have
languished in filthy, roach-infested jails, suffering the abuse and
brutality of policemen who view them as "dirty nigger-lovers." Unlike
so many of their moderate brothers and sisters, they have recognized
the urgency of the moment and sensed the need for powerful "action"
antidotes to combat the disease of segregation.

Let me take note of my other major disappointment. I have been

[9] John Bunyan (1628–1668) was an English minister and author of *The Pilgrim's
Progress*. (ED.)

[10] White Southern writers and activists who spoke out against segregation and other
forms of racial discrimination. (ED.)

so greatly disappointed with the white church and its leadership. Of course, there are some notable exceptions. I am not unmindful of the fact that each of you has taken some significant stands on this issue. I commend you, Reverend Stallings, for your Christian stand on this past Sunday, in welcoming Negroes to your worship service on a nonsegregational basis. I commend the Catholic leaders of this state for integrating Spring Hill College several years ago.

But despite these notable exceptions, I must honestly reiterate that I have been disappointed with the church. I do not say this as one of those negative critics who can always find something wrong with the church. I say this as a minister of the gospel, who loves the church; who was nurtured in its bosom; who has been sustained by its spiritual blessings and who will remain true to it as long as the cord of life shall lengthen.

When I was suddenly catapulted into the leadership of the bus protest in Montgomery, Alabama, a few years ago, I felt we would be supported by the white church. I felt that the white ministers, priests, and rabbis of the South would be among our strongest allies. Instead, some have been outright opponents, refusing to understand the freedom movement and misrepresenting its leaders; all too many others have been more cautious than courageous and have remained silent behind the anesthetizing security of stained-glass windows.

In spite of my shattered dreams, I came to Birmingham with the hope that the white religious leadership of this community would see the justice of our cause and, with deep moral concern, would serve as the channel through which our just grievances could reach the power structure. I had hoped that each of you would understand. But again I have been disappointed.

I have heard numerous southern religious leaders admonish their worshipers to comply with a desegregation decision because it is the law, but I have longed to hear white ministers declare: "Follow this decree because integration is morally right and because the Negro is your brother." In the midst of blatant injustices inflicted upon the Negro, I have watched white churchmen stand on the sideline and mouth pious irrelevancies and sanctimonious trivialities. In the midst of a mighty struggle to rid our nation of racial and economic injustice, I have heard many ministers say: "Those are social issues, with which the gospel has no real concern." And I have watched many churches commit themselves to a completely otherworldly religion which makes a strange, un-Biblical distinction between body and soul, between the sacred and the secular.

I have traveled the length and breadth of Alabama, Mississippi, and all the other southern states. On sweltering summer days and crisp autumn mornings I have looked at the South's beautiful churches with their lofty spires pointing heavenward. I have beheld the impressive outlines of her massive religious-education buildings. Over and over I have found myself asking: "What kind of people worship here? Who is their God? Where were their voices when the lips of Governor Barnett[11] dripped with words of interposition and nullification? Where were they when Governor Wallace[12] gave a clarion call for defiance and hatred? Where were their voices of support when bruised and weary Negro men and women decided to rise from the dark dungeons of complacency to the bright hills of creative protest?"

Yes, these questions are still in my mind. In deep disappointment I have wept over the laxity of the church. But be assured that my tears have been tears of love. There can be no deep disappointment where there is not deep love. Yes, I love the church. How could I do otherwise? I am in the rather unique position of being the son, the grandson, and the great-grandson of preachers. Yes, I see the church as the body of Christ. But, oh! How we have blemished and scarred that body through social neglect and through fear of being nonconformists.

There was a time when the church was very powerful—in the time when the early Christians rejoiced at being deemed worthy to suffer for what they believed. In those days the church was not merely a thermometer that recorded the ideas and principles of popular opinion; it was a thermostat that transformed the mores of society. Whenever the early Christians entered a town, the people in power became disturbed and immediately sought to convict the Christians for being "disturbers of the peace" and "outside agitators." But the Christians pressed on, in the conviction that they were "a colony of heaven," called to obey God rather than man. Small in number, they were big in commitment. They were too God-intoxicated to be "astronomically intimidated." By their effort and example

---

[11] Ross Barnett (1898–1988), Governor of Mississippi who attempted to bar the first black students attempting to register at the University of Mississippi. (ED.)

[12] George Wallace (1919–   ), Governor of Alabama who unsuccessfully tried to prevent the desegregation of the University of Alabama. (ED.)

brotherhood will shine over our great nation with all their scintillating beauty.

Yours for the cause of Peace and Brotherhood,
MARTIN LUTHER KING, JR.

JAMES BALDWIN

Why I Left America

Conversation: Ida Lewis and James Baldwin

James Baldwin (1924–1987), Harlem-born essayist, novelist, and social activist, lived much of his adult life as an expatriate in France. In *Go Tell It on the Mountain* (1953), *Notes of a Native Son* (1955), and *Nobody Knows My Name* (1961), he chronicled the effects on society wrought by racial prejudice. Other works include the novels *Giovanni's Room* (1956), *Another Country* (1962), *Tell Me How Long the Train's Been Gone* (1968), *If Beale Street Could Talk* (1974), and the short story collection *Going to Meet the Man* (1965). His essays have been collected in *The Price of the Ticket* (1985). The following selection originally appeared in *Essence*.

James Baldwin is probably the most widely quoted black writer in the past decade. He is the author of numerous works, all of which have won critical acclaim. Among these are his novels: Go Tell It on the Mountain, his first work; Giovanni's Room, which was set in Paris, and Another Country, his first critical and commercial success. His latest: Tell Me How Long the Train's Been Gone. He also wrote a number of personal essays that were collected in book form; Notes of a Native Son, was his first collection, followed by Nobody Knows My Name, which brought him literary prominence. The third volume, The Fire Next Time, was regarded as one of the most brilliant essays written on black protest. Two plays, Blues for Mister Charlie and The Amen Corner were performed on the American stage.

From boy-preacher in Harlem store-front churches to famed essayist and novelist, Baldwin is now an expatriate in Paris. Why expatriate?

---

they brought an end to such ancient evils as infanticide and gladiatorial contests.

Things are different now. So often the contemporary church is a weak, ineffectual voice with an uncertain sound. So often it is an archdefender of the status quo. Far from being disturbed by the presence of the church, the power structure of the average community is consoled by the church's silent—and often even vocal—sanction of things as they are.

But the judgment of God is upon the church as never before. If today's church does not recapture the sacrificial spirit of the early church, it will lose its authenticity, forfeit the loyalty of millions, and be dismissed as an irrelevant social club with no meaning for the twentieth century. Every day I meet young people whose disappointment with the church has turned into outright disgust.

Perhaps I have once again been too optimistic. Is organized religion too inextricably bound to the status quo to save our nation and the world? Perhaps I must turn my faith to the inner spiritual church, the church within the church, as the true *ekklesia*[13] and the hope of the world. But again I am thankful to God that some noble souls from the ranks of organized religion have broken loose from the paralyzing chains of conformity and joined us as active partners in the struggle for freedom. They have left their secure congregations and walked the streets of Albany, Georgia, with us. They have gone down the highways of the South on tortuous rides for freedom. Yes, they have gone to jail with us. Some have been dismissed from their churches, have lost the support of their bishops and fellow ministers. But they have acted in the faith that right defeated is stronger than evil triumphant. Their witness has been the spiritual salt that has preserved the true meaning of the gospel in these troubled times. They have carved a tunnel of hope through the dark mountain of disappointment.

I hope the church as a whole will meet the challenge of this decisive hour. But even if the church does not come to the aid of justice, I have no despair about the future. I have no fear about the outcome of our struggle in Birmingham, even if our motives are at present misunderstood. We will reach the goal of freedom in Birmingham and all over the nation, because the goal of America is

---

[13] In the New Testament, the Greek word for the early Christian church. (ED.)

freedom. Abused and scorned though we may be, our destiny is tied up with America's destiny. Before the pilgrims landed at Plymouth, we were here. Before the pen of Jefferson etched the majestic words of the Declaration of Independence across the pages of history, we were here. For more than two centuries our forebears labored in this country without wages; they made cotton king; they built the homes of their masters while suffering gross injustice and shameful humiliation—and yet out of a bottomless vitality they continued to thrive and develop. If the inexpressible cruelties of slavery could not stop us, the opposition we now face will surely fail. We will win our freedom because the sacred heritage of our nation and the eternal will of God are embodied in our echoing demands.

Before closing I feel impelled to mention one other point in your statement that has troubled me profoundly. You warmly commended the Birmingham police force for keeping "order" and "preventing violence." I doubt that you would have so warmly commended the police force if you had seen its dogs sinking their teeth into unarmed, nonviolent Negroes. I doubt that you would so quickly commend the policemen if you were to observe their ugly and inhumane treatment of Negroes here in the city jail; if you were to watch them push and curse old Negro women and young Negro girls; if you were to see them slap and kick old Negro men and young boys; if you were to observe them, as they did on two occasions, refuse to give us food because we wanted to sing our grace together. I cannot join you in your praise of the Birmingham police department.

It is true that the police have exercised a degree of discipline in handling the demonstrators. In this sense they have conducted themselves rather "nonviolently" in public. But for what purpose? To preserve the evil system of segregation. Over the past few years I have consistently preached that nonviolence demands that the means we use must be as pure as the ends we seek. I have tried to make clear that it is wrong to use immoral means to attain moral ends. But now I must affirm that it is just as wrong, or perhaps even more so, to use moral means to preserve immoral ends. Perhaps Mr. Connor and his policemen have been rather nonviolent in public, as was Chief Pritchett in Albany, Georgia, but they have used the moral means of nonviolence to maintain the immoral end of racial injustice. As T. S. Eliot has said, "The last temptation is the greatest treason: To do the right deed for the wrong reason."

I wish you had commended the Negro sit-inners and demonstrators of Birmingham for their sublime courage, their willingness to suffer, and their amazing discipline in the midst of great provocation.

One day the South will recognize its real heroes. They will be the James Merediths,[14] with the noble sense of purpose that enables them to face jeering and hostile mobs, and with the agonizing loneliness that characterizes the life of the pioneer. They will be old, oppressed, battered Negro women, symbolized in a seventy-two-year-old woman in Montgomery, Alabama, who rose up with a sense of dignity and with her people decided not to ride segregated buses, and who responded with ungrammatical profundity to one who inquired about her weariness: "My feets is tired, but my soul is at rest." They will be the young high school and college students, the young ministers of the gospel and a host of their elders, courageously and nonviolently sitting in at lunch counters and willingly going to jail for conscience' sake. One day the South will know that when these disinherited children of God sat down at lunch counters, they were in reality standing up for what is best in the American dream and for the most sacred values in our Judaeo-Christian heritage, thereby bringing our nation back to those great wells of democracy which were dug deep by the founding fathers in their formulation of the Constitution and the Declaration of Independence.

Never before have I written so long a letter. I'm afraid it is much too long to take your precious time. I can assure you that it would have been much shorter if I had been writing from a comfortable desk, but what else can one do when he is alone in a narrow jail cell, other than write long letters, think long thoughts, and pray long prayers?

If I have said anything in this letter that overstates the truth and indicates an unreasonable impatience, I beg you to forgive me. If I have said anything that understates the truth and indicates my having a patience that allows me to settle for anything less than brotherhood, I beg God to forgive me.

I hope this letter finds you strong in the faith. I also hope that circumstances will soon make it possible for me to meet each of you, not as an integrationist or a civil-rights leader but as a fellow clergyman and a Christian brother. Let us all hope that the dark clouds of racial prejudice will soon pass away and the deep fog of misunderstanding will be lifted from our fear-drenched communities, and in some not too distant tomorrow the radiant stars of love and

[14] James Meredith was the first black student to enter the University of Mississippi. (ED.)

What is he about now? While we were in Paris, Essence *stopped to visit him and this is what he told us.*

IDA: Jimmy, I'm here to probe, to find out what the new James Baldwin is all about?

JIMMY: Okay. I won't duck anything.

IDA: I am curious about why you are in Paris and not New York. Haven't you been this route before?

JIMMY: It's a difficult question to answer. But for exercise, let's begin back in 1948 when I first left America. Why in the world, I've been asked, did you go to a white country? When I first heard that question it threw me. But the answer is obvious; there were no black countries in 1948. Whether there are black countries today is another question, which we won't go into now. But you know I didn't *come* to Paris in '48, I simply *left* America. I would have gone to Tokyo, I would have gone to Israel, I would have *gone* anywhere. I was getting out of America.

So I found myself in Paris. I arrived here with $40, scared to death, not knowing what I was going to do, but knowing that whatever was going to happen here would not be worse than what was certainly going to happen in America. Here I was in danger of death; but in America it was not a danger, it was a certainty. Not just physical death, I mean *real* death.

IDA: Would you explain this death you speak about?

JIMMY: The death of working in the post office for 37 years; of being a civil servant for a hostile government. The death of going under and watching your family go under.

IDA: These kinds of deaths were still part of black life when you returned to the States in '57. Why did you return?

JIMMY: I went back in '57 because I got terribly tired. It was during the Algerian war.[1] My friends were Algerians and Africans. They are the people who befriended me when I arrived here broke. In a sense, we saved each other, we lived together. So when the war began, my friends began to disappear one by one. What was happening was

---

[1] The Algerian War (1954–1955) was waged by Algerians against France to gain independence. (ED.)

obvious. When hotels were raided, I was let alone, but my friends were taken away. My green American passport saved me.

I got tired and I began to be ashamed, sitting in cafés in Paris and explaining Little Rock and Tennessee. I thought it was easier to go home. It was impossible to sit there and listen to Frenchmen talk about my Algerian friends in the terms that had always been used to describe us, you know, "You rape our women. You carry knives."

IDA: In a sense, all of us became Algerians.

JIMMY: Yes, in another language, but it was the same thing. So I went home. The rest, as we say, is history.

IDA: You became the famous James Baldwin, writer and black spokesman.

JIMMY: Yes, I played two roles. I never wanted to be a spokesman, but I suppose it's something that had to happen. But that is over now. And I discovered that the time I needed to stop and start again, the necessary kind of rest to get myself together, was not possible in America because the pressures were too great. So, I had to leave once more.

IDA: Could you be more specific?

JIMMY: Because of what I had become in the minds of the public, I ceased to belong to me. Once you are in the public limelight, you must somehow find a way to deal with that mystery. You have to realize you've been paid for, and you can't goof. I kept leaving for a short time—to do this, to do that—but to save myself I finally had to leave for good.

IDA: Can you recall that moment of decision?

JIMMY: One makes decisions in funny ways; you make a decision without knowing you've made it. I suppose my decision was made when Malcolm X was killed, when Martin Luther King was killed, when Medgar Evers and John and Bobby and Fred Hampton were killed.[2] I loved Medgar. I loved Martin and Malcolm. We all worked together and kept the faith together. Now they are all dead. When you think about it, it is incredible. I'm the last witness—everybody else is dead. I couldn't stay in America, I had to leave.

---

[2] Malcolm X, Martin Luther King, Medgar Evers, and Fred Hampton were black activists and civil rights leaders in the 1950s and 1960s. "John and Bobby" is a reference to John F. and Robert F. Kennedy. (ED.)

IDA: What was buried in those graveyards?

JIMMY: That dialogue is gone. With those great men, the possibility of a certain kind of dialogue in America has ended. Maybe the possibility of it was never real, but the hope certainly was. Now, the Western world, which has always stood on very shaky foundations, is coalescing according to the principle under which it was organized, and that principle is white supremacy. From England to Sacramento, Ronald Reagan and Enoch Powell[3] are the same person.

IDA: The other reasons?

JIMMY: I was invited to Israel and I'd planned to take my first trip to Africa after that. But when the time came, I had so many things on my mind I didn't dare go to Africa. After I visited Israel, I understood the theology of Judaism—and its mythology—better than I had before. I understood the great blackmail which has been imposed on the world not by the Jew but by the Christian. We fell for it, and the Jews fell for it. Let me put it this way. When I was in Israel I thought I liked Israel. I liked the people. But to me it was obvious why the Western world created the state of Israel, which is not really a Jewish state. The West needed a handle in the Middle East. And they created the state as a European pawn. It is tragic that the Jews should allow themselves to be used in this fashion, because no one cares what happens to the Jews. No one cares what is happening to the Arabs. But they do care about the oil. That part of the world is a crucial matter if you intend to rule the world.

I'm not anti-Semitic at all, but I am anti-Zionist. I don't believe they had the right, after 3,000 years, to reclaim the land with Western bombs and guns on biblical injunction. When I was in Israel it was as though I was in the middle of *The Fire Next Time*. I didn't dare go from Israel to Africa, so I went to Turkey, just across the road, and stayed there until I finished *Another Country*.

IDA: You sound as if you had been in spiritual trouble.

JIMMY: I was. It was very useful for me to go to a place like Istanbul at that point of my life, because it was so far out of the way from what I called home and the pressures. It's a funny thing, becoming famous. If you're an actor or dancer, it is what you expect. But if you're a writer, you don't expect what happened to me. You expect

---

[3] Enoch Powell (1912–), a British politician and member of Parliament, was noted for his outspoken racist views. (ED.)

to be photographed all over the place but you don't expect the shit, the constant demands, the people's expectations. During my Istanbul stay I learned a lot about dealing with people who are neither Western nor Eastern. In a way, Turkey is a satellite on the Russian border. That's something to watch. You learn about the brutality and the power of the Western world. You're living with people whom nobody cares about, who are bounced like a tennis ball between the great powers. Not that I wasn't previously aware of the cynicism of power politics and foreign aid, but it was a revelation to see it functioning every day in that sort of a theatre.

IDA: The Turks are poor people. It seems to me that they, too, are victims of many of the same prejudices that affect black men. Did you find any comparisons?

JIMMY: It's a very curious comparison. I would say, no, because of the fact that the American black man is now the strangest creature in history, due to his long apprenticeship in the West. For example, the people of Istanbul have never seen New York. *West Side Story* is an event for them. They know nothing about what the black man has gone through in America. They still think of America as a promised land.

The American black man knows something which nobody else in the world knows. To have been where we were, to have paid the price we have paid, to have survived, and to have shaken up the world the way we have is a rare journey. No one else has made it but us. There is a reason that people are listening to James Brown, Nina Simone, and Aretha Franklin all over the world, and not to somebody from Moscow, Turkey, or England. And the reason is not in our crotch but in our heart, our soul. It's something the world denied and lied about, energy they labeled savage, inferior, and insignificant. But it has been proven that no matter what they labeled it, they cannot do without it.

The peoples of Turkey, Greece, even the peoples in Jamaica have not gone through the fire. They don't know that the drama which was America is over. I know that. What we have allowed to happen to our country is shameful. I'm ashamed of Nixon. I wouldn't hire him to become keeper of the gate in Central Park. There's no excuse for a man like Nixon to be put in charge of a country like the United States.

IDA: But don't we need all thinking and able-bodied Americans to change what has happened? We can't run away.

JIMMY: Okay, you're right. But it's like this: I believe that I've got a master stone in which I see something and I have to find a way of chiseling out what I see. I left America, finally, because I knew I could not do it there.

It doesn't matter where I do it as long as I do it. I don't believe in nations any more. Those passports, those borders are as outworn and useless as war. No one can afford them anymore. We're such a conglomerate of things. Look at the American black man, all the bloods in a single stream. Look at the history of anybody you might know. He may have been born in Yugoslavia, raised in Germany, exiled to Casablanca, killed in Spain. That's our century. It will take the human race a long time to get over this stuff.

IDA: That leaves blacks in a strange situation.

JIMMY: It certainly does. Because what has happened is that the party's over. All the pretenses of the Western world have been exposed. There is no way to convince me or any other black person in the world, to say nothing of people who are neither black nor white, that America is anything but an outlaw nation. It doesn't make any difference what one says about the Declaration of Independence, the Bill of Rights, the Magna Carta, when arms are being sold to South Africa, and the Vietnamese are being killed on their own soil by American bombs. The name of the game in America is banks and power. And one does not have to investigate too far to discover that the Western economy has been built on the backs of non-white peoples.

IDA: But to leave one's country, Jimmy, is traumatic.

JIMMY: I fought leaving for a long time. I didn't want to go. I had been based in New York for quite a while, my family and friends are there. It is my country and I'm not 24 years old any more. It was not easy to pack up and leave. What probably convinced me that I had to leave was my encounter with Hollywood.

IDA: You went to Hollywood to write a screenplay on the life of Malcolm X?

JIMMY: Yes. I never wanted to go to Hollywood. And I would never have gone had it not been for Malcolm. When I was asked to write the screenplay on my friend's life, part of me knew that it really could not be done. But I didn't believe I had the right to turn down a possible opportunity to reveal Malcolm on-screen. I knew the odds were against me, but sometimes you take outside chances. It's better than thinking for the rest of your life that perhaps it could have been done.

Believe me, my Hollywood journey was a revelation. It was incredible to find yourself in a situation where the people who perpetrated his murder attempted to dictate his love, grief, and suffering to you. I believed Malcolm trusted me and that held me there. I tried to go down with the deal. I went the route. And when that battle was over, and I realized there was no hope—that they were speaking Hindustani and I was speaking Spanish—I was through. Day followed day and week followed week, and nothing, nothing, nothing, would penetrate. Not because they were wicked but because they couldn't hear. If they could hear, they wouldn't be white. Malcolm understood this. He said that white is a state of mind—a fatal state of mind. There I was in Hollywood. The things I was asked to write in the name of Malcolm, the advice I was given about the life and death of a friend of mine was not to be believed. So I left. I split to save my life. Ida, you once said that I was an actor. I'm an actor, but I'm also very determined.

IDA: Let's turn to another subject—your family.

JIMMY: I'd love to because my family saved me. If it hadn't been for my family, all those brothers and sisters, I'd be a very different person today. Let me explain. I was the older brother. And when I was growing up I didn't like all those brothers and sisters. No kid likes to be the oldest. You get spanked for what they do. But when they turn to you for help—what can you do? You can't drop the kid on his head down the steps. There he is, right?

So when I say that they saved me I mean that they kept me so busy caring for them, keeping them from the rats, roaches, falling plaster, and all the banality of poverty that I had no time to go jumping off the roof, or to become a junkie or an alcoholic. It's either/or in the ghetto. And I was one of the lucky ones. The welfare of my family has always driven me, always controlled me. I wanted to become rich and famous simply so no one could evict my family again.

IDA: So keeping your family from being thrown into the street was your inspiration.

JIMMY: That's really the key to my will to succeed. I was simply a frightened young man who had a family to save.

IDA: Have you remained close to your family?

JIMMY: The greatest things in my life are my brothers and sisters, and my nieces and nephews. We're all friends. They continue, in their own way, to save me. They are my life.

IDA: After you left America the last time you ended up in Istanbul. What could take a black American to Turkey?

JIMMY: There are several reasons why I went to Istanbul. One was that I had a friend there, a Turkish actor who worked with me at The Actors Studio in '58. He's memorable to me because at one point in the play version of *Giovanni,* someone had to spit on the cross, and no Christian actor was willing to do it. But my friend is a Moslem, so he loved it. Then he had to go away to Turkey to do his military service and I said, "Someday I'll visit you in Turkey." But I never really thought I would.

IDA: But wars will go on and on and on. . . .

JIMMY: Unhappily, we have yet to realize that nobody can go to war anymore and win. It's impossible. It's a dirty habit that mankind has got to give up.

But what is important to us as blacks is to realize that the kinds of wars perpetrated today are quite different from those of the past. Before Vietnam, the European wars were family affairs. Hitler's Germany was no big deal until people feared that he might take over all of Europe. He had murdered millions with the people's consent. Nobody cared. Nobody. Only when Europe itself was endangered by the madman it had created did it become moral. But right from the start Vietnam has been a racist war in which all the West is implicated. It was never a family affair. America's in the vanguard but the war reveals where the West is really based. That's a crisis. I see it as the beginning of the end.

IDA: Why have you chosen France as your refuge?

JIMMY: Laziness. Habit. I speak French; I became famous here. The French are a very special sort. They will leave you alone, let you do your thing. And all I want is to be left alone to do my gig. I couldn't, after all, pick Tokyo or Rome or Barcelona or London. They don't know me as Paris does, or vice versa. Paris was actually the only place for me to come.

IDA: Have you changed much over the last 10 years? What kind of person are you now?

JIMMY: I could say that I'm sadder, but I'm not. I'm much more myself than I've ever been. I'm freer. I've lost so much, but I've gained a lot. I cannot claim that I'm a happy man. I'm terrified, but I'm not unhappy. I've lived long enough to know what I have to do—and what I will not do.

IDA: What won't you do, Jimmy?

JIMMY: I will never sell you . . . even when you want me to. You follow me. You created me. You're stuck with me for life.

IDA: Let's talk about the meaning of being black today. What does it mean to you?

JIMMY: I think that it is probably the luckiest thing that could have happened to me or to anyone who's black. I was walking with my brother David in London a couple weeks ago, and we were sort of walking fast because there were a lot of people around us. We were trying to get some place where we could sit down and have a quiet drink and talk without having to go through all that. I said, "Davy, I wouldn't dare look back. If I looked back, I'd shake." And then, we both realized that if you are not afraid to look back, it means that nothing you are facing can frighten you.

What it means to me? Nobody can do anything if you really know that you're black. And I know where I've been. I know what the world has tried to do to me as a black man. When I say me, that means millions of people. I know that it's not easy to live in a world that's determined to murder you. Because they're not trying to mistreat you, or despise you, or rebuke you or scorn you. They're trying to kill you. Not only to kill you, but kill your mother and your father, your brothers and your children. That's their intention. That's what it means to keep the Negro in his place. I have seen the game, and if you lose it, you're in trouble, not me. And the secret about the white world is out. Everybody knows it.

All that brotherly love was bullshit. All those missionaries were murderers. That old cross was bloodied with my blood. And all that money in all those banks was made by me for them. So, for me what it means to be black is what one has been forced to see through, all the pretensions and all the artifacts of the world that calls itself white. One sees a certain poverty, a poverty one would not have believed. And it doesn't make any difference what they do now.

The terrible thing about being white is that whatever you do is irrelevant. Play your games, dance your waltzes, shoot your guns, fly your helicopters, murder your natives. It's all been done. It may take another thousand years, another twenty years, another thirty years, but I've already worn you out. Whitey, you can't make it because I've got nothing to lose. What has happened is, I've stepped outside your terms. As long as it is important to be white or black in one's own head, then you had us. Nobody gives a damn any more. Western civilization's had to be defended by the people who are defending it. By the time you sank to the level of such mediocrities as presidents, whom I will not name, I'm sorry, you've had it. Civilization depends on Mr. Nixon and Mr. Agnew? We can forget about that civilization. There's not a living soul who wants to become Richard Nixon. There never will be in the entire history of the world.

IDA: What about the new black pride?

JIMMY: It's not new. Black pride, baby, is what got my father through. Drove him mad, too, and finally killed him. There's nothing new about it, and people who think it's new are making a mistake. Black pride is in all those cotton fields, all those spirituals, all those Uncle Tom bits, all that we had to go through to get through. There's something dangerous in the notion that it is new, because we can fall into the European trap, too. After all, I've been treated as badly by black people as I have by white people. And I'm not about to accept another kind of cultural dictatorship. I won't accept it from Governor Wallace, and I won't accept it from anybody else, either. I am an artist. No one will tell me what to do. You can shoot me and throw me off a tower, but you cannot tell me what to write or how to write it. Because I won't go. Most people talking about black pride and black power don't know what they're talking about. I've lived long enough to know people who were at one time so white they wouldn't talk to me. And now they're so black they won't talk to me. I kid you not.

IDA: What about all the new blacks?

JIMMY: Maybe they'll be white next week. They go with the winds, like a water wheel. I've lived nearly half a century. No dreary young S.O.B. is going to tell me what to do. Oh, nonononono. Of course, it is inevitable. On a certain level it's even healthy. But I'm somewhere else. Now, for the first time in my life, I suppose because I've paid for it, I really do know something else.

I trust myself more than ever before. And I suppose it's only because I had to accept something about the role I play, which I didn't want to accept. But now it's all right.

IDA: Well, how do you see yourself?

JIMMY: I'm a witness. That's my responsibility. I write it all down.

IDA: What's the difference between a witness and an observer?

JIMMY: An observer has no passion. It doesn't mean I saw it. It means that I was there. I don't have to observe the life and death of Martin Luther King. I am a witness to it. Follow me?

SHELBY STEELE

On Being Black and Middle Class

Shelby Steele (1946–   ), a professor of English at San Jose State University in California, was born in Chicago. Steele's writing, which focuses on racial issues in the United States, has appeared in many publications, including *The American Scholar, Black World, Harper's,* the *New York Times Book Review,* and *Commentary,* in which the following selection first appeared. His controversial first book, *The Content of Our Character: A New Vision of Race in America,* was published in 1990.

Not long ago a friend of mine, black like myself, said to me that the term "black middle class" was actually a contradiction in terms. Race, he insisted, blurred class distinctions among blacks. If you were black, you were just black and that was that. When I argued, he let his eyes roll at my naiveté. Then he went on. For us, as black professionals, it was an exercise in self-flattery, a pathetic pretension, to give meaning to such a distinction. Worse, the very idea of class threatened the unity that was vital to the black community as a whole. After all, since when had white America taken note of anything but color when it came to blacks? He then reminded me of an old Malcolm X line that had been popular in the sixties. Question: What is a black man with a Ph.D.? Answer: A nigger.

For many years I had been on my friend's side of this argument. Much of my conscious thinking on the old conundrum of race and class was shaped during my high school and college years in the race-charged sixties, when the fact of my race took on an almost religious significance. Progressively, from the mid-sixties on, more and more aspects of my life found their explanation, their justification, and their motivation in race. My youthful concerns about career, romance, money, values, and even styles of dress became a subject to consultation with various oracular sources of racial wisdom. And these ranged from a figure as ennobling as Martin Luther King, Jr., to the underworld elegance of dress I found in jazz clubs on the South Side of Chicago. Everywhere there were signals, and in those days I considered myself so blessed with clarity and direction that I pitied my white classmates who found more embarrassment than guidance in the fact of *their* race. In 1968, inflated by my new power, I took a mischievous delight in calling them culturally disadvantaged.

But now, hearing my friend's comment was like hearing a priest from a church I'd grown disenchanted with. I understood him, but my faith was weak. What had sustained me in the sixties sounded monotonous and off the mark in the eighties. For me, race had lost much of its juju, its singular capacity to conjure meaning. And today, when I honestly look at my life and the lives of many other middle-class blacks I know, I can see that race never fully explained our situation in American society. Black though I may be, it is impossible for me to sit in my single-family house with two cars in the driveway and a swing set in the back yard and *not* see the role class has played in my life. And how can my friend, similarly raised and similarly situated, not see it?

Yet despite my certainty I felt a sharp tug of guilt as I tried to explain myself over my friend's skepticism. He is a man of many comedic facial expressions and, as I spoke, his brow lifted in extreme moral alarm as if I were uttering the unspeakable. His clear implication was that I was being elitist and possibly (dare he suggest?) anti-black—crimes for which there might well be no redemption. He pretended to fear for me. I chuckled along with him, but inwardly I did wonder at myself. Though I never doubted the validity of what I was saying, I felt guilty saying it. Why?

After he left (to retrieve his daughter from a dance lesson) I realized that the trap I felt myself in had a tiresome familiarity and, in a sort of slow-motion epiphany, I began to see its outline. It was like the suddenly sharp vision one has at the end of a burdensome marriage when all the long-repressed incompatibilities come undeniably to light.

What became clear to me is that people like myself, my friend, and middle-class blacks generally are caught in a very specific double bind that keeps two equally powerful elements of our identity at odds with each other. The middle-class values by which we were raised—the work ethic, the importance of education, the value of property ownership, of respectability, of "getting ahead," of stable family life, of initiative, of self-reliance, etc.—are, in themselves, raceless and even assimilationist. They urge us toward participation in the American mainstream, toward integration, toward a strong identification with the society—and toward the entire constellation of qualities that are implied in the word "individualism." These values are almost rules for how to prosper in a democratic, free-enterprise society that admires and rewards individual effort. They tell us to work hard for ourselves and our families and to seek our opportunities whenever they appear, inside or outside the confines of whatever ethnic group we may belong to.

But the particular pattern of racial identification that emerged in the sixties and that still prevails today urges middle-class blacks (and all blacks) in the opposite direction. This pattern asks us to see ourselves as an embattled minority, and it urges an adversarial stance toward the mainstream, an emphasis on ethnic consciousness over individualism. It is organized around an implied separatism.

The opposing thrust of these two parts of our identity results in the double bind of middle-class blacks. There is no forward movement on either plane that does not constitute backward movement on the other. This was the familiar trap I felt myself in while talking with my friend. As I spoke about class, his eyes reminded me that I was betraying race. Clearly, the two indispensable parts of my identity were a threat to each other.

Of course when you think about it, class and race are both similar in some ways and also naturally opposed. They are two forms of collective identity with boundaries that intersect. But whether they clash or peacefully coexist has much to do with how they are defined. Being both black and middle class becomes a double bind when class and race are defined in sharply antagonistic terms, so that one must be repressed to appease the other.

But what is the "substance" of these two identities, and how does each establish itself in an individual's overall identity? It seems to me that when we identify with any collective we are basically identifying with images that tell us what it means to be a member of that collective. Identity is not the same thing as the fact of membership in a collective; it is, rather, a form of self-definition, facilitated by images of what we wish our membership in the collective to mean. In this sense, the images we identify with may reflect the aspirations of the collective more than they reflect reality, and their content can vary with shifts in those aspirations.

But the process of identification is usually dialectical. It is just as necessary to say what we are *not* as it is to say what we are—so that finally identification comes about by embracing a polarity of positive and negative images. To identify as middle class, for example, I must have both positive and negative images of what being middle class entails; then I will know what I should and should not be doing in order to be middle class. The same goes for racial identity.

In the racially turbulent sixties the polarity of images that came to define racial identification was very antagonistic to the polarity that defined middle-class identification. One might say that the positive images of one lined up with the negative images of the other, so that to identify with both required either a contortionist's flexibility or a dangerous splitting of the self. The double bind of the black middle class was in place.

The black middle class has always defined its class identity by means of positive images gleaned from middle- and upper-class white society, and by means of negative images of lower-class blacks. This habit goes back to the institution of slavery itself, when "house" slaves both mimicked the whites they served and held themselves above the "field" slaves. But in the sixties the old bourgeois impulse to dissociate from the lower classes (the "we-they" distinction) backfired when racial identity suddenly called for the celebration of this same black lower class. One of the qualities of a double bind is that one feels it more than sees it, and I distinctly remember the tension and strange sense of dishonesty I felt in those days as I moved back and forth like a bigamist between the demands of class and race.

Though my father was born poor, he achieved middle-class standing through much hard work and sacrifice (one of his favorite words) and by identifying fully with solid middle-class values—mainly hard work, family life, property ownership, and education for his children (all four of whom have advanced degrees). In his mind these were not so much values as laws of nature. People who embodied them made up the positive images in his class polarity. The negative images came largely from the blacks he had left behind because they were "going nowhere."

No one in my family remembers how it happened, but as time went on, the negative images congealed into an imaginary character named Sam, who, from the extensive service we put him to, quickly grew to mythic proportions. In our family lore he was sometimes a trickster, sometimes a boob, but always possessed of a catalogue of sly faults that gave up graphic images of everything we should not be. On sacrifice: "Sam never thinks about tomorrow. He wants it now or he doesn't care about it." On work: "Sam doesn't favor it too much." On children: "Sam likes to have them but not to raise them." On money: "Sam drinks it up and pisses it out." On fidelity: "Sam has to have two or three women." On clothes: "Sam features loud clothes. He likes to see and be seen." And so on. Sam's persona amounted to a negative instruction manual in class identity.

I don't think that any of us believed Sam's faults were accurate representations of lower-class black life. He was an instrument of self-definition, not of sociological accuracy. It never occurred to us that he looked very much like the white racist stereotype of blacks, or that he might have been a manifestation of our own racial self-hatred. He simply gave us a counterpoint against which to express our aspirations. If self-hatred was a factor, it was not, for us, a matter of hating lower-class blacks but of hating what we did not want to be.

Still, hate or love aside, it is fundamentally true that my middle-class identity involved a dissociation from images of lower-class black life and a corresponding identification with values and patterns of responsibility that are common to the middle class everywhere. These values sent me a clear message: be both an individual and a responsible citizen; understand that the quality of your life will approximately reflect the quality of effort you put into it; know that individual responsibility is the basis of freedom and that the limitations imposed by fate (whether fair or unfair) are no excuse for passivity.

Whether I live up to these values or not, I know that my acceptance of them is the result of lifelong conditioning. I know also that I share this conditioning with middle-class people of all races and that I can no more easily be free of it than I can be free of my race. Whether all this got started because the black middle class modeled itself on the white middle class is no longer relevant. For the middle-class black, conditioned by these values from birth, the sense of meaning they provide is as immutable as the color of his skin.

I started the sixties in high school feeling that my class-conditioning was the surest way to overcome racial barriers. My racial identity was pretty much taken for granted. After all, it was obvious to the world that I was black. Yet I ended the sixties in graduate school a little embarrassed by my class background and with an almost desperate need to be "black." The tables had turned. I knew very clearly (though I struggled to repress it) that my aspirations and my sense of how to operate in the world came from my class background, yet "being black" required certain attitudes and stances that made me feel secretly a little duplicitous. The inner compatibility of class and race I had known in 1960 was gone.

For blacks, the decade between 1960 and 1969 saw racial identification undergo the same sort of transformation that national identity undergoes in times of war. It became more self-conscious, more narrowly focused, more prescribed, less tolerant of opposition. It spawned an implicit party line, which tended to disallow competing forms of identity. Race-as-identity was lifted from the relative slumber it knew in the fifties and pressed into service in a social and political war against oppression. It was redefined along sharp adversarial lines and directed toward the goal of mobilizing the great mass of black Americans in this warlike effort. It was imbued with a strong moral authority, useful for denouncing those who opposed it and for celebrating those who honored it as a positive achievement rather than as a mere birthright.

The form of racial identification that quickly evolved to meet this challenge presented blacks as a racial monolith, a singular people with a common experience of oppression. Differences within the race, no matter how ineradicable, had to be minimized. Class distinctions were one of the first such differences to be sacrificed, since they not only threatened racial unity but also seemed to stand in contradiction to the principle of equality which was the announced goal of the movement for racial progress. The discomfort I felt in 1969, the vague but relentless sense of duplicity, was the result of a historical necessity that put my race and class at odds, that was asking me to cast aside the distinction of my class and identify with a monolithic view of my race.

If the form of this racial identity was the monolith, its substance was victimization. The civil rights movement and the more radical splinter groups of the late sixties were all dedicated to ending racial victimization, and the form of black identity that emerged to facilitate this goal made blackness and victimization virtually synonymous. Since it was our victimization more than any other variable that identified and unified us, moreover, it followed logically that the purest black was the poor black. It was images of him that clustered around the positive pole of the race polarity; all other blacks were, in effect, required to identify with him in order to confirm their own blackness.

Certainly there were more dimensions to the black experience than victimization, but no other had the same capacity to fire the indignation needed for war. So, again out of historical necessity, victimization became the overriding focus of racial identity. But this only deepened the double bind for middle-class blacks like me. When it came to class we were accustomed to defining ourselves against lower-class blacks and identifying with at least the values of middle-class whites; when it came to race we were now being asked to identify with images of lower-class blacks and to see whites, middle class or otherwise, as victimizers. Negative lining up with positive, we were called upon to reject what we had previously embraced and to embrace what we had previously rejected. To put it still more personally, the Sam figure I had been raised to define myself against had now become the "real" black I was expected to identify with.

The fact that the poor black's new status was only passively earned by the condition of his victimization, not by assertive, positive action, made little difference. Status was status apart from the means by which it was achieved, and along with it came a certain power—the power to define the terms of access to that status, to say who was black and who was not. If a lower-class black said you were not really "black"—a sellout, an Uncle Tom—the judgment was all the more devastating because it carried the authority of his status. And this judgment soon enough came to be accepted by many whites as well.

In graduate school I was once told by a white professor, "Well, but . . . you're not really black. I mean, you're not disadvantaged." In his mind my lack of victim status disqualified me from the race itself. More recently I was complimented by a black student for speaking reasonably correct English, "proper" English as he put it. "But I don't know if I really want to talk like that," he went on. "Why not?" I asked. "Because then I wouldn't be black no more," he replied without a pause.

To overcome his marginal status, the middle-class black had to identify with a degree of victimization that was beyond his actual experience. In college (and well beyond) we used to play a game called "nap matching." It was a game of one-upmanship, in which we sat around outdoing each other with stories of racial victimization, symbolically measured by the naps of our hair. Most of us were middle class and so had few personal stories to relate, but if we could not match naps with our own biographies, we would move on to those legendary tales of victimization that came to us from the public domain.

The single story that sat atop the pinnacle of racial victimization for us was that of Emmett Till, the Northern black teenager who, on a visit to the South in 1955, was killed and grotesquely mutilated for supposedly looking at or whistling at (we were never sure which, though we argued the point endlessly) a white woman. Oh, how we probed his story, finding in his youth and Northern upbringing the quintessential embodiment of black innocence, brought down by a white evil so portentous and apocalyptic, so gnarled and hideous, that it left us with a feeling not far from awe. By telling his story and others like it, we came to *feel* the immutability of our victimization, its utter indigenousness, as a thing on this earth like dirt or sand or water.

Of course, these sessions were a ritual of group identification, a means by which we, as middle-class blacks, could be at one with our race. But why were we, who had only a moderate experience of victimization (and that offset by opportunities our parents never had), so intent on assimilating or appropriating an identity that in so many ways contradicted our own? Because, I think, the sense of innocence that is always entailed in feeling victimized filled us with a corresponding feeling of entitlement, or even license, that helped us endure our vulnerability on a largely white college campus.

In my junior year in college I rode to a debate tournament with three white students and our faculty coach, an elderly English professor. The experience of being the lone black in a group of whites was so familiar to me that I thought nothing of it as our trip began. But then halfway through the trip the professor casually turned to me and, in an isn't-the-world-funny sort of tone, said that he had just refused to rent an apartment in a house he owned to a "very nice" black couple because their color would "offend" the white couple who lived downstairs. His eyebrows lifted helplessly over his hawkish nose, suggesting that he too, like me, was a victim of America's racial farce. His look assumed a kind of comradeship: he and I were above this grimy business of race, though for expediency we had occasionally to concede the world its madness.

My vulnerability in this situation came not so much from the professor's blindness to his own racism as from his assumption that I would participate in it, that I would conspire with him against my own race so that he might remain comfortably blind. Why did he think I would be amenable to this? I can only guess that he assumed my middle-class identity was so complete and all-encompassing that I would see his action as nothing more than a trifling concession to the folkways of our land, that I would in fact applaud his decision not to disturb propriety. Blind to both his own racism and to me— one blindness serving the other—he could not recognize that he was asking me to betray my race in the name of my class.

His blindness made me feel vulnerable because it threatened to expose my own repressed ambivalence. His comment pressured me to choose between my class identification, which had contributed to my being a college student and a member of the debating team, and my desperate desire to be "black." I could have one but not both; I was double-bound.

Because double binds are repressed there is always an element of terror in them: the terror of bringing to the conscious mind the buried duplicity, self-deception, and pretense involved in serving two masters. This terror is the stuff of vulnerability, and since vulnerability is one of the least tolerable of all human feelings, we usually transform it into an emotion that seems to restore the control of which it has robbed us; most often, that emotion is anger. And so, before the professor had even finished his little story, I had become a furnace of rage. The year was 1967, and I had been primed by endless hours of nap-matching to feel, at least consciously, completely at one with the victim-focused black identity. This identity gave me the license, and the impunity, to unleash upon this professor one of those volcanic eruptions of racial indignation familiar to us from the novels of Richard Wright. Like Cross Damon in *Outsider,* who kills in perfectly righteous anger, I tried to annihilate the man. I punished him not according to the measure of his crime but according to the measure of my vulnerability, a measure set by the cumulative tension of years of repressed terror. Soon I saw that terror in *his* face, as he stared hollow-eyed at the road ahead. My white friends in the back seat, knowing no conflict between their own class and race, were astonished that someone they had taken to be so much like themselves could harbor a rage that for all the world looked murderous.

Though my rage was triggered by the professor's comment, it was deepened and sustained by a complex of need, conflict, and repression in myself of which I had been wholly unaware. Out of my racial vulnerability I had developed the strong need of an identity with which to defend myself. The only such identity available was that of me as victim, him as victimizer. Once in the grip of this paradigm, I began to do far more damage to myself than he had done.

Seeing myself as a victim meant that I clung all the harder to my racial identity, which, in turn, meant that I suppressed my class identity. This cut me off from all the resources my class values might have offered me. In those values, for instance, I might have found the means to a more dispassionate response, the response less of a victim attacked by a victimizer than of an individual offended by a foolish old man. As an individual I might have reported this professor to the college dean. Or I might have calmly tried to reveal his blindness to him, and possibly won a convert. (The flagrancy of his remark suggested a hidden guilt and even self-recognition on which I might have capitalized. Doesn't confession usually signal a willingness to face oneself?) Or I might have simply chuckled and then let my silence serve as an answer to his provocation. Would not my composure, in any form it might take, deflect into his own heart the arrow he'd shot at me?

Instead, my anger, itself the hair-trigger expression of a long-repressed double bind, not only cut me off from the best of my own resources, it also distorted the nature of my true racial problem. The righteousness of this anger and easy catharsis it brought buoyed the delusion of my victimization and left me as blind as the professor himself.

As a middle-class black I have often felt myself *contriving* to be "black." And I have noticed this same contrivance in others—a certain stretching away from the natural flow of one's life to align oneself with a victim-focused black identity. Our particular needs are out of sync with the form of identity available to meet those needs. Middle-class blacks need to identify racially; it is better to think of ourselves as black and victimized than not black at all; so we contrive (more unconsciously than consciously) to fit ourselves into an identity that denies our class and fails to address the true source of our vulnerability.

For me this once meant spending inordinate amounts of time at black faculty meetings, though these meetings had little to do with my real racial anxieties or my professional life. I was new to the university, one of two blacks in an English department of over seventy, and I felt a little isolated and vulnerable, though I did not admit it to myself. But at these meetings we discussed the problems of black faculty and students within a framework of victimization. The real vulnerability we felt was covered over by all the adversarial drama the victim/victimized polarity inspired, and hence went unseen and unassuaged. And this, I think, explains our rather chronic ineffectiveness as a group. Since victimization was not our primary problem—the university had long ago opened its doors to us—we had to contrive to make it so, and there is not much energy in contrivance. What I got at these meetings was ultimately an object lesson in how fruitless struggle can be when it is not grounded in actual need.

At our black faculty meetings, the old equation of blackness with victimization was ever present—to be black was to be a victim; therefore, not to be a victim was not to be black. As we contrived to meet the terms of this formula there was an inevitable distortion of both ourselves and the larger university. Through the prism of victimization the university seemed more impenetrable than it actually was, and we more limited in our powers. We fell prey to the victim's myopia, making the university an institution from which we could seek redress but which we could never fully join. And this mind-set often led us to look more for compensations for our supposed victimization than for opportunities we could pursue as individuals.

The discomfort and vulnerability felt by middle-class blacks in the sixties, it could be argued, was a worthwhile price to pay considering the progress achieved during that time of racial confrontation. But what may have been tolerable then is intolerable now. Though changes in American society have made it an anachronism, the monolithic form of racial identification that came out of the sixties is still very much with us. It may be more loosely held, and its power to punish heretics has probably diminished, but it continues to catch middle-class blacks in a double bind, thus impeding not only their own advancement but even, I would contend, that of blacks as a group.

The victim-focused black identity encourages the individual to feel that his advancement depends almost entirely on that of the group. Thus he loses sight not only of his own possibilities but of the inextricable connection between individual effort and individual advancement. This is a profound emcumbrance today, when there is more opportunity for blacks than ever before, for it reimposes limitations that can have the same oppressive effect as those the society has only recently begun to remove.

It was the emphasis on mass action in the sixties that made the victim-focused black identity a necessity. But in the eighties and beyond, when racial advancement will come only through a multitude of individual advancements, this form of identity inadvertently adds itself to the forces that hold us back. Hard work, education, individual initiative, stable family life, property ownership—these have always been the means by which ethnic groups have moved ahead in America. Regardless of past or present victimization, these "laws" of advancement apply absolutely to black Americans also. There is no getting around this. What we need is a form of racial identity that energizes the individual by putting him in touch with both his possibilities and his responsibilities.

It has always annoyed me to hear from the mouths of certain arbiters of blackness that middle-class blacks should "reach back" and pull up those blacks less fortunate than they—as though middle-class status were an unearned and essentially passive condition in which one needed a large measure of noblesse oblige[1] to occupy one's time. My own image is of reaching back from a moving train to lift on board those who have no tickets. A noble enough senti-ment—but might it not be wiser to show them the entire structure of principles, effort, and sacrifice that puts one in a position to buy a ticket any time one likes? This, I think, is something members of the black middle class can realistically offer to other blacks. Their example is not only a testament to possibility but also a lesson in method. But they cannot lead by example until they are released from a black identity that regards that example as suspect, that sees them as "marginally" black, indeed that holds *them* back by catching them in a double bind.

To move beyond the victim-focused black identity we must learn to make a difficult but crucial distinction: between actual victimiza-tion, which we must resist with every resource, and identification with the victim's status. Until we do this we will continue to wrestle more with ourselves than with the new opportunities which so many paid so dearly to win.

MICHAEL J. ARLEN

Life and Death in the Global Village

Michael J. Arlen (1930–   ) is a London-born journalist and televi-sion critic whose books include *The Living Room War* (1969), *Pas-sage to Ararat* (1975), *The View from Highway 1* (1976), and *Thirty Seconds* (1980). The following selection originally appeared in the *New Yorker*.

He was shot in secrecy, away from cameras. No strange slow-motion scenes, as when the young Japanese student, sword in hand, rushed

---

[1] the obligation of persons of high rank to behave nobly or generously (ED.)

across the stage to lunge at a Socialist politician, or when Verwoerd,[1] the South African, was shot at and for whole crazy moments (it seems so long ago; so many people shot at since then) the cameras swirled and danced around the tumbling, stampeding bodies of the crowd—and then John Kennedy was killed, his life made to disappear right there before us, frame by frame, the projector slowing down, s-l-o-w-i-n-g d-o-w-n, s...l...o...w...i...n...g d...o...w...n as we watched (three consecutive days we watched), gathered in little tight-gutted bands around the television set, meals being cooked somehow, children put to bed, sent out to play, our thoughts of abandonment and despair and God knows what else focussing on the images of the television set, television itself taking on (we were told later) the aspect of a national icon, a shrine, an exorciser of grief; we were never so close (we were told later) than in those days just after Dallas. It could not have been quite close enough, it seems, or lasted long enough. The man who was shot in Memphis on Thursday of last week was standing on a second-floor balcony of a motel, the Lorraine, leaning over the railing of the balcony in front of his room, which was No. 306. (We have been told it was No. 306.) He was shot once and killed by a man who fired his rifle (a Remington 30.06), apparently, from inside a bathroom window of a rooming house some two hundred feet away. The address of the rooming house is 420 South Main Street. There was no film record of the act, no attendant Zapruder[2] to witness for us the body falling and other memorabilia, but most of us found out about it by television, and it is by television that most of us have been connected with whatever it is that really happened, or is happening now. Television connects— the global village. We sit at home— We had been out, actually, a party full of lawyers, and had come back early, and turned on the eleven-o'clock news. "I have a dream . . ." young Dr. King was chanting, "that one day on the red hills of Georgia . . ." C.B.S.'s Joseph Benti said that Dr. King had been shot and killed, was dead. The President was speaking. "I ask every citizen to reject the blind violence that has struck Dr. King, who lived by non-violence," he

---

[1] Hendrik Verwoerd, prime minister of South Africa from 1958 to 1966, was a strong proponent of the policy of apartheid. He was shot in a failed assassination attempt, in 1960. He was in fact assassinated six years later, when he was stabbed to death in the parliamentary chamber. (ED.)

[2] Abraham Zapruder was a Dallas businessman who filmed the assassination of John F. Kennedy with an 8 mm home-movie camera. (ED.)

said. They showed us pictures of Dr. King in Montgomery. They showed us pictures of the outside of the Lorraine Motel.

The telephone rang. A friend of my wife's. "Have you heard?" she said. I said we'd heard. "It's so horrible," she said. And then, "I can't believe it." And then, "I feel we're all mad." I held the phone against my ear, mumbling the usual things, feeling, in part, her grief, her guilt, her sense of lunacy—whatever it was—and, in part, that adrenalin desire we strangers have who have been separate in our cabins all the long sea voyage to somehow touch each other at the moment that the ship goes down. She talked some more. "I'm keeping you from watching," she said at last. I mumbled protests, and we said goodbye, and disconnected. We will all meet for dinner three weekends hence and discuss summer rentals on the Vineyard.

All over the country now the members of the global village sit before their sets, and the voices and faces out of the sets speak softly, earnestly, reasonably, sincerely to us, in order once again (have four and a half years really gone by since Dallas?) to bind us together, to heal, to mend, to take us forward. The President appears. His face looks firmer, squarer, straighter now than it has looked in months. "We can achieve nothing by lawlessness and divisiveness among the American people," he says. "It's only by joining together and only by working together we can continue to move toward equality and fulfillment for all of our people." The Vice-President speaks. "The cause for which he marched and worked I am sure will find a new strength. The plight of discrimination, poverty, and neglect must be erased from America," he says. Former Vice-President Richard Nixon is expected to release a statement soon. There are brief pictures of a coffin being slid onto a plane. The Field Foundation,[3] one hears, has just undertaken to donate a million dollars to the civil-rights movement. Dr. Ralph Bunche[4] asks for "an effort of unparalleled determination, massiveness, and urgency to convert the American ideal of equality into reality."

The television sets hum in our midst. Gray smoke, black smoke begins to rise from blocks of buildings in Washington and Chicago.

---

[3] The Field Foundation was established by Marshall Field IV, heir to the retailing fortune, in 1960. It funds urban affairs projects and cultural activities in the Chicago area. (ED.)

[4] Ralph Bunche (1904–1971) was a black United States diplomat and a member of the United Nations for twenty years. He won the Nobel Prize for peace in 1950 for his negotiation of an Arab-Israeli truce in Palestine in 1949. (ED.)

Sirens whine outside our windows in the night. The voices out of
Memphis seem to be fainter now; the pictures of that little, nondes-
cript motel, the railing, the bathroom window are already being
shown to us less frequently today. Down below us on the sidewalk,
six blue-helmeted policemen are gathered in a group. Three police
cars are parked farther down the street. The television beams out at
us a Joel McCrea movie. Detroit and Newark have been remembered.
Responsible decisions have been made in responsible places. The
President is working now "to avoid catastrophe." The cartoons are
on this morning. The air is very bright outside. The day is sunny.
All day long, the sirens sound. The television hums through its
schedule. There is a circus on Channel 4. Back from the dime store,
my daughter asks one of the helmeted policemen if anything has
happened. He seems surprised. No, nothing, he says. A squad car
drives slowly, slowly by. A bowling exhibition is taking place on
Channel 7. Another movie—and then the news. Great waves of
smoke, clouds, billowing waves are suddenly pouring out of buildings. The sounds of bells and sirens. Mayor Daley[5] speaks. Mayor
Daley declares a curfew. Six Negro boys are running down a street
carrying armfuls of clothes. Police cars streak by. More smoke. The
news is over. We are reënveloped in a movie. We sit there on the
floor and absorb the hum of television. Last summer, it inflamed our
passions, did it not? This time, the scenes of black men running past
the smoking buildings of Chicago are handled briefly, almost dream-
ily—a light caress by cameras and announcers. The coffin—one wonders where the coffin is at present, who is with it. Boston University
announces that ten new scholarships for "underprivileged students"
have just been created. The Indian Parliament pays tribute. The voices
of reason and reordering rise out of the civic temples of the land and
float through the air and the airwaves into our homes. Twenty-one
House Republicans have issued an "urgent appeal" for passage of the
new civil-rights bill. "With whom will we stand? The man who fired
the gun? Or the man who fell before it?" Senator Edward Brooke, of
Massachusetts, asks. The City Council of Chicago meets and passes
a resolution to build a "permanent memorial." Senator Robert Kennedy deplores the rise in violence.

[5] Richard Daley (1902–1976) was mayor of Chicago from 1955 until his death in
1976. He was criticized for his reluctance to stop racial segregation in housing and
public schools and for the harsh measures he took in dealing with demonstrators
during the Democratic National Convention in 1968. (ED.)

There was a moment the other evening when (just for a few seconds) everybody stopped talking, when (just for a few seconds) the television stopped its humming and soothing and filling of silences and its preachments of lessons-we-have-just-learned and how-we-must-all-march-together—and (just for a few seconds) Mrs. King appeared; she was speaking about her husband, her dead husband. She spoke; she seemed so alive with him—it's marvellous how that sometimes happens between people; he really had been alive, and one knew it then—and for a few scant moments, just at that time, and afterward, sitting there looking at the set, that very imperfect icon, that very imperfect connector of people (will somebody really have the nerve to say this week that we are a nation "united in grief"?), one could almost hear the weeping out there, of real people in real villages, and the anger, this time, of abandonment.

And then the sounds came back—the sounds of one's own life. The weatherman came on. A Negro minister on Channel 13 was talking about the need to implement the recommendations of the President's new Commission on Civil Disorders. He *had* been alive . . . hadn't he? Later that night, one could hear the sirens—very cool and clear—and, somewhere nearby (around the corner? blocks away?), the sounds of footsteps running.

MILTON FRIEDMAN

The Social Responsibility of Business Is to Increase Its Profits

Milton Friedman (1912–   ), an economist, was born in Brooklyn, New York. His books include *Essays in Positive Economics* (1966), *Bright Promises, Dismal Performance* (1983), and, with his wife, Rose Friedman, *Free to Choose: A Personal Statement* (1980). From 1966–1984 he also wrote a column for *Newsweek* magazine, and in 1976 he received the Nobel Prize in economics. The following selection first appeared in the *New York Times Magazine*.

When I hear businessmen speak eloquently about the "social responsibilities of business in a free-enterprise system," I am reminded of the wonderful line about the Frenchman who discovered at the age of 70 that he had been speaking prose all his life. The businessmen believe that they are defending free enterprise when they declaim that business is not concerned "merely" with profit but also with promoting desirable "social" ends; that business has a "social conscience" and takes seriously its responsibilities for providing employment, eliminating discrimination, avoiding pollution and whatever else may be the catchwords of the contemporary crop of reformers. In fact they are—or would be if they or anyone else took them seriously—preaching pure and unadulterated socialism. Businessmen who talk this way are unwitting puppets of the intellectual forces that have been undermining the basis of a free society these past decades.

The discussions of the "social responsibilities of business" are notable for their analytical looseness and lack of rigor. What does it mean to say that "business" has responsibilities? Only people can have responsibilities. A corporation is an artificial person and in this sense may have artificial responsibilities, but "business" as a whole cannot be said to have responsibilities, even in this vague sense. The first step toward clarity in examining the doctrine of the social responsibility of business is to ask precisely what it implies for whom.

Presumably, the individuals who are to be responsible are businessmen, which means individual proprietors or corporate executives. Most of the discussion of social responsibility is directed at corporations, so in what follows I shall mostly neglect the individual proprietors and speak of corporate executives.

In a free-enterprise, private-property system, a corporate executive is an employee of the owners of the business. He has direct responsibility to his employers. That responsibility is to conduct the business in accordance with their desire, which generally will be to make as much money as possible while conforming to the basic rules of the society, both those embodied in law and those embodied in ethical custom. Of course, in some cases his employers may have a different objective. A group of persons might establish a corporation for an eleemosynary purpose—for example, a hospital or a school. The manager of such a corporation will not have money profit as his objectives but the rendering of certain services.

In either case, the key point is that, in his capacity as a corporate executive, the manager is the agent of the individuals who own the corporation or establish the eleemosynary institution, and his primary responsibility is to them.

Needless to say, this does not mean that it is easy to judge how well he is performing his task. But at least the criterion of performance is straightforward, and the persons among whom a voluntary contractual arrangement exists are clearly defined.

Of course, the corporate executive is also a person in his own right. As a person, he may have many other responsibilities that he recognizes or assumes voluntarily—to his family, his conscience, his feelings of charity, his church, his clubs, his city, his country. He may feel impelled by these responsibilities to devote part of his income to causes he regards as worthy, to refuse to work for particular corporations, even to leave his job, for example, to join his country's armed forces. If we wish, we may refer to some of these responsibilities as "social responsibilities." But in these respects he is acting as a principal, not an agent; he is spending his own money or time or energy, not the money of his employers or the time or energy he has contracted to devote to their purposes. If these are "social responsibilities," they are the social responsibilities of individuals, not of business.

What does it mean to say that the corporate executive has a "social responsibility" in his capacity as businessman? If this statement is not pure rhetoric, it must mean that he is to act in some way that is not in the interest of his employers. For example, that he is to refrain from increasing the price of the product in order to contribute to the social objective of preventing inflation, even though a price increase would be in the best interests of the corporation. Or that he is to make expenditures on reducing pollution beyond the amount that is in the best interests of the corporation or that is required by law in order to contribute to the social objective of improving the environment. Or that, at the expense of corporate profits, he is to hire "hardcore" unemployed instead of better qualified available workmen to contribute to the social objective of reducing poverty.

In each of these cases, the corporate executive would be spending someone else's money for a general social interest. Insofar as his actions in accord with his "social responsibility" reduce returns to stockholders, he is spending their money. Insofar as his actions raise the price to customers, he is spending the customers' money. Insofar as his actions lower the wages of some employees, he is spending their money.

The stockholders or the customers or the employees could separately spend their own money on the particular action if they wished to do so. The executive is exercising a distinct "social responsibility," rather than serving as an agent of the stockholders or the customers or the employees, only if he spends the money in a different way than they would have spent it.

But if he does this, he is in effect imposing taxes, on the one hand, and deciding how the tax proceeds shall be spent, on the other.

This process raises political questions on two levels: principle and consequences. On the level of political principle, the imposition of taxes and the expenditure of tax proceeds are governmental functions. We have established elaborate constitutional, parliamentary and judicial provisions to control these functions, to assure that taxes are imposed so far as possible in accordance with the preferences and desires of the public—after all, "taxation without representation" was one of the battle cries of the American Revolution. We have a system of checks and balances to separate the legislative function of imposing taxes and enacting expenditures from the executive function of collecting taxes and administering expenditure programs and from the judicial function of mediating disputes and interpreting the law.

Here the businessman—self-selected or appointed directly or indirectly by stockholders—is to be simultaneously legislator, executive and jurist. He is to decide whom to tax by how much and for what purpose, and he is to spend the proceeds—all this guided only by general exhortations from on high to restrain inflation, improve the environment, fight poverty and so on and on.

The whole justification for permitting the corporate executive to be selected by the stockholders is that the executive is an agent serving the interests of his principal. This justification disappears when the corporate executive imposes taxes and spends the proceeds for "social" purposes. He becomes in effect a public employee, a civil servant, even though he remains in name an employee of a private enterprise. On grounds of political principle, it is intolerable that such civil servants—insofar as their actions in the name of social responsibility are real and not just window-dressing—should be selected as they are now. If they are to be civil servants, then they must be elected through a political process. If they are to impose taxes and make expenditures to foster "social" objectives, then political machinery must be set up to make the assessment of taxes and to determine through a political process the objectives to be served.

This is the basic reason why the doctrine of "social responsibility" involves the acceptance of the socialist view that political mechanisms, not market mechanisms, are the appropriate way to determine the allocation of scarce resources to alternative uses.

On the grounds of consequences, can the corporate executive in fact discharge his alleged "social responsibilities"? On the other hand, suppose he could get away with spending the stockholders' or customers' or employees' money. How is he to know how to spend it? He is told that he must contribute to fighting inflation. How is he to know what action of his will contribute to that end? He is presumably an expert in running his company—in producing a product or selling it or financing it. But nothing about his selection makes him an expert on inflation. Will his holding down the price of his product reduce inflationary pressure? Or, by leaving more spending power in the hands of his customers, simply divert it elsewhere? Or, by forcing him to produce less because of the lower price, will it simply contribute to shortages? Even if he could answer these questions, how much cost is he justified in imposing on his stockholders, customers and employees for this social purpose? What is his appropriate share and what is the appropriate share of others?

And, whether he wants to or not, can he get away with spending his stockholders', customers' or employees' money? Will not the stockholders fire him? (Either the present ones or those who take over when his actions in the name of social responsibility have reduced the corporation's profits and the price of its stock.) His customers and his employees can desert him for other producers and employers less scrupulous in exercising their social responsibilities.

This facet of "social responsibility" doctrine is brought into sharp relief when the doctrine is used to justify wage restraint by trade unions. The conflict of interest is naked and clear when union officials are asked to subordinate the interest of their members to some more general purpose. If the union officials try to enforce wage restraint, the consequence is likely to be wildcat strikes, rank-and-file revolts and the emergence of strong competitors for their jobs. We thus have the ironic phenomenon that union leaders—at least in the U.S.—have objected to Government interference with the market far more consistently and courageously than have business leaders.

The difficulty of exercising "social responsibility" illustrates, of course, the great virtue of private competitive enterprise—it forces people to be responsible for their own actions and makes it difficult for them to "exploit" other people for either selfish or unselfish purposes. They can do good—but only at their own expense.

Many a reader who has followed the argument this far may be tempted to remonstrate that it is all well and good to speak of Government's having the responsibility to impose taxes and determine expenditures for such "social" purposes as controlling pollution or training the hard-core unemployed, but that the problems are too urgent to wait on the slow course of political processes, that the exercise of social responsibility by businessmen is a quicker and surer way to solve pressing current problems.

Aside from the question of fact—I share Adam Smith's skepticism about the benefits that can be expected from "those who affected to trade for the public good"—this argument must be rejected on grounds of principle. What it amounts to is an assertion that those who favor the taxes and expenditures in question have failed to persuade a majority of their fellow citizens to be of like mind and that they are seeking to attain by undemocratic procedures what they cannot attain by democratic procedures. In a free society, it is hard for "evil" people to do "evil," especially since one man's good is another's evil.

I have, for simplicity, concentrated on the special case of the corporate executive, except only for the brief digression on trade unions. But precisely the same argument applies to the newer phenomenon of calling upon stockholders to require corporations to exercise social responsibility (the recent G.M. crusade for example). In most of these cases, what is in effect involved is some stockholders trying to get other stockholders (or customers or employees) to contribute against their will to "social" causes favored by the activists. Insofar as they succeed, they are again imposing taxes and spending the proceeds.

The situation of the individual proprietor is somewhat different. If he acts to reduce the returns of his enterprise in order to exercise his "social responsibility," he is spending his own money, not someone else's. If he wishes to spend his money on such purposes, that is his right, and I cannot see that there is any objection to his doing so. In the process, he, too, may impose costs on employees and customers. However, because he is far less likely than a large corporation or union to have monopolistic power, any such side effects will tend to be minor.

Of course, in practice the doctrine of social responsibility is frequently a cloak for actions that are justified on other grounds rather than a reason for those actions.

To illustrate, it may well be in the long-run interest of a corporation that is a major employer in a small community to devote resources to providing amenities to that community or to improving its government. That may make it easier to attract desirable employees, it may reduce the wage bill or lessen losses from pilferage and sabotage or have other worthwhile effects. Or it may be that, given the laws about the deductibility of corporate charitable contributions, the stockholders can contribute more to charities they favor by having the corporation make the gift than by doing it themselves, since they can in that way contribute an amount that would otherwise have been paid as corporate taxes.

In each of these—and many similar—cases, there is a strong temptation to rationalize these actions as an exercise of "social responsibility." In the present climate of opinion, with its widespread aversion to "capitalism," "profits," the "soulless corporation" and so on, this is one way for a corporation to generate goodwill as a byproduct of expenditures that are entirely justified in its own self-interest.

It would be inconsistent of me to call on corporate executives to refrain from this hypocritical window-dressing because it harms the foundations of a free society. That would be to call on them to exercise a "social responsibility"! If our institutions and the attitudes of the public make it in their self-interest to cloak their actions in this way, I cannot summon much indignation to denounce them. At the same time, I can express admiration for those individual proprietors or owners of closely held corporations or stockholders of more broadly held corporations who disdain such tactics as approaching fraud.

Whether blameworthy or not, the use of the cloak of social responsibility, and the nonsense spoken in its name by influential and prestigious businessmen, does clearly harm the foundations of a free society. I have been impressed time and again by the schizophrenic character of many businessmen. They are capable of being extremely far-sighted and clear-headed in matters that are internal to their businesses. They are incredibly short-sighted and muddleheaded in matters that are outside their businesses but affect the possible survival of business in general. This short-sightedness is strikingly exemplified in the calls from many businessmen for wage and price guidelines or controls or income policies. There is nothing that could do more in a brief period to destroy a market system and replace it by a centrally controlled system than effective governmental control of prices and wages.

The short-sightedness is also exemplified in speeches by businessmen on social responsibility. This may gain them kudos in the short run. But it helps to strengthen the already too prevalent view that the pursuit of profits is wicked and immoral and must be curbed and controlled by external forces. Once this view is adopted, the external forces that curb the market will not be the social consciences, however highly developed, of the pontificating executives; it will be the iron fist of Government bureaucrats. Here, as with price and wage controls, businessmen seem to me to reveal a suicidal impulse.

The political principle that underlies the market mechanism is unanimity. In an ideal free market resting on private property, no individual can coerce any other, all cooperation is voluntary, all parties to such cooperation benefit or they need not participate. There are no values, no "social" responsibilities in any sense other than the shared values and responsibilities of individuals. Society is a collection of individuals and of the various groups they voluntarily form.

The political principle that underlies the political mechanism is conformity. The individual must serve a more general social interest—whether that be determined by a church or a dictator or a majority. The individual may have a vote and say in what is to be done, but if he is overruled, he must conform. It is appropriate for some to require others to contribute to a general social purpose whether they wish to or not.

Unfortunately, unanimity is not always feasible. There are some respects in which conformity appears unavoidable, so I do not see how one can avoid the use of the political mechanism altogether.

But the doctrine of "social responsibility" taken seriously would extend the scope of the political mechanism to every human activity. It does not differ in philosophy from the most explicitly collectivist doctrine. It differs only by professing to believe that collectivist ends can be attained without collectivist means. That is why, in my book "Capitalism and Freedom," I have called it a "fundamentally subversive doctrine" in a free society, and have said that in such a society, "there is one and only one social responsibility of business—to use its resources and engage in activities designed to increase its profits so long as it stays within the rules of the game, which is to say, engages in open and free competition without deception or fraud."

JOEL ACHENBACH

Fake Up, America!

Joel Achenbach (1960–   ), formerly a reporter for the *Miami Herald*, is now a reporter for Style section of the *Washington Post*. He writes a syndicated column entitled "Why Things Are," and in

1991 published a collection of his articles in a book also entitled *Why Things Are*. His work has also appeared in *Esquire, Seventeen,* and *Mother Jones,* in which the following selection first appeared.

A while back I was watching an old movie on TV, with good guys and bad guys, and this good guy showed up and started punching and whacking and thunking and wonking the bad guys and then, brilliantly I thought, turned a fire hose on them, extinguishing their ardor for evil, and as my mind drifted I suddenly realized who the good guy was: my president! At least he *looked* like him. Talked like him. It *was* him. I was glad I had cable.

More recently I saw my president on TV in Moscow, wielding the fire hose of American righteousness. He told an anecdote that illustrated Trust. See, there were these two outlaws, Butch Cassidy and the Sundance Kid, and they were being chased by this posse, and they came to a cliff above a river, and Sundance said he didn't want to jump because he couldn't swim and Butch laughed and said the fall will probably kill you anyway, and . . . well, it all had something to do with Trust.

The night before, he had given Gorbachev a gift that supposedly had some significance: a movie. *Friendly Persuasion,* it was called. Reagan didn't mention that the screenwriter had been blacklisted for suspected Communist sympathies.

When a student asked Reagan about the treatment of the American Indian, the president once again turned to Hollywood for the answer, no doubt rifling through his mental catalog of old *Wagon Train* scripts:

"Maybe we should not have humored them" when they asked to live on reservations, he said. "Maybe we should have said, 'No, come join us. Be citizens along with the rest of us.' "

I admire the president for his strong sense of Right and Wrong. But he seems to have a tenuous grasp of Real and Make-Believe. What really scares me is that, far from being an anachronism, Ronald Reagan may be every bit the Average American fundamentally uninterested in distinguishing the real from the fake, particularly when there are still the comics to read. And then the horoscope.

It's getting worse. You can sense it everywhere. I even sense it in my Pepperidge Farm "Nantucket" Chocolate Chunk Cookies, part of the Pepperidge Farm "American Collection." Here's what it says on the package:

"Only the bakers of Pepperidge Farm could pack so much

scrumptious personality into classically American cookies. . . . They added a heaping measure of simple fuss and bother. . . . That meant making each cookie one of a kind, with an individual personality all its own. So they gave them rugged, irregular shapes, just as if some-one had lovingly shaped each cookie by hand."

What we have here, first of all, is the classic Humble Down-Home Multinational Corporation affectation. Pepperidge Farm is a billion-dollar corporate enterprise that is in turn owned by Campbell's, the world's largest soup company, yet they beg us to think of them as just regular folks who probably live in the woods in some gingerbread house.

More distressingly, they have clearly designed a machine that makes cookies that look as though a human being had made them. Then, incredibly, they admit the hoax right there on the bag. They *brag* about it. They say, yo, these cookies only *look* as though some-one had made them by hand. One thinks of those loathsome AT&T commercials in which the camera jerks around as though controlled by a spastic. People are mumbling dispiritedly, like nonactors. We are supposed to think that this is reality so stark, so *naked,* that they frantically shoved a camera in front of it and rolled the tape. With the budget for this ad campaign you could probably buy a nuclear submarine. My deep suspicion is that the camera is not hand-held at all, but is attached to a complex machine that exactly simulates the jostling motions of human camera operators. Maybe it's the same machine that makes those cookies look homemade.

I first sensed that nothing is real anymore a few years back during the Victory Tour by the Jacksons. For complex reasons I went to see them two nights in a row. The first night was great. The second night was exactly the same. And that was the strange thing: it was exactly the same. The dance steps were exactly the same. The stage chatter was exactly the same. Even the spontaneity was the same. Both nights Michael spontaneously began to cry in the middle of a certain song.

"He does it every night, the same way," a teenage girl who had been following the tour told me. "It's fantastic."

Real? Fake? Who cares?

We've made the mental adjustments, just as we did as kids when we had to deal with the fact that, on *The Flintstones,* neither Barney nor Fred had a neck.

The technology of falsehood has outraced our judgment. Alienated from nature, liberated from such barbaric responsibilities as the growing of food, the making of shelter, we have entered a mysterious phase in which we passively accept a cartoon version of reality that is projected upon us by unreliable, deceptive, and sometimes diabolical media.

Today, trends must have names, so I call this one: Creeping Surrealism.

It's a goofy term but you know what I mean. I keep a Creeping Surrealism file and toss old stuff into it. Like the *People* magazine cover story on the marriage of the *Miami Vice* characters played by Don Johnson and Sheena Easton. What is so wonderful about this is that *People* can, by definition, write on any human being, living or dead, yet it prefers to write about people who do not actually exist.

Another example is the construction near Orlando of fake movie studio back lots. Both Disney and MCA-Universal conducted market research that showed that the public would patronize a movie studio theme park even if there wasn't an actual studio. Both companies decided to add a studio anyway, because as one Disney official told me, "There's a certain amount of studio that we wanted just to make the entertainment areas credible." They're building old-fashioned back lots with streets that look like New York, or Middle America. Although they will be doing some filming on the sets, they are primarily designed for tourists to feel as though they are in the middle of an old-fashioned Hollywood studio. Back-lot facades are inherently fakes, but these approach a new level of falsity—they're all but imitation fakes, designed to create the illusion of facades.

Television has played with our minds so long, we no longer can be sure that "genuineness" is a value. Take the HBO pseudotrial of Kurt Waldheim. HBO claimed it had to stage a "commission of inquiry" of the Austrian president because no international tribunal was willing. The defendant didn't show up. "Can you believe it?" wrote the *Miami Herald* TV critic, Steve Sonsky. "That spoilsport Waldheim has declined to participate in his trial-by-TV. Who does he think he is? This is cable television calling."

My most brain-twisting encounter with Creeping Surrealism occurred last year at the American Booksellers Association convention in Washington. Posters advertised books from dozens of America's best-selling authors—Bill Cosby, Barry Manilow, Chuck Berry, Meadowlark Lemon, Elizabeth Taylor, Ben and Jerry—but if there was one heavyweight in the bunch, it was Shirley MacLaine. I managed to get a brief interview.

She said her new book, *It's All in the Playing,* was a compendium of revelations that came to her while playing herself in the TV movie based on her previous bestseller, *Out on a Limb.*

"It uses the structure of the experience of playing myself to explore—well, the notion that we're *all* the writers, directors, producers, and stars of our *own* drama. You can play your part in real life just as you can play your part in a movie."

It was obvious that she had her finger on the pulse of America: why be yourself when you can be like someone in a movie? I had to ask Ms. MacLaine the obvious question: would there soon be a movie based on her book about playing herself in the movie based on her previous book? She hesitated. Then she said, "I don't think so."

But later, her publicist, Stuart Applebaum, refused to rule anything out: "Nothing is impossible."

One final example of Creeping Surrealism: in 1987 Warren Burger and the folks at the Bicentennial Commission wanted Americans to appreciate the Constitution. An obvious tool: TV commercials. But what can you say about the old document in just half a minute? A blue-ribbon Madison Avenue firm came up with some ideas. One of the best was this: show military recruits taking their oath, which includes a vow to protect the Constitution.

The commercials needed a skilled director. Hired for the job was Steve Horn, who made the "Reach Out and Touch Someone" ads for AT&T. Horn visited an Army office in Brooklyn, to see how recruits were actually sworn in.

He was appalled. The Army office was small, sterile, poorly lit. "I can't show that on television," he told me later. "People wouldn't want to watch the ad."

So he filmed the ad in a majestic vaulted room at a Catholic college on the northern tip of Manhattan. Light streamed in from windows on high. Smoke machines filled the room with dense, tangible atmosphere. The actors—attractive, demographically diverse—were spaced apart in the gloom, each one perfectly erect, hands over hearts, illuminated in chiaroscuro. Artistic License, Horn said.

The real Army office can't be used, he said, because "that's such an undramatic room. So what I do, I do what I do best, I make it look good. I try to make it look dramatic and heroic. . . . Heightening reality makes things come across a little better. I think it helps to make it more real, more emotional."

In other words, Better Reality Through Television. It doesn't bother him a bit.

"Everything is a lie," he said, and I had to agree.

ANDRE DUBUS

The Curse

Andre Dubus (1936–   ), a former teacher and commissioned officer in the United States Marine Corps, has received both Guggenheim and MacArthur fellowships for his fiction. His work has appeared in numerous publications, such as the *New Yorker, Sewanee
Review,* and *Playboy,* where the following story originally appeared.
His books include the collections *We Don't Live Here Anymore*
(1984), *The Last Worthless Evening* (1986), *Selected Stories* (1988),
and the novel *Voices from the Moon* (1984).

Mitchell Hayes was forty-nine years old, but when the cops left him
in the bar with Bob, the manager, he felt much older. He did not
know what it was like to be very old, a shrunken and wrinkled man,
but he assumed it was like this: fatigue beyond relieving by rest, by
sleep. He also was not a small man. His weight moved up and down
in the 170s, and he was five feet, ten inches tall. But now his body
seemed short and thin. Bob stood at one end of the bar; he was a
large, black-haired man, and there was nothing in front of him but
an ashtray he was using. He looked at Mitchell at the cash register
and said, "Forget it. You heard what Smitty said."

Mitchell looked away, at the front door. He had put the chairs
upside down on the tables. He looked from the door past Bob to the
empty space of floor at the rear; sometimes people danced there, to
the jukebox. Opposite Bob, on the wall behind the bar, was a telephone; Mitchell looked at it. He had told Smitty there were five guys,
and when he moved to the phone, one of them stepped around the
corner of the bar and shoved him, one hand against Mitchell's chest,
and it pushed him backward; he nearly fell. That was when they
were getting rough with her at the bar. When they took her to the
floor, Mitchell looked once toward her sounds, then looked down at

the duckboard he stood on, or at the belly or chest of a young man in front of him.

He knew they were not drunk. They had been drinking before they came to his place, a loud popping of motorcycles outside, then walking into the empty bar, young and sunburned and carrying helmets and wearing thick leather jackets in August. They stood in front of Mitchell and drank drafts. When he took their first order, he thought they were on drugs, and later, watching them, he was certain. They were not relaxed in the way of most drinkers near closing time. Their eyes were quick, alert as wary animals, and they spoke loudly, with passion, but their passion was strange and disturbing, because they were only chatting, bantering. Mitchell knew nothing of the effects of drugs, so could not guess what was in their blood. He feared and hated drugs because of his work and because he was the stepfather of teenagers: a boy and a girl. He gave last call and served them and leaned against the counter behind him.

Then the door opened and the girl walked in from the night, a girl he had never seen, and she crossed the floor toward Mitchell. He stepped forward to tell her she had missed last call; but before he spoke, she asked for change for the cigarette machine. She was young—he guessed nineteen to twenty-one—and deeply tanned and had dark hair. She was sober and wore jeans and a dark-blue T-shirt. He gave her the quarters, but she was standing between two of the men and she did not get to the machine.

When it was over and she lay crying on the cleared circle of floor, he left the bar and picked up the jeans and T-shirt beside her and crouched and handed them to her. She did not look at him. She laid the clothes across her breasts and what Mitchell thought of now as her wound. He left her and dialed 911, then Bob's number. He woke up Bob. Then he picked up her sneakers from the floor and placed them beside her and squatted near her face, her crying. He wanted to speak to her and touch her, hold a hand or press her brow, but he could not.

The cruiser was there quickly, the siren coming east from town, then slowing and deepening as the car stopped outside. He was glad Smitty was one of them; he had gone to high school with Smitty. The other was Dave, and Mitchell knew him because it was a small town. When they saw the girl, Dave went out to the cruiser to call for an ambulance; and when he came back, he said two other cruisers had those scumbags and were taking them in. The girl was still crying and could not talk to Smitty and Dave. She was crying when a man and a woman lifted her onto a stretcher and rolled her out the door and she vanished forever in a siren.

Bob came in while Smitty and Dave were sitting at the bar drinking coffee and Smitty was writing his report; Mitchell stood behind the bar. Bob sat next to Dave as Mitchell said, "I could have stopped them, Smitty."

"That's our job," Smitty said. "You want to be in the hospital now?"

Mitchell did not answer. When Smitty and Dave left, he got a glass of Coke from the cobra and had a cigarette with Bob. They did not talk. Then Mitchell washed his glass and Bob's cup and they left, turning off the lights. Outside, Mitchell locked the front door, feeling the sudden night air after almost ten hours of air conditioning. When he had come to work, the day had been very hot, and now he thought it would not have happened in winter. They had stopped for a beer on their way somewhere from the beach; he had heard them say that. But the beach was not the reason. He did not know the reason, but he knew it would not have happened in winter. The night was cool, and now he could smell trees. He turned and looked at the road in front of the bar. Bob stood beside him on the small porch.

"If the regulars had been here . . ." Bob said.

He turned and with his hand resting on the wooden rail, he walked down the ramp to the ground. At his car, he stopped and looked over its roof at Mitchell.

"You take it easy," he said.

Mitchell nodded. When Bob got into his car and left, he went down the ramp and drove home to his house on a street that he thought was neither good nor bad. The houses were small, and there were old large houses used now as apartments for families. Most of the people had work, most of the mothers cared for their children and most of the children were clean and looked like they lived in homes, not caves like some he saw in town. He worried about the older kids, one group of them, anyway. They were idle. When he was a boy in a town farther up the Merrimack River, he and his friends committed every mischievous act he could recall on afternoons and nights when they were idle. His stepchildren were not part of that group. They had friends from the high school. The front-porch light was on for him and one in the kitchen at the rear of the house. He went in the front door and switched off the porch light and walked through the living and dining rooms to the kitchen. He got a can of beer from the refrigerator, turned out the light, and sat at the table. When he could see, he took a cigarette from Susan's pack in front of him.

Down the hall, he heard Susan move on the bed, then get up, and he hoped it wasn't for the bathroom but for him. He had met her eight years ago, when he had given up on ever marrying and having kids; then, one night, she came into the bar with two of her girlfriends from work. She made six dollars an hour going to homes of invalids, mostly what she called her little old ladies, and bathing them. She got the house from her marriage, and child support the guy paid for a few months till he left town and went south. She came barefoot down the hall and stood in the kitchen doorway and said, "Are you all right?"

"No."

She sat across from him, and he told her. Very soon, she held his hand. She was good. He knew if he had fought all five of them and was lying in pieces in the hospital bed, she would tell him he had done the right thing, as she was telling him now. He liked her strong hand on his. It was a professional hand, and he wanted from her something he had never wanted before: to lie in bed while she bathed him. When they went to bed, he did not think he would be able to sleep, but she knelt beside him and massaged his shoulders and rubbed his temples and pressed her hands on his forehead. He woke to the voices of Marty and Joyce in the kitchen. They had summer jobs, and always when they woke him, he went back to sleep till noon, but now he got up and dressed and when to the kitchen door. Susan was at the stove, her back to him, and Marty and Joyce were talking and smoking. He said, "Good morning," and stepped into the room.

"What are you doing up?" Joyce said.

She was a pretty girl with her mother's wide cheekbones, and Marty was a tall, good-looking boy, and Mitchell felt as old as he had before he slept. Susan was watching him. Then she poured him a cup of coffee and put it at his place and he sat. Marty said, "You getting up for the day?"

"Something happened last night. At the bar." They tried to conceal their excitement, but he saw it in their eyes. "I should have stopped it. I think I *could* have stopped it. That's the point. There were these five guys. They were on motorcycles, but they weren't bikers. Just punks. They came in late, when everybody else had gone home. It was a slow night, anyway. Everybody was at the beach."

"They rob you?" Marty asked.

"No. A girl came in. Young. Nice-looking. You know: just a girl, minding her business."

They nodded, and their eyes were apprehensive.

"She wanted cigarette change; that's all. Those guys were on dope. Coke or something. You know: They were flying in place."

"Did they rape her?" Joyce said.

"Yes, honey."

"The *fuckers*."

Susan opened her mouth, then closed it, and Joyce reached quickly for Susan's pack of cigarettes. Mitchell held his lighter for her and said, "When they started getting rough with her at the bar, I went for the phone. One of them stopped me. He shoved me; that's all. I should have hit him with a bottle."

Marty reached over the table with his big hand and held Mitchell's shoulder.

"No, Mitch. Five guys that mean. And coked up or whatever. No way. You wouldn't be here this morning."

"I don't know. There was always a guy with me. But just one guy, taking turns."

"Great," Joyce said. Marty's hand was on Mitchell's left shoulder; she put hers on his right hand.

"They took her to the hospital," he said. "The guys are in jail."

"They are?" Joyce said.

"I called the cops. When they left."

"You'll be a good witness," Joyce said.

He looked at her proud face.

"At the trial," she said.

The day was hot, but that night, most of the regulars came to the bar. Some of the younger ones came on motorcycles. They were a good crowd: They all worked, except the retired ones, and no one ever bothered the women, not even the young ones with their summer tans. Everyone talked about it: Some had read the newspaper story, some had heard the story in town, and they wanted to hear it from Mitchell. He told it as often as they asked, but he did not finish it, because he was working hard and could not stay with any group of customers long enough.

He watched their faces. Not one of them, even the women, looked at him as if he had not cared enough for the girl or was a coward. Many of them even appeared sympathetic, making him feel for moments that he was a survivor of something horrible; and when that feeling left him, he was ashamed. He felt tired and old, making drinks and change, talking and moving up and down the bar. At the stool at the far end, Bob drank coffee; and whenever Mitchell looked at him, he smiled or nodded and once raised his right fist, with the thumb up.

Reggie was drinking too much. He did that two or three times a month, and Mitchell had to shut him off, and Reggie always took it humbly. He was a big, gentle man with a long brown beard. But tonight, shutting off Reggie demanded from Mitchell an act of will, and when the eleven-o'clock news came on the television and Reggie ordered another shot and a draft, Mitchell pretended not to hear him. He served the customers at the other end of the bar, where Bob was. He could hear Reggie calling, "Hey, Mitch; shot and a draft, Mitch."

Mitchell was close to Bob now. Bob said softly, "He's had enough."

Mitchell nodded and went to Reggie, leaned closer to him, so he could speak quietly, and said, "Sorry, Reggie. Time for coffee. I don't want you dead out there."

Reggie blinked at him.

"OK, Mitch." He pulled some bills from his pocket and put them on the bar. Mitchell glanced at them and saw at least a ten-dollar tip. When he ran up Reggie's tab, the change was $16.50, and he dropped the coins and shoved the bills into the beer mug beside the cash register. The mug was full of bills, as it was on most nights, and he kept his hand in there, pressing Reggie's into the others, and saw the sunburned young men holding her down on the floor and one kneeling between her legs, spread and held, and he heard their cheering voices and her screaming and groaning and finally weeping and weeping and weeping, until she was the siren crying, then fading into the night. From the floor behind him, far across the room, he felt her pain and terror and grief, then her curse upon him. The curse moved into his back and spread down and up his spine, into his stomach and legs and arms and shoulders until he quivered with it. He wished he were alone so he could kneel to receive it.

RUSSELL BAKER

Big Brother Really Is Watching

Russell Baker (1925–) is an American reporter and columnist for the *New York Times* who is best known for his political satire. He won a Pulitzer Prize for distinguished commentary in 1979 and for his autobiography *Growing Up* in 1983. *So This Is Depravity* (1980), and *There's a Country in My Cellar* (1990) are collections of his columns. *The Good Times,* a second volume of memoirs, was published in 1989. The following selection originally appeared in the *New York Times.*

Washington, March 5—The number of crimes that a human being may commit against large organizations is astonishing. One of the worst is noncompliance. A large organization hates nothing so much as a human being who fails to comply. This is why large organizations fill the mails with warnings that "failure to comply may result in—" or that "the penalty for noncompliance may be—."

Fear of committing noncompliance is a heavy burden on contemporary man, surrounded as he is by circling hordes of large organizations ready to pounce upon him for any number of other offenses against organization.

Has he failed to register, failed to notify, failed to report? No? In that case, perhaps he has failed to renew, failed to file, failed to sign. Maybe he has bent, spindled or folded. Perhaps he has registered, notified, reported, renewed, filed, signed, carefully avoiding bending, spindling and folding, and even complied. Ah, but has he complied before the legal deadline?

They are hard tyrants, large organizations. When you are young they haul you in like so much meat on a hook and test you for the large-organization way of life. "Sweat, you little half-formed human beings," they gloat, distributing their infernal multiple-choice tests and magnetic pencils. "We are testing you for aptitude to perform well in a large organization created to prepare you for a life of compliance, registration, notification, reporting, renewal, filing and signing before the legal deadline without any sloppy bending, spindling or folding."

Those who pass the tests are put in custody of another large organization dedicated to making them take Physics 101 because they want to read poetry. "Failure to observe regulations against entertaining female guests in the dormitory may result in—."

COMPLIANCE TO ORGANIZATION

After compliance, commencement, and then toil. A large organization numbers them. ("What? Not want to be numbered, silly man? You will be glad we numbered you when you reach 65 and one of our large actuarial organizations makes you stop toiling and go play shuffleboard.")

Another large organization specifies what clothing styles may be worn in public without risking noncompliance. Another may decree a two-year term in the killing trade. ("Your large organization does not need to be reminded, boy, that killing is wrong. You apparently need to be reminded, however, that killing is not wrong under certain exceptions specified by a sufficiently large organization. The penalty for noncompliance may be—.")

Large organizations find that human beings become more compliable as they age, but they have discovered that it is bad policy to ease up on the terror. And so there is no peace from the time the alarm clock sounds to the gurgle of the last nightcap.

"What are the large organizations threatening us with today, Darling?" one asks at breakfast.

"Let's see. They threaten to deprive us of the use of the car unless we have it inspected within fourteen days. They threaten to fine us a large sum of money unless we amend the estimate of how much income tax we will owe next year. Oh yes, and they threaten to send us another best seller by that awful boy novelist unless you notify them immediately that you don't want this month's book club selection."

"Are they threatening to ruin our credit rating, or did I just dream I had a telephone call from a madman who said he was going to ruin me unless I paid a bill I've already paid?"

"You didn't dream it. That was the large credit organization and they promise to libel you as a cheat and a deadbeat."

"But I've paid that bill."

"Yes, but you spindled the voucher and the large computer organization refused to register your payment. It looks like it's curtains for your reputation unless the computer agrees to give you a second chance."

MORE INTIMIDATIONS

"Any large organizations testing the children today?"

"Yes, there's a large testing organization from Princeton threatening to ruin the children's opportunity to go to college by giving some sort of test at school this morning."

Outside, meanwhile, large organizations are preparing to raise the bus fare, strike the electric company, distill the perfect nerve gas, build a shoddier car, reduce the postal service and start a small war. Soon the postman will arrive with several large organizations' periodic reminders that "the penalty for noncompliance may be—."

JONATHAN KOZOL

The Homeless

Jonathan Kozol (1936–   ) won the National Book Award in 1967
for *Death at an Early Age,* which analyzed the failures of education
for young children. Other books include *On Being a Teacher*
(1981) and *Illiterate America* (1985). In *Rachel and Her Children*
(1988), from which the following selection is taken, Kozol describes the effects of homelessness on the present generation of
children.

Many homeless people, unable to get into shelters, or frightened of disease or violence, or intimidated by the regulations, look for refuge in such public places as train stations and church doorways. Scores of people sleep in the active subway tunnels of Manhattan, inches from six-hundred-volt live rails. Many more sleep on the ramps and the station platforms. Go into the subway station under Herald Square on a December night at twelve o'clock and you will see what scarce accommodations can mean. Emerging from the subway, walk along Thirty-third Street to Eighth Avenue. There you will see another form of scarce accommodations: hot-air grates outside the buildings on Eighth Avenue are highly prized. Homeless people who arrive late often find there is no vacancy, even for a cardboard box over a grate.

A man who has taken shelter from the wind that sweeps Fifth

Avenue by sleeping beneath the outstretched arms of Jesus on the bronze doors of St. Patrick's Cathedral tells a reporter he can't sleep there anymore, because shopkeepers feel that he is hurting business. He moves to the south side of the church, where he will be less visible.

Stories like this are heard in every state and every city of the nation. In Florida, a twenty-year-old man tells me that he ran away from a juvenile-detention home in Michigan when he was nine years old. He found that he was small enough to slip his body through the deposit slot of a Goodwill box next to a Salvation Army building. Getting in was easy, he explains, and it was warm, because of the clothes and quilts and other gifts that people had dropped into the box. "Getting out was not so easy," he says. "I had to reach my arms above my head, grab hold of the metal edge, twist my body into an S, and pull myself slowly out through the slot. When I was fourteen, I was too big to fit into the slot. I believe I am the only person in America who lived for five years in a Goodwill box."

Many homeless people sleep in trash compactors and in dumpsters behind restaurants. These offer perhaps the ultimate concealment, and the heat generated by the rotting food may protect a homeless person against freezing weather. In Chicago some years ago, a news report told of a man who had been sleeping in a broken trash compactor. One night, not knowing that in his absence the trash compactor had been repaired, he fell asleep, the engine was turned on, and he was compressed into a cube of refuse.

People in many cities speak of spending nights in phone booths. I have seen this only in New York in 1986. Public telephones in Grand Central are aligned in recessed areas outside the main concourse. On almost any night, before one-thirty, visitors could see a score of people stuffed into these booths with their belongings. Even phone-booth vacancies are scarce in New York City: as in public housing, people are sometimes obliged to double up. One night, I saw three people—a man, a woman, and a child—jammed into a single booth. All three were asleep.

Officials have tried a number of times to drive the homeless from Grand Central. In order to make conditions less attractive, nearly all the benches have been removed from the terminal. One set of benches has been left there, I am told, because they have been judged "historic landmarks." The terminal's three hundred lockers, used in former times by homeless people to secure their few belongings, were removed in 1986. The authorities were forced to justify this action by declaring the homeless "a threat to public safety," according to the

City Council. Shaving, washing clothes, and other forms of hygiene are prohibited in the men's room of Grand Central. A fast-food chain that wanted to distribute unsold doughnuts in the terminal was denied the right to do so, on the ground that it would draw more hungry people.

At one-thirty every morning, homeless people are ejected from Grand Central. Many initially took refuge on a ramp that leads to Forty-second Street. The ramp provides a degree of warmth, because it was protected from the street by wooden doors. The station management—Grand Central is run by Metro North—responded to this challenge in three ways. First, the ramp was mopped with a strong mixture of ammonia to produce a noxious smell. Then, when the people sleeping there brought cardboard boxes and newspapers to protect them from the fumes, the entrance doors were chained wide open. Temperatures dropped some nights to ten degrees. Finally, in early 1987, Metro North fenced off the ramp entirely.

In a case that won brief press attention in December of 1985, an elderly woman who had been living in Grand Central, on one of the few remaining benches, was removed night after night during the weeks preceding Christmas. On Christmas Eve, it became evident that she was ill, but no one called an ambulance. At one-thirty, the police compelled her to move outside. At dawn, she came inside and climbed back on a bench to sleep; she died during the morning of pneumonia.

In 1988, homeless people will not often be found sleeping on the benches in Grand Central. The benches now are cordoned off with yellow tape at 9 P.M. Police patrol the area with a dog.

At Penn Station in 1986, homeless women congregated near the entrance to the bathroom. Each hour on the hour, Amtrak police came by and herded them away. In June of 1985, Amtrak officials had issued this directive to all officers: "It is the policy of Amtrak to not allow the homeless and undesirables to remain. . . . Officers are encouraged to eject all undesirables. . . . Now is the time to train and educate them that their presence will not be tolerated as cold weather sets in." In an internal memo, an Amtrak official later went beyond this language and asked, "Can't we get rid of this trash?"

In a surprising action, the American Federation of Railroad Police, representing the station's police employees, resisted the directive, and, in 1986, brought suit against Penn Station's management. Nonetheless, as temperatures plunged during the nights after Thanksgiving, homeless men and women were ejected from the station. At two one morning that November, I watched a man who was perhaps fifty years old, about my age, carry a cardboard box outside the station and try to construct a barricade against the wind that tore across Eighth Avenue. The man was so cold his fingers shook, and when I spoke to him he tried to answer but could not.

Driving women from the toilets in a railroad station raises questions that go far beyond the issue of "deterrence." Some people may find it surprising to learn that many of the women driven out are quite young. Few are dressed in the rags that are suggested by the term "bag ladies." Some are dressed so neatly and conceal their packages and bags so skillfully that one finds it hard to differentiate them from commuters waiting for a train. Given the denial of hygienic opportunities, it is difficult to know how they are able to remain presentable. The sight of clusters of police officials, mostly male, guarding a women's toilet from being used by homeless women does not speak well for the public conscience of New York.

Several cities have devised unusual measures to make sure that homeless people will learn quickly that they are not welcome. In Laramie, Wyoming, in recent years, homeless people were given one night's shelter; the next morning, an organization called the Good Samaritan Fund gave them one-way tickets to another town. In 1986, the college town of Lancaster, Ohio, offered homeless families one-way tickets to Columbus.

In a number of states and cities, homeless people have been knifed or set on fire. Two high-school students in California have been tried for the knife murder of a homeless man they found sleeping in a park. The man, an unemployed housepainter, was stabbed seventeen times, and then his throat was slashed.

In Chicago, a man was set ablaze while he slept on a bench early in the morning, opposite a popular restaurant. Rush-hour commuters passed him and his charred possessions for hours. At noon, someone called the police. A man who reportedly had watched him burning from a third-floor apartment above the bench had refused to notify the police. The purpose of setting fire to him was "to get him out," according to a local record-store employee. The homeless man survived, according to the *Wall Street Journal,* because the fire did not penetrate his many layers of clothing. A local resident told reporters that his neighbors viewed the homeless as akin to "nuclear waste."

In Tucson, where police have used German shepherds to hunt for the homeless in the skid-row neighborhoods, a mayor was re-elected in 1983 on the promise that he would drive the homeless out of town. In Phoenix, a woman who leads an anti-homeless lobby known as Fight Back told reporters, "We're tired of it. Tired of feeling guilty about these people."

In several cities, it is a crime to sleep in public; in some, armrests have been installed in the middle of park benches to make it impossible for people to lie down. In others, trash has been defined as "public property," to make it a felony for the poor to forage in the rotted food.

Some grocers in Santa Barbara have sprinkled bleach on food that they discarded in their dumpsters. In Portland, Oregon, owners of some shops in the redeveloped Old Town have designed slow-dripping gutters (they are known as "drip lines") to prevent the homeless from attempting to take shelter under their awnings.

In Fort Lauderdale, harsher tactics have been recommended. A member of the City Council offered a proposal to spray trash containers with rat poison to discourage foraging by homeless families. The way to get rid of vermin, he remarked, is to cut their food supply. Some of these policies have been defeated, but the inclination to sequester, punish, and conceal the homeless has attracted wide support.

"We are the rejected waste of the society," Richard Lazarus[1] told me. "They use us if they think we have some use—maybe for sweeping leaves or scrubbing off graffiti in the subway stations. They don't object if we donate our blood. I've given plasma. That's one way that even worthless people can do something for democracy. We may serve another function, too. Perhaps we help to scare the people who still have a home—even a place that's got no heat, that's rat-infested, filthy. If they see us in the streets, maybe they are scared enough so they will learn not to complain. If they were thinking about asking for a better heater or a better stove, they're going to think twice. It's like farmers posting scarecrows in the fields. People see these terrifying figures in Penn Station, and they know that with one false step they could be here, too. They think, 'I better not complain.'

"The problem comes, however, when a city tries to find a place to hide us. It comes to be an engineering question: waste disposal. Store owners certainly regard us in that way. We ruin business and lower the value of good buildings. People fear that we are carriers of illness. Many times, we are. So they wear those plastic gloves if they

---

[1] Richard Lazarus is the fictitious name given by Kozol to a homeless man. (ED.)

are forced to touch us. It reminds me of the workers in the nuclear reactors—they have to wear protective clothing if they come in contact with the waste. Then, you have state governors all over the United States refusing to allow this stuff to be deposited within their borders. Now you hear them talking about dumping toxic waste into the ocean in steel cans. Could they find an island someplace for the homeless?"

Lazarus's question brings back a strange memory for me. In Boston, for years before the homeless were identified as a distinguishable category of the dispossessed, a de-facto caste of homeless people dwelt in a vast public-housing project, called Columbia Point, built on a virtual island that was linked only by one access road to the United States. The project, infested with rats because it was constructed on a former garbage dump, was so crowded, violent, and ugly that social workers were reluctant to pay visits there, few shop owners would operate a business there, and even activists and organizers were afraid to venture there at night. From the highway to Cape Cod one could see the distant profile of those high-rise structures. A friend from California asked me if it was a prison. He told me that it looked like Alcatraz. I answered that it was a housing project. The notion of shoving these people as far out into the ocean as possible does bring to mind the way that waste-disposal problems are sometimes resolved.

New York has many habitable islands. One of them has already earned a place in history as the initial stopping point for millions of European refugees who came to the United States in search of freedom. One reason for their temporary isolation was the fear that they might carry dangerous infections. New York's permanent refugees are carriers of every possible infection; most, moreover, have no prospering relatives to vouch for them, as earlier generations sometimes did, in order to assure that they will not become a burden to the state. They are already regarded as a burden. An island that once served as a quarantine for aliens who crowded to our shore might serve now as quarantine for those who huddle in train stations and in Herald Square.

Richard Lazarus may not be paranoid in speaking of himself as human waste; he may simply be reading the headlines in the press. "I just can't accommodate them," the owner of a building in midtown Manhattan says. The mayor of Newark, where a number of homeless families have been sent from New York City, speaks of his fear that displaced families from New York might be "permanently dumped in Newark." He announces a deadline after which they will presumably be dumped back in New York.

New Yorkers, according to the *Times,* "are increasingly opposing the city's attempts to open jails, shelters for the homeless, garbage incinerators" in their neighborhoods. The *Times* reports that the city has to reassure communities that they are not being singled out when they are chosen as sites "for homeless shelters and garbage-burning generating plants."

What startles most observers of the homeless is not simply that such tragedies persist in the United States but that almost all have been well documented and that even the most solid documentation does not bring about corrective action. Instead of action, a common response to this kind of problem in New York, as elsewhere, has been the appointment of a "task force" to investigate it. This is frequently the last we hear of the problem. Another substitute for action is a press event at which a city official seems to overleap immediate concerns by the unveiling of a plan to build a thousand, or a hundred thousand, homes over the next ten or twenty years at a cost of several billion dollars. The sweep of these announcements tends to dwarf the urgency of the initial issue. When, after a year or so, we learn that little has been done and the problem has grown worse, we tend to feel not outrage but exhaustion. Exhaustion, however, turns easily to a less generous reaction.

"I am about to be heartless," a columnist wrote in *Newsweek* in December of 1986. "There are people living on the streets of most American cities, turning sidewalks into dormitories. They are called the homeless, street people, vagrants, beggars, vent men, bag ladies, bums. Often they are called worse. They are America's living nightmare—tattered human bundles. They have got to go." The writer noted that it was his taxes that paid for the paving and the cleaning of the streets where some of the homeless lived. "That makes me their landlord," he wrote. "I want to evict them."

A senior at Boston University sees homeless people on the streets not far from where he goes to class. He complains to his college newspaper that measures taken recently to drive them from the area have not been sufficiently aggressive. "I would very much like to see actions more severe," he writes. Perhaps, he admits, it isn't possible to have them all arrested, though this notion seems to hold appeal for him; perhaps "a more suitable middle ground" may be arrived at to prevent this "nauseating and often criminal element" from being permitted to "run free so close to my home."

Another Bostonian says, in the weekly Boston *Phoenix,* "Our response to these street people . . . has gone from indifference to pitying . . . to hatred." I think that this is coming to be true and that it marks an incremental stage in our preparedness to view the frail, the ill, the dispossessed, the unsuccessful not as people who have certain human qualities we share but as untouchables. From harsh deterrence to punitive incarceration and then to the willful cutting off of life supports is an increasingly short journey. "I am proposing triage of a sort, triage by self-selection," Charles Murray writes in "Losing Ground." "The patient always has the right to fail. Society always has the right to let him."

Why is it that writings that present such hardened attitudes seem to prevail so easily in public policy? It may be that generous voices are more readily derided; callous attitudes are never subject to the charge of being sentimental. It is a recurrent theme in "King Lear," Michael Ignatieff writes, that "there is a truth in the brutal simplicities of the merciless which the more complicated truth of the merciful is helpless to refute. . . ." A rich man "never lacks for arguments to deny the poor his charity. 'Basest beggars' can always be found to be 'in the poorest things superfluous.' " So from pity we graduate to weariness, from weariness to impatience, from impatience to annoyance, from annoyance to dislike, and sometimes to contempt.

"No excuses are good enough," the *Times* observed in reference to the Holland Hotel in 1985, a year before I spoke with Sarah Andrews of her stay there. But excuses did suffice. The city did, and does, continue to send children to the Holland and to many similar hotels. Nearly two hundred families, with over four hundred children, were still living in the Holland last September. Can it be that these children have by now become not simply noxious or unclean in our imagination but something like an ulcer to society?

Richard Lazarus said to me, "If the point is to dispose of us most economically, why do they need to go to all this trouble and expense? Why not end this misery efficiently? Why not a lethal injection?" This question, voiced in panic and despair, is perhaps one that he would not have posed if he had been in a less tormented state of mind. The answer is that we have failed in many ways to do what conscience and American ideals demand, but we have yet to fall so far as to wish to engineer anyone's demise. Despite the grave injustices that we allow, or lack the power to confront, we do not in fact want to "dispose" of any people, or "compact" them into concentration camps or other institutions of internment. The truth is that we do not know what we want to do with these poor people. We leave them, therefore, in a limbo, and while waiting in that limbo many who are very young do cease to be a burden to society.

But the question asked by this shaken man emerging from the underground of New York's subway system to gaze up at the Grand Hyatt may suggest a slightly different question: Might a day come in the not too distant future when a notion of this sort may be proposed and not regarded as abhorrent? It has happened in other advanced societies. We know this, and we also know that no society is totally exempt from entertaining "rational" solutions of this kind. State terrorism as social-welfare policy—that, I think, is a fair description of how Lazarus, a credible witness of life at the bottom in Manhattan, has come to see things. True, it has not yet achieved acceptance in our social order, but it may no longer be regarded as beyond imagining.

NANCY MAIRS

On Being a Cripple

Nancy Mairs (1943–   ) is an American poet and essayist with multiple sclerosis who writes about such topics as chronic illness, loss, sex, parenting, love, and writing. *In All the Rooms of the Yellow House* (1984) is a volume of her poetry; *Plaintext* (1986), from which the following selection is taken, is a collection of her essays. She is also the author of a memoir, *Remembering the Bone House* (1989).

To escape is nothing. Not to escape is nothing.

Louise Bogan

The other day I was thinking of writing an essay on being a cripple. I was thinking hard in one of the stalls of the women's room in my office building, as I was shoving my shirt into my jeans and tugging up my zipper. Preoccupied, I flushed, picked up my book bag, took my cane down from the hook, and unlatched the door. So many movements unbalanced me, and as I pulled the door open I fell over backward, landing fully clothed on the toilet seat with my legs splayed in front of me: the old beetle-on-its-back routine. Saturday afternoon, the building deserted, I was free to laugh aloud as I wriggled back to my feet, my voice bouncing off the yellowish tiles from all directions. Had anyone been there with me, I'd have been still and faint and hot with chagrin. I decided that it was high time to write the essay.

First, the matter of semantics. I am a cripple. I choose this word to name me. I choose from among several possibilities, the most common of which are "handicapped" and "disabled." I made the choice a number of years ago, without thinking, unaware of my motives for doing so. Even now, I'm not sure what those motives are, but I recognize that they are complex and not entirely flattering. People—crippled or not—wince at the word "cripple," as they do not at "handicapped" or "disabled." Perhaps I want them to wince. I want them to see me as a tough customer, one to whom the fates/gods/viruses have not been kind, but who can face the brutal truth of her existence squarely. As a cripple, I swagger.

But, to be fair to myself, a certain amount of honesty underlies my choice. "Cripple" seems to me a clean word, straightforward and precise. It has an honorable history, having made its first appearance in the Lindisfarne Gospel in the tenth century. As a lover of words, I like the accuracy with which it describes my condition: I have lost the full use of my limbs. "Disabled," by contrast, suggests an incapacity, physical or mental. And I certainly don't like "handicapped," which implies that I have deliberately been put at a disadvantage, by whom I can't imagine (my God is not a Handicapper General), in order to equalize chances in the great race of life. These words seem to me to be moving away from my condition, to be widening the gap between word and reality. Most remote is the recently coined euphemism "differently abled," which partakes of the same semantic hopefulness that transformed countries from "undeveloped" to "underdeveloped," then to "less developed," and finally to "developing" nations. People have continued to starve in those countries during the shift. Some realities do not obey the dictates of language.

Mine is one of them. Whatever you call me, I remain crippled. But I don't care what you call me, so long as it isn't "differently abled," which strikes me as pure verbal garbage designed, by its ability to describe anyone, to describe no one. I subscribe to George Orwell's thesis that "the slovenliness of our language makes it easier for us to have foolish thoughts." And I refuse to participate in the degeneration of the language to the extent that I deny that I have lost anything in the course of this calamitous disease; I refuse to pretend that the only differences between you and me are the various ordinary ones that distinguish any one person from another. But call me "disabled" or "handicapped" if you like. I have long since grown accustomed to them; and if they are vague, at least they hint at the truth. Moreover, I use them myself. Society is no readier to accept crippledness than to accept death, war, sex, sweat, or wrinkles. I would never refer to another person as a cripple. It is the word I use to name only myself.

I haven't always been crippled, a fact for which I am soundly grateful. To be whole of limb is, I know from experience, infinitely more pleasant and useful than to be crippled; and if that knowledge leaves me open to bitterness at my loss, the physical soundness I once enjoyed (though I did not enjoy it half enough) is well worth the occasional stab of regret. Though never any good at sports, I was a normally active child and young adult. I climbed trees, played hopscotch, jumped rope, skated, swam, rode my bicycle, sailed. I despised team sports, spending some of the wretchedest afternoons of my life sweaty and humiliated, behind a field-hockey stick and under a basketball hoop. I tramped alone for miles along the bridle paths that webbed the woods behind the house I grew up in. I swayed through countless dim hours in the arms of one man or another under the scattered shot of light from mirrored balls, and gyrated through countless more as Tab Hunter and Johnny Mathis gave way to the Rolling Stones, Creedence Clearwater Revival, Cream. I walked down the aisle. I pushed baby carriages, changed tires in the rain, marched for peace.

When I was twenty-eight I started to trip and drop things. What at first seemed my natural clumsiness soon became too pronounced to shrug off. I consulted a neurologist, who told me that I had a brain tumor. A battery of tests, increasingly disagreeable, revealed no tumor. About a year and a half later I developed a blurred spot in one eye. I had, at last, the episodes "disseminated in space and time" requisite for a diagnosis: multiple sclerosis. I have never been sorry for the doctor's initial misdiagnosis, however. For almost a week, until the negative results of the tests were in, I thought that I was going to die right away. Every day for the past nearly ten years, then, has been a kind of gift. I accept all gifts.

Multiple sclerosis is a chronic degenerative disease of the central nervous system, in which the myelin that sheathes the nerves is somehow eaten away and scar tissue forms in its place, interrupting the nerves' signals. During its course, which is unpredictable and uncontrollable, one may lose vision, hearing, speech, the ability to walk, control of bladder and/or bowels, strength in any or all extremities, sensitivity to touch, vibration, and/or pain, potency, coordination of movements—the list of possibilities is lengthy and yes, horrifying. One may also lose one's sense of humor. That's the easiest to lose and the hardest to survive without.

In the past ten years, I have sustained some of these losses. Characteristic of MS are sudden attacks, called exacerbations, followed by remissions, and these I have not had. Instead, my disease has been slowly progressive. My left leg is now so weak that I walk with the aid of a brace and a cane; and for distances I use an Amigo, a variation on the electric wheelchair that looks rather like an electrified kiddie car. I no longer have much use of my left hand. Now my right side is weakening as well. I still have the blurred spot in my right eye. Overall, though, I've been lucky so far. My world has, of necessity, been circumscribed by my losses, but the terrain left me has been ample enough for me to continue many of the activities that absorb me: writing, teaching, raising children and cats and plants and snakes, reading, speaking publicly about MS and depression, even playing bridge with people patient and honorable enough to let me scatter cards every which way without sneaking a peek.

Lest I begin to sound like Pollyanna, however, let me say that I don't like having MS. I hate it. My life holds realities—harsh ones, some of them—that no right-minded human being ought to accept without grumbling. One of them is fatigue. I know of no one with MS who does not complain of bone-weariness; in a disease that presents an astonishing variety of symptoms, fatigue seems to be a common factor. I wake up in the morning feeling the way most people do at the end of a bad day, and I take it from there. As a result, I spend a lot of time *in extremis*[1] and, impatient with limitation, I tend to ignore my fatigue until my body breaks down in some way and forces rest. Then I miss picnics, dinner parties, poetry readings, the brief visits of old friends from out of town. The offspring of a puritanical tradition of exceptional venerability, I cannot view these lapses without shame. My life often seems a series of small failures to do as I ought.

I lead, on the whole, an ordinary life, probably rather like the one I would have led had I not had MS. I am lucky that my predilections were already solitary, sedentary, and bookish—unlike the

---

[1] in extreme circumstances (ED.)

world-famous French cellist I have read about, or the young woman I talked with one long afternoon who wanted only to be a jockey. I had just begun graduate school when I found out something was wrong with me, and I have remained, interminably, a graduate student. Perhaps I would not have if I'd thought I had the stamina to return to a full-time job as a technical editor; but I've enjoyed my studies.

In addition to studying, I teach writing courses. I also teach medical students how to give neurological examinations. I pick up freelance editing jobs here and there. I have raised a foster son and sent him into the world, where he has made me two grandbabies, and I am still escorting my daughter and son through adolescence. I go to Mass every Saturday. I am a superb, if messy, cook. I am also an enthusiastic laundress, capable of sorting a hamper full of clothes into five subtly differentiated piles, but a terrible housekeeper. I can do italic writing and, in an emergency, bathe an oil-soaked cat. I play a fiendish game of Scrabble. When I have the time and the money, I like to sit on my front steps with my husband, drinking Amaretto and smoking a cigar, as we imagine our counterparts in Leningrad and make sure that the sun gets down once more behind the sharp childish scrawl of the Tucson Mountains.

This lively plenty has its bleak complement, of course, in all the things I can no longer do. I will never run again, except in dreams, and one day I may have to write that I will never walk again. I like to go camping, but I can't follow George and the children along the trails that wander out of a campsite through the desert or into the mountains. In fact, even on the level I've learned never to check the weather or try to hold a coherent conversation: I need all my attention for my wayward feet. Of late, I have begun to catch myself wondering how people can propel themselves without canes. With only one usable hand, I have to select my clothing with care not so much for style as for ease of ingress and egress, and even so, dressing can be laborious. I can no longer do fine stitchery, pick up babies, play the piano, braid my hair. I am immobilized by acute attacks of depression, which may or may not be physiologically related to MS but are certainly its logical concomitant.

These two elements, the plenty and the privation, are never pure, nor are the delight and wretchedness that accompany them. Almost every pickle that I get into as a result of my weakness and clumsiness—and I get into plenty—is funny as well as maddening and sometimes painful. I recall one May afternoon when a friend and I were going out for a drink after finishing up at school. As we were climbing into opposite sides of my car, chatting, I tripped and fell, flat and hard, onto the asphalt parking lot, my abrupt departure interrupting him in mid-sentence. "Where'd you go?" he called as he came around the back of the car to find me hauling myself up by the door frame. "Are you all right?" Yes, I told him, I was fine, just a bit rattly, and we drove off to find a shady patio and some beer. When I got home an hour or so later, my daughter greeted me with "What have you done to yourself?" I looked down. One elbow of my white turtleneck with the green froggies, one knee of my white trousers, one white kneesock were blood-soaked. We peeled off the clothes and inspected the damage, which was nasty enough but not alarming. That part wasn't funny: The abrasions took a long time to heal, and one got a little infected. Even so, when I think of my friend talking earnestly, suddenly, to the hot thin air while I dropped from his view as though through a trap door, I find the image as silly as something from a Marx Brothers movie.

I may find it easier than other cripples to amuse myself because I live propped by the acceptance and the assistance and, sometimes, the amusement of those around me. Grocery clerks tear my checks out of my checkbook for me, and sales clerks find chairs to put into dressing rooms when I want to try on clothes. The people I work with make sure I teach at times when I am least likely to be fatigued, in places I can get to, with the materials I need. My students, with one anonymous exception (in an end-of-the-semester evaluation) have been unperturbed by my disability. Some even like it. One was immensely cheered by the information that I paint my own finger-nails; she decided, she told me, that if I could go to such trouble over fine details, she could keep on writing essays. I suppose I became some sort of bright-fingered muse. She wrote good essays, too.

The most important struts in the framework of my existence, of course, are my husband and children. Dismayingly few marriages survive the MS test, and why should they? Most twenty-two- and nineteen-year-olds, like George and me, can vow in clear conscience, after a childhood of chickenpox and summer colds, to keep one another in sickness and in health so long as they both shall live. Not many are equipped for catastrophe: the dismay, the depression, the extra work, the boredom that a degenerative disease can insinuate into a relationship. And our society, with its emphasis on fun and its association of fun with physical performance, offers little encour-agement for a whole spouse to stay with a crippled partner. Children experience similar stresses when faced with a crippled parent, and they are more helpless, since parents and children can't usually get divorced. They hate, of course, to be different from their peers, and the child whose mother is tacking down the aisle of a school auditorium packed with proud parents like a Cape Cod dinghy in a stiff breeze jolly well stands out in a crowd. Deprived of legal divorce, the child can at least deny the mother's disability, even her existence, forgetting to tell her about recitals and PTA meetings, refusing to accompany her to stores or church or the movies, never inviting friends to the house. Many do.

But I've been limping along for ten years now, and so far George and the children are still at my left elbow, holding tight. Anne and Matthew vacuum floors and dust furniture and haul trash and rake up dog droppings and button my cuffs and bake lasagne and Toll House cookies with just enough grumbling so I know that they don't have brain fever. And far from hiding me, they're forever dragging me by racks of fancy clothes or through teeming school corridors, or welcoming gaggles of friends while I'm wandering through the house in Anne's filmy pink babydoll pajamas. George generally calls before he brings someone home, but he does just as many dumb thankless chores as the children. And they all yell at me, laugh at some of my jokes, write me funny letters when we're apart—in short, treat me as an ordinary human being for whom they have some use. I think they like me. Unless they're faking. . . .

Faking. There's the rub. Tugging at the fringes of my consciousness always is the terror that people are kind to me only because I'm a cripple. My mother almost shattered me once, with that instinct mothers have—blind, I think, in this case, but unerring nonetheless—for striking blows along the fault-lines of their children's hearts, by telling me, in an attack on my selfishness, "We all have to make allowances for you, of course, because of the way you are." From the distance of a couple of years, I have to admit that I haven't any idea just what she meant, and I'm not sure that she knew either. She was awfully angry. But at the time, as the words thudded home, I felt my worst fear, suddenly realized. I could bear being called selfish: I am. But I couldn't bear the corroboration that those around me were doing in fact what I'd always suspected them of doing, professing fondness while silently putting up with me because of the way I am. A cripple. I've been a little cracked ever since.

Along with this fear that people are secretly accepting shoddy goods comes a relentless pressure to please—to prove myself worth the burdens I impose, I guess, or to build a substantial account of goodwill against which I may write drafts in times of need. Part of the pressure arises from social expectations. In our society, anyone who deviates from the norm had better find some way to compensate. Like fat people, who are expected to be jolly, cripples must bear their lot meekly and cheerfully. A grumpy cripple isn't playing by the rules. And much of the pressure is self-generated. Early on I vowed that, if I had to have MS, by God I was going to do it well. This is a class act, ladies and gentlemen. No tears, no recriminations, no faint-heartedness.

One way and another, then, I wind up feeling like Tiny Tim, peering over the edge of the table at the Christmas goose, waving my crutch, piping down God's blessing on us all. Only sometimes I don't want to play Tiny Tim. I'd rather be Caliban, a most scurvy monster. Fortunately, at home no one much cares whether I'm a good cripple or a bad cripple as long as I make vichyssoise with fair regularity. One evening several years ago, Anne was reading at the dining-room table while I cooked dinner. As I opened a can of tomatoes, the can slipped in my left hand and juice spattered me and the counter with bloody spots. Fatigued and infuriated, I bellowed, "I'm so sick of being crippled!" Anne glanced at me over the top of her book. "There now," she said, "do you feel better?" "Yes," I said, "yes, I do." She went back to her reading. I felt better. That's about all the attention my scurviness ever gets.

Because I hate being crippled, I sometimes hate myself for being a cripple. Over the years I have come to expect—even accept—attacks of violent self-loathing. Luckily, in general our society no longer connects deformity and disease directly with evil (though a charismatic once told me that I have MS because a devil is in me) and so I'm allowed to move largely at will, even among small children. But I'm not sure that this revision of attitude has been particularly helpful. Physical imperfection, even freed of moral disapprobation, still defies and violates the ideal, especially for women, whose confinement in their bodies as objects of desire is far from over. Each age, of course, has its ideal, and I doubt that ours is any better or worse than any other. Today's ideal woman, who lives on the glossy pages of dozens of magazines, seems to be between the ages of eighteen and twenty-five; her hair has body, her teeth flash white, her breath smells minty, her underarms are dry; she has a career but is still a fabulous cook, especially of meals that take less than twenty minutes to prepare; she does not ordinarily appear to have a husband or children; she is trim and deeply tanned; she jogs, swims, plays tennis, rides a bicycle, sails, but does not bowl; she travels widely, even to out-of-the-way places like Finland and Samoa, always in the company of the ideal man, who possesses a nearly identical set of characteristics. There are a few exceptions. Though usually white and often blonde, she may be black, Hispanic, Asian, or Native American, so long as she is unusually sleek. She may be old, provided she is selling a laxative or is Lauren Bacall. If she is selling a detergent, she may be married and have a flock of strikingly messy children. But she is never a cripple.

Like many women I know, I have always had an uneasy relationship with my body. I was not a popular child, largely, I think now, because I was peculiar: intelligent, intense, moody, shy, given to unexpected actions and inexplicable notions and emotions. But as I entered adolescence, I believed myself unpopular because I was homely: my breasts too flat, my mouth too wide, my hips too narrow, my clothing never quite right in fit or style. I was not, in fact, particularly ugly, old photographs inform me, though I was well off the ideal; but I carried this sense of self-alienation with me into adulthood, where it regenerated in response to the depredations of MS. Even with my brace I walk with a limp so pronounced that, seeing myself on the videotape of a television program on the disabled, I couldn't believe that anything but an inchworm could make progress humping along like that. My shoulders droop and my pelvis thrusts forward as I try to balance myself upright, throwing my frame into a bony S. As a result of contractures, one shoulder is higher than the other and I carry one arm bent in front of me, the fingers curled into a claw. My left arm and leg have wasted into pipe-stems, and I try always to keep them covered. When I think about how my body must look to others, especially to men, to whom I have been trained to display myself, I feel ludicrous, even loathsome.

At my age, however, I don't spend much time thinking about my appearance. The burning egocentricity of adolescence, which assures one that all the world is looking all the time, has passed, thank God, and I'm generally too caught up in what I'm doing to step back, as I used to, and watch myself as though upon a stage. I'm also too old to believe in the accuracy of self-image. I know that I'm not a hideous crone, that in fact, when I'm rested, well dressed, and well made up, I look fine. The self-loathing I feel is neither physically nor intellectually substantial. What I hate is not me but a disease.

I am not a disease.

And a disease is not—at least not singlehandedly—going to determine who I am, though at first it seemed to be going to. Adjusting to a chronic incurable illness, I have moved through a process similar to that outlined by Elizabeth Kübler-Ross in *On Death and Dying*. The major difference—and it is far more significant than most people recognize—is that I can't be sure of the outcome, as the terminally ill cancer patient can. Research studies indicate that, with proper medical care, I may achieve a "normal" life span. And in our society, with its vision of death as the ultimate evil, worse even than decrepitude, the response to such news is, "Oh well, at least you're not going to *die*." Are there worse things than dying? I think that there may be.

I think of two women I know, both with MS, both enough older than I to have served as models. One took to her bed several years ago and has been there ever since. Although she can sit in a high-backed wheelchair, because she is incontinent she refuses to go out at all, even though incontinence pants, which are readily available at any pharmacy, could protect her from embarrassment. Instead, she stays at home and insists that her husband, a small quiet man, a retired civil servant, stay there with her except for a quick weekly foray to the supermarket. The other woman, whose illness was diagnosed when she was eighteen, a nursing student engaged to a young doctor, finished her training, married her doctor, accompanied him to Germany when he was in the service, bore three sons and a daughter, now grown and gone. When she can, she travels with her husband; she plays bridge, embroiders, swims regularly; she works, like me, as a symptomatic-patient instructor of medical students in neurology. Guess which woman I hope to be.

At the beginning, I thought about having MS almost incessantly. And because of the unpredictable course of the disease, my thoughts were always terrified. Each night I'd get into bed wondering whether I'd get out again the next morning, whether I'd be able to see, to speak, to hold a pen between my fingers. Knowing that the day might come when I'd be physically incapable of killing myself, I thought perhaps I ought to do so right away, while I still had the strength. Gradually I came to understand that the Nancy who might one day lie inert under a bedsheet, arms and legs paralyzed, unable to feed or bathe herself, unable to reach out for a gun, a bottle of pills, was not the Nancy I was at present, and that I could not presume to make decisions for that future Nancy, who might well not want in the least to die. Now the only provision I've made for the future Nancy is that when the time comes—and it is likely to come in the form of pneumonia, friend to the weak and the old—I am not to be treated with machines and medications. If she is unable to communicate by then, I hope she will be satisfied with these terms.

Thinking all the time about having MS grew tiresome and intrusive, especially in the large and tragic mode in which I was accustomed to considering my plight. Months and even years went by without catastrophe (at least without one related to MS), and really I was awfully busy, what with George and children and snakes and students and poems, and I hadn't the time, let alone the inclination, to devote myself to being a disease. Too, the richer my life became, the funnier it seemed, as though there were some connection between largesse and laughter, and so my tragic stance began to waver until, even with the aid of a brace and cane, I couldn't hold it for very long at a time.

After several years I was satisfied with my adjustment. I had suffered my grief and fury and terror, I thought, but now I was at ease with my lot. Then one summer day I set out with George and the children across the desert for a vacation in California. Part way to Yuma I became aware that my right leg felt funny. "I think I've had an exacerbation," I told George. "What shall we do?" he asked. "I think we'd better get the hell to California," I said, "because I don't know whether I'll ever make it again." So we went on to San Diego and then to Orange, and up the Pacific Coast Highway to Santa Cruz, across to Yosemite, down to Sequoia and Joshua Tree, and so back over the desert to home. It was a fine two-week trip, filled with friends and fair weather, and I wouldn't have missed it for the world, though I did in fact make it back to California two years later. Nor would there have been any point in missing it, since in MS, once the symptoms have appeared, the neurological damage has been done, and there's no way to predict or prevent that damage.

The incident spoiled my self-satisfaction, however. It renewed my grief and fury and terror, and I learned that one never finishes adjusting to MS. I don't know now why I thought one would. One does not, after all, finish adjusting to life, and MS is simply a fact of my life—not my favorite fact, of course—but as ordinary as my nose and my tropical fish and my yellow Mazda station wagon. It may at any time get worse, but no amount of worry or anticipation can prepare me for a new loss. My life is a lesson in losses. I learn one at a time.

And I had best be patient in the learning, since I'll have to do it like it or not. As any rock fan knows, you can't always get what you want. Particularly when you have MS. You can't, for example, get cured. In recent years researchers and the organizations that fund research have started to pay MS some attention even though it isn't fatal; perhaps they have begun to see that life is something other than a quantitative phenomenon, that one may be very much alive for a very long time in a life that isn't worth living. The researchers have made some progress toward understanding the mechanism of the disease: It may well be an autoimmune reaction triggered by a slow-acting virus. But they are nowhere near its prevention, control, or cure. And most of us want to be cured. Some, unable to accept incurability, grasp at one treatment after another, no matter how bizarre: megavitamin therapy, gluten-free diet, injections of cobra venom, hypothermal suits, lymphocytopharesis, hyperbaric chambers. Many treatments are probably harmless enough, but none are curative.

The absence of a cure often makes MS patients bitter toward their doctors. Doctors are, after all, the priests of modern society, the new shamans, whose business is to heal, and many an MS patient roves from one to another, searching for the "good" doctor who will make him well. Doctors too think of themselves as healers, and for this reason many have trouble dealing with MS patients, whose disease in its intransigence defeats their aims and mocks their skills. Too few doctors, it is true, treat their patients as whole human beings, but the reverse is also true. I have always tried to be gentle with my doctors, who often have more at stake in terms of ego than I do. I may be frustrated, maddened, depressed by the incurability of my disease, but I am not diminished by it, and they are. When I push myself up from my seat in the waiting room and stumble toward them, I incarnate the limitation of their powers. The least I can do is refuse to press on their tenderest spots.

This gentleness is part of the reason that I'm not sorry to be a cripple. I didn't have it before. Perhaps I'd have developed it anyway—how could I know such a thing?—and I wish I had more of it, but I'm glad of what I have. It has opened and enriched my life enormously, this sense that my frailty and need must be mirrored in others, that in searching for and shaping a stable core in a life wrenched by change and loss, change and loss, I must recognize the same process, under individual conditions, in the lives around me. I do not deprecate such knowledge, however I've come by it.

All the same, if a cure were found, would I take it? In a minute. I may be a cripple, but I'm only occasionally a loony and never a saint. Anyway, in my brand of theology God doesn't give bonus points for a limp. I'd take a cure; I just don't need one. A friend who also has MS startled me once by asking, "Do you ever say to yourself, 'Why me, Lord?' " "No, Michael, I don't," I told him, "because whenever I try, the only response I can think of is 'Why not?' " If I could make a cosmic deal, who would I put in my place? What in my life would I give up in exchange for sound limbs and a thrilling rush of energy? No one. Nothing. I might as well do the job myself. Now that I'm getting the hang of it.

RANDY SHILTS

AIDS

Randy Shilts (1951–   ) is an investigative journalist who has covered the AIDS epidemic since 1982. His work has appeared in the *San Francisco Chronicle,* the *Washington Post,* the *Chicago Tribune, Christopher Street,* and other publications. Shilts's books include *The Mayor of Castro Street: The Life and Times of Harvey Milk* (1982) and the highly acclaimed *And the Band Played On: Politics, People, and the AIDS Epidemic* (1987), from which the following selection is taken.

JULY 4, 1976
NEW YORK HARBOR

Tall sails scraped the deep purple night as rockets burst, flared, and flourished red, white, and blue over the stoic Statue of Liberty. The whole world was watching, it seemed; the whole world was there. Ships from fifty-five nations had poured sailors into Manhattan to join the throngs, counted in the millions, who watched the greatest pyrotechnic extravaganza ever mounted, all for America's 200th birthday party. Deep into the morning, bars all over the city were crammed with sailors. New York City had hosted the greatest party ever known, everybody agreed later. The guests had come from all over the world.

This was the part the epidemiologists would later note, when they stayed up late at night and the conversation drifted toward where it had started and when. They would remember that glorious night in New York Harbor, all those sailors, and recall: From all over the world they came to New York.

CHRISTMAS EVE, 1976
KINSHASA, ZAIRE

The hot African sky turned black and sultry; it wasn't like Christmas at all.

The unrelenting mugginess of the equatorial capital made Dr. Ib Bygbjerg even lonelier for Denmark. In the kitchen, Dr. Grethe Rask, determined to assuage her young colleague's homesickness, began preparing an approximation of the dinner with which Danes traditionally began their Christmas observance, the celebration known through centuries of custom as the Feast of the Hearts.

The preparations brought back memories of the woman's childhood in Thisted, the ancient Jutland port nestled on the Lim Fiord not far from the North Sea. As the main course, Grethe Rask knew, there needed to be something that flies. In Jutland that would mean goose or duck; in Zaire, chicken would have to suffice. As she began preparing the fowl, Grethe again felt the familiar fatigue wash over her. She had spent the last two years haunted by weariness, and by now, she knew she couldn't fight it.

Grethe collapsed on her bed. She had been among the Danish doctors who came to replace the Belgian physicians who were no longer welcome in this new nation eager to forget its recent colonial incarnation as the Belgian Congo. Grethe had first gone there in 1964, returning to Europe for training in stomach surgery and tropical diseases. She had spent the last four years in Zaire but, despite all this time in Africa, she remained unmistakably from the Danish stock who proudly announce themselves as north of the fjord. To be north of the Lim Fiord was to be direct and decisive, independent and plainspoken. The Jutlanders born south of the stretch of water that divides the Danish peninsula tend toward weakness, as anyone north of the fjord might explain. Far from the kings in Copenhagen, these hardy northern people had nurtured their collective heritage for centuries. Grethe Rask from Thisted mirrored this.

It explained why she was here in Zaire, 5,000 miles from where she might forge a lucrative career as a surgeon in the sprawling modern hospitals of Copenhagen. Such a cosmopolitan career meant people looking over her shoulder, giving orders. Grethe preferred the work she had done at a primitive hospital in the remote village of Abumombazi in the north of Zaire. She alone was in charge there.

The hospital conditions in Abumombazi were not as deplorable as in other parts of the country. A prominent Zairian general came from the region. He had had the clout to attract a white doctor to the village, and there, with Belgian nuns, Grethe worked with what she could beg and borrow. This was Central Africa, after all, and even a favored clinic would never have such basics as sterile rubber gloves or disposable needles. You just used needles again and again until they wore out; once gloves had worn through, you risked dipping your hands in your patient's blood because that was what needed to be done. The lack of rudimentary supplies meant that a surgeon's work had risks that doctors in the developed world could not imagine, particularly because the undeveloped part, specifically

Central Africa, seemed to sire new diseases with nightmarish regularity. Earlier that year, not far from Abumombazi, in a village along the Ebola River on the Zaire-Sudan border, a virulent outbreak of a horrifying new disease had demonstrated the dangers of primitive medicine and new viruses. A trader from the village of Enzara, suffering from fevers and profuse, uncontrollable bleeding, had come to the teaching hospital for nurses in Maridi. The man apparently had picked up the disease sexually. Within days, however, 40 percent of the student nurses in Maridi were stricken with the fever, transmitted by contact with the patient's infected blood either through standard care procedures or through accidental needle-sticks.

Frightened African health officials swallowed their pride and called the World Health Organization, who came with a staff from the American Centers for Disease Control. By the time the young American doctors arrived, thirty-nine nurses and two doctors were dead. The CDC doctors worked quickly, isolating all patients with fevers. Natives were infuriated when the Americans banned the traditional burials of the victims since the ritual bathing of the bodies was clearly spreading the disease further. Within weeks, however, the epidemic was under control. In the end, the Ebola Fever virus, as it came to be known, killed 53 percent of the people it infected, seizing 153 lives before it disappeared as suddenly and mysteriously as it had arisen. Sex and blood were two horribly efficient ways to spread a new virus, and years later, a tenuous relief would fill the voices of doctors who talked of how fortunate it was for human-kind that this new killer had awakened in this remote corner of the world and had been stamped out so quickly. A site just a bit closer to regional crossroads could have unleased a horrible plague. With modern roads and jet travel, no corner of the earth was very remote anymore; never again could diseases linger undetected for centuries among a distant people without finding some route to fan out across the planet.

The battle between humans and disease was nowhere more bitterly fought than here in the fetid equatorial climate, where heat and humidity fuel the generation of new life forms. One historian has suggested that humans, who first evolved in Africa eons ago, migrated north to Asia and Europe simply to get to climates that were less hospitable to the deadly microbes the topics so efficiently bred.

Here, on the frontiers of the world's harshest medical realities, Grethe Rask tended the sick. In her three-years in Abumombazi, she had bullied and cajoled people for the resources to build her jungle hospital, and she was loved to the point of idolization by the local people. Then, she returned to the Danish Red Cross Hospital, the largest medical institution in the bustling city of Kinshasa, where she assumed the duties of chief surgeon. Here she met Ib Bygbjerg, who had returned from another rural outpost in the south. Bygbjerg's thick dark hair and small compact frame belied his Danish ancestry, the legacy, he figured, of some Spanish sailor who made his way to Denmark centuries ago. Grethe Rask had the features one would expect of a woman from Thisted, high cheekbones and blond hair worn short in a cut that some delicately called mannish.

To Bygbjerg's eye, on that Christmas Eve, there were troubling things to note about Grethe's appearance. She was thin, losing weight from a mysterious diarrhea. She had been suffering from the vague yet persistent malaise for two years now, since her time in the impoverished northern villages. In 1975, the problem had receded briefly after drug treatments, but for the past year, nothing had seemed to help. The surgeon's weight dropped further, draining and weakening her with each passing day.

Even more alarming was the disarray in the forty-six-year-old woman's lymphatic system, the glands that play the central role in the body's never-ending fight to make itself immune from disease. All of Grethe's lymph glands were swollen and had been for nearly two years. Normally, a lymph node might swell here or there to fight this or that infection, revealing a small lump on the neck, under an arm, or perhaps, in the groin. There didn't seem to be any reason for her glands to swell; there was no precise infection anywhere, much less anything that would cause such a universal enlargement of the lymph nodes all over her body.

And the fatigue. It was the most disconcerting aspect of the surgeon's maliase. Of course, in the best of times, this no-nonsense woman from north of the fjord did not grasp the concept of relaxa-tion. Just that day, for example, she had not been scheduled to work, but she put in a full shift, anyway; she was always working, and in this part of the world nobody could argue because there was always so much to be done. But the weariness, Bygbjerg could tell, was not bred by overwork. Grethe had always been remarkably healthy, throughout her arduous career. No, the fatigue was something darker; it had become a constant companion that weighted her every move, mocking the doctor's industry like the ubiquitous cackling of the hyena on the savannah.

Though she was neither sentimental nor particularly Christian, Grethe Rask had wanted to cheer her young colleague; instead, she lay motionless, paralyzed again. Two hours later, Grethe stirred and began, halfheartedly, to finish dinner. Bygbjerg was surprised that she was so sick then that she could not muster the strength to stay awake for something as special as the Feast of the Hearts.

NOVEMBER 1977
HJARDEMAAL, DENMARK

A cold Arctic wind blistered over the barren heath outside a whitewashed cottage that sat alone, two miles from the nearest neighbors in the desolate region of Denmark north of the Lim Fiord. Sweeping west, from the North Sea over the sand dunes and low, bowed pines, the gusts made a whoosh-whooshing sound. Inside the little house, under a neat red-tiled roof, Grethe Rask gasped her short, sparse breaths from an oxygen bottle.

"I'd better go home to die," Grethe had told Ib Bygbjerg matter-of-factly.

The only thing her doctors could agree on was the woman's terminal prognosis. All else was mystery. Also newly returned from Africa, Bygbjerg pondered the compounding mysteries of Grethe's health. None of it made sense. In early 1977, it appeared that she might be getting better; at least the swelling in her lymph nodes had gone down, even as she became more fatigued. But she had continued working, finally taking a brief vacation in South Africa in early July.

Suddenly, she could not breathe. Terrified, Grethe flew to Copenhagen, sustained on the flight by bottled oxygen. For months now, the top medical specialists of Denmark had tested and studied the surgeon. None, however, could fathom why the woman should, for no apparent reason, be dying. There was also the curious array of health problems that suddenly appeared. Her mouth became covered with yeast infections. Staph infections spread in her blood. Serum tests showed that something had gone awry in her immune system; her body lacked T-cells, the quarterbacks in the body's defensive line against disease. But biopsies showed she was not suffering from a lymph cancer that might explain not only the T-cell deficiency but her body's apparent inability to stave off infection. The doctors could only gravely tell her that she was suffering from progressive lung disease of unknown cause. And, yes, in answer to her blunt questions, she would die.

Finally, tired of the poking and endless testing by the Copenhagen doctors, Grethe Rask retreated to her cottage near Thisted. A local doctor fitted out her bedroom with oxygen bottles. Grethe's longtime female companion, who was a nurse in a nearby hospital, tended her. Grethe lay in the lonely whitewashed farmhouse and remembered her years in Africa while the North Sea winds piled the first winter snows across Jutland.

In Copenhagen, Ib Bygbjerg, now at the State University Hospital, fretted continually about his friend. Certainly, there must be an answer to the mysteries of her medical charts. Maybe if they ran more tests. . . . It could be some common tropical culprit they had overlooked, he argued. She would be cured, and they would all chuckle over how easily the problem had been solved when they sipped wine and ate goose on the Feast of the Hearts. Bygbjerg pleaded with the doctors, and the doctors pleaded with Grethe Rask, and reluctantly the wan surgeon returned to the old *Rigshospitalet* in Copenhagen for one last chance.

Bygbjerg would never forgive himself for taking her away from the cottage north of the fjord. The virulent microbes that were haunting her body would not reveal themselves in the bombardment of tests she endured in those last days. On December 12, 1977, just twelve days before the Feast of the Hearts, Margrethe P. Rask died. She was forty-seven years old.

Later, Bygbjerg decided he would devote his life to studying tropical medicine. Before he died, he wanted to know what microscopic marauder had come from the African jungles to so ruthlessly rob the life of his best friend, a woman who had been so intensely devoted to helping others.

An autopsy revealed that Grethe Rask's lungs were filled with millions of organisms known as *Pneumocystis carinii;* they had caused a rare pneumonia that had slowly suffocated the woman. The diagnosis raised more questions than answers: Nobody died of *Pneumocystis.* Intrigued, Bygbjerg wanted to start doing research on the disease, but he was dissuaded by wizened professors, who steered him toward work in malaria. Don't study *Pneumocystis,* they told him; it was so rare that there would be no future in it.

FRANK CONROY

Think about It

Frank Conroy (1936–   ) directs the Iowa Writer's Workshop and frequently writes about music. His stories and essays have appeared in *GQ, Esquire,* the *New York Times Magazine,* and *Harper's,* where the following selection first appeared. His books include *Stop-Time* (1969), a memoir, and *Midair* (1985), a collection of stories.

When I was sixteen I worked selling hot dogs at a stand in the Fourteenth Street subway station in New York City, one level above the trains and one below the street, where the crowds continually flowed back and forth. I worked with three Puerto Rican men who could not speak English. I had no Spanish, and although we understood each other well with regard to the tasks at hand, sensing and adjusting to each other's body movements in the extremely confined space in which we operated, I felt isolated with no one to talk to. On my break I came out from behind the counter and passed the time with two old black men who ran a shoeshine stand in a dark corner of the corridor. It was a poor location, half ridden by columns, and they didn't have much business. I would sit with my back against the wall while they stood or moved around their ancient elevated stand, talking to each other or to me, but always staring into the distance as they did so.

As the weeks went by I realized that they never looked at anything in their immediate vicinity—not at me or their stand or anybody who might come within ten or fifteen feet. They did not look at approaching customers once they were inside the perimeter. Save for the instant it took to discern the color of the shoes, they did not even look at what they were doing while they worked, but rubbed in polish, brushed, and buffed by feel while looking over their shoulders, into the distance, as if awaiting the arrival of an important person. Of course there wasn't all that much distance in the underground station, but their behavior was so focused and consistent they seemed somehow to transcend the physical. A powerful mood was created, and I came almost to believe that these men could see through walls, through girders, and around corners to whatever hyperspace it was where whoever it was they were waiting and watching for would finally emerge. Their scattered talk was hip, elliptical, and hinted at mysteries beyond my white boy's ken, but it was the staring off, the long, steady staring off, that had me hypnotized. I left for a better job, with handshakes from both of them, without understanding what I had seen.

Perhaps ten years later, after playing jazz with black musicians in various Harlem clubs, hanging out uptown with a few young artists and intellectuals, I began to learn from them something of the extraordinarily varied and complex riffs and rituals embraced by different people to help themselves get through life in the ghetto. Fantasy of all kinds—from playful to dangerous—was in the very air of Harlem. It was the spice of uptown life.

Only then did I understand the two shoeshine men. They were trapped in a demeaning situation in a dark corner in an underground corridor in a filthy subway system. Their continuous staring off was a kind of statement, a kind of dance. Our bodies are here, went the statement, but our souls are receiving nourishment from distant sources only we can see. They were powerful magic dancers, sorcerers almost, and thirty-five years later I can still feel the pressure of their spell.

The light bulb may appear over your head, is what I'm saying, but it may be a while before it actually goes on. Early in my attempts to learn jazz piano, I used to listen to recordings of a fine player named Red Garland, whose music I admired. I couldn't quite figure out what he was doing with his left hand, however; the chords eluded me. I went uptown to an obscure club where he was playing with his trio, caught him on his break, and simply asked him. "Sixths," he said cheerfully. And then he went away.

I didn't know what to make of it. The basic jazz chord is the seventh, which comes in various configurations, but it is what it is. I was a self-taught pianist, pretty shaky on theory and harmony, and when he said sixths I kept trying to fit the information into what I already knew, and it didn't fit. But it stuck in my mind—a tantalizing mystery.

A couple of years later, when I began playing with a bass player, I discovered more or less by accident that if the bass played the root and I played a sixth based on the fifth note of a scale, a very interesting chord involving both instruments emerged. Ordinarily, I suppose I would have skipped over the matter and not paid much attention, but I remembered Garland's remark and so I stopped and spent a week or two working out the voicings, and greatly strengthened my foundations as a player. I had remembered what I hadn't understood, you might say, until my life caught up with the information and the light bulb went on.

I remember another, more complicated example from my sophomore year at the small liberal-arts college outside Philadelphia. I seemed never to be able to get up in time for breakfast in the dining hall. I would get coffee and a doughnut in the Coop instead—a basement area with about a dozen small tables where students could get something to eat at odd hours. Several mornings in a row I noticed a strange man sitting by himself with a cup of coffee. He was in his sixties, perhaps, and sat straight in his chair with very little extraneous movement. I guessed he was some sort of distinguished visitor to the college who had decided to put in some time at a student hangout. But no one ever sat with him. One morning I approached his table and asked if I could join him.

"Certainly," he said. "Please do." He had perhaps the clearest eyes I had ever seen, like blue ice, and to be held in their steady gaze was not, at first, an entirely comfortable experience. His eyes gave nothing away about himself while at the same time creating in me the eerie impression that he was looking directly into my soul. He asked a few quick questions, as if to put me at my ease, and we fell into conversation. He was William O. Douglas from the Supreme Court, and when he saw how startled I was he said, "Call me Bill. Now tell me what you're studying and why you get up so late in the morning." Thus began a series of talks that stretched over many weeks. The fact that I was an ignorant sophomore with literary pretensions who knew nothing about the law didn't seem to bother him. We talked about everything from Shakespeare to the possibility of life on other planets. One day I mentioned that I was going to have dinner with Judge Learned Hand. I explained that Hand was my girlfriend's grandfather. Douglas nodded, but I could tell he was surprised at the coincidence of my knowing the chief judge of the most important court in the country save the Supreme Court itself. After fifty years on the bench Judge Hand had become a famous man, both in and out of legal circles—a living legend, to his own dismay. "Tell him hello and give him my best regards," Douglas said.

Learned Hand, in his eighties, was a short, barrel-chested man with a large, square head, huge, thick, bristling eyebrows, and soft brown eyes. He radiated energy and would sometimes bark out remarks or questions in the living room as if he were in court. His humor was sharp, but often leavened with a touch of self-mockery. When something caught his funny bone he would burst out with explosive laughter—the laughter of a man who enjoyed laughing. He had a large repertoire of dramatic expressions involving the use of his eyebrows—very useful, he told me conspiratorially, when looking down on things from behind the bench. (The court stenographer could not record the movement of his eyebrows.) When I told him I'd been talking to William O. Douglas, they first shot up in exaggerated surprise, and then lowered and moved forward in a glower.

"*Justice* William O. Douglas, young man," he admonished. "Justice Douglas, if you please." About the Supreme Court in general, Hand insisted on a tone of profound respect. Little did I know that in private correspondence he had referred to the Court as "The Blessed Saints, Cherubim and Seraphim," "The Jolly Boys," "The Nine Tin Jesuses," "The Nine Blameless Ethiopians," and my particular favorite, "The Nine Blessed Chalices of the Sacred Effluvium."

Hand was badly stooped and had a lot of pain in his lower back. Martinis helped, but his strict Yankee wife approved of only one before dinner. It was my job to make the second and somehow slip it to him. If the pain was particularly acute he would get out of his chair and lie flat on the rug, still talking, and finish his point without missing a beat. He flattered me by asking for my impression of Justice Douglas, instructed me to convey his warmest regards, and then began talking about the Dennis case, which he described as a particularly tricky and difficult case involving the prosecution of eleven leaders of the Communist party. He had just started in on the First Amendment and free speech when we were called in to dinner.

William O. Douglas loved the outdoors with a passion, and we fell into the habit of having coffee in the Coop and then strolling under the trees down toward the duck pond. About the Dennis case, he said something to this effect: "Eleven Communists arrested by the government. Up to no good, said the government; dangerous people, violent overthrow, etc. First Amendment, said the defense, freedom of speech, etc." Douglas stopped walking. "Clear and present danger."

"What?" I asked. He often talked in a telegraphic manner, and one was expected to keep up with him. It was sometimes like listening to a man thinking out loud.

"Clear and present danger," he said. "That was the issue. Did they constitute a clear and present danger? I don't think so. I think everybody took the language pretty far in Dennis." He began walking, striding along quickly. Again, one was expected to keep up with him. "The FBI was all over them. Phones tapped, constant surveillance. How could it be clear and present danger with the FBI watching every move they made? That's a ginkgo," he said suddenly, pointing to a tree. "A beauty. You don't see those every day. Ask Hand about clear and present danger."

I was in fact reluctant to do so. Douglas's argument seemed to me to be crushing—the last word, really—and I didn't want to embarrass Judge Hand. But back in the living room, on the second martini, the old man asked about Douglas. I sort of scratched my nose and recapitulated the conversation by the ginkgo tree.

"What?" Hand shouted. "Speak up, sir, for heaven's sake."

"He said the FBI was watching them all the time so there couldn't be a clear and present danger," I blurted out, blushing as I said it.

A terrible silence filled the room. Hand's eyebrows writhed on his face like two huge caterpillars. He leaned forward in the wing chair, his face settling, finally, into a grim expression. "I am astonished," he said softly, his eyes holding mine, "at Justice Douglas's newfound faith in the Federal Bureau of Investigation." His big, granite head moved even closer to mine, until I could smell the martini. "I had understood him to consider it a politically corrupt, incompetent organization, directed by a power-crazed lunatic." I realized I had been holding my breath throughout all of this, and as I relaxed, I saw the faintest trace of a smile cross Hand's face. Things are sometimes more complicated than they first appear, his smile seemed to say. The old man leaned back. "The proximity of the danger is something to think about. Ask him about that. See what he says."

I chewed the matter over as I returned to campus. Hand had pointed out some of Douglas's language about the FBI from other sources that seemed to bear out his point. I thought about the words "clear and present danger," and the fact that if you looked at them closely they might not be as simple as they had first appeared. What degree of danger? Did the word "present" allude to the proximity of the danger, or just the fact that the danger was there at all—that it wasn't an anticipated danger? Were there other hidden factors these great men were weighing of which I was unaware?

But Douglas was gone, back to Washington. (The writer in me is tempted to create a scene here—to invent one for dramatic purposes—but of course I can't do that.) My brief time as a messenger boy was over, and I felt a certain frustration, as if, with a few more exchanges, the matter of *Dennis* v. *United States* might have been resolved to my satisfaction. They'd left me high and dry. But, of course, it is precisely because the matter did not resolve that has caused me to think about it, off and on, all these years. "The Constitution," Hand used to say to me flatly, "is a piece of paper. The

Bill of Rights is a piece of paper." It was many years before I understood what he meant. Documents alone do not keep democracy alive, nor maintain the state of law. There is no particular safety in them. Living men and women, generation after generation, must continually remake democracy and the law, and that involves an ongoing state of tension between the past and the present which will never completely resolve.

Education doesn't end until life ends, because you never know when you're going to understand something you hadn't understood before. For me, the magic dance of the shoeshine men was the kind of experience in which understanding came with a kind of click, a resolving kind of click. The same with the experience at the piano. What happened with Justice Douglas and Judge Hand was different, and makes the point that understanding does not always mean resolution. Indeed, in our intellectual lives, our creative lives, it is perhaps those problems that will never resolve that rightly claim the lion's share of our energies. The physical body exists in a constant state of tension as it maintains homeostasis, and so too does the active mind embrace the tension of never being certain, never being absolutely sure, never being done, as it engages the world. That is our special fate, our inexpressibly valuable condition.

SIX

Culture and Tradition

[Tradition] cannot be inherited, and if you want it you must obtain it
by great labor.

T. S. Eliot

All that we are is a result of all that has gone before us. If we
really want to see where we are going as a culture, we need to look
to our past. For example, we may well ask what contribution the
ancient Greeks have given us. After all, this civilization thrived so
long ago that it might seem to bear no resemblance to our contemporary world and its problems. Yet closer examination reveals that
we owe a great debt to the ancient Greeks, for they gave us the
essential tools with which we have built our world. The rational,
scientific approach that the Greeks developed has allowed human
beings to rise above superstition, ignorance, and fear. To study ancient Greek culture is to study ourselves, to study who we are and
from whence we have come.

Socrates' "Apology" rings through the ages as the classic defense
of the dissenter, the outsider, the questioner of society and the status
quo. As Socrates says, he merely asked questions and engaged in
conversation, and for that others found him to be a gadfly, an irritant.
What crime has he committed, he asks of his judges? But Socrates
was condemned to death, and although his tradition of dissent continues and is now protected in our Bill of Rights (see Section 4), we
still often do not value dissenters. While we don't execute them, we
rarely honor them, either. Still, the tradition of dissent is an important
one in our society, and it is a tradition we owe in part to Socrates
and the ancient Greeks.

Yet there is more to our past than we may have recognized. Other
cultures and other peoples have contributed to who we are, as a
culture, today. As Arthur Danto discusses in his essay, we need to
approach the world's literature as a repository of universal value. We
need to search out that which we have neglected or ignored. This is
perhaps what T. S. Eliot meant by obtaining tradition through "great
labor." Tradition, our legacy from the past, can easily be diminished
by ignoring that which other cultures have left for us. Discovering
what has been ignored is not easy, but the reward is great. Scholars
today are busy searching for and discovering rich treasures in the
literature of many cultures that have been overlooked. As this literature is restored to its proper place of study and enjoyment, we will
increase our cultural inheritance.

As Mark Mathabane points out in his essay, for example, the significant contributions of Africans and African-Americans to our culture have only recently been recognized. We can too easily make the mistake of defining our culture too narrowly. While we owe much to ancient Greece and other European countries, we also owe a great deal to many nonwestern cultures.

Still, there are potential pitfalls in focusing on these various cultural contributions, as discussed by Diane Ravitch in her essay. Just as we recognize the great contributions made by so many cultures to our nation, so too do we recognize that we are one nation made up of many cultural contributions and traditions. Our strength is in our diversity, but in a diversity that brings us together, rather than splintering us into separate, antagonistic groups. All of us share the concerns of liberty as discussed by John Stuart Mill. Liberty is not an issue of culture but an issue of the human condition. What different cultures have contributed to our national culture matters not simply because of the source of the contribution, but because of the *value* of that contribution.

As wide-ranging as the essays in this selection might appear, they are all united in discussing important aspects of our tradition and culture, of who we are today. As you read these essays look not only for the threads that unite them, but also for the links between the ideas they express and our present culture.

While reading these selections, keep a log of your questions about and reactions to each selection. From time to time look back over your notes; if there are any questions or reactions that keep occurring, note them. When you are finished reading, you can use one or two such questions or reactions as the basis for a paper that either answers a question or analyzes a reaction.

R. W. LIVINGSTONE

The Rainbow Bridge

R. W. Livingstone (1880–1960) was an English scholar and educator known for his commitment to the classical liberal arts curriculum. As president of Corpus Christi College at Oxford from 1933
to 1944, Livingstone expanded educational opportunities for adults
and established a residential college for women. His books *A Defense of Classical Education* (1916), *The Future in Education* (1941),
and *The Rainbow Bridge* (1959), from which the following selection
is taken, exemplify his belief in the importance of classical literature in education.

The chief task of education is to make human beings, to develop the
aptitudes and attitudes necessary for successful living. How can a
classical education develop them? That is the subject of this article.
"Of course, it cannot," is the obvious and I would add, unthinking
reply. "Why, these people are antiquated. Their problems were different. Their civilization, compared to ours, was primitive. They had
no aeroplanes, automobiles, railroads, no atomic power or electricity,
not even steam." All these things can also be said of the New Testament, of Shakespeare, of Molière,[1] even of Goethe.[2] But are they
for that reason antiquated? The criticism of the classics which I have
mentioned is due to a failure to distinguish knowledge and wisdom.
Knowledge gets out-of-date—often very quickly—especially scientific
knowledge. But wisdom does not. Like gold, it keeps its value,
however long ago some human mind dug it up.

"Still," it may be said, "a classical education is no equipment for
the modern world. Perhaps it is suitable for a life of thought, of
literature, of teaching; but not for politics, for a public career, and
still less for business." I have given elsewhere an answer to this
objection. Facts show that one cannot argue that a good classical

---

[1] Moliere was the pseudonym of Jean Baptiste Poquelin (1622–1673), a French actor
and playwright known for his comedies, including *The Misanthrope* and *Tartuffe*. (ED.)

[2] Johann Wolfgang von Goethe (1749–1832) was a German poet, novelist, playwright,
philosopher, and scientist. His works include *The Sorrows of Young Werther* and *Faust*.
(ED.)

education is in fact a bad preparation for life in the world. But what is the explanation of this paradox? How can the study of two long-dead peoples be any preparation for living in our modern age? This is an interesting problem, not only in itself but because it raises the general questions: What is a good education? What ought we to be seeking when we go to school or college or when we educate ourselves? What insights, what outlook, what training of the mind?

There are two types of teachers to whom we have reason to be grateful. There are those who teach us facts, who introduce us in a methodical way to a subject, lay solid foundations in it, and on these foundations raise the tower of knowledge, foursquare and firmly built. We owe much to them. But there is another, rarer type, to whom we owe more still—those teachers who have an attitude to life, an outlook on the world, that we have not met before, who open our eyes to a new point of view and teach us to see life in a new way. That is the most valuable education one ever gets; and one can recognize it not so much perhaps by the impression it makes at the moment as by the way in which the mind recurs with growing understanding and gratitude to an inspiration which the passage of time does nothing to dim. The Greeks belong to this rarer type of teachers. They give, or can give, two things which everyone needs, two things which education must give if it is to be education at all; first, a certain intellectual habit and attitude of mind; second, a view of life. If education can give these two things, a right view of life and the right mental habits, it will have given us the chief equipment which we need for our voyage through the world. My suggestion is that Greek can give these two things. If so, it has a very important connection with the modern world, and it is the connection between ancient Greece and modern civilization with which this article deals—the mental habits and the attitude to life which can be learned from the Greeks. First their mental habits. What were they?

If we wish to know the nature and quality of a man's mind, we can discover it by studying his life and observing what he has achieved. So too with a nation. If we wish to know its quality, capacity, nature, genius, we have only to study what it has done, and then to ask what the nation must have been like to do this. What did the Greeks do?

In Norse mythology there is a legend of a rainbow bridge, made by the gods so that men who had earned the right could cross the deep and sundering gulf between Midgard, which is the earth, and Asgard, which is heaven. That legend reflects man's sense of the two worlds, human and superhuman, to both of which he belongs, and his instinct, often sleeping, never dead, to pass from the lower to the higher world. Earth and heaven, barbarism and civilization; those are worlds between which a deep gulf lies. But the gulf can be bridged. In Norse mythology the bridge is built by Odin[3] and the Aesir; in history and fact it was built by the Greeks with a double-span, the bridge of goodness and the bridge of wisdom, by which men pass from barbarism to civilization, if not from earth to heaven.

It was not an easy bridge to build. Consider, very briefly, the Greek achievement—in the form of two contrasts. If we had lived in Greece in 650 B.C. we would have thought that the sun and moon were gods, that thunder and lightning were divine weapons, that the arrows of Apollo caused influenza, that corn was the gift of Demeter, that each mountain, tree, and river was the home of a spirit. Four hundred years later we would have known that the earth was a sphere rotating on its own axis and revolving round the sun; the circumference of the earth had been determined accurately within fifty miles; a recent astronomer had catalogued eight hundred fixed stars; and two hundred years earlier a scientist had argued that the universe was constructed of atoms in infinite space. There we have one of the great transformations of the world, one of the great steps forward in the history of man: the creation of a rational, scientific attitude to the universe. That is a bridge which the Greeks built between 600 and 300 B.C.

Human history shows nothing comparable. It is not of course the actual amount of knowledge achieved, of facts discovered. It is to have created, out of ignorance and superstition, the idea of science, the notion of a rational world. We have done infinitely more in detailed scientific discovery. But ours has been development; theirs was origination. Greek science—by which I mean the idea that the universe is rational and is capable of being explained and under-stood—was created in a world in which science, as we understand the word, did not exist; and to have originated science is greater than to have developed it.

That, to recur to my metaphor, is one span of the bridge leading from barbarism to civilization which the Greeks built for us—the span of reason which leads to knowledge. Now let me turn to the other span. The fact that in the dark chaos of ignorance and super-stition the Greeks conceived the idea of looking at the universe and

---

[3] Odin was an important god in Norse mythology. The Aesir were the principal race of Norse gods. (ED.)

life with the eye of reason shows that they must have had unique intellectual genius. But they created something else besides science and philosophy: they created a great human ideal; and from that fact we can divine that they had a rare spiritual genius too. We have seen the contrast between man's attitude to the universe before and after Greek thought, and how the Greeks built the bridge by which mankind crossed from a non-scientific view of the world to a scientific view. But they built an even more important bridge—the bridge by which it passed from barbarism to the life which caused Goethe to say that of all men the Greeks had dreamed the dream of life best.

Think of the early Greek world as we see it in the poems of Homer, a world with its splendid virtues, but also full of injustice, cruelty, and superstition, a world that knew human sacrifice and believed in gods who, even as men, would have been discreditable. And then contrast with it the Greek world of the fifth century B.C., and see how in the interval the Greeks had created out of a primitive society a great spiritual life. It may seem a surprising suggestion that Greece can help us in the field of conduct, of morals. People don't always think of her in that light; art, literature, thought—yes; morality—no. But Greece and Christianity are the two supreme masters of the ethical, the spiritual life. There and nowhere else in Western civilization do we find what the modern world has largely lost; a clear philosophy of living.

Think, as I suggested, of the world of Homer; then look at two pictures: the first an ideal for the state, the second an ideal for the individual. The first, from the second book of Thucydides, is Pericles' political ideal for Athens:[4]

> Our constitution is called a democracy because it is in the hands not of the few but of the many. But the laws secure equal justice for all in their private disputes. As for social standing, our practice is that a citizen who has recognized ability in some field gets public preferment—it is a question of his abilities, not of his rank. As for poverty, our practice is that if a man can do good work for the community, humbleness of condition is no bar. . . . Open and friendly in our private intercourse, in our public conduct we keep strictly within the control of law . . . we are obedient to those in authority and to the laws, more especially to those which offer protection to the oppressed.

---

[4] *Thucydides* (460–400 B.C.?), a Greek writer and historian, wrote *The History of the Peloponnesian War*. *Pericles* (495–429 B.C.) was an Athenian statesman largely responsible for the development of Athens as a political and cultural force in Greece. (ED.)

Has any finer definition of the democratic ideal ever been written? Has any nation gone beyond that? Or contrast with the ideals of the Homeric age this conception, from the *Theaetetus* of Plato, of what human life should be. "Evil, Theodorus, can never pass away, for there must always be an opposite to good. It has no place in heaven, so of necessity it haunts the mortal nature and this earthly sphere. Therefore we ought to escape from earth to heaven as quickly as we can; and the way to escape is to become like God, as far as this is possible; and the way to become like him is to become holy, good and wise."

Between 700 and 400 B.C., beside the transformation of human outlook by the creation of the scientific spirit, is another of the great transformations of the world—the creation of a rational and worthy spiritual ideal for men. During those years a real civilization emerged with incredible rapidity; amid heavy clouds a patch of the clearest sky appeared, in which of the three great lights of the human firmament—Goodness, Beauty, Truth—two at least, Beauty and Truth, shine as brightly as they have ever shone since. There is only one other movement in the spiritual history of Western civilization in any degree comparable to it in importance—what was done in Palestine between the age of the Book of Judges and the age of the New Testament.

What qualities make the Greek achievement possible? How could a people pass, in a few centuries, from Homeric to Platonic morality, from primitive views about the universe to thinking that it was composed of atoms in infinite space?

Two qualities do much to explain this achievement; and they can be divined in some Greek sayings taken from the sixth and fifth centuries B.C., if we look behind the saying to the outlook of the man who said it. "I would rather discover one scientific fact than be King of Persia" (as we might say, a Rockefeller or a Ford). "Why are we born? To contemplate the works of Nature." What sort of men were the speakers of these words, Democritus and Anaxagoras?[5] What do these phrases reveal? A passionate interest in the world and curiosity about it—their own word to describe their feeling, "won-

---

[5] *Democritus* (460–370 B.C.) was a Greek philosopher who extended an atomistic theory of the universe. *Anaxagoras* (500–428 B.C.), also a Greek philosopher, is remembered for his discovery of the true cause of an eclipse and for the doctrine of cosmology. (ED.)

der," is better. These men do not want money or fame or pleasure, but they find the world about them extraordinarily interesting, and it seems to them a sufficient occupation to contemplate and study it. People who felt like that were singularly well-equipped to create science and philosophy. We recognize in those sayings the secret of perpetual youth, and feel in them the greatness of man—something divine and immortal emerging in this frail, sensuous, mundane, petty creature. The Greeks say in effect about the pursuit of knowledge what Antony in Shakespeare says about something very different: "The nobleness of life is to do this." That attitude of wonder in the presence of the world is a continuous quantity of Greek thought.

Then there is a second quality, which again is revealed in two sentences, if, as before, we look behind the words to the spirit of the man who uttered them. The first is: "Wisdom consists in saying what is true, and in acting according to Nature, listening to her" (Heraclitus, sixth century B.C.). The second instance is a sentence from Plato:

> I am one of the people who would like to be proved wrong if they say anything which is not correct, and would like to prove others wrong if they are in error; and I should not find it more disagreeable to have my own errors pointed out than to prove others wrong, for it is a greater gain to be set free from the greatest of evils (error) than to set others free.

The speaker of these words was not a common type—how many of us think it an advantage to be shown wrong? In those two passages another secret of how the Greeks came to create science and philosophy and a rational view of life is apparent. They found the world and life intensely interesting, but also they desired to see both as they really are. That again is a continuous quality of Greek literature, the instinct to see things accurately—not to rest in prejudices and preconceptions. How difficult, how salutary, how liberating! Few things are more needed in politics, amid the cant of party, in the work of education or administration—indeed everywhere—than this desire, without bitterness or cynicism, to see things as they are. There again we see the divine in man, something human and also superhuman.

These attitudes: curiosity, the capacity for intense interest, and the power

> To bear all naked truths,
> And to envisage circumstance, all calm,

are the essential qualities for achievement in science and philosophy. (But in what field of life are they not of supreme importance?) No people have ever used the eye of the mind so steadily and effectively as the Greeks. It meets us everywhere from Homer to Epictetus.[6] Even the earliest Greek literature shows that instinct to see things without prejudice or prepossession, which is a forerunner of reason. Thus Homer writes of a war between Greeks and barbarians, but we could not tell from the *Iliad* whether he was Greek or Trojan. Thus Thucydides narrates the war in which his country was ruined; but it would be difficult to tell, except for the rare passages in which he speaks in the first person, whether he was an Athenian or a Spartan.

It is by the use of reason that the Ionians[7] broke loose from a savage's view of the universe and argued their way through a series of hypotheses to the atomism of Democritus. It is by reason that the Greeks achieved the most difficult of all tasks, that of seeing further than the accepted conventions of their age; thus Plato, in a state where women had no education or share in public life, declared that they should have the same upbringing as men and follow the same pursuits and occupations; thus, in an age when slavery was universally accepted, Alcidamas (fifth century B.C.) wrote: "God has set all men free; nature has made no one a slave"; thus, two centuries later in a world divided by race, culture, and government, Diogenes, when asked what was his country, replied: "I am a citizen of the world"; and Zeno, the founder of Stoicism, said: "Let us look on all men as fellow countrymen and fellow citizens, and let there be unity in our life, like that of a flock feeding together in a common pasture."

The Greeks reached these truths—Plato, the emancipation of women; Alcidamas, the abolition of slavery; Zeno, the unity of mankind—not under the pressure of social or economic trends, but by the power of reason, breaking the thought barrier of their time. It has taken mankind a long time to see as far; even today we have not seen as far as Zeno.

Yes, it may be said, but what exactly do we get by reading this literature and studying this civilization? In what way does it prepare

---

[6] Epictetus (55–135) was a Greek slave who became a freed man. He was a philosopher with a special interest in ethics and he professed that man must believe in a god whose thoughts direct the universe. (ED.)

[7] People from the western coast of Anatolia, where much of early Greek philosophy originated. (ED.)

us to live in the modern world? No doubt the Greek achievement was remarkable, indeed unique. But how does it help us now?

My reply would be that the people who did these things must have been a very remarkable people, a people with extraordinary qualities of mind, the sort of people one likes to meet, the sort of people one cannot meet without learning something from them; and when one reflects that the Greeks brought into the world the idea of science and the ideal of democracy, and when one considers their achievement in philosophy, in political thought, in poetry, in sculpture, in architecture, in the creation of an ideal of life, are not the men who did these things worth meeting? Are they not likely to be able to teach us much, not in actual facts, but if we ask from them what Elisha asked from Elijah[8]—a portrait of his spirit? The most important thing in education is to live with the right people—in life, if we can find them; in the past, where they are easy to find. The Greeks, I think, stand highest among the right people.

No race has ever been so gifted, and, taking them individually, some of its writers have no rivals. Can we think of anyone equal to Homer in epic, to Thucydides in history, to Aristophanes in his special field of comedy? There have been great philosophers since their time, but it would be difficult to maintain that any of them are equal to Aristotle and still less to Plato, of whom Whitehead said that "the safest general characterization of the European philosophical tradition is that it consists of a series of footnotes to Plato." Shakespeare no doubt is supreme among dramatists, but each of the three great Greek tragic poets is his superior in a particular field.

Greek studies are a training of the eye of the mind to see rightly, and that is a sufficient reason for regarding them as a good training for life. Only a small minority of those who pass through school and college will learn Greek, though it might well be a larger minority than it is today. But any educated person can read at least some of the Greek masterpieces in English. He will of course lose much; poetry can never be transmuted from one tongue into another without change and loss. And he will not know the Greek language, "A language doubtless the most perfect that has been contrived by the art of man" (Gibbon). "Their language . . . in variety, in simplicity, in flexibility, and in copiousness, excels every other language of the

---

[8] *Elijah* was a Hebrew prophet who, according to tradition, was taken up to heaven in a chariot, thus showing the possibility of life beyond earth. *Elisha* was a pupil of Elijah. (ED.)

western world" (Shelley). "Greek, which contains all the excellences of all the languages" (Coleridge). Not to know a language, of which such critics speak as they do, is to miss one of the great achievements of the human mind.

ARTHUR DANTO

The Canon and the Wisdom of the East

Arthur Danto (1924–   ), a professor of philosophy at Columbia University, was born in Ann Arbor, Michigan. Danto has been a co-director of the Center for the Study of Human Rights since 1978 and is currently an art critic for *The Nation*. His books reveal his interest in the connections between philosophy and art; they include *What Philosophy Is* (1968), *Mysticism and Morality: Oriental Thought and Moral Philosophy* (1972), *The Philosophical Disenfranchisement of Art* (1986), and *Encounters and Reflections: Art in the Historical Present* (1990). The following selection first appeared in *Harper's* magazine.

Not long ago I was sitting in the lobby of the Asoka Hotel in New Delhi, discussing with my hosts, in the spirit of philosophical small talk in India, the evidence for levitation. It was lunchtime, and the lobby was filled with the bright and busy personalities one expects to find in such spaces, waiting for whomever they had made dates with. At one point the elevator opened and a Sikh came out with a book balanced on his head. He was flanked by four other Sikh men and some women in brilliant saris. An especially tall and fierce Sikh swatted the air over the book with a kind of whisk, as if to keep insects from alighting. The company swept out of the elevator and through the lobby, and not a head was turned. I, on the other hand, was amazed. "Good heavens," I remember saying to my Indian colleague, Professor Chattopadhyaya, "what was *that*?" Chattopadhyaya, a suave and urbane man, seemed surprised at my surprise. "Oh, just the *Granth Sahib*," he told me. "Somebody sent for it no doubt." He was anxious to return to the anecdotal basis for belief in levitation, but I told him that I would find somebody levitating in the lobby of the Asoka Hotel measurably less astounding than the knot of book bearers that had appeared like a vision in the lobby of that elegant building.

This experience comes to mind whenever I'm asked about the canon and whether college humanities courses should be expanded to include non-Western literature. I have great difficulty responding to that question because I really do not know what my relationship is to such books, or what it means to read them—or even to what degree the physical reality of a sacred text such as the *Granth Sahib* is connected to its contents.

I have read that the Guru Angad, the "author" of this work (to the degree that even the concept of authorship can be taken for granted), invented a special script, a variation on the traditional Sharada alphabet, in order to convey the sacred character of the text. What becomes of that sacred character, I wonder, when the book is translated into English, arranged in columns of type, and then carted off by students in Velcro-fastened jackets, along with a stack of other oriental classics, a couple of Grateful Dead cassettes, a filofax, and a pack of Doublemint gum?

Many of these books were intended to be the only book one had to know in order to live one's life. These sacred texts were distant Himalayas of knowledge—their intuitions glacial, their perspectives sweeping—in which the world was revealed in its true proportion, as were the readers themselves. Though these books imparted knowledge for living one's life, the living of that life, paradoxically, was a prerequisite to understanding how to read the book. What remains, then, of these books' true identities when they are brought into our classrooms and praised for their "literary value"?

Let me offer a comparison. I have lately been interested in the issue of how primitive art, as it is called, should be looked at. Beyond question, these objects stand up artistically, once we remove the criterion of naturalistic representation from our judgment. We consider them aesthetically worthy of exhibition in our institutions, and so place them in an artistic tradition defined by visual excellence. But if we examine these works within their *own* cultures, they offer other dimensions—the magical and spiritual, to mention only two examples—that are far more important than being pleasing to the eye or exhibiting formal excellence. These dimensions are lost, however, when a museum attempts to universalize art. Inadvertently, the museum blinds us to nonvisual artistic traditions, ones in which art does not exist for the reasons it may exist among us.

A similar problem arises when we talk about "opening the canon," a concept that approaches the world's literature, as the museum approaches the world's art, as if it were all of a piece, a repository of universal value. Indeed, we may have an even harder time preserving a book's cultural context than we do with a work of art, since the very way books look—the uniform appearance of words on a page— can imply similarities among Great Books where in fact there may be none.

This creates a dilemma: We want to have access to non-Western books at the university and elsewhere, but the price of that access may be that we make these books, in their own terms, *inaccessible.* By reading these texts on assignment and then sitting in a classroom discussing them, we actually move further from understanding their meaning. In Muslim culture, for example, the Koran is read repeat- edly, it is memorized, it is recited through the night, but it is never "discussed" the way it is in the university classroom, as a "great book" or an important one. Our attempt to treat non-Western works simply as voices in one great multicultural discussion may reveal as much about our own premises as treating them as the Wisdom of the East revealed about the premises of Victorian culture—a culture convinced that drops of moral medicine, curative and restorative, could be distilled from these odd texts.

As a philosopher who has spent more than the common time of his profession among these texts, I have often been struck by certain powerful similarities between some of what they appear to say and some of what our texts do. For example, certain images in Buddhist literature are powerfully reminiscent of what Hume[1] says about the self in the well-known and troubling passage in *A Treatise of Human Nature;* while the celebrated last proposition of Wittgenstein's *Tractatus*[2] sounds much like the famous first verse of the *Tao Te Ching.*[3] But despite appearances, I don't think these common themes entail anything more than a specious similarity.

The difficulty with our approach to non-Western literature is that it fails to adequately address the issue of these texts' Otherness. I am

---

[1] David Hume (1711–1776) was a Scottish philosopher and historian who maintained that human knowledge is limited to the experience of ideas and impressions that cannot be verified as true. (ED.)

[2] Ludwig Wittgenstein (1889–1951) was an Austrian-born English philosopher whose book *Tractatus* is notable for its analysis of language and meaning. (ED.)

[3] Source of Taoism, a Chinese philosophy and religion; probably written in the third century B.C. (ED.)

not arguing for relativism of any sort. But in non-Western cultures there are values other than truth and ways of addressing books other than by analyzing their content. For texts are things that have to be lived, as many books of the Orient are lived—their vitality as writing bound up with their being vitally a part of the lives of their readers in a way that they cannot be with ours.

PLATO

Apology[1]

Plato (c. 428–c. 348 B.C.) was a Greek philosopher whose ideas, along with those of Socrates (his teacher) and Aristotle (his student), form the foundation of Western intellectual thought. Born into a wealthy Athenian family, Plato followed his mentor Socrates' footsteps, dedicating his life to philosophy and education. His idealistic philosophy, emphasizing rationality and morality, is evident throughout his works, which include the *Apology, Crito, Phaedrus,* the *Symposium,* and the *Republic.* Plato's writing takes the form of dialogues, which he apparently believed were more representative of thought in action than expository prose. Socrates, who left no written work, serves as Plato's spokesman in these dialogues.

How you, O Athenians, have been affected by my accusers, I cannot tell; but I know that they almost made me forget who I was— so persuasively did they speak; and yet they have hardly uttered a word of truth. But of the many falsehoods told by them, there was one which quite amazed me;—I mean when they said that you should be upon your guard and not allow yourselves to be deceived by the force of my eloquence. To say this, when they were certain to be detected as soon as I opened my lips and proved myself to be anything but a great speaker, did indeed appear to me most shameless—unless by the force of eloquence they mean the force of truth; for if such is

Translated by Benjamin Jowett.

[1] a defense or explanation of the truth or justice of something (ED.)

their meaning, I admit that I am eloquent. But in how different a way from theirs! Well, as I was saying, they have scarcely spoken the truth at all; but from me you shall hear the whole truth; not, however, delivered after their manner in a set oration duly ornamented with words and phrases. No, by heaven! but I shall use the words and argument which occur to me at the moment; for I am confident in the justice of my cause: at my time of life I ought not to be appearing before you, O men of Athens, in the character of a juvenile orator—let no one expect it of me. And I must beg of you to grant me a favour:—if I defend myself in my accustomed manner, and you hear me using the words which I have been in the habit of using in the agora,[2] at the tables of the money-changers, or anywhere else, I would ask you not to be surprised, and not to interrupt me on this account. For I am more than seventy years of age, and appearing now for the first time in a court of law, I am quite a stranger to the language of the place; and therefore I would have you regard me as if I were really a stranger, whom you would excuse if he spoke in his native tongue, and after the fashion of his country:— Am I making an unfair request of you? Never mind the manner, which may or may not be good; but think only of the truth of my words, and give heed to that: let the speaker speak truly and the judge decide justly.

And first, I have to reply to the older charges and to my first accusers, and then I will go on to the later ones. For of old I have had many accusers, who have accused me falsely to you during many years; and I am more afraid of them than of Anytus and his associates, who are dangerous, too, in their own way. But far more dangerous are the others, who began when you were children, and took possession of your minds with their falsehoods, telling of one Socrates, a wise man, who speculated about the heaven above, and searched into the earth beneath, and made the worse appear the better cause. The disseminators of this tale are the accusers whom I dread; for their hearers are apt to fancy that such enquirers do not believe in the existence of the gods. And they are many, and their charges against me are of ancient date, and they were made by them in the days when you were more impressible than you are now—in childhood, or it may have been in youth—and the cause when heard went by default, for there was none to answer. And hardest of all, I do not

---

[2] the marketplace in ancient Greek cities (ED.)

know and cannot tell the names of my accusers; unless in the chance case of a comic poet. All who from envy and malice have persuaded you—some of them having first convinced themselves—all this class of men are most difficult to deal with; for I cannot have them up here, and cross-examine them, and therefore I must simply fight with shadows in my own defence, and argue when there is no one who answers. I will ask you then to assume with me, as I was saying, that my opponents are of two kinds; one recent, the other ancient: and I hope that you will see the propriety of my answering the latter first, for these accusations you heard long before the others, and much oftener.

I will begin at the beginning, and ask what is the accusation which has given rise to the slander of me, and in fact has encouraged Meletus to prefer this charge against me. Well, what do the slanderers say? They shall be my prosecutors, and I will sum up their words in an affidavit: "Socrates is an evildoer, and a curious person, who searches into things under the earth and in heaven, and he makes the worse appear the better cause; and he teaches the aforesaid doctrines to others." Such is the nature of the accusation: it is just what you have yourselves seen in the comedy of Aristophanes, who has introduced a man whom he calls Socrates, going about and saying that he walks in air, and talking a deal of nonsense concerning matters of which I do not pretend to know either much or little— not that I mean to speak disparagingly of any one who is a student of natural philosophy. I should be very sorry if Meletus could bring so grave a charge against me. But the simple truth is, O Athenians, that I have nothing to do with physical speculations. Very many of those here present are witnesses to the truth of this, and to them I appeal. Speak then, you who have heard me, and tell your neighbours whether any of you have ever known me hold forth in few words or in many upon such matters. . . . You hear their answer. And from what they say of this part of the charge you will be able to judge of the truth of the rest.

I dare say, Athenians, that some one among you will reply, "Yes, Socrates, but what is the origin of these accusations which are brought against you; there must have been something strange which you have been doing? All these rumours and this talk about you would never have arisen if you had been like other men: tell us, then, what is the cause of them, for we should be sorry to judge hastily of you." Now, I regard this as a fair challenge, and I will endeavor to explain to you the reason why I am called wise and have such an evil fame. Please to attend then. And although some of you may think that I am joking, I declare that I will tell you the entire truth. Men of Athens, this reputation of mine has come of a certain sort of wisdom which I possess. If you ask me what kind of wisdom, I reply, wisdom such as may perhaps be attained by man, for to that extent I am inclined to believe that I am wise; whereas the persons of whom I was speaking have a superhuman wisdom, which I may fail to describe, because I have it not myself; and he who says that I have, speaks falsely, and is taking away my character. And here, O men of Athens, I must beg you not to interrupt me, even if I seem to say something extravagant. For the word which I will speak is not mine. I will refer you to a witness who is worthy of credit; that witness shall be the God of Delphi[3]—he will tell you about my wisdom, if I have any, and of what sort it is. You must have know Chaerephon; he was early a friend of mine, and also a friend of yours, for he shared in the recent exile of the people, and returned with you. Well, Chaerephon, as you know, was very impetuous in all his doings, and he went to Delphi and boldly asked the oracle to tell him whether—as I was saying, I must beg you not to interrupt—he asked the oracle to tell him whether any one was wiser than I was, and the Pythian prophetess[4] answered, that there was no man wiser. Chaerephon is dead himself; but his brother, who is in court, will confirm the truth of what I am saying.

Why do I mention this? Because I am going to explain to you why I have such an evil name. When I heard the answer, I said to myself, What can the God mean? and what is the interpretation of his riddle? for I know that I have no wisdom, small or great. What then can he mean when he says that I am the wisest of men? And yet he is a god, and cannot lie; that would be against his nature. After long consideration, I thought of a method of trying the question. I reflected that if I could only find a man wiser than myself, then I might go to the god with a refutation in my hand. I should say to him, "Here is a man who is wiser than I am; but you said that I was the wisest." Accordingly I went to one who had the reputation of wisdom, and observed him—his name I need not mention; he was a politician whom I selected for examination—and the result was as

---

[3] Apollo, god of the Sun, whose shrine was at Delphi, in Greece. (ED.)

[4] Priestess who voiced the gods's answers at Apollo's shrine. (ED.)

follows: When I began to talk with him, I could not help thinking that he was not really wise, although he was thought wise by many, and still wiser by himself; and thereupon I tried to explain to him that he thought himself wise, but was not really wise; and the consequence was that he hated me, and his enmity was shared by several who were present and heard me. So I left him, saying to myself, as I went away: Well, although I do not suppose that either of us knows anything really beautiful and good, I am better off than he is—for he knows nothing, and thinks that he knows; I neither know nor think that I know. In this latter particular, then, I seem to have slightly the advantage of him. Then I went to another who had still higher pretensions to wisdom, and my conclusion was exactly the same. Whereupon I made another enemy of him, and of many others besides him.

Then I went to one man after another, being not unconscious of the enmity which I provoked, and I lamented and feared this: but necessity was laid upon me,—the word of God, I thought, ought to be considered first. And I said to myself, Go I must to all who appear to know, and find out the meaning of the oracle. And I swear to you, Athenians, by the dog I swear!—for I must tell you the truth—the result of my mission was just this: I found that the men most in repute were all but the most foolish; and that others less esteemed were really wiser and better. I will tell you the tale of my wanderings and of the "Herculean" labours, as I may call them, which I endured only to find at last the oracle irrefutable. After the politicians, I went to the poets; tragic, dithyrambic, and all sorts. And there, I said to myself, you will be instantly detected; now you will find out that you are more ignorant than they are. Accordingly I took them some of the most elaborate passages in their own writings, and asked what was the meaning of them—thinking that they would teach me something. Will you believe me? I am almost ashamed to confess the truth, but I must say that there is hardly a person present who would not have talked better about their poetry than they did themselves. Then I knew that not by wisdom do poets write poetry, but by a sort of genius and inspiration; they are like diviners or soothsayers who also say many fine things, but do not understand the meaning of them. The poets appeared to me to be much in the same case; and I further observed that upon the strength of their poetry they believed themselves to be the wisest of men in other things in which they were not wise. So I departed, conceiving myself to be superior to them for the same reason that I was superior to the politicians.

At last I went to the artisans. I was conscious that I knew nothing at all, as I may say, and I was sure that they knew many fine things; and here I was not mistaken, for they did know many things of which I was ignorant, and in this they certainly were wiser than I was. But I observed that even the good artisans fell into the same error as the poets;—because they were good workmen they thought that they also knew all sorts of high matters, and this defect in them overshadowed their wisdom; and therefore I asked myself on behalf of the oracle, whether I would like to be as I was, neither having their knowledge nor their ignorance, or like them in both; and I made answer to myself and to the oracle that I was better off as I was.

This inquisition has led to my having many enemies of the worst and most dangerous kind, and has given occasion also to many calumnies. And I am called wise, for my hearers always imagine that I myself possess the wisdom which I find wanting in others; but the truth is, O men of Athens, that God only is wise; and by his answer he intends to show that the wisdom of men is worth little or nothing; he is not speaking of Socrates, he is only using my name by way of illustration, as if he said, He, O men, is the wisest, who, like Socrates, knows that his wisdom is in truth worth nothing. And so I go about the world obedient to the god, and search and make enquiry into the wisdom of any one, whether citizen or stranger, who appears to be wise; and if he is not wise, then in vindication of the oracle I show him that he is not wise; and my occupation quite absorbs me, and I have no time to give either to any public matter of interest or to any concern of my own, but I am in utter poverty by reason of my devotion to the god.

There is another thing:—young men of the richer classes, who have not much to do, come about me of their own accord; they like to hear the pretenders examined, and they often imitate me, and proceed to examine others; there are plenty of persons, as they quickly discover, who think that they know something, but really know little or nothing; and then those who are examined by them instead of being angry with themselves are angry with me: This confounded Socrates, they say; this villainous misleader of youth!— and then if somebody asks them, Why, what evil does he practise or teach? they do not know, and cannot tell; but in order that they may not appear to be at a loss, they repeat the ready-made charges which are used against all philosophers about teaching things up in the clouds and under the earth, and having no gods, and making the worst appear the better cause; for they do not like to confess that their pretence of knowledge has been detected—which is the truth;

and as they are numerous and ambitious and energetic, and are drawn up in battle array and have persuasive tongues, they have filled your ears with their loud and inveterate calumnies. And this is the reason why my three accusers, Meletus and Anytus and Lycon, have set upon me; Meletus, who has a quarrel with me on behalf of the poets; Anytus, on behalf of the craftsmen and politicians; Lycon, on behalf of the rhetoricians: and, as I said at the beginning, I cannot expect to get rid of such a mass of calumny all in a moment. And this, O men of Athens, is the truth and the whole truth; I have concealed nothing, I have dissembled nothing. And yet, I know that my plainness of speech makes them hate me, and what is their hatred but a proof that I am speaking the truth? Hence has arisen the prejudice against me; and this is the reason of it, as you will find out either in this or in any future enquiry.

I have said enough in my defence against the first class of my accusers; I turn to the second class. They are headed by Meletus, that good man and true lover of his country, as he calls himself. Against these, too, I must try to make a defence:—Let their affidavit be read: it contains something of this kind: It says that Socrates is a doer of evil, who corrupts the youth; and who does not believe in the gods of the State, but has other new divinities of his own. Such is the charge; and now let us examine the particular counts. He says that I am a doer of evil, and corrupt the youth; but I say, O men of Athens, that Meletus is a doer of evil, in that he pretends to be in earnest when he is only in jest, and is so eager to bring men to trial from a pretended zeal and interest about matters in which he really never had the smallest interest. And the truth of this I will endeavour to prove to you.

Come hither, Meletus, and let me ask a question of you. You think a great deal about the improvement of youth?

Yes, I do.

Tell the judges, then, who is their improver; for you must know, as you have taken the pains to discover their corrupter, and are citing and accusing me before them. Speak, then, and tell the judges who their improver is.—Observe, Meletus, that you are silent, and have nothing to say. But is not this rather disgraceful, and a very considerable proof of what I was saying that you have no interest in the matter? Speak up, friend, and tell us who their improver is.

The laws.

But that, my good sir, is not my meaning. I want to know who the person is, who, in the first place, knows the laws.

The judges, Socrates, who are present in court.

What, do you mean to say, Meletus, that they are able to instruct and improve youth?

Certainly they are.

What, all of them, or some only and not others?

All of them.

By the goddess Here, that is good news! There are plenty of improvers, then. And what do you say of the audience,—do they improve them?

Yes, they do.

And the senators?

Yes, the senators improve them.

But perhaps the members of the assembly corrupt them?—or do they improve them?

They improve them.

Then every Athenian improves and elevates them; all with the exception of myself; and I alone am their corrupter? Is that what you affirm?

That is what I stoutly affirm.

I am very unfortunate if you are right. But suppose I ask you a question: How about horses? Does one man do them harm and all the world good? Is not the exact opposite the truth? One man is able to do them good, or at least not many;—the trainer of horses, that is to say, does them good, and others who have to do with them rather injure them? Is not that true, Meletus, of horses, or of any other animal? Most assuredly it is; whether you and Anytus say yes or no. Happy indeed would be the condition of youth if they had one corrupter only, and all the rest of the world were their improvers. But you, Meletus, have sufficiently shown that you never had a thought about the young: your carelessness is seen in your not caring about the very things which you bring against me.

And now, Meletus, I will ask you another question—by Zeus I will: Which is better, to live among bad citizens, or among good ones? Answer, friend, I say; the question is one which may be easily answered. Do not the good do their neighbours good, and the bad do them evil?

Certainly.

And is there any one who would rather be injured than benefited by those who live with him? Answer, my good friend, the law requires you to answer—does any one like to be injured?

Certainly not.

And when you accuse me of corrupting and deteriorating the

youth, do you allege that I corrupt them intentionally or unintentionally?

Intentionally, I say.

But you have just admitted that the good do their neighbours good, and the evil do them evil. Now, is that a truth which your superior wisdom has recognized thus early in life, and am I, at my age, in such darkness and ignorance as not to know that if a man with whom I have to live is corrupted by me, I am very likely to be harmed by him; and yet I corrupt him, and intentionally, too—so you say, although neither I nor any other human being is ever likely to be convinced by you. But either I do not corrupt them, or I corrupt them unintentionally; and on either view of the case you lie. If my offence is unintentional, the law has no cognizance of unintentional offences: you ought to have taken me privately, and warned and admonished me; for if I had been better advised, I should have left off doing what I only did unintentionally—no doubt I should; but you would have nothing to say to me and refused to teach me. And now you bring me up in this court, which is a place not of instruction, but of punishment.

It will be very clear to you, Athenians, as I was saying, that Meletus has no care at all, great or small, about the matter. But still I should like to know, Meletus, in what I am affirmed to corrupt the young. I suppose you mean, as I infer from your indictment, that I teach them not to acknowledge the gods which the State acknowledges, but some other new divinities or spiritual agencies in their stead. These are the lessons by which I corrupt the youth, as you say.

Yes, that I say emphatically.

Then, by the gods, Meletus, of whom we are speaking, tell me and the court, in somewhat plainer terms, what you mean! For I do not as yet understand whether you affirm that I teach other men to acknowledge some gods, and therefore that I do believe in gods, and am not an entire atheist—this you do not lay to my charge,—but only you say that they are not the same gods which the city recognizes—the charge is that they are different gods. Or, do you mean that I am an atheist simply, and a teacher of atheism?

I mean the latter—that you are a compete atheist.

What an extraordinary statement! Why do you think so, Meletus? Do you mean that I do not believe in the godhead of the sun or moon, like other men?

I assure you judges, that he does not: for he says that the sun is stone, and the moon earth.

Friend Meletus, you think that you are accusing Anaxagoras:[5] and you have but a bad opinion of the judges, if you fancy them illiterate to such a degree as not to know that these doctrines are found in the books of Anaxagoras the Clazomenian, which are full of them. And so, forsooth, the youth are said to be taught them by Socrates, when there are not infrequently exhibitions of them at the theatre (price of admission one drachma at the most); and they might pay their money, and laugh at Socrates if he pretends to father these extraordinary views. And so, Meletus, you really think that I do not believe in any god?

I swear by Zeus that you believe absolutely in none at all.

Nobody will believe you, Meletus, and I am pretty sure that you do not believe yourself. I cannot help thinking, men of Athens, that Meletus is reckless and impudent, and that he has written this indictment in a spirit of mere wantonness and youthful bravado. Has he not compounded a riddle, thinking to try me? He said to himself:—I shall see whether the wise Socrates will discover my facetious contradiction, or whether I shall be able to deceive him and the rest of them. For he certainly does appear to me to contradict himself in the indictment as much as if he said that Socrates is guilty of not believing in the gods, and yet of believing in them—but this is not like a person who is in earnest.

I should like you, O men of Athens, to join me in examining what I conceive to be his inconsistency; and do you, Meletus, answer. And I must remind the audience of my request that they would not make a disturbance if I speak in my accustomed manner:

Did ever man, Meletus, believe in the existence of human things, and not of human beings? . . . I wish, men of Athens, that he would answer, and not be always trying to get up an interruption. Did ever any man believe in horsemanship, and not in horses? or in flute-playing, and not in flute-players? No, my friend; I will answer to you and to the court, as you refuse to answer for yourself. There is no man who ever did. But now please to answer the next question: Can a man believe in spiritual and divine agencies, and not in spirits or demigods?

He cannot.

How lucky I am to have extracted that answer, by the assistance

---

[5] Anaxagoras (500–428 B.C.) was a Greek philosopher who maintained that the mind, or the intelligence, causes matter to combine and recombine to make objects and create change in the universe. (ED.)

of the court! But then you swear in the indictment that I teach and believe in divine or spiritual agencies (new or old, no matter for that); at any rate, I believe in spiritual agencies,—so you say and swear in the affidavit; and yet if I believe in divine beings, how can I help believing in spirits or demigods;—must I not? To be sure I must; and therefore I may assume that your silence gives consent. Now what are spirits or demigods? are they not either gods or the sons of gods?

Certainly they are.

But this is what I call the facetious riddle invented by you: the demigods or spirits are gods, and you say first that I do not believe in gods, and then again that I do believe in gods; that is, if I believe in demigods. For if the demigods are the illegitimate sons of gods, whether by the nymphs or by any other mothers, of whom they are said to be the sons—what human being will ever believe that there are no gods if they are the sons of Gods? You might as well affirm the existence of mules, and deny that of horses and asses. Such nonsense, Meletus, could only have been intended by you to make trial of me. You have put this into the indictment because you had nothing real of which to accuse me. But no one who has a particle of understanding will ever be convinced by you that the same men can believe in divine and superhuman things, and yet not believe that there are gods and demigods and heroes.

I have said enough in answer to the charge of Meletus: any elaborate defence is unnecessary; but I know only too well how many are the enmities which I have incurred, and this is what will be my destruction if I am destroyed;—not Meletus, nor yet Anytus, but the envy and detraction of the world, which has been the death of many good men, and will probably be the death of many more; there is no danger of my being the last of them.

Some will say: And are you not ashamed, Socrates, of a course of life which is likely to bring you to an untimely end? To him I may fairly answer: There you are mistaken: a man who is good for anything ought not to calculate the chance of living or dying; he ought only to consider whether in doing anything he is doing right or wrong—acting the part of a good man or of a bad. Whereas, upon your view, the heroes who fell at Troy were not good for much, and the son of Thetis above all, who altogether despised danger in comparison with disgrace; and when he was so eager to slay Hector, his goddess mother said to him, that if he avenged his companion Patroclus, and slew Hector, he would die himself—"Fate," she said, in these or the like words, "waits for you next after Hector"; he, receiving this warning, utterly despised danger and death, and instead of fearing them, feared rather to live in dishonour, and not to avenge his friend.[6] "Let me die forthwith," he replied, "and be avenged of my enemy, rather than abide here by the beaked ships, a laughing-stock and a burden of the earth." Had Achilles any thought of death and danger? For wherever a man's place is, whether the place which he has chosen or that in which he has been placed by a commander, there he ought to remain in the hour of danger; he should not think of death or of anything but of disgrace. And this, O men of Athens, is a true saying.

Strange, indeed, would be my conduct, O men of Athens, if I, who, when I was ordered by the generals whom you chose to com-mand me at Potidaea and Amphipolis and Delium, remained where they placed me, like any other man, facing death—if now, when, as I conceive and imagine, God orders me to fulfill the philosopher's mission of searching into myself and other men, I were to desert my post through fear of death, or any other fear; that would indeed be strange, and I might justly be arraigned in court for denying the existence of the gods, if I disobeyed the oracle because I was afraid of death, fancying that I was wise when I was not wise. For the fear of death is indeed the pretence of wisdom, and not real wisdom, being a pretence of knowing the unknown; and no one knows whether death, which men in their fear apprehend to be the greatest evil, may not be the greatest good. Is not this ignorance of a dis-graceful sort, the ignorance which is the conceit that a man knows what he does not know? And in this respect only I believe myself to differ from men in general, and may perhaps claim to be wiser than they are:—that whereas I know but little of the world below, I do not suppose that I know: but I do know that injustice and disobe-dience to a better, whether God or man, is evil and dishonourable, and I will never fear or avoid a possible good rather than a certain evil. And therefore if you let me go now, and are not convinced by Anytus, who said that since I had been prosecuted I must be put to death; (or if not that I ought never to have been prosecuted at all); and that if I escape now, your sons will all be utterly ruined by listening to my words—if you say to me, Socrates, this time we will not mind Anytus, and you shall be let off, but upon one condition,

---

[6] The "*son of Thetis*" refers to the Greek hero Achilles, son of the sea goddess Thetis. *Hector* was a captain and chief hero of the Trojan forces in the Trojan War. *Patroclus,* the beloved friend of Achilles, was killed by Hector in that war. (ED.)

that you are not to enquire and speculate in this way any more, and that if you are caught doing so again you shall die;—if this was the condition on which you let me go, I should reply: Men of Athens, I honour and love you; but I shall obey God rather than you, and while I have life and strength I shall never cease from the practice and teaching of philosophy, exhorting any one whom I meet and saying to him after my manner: You, my friend,—a citizen of the great and mighty and wise city of Athens,—are you not ashamed of heaping up the greatest amount of money and honour and reputation, and caring so little about wisdom and truth and the greatest improvement of the soul, which you never regard or heed at all? And if the person with whom I am arguing, says: Yes, but I do care; then I do not leave him or let him go at once; but I proceed to interrogate and examine and cross-examine him, and if I think that he has no virtue in him, but only says that he has, I reproach him with undervaluing the greater, and overvaluing the less. And I shall repeat the same words to every one whom I meet, young and old, citizen and alien, but especially to the citizens, inasmuch as they are my brethren. For know that this is the command of God; and I believe that no greater good has ever happened in the State than my service to the God. For I do nothing but go about persuading you all, old and young alike, not to take thought for your persons or your properties, but first and chiefly to care about the greatest improvement of the soul. I tell you that virtue is not given by money, but that from virtue comes money and every other good of man, public as well as private. This is my teaching, and if this is the doctrine which corrupts the youth, I am a mischievous person. But if any one says that this is not my teaching, he is speaking an untruth. Wherefore, O men of Athens, I say to you, do as Anytus bids or not as Anytus bids, and either acquit me or not; but whichever you do, understand that I shall never alter my ways, not even if I have to die many times.

Men of Athens, do not interrupt, but hear me; there was an understanding between us that you should hear me to the end: I have something more to say, at which you may be inclined to cry out; but I believe that to hear me will be good for you, and therefore I beg that you will not cry out. I would have you know, that if you kill such an one as I am, you will injure yourselves more than you will injure me. Nothing will injure me, not Meletus nor yet Anytus—they cannot, for a bad man is not permitted to injure a better than himself. I do not deny that Anytus may, perhaps, kill him, or drive him into exile, or deprive him of civil rights; and he may imagine, and others may imagine, that he is inflicting a great injury upon him:

but there I do not agree. For the evil of doing as he is doing—the evil of unjustly taking away the life of another—is greater far.

And now, Athenians, I am not going to argue for my own sake, as you may think, but for yours, that you may not sin against the God by condemning me, who am his gift to you. For if you kill me you will not easily find a successor to me, who, if I may use such a ludicrous figure of speech, am a sort of gadfly, given to the State by God; and the State is a great and noble steed who is tardy in his motions owing to his very size, and requires to be stirred into life. I am that gadfly which God has attached to the State, and all day long and in all places am always fastening upon you, arousing and persuading and reproaching you. You will not easily find another like me, and therefore I would advise you to spare me. I dare say that you may feel out of temper (like a person who is suddenly awakened from sleep), and you think that you might easily strike me dead as Anytus advises, and then you would sleep on for the remainder of your lives, unless God in his care of you sent you another gadfly. When I say that I am given to you by God, the proof of my mission is this:—if I had been like other men, I should not have neglected all my own concerns or patiently seen the neglect of them during all these years, and have been doing yours, coming to you individually like a father or elder brother, exhorting you to regard virtue; such conduct, I say, would be unlike human nature. If I had gained anything, or if my exhortations had been paid, there would have been some sense in my doing so; but now, as you will perceive, not even the impudence of my accusers dares to say that I have ever exacted or sought pay of any one; of that they have no witness. And I have a sufficient witness to the truth of what I say—my poverty.

Now, do you really imagine that I could have survived all these years, if I had led a public life, supposing that like a good man I had always maintained the right and had made justice, as I ought, the first thing? No, indeed, men of Athens, neither I nor any other man. But I have been always the same in all my actions, public as well as private, and never have I yielded any base compliance to those who are slanderously termed my disciples, or to any other. Not that I have any regular disciples. But if any one likes to come and hear me while I am pursuing my mission, whether he be young or old, he is not excluded. Nor do I converse only with those who pay; but any one, whether he be rich or poor, may ask and answer me and listen to my words; and whether he turns out to be a bad man or a good one, neither result can be justly imputed to me; for I never taught or professed to teach him anything. And if any one says that he has ever learned or heard anything from me in private which all the world has not heard, let me tell you that he is lying.

Well, Athenians, this and the like of this is all the defence which I have to offer. Yet a word more. Perhaps there may be some one who is offended at me, when he calls to mind how he himself on a similar, or even a less serious occasion, prayed and entreated the judges with many tears, and how he produced his children in court, which was a moving spectacle, together with a host of relations and friends; whereas I, who am probably in danger of my life, will do none of these things. The contrast may occur to his mind, and he may be set against me, and vote in anger because he is displeased at me on this account. Now, if there be such a person among you,— mind, I do not say that there is,—to him I may fairly reply: My friend, I am a man, and like other men, a creature of flesh and blood, and not "of wood or stone," as Homer[7] says; and I have a family, yes, and sons, O Athenians, three in number, one almost a man, the two others who are still young; and yet I will not bring any of them hither in order to petition you for an acquittal. And why not? Not from any self-assertion or want of respect for you. Whether I am or am not afraid of death is another question, of which I will not now speak. But, having regard to public opinion, I feel that such conduct would be discreditable to myself, and to you, and to the whole State. One who has reached my years, and who has a name for wisdom, ought not to demean himself. Whether this opinion of me be deserved or not, at any rate the world has decided that Socrates is in some way superior to other men. And if those among you who are said to be superior in wisdom and courage, and any other virtue, demean themselves in this way, how shameful is their conduct! I have seen men of reputation, when they have been condemned, behaving in the strangest manner; they seem to fancy that they were going to suffer something dreadful if they died, and that they could be immortal if you only allowed them to live; and I think that such are a dishonour to the State, and that any stranger coming in would have said of them that the most eminent men of Athens, to whom the Athenians themselves give honour and command, are no better than women. And I say that these things ought not to be done by those

---

[7] Homer (9th–8th century B.C.?) was a Greek poet who, according to tradition, wrote the *Iliad* and the *Odyssey*. (ED.)

of us who have a reputation; and if they are done, you ought not to permit them; you ought rather to show that you are far more disposed to condemn the man who gets up a doleful scene and makes the city ridiculous, than him who holds his peace.

But, setting aside the question of public opinion, there seems to be something wrong in asking a favour of a judge, and thus procuring an acquittal, instead of informing and convincing him. For his duty is, not to make a present of justice, but to give judgment; and he has sworn that he will judge according to the laws, and not according to his own good pleasure; and we ought not to encourage you, nor should you allow yourselves to be encouraged, in this habit of perjury—there can be no piety in that. Do not then require me to do what I consider dishonourable and impious and wrong, especially now, when I am being tried for impiety on the indictment of Meletus. For if, O men of Athens, by force of persuasion and entreaty I could overpower your oaths, then I should be teaching you to believe that there are no gods, and in defending should simply convict myself of the charge of not believing in them. But that it is not so—far otherwise. For I do believe that there are gods, and in a sense higher than that in which any of my accusers believe in them. And to you and to God I commit my cause, to be determined by you as is best for you and me.

[*The vote is taken and Socrates is convicted. Socrates is condemned to death.*]

Not much time will be gained, O Athenians, in return for the evil name which you will get from the detractors of the city, who will say that you killed Socrates, a wise man; for they will call me wise, even though I am not wise, when they want to reproach you. If you had waited a little while, your desire would have been fulfilled in the course of nature. For I am far advanced in years, as you may perceive, and not far from death. I am speaking now not to all of you, but only to those who have condemned me to death. And I have another thing to say to them: You think that I was convicted because I had no words of the sort which would have procured my acquittal—I mean, if I had thought fit to leave nothing undone or unsaid. Not so; the deficiency which led to my conviction was not of words—certainly not. But I had not the boldness or impudence or inclination to address you as you would have liked me to do, weeping and wailing and lamenting, and saying and doing many things which you have been accustomed to hear from others, and which, as I maintain, are unworthy of me. I thought at the time that I ought not to do anything common or mean when in danger: nor do I now repent of the style of my defence; I would rather die having spoken after my manner, than speak in your manner and live. For neither in war nor yet at law ought I or any man to use every way of escaping death. Often in battle there can be no doubt that if a man will throw away his arms, and fall on his knees before his pursuers, he may escape death; and in other dangers there are other ways of escaping death; if a man is willing to say and do anything. The difficulty, my friends, is not to avoid death, but to avoid unrighteousness; for that runs faster than death. I am old and move slowly, and the slower runner has overtaken me, and my accusers are keen and quick, and the faster runner, who is unrighteousness, has overtaken them. And now I depart hence condemned by you to suffer the penalty of death,—they too go their ways condemned by the truth to suffer the penalty of villainy and wrong; and I must abide by my award—let them abide by theirs. I suppose that these things may be regarded as fated,—and I think that they are well.

And now, O men who have condemned me, I would fain prophesy to you; for I am about to die, and in the hour of death men are gifted with prophetic power. And I prophesy to you who are my murderers, that immediately after my departure punishment far heavier than you have inflicted on me will surely await you. Me you have killed because you wanted to escape the accuser, and not to give an account of your lives. But that will not be as you suppose: far otherwise. For I say that there will be more accusers of you than there are now; accusers whom hitherto I have restrained: and as they are younger they will be more inconsiderate with you, and you will be more offended at them. If you think that by killing men you can prevent some one from censuring your evil lives, you are mistaken; that is not a way of escape which is either possible or honourable; the easiest and the noblest way is not to be disabling others, but to be improving yourselves. This is the prophecy which I utter before my departure to the judges who have condemned me.

Friends, who would have acquitted me, I would like also to talk with you about the thing which has come to pass, while the magistrates are busy, and before I go to the place at which I must die. Stay then a little, for we may as well talk with one another while there is time. You are my friends, and I should like to show you the meaning of this event which has happened to me. O my judges—for you I may truly call judges—I should like to tell you of a wonderful circumstance. Hitherto the divine faculty of which the internal oracle is the source has constantly been in the habit of opposing me even about trifles, if I was going to make a slip or error in any matter; and now as you see there has come upon me that which may be thought, and is generally believed to be, the last and worst evil. But the oracle made no sign of opposition, either when I was leaving my house in the morning, or when I was on my way to the court, or while I was speaking, at anything which I was going to say; and yet I have often been stopped in the middle of a speech, but now in nothing I either said or did touching the matter in hand has the oracle opposed me. What do I take to be the explanation of this silence? I will tell you. It is an intimation that what has happened to me is a good, and that those of us who think that death is an evil are in error. For the customary sign would surely have opposed me had I been going to evil and not to good.

Let us reflect in another way, and we shall see that there is great reason to hope that death is a good; for one of two things—either death is a state of nothingness and utter unconsciousness, or, as men say, there is a change and migration of the soul from this world to another. Now, if you suppose that there is no consciousness, but a sleep like the sleep of him who is undisturbed even by dreams, death will be an unspeakable gain. For if a person were to select the night in which his sleep was undisturbed even by dreams, and were to compare with this the other days and nights of his life, and then were to tell us how many days and nights he had passed in the course of his life better and more pleasantly than this one, I think that any man, I will not say a private man, but even the great king will not find many such days or nights, when compared with the others. Now, if death be of such a nature, I say that to die is gain; for eternity is then only a single night. But if death is the journey to another place, and there, as men say, all the dead abide, what good, O my friends and judges, can be greater than this? If, indeed, when the pilgrim arrives in the world below, he is delivered from the professors of justice in this world, and finds the true judges who are said to give judgment there, Minos and Rhadamanthus and Aeacus and Triptolemus,[8] and other sons of God who were righteous in their own life, that pilgrimage will be worth making. What would not a man give if he might converse with Orpheus and Musaeus and Hesiod

---

[8] Heroes of Greek mythology. *Minos,* his brother *Rhadamanthus,* and *Aeacus* were the judges of Hades, the Greek underworld. *Triptolemus* is credited with providing grain and teaching humanity to plow. (ED.)

and Homer?[9] Nay, if this be true, let me die again and again. I myself, too, shall have a wonderful interest in there meeting and conversing with Palamedes, and Ajax the son of Telamon,[10] and any other ancient hero who has suffered death through an unjust judgment; and there will be no small pleasure, as I think, in comparing my own sufferings with theirs. Above all, I shall then be able to continue my search into true and false knowledge; as in this world, so also in the next; and I shall find out who is wise, and who pretends to be wise, and is not. What would not a man give, O judges, to be able to examine the leader of the great Trojan expedition; or Odysseus or Sisyphus,[11] or numberless others, men and women too! What infinite delight would there be in conversing with them and asking them questions! In another world they do not put a man to death for asking questions; assuredly not. For besides being happier than we are, they will be immortal, if what is said is true.

Wherefore, O judges, be of good cheer about death, and know of a certainty, that no evil can happen to a good man, either in life or after death. He and his are not neglected by the gods; nor has my own approaching end happened by mere chance. But I see clearly that the time had arrived when it was better for me to die and be released from trouble; wherefore the oracle gave no sign. For which reason, also, I am not angry with my condemners, or with my accusers; they have done me no harm, although they did not mean to do me any good; and for this I may gently blame them.

Still, I have a favour to ask of them. When my sons are grown up, I would ask you, O my friends, to punish them; and I would have you trouble them, as I have troubled you, if they seem to care about riches, or anything, more than about virtue; or if they pretend to be something when they are really nothing,—then reprove them, as I have reproved you, for not caring about that for which they ought to care, and thinking that they are something when they are

[9] In Greek mythology, *Orpheus* was a musician from Thrace who played his lyre so sweetly that the birds and animals followed him. *Musaeus, Hesiod,* and *Homer* were ancient Greek poets. (ED.)

[10] *Palamedes* and *Ajax* were heroes of the Trojan War. *Telamon* sailed on the Argo in search of the Golden Fleece. (ED.)

[11] *Odysseus* is the hero of Homer's *Odyssey. Sisyphus,* a figure in Greek legend, was sentenced after his death to roll a large rock up to the top of a hill repeatedly, only to have it roll back down again. (ED.)

really nothing. And if you do this, both I and my sons will have received justice at your hands.

The hour of departure has arrived, and we go our ways—I to die, and you to live. Which is better God only knows.

I. F. STONE

Socrates and His Accusers: Their Basic Differences

I. F. Stone (1907–1989) was a reporter and editorial writer for several periodicals including *The Nation* and the *New York Post*. He published *I.F. Stone's Weekly* from 1953 to 1968 and *I.F. Stone's Bi-Weekly* from 1969 to 1971. His books, which focus on philosophy, politics, and government, include *Underground to Palestine* (1946), *The Haunted Fifties* (1963), *The Hidden History of the Korean War* (1969), *Polemics and Prophecies* (1970), and *The Trial of Socrates* (1988), from which the following selection is taken.

To judge only by Plato, one might conclude that Socrates got into trouble with his fellow citizens by exhorting them to virtue, never an endearing occupation. But if we turn away from the *Apology* for a wider view, we will see that the conflict between Socrates and his native city began because he differed so profoundly from most of his fellow Athenians and, indeed, from the ancient Greeks generally, on three basic philosophical questions. These differences were not mere distant abstractions, of no concern to ordinary mortals, but challenged the very foundations of the self-government they enjoyed.

The first and most fundamental disagreement was on the nature of the human community. Was it, as Greeks would have said, a *polis*—a free city? Or was it, as Socrates so often said, a herd?

A good place to start is with one of the most famous observations of antiquity—Aristotle's remark, at the very beginning of his treatise on politics, that man is a political animal.

The English translation is unfortunate. The English words *political animal* are, it is true, an exact and literal rendering of the Greek term, *zoon politikon*. But in English this conjures up the picture of a ward heeler who spends his life in the seedy chores of a modern political machine.

The Greek word *polis,* or city, and its various derivatives carried very different connotations. To be a *polites,* a citizen of a *polis,* was a badge of honor. It implied that the citizen had a right to debate, and a right to vote on, the decisions that affected his life and that of his city.

A *polis* meant something more to the ancient Greeks than "city" does to us in a modern nation-state. It did not mean merely to live in an urban rather than a rural area. The *polis* was an independent and sovereign "state" in the full modern sense. The *polis* made law within its borders, and—outside them—it made war or peace as it saw fit.

But when Aristotle began his *Politics* with the proposition that man was a "political animal," he was not concerned with the *polis* in its outward manifestations as a sovereign body but in the inner relations that made the city possible. Aristotle's point was that man alone had the qualities that made a communal existence possible, and for him as for most Greeks the highest form of such *koinonia*— literally "community"—was the *polis.* It was made possible, Aristotle said, because of all the animals man alone had the *logos.*[1] The *logos* was more than the power of speech. It also denoted reason and morality.

There are, as Aristotle observed, other social or gregarious forms of life. Certain insects lead a communal existence in hives and certain wild animals live together in herds. But it is man's "special distinction from the other animals that he alone has perception of good and bad and of the just and the unjust." It is this intrinsic sense of justice that gives man his social instinct, his "impulse" as Aristotle calls it, to a social life, and makes man "a political animal in a greater measure than any bee or any gregarious animal."[2]

When Aristotle said that the *polis* exists "by nature," he meant that it springs from the nature of man, from an intrinsic sense of justice.

For the Greeks, *polis* had a special characteristic that distinguished it from other forms of human community. It was, as Aristotle says, "an association of free men," as distinguished from such other

[1] Aristotle, *Politics,* 1.1.10.

[2] Ibid., 2.1.9–10.

and earlier forms of association as the family, which was ruled by its patriarch, or monarchy, or the relation of master and slave. The *polis* governed itself. The ruled were the rulers. As Aristotle described it, the citizen "takes turns to govern and be governed"[3] Whether in oligarchies, where citizenship was restricted, or in democracies like Athens, where all freeborn males were citizens, major offices were filled by election but many others were filled by lot to give all citizens an equal chance to participate in their government. Every citizen had the right to vote and speak in the assembly where the laws were enacted, and to sit in the jury courts where those laws were applied and interpreted. These were the basic characteristics of Greek *politics*—the administration of its cities—long before Aristotle described them in the fourth century B.C. They governed the life of Athens in the lifetime of Socrates, and it was with these premises that Socrates and his disciples disagreed.

The difference was fundamental. Politics in Athens and the Greek city-states generally, as in Rome under the Republic, was a kind of two-party class struggle. Both sides agreed that the city should be governed by its citizens. They divided over how wide that citizenship should be. Was citizenship to be restricted, as in the oligarchies, or widespread, as in the democracies? Was the city to be ruled by the few or the many, which also meant the rich or the poor? But for both sides, politics—the very life of the city—lay in self-government, and to oppose self-government was to be not just antidemocratic but anti*political*. This is how Socrates looked to most of his contemporaries.

Socrates was neither an oligarch nor a democrat. He stood apart from either side. His ideal, as we see it variously expressed in both Xenophon[4] and Plato and reflected in what we know of the other Socratics, was rule neither by the few nor the many but by—as he put it in Xenophon's *Memorabilia*—"the one who knows."[5] This must have looked to his contemporaries as a reversion to kingship in its most absolute form. And to advocate kingship was to set oneself

---

[3] Ibid., 2.1.2.

[4] Xenophon (431–350 B.C.) was a Greek historian and student of Socrates. His *Memorabilia* is an account of Socrates' life and teachings. (ED.)

[5] Xenophon, 7 vols. (Loeb Classical Library, 1918–1925), *Memorabilia*, 3.8.10–11 (4:229).

wholly in opposition to the *polis*. In fifth- and fourth-century Athens, advocacy of kingship must have looked as quirky as a monarchist political party would in twentieth-century America—too quaint and eccentric even to be alarming.

Neither the few nor the many wanted to revive kingship, wanted to give up control over the government of their own lives. They differed bitterly—and fought miniature civil wars—over who should be counted in the citizenry. But they agreed that the citizens should rule their city.

The controversy is not so comfortably ancient as it may at first seem. The twentieth century has seen—and still sees—new forms of one-man rule in the totalitarianisms of right and left. Indeed, the germ of totalitarianism is already evident in the way Socrates formulated his theory of government in the *Memorabilia,* the earliest and fullest expression of his views.

Socrates would have argued that he was proposing not kingship in its ancient form but a new kind of one-man rule, the basis of an ideal society. In the *Memorabilia,* Socrates set himself up as an opponent of all forms of existing government. He itemized—and rejected—them one by one.

"Kings and rulers," he said, "are not those who hold the sceptre," the symbol of their high office, which they often claimed to have received from Zeus himself. That took care of monarchy in its conventional form. Nor are they, he continued, "those who are chosen by the multitude." That took care of democracy. "Nor those on whom the lot falls"—that rejected public officials chosen by lot. "[N]or those who owe their power to force or deception"—that took care of "tyrants." The true or ideal "kings and rulers" are "those who know how to rule."

An Athenian democrat would have said that it is just such men who are sought out by popular vote and—to guard against mistaken judgment and abuse of authority—are limited in their powers and terms of office. But Socrates did not envisage any such safeguarding limits on the rulers. His basic premise—according to Xenophon— was "that it is the business of the ruler to give orders and of the ruled to obey." This must have looked like the old kingship refurbished and made absolute. But Socrates would have said that he was advocating a new form of rule—rule, as we would say, by experts. In Xenophon, Socrates defended his advocacy of absolute rule with analogies also familiar in the Platonic dialogues. Socrates "went on to show," Xenophon recalls, "that on a ship the one who knows, rules, and the owner [of the ship] and all the others [on board] obey the one who knows." Similarly, Socrates argued, "in farming the landowners, in illness the patients" and "in training" the athletes send for experts, "those who know," that "they may obey them and do the right thing." He even added a little joke, in that era of male supremacy, saying that "in spinning wool . . . the women govern the men because they know how to do it and men do not."[6]

These are all imperfect analogies, from which fallacious conclusions are drawn. A Greek democrat could argue that the shipowner, the patient, the landowner, and the athlete were free to pick their "experts," and if these experts proved unsatisfactory they could be discharged and others hired in their place. This was what a free city did in picking—and replacing—its officials. Otherwise, behind the façade of "the one who knows" there lurked the face of tyranny. The problem was not only to find the right expert but to have the means to get rid of him if he turned out badly.

To understand the first grapplings with his problem in the Greek city-states—the first beginnings of what we call political science—we are largely dependent on the pages of Plato and Aristotle. To evaluate their contribution one must begin with an essential difference between them.

Plato was a theorist, Aristotle a scientific observer. Aristotle prized practical over theoretical knowledge in dealing with human affairs. Aristotle had a strong bias in favor of experience and common sense. In contrast, Plato in a famous passage of the *Republic* proposed to limit the study of "the dialectic"—and thus the future rulers of his utopia—to those who could "let go of the eyes and the other senses and rise to the contemplation of *to on*"—"pure being" or "being itself."[7] This would no doubt be a contemplative joy to the mystic, but it hardly offers guidance to the statesman, forced to deal with tangled affairs and obdurate human nature.

Aristotle takes issue with Plato at the very beginning of his own masterwork on philosophy, the *Metaphysics*. It starts off by saying, "All men naturally desire knowledge. An indication of this is our esteem for the senses." Without them, and especially sight, Aristotle asks, how can we know and act? In the same way, at the beginning of the *Politics* Aristotle makes it clear that he is taking issue with the political views of Plato and Socrates. There, as in the *Metaphysics,*

[6] Ibid.

[7] Plato, *Republic,* 7.537D7ff.

he does not mention them by name. But the reference is unmistakable. "Those then who think," Aristotle writes, "that the nature of the statesman, the royal ruler, the head of an estate and the master of a family are the same, are mistaken."[8] The *polis* commanded the loyalty of free men because it embodied the consent of the governed. To the Greek, all this would have seemed indisputable.

The *politikos*, the political leader or statesman in a *polis,* was an elected official, subject to a limited term—usually a year—of office, answerable in a popular assembly and the popular jurycourts for the conduct of his office, and invested even in time of war with far less than absolute power. The citizens he led were not his inferiors in legal status or rank but (as Aristotle observed in his *Politics*) "equal and like."[9] They shared a common humanity.

Here lay the first and most fundamental of the conflicts between Socrates and Athens.

The various followers of Socrates disagreed, often as violently as modern scholars, as to just what Socrates *had* taught them, even—and especially—on the nature of virtue. But on one matter they agreed: They all rejected the *polis.* They all saw the human community not as a self-governing body of citizens with equal rights but as a herd that required a shepherd or king. They all treated democracy with condescension or contempt.

Xenophon's ideal, as set forth in his own utopia, the *Cyropaedia,* or *Education of Cyrus,* was monarchy under law. This was the Persian model as Xenophon imagined its establishment by Cyrus the Great, founder of the Persian empire.

Antisthenes, the oldest disciple of Socrates, considered monarchy the ideal form of government and agreed with Xenophon that Cyrus was the ideal monarch.[10] These views were presumably expressed in his lost dialogue, the *Statesman,* mentioned by Athenaeus.[11]

Antisthenes was the founder of Cynicism, and he was especially cynical about democracy. Two stories gibing at it are attributed to

[8] Aristotle, *Politics* (Loeb Classical Library, 1932), 1.2.1 (3).

[9] Ibid., 3.9.9.

[10] Kurt von Fritz in the *Oxford Classical Dictionary,* edited by H. G. L. Hammond and H. H. Scullard, 2nd ed. (Oxford: Clarendon Press, 1970), on Antisthenes.

[11] Athenaeus, 5.221d. [Athenaeus (200 A.D.) was a Greek grammarian whose *The Gastronomers* reports on fictional conversations among Greek notables, providing numerous quotations from other works that have been lost. (ED.)]

Antisthenes, one by Diogenes Laertius,[12] the other by Aristotle. In the first, Antisthenes is supposed to have asked the Athenians why they did not vote that asses were horses since (as he said) they sometimes elected generals who had as little resemblance to real commanders as an ass did to a horse![13] This satirical comparison may have originated with Socrates himself, since in Plato's *Phaedrus,* Socrates speaks of a popular orator palming off an ass as a horse on an ignorant city.[14]

Aristotle in his *Politics* attributed to Antisthenes a sardonic fable about the lions and the hares. "When the hares made speeches in the assembly and demanded that all should have equality," Antisthenes related, "the lions replied, 'Where are your claws and teeth?' "[15] This was the cynical reply to the democratic demand for egalitarianism.

Plato sketched several utopias. All but one of them, the *Laws,* was based on one form or another of monarchy. In the *Politicus,* or *Statesman,* as we have seen, the ideal rule was absolute monarchy. In the *Republic,* it was absolute rule by one or several "philosopher kings." In the *Timaeus* and its sequel, the *Critias,* Plato pictured the Golden Age of man as a time when the gods tended their human herds as men later tended their cattle.

Even in the "moderate" utopia of Plato's old age, the *Laws,* the narrowly restricted citizen body would have operated under the watchful eye of a Nocturnal Council, an inquisitorial body empowered to root out dissent, the archetype of our late but unlamented House Un-American Activities Committee. Travel abroad was severely restricted to keep the community from "spiritual pollution"— as the Chinese Communists now say—by foreign ideas. These Platonic innovations in thought-control went beyond any kingship the Greeks had ever known. They were in fact the first sketches of what we now call totalitarian societies.

In Plato's *Gorgias,* Socrates makes clear that no form of the *polis* met with his approval. There the two most famous conservative

---

[12] Diogenes Laertius was a Greek author of the third century A.D. noted for his history of Greek philosophy, *Lives, Teachings, Sayings of Famous Philosophers.* (ED.)

[13] Diogenes Laertius, *Lives of Eminent Philosophers,* 2 vols. (Loeb Classical Library, 1925), 6.8 (2:9).

[14] Plato, *Phaedrus,* 260C.

[15] *Politics,* 3.7.2 (Loeb, 241–243 and note, 240).

statesmen of Athens, Cimon and Miltiades, are treated with the same impartial scorn as the two most famous democratic leaders, Themistocles and Pericles. Socrates said of Pericles, who had recently died, that he must be judged a failure as a statesman because he had left the human herd in his care "wilder than when he took them in hand. . . . [W]e know of nobody," Socrates concludes, "who has shown himself a good statesman in this city of ours."[16] "I think," Plato has him say, "I am one of few, not to say the only one, in Athens who attempts the true art of statesmanship."[17] It was not his most modest moment.

Socrates laid it down as his basic principle of government in the *Memorabilia* "that it is the business of the ruler to give orders and of the ruled to obey." Not the consent of the governed but their submission was required. This was of course an authoritarian principle most Greeks, and particularly the Athenians, rejected.

Fundamental to all the Greek city-states was the equality of the citizenry, whether restricted to the few or the many. The Socratic premise was a basic inequality; nobody was a citizen, all were subjects. A gulf separated the ruler from the ruled.

In one respect the Socrates of Xenophon differs from the Socrates of Plato. In Xenophon's *Memorabilia* Socrates advocates kingship within the limits of law, but in Plato's *Republic* Socrates imposes no such restriction upon the philosopher kings. This may reflect the differences between the two disciples. Absolutism is the hallmark of the Platonic utopias, whereas Xenophon, in the *Education of Cyrus,* puts forward as his ideal a kingship exercised within the bounds of law. Xenophon and Plato may have "heard" Socrates differently on the subject in accordance with their own preconceptions, as disciples so often do.

At one point in Xenophon's *Memorabilia* Socrates even speaks not only of law but of popular consent as necessary ingredients of a true monarchy. Xenophon wrote that Socrates distinguished between "kingship and despotism" by saying that the "government of men with their consent and in accordance with the laws of the state was kingship; while government of unwilling subjects and not controlled

---

[16] Plato, 8 vols. (Loeb Classical Library, 1925–1931), *Gorgias* 516C, 517A (5:497–499).

[17] Ibid., 521D (Loeb 5:515).

by laws, but imposed by the will of the ruler, was despotism."[18] But what if a lawful king began to act lawlessly? Did his subjects then have a right to overthrow him, as a shipowner might discharge a pilot who had become alcoholic or a patient change a physician who had abused his trust? Socrates is forced to confront the problem of what to do about a bad ruler or one who turns bad. After he has just laid down the proposition that "it is the business of the ruler to give orders and of the ruled to obey," two questions are put to him. What if the ruler disregards good advice? What if he kills a loyal subject, who dared to give him such advice?

Socrates is evasive and answers with a question of his own: "How can he [the ruler] refuse when a penalty waits on disregard of good counsel? All disregard of good counsel is bound surely to result in error, and his error will not go unpunished."

To the second question, about killing a loyal subject, Socrates offers a similar reply. "Do you think," he asks, "that he who kills the best of his allies suffers no loss, or that his loss is trifling? Do you think that this conduct brings him safety, or rather swift destruction?"[19]

These simplistic replies would have satisfied few of his contemporaries. What Socrates did not say is more impressive than what he did say. Nowhere does he affirm the right of citizens to get rid of a ruler who rejects good advice and kills those who offer it. He asks them to rely, like a free-market theorist, on the supposedly inevitable consequences of bad judgment and misconduct. The "destruction" Socrates predicts for the bad ruler is no consolation to the ruled. The city and the citizens may be destroyed along with the stubborn and willful ruler. Or he may decamp, like a Marcos or a Duvalier, with the wealth he stole from his subjects. Tyrants all too often get away with their plunder.

Socrates thinks like a loyal monarchist. His basic view is expressed at another point in the *Memorabilia,* when he asks why in Homer King Agamemnon is called "shepherd of the people"? Answering his own question, he replies: "Because a shepherd must see that his sheep are safe and fed."[20]

The good shepherd does indeed see that his flock is safe and fed,

---

[18] *Memorabilia,* 4.6.12 (Loeb 4:343–345).

[19] Ibid., 3.9.11–13 (Loeb 4:229–231).

[20] Ibid., 3.2.1.

and to that degree there is a common interest uniting them. But the ultimate purpose of the shepherd is to shear the sheep for their wool and eventually to sell them for mutton. The herd is destined for the meat market, and the sheep are not consulted by the shepherd when he decides their time has come. The lesson the Greeks drew from the shepherd analogy is that the sheep cannot trust their shepherd, nor a community entrust itself to one man's absolute will, however benevolent he claims his purpose to be. They preferred to become a *polis* rather than be treated as a herd.

By the time of Socrates, kingship had disappeared from the Greek city-states, and lived on only among the barbarians or in semibarbarous areas like Macedonia. Aristotle, surveying the Greek city-states two generations after the death of Socrates, could say, "There are now no royalties. Monarchies, where they exist, are tyrannies."[21]

In Sparta, which the Socratics admired, the one Hellenic city-state in which there were still hereditary kings, their authority had dwindled to no more than that of military commanders in time of war. Even then they had to operate under the watchful eye of annually elected "ephors" or overseers, Sparta's highest executive officers. And there were two kings, from two different royal families; division of authority and rivalry kept them in check.

Elsewhere the name of *basileus,* or king, survived as an anachronistic relic. Certain religious rites were still administered by priests chosen from ancient royal families. In Athens there were nine annually elected *archons,* or magistrates. The *archon basileus,* or king magistrate, also exercised quasi-religious functions. He was chosen from certain priestly families who claimed royal ancestry. But his authority was in no way kingly. He was not the head of the state even for ceremonial purposes. Thus the last vestige of kingship in the Athens of Socrates figures in his trial. We meet Socrates in Plato's *Euthyphro* on the portico of the *archon basileus.* The old philosopher has come there for the preliminary examination before trial because one charge against him was impiety, and the king magistrate was the *archon* who presided over such cases.

Even when Athenian democracy was twice overthrown in the lifetime of Socrates, the antidemocrats tried to substitute not kingship but an oligarchy much like the patrician Senate in Republican Rome.

In Rome, as in the Greek city-states, kingship was overthrown

---

[21] *Politics,* 5.9.1.

by the aristocracy many generations before Socrates. The very word
rex, or king, was in such disrepute in Rome that when the Republic
was finally overthrown, the new monarchs did not call themselves
kings but caesars, from the name of the aristocrat who had toppled
the oligarchic Republic. Socrates and his followers were totally out
of step with their time in advocating kingship of any kind.

JOHN STUART MILL

On Liberty

John Stuart Mill (1806–1873) was an English philosopher and
economist. His major publications are *A System of Logic* (1843),
Utilitarianism (1863), *The Subjection of Women,* (1869), which expresses his interest in women's rights, and *On Liberty* (1859),
which is a classic discussion of ethics and politics.

OF THE LIBERTY OF THOUGHT AND DISCUSSION

The time, it is to be hoped, is gone by, when any defence
would be necessary of the "liberty of the press" as one of the securities
against corrupt or tyrannical government. No argument, we may
suppose, can now be needed, against permitting a legislature or an
executive, not identified in interest with the people, to prescribe
opinions to them, and determine what doctrines or what arguments
they shall be allowed to hear. This aspect of the question, besides,
has been so often and so triumphantly enforced by preceding writers,
that it needs not be specially insisted on in this place. Though the
law of England, on the subject of the press, is as servile to this day
as it was in the time of the Tudors,[1] there is little danger of its being
actually put in force against political discussion, except during some
temporary panic, when fear of insurrection drives ministers and
judges from their propriety; and, speaking generally, it is not, in
constitutional countries, to be apprehended, that the government,

---

[1] English royal dynasty that ruled from 1485 to 1603; it included Henry VII, Henry
VIII, Edward VI, Mary I, and Elizabeth I. (ED.)

whether completely responsible to the people or not, will often attempt to control the expression of opinion, except when in doing so it makes itself the organ of the general intolerance of the public. Let us suppose, therefore, that the government is entirely at one with the people, and never thinks of exerting any power of coercion unless in agreement with what it conceives to be their voice. But I deny the right of the people to exercise such coercion, either by themselves or by their government. The power itself is illegitimate. The best government has no more title to it than the worst. It is as noxious, or more noxious, when exerted in accordance with public opinion, than when in opposition to it. If all mankind minus one were of one opinion, and only one person were of the contrary opinion, mankind would be no more justified in silencing that one person, than he, if he had the power, would be justified in silencing mankind. Were an opinion a personal possession of no value except to the owner; if to be obstructed in the enjoyment of it were simply a private injury, it would make some difference whether the injury was inflicted only on a few persons or on many. But the peculiar evil of silencing the expression of an opinion is, that it is robbing the human race; posterity as well as the existing generation; those who dissent from the opinion, still more than those who hold it. If the opinion is right, they are deprived of the opportunity of exchanging error for truth: if wrong, they lose, what is almost as great a benefit, the clearer perception and livelier impression of truth, produced by its collision with error. . . .

We have now recognised the necessity to the mental well-being of mankind (on which all their other well-being depends) of freedom of opinion, and freedom of the expression of opinion, on four distinct grounds; which we will now briefly recapitulate.

First, if any opinion is compelled to silence, that opinion may, for aught we can certainly know, be true. To deny this is to assume our own infallibility.

Secondly, though the silenced opinion be an error, it may, and very commonly does, contain a portion of truth; and since the general or prevailing opinion on any subject is rarely or never the whole truth, it is only by the collision of adverse opinions that the remainder of the truth has any chance of being supplied.

Thirdly, even if the received opinion be not only true, but the whole truth; unless it is suffered to be, and actually is, vigorously and earnestly contested, it will, by most of those who receive it, be held in the manner of a prejudice, with little comprehension or feeling of its rational grounds. And not only this, but, fourthly, the meaning of the doctrine itself will be in danger of being lost, or enfeebled, and deprived of its vital effect on the character and conduct; the dogma becoming a mere formal profession, inefficacious for good, but cumbering the ground, and preventing the growth of any real and heartfelt conviction, from reason or personal experience.

Before quitting the subject of freedom of opinion, it is fit to take some notice of those who say that the free expression of all opinions should be permitted, on condition that the manner be temperate, and do not pass the bounds of fair discussion. Much might be said on the impossibility of fixing where these supposed bounds are to be placed; for if the test be offence to those whose opinions are attacked, I think experience testifies that this offence is given whenever the attack is telling and powerful, and that every opponent who pushed them hard, and whom they find it difficult to answer, appears to them, if he shows any strong feeling on the subject, an intemperate opponent. But this, though an important consideration in a practical point of view, merges in a more fundamental objection. Undoubtedly the manner of asserting an opinion, even though it be a true one, may be very objectionable, and may justly incur severe censure. But the principal offences of the kind are such as it is mostly impossible, unless by accidental self-betrayal, to bring home to conviction. The gravest of them is, to argue sophistically, to suppress facts or arguments, to misstate the elements of the case, or misrepresent the opposite opinion. But all this, even to the most aggravated degree, is so continually done in perfect good faith, by persons who are not considered, and in many other respects may not deserve to be considered, ignorant or incompetent, that it is rarely possible, on adequate grounds, conscientiously to stamp the misrepresentation as morally culpable; and still less could law presume to interfere with this kind of controversial misconduct. With regard to what is commonly meant by intemperate discussion, namely invective, sarcasm, personality, and the like, the denunciation of these weapons would deserve more sympathy if it were ever proposed to interdict them equally to both sides; but it is only desired to restrain the employment of them against the prevailing opinion: against the unprevailing they may not only be used without general disapproval, but will be likely to obtain for him who uses them the praise of honest zeal and righteous indignation. Yet whatever mischief arises from their use is greatest when they are employed against the comparatively defenceless; and whatever unfair advantage can be derived by any opinion from this mode of asserting it, accrues almost exclusively to receivedopinions. The worst offence of this kind which can be committed by a polemic is to stigmatise those who hold the contrary opinion as bad and immoral men. To calumny of this sort, those who hold any unpopular opinion are peculiarly exposed, because they are in general few and uninfluential, and nobody but themselves feels much interested in seeing justice done them; but this weapon is, from the nature of the case, denied to those who attack a prevailing opinion: they can neither use it with safety to themselves, nor, if they could, would it do anything but recoil on their own cause. In general, opinions contrary to those commonly received can only obtain a hearing by studied moderation of language, and the most cautious avoidance of unnecessary offence, from which they hardly ever deviate even in a slight degree, without losing ground: while unmeasured vituperation employed on the side of the prevailing opinion really does deter people from professing contrary opinions, and from listening to those who profess them. For the interest, therefore, of truth and justice, it is far more important to restrain this employment of vituperative language than the other; and, for example, if it were necessary to choose, there would be much more need to discourage offensive attacks on infidelity than on religion. It is, however, obvious that law and authority have no business with restraining either, while opinion ought, in every instance, to determine its verdict by the circumstances of the individual case; condemning every one, on whichever side of the argument he places himself, in whose mode of advocacy either want of candour, or malignity, bigotry, or intolerance of feeling manifest themselves; but not inferring these vices from the side which a person takes, though it be the contrary side of the question to our own; and giving merited honour to every one, whatever opinion he may hold, who has calmness to see and honesty to state what his opponents and their opinions really are, exaggerating nothing to their discredit, keeping nothing back which tells, or can be supposed to tell, in their favour. This is the real morality of public discussion: and if often violated, I am happy to think that there are many controversialists who to a great extent observe it, and a still greater number who conscientiously strive towards it.

OF THE LIMITS TO THE AUTHORITY OF SOCIETY OVER THE INDIVIDUAL

What, then, is the rightful limit to the sovereignty of the individual over himself? Where does the authority of society begin? How much of human life should be assigned to individuality, and how much to society?

Each will receive its proper share, if each has that which more particularly concerns it. To individuality should belong the part of life in which it is chiefly the individual that is interested; to society, the part which chiefly interests society.

Though society is not founded on a contract, and though no good purpose is answered by inventing a contract in order to deduce social obligations from it, every one who receives the protection of society owes a return for the benefit, and the fact of living in society renders it indispensable that each should be bound to observe a certain line of conduct towards the rest. This conduct consists, first, in not injuring the interests of one another; or rather certain interests, which, either by express legal provision, or by tacit understanding, ought to be considered as rights; and secondly, in each person's bearing his share (to be fixed on some equitable principle) of the labours and sacrifices incurred for defending the society or its members from injury and molestation. These conditions society is justified in enforcing, at all costs to those who endeavour to withhold fulfilment. Nor is this all that society may do. The acts of an individual may be hurtful to others, or wanting in due consideration for their welfare, without going to the length of violating any of their constitutional rights. The offender may then be justly punished by opinion, though not by law. As soon as any part of a person's conduct affects prejudicially the interests of others, society has jurisdiction over it, and the question whether the general welfare will or will not be promoted by interfering with it, becomes open to discussion. But there is no room for entertaining any such question when a person's conduct affects the interests of no persons besides himself, or needs not affect them unless they like (all the persons concerned being of full age, and the ordinary amount of understanding). In all such cases, there should be perfect freedom, legal and social, to do the action and stand the consequences.

It would be a great misunderstanding of this doctrine to suppose that it is one of selfish indifference, which pretends that human beings have no business with each other's conduct in life, and that they should not concern themselves about the well-doing or well-being of one another, unless their own interest is involved. Instead of any diminution, there is need of a great increase of disinterested exertion to promote the good of others. But disinterested benevolence can find other instruments to persuade people to their good than whips and scourges, either of the literal or the metaphorical sort. I am the last person to undervalue the self-regarding virtues; they are only second in importance, if even second, to the social. It is equally the business of education to cultivate both. But even education works by conviction and persuasion as well as by compulsion, and it is by the former only that, when the period of education is passed, the self-regarding virtues should be inculcated. Human beings owe to each other help to distinguish the better from the worse, and encouragement to choose the former and avoid the latter. They should be forever stimulating each other to increased exercise of their higher faculties, and increased direction of their feelings and aims towards wise instead of foolish, elevating instead of degrading, objects and contemplations. But neither one person, nor any number of persons, is warranted in saying to another human creature of ripe years, that he shall not do with his life for his own benefit what he chooses to do with it. He is the person most interested in his own well-being: the interest which any other person, except in cases of strong personal attachment, can have in it, is trifling, compared with that which he himself has; the interest which society has in him individually (except as to his conduct to others) is fractional, and altogether indirect; while with respect to his own feelings and circumstances, the most ordinary man or woman has means of knowledge immeasurably surpassing those that can be possessed by any one else. The interference of society to overrule his judgment and purposes in what only regards himself must be grounded on general presumptions; which may be altogether wrong, and even if right, are as likely as not to be misapplied to individual cases, by persons no better acquainted with the circumstances of such cases than those are who look at them merely from without. In this department, therefore, of human affairs, Individuality has its proper field of action. In the conduct of human beings towards one another it is necessary that general rules should for the most part be observed, in order that people may know what they have to expect: but in each person's own concerns his individual spontaneity is entitled to free exercise. Considerations to aid his judgment, exhortations to strengthen his will, may be offered to him, even obtruded on him, by others: but he himself is the final judge. All errors which he is likely to commit against advice and warning are far outweighed by the evil of allowing others to constrain him to what they deem his good.

I do not mean that the feelings with which a person is regarded by others ought not to be in any way affected by his self-regarding qualities or deficiencies. This is neither possible nor desirable. If he is eminent in any of the qualities which conduce to his own good, he is, so far, a proper object of admiration. He is so much the nearer to the ideal perfection of human nature. If he is grossly deficient in those qualities, a sentiment the opposite of admiration will follow.

There is a degree of folly, and a degree of what may be called (though the phrase is not unobjectionable) lowness or depravation of taste, which, though it cannot justify doing harm to the person who manifests it renders him necessarily and properly a subject of distaste, or, in extreme cases, even of contempt: a person could not have the opposite qualities in due strength without entertaining these feelings. Though doing no wrong to any one, a person may so act as to compel us to judge him, and feel to him, as a fool, or as a being of an inferior order: and since this judgment and feeling are a fact which he would prefer to avoid, it is doing him a service to warn him of it beforehand, as of any other disagreeable consequence to which he exposes himself. It would be well, indeed, if this good office were much more freely rendered than the common notions of politeness at present permit, and if one person could honestly point out to another that he thinks him in fault, without being considered unmannerly or presuming. We have a right, also, in various ways, to act upon our unfavourable opinion of any one, not to the oppression of his individuality, but in the exercise of ours. We are not bound, for example, to seek his society; we have a right to avoid it (though not to parade the avoidance), for we have a right to choose the society most acceptable to us. We have a right, and it may be our duty, to caution others against him, if we think his example or conversation likely to have a pernicious effect on those with whom he associates. We may give others a preference over him in optional good offices, except those which tend to his improvement. In these various modes a person may suffer very severe penalties at the hands of others for faults which directly concern only himself; but he suffers these penalties only in so far as they are the natural, and, as it were, the spontaneous consequences of the faults themselves, not because they are purposely inflicted on him for the sake of punishment. A person who shows rashness, obstinacy, self-conceit—who cannot live within moderate means—who cannot restrain himself from hurtful indulgences—who pursues animal pleasures at the expense of those of feeling and intellect—must expect to be lowered in the opinion of others, and to have a less share of their favourable sentiments; but of this he has no right to complain, unless he has merited their favour by special excellence in his social relations, and has thus established a title to their good offices, which is not affected by his demerits towards himself. . . .

The distinction here pointed out between the part of a person's life which concerns only himself, and that which concerns others, many persons will refuse to admit. How (it may be asked) can any part of the conduct of a member of society be a matter of indifference to the other members? No person is an entirely isolated being; it is impossible for a person to do anything seriously or permanently hurtful to himself, without mischief reaching at least to his near connections, and often far beyond them. If he injures his property, he does harm to those who directly or indirectly derived support from it, and usually diminishes, by a greater or less amount, the general resources of the community. If he deteriorates his bodily or mental faculties, he not only brings evil upon all who depended on him for any portion of their happiness, but disqualifies himself for rendering the services which he owes to his fellow-creatures generally; perhaps becomes a burthen on their affection or benevolence; and if such conduct were very frequent, hardly any offence that is committed would detract more from the general sum of good. Finally, if by his vices or follies a person does no direct harm to others, he is nevertheless (it may be said) injurious by his example; and ought to be compelled to control himself, for the sake of those whom the sight or knowledge of his conduct might corrupt or mislead.

And even (it will be added) if the consequences of misconduct could be confined to the vicious or thoughtless individual, ought society to abandon to their own guidance those who are manifestly unfit for it? If protection against themselves is confessedly due to children and persons under age, is not society equally bound to afford it to persons of mature years who are equally incapable of self-government? If gambling, or drunkenness, or incontinence, or idleness, or uncleanliness, are as injurious to happiness, and as great a hindrance to improvement, as many or most of the acts prohibited by law, why (it may be asked) should not law, so far as it is consistent with practicability and social convenience, endeavour to repress these also? And as a supplement to the unavoidable imperfections of law, ought not opinion at least to organise a powerful police against these vices, and visit rigidly with social penalties those who are known to practise them? There is no question here (it may be said) about restricting individuality, or impeding the trial of new and original experiments in living. The only things it is sought to prevent are things which have been tried and condemned from the beginning of the world until now; things which experience has shown not to be useful or suitable to any person's individuality. There must be some length of time and amount of experience after which a moral or prudential truth may be regarded as established: and it is merely desired to prevent generation after generation from falling over the same precipice which has been fatal to their predecessors.

I fully admit that the mischief which a person does to himself may seriously affect, both through their sympathies and their interests, those nearly connected with him and, in a minor degree, society at large. When, by conduct of this sort, a person is led to violate a distinct and assignable obligation to any other person or persons, the case is taken out of the self-regarding class, and becomes amenable to moral disapprobation in the proper sense of the term. If, for example, a man, through intemperance or extravagance, becomes unable to pay his debts, or, having undertaken the moral responsibility of a family, becomes from the same cause incapable of supporting or educating them, he is deservedly reprobated, and might be justly punished; but it is for the breach of duty to his family or creditors, not for the extravagance. If the resources which ought to have been devoted to them, had been diverted from them for the most prudent investment, the moral culpability would have been the same. George Barnwell murdered his uncle to get money for his mistress, but if he had done it to set himself up in business, he would equally have been hanged. Again, in the frequent case of a man who causes grief to his family by addiction to bad habits, he deserves reproach for his unkindness or ingratitude; but so he may for cultivating habits not in themselves vicious, if they are painful to those with whom he passes his life, or who from personal ties are dependent on him for their comfort. Whoever fails in the consideration generally due to the interests and feelings of others, not being compelled by some more imperative duty, or justified by allowable self-preference, is a subject of moral disapprobation for that failure, but not for the cause of it, not for the errors, merely personal to himself, which may have remotely led to it. In like manner, when a person disables himself, by conduct purely self-regarding, from the performance of some definite duty incumbent on him to the public, he is guilty of a social offence. No person ought to be punished simply for being drunk; but a soldier or a policeman should be punished for being drunk on duty. Whenever, in short, there is a definite damage, or a definite risk of damage, either to an individual or to the public, the case is taken out of the province of liberty, and placed in that of morality or law. . . .

But the strongest of all the arguments against the interference of the public with purely personal conduct is that, when it does interfere, the odds are that it interferes wrongly, and in the wrong place. On questions of social morality, of duty to others, the opinion of the public, that is, of an overruling majority, though often wrong, is likely to be still oftener right; because on such questions they are only required to judge of their own interests; of the manner in which some mode of conduct, if allowed to be practised, would affect themselves. But the opinion of a similar majority, imposed as a law on the minority, on questions of self-regarding conduct, is quite as likely to be wrong as right; for in these cases public opinion means, at the best, some people's opinion of what is good or bad for other people; while very often it does not even mean that; the public, with the most perfect indifference, passing over the pleasure or convenience of those whose conduct they censure, and considering only their own preference. There are many who consider as an injury to themselves any conduct which they have a distaste for, and resent it as an outrage to their feelings; as a religious bigot, when charged with disregarding the religious feelings of others, has been known to retort that they disregard his feelings, by persisting in their abominable worship or creed. But there is no parity between the feeling of a person for his own opinion, and the feeling of another who is offended at his holding it; no more than between the desire of a thief to take a purse, and the desire of the right owner to keep it. And a person's taste is as much his own peculiar concern as his opinion or his purse. It is easy for any one to imagine an ideal public which leaves the freedom and choice of individuals in all uncertain matters undisturbed, and only requires them to abstain from modes of conduct which universal experience has condemned. But where has there been seen a public which set any such limit to its censorship? or when does the public trouble itself about universal experience? In its interferences with personal conduct it is seldom thinking of anything but the enormity of acting or feeling differently from itself; and this standard of judgment, thinly disguised, is held up to mankind as the dictate of religion and philosophy, by nine-tenths of all moralists and speculative writers. These teach that things are right because they are right; because we feel them to be so. They tell us to search in our own minds and hearts for laws of conduct binding on ourselves and on all others. What can the poor public do but apply these instructions, and make their own personal feelings of good and evil, if they are tolerably unanimous in them, obligatory on all the world?

The evil here pointed out is not one which exists only in theory; and it may perhaps be expected that I should specify the instances in which the public of this age and country improperly invests its own preferences with the character of moral laws. I am not writing an essay on the aberrations of existing moral feeling. That is too weighty a subject to be discussed parenthetically, and by way of illustration. Yet examples are necessary to show that the principle I maintain is of serious and practical moment, and that I am not endeavouring to erect a barrier against imaginary evils. And it is not difficult to show, by abundant instances, that to extend the bounds of what may be called moral police, until it encroaches on the most unquestionable legitimate liberty of the individual, is one of the most universal of all human propensities. . . .

But, without dwelling upon supposititious cases, there are, in our own day, gross usurpations upon the liberty of private life actually practised, and still greater ones threatened with some expectation of success, and opinions propounded which assert an unlimited right in the public not only to prohibit by law everything which it thinks wrong, but, in order to get at what it thinks wrong, to prohibit a number of things which it admits to be innocent.

Under the name of preventing intemperance, the people of one English colony, and of nearly half the United States, have been interdicted by law from making any use whatever of fermented drinks, except for medical purposes: for prohibition of their sale is in fact, as it is intended to be, prohibition of their use. And though the impracticability of executing the law has caused its repeal in several of the States which had adopted it, including the one from which it derives its name, an attempt has notwithstanding been commenced, and is prosecuted with considerable zeal by many of the professed philanthropists, to agitate for a similar law in this country. The association, or "Alliance" as it terms itself, which has been formed for this purpose, has acquired some notoriety through the publicity given to a correspondence between its secretary and one of the very few English public men who hold that a politician's opinions ought to be founded on principles. Lord Stanley's[2] share in this correspondence is calculated to strengthen the hopes already built on him, by those who know how rare such qualities as are manifested in some of his public appearances unhappily are among those who figure in political life. The organ of the Alliance, who would "deeply deplore the recognition of any principle which could be wrested to justify bigotry and persecution," undertakes to point out the "broad and impassable barrier" which divides such principles from those of the association. "All matters relating to thought, opinion, conscience, appear to me," he says, "to be without the sphere of legislation; all pertaining to social act, habit, relation, subject only to a discretionary power vested in the State itself, and not in the

---

[2] Edward Henry Smith Stanley (1826–1893) was an English politican who held a number of significant government positions. (ED.)

individual, to be within it." No mention is made of a third class, different from either of these, viz., acts and habits which are not social, but individual; although it is to this class, surely, that the act of drinking fermented liquors belongs. Selling fermented liquors, however, is trading, and trading is a social act. But the infringement complained of is not on the liberty of the seller, but on that of the buyer and consumer; since the State might just as well forbid him to drink wine as purposely make it impossible for him to obtain it. The secretary, however, says, "I claim, as a citizen, a right to legislate whenever my social rights are invaded by the social act of another." And now for the definition of these "social rights." "If anything invades my social rights, certainly the traffic in strong drink does. It destroys my primary right of security, by constantly creating and stimulating social disorder. It invades my right of equality, by deriving a profit from the creation of a misery I am taxed to support. It impedes my right to free moral and intellectual development, by surrounding my path with dangers, and by weakening and demoralising society, from which I have a right to claim mutual aid and intercourse." A theory of "social rights" the like of which probably never before found its way into distinct language: being nothing short of this—that it is the absolute social right of every individual, that every other individual shall act in every respect exactly as he ought; that whosoever fails thereof in the smallest particular violates my social right, and entitles me to demand from the legislature the removal of the grievance. So monstrous a principle is far more dangerous than any single interference with liberty; there is no violation of liberty which it would not justify; it acknowledges no right to any freedom whatever, except perhaps to that of holding opinions in secret, without ever disclosing them: for, the moment an opinion which I consider noxious passes any one's lips, it invades all the "social rights" attributed to me by the Alliance. The doctrine ascribes to all mankind a vested interest in each other's moral, intellectual, and even physical perfection, to be defined by each claimant according to his own standard.

Another important example of illegitimate interference with the rightful liberty of the individual, not simply threatened, but long since carried into triumphant effect, is Sabbatarian legislation. Without doubt, abstinence on one day in the week, so far as the exigencies of life permit from the usual daily occupation, though in no respect religiously binding on any except Jews, is a highly beneficial custom. And inasmuch as this custom cannot be observed without a general consent to that effect among the industrious classes, therefore, in so far as some persons by working may impose the same necessity on others, it may be allowable and right that the law should guarantee to each the observance by others of the custom, by suspending the greater operations of industry on a particular day. But this justification, grounded on the direct interest which others have in each individual's observance of the practice, does not apply to the self-chosen occupations in which a person may think fit to employ his leisure; nor does it hold good, in the smallest degree, for legal restrictions on amusements. It is true that the amusement of some is the day's work of others; but the pleasure, not to say the useful recreation, of many, is worth the labour of a few, provided the occupation is freely chosen, and can be freely resigned. The operatives are perfectly right in thinking that if all worked on Sunday, seven days' work would have to be given for six days' wages; but so long as the great mass of employments are suspended, the small number who for the enjoyment of others must still work, obtain a proportional increase of earnings; and they are not obliged to follow those occupations if they prefer leisure to emolument. If a further remedy is sought, it might be found in the establishment by custom of a holiday on some other day of the week for those particular classes of persons. The only ground, therefore, on which restrictions on Sunday amusements can be defended, must be that they are religiously wrong; a motive of legislation which can never be too earnestly protested against. "Deorum injuriæ Diis Curæ."[3] It remains to be proved that society or any of its officers holds a commission from on high to avenge any supposed offence to Omnipotence, which is not also a wrong to our fellow-creatures. The notion that it is one man's duty that another should be religious, was the foundation of all the religious persecutions ever perpetrated, and, if admitted, would fully justify them. Though the feeling which breaks out in the repeated attempts to stop railway travelling on Sunday, in the resistance to the opening of Museums, and the like, has not the cruelty of the old persecutors, the state of mind indicated by it is fundamentally the same. It is a determination not to tolerate others in doing what is permitted by their religion, because it is not permitted by the persecutor's religion. It is a belief that God not only abominates the act of the misbeliever, but will not hold us guiltless if we leave him unmolested.

---

[3] "Injuries to the gods can be cured by the gods." (ED.)

NICCOLO MACHIAVELLI

Should Princes Tell the Truth?

Niccolo Machiavelli (1469–1527) was a statesman and political philosopher from Florence, Italy who served the Florentine Republic from 1498–1512, when the Medicis returned to power. Machiavelli was imprisoned, exiled, and then spent the rest of his life writing. *The Prince,* from which the following selection is excerpted, was written in 1513 but not published until 1532. Machiavelli is best known for this work, in which he outlines what he considers the necessary behavior for a successful political leader. Other works include *Discourses on Livy* (1531) and *History of Florence* (1532).

How praiseworthy it is for a prince to maintain faith and to live by integrity and not by cunning, everyone understands; nevertheless one sees by experience, in our times, that those princes who have done great things have kept little account of faith, and have also known with cunning how to go round the brains of men; and in the end they have surpassed those who have founded themselves on loyalty.

You ought to know, then, that there are two kinds of fighting: one with the laws, the other with force. The first one is proper to man; the second to the beasts; but because the first proves many times to be insufficient, one needs must resort to the second. Therefore it is necessary for a prince to know well how to use the beast and the man. This part has been covertly taught to princes by the ancient writers, who wrote that Achilles and many other ancient princes were given to the care of Chiron the centaur, so that he might look after them under his discipline. To say this is simply to wish to say that one has to have as a preceptor one who is half-beast and half-man, that it is needful for a prince to know how to use the one and the other nature, and that the one without the other is not durable.

Since a prince must of necessity know well how to use the beast, he ought of the beasts to pick the fox and the lion; for the lion cannot defend himself from snares, and the fox cannot defend himself from wolves. One needs, then, to be fox to know snares, and lion to terrify wolves. Those who rely simply on the lion do not understand this. A prudent lord, therefore, cannot, nor ought he, observe faith, when such observance turns against him and the causes which made him give his promise are extinguished. And if all men were good, this precept would not be good; but since they are wicked, and would not be faithful to you, you also do not have to be faithful to them. Nor does a prince ever lack legitimate causes to color his inobservance. Of this one could give infinite modern examples and show how many peace treaties and how many promises have been of no effect and made vain by the infidelity of princes—and those who have known best how to use the fox, have turned out best. But it is necessary to this nature to know how to color it, and to be a great hypocrite and deceiver, and men are so simple, and so obedient to present necessity, that he who deceives will always find one who will let himself be deceived.

I do not wish to be silent about one of these recent examples. Alexander VII never did anything else and he never thought about anything else but how to deceive men, and he always found a subject for his practice. And there never was a man who was more efficacious in asseverating, or with greater oaths affirmed a thing, who less observed [his faith]. Nevertheless, he always succeeded in deceiving at will, because he knew so well this part of the world.

It is not necessary, then, for a prince to have in fact all of the qualities written above, but it is indeed necessary to appear to have them. I shall rather dare to say this: that having them and observing them always, they are harmful, but in appearing to have them, they are useful—so as to appear to be full of pity, faithful, human, open, religious, and to be so, but with one's mind constructed in such a mode that when the need not to be arises, you can, and know how to, change to the contrary. And this has to be understood, that a prince, and especially a new prince, cannot observe all those things by which men are held to be good, for they are often necessitated to work against faith, against charity, against humanity, against religion, in order to maintain the state. And therefore, it is needful that he have a mind so disposed that he can turn as the winds of fortune and the variations of things command him; and, as has been said above, [he ought] not to depart from the good, if he is able, but [he ought] to know how to enter the bad, when necessitated to do so.

A prince, then, ought to take great care that nothing goes out of his mouth which is not full of the five qualities written above, and that he appears to be, when one sees and hears him, all pity, all faith, all integrity, all humanity, and all religion. Nothing is more necessary than to have this last quality. For men, universally, judge more by the eyes than by the hands, because it is given to everyone that they see, but to few that they can touch. Everyone sees what you seem to be, but few touch what you are, and those few will not dare to oppose themselves to the opinions of the many who have the majesty of the state defending them. And with respect to all human actions, and especially those of princes where there is no judge to whom to appeal, one looks to the end. Let a prince then win and maintain the state— the means will always be judged honorable and will be praised by everyone; for the vulgar are always taken in by the appearance and the outcome of a thing, and in this world there is no one but the vulgar. The few have no place while the many have a great number of places upon which they may perch. A certain present-day prince, whom it is not good to name, never preaches anything but peace and faith, and is the greatest enemy of the one and of the other; and one as well as the other, if he had observed them, would many times have taken from him either his reputation or his state.

ALLAN BLOOM

Western Civ

Allan Bloom (1930–   ) is codirector of the John M. Olin Center for Inquiry into the Theory and Practice of Democracy at the University of Chicago, where he is also a professor on the Committee on Social Thought. His controversial and best-selling *The Closing of the American Mind: How Higher Education Has Failed Democracy and Impoverished the Souls of Today's Students* (1987) is a critique of the contemporary university. "Western Civ" is from *Giants and Dwarfs,* a collection of his essays published in 1990.

Fellow elitists:

If I were E. D. Hirsch[1]—people do tend to mix us up—I might ask, "What is the literary influence on my salutation?" The answer is Franklin D. Roosevelt's salutation to another select audience, the

---

[1] Author of *Cultural Literacy* (1987), a book that attempts to organize information the author thinks literate Americans should know. (ED.)

Daughters of the American Revolution. He began his address, "Fellow Immigrants."

Roosevelt was gently ridiculing those ladies for believing that in America old stock constitutes any title whatsoever to privilege. That notion is a relic of the aristocratic past which this democracy supplanted in favor of equality or of privilege based on merit. Roosevelt was urbane and witty, this century's greatest virtuoso of democratic leadership. We, the immigrants or the children of immigrants, loved his act; he was on our side. Our enjoyment of his joke was enhanced by the acid of vengeance against those who thought they were better than us. F.D.R. knew how to manipulate such sentiments, and his slap at the D.A.R. was not entirely disinterested insofar as there were a lot more of us than there were of them. Moreover Roosevelt's enjoyment was quite different from ours. He was really one of them. His family's claims to antiquity, wealth, and distinction were as good as practically anyone's. It was certainly more pleasant to poke fun at his equals or inferiors than to show resentment toward his superiors. His was an aristocratic condescension. He condescended to rule in a democracy, to be, as was often said about him at the time, "a traitor to his class"—a neat mixture of man's perpetual striving to be first and the demands of a society where all are held to be equal. The psychology of democracy is complex and fascinating.

That psychology determined the very unusual intensity of the response to *The Closing of the American Mind*, focusing on my alleged elitism. I was suspect as an enemy of our democratic regime. And the first and loudest voices in this chorus came from the Ivy League, particularly from those with some connection to Harvard—to the point where I thought of the old joke about the farmer who hears a thief in the chicken coop. Substituting the Harvard Coop, I imagined myself yelling, "Who's in there?" and getting the answer, "There's nobody in here but us antielitists." Everybody knows that Harvard is in every respect—its students, its faculty, its library, and its endowment—the best university in the world. Long ago when I, a Middle-Westerner, taught for a year at Yale, I was amazed at the little Harvard worm that was eating away at the souls of practically all the professors and students there, except for the ones who had turned down the opportunity to be at Harvard. *Elite* is not a word I care for very much—imprecise and smacking of sociological abstraction—but if any American institution of any kind merits that name, it is Harvard, and it lends that tincture to everyone associated with it.

Why, then, this passion to accuse others of the crime of elitism? One is tempted to attribute it to simple self-protectiveness. "If we say he is one, they won't notice us." But I suspect some, or many, acted from a more tortuous, more ambiguous motive: guilt. The leading principle of our regime is the equal worth of all persons, and facts or sentiments that appear to contradict that principle are experienced by a democrat as immoral. Bad conscience accompanies the democrat who finds himself part of an elite. He tries to suppress or deny to himself whatever covert feelings he might experience—I am sure that none of you has had them—of delight or superiority in the fact that he has been distinguished by Harvard, of how much better off he or she is than the poor jerks at Kalamazoo College, even that he or she deserves it, that superior gifts merit superior education, position, and esteem. A few might consciously believe such things, but since they would be at odds with the egalitarian opinions of democracy, they tend to become spiritual outlaws, hypocrites, and cynically indifferent to the only American principle of justice. The rest, to soothe their consciences, have to engage in casuistry, not to say sophistry. The simple democratic answer would be open admissions, just as there would be if Harvard were located in Europe, where such elitism is less tolerated. But nobody here really considers that. Harvard, I gather, intends to remain adamantly exclusive, implying thereby that there are significant natural differences among human beings. President Bok's[2] way of squaring such elitism with democratic right-thinking is, apparently, to teach that the Harvard person is a doer of good works for society as a whole. This is in the spirit of Harvard's John Rawls,[3] who permits people to possess and cultivate superior talents if they can be proved to benefit the most disadvantaged part of society. Whether this solution is reason or rationalization is open to discussion.

All this suggests the intricate psychology of the democrat, which we must be aware of in order to know ourselves and which we are not likely to be aware of without the help of significant thinkers like Tocqueville, Burke,[4] and Plato, who see us from the outside and

---

[2] Derek Bok (1930–   ) was president of Harvard from 1971 until 1990. (ED.)

[3] Philosophy professor at Harvard who proposes that the government has a duty to raise the status of society's poor, even at the expense of the other classes. (ED.)

[4] *Alexis de Tocqueville* (1805–1859) was a French historian and political philosopher whose *Democracy in America* studied and evaluated political and social institutions in the United States. *Edmund Burke* (1729–1797) was an English statesman and political thinker during the reign of George III; he argued in the British Parliament for more liberal treatment of the American colonies. (ED.)

judge us in terms of serious alternatives to democracy. The charge of elitism reflects the moral temper of our regime, as the charge of atheism would have done in an earlier age. You couldn't get much of a response in a university today by saying that Allan Bloom doesn't believe in God. But you can get a lot of people worked up by saying that I don't believe in equality. And this tells us a lot about our times, and explains how tempting a career is offered to egalitarian Tartufferie.[5] "Elitist" is not a very precise charge; but compared with the Ivy League, I would have at worst to be called a moderate elitist, and by persons other than those who are now making the charge.

The real disagreement concerns the content of today's and tomorrow's elite education. We are now witnessing the introduction of a new "nonelitist," "nonexclusionary" curriculum in the humanities and in parts of the social sciences, and with it a program for reforming the human understanding. This is an extremely radical project whose supporters pass it off as mainstream by marching under the colors of all the movements toward a more equal society which almost all Americans endorse. Not recognized for what it is, this radicalism can thus marshal powerful and sometimes angry passions alongside its own fanatic ones. *The Closing of the American Mind* was brought before this inquisition and condemned to banishment from the land of the learned. The American Council of Learned Societies even issued a report written by a panel of the new men and women which declared that there is now a scholarly consensus, nay, a proof, that all classic texts must be studied using a single approved method. Such texts are, we are ordered to believe, expressions of the unconscious class, gender, or race prejudices of their authors. The calling of the humanities in our day is to liberate us from the sway of those authors and their prejudices; Shakespeare and Milton, among others, are mentioned in the report. This puts humanists at the cutting edge of the battle against Eurocentrism. The battle is not primarily, or even at all, scholarly but moral and political, and members of the reactionary rear guard are the objects of special fury, the enemies of historic destiny. What kind of a man could stand in the way of deconstructionism,[6] which according to Hillis Miller, one of its proponents, will bring the millennium of peace and justice to all man-

---

[5] hypocrisy—from the name Tartuffe, a character in Moliere's play by the same name (ED.)

[6] A method of literary criticism that maintains the impossibility of determining one exclusive meaning for a literary text. (ED.)

kind? Consequently the report deplored the "disturbing" success of *The Closing of the American Mind* and attributed it to that old bogey, "American anti-intellectualism" (of the Know-Nothing or Mc-Carthyite variety, you see). The characters who wrote this report were sent by central casting for the movie version of *The Closing of the American Mind.*

Such responses were inevitable, since I am very much a critic of the radical reform being imposed on us, although I have always been a supporter and a beneficiary of the movements toward practical equality.

For my sins I have reaped an unabating whirlwind of abuse, paralleled in my experience only by Sartre's diatribes against his enemies and critics in *Les Temps Modernes* in the forties and fifties. (As I argued in my book, that Sartrean world was the conveyer belt for many of the views affecting us now.) I suspect that Sartre is the model for *engagé* critics who charged that my opinions stain my hands with the blood of innocents in Nicaragua, *les mains sales,* and called me, in a striking reminder of our McCarthyite heritage, "un-American."

People's angers teach much about what concerns them. Anger almost always disguises itself as moral indignation and, as Aristotle teaches, is the only one of the passions that requires speech and reason—to provide arguments which justify it and without which it is frustrated and withers. Anger proves man's rationality while it obscures and endangers reason. The arguments it adduces always lead back to a general principle of morality and then issue in blame—they would also lead to book-burning if the angry were not strongly constrained by our liberal society. Here is an example as reported by Richard Bernstein in *The New York Times* (September 25, 1988):

A "Minute of Hatred" in Chapel Hill:
Academia's Liberals Defend Their Carnival of Canons
Against Bloom's "Killer B's"

> In some respects, the scenes in North Carolina last weekend recalled the daily "minute of hatred" in George Orwell's *1984,* when citizens are required to rise and hurl invective at pictures of a man known only as Goldstein, the Great Enemy of the state.
>
> At a conference on the future of liberal education sponsored by Duke University and the University of North Carolina at Chapel Hill, speaker after speaker denounced what they called "the cultural conservatives" who, in the words of a Duke English professor, Stanley Fish, have mounted "dyspeptic attacks on the humanities."

> There were no pictures of these "cultural conservatives" on the wall, but they were derided, scorned, laughed at . . .

I appreciate the *Times'* making explicit the resemblance to Stalinist thought control. Such sentiments represent the current establishment in the humanities, literature, and history. These professors are from hot institutions like Stanford and Duke which have most openly dedicated themselves to the new educational dawn called *openness,* a dawn whose rosy fingers are currently wrapped tightly around the throat of the curriculum in most universities.

The attack on *The Closing of the American Mind* brings this movement into focus, though it has misrepresented both the book and me. There is a desire to make me into something other than what I am so that I can be more easily categorized and demolished. In the first place I am not a conservative—neo- or paleo-. I say this not to curry favor in a setting where conservatism is out of favor. Conservatism is a respectable outlook, and its adherents usually have to have some firmness of character to stick by what is so unpopular in universities. I just do not happen to be that animal. Any superficial reading of my book will show that I differ from both theoretical and practical conservative positions. My teachers—Socrates, Machiavelli, Rousseau, and Nietzsche—could hardly be called conservatives. All foundings are radical, and conservatism always has to be judged by the radical thought or events it intends to conserve. At first I was not, to use Marxist language, even considered an objective ally of the Right—as the very favorable opinions of the book expressed by Left liberals such as Christopher Lehmann-Haupt, Richard Reeves, Robert Skidelsky, and Conor Cruise O'Brien prove. But that was before the elite intellectuals weighed in. Their misunderstanding has something to do with the fact that I am also not in any current sense a liberal, although the preservation of liberal society is of central concern to me. The permanent human tendency is to doubt that the theoretical stance is authentic and suspect that it is only a covert attachment to a party. And this tendency is much strengthened in our time when philosophy is itself understood to be *engagé,* the most extreme partisanship. The necessity of parties in politics has been extrapolated to the point where it now seems that the mind itself must be dominated by the spirit of party. From this perspective, theory looks pallid, weak, dishonest, and sinister.

Arthur Schlesinger, Jr., criticized me in a way which shows how naïve the views of contemporary intellectuals have become. He said, with a somewhat unsure grasp of what I wrote, that I am an absolutist whereas the authentic American tradition is relativist. To support this latter contention he cited—hold on to your seats—the Declaration of Independence's "We hold these truths to be self-evident, that all men are created equal and are endowed by their Creator with certain inalienable rights . . ." He takes this statement of fundamental principle, *mirabile dictu,*[7] to be evidence of the American Founders' relativism. Schlesinger[8] made this astounding argument in a commencement address at Brown University, where he apparently thinks the students will believe anything.

It is a waste of time to defend myself when the charges allege that I said things I did not say, but it is perhaps useful to instruct Professor Schlesinger about the real question. I never stated, nor do I believe, that man is, or can be, in possession of absolutes. My language is not that of absolutes, a language not present in my writings. I tried to teach, evidently not very successfully in his case, that there are two threats to reason, the opinion that one knows the truth about the most important things and the opinion that there is no truth about them. Both of these opinions are fatal to philosophy; the first asserts that the quest for the truth is unnecessary, while the second asserts that it is impossible. The Socratic knowledge of ignorance, which I take to be the beginning point of all philosophy, defines the sensible middle ground between two extremes, the proofs of which demand much more than we know. Pascal's formula about our knowing too little to be dogmatists and too much to be skeptics perfectly describes our human condition as we really experience it, although men have powerful temptations to obscure it and often find it intolerable.

Socrates' way of life is the consequence of his recognition that we can know what it is that we do not know about the most important things and that we are by nature obliged to seek that knowledge. We must remain faithful to the bit of light which pierces through our circumambient darkness.

It is the theoretical life I admire, not some moralism or other, and I seek to defend it against the assaults peculiar to our time. Philosophy, the enemy of illusions and false hopes, is never really popular and is always suspect in the eyes of the supporters of which-

---

[7] amazing as it may seem (ED.)

[8] Arthur Schlesinger, Jr. (1917–) is an American historian who has won two Pulitzer Prizes, one in history for his book *The Age of Jackson* (1945), and one in biography for his book *A Thousand Days* (1965), on the Kennedy Administration. (ED.)

ever of the extremes happens to dominate. Mr. Schlesinger is an average representative of the relativism which is today's consensus on the Left. However, so eminent and perceptive an observer as Walker Percy, looking from the Right, says that he suspects that I am a nihilist, and he is supported in that view by much less responsible persons from the same quarter. I would respond to him with exactly the same arguments I made to Arthur Schlesinger. This equilibrium of criticism reassures me that I am in the right way, and it confirms my apprehensions about philosophy. It is neither understood nor desired. To the ones it is absolutism, to the others it is relativism; there is no middle; each camp shoves it over into the other. I am now even more persuaded of the urgent need to study why Socrates was accused. The dislike of philosophy is perennial, and the seeds of the condemnation of Socrates are present at all times, not in the bosoms of pleasure seekers, who don't give a damn, but in those of high-minded and idealistic persons who do not want to submit their aspirations to examination. Certainly Socrates is the source of a profound liberalism in relation to which Professor Schlesinger's version of it looks like a parody.

I conclude this digression by remarking that Professor Schlesinger's relativism is not real relativism but a curious mixture of absolutism and relativism typical of our time. Professor Schlesinger is absolutely and unquestioningly committed to democracy and wants to avoid people quibbling about it. He coyly says he does not believe in anything and that good and evil are just preferences, and then he entrusts democracy's fate to a hidden or, rather, a divine hand. I, for my part, doubt that there is any substitute for rational argument for all of its risks and uncertainties. Professor Schlesinger, no stranger to the fabrication of myths or ideologies, appears to be providing one for the tyranny of the majority.

Further, I am also not the leader or member of an educational reform movement, or any movement whatsoever. I respect persons like Sidney Hook[9] who give the best of their energies to fighting threats to academic integrity. But that is not me. I have always been content to hang around the fringes of the intellectual establishment and look in, and am continually surprised that I can support myself that way. To attempt to change things would take me away from my natural activity, would delay gratification now for the sake of unsure

---

[9] Sidney Hook (1902–1989), was an American educator and social philosopher who intellectually defended liberal democracy as an alternative to Marxism. (ED.)

futures. I suppose I think the most important thing is to think things through. My book is a statement—as serious as I could make it— about the contemporary situation seen from the perspective of our quest for self-knowledge. Not in my wildest imagination did I think it would appeal to anyone but a few friends and potential friends, a few students and potential students. When it became a hit, the genial American can-do traits surfaced. The prospect I described is publicly unendurable, and I was both criticized for not providing a cure and praised for having prescribed one. Perhaps a public debate about education is a good thing. But I am not a very active participant in it. I suspect that any confrontation with currently stronger forces only precipitates greater defeats for liberal education. Above all, I wish to avoid the self-absorption and corrosion I have seen in others who were principals in *causes célèbres.*[10]

I have gotten a great kick out of becoming the academic equivalent of a rock star. This is partly because the eternal American child in me found it agreeable to experience peculiarly American success from the inside—to find out whether I had been missing anything. But mostly it was because I was afforded a close-up look at the closing of the American mind. I have had to learn, however, to watch out as it slams shut on me.

To the extent I am passionately affected by the spectacle I describe in the book, I feel sorrow or pity for young people whose horizon has become so dark and narrow that, in this enlightened country, it has begun to resemble a cave. Self-consciousness, self-awareness, the Delphic "know thyself" seems to me to be the serious business of education. It is, I know, very difficult even to know what that means, let alone achieve it. But one thing is certain. If one's head is crammed with ideas that were once serious but have become clichés, if one does not even know that these clichés are not as natural as the sun and moon, and if one has no notion that there are alternatives to them, one is doomed to be the puppet of other people's ideas. Only the search back to the origins of one's ideas in order to see the real arguments for them, before people became so certain of them that they ceased thinking about them at all, can liberate us. Our study of history has taught us to laugh at the follies of the whole past, the monarchies, oligarchies, theocracies, and aristocracies with their fanaticism for empire or salvation, once taken so seriously. But we

---

[10] situations attracting intense and widespread interest (ED.)

have very few tools for seeing ourselves in the same way, as others will see us. Each age always conspires to make its own way of thinking appear to be the only possible or just way, and our age has the least resistance to the triumph of its own way. There is less real presence of respectable alternatives and less knowledge of the titanic intellectual figures who founded our way. Moreover we are also affected by historicism, which tells us one cannot resist one's way, and relativism, which asks, "What's the use, anyway?" All this has the effect of crippling the natural longing to get out.

In *The Closing of the American Mind* I criticized doctrinaire historicism and relativism as threats to the self-awareness of those who honestly seek it. I pointed to the great sources of those serious ideas which have become dogmas and urged that we turn to serious study of them in order to purge ourselves of our dogmatism. For this I have been violently attacked as nostalgic, ideological, doctrinaire. The meaning is really "Don't touch our belief structure; it hurts." We ought to know, on the basis of historical observation, that what epochs consider their greatest virtue is most often really their greatest temptation, vice, or danger—Roman manliness, Spanish piety, British class, German authenticity. We have to learn to put the scalpel to our virtues. Plato suggests that if you're born in a democracy you are likely to be a relativist. It goes with the territory. Relativism may be true, but, since you are by birthright inclined to it, you especially had better think it over—not for the sake of good morals or good social order, at least in any usual sense of those terms, but for the sake of your freedom and your self-awareness.

Since I first addressed the issue of relativism, I have learned with what moral fervor it is protected and its opposite, ethnocentrism, attacked. This fervor does not propose an investigation but a crusade. The very idea that we ought to look for standards by which to judge ourselves is scandalous. You simply have to believe in the current understanding of openness if you are to believe in democracy and be a decent person.

This openness dogma was epitomized by one intellectual who, unencumbered by acquaintance with my book, ridiculed me for not simply accepting that all cultures are equal. He said that his opinion must be standard equipment for all those who expect to cope with "the century of the Pacific" which is upon us. His formulation set my imagination in motion. I decided it might be interesting to experience a Gulliver's travel to Japan to see whether we really want to set our bark on the great Pacific with a relativist compass and without an "ethnocentric" life jacket. We can weigh anchor at the new, new Stanford, whose slogan is now "Join Stanford and see the world." When we arrive in Japan we shall see a thriving nation. Its success clearly has something to do with its society, which asks much of itself and gets it. It is a real community; its members have roots. Japanese society is often compared to a family. These characteristics are in tune with much of current liberal thought in America. (Remember Governor Cuomo's keynote speech to the Democratic Convention in 1984.)

But the family is exclusive. For in it there is an iron wall separating insiders from outsiders, and its members feel contrary sentiments toward the two. So it is in Japanese society, which is intransigently homogeneous, barring the diversity which is the great pride of the United States today. To put it brutally, the Japanese seem to be racists. They consider themselves superior; they firmly resist immigration; they exclude even Koreans who have lived for generations among them. They have difficulty restraining cabinet officers from explaining that American's failing economy is due to blacks.

Should we open ourselves up to this new culture? Sympathize with its tastes? Should we aim for restrictiveness rather than diversity? Should we experiment with a more effective racism? All these things could be understood as part of our interest in keeping up with the Japanese economic miracle. Or they could, in a tonier vein, help us in our search for community and roots. We recoil in horror at even having such thoughts. But how can we legitimate our horror? It is only the result of our acculturation, excess baggage brought with us on such voyages of discovery. If there are no transcultural values, our reaction is ethnocentric. And the one thing we know absolutely is that ethnocentrism is bad. So we have painted ourselves into a corner. And it is important to understand this. Those who shrug off such difficulties fail to recognize how important it is to have justice in addition to feeling on our side. Without justice we shall soon succumb to some dangerous temptations and have perhaps already begun to do so.

Many such lessons are to be learned on future voyages to the non-Western world. Discovery requires courage and resoluteness, as Heidegger will teach you. I wonder whether all the *engagé* critics who use his language are aware of what he means when he says that one has to face storms in the ocean of becoming. When little children speak of how bad ethnocentrism is, I know that they have been propagandized. It is too complicated a thing for them to understand. Condemning ethnocentrism is frequently a sign of intellectual, although not necessarily moral, progress. But it is only a first step. To recognize that some of the things our culture believes are not true imposes on us the duty of finding out which are true and which are not, a business altogether more difficult than the wholesale jettisoning of all that one thought one knew. Such jettisoning always ends up with the selective and thoughtless return to old ethnocentric ideas on the basis of what one needs right now, of what pleases one, of pure feeling.[11] But to travel one must spend a little time thinking about one's compass as well as the land one wishes to reach.

This problem has been nicely illustrated these last months by the case of Salman Rushdie, author of *The Satanic Verses,* which insulted the Muslim faith and occasioned the Ayatollah Khomeini's command to have Rushdie killed in England, or wherever he is to be found. There was general shock throughout the Western world at this, and writers, whose ox was being gored, rushed before the TV cameras to denounce this blatant attack on the inviolable principle of freedom of speech. All well and good. But the kicker is that most of these very same writers have for many years been teaching that we must respect the integrity of other cultures and that it is arrogant ethnocentrism to judge other cultures according to our standards, which are themselves merely products of our culture. In this case, however, all such reasonings were forgotten, and freedom of speech was treated as though its claims to transcultural status, its claims to be valid everywhere and always, are true. A few days earlier such claims were treated as instruments of American imperialism; miraculously they were transformed into absolutes. Leaving aside the intellectual incoherence here, this floating means to say we do not know from moment to moment what we will do when there are conflicts, which there inevitably will be, between human rights and the imperatives of the culturally sacred. You may have noticed that there has recently been silence about the case; this is partially because it is an embarrassment, and our convictions are weak. The serious arguments that established the right of freedom of speech were made by philosophers—most notably Locke, Milton, and Mill—and our contemporaries do not return to them to refresh their memories and to see whether the arguments are really good. And this is due not only to laziness but also to the current attack on the very idea of such study.

The educational project of reforming the mind in the name of openness has gained strength in the last couple of years and is

---

[11] Following this lecture, Henry Rosovsky, the legendary dean of Harvard College, exasperated by me, announced that he is a relativist. In the next instant he was complaining that I only look for the bad things in Japan and not the good ones.

succeeding in changing curricula all over the country. These changes
are as great as any of the sixties but not nearly so noticeable because
so easily accepted and now apparently so obviously right. From the
slogans and the arguments echoed so frequently in the universities
and the press one can judge the intentions of the reform and what
is at stake. The key word is *canon*. What we are witnessing is the
Quarrel of the Canons, the twentieth century's farcical version of the
seventeenth century's Quarrel between the Ancients and the Moderns—the greatest document of which is Swift's[12] "Battle of the
Books." Would that he were here to describe ours as he described
theirs! The issue is what food best nourishes the hungers of young
souls. "The canon" is the newly valued, demagogically intended,
expression for the books taught and read by students at the core of
their formal education. But as soon as one adopts the term, as both
sides have—foolishly so for those who defend Dante, Shakespeare,
and Kant—the nature of the debate has thereby been determined.
For canon means what is established by authority, by the powers,
hence not by criteria that are rationally defensible. The debate shifts
from the content of books to how they become powerful, the motives
for which they are used. Canons are, by definition, instruments of
domination. They are there to be overthrown, *deconstructed,* in the
name of liberation. Those who seek *empowerment* must overcome the
prevailing canon, the main source of their enslavement. Curiously
books are invested with a very great significance in all this. They are
the causes, not mere epiphenomena, as Marxism would have it.
Change the books, not the ownership of the means of production,
and you change the world: "Readers of the world, you have nothing
to lose but your canon." The language is the language of power.
"Philosophy is the most spiritualized will to power." That is from
Nietzsche, as is, more or less, all the current talk about the canon.
"It's all about power," as they say, and in a more metaphysical sense
than most know. Philosophy in the past was about knowing; now it
is about power. This is the source of the deep drama being played
out so frivolously about us. Intellectual life is the struggle of wills to
power. Edward Said said at Stanford that the new university reforms
were the triumph of postmodernism, meaning, among other things,
that the curriculum which taught that the theoretical life is highest
has been overcome. Underlying the discussion about non-Western

---

[12] Jonathan Swift (1667–1745) was an English writer who was born in Ireland. He is
known chiefly for his satire, including "The Battle of the Books" (1704), an essay on
the debate over ancient and modern learning in Britain at the time. (ED.)

content is a discussion among Westerners using entirely Western categories about the decline or end of the West. The suicide of the West is, by definition, accomplished by Western hands.

The *Times* report of the North Carolina conference gives the flavor of the public discussion: ". . . the conference's participants denounced what they said was a narrow, outdated interpretation of the humanities and of culture itself, one based, they frequently pointed out, on works written by 'dead white European males.' " That is *the* slogan. Above all, the campaign is against Eurocentrism:

> The message of the North Carolina conference was that American society has changed too much for this view to prevail any longer. Blacks, women, Latinos and homosexuals are demanding recognition for their own canons. "Projects like those of Bennett, Hirsch and Bloom all look back to the recovery of the earlier vision of American culture, as opposed to the conception of a kind of ethnic carnival or festival of cultures or ways of life or customs," Professor Fish said.

Replace the old, cold Greek temple with an oriental bazaar. This might be called the Chicago politics model. Overthrow the Waspocracy by means of a Rainbow Coalition. This has more or less plausibility as a political "strategy." Whether it should be the polar star in the formation of young minds is another question. It promises continuing wondrous curricular variations as different specialties and groups vie for power. I would need the pen of Flaubert to characterize it fully. I am grateful to Professor Fish for having described it so candidly.[13]

This is the popular surface of the movement, the publicly acceptable principle of everyone's getting a piece of the action in a nation that has bought into group politics. But there is a deeper, stronger, and more revealing side: "The conference buzzed with code

---

[13] During the question period I discovered that this project has been a roaring success with at least some students. A Chinese, a black, an Armenian, and a person speaking for homosexuals wondered whether they were being "excluded," inasmuch as books by members of their "communities" are not represented in curricula in proportion to their numbers in the population. They seemed to think that Greeks and Italians have been in control of universities and that now their day is coming. One can imagine a census which would redistribute the representation of books. The premise of these students' concerns is that "where you come from," your culture, is more important than where you are going. They are rather like Plato's noble guardian dogs in the *Republic* who love what is familiar, no matter how bad it is, and hate all that is strange or foreign. This kind of demand is entirely new: you do not go to college to discover for yourself what is good but to be confirmed in your origins.

words. When the speakers talked about 'the hegemonic culture,' they meant undemocratic domination by white men. The scholars particularly scorned the idea that certain great works of literature have absolute value or represent some eternal truth. Just about everything, they argued, is an expression of race, class or gender." This is academic jargon, one-third Marxist, two-thirds Nietzschean; but it points toward the metaphysics of the cosmic power struggle in terms of which we interpret everything nowadays. All books have to be reinterpreted to find the conscious or unconscious power motive of their authors. As Nietzsche puts it, "Every philosophy is the author's secret confession."

The other side in this struggle can be found in the words of W. E. B. Du Bois at the turn of the century:

> I sit with Shakespeare and he winces not. Across the color line I move arm in arm with Balzac and Dumas, where smiling men and welcoming women glide in gilded halls. From out the caves of evening that swing between the strong-limbed earth and the tracery of the stars, I summon Aristotle and Aurelius and what soul I will, and they come all graciously with no scorn or condescension. So, wed with Truth, I dwell above the Veil.[14]

I confess that this view is most congenial to me. Du Bois found our common transcultural humanity not in a canon, but in certain works from which he learned about himself and gained strength for his lonely journey, beyond the Veil. He found community rather than war. He used the books to think about his situation, moving beyond the corrosive of prejudice to the independent and sublime dignity of the fully developed soul. He recapitulates the ever-renewed experience of books by intelligent poor and oppressed people seeking for a way out.

But during the recent Stanford curriculum debate, a leader of the black student group declared that the implicit message of the Western civilization curriculum is "nigger go home." Du Bois from this perspective was suffering from false consciousness, a deceptive faith in theoretical liberation offered by the inventors of practical slavery. *No Exit.*

These opposing quotes truly reflect the meaning of the debate over what is called the canon. The word has religious overtones. *The*

---

[14] W. E. Burghardt Du Bois, *The Souls of Black Folk* (New York: The New American Library, Inc., 1969), p. 139.

Canon is the list of books of the Bible accepted by the Catholic
Christian church as genuine and inspired. These books are supposed
to compel our faith without reason or evidence. Using a word like
canon arouses our passion for liberation from authority. This kind
of pseudoreligious characterization of practically everything is epidemic in the post-Nietzschean period. God is dead, and he is the
only founder. All kinds of abstract words, like *charisma,* determine
our perspective on phenomena before we look at them, and harden
the opinion that power is the only thing, in the intellectual arena as
well as in the political arena. A canon is regarded as the means of
indoctrination used by a ruling elite, and study is the process of
entitlement for entry into the elite, for distinguishing the dominators
from the dominated. In other words, the priests who teach the canon
are empowered by the canon, and they protect their privileged position by their teaching. They establish the canon and are established
by it. So you see why a professor like me defends the canon so
ferociously.

One can go on weaving these webs of fantasy endlessly, and there
is an element of truth in them. Obviously books are used by nations
and religions to support their way and to train the young to it. But
that is not the whole story. Many books, perhaps the most important
ones, have an independent status and bring us light from outside our
cave, without which we would be blind. They are frequently the acid
which reveals the outlines of abusive power. This is especially true
in a liberal society like our own, where it is hard to find a "canonical"
book which truly supports our way unqualifiedly. It is at least as
plausible that the books which have a continuing good reputation
and used to be read in colleges have made it on their intrinsic merits.
To be sure, traditions tend to ossify and also to aggregate superfluous
matters, to be taught authoritatively by tiresome persons who don't
know why they are important and who hold their jobs because they
are virtuosos of trivia. But this only means that the traditions have
to be renewed from time to time and the professors made to give an
account of themselves.

One of the most obvious cases of a writer used as an authority
to bolster what might be called a structure of power is Aristotle
during the Christian Middle Ages. Scholasticism[15] was a stifling force

---

[15] Philosophy linking faith and reason that dominated Western Christian civilization
during the Middle Ages. (ED.)

which had to be rebelled against in order to free the mind. But to take that Will Durant[16]-like interpretation as exhaustive would be naïve. In the first place, Aristotle is something on his own. He survived the wreckage of Scholasticism quite nicely and needed no power structure prior to that time or afterward to insure the continuing interest enlightened men and women take in his works. Moreover, Aristotle's accession to power was a result of a revolution in Christianity which rationalized it and made it move a long way from revelation toward reason. It was the explosion of Greek philosophy into Christian Europe. That philosophy had been preserved and renewed among the Muslims. The challenge of reason presented by the Muslim philosophers precipitated a crisis in Christianity that was appeased but not entirely resolved by Thomas Aquinas. Aristotle sat among the Christian sages, but he inspired many to turn against them. Here we have a truly interesting case of the relation between the allegedly Western and the allegedly non-Western. Such cases speak against the canonical thesis rather than for it and are covered over by it.

It is a grave error to accept that the books of the dead white Western male canon are essentially Western—or any of those other things. The fact that I am doubtful about the non-Western craze suggests automatically, even to sympathetic critics, that I am promoting Western Civ or the like. Yet the very language used shows how enslaved we have become to the historicist assertion that all thought is decisively culture-bound. When Averroës[17] and Thomas Aquinas[18] read Aristotle they did not think of him as Greek and put him into his historical context. They had no interest in Greek Civ but treated him as a wise man, hence a contemporary at all times. We smile at this naïveté, but they understood Aristotle better than do our scholars, as one can see simply by perusing the commentaries.

---

[16] Will Durant (1885–1981) was an American historian and philosopher. He and his wife Ariel compiled the *Story of Civilization* (1935–1975), an eleven-volume work. (ED.)

[17] Averroës (1126–1198) was an Islamic-Iberian philosopher whose real name was Muhammad ibn Rushd. His summary and commentary on Aristotle influenced much of Western medieval thought, especially that of Aquinas. (ED.)

[18] St. Thomas Aquinas (1224–1274), an Italian Dominican friar and religious philosopher, brought together the scientific rationalism of Aristotle and the faith of Christianity. (ED.)

Plato and Kant claim that they speak to all men everywhere and forever, and I see no reason to reject those claims *a priori*.[19] But that is precisely what is done when they are taken to be parts of Western Civ. To the extent they are merely that, the appeals against them are justified, for Western Civ is clearly partial, demanding the supplement of all the other Civs. The strength of these appeals is in their demand for wholeness or completeness of understanding. Therefore, to begin with, historicism, the alleged primacy of culture, has to be called into question, though it is one of those opinions that has so completely captured modern minds that it appears indubitable. The quarrel is *not* about Western and non-Western but about the possibility of philosophy. The real issue is being obscured due to a political dispute. If we give in we shall allow very modern philosophy to swallow up all philosophers from Socrates up to and including Marx. Postmodernism is an attempt to annihilate the inspiration of Greek philosophy that is more effective than that of the barbarians with their Dark Ages after the fall of Rome, more effective because it is being accomplished by the force and the guile of philosophy itself. I am not asserting the truth of philosophy's old claim to break through the limits of culture and history, but I am asserting that it is the only question. It is neither a Western nor a non-Western question.

Nobody, or practically nobody, argues that natural science is essentially Western. Some efforts have been made in that direction, just as some feminists have tried to show that science is essentially male, but these efforts, aside from their admirable sense of the need for theoretical consistency, have not proved persuasive. There is that big rock of transcultural knowledge or truth, natural science, standing amidst us while we chatter on about the cultural basis of all knowledge. A serious non-Western putsch would require that students learn fifty percent non-Western math, fifty percent non-Western physics, fifty percent non-Western biology, and so forth for medicine and engineering. The reformers stop there because they know they would smack up against a brick wall and discredit their whole movement. Philosophy, they say, is not like that. Perhaps, but I have yet to see a serious discussion about wherein it differs. Differ it does today. But qualitatively? That question ought to keep us busy for a long time. Science is surely somehow transcultural. Religion seems pretty much limited to cultures, even to define them. Is phi-

---

[19] presumptively, without closer analysis (ED.)

losophy like science, or is it like religion? What we are witnessing is an attempt to drag it away definitively to the camp of religion.

The universities have dealt with this problem by ceding the despised historicized humanities to the political activists and extremists, leaving undisturbed their nonhistoricized disciplines, which is where the meat and the money are. It is a windfall for administrators to be able to turn all the affirmative-action complaints over to the humanities, which act as a lightning rod while their ship continues its stately progress over undisturbed waters. Stanford shows its concerned, humane, radical face to its inner community, and its serious technical face to the outside community, particularly to its donors. The humanities radicals will settle for this on the calculation that if they can control the minds of the young, they will ultimately gain political control over the power of science.

The essential liberating texts have survived because they are useful. When I spoke of democracy and relativism in *The Closing of the American Mind,* I said only what I learned from Plato and a few others. I appreciate and need further information. So do we all. The serious scholars in non-Western thought should bring us the powerful *texts* they know of to help us. The true canon aggregates around the most urgent questions we face. That is the only ground for the study of books. Idle cultural reports, Eastern or Western, cannot truly concern us, except as a hobby. Edgar Z. Friedenberg once said that social scientists are always giving themselves hernias trying to see something about America Tocqueville did not see. That is why we need Tocqueville, and our neglecting to read him can be interpreted as an effort at hernia prevention. Nietzsche did not seek out Socrates because he was part of the classical canon German boys learned in school. He did so in spite of that fact. Socrates was necessary to him as the profoundest statement of what philosophy is and as the worthiest of rivals. Machiavelli was impelled by real need, not by conformism, when he sought out Xenophon. Male, female, black, white, Greek, barbarian: that was all indifferent, as it should be. Nietzsche reflected on Buddha when he wanted to test the principle of contradiction. That is a model of the way things should be. The last thing we need is a sort of philosophic U.N. run by bureaucrats for the sake of representation for all peoples.

Each must ultimately judge for himself about the important books, but a good beginning would be to see what other thinkers the thinkers who attract him turn to. That will quickly lead to the top. There are very few who remain there, and they recognize one another. There is no conspiracy, only the desire to know. If we allow ourselves to be seduced by the plausible theses of our day, and turn our backs on the great dialogue, our loss will be irreparable.

In my book I connected this radical historicism with fascism and asserted that the thinking of the European Right had wandered over to the Left in America. This earned me severe and unthinking criticism (with the honorable exception of Richard Rorty).[20] It seems to such critics that I am one of those persons who trivialize unique and terrible phenomena by calling anyone whom I don't like a fascist or a Nazi. But I did not call persons active in the sixties those names. I said that the language of the New Left was no longer truly Marxist and had become imbued with the language of fascism. And anyone with an ear for the speech of intellectuals in Weimar Germany[21] will hear echoes all around us of the dangerous ideas to which they became accustomed. Since the publication of *The Closing of the American Mind,* fortuitously there has been fresh attention paid to the Nazism of Martin Heidegger,[22] more and more widely recognized as the most intelligent figure contributing to the postmodernist movement. At the same time Paul de Man,[23] who introduced deconstructionism into the United States, was revealed to have written, as a young man, pro-Nazi articles for a collaborationist Belgian newspaper. In reading these articles I was struck by the fact that if one suppresses the references to Hitler and Hitlerism, much of it sounds

---

[20] Richard Rorty, University Professor of Humanities at the University of Virginia, has published *Objectivity, Relativity, and Truth* and *Essays on Heidegger and Others.* (ED.)

[21] The Weimar Republic in Germany began with the abolition of the German monarchy and the meeting of a new National Assembly in 1919. It lasted until 1933, when Adolf Hitler and his National Socialist (Nazi) party came into power. It was during the Weimar Republic that certain extremist parties, including the Nazis and the Communists, gained power and influence in Germany; the rise of the Nazis was fueled, in particular, by the economic depression that began in 1929. (ED.)

[22] Martin Heidegger (1889–1976) was a German philosopher who was interested in the nature and meaning of Being. His books include *Being and Time* and *What Is Metaphysics?* His career was marked by controversy, however, due to his membership in the Nazi party and the pro-Nazi sentiments expressed in some of his speeches as rector of the University of Freiburg in the early 1930s. (ED.)

[23] Paul de Man (1919–1983), a Belgian-born philosopher and deconstructionist literary theorist, taught at Harvard, Cornell, Johns Hopkins, and Yale Universities. In 1987, a graduate student came upon articles de Man had written from 1940 to 1943 for two German-controlled publications; some of these articles were found to express anti-Semitic sentiments, prompting some of de Man's critics to question the value of his work. (ED.)

like what one reads in advanced literary reviews today. The lively debate around these questions has not been very helpful, for it focuses more on questions of personal guilt than on the possible relation of their thought to the foulest political extremism. The fact that de Man had become a Leftist doesn't prove a thing. He never seems to have passed through a stage where he was attracted by reason or liberal democracy. Those who chose culture over civilization, the real opposition, which we have forgotten, were forced to a position beyond good and evil, for good and evil are products of cultures. The really great thinkers who thought through what the turn to culture means, starting from power, said that immoderation, violence, blood, and soil are its means. These are the consequence of the will to power. I am inclined to take the views of men of such stature seriously. Very few of America's end-of-the-West people are attracted by these aspects of the problem of culture, although there are some, I suspect, who do experience a terrible frisson of joy when they hear them. However that may be, one always ends up by paying a price for the consequences of what one thinks.

This is how the American intellectual scene looks. Much greater events occurring outside the United States, however, demonstrate the urgency of our task. Those events are epitomized by the Statue of Liberty erected by the Chinese students in Tiananmen Square. Apparently, after some discussion about whether it should be altered to have Chinese rather than *Eurocentric* features, there was a consensus that it did not make any difference.

The terror in China continues, and we cannot yet know what will become of those courageous young persons. But we do know the justice of their cause; and although there is no assurance that it will ultimately triumph, their oppressors have won the universal execration of mankind. With Marxist ideology a wretched shambles everywhere, nobody believes any longer in communist legitimacy. Everywhere in the communist world what is wanted is rational liberal democracy that recognizes men's natural freedom and equality and the rights dependent on them. The people of that world need and want education in democracy and the institutions that actualize it. That education is one of the greatest services the democracies can offer to the people who live under communist tyrannies and long for liberty. The example of the United States is what has impressed them most, and their rulers have been unable to stem the infection. Our example, though, requires explanations, the kind the Founders gave to the world. And this is where we are failing: the dominant schools in American universities can tell the Chinese students only that they should avoid Eurocentrism, that rationalism has failed, that they should study non-Western cultures, and that *bourgeois* liberalism is the most despicable of regimes. Stanford has replaced John Locke, *the* philosopher of liberalism, with Frantz Fanon, an ephemeral writer once promoted by Sartre because of his murderous hatred of Europeans and his espousal of terrorism. However, this is not what the Chinese need. They have Deng Xiaoping to deconstruct their Statue of Liberty. We owe them something much better.

It is in this atmosphere, the awareness that we tread near the edge of the abyss, that I think and write. The American intellectual scene is bleak and ominous but certainly provides great theoretical exhilaration, if one can bear to observe it closely.

WENDY STEINER

"The Academic Equivalent of a Rock Star"

Wendy Steiner (1949–   ) is an author whose works include *Exact Resemblances to Exact Resemblance: The Literary Portraiture of Gertrude Stein* (1978), *The Colors of Rhetoric: Problems in the Relation between Modern Literature and Painting* (1982), and *Pictures of Romance: Form against Context in Painting and Literature* (1988). The following selection originally appeared in the *New York Times Book Review.*

According to Allan Bloom, Socrates computed the pleasure of the philosopher's life at 729 times that of the tyrant. With such an edge, the philosopher should engage in a little charitable redistribution, helping the tyrant toward glimpses of the good life and innocent citizens to a bit of bliss. But Mr. Bloom's doctrine has no such effect. No doubt, the spiritual crisis of our age—which he paints in the direst hues—is responsible for his insulting the reader with illogic, contradiction and infuriating double binds.

Mr. Bloom, a professor of political philosophy, reached public notice in 1987 with the best seller *The Closing of the American Mind.* Its thesis is that American youth is being cheated of its intellectual

birthright by irresponsible academics who ignore the best that has
been thought and written in their zeal to boost women, minorities
and exotic cultures. When liberal educators admit the foreign, the
skeptical and the deconstructive into the great Western tradition,
they are promoting ideas that contradict the very liberalism that
motivates them; instead, they should teach liberalism by excluding
everything that is not liberal. The argument of that book is tortuous,
but it is accompanied by flights of such high-minded conviction and
humble self-deprecation—the mild-mannered Clark Kent of philosophy called forth from his University of Chicago seclusion to save
American society from the deadly grip of deconstruction—that he
has become, in his own words, "the academic equivalent of a rock
star." Now not only the William Bennetts[1] of America rampage
against the professoriate, but a voice crying out of the putrid ranks
themselves.

In time to capitalize on the success of *Closing,* Mr. Bloom's
publisher has released a collection of his essays written over the past
30 years, *Giants and Dwarfs.* It contains an introductory response to
his critics, readings of great books, florid tributes to favorite teachers
and denunciations of egalitarianism. The contradictions and biases
of *The Closing of the American Mind* are here vividly apparent. Mr.
Bloom reads *The Merchant of Venice,* for example, as a caution that
people of different religions and cultures cannot cooperate unless
they abandon their ethnic identities.[2] "In Venice and modern
thought, there was an attempt to . . . unite men, not on the level of
their truly human sameness, but on that of the politically beneficial—
a unity expressed in men's universal desire for gain." It is not clear
why, if the desire for gain is universal, the appeal to men on this
basis ignores their "truly human sameness." Moreover, we are never

---

[1] William Bennett (1943–   ) has held several federal positions in the United States.
As secretary of the Department of Education from 1985 to 1988, he was known for
his vocal opposition to plans to reshape college curricula in American universities to
require more courses with a non-Western emphasis (particularly a plan adopted at
Stanford University in the late 1980s). He was the director of the Office for National
Drug Control Policy from 1989 to 1990. (ED.)

[2] In Shakespeare's *The Merchant of Venice,* Shylock, a Jewish moneylender, lends
money to his rival Antonio, a Christian merchant, on the condition that if the amount
is not repaid by the agreed-upon day, Antonio must forfeit a pound of his own flesh.
When Antonio's merchant ships are delayed and he is unable to repay Shylock by the
deadline, Shylock takes him to court in an attempt to extract his payment of flesh.
(ED.)

told what that sameness is; of course, if we have to be told, maybe we are unworthy of knowing. But it seems clear that if Antonio and Shylock had only gone to college together rather than teaming up on a business venture, their association would have met a better end—provided it was a Greek academy they attended and not an American university.

Mr. Bloom's disapproval of cultural miscegenation leads him to denounce the most remarkable achievement of recent educational reform—the attempt to revise, expand and diversify the canon of texts regularly studied in American universities. He is particularly worried about teaching foreign works, for example those by the Japanese, who, he warns, are racially intolerant. This may sound like the pot calling the kettle black, but Mr. Bloom does not notice. "Should we open ourselves up to this new culture? Sympathize with its tastes? Should we aim for restrictiveness rather than diversity? Should we experiment with a more effective racism?" As I recall, the ancient Greeks, who form the basis of Mr. Bloom's ideal curriculum, kept slaves, marginalized women and left unwanted babies to perish on mountainsides. Mr. Bloom's logic would suggest that the long dominance of the classical tradition in Western higher education is responsible for the prevalence of American racism, sexism and child abuse.

But it is not just foreign influences in education that scare him. Ethnicity and historicism are antithetical to his notion of the human. He complains when Chinese, black, Armenian and gay students demand to have books by members of their communities included in the curriculum. "The premise of these students' concerns is that 'where you come from,' your culture, is more important than where you are going . . . [that] you do not go to college to discover for yourself what is good but to be confirmed in your origins." This statement fits squarely into the ideology of the second-generation American, the assimilationist who makes a virtue of cutting loose from his or her origins in order to embrace an ethnically unmarked Americanness. Like a latter-day Horatio Alger,[3] Mr. Bloom sees himself as having gone somewhere better than where he began.

He does value one origin, however, and that is ancient Greece.

---

[3] Horatio Alger (1832–1899) was a popular writer of boys' stories in the later nineteenth century. The characters in Alger's stories made him famous as the creator of the American mythical figure of the "Alger hero"—a poor but honest and hard-working youth who overcomes the obstacles of poverty to rise to wealth and fame. (ED.)

This is what the deconstructionists mean by the "privileging" of a given tradition, and Mr. Bloom performs all the mystification typical of such special pleading. He mocks those who argue that the canon is an instrument of control and an expression of (perhaps unconscious) class, gender and racial prejudices. Though he admits that sometimes books promote such views, he clearly thinks that some great works of literature have absolute value or represent eternal truth. "How enslaved we have become to the historicist assertion that all thought is decisively culture-bound," he exclaims. Plato's allegory of the cave provides the imagery for release from the specificity of history and context: "Many books, perhaps the most important ones, have an independent status and bring us light from outside our cave, without which we would be blind."

These claims appear in Mr. Bloom's introduction, but in the book's earlier essays on canonic literary works he sets out to demonstrate just the opposite, that Plato's *Republic,* Shakespeare's *Richard II* and Rousseau's *Emile* are grounded in history and instrumental in creating politically malleable citizens. "Poetry . . . shapes the men on whom the statesman's rhetoric can work. . . . Poetry is not autonomous; its life is infused by its attachment to the same objects which motivate the best of acting men." One wonders how Mr. Bloom can unblinkingly assert completely contradictory positions. He would clearly not like us to conclude that he is not acute enough to recognize such gross errors, but unless we come to such a conclusion, *Giants and Dwarfs* sets off that nasty tingling sensation one has in the presence of Orwellian doublespeak.

Indeed, Mr. Bloom gives us every reason to suspect that he is capable of using it, for he opposes the egalitarian basis of American democracy. "A man's mind is almost necessarily a prisoner of the horizon of his particular time and place, and in a democracy that means of the most fundamental premises or prejudices of public opinion." The giants of his title are the great thinkers of the past and present, whereas the dwarfs are the rest of the human species. He marvels at Raymond Aron's[4] "strange spiritual asceticism . . . in believing in the right of others to think as they please." Accused of promoting elitism in *The Closing of the American Mind,* Mr. Bloom presents himself as a victim of the democratic prejudice in favor of

---

[4] Raymond Aron (1905–1983) was a French sociologist, philosopher, and political commentator known for his mistrust of strict adherence to ideological principles. (ED.)

equality: "The leading principle of our regime is the equal worth of all persons, and facts or sentiments that appear to contradict that principle are experienced by a democrat as immoral." Here he comes perilously close to the specter of the Japanese racists he conjures up seven pages later.

Mr. Bloom denies being either a liberal or a conservative, though in one essay or another he praises tenets of both. But of course, a consistent identification with one political position might enclose him within the cave, and Mr. Bloom must be free to bask in the Greek light. What is it like to inhabit this sunny climate? Like all Mediterranean sojourns, it requires a talent for inactivity. Mr. Bloom praises the philosopher Leo Strauss[5] for having "a life in which the only real events were thoughts," and he pictures friendship as men spending "their lives together reading and talking about the life they would like to lead while they are leading it." But along with this inactivity comes isolation and the disapproval of one's fellow men. Philosophy, Mr. Bloom says, "is neither understood nor desired. . . . I am now even more persuaded of the urgent need to study why Socrates was accused."

Mr. Bloom's life falls short of true contemplative catatonia, for he has gone public. "I have gotten a great kick," he writes, "out of becoming the academic equivalent of a rock star." Accordingly, though the teachers he most admires were ignored by the world, Mr. Bloom sees himself as a tragic Socrates condemned by a professorial rabble hostile to the teaching of their gadfly. Maybe his mistake was to forget Leo Strauss' example of dedication "to an intransigent seriousness as opposed to popularization." Had he kept out of the limelight, his epic diction—"an inner need to pay [Strauss] tribute and a kind of filial piety urge me on"—would perhaps not sound so comical. But popularization unavoidably turned this philosopher into a martyr—if not to the hemlock-wielding public, then to his own bathetic self-dramatizing. In separating the giants from the dwarfs, the philosopher is well advised to heed the ancient wisdom: "Know thyself."

---

[5] Leo Strauss (1899–1973) was a German-born American political philosopher who interpreted classical political theory in his scholarly works, such as *On Tyranny* and *Natural Right and History*. (ED.)

MARK MATHABANE

The African Contribution

Mark Mathabane (1960–   ) was born in South Africa under the discriminatory system of apartheid. He recounts his early experiences in *Kaffir Boy* (1986). In *Kaffir Boy in America* (1989), from which the following selection is taken, he writes about his experiences while in the United States on a tennis scholarship. In his second book, he notes that, "the word *Kaffir* is of Arabic origin. It means 'infidel.' In South Africa, it is used pejoratively by whites to refer to blacks. It is the equivalent of the term 'nigger.'"

In the library one afternoon, having completed my homework, I began browsing among the bookshelves. I came upon a paperback copy of *Black Boy*, Richard Wright's searing autobiography. My attention was arrested by the title and by the following defiant words on the back cover of the book: "The white South said that it knew 'niggers,' and I was what the white South called 'nigger.' Well, the white South had never known me—never known what I thought, what I felt."

I mentally replaced "white South" with "white South Africa," and "nigger" with "Kaffir," and was intrigued by how Richard Wright's feelings mirrored my own. I immediately sat down in a chair by the window and began reading the book. I was overwhelmed; I could not put the book down. I even missed my economics class because I was so engrossed. When the library closed I was three-quarters of the way through the book. Bleary-eyed, I went back to my room and read the rest.

The next day I went back to the library and asked the head librarian—a good-natured Franciscan priest with white hair and a charming smile—if the library had more books by black authors. He guided me to the treasure. I checked out Richard Wright's *Native Son*, Eldridge Cleaver's *Soul on Ice*, W. E. B. Du Bois's *Souls of Black Folks*, *The Autobiography of Malcolm X*, Franz Fanon's *The Wretched of the Earth*, Claude Brown's *Manchild of the Promised Land*, James Baldwin's *The Fire Next Time* and *Notes of a Native Son*, Maya Angelou's *I Know Why the Caged Bird Sings*, James Weldon Johnson's *The Autobiography of an Ex-Colored Man*, and the autobiography and incendiary speeches of Frederick Douglass. I devoured the books with relish.

After this momentous discovery I knew that my life would never be the same. Here were black men and women, rebels in their own right, who had felt, thought, and suffered deeply, who had grown up under conditions that had threatened to destroy their very souls; here they were, baring their bleeding hearts on paper, using words as weapons, plunging into realms of experience I had never before thought reachable, and wrestling with fate itself in an heroic attempt to make the incomprehensible—man's inhumanity to man—comprehensible. Most astonishing was that these men and women had written about what I felt and thought, what I had been through as a black man, what I desired, what I dreamed about, and what I refused to compromise.

"These are soul mates," I said to myself, "these are my true brothers and sisters." Where had they been all those years when I was lost in the wilderness, feeling so alone, wondering why I was being misunderstood by the world, why I seemed so at odds with complacent reality? I had to learn to write like them, to purge myself of what they had purged themselves of so eloquently. Here was a way through which I could finally understand myself, perform the duty I'd pledged to my countrymen and to my mother.

Inspired by these black writers, I bought myself a pair of notebooks and sat down one evening and began to write. I chose as a topic an issue of which I had only superficial knowledge, but one which appealed to my fancy. Words came very easily to the pen, but when I paused to evaluate what I had written and compared it to the masters I was determined to emulate, I found my effort ridiculous. The language was verbose, the ideas vague and incoherent. What was I doing wrong? Maybe I needed some expert advice. One day Mr. Allan, my English teacher, asked us to write a short story.

My story—a vivid, fictional description of Africa—was considered the best by Mr. Allan, who was a hard-to-please but excellent critic and teacher of English. He was stingy with A's, no matter how well the job done. I received an A for my essay; my previous assignments had merited C's and B-minuses.

I carefully analyzed the essay to determine what exactly had so impressed the scrupulous teacher. I came up with the following answer: to write well, write about what you know, for experience is the best teacher, and writing is a means of self-expression.

Flushed with confidence from writing the essay, I jotted down ideas for more essays and possibly novels. I filled notebooks with

descriptions and characters and plots. Maybe writing is my calling
in life, I thought. Determined to hone my skills, I went back to my
favorite writers for tips on how to go about the arduous task of
learning how to move the world with the right word and the right
accent. Every one of the writers I admired had been a voracious
reader of books. I was already one. They had felt deeply. I felt deeply,
too. They possessed an inborn obsession to share with the rest of
humanity, through the written word, their innermost feelings, their
vision of life, its agony and ecstasy, its manifold pains and sorrows
and joys, its loves and hatreds—all of which they had extracted by
looking deeply and with compassion into the human heart.

Such a temperament I believed I still lacked because I had yet to
acquire a sound liberal arts education. The college library had an
impressive record collection of Shakespeare's plays; the dramas of
Sophocles, Euripides, and Aristophanes; the *Dialogues* of Plato; the
poems of Milton; and the plays of Dryden and Goldsmith, read by
such giants of the stage as Paul Robeson, Claire Bloom, Sir Laurence
Olivier, Anthony Quayle, Richard Burton, Sir John Gielgud, and Paul
Schofield, among others. I checked out these records at the rate of
three a day, and listened to them over and over again. The head
librarian expressed pleasure at seeing me madly in love with Shakespeare and soon I was being talked about.

I took an English course with Professor Ann Klein. She instantly
detected my enthusiastic love for poetry and helped me improve my
taste and understanding of Keats, Shelley, Wordsworth, Coleridge,
and Byron. Whereas heretofore my enjoyment of classical music had
been visceral, I enrolled in a piano class out of a belief that the best
way to understand classical music was to play an instrument.

Other subjects I now enjoyed were economics and philosophy.
In the latter, taught by the easygoing, amiable Father Lucan, I was
introduced to the brilliant ideas and provocative arguments for
greater liberty, toleration, and individuality by Locke, Rousseau, and
John Stuart Mill. The notably eclectic course Personal and Moral Life
merely mentioned in passing their great ideas, but I went out in
search of the complete works and read them avidly. I was fascinated
by Rousseau's *The Social Contract,* especially his famous assertion
"Man is born free, and everywhere he is in chains. One thinks himself
the master of others and still remains a greater slave than they." But
I found some of his arguments elliptical and contradictory. Mill and
Locke became my favorite philosophers. I was amazed to discover,
with repeated readings of their seminal works, that they basically
confirmed what I had believed instinctively about the nature of

freedom, individuality, and natural and civil rights. Locke's "Treatise on Toleration," his "Second Essay on Government," and Mill's *On Liberty* and *The Subjection of Women* left a decisive influence on my mind. This immersion in books alleviated the stress of constantly worrying about the condition of my mother and family.

Once again my love affair with the world of books landed me in trouble. I now walked about with a mind pregnant with thoughts inspired by reading. I longed to live only in the world of the imagination and ideas because physical reality suddenly seemed artificial, cold, dead. I became absentminded. Some of the black students on campus wondered why I no longer came to their parties, why I occasionally sat alone in the cafeteria, deep in thought.

"He's too proud," someone said.

"He's trying to be white," another said.

"He thinks he is better than us."

"He's stir-crazy."

They never understood my need for solitude, that "to fly from, need not be to hate, mankind." They never understood why I found great pleasure in watching squirrels racing up and down trees, in walking down to the Mississippi River and spending the afternoon staring at its murky waters, at the falling autumn leaves along its banks, at clouds sailing across the sky, and at the sleepy town of Hannibal on the other side, where Mark Twain was born. They never understood why I loved memorizing poetry, why I used quotations from books to illustrate a point, or why I urged them to become more politically active on campus so they could better protect their interests and make their presence felt as blacks. I tried establishing ties of solidarity with them, given our common experiences growing up in the ghetto, but we kept drifting apart because of our divergent attitudes. I was eager to fight, to protest, as black Americans had done in the 1960s, during those unforgettable days of Martin Luther King, Jr., Malcolm X, and Stokely Carmichael's misunderstood credo of Black Power. They were eager to accommodate, to live for the moment, to make their peace with the status quo, to wallow in apathy and self-pity. At times it appeared that I had come to America a generation too late. In fairness to many of these black students, they were concerned that an activist attitude might lose them their athletic scholarships or financial aid.

In celebration of black history month, in February 1980, I wrote the following poem, entitled "Longing for My Roots." It was a nostalgic poem, inspired by thoughts of home and of my ailing mother.

when I was a little child
living amidst innocence among
the chaste hills
and the pure forests and purer
streams
i never for a single moment paused
to think
that there might come a
time
when all i would have to live with
was to be just a memory

all the enchanting silhouettes of
the africa
i used to so lovingly know
all the natural beauty of her
beasts
the magnificent plumage of her
wild birds
the blithesomeness of her
black people
the eternal feeling of freedom
among singing titihoyes
the rivers that seem to eddy whirl
their courses
through hills and plains

all the everlasting elegance of
the springbok
the gentle tip-tappering of
summer's rain
the haunting murmur of
the windsong
the thundering of hooves
upon the serengeti

all that i am now without
all that boundless joy
i once so much cherished
i have prematurely left behind
to die and to decay

yet an african still am i
a proud man as such

i am black (soot black)
a handsome black warrior as such
i am still the proud possessor
of that undaunted spirit
reminiscent of endless freedom
among the misty hills
where the zebra used to cry
with ecstatic joy

i still remember the kraal
the grassy citadel of
my forefathers
i still can smell
the scent of fresh cowdung
and in hours of solitude
i still can hear
the bewitching sound of cowhide drums
and see through the haze of time
valiant, plumed warriors
as they leap and fall
while others
fall
never to leap again

even now
far, far away from home
oceans of water away
i still can see the misty hills
i can still hear mama's voice
echoing through the valley of
a thousand hills
calling me to come home
for supper around the fireside

I showed the poem to several black students. Some of them, apparently ignorant or ashamed of their heritage as African-Americans, regarded it as confirmation of Africa's primitiveness. But I was proud of it. I knew that Africa, despite its many and serious problems, despite the Western tendency to stereotype it, remained a place of immense natural and cultural beauty, and that its diverse, proud, brave, resilient, and beautiful peoples are descended from some of the oldest civilizations on earth, which have made valuable contributions to literature, art, music, dance, science, religion, and other fields of human endeavor.

DIANE RAVITCH

Multiculturalism

Diane Ravitch (1938–) teaches history and education at Columbia University's Teacher's College. She has contributed to such periodicals as *Commentary, New Leader,* the *New York Times,* and *The American Scholar,* where the following selection originally appeared. Her works include *The Great School Wars: A History of the New York City Public Schools,* 2nd ed. (1988), *The Schools We Deserve: Reflections on the Educational Crisis of Our Time* (1985), and, with Chester E. Finn, Jr., *What Do Our Seventeen-Year-Olds Know? The First National Assessment of What American Students Know about History and Literature* (1987). She is currently the assistant secretary for educational research and improvement and counselor to the secretary of education.

Questions of race, ethnicity, and religion have been a perennial source of conflict in American education. The schools have often attracted the zealous attention of those who wish to influence the future, as well as those who wish to change the way we view the past. In our history, the schools have been not only an institution in which to teach young people skills and knowledge, but an arena where interest groups fight to preserve their values, or to revise the judgments of history, or to bring about fundamental social change. In the nineteenth century, Protestants and Catholics battled over which version of the Bible should be used in school, or whether the Bible should be used at all. In recent decades, bitter racial disputes—provoked by policies of racial segregation and discrimination—have generated turmoil in the streets and in the schools. The secularization of the schools during the past century has prompted attacks on the curricula and textbooks and library books by fundamentalist Christians, who object to whatever challenges their faith-based views of history, literature, and science.

Given the diversity of American society, it has been impossible to insulate the schools from pressures that result from differences and tensions among groups. When people differ about basic values, sooner or later those disagreements turn up in battles about how schools are organized or what the schools should teach. Sometimes these battles remove a terrible injustice, like racial segregation. Sometimes, however, interest groups politicize the curriculum and attempt to impose their views on teachers, school officials, and textbook publishers. Across the country, even now, interest groups are pressuring local school boards to remove myths and fables and other imaginative literature from children's readers and to inject the teaching of creationism in biology. When groups cross the line into extremism, advancing their own agenda without regard to reason or to others, they threaten public education itself, making it difficult to teach any issues honestly and making the entire curriculum vulnerable to political campaigns.

For many years, the public schools attempted to neutralize controversies over race, religion, and ethnicity by ignoring them. Educators believed, or hoped, that the schools could remain outside politics; this was, of course, a vain hope since the schools were pursuing policies based on race, religion, and ethnicity. Nonetheless, such divisive questions were usually excluded from the curriculum. The textbooks minimized problems among groups and taught a sanitized version of history. Race, religion, and ethnicity were presented as minor elements in the American saga; slavery was treated as an episode, immigration as a sidebar, and women were largely absent. The textbooks concentrated on presidents, wars, national politics, and issues of state. An occasional "great black" or "great woman" received mention, but the main narrative paid little attention to minority groups and women.

With the ethnic revival of the 1960s, this approach to the teaching of history came under fire, because the history of national leaders— virtually all of whom were white, Anglo-Saxon, and male—ignored the place in American history of those who were none of the above. The traditional history of elites had been complemented by an assimilationist view of American society, which presumed that everyone in the American melting pot would eventually lose or abandon those ethnic characteristics that distinguished them from mainstream Americans. The ethnic revival demonstrated that many groups did not want to be assimilated or melted. Ethnic studies programs popped up on campuses to teach not only that "black is beautiful," but also that every other variety of ethnicity is "beautiful" as well; everyone who had "roots" began to look for them so that they too could recover that ancestral part of themselves that had not been homogenized.

As ethnicity became an accepted subject for study in the late 1960s, textbooks were assailed for their failure to portray blacks accurately; within a few years, the textbooks in wide use were carefully screened to eliminate bias against minority groups and women. At the same time, new scholarship about the history of women, blacks, and various ethnic minorities found its way into the textbooks. At first, the multicultural content was awkwardly incorporated as little boxes on the side of the main narrative. Then some of the new social historians (like Stephan Thernstrom, Mary Beth Norton, Gary Nash, Winthrop Jordan, and Leon Litwack) themselves wrote textbooks, and the main narrative itself began to reflect a broadened historical understanding of race, ethnicity, and class in the American past. Consequently, today's history textbooks routinely incorporate the experiences of women, blacks, American Indians, and various immigrant groups.

As a result of the political and social changes of recent decades, cultural pluralism is now generally recognized as an organizing principle of this society. In contrast to the idea of the melting pot, which promised to erase ethnic and group differences, children now learn that variety is the spice of life. They learn that America has provided a haven for many different groups and has allowed them to maintain their cultural heritage or to assimilate, or—as is often the case—to do both; the choice is theirs, not the state's. They learn that cultural pluralism is one of the norms of a free society; that differences among groups are a national resource rather than a problem to be solved. Indeed, the unique feature of the United States is that its common culture has been formed by the interaction of its subsidiary cultures. It is a culture that has been influenced over time by immigrants, American Indians, Africans (slave and free) and by their descendants. American music, art, literature, language, food, clothing, sports, holidays, and customs all show the effects of the commingling of diverse cultures in one nation. Paradoxical though it may seem, the United States has a common culture that is multicultural.

Our schools and our institutions of higher learning have in recent years begun to embrace what Catherine R. Stimpson of Rutgers University has called "cultural democracy," a recognition that we must listen to a "diversity of voices" in order to understand our culture, past and present. This understanding of the pluralistic nature of American culture has taken a long time to forge. It is based on sound scholarship and has led to major revisions in what children are taught and what they read in school. The new history is—indeed, must be—a warts-and-all history; it demands an unflinching examination of racism and discrimination in our history. Making these changes is difficult, raises tempers, and ignites controversies, but gives a more interesting and accurate account of American history.

Accomplishing these changes is valuable, because there is also a useful lesson for the rest of the world in America's relatively successful experience as a pluralistic society. Throughout human history, the clash of different cultures, races, ethnic groups, and religions has often been the cause of bitter hatred, civil conflict, and international war. The ethnic tensions that now are tearing apart Lebanon, Sri Lanka, Kashmir, and various republics of the Soviet Union remind us of the costs of unfettered group rivalry. Thus, it is a matter of more than domestic importance that we closely examine and try to understand that part of our national history in which different groups competed, fought, suffered, but ultimately learned to live together in relative peace and even achieved a sense of common nationhood.

Alas, these painstaking efforts to expand the understanding of American culture into a richer and more varied tapestry have taken a new turn, and not for the better. Almost any idea, carried to its extreme, can be made pernicious, and this is what is happening now to multiculturalism. Today, pluralistic multiculturalism must contend with a new, particularistic multiculturalism. The pluralists seek a richer common culture; the particularists insist that no common culture is possible or desirable. The new particularism is entering the curriculum in a number of school systems across the country. Advocates of particularism propose an ethnocentric curriculum to raise the self-esteem and academic achievement of children from racial and ethnic minority backgrounds. Without any evidence, they claim that children from minority backgrounds will do well in school *only* if they are immersed in a positive, prideful version of their ancestral culture. If children are of, for example, Fredonian ancestry, they must hear that Fredonians were important in mathematics, science, history, and literature. If they learn about great Fredonians and if their studies use Fredonian examples and Fredonian concepts, they will do well in school. If they do not, they will have low self-esteem and will do badly.

At first glance, this appears akin to the celebratory activities associated with Black History Month or Women's History Month, when schoolchildren learn about the achievements of blacks and women. But the point of those celebrations is to demonstrate that neither race nor gender is an obstacle to high achievement. They teach all children that everyone, regardless of their race, religion, gender, ethnicity, or family origin, can achieve self-fulfillment, honor, dignity in society if they aim high and work hard.

By contrast, the particularistic version of multiculturalism is unabashedly filiopietistic[1] and deterministic. It teaches children that their identity is determined by their "cultural genes." That something in their blood or their race memory or their cultural DNA defines who they are and what they may achieve. That the culture in which they live is not their own culture, even though they were born here. That American culture is "Eurocentric," and therefore hostile to anyone whose ancestors are not European. Perhaps the most invidious implication of particularism is that racial and ethnic minorities are not and should not try to be part of American culture; it implies that American culture belongs only to those who are white and European; it implies that those who are neither white nor European are alienated from American culture by virtue of their race or ethnicity; it implies that the only culture they do belong to or can ever belong to is the culture of their ancestors, even if their families have lived in this country for generations.

The war on so-called Eurocentrism is intended to foster self-esteem among those who are not of European descent. But how, in fact, is self-esteem developed? How is the sense of one's own possibilities, one's potential choices, developed? Certainly, the school curriculum plays a relatively small role as compared to the influence of family, community, mass media, and society. But to the extent that curriculum influences what children think of themselves, it should encourage children of all racial and ethnic groups to believe that they are part of this society and that they should develop their talents and minds to the fullest. It is enormously inspiring, for example, to learn about men and women from diverse backgrounds who overcame poverty, discrimination, physical handicaps, and other obstacles to achieve success in a variety of fields. Behind every such biography of accomplishment is a story of heroism, perseverance, and self-discipline. Learning these stories will encourage a healthy spirit of pluralism, of mutual respect, and of self-respect among children of different backgrounds. The children of American society today will live their lives in a racially and culturally diverse nation, and their education should prepare them to do so.

The pluralist approach to multiculturalism promotes a broader interpretation of the common American culture and seeks due recognition for the ways that the nation's many racial, ethnic, and

---

[1] based on an excessive reverence for one's ancestors or cultural tradition (ED.)

cultural groups have transformed the national culture. The pluralists say, in effect, "American culture belongs to us, all of us; the U.S. is us, and we remake it in every generation." But particularists have no interest in extending or revising American culture; indeed, they deny that a common culture exists. Particularists reject any accommodation among groups, any interactions that blur the distinct lines between them. The brand of history that they espouse is one in which everyone is either a descendant of victims or oppressors. By doing so, ancient hatreds are fanned and recreated in each new generation. Particularism has its intellectual roots in the ideology of ethnic separatism and in the black nationalist movement. In the particularist analysis, the nation has five cultures: African American, Asian American, European American, Latino/Hispanic, and Native American. The huge cultural, historical, religious, and linguistic differences within these categories are ignored, as is the considerable intermarriage among these groups, as are the linkages (like gender, class, sexual orientation, and religion) that cut across these five groups. No serious scholar would claim that all Europeans and white Americans are part of the same culture, or that all Asians are part of the same culture, or that all people of Latin-American descent are of the same culture, or that all people of African descent are of the same culture. Any categorization this broad is essentially meaningless and useless.

Particularism is a bad idea whose time has come. It is also a fashion spreading like wildfire through the education system, actively promoted by organizations and individuals with a political and professional interest in strengthening ethnic power bases in the university, in the education profession, and in society itself. One can scarcely pick up an educational journal without learning about a school district that is converting to an ethnocentric curriculum in an attempt to give "self-esteem" to children from racial minorities. A state-funded project in a Sacramento high school is teaching young black males to think like Africans and to develop the "African Mind Model Technique," in order to free themselves of the racism of American culture. A popular black rap singer, KRS-One, complained in an op-ed article in the *New York Times* that the schools should be teaching blacks about their cultural heritage, instead of trying to make everyone Americans. "It's like trying to teach a dog to be a cat," he wrote. KRS-One railed about having to learn about Thomas Jefferson and the Civil War, which had nothing to do (he said) with black history.

Pluralism can easily be transformed into particularism, as may be seen in the potential uses in the classroom of the Mayan contribution to mathematics. The Mayan example was popularized in a movie called *Stand and Deliver,* about a charismatic Bolivian-born mathematics teacher in Los Angeles who inspired his students (who are Hispanic) to learn calculus. He told them that their ancestors invented the concept of zero; but that wasn't all he did. He used imagination to put across mathematical concepts. He required them to do homework and to go to school on Saturdays and during the Christmas holidays, so that they might pass the Advanced Placement mathematics examination for college entry. The teacher's reference to the Mayans' mathematical genius was a valid instructional device: It was an attention-getter and would have interested even students who were not Hispanic. But the Mayan example would have had little effect without the teacher's insistence that the class study hard for a difficult examination.

Ethnic educators have seized upon the Mayan contribution to mathematics as the key to simultaneously boosting the ethnic pride of Hispanic children and attacking Eurocentrism. One proposal claims that Mexican-American children will be attracted to science and mathematics if they study Mayan mathematics, the Mayan calendar, and Mayan astronomy. Children in primary grades are to be taught that the Mayans were first to discover the zero and that Europeans learned it long afterwards from the Arabs, who had learned it in India. This will help them see that Europeans were latecomers in the discovery of great ideas. Botany is to be learned by study of the agricultural techniques of the Aztecs, a subject of somewhat limited relevance to children in urban areas. Furthermore, "ethnobotanical" classifications of plants are to be substituted for the Eurocentric Linnaean system. At first glance, it may seem curious that Hispanic children are deemed to have no cultural affinity with Spain; but to acknowledge the cultural tie would confuse the ideological assault on Eurocentrism.

This proposal suggests some questions: Is there any evidence that the teaching of "culturally relevant" science and mathematics will draw Mexican-American children to the study of these subjects? Will Mexican-American children lose interest or self-esteem if they discover that their ancestors were Aztecs or Spaniards, rather than Mayans? Are children who learn in this way prepared to study the science and mathematics that are taught in American colleges and universities and that are needed for advanced study in these fields? Are they even prepared to study the science and mathematics taught in *Mexican* universities? If the class is half Mexican-American and half something else, will only the Mexican-American children study in a Mayan and Aztec mode or will all the children? But shouldn't all children study what is culturally relevant for them? How will we train teachers who have command of so many different systems of mathematics and science?

Every field of study, it seems, has been tainted by Eurocentrism, which was defined by a professor at Manchester University, George Ghevarughese Joseph, in *Race and Class* in 1987, as "intellectual racism." Professor Joseph argues that the history of science and technology—and in particular, of mathematics—in non-European societies was distorted by racist Europeans who wanted to establish the dominance of European forms of knowledge. The racists, he writes, traditionally traced mathematics to the Greeks, then claimed that it reached its full development in Europe. These are simply Eurocentric myths to sustain an "imperialist/racist ideology," says Professor Joseph, since mathematics was found in Egypt, Babylonia, Mesopotamia, and India long before the Greeks were supposed to have developed it. Professor Joseph points out too that Arab scientists should be credited with major discoveries traditionally attributed to William Harvey, Isaac Newton, Charles Darwin, and Sir Francis Bacon. But he is not concerned only to argue historical issues; his purpose is to bring all of these different mathematical traditions into the school classroom so that children might study, for example, "traditional African designs, Indian *rangoli* patterns and Islamic art" and "the language and counting systems found across the world."

Particularism is akin to cultural Lysenkoism,[2] for it takes as its premise the spurious notion that cultural traits are inherited. It implies a dubious, dangerous form of cultural predestination. Children are taught that if their ancestors could do it, so could they. But what happens if a child is from a cultural group that made no significant contribution to science or mathematics? Does this mean that children from that background must find a culturally appropriate field in which to strive? How does a teacher find the right cultural buttons for children of mixed heritage? And how in the world will teachers use this technique when the children in their classes are drawn from many different cultures, as is usually the case? By the time that every culture gets its due, there may be no time left to teach the subject itself. This explosion of filiopietism (which, we

[2] Doctrine of Trofim Lysenko (1898–1976), a controversial Russian scientist, who asserted that, contrary to accepted genetic theory, traits acquired through environmental influences are passed on through heredity. (ED.)

should remember, comes from adults, not from students) is reminiscent of the period some years ago when the Russians claimed that they had invented everything first; as we now know, this nationalistic braggadocio did little for their self-esteem and nothing for their economic development. We might reflect, too, on how little social prestige has been accorded in this country to immigrants from Greece and Italy, even though the achievements of their ancestors were at the heart of the classical curriculum.

Particularism can easily be carried to extremes. Students of Fredonian descent must hear that their ancestors were seminal in the development of all human civilization and that without the Fredonian contribution, we would all be living in caves or trees, bereft of art, technology, and culture. To explain why Fredonians today are in modest circumstances, given their historic eminence, children are taught that somewhere, long ago, another culture stole the Fredonians' achievements, palmed them off as their own, and then oppressed the Fredonians.

I first encountered this argument almost twenty years ago, when I was a graduate student. I shared a small office with a young professor, and I listened as she patiently explained to a student why she had given him a D on a term paper. In his paper, he argued that the Arabs had stolen mathematics from the Nubians in the desert long ago (I forget in which century this theft allegedly occurred). She tried to explain to him about the necessity of historical evidence. He was unconvinced, since he believed that he had uncovered a great truth that was beyond proof. The part I couldn't understand was how anyone could lose knowledge by sharing it. After all, cultures are constantly influencing one another, exchanging ideas and art and technology, and the exchange usually is enriching, not depleting.

It is hardly surprising that America's schools would recognize strong cultural ties with Europe since our nation's political, religious, educational, and economic institutions were created chiefly by people of European descent, our government was shaped by European ideas, and nearly 80 percent of the people who live here are of European descent. The particularists treat all of this history as a racist bias toward Europe, rather than as the matter-of-fact consequences of European immigration. Even so, American education is not centered on Europe. American education, if it is centered on anything, is centered on itself. It is "Americentric." Most American students today have never studied any world history; they know very little about Europe, and even less about the rest of the world. Their minds are rooted solidly in the here and now. When the Berlin Wall was opened

in the fall of 1989, journalists discovered that most American teenagers had no idea what it was, nor why its opening was such a big
deal. Nonetheless, Eurocentrism provides a better target than Amer-
icentrism.

In school districts where most children are black and Hispanic,
there has been a growing tendency to embrace particularism rather
than pluralism. Many of the children in these districts perform poorly
in academic classes and leave school without graduating. They would
fare better in school if they had well-educated and well-paid teachers,
small classes, good materials, encouragement at home and school,
summer academic programs, protection from the drugs and crime
that ravage their neighborhoods, and higher expectations of satisfying
careers upon graduation. These are expensive and time-consuming
remedies that must also engage the larger society beyond the school.
The lure of particularism is that it offers a less complicated anodyne,
one in which the children's academic deficiencies may be addressed—
or set aside—by inflating their racial pride. The danger of this remedy
is that it will detract attention from the real needs of schools and the
real interests of children, while simultaneously arousing distorted
race pride in children of all races, increasing racial antagonism and
producing fresh recruits for white and black racist groups.

The rising tide of particularism encourages the politicization of all
curricula in the schools. If education bureaucrats bend to the political
and ideological winds, as is their wont, we can anticipate a generation
of struggle over the content of the curriculum in mathematics, science, literature, and history. Demands for "culturally relevant" studies, for ethnostudies of all kinds, will open the classroom to unending
battles over whose version is taught, who gets credit for what, and
which ethno-interpretation is appropriate. Only recently have districts begun to resist the demands of fundamentalist groups to censor
textbooks and library books (and some have not yet begun to do
so).

The spread of particularism throws into question the very idea
of American public education. Public schools exist to teach children
the general skills and knowledge that they need to succeed in American society, and the specific skills and knowledge that they need in
order to function as American citizens. They receive public support
because they have a public function. Historically, the public schools
were known as "common schools" because they were schools for all,
even if the children of all the people did not attend them. Over the
years, the courts have found that it was unconstitutional to teach

religion in the common schools, or to separate children on the basis of their race in the common schools. In their curriculum, their hiring practices, and their general philosophy, the public schools must not discriminate against or give preference to any racial or ethnic group. Yet they are permitted to accommodate cultural diversity by, for example, serving food that is culturally appropriate or providing library collections that emphasize the interests of the local community. However, they should not be expected to teach children to view the world through an ethnocentric perspective that rejects or ignores the common culture. For generations, those groups that wanted to inculcate their religion or their ethnic heritage have instituted private schools—after school, on weekends, or on a full-time basis. There, children learn with others of the same group—Greeks, Poles, Germans, Japanese, Chinese, Jews, Lutherans, Catholics, and so on—and are taught by people from the same group. Valuable as this exclusive experience has been for those who choose it, this has not been the role of public education. One of the primary purposes of public education has been to create a national community, a definition of citizenship and culture that is both expansive and *inclusive.*

The curriculum in public schools must be based on whatever knowledge and practices have been determined to be best by professionals—experienced teachers and scholars—who are competent to make these judgments. Professional societies must be prepared to defend the integrity of their disciplines. When called upon, they should establish review committees to examine disputes over curriculum and to render judgment, in order to help school officials fend off improper political pressure. Where genuine controversies exist, they should be taught and debated in the classroom. Was Egypt a black civilization? Why not raise the question, read the arguments of the different sides in the debate, show slides of Egyptian pharoahs and queens, read books about life in ancient Egypt, invite guest scholars from the local university, and visit museums with Egyptian collections? If scholars disagree, students should know it. One great advantage of this approach is that students will see that history is a lively study, that textbooks are fallible, that historians disagree, that the writing of history is influenced by the historian's politics and ideology, that history is written by people who make choices among alternative facts and interpretations, and that history changes as new facts are uncovered and new interpretations win adherents. They will also learn that cultures and civilizations constantly interact, exchange ideas, and influence one another, and that the idea of racial or ethnic purity is a myth. Another advantage is that students might once again study ancient history, which has all but disappeared from the curricula of American schools. (California recently introduced a required sixth grade course in ancient civilizations, but ancient history is otherwise *terra incognita* in American education.)

The multicultural controversy may do wonders for the study of history, which has been neglected for years in American schools. At this time, only half of our high school graduates ever study any world history. Any serious attempt to broaden students' knowledge of Africa, Europe, Asia, and Latin America will require at least two, and possibly three years of world history (a requirement thus far only in California). American history, too, will need more time than the one-year high-school survey course. Those of us who have insisted for years on the importance of history in the curriculum may not be ready to assent to its redemptive power, but hope that our new allies will ultimately join a constructive dialogue that strengthens the place of history in the schools.

As cultural controversies arise, educators must adhere to the principle of "E Pluribus Unum." That is, they must maintain a balance between the demands of the one—the nation of which we are common citizens—and the many—the varied histories of the American people. It is not necessary to denigrate either the one or the many. Pluralism is a positive value, but it is also important that we preserve a sense of an American community—a society and a culture to which we all belong. If there is no overall community with an agreed-upon vision of liberty and justice, if all we have is a collection of racial and ethnic cultures, lacking any common bonds, then we have no means to mobilize public opinion on behalf of people who are not members of our particular group. We have, for example, no reason to support public education. If there is no larger community, then each group will want to teach its own children in its own way, and public education ceases to exist.

History should not be confused with filiopietism. History gives no grounds for race pride. No race has a monopoly on virtue. If anything, a study of history should inspire humility, rather than pride. People of every racial group have committed terrible crimes, often against others of the same group. Whether one looks at the history of Europe or Africa or Latin America or Asia, every continent offers examples of inhumanity. Slavery has existed in civilizations around the world for centuries. Examples of genocide can be found around the world, throughout history, from ancient times right through to our own day. Governments and cultures, sometimes by edict, sometimes simply following tradition, have practiced not only slavery, but human sacrifice, infanticide, cliterodectomy, and mass murder. If we teach children this, they might recognize how absurd both racial hatred and racial chauvinism are.

What must be preserved in the study of history is the spirit of inquiry, the readiness to open new questions and to pursue new understandings. History, at its best, is a search for truth. The best way to portray this search is through debate and controversy, rather than through imposition of fixed beliefs and immutable facts. Perhaps the most dangerous aspect of school history is its tendency to become Official History, a sanctified version of the Truth taught by the state to captive audiences and embedded in beautiful mass-market textbooks as holy writ. When Official History is written by committees responding to political pressures, rather than by scholars synthesizing the best available research, then the errors of the past are replaced by the politically fashionable errors of the present. It may be difficult to teach children that history is both important and uncertain, and that even the best historians never have all the pieces of the jigsaw puzzle, but it is necessary to do so. If state education departments permit the revision of their history courses and textbooks to become an exercise in power politics, then the entire process of state-level curriculum-making becomes suspect, as does public education itself.

The question of self-esteem is extraordinarily complex, and it goes well beyond the content of the curriculum. Most of what we call self-esteem is formed in the home and in a variety of life experiences, not only in school. Nonetheless, it has been important for blacks—and for other racial groups—to learn about the history of slavery and of the civil rights movement; it has been important for blacks to know that their ancestors actively resisted enslavement and actively pursued equality; and it has been important for blacks and others to learn about black men and women who fought courageously against racism and who provide models of courage, persistence, and intellect. These are instances where the content of the curriculum reflects sound scholarship, and at the same time probably lessens racial prejudice and provides inspiration for those who are descendants of slaves. But knowing about the travails and triumphs of one's forebears does not necessarily translate into either self-esteem or personal accomplishment. For most children, self-esteem—the self-confidence that grows out of having reached a goal—comes not from hearing about the monuments of their ancestors but as a consequence of what they are able to do and accomplish through their own efforts.

As I reflected on these issues, I recalled reading an interview a few years ago with a talented black runner. She said that her model is Mikhail Baryshnikov. She admires him because he is a magnificent athlete. He is not black; he is not female; he is not American-born; he is not even a runner. But he inspires her because of the way he trained and used his body. When I read this, I thought how narrow-minded it is to believe that people can be inspired *only* by those who are exactly like them in race and ethnicity.

CARL JUNG

The Concept of the Collective Unconscious

Carl Gustav Jung (1875–1961) was a Swiss psychiatrist and the founder of analytic psychology. Jung pioneered the study of schizophrenia and introduced the terms *extrovert, introvert,* and *complex* into the language of psychology. His collected works consist of eighteen volumes, including *The Psychology of Dementia* (1906), *The Psychology of the Unconscious* (1912), and *Modern Man in Search of a Soul* (1933).

Probably none of my empirical concepts has met with so much misunderstanding as the idea of the collective unconscious. In what follows I shall try to give (1) a definition of the concept, (2) a description of what it means for psychology, (3) an explanation of the method of proof, and (4) an example.

DEFINITION

The collective unconscious is a part of the psyche which can be negatively distinguished from a personal unconscious by the fact that it does not, like the latter, owe its existence to personal experience and consequently is not a personal acquisition. While the personal unconscious is made up essentially of contents which have at one time been conscious but which have disappeared from consciousness through having been forgotten or repressed, the contents of the collective unconscious have never been in consciousness, and therefore have never been individually acquired, but owe their existence exclusively to heredity. Whereas the personal unconscious consists for the most part of complexes, the content of the collective unconscious is made up essentially of archetypes.

The concept of the archetype, which is an indispensable correlate of the idea of the collective unconscious, indicates the existence of definite forms in the psyche which seem to be present always and everywhere. Mythological research calls them "motifs"; in the psychology of primitives they correspond to Lévy-Bruhl's concept of "représentations collectives," and in the field of comparative religion they have been defined by Hubert and Mauss as "categories of the imagination." Adolf Bastian long ago called them "elementary" or "primordial thoughts."[1] From these references it should be clear enough that my idea of the archetype—literally a pre-existent form— does not stand alone but is something that is recognized and named in other fields of knowledge.

My thesis, then, is as follows: In addition to our immediate consciousness, which is of a thoroughly personal nature and which we believe to be the only empirical psyche (even if we tack on the personal unconscious as an appendix), there exists a second psychic system of a collective, universal, and impersonal nature which is identical in all individuals. This collective unconscious does not develop individually but is inherited. It consists of preexistent forms, the archetypes, which can only become conscious secondarily and which give definite form to certain psychic contents.

THE PSYCHOLOGICAL MEANING OF THE COLLECTIVE UNCONSCIOUS

Medical psychology, growing as it did out of professional practice, insists on the personal nature of the psyche. By this I mean the views of Freud and Adler. It is a psychology of the person, and its aetiological or causal factors are regarded almost wholly as personal in nature. Nonetheless, even this psychology is based on certain general biological factors, for instance on the sexual instinct or on the urge for self-assertion, which are by no means merely personal peculiarities. It is forced to do this because it lays claim to being an explanatory science. Neither of these views would deny the existence

---

[1] *Lucien Lévy-Bruhl* (1857–1939) was a French philosopher and sociologist. *Henri Hubert* (1872–1927) and *Marcel Mauss* (1872–1950), French sociologists, were the coauthors of books on religion. *Adolf Bastian* (1826–1905) was a German ethnologist who proposed that the cultural traits, folklore, myths, and beliefs of various ethnic groups are essentially the same, merely differing in form because of geography. (ED.)

of a priori instincts common to man and animals alike, or that they have a significant influence on personal psychology. Yet instincts are impersonal, universally distributed, hereditary factors of a dynamic or motivating character, which very often fail so completely to reach consciousness that modern psychotherapy is faced with the task of helping the patient to become conscious of them. Moreover, the instincts are not vague and indefinite by nature, but are specifically formed motive forces which, long before there is any consciousness, and in spite of any degree of consciousness later on, pursue their inherent goals. Consequently they form very close analogies to the archetypes, so close, in fact, that there is good reason for supposing that the archetypes are the unconscious images of the instincts themselves, in other words, that they are patterns of instinctual behaviour.

The hypothesis of the collective unconscious is, therefore, no more daring than to assume there are instincts. One admits readily that human activity is influenced to a high degree by instincts, quite apart from the rational motivations of the conscious mind. So if the assertion is made that our imagination, perception, and thinking are likewise influenced by inborn and universally present formal elements, it seems to me that a normally functioning intelligence can discover in this idea just as much or just as little mysticism as in the theory of instincts. Although this reproach of mysticism has frequently been levelled at my concept, I must emphasize yet again that the concept of the collective unconscious is neither a speculative nor a philosophical but an empirical matter. The question is simply this: are there or are there not unconscious, universal forms of this kind? If they exist, then there is a region of the psyche which one can call the collective unconscious. It is true that the diagnosis of the collective unconscious is not always an easy task. It is not sufficient to point out the often obviously archetypal nature of unconscious products, for these can just as well be derived from acquisitions through language and education. Cryptomnesia[2] should also be ruled out, which it is almost impossible to do in certain cases. In spite of all these difficulties, there remain enough individual instances showing the autochthonous revival of mythological motifs to put the matter beyond any reasonable doubt. But if such an unconscious exists at all, psychological explanation must take account of it and submit certain alleged personal aetiologies to sharper criticism.

What I mean can perhaps best be made clear by a concrete

---

[2] Apparently creative thinking in which organized ideas derived from past experiences seem to be new because the past experience is not recalled for some reason. (ED.)

example. You have probably read Freud's discussion of a certain picture by Leonardo da Vinci: St. Anne with the Virgin Mary and the Christ-child. Freud interprets this remarkable picture in terms of the fact that Leonardo himself had two mothers. This causality is personal. We shall not linger over the fact that this picture is far from unique, nor over the minor inaccuracy that St. Anne happens to be the grandmother of Christ and not, as required by Freud's interpretation, the mother, but shall simply point out that interwoven with the apparently personal psychology there is an impersonal motif well known to us from other fields. This is the motif of the *dual mother*, an archetype to be found in many variants in the field of mythology and comparative religion and forming the basis of numerous "representations collectives." I might mention, for instance, the motif of the *dual descent*, that is, descent from human and divine parents, as in the case of Heracles, who received immortality through being unwittingly adopted by Hera. What was a myth in Greece was actually a ritual in Egypt: Pharoah was both human and divine by nature. In the birth chambers of the Egyptian temples Pharaoh's second, divine conception and birth is depicted on the walls; he is "twice-born." It is an idea that underlies all rebirth mysteries, Christianity included. Christ himself is "twice-born": through his baptism in the Jordan he was regenerated and reborn from water and spirit. Consequently, in the Roman liturgy the font is designated the "uterus ecclesiae," and, as you can read in the Roman missal, it is called this even today, in the "benediction of the font" on Holy Saturday before Easter. Further, according to an early Christian-Gnostic idea, the spirit which appeared in the form of a dove was interpreted as Sophia-Sapientia—Wisdom and the Mother of Christ. Thanks to this motif of the dual birth, children today, instead of having good and evil fairies who magically "adopt" them at birth with blessings or curses, are given sponsors—a "godfather" and a "godmother."

The idea of a second birth is found at all times and in all places. In the earliest beginnings of medicine it was a magical means of healing; in many religions it is the central mystical experience; it is the key idea in medieval, occult philosophy, and, last but not least, it is an infantile fantasy occurring in numberless children, large and small, who believe that their parents are not their real parents but merely foster-parents to whom they were handed over. Benvenuto Cellini[3] also had this idea, as he himself relates in his autobiography.

---

[3] Benvenuto Cellini (1500–1571) was a Florentine goldsmith and sculptor whose *Autobiography* is an important account of Renaissance life in Italy. (ED.)

Now it is absolutely out of the question that all the individuals who believe in a dual descent have in reality always had two mothers, or conversely that those few who shared Leonardo's fate have infected the rest of humanity with their complex. Rather, one cannot avoid the assumption that the universal occurrence of the dual-birth motif together with the fantasy of the two mothers answers an omnipresent human need which is reflected in these motifs. If Leonardo da Vinci did in fact portray his two mothers in St. Anne and Mary—which I doubt—he nonetheless was only expressing something which countless millions of people before and after him have believed. The vulture symbol (which Freud also discusses in the work mentioned) makes this view all the more plausible. With some justification he quotes as the source of the symbol the *Hieroglyphica* of Horapollo, a book much in use in Leonardo's time. There you read that vultures are female only and symbolize the mother. They conceive through the wind *(pneuma)*. This word took on the meaning of "spirit" chiefly under the influence of Christianity. Even in the account of the miracle at Pentecost the pneuma still has the double meaning of wind and spirit. This fact, in my opinion, points without doubt to Mary, who, a virgin by nature, conceived through the pneuma, like a vulture. Furthermore, according to Horapollo, the vulture also symbolizes Athene, who sprang, unbegotten, directly from the head of Zeus, was a virgin, and knew only spiritual motherhood. All this is really an allusion to Mary and the rebirth motif. There is not a shadow of evidence that Leonardo meant anything else by his picture. Even if it is correct to assume that he identified himself with the Christ-child, he was in all probability representing the mythological dual-mother motif and by no means his own personal prehistory. And what about all the other artists who painted the same theme? Surely not all of them had two mothers?

Let us now transpose Leonardo's case to the field of the neuroses, and assume that a patient with a mother complex is suffering from the delusion that the cause of his neurosis lies in his having really had two mothers. The personal interpretation would have to admit that he is right—and yet it would be quite wrong. For in reality the cause of his neurosis would lie in the reactivation of the dual-mother archetype, quite regardless of whether he had one mother or two mothers, because as we have seen, this archetype functions individually and historically without any reference to the relatively rare occurrence of dual motherhood.

In such a case, it is of course tempting to presuppose so simple and personal a cause, yet the hypothesis is not only inexact but totally false. It is admittedly difficult to understand how a dual-mother motif—unknown to a physician trained only in medicine—could have so great a determining power as to produce the effect of a traumatic condition. But if we consider the tremendous powers that lie hidden in the mythological and religious sphere in man, the aetiological significance of the archetype appears less fantastic. In numerous cases of neurosis the cause of the disturbance lies in the very fact that the psychic life of the patient lacks the co-operation of these motive forces. Nevertheless a purely personalistic psychology, by reducing everything to personal causes, tries its level best to deny the existence of archetypal motifs and even seeks to destroy them by personal analysis. I consider this a rather dangerous procedure which cannot be justified medically. Today you can judge better than you could twenty years ago the nature of the forces involved. Can we not see how a whole nation is reviving an archaic symbol, yes, even archaic religious forms, and how this mass emotion is influencing and revolutionizing the life of the individual in a catastrophic manner? The man of the past is alive in us today to a degree undreamt of before the war, and in the last analysis what is the fate of great nations but a summation of the psychic changes in individuals?

So far as a neurosis is really only a private affair, having its roots exclusively in personal causes, archetypes play no role at all. But if it is a question of a general incompatibility or an otherwise injurious condition productive of neuroses in relatively large numbers of individuals, then we must assume the presence of constellated archetypes. Since neuroses are in most cases not just private concerns, but *social* phenomena, we must assume that archetypes are constellated in these cases too. The archetype corresponding to the situation is activated, and as a result those explosive and dangerous forces hidden in the archetype come into action, frequently with unpredictable consequences. There is no lunacy people under the domination of an archetype will not fall a prey to. If thirty years ago anyone had dared to predict that our psychological development was tending towards a revival of the medieval persecutions of the Jews, that Europe would again tremble before the Roman fasces and the tramp of legions, that people would once more give the Roman salute, as two thousand years ago, and that instead of the Christian Cross an archaic swastika would lure onward millions of warriors ready for death—why, that man would have been hooted at as a mystical fool. And today? Surprising as it may seem, all this absurdity is a horrible reality. Private life, private aetiologies, and private neuroses have become almost a fiction in the world of today. The man of the past who lived in a world of archaic "representations collectives" has risen again into very visible and painfully real life, and this not only in a few unbalanced individuals but in many millions of people.

There are as many archetypes as there are typical situations in life. Endless repetition has engraved these experiences into our psychic constitution, not in the form of images filled with content, but at first only as *forms without content,* representing merely the possibility of a certain type of perception and action. When a situation occurs which corresponds to a given archetype, that archetype becomes activated and a compulsiveness appears, which, like an instinctual drive, gains its way against all reason and will, or else produces a conflict of pathological dimensions, that is to say, a neurosis.

METHOD OF PROOF

We must now turn to the question of how the existence of archetypes can be proved. Since archetypes are supposed to produce certain psychic forms, we must discuss how and where one can get hold of the material demonstrating these forms. The main source, then, is *dreams,* which have the advantage of being involuntary, spontaneous products of the unconscious psyche and are therefore pure products of nature not falsified by any conscious purpose. By questioning the individual one can ascertain which of the motifs appearing in the dream are known to him. From those which are unknown to him we must naturally exclude all motifs which might be known to him, as for instance—to revert to the case of Leonardo— the vulture symbol. We are not sure whether Leonardo took this symbol from Horapollo or not, although it would have been perfectly possible for an educated person of that time, because in those days artists were distinguished for their wide knowledge of the humanities. Therefore, although the bird motif is an archetype par excellence, its existence in Leonardo's fantasy would still prove nothing. Consequently, we must look for motifs which could not possibly be known to the dreamer and yet behave functionally in his dream in such a manner as to coincide with the functioning of the archetype known from historical sources.

Another source for the material we need is to be found in "active imagination." By this I mean a sequence of fantasies produced by deliberate concentration. I have found that the existence of unrealized, unconscious fantasies increases the frequency and intensity of dreams, and that when these fantasies are made conscious the dreams change their character and become weaker and less frequent. From this I have drawn the conclusion that dreams often contain fantasies which "want" to become conscious. The sources of dreams are often repressed instincts which have a natural tendency to influence the conscious mind. In cases of this sort, the patient is simply given the task of contemplating any one fragment of fantasy that seems significant to him—a chance idea, perhaps, or something he has become conscious of in a dream—until its context becomes visible, that is to say, the relevant associative material in which it is embedded. It is not a question of the "free association" recommended by Freud for the purpose of dream-analysis, but of elaborating the fantasy by observing the further fantasy material that adds itself to the fragment in a natural manner.

This is not the place to enter upon a technical discussion of the method. Suffice it to say that the resultant sequence of fantasies relieves the unconscious and produces material rich in archetypal images and associations. Obviously, this is a method that can only be used in certain carefully selected cases. The method is not entirely without danger, because it may carry the patient too far away from reality. A warning against thoughtless application is therefore in place.

Finally, very interesting sources of archetypal material are to be found in the delusions of paranoiacs, the fantasies observed in trance-states, and the dreams of early childhood, from the third to the fifth year. Such material is available in profusion, but it is valueless unless one can adduce convincing mythological parallels. It does not, of course, suffice simply to connect a dream about a snake with the mythological occurrence of snakes, for who is to guarantee that the functional meaning of the snake in the dream is the same as in the mythological setting? In order to draw a valid parallel, it is necessary to know the functional meaning of the individual symbol, and then to find out whether the apparently parallel mythological symbol has a similar context and therefore the same functional meaning. Establishing such facts not only requires lengthy and wearisome researches, but is also an ungrateful subject for demonstration. As the symbols must not be torn out of their context, one has to launch forth into exhaustive descriptions, personal as well as symbological, and this is practically impossible in the framework of a lecture. I have repeatedly tried it at the risk of sending one half of my audience to sleep.

But as to whether this supra-individual psychic activity actually exists, I have so far given no proof that satisfies all the requirements.

I should now like to do this once more in the form of an example. The case is that of a man in his thirties, who was suffering from a paranoid form of schizophrenia. He became ill in his early twenties. He had always presented a strange mixture of intelligence, wrong-headedness, and fantastic ideas. He was an ordinary clerk, employed in a consulate. Evidently as a compensation for his very modest existence he was seized with megalomania[4] and believed himself to be the Saviour. He suffered from frequent hallucinations and was at times very much disturbed. In his quiet periods he was allowed to go unattended in the corridor. One day I came across him there, blinking through the window up at the sun, and moving his head from side to side in a curious manner. He took me by the arm and said he wanted to show me something. He said I must look at the sun with eyes half shut, and then I could see the sun's phallus. If I moved my head from side to side the sun-phallus would move too, and that was the origin of the wind.

I made this observation about 1906. In the course of the year 1910, when I was engrossed in mythological studies, a book of Dieterich's came into my hands. It was part of the so-called Paris magic papyrus and was thought by Dieterich to be a liturgy of the Mithraic cult.[5] It consisted of a series of instructions, invocations, and visions. One of these visions is described in the following words: "And likewise the so-called tube, the origin of the ministering wind. For you will see hanging down from the disc of the sun something that looks like a tube. And towards the regions westward it is as though there were an infinite east wind. But if the other wind should prevail towards the regions of the east, you will in like manner see the vision veering in that direction." The Greek word for "tube," $\alpha\nu\lambda\delta\varsigma$ means a wind-instrument, and the combination $\alpha\dot{\nu}\lambda\grave{o}\varsigma\,\pi\alpha\chi\grave{\nu}\varsigma$ in Homer means "a thick jet of blood." So evidently a stream of wind is blowing through the tube out of the sun.

The vision of my patient in 1906, and the Greek text first edited in 1910, should be sufficiently far apart to rule out the possibility of cryptomnesia on his side and of thought-transference on mine. The

---

[4] a mental disorder characterized by irrational feelings of personal power and grandeur (ED.)

[5] The religion of Mithraism, imported to Rome in approximately 75 B.C., had elaborate rites and ceremonies and was a competitor with Christianity for two hundred years, especially among Roman soldiers. The name comes from Mithras, a Persian god of truth and justice who opposed evil. (ED.)

obvious parallelism of the two visions cannot be disputed, though one might object that the similarity is purely fortuitous. In that case we should expect the vision to have no connections with analogous ideas, nor any inner meaning. But this expectation is not fulfilled, for in certain medieval paintings this tube is actually depicted as a sort of hose-pipe reaching down from heaven under the robe of Mary. In it the Holy Ghost flies down in the form of a dove to impregnate the Virgin. As we know from the miracle of Pentecost, the Holy Ghost was originally conceived as a mighty rushing wind, the πνεῦμα, "the wind that bloweth where it listeth." In a Latin text we read: "Animo descensus per orbem solis tribuitur" (They say that the spirit descends through the disc of the sun). This conception is common to the whole of late classical and medieval philosophy.

I cannot, therefore, discover anything fortuitous in these visions, but simply the revival of possibilities of ideas that have always existed, that can be found again in the most diverse minds and in all epochs, and are therefore not to be mistaken for inherited ideas.

ARNOLD TOYNBEE

Why I Dislike Western Civilization

Arnold Toynbee (1889–1975) was an English writer and historian whose subjects included Graeco-Roman studies, contemporary affairs, travel, religion, biography, and autobiography. He is noted for *A Study of History* (1934–1961), a twelve volume comparison of historical patterns of twenty-six civilizations. The following selection appeared first in the *New York Times.*

When I say baldly that I dislike contemporary Western civilization, I am, of course, saying this partly to tease my fellow Westerners. The stand that I take is partly a joke, but it is also partly serious.

My dislike of the West, though genuine as far as it goes, cannot really be unmitigated. If it were, I should not feel lost—as I know that I should—if I did not have a *pied-à-terre*[1] in London. I am a

---

[1] temporary lodging (ED.)

Londoner born and bred, but I have not reacted against my native city; and, though I dislike the congestion of the mechanized traffic there, I know that this pest is just as bad in all the other great cities of the postwar world.

If I were to be hounded out of London by some (nonexistent) British counterpart of the House Committee on Un-American Activities, I expect I could make myself at home in Edinburgh or Melbourne or Rome or Hamburg or Boston, Mass. (my great-grandfather's farm was in sight of Boston Stump, the tapering tower of St. Botolph's Church in Boston, England). I should not feel at home as a permanent resident in New York or Chicago or Pittsburgh or Glasgow or Manchester or Milan. And I do not suppose that I could strike root in Kyoto or in Damascus or in Istanbul or even in Athens, though I love and admire each of these beautiful non-Western cities.

In ancient Greece, the navel of the earth was marked by a monolith at Delphi. The navel of my earth is not in Greece (though my heart and mind reside there). My world-navel is the Albert Memorial in Kensington Gardens. This British monument may be comically ugly but, to me, it is reassuringly familiar. I used to play around its steps when I was a tiny child. Its frieze taught me the names of the great poets, artists and thinkers of the past; the group of figures at the four corners put the four continents on the map for me.

Yes, one is a prisoner of one's time and place. I belong to the presyncopation age. Classical Western music is music for my ears. When I hear jazz, I become uneasy and turn hostile. I feel my traditional world being victoriously invaded by tropical Africa. Politically, I am on the side of Africa against the Western colonial powers, but when it comes to music, Africa's cultural colonialism makes me cherish the West's pre-African musical past.

To be the prisoner of one's time and place is one of our human limitations. A human being has roots, like a tree, and these roots tether him—though, unlike a tree's roots, they are emotional and intellectual roots. However, it is characteristic of our human nature that we rebel against our human limitations and try to transcend them. I myself, besides being human, happen to be a historian, and a historian's special form of human rebellion is to try to shake himself free of his own parochial blood and soil (to use Hitler's hateful but expressive words). A historian's métier is to move freely through time and space.

What a bore one's own native civilization is. It is dull just because it is familiar. I had the good fortune to be educated in Greek and Latin. This education served me as a magic carpet on which I wafted myself from the twentieth century of the Christian era to the third century B.C., and from the North Atlantic to the Eastern Mediterranean. I hated having to learn the names and dates of the Kings of England. The kings of Israel and Judah were almost as bad, since the Old Testament in the King James version has become virtually part of English literature. But I enjoyed finding my way among the Ptolemies and the Seleucuses.[2] English constitutional history? One glance at the syllabus of the Oxford school of medieval and modern history was enough to put me off reading for that. But the history of Islam, the history of Buddhism—these opened up fascinating new worlds.

Contemporary Western civilization annoys me, not because it is Western, but because it is mine and because I am a historian. If I had happened to be born in 1889 in China instead of England, no doubt I should be annoyed today with the China of Pu Yi and Chiang Kai-shek and Chou En-lai.[3] But being, as I am, a Western historian, I am inevitably annoyed by the contemporary West. It holds me fast entangled in its coils. It prevents me from getting back behind the machine age and from getting out into Russia, Dar-el-Islam, the Hindu world, Eastern Asia. My inescapable Westernness makes it impossible for me to become culturally acclimatized in any of these other contemporary civilizations. This is a limitation on my human freedom that I resent.

However, I have a more formidable reason for disliking the West than any that I have mentioned so far. Since I have been grown-up (I am now turned 75), the West has produced two world wars; it has produced Communism, Fascism and National Socialism; it has produced Mussolini and Hitler and McCarthy. These Western enormities make me, as a Westerner, feel insecure. Now that my German fellow-Westerners have murdered six million Jews, how can I be certain that my English fellow-countrymen might not do something equally criminal? We did murder some thousands of defenseless

---

[2] *Ptolemy* (A.D. 127–145) was an Alexandrian astronomer, geographer, and mathematician who proposed that the earth was the center of the universe of planets. *Seleucus* was the first of a dynasty of rulers of Babylonia and adjacent areas, from 312 to 64 B.C. (ED.)

[3] *Pu Yi* (1906–1967) was the tenth and last emporer of the Quing dynasty of China, from 1908 to 1912. *Chiang Kai-shek* (1887–1975) was a Nationalist Chinese leader who fled to Taiwan in 1949 when the Communists took over mainland China. *Chou En-lai* (1898–1976) was Premier of China under Mao Tse-tung, from 1949 to 1976. (ED.)

civilians at Port Said in 1956.[4] What might we not go on to do after that? What might I not be capable of doing myself, if this contemporary Western criminal lunacy were to waylay me?

I shiver and shake. Old-fashioned Christian humility, please come to my rescue. Please save me from contemporary post-Christian Western self-complacent sinfulness. I should feel my spirits rise if, instead of being Hitler's fellow-Westerner—as I am—I could be Gandhi's fellow-Hindu. Yes, I believe I could even stomach Benares[5] as the price of being liberated from Hitler's company. But I cannot escape Hitler. This fellow-Westerner of mine (of the same age to within a week) is going to haunt me for the rest of my West-bound life.

Apart from contemporary Western crimes, there are other blemishes on contemporary Western life that I find repulsive. Though I dislike the former enslavement of the individual to the community in Japan, I also dislike, and this perhaps even more, the lengths to which contemporary Western individualism has gone. The contemporary West is callous toward the aged. This is, I believe, the first civilization, so far, in which the aged have not had a place, as a matter of course, in their adult children's homes. Looking at this Western callousness with de-Westernized eyes, I find it shocking.

I also dislike the contemporary Western advertising business. It has made a fine art out of taking advantage of human silliness. It rams unwanted material goods down surfeited throats when two-thirds of all human beings now alive are in desperate need of the bare necessities of life. This is an ugly aspect of the affluent society; and, if I am told that advertising is the price of affluence, I reply without hesitation, that affluence has been bought too dear. Another item in the price of affluence is the standardization of mass-produced goods and services. This is, in itself, a deplorable impoverishment of the material side of human culture, and it brings spiritual standardization with it, which is still worse.

Looking back into the past history of the West—a past which was still present when I was a child—I admire the nineteenth-century West's success in postponing the age of sexual awakening, of sexual experience and sexual infatuation far beyond the age of physical

---

[4] Port Said is an Egyptian city that lies at the junction of the Suez Canal and the Mediterranean Sea; it was invaded by British and French troops in 1956 as part of a conflict over the Suez Canal. (ED.)

[5] Ancient holy Hindu city in India on the banks of the Ganges River. (ED.)

puberty. You may tell me that this was against nature; but to be human consists precisely in transcending nature—in overcoming the biological limitations that we have inherited from our prehuman ancestors.

All human societies overcome death by creating and maintaining institutions that are handed on from one generation to another. Sex is a still more awkward feature of our biological inheritance than death, and our nineteenth-century Western society handled sex with relative success. By postponing the age of sexual awakening, it prolonged the length of the period of education. It is this, together with the seventeenth-century Western achievement of learning to think for oneself instead of taking tradition on trust, that accounts for the West's preeminence in the world during the last few centuries.

Nineteenth-century Westerners condemned with justice the Hindu institution of child-marriage, and they deplored, also with justice, the spectacle of an intellectually promising Moslem boy being allowed to commit intellectual suicide by sexual indulgence at the age of puberty. The twentieth-century West is now imitating the non-Western habits that the nineteenth-century West rightly—though perhaps self-righteously—condemned.

Our irrational contemporary Western impatience and our blind adulation of speed for speed's sake are making havoc, today, of the education of our children. We force their growth as if they were chicks in a pullet factory. We drive them into a premature awareness of sex even before physical puberty has overtaken them. In fact, we deprive our children of the human right of having a childhood. This forcing of sex-consciousness started in the United States; it has spread to Britain, and who knows how many other Western countries this perverse system of miseducation is going to invade and demoralize?

Our whole present policy in the upbringing of the young is paradoxical. While we are lowering the age of sexual awareness—and frequently the age of sexual experience, too—to a veritably Hindu degree, we are at the same time prolonging the length of education. We force our boys and girls to become sex-conscious at twelve or thirteen, and then we ask them to prolong their postgraduate studies till they are nearly thirty. How are they to be expected to give their minds to education during those last sixteen or seventeen sex-haunted years?

We are proud of ourselves for providing secondary education, college education, postgraduate education for everybody. But we shall be plowing the sands if we do not simultaneously revert to our grandparents' practice of prolonging the age of sexual innocence. If we persist, in this vital matter, on our present Hindu course, our brand-new would-be institutions for higher education will become, in practice, little more than social clubs for sexual mating.

This relapse into precocious sexuality is one of the moral blemishes of the contemporary Western civilization. One of its intellectual blemishes is its insistence on splitting up the universe into smaller and smaller splinters. It has split up the human race into a host of sovereign independent national states. It has split up knowledge and understanding into a host of separate watertight "disciplines." I dislike nationalism and I dislike specialization, and both are characteristically Western aberrations.

When I was about sixteen years old, I stayed with an uncle who was a specialist on Dante, while his wife was a specialist on Horace Walpole.[6] Their library was less specialized than they themselves were, and I browsed in it with excitement and delight. When I was due to leave, my uncle said to me: "Arnold, your aunt and I think you are allowing your interest to be too general. You ought to specialize." I said nothing, but I was instantaneously certain that I was not going to follow this advice; and, in fact, I have consistently done the opposite throughout the sixty years that have passed since then.

What a world to find oneself born into. Since as early as I first became conscious of my native Western environment, Western technology has been inventing new and ever more complicated machines. I did learn to ride a bicycle. How can one be expected, in just one lifetime, to go on to learn to ride a motorcycle or to drive a car? I started shaving in the age of the cutthroat razor, and Mr. Gillette's invention came as a great relief to me. But how can I be expected to go on to use an electric razor? How could I know about volts and ohms and transformers? An American friend did give me an electric razor. This lies safely tucked away in a drawer, and whenever I unearth it, it alarms me.

I do now travel about the world in cars and airplanes. The better these get at covering the distance, the worse they get at allowing an inquisitive passenger to see the view. I did my first traveling in Greece in 1911–12. I did it on foot with a rucksack on my back. I was as free as a bird. I could go where even mules could not go. I could see the world as I pleased. I have never traveled so satisfactorily as that since then.

---

[6] Horace Walpole (1717–1797) was an English writer who became famous for his horror tale *The Castle of Otranto,* which initiated interest in Gothic romance novels. (ED.)

The other day, I had a three-hour mule ride from an airstrip to the rock-cut churches at Lalibela in Ethiopia. Once again I was seeing the real world, the unmechanized pre-Western world in which I feel truly at home. Machinery perplexes and dismays me, and I have been born into the Western machine age. Why was I not born in the third-century-B.C. Syria or seventh-century-A.D. China? I should not then have been harassed by machinery as I am in the contemporary West. I heartily dislike this side of contemporary Western life, and, in the eyes of the rest of the world, mechanization is what the contemporary West stands for.

Well, these are some of the reasons why I dislike the contemporary Western civilization. But, as I have said at the beginning of this article, my dislike is not undiluted. My grandchildren, after all, are Westerners, and I certainly like them. Moreover, I want them, in their turn, to have grandchildren who will have grandchildren. I should be desolated if I believed that Western man was going to commit mass suicide by engaging in a third world war that, this time, would be fought with atomic weapons.

To discover the existence of the atom and to go on to discover how to split it has been the *chef d'oeuvre*[7] of Western science and technology. I do not love Western science for having made these deadly inventions; but I have just enough faith in Western man's political commonsense to expect that he will not liquidate himself. So perhaps, after all, I do not rate my native Western civilization so low as I fancy that I do in my moments of acute exasperation at the West's more uncongenial vagaries.

LU XUN

The Fair of the Five Fierce Gods

Lu Xun (pronounced Lu Shoon) (1881–1936) is chief among the major figures of modern Chinese literature. His most famous work, "The Story of Au Q" is essentially an allegory about the decline of China from its long-held position as one of the great centers of

---

[7] masterpiece (ED.)

Translated by Gladys Yang.

world civilization. Lu Xun also wrote about traditional Chinese family life, bringing into focus tensions between traditional values and social change. *The Selected Stories of Lu Xun* was published in the United States in 1960.

In addition to New Year and the other festivals, we children looked forward to the temple fairs in honour of certain gods. But because my home was rather out of the way, not till the afternoon did the processions pass our door, by which time the retinue had dwindled away until there was almost nothing left of it. Often, after hours of craning our necks and waiting, all we saw was some dozen men running hastily past carrying an effigy of a god with a golden, blue, or crimson face. And that was all.

I always hoped that *this* procession would be bigger and better than the last, but the result was invariably more or less the same. And all I was left with was a souvenir bought for one copper before the god passed by—a whistle made of a bit of clay, a scrap of coloured paper, a split bamboo, and two or three cock's feathers. This whistle, known as a 'tootle-toot', produced a piercing blast, and I blew it lustily for two or three days.

Now when I read Zhang Dai's[1] *Reminiscences,* I am struck by the splendour of temple fairs in his time, even if these Ming dynasty writers do tend to exaggerate. We still welcome the dragon king today when we pray for rain, but it is very simply done, with only some dozen men carrying a dragon and making it twist and coil, while village boys dress up as sea monsters. In the old days they acted plays, and it was most spectacular. Here is Zhang Dai's description of a pageant with characters from *Heroes of the Marshland:*

> . . . They went out in all directions to find one fellow who was short and swarthy, another who was tall and hefty, a mendicant friar, a fat monk, a stout woman and a slender one. They looked for a pale face too and a head set askew, a red moustache and a handsome beard, a strong dark man and one with ruddy cheeks and a long beard. They searched high and low in the town, and if they failed to find any character they went outside the city walls, to the villages and hamlets in the hills, even to neighbouring prefectures and counties. A high price was paid to the thirty-six men who played the heroes of Liangshan; but each looked his part to the life, and they went out in force on horseback and on foot. . . .

[1] A seventeenth-century writer.

Who could resist watching such a lifelike pageant of the men and women of days gone by? The pity is that such brave shows disappeared long ago along with the Ming dynasty.

Though these processions were not prohibited by the authorities—unlike women's long gowns in Shanghai today or the discussion of politics in Peking—still, women and children were not allowed to watch them, and educated people or the so-called literati seldom went to look on either. Only layabouts and idlers would gather before the temple or yamen to watch the fun; and since most of my knowledge of these festivities comes from their accounts it is not the firsthand observation so much valued by researchers. I do, however, remember once witnessing a rather fine show myself. First came a boy on horseback called The Announcer. Then, after a considerable interval, the High Pole arrived. This was a great bamboo pole to which a long banner was attached, and it was carried in both hands by a huge fat man dripping with perspiration. When in the mood he would balance the pole on his head or teeth, or even on the tip of his nose. He was followed by stilt-walkers, children on platforms carried by men, and other children on horseback, all masquerading as characters from operas. There were people dressed in red like felons too, loaded with cangues and chains, some of whom were also children. To me each part was glorious and each participant extremely lucky—I no doubt envied them this chance to show off. I used to wish I could have some serious illness, so that my mother would go to the temple to promise the god that I would masquerade as a felon. . . . So far, though, I have failed to have any association with these processions.

Once I was to go to Dongguan Village for the Fair of the Five Fierce Gods. This was a great occasion in my childhood, for this fair was the grandest in the whole county and Dongguan Village was very far from my home, more than twenty miles by boat from the town. There were two remarkable temples there. One was the Temple to Lady Mei, the virgin mentioned in the *Tales of Liao Zhai*[2] who remained unmarried after the death of her betrothed and became a goddess after she died, but then appropriated someone else's husband. On the shrine, sure enough, the images of a young man and woman were smiling at each other, counter to all the laws of propriety. The other was the Temple of the Five Fierce Gods, the very

[2] A collection of short stories by Pu Songling (1640–1715).

name of which was strange enough. According to those with a passion for research, these were the Wu Tong gods. There is no conclusive proof of this, however. The images were five men, who did not look particularly fierce, and behind them sat five wives in a row, this intermingling of sexes falling far short of the strict segregation practised in Peking theatres. In fact, this was counter to all the laws of propriety too; but since these were the Five Fierce Gods, nothing could be done about it. They were obviously an exception to the rule.

Since Dongguan Village was a long way from the town, we all got up at dawn. The big boat with three windows booked the night before was already moored in the harbour, and to it our man started carrying the chairs, food, a stove for brewing tea, and a hamper of cakes. Laughing and skipping, I urged him to get a move on. Suddenly from his respectful expression I knew there was something up. I looked round and saw my father standing behind me.

'Go and fetch your book,' he said slowly.

The book he meant was the *Rhymed History*[3] which served as my primer. I had no other book. In our district children started school when their years were odd not even: that is how I know I must have been seven at the time.

With trepidation I fetched the book. He made me sit beside him at the table in the centre of the hall and read to him sentence by sentence. Inwardly quaking, I read to him sentence by sentence.

Two sentences made one line, and I must have read twenty or thirty lines.

'Learn them by heart,' he said. 'If you cannot recite them correctly, you will not be allowed to go to the fair.'

This said, he stood up and walked into his room.

I felt as if someone had doused me with icy water. But what could I do? Naturally I had to read and re-read, and force myself to memorize—I would have to recite it too.

> In the beginning was Pan Gu,
> Born of primeval void;
> He was the first to rule the world,
> The chaos to divide.

---

[3] A rhymed account of Chinese history to the end of the Ming dynasty written by Wang Shiyun. (ED.)

That is the kind of book it was. The first four lines are all I can remember. I have forgotten the rest, including of course the twenty or thirty lines I was forced to memorize that day. I remember hearing it said at the time that studying the *Rhymed History* was more useful than studying the *Thousand Characters* or the *Hundred Surnames*,[4] for from it you could learn the outline of all history past and present. It is naturally a very good thing to know the outline of all history past and present. My trouble was that I could not understand a word.

'In the beginning was Pan Gu,' I read.

> In the beginning was Pan Gu. . . .

I read on and learned it by heart.

> In the beginning was Pan Gu,
> Born of primeval void. . . .

Everything needed had been carried to the boat. The noise and bustle at home had turned to silence. The morning sun shone on the western wall. The weather was clear and fine. Mother, the servant, my nurse Mama Chang or Ah Chang—none of them could rescue me. They had to wait in silence till I had learned my lesson and could recite it. In the utter stillness it seemed as if iron pincers would thrust out from my head to seize that 'Born of primeval void' and all the other lines. And I could hear my voice quaver as I read desperately on, quaver like a cricket's chirping on a late autumn night.

Everybody was waiting. The sun had risen even higher.

Suddenly I felt a surge of confidence. I stood up, picked up the book, and went to my father's study to recite all those lines in one breath. I recited as if in a dream.

'Good. You may go.' Father nodded his head as he spoke.

At once everyone sprang into action, breaking into smiles as we set out for the harbour. The servant carried me high as if to congratulate me on my success as he strode ahead of the rest.

I was not as happy as they were, though. After the boat cast off, the riverside scenery, the cakes in the hamper, the bustle of the fair when we reached Dongguan Village—none of these seemed to me very interesting.

---

[4] Two books used in school. (ED.)

Now everything else is forgotten, vanished without a trace. Only my recitation from the *Rhymed History* is as clear in my mind as if it happened yesterday.

Even now, when I think of it, I still wonder why my father made me learn a lesson by heart at a time like that.

S E V E N

The Politics of Language

Perhaps of all the creations of man language is the most astonishing.

Lytton Strachey

Use what language you will, you can never say anything but what you are.

Ralph Waldo Emerson

Language is the most versatile and powerful tool ever developed by the human race. It is not just a vehicle for expressing our thoughts; it is the dress of thought. Language and thought are so entwined that they become, for all practical purposes, inseparable. Just as we cannot separate "the dancer from the dance," so we cannot separate the thought from the language that expresses the thought.

Language has allowed us not just to build our cities but to create entire societies; it has allowed us to express our values in great and enduring literature. But like any tool, language can be misused. It can be used to divide rather than unite, to destroy rather than build, to deceive and manipulate instead of educating and inspiring, to corrupt or prevent thought instead of fostering it.

Language is also a means for learning about ourselves—for discovering ourselves, our world, and our place in that world. As Michelle Cliff recounts in the opening essay of this section, language allowed her to discover what it means to be a Jamaican and a Caribbean—an identity she forges through language by discovering a voice that gives expression to that identity. Cliff's essay recounts her particular journey through language into a new awareness of her self, but her essay also suggests that each of us can use language to explore who we are, what our world is, and what our place is in that world.

Roger Scruton and Henry Louis Gates, Jr. explore, respectively, the issues of gender and race in language, issues which they find not only complex but far subtler than we would expect. Scruton takes issue with the strategies of "gender elimination" in English. Gates argues that those who have developed the language of literary criticism have done so at the expense of black literature and black culture. Both of these critics recognize the power of language to shape our thoughts, our way of viewing and defining our world, and the way we respond to that world. Both writers address struggles among various opposing groups, all seeking to control certain aspects of language.

After reading these essays, you might identify other areas that have engendered similar battles about the language used to discuss them. For example, you might explore the language used to describe and discuss AIDS, homelessness, pollution, environmental problems, poverty, crime, and other social issues. You could make a brief list of the most important words used to discuss one of these issues, then make a list of other words that could be used instead. Analyze the two lists. How does the language used to discuss such issues affect the way you perceive them?

Both William Lutz and Edward White write about the use of language to manipulate and even prevent thought, about language used as a weapon. Both essays illustrate the dangers of such language and the need for us to be on guard against it. You might want to develop your own list of examples of doublespeak and singlespeak. George Orwell's essay "Politics and the English Language" has come to be considered the classic statement, not just on clarity in language, but on the use of language to mislead, obfuscate, and deceive. It is an essay that can teach us much about writing that is clear, honest, and effective.

Harry Brent considers Orwell's comments on language in the context of Orwell's wartime experiences. As Brent points out, Orwell learned the connection between words and reality during his service in the Spanish Civil War. Noble-sounding words quickly gained new meaning for Orwell in the midst of the grim experiences of war— experiences that contributed significantly to his attitudes toward and use of language.

Some might think it odd that a nuclear physicist would be concerned with language, but as Werner Heisenberg observes in his essay, language is an important tool for thinking in *all* fields. Heisenberg discusses the problems inherent in the very nature and structure of language itself, and how the physicist has to struggle to overcome these problems. Yet, as Heisenberg also points out, language is an indispensable tool for the advancement of science. While making new discoveries in science, the physicist is also creating new language to discuss these new realities. The tool of language must be changed and adapted continuously to the new tasks demanded of it.

Since language fills the world around us, we have an endless supply of material for observation and study. Yet it is precisely

687

because our daily life is so filled with language that we tend not to notice it. The selections in this section should help you to think, perhaps for the first time, about the role language has played in your own life. The writing you do in response to these selections will help you to explore that role.

MICHELLE CLIFF

A Journey into Speech

Michelle Cliff (1946–   ) is a Jamaican-born novelist, essayist, and poet who was educated in London and now lives in the United States. In her writing, Cliff deals with the extent to which the history of blacks has been submerged by historians, and the ways in which black American women have transmitted values and assumed important social responsibilities. Her books include the novels *Abeng* (1984) and *No Telephone to Heaven* (1987), the poetry collection *Claiming an Identity They Taught Me to Despise* (1980), and *The Land of Look Behind* (1985), a collection of poetry and prose from which the following selection is taken.

The first piece of writing I produced, beyond a dissertation on intellectual game-playing in the Italian Renaissance, was entitled "Notes on Speechlessness," published in *Sinister Wisdom*, no. 5. In it I talked about my identification with Victor, the wild boy of Aveyron, who, after his rescue from the forest and wildness by a well-meaning doctor of Enlightenment Europe, became "civilized," but never came to speech. I felt, with Victor, that my wildness had been tamed—that which I had been taught was my wildness.

My dissertation was produced at the Warburg Institute, University of London, and was responsible for giving me an intellectual belief in myself that I had not had before, while at the same time distancing me from who I am, almost rendering me speechless about who I am. At least I believed in the young woman who wrote the dissertation—still, I wondered who she was and where she had come from.

I could speak fluently, but I could not reveal. I immersed myself in the social circles and academies of Siena, Florence, Urbino, as well as Venice, creating a place for myself there, and describing this ideal world in eloquent linear prose.

When I began, finally, partly through participation in the feminist movement, to approach myself as a subject, my writing was jagged, nonlinear, almost shorthand. The "Notes on Speechlessness" were indeed notes, written in snatches on a nine-to-five job. I did not choose the note form consciously; a combination of things drew me to it. An urgency for one thing. I also felt incompetent to construct an essay in which I would describe the intimacies, fears, and lies I wrote of in "Speechlessness." I felt my thoughts, things I had held within for a lifetime, traversed so wide a terrain, had so many stops and starts, apparent non sequiturs, that an essay—with its cold-blooded dependence on logical construction, which I had mastered practically against my will—could not work. My subject could not respond to that form, which would have contradicted the idea of speechlessness. This tender approach to myself within the confines and interruptions of a forty-hour-a-week job and against a history of forced fluency was the beginning of a journey into speech.

To describe this journey further, I must begin at the very beginning, with origins, and the significance of these origins. How they have made me the writer I am.

I originate in the Caribbean, specifically on the island of Jamaica, and although I have lived in the United States and in England, I travel as a Jamaican. It is Jamaica that forms my writing for the most part, and which has formed for the most part, myself. Even though I often feel what Derek Walcott expresses in his poem "The Schooner *Flight*": "I had no nation now but the imagination." It is a complicated business.

Jamaica is a place halfway between Africa and England, to put it simply, although historically one culture (guess which one) has been esteemed and the other denigrated (both are understatements)—at least among those who control the culture and politics of the island—the Afro-Saxons. As a child among these people, indeed of these people, as one of them, I received the message of anglocentrism, of white supremacy, and I internalized it. As a writer, as a human being, I have had to accept that reality and deal with its effect on me, as well as finding what has been lost to me from the darker side, and what may be hidden, to be dredged from memory and dream. And it *is* there to be dredged. As my writing delved longer and deeper into this part of myself, I began to dream and imagine. I was able to clearly envision Nanny, the leader of a group of guerrilla fighters known as the Windward Maroons, as she is described: an old Black woman naked except for a necklace made from the teeth of white men. I began to love her.

It is a long way from the court of Urbino to Nanny the Coro-mantyn warrior. (Coromantyn, or Coromantee, was used by the British in Jamaica to describe slaves from the Gold Coast of Africa, especially slaves who spoke Akan.)

One of the effects of assimilation, indoctrination, passing into the anglocentrism of British West Indian culture is that you believe absolutely in the hegemony of the King's English and in the form in which it is meant to be expressed. Or else your writing is not literature; it is folklore, and folklore can never be art. Read some poetry by West Indian writers—some, not all—and you will see what I mean. You have to dissect stanza after extraordinarily anglican stanza for Afro-Caribbean truth; you may never find the latter. But this has been our education. The anglican ideal—Milton, Wordsworth, Keats—was held before us with an assurance that we were unable, and would never be enabled, to compose a work of similar correctness. No reggae spoken here.

To write as a complete Caribbean woman, or man for that matter, demands of us retracing the African part of ourselves, reclaiming as our own, and as our subject, a history sunk under the sea, or scattered as potash in the canefields, or gone to bush, or trapped in a class system notable for its rigidity and absolute dependence on color stratification. On a past bleached from our minds. It means finding the art forms of these of our ancestors and speaking in the *patois*[1] forbidden us. It means realizing our knowledge will always be wanting. It means also, I think, mixing in the forms taught us by the oppressor, undermining his language and co-opting his style, and turning it to our purpose. In my current work-in-progress, a novel, I alternate the King's English with *patois,* not only to show the class background of characters, but to show how Jamaicans operate within a split consciousness. I would be as dishonest to write the novel entirely in *patois* as to write entirely in the King's English. Neither is the novel a linear construction; its subject is the political upheavals of the past twenty years. Therefore, I have mixed time and incident and space and character and also form to try to mirror the historical turbulence.

For another example, I wrote a long poem, actually half-poem, half-prose, in which I imagine the visit of Botha of South Africa to the heads of western Europe in the summer of 1984. I wrote this as a parody of Gilbert and Sullivan because their work epitomizes salient aspects of the British Empire which remain vibrant. And because as a child I was sick to death of hearing "I am the very model of a modern major general." I enjoyed writing this, playing with rhyme and language—it was like spitting into their cultural soup.

We are a fragmented people. My experience as a writer coming from a culture of colonialism, a culture of Black people riven from

---

[1] a nonstandard dialect spoken by a particular group (ED.)

each other, my struggle to get wholeness from fragmentation while working within fragmentation, producing work which may find its strength in its depiction of fragmentation, through form as well as content, is similar to the experience of other writers whose origins are in countries defined by colonialism.

Ama Ata Aidoo, the Ghanaian writer, in her extraordinary book, *Our Sister Killjoy or Reflections from a Black-Eyed Squint* (NOK Publishers, Lagos and New York, 1979), plots this fragmentation, and shows how both the demand and solace of the so-called mother country can claim us, while we long for our homeland and are shamed for it and ourselves at the same time. The form Aidoo uses to depict this dilemma of colonial peoples—part prose, fictional and epistolary, part poetry—illustrates the fragmentation of the heroine and grasps the fury of the heroine, living in Europe but drawn back to Ghana, knowing she can never be European. She will only be a been-to; that is, one who has been to the mother country. *Our Sister Killjoy* affected me directly, not just because like Aidoo's heroine I was a been-to. I was especially drawn by the way in which Aidoo expresses rage against colonialism—crystallized for her by the white man she calls the "Christian Doctor" throughout, excising Black African hearts to salvage white South African lives. In her expression of the rage she feels her prose breaks apart sharply into a staccato poetry—direct, short, brilliantly bitter—as if measured prose would disintegrate under her fury.

I wanted that kind of directness in my writing, as I came into closer contact with my rage, and a realization that rage could fuel and shape my work. As a light-skinned colonial girlchild, both in Jamaica and in the Jamaican milieu of my family abroad, rage was the last thing expected of me.

After reading Aidoo I knew I wanted to tell exactly how things were, what had been done, to us and by us, without muddying the issue with conventional beauty, avoiding becoming trapped in the grace of language for its own sake, which is always seductive.

In *Claiming an Identity They Taught Me to Despise,* a piece published before I read Aidoo, halfway between poetry and prose, as I am halfway between Africa and England, patriot and expatriate, white and Black, I felt my use of language and imagery had sometimes masked what I wanted to convey. It seemed sometimes that the reader was able to ignore what I was saying while admiring the way in which it was said.

And yet, *Claiming* is an honest self-portrait of who I was at the time. Someone who was unable, for the most part, to recapture the native language of Jamaica, and who relied on the King's English and

European allusions, but who wrote from a feminist consciousness and a rapidly evolving consciousness of colonialism, and a knowledge of self-hatred. Someone who also dreamed in Latin—as I did and as I recorded in the title section, included here. *Claiming*'s strengths, I think, are in the more intimate, private places of the piece, which I constructed much as the "Notes on Speechlessness" are constructed. Shorthand—almost—as memory and dream emerge; fast, at once keen, at once incomplete. I was also, in those sections, laboring under the ancient taboos of the assimilated: don't tell outsiders anything real about yourself. Don't reveal *our* secrets to *them*. Don't make us seem foolish, or oppressed. Write it quickly before someone catches you. Before you catch yourself.

After reading *Our Sister Killjoy,* something was set loose in me, I directed rage outward rather than inward, and I was able to write a piece called "If I Could Write This in Fire I Would Write This in Fire." In it I let myself go, any thought of approval for my words vanished; I strung together myth, dream, historical detail, observation, as I had done before, but I added native language, tore into the indoctrination of the colonizer, surprised myself with the violence of my words.

That piece of writing led to other pieces in which I try to depict personal fragmentation and describe political reality, according to the peculiar lens of the colonized.

ROGER SCRUTON

Ideologically Speaking

Roger Scruton (1944–   ) is a British lecturer and philosopher who writes about art, culture, and social and political issues. His books include *Art and Imagination: A Study in the Philosophy of the Mind* (1974), *The Aesthetics of Architecture* (1979), *The Meaning of Conservatism* (1980), and *The Philosopher on Dover Beach* (1991). The following selection appears in *The State of the Language* (1989), Christopher Ricks and Leonard Michaels, editors.

I cannot prevent myself from feeling an inner revulsion whenever the word *person* is self-consciously summoned to take the place once occupied by *man,* or when the flow of a sentence is interrupted by a

distracting use of *he or she* where *he* would once have been manda-
tory. Far from serving to remove the "irrelevant" reference to gender
from the English language, such practices heighten that reference,
and transform it from a harmless quirk of grammar to a vigilant
ideological presence. I resent this ideological intrusion, and its in-
solent dealings with our mother (perhaps I should say "parent")
tongue. But like many who share such reactionary sentiments, I find
it difficult to justify them except in ways which are too *ad hoc,* or
too *ad feminam,*[1] to gain a hearing from those who do not already
share them. It seems to me, therefore, that a great service would be
done to the dwindling body of linguistic reactionaries if an argument
could be found for their position which is something more than a
mere reiteration of it. In this article I search for that argument—
though with a despairing sense that it lies, in the end, too deep for
words, being presupposed in every word that is used to utter it.

I have mentioned two strategies of "gender elimination": the
substitution of *person* for *man,* and of *he or she* for *he.* They are only
superficially similar. A moment's reflection tells us that while the
second change is stylistic, the first is also semantic. The word *person*
comes to us from the Latin *persona*—originally meaning "a mask,"
but transformed by Roman law to designate the bearer of rights and
duties, who comes before the law in order that his rights and duties
should be determined (or rather, in order that *her* rights and duties
should be determined, for *persona,* of course, is feminine). As Sir
Ernest Barker beautifully put it: "it is not the natural Ego which
enters a court of law. It is a right-and-duty bearing person, created
by the law, which appears before the law."[2] The Roman-law conception passed into jurisprudential and philosophical usage, so that
already in Boethius[3] the word *persona* is used to denote the human
individual, in his quality as rational agent. It is now quite normal
among philosophers to assume that "personality" belongs to our
essence, and that this puzzling fact is independent not only of law,
but of all human institutions. Personality is no longer something
bestowed upon himself by man, but something discovered in him,

---

[1] *Ad hoc* translates to mean for a particular purpose; *ad feminam* means to the woman,
appealing to a woman's interests or prejudices. (ED.)

[2] Sir Ernest Barker, introduction to O. Gierke, *Natural Law and the Theory of Society,
1500–1800,* trans. Barker (Cambridge, 1934), p. lxxi.

[3] Anicius Manlius Severinus Boethius (c. 480–524) was a Roman philosopher and
author of *The Consolation of Philosophy.* (ED.)

by all who would treat him as he really is. It was from this concept of personality that Kant[4] distilled the Enlightenment morality which has all but replaced the morality of Christendom. And it is the classless, genderless—indeed sexless—morality of Kant whose brilliant rays are dimly reflected in the sermons of the modern feminist.

Not all persons are human. There are corporate persons, such as churches and firms; there are (or may be) divine persons, angels and devils. Moreover, not everything that belongs to our humanity belongs also to our personality. The embodiment of the person in the human organism brings with it a "human condition": a bond by which the free being and the animal are inseparably united, so as to confront the world from the same eyes, and with the same mystifying countenance, and therein to wrestle with each other till death do them part. The human being suffers and dies; he is at one with nature and with the animals, attached to his flesh and to the flesh of others. He rejoices in the sight, sound, smell, and touch of things: of his child, his dog, his horse, and his lover. And all those ineffable experiences are invoked when we refer to him not as *person,* but as *man.* This term returns us to our incarnation, and places the flesh where it should be, in the center of our moral view:

> man, proud man,
> Drest in a little brief authority,
> Most ignorant of what he's most assur'd,
> His glassy essence, like an angry ape,
> Plays such fantastic tricks before high heaven,
> As make the angels weep.

Even if we considered personality to be the most important fact of our condition, this could not lead us to the conclusion that we should refer to ourselves always as persons, or that we do not need a word to designate our incarnation and to locate us not in the hierarchy of angels, but amid the throngs of life. To use the word *person,* where our poets and liturgical writers have chosen *man,* is to deny the need to capture our destiny in words of our own.

But why the word *man?* For does this not imply some preference for the masculine gender, some lingering attachment to the view that, when the chips are down, it is men, and not women, who count? If not *person,* why not some other word which is semantically equiva-

---

[4] Immanuel Kant (1724–1804) was a German philosopher and metaphysician and author of the *Critique of Pure Reason* (1781). (ED.)

lent to *man* in its generic use, and yet free from every resonance of gender? Slavonic languages have such a word—*chelovek* in Russian, *člověk* in Czech, *człowiek* in Polish—whose etymology has nothing to do with man or woman. Why do we not follow suit, perhaps inventing a word for the purpose?

We could indeed adopt this strategy. But think of the cost. All at once we cease to use the word reserved by our language for the most important of the world's phenomena. More: we begin to treat the word as somehow polluted and unclean, to be avoided in polite society and reserved for onanistic use. Our past literature becomes tainted for us, something to be read or uttered with secret pangs of guilt and naughty titters—something that is no longer part of us, as antiquated and absurd as the Roman toga or the Morris dance. The result would be a massive "deculturation," as we cease to hear the language of Shakespeare and the King James Bible as addressed directly to the modern ear. And, in all probability, the experiment would fail. In a few decades the new word for man would be uttered always in inverted commas, like *citoyen* in post-Restoration France, or *comrade* in the modern communist state.

What is at stake becomes clearer when we consider the other example of "gender elimination": the use of *he or she* where *he* was once the norm. That this usage is inelegant will be freely admitted, even by those who advocate it. One philosopher has even suggested (and used) the alternative device of randomization, so that in neighboring sentences the impersonal pronoun is now masculine, now feminine.[5] The result is a stylistic catastrophe of unprecedented proportions. In such an idiom, neither the well-turned counsel, nor the poignant perception, can find utterance. Others still have advocated the use of *they* as a genderless third-person pronoun—a usage which has a certain popular authority. Dale Spender even argues that this usage was once universal, and that the rule requiring *he* is the invention of "patriarchal" grammarians in the nineteenth century.[6] If that were so, then we should have to thank the Victorians for a considerable stylistic gain: try to use the generic *they* consistently, and observe the confusion of syntax and number that immediately follows. In fact, however, the truth seems (as so often) to be the opposite of what is confidently affirmed by Dale Spender. It is true

---

[5] D. Gauthier, *Morals by Agreement* (Oxford, 1985).

[6] Dale Spender, *Man-Made Language,* 2nd ed. (London, 1985), p. 149.

that there are early instances of the generic use of *they*: "Each of theym sholde make themselfe ready," writes Caxton in *Sonnes of Aymon* (c. 1489), while Shakespeare has "God send everyone their heart's desire" (*As You Like It*, 1598). Nevertheless, some of the first examples of the systematic use of *they* as a generic pronoun are in the polemical works of John Stuart Mill, where the author's usual eloquence is expressly constrained by his feminist principles. Seventeenth- and eighteenth-century English almost invariably seems to use *he* as a generic pronoun, and this is what we find in the works that did most to create the literary English of modernity: the King James Bible and the Book of Common Prayer. As these works abundantly demonstrate, the generic pronoun owes much of its power to the fact that it places before us an image of the human *individual*, but in the *general* condition which defines him. It reminds us that all counsels go unheard, until the individual life is touched by them: "He that findeth his life shall lose it: and he that loseth his life for my sake shall find it" (Matt. 7:39). The occurrence of the generic pronoun in the New Testament is of course influenced by the Greek. But the style of that sentence is the style of the surrounding English language: "He that is too much in any thing, so that he give another occasion of satiety, maketh himself cheap" (Francis Bacon). Consider what would happen to the writings of Addison, Johnson, Arnold, Ruskin, Dickens, or George Eliot, if every generic pronoun were plural, or if it should appear, when singular, always yoked to its feminine partner, struggling against it in a marriage of inconvenience. Even the law, which speaks not of man but of persons, has need of an individualizing generic pronoun, and therefore employs the standard *he*: "The words of a testator's will necessarily refer to facts and circumstances respecting his property and his family and other persons and things . . ."—which impeccably tautologous utterance comes to us with the authority of Halsbury's *Laws of England*.

Logically speaking, the pronoun is the equivalent of the mathematician's variable: it stands "in place of" the noun which fixes its referent. That it should bear a gender of its own is a grammatical fact of no semantic consequence. For semantically, its gender is the gender of the noun for which it stands proxy. The impersonal *he* stands proxy as a rule for *man*: for the general noun which describes us as instances of human life rather than as persons. And once again the complaint will be made that the resonance of gender here involves a reaffirmation of the discredited belief in the precedence of the male sex.

How can such a complaint be answered? First, we should not

neglect the fact that linguistic gender distinctions are far from universal. The Finno-Ugric and Turkic languages provide us with the nearest examples, culturally speaking, of genderlessness, and it is instructive to compare them with the Indo-European languages whose grammar has given so much cause for offense. No doubt there is difficulty in conducting the necessary investigations. But at least the genderless languages give us a point of comparison. And if they tell us anything, it is that the masculine pronoun has little power to oppress the female sex. The historical emancipation of the Finnish woman is part of a wider Scandinavian phenomenon—one welcomed by Ibsen and bitterly complained of by Strindberg. It was neither advanced by the Finnish language, nor retarded by the Swedish and Norwegian. The historical subjection of the Turkish woman was an *Islamic* phenomenon, and her partial emancipation, when it came, was not the result of a "genderless" perspective, but the effect of secularization, and of a quaint old-fashioned belief in modernity. As for the position of Hungarian women, how are we to distinguish it, in general, from the position of women in Bohemia, Moravia, and Austria? Even if we accept the feminist view of traditional Europe as a society based on "patriarchal" oppression, there seems to be little evidence that pronominal gender has done anything either to reinforce or to legitimize the ancestral power of men.

The feminists would, I imagine, be unimpressed by those considerations. The "emancipation" of European women, they will argue, was a matter of local adjustment, whereby the chains of male domination were made to chafe less severely, precisely so that the victim should cease to struggle against them. The true oppression is "structural": it runs through all institutions, not showing itself in overt violence, but maintaining, nevertheless, a persistent and tacit preference for all that belongs to the male. To such a "capillary" oppression language cannot but add its justifying signature, and what better way for women to free themselves than to cancel masculine dominance in this, its longest-standing citadel?

Our language is particularly unfortunate. For gender usually becomes apparent in English only at the pronominal level. In Romance and Slavonic languages, as in Greek, German, Hebrew, and Arabic, gender attaches to every adjective and every noun. The idea that gender has something to do with the sexuality of the thing described is apt to strike the speaker of such a language as faintly ridiculous. Having introduced the moon as *la lune* I must naturally refer to it thereafter as *elle*. But consider some of the vagaries of gender in those languages which are structured by it. In Arabic, for example, all adjectives qualifying plural nouns which refer to nonhuman things must occur in the feminine singular, while the numeral adjectives from three to nine are used in the masculine gender with feminine nouns and in the feminine with masculine nouns. In Czech there are two masculine genders, one for words which describe "animate" objects, and one for words which describe "inanimate" objects; in French the generic pronoun can be either *il* (standing for *quelqu'un*) or *elle* (standing for *une personne*); the Germans refer to girls in the neuter (*das Mädchen*), and agree with the Arabs, French, and Italians in seeing towns as feminine. And so on. All such facts, however interesting in themselves, have not the slightest bearing on sexual politics, and serve only to emphasize the semantic arbitrariness of gender.

In English, however, with a few rare exceptions (such as the personifying *she*), *he* and *she* are used exclusively of things with male or female *sex*. Gender in language is therefore seldom attributed to deeprooted habits of grammar which are perceptibly beyond the reach of conscious change. It really may seem, to someone faced with the choice of using *he* as opposed to *he or she,* that he is confronting a question of sexual morality, rather than one of conventional usage.

There is an intellectual device that runs through all Marxist and feminist criticism and that is probably the mainstay of radical social analysis in our time. This is the theory of ideology, as adumbrated by Marx and Engels, and the "hermeneutics[7] of suspicion" (to use Paul Ricoeur's[8] apt expression) which derives from it. According to this theory, historical societies have been characterized by distinctive economic structures, by political superstructures which derive therefrom, and by ruling "ideologies." These ideologies arise spontaneously from the social process and render natural and authoritative the prevailing disposition of social and economic power. Ideology includes systems of belief, such as religion, but it is always more than that. It is a form of what Marx called "consciousness," and what current Foucauldian[9] jargon prefers to call "discourse": a mode of

[7] a philosophical theory of the process of interpretation and understanding (ED.)

[8] Paul Ricoeur (1913–) is a French phenomenologist, philosopher, and historian. (ED.)

[9] Michel Foucault (1926–1984) was a French philosopher and author of *The Order of Discourse* (1971). (ED.)

systematic representation of the world. This mode of representation may also be systematically false, in the way that lenses can be systematically false—not so much by authorizing this or that erroneous conclusion, but by employing concepts and categories that distort the whole of reality in a direction useful to the prevailing power. Marx believed that there could be a scientific, or unideological, consciousness, and that such a consciousness would be true to reality, in the manner of lensless spectacles. Recent offsprings of the theory have tended to forego that interesting claim, using the theory more as an instrument of criticism than as a prescription for any "correct" understanding of the world. For the Foucauldian, suspicion is all, and power, stark power, lurks behind every discourse, even the discourse which tells us so.

Such a theory has almost unlimited capacity to disestablish existing authorities. Whatever you say, it can penetrate behind your utterance and establish conflagration in your camps. No claim to truth or objectivity can survive its proof that your very *choice of words* is steeped in self-serving falsehood. What matters is not the objective truth-value of a judgment, but the ideological quality of the "discourse" which is employed in it, the implication being that objectivity and truth either have no independent authority, or else are but another "mask." Truth and objectivity are created *within* a given discourse, which are therefore unable to assess it from any point of view that is not its own. "Truth" is but another name for self-serving error. Nietzsche came close to believing this self-refuting proposition. Feminists frequently embrace it in all its absurdity:

> Piercing through to the essence of this debate, Adrienne Rich (1979) summed it up succinctly when she stated that "objectivity" is nothing other than male "subjectivity". The patriarchal order is the produce of male subjectivity and it has been legitimated and made "unquestionable" by conceptualizing it as "objectivity" . . . The meanings encoded under the rubric of psychology, or history, or even biology, for example, have also been political, although not necessarily frankly so. That these meanings have not been open to question, that they have been justified on grounds of "objectivity", is no longer a defence, for "objectivity"—as it has been defined and appropriated by males—is just as much a political act as any feminists are currently engaged in.[10]

This seductive way of thinking does not stand up to a moment's philosophical analysis: if the patriarchal order has been made "un-

---

[10] Spender, *Man-Made Language,* pp. 61 and 63.

questionable" by our discourse, how is it that Dale Spender and her colleagues are able to question it? If "objectivity" is another patriarchal mask, what of the theory that tells us so: is it objectively valid, or not? (Neither answer is available; and yet there is no third possibility.) And so on. Nevertheless, ideological criticism seems to offer a method and a goal to the study of literature. In every age critics have recognized that their concern is not with the literal truth or falsehood of a text, but with the values, emotions, and resonances that are conveyed by it. But why are they so concerned? Ideological criticism offers an answer, and one which justifies the critic as no other answer has justified him. Criticism exists, it tells us, precisely to go behind the spurious claims of truth, and to discover the power which is seeking to make use of them. By doing that, we show to be artificial what had been previously perceived as natural, and we expose the reality of choice where choice has been denied. Stripped of ideology, the world becomes a "field of action": the disinterpreted world is *ready for change.*

Ideological criticism has immense charm. For it too can play its part in that "brokerage of power" which it denounces. It promises precisely to *transfer* power, from the one who now possesses it to the one who unmasks him, from the speaker of prevailing discourse to the zealous critic who lays bare the realm of choice. This is why ideological criticism has all but conquered the academic world and become the intellectual center of the humanities. It is the final vindication of the donnish life; the instrument which gives to the teeth-gnashing fantasist his longed-for power over the world of real things. The ideological critic can never stop short at criticism, however. Always he seeks to legislate: to fill the consciousness of men with the ultimate choices that he discerns, and to force open every door against which ordinary humanity has stacked its moral baggage. What is the consequence of this legislative impulse?

When Lenin and his band of bolsheviks took power, they were in the grip of Marxist theory, and sincerely believed that their task would be impeded not only by the bourgeoisie, but also by the Russian language, which had hitherto been steeped in bourgeois ideology. They therefore began to devise a new "discourse," one that would be transparent to the truth of history, and from which the lurking ideology of the "class enemy" would have been expelled. Each thing was to be referred to by its proper (that is, Marxist-Leninist) name. People were divided into "exploiters" and "the proletariat"; references to authority, to the sacred, and to law were either put in inverted commas or else qualified with some pejorative adjective like "bourgeois." "Revolutionary legality," when it came, bore only a superficial resemblance to that "bourgeois legality" which it replaced, just as the newly invented "masses" had no connection with the "common man" of bourgeois thinking. The old language of human relations was also to be purified: "proletarian solidarity" took the place of individual friendship (indeed, friendship between individuals became something like a contradiction in terms); and terms like "peace" and "friendship" were to be applied henceforth not to negotiated relations between those with unequal power, but only to relations of *equality,* in a world in which the "class struggle" had come to an end. (The resulting semantic transformation of the word *peace*—according to which there can be peace only when both parties to it have "accepted socialism"—has had fatal diplomatic consequences.)

It is of no great consequence that the "scientific" theories which inspired the new language are false. Human error has been built into language from time immemorial without destroying man's capacity to correct it: the capacity to say of witches, that there are none; of the Emperor, that he has no clothes; and of patriarchy, that its days are numbered. Of more consequence is the emergence of a phenomenon which is perhaps peculiar to the modern world: the phenomenon which the French and Russians call "wooden language," and which we might call, in honor of Orwell's satire, newspeak. Recent studies by Petr Fidelius and Françoise Thom cast interesting light on the syntax and vocabulary of communist language and both suggest that the revolutionary attempt to *impose* an interpretation on events, by embodying it in discourse, has in fact diverted language from its referential function.[11] It makes no difference that the purpose was to *emancipate*—to reveal the choices that had hitherto been canceled by ideology. Vocabulary, syntax, logic, and style all take on a new purpose, which is not to describe the world, nor even to interpret it, but to *uphold the interpreting power.* The interpretation is no longer understood in relation to the world (the world is of no relevance to the "correct" use of language), but in relation to the political power which decreed it. Linguistic deviations are assessed according to whether they accept or question the tacit claims of power. Hence what matters in any criticism is not its truth or falsehood, but whether it accepts or rejects the legitimizing language.

---

[11] Petr Fidelius, *Jazyk a Moc* ("Language and Power") (Munich, 1983), translated by Erika Abrams as *L'Esprit post-totalitaire* (Paris, 1986); Françoise Thom, *La Langue de bois* (Paris, 1987); translated as *Newspeak* (London, 1984).

In Czechoslovakia, for example, you could write that the "fraternal assistance offered by the Soviet Union to the people of Czechoslovakia in 1968 did not lead to effective normalization, and only partially eliminated the counterrevolutionary forces," and the implied criticism would be assigned to some bureaucratic category and ignored. But were you to write "the Soviet invasion of our country conferred the greatest benefit in reestablishing the Leninist system of party dictatorship," you would be arrested at once: not for praising the invasion, but for using language transparent to the thing described. You would have broken the circle of newspeak, whereby words rise free of reality and return always to their dominating purpose, which is to conceal and render "natural" the ruling power. Facts are of secondary importance, and can be amended as linguistic propriety requires. While no party ideologist believes the theories of Marx, all recognize that truth and reference have no serious part in the public discourse of communism. Language is used in another way. Actual events are therefore generally described in abstract terms, as peculiar impersonal processes, contending in a nebulous region of pure power; people are seldom mentioned by name, and actions are assigned to no real personality. Reality appears always as a contest of opposites: "positive" and "negative," "progressive" and "reactionary." But only one thing remains clear: that the power which speaks these terms is "correct," and in no need of criticism from those who are not already absorbed by it.

Here is an example, taken from Mikhail Gorbachev's "new thinking for our country and the world":

> Many competent specialists admit that social and economic development in Soviet society can be accelerated and that success in the current drive for restructuring will have positive international consequences. They justly reason that the world community can only stand to gain from the growing well-being of the Soviet people and further progress of democracy. The scope and scale of the social and economic programs undertaken by the Soviet Union bear evidence of, and offer material guarantees for, its peaceful foreign policy. . . . Leaving aside many evaluations and estimates that we see as disputable, we, on the whole, regard this position as realistic and welcome its predominantly constructive orientation.[12]

This passage, chosen at random from a book which proceeds in that vein for 250 pages, could have been written by a party computer;

---

[12] Mikhail Gorbachev, *Perestroika: New Thinking for Our Country and the World* (London, 1987), p. 126.

perhaps it was. No people are identified: only "competent specialists," "evaluations," and "estimates"; no events are described: only a vaguely characterized "development," "restructuring," and "further progress in democracy" (further than what?). We are offered a glimpse of "social and economic programmes," and are invited to admire their scope and scale: but what they are, and who is in charge of them, we cannot tell. Everything is bent to the sole task of emphasizing that the Soviet Union is not a threat (it has a "peaceful foreign policy"), and that to recognize this fact is "positive," showing a "predominantly constructive orientation." The passage is succeeded by another, following the Manichaean[13] logic of newspeak, in which those who say that *perestroika* is simply a device to enhance and consolidate the power of the Party are liars and warmongers, propagators of "scares concerning dynamism in domestic and foreign policies," who "hope to cause our people's mistrust towards the leadership." These enemies of the people, we learn, are "ready to use anything to achieve their ends."[14]

The enemy—thus vaguely and abstractly characterized—has no other quality than his determination to speak referentially: he is the one who refuses to enter the charmed circle of newspeak and decides instead to call things by their names. Interestingly enough, Gorbachev concludes his invective by confronting the enemy directly, and in the course of doing so, covertly admits that what the enemy says is true: *perestroika* is indeed another word of newspeak, designed to name and legitimize the Party's monopoly of power:

> today members of the Politburo and the Central Committee are unanimous as they have never been before, and there is nothing that can make that unanimity waver. Both in the army, in the State Security Committee (the KGB), and in every other government department, the Party wields the highest authority and has a decisive voice politically. The drive for perestroika has only consolidated the Party's position, adding a new dimension to its moral and political role in society and the state.[15]

The language here is no different from that used by previous leaders, and is as devoid of referential purpose as theirs. But woe betide the

---

[13] believing in dualism between good and evil (ED.)

[14] Gorbachev, *Perestroika*, pp. 127, 128.

[15] Gorbachev, *Perestroika*, p. 128.

person who refuses to speak it, and who, in defiance of the Party, insists on calling a spade a spade.

A student of communist newspeak will be struck by an extraordinary paradox. The attempt to chase ideology from language, to achieve a discourse transparent to social truth, has in fact produced the opposite: a discourse that is *opaque* to truth, precisely because it is devoted to uprooting "class ideology." Such a discourse has *become* an ideology, in the Marxist sense: an instrument for legitimizing power. But it is nothing *else*. As Thom and Fidelius have demonstrated, its referential function has all but "withered away"; so too have the possibilities of deliberation. It is impossible to use such a language to suggest that things might be *fundamentally* changed. It is, moreover, a language in which honest communication is next to impossible, and in which all agreements are canceled in the very act of making them, since neither the subject nor the object of agreement can be defined.

The example returns me to the feminist attempt to expropriate the language of dissent. The feminist, like the Marxist, is deeply suspicious of power—at least, of power in the hands of others—and shares the Marxist conviction that power lurks within the structures of our thought and language and must first be expelled from *there*. Modern English is a "patriarchal" discourse and this, for the feminist, is the most important fact about it. The need arises to expose the underlying patriarchal assumptions, and to offer another language, free from ideology and transparent to social truth. As with Leninism, what is offered is *emancipation,* an opening of the world to previously canceled choices. And, I suspect, the long-term consequences could well be the same as those of Leninism: a complete *ideologization* of language, and a displacement of its primary referential function, so that it ceases to be a medium of rational decision-making, or a means to conversation with one's kind.

Langue de bois emerges only with the seizure of power, and the subsequent emergence of a public discourse of warning. But the way is already prepared for this event by a theory which sees nothing in language *besides* power, and which represents all decisions of style, syntax, and semantics as ultimately reducible to transactions in an ideological "struggle." In this respect, the language of modern feminism can be compared with that of Lenin: a vigilant, depersonalized meditation on a world gripped by hostile powers: "an acute and impassioned *attentiveness* to the ways in which primarily male structures of power are inscribed (or encoded) within our literary inheritance," as one feminist critic has expressed it.[16] The feminist, like the Marxist, wishes to uproot and destroy the power that hides itself in language.

Marxist suspicion was directed towards what Hayek[17] would call the "catallactic" aspects of thought: the aspects which arise "by an invisible hand" and which, while the result of many choices, are themselves never chosen. Like prices in a market, the structures of language are unchosen outcomes of a myriad individual decisions. In this, the follower of Adam Smith might argue, lies their wisdom. They provide solutions to problems that are generated and solved socially. These problems cannot be fully understood by one person, and could never be solved by a plan. Nor can the natural solutions that mankind has hit upon be improved by some steering committee of experts. Such a committee would wish to impose as *law,* and in the teeth of human instinct, a solution which can exist only as a tacit convention. Just as the Leninists ended by displacing the primary functions of discourse and producing a monstrous, all-encompassing version of the very evils that they claimed to fear, so, I suspect, will the feminists produce a new *langue de bois* of their own. The sole study of the user of this language will be to dispose his words and thoughts in accordance with the rules of ideological correctness. Truth, reference, deliberation, and honest feeling: these would take a secondary place, and be recognized, if at all, largely as masks adopted by the patriarchal enemy. When this happens, the writings of English-speaking feminists will be as unreadable as the speeches of Gorbachev.

---

[16] Annette Kolodny, "Dancing through the Minefield: Some Observations on the Theory, Practice and Politics of a Feminist Literary Criticism," in *Feminist Literary Theory: A Reader,* ed. Mary Eagleton (Oxford, 1986), p. 186.

[17] Friedrich August von Hayek (1899–) is an Austrian-born British economist who believes that governments should not intervene in the marketplace in order to forestall the natural cycles of inflation, unemployment, or depression. (ED.)

HENRY LOUIS GATES, JR.

Talking Black

Henry Louis Gates, Jr. (1950–) is an author and professor of English and Afro-American Studies. In 1982, he created "The Image of the Black in the Western Imagination," a series for public television. He is the author of *The Signifying Monkey: A Theory of Afro-American Literary Criticism* (1988), which won an American Book Award in 1989, and the editor of *Reading Black, Reading Feminist: A Critical Anthology* (1990). He has taught at Yale, Cornell, and Duke Universities, and is now at Harvard.

For a language acts in divers ways, upon the spirit of a people; even as the spirit of a people acts with a creative and spiritualizing force upon a language.
Alexander Crummell, 1860

A new vision began gradually to replace the dream of political power—a powerful movement, the rise of another ideal to guide the unguided, another pillar of fire by night after a clouded day. It was the ideal of "book-learning"; the curiosity, born of compulsory ignorance, to know and test the power of the cabalistic letters of the white man, the longing to know.
W. E. B. Du Bois, 1903

The knowledge which would teach the white world was Greek to his own flesh and blood. . . . and he could not articulate the message of another people.
W. E. B. Du Bois, 1903

Alexander Crummell, a pioneering nineteenth-century Pan-Africanist, statesman, and missionary who spent the bulk of his creative years as an Anglican minister in Liberia, was also a pioneering intellectual and philosopher of language, founding the American Negro Academy in 1897 and serving as the intellectual godfather of W. E. B. De Bois. For his first annual address as president of the academy, delivered on 28 December 1897, Crummell selected as his topic "The Attitude of the American Mind toward the Negro Intellect." Given the occasion of the first annual meeting of the great intellectuals of the race, he could not have chosen a more timely or appropriate subject.

Crummell wished to attack, he said, "the denial of intellectuality in the Negro; the assertion that he was not a human being, that he

did not belong to the human race." He argued that the desire "to
becloud and stamp out the intellect of the Negro" led to the enact-
ment of "laws and Statutes, closing the pages of every book printed
to the eyes of Negroes; barring the doors of every school-room against
them!" This, he concluded, "was the systematized method of the
intellect of the South, to stamp out the brains of the Negro!"—a
program that created an "almost Egyptian darkness [which] fell upon
the mind of the race, throughout the whole land."

Crummell next shared with his audience a conversation between
two Boston lawyers which he had overheard when he was "an errand
boy in the Anti-slavery office in New York City" in 1833 or 1834:

> While at the Capitol they happened to dine in the company of the great
> John C. Calhoun, then senator from South Carolina. It was a period of
> great ferment upon the question of Slavery, States Rights, and Nullifi-
> cation; and consequently the Negro was the topic of conversation at the
> table. One of the utterances of Mr. Calhoun was to this effect—"That if
> he could find a Negro who knew the Greek syntax, he would then
> believe that the Negro was a human being and should be treated as a
> man."

"Just think of the crude asininity," Crummell concluded rather generously, "of even a great man!"[1]

The salient sign of the black person's humanity—indeed, the only
sign for Calhoun—would be the mastering of the very essence of
Western civilization, of the very foundation of the complex fiction
upon which white Western culture had been constructed. It is likely
that "Greek syntax," for John C. Calhoun, was merely a hyperbolic
figure of speech, a trope of virtual impossibility; he felt driven to the
hyperbolic mode, perhaps, because of the long racist tradition in
Western letters of demanding that black people *prove* their full humanity. We know this tradition all too well, dotted as it is with the
names of great intellectual Western racialists, such as Francis Bacon,
David Hume, Immanuel Kant, Thomas Jefferson, and G. W. F. Hegel.[2]

---

[1] Alexander Crummell, "The Attitude of the American Mind toward the Negro Intellect," *The American Negro Academy, Occasional Papers, no. 3* (Washington, D.C., 1898),
pp. 10, 10–11, 11.

[2] *Francis Bacon* (1561–1626) was an English philosopher best known for his ideas on
inductive methods of acquiring natural knowledge. *David Hume* (1711–1776) was a
Scottish philosopher and historian famous for his philosophical skepticism, denying
the possibility of verifying the truth of human knowledge. *Immanuel Kant* (1724–
1804) was a German philosopher and metaphysician and author of the *Critique of*

Whereas each of these figures demanded that blacks write poetry to prove their humanity, Calhoun—writing in a post-Phillis Wheatley[3] era—took refuge in, yes, Greek syntax.

In typical African-American fashion, a brilliant black intellectual accepted Calhoun's bizarre challenge. The anecdote Crummell shared with his fellow black academicians turned out to be his shaping scene of instruction. For Crummell himself jumped on a boat, sailed to England, and matriculated at Queen's College, Cambridge, where he mastered (naturally enough) the intricacies of Greek syntax. Calhoun, we suspect, was not impressed.

Crummell never stopped believing that mastering the master's tongue was the sole path to civilization, intellectual freedom, and social equality for the black person. It was Western "culture," he insisted, that the black person "must claim as his rightful heritage, as a man—not stinted training, not a caste education, not," he concluded prophetically, "a Negro curriculum."[4] As he argued so passionately in his speech of 1860, "The English Language in Liberia," the acquisition of the English language, along with Christianity, is the wonderful sign of God's providence encoded in the nightmare of African enslavement in the racist wilderness of the New World. English, for Crummell, was "the speech of Chaucer and Shakespeare, of Milton and Wordsworth, of Bacon and Burke, of Franklin and Webster," and its potential mastery was "this one item of compensation" that "the Almighty has bestowed upon us" in exchange for "the exile of our fathers from their African homes to America." In the English language are embodied "the noblest theories of liberty" and "the grandest ideas of humanity." If black people master the master's tongue, these great and grand ideas will become African ideas, because "ideas conserve men, and keep alive the vitality of nations."

In dark contrast to the splendors of the English language, Crummell set the African vernacular languages, which, he wrote, have "definite marks of inferiority connected with them all, which place them at the widest distances from civilized languages." Any effort to

---

Pure Reason (1781). Georg Hegel (1770–1831) was a German philosopher who created a universal system of historical progression known as the Hegelian dialectic. (ED.)

[3] Phillis Wheatley (1753?–1784) was an American poet born in Africa and sold as a slave to John Wheatley of Boston. Her book *Poems on Various Subjects, Religious and Moral* was published in 1773. (ED.)

[4] Crummell, "The Attitude of the American Mind toward the Negro Intellect," p. 16.

render the master's discourse in our own black tongue is an egregious error, for we cannot translate sublime utterances "in[to] broken English—a miserable caricature of their noble tongue." We must abandon forever both indigenous African vernacular languages and the neo-African vernacular languages that our people have produced in the New World:

> All low, inferior, and barbarous tongues are, doubtless, but the lees and dregs of noble languages, which have gradually, as the soul of a nation has died out, sunk down to degradation and ruin. We must not suffer this decay on these shores, in this nation. We have been made, providentially, the deposit of a noble trust; and we should be proud to show our appreciation of it. Having come to the heritage of this language we must cherish its spirit, as well as retain its letter. We must cultivate it among ourselves; we must strive to infuse its spirit among our reclaimed and aspiring natives.[5]

I cite the examples of John C. Calhoun and Alexander Crummell as metaphors for the relation between the critic of black writing and the larger institution of literature. Learning the master's tongue, for our generation of critics, has been an act of empowerment, whether that tongue be New Criticism, humanism, stucturalism, Marxism, poststructuralism, feminism, new historicism, or any other -ism. But even as Afro-American literature and criticism becomes institutionalized, our pressing question now becomes this: in what tongue shall we choose to speak, and write, our own criticisms? What are we now to do with the enabling masks of empowerment that we have donned as we have practiced one mode of "white" criticism or another?

The Afro-American literary tradition is distinctive in that it evolved in response to allegations that its authors did not, and could not, create literature, a capacity that was considered the signal measure of a race's innate "humanity." The African living in Europe or in the New World seems to have felt compelled to create a literature not only to demonstrate that blacks did indeed possess the intellectual ability to create a written art, but also to indict the several social and economic institutions that delimited the "humanity" of all black people in Western cultures.

So insistent did these racist allegations prove to be, at least from

---

[5] Alexander Crummell, "The English Language in Liberia," in *The Future of Africa* (New York, 1862), pp. 10, 50.

the eighteenth to the early twentieth century, that it is fair to describe the subtext of the history of black letters in terms of the urge to refute them. Even as late as 1911, when J. E. Casely-Hayford published *Ethiopia Unbound* (the "first" African novel), he felt it necessary to address this matter in the first two paragraphs of his text. "At the dawn of the twentieth century," the novel opens, "men of light and leading both in Europe and in America had not yet made up their minds as to what place to assign to the spiritual aspirations of the black man."[6] Few literary traditions have begun with such a complex and curious relation to criticism: allegations of an absence led directly to a presence, a literature often inextricably bound in a dialogue with its harshest critics.

Black literature and its criticism, then, have been put to uses that were not primarily aesthetic: rather, they have formed part of a larger discourse on the nature of the black, and his or her role in the order of things. Even so, a sense of integrity has arisen in the Afro-American tradition, though it has less to do with the formal organicism of the New Critics than with an intuitive notion of "ringing true," or Houston Baker's concept of "sounding." (One of the most frequently used critical judgments in the African-American tradition is "That shit don't sound right," or, as Alice Walker puts it in *The Color Purple,* "Look like to me only a fool would want to talk in a way that feel peculiar to your mind."[7] That is the sense I am calling on here, understanding how problematic even this can be. Doubleness, alienation, equivocality: since the turn of the century at least, these have been recurrent tropes for the black tradition.

To be sure, this matter of the language of criticism and the integrity of its subject has a long and rather tortured history in all black letters. It was David Hume, after all, who called Francis Williams, the Jamaican poet of Latin verse, "a parrot who merely speaks a few words plainly." Phillis Wheatley, too, has long suffered from the spurious attacks of black and white critics alike for being the *rara avis*[8] of a school of so-called mockingbird poets, whose use of European and American literary conventions has been considered a corruption of a "purer" black expression, found in forms such as the

---

[6] J. E. Caseley-Hayford, *Ethiopia Unbound: Studies in Race Emancipation* (London, 1911), pp. 1–2.

[7] Alice Walker, *The Color Purple* (New York, 1982), p. 194.

[8] a rare person or thing (ED.)

blues, signifying, spirituals, and Afro-American dance. Can we, as critics, escape a "mockingbird" posture?

Only recently have some scholars attempted to convince critics of black literature that we can. Perhaps predictably, a number of these attempts share a concern with that which has been most repressed in the received tradition of Afro-American criticism: close readings of the texts themselves. And so we are learning to read a black text within a black formal cultural matrix. That means reading a literary culture that remains, for the most part, intransigently oral. If the black literary imagination has a privileged medium, it is what Douglass called the "live, calm, grave, clear, pointed, warm, sweet, melodious and powerful human voice." And the salient contribution of black literature may lie in its resolute vocality. But there is no black voice; only voices, diverse and mutable. Familiarly, there's the strut, confidence laced with bitters—

> I am a Waiter's Waiter. I know all the moves, all the pretty, fine moves that big book will never teach you . . . I built the railroad with my moves. (James Alan McPherson, "Solo Song")[9]

Or the boisterous revelator:

> When he was on, Reverend Jones preached his gospel hour in a Texas church that held no more than 250 people, but the way he had the old sisters banging on them bass drums and slapping them tambourines, you'd think that God's Own Philharmonic was carrying on inside that old church where the loudspeaks blasted Jones's message to the thousands who stood outside. At the conclusion of Reverend Jones's sermon, the church didn't need no fire, because it was being warmed by the spirit of the Lord. By the spirit of Jesus. (Ishmael Reed, *The Terrible Threes*)[10]

Yet how tonally remote they are from this cento of Baldwin,[11] a preacher's son for whom King Jamesian inversions were second nature:

> In the case of the Negro the past was taken from him whether he would or no; yet to forswear it was meaningless and availed him nothing, since

---

[9] James Alan McPherson, "A Solo Song for Doc," in *Hue and Cry* (Boston, 1969), p. 43.

[10] Ishmael Reed, *The Terrible Threes* (New York, 1989), p. 17.

[11] James Baldwin (1924–1987) was a black American writer whose works include *Go Tell It on the Mountain* (1953) and *Notes of a Native Son* (1955). (ED.)

his shameful history was carried, quite literally, on his brow. Shameful; for he was heathen as well as black and would never have discovered the healing blood of Christ had not we braved the jungles to bring him these glad tidings. . . .

Where the Negro face appears, a tension is created, the tension of a silence filled with things unutterable. ("Many Thousands Gone")[12]

Baldwin wrote of "something ironic and violent and perpetually understated in Negro speech," and in this he was describing his own careful, ungentle cadences. Contrast, again, the homeliest intimacies of nuance that Morrison will unexpectedly produce:

There is a loneliness that can be rocked. Arms crossed, knees drawn up; holding, holding on, this motion, unlike a ship's, smooths and contains the rockers. It's an inside kind—wrapped tight like skin. (*Beloved*)[13]

There's no hidden continuity or coherence among them. History makes them like beads on a string: there's no necessary resemblance; but then again, no possible separation.

And so we've had to learn to "read black" as a textual effect because the existence of a black canon is a historically contingent phenomenon; it is not inherent in the nature of "blackness," not vouchsafed by the metaphysics of some racial essence. The black tradition exists only insofar as black artists enact it. Only because black writers have read and responded to other black writers with a sense of recognition and acknowledgment can we speak of a black literary inheritance, with all the burdens and privileges that has entailed. Race is a text (an array of discursive practices), not an essence. It must be *read* with painstaking care and suspicion, not imbibed.

The disjunction between the language of criticism and the language of its subject helps defamiliarize the texts of the black tradition: ironically, it is necessary to create distance between reader and texts in order to go beyond reflexive responses and achieve critical insight into and intimacy with their formal workings. I have done this to respect the integrity of these texts, by trying to avoid confusing my experiences as an Afro-American with the black act of language that defines a text. This is the challenge of the critic of black literature

[12] James Baldwin, "Many Thousands Gone," in *Notes of a Native Son* (Boston, 1957), p. 29.

[13] Toni Morrison, *Beloved* (New York, 1987), p. 276.

in the 1980s: not to shy away from white power—that is, a new critical vocabulary—but to translate it into the black idiom, *renaming* principles of criticism where appropriate, but especially naming indigenous black principles of criticism and applying them to our own texts. *Any* tool that enables the critic to explain the complex workings of the language of a text is appropriate here. For it is language, the black language of black texts, that expresses the distinctive quality of our literary tradition. Once it may have seemed that the only critical implements black critics needed were the pom-pom and the twirled baton; in fact, there is no deeper form of literary disrespect. We will not protect the integrity of our tradition by remaining afraid of, or naive about, literary analysis; rather, we will inflict upon it the violation of reflexive, stereotypical reading—or nonreading. We are the keepers of the black literary tradition. No matter what approach we adopt, we have more in common with each other than we do with any other critic of any other literature. We write for each other, and for our own contemporary writers. This relation is a critical trust.

It is also a *political* trust. How can the demonstration that our texts sustain ever closer and more sophisticated readings *not* be political at a time when all sorts of so-called canonical critics mediate their racism through calls for "purity" of "the tradition," demands as implicitly racist as anything the Southern Agrarians said? How can the deconstruction of the forms of racism itself not be political? How can the use of literary analysis to explicate the racist social text in which we still find ourselves be anything *but* political? To be political, however, does not mean that I have to write at the level of a Marvel comic book. My task, as I see it, is to help guarantee that black and so-called Third World literature is taught to black and Third World and white students by black and Third World and white professors in heretofore white mainstream departments of literature, and to train students to think, to read, and to write clearly, to expose false uses of language, fraudulent claims, and muddled arguments, propaganda, and vicious lies—from all of which our people have suffered just as surely as we have from an economic order in which we were zeroes and a metaphysical order in which we were absences. These are the "values" which should be transmitted through the languages of cultural and literary study.

In the December 1986 issue of the *Voice Literary Supplement,* in an essay entitled "Cult-Nats Meet Freaky-Deke," Greg Tate argued cogently and compellingly that "black aestheticians need to develop a coherent criticism to communicate the complexities of our culture. There's no periodical on black cultural phenomena equivalent to *The Village Voice* or *Artforum,* no publication that provides journalism on black visual art, philosophy, politics, economics, media, literature, linguistics, psychology, sexuality, spirituality, and pop culture. Though there are certainly black editors, journalists, and academics capable of producing such a journal, the disintegration of the black cultural nationalist movement and the brain-drain of black intellectuals to white institutions have destroyed the vociferous public dialogue that used to exist between them." While I would argue that *Sage, Callaloo,* and *Black American Literature Forum* are indeed fulfilling that function for academic critics, I am afraid that the truth of Tate's claim is irresistible.

But his most important contribution to the future of black criticism is to be found in his most damning allegation. "What's unfortunate," he writes, "is that while black artists have opened up the entire 'text of blackness' for fun and games, not many black critics have produced writing as fecund, eclectic, and freaky-deke[14] as the art, let alone the culture, itself. . . . For those who prefer exegesis with a polemical bent, just imagine how critics as fluent in black and Western culture as the postliberated artists could strike terror into that bastion of white supremacist thinking, the Western art [and literary] world[s]." To which I can only say, "Amen, Amen."

Tate's challenge is a serious one because neither ideology nor criticism nor blackness can exist as entities of themselves, outside their forms or their texts. This is the central theme of Ralph Ellison's *Invisible Man* and Ishmael Reed's *Mumbo Jumbo,* for example. But how can we write or read the text of "Blackness"? What language(s) do black people use to represent their critical or ideological positions? In what forms of language do we speak or write? Can we derive a valid, integral "black" text of criticism or ideology from borrowed or appropriated forms? Can a black woman's text emerge authentically as borrowed, or "liberated," or revised, from the patriarchal forms of the slave narratives, on the one hand, or from the white matriarchal forms of the sentimental novel, on the other, as Harriet Jacobs and Harriet Wilson[15] attempted to do in *Incidents in the Life of a Slave*

---

[14] unconventional in attitude and behavior (ED.)

[15] *Harriet Brent Jacobs* (1813–1897) was a runaway slave who wrote an autobiography entitled *Incidents in the Life of a Slave Girl* (1861). *Harriet Wilson* (1828?–1870?) was

Girl (1861) and *Our Nig* (1859)? Where lies the liberation in revision, the ideological integrity of defining freedom in the modes and forms of difference charted so cogently by so many poststructural critics of black literature?

For it is in these spaces of difference that black literature has dwelled. And while it is crucial to read these patterns of difference closely, we should understand as well that the quest was lost, in an important sense, before it had even begun, simply because the terms of our own self-representation have been provided by the master. It is not enough for us to show that refutation, negation, and revision exist, and to define them as satisfactory gestures of ideological independence. Our next concern will be to address the black political signified, that is, the cultural vision and the black critical language that underpin the search through literature and art for a profound reordering and humanizing of everyday existence. We encourage our writers and critics to undertake the fullest and most ironic exploration of the manner and matter, the content and form, the structure and sensibility so familiar and poignant to us in our most sublime form of art, black music, where ideology and art are one, whether we listen to Bessie Smith or to postmodern and poststructural John Coltrane.

Just as we encourage our writers to meet this challenge, we as critics can turn to our own peculiarly black structures of thought and feeling to develop our own language of criticism. We do so by drawing on the black vernacular, the language we use to speak to each other when no white people are around. Unless we look to the vernacular to ground our modes of reading, we will surely sink in the mire of Nella Larsen's[16] quicksand, remain alienated in the isolation of Harriet Jacobs' garret, or masked in the received stereotype of the Black Other helping Huck to return to the raft, singing "China Gate" with Nat King Cole under the Da Nang moon, or reflecting our balded heads in the shining flash of Mr. T's signifying gold chains.

We can redefine reading itself from within our own black cultures, refusing to grant the racist premise that criticism is something that white people do, so that we are doomed to imitate our white colleagues, like reverse black minstrel critics done up in whiteface.

---

a black American slave and author of *Our Nig: Sketches from the Life of a Free Black* (1859). (ED.)

[16] Nella Larsen (1891–1964) was a black American novelist during the Harlem Renaissance of the 1920s. (ED.)

We should not succumb, as did Alexander Crummell, to the tragic lure of white power, the mistake of accepting the empowering language of white criticism as "universal" or as our own language, the mistake of confusing its enabling mask with our own black faces. Each of us has, in some literal or figurative manner, boarded a ship and sailed to a metaphorical Cambridge, seeking to master the master's tools. (I myself, being quite literal-minded, booked passage some fourteen years ago on the QE2.) Now we can at last don the empowering mask of blackness and talk *that* talk, the language of black difference. While it is true that we must, as Du Bois said so long ago, "know and test the power of the cabalistic letters of the white man," we must also know and test the dark secrets of a black discursive universe that awaits its disclosure through the black arts of interpretation. The future of our language and literature may prove black indeed.

DAVID DABYDEEN

On Not Being Milton: Nigger Talk in England Today

David Dabydeen (1955–   ), a Caribbean poet, was born into a family of canecutters in Guyana and moved to England at the age of fourteen. His acclaimed collection *Slave Song* (1984), about peasants working on the sugar plantations in Guyana, is written in Guyanese Creole, a mixture of East Indian, African, French, Spanish, and English dialects. As an editor of *The Black Presence in English Literature* (1982), he assembled essays addressing the often-ignored contributions of blacks to familiar works of literature. He has served as the director of Caribbean literature at Warwick University in England. He has published *Carribean Literature: A Teacher's Handbook* (1986); the following selection is from *The State of Language* (1989), Christopher Ricks and Leonard Michaels, editors.

It's hard to put two words together in creole without swearing. Words are spat out from the mouth like live squibs, not pronounced with elocution. English diction is cut up, and this adds to the abruptness of the language: *what* for instance becomes *wha* (as in *whack*), the splintering making the language more barbaric. Soft vowel sounds are habitually converted: the English tend to be polite in *war,* whereas the creole *warre* produces an appropriate snarling sound; *scorn* becomes *scaan, water wata,* and so on.

In 1984 I published a first collection of poems entitled *Slave Song,* written in a Caribbean creole and dealing with the Romance of the Cane, meaning the perverse eroticism of black labor and the fantasy of domination, bondage, and sadomasochism. The British Empire, as the Thistlewood Diaries show, was as much a pornographic as an economic project.[1] The subject demanded a language capable of describing both a lyrical and a corrosive sexuality. The creole language is angry, crude, energetic. The canecutter chopping away at the crops bursts out in a spate of obscene words, a natural gush from the gut.

In the preface to *Slave Song* I speak of the brokenness of the language which reflects the brokenness and suffering of its original users. Its potential as a naturally tragic language is there in its brokenness and rawness, which is like the rawness of a wound. If one has learnt and used Queen's English for some years, the return to creole is painful, almost nauseous, for the language is uncomfortably raw. One has to shed one's protective sheath of abstracts and let the tongue move freely in blood again.

In writing *Slave Song* I had no Caribbean literary models to imitate, since I knew none. Apart from early childhood in Guyana I was brought up in England and no Caribbean literature was taught in schools. So I was wholly ignorant of the creole poetry of Edward Brathwaite or Claude McKay, the latter influenced by the balladry of Burns. What in fact triggered off *Slave Song* were the years spent as an undergraduate at Cambridge reading English literature. There was the discovery of the "gaudy and inane phraseology" of much of eighteenth-century poetry, the wrapping of stark experiences in a napkin of poetic diction. James Grainger's poem *The Sugar Cane,* for instance, in which the toil of plantation life is erased or converted into pastoral. Instead of *overseer* Grainger uses the term "Master Swain"; instead of *slaves,* "assistant planters." The black condition is

---

[1] Thomas Thistlewood was a small landowner in Western Jamaica during the eighteenth century. He chronicles the daily life around him until his death in 1786. A selection of his writings can be found in *Miserable Slavery: Thomas Thistlewood in Jamaica, 1750-1786,* ed. Douglas Hall (London, 1988).

further embellished by calling the slaves "Afric's sable progeny." Grainger's poem is a classic example in English poetry of the refusal to call a spade a spade. Then there were all those antislavery pieces in a highfalutin Miltonic rhetoric and cadence, in which the poets used the black experience merely as a vehicle for lofty, moral pronouncements on good and evil. Or Coleridge's Greek Ode against slavery, which won him the Browne Gold Medal at Cambridge: the African here is subject to the exercise of classical erudition.

The real discovery, however, was of medieval alliterative verse. Reading *Sir Gawain and the Green Knight* was a startling moment. The sheer naked energy and brutality of the language, its "thew & sinew," reminded me immediately of the creole of my childhood. John of Trevisa, a fourteenth-century translator, described the alliterative poetry of the North of England as "harsh, piercing and formless." This quality of lawlessness and the primarily oral form of delivery bore a curious resemblance to Guyanese creole. I began to see, albeit naively, the ancient divide between north and south in Britain, the Gawain poet standing in opposition to Chaucer in terms of a native idiom versus an educated, relaxed poetic line tending towards the form of the iambic pentameter. The north/south divide is of course evocative of the divide between the so-called Caribbean periphery and the metropolitan center of London. London is supposed to provide the models of standard English, and we in the Caribbean our dialect versions.

The comparison between England and the modern Caribbean is not altogether fanciful, for in a sense we West Indians live in the Middle Ages in terms of rudimentary material resources. The British Empire was after all a feudal structure with robber barons and serfs. Transportation by horse, mule, or canoe, peasant farming, manual labor, villages lying in patches of land encircled by bush in the way that dense forest lay just outside English castle walls, these features and others of Guyana's countryside conjure up medieval life. And if, as Johan Huizinga states in *The Waning of the Middle Ages,* the sound of church bells dominated the air of England, so too in Guyana is religion a vital, noisy force. And out of this matrix of spirit and earth is born a language that is both lyrical and barbaric. But the very unsystematic and unscientific nature of the language which is a source of strength to writers like myself is cause for summary dismissal or parody for others. Peter Porter, for instance, speaks dismissively of the "difficulty" of understanding creole; presumably Porter has no time for Shakespeare or Joyce either. In *Slave Song,* in anticipation of such automatic responses, I clothed the creole poems

in an elaborate set of "notes" and "translations" as an act of coun-
terparody, in the way that Eliot had annotated his *Waste Land* supposedly for the benefit of his lazier readers. The more common
English response to creole, however, is to be found from Alan Coren's
pen. Coren in 1975 published the second volume of the collected
thoughts of Idi Amin, which had been appearing in *Punch* magazine
for some months. In the introduction Amin is made to reveal the
burden of words:

> One trouble wid de bes' seller business: you gittin' boun' to de wheel o'
> fire. No sooner you dishin' out one giant masterpiece to de gobblin'
> pubberlic, they comin' round yo' premises an' hammerin' on de door fo'
> de nex'. "Come on out, John Milton!" de mob yellin', "We know yo' in
> there! We jus' finishin' de *Parachute Lost* an' we twiddlin' de thums, wot
> about dis year's jumbo pome you lazy bum?"
>
> It hardly surprisin' E. N. Fleming packin' up de Jane Bond racket
> an' turnin' to de penicillin business. Dam sight easier scrapin' de mold
> off bread an' floggin' it up de chemist than bashin' de fingers flat day an'
> nights on de Olivetti an' wonderin' where yo' nex' plot comin' fom.
>
> Natcherly, de same happenin' wid de present writer. Las' year, de
> astoundin' fust book hittin' de shops, an' befo' anyone know wot hap-
> penin' de made fans smashin' down de premises o' W. H. Smith an'
> carryin' de amazin' tomes off by de crate! De pubberlisher rushin' out
> four impressions in four munce, an still de cravin' not satisfied. "It no
> good", de pubberlisher informin' me. "Only one way to shut de slaverin'
> buggers' gobs, yo' imperial majesty: you havin' to cobble together another
> great milestone in de history o' literature, how about Wensdy week?"
>
> So here I sittin', shovin' de affairs o' state on one side, an' puttin'
> together a noo volume o' de famous weekly bulletins fom downtown
> Kampala, Hub o' de Universe.

Two ancient images of black people emerge from Coren's pen.
First, the sense that they are scientifically illiterate. This idea can be
traced back to seventeenth- and eighteenth-century European writings which describe African societies as being devoid of intellectual
capacities ("No ingenious manufacture amongst them, no arts, no
sciences," as David Hume declared). They squat in mud huts and
gnaw bones. They know neither compass nor telescope. European
literature is littered with blacks like Man Friday, who falls to earth
to worship Crusoe's magical gun, or the savage in Conrad's steamship
who acted as fireman:

> He was an improved specimen; he could fire up a vertical boiler. He was
> there below me, and, upon my word, to look at him was as edifying as
> seeing a dog in a parody of breeches and a feather hat, walking on his

hind-legs. A few months of training had done for that really fine chap. He squinted at the steam-gauge and at the water-gauge with an evident effort of intrepidity—and he had filed teeth, too, the poor devil, and the wool of his pate shaved into queer patterns, and three ornamental scars on each of his cheeks. He ought to have been clapping his hands and stamping his feet on the bank, instead of which he was hard at work, a thrall to strange witchcraft, full of improving knowledge. He was useful because he had been instructed; and what he knew was this—that should the water in that transparent thing disappear, the evil spirit inside the boiler would get angry through the greatness of his thirst, and take a terrible vengeance. So he sweated and fired up and watched the glass fearfully (with an impromptu charm, made of rags, tied to his arm, and a piece of polished bone, as big as a watch, stuck flat-ways through his lower lip), while the wooded banks slipped past us slowly, the short noise was left behind, the interminable miles of silence—and we crept on, towards Kurtz.

Secondly, the sense that they are linguistically illiterate. Just as they are ignorant of the rules of scientific formulae, so they are ignorant of the rules of grammar. Their language is mere broken, stupid utterance. Again this view of black expression is firmly entrenched in European conceptualization. In seventeenth-century travel literature and anthropological writings the bestiality of the natives is reflected in their language. Sir Thomas Herbert in 1634 suggested that Africans and apes mated with each other, the evidence for this being that African speech sounded "more like that of Apes than Men . . . their language is rather apishly than articulately founded." Many passages focus on the monstrosity of their organs of speech as well as their organs of propagation. Whilst John Ogilby (1670) is writing about the "large propagators" sported by the men of Guinea, and Richard Jobson (1623) on male Mandingoes being "furnished with such members as are after a sort burdensome unto them," William Strachey (1612) focuses on their "great big lips and wide mouths." Thick lips and monstrously misshapen mouths, sometimes, as in the case of the anthropophagi,[2] located in their chests, indicated an inability to make proper speech. When we find eloquent and civilized blacks in English literature of the period, as in the case of Mrs. Aphra Behn's Oroonoko, their physical features are more European than African: "His mouth, the finest shaped that could be

---

[2] cannibals (ED.)

seen; far from those great turn'd lips which are so natural to the rest of the Negroes."

In the eighteenth century, which was the Age of Slavery as well as the Age of the Dictionary, such attitudes to Africans were sustained, the link between barbarism and lack of speech made explicit. *Spectator* No. 389 of May 1712 described Hottentots[3] as "Barbarians, who are in every respect scarce one degree above Brutes, having no language among them but a confused Gabble, which is neither well understood by themselves or others." Given the centrality of the Word in eighteenth-century English civilization (Pope's "What oft was thought, but ne'er so well expressed"; Hogarth's *Conversation Pieces;* Steele's *Tatler;* Johnson's *Dictionary*), the apparent wordlessness of the Africans was deemed to be incontrovertible evidence of their barbarism.

The equation between African and animal, sustained by the issue of language, which gave moral validity to the slave trade, continued in the nineteenth century, the Age of Imperialism and Anthropometrics, African's skulls, lips, teeth, and mouths were scrupulously measured by leading white scientists to reveal black cultural and moral primitivism and therefore the necessity of continuing colonial rule. Science underpinned the imperial process. It was also quite obvious, however, that Africans had language, and this posed a problem to white conceptualization since language was an undeniable *human* characteristic. Professor Bernth Lindfors illustrates the problem by reference to the case of the San people of South Africa, a group of whom were brought to Britain between 1846 and 1850 to be displayed at circuses and fairgrounds.[4] The speech of the San visitors was their most noticeable feature: 70 percent of it consisted of a set of implosive consonants, commonly called "clicks," which were absent from the English phonological system. Lindfors states that "the number and variety of these click consonants, complicated still further by subtle vowel colourings and significant variations in tone make it, from the phonetic point of view, among the world's most complex languages." To the Victorians, however, hardly interested in such analysis, San speech merely sounded like animal noises. The *Liverpool Chronicle* reported that "the language resembles more

[3] A people of southwestern Africa uprooted by Dutch colonialists in the seventeenth century (ED.)

[4] Bernth Lindfors, "The Hottentot Venus" (paper given at London University's International Conference on the History of Blacks in Britain, 1981).

the cluck of turkeys than the speech of human beings" (5 December 1846), and the *Era* described the language as "wholly incomprehensible, for nobody can interpret it. . . . The words are made up of coughs and clucks, such as a man uses to his nag. Anything more uncivilised can scarcely be conceived" (6 June 1847). Even when admission of the humanity of the San people was grudgingly conceded, the classics of white literature were raised against them: the *Observer* wrote that "their distinguishing characteristic as men is their use of language, but besides that, they have little in common . . . with that race of beings which boasts of a Newton and a Milton" (21 June 1847). The science of Newton and the literature of Milton are sufficient to put black people in their place. Idi Amin's (Alan Coren's) reference to Milton is not a loose one. Milton's ornate, highly structured, Latinate expressions, so unattractive to modern tastes influenced by Eliot and Yeats, are still the exemplars of English civilization against which the barbaric, broken utterances of black people are judged.

In January 1978 Margaret Thatcher made a speech broadcast on prime-time television which reinforced the notions of "otherness" so prevalent in British writings on blacks. It was rhetoric which decimated the neo-fascist National Front party as an electoral force by winning the far-right of the Tory party:

> If we went on as we are, then by the end of the century there would be four million people of the New Commonwealth or Pakistan here. Now that is an awful lot and I think it means that people are really rather afraid that this country might be swamped by people with a different culture. And you know, the British character has done so much for democracy, for law, and done so much throughout the world, that if there is a fear that it might be swamped, people are going to react and be rather hostile to those coming in.

Her pronouncement, however, was very outdated, for the native British some four decades earlier had already exhibited "rather hostile" (note how the upper-class term "rather" softens the sinisterness of "hostile" and "afraid") behavior towards fellow black citizens. In September 1948, two months after the first boatload of postwar West Indian immigrants arrived on the *S.S. Empire Windrush,* race riots broke out in the streets of England. A decade later, in 1958, antiblack riots erupted in Nottingham and in the Notting Hill area of London, with gangs of white teenagers engaged in "nigger hunting," the working-class version of fox-hunting. In the next decade onwards, communal violence based on Catholic-Protestant/Irish-English hostilities became a daily feature of British life. The killing of civilians, policemen, soldiers, politicians, and one member of the Royal Family dominated television screens. In the eighties, race riots in Bristol, Liverpool, and London (the old slave ports) led to the police use of plastic bullets for the first time on the British mainland. Today, even Home Office statistics reveal that the number of physical racial attacks on black people runs into the thousands annually, while the nighttime burning down of homes is a routine experience for some immigrant communities. When E. P. Thompson declared that "England is the last colony of the British Empire," it was to such neo-colonial violence and community strife that he was referring.

One of the many ways in which young British blacks have resisted white domination is in the creation of a patois evolved from the West Indian creole of their parents. The poetry that has emerged from the black communities is expressed in the language of this patois, and one of its greatest exponents is Linton Kwesi Johnson:

> Shock-black bubble-doun-beat bouncing
> rock-wise tumble-doun sound music:
> foot-drop find drum, blood story,
> bass history is a moving
>   is a hurting black story.
>   ("Reggae Sounds")[5]

Johnson's poetry is recited to music from a reggae band. The paraphernalia of sound systems, amplifiers, speakers, microphones, electric guitars, and the rest which dominates the stage and accompanies what one critic has dismissed as "jungle-talk" is a deliberate "misuse" of white technology. "Sound systems," essential to "dub-poetry," are often homemade contraptions, cannibalized parts of diverse machines reordered for black expression. This de/reconstruction is in itself an assertive statement, a denial of the charge of black incapacity to understand technology. The mass-produced technology is remade for self-use in the way that the patois is a "private" reordering of "standard" English. The deliberate exploitation of high-tech to serve black "jungle-talk" is a reversal of colonial history. Caliban is tearing up the pages of Prospero's magic book and repasting it in his own order, by his own method, and for his own purpose.

A feature of Black British poetry is a sheer delight in the rhythms

---

[5] L. K. Johnson, *Dread Beat and Blood* (London, 1975), p. 56.

and sound of language that survives technology, and this joyousness is revealed in poems like Mikey Smith's "R-ooTs" (the line "lawwwwwwd," as Edward Brathwaite says, sounding like the exhaust roar of a motorcycle) or in the writings of Jimi Rand. There is a deliberate celebration of the "primitive" consciousness of sound in Smith's "Nock-Nock":

> Me was fas asleep in me bed
> wen a nok come pun me door,
> bright and early, fore day morning
> before dawn bruk.
> Nock nock—nock nock,
> badoombadoom nock nock
> badoombadoom nock nock
> badoombadoom nock badoom nock.
> Who dat; a who dat nock?[6]

This deliberate wearing of the "primitive" label is even more explicit in his "Nigger Talk" poem:

> Funky talk
> Nitty gritty grass-root talk
> Dat's wha I da talk
> Cause de talk is togedder talk,
> Like right on, out-a-sight, kind-a-too-much.
> Ya hip to it yet?
> Ya dig de funky way to talk
> Talk talk?
> Dis na white talk;
> Na white talk dis.
> It is coon, nignog samba wog talk.[7]

The use of language is inextricably bound up with a sense of being black. Hence John Agard's poem "Listen Mr Oxford Don" is conscious of the way creole suffers from the charge of being surly and indecent ("Mugging de Queen's English"), and Agard links this literary indictment to attitudes in the wide society where blacks are accused of a host of criminal activities:

> Dem accuse me of assault
> on de Oxford dictionary/

---

[6] Mikey Smith, *News for Babylon,* ed. James Berry (London, 1984), p. 108.

[7] *News for Babylon,* p. 113.

imagine a concise peaceful man like me/
dem want me serve time
for inciting rhyme to riot
so mek dem send one big word after me
i ent serving no jail sentence
I slashing suffix in self-defence
I bashing future wit present tense
and if necessary

I making de Queen's English accessory/to my offence[8]

Johnson, Agard, and others are reacting against the "rational structure and comprehensible language" which Robert Conquest saw as a distinguishing feature of the Movement poets and which still afflicts contemporary English verse. The charge that Alvarez leveled against the Movement—the disease of gentility—is still relevant today. Andrew Motion, for instance, can visit Anne Frank's room and on emerging conclude that all Anne Frank wanted was to

leave as simply
as I do, and walk at ease
up dusty tree-lined avenues, or watch
a silent barge come clear of bridges
settling their reflections in the blue canal.[9]

There is glibness and gentility here, disguised as understatements but really amounting to a kind of obscenity. As Michael Hulse has commented, "to go as a tourist to a house which, like many similar houses in Amsterdam, focussed human hope and suffering, and then to parade the delicacy of one's response, savours somewhat of an opportunism that is slightly obscene." The quiet understatement of Motion's response to human tragedy is as obscene as Conrad's heated, insistent rhetoric ("It was the stillness of an implacable force brooding over an inscrutable intention," etc.): both belong to a tradition of colonizing the experience of others for the gratification of their own literary sensibilities.

The pressure of the same racism that destroyed Anne Frank and encounter with the thuggery that lurks beneath the polite surface of English life and letters force black writers into poetry that is disturbing and passionate. The play of the light of memory upon pine

---

[8] J. Agard, *Mangoes and Bullets* (London, 1985), p. 44.

[9] A. Motion, *Dangerous Play* (Middlesex, 1985), p. 41.

furniture touching vignettes of domestic life, elegiac recollections of dead relatives, wonderment at the zig-zag fall of an autumnal leaf, none of these typical contemporary English poetic concerns are of special relevance to them. They participate in a West Indian literary tradition which seeks to subvert English canons by the use of lived nigger themes in lived nigger language. Their strategies of "rants, rudeness and rhymes" look back half a century to the West Indian struggle to establish "black" expression. In March 1931 a new Trinidadian journal, *The Beacon,* attempted to instigate a movement for "local" literature, encouraging writing that was authentic to the West Indian landscape and to the daily speech of its inhabitants. "We fail utterly to understand," an editorial of January/February 1932 commented on the quality of short stories received for publication, "why anyone should want to see Trinidad as a miniature Paradiso, where gravediggers speak like English M.P.'s." Emphasis was placed on the use of creole, and on a realistic description of West Indian life, for political and aesthetic reasons. To write in creole was to validate the experience of black people against the contempt and dehumanizing dismissal by white people. Celebration of blackness necessitated celebration of black language, for how could black writers be true to their blackness using the language of their colonial masters? The aesthetic argument was bound up with this political argument, and involved an appreciation of the energy, vitality, and expressiveness of creole, an argument that Edward Brathwaite has rehearsed in his book *The History of the Voice* (1984). For Brathwaite the challenge to West Indian poets was how to shatter the frame of the iambic pentameter which had prevailed in English poetry from the time of Chaucer onwards. The form of the pentameter is not appropriate to a West Indian environment: "The hurricane does not roar in pentameters. And that's the problem: how do you get a rhythm which approximates the *natural* experience, the *environmental* experience?"[10] The use of creole, or Nation language, as he terms it, involves recognition of the vitality of the oral tradition surviving from Africa, the earthiness of proverbial folk speech, the energy and power of gestures which accompany oral delivery, and the insistence of the drumbeat to which the living voice responds.

England today is the largest West Indian island after Jamaica and Trinidad—there are over half a million of us here—and our genera-

---

[10] E. Brathwaite, *The History of the Voice* (London, 1984), p. 10.

tion is confronted by the same issues that Brathwaite and other writers faced in their time. If a writer was to be recognized, the pressure then was to slavishly imitate the expressions of the Mother Country. Hence the vague Miltonic cadence of Walter Mac M. Lawrence, one of our early Guyanese writers, in describing, quite inappropriately, the native thunder of the Kaiteur Falls:

> And falling in splendour sheer down from the heights
> that should gladden the heart of our eagle to scan,
> That lend to the towering forest beside thee the semblance
> of shrubs trimmed and tended by man—
> That viewed from the brink where the vast, amber volume
> that once was a stream cataracts into thee,
> Impart to the foothills surrounding the maelstrom beneath
> thee that rage as this troublous sea.[11]

Brathwaite and others eventually rescued us from this cascade of nonsense sounds. The pressure now is also towards mimicry. Either you drop the epithet "black" and think of yourself as a "writer" (a few of us foolishly embrace this position, desirous of the status of "writing" and knowing that "black" is blighted)—that is, you cease dwelling on the nigger/tribal/nationalistic theme, you cease *folking* up the literature, and you become "universal"—or else you perish in the backwater of small presses, you don't get published by the "quality" presses, and you don't receive the corresponding patronage of mediahype. This is how the threat against us is presented. Alison Daiches, summarizing these issues, puts them in a historical context: the pressure is to become a mulatto and house-nigger (Ariel) rather than stay a field-nigger (Caliban).[12]

I cannot feel or write poetry like a white man, however, much less serve him. And to become mulattos, black people literally have to be fucked (and fucked up) first. Which brings us back to the pornography of Empire. I feel that I am different, not wholly, but sufficiently for me to want to contemplate that which is other in me, that which owes its life to particular rituals of ancestry. I know that the concept of "otherness" is the fuel of white racism and dominates current political discourse, from Enoch Powell's "In these great num-

---

[11] Walter Mac M. Lawrence, cited in M. Gilkes, *Creative Schizophrenia: The Caribbean Culture Challenge* (University of Warwick, Centre for Caribbean Studies, Third Walter Rodney Memorial Lecture, 1986), p. 3.

[12] Alison Daiches, in *Third World Impact,* ed. A. Ali (London, 1988), p. 74.

bers blacks are, and remain, alien here. With the growth of consecrated numbers, their alienness grows not by choice but by necessity,"
to Margaret Thatcher's "swamped by people of a different culture."
I also know that the concept of "otherness" pervades English literature, from Desdemona's[13] fatal attraction to the body of alien experience in preference to the familiarity of her own culture to
Marlow's[14] obsession with the thought that Africans are in one sense
alien but in a more terrible sense the very capacities within Europeans
for the gratification of indecent pleasures. But these are not my
problem. I'm glad to be peculiar, to modify the phrase. I'd prefer to
be simply peculiar, and to get on with it, to live and write accordingly,
but gladness is a forced response against the weight of insults, a
throwing off of white men's burdens.

As to "universality," let Achebe have the last word, even if in the
most stylish of English:

> In the nature of things the work of a Western writer is automatically
> informed by universality. It is only others who must strain to achieve it.
> So-and-so's work is universal; he has truly arrived! As though univer-
> sality were some distant bend in the road which you may take if you
> travel out far enough in the direction of Europe or America, if you put
> adequate distance between yourself and your home. I should like to see
> the word "universal" banned altogether from discussion of African lit-
> erature until such a time as people cease to use it as a synonym for the
> narrow, self-serving parochialism of Europe, until their horizon extends
> to include all the world.[15]

---

[13] In Shakespeare's *Othello,* Desdemona, the daughter of a Venetian senator, is secretly
married to Othello, a Moor. He murders her in a fit of jealousy after Iago leads him
to suspect Desdemona of infidelity. (ED.)

[14] In Joseph Conrad's *Heart of Darkness,* Marlow journeys into Africa and discovers
the ghastly transformation of a white trader, Mr. Kurtz, into a barbaric ruler over the
native inhabitants. (ED.)

[15] C. Achebe, *Hopes and Impediments* (Oxford, 1988), p. 52. [Chinua Achebe (1930–   )
is a Nigerian novelist who writes about the effects of colonialism and modernization
on the traditional culture of Africa. (ED.)]

WILLIAM LUTZ

Doublespeak

William Lutz (1940–   ) is a professor and former chair of the Department of English at Rutgers University at Camden. He edits the *Quarterly Review of Doublespeak* and is the author of *Doublespeak: From Revenue Enhancement to Terminal Living* (1989), from which the following selection is taken.

There are no potholes in the streets of Tucson, Arizona, just "pavement deficiencies." The Reagan Administration didn't propose any new taxes, just "revenue enhancement" through new "user's fees." Those aren't bums on the street, just "non-goal oriented members of society." There are no more poor people, just "fiscal underachievers." There was no robbery of an automatic teller machine, just an "unauthorized withdrawal." The patient didn't die because of medical malpractice, it was just a "diagnostic misadventure of a high magnitude." The U.S. Army doesn't kill the enemy anymore, it just "services the target." And the doublespeak goes on.

Doublespeak is language that pretends to communicate but really doesn't. It is language that makes the bad seem good, the negative appear positive, the unpleasant appear attractive or at least tolerable. Doublespeak is language that avoids or shifts responsibility, language that is at variance with its real or purported meaning. It is language that conceals or prevents thought; rather than extending thought, doublespeak limits it.

Doublespeak is not a matter of subjects and verbs agreeing; it is a matter of words and facts agreeing. Basic to doublespeak is incongruity, the incongruity between what is said or left unsaid, and what really is. It is the incongruity between the word and the referent, between seem and be, between the essential function of language— communication— and what doublespeak does—mislead, distort, deceive, inflate, circumvent, obfuscate.

HOW TO SPOT DOUBLESPEAK

How can you spot doublespeak? Most of the time you will recognize doublespeak when you see or hear it. But, if you have any doubts, you can identify doublespeak just by answering these questions: Who is saying what to whom, under what conditions and circumstances, with what intent, and with what results? Answering these questions will usually help you identify as doublespeak language that appears to be legitimate or that at first glance doesn't even appear to be doublespeak.

First Kind of Doublespeak

There are at least four kinds of doublespeak. The first is the euphemism, an inoffensive or positive word or phrase used to avoid a harsh, unpleasant, or distasteful reality. But a euphemism can also be a tactful word or phrase which avoids directly mentioning a painful reality, or it can be an expression used out of concern for the feelings of someone else, or to avoid directly discussing a topic subject to a social or cultural taboo.

When you use a euphemism because of your sensitivity for someone's feelings or out of concern for a recognized social or cultural taboo, it is not doublespeak. For example, you express your condolences that someone has "passed away" because you do not want to say to a grieving person, "I'm sorry your father is dead." When you use the euphemism "passed away," no one is misled. Moreover, the euphemism functions here not just to protect the feelings of another person, but to communicate also your concern for that person's feelings during a period of mourning. When you excuse yourself to go to the "rest room," or you mention that someone is "sleeping with" or "involved with" someone else, you do not mislead anyone about your meaning, but you do respect the social taboos about discussing bodily functions and sex in direct terms. You also indicate your sensitivity to the feelings of your audience, which is usually considered a mark of courtesy and good manners.

However, when a euphemism is used to mislead or deceive, it becomes doublespeak. For example, in 1984 the U.S. State Department announced that it would no longer use the word "killing" in its annual report on the status of human rights in countries around the world. Instead, it would use the phrase "unlawful or arbitrary deprivation of life," which the department claimed was more accurate. Its real purpose for using this phrase was simply to avoid discussing the embarrassing situation of government-sanctioned killings in countries that are supported by the United States and have been certified by the United States as respecting the human rights of their citizens. This use of a euphemism constitutes doublespeak, since it is designed to mislead, to cover up the unpleasant. Its real intent is at variance with its apparent intent. It is language designed to alter our perception of reality.

The Pentagon, too, avoids discussing unpleasant realities when it refers to bombs and artillery shells that fall on civilian targets as "incontinent ordnance." And in 1977 the Pentagon tried to slip funding for the neutron bomb unnoticed into an appropriations bill by calling it a "radiation enhancement device."

Second Kind of Doublespeak

A second kind of doublespeak is jargon, the specialized language of a trade, profession, or similar group, such as that used by doctors, lawyers, engineers, educators, or car mechanics. Jargon can serve an important and useful function. Within a group, jargon functions as a kind of verbal shorthand that allows members of the group to communicate with each other clearly, efficiently, and quickly. Indeed, it is a mark of membership in the group to be able to use and understand the group's jargon.

But jargon, like the euphemism, can also be doublespeak. It can be—and often is—pretentious, obscure, and esoteric terminology used to give an air of profundity, authority, and prestige to speakers and their subject matter. Jargon as doublespeak often makes the simple appear complex, the ordinary profound, the obvious insightful. In this sense it is used not to express but impress. With such doublespeak, the act of smelling something becomes "organoleptic analysis," glass becomes "fused silicate," a crack in a metal support beam becomes a "discontinuity," conservative economic policies become "distributionally conservative notions."

Lawyers, for example, speak of an "involuntary conversion" of property when discussing the loss or destruction of property through theft, accident, or condemnation. If your house burns down or if your car is stolen, you have suffered an involuntary conversion of your property. When used by lawyers in a legal situation, such jargon is a legitimate use of language, since lawyers can be expected to understand the term.

However, when a member of a specialized group uses its jargon to communicate with a person outside the group, and uses it knowing that the nonmember does not understand such language, then there is doublespeak. For example, on May 9, 1978, a National Airlines 727 airplane crashed while attempting to land at the Pensacola, Florida airport. Three of the fifty-two passengers aboard the airplane were killed. As a result of the crash, National made an after-tax insurance benefit of $1.7 million, or an extra 18¢ a share dividend for its stockholders. Now National Airlines had two problems: It did not want to talk about one of its airplanes crashing, and it had to account for the $1.7 million when it issued its annual report to its stockholders. National solved the problem by inserting a footnote in its annual report which explained that the $1.7 million income was due to "the involuntary conversion of a 727." National thus acknowledged the crash of its airplane and the subsequent profit it made from the crash, without once mentioning the accident or the deaths. However, because airline officials knew that most stockholders in the company, and indeed most of the general public, were not familiar with legal jargon, the use of such jargon constituted doublespeak.

Third Kind of Doublespeak

A third kind of doublespeak is gobbledygook or bureaucratese. Basically, such doublespeak is simply a matter of piling on words, of overwhelming the audience with words, the bigger the words and the longer the sentences the better. Alan Greenspan, then chair of President Nixon's Council of Economic Advisors, was quoted in *The Philadelphia Inquirer* in 1974 as having testified before a Senate committee that "It is a tricky problem to find the particular calibration in timing that would be appropriate to stem the acceleration in risk premiums created by falling incomes without prematurely aborting the decline in the inflation-generated risk premiums."

Nor has Mr. Greenspan's language changed since then. Speaking to the meeting of the Economic Club of New York in 1988, Mr. Greenspan, now Federal Reserve chair, said, "I guess I should warn you, if I turn out to be particularly clear, you've probably misunderstood what I've said." Mr. Greenspan's doublespeak doesn't seem to have held back his career.

Sometimes gobbledygook may sound impressive, but when the quote is later examined in print it doesn't even make sense. During the 1988 presidential campaign, vice-presidential candidate Senator Dan Quayle explained the need for a strategic-defense initiative by saying, "Why wouldn't an enhanced deterrent, a more stable peace, a better prospect to denying the ones who enter conflict in the first place to have a reduction of offensive systems and an introduction to defensive capability? I believe this is the route the country will eventually go."

The investigation into the Challenger disaster in 1986 revealed the doublespeak of gobbledygook and bureaucratese used by too many involved in the shuttle program. When Jesse Moore, NASA's associate administrator, was asked if the performance of the shuttle program had improved with each launch or if it had remained the same, he answered, "I think our performance in terms of the liftoff performance and in terms of the orbital performance, we knew more about the envelope we were operating under, and we have been pretty accurately staying in that. And so I would say the performance has not by design drastically improved. I think we have been able to characterize the performance more as a function of our launch experience as opposed to it improving as a function of time." While this language may appear to be jargon, a close look will reveal that it is really just gobbledygook laced with jargon. But you really have to wonder if Mr. Moore had any idea what he was saying.

Fourth Kind of Doublespeak

The fourth kind of doublespeak is inflated language that is designed to make the ordinary seem extraordinary; to make everyday things seem impressive; to give an air of importance to people, situations, or things that would not normally be considered important; to make the simple seem complex. Often this kind of doublespeak isn't hard to spot, and it is usually pretty funny. While car mechanics may be called "automotive internists," elevator operators members of the "vertical transportation corps," used cars "preowned" or "experienced cars," and black-and-white television sets described as having "non-multicolor capability," you really aren't misled all that much by such language.

However, you may have trouble figuring out that, when Chrysler "initiates a career alternative enhancement program," it is really laying off five thousand workers; or that "negative patient care outcome" means the patient died; or that "rapid oxidation" means a fire in a nuclear power plant.

The doublespeak of inflated language can have serious consequences. In Pentagon doublespeak, "pre-emptive counterattack" means that American forces attacked first; "engaged the enemy on all sides" means American troops were ambushed; "backloading of augmentation personnel" means a retreat by American troops. In the doublespeak of the military, the 1983 invasion of Grenada was conducted not by the U.S. Army, Navy, Air Force, and Marines, but by the "Caribbean Peace Keeping Forces." But then, according to the Pentagon, it wasn't an invasion, it was a "predawn vertical insertion."

DOUBLESPEAK THROUGHOUT HISTORY

Doublespeak is not a new use of language peculiar to the politics or economics of the twentieth century. In the fifth century B.C., the Greek historian Thucydides wrote in *The Peloponnesian War* that

> revolution thus ran its course from city to city. . . . Words had to change their ordinary meanings and to take those which were now given them. Reckless audacity came to be considered the courage of a loyal ally; prudent hesitation, specious cowardice; moderation was held to be a cloak for unmanliness; ability to see all sides of a question, inaptness to act on any. Frantic violence became the attribute of manliness; cautious plotting, a justifiable means of self-defense. The advocate of extreme measures was always trustworthy; his opponent, a man to be suspected.

Julius Caesar, in his account of the Gallic Wars, described his brutal and bloody conquest and subjugation of Gaul as "pacifying" Gaul. "Where they make a desert, they call it peace," said an English nobleman quoted by the Roman historian Tacitus. When traitors were put to death in Rome, the announcement of their execution was made in the form of saying "they have lived." "Taking notice of a man in the ancestral manner" meant capital punishment; "the prisoner was then led away" meant he was executed.

In his memoirs, *V-2*, Walter Dornberger, commanding officer of the Peenemünde Rocket Research Institute in Germany during World War II, describes how he and his staff used language to get what they needed from the Bureau of Budget for their rocket experiments. A pencil sharpener was an "Appliance for milling wooden dowels up to 10 millimeters in diameter," and a typewriter was an "Instrument for recording test data with rotating roller." But it was the Nazis who were the masters of doublespeak, and they used it not just to achieve and maintain power but to perpetrate some of the most heinous crimes in the history of the human race.

In the world of Nazi Germany, nonprofessional prostitutes were called "persons with varied sexual relationships"; "protective custody" was the very opposite of protective; "Winter Relief" was a compulsory tax presented as a voluntary charity; and a "straightening of the front" was a retreat, while serious difficulties became "bottlenecks." Minister of Information (the very title is doublespeak) Josef Goebbels spoke in all seriousness of "simple pomp" and "the liberalization of the freedom of the press."

Nazi doublespeak reached its peak when dealing with the "Final

Solution," a phrase that is itself the ultimate in doublespeak. The notice, "The Jew X.Y. lived here," posted on a door, meant the occupant had been "deported," that is, killed. When mail was returned stamped "Addressee has moved away," it meant the person had been "deported." "Resettlement" also meant deportation, while "work camp" meant concentration camp or incinerator, "action" meant massacre, "Special Action Groups" were army units that conducted mass murder, "selection" meant gassing, and "shot while trying to escape" meant deliberately killed in a concentration camp.

GEORGE ORWELL AND LANGUAGE

In his famous and now-classic essay, "Politics and the English Language," which was published in 1946, George Orwell wrote that the "great enemy of clear language is insincerity. When there is a gap between one's real and one's declared aims, one turns as it were instinctively to long words and exhausted idioms, like a cuttlefish squirting out ink." For Orwell, language was an instrument for "expressing and not for concealing or preventing thought." In his most biting comment, he observed that, "in our time, political speech and writing are largely the defense of the indefensible. . . . [P]olitical language has to consist largely of euphemism, question-begging and sheer cloudy vagueness. . . . Political language . . . is designed to make lies sound truthful and murder respectable, and to give an appearance of solidity to pure wind."

Orwell understood well the power of language as both a tool and a weapon. In the nightmare world of his novel, *Nineteen Eighty-Four,* Orwell depicted a society where language was one of the most important tools of the totalitarian state. Newspeak, the official state language in the world of *Nineteen Eighty-Four,* was designed not to extend but to *diminish* the range of human thought, to make only "correct" thought possible and all other modes of thought impossible. It was, in short, a language designed to create a reality that the state wanted.

Newspeak had another important function in Orwell's world of *Nineteen Eighty-Four.* It provided the means of expression for doublethink, the mental process that allows you to hold two opposing ideas in your mind at the same time and believe in both of them. The classic example in Orwell's novel is the slogan, "War Is Peace." Lest you think doublethink is confined only to Orwell's novel, you need only recall the words of Secretary of State Alexander Haig when he testified before a congressional committee in 1982 that a continued weapons build-up by the United States is "absolutely essential to our hopes for meaningful arms reduction." Or remember what Senator Orin Hatch said in 1988: "Capital punishment is our society's recognition of the sanctity of human life."

At its worst, doublespeak, like newspeak, is language designed to limit, if not eliminate, thought. Like doublethink, doublespeak enables speaker and listener, writer and reader, to hold two opposing ideas in their minds at the same time and believe in both of them. At its least offensive, doublespeak is inflated language that tries to give importance to the insignificant.

THE DOUBLESPEAK ALL AROUND US

Orwell was concerned primarily with political language because it is the language of power, but it is not just political language that is so misleading these days. Everywhere you turn you encounter the language with which Orwell was so concerned. It's not an economic recession but, according to the Reagan Administration, a "period of accelerated negative growth" or simply "negative economic growth." There's no such thing as acid rain; according to the Environmental Protection Agency, it's just "poorly buffered precipitation" or, more impressively, "atmospheric deposition of anthropogenetically-derived acidic substances." And those aren't gangsters, mobsters, the Mafia or La Cosa Nostra in Atlantic City according to the "New Jersey Division of Gaming Enforcement" (a doublespeak title that avoids the use of that dreaded word, "gambling") they're just "members of a career-offender cartel."

Military Doublespeak

Military doublespeak seems to have always been around. In 1947 the name of the Department of War was changed to the more pleasing if misleading Department of Defense. How much easier it is to spend hundreds of billions of dollars for defense instead of war. During the Vietnam War the American public learned that it was an "incursion" into Cambodia, not an invasion; a "protective reaction strike" or "a limited duration protective reaction strike" or "air support," not bombing.

When asked why U.S. forces lacked intelligence information on Grenada before they invaded the island in 1983, Admiral Wesley L. McDonald told reporters that "We were not micromanaging Grenada intelligence-wise until about that time frame." In today's armed forces it's not a shovel but a "combat emplacement evacuator," not a bullet hole but a "ballistically induced aperture in the subcutaneous environment."

Business Doublespeak

The world of business has produced large amounts of doublespeak. If an airplane crash is one of the worst things that can happen to an airline company, a recall of automobiles because of a safety defect is one of the worst things that can happen to an automobile company. In April of 1972, when the Ford Motor Company had to recall 423,000 1972 Torino and Mercury Montego models to correct "mechanical deficiencies," the company sent a letter to all those who had bought the defective cars. In its letter, Ford said that the rear axle bearings of the cars "can deteriorate" and went on to say "Continued driving with a failed bearing could result in disengagement of the axle shaft and adversely affect vehicle control." This is the language of nonresponsibility. What are "mechanical deficiencies"—poor design, bad workmanship? The rear axle bearings "can deteriorate," but will they deteriorate? If they do deteriorate, what causes the deterioration? Note that "continued driving" is the subject of the sentence, which suggests that it is not Ford's poor manufacturing that is at fault but the driver who insists on driving the defective car. Note, too, the expression "failed bearing," which implies that the bearing failed, not Ford. Finally the phrase "adversely affect vehicle control" means simply that, because of the mechanical defect, the driver could lose control of the car and get killed.

If you ask the questions for examining language to see if it's doublespeak (who is saying what to whom, under what conditions and circumstances, with what intent, and with what results), you can quickly discover the doublespeak here. What Ford should be saying to its customers is that the car Ford sold them has a serious defect that should be corrected immediately, otherwise the customer runs the risk of being seriously injured or killed. But you have to find this message beneath the doublespeak that Ford has used to disguise its embarrassing and unpleasant message. We will never know how many customers didn't bring their cars in for repairs because they didn't understand from that letter just how serious the problem was and that they'd better get their car to the service department fast.

When it comes time to fire or lay off employees, business has produced more than enough doublespeak to deal with the unpleasant situation. Employees are, of course, never fired or laid off. They are "selected out," "placed out," "non-retained," "released," "dehired," or "non-renewed." A corporation will "eliminate the redundancies in the human resources area," assign "candidates for derecruitment" to a "mobility pool," "revitalize the department" by placing executives on "special assignment," "enhance the efficiency of operations," "streamline the field sales organization," or "further rationalize marketing efforts." The reality behind all this doublespeak is that companies are firing or laying off employees, but no one wants to acknowledge to the stockholders, public, or competition that times are tough, business is bad, and people have to go.

When the oil industry was hit hard by declining sales and a surplus of oil, after years of great prosperity and a shortage of oil, the doublespeak flowed thicker than crude oil. Because of "reduced demand for product," which results in "space refining capacity" and problems in "down-stream operations," oil companies have been forced to "re-evaluate and consolidate their operations" and take "appropriate cost-reduction actions," in order to "enhance the efficiency of operations," which has meant the "elimination of marginal outlets," "accelerating our divestment program," and the "disposition of low throughput marketing units." This doublespeak really means that oil companies have fired employees, cut back on expenses, and closed gas stations and oil refineries because there's a surplus of oil and people are not buying as much gas and oil as in the past.

One oil company faced with declining business sent a memorandum to its employees advising them that the company's "business plans are under revision and now reflect a more moderate approach toward our operating and capital programs." The result of this "more moderate approach" is a "surplus of professional/technical employees." To "assist in alleviating the surplus, selected professional and technical employees" have been "selected to participate" in a "Voluntary Program" providing "incentives" for employees who "resign voluntarily." What this memorandum means, of course, is that expenses must be cut because of declining business, so some employees will have to go.

Wall Street produces doublespeak right along with the junk bonds. It is rare to read in a trade publication that the stock market "fell." Others might say the stock market fell, but those who work on Wall Street prefer to say that the stock market "retreated," "eased," made a "technical adjustment" or a "technical correction," or perhaps that "prices were off due to profit taking," or "off in light trading" or "lost ground." In October 1987, when the stock market collapsed, losing billions of dollars, one brokerage house called the collapse a "fourth quarter equity retreat." As a side note, it is interesting to observe that the stock market never rises because of a "technical adjustment" or "correction," nor does it ever "ease" upward. Stock prices always "climb," "advance," "move forward," "edge up," or "surge."

Business magazines, corporate reports, executive speeches, and the business sections of newspapers are filled with words and phrases such as "marginal rates of substitution," "equilibrium price," "getting off margin," "distributional coalition," "non-performing assets," and "encompassing organizations." Much of this is jargon or inflated language designed to make the simple seem complex, but there are other examples of business doublespeak that misleads or is designed to avoid a harsh reality. What should you make of such expressions as "negative deficit" or "revenue excesses" (i.e., profit), "invest in" (spend money or buy something), "price enhancement" or "price adjustment" (price increase), "shortfall" (mistake in planning), or "period of accelerated negative growth" or "negative economic growth" (recession)?

Business doublespeak often attempts to give substance to pure wind (to use Orwell's term), to make ordinary actions seem complex. Executives "operate" in "timeframes" within the "context" of which a "task force" will serve as the proper "conduit" for all the necessary "input" to "program a scenario" that, within acceptable "parameters," and with the proper "throughput," will "generate" the "maximum output" for a "print out" of "zero defect terminal objectives" which will "enhance the bottom line."

Education Doublespeak

Politicians, members of the military, and businesspeople are not the only ones who use doublespeak. People in all parts of society use it. Education has more than its share of doublespeak. On some college campuses, what was once the Department of Physical Education is now the "Department of Human Kinetics" or the "College of Applied Life Studies." You may have called it Home Economics, but now it's the "School of Human Resources and Family Studies." These days, you don't go to the library to study; you go to the "Learning Resources Center."

Those aren't desks in the elementary school classroom, they're "pupil stations." Teachers, who are "classroom managers" applying an "action plan" to a "knowledge base," are concerned with the "basic fundamentals," which are "inexorably linked" to the "education user's" "time-on-task." Students don't take simple tests; now it's "criterion-referenced testing" that measures whether a student has achieved the "operational curricular objectives." A school system in Pennsylvania, making absolutely no mention of whether the student learned anything, uses the following grading system on its report cards: "no effort, less than minimal effort, minimal effort, more than minimal effort, less than full effort, full effort, better than full effort, effort increasing, effort decreasing."

B. W. Harlston, president of City College in New York, said in 1982 that some college students in New York come from "economically nonaffluent" families, while a spokesperson at Duke University said in 1982 that coach Red Wilson wasn't being fired, "He just won't be asked to continue in that job." An article in a scholarly journal suggests teaching students three approaches to writing to help them become better writers: "concretization of goals, procedural facilitation, and modeling planning."

In its August 3, 1981 issue, *Newsweek* magazine reported that the prestigious National Bureau of Economic Research published a working paper by Brown University economist Herschel I. Grossman entitled "Familial Love and Intertemporal Optimality." Professor Grossman reached this conclusion about family love: "An altruistic utility function promotes intertemporal efficiency. However, altruism creates an externality that implies that satisfying the conditions for efficiency does not insure intertemporal optimality."

A research report issued by the U.S. Office of Education in 1966 contains this sentence: "In other words, feediness is the shared information between toputness, where toputness is at a time just prior to the inputness." At times, doublespeak seems to be the primary product of educators.

DEADLY DOUBLESPEAK

There are instances, however, where doublespeak becomes more than amusing, more than a cause for a laugh. At St. Mary's Hospital in Minneapolis in 1982, an anesthetist turned the wrong knob during a Cesarean delivery, giving a fatal dose of nitrous oxide which killed the mother and unborn child. The hospital called it a "therapeutic misadventure." In its budget request to Congress in 1977, the Pentagon called the neutron bomb "an efficient nuclear weapon that eliminates an enemy with a minimum degree of damage to friendly territory." The Pentagon also calls the expected tens of millions of civilian dead in a nuclear war "collateral damage," a term the Pentagon also applies to the civilians killed in any war. And in 1977 people watching the Dick Cavett show on television learned from former Green Beret Captain Bob Marasco that during the Vietnam war the Central Intelligence Agency created the phrase "eliminate with extreme prejudice" to replace the more direct verb "kill."

President Reagan and the Doublespeak of Politics

Identifying doublespeak can at times be difficult. For example, on July 27, 1981, President Ronald Reagan said in a speech televised to the American public that "I will not stand by and see those of you who are dependent on Social Security deprived of the benefits you've worked so hard to earn. You will continue to receive your checks in the full amount due you." This speech had been billed as President Reagan's position on Social Security, a subject of much debate at the time. After the speech, public opinion polls revealed that the great majority of the public believed that the president had affirmed his support for Social Security and that he would not support cuts in benefits. However, only days after the speech, on July 31, 1981, an article in the *Philadelphia Inquirer* quoted White House spokesperson David Gergen as saying that President Reagan's words had been "carefully chosen." What President Reagan had meant, according to Gergen, was that he was reserving the right to decide who was "dependent" on those benefits, who had "earned" them, and who, therefore, was "due" them.

The subsequent remarks of David Gergen reveal the real intent of President Reagan as opposed to his apparent intent. Thus, the criteria for analyzing language to determine whether it is doublespeak (who is saying what to whom, under what conditions and circumstances, with what intent, and with what results), when applied in light of David Gergen's remarks, reveal the doublespeak of President Reagan. Here, indeed, is the insincerity of which Orwell wrote. Here, too, is the gap between the speaker's real and declared aim.

Doublespeak and Political Advertisements

During the 1982 congressional election campaign, the Republican National Committee sponsored a television advertisement that pictured an elderly, folksy postman delivering Social Security checks "with the 7.4% cost-of-living raise that President Reagan promised." The postman then adds that "he promised that raise and he kept his promise, in spite of those sticks-in-the-mud who tried to keep him from doing what we elected him to do." The commercial was, in fact, deliberately misleading. The cost-of-living increases had been provided automatically by law since 1975, and President Reagan had tried three times to roll them back or delay them but was overruled by congressional opposition. When these discrepancies were pointed out to an official of the Republican National Committee, he called the commercial "inoffensive" and added, "Since when is a commercial supposed to be accurate? Do women really smile when they clean their ovens?"

Again, applying the criteria for identifying doublespeak to this advertisement reveals the doublespeak in it, once you know the facts of past actions by President Reagan. Moreover, the official for the Republican National Committee assumes that all advertisements, whether for political candidates or commercial products, do not tell the truth; in his doublespeak, they do not have to be "accurate." Thus, the real intent of the advertisement was to mislead, while the apparent purpose of the commercial was to inform the public of President Reagan's position on possible cuts in Social Security benefits. Again there is insincerity, and again there is a gap between the speaker's real and declared aims.

Alexander Haig and Doublespeak

One of the most chilling and terrifying uses of doublespeak in recent memory occurred in 1981 when then Secretary of State Alexander Haig was testifying before congressional committees about the murder of three American nuns and a Catholic lay worker in El Salvador. The four women had been raped and then shot at close range, and there was clear evidence that the crime had been committed by soldiers of the Salvadoran government. Before the House Foreign Affairs committee, Secretary Haig said:

> I'd like to suggest to you that some of the investigations would lead one to believe that perhaps the vehicle the nuns were riding in may have tried to run a roadblock, or may accidentally have been perceived to have been doing so, and there'd been an exchange of fire and then perhaps those who inflicted the casualties sought to cover it up. And this could have been at a very low level of both competence and motivation in the context of the issue itself. But the facts on this are not clear enough for anyone to draw a definitive conclusion.

The next day, before the Senate Foreign Relations Committee, Secretary Haig claimed that press reports on his previous testimony were "inaccurate." When Senator Claiborne Pell asked whether the secretary was suggesting the possibility that "the nuns may have run through a roadblock," he replied, "You mean that they tried to violate . . . ? Not at all, no, not at all. My heavens! The dear nuns who raised me in my parochial schooling would forever isolate me from their affections and respect." Then Senator Pell asked Secretary Haig, "Did you mean that the nuns were firing at the people, or what did 'an exchange of fire' mean?" The secretary replied, "I haven't met any pistol-packing nuns in my day, Senator. What I meant was that if one fellow starts shooting, then the next thing you know they all panic." Thus did the secretary of state of the United States explain official government policy on the murder of four American citizens in a foreign land.

Secretary Haig's testimony implies that the women were in some way responsible for their own fate. By using such vague wording as "would lead one to believe" and "may accidentally have been perceived to have been doing so," he avoids any direct assertion. The use of the phrase "inflicted the casualties" not only avoids using the word "kill" but also implies that at the worst the killings were accidental or justifiable. The result of this testimony is that the secretary of state has become an apologist for rape and murder. This is indeed language in defense of the indefensible; language designed to make lies sound truthful and murder respectable; language designed to give an appearance of solidity to pure wind.

THE DANGERS OF DOUBLESPEAK

These previous three examples of doublespeak should make it clear that doublespeak is not the product of carelessness or sloppy thinking. Indeed, most doublespeak is the product of clear thinking and is carefully designed and constructed to appear to communicate when in fact it doesn't. It is language designed not to lead but mislead. It is language designed to distort reality and corrupt thought. In the world created by doublespeak, if it's not a tax increase, but rather "revenue enhancement" or "tax base broadening," how can you complain about higher taxes? If it's not acid rain, but rather "poorly buffered precipitation," how can you worry about all those dead trees? If that isn't the Mafia in Atlantic City, but just "members of a career-offender cartel," why worry about the influence of organized crime in the city? If Supreme Court Justice William Rehnquist wasn't addicted to the pain-killing drug his doctor prescribed, but instead it was just that the drug had "established an interrelationship with the body, such that if the drug is removed precipitously, there is a reaction," you needn't question that his decisions might have been influenced by his drug addiction. If it's not a Titan II nuclear-armed intercontinental ballistic missile with a warhead 630 times more powerful than the atomic bomb dropped on Hiroshima, but instead, according to Air Force Colonel Frank Horton, it's just a "very large, potentially disruptive reentry system," why be concerned about the threat of nuclear destruction? Why worry about the neutron bomb escalating the arms race if it's just a "radiation enhancement weapon"? If it's not an invasion, but a "rescue mission" or a "predawn vertical insertion," you won't need to think about any violations of U.S. or international law.

Doublespeak has become so common in everyday living that many people fail to notice it. Even worse, when they do notice doublespeak being used on them, they don't react, they don't protest. Do you protest when you are asked to check your packages at the desk "for your convenience," when it's not for your convenience at all but for someone else's? You see advertisements for "genuine imitation leather," "virgin vinyl," or "real counterfeit diamonds," but do you question the language or the supposed quality of the product? Do you question politicians who don't speak of slums or ghettos but of the "inner city" or "substandard housing" where the "disadvantaged" live and thus avoid talking about the poor who have to live in filthy, poorly heated, ramshackle apartments or houses? Aren't you amazed that patients don't die in the hospital anymore, it's just "negative patient-care outcome"?

Doublespeak such as that noted earlier that defines cab drivers as "urban transportation specialists," elevator operators as members of the "vertical transportation corps," and automobile mechanics as "automotive internists" can be considered humorous and relatively harmless. However, when a fire in a nuclear reactor building is called "rapid oxidation," an explosion in a nuclear power plant is called an "energetic disassembly," the illegal overthrow of a legitimate government is termed "destabilizing a government," and lies are seen as "inoperative statements," we are hearing doublespeak that attempts to avoid responsibility and make the bad seem good, the negative appear positive, something unpleasant appear attractive; and which seems to communicate but doesn't. It is language designed to alter our perception of reality and corrupt our thinking. Such language does not provide us with the tools we need to develop, advance, and preserve our culture and our civilization. Such language breeds suspicion, cynicism, distrust, and, ultimately, hostility.

Doublespeak is insidious because it can infect and eventually destroy the function of language, which is communication between people and social groups. This corruption of the function of language can have serious and far-reaching consequences. We live in a country that depends upon an informed electorate to make decisions in selecting candidates for office and deciding issues of public policy. The use of doublespeak can become so pervasive that it becomes the coin of the political realm, with speakers and listeners convinced that they really understand such language. After awhile we may really believe that politicians don't lie but only "misspeak," that illegal acts are merely "inappropriate actions," that fraud and criminal conspiracy are just "miscertification." President Jimmy Carter in April of 1980 could call the aborted raid to free the American hostages in Teheran an "incomplete success" and really believe that he had made a statement that clearly communicated with the American public. So, too, could President Ronald Reagan say in 1985 that "ultimately our security and our hopes for success at the arms reduction talks hinge on the determination that we show here to continue our program to rebuild and refortify our defenses" and really believe that greatly increasing the amount of money spent building new weapons would lead to a reduction in the number of weapons in the world. If we really believe that we understand such language and that such language communicates and promotes clear thought, then the world of *Nineteen Eighty-Four,* with its control of reality through language, is upon us.

EDWARD M. WHITE

Singlespeak

Edward M. White (1933–   ) is a professor of English at California State University, San Bernardino. He writes on topics ranging from ethnic concerns to literature, literary theory, writing, and journalism. His most recent books are *Teaching and Assessing Writing* (1985) and *Developing Successful College Writing Programs* (1989).

Oh God us keep
From Single Vision and Newton's Sleep.

                                                            William Blake

The evils of doublespeak are plain, and no sensible person concerned about the moral uses of prose can defend language designed to deceive. The pages of the *Quarterly Review of Doublespeak* are certainly filled with enough egregious examples of deliberate dishonesty in usage, of language "with pernicious social and political consequences" (to quote from the statement accompanying the Doublespeak Award), to earn the amused contempt of all morally sensitive readers.

But let us turn our attention to a less obvious evil, one that normally stands virtuously beside us in our opposition to the dishonest use of language. If we spend time on such matters as doublespeak in college composition classes, we are often surprised to find that our students are perfectly ready to condemn as doublespeak any metaphor at all, any prose of substantial complexity, any long words or long ideas. For many of our students, the distinction between the evils of doublespeak and the virtues of art (a distinction we tend to assume is real and important) simply does not exist. These well-meaning and supportive students have some theoretical justification for confusing art with deceit. When Picasso argues that "Art is a lie that tells the truth," he suggests that duplicity of a certain kind is a necessary part of an artist's work. But the simplemindedness and literal-mindedness that I am calling Singlespeak maintains itself in virtuous opposition to art or to any but the simplest meanings. When Blake calls the single vision "Newton's Sleep" (and, elsewhere, simply, "blindness"), he identifies the profound simplemindedness that is unable to notice or respond to complex visions; a reductionism far from the unequivocal virtue that simplistic notions of doublespeak might suggest as its opposite.[1]

The singlespeak that is at least as pernicious as doublespeak is that particularly complacent form of simplicity that sees language as ideally a clear glass; because all meanings must be simple, or single, any language that suggests complexity or ambiguity is like a dirty window, to be cleaned or broken. Writing and speaking are seen as transmissions of already-shaped (encoded) ideas which are then to be decoded by readers or hearers with as little interference as possible. Writing itself is imagined to be a simple product, not a process of inquiry or discovery; abstractions and metaphors interfere with unambiguous communication and should be replaced by simple, concrete nouns; all concepts can be and ought to be reduced to a briefing paragraph for a busy executive; Henry James is unreadable. The prose

---

[1] William Blake, letter to Thomas Butts, 22 November 1802, lines 84–88, in *The Letters of William Blake,* 3rd edition, ed. Geoffrey Keynes (Oxford: Clarendon Press, 1980).

model is Hemingway, whose hero in *A Farewell to Arms* finds abstractions "obscene" and can find comfort only in the names of places and dates.[2]

George Orwell, the patron saint of opposition to doublespeak, seems to use the same window metaphor for prose when he says, in "Why I Write," "Good prose is like a window pane." But the context makes clear that he is not arguing for simplicity, but rather for a clear fusion of "political purpose and artistic purpose into one whole." The "window pane" of his metaphor should be as clear as possible, but it offers at best a streaked view into an artistic unknown: "All writers are vain, selfish and lazy, and at the very bottom of their motives there lies a mystery."[3] Indeed, it is hard to say which he opposes more strongly: the obfuscation of doublespeak or the simplemindedness of slogans and false simplicity that reveal singlespeak. The Newspeak dictionary in *Nineteen Eighty-Four,* after all, is designed to give authority to the lies created when a complex language disappears. It is true, however, that Orwell's most overt statement on the subject, the ubiquitous "Politics and the English Language," argues so strongly against political doubletalk that it overstates the need for simple, concrete expression.[4] We need occasional reminders, such as Richard Ohmann's sarcastically entitled article, "Use Definite, Specific, Concrete Language" (1979), that abstract words are also important tools for thought and vision.[5]

The underlying "blindness" that Blake warns us against is the insistence that reality is simple and knowable, and that language should reflect that simplicity. For Blake, the name that came to mind was Newton; for others it is more likely to be the archetypal strong, silent type, one of few words and unerring judgment. James Fenimore Cooper's Natty Bumppo and his successors, the stolid sheriffs and solitary soldiers of fortune of our Westerns and war movies, neither reflect nor read. Such myths enforce the view that simple and unlet-

---

[2] Ernest Hemingway, *A Farewell to Arms* (New York: Scribner's, 1957).

[3] George Orwell, "Why I Write," in *An Age Like This (1920–1940),* 1–7, vol. 1 of *The Collected Essays, Journalism and Letters of George Orwell,* 4 vols., ed. Sonia Orwell and Ian Angus (London: Secker & Warburg, 1968), 7.

[4] George Orwell, "Politics and the English Language," in *In Front of Your Nose (1945–1950),* 127–40, vol. 4 of *The Collected Essays, Journalism and Letters of George Orwell,* 4 vols., ed. Sonia Orwell and Ian Angus (London: Secker & Warburg, 1968).

[5] R. Ohmann, "Use Definite, Specific, Concrete Language," *College English* 41 (1979): 390–97.

tered good sense is to be preferred to sophisticated wisdom which, like sophisticated wine, smells of corruption. It is precisely this appeal to the stolid virtues of the Frontier that makes singlespeak even more dangerous than doublespeak.

Doublespeak at its most appalling needs only to be cited to be exposed; singlespeak masquerades as opposition to doublespeak, as simple good sense, as clarity. To many of our students cursed with singlespeak, our admiration for such verbal reflections of complexity as irony, metaphor, and literature itself, appears to be admiration of doublespeak. Why can't Swift just *say* what he means? Who has the time to figure out what Austen really has in mind? If Marvell wants to take his coy mistress to bed, why doesn't he just tell her so, or, better still, just do it and not talk about it?

Thus, both double- and singlespeak are manifestations of the same kind of solipsistic naiveté: the use of language to adapt reality to our own ends, without awareness that both reality and language are very complex. But there are important differences, such as those I have begun to suggest here. I suspect that subsuming singlespeak under the umbrella of doublespeak blurs these differences, making it a bit too easy for those who would dismiss valid complexity as doublespeak, and letting singlespeakers cloak themselves in too-easy virtue.

In our zeal to ferret out and expose the dishonesty of doublespeak, we need to be particularly careful not to endorse or reward the blindness of singlespeak. As we shake our heads over the *pre-dawn vertical insertion* that invaded Grenada, let us remember the *America—Love It or Leave It* that prepared the way. The direct diction of *I Found It* on the bumpers of heaven-bound chariots is part of the seamless web of theological obfuscation that shapes the bountiful collection baskets and public hypocrisies of TV preachers. The supposed law of supply and demand is singlespeak, behind which lurks a thousand dishonest explanations for outrageous conduct: A "bribe" is a rebate, is it not? High authority does not excuse singlespeak, indeed it adds to the offense: *Avoid foreign entanglements; A poem should not mean but be.* Wherever common sense asserts false and simple answers to complex questions, singlespeak declares its blindness to be most excellent vision.

The student allegiance to singlespeak, of course, reflects the admiration for simplemindedness that afflicts much of our society. We find it everywhere, though usually in the guise of "straight talk" or something called "realism." Since it hides more readily than doublespeak in its mask of rude virtue, we must be unusually vigilant to identify singlespeak and expose it for what it is.

Take, for instance, the following editorial from *The Wall Street Journal* of December 11, 1986. Entitled "Seeing Red," it seeks to set straight those who feel that the issues of American military intervention in Nicaragua are complicated:

> An intriguing Media General-Associated Press poll reports that 60% of the people interviewed oppose military aid to the Nicaraguan contras, but 42% don't even know which side the U.S. is on. Meanwhile, 58% think communist governments in Latin American threaten U.S. security. We think we see the problem here: It's hard to tell anymore who the communists are and who the good guys are. Years ago such struggles were divided into communists and anti-communists. This view was ridiculed as ignorant of various "indigenous liberation movements." Flattered, the communists started giving themselves colorful names: the Sandinistas, the Tupemaros, Shining Path, M-19. The Sandinistas shrewdly called their anti-communist opponents "contras," a word without content for most Americans. If clarity of meaning is important, perhaps we should return to the ancient but clear classifications. Communists are communists. The people who are against them are anti-communists. Anyone who still can't figure out which side he's on is entitled to be listed under the column labeled "Don't Know."[6]

If this were the house organ of some right-wing military splinter group, we could smile and let it go. But this is, after all, *The Wall Street Journal,* the voice of responsibility for American capitalism. So we must notice the skill and force calling for singlespeak. If we follow the editorial, we must not, despite all knowledge of differences among those who call themselves communists, think that those people are different from one another; the Soviets, the Chinese, the Hungarians, the Cubans, the Italian or French Eurocommunists, the opponents of dictators wherever they may be—all, all of them are to be seen as the same. If they seem to have different names, they have "shrewdly" chosen them solely to confuse Americans, a gullible tribe who have trouble with clear classifications. Everything is simple, if people would only realize that there are only two possible positions in the world. The singlespeaker is ever ready to provide the scorecard with the lineup on it, so we can tell our team from theirs. Doublespeak may cover over what happens in military action, but it is singlespeak that starts the war in the first place.

We ought not to be surprised to find that professional educators have a particular affinity for singlespeak. Their job is to make com-

---

[6] Editorial, "Seeing Red," *The Wall Street Journal,* 11 December 1986: 32.

plicated matters accessible to the untrained and it seems all too easy for them to fall into the grossest kinds of oversimplifications. Nonetheless, when such a habit of mind shows itself "resolving" educational problems barely perceived, we experience the shock of the singlespeaker.

I recall an official from the California State Department of Education saying at a meeting, "Now that we have solved the problem of reading, it is time to turn our attention to writing." I smile privately at the outraged parent holding forth at a school board meeting, berating the schoolteachers who had allowed children to raise questions on forbidden subjects: "We're paying you to educate our kids, so stop messing with their *minds!*"

Perhaps the neatest example of educational singlespeak as I write this is the concept of "value-added education." That slogan has momentarily replaced "merit pay for teachers" as the simple answer to the complex problem of improving education. By the time you read this, no doubt a new slogan will be in the news; nonetheless, we might as well look at this one, since it so nicely embodies the aspects of singlespeak which educational slogans have in common.

Value-added education, as espoused by educational politicians such as Governor Ashcroft of Missouri, is based on the commercial concept of molding raw materials into processed goods. Thus, when raw rubber is turned into automobile tires at a manufacturing plant, the tires are worth more than the rubber. A "value-added tax" (common in many European countries) is then assessed on the difference in cost.

While the value-added tax may be European, the concept of value-added education is truly American. It not only uses the analogy of molding raw material as a way of thinking about education, but it also assumes that a readily ascertainable and measurable difference from raw material to molded product in fact defines education. It thus sees education as something that is done to students (not something students do or become) and restricts the value of education to that which can be measured by pre- and posttesting. Since anyone can see that rubber tires are different from raw rubber, our seniors should be similarly and obviously different from our freshmen. The difference, when quantified, becomes the value of the education they have received, and that derived statistic becomes the basis for funding educational institutions.

Newton's Sleep, indeed! It is the essence of singlespeak to reduce complex phenomena or activities to the readily quantifiable. Even sophisticated thinkers find that task daunting. A generation ago,

Albert Kitzhaber (1963) tried to assess the difference between the writing of freshmen and seniors at Dartmouth College. Unfortunately, he did not have the refined techniques of essay testing that are now available, so he chose a series of error counts as his assessment device. To his dismay, he found that the seniors wrote "worse" than the freshmen; that is, that the seniors made more errors in their writing.[7] Later research has demonstrated that most writers make more errors in first draft work as their writing tasks become more complex and ambitious. (For example, if you write only simple sentences and use only a basic vocabulary, you are not as likely to make sentence or spelling errors as you will with more advanced verbal materials.) The Dartmouth seniors were, in fact, writing far more advanced work than they did as freshmen, but the measurement of that advance was wholly beyond the tools available. The measurement that was available "proved" what everyone knew to be untrue. If Dartmouth had been foolish enough to use those results to revise its curriculum, we would now see its general education program reduced to exercises in spelling and sentence structure. Unhappily, less enlightened institutions deceived by educational singlespeak are cheerfully following that path. Those institutions now committed to "value-added" education are, in fact, using their relatively simple-minded evaluation devices to shape and reduce their curricula.

In theory, of course, we could come up with evaluation devices sufficiently complex to measure the real value of education—but don't count on it. Such devices are costly, complicated, and hard to quantify. The singlespeak metaphor of "value-added" demands quick weights and measures, practical budgetary action, and unambiguous decision-making: Either you have learned double entry bookkeeping or you have not; don't bother with poetry if you can't come up with similar numbers. Singlespeak requires simplicity and has no interest in Einstein's qualifier: "Everything," he said, "should be as simple as possible—but no simpler."

Singlespeak, thus, is the vocabulary of those who need no Newspeak for self-deception; Oldspeak does the job perfectly well. Doublethink is unnecessary and rather too much trouble because half-think manages the world very nicely, thank you. Singlespeak is sometimes comic (the character Zero in the *Beetle Bailey* comic strip forever at attention before the sign "Watch this space for important

---

[7] Albert R. Kitzhaber, *Themes, Theories, and Therapy: The Teaching of Writing in College* (New York: McGraw-Hill, 1963).

announcements"), but usually it is serious and quiet. Singlespeak is most deceptive when it pretends to simple honesty; most dangerous as it asserts its simple virtue. We may at last have a committee to defend us from doublespeak, but where is the task force to protect us from the more subtle, pernicious, and pervasive power of single-speak?

GEORGE ORWELL

Politics and the English Language

George Orwell (1903–1950) was the pen name of Eric Blair, English journalist, essayist, novelist, and critic who was born in Bengal, India. His classic novels *Animal Farm* (1945) and *Nineteen Eighty-four* (1949) examine the roots of totalitarianism. His other important works include *Down and Out in Paris and London* (1933) and his account of his participation in the Spanish Civil War in *Homage to Catalonia* (1938). He is generally regarded as one of this century's leading commentators on literature and politics. He published articles, reviews, and several collections of essays, including *Shooting an Elephant* (1950) in which the following selection appears.

Most people who bother with the matter at all would admit that the English language is in a bad way, but it is generally assumed that we cannot by conscious action do anything about it. Our civilization is decadent and our language—so the argument runs—must inevitably share in the general collapse. It follows that any struggle against the abuse of language is a sentimental archaism, like preferring candles to electric light or hansom cabs to aeroplanes. Underneath this lies the half-conscious belief that language is a natural growth and not an instrument which we shape for our own purposes.

Now, it is clear that the decline of a language must ultimately have political and economic causes: it is not due simply to the bad influence of this or that individual writer. But an effect can become a cause, reinforcing the original cause and producing the same effect in an intensified form, and so on indefinitely. A man may take to drink because he feels himself to be a failure, and then fail all the more completely because he drinks. It is rather the same thing that is happening to the English language. It becomes ugly and inaccurate because our thoughts are foolish, but the slovenliness of our language makes it easier for us to have foolish thoughts. The point is that the process is reversible. Modern English, especially written English, is full of bad habits which spread by imitation and which can be avoided if one is willing to take the necessary trouble. If one gets rid of these habits one can think more clearly, and to think clearly is a necessary first step towards political regeneration: so that the fight against bad English is not frivolous and is not the exclusive concern of professional writers. I will come back to this presently, and I hope that by that time the meaning of what I have said here will have become clearer. Meanwhile, here are five specimens of the English language as it is now habitually written.

These five passages have not been picked out because they are especially bad—I could have quoted far worse if I had chosen—but because they illustrate various of the mental vices from which we now suffer. They are a little below the average, but are fairly representative samples. I number them so that I can refer back to them when necessary:

"(1) I am not, indeed, sure whether it is not true to say that the Milton who once seemed not unlike a seventeeth-century Shelley had not become, out of an experience ever more bitter in each year, more alien [sic] to the founder of that Jesuit sect which nothing could induce him to tolerate."
                    Professor Harold Laski (Essay in *Freedom of Expression*).

"(2) Above all, we cannot play ducks and drakes with a native battery of idioms which prescribes such egregious collocations of vocables as the Basic *put up with* for *tolerate* or *put at a loss* for *bewilder*."
                                        Professor Lancelot Hogben (*Interglossa*).

"(3) On the one side we have the free personality: by definition it is not neurotic, for it has neither conflict nor dream. Its desires, such as they are, are transparent, for they are just what institutional approval keeps in the forefront of consciousness; another institutional pattern would alter their number and intensity; there is little in them that is natural, irreducible, or culturally dangerous. But *on the other side,* the social bond itself is nothing but the mutual reflection of these self-secure integrities. Recall the definition of love. Is not this the very picture of a small academic? Where is there a place in this hall of mirrors for either personality or fraternity?"
                    Essay on psychology in *Politics* (New York).

"(4) All the 'best people' from the gentlemen's clubs, and all the frantic fascist captains, united in common hatred of Socialism and bestial horror of the rising tide of the mass revolutionary movement, have turned to acts of provocation, to foul incendiarism, to medieval legends of poisoned wells, to legalize their own destruction of proletarian organizations, and rouse the agitated petty-bourgeoisie to chauvinistic fervour on behalf of the fight against the revolutionary way out of the crisis."

Communist pamphlet.

"(5) If a new spirit *is* to be infused into this old country, there is one thorny and contentious reform which must be tackled, and that is the humanization and galvanization of the B.B.C. Timidity here will bespeak cancer and atrophy of the soul. The heart of Britain may be sound and of strong beat, for instance, but the British lion's roar at present is like that of Bottom in Shakespeare's *Midsummer Night's Dream*—as gentle as any sucking dove. A virile new Britain cannot continue indefinitely to be traduced in the eyes or rather ears, of the world by the effete languors of Langham Place, brazenly masquerading as 'standard English.' When the Voice of Britain is heard at nine o'clock, better far and infinitely less ludicrous to hear aitches honestly dropped than the present priggish, inflated, inhibited, school-ma'amish arch braying of blameless bashful mewing maidens!"

Letter in *Tribune.*

Each of these passages has faults of its own, but, quite apart from avoidable ugliness, two qualities are common to all of them. The first is staleness of imagery: the other is lack of precision. The writer either has a meaning and cannot express it, or he inadvertently says something else, or he is almost indifferent as to whether his words mean anything or not. This mixture of vagueness and sheer incompetence is the most marked characteristic of modern English prose, and especially of any kind of political writing. As soon as certain topics are raised, the concrete melts into the abstract and no one seems able to think of turns of speech that are not hackneyed: prose consists less and less of *words* chosen for the sake of their meaning, and more and more of *phrases* tacked together like the sections of a prefabricated hen-house. I list below, with notes and examples, various of the tricks by means of which the work of prose-construction is habitually dodged:

DYING METAPHORS

A newly invented metaphor assists thought by evoking a visual image, while on the other hand a metaphor which is technically "dead" (e.g. *iron resolution*) has in effect reverted to being an ordinary word and can generally be used without loss of vividness. But in between these two classes there is a huge dump of worn-out metaphors which have lost all evocative power and are merely used because they save people the trouble of inventing phrases for themselves. Examples are: *Ring the changes on, take up the cudgels for, toe the line, ride roughshod over, stand shoulder to shoulder with, play into the hands of, no axe to grind, grist to the mill, fishing in troubled waters, on the order of the day, Achilles' heel, swan song, hotbed.* Many of these are used without knowledge of their meaning (what is a "rift," for instance?), and incompatible metaphors are frequently mixed, a sure sign that the writer is not interested in what he is saying. Some metaphors now current have been twisted out of their original meaning without those who use them even being aware of the fact. For example, *toe the line* is sometimes written *tow the line.* Another example is *the hammer and the anvil,* now always used with the implication that the anvil gets the worst of it. In real life it is always the anvil that breaks the hammer, never the other way about: a writer who stopped to think what he was saying would be aware of this, and would avoid perverting the original phrase.

OPERATORS OR VERBAL FALSE LIMBS

These save the trouble of picking out appropriate verbs and nouns, and at the same time pad each sentence with extra syllables which give it an appearance of symmetry. Characteristic phrases are: *render inoperative, militate against, make contact with, be subjected to, give rise to, give grounds for, have the effect of, play a leading part (role) in, make itself felt, take effect, exhibit a tendency to, serve the purpose of, etc., etc.* The keynote is the elimination of simple verbs. Instead of being a single word, such as *break, stop, spoil, mend, kill,* a verb becomes a *phrase,* made up of a noun or adjective tacked on to some general-purposes verb such as *prove, serve, form, play, render.* In addition, the passive voice is wherever possible used in preference to the active, and noun constructions are used instead of gerunds (*by examination of* instead of *by examining*). The range of verbs is further cut down by means of the *-ize* and *de-* formation, and the banal statements are given an appearance of profundity by means of the *not un-* formation. Simple conjunctions and prepositions are replaced by such phrases as *with respect to, having regard to, the fact that, by dint of, in view of, in the interests of, on the hypothesis that;* and the ends of sentences are saved from anticlimax by such resounding commonplaces as *greatly to be desired, cannot be left out of account,* *a development to be expected in the near future, deserving of serious consideration, brought to a satisfactory conclusion,* and so on and so forth.

PRETENTIOUS DICTION

Words like *phenomenon, element, individual* (as noun), *objective, categorical, effective, virtual, basic, primary, promote, constitute, exhibit, exploit, utilize, eliminate, liquidate,* are used to dress up simple statements and give an air of scientific impartiality to biased judgments. Adjectives like *epoch-making, epic, historic, unforgettable, triumphant, age-old, inevitable, inexorable, veritable,* are used to dignify the sordid processes of international politics, while writing that aims at glorifying war usually takes on an archaic colour, its characteristic words being: *realm, throne, chariot, mailed fist, trident, sword, shield, buckler, banner, jackboot, clarion.* Foreign words and expressions such as *cul de sac, ancien régime, deus ex machina, mutatis mutandis, status quo, gleichschaltung, weltanschauung,* are used to give an air of culture and elegance. Except for the useful abbreviations *i.e., e.g.,* and *etc.,* there is no real need for any of the hundreds of foreign phrases now current in English. Bad writers, and especially scientific, political and sociological writers, are nearly always haunted by the notion that Latin or Greek words are grander than Saxon ones, and unnecessary words like *expedite, ameliorate, predict, extraneous, deracinated, clandestine, subaqueous* and hundreds of others constantly gain ground from their Anglo-Saxon opposite numbers.[1] The jargon peculiar to Marxist writing (*hyena, hangman, cannibal, petty bourgeois, these gentry, lacquey, flunkey, mad dog, White Guard,* etc.) consists largely of words and phrases translated from Russian, German or French; but the normal way of coining a new word is to use a Latin or Greek root with the appropriate affix and, where necessary, the *-ize* formation. It is often easier to make up words of this kind (*deregionalize, impermissible, extramarital, nonfragmentatory* and so forth) than to think up the English words that will cover one's meaning. The result, in general, is an increase in slovenliness and vagueness.

---

[1] An interesting illustration of this is the way in which the English flower names which were in use till very recently are being ousted by Greek ones, *snapdragon* becoming *antirrhinum, forget-me-not* becoming *myosotis,* etc. It is hard to see any practical reason for this change of fashion: it is probably due to an instinctive turning-away from the more homely word and a vague feeling that the Greek word is scientific.

MEANINGLESS WORDS

In certain kinds of writing, particularly in art criticism and literary criticism, it is normal to come across long passages which are almost completely lacking in meaning.[2] Words like *romantic, plastic, values, human, dead, sentimental, natural, vitality,* as used in art criticism, are strictly meaningless in the sense that they not only do not point to any discoverable object, but are hardly ever expected to do so by the reader. When one critic writes, "The outstanding feature of Mr. X's work is its living quality", while another writes, "The immediately striking thing about Mr. X's work is its peculiar deadness", the reader accepts this as a simple difference of opinion. If words like *black* and *white* were involved, instead of the jargon words *dead* and *living,* he would see at once that language was being used in an improper way. Many political words are similarly abused. The word *Fascism* has now no meaning except in so far as it signifies "something not desirable." The words *democracy, socialism, freedom, patriotic, realistic, justice,* have each of them several different meanings which cannot be reconciled with one another. In the case of a word like *democracy,* not only is there no agreed definition, but the attempt to make one is resisted from all sides. It is almost universally felt that when we call a country democratic we are praising it: consequently the defenders of every kind of régime claim that it is a democracy, and fear that they might have to stop using the word if it were tied down to any one meaning. Words of this kind are often used in a consciously dishonest way. That is, the person who uses them has his own private definition, but allows his hearer to think he means something quite different. Statements like *Marshal Pétain was a true patriot, The Soviet Press is the freest in the world, The Catholic Church is opposed to persecution,* are almost always made with intent to deceive. Other words used in variable meanings, in most cases more or less dishonestly, are: *class, totalitarian, science, progressive, reactionary, bourgeois, equality.*

Now that I have made this catalogue of swindles and perversions, let me give another example of the kind of writing that they lead to.

---

[2] Example: "Comfort's catholicity of perception and image, strangely Whitmanesque in range, almost the exact opposite in aesthetic compulsion, continues to evoke that trembling atmospheric accumulative hinting at a cruel, an inexorably serene timelessness . . . Wrey Gardiner scores by aiming at simple bull's-eyes with precision. Only they are not so simple, and through this contented sadness runs more than the surface bittersweet of resignation" (*Poetry Quarterly*).

This time it must of its nature be an imaginary one. I am going to translate a passage of good English into modern English of the worst sort. Here is a well-known verse from *Ecclesiastes*:

> "I returned and saw under the sun, that the race is not to the swift, nor the battle to the strong, neither yet bread to the wise, nor yet riches to men of understanding, nor yet favour to men of skill; but time and chance happeneth to them all."

Here it is in modern English:

> "Objective consideration of contemporary phenomena compels the conclusion that success or failure in competitive activities exhibits no tendency to be commensurate with innate capacity, but that a considerable element of the unpredictable must invariably be taken into account."

This is a parody, but not a very gross one. Exhibit (3), above, for instance, contains several patches of the same kind of English. It will be seen that I have not made a full translation. The beginning and ending of the sentence follow the original meaning fairly closely, but in the middle and concrete illustrations—race, battle, bread—dissolve into the vague phrase "success or failure in competitive activities." This had to be so, because no modern writer of the kind I am discussing—no one capable of using phrases like "objective consideration of contemporary phenomena"—would ever tabulate his thoughts in that precise and detailed way. The whole tendency of modern prose is away from concreteness. Now analyse these two sentences a little more closely. The first contains forty-nine words but only sixty syllables, and all its words are those of everyday life. The second contains thirty-eight words of ninety syllables: eighteen of its words are from Latin roots, and one from Greek. The first sentence contains six vivid images, and only one phrase ("time and chance") that could be called vague. The second contains not a single fresh, arresting phrase, and in spite of its ninety syllables it gives only a shortened version of the meaning contained in the first. Yet without a doubt it is the second kind of sentence that is gaining ground in modern English. I do not want to exaggerate. This kind of writing is not yet universal, and outcrops of simplicity will occur here and there in the worst-written page. Still, if you or I were told to write a few lines on the uncertainty of human fortunes, we should probably come much nearer to my imaginary sentence than to the one from *Ecclesiastes*.

As I have tried to show, modern writing at its worst does not consist in picking out words for the sake of their meaning and inventing images in order to make the meaning clearer. It consists in gumming together long strips of words which have already been set in order by someone else, and making the results presentable by sheer humbug. The attraction of this way of writing is that it is easy. It is easier—even quicker, once you have the habit—to say *In my opinion it is a not unjustifiable assumption that* than to say *I think*. If you use ready-made phrases, you not only don't have to hunt about for words; you also don't have to bother with the rhythms of your sentences, since these phrases are generally so arranged as to be more or less euphonious. When you are composing in a hurry—when you are dictating to a stenographer, for instance, or making a public speech—it is natural to fall into a pretentious, Latinized style. Tags like a *consideration which we should do well to bear in mind* or *a conclusion to which all of us would readily assent* will save many a sentence from coming down with a bump. By using stale metaphors, similes and idioms, you save much mental effort, at the cost of leaving your meaning vague, not only for your reader but for yourself. This is the significance of mixed metaphors. The sole aim of a metaphor is to call up a visual image. When these images clash—as in *The Fascist octopus has sung its swan song, the jackboot is thrown into the melting pot*—it can be taken as certain that the writer is not seeing a mental image of the objects he is naming; in other words he is not really thinking. Look again at the examples I gave at the beginning of this essay. Professor Laski (1) uses five negatives in fifty-three words. One of these is superfluous, making nonsense of the whole passage, and in addition there is the slip *alien* for akin, making further nonsense, and several avoidable pieces of clumsiness which increase the general vagueness. Professor Hogben (2) plays ducks and drakes with a battery which is able to write prescriptions, and, while disapproving of the everyday phrase *put up with,* is unwilling to look *egregious* up in the dictionary and see what it means. (3), if one takes an uncharitable attitude towards it, is simply meaningless: probably one could work out its intended meaning by reading the whole of the article in which it occurs. In (4), the writer knows more or less what he wants to say, but an accumulation of stale phrases chokes him like tea leaves blocking a sink. In (5), words and meaning have almost parted company. People who write in this manner usually have a general emotional meaning—they dislike one thing and want to express solidarity with another—but they are not interested in the detail of what they are saying. A scrupulous writer, in every sentence that he writes, will ask himself at least four questions, thus: What am I trying to say? What words will express it? What image or idiom will make it clearer? Is this image fresh enough to have an effect? And he will probably ask himself two more: Could I put it more shortly? Have I said anything that is avoidably ugly? But you are not obliged to go to all this trouble. You can shirk it by simply throwing your mind open and letting the ready-made phrases come crowding in. They will construct your sentences for you—even think your thoughts for you, to a certain extent—and at need they will perform the important service of partially concealing your meaning even from yourself. It is at this point that the special connection between politics and the debasement of language becomes clear.

In our time it is broadly true that political writing is bad writing. Where it is not true, it will generally be found that the writer is some kind of rebel, expressing his private opinions and not a "party line." Orthodoxy, of whatever colour, seems to demand a lifeless, imitative style. The political dialects to be found in pamphlets, leading articles, manifestos, White Papers and the speeches of under-secretaries do, of course, vary from party to party, but they are all alike in that one almost never finds in them a fresh, vivid, home-made turn of speech. When one watches some tired hack on the platform mechanically repeating the familiar phrases—*bestial atrocities, iron heel, blood-stained tyranny, free peoples of the world, stand shoulder to shoulder*—one often has a curious feeling that one is not watching a live human being but some kind of dummy: a feeling which suddenly becomes stronger at moments when the light catches the speaker's spectacles and turns them into blank discs which seem to have no eyes behind them. And this is not altogether fanciful. A speaker who uses that kind of phraseology has gone some distance towards turning himself into a machine. The appropriate noises are coming out of his larynx, but his brain is not involved as it would be if he were choosing his words for himself. If the speech he is making is one that he is accustomed to make over and over again, he may be almost unconscious of what he is saying, as one is when one utters the responses in church. And this reduced state of consciousness, if not indispensable, is at any rate favourable to political conformity.

In our time, political speech and writing are largely the defence of the indefensible. Things like the continuance of British rule in India, the Russian purges and deportations, the dropping of the atom bombs on Japan, can indeed be defended, but only by arguments which are too brutal for most people to face, and which do not square with the professed aims of political parties. Thus political language has to consist largely of euphemism, question-begging and sheer cloudy vagueness. Defenceless villages are bombarded from the air, the inhabitants driven out into the countryside, the cattle machine-gunned, the huts set on fire with incendiary bullets: this is called *pacification*. Millions of peasants are robbed of their farms and sent trudging along the roads with no more than they can carry: this is called *transfer of population* or *rectification of frontiers*. People are imprisoned for years without trial, or shot in the back of the neck or sent to die of scurvy in Arctic lumber camps: this is called *elimination of unreliable elements*. Such phraseology is needed if one wants to name things without calling up mental pictures of them. Consider for instance some comfortable English professor defending Russian totalitarianism. He cannot say outright, "I believe in killing off your opponents when you can get good results by doing so." Probably, therefore, he will say something like this:

"While freely conceding that the Soviet régime exhibits certain features which the humanitarian may be inclined to deplore, we must, I think, agree that a certain curtailment of the right to political opposition is an unavoidable concomitant of transitional periods, and that the rigors which the Russian people have been called upon to undergo have been amply justified in the sphere of concrete achievement."

The inflated style is itself a kind of euphemism. A mass of Latin words falls upon the facts like soft snow, blurring the outlines and covering up all the details. The great enemy of clear language is insincerity. When there is a gap between one's real and one's declared aims, one turns as it were instinctively to long words and exhausted idioms, like a cuttlefish squirting out ink. In our age there is no such thing as "keeping out of politics." All issues are political issues, and politics itself is a mass of lies, evasions, folly, hatred and schizophrenia. When the general atmosphere is bad, language must suffer. I should expect to find—this is a guess which I have not sufficient knowledge to verify—that the German, Russian and Italian languages have all deteriorated in the last ten or fifteen years, as a result of dictatorship.

But if thought corrupts language, language can also corrupt thought. A bad usage can spread by tradition and imitation, even among people who should and do know better. The debased language that I have been discussing is in some ways very convenient. Phrases like *a not unjustifiable assumption, leaves much to be desired, would serve no good purpose, a consideration which we should do well to bear in mind,* are a continuous temptation, a packet of aspirins always at one's elbow. Look back through this essay, and for certain you will find that I have again and again committed the very faults I am protesting against. By this morning's post I have received a pamphlet dealing with conditions in Germany. The author tells me that he "felt impelled" to write it. I open it at random, and here is almost the first sentence that I see: "(The Allies) have an opportunity not only of achieving a radical transformation of Germany's social and political structure in such a way as to avoid a nationalistic reaction in Germany itself, but at the same time of laying the foundations of a cooperative and unified Europe." You see, he "feels impelled" to write—feels, presumably, that he has something new to say—and yet his words, like cavalry horses answering the bugle, group themselves automatically into the familiar dreary pattern. This invasion of one's mind by ready-made phrases (*lay the foundations, achieve a radical transformation*) can only be prevented if one is constantly on guard against them, and every such phrase anaesthetizes a portion of one's brain.

I said earlier that the decadence of our language is probably curable. Those who deny this would argue, if they produced an argument at all, that language merely reflects existing social conditions, and that we cannot influence its development by any direct tinkering with words and constructions. So far as the general tone or spirit of a language goes, this may be true, but it is not true in detail. Silly words and expressions have often disappeared, not through any evolutionary process but owing to the conscious action of a minority. Two recent examples were *explore every avenue* and *leave no stone unturned,* which were killed by the jeers of a few journalists. There is a long list of flyblown metaphors which could similarly be got rid of if enough people would interest themselves in the job; and it should also be possible to laugh the *not un-* formation out of existence,[3] to reduce the amount of Latin and Greek in the average sentence, to drive out foreign phrases and strayed scientific words, and, in general, to make pretentiousness unfashionable. But all these are minor points. The defence of the English language implies more than this, and perhaps it is best to start by saying what it does *not* imply.

To begin with it has nothing to do with archaism, with the salvaging of obsolete words and turns of speech, or with the setting up of a "standard English" which must never be departed from. On the contrary, it is especially concerned with the scrapping of every word or idiom which has outworn its usefulness. It has nothing to do with correct grammar and syntax, which are of no importance so

---

[3] One can cure oneself of the *not un-*formation by memorizing this sentence: *A not unblack dog was chasing a not unsmall rabbit across a not ungreen field.*

long as one makes one's meaning clear, or with the avoidance of Americanisms, or with having what is called a "good prose style." On the other hand it is not concerned with fake simplicity and the attempt to make written English colloquial. Nor does it even imply in every case preferring the Saxon word to the Latin one, though it does imply using the fewest and shortest words that will cover one's meaning. What is above all needed is to let the meaning choose the word, and not the other way about. In prose, the worst thing one can do with words is to surrender to them. When you think of a concrete object, you think wordlessly, and then, if you want to describe the thing you have been visualizing you probably hunt about till you find the exact words that seem to fit. When you think of something abstract you are more inclined to use words from the start, and unless you make a conscious effort to prevent it, the existing dialect will come rushing in and do the job for you, at the expense of blurring or even changing your meaning. Probably it is better to put off using words as long as possible and get one's meaning as clear as one can through pictures or sensations. Afterwards one can choose—not simply *accept*—the phrases that will best cover the meaning, and then switch round and decide what impression one's words are likely to make on another person. This last effort of the mind cuts out all stale or mixed images, all prefabricated phrases, needless repetitions, and humbug and vagueness generally. But one can often be in doubt about the effect of a word or a phrase, and one needs rules that one can rely on when instinct fails. I think the following rules will cover most cases:

> (i)   Never use a metaphor, simile or other figure of speech which you are used to seeing in print.
> (ii) Never use a long word where a short one will do.
> (iii) If it is possible to cut a word out, always cut it out.
> (iv) Never use the passive where you can use the active.
> (v)   Never use a foreign phrase, a scientific word or a jargon word if you can think of an everyday English equivalent.
> (vi) Break any of these rules sooner than say anything outright barbarous.

These rules sound elementary, and so they are, but they demand a deep change of attitude in anyone who has grown used to writing in the style now fashionable. One could keep all of them and still write bad English, but one could not write the kind of stuff that I quoted in those five specimens at the beginning of this article.

I have not here been considering the literary use of language, but merely language as an instrument for expressing and not for concealing or preventing thought. Stuart Chase and others have come near to claiming that all abstract words are meaningless, and have used this as a pretext for advocating a kind of political quietism. Since you don't know what Fascism is, how can you struggle against Fascism? One need not swallow such absurdities as this, but one ought to recognize that the present political chaos is connected with the decay of language, and that one can probably bring about some improvement by starting at the verbal end. If you simplify your English, you are freed from the worst follies of orthodoxy. You cannot speak any of the necessary dialects, and when you make a stupid remark its stupidity will be obvious, even to yourself. Political language—and with variations this is true of all political parties, from Conservatives to Anarchists—is designed to make lies sound truthful and murder respectable, and to give an appearance of solidity to pure wind. One cannot change this all in a moment, but one can at least change one's own habits, and from time to time one can even, if one jeers loudly enough, send some worn-out and useless phrase—some *jackboot, Achilles' heel, hotbed, melting pot, acid test, veritable inferno* or other lump of verbal refuse—into the dustbin where it belongs.

HARRY BRENT

"Bullets Hurt, Corpses Stink": George Orwell and the Language of Warfare

Harry Brent (1943–   ) is a professor and former chair of the Department of English at Baruch College of the City University of New York. He is also former chair of the College Section of the National Council of Teachers of English. The following selection appears in *Beyond 1984* (1989) edited by William Lutz.

Although most educated people in the United States can claim some familiarity with George Orwell's *Nineteen Eighty-Four,* many of them are probably unaware that Big Brother, The Ministry of Truth, and Newspeak are not abstractions chiefly associated, as the Left would have it, with Hitler or, as the Right would have it, with Stalin. More important in Orwell's experience than either the German or the Georgian was the Spaniard, Generalissimo Franco. The dynamics of *Nineteen Eighty-Four* have their roots in Orwell's actual experience, specifically in his service to the Republican cause during the Spanish Civil War.

This essay will explore some of the connections that Orwell began to make in Spain between language and warfare, connections we see in *Homage to Catalonia*. I believe that Orwell's experiences in Spain not only helped lay the groundwork for *Nineteen Eighty-Four,* but also made him especially aware of the necessity for language to reflect reality accurately, a principle that was to guide the rest of his writing and his life.

In 1942, in his essay entitled "Looking Back on the Spanish War," Orwell asked

> How will the history of the Spanish war be written? If Franco remains in power his nominees will write the history books. . . .
> . . . If the Leader says of such and such an event, "It never happened"—well, it never happened. If he says that two and two are five—well, two and two are five. This prospect frightens me much more than bombs.[1]

Here we see some of the roots of *Nineteen Eighty-Four* in Orwell's fears for the emergence of a system of political engineering in which history would become whatever the ruler wanted it to be.

The Spanish Civil War was significant for Orwell because he participated in the frontline fighting against the Fascists. It was in Spain that Orwell came close to death (he was wounded in the neck by a bullet) and where he experienced day-to-day hardships which, unlike those recorded in *Down and Out in Paris and London,* he could not leave at will. The daily experience of being close to immediate death prompted Orwell to use language with great precision. In Spain he learned the truth of war firsthand, that "a louse is a louse and a bomb a bomb," and that "bullets hurt, corpses stink" (2:250).[2]

Orwell recorded his experiences in Spain in *Homage to Catalonia.*

---

[1] George Orwell, "Looking Back on the Spanish Civil War," in *My Country Right or Left (1940–43),* vol. 2 of *The Collected Essays, Journalism and Letters of George Orwell,* ed. Sonia Orwell and Ian Angus, 4 vol. (New York: Harcourt, Brace & World, 1968), 2:258–59.

[2] Orwell, "Looking Back," 2:250.

The book is the story of his military service with the Republican cause in 1937 on the Zaragoza front in Catalonia (the northeastern region of Spain) and his unlucky adventures in Barcelona, where he found himself enlisted by sheer accident as part of the minority in the internecine strife that characterized life on the Republican side.

Let us begin at the end of *Homage to Catalonia.* Orwell has just left Spain by way of the French border and has reached the seaside town of Banyuls.

Banyuls is not a particularly friendly town. Located in the extreme south of France, it is the last place of any importance before the Spanish border. Hunted by the leadership of his own Republican side, Orwell stopped there, glad to be out of the fighting and wanting a rest. In *Homage to Catalonia* he remarks that "the little town seemed solidly pro-Franco," that the waiter in the local café, aware of Orwell's Republican associations, glowered at him, and that he and his wife remarked to each other that they wished they were back in Spain.[3]

What is striking about the passage is an evident nostalgia for danger. What may not be as evident is that Banyuls, for Orwell, is much less sharply defined than the Barcelona he has just left. Orwell says of his entry into France that "With every mile that you went northward France grew greener and softer." He contrasts France with Spain, remarking that in Spain things seemed clearer, more well-defined. The softness of the French landscape leads him to comment on the nature of perception itself: "It is difficult to be certain of anything except what you have seen with your own eyes."[4] Orwell warned his readers to "beware of my partisanship, my mistakes of fact and the distortion inevitably caused by my having seen only one corner of events."[5] It is as if his leaving Spain, where "mountain and vine" clearly defined the landscape, gave Orwell cause to question his own vision. The soft focus of the French landscape made him wonder about the accuracy of his perceptions and the possibilities for precision in language. It is almost as if Orwell is telling us that one must go to Spain, or at least have an experience like "Spain" to talk about life in a sharply defined way.

Orwell was forever going places, to Burma in his first attempt at

---

[3] George Orwell, *Homage to Catalonia* (New York: Harcourt, Brace & World, 1952), 229.

[4] Orwell, *Homage to Catalonia,* 230–31.

[5] Orwell, *Homage to Catalonia,* 211.

a profession, to Paris to write about being "down and out," and to Spain to fight for a cause he believed in. Part of his motive for these journeys was to see to the essence of things: the roots of poverty in Paris, the roots of war in Spain. Orwell's need for direct experience is reflected in his preference for direct language. Though possessed of great ironic perception, he was not a man of much verbal irony, a characteristic that cost him a greater literary reputation. This point is illustrated by one of his encounters with Henry Miller.

Miller gave Orwell a corduroy jacket when Orwell, on his way to Spain, visited him in Paris. To push the gift on Orwell, Miller jestingly told him that it was a contribution to the Republican cause. Later, however, Miller remarked that he would still have given Orwell the jacket had he been going to help the Fascists.[6] Orwell refers to this meeting in his essay, "Inside the Whale," which includes a critique of Miller's *Tropic of Cancer*:

> I first met Miller at the end of 1936, when I was passing through Paris on my way to Spain. What most intrigued me about him was to find that he felt no interest in the Spanish war whatever. He merely told me in forcible terms that to go to Spain at that moment was the act of an idiot. He could understand anyone going there from purely selfish motives, out of curiosity, for instance, but to mix oneself up in such things *from a sense of obligation* was sheer stupidity. In any case my ideas about combating Fascism, defending democracy, etc etc were all baloney.[7]

Orwell's criticism of Henry Miller is very much like his criticism of Miller's novel:

> Miller's outlook is deeply akin to that of Whitman, and nearly everyone who has read him has remarked on this. *Tropic of Cancer* ends with an especially Whitmanesque passage, in which, after the lecheries, the swindles, the fights, the drinking bouts and the imbecilities, he simply sits down and watches the Seine flowing past, in a mystical acceptance of the thing-as-it-is. Only, what is he accepting? In the first place, not America, but the ancient boneheap of Europe, where every grain of soil has passed through innumerable human bodies. Secondly, not an epoch of expansion and liberty, but an epoch of fear, tyranny and regimentation. To say "I accept" in an age like ours is to say that you accept concen-

---

[6] Alfred Perles, *My Friend Henry Miller* (London: Neville Spearman, 1955), 156–59.

[7] George Orwell, "Inside the Whale," in *An Age Like This (1920–40)*, vol. 1 of *The Collected Essays, Journalism and Letters of George Orwell*, ed. Sonia Orwell and Ian Angus, 4 vol. (New York: Harcourt, Brace & World, 1968), 1:519.

tration camps, rubber truncheons, Hitler, Stalin, bombs, aeroplanes, tinned food, machine guns, putsches, purges, slogans.[8]

Perhaps those who looked down on Orwell in the Fifties, who noted his lack of verbal irony, dismissed these words as pseudo-Marxist cant. No doubt many of those same people also dismissed Miller for prurient opportunism. I suggest, however, that ironically, the attitude Orwell exhibits here has something very much in common with Miller, and, by extension, with Whitman; i.e., an appreciation of simplicity and directness in language cultivated through a keen eye to see "the thing-as-it-is" and to call it such. Perhaps Orwell's great failing was his reluctance or inability to use verbal irony, to get himself perceived as a possessor of "wit." He fails to comment with "wit" about Miller's gesture of the coat or about the language of *Tropic of Cancer.* Orwell's "failure" resides in either his inability or his refusal to use the language of indirection. Certainly his great success (as was true of Miller) was to see through obfuscation in language, through the talk that covers up. Orwell's concern for directness and honesty in language cannot be easily separated from his admiration of these virtues in life.

Long before *Nineteen Eighty-Four* or "Politics and the English Language," Orwell began to hone a hatred of obfuscation. The language of *Burmese Days* and *Down and Out in Paris and London* already marked him as a writer who cultivated simplicity and directness; however, it was in *Homage to Catalonia* that tensions between directness and honesty, on the one hand, and complexity and untruth on the other, received more constant attention. Perhaps it was the experience of war, of almost being killed, that gave Orwell the extra push that was to make him the twentieth century's champion of stylistic clarity. It is hard to sound witty and truthful at the same time when recounting such experiences. Whatever the case, *Homage to Catalonia* shows that warfare provided him with the arena to take language to its bones.

In the opening passage of *Homage to Catalonia,* Orwell speaks of his encounter with an Italian volunteer who had also come to aid the Republican side:

> He was a tough-looking youth of twenty-five or six, with reddish-yellow hair and powerful shoulders. His peaked leather cap was pulled fiercely over one eye. He was standing in profile to me, his chin on his breast,

---

[8] Orwell, "Inside the Whale," 1:499.

gazing with a puzzled frown at a map which one of the officers had open on the table. Something in his face deeply moved me. It was the face of a man who would commit murder and throw away his life for a friend— the kind of face you would expect in an Anarchist, though as likely as not he was a Communist. There were both candor and ferocity in it; also the pathetic reverence that illiterate people have for their supposed superiors. Obviously he could not make head or tail of the map; obviously he regarded map-reading as a stupendous intellectual feat. I hardly know why, but I have seldom seen anyone—any man, I mean— to whom I have taken such an immediate liking. While they were talking round the table some remark brought it out that I was a foreigner. The Italian raised his head and said quickly:

"Italiano?"

I answered in my bad Spanish:

"No, Ingles. Y tu?"

"Italiano."

As we went out he stepped across the room and gripped my hand very hard. Queer, the affection you can feel for a stranger. . . . One was always making contacts of that kind in Spain.[9]

In the Eighties, this is not the way to start a good book. Orwell's sensibility as reflected here lacks the irony and ambiguity that literary criticism of our age associates with complexity of thought. As Orwell chose to be on that "other" side in the Spanish Civil War, he also chose that great otherness of a writer who uses the language of direction at the expense of irony and ambiguity: he speaks with simplicity and truth. This is why Orwell is generally seen as a sort of second-rate novelist by the critics of our time. It is also why we instinctively regard him as *the* great critic of language in our age.

Orwell was aware of his place in the twentieth century literary tradition, and if he was able to endure condescension, he was also capable of meting out his own rather harsh literary judgments. In "Inside the Whale" Orwell has some unkind words for the intellectuals of his day who, in his frame of reference, had abandoned their independence for the security of larger movements, such as the Communist Party, and the Roman Catholic Church. His few good words are for T. S. Eliot, whose acceptance of Anglo as opposed to Roman Catholicism, "embraced the ecclesiastical equivalent of Trotskyism."[10] An ardent internationalist, Orwell was nonetheless wed in

---

[9] Orwell, *Homage to Catalonia,* 1–2.

[10] Orwell, "Inside the Whale," 1:515.

his heart to his native land. Perhaps this is why he could spare the Anglican Eliot. He showed no such mercy to W. H. Auden.

As the subject of "Inside the Whale," Auden was initially selected for praise. Orwell quotes an extract from his poem, "Spain," calling it "one of the few decent things that have been written about the Spanish War":

> Tomorrow for the young, the poets exploding
>   like bombs,
> The walks by the lake, the weeks of perfect
>   communion;
>   Tomorrow the bicycle races
> Through the suburbs on summer evenings. But
>   today the struggle.
> Today the deliberate increase in the chances
>   of death,
> The conscious acceptance of guilt in the
>   necessary murder;
>   Today the expending of powers
> On the flat ephemeral pamphlet and the boring
>   meeting.[11]

Halfway through his evaluation of Auden's poem, however, praise suddenly changes to invective, as if a sudden truth had caught Orwell and spun him one hundred-eighty degrees in midsentence:

> The second stanza is intended as a sort of thumbnail sketch of a day in the life of a "good party man." In the morning a couple of political murders, a ten-minutes' interlude to stifle "bourgeois" remorse, and then a hurried luncheon and a busy afternoon and evening chalking walls and distributing leaflets. All very edifying. But notice the phrase "necessary murder." It could only be written by a person to whom murder is at most a *word*.[12]

Orwell goes on at some length to castigate "Mr. Auden's brand of amoralism."

Although Orwell is being unfair to Auden (there is sufficient ambiguity in the poem to lead to many supportable conclusions about the meaning of "necessary murder"; indeed, Auden revised the poem several times), what is most remarkable is that Orwell begins by using Auden's poem to buttress his own criticism of the political

[11] Orwell, "Inside the Whale," 1:516.

[12] Orwell, "Inside the Whale," 1:516.

timidity of twentieth-century writers and then—in the process of making that argument—he changes it into an attack on Auden's use of language. Orwell seems comfortable enough with Auden's ideas until Auden uses language to misrepresent reality, horrible reality. What Orwell objects to is the phrasing. He has a mind directed to language.

But there is more to it than that. Through language, Orwell is able to sense that Auden, in the very act of criticizing the same people as does Orwell himself, obliquely identifies with murderers and thereby apologizes for murder itself. Orwell is not one to talk about ambiguity, but about truths, central truths, even where they exist in ambiguous contexts. And Orwell, always one to speak in plain terms, has no patience with abstract ambiguities that predicate a necessity for murder. It is a strange line that Orwell treads, between the tunnel vision of "party men" and the "multiple perspectives" of new critics. Orwell, it seems, is too much interested in truth and it is his contempt for language misused, for "necessary" murder, that prods him toward the allegorical truth of Nineteen Eighty-Four.

Perhaps Orwell's attack upon Auden was prompted by Auden's use of Spain as the background metaphor in his poem. There is a certain universal distaste for those who write about real tragedy from the vantage of comfort, and this is felt most acutely by those who have seen or experienced the same tragedy firsthand. Orwell was no stranger to the things Auden was writing about, and it must have galled him that this young, intellectual poet and sometime political activist would dare to write in such a judgmental way about something that Orwell had actually experienced.

Homage to Catalonia is the antithesis of Auden's "Spain." A record of Orwell's experiences in the Spanish Civil War, its perspective and tone show Orwell's deep regard for the direct, the immediate and the real. There is virtually no hypothesizing in his book. From time to time, Orwell gives brief explanations of the political background that turned one Republican faction against another, but for the most part the book is a narrative of his day-to-day experiences as a volunteer—experiences that included several brushes with death, and that threw into high relief the ordinary things of life; experiences that helped Orwell to develop that clarity of style which marks his later writings. It is a book with little speculation and much direct talk.

Homage to Catalonia is not a good book to read to get an idea of the history of the Spanish Civil War. Orwell was somewhat confused about the general political divisions of even the Republican side. His enlistment on the side of the vaguely Trotskyist but mostly anarchist

P.O.U.M. (*Partido Obrera Unificación Marxista*—Party of Marxist Uni-fication) happened by chance, Orwell having brought to the Spanish front a letter of introduction from an English friend with connections to it. Indeed, when the P.O.U.M. was suppressed by the Communists and Orwell found himself fired upon by former comrades, he was somewhat at a loss to understand why.

From the very beginning of *Homage to Catalonia,* Orwell concen-trates on those details of daily life in the barracks and trenches that evoke our response to the humanity, or lack of it, inherent in the situation of war. His attention to detail in the reality he saw, his horror in the little things and his recognition that humans can put up with such horror, paved the way for similar details in the world of *Nineteen Eighty-Four.*

From the very first chapter of *Homage to Catalonia* Orwell seems to assume that his readers will know what the Civil War is about. He gives no introduction to the politics of the situation; no general overview of the military positions of the two sides. What interests Orwell is that the post he reports to had once been a riding school, that the parade field is covered with gravel, and that "the whole place still smelt of horse-piss and rotten oats."[13] Orwell is concerned with the changing position of women in the revolution, but instead of discussing the issue abstractly, he tells us that on his arrival the militiamen laughed at women at drill, while "a few months earlier no one would have seen anything comic in a woman handling a gun."[14] He always chooses the illustration over the abstraction.

Orwell's attention to the truth of detail forms a web of coherence for the entire narrative. Early in the story, he comments about lice:

> The human louse somewhat resembles a tiny lobster, and he lives chiefly in your trousers. Short of burning all your clothes there is no known way of getting rid of him. Down the seams of your trousers he lays his glittering white eggs, like tiny grains of rice, which hatch out and breed families of their own at horrible speed. I think the pacifists might find it helpful to illustrate their pamphlets with enlarged photographs of lice. Glory of war, indeed! In war *all* soldiers are lousy, at least when it is warm enough. The men who fought at Verdun, at Waterloo, at Flodden, at Senlac, at Thermopylae—every one of them had lice crawling over his testicles.[15]

[13] Orwell, *Homage to Catalonia,* 7.

[14] Orwell, *Homage to Catalonia,* 7.

[15] Orwell, *Homage to Catalonia,* 76.

Orwell mistakenly attributes ovaries to male lice, but in all other respects his description is essentially accurate; an accuracy that most people writing about war tend to miss. All through the book, his focus is on the small details that tell us the truth of war as accurately as the photographs of Cappa, or (as with the lice) with greater accuracy than any photograph is capable. Even when recounting the very complex factional warfare in Barcelona, Orwell notes that he was glad to buy some goat's cheese and that behind the barricades "men were frying eggs."[16]

Orwell writes with much the same attitude as Robert Graves in *Goodbye to All That,* an autobiography centered on the First World War in which it is assumed that the reader knows the essence of the conflict, at least from the Allied side. Both authors also focus on one-to-one encounters with the enemy. Graves, while on duty as a sniper, tells us that he just could not pull the trigger on a German soldier taking a bath.[17] Orwell, however, seems the harder man; at least the language he uses and the picture he paints with it has harder edges. After he and his comrades breached the Spanish line, Orwell found himself chasing one of the defenders through a communications trench:

> He was bareheaded and seemed to have nothing on except a blanket which he was clutching round his shoulders. . . . [M]y mind leapt backwards twenty years, to our boxing instructor at school, showing me in vivid pantomime how he had bayoneted a Turk at the Dardanelles. I gripped my rifle by the small of the butt and lunged at the man's back. He was just out of my reach. And for a little distance we proceeded like this, he rushing up the trench and I after him on the ground above, prodding at his shoulderblades and never quite getting there—a comic memory for me to look back upon, though I suppose it seemed less comic to him.[18]

If the retrospective irony here is uncharacteristic of Orwell, his attention to detail is not. For Orwell, the language of warfare eschews any specifically military terminology, or even any abstract terminology. It is simple and direct, the language of everyday life. What makes the foregoing passage so eerie is that Orwell describes his

[16] Orwell, *Homage to Catalonia,* 127.

[17] Robert Graves, *Goodbye to All That* (New York: Jonathan Cape & Harrison Smith, 1930), 164.

[18] Orwell, *Homage to Catalonia,* 92.

trying to bayonet a man to death with the same kind of tone he might use to describe an athletic exercise like trying to row a boat. The man who called Auden out for abstractly predicating a necessity for murder now speaks with a strangely detached enthusiasm about almost having committed a "necessary murder" himself. Orwell reports the facts even when they are inconsistent with his vision of himself.

Later in the novel, when fighting has broken out among various factions in Barcelona, Orwell finds himself confronting one of his former comrades (erroneously identified by Orwell as a Civil Guard) across the rooftops. Orwell trains his rifle on the man he thinks is about to begin shooting at him. They exchange words. The "civil guard" explains that he was not going to shoot at Orwell but at a third individual who had fired on him first. Orwell then asks, "Have you got any more beer left?" His tentative comrade answers: "No, it's all gone."[19] Even in life-threatening situations, Orwell focuses on the little things. Ironies in his works come not from his imagination, but from his eyes and his ears. Orwell does not usually write like Hemingway. It is only when he is faced with life and death situations that "the ordinary" takes over, in his syntax and in his reports. In *Homage to Catalonia,* we see the ordinary as special because death is always just at hand.

Even the passage in which Orwell is shot through the neck is simple and direct. Without the speculation on ultimate matters one might expect in a description of such a moment, Orwell speaks of the event almost as if he is recounting a minor skiing accident:

> Roughly speaking it was the sensation of being *at the centre* of an explosion. There seemed to be a loud bang and a blinding flash of light all round me, and I felt a tremendous shock—no pain, only a violent shock, such as you get from an electric terminal. . . . I fancy you would feel the same way if you were hit by lightening.[20]

Warfare is simple, stark, real. The language of warfare avoids embellishment and apology. It is not the language of Auden.

The starkness and simplicity of his language reflects the simple bravery of Orwell's action on the battlefield. Bernard Crick, Orwell's biographer, records the reminiscences of Bob Edwards regarding Orwell:

[19] Orwell, *Homage to Catalonia,* 133.

[20] Orwell, *Homage to Catalonia,* 185.

He was absolutely fearless. About seven hundred yards from our lines and very close to a Fascist machine-gun post was a huge crop of potatoes. The war had interfered with the harvesting and there were these lovely potatoes. Orwell worked it out that a man, crawling on his stomach, could just not be hit by machine-gunners at that distance. With a sack— about three times a week, yes—he'd say, "I'm out for potatoes" and I'd say "For goodness sake, you know, it's not worth the risk." He said, "They can't hit me. I've already proved it." And they shot at him, you know, every time he went out for potatoes, they were shooting all the time. But he'd worked it out that they just couldn't hit a man at this distance.[21]

In *Homage to Catalonia,* Orwell modestly implies that he was not the only one who went for potatoes:

> We discovered another patch farther on, where there was practically no cover and you had to lift the potatoes lying on your belly—a fatiguing job. If their machine-gunners spotted you, you had to flatten yourself out like a rat when it squirms under a door, with the bullets cutting up the clods a few yards behind you. It seemed worth it at the time. Potatoes were getting very scarce. If you got a sackful you could take them down to the cook-house and swap them for a water-bottleful of coffee.[22]

It is hard to question the sincerity or the simplicity of a man who risks machinegun fire to gather potatoes. Yet, as with all abstractions, Orwell was beyond "sincerity." In a world that talked a lot about action, he simply acted. In the world of language, he simply spoke the truth, whether about being hit by a bullet or about trying to bayonet a man to death.

If Orwell could be brave for necessity—to gather potatoes—he could also kill for the same reason (his criticism of Auden notwithstanding), as we saw in his account of the bayonet chase. At another point in *Homage to Catalonia* the Fascists launch an earnest attack on the P.O.U.M. position. Orwell and his comrades respond with grenades:

> I flung it and threw myself on my face. By one of those strokes of luck that happen about once in a year I had managed to drop the bomb almost exactly where the rifle had flashed. There was the roar of the explosion and then, instantly, a diabolical outcry of screams and groans. We had got one of them, anyway; I don't know whether he was killed,

[21] Bernard Crick, *George Orwell: A Life* (Boston: Little, Brown, 1980), 325.

[22] Orwell, *Homage to Catalonia,* 74.

but certainly he was badly hurt. Poor wretch! I felt a vague sorrow as I heard him screaming.[23]

For Orwell, action and language existed on the same plane of reality. His objection to Auden was not so much that Auden countenanced political killing, but that he used mere language to apologize for it, or to make it seem understandable from the perspective of the political activist in the poem. As we have seen in the episodes of the grenade and the bayonet, Orwell himself was capable of killing for his own political beliefs. The difference between him and the character Auden created is that Orwell would talk about his actions from experience.

One should not get the impression that Orwell was some kind of cold-blooded killer who tried to justify the taking of life simply by owning up to the deed in straightforward language. If he was capable of killing in battle, he still felt the reluctance and repugnance associated with such an action. In "Looking Back at the Spanish Civil War," he mentions that at one point he had an easy shot at an enemy:

> At this moment a man, presumably carrying a message to an officer, jumped out of the [Fascist] trench and ran along the top of the parapet in full view. He was half-dressed and was holding up his trousers with both hands as he ran. I refrained from shooting at him. It is true that I am a poor shot and unlikely to hit a running man at a hundred yards, and also that I was thinking chiefly about getting back to our trench while the Fascists had their attention fixed on the aeroplanes. Still, I did not shoot partly because of that detail about the trousers. I had come here to shoot at Fascists; but a man who is holding up his trousers isn't a Fascist, he is visibly a fellow creature, similar to yourself, and you don't feel like shooting at him.[24]

Details matter to Orwell; details like the trousers. He tells the simple truth, whether it be about his attempt to use a bayonet on another human being, or about his reluctance to shoot an enemy holding up his pants, or about gathering potatoes under fire. The ambiguity for Orwell is in the heart, never in the words. The words simply and truthfully tell what happened.

Perhaps the final word on Orwell's experiences in Spain, and on his use of language in relation to warfare, is that his concern for simple and immediate truth transcended whatever larger political

[23] Orwell, *Homage to Catalonia,* 97.

[24] Orwell, "Looking Back," 2:254.

commitments he held. We know that Orwell was against Fascism, but what of his attitude toward the Fascists themselves? In *Homage to Catalonia* he says:

> In trench warfare five things are important: firewood, food, tobacco, candles and the enemy. In winter on the Zaragoza front they were important in that order, with the enemy a bad last. . . . The real preoccupation of both armies was trying to keep warm.[25]

Slightly later, he explains that the Republicans frequently aimed propaganda at the Fascist lines by shouting revolutionary messages. One of them was especially interesting to Orwell:

> Sometimes, instead of shouting revolutionary slogans he simply told the Fascists how much better we were fed than they were. His account of the Government rations was apt to be a little imaginative. "Buttered toast!"—you could hear his voice echoing across the lonely valley— "We're just sitting down to buttered toast over here! Lovely slices of buttered toast!"[26]

As Orwell himself points out, neither he nor the man shouting had tasted butter in weeks. Yet for Orwell this small lie contained one of the greatest truths of the war; that Fascist or Communist, men know that bullets hurt, that corpses stink, and that in cold, wet trenches buttered toast tastes good.

WERNER HEISENBERG

Language and Reality in Modern Physics

Werner Heisenberg (1901–1976) was a German physicist best known for his theory of the "uncertainty" or "indeterminacy" principle which raised philosophical questions about the limits of human knowledge. He wrote numerous essays and articles on quantum mechanics and atomic physics. He published *The Physical*

---

[25] Orwell, *Homage to Catalonia,* 23.

[26] Orwell, *Homage to Catalonia,* 43.

Principles of the Quantum Theory in 1930 and won the Nobel Prize for physics in 1932. The following selection is from his book *Physics and Philosophy* (1958).

Throughout the history of science new discoveries and new ideas have always caused scientific disputes, have led to polemical publications criticizing the new ideas, and such criticism has often been helpful in their development; but these controversies have never before reached that degree of violence which they attained after the discovery of the theory of relativity and in a lesser degree after quantum theory. In both cases the scientific problems have finally become connected with political issues, and some scientists have taken recourse to political methods to carry their views through. This violent reaction on the recent development of modern physics can only be understood when one realizes that here the foundations of physics have started moving; and that this motion has caused the feeling that the ground would be cut from science. At the same time it probably means that one has not yet found the correct language with which to speak about the new situation and that the incorrect statements published here and there in the enthusiasm about the new discoveries have caused all kinds of misunderstanding. This is indeed a fundamental problem. The improved experimental technique of our time brings into the scope of science new aspects of nature which cannot be described in terms of the common concepts. But in what language, then, should they be described? The first language that emerges from the process of scientific clarification is in theoretical physics usually a mathematical language, the mathematical scheme, which allows one to predict the results of experiments. The physicist may be satisfied when he has the mathematical scheme and knows how to use it for the interpretation of the experiments. But he has to speak about his results also to nonphysicists who will not be satisfied unless some explanation is given in plain language, understandable to anybody. Even for the physicist the description in plain language will be a criterion of the degree of understanding that has been reached. To what extent is such a description at all possible? Can one speak about the atom itself? This is a problem of language as much as of physics, and therefore some remarks are necessary concerning language in general and scientific language specifically.

Language was formed during the prehistoric age among the human race as a means for communication and as a basis for thinking.

We know little about the various steps in its formation; but language now contains a great number of concepts which are a suitable tool for more or less unambiguous communication about events in daily life. These concepts are acquired gradually without critical analysis by using the language, and after having used a word sufficiently often we think that we more or less know what it means. It is of course a well-known fact that the words are not so clearly defined as they seem to be at first sight and that they have only a limited range of applicability. For instance, we can speak about a piece of iron or a piece of wood, but we cannot speak about a piece of water. The word "piece" does not apply to liquid substances. Or, to mention another example: In discussions about the limitations of concepts, Bohr[1] likes to tell the following story: "A little boy goes into a grocer's shop with a penny in his hand and asks: 'Could I have a penny's worth of mixed sweets?' The grocer takes two sweets and hands them to the boy saying: 'Here you have two sweets. You can do the mixing yourself.'" A more serious example of the problematic relation between words and concepts is the fact that the words "red" and "green" are used even by people who are colorblind, though the ranges of applicability of these terms must be quite different for them from what they are for other people.

This intrinsic uncertainty of the meaning of words was of course recognized very early and has brought about the need for definitions, or—as the word "definition" says—for the setting of boundaries that determine where the word is to be used and where not. But definitions can be given only with the help of other concepts, and so one will finally have to rely on some concepts that are taken as they are, unanalyzed and undefined.

In Greek philosophy the problem of the concepts in language has been a major theme since Socrates, whose life was—if we can follow Plato's artistic representation in his dialogues—a continuous discussion about the content of the concepts in language and about the limitations in modes of expression. In order to obtain a solid basis for scientific thinking, Aristotle in his logic started to analyze the forms of language, the formal structure of conclusions and deductions independent of their content. In this way he reached a degree of abstraction and precision that had been unknown up to that time in

---

[1] Niels Bohr (1885–1962) was a Danish physicist who, using quantum theory, created a concept of atomic structure which won him the Nobel Prize in physics in 1922. (ED.)

Greek philosophy and he thereby contributed immensely to the clarification, to the establishment of order in our methods of thought. He actually created the basis for the scientific language.

On the other hand, this logical analysis of language again involves the danger of an oversimplification. In logic the attention is drawn to very special structures, unambiguous connections between premises and deductions, simple patterns of reasoning, and all the other structures of language are neglected. These other structures may arise from associations between certain meanings of words; for instance, a secondary meaning of a word which passes only vaguely through the mind when the word is heard may contribute essentially to the content of a sentence. The fact that every word may cause many only half-conscious movements in our mind can be used to represent some part of reality in the language much more clearly than by the use of the logical patterns. Therefore, the poets have often objected to this emphasis in language and in thinking on the logical pattern, which—if I interpret their opinions correctly—can make language less suitable for its purpose. We may recall for instance the words in Goethe's *Faust* which Mephistopheles speaks to the young student (quoted from the translation by Anna Swanwick):

> Waste not your time, so fast it flies;
> Method will teach you time to win;
> Hence, my young friend, I would advise,
> With college logic to begin.
> Then will your mind be so well brac'd,
> In Spanish boots so tightly lac'd,
> That on 'twill circumspectly creep,
> Thought's beaten track securely keep,
> Nor will it, ignis-fatuus like,
> Into the path of error strike.
> Then many a day they'll teach you how
> The mind's spontaneous acts, till now
> As eating and as drinking free,
> Require a process;—one, two, three!
> In truth the subtle web of thought
> Is like the weaver's fabric wrought,
> One treadle moves a thousand lines,
> Swift dart the shuttles to and fro,
> Unseen the threads unnumber'd flow,
> A thousand knots one stroke combines.
> Then forward steps your sage to show,
> And prove to you it must be so;
> The first being so, and so the second.

The third and fourth deduc'd we see;
And if there were no first and second,
Nor third nor fourth would ever be.
This, scholars of all countries prize,
Yet 'mong themselves no weavers rise.
Who would describe and study aught alive,
Seeks first the living spirit thence to drive:
Then are the lifeless fragments in his hand,
There only fails, alas!—the spirit-band.

This passage contains an admirable description of the structure of language and of the narrowness of the simple logical patterns.

On the other hand, science must be based upon language as the only means of communication and there, where the problem of unambiguity is of greatest importance, the logical patterns must play their role. The characteristic difficulty at this point may be described in the following way. In natural science we try to derive the particular from the general, to understand the particular phenomenon as caused by simple general laws. The general laws when formulated in the language can contain only a few simple concepts—else the law would not be simple and general. From these concepts are derived an infinite variety of possible phenomena, not only qualitatively but with complete precision with respect to every detail. It is obvious that the concepts of ordinary language, inaccurate and only vaguely defined as they are, could never allow such derivations. When a chain of conclusions follows from given premises, the number of possible links in the chain depends on the precision of the premises. Therefore, the concepts of the general laws must in natural science be defined with complete precision, and this can be achieved only by means of mathematical abstraction.

In other sciences the situation may be somewhat similar in so far as rather precise definitions are also required; for instance, in law. But here the number of links in the chain of conclusions need not be very great, complete precision is not needed, and rather precise definitions in terms of ordinary language are sufficient.

In theoretical physics we try to understand groups of phenomena by introducing mathematical symbols that can be correlated with fact, namely, with the results of measurements. For the symbols we use names that visualize their correlation with the measurement. Thus the symbols are attached to the language. Then the symbols are interconnected by a rigorous system of definitions and axioms, and finally the natural laws are expressed as equations between the symbols. The infinite variety of solutions of these equations then corresponds to the infinite variety of particular phenomena that are possible in this part of nature. In this way the mathematical scheme represents the group of phenomena so far as the correlation between the symbols and the measurements goes. It is this correlation which permits the expression of natural laws in the terms of common language, since our experiments consisting of actions and observations can always be described in ordinary language.

Still, in the process of expansion of scientific knowledge the language also expands; new terms are introduced and the old ones are applied in a wider field or differently from ordinary language. Terms such as "energy," "electricity," "entropy" are obvious examples. In this way we develop a scientific language which may be called a natural extension of ordinary language adapted to the added fields of scientific knowledge.

During the past century a number of new concepts have been introduced in physics, and in some cases it has taken considerable time before the scientists have really grown accustomed to their use. The term "electromagnetic field," for instance, which was to some extent already present in Faraday's[2] work and which later formed the basis of Maxwell's[3] theory, was not easily accepted by the physicists, who directed their attention primarily to the mechanical motion of matter. The introduction of the concept really involved a change in scientific ideas as well, and such changes are not easily accomplished.

Still, all the concepts introduced up to the end of the last century formed a perfectly consistent set applicable to a wide field of experience, and, together with the former concepts, formed a language which not only the scientists but also the technicians and engineers could successfully apply in their work. To the underlying fundamental ideas of this language belonged the assumptions that the order of events in time is entirely independent of their order in space, that Euclidean geometry is valid in real space, and that the events "happen" in space and time independently of whether they are observed or not. It was not denied that every observation had some influence on the phenomenon to be observed but it was generally assumed that by doing the experiments cautiously this influence could be

---

[2] Michael Faraday (1791–1867) was an English scientist whose work formed the basis of classical field theory and who discovered electromagnetic induction. (ED.)

[3] James Clerk Maxwell (1831–1879) was a Scottish physicist known for his work in electricity and magnetism, namely his development of the theory of the electromagnetic field. (ED.)

made arbitrarily small. This seemed in fact a necessary condition for the ideal of objectivity which was considered as the basis of all natural science.

Into this rather peaceful state of physics broke quantum theory and the theory of special relativity as a sudden, at first slow and then gradually increasing, movement in the foundations of natural science. The first violent discussions developed around the problems of space and time raised by the theory of relativity. How should one speak about the new situation?

The problems of language here are really serious. We wish to speak in some way about the structure of the atoms and not only about the "facts"—the latter being, for instance, the black spots on a photographic plate or the water droplets in a cloud chamber. But we cannot speak about the atoms in ordinary language.

The analysis can now be carried further in two entirely different ways. We can either ask which language concerning the atoms has actually developed among the physicists in the thirty years that have elapsed since the formulation of quantum mechanics. Or we can describe the attempts for defining a precise scientific language that corresponds to the mathematical scheme.

In answer to the first question one may say that the concept of complementarity introduced by Bohr into the interpretation of quantum theory has encouraged the physicists to use an ambiguous rather than an unambiguous language, to use the classical concepts in a somewhat vague manner in conformity with the principle of uncertainty, to apply alternatively different classical concepts which would lead to contradictions if used simultaneously. In this way one speaks about electronic orbits, about matter waves and charge density, about energy and momentum, etc., always conscious of the fact that these concepts have only a very limited range of applicability. When this vague and unsystematic use of the language leads into difficulties, the physicist has to withdraw into the mathematical scheme and its unambiguous correlation with the experimental facts.

This use of the language is in many ways quite satisfactory, since it reminds us of a similar use of the language in daily life or in poetry. We realize that the situation of complementarity is not confined to the atomic world alone; we meet it when we reflect about a decision and the motives for our decision or when we have the choice between enjoying music and analyzing its structure. On the other hand, when the classical concepts are used in this manner, they always retain a certain vagueness, they acquire in their relation to "reality" only the same statistical significance as the concepts of classical thermodynamics in its statistical interpretation.

All these difficult definitions and distinctions can be avoided if one confines the language to the description of facts, i.e., experimental results. However, if one wishes to speak about the atomic particles themselves one must either use the mathematical scheme as the only supplement to natural language or one must combine it with a language that makes use of a modified logic or of no well-defined logic at all. In the experiments about atomic events we have to do with things and facts, with phenomena that are just as real as any phenomena in daily life. But the atoms or the elementary particles themselves are not as real; they form a world of potentialities or possibilities rather than one of things or facts.

EIGHT

The Pleasures of Art, Reading, and Music

The perfection of art is to conceal art.

Quintilian

Art has nothing to do with communication between person and person, only with communication between different parts of a person's mind.

Rebecca West

How do we know that something has value? We do not mean *value* in the sense of monetary worth, but in the sense of enduring appeal, of permanence and importance to culture. To say that something has value, as Bernard Berenson does in his essay entitled "Value," is to make a judgment, and today the very act of making judgments has become open to question. Who is to say, one might ask, whether a painting by Picasso is superior to the work of a subway graffiti artist? Who is to say that Mozart is superior to your own improvised jazz? In short, can we define the word *good* as it is used in the title of Marya Mannes's "How Do You Know It's Good?" Or do all artistic value judgments involve what Arthur Koestler calls "Cultural Snobbery"?

One does not have to be a snob to recognize that art is all around us; indeed this is one of the themes of Helen Gardner's "Art in Everyday Life." If you doubt this premise, take a walk around your campus or town and take note of what you see that can be considered "art." Not only do obvious "works of art" fit this category, but so do buildings, plants and shrubs, benches, and other things. Indeed, the particular placement and juxtaposition of all these objects might be said to constitute "art."

The essays in this section address the cultural boundaries of what constitutes art. As any visit to a large art museum will likely show, definitions of beauty vary from culture to culture and from one historical period to another. Given these differences, can we say that there are universal ideas that underlie beauty itself? Or is beauty determined by the contexts of time and culture? Questions such as these are asked in Edith Hamilton's "The Way of the East and the West in Art."

What Hamilton does with art, Walter Benjamin does with books in "Unpacking My Library." This essay is on one hand very personal, but it also raises questions about the human need to classify even the "artistic" things in life. Classification also operates as a principle in Aaron Copland's "How We Listen to Music," in which the author takes us on a tour of our own reactions to one of life's greatest pleasures.

Finally, Vladimir Nabokov, in "Philistines and Philistinism," suggests that the same works of art may be viewed by different people at different times in remarkably different ways. Again, we are brought back to the question of value. Is yesterday's popular and respected art any less "good" simply because it has gone out of fashion, or because it is admired now only by people with outdated taste? If so, then what of today's art? Is there any hope for setting standards that help define artistic worth?

To begin answering these questions, you might visit your library and read through back issues of periodicals, especially those with many pictures, such as *Life* magazine. (The old *Life,* which appeared on a weekly basis, often contained popular articles on various trends of the time, many of which were influenced by changes in the art world.) Look at the furniture, the clothes, the architecture, not only in photo essays, but in advertisements as well. Record your reactions to the styles of the past. Which have survived? Which have gone their way? Which have come back?

You could conduct the same kind of research with respect to reading and music. Look at old issues of the *New York Times Book Review,* for example, or listen to old recordings. In what ways, in your opinion, have changes been for the better? In what ways for the worse?

BERNARD BERENSON

Value

Bernard Berenson (1865–1959) was an American art critic and historian who lived as an expatriate in Italy. Berenson, best known for his expertise in Italian Renaissance painting, advised numerous museums and private collectors. His villa, *I Tatti,* is widely known for its art collection and library. His book *Italian Painters of the Renaissance* (1932) is a revised and collected version of four of his earlier works on this subject. The following selection is from *Aesthetics and History* (1948), which is considered a classic in the field of art.

What is aught but as 'tis valued?

Shakespeare: Troilus and Cressida

A great historian, Leopold von Ranke, thought that the business of history was to find out what happened at a given time and place. Agreed! Yet for whom, and why, and to whose advantage? All sorts of things happen, an infinity of things, everywhere and all the time. Few attract attention, and fewer still are recorded. Our mind's eye is blinkered to everything except those rare events of the past that still smoulder with passions not wholly spent, or those that feed curiosity touching matters that the tendencies of the moment happen to stimulate. Let us take as an example the Crusades. We know what Villehardouin and Robert de Clary say about the conquest of Constantinople by the Latin Christians. Byzantine and Muslim chronicles supply a different picture. We expect a dramatically contrasted appreciation of the results, but are not prepared to find that the links of the chain leading up to the catastrophe, the events themselves, are neither the same, nor, when the same, are they given in the same order and with the same emphasis.

Or take the various French epics about Antioch, Jerusalem, Reynaud de Châtillon and Saladin, St. Louis and his paladins. We read Arab accounts of the presumably identical happenings and personages. We admire and love St. Louis, but heretics and Jews had good reason for a less enthusiastic appraisal of a charity from which they were cruelly excluded. What about such hallowed figures as St.

Ambrose,[1] St. John Chrysostom[2]—very wolves to Jews! Not that the Jews were any better. And then the Emperor Titus[3] to the rest of the world the delight of the human race; to the Jews the uniquely wicked. It is like diagrams that you can read off as concave or convex.

I cannot resist referring to the war that is going on between the East and the West—I say the East because whether for good or for evil the East begins with the Rhine. I read dailies from Berlin, Paris, and London as well as from Switzerland and Italy. Not only are the evaluations of the events all but diametrically opposed; the accounts themselves are so coloured by passion that but for identity of place-names and dates, one might fail to recognize that they dealt with the same happenings.

In the course of war, emotions are deepened and passions height-ened. They are always there, however, smouldering under the thresh-old of consciousness. They shape the story that at the moment they want to force others to believe. In the full sense of the words, then, Napoleon's definition of history as a fable agreed upon is correct—agreed upon by the winning side.

If we were able to attain accurate knowledge of what happened in the past, we could not cope with it. Time would not suffice, patience would not hold out. Long before either of them failed, curiosity would be satiated to the point of distaste. The most jejune[4] chronicle has to be a selection, and is not so candid as may seem to the lovers of the quaint. It is a selection motivated by a definite interest with its smoke screen of ideals, even when made without malice. For in all probability the compiler, half aware perhaps that he was lying or inventing, remained imperturbably unaware of what was shaping his composition.

Were the historians of the nineteenth century so very different from those of the barbarous or Dark Ages? The best of them un-doubtedly avoided what they themselves recognized as untruths and fancies. They were nevertheless almost as naive in accepting with

---

[1] St. Ambrose (340?–397) was bishop of Milan, a popular leader among the Milanese, and a major influence upon St. Augustine. (ED.)

[2] St. John Chrysostom (c. 347–407) was an early Church leader and patriarch of Constantiople. (ED.)

[3] Emperor Titus (A.D. 39–81) ruled Rome from A.D. 79–81. He conquered Jerusalem in A.D. 70 during the rule of his father, Vespasian. (ED.)

[4] lacking significance (ED.)

scarcely a question their Platonic idea, their hastily conceived or preconceived notion of the period or person they were portraying. More often than not the documents they so painstakingly recovered and so eagerly displayed could be used for a different distribution of light and shade from the one in their picture. It has been done since, but in that age of faith which the last century so pre-eminently was, it would have been difficult, perhaps impossible. And what of all the documents that they more or less deliberately put aside because they did not fit into the desired pattern! And whence the pattern?

Until a few decades ago nobody questioned that events of every nature had qualities attached to them as definite as to things to eat or drink or smell. It was admitted that what was one man's meat might be another man's poison, that one man will prefer pork fat and another metaphysical poetry, that Pius V and his court will rejoice over the massacre of St. Bartholomew and Milton cry for vengeance 'on the late massacre in Piedmont', that some would prefer the art of the fifth century before Christ, and others be so exclusive as to find perfection in one and only one particular Byzantine coin; that there might be transvaluers who put Greco above Velasquez and Luca Giordano above Titian, the Carracci above Michelangelo, and Magnasco above Tintoretto;[5] and so on and so on in hundreds, and thousands, and tens of thousands of instances from every realm of being. But it is something new in the world that value, choice, preference, no matter how freakish and how preverse, should be excluded altogether. Not only is value to be tabooed in questions of art but in questions of history and even of life itself. Thus I have heard of an Italian nobleman in the best society, who could not understand why there should be such an outcry over the treatment of Jews in Naziland and none over the forcible feeding of geese in Strassburg. And I once knew a lady who doubted our right to destroy noxious animals, including microbes, and regarded our clamours for help in the war against them as impertinent, and our claim for sympathy as impudent.

Behind this attitude there is, no doubt, the uncomfortable feeling that every entity has a right to exist on its own account, regardless

---

[5] Renowned Spanish (*El Greco, Velasquez*) and Italian (*Giordano, Titian*, the *Carracci, Michelangelo, Magnasco, Tintoretto*) painters of the sixteenth and seventeenth centuries. (ED.)

of its effect upon other entities, and furthermore that there is good in things most evil, and beauty in shapes most ugly.

No doubt in a universe of everlasting ecstasy each entity would realize itself completely, without interfering with any other entity. Its intrinsic qualities would be allowed full play and never at the expense of others. No meanest being would be called upon to wither that others might flourish, to die that others might live.

But strict economy must be practised by us if we are to find shelter yet a while in the exquisitely contrived House of Life that we have been constructing in the course of millenniums.

No hawks from without, no vermin from within. 'Hawks' are the hostile forces from the outside, 'vermin' the destructive, disintegrating, cancerous energies within; from the microbes that still frustrate our most patient attempts to sterilize them, to the undesirables of our own species.

Nor are we unmindful of the fragility of our abode and the precariousness of our tenure. There probably has never been a moment when mankind was more ready to secure its position by casting out those of its own species who seemed parasitical or dangerous. In Germany it was the Jew, in Russia whoever is not a proletarian, in Spain the Reds, in Mexico the priest, in the United States the declared Communist, and in all countries militant rebels against the policy of the oligarchy in control.

Crushed under the weight of decrees piled high by police-minded bipeds, with their gross utilitarianism, and their zoological hopes and fears for a society in which they are to hold the highest places, some few succeed in wriggling out, and in unconscious reaction to values too brutalizingly narrow, take refuge in a realm of 'unchartered freedom' where there are no values at all, no standards, no criticisms, no judgements. As if there could exist anything human, as distinct from the zoological, that was not a question of value.

In our domain, in the field of visual representation, those philologers known as 'classical archaeologists' attempted to avoid this Polish anarchy, this *liberum veto,* by estimating a work of art according to the quantity of light it shed upon a text, a problem in ancient history, or on how much it served as an illustration to myth, fable, and history. A Winckelmann[6] came to judgement in the middle of the eighteenth century. From materials already collected and even

---

[6] Johann Winckelmann (1717–1768) was a German archaeologist and art critic who compiled a systematic study of ancient Greek and Roman art. (ED.)

then being excavated not only in and near Rome but in recently
rediscovered Herculaneum and Pompeii, Winckelmann tried to pick
out certain shapes, profiles, and proportions, and to standardize them
as canons of plastic beauty. We are all acquainted with his ideal
embodied in the 'Apollo Belvedere', the 'Laocoön', the Ludovisi 'Juno',
Goethe's favourite, etc.

In Winckelmann these standards had much that was artistic. But
for most archaeologists these shapes and patterns derived their authority rather from ancient writers, Pliny and Pausanias[7] chiefly. The
direct appeal of the object as an experience in art and taste was
ignored. For example, an Apollo at Munich used to be admired
because it was supposed to be a statue mentioned by Horace. When
this identification was disproved philologers and archaeologists lost
no time in deserting their former idol.

Happily, few writers to-day are such archaeologists, but their
authority and dictatorship used to influence us all. Just as the most
free and easy politician or journalist may talk Plato or Hegel without
having read a word of either, so the most frivolous, irresponsible art
critic may talk Winckelmann or Mengs, and remain as unaware of
what he is doing as Monsieur Jourdain was that he was speaking
prose.

With the triumph of the Romantic movement a certain tendency
appeared among the most advanced French painters to emancipate
themselves from the Winckelmannian and archaeological canons of
art, but it made no great headway, even in France. Feebler still was
the Pre-Raphaelite and Ruskinian[8] movement. After 1870 'Philologia',
goddess of victorious Germans, inspired and domineered over archaeology wherever classical studies were pursued.

How the revolt against this tyranny started and how quickly it
carried every position so long held by archaeologists, would make as
interesting reading as the story of the recent disappearance of Orthodoxy from Holy Russia. Somewhere between 1900 and 1910 the
classical archaeologist himself lost faith in his standards and systems.
He discovered that he was being overwhelmed by wave upon wave

---

[7] *Pliny the Elder* (A.D. c.23–79) was a Roman naturalist and author of the thirty-seven
volume *Natural History*. *Pausanias* (flourished A.D. 143–176) was a Greek geographer
and author of *Periegesis of Greece*. (ED.)

[8] The *Pre-Raphaelite* movement was established in 1848 by English painters and poets
who wanted to recapture the purity of medieval imagery by imitating the style of
Italian art prior to Raphael. *Ruskinian* thought, originating with John Ruskin (1819–
1900), a prominent English art critic, defended the Pre-Raphaelites. (ED.)

of art objects which could not be appraised by reference to Winckelmannian shapes and proportions. These objects were brought from
the Far East and the isles of the sea, from the hearts of inner and of
near Asia, from darkest Africa and Central America, from regions in
short, hitherto without a place in art studies, also from periods absent
in art books, the Aurignacian, the Capsian, the neolithic, the early
dynasties of Egypt, the Byzantine, the Latin Middle Ages, not to
speak of such revelations in the Greek world itself as the Minoan,
the Mycenean. Finally in the holy of holies of more recent classical
archaeology formerly restricted to the later fifth century, there came
the rediscovery and revaluation of archaic marbles from Delphi, from
the Acropolis, and from the Attic plain.

The archaeologist dared not deny, as in my youth he still used
to, that these were works of art, but he could not find a way to
subsume them under a common denominator. The only one he had
was that of Winckelmann, and that did not work. As we have seen,
his whole training had been in philology and not in art appreciation.
There was nothing left for him to do but to give appraisal and join
the merry rout for whom there were no standards, who ignored or
refused to recognize the existence of means for judging the work of
art. All was reduced to the same level. Everything was equally interesting intrinsically, or as a link in a chain of events. There were to
be no more invidious distinctions. A bronze mass product—say,
buckles from Minnusinsk—was put on a level both historically and
aesthetically with the Theseus of the Parthenon, and scrawls at Dura-
Europos with the frescoes at the Villa dei Misteri or the Casa di
Menandro at Pompeii. And as the archaeologist, although he deserted
his own ship, still enjoys, or until the other day did enjoy, the
authority of a pilot, his negation of value chimed in only too well
with the absence of standards among the financially and sartorially
higher but intellectually lower society, for whom the work of art is
never more than mere news, and trivial news at that. Thus I have
seen and heard solemn professors join fashionable museum directors
and those incarnations of conspicuous waste, smart society women,
in exalting the humble artifacts of Fuzzy-Wuzzyland.

The folk just referred to would be far from ridiculous if they
could feel and appreciate the positive qualities of these outlandish
products. For the up-to-daters I have in mind, these products have
a merely negative merit, the one of not being objects raved about
yesterday.

When Negro sculpture first came to Paris, some five and thirty
years ago, the dealer who launched it hoped to win us over by saying

that no Greek masterpiece could hold up its head against it, and that it was in the round. This cry, that Negro sculpture was in the round, you heard for a season at all the Paris dealers, and collectors, and in all Paris social gatherings, and the next season everywhere in New York, and finally after a decent interval you read in luscious language in London dailies, weeklies, and monthlies, and heard at all London luncheon parties and tea-tables: 'The great thing about Negro sculpture is that it is in the round.' It occurred to nobody to ask the pioneer dealers and their disciples, the London critics and dilettanti: 'What of it? What if they are in the round?' And what has their roundness to do with their being great works of art? Are not gasometers in the round, and the enormous pipes that disfigure lovely subalpine valleys? 'Ah, but they are cylindrical,' and no epithet could be more decisive, more majestically final.

These writers and amateurs would have been hard put to it to furnish a satisfactory answer, and so would the critics who ask us to admire a piece of sculpture because it is well carved, highly polished, or on the contrary far from finished; or a painting because it is minutely drawn, or, the exact opposite, freely dashed in, daintily or boldly painted, because it is all cylinders, all pyramids, or all diagonals. What of that? What concern is it of mine? I am neither painter nor sculptor, and to one who is not a craftsman, displays of skill in the visual arts are nothing like so exciting as similar displays in the circus, the boxing match, the cock-fight, or the bull-ring. As for cylinders, cubes, and diagonals, what are they that I should be impressed and bow down and worship them? Are they perchance ultimates? If they are, prove that they are, and I too will adore them.

A relative indifference to value may be tolerated in ordinary history. Its past events have been sifted by time, and if remembered it is for the interest they still can claim. They have ceased to be distinguishable as the energies they were in their time, and if in any measure operative, still it is only as merged in the ocean stream which is propelling us forward.

But works of art in general, and visual ones in particular, are still with us. Not only are they still with us, but they count as the only primary documents for art history. In that field written documents are ancillary and have no meaning except in connection with surviving works of art.

Nothing that survives, that is still alive, can be treated impassively. Willynilly, it affects us. One has to be either insensible, unconscious, or both to assume objectivity toward works of art. We cannot help being attracted or repelled by them, feeling them as forces to befriend or to avoid as with other living creatures. Whatever has life, and as long as it retains life, has a capacity for doing good or doing harm that we cannot and do not ignore.

Objects made by the hand of man are of two classes. Those that are without life, like most products of primitive mankind, we call artifacts. On the other hand, visual objects that are alive are works of art. An artifact is anything in any material done by human hands. A pot, a pan, a shovel, a spoon, a knife is seldom nowadays more than an artifact although it always could be, and in the past has been, a work of art as well. So a grocer's bill is not literature, nor, although on a higher plane, is the best expository prose *Dichtung*. A steam whistle is an auditory artifact, a bugle call is already music.

The chief reason for indifference to value has been that students, when historians, are busy exploring the archives for documents and as classical archaeologists intent on discovering what could throw light on antiquity. There would be no harm done if we, being human, were not apt to fall in love with the products of our activities and credit them with values, intellectual, spiritual, and artistic, which seldom pass current outside our private universe. The expert palaeographer and hunter of archives gets no training in the appreciation of quality, or in understanding what in a given style is creative and pioneering and what is imitative, stagnant, or even retrograde. In other words the palaeographer will not be able to judge whether to place the work of art in question at the beginning or at the end of style. Furthermore archaeological interest threatens to wipe out the distinction between fine arts and industrial arts, between monumental and minor arts, between art objects and objects of curiosity.

By now archives have been ransacked and archaeological fields the world over ploughed and excavated. It is improbable that, within the range of our interests, discoveries are still awaiting us as mind-opening as those made in the last two hundred years. We need no longer seize upon an unpublished piece of script and show it off in triumph as even a real historian like the late Bishop Creighton did, at the end of his illuminating volumes on the Papacy during the humanistic period; or as some colleagues of mine will write up elaborately a rubber-stamped Bernardo Daddi or Andrea del Brescianino.[9] There is no further reason for neglecting values in order that explorations may at all costs be encouraged. We can now afford to

---

[9] *Bernardo Daddi* (fl. 1312–48) and *Andrea del Brescianino* (fl. 1505–1525) were Italian Renaissance painters. (ED.)

appraise objects and artifacts according to their significance, first as
to the degree that they enable us to reconstruct the past in general;
then to reconstruct the history of a given art; and finally to select
and interpret the history of the past which can still vitalize and
humanize us.

The past that history is called upon to reconstruct is not the past
of the Andaman Islanders, of the Lolos, or of the Redskins, nor even
of such highly civilized people as the Chinese and their cultural
dependents, Annamese, Japanese, Siamese, and Koreans. The past
that concerns us Mediterranean-Atlantic folk, no matter what continent we now inhabit, the past that is history for us is the succession
of events—fears, passions, illusions, and hopes—that have made us
what we think we now are. In a sense there are as many histories to
be written as there are individuals; and every tribe, every association,
every church, will have its own private history. In other words history
is the biography of a community, large or small, as wide-flung as the
white race, as limited as the parish pump. It follows that past events
concern us in the measure that they contribute to our sense of the
past, as at the present moment we want to define it.

In ordinary human history, including the biographies of artists,
values whether political or ethical are connected with formative
events and creative personalities celebrated by Plutarch in antiquity,
by the lives of worthies in the Middle Ages, and in many books
nearer our own day. In art history, on the other hand, value is derived
from qualities which presently will be discussed at some length. In
one overwhelmingly important respect it differs from other types of
history: its events—that is to say, its masterpieces—are to some
extent still with us and not merely known to us by hearsay as is the
case with kings, conquerors, statesmen, preachers, founders in general, fiddlers, singers, play-actors, in short spellbinders of every kind.
Works of art speak to us, appeal to us, act on us as living entities.

All the arts enjoy this advantage, but none so much as the visual
arts. How much easier it is to learn the language of the Aeginetan
marbles, the Acropolis Korae, or the Olympian pediments, not to
speak of more modern-seeming sculptures like those of Paeonius,
Lysippus, Praxiteles, and later Hellenistic sculptors, than it is to
enjoy, in the original Greek, the odes of Pindar, the tragedies of
Aeschylus, Sophocles, and Euripides, or the idylls of Theocritus. You
can read them in translation, but even the best version in another
language gives but a faint sense of their real quality, whereas a Greek
statue can be so well copied that, as in the case of Hermes of

Praxiteles, it remains doubtful whether it is or is not that fascinating
sculptor's own handiwork.

MARYA MANNES

How Do You Know It's Good?

Marya Mannes (1904–   ) is a New York City-born journalist, editor, and social critic. Mannes has been an editor and cultural
writer for such publications as *Vogue, Mademoiselle,* and the *New
York Times.* In her 1964 book *But Will It Sell?* the author criticized
pop art, commercial television, and American society's obsession
with violence. Her novel *They* (1968) deals with the alienation of
elderly people devalued by a youth-oriented culture. In 1974, she
published the controversial *Last Rights,* which argued for euthana-
sia. The following selection first appeared in *Glamour* magazine in
1962.

Suppose there were no critics to tell us how to react to a picture, a
play, or a new composition of music. Suppose we wandered innocent
as the dawn into an art exhibition of unsigned paintings. By what
standards, by what values would we decide whether they were good
or bad, talented or untalented, successes or failures? How can we
ever know that what we think is right?

For the last fifteen or twenty years the fashion in criticism or
appreciation of the arts has been to deny the existence of any valid
criteria and to make the words "good" or "bad" irrelevant, immaterial,
and inapplicable. There is no such thing, we are told, as a set of
standards, first acquired through experience and knowledge and later
imposed on the subject under discussion. This has been a popular
approach, for it relieves the critic of the responsibility of judgment
and the public of the necessity of knowledge. It pleases those re-
sentful of disciplines, it flatters the empty-minded by calling them
open-minded, it comforts the confused. Under the banner of democracy and the kind of equality which our forefathers did *not* mean, it
says, in effect, "Who are you to tell us what *is* good or bad?" This
is the same cry used so long and so effectively by the producers of

mass media who insist that it is the public, not they, who decides what it wants to hear and see, and that for a critic to say that *this* program is bad and *this* program is good is purely a reflection of personal taste. Nobody recently has expressed this philosophy more succinctly than Dr. Frank Stanton, the highly intelligent president of CBS television. At a hearing before the Federal Communications Commission, this phrase escaped him under questioning: "One man's mediocrity is another man's good program."

There is no better way of saying "No values are absolute." There is another important aspect to this philosophy of *laissez faire:* It is the fear, in all observers of all forms of art, of guessing wrong. This fear is well come by, for who has not heard of the contemporary outcries against artists who later were called great? Every age has its arbiters who do not grow with their times, who cannot tell evolution from revolution or the difference between frivolous faddism, amateurish experimentation, and profound and necessary change. Who wants to be caught *flagrante delicto*[1] with an error of judgment as serious as this? It is far safer, and certainly easier, to look at a picture or a play or a poem and to say "This is hard to understand, but it may be good," or simply to welcome it as a new form. The word "new"—in our country especially—has magical connotations. What is new must be good; what is old is probably bad. And if a critic can describe the new in language that nobody can understand, he's safer still. If he has mastered the art of saying nothing with exquisite complexity, nobody can quote him later as saying anything.

But all these, I maintain, are forms of abdication from the responsibility of judgment. In creating, the artist commits himself; in appreciating, you have a commitment of your own. For after all, it is the audience which makes the arts. A climate of appreciation is essential to its flowering, and the higher the expectations of the public, the better the performance of the artist. Conversely, only a public ill-served by its critics could have accepted as art and as literature so much in these last years that has been neither. If anything goes, everything goes; and at the bottom of the junkpile lie the discarded standards too.

But what are these standards? How do you get them? How do you know they're the right ones? How can you make a clear pattern

[1] in the act of committing an offense (ED.)

out of so many intangibles, including that greatest one, the very private I?

Well for one thing, it's fairly obvious that the more you read and see and hear, the more equipped you'll be to practice that art of association which is at the basis of all understanding and judgment. The more you live and the more you look, the more aware you are of a consistent pattern—as universal as the stars, and the tides, as breathing, as night and day—underlying everything. I would call this pattern and this rhythm an order. Not order—*an* order. Within it exists an incredible diversity of forms. Without it lies chaos—the wild cells of destruction—sickness. It is in the end up to you to distinguish between the diversity that is health and the chaos that is sickness, and you can't do this without a process of association that can link a bar of Mozart with the corner of a Vermeer painting, or a Stravinsky score with a Picasso abstraction; or that can relate an aggressive act with a Franz Kline painting and a fit of coughing with a John Cage composition.

There is no accident in the fact that certain expressions of art live for all time and that others die with the moment, and although you may not always define the reasons, you can ask the questions. What does an artist say that is timeless; how does he say it? How much is fashion, how much is merely reflection? Why is Sir Walter Scott so hard to read now, and Jane Austen not? Why is baroque right for one age and too effulgent for another?

Can a standard of craftsmanship apply to art of all ages, or does each have its own, and different, definitions? You may have been aware, inadvertently, that craftsmanship has become a dirty word these years because, again, it implies standards—something done well or done badly. The result of this convenient avoidance is a plentitude of actors who can't project their voices, singers who can't phrase their songs, poets who can't communicate emotion, and writers who have no vocabulary—not to speak of painters who can't draw. The dogma now is that craftsmanship gets in the way of expression. You can do better if you don't know *how* you do it, let alone *what* you're doing.

I think it is time you helped reverse this trend by trying to rediscover craft: the command of the chosen instrument, whether it is a brush, a word, or a voice. When you begin to detect the difference between freedom and sloppiness, between serious experimentation and egotherapy, between skill and slickness, between strength and violence, you are on your way to separating the sheep from the goats, a form of segregation denied us for quite a while. All you need to restore it is a small bundle of standards and a Geiger counter that detects fraud, and we might begin our tour of the arts in an area where both are urgently needed: contemporary painting.

I don't know what's worse: to have to look at acres of bad art to find the little good, or to read what the critics say about it all. In no other field of expression has so much double-talk flourished, so much confusion prevailed, and so much nonsense been circulated: further evidence of the close interdependence between the arts and the critical climate they inhabit. It will be my pleasure to share with you some of this double-talk so typical of our times.

Item one: preface for a catalogue of an abstract painter:

"Time-bound meditation experiencing a life; sincere with plastic piety at the threshold of hallowed arcana; a striving for pure ideation giving shape to inner drive; formalized patterns where neural balances reach a fiction." End of quote. Know what this artist paints like now?

Item two: a review in the *Art News:*

". . . a weird and disparate assortment of material, but the monstrosity which bloomed into his most recent cancer of aggregations is present in some form everywhere. . . ." Then, later, "A gluttony of things and processes terminated by a glorious constipation."

Item three, same magazine, review of an artist who welds automobile fragments into abstract shapes:

"Each fragment . . . is made an extreme of human exasperation, torn at and fought all the way, and has its rightness of form as if by accident. *Any technique that requires order or discipline would just be the human ego.* No, these must be egoless, uncontrolled, undesigned and different enough to give you a bang—fifty miles an hour around a telephone pole. . . ."

"Any technique that requires order or discipline would just be the human ego." What does he mean—"just be"? What are they really talking about? Is this journalism? Is it criticism? Or is it that other convenient abdication from standards of performance and judgment practiced by so many artists and critics that they, like certain writers who deal only in sickness and depravity, "reflect the chaos about them"? Again, whose chaos? Whose depravity?

I had always thought that the prime function of art was to create order *out* of chaos—again, not the order of neatness or rigidity or convention or artifice, but the order of clarity by which one will and one vision could draw the essential truth out of apparent confusion. I still do. It is not enough to use parts of a car to convey the brutality

of the machine. This is as slavishly representative, and just as easy,
as arranging dried flowers under glass to convey nature.

Speaking of which, i.e., the use of the real materials (burlap, old
gloves, bottletops) in lieu of pigment, this is what one critic had to
say about an exhibition of Assemblage[2] at the Museum of Modern
Art last year.

> Spotted throughout the show are indisputable works of art, accounting
> for a quarter or even a half of the total display. But the remainder are
> works of non-art, anti-art, and art substitutes that are the aesthetic
> counterparts of the social deficiencies that land people in the clink on
> charges of vagrancy. These aesthetic bankrupts . . . have no legitimate
> ideological roof over their heads and not the price of a square intellectual
> meal, much less a spiritual sandwich, in their pockets.

I quote these words of John Canaday of *The New York Times* as
an example of the kind of criticism which puts responsibility to an
intelligent public above popularity with an intellectual coterie. Canaday has the courage to say what he thinks and the capacity to say
it clearly: two qualities notably absent from his profession.

Next to art, I would say that appreciation and evaluation in the
field of music is the most difficult. For it is rarely possible to judge
a new composition at one hearing only. What seems confusing or
fragmented at first might well become clear and organic a third time.
Or it might not. The only salvation here for the listener is, again, an
instinct born of experience and association which allows him to
separate intent from accident, design from experimentation, and pretense from conviction. Much of contemporary music is, like its sister
art, merely a reflection of the composer's own fragmentation: an
absorption in self and symbols at the expense of communication with
others. The artist, in short, says to the public: If you don't understand
this, it's because you're dumb. I maintain that you are not. You may
have to go part way or even halfway to meet the artist, but if you
must go the whole way, it's his fault, not yours. Hold fast to that.
And remember it too when you read new poetry, that estranged sister
of music.

> A multitude of causes, unknown to former times, are now acting with a
> combined force to blunt the discriminating powers of the mind, and,
> unfitting it for all voluntary exertion, to reduce it to a state of almost

---

[2] an artistic technique in which bits of material and other objects are pasted together
replacing the traditional canvas (ED.)

savage torpor. The most effective of these causes are the great national events which are daily taking place and the increasing accumulation of men in cities, where the uniformity of their occupations produces a craving for extraordinary incident, which the rapid communication of intelligence hourly gratifies. To this tendency of life and manners, the literature and theatrical exhibitions of the country have conformed themselves.

This startlingly applicable comment was written in the year 1800 by William Wordsworth in the preface to his "Lyrical Ballads"; and it has been cited by Edwin Muir in his recently published book "The Estate of Poetry." Muir states that poetry's effective range and influence have diminished alarmingly in the modern world. He believes in the inherent and indestructible qualities of the human mind and the great and permanent objects that act upon it, and suggests that the audience will increase when "poetry loses what obscurity is left in it by attempting greater themes, for great themes have to be stated clearly." If you keep that firmly in mind and resist, in Muir's words, "the vast dissemination of secondary objects that isolate us from the natural world," you have gone a long way toward equipping yourself for the examination of any work of art.

When you come to theatre, in this extremely hasty tour of the arts, you can approach it on two different levels. You can bring to it anticipation and innocence, giving yourself up, as it were, to the life on the stage and reacting to it emotionally, if the play is good, or listlessly, if the play is boring; a part of the audience organism that expresses its favor by silence or laughter and its disfavor by coughing and rustling. Or you can bring to it certain critical faculties that may heighten, rather than diminish, your enjoyment.

You can ask yourselves whether the actors are truly in their parts or merely projecting themselves; whether the scenery helps or hurts the mood; whether the playwright is honest with himself, his characters, and you. Somewhere along the line you can learn to distinguish between the true creative act and the false arbitrary gesture; between fresh observation and stale cliché; between the avant-garde play that is pretentious drivel and the avant-garde play that finds new ways to say old truths.

Purpose and craftsmanship—end and means—these are the keys to your judgment in all the arts. What is this painter trying to say when he slashes a broad band of black across a white canvas and lets the edges dribble down? Is it a statement of violence? Is it a self-portrait? If it is *one* of these, has he made you believe it? Or is this a gesture of the ego or a form of therapy? If it shocks you, what does it shock you into?

And what of this tight little painting of bright flowers in a vase? Is the painter saying anything new about flowers? Is it different from a million other canvases of flowers? Has it any life, any meaning, beyond this statement? Is there any pleasure in its forms or texture? The question is not whether a thing is abstract or representational, whether it is "modern" or conventional. The question, inexorably, is whether it is good. And this is a decision which only you, on the basis of instinct, experience, and association, can make for yourself. It takes independence and courage. It involves, moreover, the risk of wrong decision and the humility, after the passage of time, of recognizing it as such. As we grow and change and learn, our attitudes can change too, and what we once thought obscure or "difficult" can later emerge as coherent and illuminating. Entrenched prejudices, obdurate opinions are as sterile as no opinions at all.

Yet standards there are, timeless as the universe itself. And when you have committed yourself to them, you have acquired a passport to that elusive but immutable realm of truth. Keep it with you in the forests of bewilderment. And never be afraid to speak up.

ARTHUR KOESTLER

Cultural Snobbery

Arthur Koestler (1905–1983) was a Hungarian-born British novelist, essayist, and reporter. A member of the Communist party until 1938, he became disillusioned during the Moscow "purge" trials. Koestler's best known novel, *Darkness at Noon* (1940), is a fictionalized account of those trials. He was captured as a spy at the beginning of World War II, an experience that inspired his 1941 novel, *Scum of the Earth*. His later books include *The Act of Creation* (1964), *The Ghost in the Machine* (1967), and *Janus: A Summing Up* (1978), about his own life. Koestler, who had leukemia and Parkinson's Disease, committed suicide in 1983.

A friend of mine, whom I shall call Brenda, was given for her birthday by one of her admirers a Picasso line drawing in a simple modern frame. It was an admirable and typical sample of Picasso's "classical" period: a Greek youth carrying a girl in his arms, the contours of the two figures somehow mixed up and partly indistinguishable like those of Siamese twins with shared limbs, yet adding up to a charming and harmonious total effect. It looked like a lithograph, but it bore no serial number, so Brenda took it to be a reproduction and hung it, somewhat disappointed with the gift, over her staircase. On my next visit, several weeks later, it was hanging over her drawing room mantelpiece. "I see the Picasso reproduction has been promoted," I said. "*Reproduction!*" she cried indignantly. "It turned out it's an *original!* Isn't it lovely? Look at that line along the girl's hip. . . ." etc.

As a matter of fact, it *was* an original—a shyly understated gift of the mumbling and devoted admirer. But as it was a line drawing consisting of nothing but black contour on white paper, it needed an expert, or at least a good magnifying lens, to decide whether it was an original, a lithograph, or a reproduction. Neither Brenda nor any of her visitors could tell the difference. But they took it for granted, as we all do, that an original deserves a proud display, whereas a reproduction belongs, at best, over the staircase.

I shall now try to analyze, in a pedantic way, the reason for this apparently so natural attitude. The original is of course many times more expensive than a reproduction; but we would indignantly reject the idea of displaying a picture simply because it is expensive; we pretend to be guided in these matters by purely aesthetic considerations. Next, one might surmise that our contempt for reproductions originates in the poor quality and even poorer choice of subjects of the Victorian print. But modern printing techniques have achieved miracles, and some Ganymede[1] reproductions are almost indistinguishable from the original. In the extreme case of the line drawing, we have complete aesthetic equivalence between original and reproduction.

And yet there is something revolting in this equivalence. It even takes a certain courage to admit to oneself that the aesthetic effect of a copy might be indistinguishable from that of the original. We live in an age of stereotyped mass production; and after mass-produced furniture, mass-produced and pre-fabricated houses, the idea of mass-produced Piero della Francescas[2] is indeed revolting. But then, we have no similar objection to mass-produced gramophone records. Nor to mass-produced books, and yet they too fall into the

---

[1] in Greek mythology, a beautiful boy who is abducted by Zeus (ED.)

[2] Piero della Francesca (c. 1420–1492) was an Italian Renaissance painter. (ED.)

category of "reproductions." Why then do you prefer, according to your income, a more or less second-rate original picture on the wall to a first-rate reproduction of a masterpiece? Would you rather read a mediocre young poet in manuscript than Shakespeare in a paper-cover edition?

Our argument seems to have become bogged down. Let us find out what Brenda herself has to say to explain her behavior, in a dialogue with the writer:

BRENDA: "I simply can't understand what all this fuss and talk is about. But *of course* my attitude to the drawing has changed since I know that Picasso himself did it. That's nothing to do with snobbery—it's just that I wasn't told before."

K: "Your attitude has changed—but has that thing on the wall changed?"

B: "Of course it hasn't, but now I *see* it differently!"

K: "I would like to understand what it is that determines your attitude to a picture in general."

B: "Its quality, of course."

K: "And what determines its quality?"

B: "Oh, don't be such a pedant. Color, composition, balance, harmony, power, what have you."

K: "So, in looking at a picture, you are guided by purely aesthetic value judgments, depending on the qualities you mentioned?"

B: "Of course I am."

K: "Now, as that picture hasn't changed, and its qualities haven't changed, how can your attitude have changed?"

B: "But I have told you before, you idiot. Of course my attitude to it is now different, since I know it isn't one reproduction in a million, but done by Picasso himself. Can't you see?"

K: "No, I can't; you are contradicting yourself. The rarity of the object, and your knowledge of the manner in which it came into being, do not alter the qualities of that object, and accordingly should not alter your judgment of it, if it were really based on purely aesthetic criteria—as you believe it to be. But it isn't. Your judgment is not based on what you *see,* but on a purely accidental bit of information, which might be right or wrong and is entirely extraneous to the issue."

B: "Wrong? How *dare* you insinuate that my Picasso isn't an original? And how *dare* you say that the question whether he drew it himself is 'extraneous' to the issue?"

And so it will go on indefinitely. Yet Brenda is not stupid; she is merely confused in believing that her attitude to an object of art is determined by purely aesthetic considerations, whereas in fact it is decisively influenced by factors of a quite different order. She is unable to see her picture isolated from the context of her knowledge of its origin. For, in our minds, the question of origin, authorship, or authenticity, *though in itself extraneous to aesthetic value,* is so intimately and indistinguishably fused with our attitude to the object that we find it well-nigh impossible to isolate the two. Thus, Brenda unconsciously projects one scale of values onto a system of quite different values.

Is Brenda, then, a snob? It depends on the definition of snobbery at which we hope to arrive at the end. But as a working hypothesis, I would like to suggest that this process of unconsciously applying to any given field a judgment derived from an alien system of values constitutes the essence of the phenomenon of snobbery. By these standards Brenda would *not* be a snob if she had said: "The reproduction in this case is just as beautiful as the original. But one gives me a greater thrill than the other for reasons which have nothing to do with beauty." She is an unconscious snob because she is unable to distinguish between the two elements of her experience, unable to name the extraneous cause of her biased aesthetic judgment, or to see that it is biased.

I am aware of pedantically laboring an apparently obvious point. But it will become at once less obvious if we turn to a different yet related problem.

In 1948, a German art restorer named Dietrich Fey, engaged in reconstruction work on Lübeck's[3] ancient St. Marien Church, stated that his workmen had discovered traces of old Gothic wall paintings dating back to the thirteenth century, under a coating of chalk on the church walls. The restoration of the paintings was entrusted to Fey's assistant, Lothar Malskat, who finished the job two years later. In 1950, Chancellor Adenauer presided over the ceremonies marking

[3] a city in northwest Germany whose medieval Gothic architecture was restored after World War II (ED.)

the completion of the restoration work in the presence of art experts from all parts of Europe. Their unanimous opinion, voiced by Chancellor Adenauer, was that the twenty-one thirteenth-century Gothic saints on the church walls were "a valuable treasure and a fabulous discovery of lost masterpieces."

None of the experts on that or any later occasion expressed doubt as to the authenticity of the frescoes. It was Herr Malskat himself who, two years later, disclosed the fraud. He presented himself on his own initiative at Lübeck police headquarters, where he stated that the frescoes were entirely his own work, undertaken by order from his boss, Herr Fey, and asked to be tried for forgery. The leading German art experts, however, stuck to their opinion: the frescoes, they said, were no doubt genuine, and Herr Malskat was merely seeking cheap publicity. An official Board of Investigation was appointed which came to the conclusion that the restoration of the wall paintings was a hoax—but only after Herr Malskat had confessed that he had also manufactured hundreds of Rembrandts, Watteaus, Toulouse-Lautrecs, Picassos, Henri Rousseaus, Corots, Chagalls, Vlamincks, and other masters and sold them as originals—some of which were actually found by the police in Herr Fey's house. Without this evidence, it is doubtful whether the German experts would ever have admitted having been fooled.

My point is not the fallibility of the experts. Herr Malskat's exploit is merely the most recent of a number of similarly successful hoaxes and forgeries—of which the most fabulous were probably van Megeeren's false Vermeers. The disturbing question which they raise is whether the Lübeck saints are less beautiful, and have ceased to be "a valuable treasure of masterpieces," simply because they had been painted by Herr Malskat and not by somebody else?

There are several answers to this line of argument, but before going into them I want to continue in the part of *advocatus diaboli*[4] by considering an example of a forgery in a different field: Macpherson's *Ossian*. The case is so notorious that the facts need only be briefly mentioned. James Macpherson (1736–96), a Scottish poet and adventurer, alleged that in the course of his wanderings, in the Highlands he had discovered some ancient Gaelic manuscripts. Enthusiastic Scottish littérateurs put up a subscription to enable Macpherson to pursue his researches, and in 1761 he published *Fingal*,

[4] devil's advocate (ED.)

an Ancient Epic Poem in Six Books, together with Several Other Poems composed by Ossian, the Son of Fingal. Ossian is the legendary third-century hero and bard of Celtic literature. *Fingal* was soon followed by the publication of a still larger Ossianic epic called *Temora,* and this by a collected edition, *The Works of Ossian.* The authenticity of Macpherson's text was at once questioned in England, particularly by Dr. Johnson[5] (whom Macpherson answered by sending him a challenge to a duel), and to his death Macpherson refused, under various unconvincing pretexts, to publish his alleged Gaelic originals. By the turn of the century the controversy was settled and it was established that, while Macpherson had used fragments of ancient Celtic lore, most of the "Ossianic" texts were of his own making.

Yet here again the question arises whether the poetic quality of the work itself is altered by the fact that it was written not by Ossian, the son of Fingal, but by James Macpherson? The "Ossianic" texts were translated into many languages, and had a considerable influence on the literature and cultural climate of Europe at the late eighteenth and early nineteenth centuries. This is how the *Encyclopedia Britannica* sums up its evaluation of Macpherson:

> The varied sources of his work and its worthlessness as a transcript of actual Celtic poems do not alter the fact that he produced a work of art which . . . did more than any single work to bring about the romantic movement in European, and especially in German, literature. . . . Herder and Goethe . . . were among its profound admirers.

These examples could be continued indefinitely. Antique furniture, Roman statuary, Greek tanagra figures, and Italian madonnas are being forged, copied, counterfeited all the time, and the value we set on them is not determined by aesthetic appreciation and pleasure to the eye, but by the precarious and often uncertain judgment of experts. A mediocre but authenticated picture by a known master is held in a higher esteem than an artistically superior work of his unknown pupil or "school"—not only by art dealers guided by "investment," but by all of us, including this writer. Are we, then, all snobs to whom a signature, an expert testimonial, or the postmark of a given period is more important than the intrinsic beauty of the object itself?

---

[5] Samuel Johnson (1709–1784) was a leading English writer, scholar, and critic. His works include the *Dictionary of the English Language* (1755), *Lives of the Poets* (1779–81), and an edition of Shakespeare's plays. (ED.)

I now propose to present the case for the defense. It can be summed up in a single sentence: our appraisal of any work of literature or art is never a unitary act, but the result of two independent and simultaneous processes which tend to distort each other.

When we look at an Egyptian fresco, we do not enjoy the painting at its face value, but by means of an unconscious reattunement of the mind to the values of the period. We know, for instance, that the Egyptians had not discovered the technique of perspective in depth. We know that on certain Egyptian murals the size of the figures is determined by their relative social rank. Similarly, we look at every picture through a double frame: the solid frame which isolates it from its surroundings and creates for it a hole in space, as it were; and the unconscious frame of reference in our minds which creates for it a hole in time and locates it in its period and cultural climate. Every time we think that we are making a purely aesthetic judgment based on pure sensory perception, we are in fact judging relative to this second frame or context or mental field.

Any work of art, or literature, or music, can only be appreciated against the background of its period, and that is what we unconsciously do: when we naïvely believe that we are applying absolute criteria, we are in fact applying relative ones. When we contemplate the false Vermeer the first time believing it to be authentic and the second time knowing that it is a fake, our aesthetic experience will indeed completely change, though the picture has remained the same. For it is now seen in a different frame of reference and therefore, in fact, differently. The same considerations apply to the perpetrator of the fake. He may be able to imitate the technique of the seventeenth-century Dutch School, but he could not spontaneously start painting like Vermeer—because his visual organization is different, his perception of reality is different, and because he cannot, except by an artificial effort, erase from his mind the accumulated experience of everything that happened in painting since Vermeer. And if, by a tour de force, a contemporary artist succeeded in reconditioning his own vision to that of the Dutch seventeenth century or the Italian *quattrocento,* he would have to use mass hypnosis to recondition the vision of his customers in a similar manner.

We can add to our knowledge and experience, but we cannot subtract from it. When Picasso decides to disregard the laws of perspective, that means that he has passed through and beyond a certain technique—unlike the Egyptian painter, who has never acquired it. Evolution is an irreversible process; the culture of a period might apparently point into the same direction as an earlier one, but it does so from a different turn of the spiral. A modern primitive is different from a primitive primitive; contemporary classicism is different from any classical classicism; only the mentally insane are able to amputate part of their past.

And yet when we contemplate works of the past, we must perform just such a process of mental subtraction, by attuning our minds to the climate and experience of the period. In order to appreciate them, we must enter into their spirit, by forgetting our modern experience and all that we have learnt since that Homeric epic of Byzantine mosaic was created. We must descend into the past, making our mind a blank; and as we do so, we unconsciously condescend. We close our eyes to crudities of technique, naïveties of perception, prevailing superstitions, limitations of knowledge, factual errors. We make allowances. A little honest introspection will always reveal the element of condescension contained in our admiration for the classics; and part of our enjoyment when listening to the voices of the past is derived from this half-consciously patronizing attitude—"how clever of them to know that at their age." We feel that we have descended a turn of the spiral; we are looking up in awe and wonder at Dante's dreadful Paradise, but at the same time we seem to be bending down, with a tender antiquarian stoop.

This legitimate kind of aesthetic double-think degenerates into snobbery at the point where the frame of reference becomes more important than the picture, when the thrill derived from the gesture of bending over the past dominates the aesthetic experience. The result is a widespread confusion of critical judgment—overestimation of the dead and belittlement of the living, indiscriminate reverence for anything that is "classical," "antique," "primitive," or simply old. In its extreme form this tendency prompts people to have their wall brackets and picture frames artifically dirtied to lend them the patina of age; so let us call it the "patina snobbery."

The process that leads to these distortions of judgment is basically the same as outlined before: the projection of one scale of values to a psychologically related but objectively alien field of experience. The essence of snobbery is to assess value according to a wrong type of scale; the snob is always trying to measure beauty with a thermometer or weight with a clock.

The thirteen-year-old daughter of a friend was recently taken to the Greenwich Museum. When she was asked which was the most beautiful thing she had seen in the Museum, she said unhesitatingly: "Nelson's shirt." When asked what was so beautiful about it, she

explained: "That shirt with the blood on it was jolly nice. Fancy real blood on a real shirt, which belonged to somebody really historic!"

The child's thrill is obviously derived from the same source as the magic that emanates from Napoleon's inkpot, the lock of hair on the Egyptian mummy's head, the relic of the saint carried in annual procession, the strand of the rope by which a famous murderer was hanged, and from Tolstoi's laundry bill. In the mentality of the primitive, an object which had been in contact with a person is not merely a souvenir: it becomes magically imbued with the substance of that personality and in turn magically emanates something of that substance.

"There is, I am sure, for most of us, a special pleasure in sinking your teeth into a peach produced on the estate of an earl who is related to the Royal Family," a London columnist wrote recently in the *Daily Express.*

Primitive magic survives in the subconscious; the strand of hair carried in the locket, grandmother's wedding dress, the faded fan of the first ball, the regimental badge, all have a half-conscious fetish character. The bobby-soxers who tear shreds off the crooner's garb are the vulgarized twentieth-century version of the worshipers cherishing a splinter from a saint's bone. The value that we set on original manuscripts, on "signed" pieces of furniture, on Dickens' quill and Kepler's telescope, are more dignified manifestations of the same unconscious tendency. It is, as the child said, "jolly nice" to behold a fragment of a marble by Praxiteles—even if it is battered out of human shape, with a leper's nose and broken ears. The contact with the master's hand has imbued it with a magic quality which has lingered on and radiates at us, conveying the same thrill as "the real blood on Nelson's real shirt."

The change in our attitude—and in the art dealer's price—when it is learned that a cracked and blackened piece of canvas is an "authenticated" work by X has nothing to do with beauty, aesthetics, or what have you—it is the working of sympathetic magic in us. (See Brenda and her Picasso drawing.) The inordinate importance that we attribute to the original, the authenticated, in those borderline cases where only the expert could tell the difference, is a derivative from the primitive fetishism. And as every honest art dealer will admit, these borderline cases are so frequent as to be almost the rule. Moreover, it was a general practice in the past for the master to let his pupils assist in the execution of larger undertakings. It is not the eye that guides the average museum visitor, but the magic of names and the magic of age. The bedevilment of aesthetic experience by

unconscious fetish worship and patina snobbery is so general that it
has become a major factor in our attitude to the art of past epochs—
an attitude as remote from spontaneous appreciation as the "Emper-
or's Clothes" fallacy regarding hyper-modern art forms.

HELEN LOUISE GARDNER

Art in Everyday Life

Helen Louise Gardner (1908–   ) is a British scholar and literary
critic. Her works include *The Art of T.S. Eliot* (1949), *The Business
of Criticism* (1959), *The Divine Poems of John Donne* (1978), and
interpretations of Milton's *Paradise Lost* and Shakespeare's *Othello*
and *King Lear*. She is also the editor of *The New Oxford Book of
English Verse 1250–1950* (1987).

We are all potential artists—almost all of us. There are but a few
who seem entirely wanting in capacity for understanding or creating;
many have considerable ability; a few become great artists. It is a
matter of degree. Art and the way of art exist for most of us—not
only exist but permeate all life, today as well as yesterday. Today life
is most complex and its activities and contacts, however much they
differ in number and breadth with the individual, are varied and
pressing. With this immediate present we are concerned primarily.

A current opinion, far too common, holds that art is a luxury, a
monopoly of wealth, a matter of museums, something to be indulged
in only in one's leisure, and quite inessential to and divorced from
one's daily activities. How far from the truth! It *is* true that to
understand a great painting one must look at it long and contempla-
tively; that to understand a sonata one must hear it, undistractedly,
many times. Few poems reveal all their beauty and meaning in one
reading. Real understanding requires concentration of eye or ear,
feelings, and intelligence. Granted, however, that great art is relatively
rare and requires contemplation and leisure for its true appreciation,
still art and a way of art permeate the world in which we live.

But what, you ask, has a *Skyscraper* or a *Navajo Blanket* or
Leonardo's *The Last Supper* to do with my everyday life, my humdrum
seven days a week? To be sure, our study of some of the arts has

been restricted to the work of great masters, often of foreign lands, and far-away ages. But in them all, as we begin "to see what we know how to look for," we begin to discern certain qualities and characteristics so constantly recurrent that we conclude that they are the result of some fundamental, universal principles. What words have we used constantly in our discussion, whether it be of buildings or statues or paintings, of books or textiles or pottery? *Unity, variety, harmony, rhythm, balance, contrast, proportion, emphasis.* What words do we use in discussing music, the dance, literature? Are they not the same? Are there not, then, some guides to point out the way to art in everyday life?

Let us be specific. The way we look at things may or may not be an art. Recalling our discussion in the first chapter of seeing as the artist sees, consider the view framed by your own window—a yard, a street, a lake bordered by woods, a group of roofs. Can you apply to it the words we have just mentioned? Is it lacking in contrasting lines and masses, or colors? Would you shift the position of some objects, imaginatively, or by shifting your own position can you obtain a better balance? Everything in the view has a form.[1] When we look at these forms as artists, we re-form them. Is this not what we have seen the artist doing in all his works that we have studied? We have found him nowhere imitating what he sees, but everywhere taking the forms that he sees as his raw material and out of them creating new forms that are more beautiful, more real and significant than the originals. Sometimes the new form is close to the original; sometimes far removed. To see everything as form or a group of forms and with imaginative insight to re-form these forms into something which has harmony, unity with variety, balance, rhythm—this is to see the world as an artist. Thus everything we see, from the small objects about our rooms to skyscrapers and mountains, we see, if we are artists, as forms and unities of forms which give us a far greater sense of their reality and significance than any exact copy of their appearance can give. To see significant aspects of commonplace

---

[1] Form is used not as a synonym for shape, but in a wider sense, including shape, proportions, contours, weight, material, texture, color—every element that enters into the composition of an object which can come to us through our senses. Everything has form; and this form is not unchangeable. Seen in the full sunshine, because of light, shadow, and color, it gives an illusion of depth; seen against the setting sun or in moonlight, it appears to flatten out into a silhouette; in varying lights its colors vary; at varying distances color, size, and other elements change.

things[2] is to transform what is mediocre, if not ugly, into something that is lovely and worth our while.

> She had a sensitivity that was very wide, eager and free . . . it lighted on small things and showed that perhaps they were not small after all. It brought buried things to light and made one wonder what need there had been to bury them.[3]

Do not the same principles hold in what we hear? In our music? As I sit writing on my porch someone on the road below is whistling a melody. He repeats it again and again. The monotony becomes irritating. Ah! He changes the key. This change brings in a pleasing variety. The whistler is the potential artist creating through the medium of tones a form for his melody. I listen for him to create a still more complex form, perhaps by the addition of another melody. In imagination I hear him interweave and contrast these two melodies (each a form) and unite them into a harmonious form which is the entire song. Just as the weaver of the *Navajo Blanket* selected two motifs, the step and the zigzag, which he varied and united into the harmonious form, which is the work of art. Thus the whistler and I are two potential artists working together: one an artist in under-standing because the ear can hear forms; the other an artist in creating because he can use forms. The eye too, to a limited extent, reinforces the ear in the comprehension of a musical form if one looks at the score.[4] The pattern which a simple folk melody makes on the printed page contrasts in appearance as well as in sound with that of a theme which consists of a group of melodies in much the same way in which the simple boldness of the *Navajo Blanket* contrasts with the complex richness of the royal *Persian Carpet.*

To see and to hear as an artist is a necessary foundation stone for doing things in an art way—creative activity. For this too most of us have some capacity, if it is not left latent. Let us consider a few of our daily activities. Can we be creative artists in their pursuance? Can we make out of them works of art? We might select four, almost

---

[2] See Walt Whitman's description of a ride on a Brooklyn ferry and in a Broadway streetcar, quoted by William James in *Talks to Teachers,* "On a Certain Blindness in Human Beings," Henry Holt and Company, New York, 1901.

[3] V. Woolf, *A Room of One's Own,* Harcourt, Brace and Company, New York, 1929, p. 161.

[4] See T. W. Surette and D. G. Mason, *Appreciation of Music,* Gray, New York, 1924, vol. i, p. 32.

at random: writing letters, furnishing our rooms, selecting our clothes, and using our leisure.

Can letter writing be an art? Are not some letters more pleasing than others? Why? Probably for at least two reasons. First, because the letter presents to the eye a pleasing form. The writing is legible and is thoughtfully spaced with ample margins; and page follows page in a logical, harmonious way. The effect of the form is an enhancement of the content. A pleasing form alone arouses in the recipient an emotional response. But how much greater the response if, in the second place, the content too has a pleasing form! To write a letter, in fact any kind of literature, one starts with an idea, which he expresses through the medium of words. Words are to the writer what stone is to the builder or sculptor, tone to the musician, pigment to the painter, or clay to the potter. By means of words he creates a form for the conveyance of his idea. The better the form, the more forceful the expression, provided the idea is worth expressing. He may elaborate the idea, add other ideas for emphasis or contrast, just as the musician contrasts his melodies (musical ideas) or Leonardo, the figure of Christ (an idea of repose) with those of the disciples (an idea of agitation).

In any kind of literature as well as in the letter, the visual form of the printed words bears a direct relation to the form of the content, just as does the visual score to the audible form of the music. The grouping of words into paragraphs and the separation of paragraphs by space devices is a simple illustration of how the eye assists the mind to grasp a break in the thought.[5] Many poems by Carl Sandburg[6] will afford a more complex illustration in which the grouping of the printed words on the page creates as definite a pattern of light and dark as do the light and dark colors in the Sienese *Madonna*. In both cases the purpose and the result are the same: a form presented to the eye reinforces the idea presented to the mind. Thus we see that the fundamental principles of music and painting (we might carry the comparison further) are the fundamental principles of letter-writing also—in fact of any kind of writing, from the simple memorandum to a complete story or drama.

To turn to our second activity, do we find these principles at

[5] Compare a page of a modern book with a classical manuscript in which all the letters are capitals and follow each other with no punctuation and no paragraphing.

[6] See E. Rickert, *New Methods for the Study of Literature,* University of Chicago Press, Chicago, 1927, chap. vii.

work in the furnishing of our rooms? Everyone lives in an abode. Does he enjoy it or dislike it? Does he have a feeling of "rightness" about it? Or is he indifferent to it? To which of the two types does your room belong? Is it overloaded with furnishings that are largely useless, and irritating in their demand of time for their care? Or is it reposeful and harmonious, a place in which one really likes to live?

Interior architecture is a complex art with many branches, involving the purpose of the room; its space design by the placement and proportions of walls, ceilings, and openings—the permanent elements; and the furnishings and people—the changeable elements. Its ultimate character is dependent upon not one but all of these elements; working in accord, if harmony results; at cross purposes, if discord results.

For many of us our room is already built. It may be furnished or partly so. If it is ugly to start with, is our objective hopeless? By no means. The room may be small and disproportionately low; a door and windows break three sides and leave the fourth a long monotonous wall surface. Let us consult, imaginatively, our sense of balance. If the room is too small, a quiet, inconspicuous, lightly broken wall treatment of retreating color will add a feeling of spaciousness; while an advancing color and wallpaper of strongly contrasted light and dark would make the room appear even smaller. If it is too low, an emphasis upon verticality (as in the hangings and other furnishings) and a suppression of horizontality (as in the avoidance of horizontal moldings and borders) will increase the appearance of height. The *Parthenon* is long and low, but the insistent verticals of the fluted columns create a balance and a feeling of "rightness." *Chartres*[7] is very vertical, hardly held in restraint by horizontals. Here too is "rightness." Both are "right." Behind the design lie the purpose and the people with their ideas and feelings. Balance for the Greek was different from balance for the Gothic. One must not be dogmatic. Each must determine for himself what constitutes balance in his own room. But balance there must be; without it everything collapses.

What then of the monotonous wall space? It may be needed to balance the broken walls of the other sides. If, on the other hand, the wall still remains monotonous and overbalances with its unbroken space, the furnishings (perhaps a picture or hanging) can be used to break the large area and establish a balance.

---

[7] a magnificent gothic cathedral in the city of Chartres in northern France (ED.)

In the furnishings, the first question is that of function: what is there in the room that has no use in function or design? What can be eliminated without sacrificing efficient use and pleasing appearance? Having reduced the furnishings to the necessary minimum with a modicum for that which delights by indulging the personal tastes of the owner (for too much impersonality is as bad as none), one may then consider each piece, first as a form and then as related to the other forms and to the form of the room as a unit. A good chair, for instance, *looks* its use. The supporting parts are proportioned to the weight; the back and arms are related to the seat so as to insure comfort. The materials fittingly harmonize and contrast. The upholstery, in pattern, color, and texture, depends upon the material of the frame: massive wood, woven reed, light metal. The construction of a good chair is dependent upon the same guiding principles as the *University Chapel*. In both it is a matter of materials, the way in which they are used, and the purpose for which they are used, subject to the creative sensitivity of the artist who can proportion and balance, contrast and unify. In the *Chapel* the thick stone walls, the great windows, the relative open and solid stone areas of the tower, the relative proportions of all parts—every detail presents itself to our eyes as a contributing element to the unified and harmonious whole; and the visual impression of strength and aspiration dignifies every event which takes place in the building. It is true that the *Chapel* gains in majesty and power through its size. A fine chair, though small in comparison, is as architectural in principle and may appeal to some as strongly as the *Chapel*.

To return to our room, though the chair may be fine of itself, does it belong in the room? Have you not seen a chair look ugly in one place and "just fit" in another? Study that chair, not in itself but in its relation to its surroundings, and you will probably find the explanation. Its form or some details of its form—its materials, their color or texture, its shape, size, or proportions—clash too dissonantly or harmonize too mildly with the table, for example, or with the room as a whole. Our objective, the harmony of the whole, is a stern master. Yet by it every piece of furnishing in a good room—furniture, hangings, wall decorations, rugs, pictures, ornaments, lighting fixtures—is measured. Each is a form of a definite material—wood, stucco, tile, metal, textiles, glass—subject to its own guiding principles of material, function, and design, and each is also a contributing element to the whole.

If we can make of our rooms works of art, can we not do the same with ourselves in our personal appearance? Just as we began

with what was given us, in making a work of art out of our room,
so in the matter of ourselves we begin with what nature has given
us. It may or may not be beautiful. We reformed the ugly room into
an attractive one by infusing into it, by means of the furnishings,
qualities of balance, proportion, unity, and harmony in accordance
with our own personal interpretations of those qualities. In the same
way the physical self is re-formed by clothing into something attractive or unattractive in proportion as the garments are selected to
secure these qualities. Have you watched people on the street with
this observation in mind? How often does a tall gaunt person wear
garments that accent verticality! And the stout person, those which
emphasize horizontality! A pale type—pale complexion, light eyes
and hair—often selects a pale uncontrasted color when it should
have a color that in hue and intensity brings in the needed contrasting
strength. Some types need brown; some, blue. Not the prevailing
style but suitability to myself. My physical self and my personality
(ideas to be expressed) are the basic forms to be re-formed and hence
set forth in their essential qualities, not obliterated. Each article of
clothing is partly a form in itself and largely a contributing element
to the whole. How attractive is a hat in a shop window! How ugly
on me!

One more activity may be mentioned for discussion—the way in
which we use our leisure. Here too can we see the way of art? It
depends upon whether we see life itself as an art—a balanced, unified,
harmonious whole. If we do, then we know that variety is essential
for this harmony.

> After all, there is not only variety, but also unity. The diversity of the
> Many is balanced by the stability of the One. That is why life must
> always be a dance, for that is what a dance is: perpetual slightly varied
> movements which are yet always held true to the shape of the whole.[8]

The great wall of the *Egyptian Temple* is more unified when
broken by carving and color. The rapid zigzag motif of the *Navajo
Blanket* brings in so refreshing a contrast to the more austere step
pattern that the unity of the entire design is greater. In Leonardo's
The Last Supper the reposeful room and the poiseful central figure
would be uninteresting were they not set over against and united
with the restless, moving masses of the disciples. Is there a work of
art which does not illustrate this principle of variety in unity? If life,

[8] H. Ellis, *The Dance of Life,* Houghton Mifflin Company, Boston, 1923, p. viii.

then, is a work of art, may we not see in leisure a vitalizing variety to the main business of life? May we not look upon leisure as a form and ask whether the character of the form is such that it exists partly for itself and partly for the intensification which its contrasts bring to the larger whole? The pattern of life may be like that of the *Navajo Blanket:* simple and forceful; or like that of the royal *Persian Carpet:* complex and rich. It is a difference not of value but of kind. One thing, however, is certain: neither the *Navajo Blanket,* nor the *Persian Carpet,* nor any kind of life is a work of art without wisely placed, balanced variety. As for life, the activities of our leisure time form one of the chief sources of this variety.

There is a tendency, in these days of specialization, to pigeonhole our activities—work, play, religion, civics, art—and when engaged in one, to banish all others to their tight compartments. An illustration of the possibility of breaking down these partitions is the late Prof. A. A. Michelson, one of the world's great physicists, who when asked why he persisted in his attempt to measure the velocity of light even more precisely when the present measurement was an acknowledged absolute, said that it "amused" him. A profound scholar, relentless in his demands for accuracy, found "amusement" in his work. Fittingly he has been called the "scientist-artist."

If we conclude that it *is* possible to look at everything with the artist's vision and to pursue all activities in accordance with art principles, let us restate what is involved. Life is the raw material of the artist, as it is of everyone's living. The artist, in the first place, as he looks out upon the world, sees things, people, and incidents as forms and grasps their significance, both outward and inward, and the significant aspects of commonplace things, in proportion as he has within himself the capacity to perceive and feel such significance. In the second place, he creates an appropriate form in appropriate material for a convincing expression of this significance. In the third place, he is a craftsman grounded in the technique of his craft. Some of these activities he pursues consciously, some subconsciously. No one of them is *a priori,* nor are they to be isolated. Each acts on and is inextricably fused with the others. They do not account entirely for the artist. Other forces are at work—social, economic, religious, geographic. But these three are distinguishable and essential wherever we find great art. There is, it is true, a difference in degree between profound, imaginative, universal art and the art of our daily activities—but not in kind. We are all potential artists.

EDITH HAMILTON

The Way of the East
and the West in Art

Edith Hamilton (1867–1963) was an American classicist, educator
and writer. She began writing and giving lectures after her retire-
ment. Her book *Mythology* (1942) is considered one of the most
complete texts on Greek myth. She is also the author of *The Greek
Way* (1930), from which the following selection is taken, *The Roman Way* (1932), and *Witness to the Truth: Christ and His Interpreters* (1948).

The way a nation goes, whether that of the mind or that of the spirit,
is decisive in its effect upon art. A brief consideration will show that
it must be so. The spirit has not essentially anything to do with what
is outside of itself. It is the mind that keeps hold of reality. The way
of the spirit is by withdrawal from the world of objects to contemplation of the world within and there is no need of any correspondence between what goes on without and what goes on within. Not
the mind but the spirit is its own place, and can make a Hell of
Heaven, a Heaven of Hell. When the mind withdraws into itself and
dispenses with facts it makes only chaos.

In the early days of the Restoration a great discussion was held
by the learned men in the presence of the king on why, if a live fish
were put into a brimming pail, the water would not overflow, while
if the fish were dead, it would. Many elevating reasons that had to
do with the inner significance of life and death were adduced for this
spiritually suggestive property of water—or fish, until the king asked
that two such pails be brought in and the fish added to them before
his eyes. When it turned out that the water reacted in the same way
to the fish alive or dead, the scientists received a lesson that had far-
reaching results on the advisability of the mind's not going the way
of the spirit and withdrawing into itself to exercise the pure reason
free and unhampered, but of remaining strictly within the limits of
the outside world. Abide by the facts, is the dictum of the mind; a
sense for fact is its salient characteristic.

In proportion as the spirit predominates, this sense disappears.
So in the Middle Ages when the West was turning more and more

to the way of the spirit, the foremost intellects could employ their great powers in questioning how many angels could stand on a needle's point, and the like. Carry this attitude toward the world of fact a few steps farther and the result is the Buddhist devotee swaying before the altar and repeating *Amida* a thousand, thousand times until he loses all consciousness of altar, *Amida,* and himself as well. The activity of the mind has been lulled to rest and the spirit, absorbed, is seeking the truth within itself. "Let a man," say the Upanishads, the great Brahman document, "meditate on the syllable Om. This is the imperishable syllable and he who knowing this, loudly repeats that syllable, enters into it and becomes immortal." "God offers to everyone," says Emerson, "his choice between truth and repose. Take which you please—you can never have both." That is the West speaking and the way of the mind. Truth means, from this point of view, finding out about things—very active exercise.

The practical effect of the divergence is of course immediately apparent in the intellectual realm. Those whose aim is to be completely independent of "this muddy vesture of decay" do not become scientists or archæologists or anything that has to do with actualities past or present. In art the result, though less immediately apparent, is no less decisive. In proportion as the spirit predominates, the real shapes and looks of things become unimportant and when the spirit is supreme, they are of no importance at all.

In Egypt, as has been said, the reality of the unseen world slowly overshadowed that of the seen, but invisible though it was, it remained substantial. The dead bodies must be preserved from returning to dust; they must be placed in tombs that were underground fortresses safe from disturbance; they must be surrounded by all the furnishings they had made use of in life. The body was enormously important and there was no idea that the abundance of the things a man possessed were not eternally important too. The art of such a people would keep a firm hold on reality. The pyramids are as real as the hills. They look to be nothing made by hands but a part of the basic structure of the earth. Where the wind lifts the sand into shades of a gigantic geometry—triangles which, as one watches, pass into curves and break again into sharp-pointed outlines, a cycle of endless change as fixed as the movement of the stars, against the immensity of the desert which never changes—the pyramids, immutable, immovable, are the spirit of the desert incased in granite. All the tremendous art of Egyptian sculpture has something of this unity with the physical world. The colossal statues have only just emerged from the rocks of the hills. They keep the marks of their origin as securely as the marks of the artist's tools that shaped them from their background.

This hold on reality is something completely different from that grasped by the mind. It has nothing to do with the action of the mind; it is a profound intuition on the part of people whose consciousness has not yet divided them from the ways of nature. This intuitive feeling is as different from the conception of reality which the mind attains to as an Egyptian tomb, where life and death are hardly differentiated, is from that prison in which Socrates sat, trying to think out what was true in the hope of immortality.

What Egyptian art would have resulted in if it had been allowed a free development, is one of those questions that forever engage the attention through the realization of an immense loss to the world. But the priests stepped in, and that direct experience of nature which was being illumined more and more by the experience of the spirit was arrested at a certain point and held fast. The priests set a fixed pattern for art all must conform to. Art can work in chains for a long time as the mind cannot, and it was centuries before the full effect appeared of the control of the artist's spirit by the priests' dogma; but by the time it was apparent Egyptian art was ended. Plato's comment is to all intents and purposes its funeral oration:

In Egypt the forms of excellence were long since fixed and patterns of them displayed in the temples. No painter or artist is allowed to innovate on the traditional forms or invent new ones. To this day, no alteration is allowed—none at all. Their works of art are painted or modeled in the same forms which they had 10,000 years ago.

But in the East there was no arrested development. There the spirit was free—it alone was free—to work unhampered. Hindoo art was produced by men who had been trained from earliest youth to look at all outside them as illusion. The belief in a solid, durable stuff which the senses induce, was the fundamental falsehood men must clear themselves from. That which appears solid and durable is only a perpetually shifting appearance, a kaleidoscope always moving, where each pattern is forever dissolving into another and all are no more significant than a spectacle for a child. Reality, permanence, importance, belong alone to the world within where truth is absolutely known because it is experienced and where the man who wills can achieve complete mastery. This is the fundamental dogma of the Upanishads:

The infinite is the Self. He who perceives this, is lord and master of all the world. Air, fire, water, food, appearances, disappearances—all spring from the Self. He who sees this sees everything and obtains everything.

It is difficult for us to associate this idea with the production of art. Art is to us of the West the unifier of what is without and what is within. It is as firmly rooted in the one as in the other. And it is quite true that the complete mystic, if such a one could be, would never even desire to put into any concrete form the beatific vision. He would remain in utter quiescence, desiring nothing:

> When to a man who understands, the Self has become all things, what sorrow, what seeking, can there be, to him who once beholds that unity?

But mystical rapture even in the East is for the few. To all the rest, reality, however illusory it is conceived of as being, remains to be reckoned with. The great Hindoo artists were not prevented from expressing themselves through it as all artists will forever, but their conception of it shaped the mold of their art. The procedure laid down for a Buddhist artist before beginning his work is applicable in what it aims at to all Hindoo art. He was to proceed to a place of solitude. There he must prepare himself, first, by performing "the Sevenfold Office" and offering to the hosts of Buddhas "real or imaginary flowers." (It is clear that the first had no superiority over the second.) Next, he must realize "the four infinite moods" and meditate upon the emptiness and non-existence of all things, until "by the fire of the idea of the abyss" he lost all consciousness of self and was able to identify himself with the divinity he desired to portray. Then, at last, calling upon him he would behold him. There would come to him visibly the very image of the god, "like a bright reflection," to serve him for his model. It would appear in no human shape, we may be sure. The whole procedure was designed to make that impossible. The conviction had been bred within the artist that the truth of his art was above and apart from all reality. In his solitary watch he had sought to purify it from all that had to do with the flesh, to banish earthly memories and through the spirit undefiled find the manifestation of the eternal. The prerequisite of the statue would be its non-humanity. Scrolls of bright blue hair must mark it off from a mere man, or many heads or arms; or an impression of inhuman force, given by a woman brandishing a human head torn from a mangled body underfoot.

It is said of Polygnotus that when he wished to paint Helen of Troy, he went to Crotona, famed for the beauty of its women, and asked to see all those who were thought to be the most beautiful. These he studied long before painting his picture, and yet when it was done it was not a representation of any one of those lovely faces he had seen but fairer by far than the fairest of them all. The Greek artist, the story would tell us, was not a photographer, any more than his Buddhist confrère; he too in the end withdrew from the visible forms of the women before him and created within himself his own form of beauty; but the story points the difference between the two as well. The studio of the Greek was not a lonely cave of meditation, but the world of moving life. His picture was based on the women he had studied; it was conditioned by their actual bodily shapes; it was superindividual but not supernatural.

The Hindoo artist was subject to no conditions; of all artists he was the freest. The Egyptian was submissive to the ways of nature and the dogma of the priest; the Greek was limited by his mind that would not let him lose sight of the things that are seen; the Hindoo was unhampered by anything outside of himself except the material he worked in, and even there he often refused to recognize a limitation. The art of India and of all the nations of the East she influenced shows again and again sculpture that seems to struggle to be free of the marble. No artists have ever made bronze and stone move as these did. There was nothing fixed and rigid for them; nothing in the world of the spirit is fixed and rigid. Hindoo art is the result of unchecked spiritual force, a flood held back by no restraints save those the artist chose to impose upon himself.

But, even though the visible world had no hold upon his conscious attention, he could not, of course—no human being can—create purely within the depths of the spirit what had no connection with facts, no semblance of anything he had seen. His artistic vision was conditioned by actualities, but only indirectly since his aim was to detach himself from them. Reality and probability appeal to the mind alone and to that appeal he was completely indifferent; he was concentrated upon spiritual significance. To him the multitudinous hands and arms of the god who appeared to him in his trance were symbolic; they stood for a truth of the spirit and expressed the only kind of reality worth an artist's while.

Presuppose a complete lack of significance in the visible world and there is only one way out for the artist, the way of symbolism. He of all men is least capable of complete abstraction. The mathematician and the philosopher can deal with pure concepts; to the artist the world of abstract ideas offers nothing at all. In symbolism he can hold to something solid and concrete even while affirming that the real has nothing to do with that which the senses perceive. Symbols are always real things invested with unreality. They are the reflection in the mirror through which we in the flesh can see, if darkly. In symbolism realities are important, even if their only importance is that they stand for something other than what they are. The mystical artist is free to make use of reality and to dispense with it as he pleases. He is at liberty also to improvise his own symbolism which can be of the simplest: many arms to express multiform power; many breasts to show spiritual nourishment; a sublimated pictorial writing. His only restraint comes from within his own self, but, despising as he does the outside world, predisposed against seeing real things as beautiful, the artist within him, who must find spiritual significance somewhere, is irresistibly impelled toward the pattern which he can make symbolic and, so, significant.

The mystical artist always sees patterns. The symbol, never quite real, tends to be expressed less and less realistically, and as the reality becomes abstracted the pattern comes forward.

The wings on Blake's angels do not look like real wings, nor are they there because wings belong to angels. They have been flattened, stylized, to provide a curving pointed frame, the setting required by the pattern of the composition. In Hindoo art and its branches, stylization reaches its height. Human figures are stylized far beyond the point of becoming a type; they too are made into patterns, schematic designs of the human body, an abstraction of humanity. In the case of an Eastern rug all desire to express any semblance of reality has gone. Such a work of art is pure decoration. It is the expression of the artist's final withdrawal from the visible world, essentially his denial of the intellect.

Dismiss the real world, see it as hateful and hopeless, and the effect upon art is fundamentally the same whether the result is a Fra Angelico[1] angel or a monster-god. Winged angels radiant against a golden background, a many-handed god, both belong to the same conception of the world. The artist has turned his back upon the things that are seen. He has shut the eyes of his mind. The art of the West, after Rome fell and the influence of Greece was lost, went the way of the East as all else did. Pictures grew more and more decorative. The flat unreality of the primitive developed into the flat unreality of the stylized, until at the Renaissance the visible world was re-discovered with the re-discovery of Greece.

Two thousand years after the golden days of Phidias and Praxi-

---

[1] Fra Angelico (c. 1400–1455) was a Florentine painter whose works depict only religious subjects. (ED.)

teles, of Zeuxis and Apelles, when their statues were defaced and broken and all but irretrievably lost, and their paintings were completely gone forever, men's minds were suddenly directed to what was left of the literature of Greece and Rome. A passion for learning like that of Plato's time swept Italy. To study the literature of Greece was to discover the idea of the freedom of the mind and to use the mind as it had not been used since the days of Greece. Once again there was a fusion of rational and spiritual power. In the Italian Renaissance a great artistic development coincided with a great intellectual awakening and the art that resulted is in its essence more like that of Greece than any other before or since. In Florence, where great painters had great minds, the beauty of the real world was discovered and men painted what they saw with their eyes. Italian painters found the laws of perspective—of course. Not because Signorelli was greater than Simone Martini[2] but only because he and his like were looking at real things and desiring to paint realities, not heavenly visions.

Whether the Greek artists used perspective or not can never be known; not a trace is left of their work; but what they felt about painting things as they are can be known without the possibility of a doubt. Their attitude is revealed in many an allusion.

A famous Greek painter exhibited a picture of a boy holding a bunch of grapes so lifelike, the birds flew down to peck at them, and the people acclaimed him as the master-artist. "If I were," he answered, "the boy would have kept the birds away." The little tale with its delightful assumption of intelligent birds is completely Greek in its fundamental assumption. Grapes were to be painted to look like grapes and boys to look like boys, and the reason was that nothing could be imagined so beautiful and so significant as the real. "Say not, who shall ascend unto Heaven or who shall descend into Hell: for lo, the Word is very nigh thee, in thy mouth and in thy heart." The Greek artist thought neither of Heaven nor of Hell; the word was very nigh unto him; he felt the real world completely sufficient for the demands of the spirit. He had no wish to mark the images of his gods with strange, unearthly attributes to lift them away from earth. He had no wish to alter them at all from what he saw as most beautiful, the shapes of the human beings around him.

---

[2] *Luca Signorelli* (1441?–1523) was an Italian painter whose realistic treatment of the human form influenced Michelangelo. *Simone Martini* (c. 1283–1344) was a Sienese painter whose greatest work is the *Annunciation*. (ED.)

A Brahman bronze of Shiva[3] stands poised in the dance, arrested for a moment in an irresistible movement. Many arms and hands curving outward from his body add to the sense of an endless rhythmic motion. The shape, light, slim-waisted, is refined away from the human. Strange symbolic things surround him, deck him, a weaving cobra, a skull, a mermaid creature, long pendants waving from hair and ears, a writhing monster beneath his feet. His beauty is like nothing beautiful ever seen upon the earth.

The Olympic Hermes is a perfectly beautiful human being, no more, no less. Every detail of his body was shaped from a consummate knowledge of actual bodies. Nothing is added to mark his deity, no aureole around his head, no mystic staff, no hint that here is he who guides the soul to death. The significance of the statue to the Greek artist, the mark of the divinity, was its beauty, only that. His art had taken form within him as he walked the streets, watched the games, noted perpetually the people he lived among. To him what he saw in those human beings was enough for all his art; he had never an impulse to fashion something different, something truer than this truth of nature. In his eyes the Word had become flesh; he made his image of the eternal what men could be. The Winged Victory is later Greek; the temple on the Acropolis was built to the Wingless Victory.

The endless struggle between the flesh and the spirit found an end in Greek art. The Greek artists were unaware of it. They were spiritual materialists, never denying the importance of the body and ever seeing in the body a spiritual significance. Mysticism on the whole was alien to the Greeks, thinkers as they were. Thought and mysticism never go well together and there is little symbolism in Greek art. Athena was not a symbol of wisdom but an embodiment of it and her statues were beautiful grave women, whose seriousness might mark them as wise, but who were marked in no other way. The Apollo Belvedere is not a symbol of the sun, nor the Versailles Artemis of the moon. There could be nothing less akin to the ways of symbolism than their beautiful, normal humanity. Nor did decoration really interest the Greeks. In all their art they were preoccupied with what they wanted to express, not with ways of expressing it,

---

[3] In Hindu religion, Brahman is the divine force of the universe whose three forms are Brahma, the creator of the universe, Vishnu, the preserver of the universe, and Shiva, the destroyer. (ED.)

and lovely expression, merely as lovely expression, did not appeal to them at all.

Greek art is intellectual art, the art of men who were clear and lucid thinkers, and it is therefore plain art. Artists than whom the world has never seen greater, men endowed with the spirit's best gift, found their natural method of expression in the simplicity and clarity which are the endowment of the unclouded reason. "Nothing in excess," the Greek axiom of art, is the dictum of men who would brush aside all obscuring, entangling superfluity, and see clearly, plainly, unadorned, what they wished to express. Structure belongs in an especial degree to the province of the mind in art, and architectonics were pre-eminently a mark of the Greek. The power that made a unified whole of the trilogy of a Greek tragedy, that envisioned the sure, precise, decisive scheme of the Greek statue, found its most conspicuous expression in Greek architecture. The Greek temple is the creation, *par excellence,* of mind and spirit in equilibrium.

A Hindoo temple is a conglomeration of adornment. The lines of the building are completely hidden by the decorations. Sculptured figures and ornaments crowd its surface, stand out from it in thick masses, break it up into a bewildering series of irregular tiers. It is not a unity but a collection, rich, confused. It looks like something not planned but built this way and that as the ornament required. The conviction underlying it can be perceived: each bit of the exquisitely wrought detail had a mystical meaning and the temple's exterior was important only as a means for the artist to inscribe thereon the symbols of the truth. It is decoration, not architecture.

Again, the gigantic temples of Egypt, those massive immensities of granite which look as if only the power that moves in the earthquake were mighty enough to bring them into existence, are something other than the creation of geometry balanced by beauty. The science and the spirit are there, but what is there most of all is force, unhuman force, calm but tremendous, overwhelming. It reduces to nothingness all that belongs to man. He is annihilated. The Egyptian architects were possessed by the consciousness of the awful, irresistible domination of the ways of nature; they had no thought to give to the insignificant atom that was man.

Greek architecture of the great age is the expression of men who were, first of all, intellectual artists, kept firmly within the visible world by their mind, but, only second to that, lovers of the human world. The Greek temple is the perfect expression of the pure intellect illumined by the spirit. No other great buildings anywhere approach its simplicity. In the Parthenon straight columns rise to plain capitals; a pediment is sculptured in bold relief; there is nothing more. And yet—here is the Greek miracle—this absolute simplicity of structure is alone in majesty of beauty among all the temples and cathedrals and palaces of the world. Majestic but human, truly Greek. No superhuman force as in Egypt; no strange supernatural shapes as in India; the Parthenon is the home of humanity at ease, calm, ordered, sure of itself and the world. The Greeks flung a challenge to nature in the fullness of their joyous strength. They set their temples on the summit of a hill overlooking the wide sea, outlined against the circle of the sky. They would build what was more beautiful than hill and sea and sky and greater than all these. It matters not at all if the temple is large or small; one never thinks of the size. It matters not—really—how much it is in ruins. A few white columns dominate the lofty height at Sunion as securely as the great mass of the Parthenon dominates all the sweep of sea and land around Athens. To the Greek architect man was the master of the world. His mind could understand its laws; his spirit could discover its beauty.

The Gothic cathedral was raised in awe and reverence to Almighty God, the expression of the aspiration of the lowly:

> We praise thee, O God, we who are as nothing save
> in our power to praise thee.

The Parthenon was raised in triumph, to express the beauty and the power and the splendor of man:

> Wonders are there many—none more wonderful
> than man.
> His the might that crosses seas swept white by storm
> winds . . .
> He the master of the beast lurking in the wild
> hills . . .
> His is speech and wind-swift thought—

Divinity was seen incarnate; through perfected mortality man was immortal.

WALTER BENJAMIN

Unpacking My Library

Walter Benjamin (1892–1940), a German literary critic considered
to be part of the Marxist tradition, mixed social criticism, linguistic
analysis, and historical anecdotes in his discussions of literature.
His essays on literary topics were collected in 1961 in *Illuminations*
(translated into English in 1968), from which the following selection is taken.

I am unpacking my library. Yes, I am. The books are not yet on the
shelves, not yet touched by the mild boredom of order. I cannot
march up and down their ranks to pass them in review before a
friendly audience. You need not fear any of that. Instead, I must ask
you to join me in the disorder of crates that have been wrenched
open, the air saturated with the dust of wood, the floor covered with
torn paper, to join me among piles of volumes that are seeing daylight
again after two years of darkness, so that you may be ready to share
with me a bit of the mood—it is certainly not an elegiac mood but,
rather, one of anticipation—which these books arouse in a genuine
collector. For such a man is speaking to you, and on closer scrutiny
he proves to be speaking only about himself. Would it not be pre-
sumptuous of me if, in order to appear convincingly objective and
down-to-earth, I enumerated for you the main sections or prize pieces
of a library, if I presented you with their history or even their
usefulness to a writer? I, for one, have in mind something less
obscure, something more palpable than that; what I am really concerned with is giving you some insight into the relationship of a
book collector to his possessions, into collecting rather than a collection. If I do this by elaborating on the various ways of acquiring
books, this is something entirely arbitrary. This or any other procedure is merely a dam against the spring tide of memories which
surges toward any collector as he contemplates his possessions. Every
passion borders on the chaotic, but the collector's passion borders
on the chaos of memories. More than that: the chance, the fate, that
suffuse the past before my eyes are conspicuously present in the
accustomed confusion of these books. For what else is this collection
but a disorder to which habit has accommodated itself to such an
extent that it can appear as order? You have all heard of people

whom the loss of their books has turned into invalids, or of those who in order to acquire them became criminals. These are the very areas in which any order is a balancing act of extreme precariousness. "The only exact knowledge there is," said Anatole France,[1] "is the knowledge of the date of publication and the format of books." And indeed, if there is a counterpart to the confusion of a library, it is the order of its catalogue.

Thus there is in the life of a collector a dialectical tension between the poles of disorder and order. Naturally, his existence is tied to many other things as well: to a very mysterious relationship to ownership, something about which we shall have more to say later; also, to a relationship to objects which does not emphasize their functional, utilitarian value—that is, their usefulness—but studies and loves them as the scene, the stage, of their fate. The most profound enchantment for the collector is the locking of individual items within a magic circle in which they are fixed as the final thrill, the thrill of acquisition, passes over them. Everything remembered and thought, everything conscious, becomes the pedestal, the frame, the base, the lock of his property. The period, the region, the craftsmanship, the former ownership—for a true collector the whole background of an item adds up to a magic encyclopedia whose quintessence is the fate of his object. In this circumscribed area, then, it may be surmised how the great physiognomists—and collectors are the physiognomists of the world of objects—turn into interpreters of fate. One has only to watch a collector handle the objects in his glass case. As he holds them in his hands, he seems to be seeing through them into their distant pass as though inspired. So much for the magical side of the collector—his old-age image, I might call it.

Habent sua fata libelli:[2] these words may have been intended as a general statement about books. So books like *The Divine Comedy,* Spinoza's *Ethics,* and *The Origin of Species* have their fates. A collector, however, interprets this Latin saying differently. For him, not only books but also copies of books have their fates. And in this sense, the most important fate of a copy is its encounter with him, with his own collection. I am not exaggerating when I say that to a true collector the acquisition of an old book is its rebirth. This is the childlike element which in a collector mingles with the element of

---

[1] Anatole France (1844–1924) was a French writer, skeptic, and critic. (ED.)

[2] Little stories have their fates. (ED.)

old age. For children can accomplish the renewal of existence in a hundred unfailing ways. Among children, collecting is only one process of renewal; other processes are the painting of objects, the cutting out of figures, the application of decals—the whole range of childlike modes of acquisition, from touching things to giving them names. To renew the old world—that is the collector's deepest desire when he is driven to acquire new things, and that is why a collector of older books is closer to the wellsprings of collecting than the acquirer of luxury editions. How do books cross the threshold of a collection and become the property of a collector? The history of their acquisition is the subject of the following remarks.

Of all the ways of acquiring books, writing them oneself is regarded as the most praiseworthy method. At this point many of you will remember with pleasure the large library which Jean Paul's poor little schoolmaster Wutz gradually acquired by writing, himself, all the works whose titles interested him in bookfair catalogues; after all, he could not afford to buy them. Writers are really people who write books not because they are poor, but because they are dissatisfied with the books which they could buy but do not like. You, ladies and gentlemen, may regard this as a whimsical definition of a writer. But everything said from the angle of a real collector is whimsical. Of the customary modes of acquisition, the one most appropriate to a collector would be the borrowing of a book with its attendant non-returning. The book borrower of real stature whom we envisage here proves himself to be an inveterate collector of books not so much by the fervor with which he guards his borrowed treasures and by the deaf ear which he turns to all reminders from the everyday world of legality as by his failure to read these books. If my experience may serve as evidence, a man is more likely to return a borrowed book upon occasion than to read it. And the non-reading of books, you will object, should be characteristic of collectors? This is news to me, you may say. It is not news at all. Experts will bear me out when I say that it is the oldest thing in the world. Suffice it to quote the answer which Anatole France gave to a philistine who admired his library and then finished with the standard question, "And you have read all these books, Monsieur France?" "Not one-tenth of them. I don't suppose you use your Sèvres china every day?"

Incidentally, I have put the right to such an attitude to the test. For years, for at least the first third of its existence, my library consisted of no more than two or three shelves which increased only by inches each year. This was its militant age, when no book was allowed to enter it without the certification that I had not read it. Thus I might never have acquired a library extensive enough to be worthy of the name if there had not been an inflation. Suddenly the emphasis shifted; books acquired real value, or, at any rate, were difficult to obtain. At least this is how it seemed in Switzerland. At the eleventh hour I sent my first major book orders from there and in this way was able to secure such irreplaceable items as *Der blaue Reiter* and Bachofen's *Sage von Tanaquil,* which could still be obtained from the publishers at that time.

Well—so you may say—after exploring all these byways we should finally reach the wide highway of book acquisition, namely, the purchasing of books. This is indeed a wide highway, but not a comfortable one. The purchasing done by a book collector has very little in common with that done in a bookshop by a student getting a textbook, a man of the world buying a present for his lady, or a businessman intending to while away his next train journey. I have made my most memorable purchases on trips, as a transient. Property and possession belong to the tactical sphere. Collectors are people with a tactical instinct; their experience teaches them that when they capture a strange city, the smallest antique shop can be a fortress, the most remote stationery store a key position. How many cities have revealed themselves to me in the marches I undertook in the pursuit of books!

By no means all of the most important purchases are made on the premises of a dealer. Catalogues play a far greater part. And even though the purchaser may be thoroughly acquainted with the book ordered from a catalogue, the individual copy always remains a surprise and the order always a bit of a gamble. There are grievous disappointments, but also happy finds. I remember, for instance, that I once ordered a book with colored illustrations for my old collection of children's books only because it contained fairy tales by Albert Ludwig Grimm and was published at Grimma, Thuringia. Grimma was also the place of publication of a book of fables edited by the same Albert Ludwig Grimm. With its sixteen illustrations my copy of this book of fables was the only extant example of the early work of the great German book illustrator Lyser, who lived in Hamburg around the middle of the last century. Well, my reaction to the consonance of the names had been correct. In this case too I discovered the work of Lyser, namely *Linas Märchenbuch,* a work which has remained unknown to his bibliographers and which deserves a more detailed reference than this first one I am introducing here.

The acquisition of books is by no means a matter of money or

expert knowledge alone. Not even both factors together suffice for
the establishment of a real library, which is always somewhat impenetrable and at the same time uniquely itself. Anyone who buys from
catalogues must have flair in addition to the qualities I have mentioned. Dates, place names, formats, previous owners, bindings, and
the like: all these details must tell him something—not as dry, isolated facts, but as a harmonious whole; from the quality and intensity
of this harmony he must be able to recognize whether a book is for
him or not. An auction requires yet another set of qualities in a
collector. To the reader of a catalogue the book itself must speak, or
possibly its previous ownership if the provenance of the copy has
been established. A man who wishes to participate at an auction must
pay equal attention to the book and to his competitors, in addition
to keeping a cool enough head to avoid being carried away in the
competition. It is a frequent occurrence that someone gets stuck with
a high purchase price because he kept raising his bid—more to assert
himself than to acquire the book. On the other hand, one of the
finest memories of a collector is the moment when he rescued a book
to which he might never have given a thought, much less a wishful
look, because he found it lonely and abandoned on the market place
and bought it to give it its freedom—the way the prince bought a
beautiful slave girl in *The Arabian Nights*. To a book collector, you
see, the true freedom of all books is somewhere on his shelves.

To this day, Balzac's *Peau de chagrin* stands out from long rows
of French volumes in my library as a memento of my most exciting
experience at an auction. This happened in 1915 at the Rümann
auction put up by Emil Hirsch, one of the greatest of book experts
and most distinguished of dealers. The edition in question appeared
in 1838 in Paris, Place de la Bourse. As I pick up my copy, I see not
only its number in the Rümann collection, but even the label of the
shop in which the first owner bought the book over ninety years ago
for one-eightieth of today's price. "Papeterie I. Flanneau," it says. A
fine age in which it was still possible to buy such a de luxe edition
at a stationery dealer's! The steel engravings of this book were designed by the foremost French graphic artist and executed by the
foremost engravers. But I was going to tell you how I acquired this
book. I had gone to Emil Hirsch's for an advance inspection and had
handled forty or fifty volumes; that particular volume had inspired
in me the ardent desire to hold on to it forever. The day of the
auction came. As chance would have it, in the sequence of the auction
this copy of *La Peau de chagrin* was preceded by a complete set of
its illustrations printed separately on India paper. The bidders sat at

a long table; diagonally across from me sat the man who was the
focus of all eyes at the first bid, the famous Munich collector Baron
von Simolin. He was greatly interested in this set, but he had rival
bidders; in short, there was a spirited contest which resulted in the
highest bid of the entire auction—far in excess of three thousand
marks. No one seemed to have expected such a high figure, and all
those present were quite excited. Emil Hirsch remained unconcerned,
and whether he wanted to save time or was guided by some other
consideration, he proceeded to the next item, with no one really
paying attention. He called out the price, and with my heart pounding
and with the full realization that I was unable to compete with any
of those big collectors I bid a somewhat higher amount. Without
arousing the bidders' attention, the auctioneer went through the usual
routine—"Do I hear more?" and three bangs of his gavel, with an
eternity seeming to separate each from the next—and proceeded to
add the auctioneer's charge. For a student like me the sum was still
considerable. The following morning at the pawnshop is no longer
part of this story, and I prefer to speak about another incident which
I should like to call the negative of an auction. It happened last year
at a Berlin auction. The collection of books that was offered was a
miscellany in quality and subject matter, and only a number of rare
works on occultism and natural philosophy were worthy of note. I
bid for a number of them, but each time I noticed a gentleman in
the front row who seemed only to have waited for my bid to counter
with his own, evidently prepared to top any offer. After this had been
repeated several times, I gave up all hope of acquiring the book
which I was most interested in that day. It was the rare *Fragmente
aus dem Nachlass eines jungen Physikers* [Posthumous Fragments of
a Young Physicist] which Johann Wilhelm Ritter published in two
volumes at Heidelberg in 1810. This work has never been reprinted,
but I have always considered its preface, in which the author-editor
tells the story of his life in the guise of an obituary for his supposedly
deceased unnamed friend—with whom he is really identical—as the
most important sample of personal prose of German Romanticism.
Just as the item came up I had a brain wave. It was simple enough:
since my bid was bound to give the item to the other man, I must
not bid at all. I controlled myself and remained silent. What I had
hoped for came about: no interest, no bid, and the book was put
aside. I deemed it wise to let several days go by, and when I appeared
on the premises after a week, I found the book in the secondhand
department and benefited by the lack of interest when I acquired it.

Once you have approached the mountains of cases in order to

mine the books from them and bring them to the light of day—or, rather, of night—what memories crowd in upon you! Nothing highlights the fascination of unpacking more clearly than the difficulty of stopping this activity. I had started at noon, and it was midnight before I had worked my way to the last cases. Now I put my hands on two volumes bound in faded boards which, strictly speaking, do not belong in a book case at all: two albums with stick-in pictures which my mother pasted in as a child and which I inherited. They are the seeds of a collection of children's books which is growing steadily even today, though no longer in my garden. There is no living library that does not harbor a number of booklike creations from fringe areas. They need not be stick-in albums or family albums, autograph books or portfolios containing pamphlets or religious tracts; some people become attached to leaflets and prospectuses, others to handwriting facsimiles or typewritten copies of unobtainable books; and certainly periodicals can form the prismatic fringes of a library. But to get back to those albums: Actually, inheritance is the soundest way of acquiring a collection. For a collector's attitude toward his possessions stems from an owner's feeling of responsibility toward his property. Thus it is, in the highest sense, the attitude of an heir, and the most distinguished trait of a collection will always be its transmissibility. You should know that in saying this I fully realize that my discussion of the mental climate of collecting will confirm many of you in your conviction that this passion is behind the times, in your distrust of the collector type. Nothing is further from my mind than to shake either your conviction or your distrust. But one thing should be noted: the phenomenon of collecting loses its meaning as it loses its personal owner. Even though public collections may be less objectionable socially and more useful academically than private collections, the objects get their due only in the latter. I do know that time is running out for the type that I am discussing here and have been representing before you a bit *ex officio*.[3] But, as Hegel put it, only when it is dark does the owl of Minerva[4] begin its flight. Only in extinction is the collector comprehended.

Now I am on the last half-emptied case and it is way past midnight. Other thoughts fill me than the ones I am talking about—not

---

[3] by virtue of an office (ED.)

[4] Minerva was the Roman goddess of the arts who frequently changed herself into an owl in order to visit humans and came to be symbolized by the owl. (ED.)

thoughts but images, memories. Memories of the cities in which I found so many things: Riga, Naples, Munich, Danzig, Moscow, Florence, Basel, Paris; memories of Rosenthal's sumptuous rooms in Munich, of the Danzig Stockturm where the late Hans Rhaue was domiciled, of Süssengut's musty book cellar in North Berlin; memories of the rooms where these books had been housed, of my student's den in Munich, of my room in Bern, of the solitude of Iseltwald on the Lake of Brienz, and finally of my boyhood room, the former location of only four or five of the several thousand volumes that are piled up around me. O bliss of the collector, bliss of the man of leisure! Of no one has less been expected, and no one has had a greater sense of well-being than the man who has been able to carry on his disreputable existence in the mask of Spitzweg's "Bookworm." For inside him there are spirits, or at least little genii, which have seen to it that for a collector—and I mean a real collector, a collector as he ought to be—ownership is the most intimate relationship that one can have to objects. Not that they come alive in him; it is he who lives in them. So I have erected one of his dwellings, with books as the building stones, before you, and now he is going to disappear inside, as is only fitting.

AARON COPLAND

How We Listen to Music

Aaron Copland (1900–1991), born in Brooklyn, New York, was a celebrated American composer and pianist who relied upon jazz and folk music in his compositions. He won a Pulitzer Prize for his ballet *Appalachian Spring* in 1945. His books include *What to Listen for in Music* (1939, revised in 1957), from which the following selection is taken, *Music and Imagination* (1952), and *Copland on Music* (1960).

We all listen to music according to our separate capacities. But, for the sake of analysis, the whole listening process may become clearer if we break it up into its component parts, so to speak. In a certain sense we all listen to music on three separate planes. For lack of a better terminology, one might name these: (1) the sensuous plane,

(2) the expressive plane, (3) the sheerly musical plane. The only advantage to be gained from mechanically splitting up the listening process into these hypothetical planes is the clearer view to be had of the way in which we listen.

The simplest way of listening to music is to listen for the sheer pleasure of the musical sound itself. That is the sensuous plane. It is the plane on which we hear music without thinking, without considering it in any way. One turns on the radio while doing something else and absent-mindedly bathes in the sound. A kind of brainless but attractive state of mind is engendered by the mere sound appeal of the music.

You may be sitting in a room reading this book. Imagine one note struck on the piano. Immediately that one note is enough to change the atmosphere of the room—proving that the sound element in music is a powerful and mysterious agent, which it would be foolish to deride or belittle.

The surprising thing is that many people who consider themselves qualified music lovers abuse that plane in listening. They go to concerts in order to lose themselves. They use music as a consolation or an escape. They enter an ideal world where one doesn't have to think of the realities of everyday life. Of course they aren't thinking about the music either. Music allows them to leave it, and they go off to a place to dream, dreaming because of and apropos of the music yet never quite listening to it.

Yes, the sound appeal of music is a potent and primitive force, but you must not allow it to usurp a disproportionate share of your interest. The sensuous plane is an important one in music, a very important one, but it does not constitute the whole story.

There is no need to digress further on the sensuous plane. Its appeal to every normal human being is self-evident. There is, however, such a thing as becoming more sensitive to the different kinds of sound stuff as used by various composers. For all composers do not use that sound stuff in the same way. Don't get the idea that the value of music is commensurate with its sensuous appeal or that the loveliest sounding music is made by the greatest composer. If that were so, Ravel would be a greater creator than Beethoven. The point is that the sound element varies with each composer, that his usage of sound forms an integral part of his style and must be taken into account when listening. The reader can see, therefore, that a more conscious approach is valuable even on this primary plane of music listening.

The second plane on which music exists is what I have called the expressive one. Here, immediately, we tread on controversial ground. Composers have a way of shying away from any discussion of music's expressive side. Did not Stravinsky himself proclaim that his music was an "object," a "thing," with a life of its own, and with no other meaning than its own purely musical existence? This intransigent attitude of Stravinsky's may be due to the fact that so many people have tried to read different meanings into so many pieces. Heaven knows it is difficult enough to say precisely what it is that a piece of music means, to say it definitely, to say it finally so that everyone is satisfied with your explanation. But that should not lead one to the other extreme of denying to music the right to be "expressive."

My own belief is that all music has an expressive power, some more and some less, but that all music has a certain meaning behind the notes and that the meaning behind the notes constitutes, after all, what the piece is saying, what the piece is about. This whole problem can be stated quite simply by asking, "Is there a meaning to music?" My answer to that would be, "Yes." And "Can you state in so many words what the meaning is?" My answer to that would be, "No." Therein lies the difficulty.

Simple-minded souls will never be satisfied with the answer to the second of these questions. They always want music to have a meaning, and the more concrete it is the better they like it. The more the music reminds them of a train, a storm, a funeral, or any other familiar conception the more expressive it appears to be to them. This popular idea of music's meaning—stimulated and abetted by the usual run of musical commentator—should be discouraged wherever and whenever it is met. One timid lady once confessed to me that she suspected something seriously lacking in her appreciation of music because of her inability to connect it with anything definite. That is getting the whole thing backward, of course.

Still, the question remains, How close should the intelligent music lover wish to come to pinning a definite meaning to any particular work? No closer than a general concept, I should say. Music expresses, at different moments, serenity or exuberance, regret or triumph, fury or delight. It expresses each of these moods, and many others, in a numberless variety of subtle shadings and differences. It may even express a state of meaning for which there exists no adequate word in any language. In that case, musicians often like to say that it has only a purely musical meaning. They sometimes go farther and say that *all* music has only a purely musical meaning. What they really mean is that no appropriate word can be found to express the music's meaning and that, even if it could, they do not feel the need of finding it.

But whatever the professional musician may hold, most musical novices still search for specific words with which to pin down their musical reactions. That is why they always find Tschaikovsky easier to "understand" than Beethoven. In the first place, it is easier to pin a meaning-word on a Tschaikovsky piece than on a Beethoven one. Much easier. Moreover, with the Russian composer, every time you come back to a piece of his it almost always says the same thing to you, whereas with Beethoven it is often quite difficult to put your finger right on what he is saying. And any musician will tell you that that is why Beethoven is the greater composer. Because music which always says the same thing to you will necessarily soon become dull music, but music whose meaning is slightly different with each hearing has a greater chance of remaining alive.

Listen, if you can, to the forty-eight fugue themes of Bach's *Well Tempered Clavichord*. Listen to each theme, one after another. You will soon realize that each theme mirrors a different world of feeling. You will also soon realize that the more beautiful a theme seems to you the harder it is to find any word that will describe it to your complete satisfaction. Yes, you will certainly know whether it is a gay theme or a sad one. You will be able, in other words, in your own mind, to draw a frame of emotional feeling around your theme. Now study the sad one a little closer. Try to pin down the exact quality of its sadness. Is it pessimistically sad or resignedly sad; is it fatefully sad or smilingly sad?

Let us suppose that you are fortunate and can describe to your own satisfaction in so many words the exact meaning of your chosen theme. There is still no guarantee that anyone else will be satisfied. Nor need they be. The important thing is that each one feel for himself the specific expressive quality of a theme or, similarly, an entire piece of music. And if it is a great work of art, don't expect it to mean exactly the same thing to you each time you return to it.

Themes or pieces need not express only one emotion, of course. Take such a theme as the first main one of the *Ninth Symphony*, for example. It is clearly made up of different elements. It does not say only one thing. Yet anyone hearing it immediately gets a feeling of strength, a feeling of power. It isn't a power that comes simply because the theme is played loudly. It is a power inherent in the theme itself. The extraordinary strength and vigor of the theme results in the listener's receiving an impression that a forceful statement has been made. But one should never try to boil it down to "the fateful hammer of life," etc. That is where the trouble begins. The musician, in his exasperation, says it means nothing but the notes themselves, whereas the nonprofessional is only too anxious to hang on to any explanation that gives him the illusion of getting closer to the music's meaning.

Now, perhaps, the reader will know better what I mean when I say that music does have an expressive meaning but that we cannot say in so many words what that meaning is.

The third plane on which music exists is the sheerly musical plane. Besides the pleasurable sound of music and the expressive feeling that it gives off, music does exist in terms of the notes themselves and of their manipulation. Most listeners are not sufficiently conscious of this third plane. It will be largely the business of this book to make them more aware of music on this plane.

Professional musicians, on the other hand, are, if anything, too conscious of the mere notes themselves. They often fall into the error of becoming so engrossed with their arpeggios and staccatos that they forget the deeper aspects of the music they are performing. But from the layman's standpoint, it is not so much a matter of getting over bad habits on the sheerly musical plane as of increasing one's awareness of what is going on, in so far as the notes are concerned.

When the man in the street listens to the "notes themselves" with any degree of concentration, he is most likely to make some mention of the melody. Either he hears a pretty melody or he does not, and he generally lets it go at that. Rhythm is likely to gain his attention next, particularly if it seems exciting. But harmony and tone color are generally taken for granted, if they are thought of consciously at all. As for music's having a definite form of some kind, that idea seems never to have occurred to him.

It is very important for all of us to become more alive to music on its sheerly musical plane. After all, an actual musical material is being used. The intelligent listener must be prepared to increase his awareness of the musical material and what happens to it. He must hear the melodies, the rhythms, the harmonies, the tone colors in a more conscious fashion. But above all he must, in order to follow the line of the composer's thought, know something of the principles of musical form. Listening to all of these elements is listening on the sheerly musical plane.

Let me repeat that I have split up mechanically the three separate planes on which we listen merely for the sake of greater clarity.

Actually, we never listen on one or the other of these planes. What we do is to correlate them—listening in all three ways at the same time. It takes no mental effort, for we do it instinctively.

Perhaps an analogy with what happens to us when we visit the theater will make this instinctive correlation clearer. In the theater, you are aware of the actors and actresses, costumes and sets, sounds and movements. All these give one the sense that the theater is a pleasant place to be in. They constitute the sensuous plane in our theatrical reactions.

The expressive plane in the theater would be derived from the feeling that you get from what is happening on the stage. You are moved to pity, excitement, or gayety. It is this general feeling, generated aside from the particular words being spoken, a certain emotional something which exists on the stage, that is analogous to the expressive quality in music.

The plot and plot development is equivalent to our sheerly musical plane. The playwright creates and develops a character in just the same way that a composer creates and develops a theme. According to the degree of your awareness of the way in which the artist in either field handles his material will you become a more intelligent listener.

It is easy enough to see that the theatergoer never is conscious of any of these elements separately. He is aware of them all at the same time. The same is true of music listening. We simultaneously and without thinking listen on all three planes.

In a sense, the ideal listener is both inside and outside the music at the same moment, judging it and enjoying it, wishing it would go one way and watching it go another—almost like the composer at the moment he composes it; because in order to write his music, the composer must also be inside and outside his music, carried away by it and yet coldly critical of it. A subjective and objective attitude is implied in both creating and listening to music.

What the reader should strive for, then, is a more *active* kind of listening. Whether you listen to Mozart or Duke Ellington, you can deepen your understanding of music only by being a more conscious and aware listener—not someone who is just listening, but someone who is listening *for* something.

VLADIMIR NABOKOV

Philistines and Philistinism

Vladimir Nabokov (1899–1977) emigrated from Russia in 1919, after the Bolshevik Revolution. He moved to the United States from Europe in 1940, becoming an American citizen in 1945. His controversial novel *Lolita* (1958) brought him both critical acclaim and notoriety. Among Nabokov's other works are *Nabokov's Dozen* (1958), the novels *Pale Fire* (1962) and *Ada* (1969), and *Speak, Memory: An Autobiography Revisited* (1966). The following selection appears in *Lectures on Literature,* a collection of his essays and classroom presentations published in 1980.

A philistine is a full-grown person whose interests are of a material and commonplace nature, and whose mentality is formed of the stock ideas and conventional ideals of his or her group and time. I have said "full-grown person" because the child or the adolescent who may look like a small philistine is only a small parrot mimicking the ways of confirmed vulgarians, and it is easier to be a parrot than to be a white heron. "Vulgarian" is more or less synonymous with "philistine": the stress in a vulgarian is not so much on the conventionalism of a philistine as on the vulgarity of some of his conventional notions. I may also use the terms *genteel* and *bourgeois. Genteel* implies the lace-curtain refined vulgarity which is worse than simple coarseness. To burp in company may be rude, but to say "excuse me" after a burp is genteel and thus worse than vulgar. The term *bourgeois* I use following Flaubert, not Marx. *Bourgeois* in Flaubert's sense is a state of mind, not a state of pocket. A bourgeois is a smug philistine, a dignified vulgarian.

A philistine is not likely to exist in a very primitive society although no doubt rudiments of philistinism may be found even there. We may imagine, for instance, a cannibal who would prefer the human head he eats to be artistically colored, just as the American philistine prefers his oranges to be painted orange, his salmon pink, and his whisky yellow. But generally speaking philistinism presupposes a certain advanced state of civilization where throughout the ages certain traditions have accumulated in a heap and have started to stink.

Philistinism is international. It is found in all nations and in all classes. An English duke can be as much of a philistine as an American Shriner or a French bureaucrat or a Soviet citizen. The mentality of a Lenin or a Stalin or a Hitler in regard to the arts and the sciences was utterly bourgeois. A laborer or a coal miner can be just as bourgeois as a banker or a housewife or a Hollywood star.

Philistinism implies not only a collection of stock ideas but also the use of set phrases, clichés, banalities expressed in faded words. A true philistine has nothing but these trivial ideas of which he entirely consists. But it should be admitted that all of us have our cliché side; all of us in everyday life often use words not as words but as signs, as coins, as formulas. This does not mean that we are all philistines, but it does mean that we should be careful not to indulge too much in the automatic process of exchanging platitudes. On a hot day every other person will ask you, "Is it warm enough for you?" but that does not necessarily mean that the speaker is a philistine. He may be merely a parrot or a bright foreigner. When a person asks you "Hullo, how *are* you?" it is perhaps a sorry cliché to reply, "Fine"; but if you made to him a detailed report of your condition you might pass for a pedant and a bore. It also happens that platitudes are used by people as a kind of disguise or as the shortest cut for avoiding conversation with fools. I have known great scholars and poets and scientists who in the cafeteria sank to the level of the most commonplace give and take.

The character I have in view when I say "smug vulgarian" is, thus, not the part-time philistine, but the total type, the genteel bourgeois, the complete universal product of triteness and mediocrity. He is the conformist, the man who conforms to his group, and he also is typified by something else: he is a pseudo-idealist, he is pseudo-compassionate, he is pseudo-wise. The fraud is the closest ally of the true philistine. All such great words as "Beauty," "Love," "Nature," "Truth," and so on become masks and dupes when the smug vulgarian employs them. In *Dead Souls* you have heard Chichikov. In *Bleak House* you have heard Skimpole. You have heard Homais in *Madame Bovary*. The philistine likes to impress and he likes to be impressed, in consequence of which a world of deception, of mutual cheating, is formed by him and around him.

The philistine in his passionate urge to conform, to belong, to join, is torn between two longings: to act as everybody does, to admire, to use this or that thing because millions of people do; or else he craves to belong to an exclusive set, to an organization, to a club, to a hotel patronage or an ocean liner community (with the captain in white and wonderful food), and to delight in the knowledge that there is the head of a corporation or a European count sitting next to him. The philistine is often a snob. He is thrilled by riches and rank—"Darling, I've actually talked to a duchess!"

A philistine neither knows nor cares anything about art, including literature—his essential nature is anti-artistic—but he wants information and he is trained to read magazines. He is a faithful reader of the *Saturday Evening Post,* and when he reads he identifies himself with the characters. If he is a male philistine he will identify himself with the fascinating executive or any other big shot—aloof, single, but a boy and a golfer at heart; or if the reader is a female philistine— a philistinette—she will identify herself with the fascinating strawberry-blonde secretary, a slip of a girl but a mother at heart, who eventually marries the boyish boss. The philistine does not distinguish one writer from another; indeed, he reads little and only what may be useful to him, but he may belong to a book club and choose beautiful, *beautiful* books, a jumble of Simone de Beauvoir, Dostoevski, Marquand, Somerset Maugham, *Dr. Zhivago,* and Masters of the Renaissance. He does not much care for pictures, but for the sake of prestige he may hang in his parlor reproductions of Van Gogh's or Whistler's respective mothers, although secretly preferring Norman Rockwell.

In his love for the useful, for the material goods of life, he becomes an easy victim of the advertisement business. Ads may be very good ads—some of them are very artistic—that is not the point. The point is that they tend to appeal to the philistine's pride in possessing things whether silverware or underwear. I mean the following kind of ad: just come to the family is a radio set or a television set (or a car, or a refrigerator, or table silver—anything will do). It has just come to the family: mother clasps her hands in dazed delight, the children crowd around all agog: junior and the dog strain up to the edge of the table where the Idol is enthroned; even Grandma of the beaming wrinkles peeps out somewhere in the background; and somewhat apart, his thumbs gleefully inserted in the armpits of his waistcoat, stands triumphant Dad or Pop, the Proud Donor. Small boys and girls in ads are invariably freckled, and the smaller fry have front teeth missing. I have nothing against freckles (in fact I find them very becoming in live creatures) and quite possibly a special survey might reveal that the majority of small American-born Americans *are* freckled, or else perhaps another survey might reveal that all successful executives and handsome housewives had been freckled in their childhood. I repeat, I have really nothing against freckles as such. But I do think there is considerable philistinism involved in the use made of them by advertisers and other agencies. I am told that when an unfreckled, or only slightly freckled, little boy actor has to appear on the screen in television, an artificial set of freckles is applied to the middle of his face. Twenty-two freckles is the minimum: eight over each cheekbone and six on the saddle of the pert nose. In the comics, freckles look like a case of bad rash. In one series of comics they appear as tiny circles. But although the good cute little boys of the ads are blond or redhaired, with freckles, the handsome young men of the ads are generally dark haired and always have thick dark eyebrows. The evolution is from Scotch to Celtic.

The rich philistinism emanating from advertisement is due not to their exaggerating (or inventing) the glory of this or that service-able article but to suggesting that the acme of human happiness is purchasable and that its purchase somehow ennobles the purchaser. Of course, the world they create is pretty harmless in itself because everybody knows that it is made up by the seller with the under-standing that the buyer will join in the make-believe. The amusing part is not that it is a world where nothing spiritual remains except the ecstatic smiles of people serving or eating celestial cereals, or a world where the game of the senses is played according to bourgeois rules, but that it is a kind of satellite shadow world in the actual existence of which neither sellers nor buyers really believe in their heart of hearts—especially in this wise quiet country.

Russians have, or had, a special name for smug philistinism—*poshlust*. *Poshlism* is not only the obviously trashy but mainly the falsely important, the falsely beautiful, the falsely clever, the falsely attractive. To apply the deadly label of *poshlism* to something is not only an esthetic judgment but also a moral indictment. The genuine, the guileless, the good is never *poshlust*. It is possible to maintain that a simple, uncivilized man is seldom if ever a *poshlust* since *poshlism* presupposes the veneer of civilization. A peasant has to become a townsman in order to become vulgar. A painted necktie has to hide the honest Adam's apple in order to produce *poshlism*.

It is possible that the term itself has been so nicely devised by Russians because of the cult of simplicity and good taste in old Russia. The Russia of today, a country of moral imbeciles, of smiling slaves and poker-faced bullies, has stopped noticing *poshlism* because Soviet Russia is so full of its special brand, a blend of despotism and pseudo-culture; but in the old days a Gogol, a Tolstoy, a Chekhov in quest of the simplicity of truth easily distinguished the vulgar side of things as well as the trashy systems of pseudo-thought. But *poshlists* are found everywhere, in every country, in this country as well as in Europe—in fact *poshlism* is more common in Europe than here, despite our American ads.

N I N E

Sports: Mens Sana in Corpore Sano

If all the year were playing holidays
To sport would be as tedious as to work.

Shakespeare: I Henry IV

Sports are a subtle barometer of change in our society. They measure how we feel about ourselves as individuals and as members of various groups. Chances are you are a fan of one sport or another. You may even be a participant. Have you ever thought of precisely *why* you may be interested or involved in a particular sport? Is your involvement based upon traditions in your family or other social groupings to which you belong? Do you see patterns of inclusion and exclusion in certain sports? What do these patterns say about our society?

To answer these questions, you might first read the short story by Ellen Gilchrist that opens this section, a story that explores the exclusion of women from many sporting activities. Or you may want to consider a woman writer's perspective on a traditionally male sport by reading Joyce Carol Oates's essay, "On Boxing."

As the great historian Johan Huizinga points out in "The Nature and Significance of Play," sport, or at least *play,* is fundamental to human nature and helps to define the essence of human society and social interaction. Sometimes, as we see in Roland Barthes's essay, "The World of Wrestling," sport permits us to exaggerate the capabilities of human nature itself, allowing us to become, vicariously, more than we can actually be.

Indeed, as Jeffrey Schrank suggests in "Sport and the American Dream," sport helps to define what we might call "the American way of life." This essay also provides a good starting point for some research. Note how Schrank, using football, baseball, and golf, handles comparisons among the three. Pick two or three other sports and make your own comparisons. If you have one sport that is your passion, read George Sheehan's "Surf's Up! Head for the Waves" and apply his writing techniques to a description of your own sport.

For many people, sports are less passions than starting points. Involvement in sports leads to meeting people and exploring new places and ideas. Sometimes sports become metaphors for other aspects of our lives. John Cheever's "The Swimmer" is a touchstone for exploring the directions we can take in life, directions that can be metaphorically defined by sports.

Then too, sports can be controversial. Especially so is hunting, a subject explored by Edward Abbey in "Blood Sport." You may have your own thoughts on one side or the other of the arguments Abbey advances. Can you make your own argument cogently, taking opposing views into account?

As you read these selections, ask yourself what it is in sports that attracts you or repels you. But try to get beyond your initial response. Perhaps you will want to interview people who participate in sports you instinctively dislike. You may find, for example, that there is a deeply philosophical side to karate and that people who practice that art are really nothing like the characters in typical martial arts films. Take your notebook to a martial arts gym and interview the people you find there. Or go to a beach and ask surfers why they surf. You may indeed find some "macho" characters, but you may also find some reflective souls. The same exercise could be done for skiing, scuba diving, tennis, golf, and many other sports.

What do sports have in common with heroism? Ask this question after you have read Jan Morris's "To Everest." Do you have a sports hero? What specific characteristics of that person elicit your admiration? Are you able to identify with sports heroes from a variety of backgrounds? If you are a man, are you able to identify with women sports figures? If a woman, with men? Everybody can identify with youthful sports heroes, for we all have been young once. If you are still young, however, can you identify with older sports heroes, such as golfer Hale Irwin, who won the U.S. Open at age forty-five? If you are middle-aged, what does an experience like Irwin's say to you? Finally, what do sports teach us about life and about ourselves? Keep such questions in mind as you read the selections that follow.

ELLEN GILCHRIST

Revenge

Ellen Gilchrist (1935–) is a Mississippi-born writer who often
sets her work in New Orleans. Gilchrist often relies on dialogue to
promote story lines in her writing; she is known for her complex
female protagonists. Her books include the novels *The Annunciation*
(1983) and *The Anna Papers* (1988), the poetry collection *The Land
Surveyor's Daughter* (1979), and the short story collections, *In the
Land of Dreamy Dreams* (1981), in which the following selection
appears, *Victory over Japan* (1984), and *I Cannot Get You Close
Enough* (1990).

It was the summer of the Broad Jump Pit.

The Broad Jump Pit, how shall I describe it! It was a bright
orange rectangle in the middle of a green pasture. It was three feet
deep, filled with river sand and sawdust. A real cinder track led up
to it, ending where tall poles for pole-vaulting rose forever in the
still Delta air.

I am looking through the old binoculars. I am watching Bunky
coming at a run down the cinder path, pausing expertly at the jump-
off line, then rising into the air, heels stretched far out in front of
him, landing in the sawdust. Before the dust has settled Saint John
comes running with the tape, calling out measurements in his high,
excitable voice.

Next comes my thirteen-year-old brother, Dudley, coming at a
brisk jog down the track, the pole-vaulting pole held lightly in his
delicate hands, then vaulting, high into the sky. His skinny tanned
legs make a last, desperate surge, and he is clear and over.

Think how it looked from my lonely exile atop the chicken house.
I was ten years old, the only girl in a house full of cousins. There
were six of us, shipped to the Delta for the summer, dumped on my
grandmother right in the middle of a world war.

They built this wonder in answer to a V-Mail[1] letter from my
father in Europe. The war was going well, my father wrote, within a

---

[1] In World War II, V- (short for Victory) mail letters were sent photographed on
microfilm and enlarged onto paper for delivery. (ED.)

year the Allies would triumph over the forces of evil, the world would be at peace, and the Olympic torch would again be brought down from its mountain and carried to Zurich or Amsterdam or London or Mexico City, wherever free men lived and worshiped sports. My father had been a participant in an Olympic event when he was young.

Therefore, the letter continued, Dudley and Bunky and Philip and Saint John and Oliver were to begin training. The United States would need athletes now, not soldiers.

They were to train for broad jumping and pole-vaulting and discus throwing, for fifty-, one-hundred-, and four-hundred-yard dashes, for high and low hurdles. The letter included instructions for building the pit, for making pole-vaulting poles out of cane, and for converting ordinary sawhorses into hurdles. It ended with a page of tips for proper eating and admonished Dudley to take good care of me as I was my father's own dear sweet little girl.

The letter came one afternoon. Early the next morning they began construction. Around noon I wandered out to the pasture to see how they were coming along. I picked up a shovel.

"Put that down, Rhoda," Dudley said. "Don't bother us now. We're working."

"I know it," I said. "I'm going to help."

"No, you're not." Bunky said. "This is the Broad Jump Pit. We're starting our training."

"I'm going to do it too," I said. "I'm going to be in training."

"Get out of here now," Dudley said. "This is only for boys, Rhoda. This isn't a game."

"I'm going to dig it if I want to," I said, picking up a shovelful of dirt and throwing it on Philip. On second thought I picked up another shovelful and threw it on Bunky.

"Get out of here, Ratface," Philip yelled at me. "You German spy." He was referring to the initials on my Girl Scout uniform.

"You goddamn niggers," I yelled. "You niggers. I'm digging this if I want to and you can't stop me, you nasty niggers, you Japs, you Jews." I was throwing dirt on everyone now. Dudley grabbed the shovel and wrestled me to the ground. He held my arms down in the coarse grass and peered into my face.

"Rhoda, you're not having anything to do with this Broad Jump Pit. And if you set foot inside this pasture or come around here and touch anything we will break your legs and drown you in the bayou with a crowbar around your neck." He was twisting my leg until it creaked at the joints. "Do you get it, Rhoda? Do you understand me?"

"Let me up," I was screaming, my rage threatening to split open my skull. "Let me up, you goddamn nigger, you Jap, you spy. I'm telling Grannie and you're going to get the worst whipping of your life. And you better quit digging this hole for the horses to fall in. Let me up, let me up. Let me go."

"You've been ruining everything we've thought up all summer," Dudley said, "and you're not setting foot inside this pasture."

In the end they dragged me back to the house, and I ran screaming into the kitchen where Grannie and Calvin, the black man who did the cooking, tried to comfort me, feeding me pound cake and offering to let me help with the mayonnaise.

"You be a sweet girl, Rhoda," my grandmother said, "and this afternoon we'll go over to Eisenglas Plantation to play with Miss Ann Wentzel."

"I don't want to play with Miss Ann Wentzel," I screamed. "I hate Miss Ann Wentzel. She's fat and she calls me a Yankee. She said my socks were ugly."

"Why, Rhoda," my grandmother said. "I'm surprised at you. Miss Ann Wentzel is your own sweet friend. Her momma was your momma's roommate at All Saint's. How can you talk like that?"

"She's a nigger," I screamed. "She's a goddamned nigger German spy."

"Now it's coming. Here comes the temper," Calvin said, rolling his eyes back in their sockets to make me madder. I threw my second fit of the morning, beating my fists into a door frame. My grandmother seized me in soft arms. She led me to a bedroom where I sobbed myself to sleep in a sea of down pillows.

The construction went on for several weeks. As soon as they finished breakfast every morning they started out for the pasture. Wood had to be burned to make cinders, sawdust brought from the sawmill, sand hauled up from the riverbank by wheelbarrow.

When the pit was finished the savage training began. From my several vantage points I watched them. Up and down, up and down they ran, dove, flew, sprinted. Drenched with sweat they wrestled each other to the ground in bitter feuds over distances and times and fractions of inches.

Dudley was their self-appointed leader. He drove them like a demon. They began each morning by running around the edge of the pasture several times, then practicing their hurdles and dashes, then on to discus throwing and calisthenics. Then on to the Broad Jump Pit with its endless challenges.

They even pressed the old mare into service. Saint John was from New Orleans and knew the British ambassador and was thinking of being a polo player. Up and down the pasture he drove the poor old creature, leaning far out of the saddle, swatting a basketball with my grandaddy's cane.

I spied on them from the swing that went out over the bayou, and from the roof of the chicken house, and sometimes from the pasture fence itself, calling out insults or attempts to make them jealous.

"Guess what," I would yell, "I'm going to town to the Chinaman's store." "Guess what, I'm getting to go to the beauty parlor." "Doctor Biggs says you're adopted."

They ignored me. At meals they sat together at one end of the table, making jokes about my temper and my red hair, opening their mouths so I could see their half-chewed food, burping loudly in my direction.

At night they pulled their cots together on the sleeping porch, plotting against me while I slept beneath my grandmother's window, listening to the soft assurance of her snoring.

I began to pray the Japs would win the war, would come marching into Issaquena County and take them prisoners, starving and torturing them, sticking bamboo splinters under their fingernails. I saw myself in the Japanese colonel's office, turning them in, writing their names down, myself being treated like an honored guest, drinking tea from tiny blue cups like the ones the Chinaman had in his store.

They would be outside, tied up with wire. There would be Dudley, begging for mercy. What good to him now his loyal gang, his photographic memory, his trick magnet dogs, his perfect pitch, his camp shorts, his Baby Brownie camera.

I prayed they would get polio, would be consigned forever to iron lungs. I put myself to sleep at night imagining their labored breathing, their five little wheelchairs lined up by the store as I drove by in my father's Packard, my arm around the jacket of his blue uniform, on my way to Hollywood for my screen test.

Meanwhile, I practiced dancing. My grandmother had a black housekeeper named Baby Doll who was a wonderful dancer. In the mornings I followed her around while she dusted, begging for dancing lessons. She was a big woman, as tall as a man, and gave off a dark rich smell, an unforgettable incense, a combination of Evening in Paris and the sweet perfume of the cabins.

Baby Doll wore bright skirts and on her blouses a pin that said REMEMBER, then a real pearl, then HARBOR. She was engaged to a sailor and was going to California to be rich as soon as the war was over.

I would put a stack of heavy, scratched records on the record player, and Baby Doll and I would dance through the parlors to the music of Glenn Miller or Guy Lombardo or Tommy Dorsey.

Sometimes I stood on a stool in front of the fireplace and made up lyrics while Baby Doll acted them out, moving lightly across the old dark rugs, turning and swooping and shaking and gliding.

Outside the summer sun beat down on the Delta, beating down a million volts a minute, feeding the soybeans and cotton and clover, sucking Steele's Bayou up into the clouds, beating down on the road and the store, on the pecans and elms and magnolias, on the men at work in the fields, on the athletes at work in the pasture.

Inside Baby Doll and I would be dancing. Or Guy Lombardo would be playing "Begin the Beguine" and I would be belting out lyrics.

> "Oh, let them begin . . . we don't care,
> America all . . . ways does its share,
> We'll be there with plenty of ammo,
> Allies . . . don't ever despair . . ."

Baby Doll thought I was a genius. If I was having an especially creative morning she would go running out to the kitchen and bring anyone she could find to hear me.

"Oh, let them begin any warrr . . ." I would be singing, tapping one foot against the fireplace tiles, waving my arms around like a conductor.

> "Uncle Sam will fight
> for the underrr . . . doggg.
> Never fear, Allies, never fear."

A new record would drop. Baby Doll would swoop me into her fragrant arms, and we would break into an improvisation on Tommy Dorsey's "Boogie-Woogie."

But the Broad Jump Pit would not go away. It loomed in my dreams. If I walked to the store I had to pass the pasture. If I stood on the porch or looked out my grandmother's window, there it was, shimmering in the sunlight, constantly guarded by one of the Olympians.

Things went from bad to worse between me and Dudley. If we so much as passed each other in the hall a fight began. He would hold up his fists and dance around, trying to look like a fighter. When I came flailing at him he would reach underneath my arms and punch me in the stomach.

I considered poisoning him. There was a box of white powder in the toolshed with a skull and crossbones above the label. Several times I took it down and held it in my hands, shuddering at the power it gave me. Only the thought of the electric chair kept me from using it.

Every day Dudley gathered his troops and headed out for the pasture. Every day my hatred grew and festered. Then, just about the time I could stand it no longer, a diversion occurred.

One afternoon about four o'clock an official-looking sedan clattered across the bridge and came roaring down the road to the house.

It was my cousin, Lauralee Manning, wearing her WAVE[2] uniform and smoking Camels in an ivory holder. Lauralee had been widowed at the beginning of the war when her young husband crashed his Navy training plane into the Pacific.

Lauralee dried her tears, joined the WAVES, and went off to avenge his death. I had not seen this paragon since I was a small child, but I had memorized the photograph Miss Onnie Maud, who was Lauralee's mother, kept on her dresser. It was a photograph of Lauralee leaning against the rail of a destroyer.

Not that Lauralee ever went to sea on a destroyer. She was spending the war in Pensacola, Florida, being secretary to an admiral.

Now, out of a clear blue sky, here was Lauralee, home on leave with a two-carat diamond ring and the news that she was getting married.

"You might have called and given some warning," Miss Onnie Maud said, turning Lauralee into a mass of wrinkles with her embraces. "You could have softened the blow with a letter."

"Who's the groom," my grandmother said. "I only hope he's not a pilot."

"Is he an admiral?" I said, "or a colonel or a major or a commander?"

---

[2] (Women Accepted for Volunteer Emergency Service) a women's unit in the United States Navy (ED.)

"My fiancé's not in uniform, Honey," Lauralee said. "He's in real estate. He runs the war-bond effort for the whole state of Florida. Last year he collected half a million dollars."

"In real estate!" Miss Onnie Maud said, gasping. "What religion is he?"

"He's Unitarian," she said. "His name is Donald Marcus. He's best friends with Admiral Semmes, that's how I met him. And he's coming a week from Saturday, and that's all the time we have to get ready for the wedding."

"Unitarian!" Miss Onnie Maud said. "I don't think I've ever met a Unitarian."

"Why isn't he in uniform?" I insisted.

"He has flat feet," Lauralee said gaily. "But you'll love him when you see him."

Later that afternoon Lauralee took me off by myself for a ride in the sedan.

"Your mother is my favorite cousin," she said, touching my face with gentle fingers. "You'll look just like her when you grow up and get your figure."

I moved closer, admiring the brass buttons on her starched uniform and the brisk way she shifted and braked and put in the clutch and accelerated.

We drove down the river road and out to the bootlegger's shack where Lauralee bought a pint of Jack Daniel's and two Cokes. She poured out half of her Coke, filled it with whiskey, and we roared off down the road with the radio playing.

We drove along in the lengthening day. Lauralee was chain-smoking, lighting one Camel after another, tossing the butts out the window, taking sips from her bourbon and Coke. I sat beside her, pretending to smoke a piece of rolled-up paper, making little noises into the mouth of my Coke bottle.

We drove up to a picnic spot on the levee and sat under a tree to look out at the river.

"I miss this old river," she said. "When I'm sad I dream about it licking the tops of the levees."

I didn't know what to say to that. To tell the truth I was afraid to say much of anything to Lauralee. She seemed so splendid. It was enough to be allowed to sit by her on the levee.

"Now, Rhoda," she said, "your mother was matron of honor in my wedding to Buddy, and I want you, her own little daughter, to be maid of honor in my second wedding."

I could hardly believe my ears! While I was trying to think of something to say to this wonderful news I saw that Lauralee was crying, great tears were forming in her blue eyes.

"Under this very tree is where Buddy and I got engaged," she said. Now the tears were really starting to roll, falling all over the front of her uniform. "He gave me my ring right where we're sitting."

"The maid of honor?" I said, patting her shoulder, trying to be of some comfort. "You really mean the maid of honor?"

"Now he's gone from the world," she continued, "and I'm marrying a wonderful man, but that doesn't make it any easier. Oh, Rhoda, they never even found his body, never even found his body."

I was patting her on the head now, afraid she would forget her offer in the midst of her sorrow.

"You mean I get to be the real maid of honor?"

"Oh yes, Rhoda, Honey," she said. "The maid of honor, my only attendant." She blew her nose on a lace-trimmed handkerchief and sat up straighter, taking a drink from the Coke bottle.

"Not only that, but I have decided to let you pick out your own dress. We'll go to Greenville and you can try on every dress at Nell's and Blum's and you can have the one you like the most."

I threw my arms around her, burning with happiness, smelling her whiskey and Camels and the dark Tabu perfume that was her signature. Over her shoulder and through the low branches of the trees the afternoon sun was going down in an orgy of reds and blues and purples and violets, falling from sight, going all the way to China.

Let them keep their nasty Broad Jump Pit I thought. Wait till they hear about this. Wait till they find out I'm maid of honor in a military wedding.

Finding the dress was another matter. Early the next morning Miss Onnie Maud and my grandmother and Lauralee and I set out for Greenville.

As we passed the pasture I hung out the back window making faces at the athletes. This time they only pretended to ignore me. They couldn't ignore this wedding. It was going to be in the parlor instead of the church so they wouldn't even get to be altar boys. They wouldn't get to light a candle.

"I don't know why you care what's going on in that pasture," my grandmother said. "Even if they let you play with them all it would do is make you a lot of ugly muscles."

"Then you'd have big old ugly arms like Weegie Toler," Miss Onnie Maud said. "Lauralee, you remember Weegie Toler, that was a swimmer. Her arms got so big no one would take her to a dance, much less marry her."

"Well, I don't want to get married anyway," I said. "I'm never getting married. I'm going to New York City and be a lawyer."

"Where does she get those ideas?" Miss Onnie Maud said.

"When you get older you'll want to get married," Lauralee said. "Look at how much fun you're having being in my wedding."

"Well, I'm never getting married," I said. "And I'm never having any children. I'm going to New York and be a lawyer and save people from the electric chair."

"It's the movies," Miss Onnie Maud said. "They let her watch anything she likes in Indiana."

We walked into Nell's and Blum's Department Store and took up the largest dressing room. My grandmother and Miss Onnie Maud were seated on brocade chairs and every saleslady in the store came crowding around trying to get in on the wedding.

I refused to even consider the dresses they brought from the "girls'" department.

"I told her she could wear whatever she wanted," Lauralee said, "and I'm keeping my promise."

"Well, she's not wearing green satin or I'm not coming," my grandmother said, indicating the dress I had found on a rack and was clutching against me.

"At least let her try it on," Lauralee said. "Let her see for herself." She zipped me into the green satin. It came down to my ankles and fit around my midsection like a girdle, making my waist seem smaller than my stomach. I admired myself in the mirror. I was almost perfect. I looked exactly like a nightclub singer.

"This one's fine," I said. "This is the one I want."

"It looks marvelous, Rhoda," Lauralee said, "but it's the wrong color for the wedding. Remember I'm wearing blue."

"I believe the child's color-blind," Miss Onnie Maud said. "It runs in her father's family."

"I am not color-blind," I said, reaching behind me and unzipping the dress. "I have twenty-twenty vision."

"Let her try on some more," Lauralee said. "Let her try on everything in the store."

I proceeded to do just that, with the salesladies getting grumpier and grumpier. I tried on a gold gabardine dress with a rhinestone-studded cumberbund. I tried on a pink ballerina-length formal and a lavender voile tea dress and several silk suits. Somehow nothing looked right.

"Maybe we'll have to make her something," my grandmother said.

"But there's no time," Miss Onnie Maud said. "Besides first we'd have to find out what she wants. Rhoda, please tell us what you're looking for."

Their faces all turned to mine, waiting for an answer. But I didn't know the answer.

The dress I wanted was a secret. The dress I wanted was dark and tall and thin as a reed. There was a word for what I wanted, a word I had seen in magazines. But what was that word? I could not remember.

"I want something dark," I said at last. "Something dark and silky."

"Wait right there," the saleslady said. "Wait just a minute." Then, from out of a prewar storage closet she brought a black-watch plaid recital dress with spaghetti straps and a white piqué jacket. It was made of taffeta and rustled when I touched it. There was a label sewn into the collar of the jacket. *Little Miss Sophisticate,* it said. *Sophisticate,* that was the word I was seeking.

I put on the dress and stood triumphant in a sea of ladies and dresses and hangers.

"This is the dress," I said. "This is the dress I'm wearing."

"It's perfect," Lauralee said. "Start hemming it up. She'll be the prettiest maid of honor in the whole world."

All the way home I held the box on my lap thinking about how I would look in the dress. Wait till they see me like this, I was thinking. Wait till they see what I really look like.

I fell in love with the groom. The moment I laid eyes on him I forgot he was flat-footed. He arrived bearing gifts of music and perfume and candy, a warm dark-skinned man with eyes the color of walnuts.

He laughed out loud when he saw me, standing on the porch with my hands on my hips.

"This must be Rhoda," he exclaimed, "the famous red-haired maid of honor." He came running up the steps, gave me a slow, exciting hug, and presented me with a whole album of Xavier Cugat records. I had never owned a record of my own, much less an album.

Before the evening was over I put on a red formal I found in a trunk and did a South American dance for him to Xavier Cugat's "Poinciana." He said he had never seen anything like it in his whole life.

The wedding itself was a disappointment. No one came but the immediate family and there was no aisle to march down and the only music was Onnie Maud playing "Liebestraum."

Dudley and Philip and Saint John and Oliver and Bunky were dressed in long pants and white shirts and ties. They had fresh military crew cuts and looked like a nest of new birds, huddled together on the blue velvet sofa, trying to keep their hands to themselves, trying to figure out how to act at a wedding.

The elderly Episcopal priest read out the ceremony in a gravelly smoker's voice, ruining all the good parts by coughing. He was in a bad mood because Lauralee and Mr. Marcus hadn't found time to come to him for marriage instruction.

Still, I got to hold the bride's flowers while he gave her the ring and stood so close to her during the ceremony I could hear her breathing.

The reception was better. People came from all over the Delta. There were tables with candles set up around the porches and sprays of greenery in every corner. There were gentlemen sweating in linen suits and the record player playing every minute. In the back hall Calvin had set up a real professional bar with tall, permanently frosted glasses and ice and mint and lemons and every kind of whiskey and liqueur in the world.

I stood in the receiving line getting compliments on my dress, then wandered around the room eating cake and letting people hug me. After a while I got bored with that and went out to the back hall and began to fix myself a drink at the bar.

I took one of the frosted glasses and began filling it from different bottles, tasting as I went along. I used plenty of crème de menthe and soon had something that tasted heavenly. I filled the glass with crushed ice, added three straws, and went out to sit on the back steps and cool off.

I was feeling wonderful. A full moon was caught like a kite in the pecan trees across the river. I sipped along on my drink. Then, without planning it, I did something I had never dreamed of doing. I left the porch alone at night. Usually I was in terror of the dark. My grandmother had told me that alligators come out of the bayou to eat children who wander alone at night.

I walked out across the yard, the huge moon giving so much light I almost cast a shadow. When I was nearly to the water's edge I turned and looked back toward the house. It shimmered in the moonlight like a jukebox alive in a meadow, seemed to pulsate with music and laughter and people, beautiful and foreign, not a part of me.

I looked out at the water, then down the road to the pasture. The Broad Jump Pit! There it was, perfect and unguarded. Why had I never thought of doing this before?

I began to run toward the road. I ran as fast as my Mary Jane pumps would allow me. I pulled my dress up around my waist and climbed the fence in one motion, dropping lightly down on the other side. I was sweating heavily, alone with the moon and my wonderful courage.

I knew exactly what to do first. I picked up the pole and hoisted it over my head. It felt solid and balanced and alive. I hoisted it up and down a few times as I had seen Dudley do, getting the feel of it.

Then I laid it ceremoniously down on the ground, reached behind me, and unhooked the plaid formal. I left it lying in a heap on the ground. There I stood, in my cotton underpants, ready to take up pole-vaulting.

I lifted the pole and carried it back to the end of the cinder path. I ran slowly down the path, stuck the pole in the wooden cup, and attempted throwing my body into the air, using it as a lever.

Something was wrong. It was more difficult than it appeared from a distance. I tried again. Nothing happened. I sat down with the pole across my legs to think things over.

Then I remembered something I had watched Dudley doing through the binoculars. He measured down from the end of the pole with his fingers spread wide. That was it, I had to hold it closer to the end.

I tried it again. This time the pole lifted me several feet off the ground. My body sailed across the grass in a neat arc and I landed on my toes. I was a natural!

I do not know how long I was out there, running up and down the cinder path, thrusting my body further and further through space, tossing myself into the pit like a mussel shell thrown across the bayou.

At last I decided I was ready for the real test. I had to vault over a cane barrier. I examined the pegs on the wooden poles and chose one that came up my shoulder.

I put the barrier pole in place, spit over my left shoulder, and marched back to the end of the path. Suck up your guts, I told myself. It's only a pole. It won't get stuck in your stomach and tear out your insides. It won't kill you.

I stood at the end of the path eyeballing the barrier. Then, above the incessant racket of the crickets, I heard my name being called. Rhoda . . . the voices were calling. Rhoda . . . Rhoda . . . Rhoda . . . Rhoda.

I turned toward the house and saw them coming. Mr. Marcus and Dudley and Bunky and Calvin and Lauralee and what looked like half the wedding. They were climbing the fence, calling my name, and coming to get me. Rhoda . . . they called out. Where on earth have you been? What on earth are you doing?

I hoisted the pole up to my shoulders and began to run down the path, running into the light from the moon. I picked up speed, thrust the pole into the cup, and threw myself into the sky, into the still Delta night. I sailed up and was clear and over the barrier.

I let go of the pole and began my fall, which seemed to last a long, long time. It was like falling through clear water. I dropped into the sawdust and lay very still, waiting for them to reach me.

Sometimes I think whatever has happened since has been of no real interest to me.

JAN MORRIS

To Everest

Jan Morris (1926–   ) is a British journalist, novelist, and travel writer who accompanied Sir Edmund Hillary on his ascent of Mt. Everest in 1953. He also wrote several volumes on the history of the British Empire. In 1972, after years of hormone therapy, Morris (born "James") underwent sex change surgery and became "Jan." *Conundrum* (1974), from which the following selection is excerpted, is an autobiographical account of that experience. Later works include *Travels* (1976), *Journeys* (1984), *Hong Kong* (1988), and *Pleasures of a Tangled Life* (1989), a sequel to *Conundrum*.

Though I resented my body, I did not dislike it. I rather admired it, as it happened. It might not be the body beautiful, but it was lean and sinewy, never ran to fat, and worked like a machine of quality, responding exuberantly to a touch of the throttle or a long haul home. Women, I think, never have quite this feeling about their bodies, and I shall never have it again. It is a male prerogative, and contributes no doubt to the male arrogance. In those days, though for that very reason I did not want it, still I recognized the merits of my physique, and had pleasure from its exercise.

I first felt its full power, as one might realize for the first time the potential of a run-in car, in 1953, when I was assigned by *The Times* to join the British expedition shortly to make the first ascent of Mount Everest. This was essentially a physical undertaking. The paper had exclusive rights to dispatches from the mountain, and I was to be the only correspondent with the team, my job being partly to see that dispatches from the expedition's leader got safely home to London, but chiefly to write dispatches of my own. The competition would be intense and very likely violent, communications were primitive to a degree, and the only way to do the job was to climb fairly high up the mountain myself and periodically, to put a complex operation simply, run down it again with the news. It was not particularly to my credit that I was given the assignment—at an agile twenty-six I was patently better suited for it than most of my colleagues at Printing House Square. I took exercise daily (as I still do), did not smoke (and still don't), and though excessively fond of wine, seldom drank spirits, not much liking the taste of them.

I was also, being some years out of the 9th Lancers,[1] furiously keen. There is something about the newspaper life, however specious its values and ridiculous its antics, that brings out the zest in its practitioners. It may be nonsense, but it is undeniably fun. I was not especially anxious to achieve fame in the trade, for I already felt instinctively that it would not be my life's occupation, but even so I would have stooped to almost any skulduggery to achieve what was, self-consciously even then, quaintly called a scoop. The news from Everest was to be mine, and anyone who tried to steal it from me should look out for trouble.

In such a mood, at such an age, at the peak of a young man's physical condition, I found myself in May, 1953, high on the flank of the world's greatest mountain.

Let me try to describe the sensation for my readers, as it seems to me today—and especially for my women readers, who are unlikely I now see to have experienced such a conjunction of energies.

Imagine first the setting. This is theatrically changeable. In the

---

[1] a British regiment in which Morris was enlisted from 1943–47 (ED.)

morning it is like living, reduced to minuscule proportions, in a bowl of broken ice cubes in a sunny garden. Somewhere over the rim, one assumes, there are green trees, fields and flowers; within the bowl everything is a brilliant white and blue. It is silent in there. The mountain walls deaden everything and cushion the hours in a disciplinary hush. The only noise is a drip of water sometimes, the howl of a falling boulder or the rumble of a distant avalanche. The sky above is a savage blue, the sun glares mercilessly off the snow and ice, blistering one's lips, dazzling one's eyes, and filling that mountain declivity with its substance.

In the afternoon everything changes. Then the sky scowls down, high snow-clouds billow in from Tibet, a restless cruel wind blows up, and before long the snow is falling in slanted parallel across the landscape, blotting out sky, ridges, and all, and making you feel that your ice-bowl has been put back into the refrigerator. It is terribly cold. The afternoon is filled with sounds, the rush of wind, the flapping of tent-canvas, the squeak and creak of guy-ropes; and as the evening draws on the snow piles up around your tent, half burying it infinitesimally in the hulk of Everest, as though you have been prematurely incarcerated, or perhaps trapped in a sunken submarine—for you can see the line of snow slowly rising through the nylon walls of the tent, like water rising to submerge you.

But imagine now the young man's condition. First, he is constant against this inconstant background. His body is running not in gusts and squalls, but at a steady high speed. He actually tingles with strength and energy, as though sparks might fly from his skin in the dark. Nothing sags in him. His body has no spare weight upon it, only muscles made supple by exercise. When, in the bright Himalayan morning, he emerges from his tent to make the long trek down the mountain to the Khumbu glacier below, it is as though he could leap down there in gigantic strides, singing as he goes. And when, the same evening perhaps, he labors up again through the driving snow, it is not a misery but a challenge to him, something to be outfaced, something actually to be enjoyed, as the deep snow drags at his feet, the water trickles down the back of his neck, and his face thickens with cold, ice, and wind.

There is no hardship to it, for it is not imposed upon him. He is the master. He feels that anything is possible to him, and that his relative position to events will always remain the same. He does not have to wonder what his form will be tomorrow, for it will be the same as it is today. His mind, like his body, is tuned to the job, and will not splutter or falter. It is this feeling of unfluctuating control,

I think, that women cannot share, and it springs of course not from the intellect or the personality, nor even so much from upbringing, but specifically from the body. The male body may be ungenerous, even uncreative in the deepest kind, but when it is working properly it is a marvelous thing to inhabit. I admit it in retrospect more than I did at the time, and I look back to those moments of supreme male fitness as one remembers champagne or a morning swim. Nothing could beat me, I knew for sure; and nothing did.

I think for sheer exuberance the best day of my life was my last on Everest. The mountain had been climbed, and I had already begun my race down the glacier towards Katmandu, leaving the expedition to pack its gear behind me. By a combination of cunning and ingenuity I had already sent a coded message through an Indian Army radio transmitter at Namche Bazar, twenty miles south of Everest, its operators being unaware of its meaning; but I did not know if it had reached London safely, so I was myself hastening back to Katmandu and the cable office with my own final dispatch. How brilliant I felt, as with a couple of Sherpa porters I bounded down the glacial moraine towards the green below! I was brilliant with the success of my friends on the mountain, I was brilliant with my knowledge of the event, brilliant with muscular tautness, brilliant with conceit, brilliant with awareness of the subterfuge, amounting very nearly to dishonesty, by which I hoped to have deceived my competitors and scooped the world. All those weeks at high altitude had suited me, too, and had given me a kind of heightened fervor, as though my brain had been quickened by drugs to keep pace with my body. I laughed and sang all the way down the glacier, and when next morning I heard from the radio that my news had reached London providentially on the eve of Queen Elizabeth's coronation, I felt as though I had been crowned myself.

I never mind the swagger of young men. It is their right to swank, and I know the sensation!

Once more on Everest I was the outsider—formally this time, as well as tacitly. None of the climbers would have guessed, I am sure, how irrevocably distinct I felt from them; but they were aware that I was not a climber, and had been attached to the expedition only to watch. At first I was supposed to provide my own victuals and equipment, but it seemed rather silly to maintain such segregation twenty thousand feet above nowhere, so I soon pooled my resources with theirs, and pitched my tent among them.

On Everest, nevertheless, I realized more explicitly some truths about myself. Though I was as fit as most of those men, I responded to different drives. I would have suffered almost anything to get those dispatches safely back to London, but I did not share the mountaineers' burning urge to see that mountain climbed. Perhaps it was too abstract an objective for me—certainly I was not animated by any respect for inviolate nature, which I have always disliked, preferring like George Leigh-Mallory a blend of tame and wild. I was pleased when they did climb Everest, but chiefly for a less than elevated reason—patriotic pride, which I knew to be unworthy of their efforts, but which I could not suppress.

I well understood the masochistic relish of challenge which impelled them, and which stimulated me too, but the blankness of the achievement depressed me. One of the older Everesters, H. W. Tilman, once quoted G. K. Chesterton to illustrate the urge of alpinism: "I think the immense act has something about it human and excusable; and when I endeavor to analyze the reason of this feeling I find it to lie, not in the fact that the thing was big or bold or successful, but in the fact that the thing was perfectly useless to everybody, including the person who did it." Leigh-Mallory presumably meant much the same, when he talked of climbing Everest simply "because it was there." But this elusive prize, this snatching at air, this nothingness, left me dissatisfied, as I think it would leave most women. Nothing had been discovered, nothing made, nothing improved.

I have always discounted the beauty of clouds, because their airy impermanence seems to me to disqualify them from the truest beauty, just as I have never responded to kinetic art, and love the shifting light of nature only because it reveals new shapes and meaning in the solids down below. Nor do I like sea views, unless there is land to be seen beyond them. A similar distrust of the ephemeral or the un-finite weakened my response to the triumph of Everest in 1953. It was a grand adventure, I knew, and my part in relaying its excitements to the world was to transform my professional life, and dog me ever after; yet even now I dislike that emptiness at its climax, that perfect uselessness, and feel in a slightly ashamed and ungrateful way that it was really all rather absurd.

For it was almost like a military expedition—the colonel in command, not so long from Montgomery's[2] staff, the little army of porters who wound their way bent-back with their loads over the hills from

---

[2] Bernard Law Montgomery (1887–1976) was a British field marshal in World War II, famous for his victories in North Africa and Europe. (ED.)

Katmandu, the meticulously packed and listed stores, the briefings, the air of ordered determination. It was a superbly successful expedition—nobody killed, nobody disgraced—and looking back upon it now I see its cohesion as a specifically male accomplishment. Again constancy was the key. Men more than women respond to the team spirit, and this is partly because, if they are of an age, of a kind, and in a similar condition, they work together far more like a mechanism. Elations and despondencies are not so likely to distract them. Since their pace is more regular, all can more easily keep to it. They are distinctly more rhythm than melody.

In 1953 the rhythm was steadier than it might be now, for it was conscious then as well as constitutional. Stiff upper lip and fair play were integral to the British masculine ethos, and shame was a powerful impulse towards achievement. Social empathy, too, strongly reinforced the sense of maleness. The functional efficiency of class I had already discovered in the Army, and it was the same on Everest. Hunt's climbers were men of the officer class, as they would then have been called, and they were bound by common tastes and values. They spoke the same language, shared the same kind of past, enjoyed the same pleasures. Three of them had been to the same school. In a social sense they formed a kind of club; in an imperial sense, and this was almost the last of the imperial adventures, they were a company of sahibs attended by their multitudinous servants.

One could not, I think, apply these categories to women of equal intelligence in similar circumstances, and less and less can one now apply them to men. Class has lost its binding function; patriotism has lost its elevating force; young men are no longer ashamed of weaknesses; the stiff upper lip is no longer an ideal, only a music hall sally. The barrier between the genders is flimsier now, and no expedition will ever again go to the Himalayas so thoroughly masculine as Hunt's. It embarrasses me rather to have to admit that from that day to this, none has gone there more successfully.

I need not belabor my sense of alienation from this formidable team. I liked most of its members very much, and have remained friends with some to this day, but my sense of detachment was extreme, and though I shamelessly accepted their help throughout the adventure, still I was always at pains to cherish my separateness. I hated to think of myself as one of them, and when in England we were asked to sign menus, maps, or autograph books, I used carefully to sign myself James Morris of *The Times*—until the climbers, fancying I fear altogether different motives in me, asked me not to. At the same

time a wayward self-consciousness—for I was a child of the age,
too—compelled me to keep up male appearances, perhaps as much
for my own persuasion as for anyone else's. I even overdid it rather.
I grew a beard, and when at the end of the expedition I walked into
the communications room at the British Embassy in Katmandu with
my tin mug jangling from the belt of my trousers, the wireless
operator asked acidly if I *had* to look so jungly. He did not know
how cruelly the jibe hurt, for in a few words it cut this way and that
through several skins of self-protection.

Everest taught me new meanings of maleness, and emphasized
once more my own inner dichotomy. Yet paradoxically my most
evocative memory of the experience haunts me with a truth of an
altogether different kind. Often when there was a lull on the mountain I would go down the glacier and wander among the moraines.
Sometimes I went south, towards the distant Buddhist temple at
Thyangboehe where the deodars shaded the green turf, and the bells,
gongs, and trumpets of the monks sounded from their shambled
refectory. Sometimes I clambered into the snows of the north, towards the great wall of the Lho La, over whose ominous white ridge
stood the peaks of Tibet. I vaguely hoped to catch a glimpse of an
abominable snowman, and I was looking too for traces of the lemurs
and mountain hares which sometimes, I had been told, penetrated
those high deserts.

I saw no animals ever. What I found instead was a man. I saw
him first in the extreme distance, across an absolutely blank snowfield
at about nineteen thousand feet, to which I had climbed from the
glacier below for the sake of the view. At first I was frightened, for
I could not make out what he was—only a small black swaying
speck, indescribably alone in the desolation. As he came closer I saw
that he could only be human, so I plunged through the loose snow
to meet him, and presently, there near the top of the world, thousands
of feet and many miles above the trees, the streams, or human
habitation, we met face to face. It was the strangest encounter of my
life.

He was a holy man, wandering in the mountains, I suppose, for
wandering's sake. His brown, crinkled, squashed-up face looked back
at me expressionless from beneath a yellow hood, and found it
seemed nothing strange in my presence there. He wore a long yellow
cloak and hide boots, and from his waist there hung a spoon and a
cloth satchel. He carried nothing else, and he wore no gloves. I
greeted him as best I could, but he did not answer, only smiling at
me distantly and without surprise. Perhaps he was in a trance. I

offered him a piece of chocolate, but he did not take it, simply standing there before me, slightly smiling, almost as though he were made of ice himself. Presently we parted, and without a word he continued on his unfaltering journey, apparently making for Tibet without visible means of survival, and moving with a proud, gliding, and effortless motion that seemed inexorable. He did not appear to move fast, but when I looked around he had almost disappeared, and was no more than that small black speck again, inexplicably moving over the snows.

I envied him his insouciant speed, and wondered if he too felt that tingling of the body, that sense of mastery, which had so deepened my sense of duality upon the slopes of Everest. But the more I thought about it, the more clearly I realized that he had no body at all.

JOYCE CAROL OATES

On Boxing

Joyce Carol Oates (1938–) is an American novelist, poet, essayist, short story writer, and critic. Her novels include *them* (1969), *American Appetites* (1989), *I Lock the Door upon Myself* (1990), *Because It Is Bitter, and Because It Is My Heart* (1990), and *The Rise of Life on Earth* (1991). Her short story collections include *Where Are You Going, Where Have You Been?: Stories of Young America* (1974) and *Raven's Wing* (1986). The characters in Oates's fiction often inhabit a world filled with violence and mental illness. She has also published nonfiction works, including the book *On Boxing* (1987), from which the following selection is taken.

They are young welterweight boxers so evenly matched they might be twins—though one has a redhead's pallor and the other is a dusky-skinned Hispanic. Circling each other in the ring, they try jabs, tentative left hooks, right crosses that dissolve in midair or turn into harmless slaps. The Madison Square Garden crowd is derisive, impatient. "Those two! What'd they do, wake up this morning and decide they were boxers?" a man behind me says contemptuously.

(He's dark, nattily dressed, with a neatly trimmed mustache and tinted glasses. A sophisticated fight fan. Two hours later he will be crying, "Tommy! Tommy! Tommy!" over and over in a paroxysm of grief as, on the giant closed-circuit television screen, middleweight champion Marvelous Marvin Hagler batters his challenger, Thomas Hearns, into insensibility.)

The young boxers must be conscious of the jeers and boos in this great cavernous space reaching up into the $20 seats in the balconies amid the constant milling of people in the aisles, the smells of hotdogs, beer, cigarette and cigar smoke, hair oil. But they are locked desperately together, circling, jabbing, slapping, clinching, now a flurry of light blows, clumsy footwork, another sweaty stumbling despairing clinch into the ropes that provokes a fresh wave of derision. Why are they here in the Garden of all places, each fighting what looks like his first professional fight? What are they doing? Neither is angry at the other. When the bell sounds at the end of the sixth and final round, the crowd boos a little louder. The Hispanic boy, silky yellow shorts, damp, frizzy, floating hair, strides about his corner of the ring with his gloved hand aloft—not in defiance of the boos, which increase in response to his gesture, or even in acknowledgment of them. It's just something he has seen older boxers do. He seems to be saying "I'm here, I made it, I did it." When the decision is announced as a draw, the crowd's derision increases in volume. "Get out of the ring!" "Go home!" Contemptuous male laughter follows the boys in their robes, towels about their heads, sweating, breathless. Why had they thought they were boxers?

How can you enjoy so brutal a sport, people ask. Or don't ask.

And it's too complicated to answer. In any case, I don't "enjoy" boxing, and never have; it isn't invariably "brutal"; I don't think of it as a sport.

Nor do I think of it in writerly terms as a metaphor for something else. (For *what* else?) No one whose interest in boxing began in childhood—as mine did as an offshoot of my father's interest—is likely to suppose it is a symbol of something beyond itself, though I can entertain the proposition that life is a metaphor for boxing—for one of those bouts that go on and on, round following round, small victories, small defeats, nothing determined, again the bell and again the bell and you and your opponent so evenly matched it's clear your opponent *is* you and why are the two of you jabbing and punching at each other on an elevated platform enclosed by ropes as in a pen beneath hot crude all-exposing lights in the presence of an indifferent crowd: that sort of writerly metaphor. But if you have seen five hundred boxing matches, you have seen five hundred boxing matches, and their common denominator, which surely exists, is not of primary interest to you. "If the Host is only a symbol," the Catholic writer Flannery O'Connor said, "I'd say the hell with it."

Each boxing match is a story, a highly condensed, highly dramatic story—even when nothing much happens: then failure is the story. There are two principal characters in the story, overseen by a shadowy third. When the bell rings no one knows what will happen. Much is speculated, nothing known. The boxers bring to the fight everything that is themselves, and everything will be exposed: including secrets about themselves they never knew. There are boxers possessed of such remarkable intuition, such prescience, one would think they had fought this particular fight before. There are boxers who perform brilliantly, but mechanically, who cannot improvise in midfight; there are boxers performing at the height of their skill who cannot quite comprehend that it won't be enough; to my knowledge there was only one boxer who possessed an extraordinary and disquieting awareness, not only of his opponent's every move or anticipated move, but of the audience's keenest shifts in mood as well— Muhammad Ali, of course.

In the ring, death is always a possibility, which is why I prefer to see films or tapes of fights already past—already crystallized into art. In fact, death is a statistically rare possibility of which no one likes to think—like your possible death tomorrow morning in an automobile crash, or in next month's airplane crash, or in a freak accident involving a fall on the stairs—a skull fracture, subarachnoid hemorrhage.

A boxing match is a play without words, which doesn't mean that it has no text or no language, only that the text is improvised in action, the language a dialogue between the boxers in a joint response to the mysterious will of the crowd, which is always that the fight be a worthy one so that the crude paraphernalia of the setting—the ring, the lights, the onlookers themselves—be obliterated. To go from an ordinary preliminary match to a "Fight of the Century"—like those between Joe Louis and Billy Conn, Muhammad Ali and Joe Frazier, most recently Marvin Hagler and Thomas Hearns—is to go from listening or half-listening to a guitar being idly plucked to hearing Bach's "Well-Tempered Clavier" being perfectly played, and that too is part of the story. So much is happening so swiftly and so subtly you cannot absorb it except to know that something memorable is happening and it is happening in a place beyond words.

The fighters in the ring are time-bound—is anything so excruciatingly long as a fiercely contested three-minute round?—but the fight itself is timeless. By way of films and tapes, it has become history, art. If boxing is a sport, it is the most tragic of all sports because, more than any human activity, it consumes the very excellence it displays: Its very drama is this consumption. To expend oneself in fighting the greatest fight of one's life is to begin immediately the downward turn that next time may be a plunge, a sudden incomprehensible fall. *I am the greatest,* Muhammad Ali says. *I am the greatest,* Marvin Hagler says. You always think you're going to win, Jack Dempsey wryly observed in his old age, otherwise you can't fight at all. The punishment—to the body, the brain, the spirit— a man must endure to become a great boxer is inconceivable to most of us whose idea of personal risk is largely ego related or emotional. But the punishment, as it begins to show in even a young and vigorous boxer, is closely assessed by his rivals. After junior-welterweight champion Aaron Pryor won a lackluster fight on points a few months ago, a younger boxer in his weight division, interviewed at ringside, said: "My mouth is watering."

So the experience of seeing great fighters of the past—and great sporting events are always *past*—is radically different from having seen them when they were reigning champions. Jack Johnson, Jack Dempsey, Joe Louis, Sugar Ray Robinson, Willie Pep, Rocky Marciano, Muhammad Ali—as spectators we know not only how a fight ends but how a career ends. Boxing is always particulars, second by incalculable second, but in the abstract it suggests these haunting lines by Yeats:

> Everything that man esteems
> Endures a moment or a day.
> Love's pleasure drives his love away,
> The painter's brush consumes his dreams;
> The herald's cry, the soldier's tread
> Exhaust his glory and his might:
> Whatever flames upon the night
> Man's own resinous heart has fed.
> from "The Resurrection"

The referee, the third character in the story, usually appears to be a mere observer, even an intruder, a near-ghostly presence as fluid in motion and quick-footed as the boxers themselves (he is frequently a former boxer). But so central to the drama of boxing is the referee that the spectacle of two men fighting each other unsupervised in an elevated ring would appear hellish, obscene—life rather than art. The referee is our intermediary in the fight. He is our moral conscience, extracted from us as spectators so that, for the duration of the fight, "conscience" is not a factor in our experience; nor is it a factor in the boxers' behavior.

Though the referees' role is a highly demanding one, and it has been estimated that there are perhaps no more than a dozen really skilled referees in the world, it seems to be necessary in the intense dramatic action of the fight that the referee have no dramatic identity. Referee's names are quickly forgotten, even as they are announced over the microphone preceding a fight. Yet, paradoxically, the referee's position is one of crucial significance. The referee cannot control what happens in the ring, but he can frequently control, to a degree, *that* it happens: he is responsible for the fight, if not for the individual fighter's performance. It is the referee solely who holds the power of life and death at certain times; whose decision to terminate a fight, or to allow it to continue, determines a man's fate. (One should recall that a well-aimed punch with a boxer's full weight behind it can have an astonishing impact—a blow that must be absorbed by the brain in its jelly sac.)

In a recent heavyweight fight in Buffalo, 220-pound Tim Witherspoon repeatedly struck his 260-pound opponent, James Broad, caught in the ropes, while the referee looked on without acting—though a number of spectators called for the fight to be stopped. In the infamous Benny Paret–Emile Griffith fight of March 24, 1962, the referee Ruby Goldstein was said to have stood paralyzed as Paret, trapped in the ropes, suffered as many as 18 powerful blows to the head before he fell. (He died ten days later.) Boxers are trained not to quit; if they are knocked down they will try to get up to continue the fight, even if they can hardly defend themselves. The primary rule of the ring—to defend oneself at all times—is both a parody and a distillation of life.

Boxing is a purely masculine world. (Though there are female boxers—the most famous is the black champion Lady Tyger Trimiar with her shaved head and tiger-striped attire—women's role in the sport is extremely marginal.) The vocabulary of boxing is attuned to a quintessentially masculine sensibility in which the role of patriarch/protector can only be assured if there is physical strength underlying it. First comes this strength—"primitive," perhaps; then comes civilization. It should be kept in mind that "boxing" and "fighting," though always combined in the greatest of boxers, can be entirely different and even unrelated activities. If boxing can be, in the lighter weights especially, a highly complex and refined skill belonging solely to civilization, fighting seems to belong to something predating civilization, the instinct not merely to defend oneself—for when has the masculine ego ever been assuaged by so minimal a gesture?—but to attack another and to force him into absolute submission. Hence the electrifying effect upon a typical fight crowd when fighting emerges suddenly out of boxing—the excitement when a boxer's face begins to bleed. The flash of red is the visible sign of the fight's authenticity in the eyes of many spectators, and boxers are right to be proud—if they are—of their facial scars.

To the untrained eye, boxers in the ring usually appear to be angry. But, of course, this is "work" to them; emotion has no part in it, or should not. Yet in an important sense—in a symbolic sense—the boxers *are* angry, and boxing is fundamentally about anger. It is the only sport in which anger is accommodated, ennobled. Why are boxers angry? Because, for the most part, they belong to the disenfranchised of our society, to impoverished ghetto neighborhoods in which anger is an appropriate response. ("It's hard being black. You ever been black? I was black once—when I was poor," Larry Holmes has said.) Today, when most boxers—most good boxers—are black or Hispanic, white men begin to look anemic in the ring. Yet after decades of remarkable black boxers—from Jack Johnson to Joe Louis to Muhammad Ali—heavyweight champion Larry Holmes was the object of racist slurs and insults when he defended his title against the over-promoted white challenger Gerry Cooney a few years ago.

Liberals who have no personal or class reason to feel anger tend to disparage, if not condemn, such anger in others. Liberalism is also unfairly harsh in its criticism of all that predates civilization—or "liberalism" itself—without comprehending that civilization is a concept, an idea, perhaps at times hardly more than a fiction, attendant upon, and always subordinate to, physical strength: missiles, nuclear warheads. The terrible and tragic silence dramatized in the boxing ring is the silence of nature before language, when the physical *was* language, a means of communication swift and unmistakable.

The phrase "killer instinct" is said to have been coined in reference to Jack Dempsey in his famous early fights against Jess Willard, Georges Carpentier, Luis Firpo ("The Wild Bull of the Pampas"), and any number of other boxers, less renowned, whom he savagely beat. The ninth of eleven children born to an impoverished Mormon sharecropper and itinerant railroad worker, Dempsey seems to have been, as a young boxer in his prime, the very embodiment of angry hunger; and if he remains the most spectacular heavyweight champion in history, it is partly because he fought when rules governing boxing were somewhat casual by present-day standards. Where aggression must be learned, even cultivated, in some champion boxers (Tunney, Louis, Marciano, Patterson, for example), Dempsey's aggression was direct and natural: Once in the ring he seems to have wanted to kill his opponent.

Dempsey's first title fight in 1919, against the aging champion Jess Willard, was called "pugilistic murder" by some sportswriters and is said to have been one of boxing's all-time blood baths. Today, this famous fight—which brought the nearly unknown twenty-four-year-old Dempsey to national prominence—would certainly have been stopped in the first minute of the first round. Badly out of condition, heavier than Dempsey by almost sixty pounds, the thirty-seven-year-old Willard had virtually no defense against the challenger. By the end of the fight, Willard's jaw was broken, his cheekbone split, nose smashed, six teeth broken off at the gum, an eye was battered shut, much further damage was done to his body. Both boxers were covered in Willard's blood. Years later Dempsey's estranged manager Kearns confessed—perhaps falsely—that he had "loaded" Dempsey's gloves—treated his hand tape with a talcum substance that turned concrete-hard when wet.

For the most part, boxing matches today are scrupulously monitored by referees and ring physicians. The devastating knockout blow is frequently the one never thrown. In a recent televised junior-middleweight bout between Don Curry and James Green, the referee stopped the fight because Green seemed momentarily disabled: His logic was that Green had dropped his gloves and was therefore in a position to be hurt. (Green and his furious trainer protested the decision but the referee's word is final: No fight, stopped, can be resumed.) The drama of the ring begins to shift subtly as more and more frequently one sees a referee intervene to embrace a weakened or defenseless man in a gesture of paternal solicitude that in itself carries much theatrical power—a gesture not so dramatic as the killing blow but one that suggests that the ethics of the ring are moving toward those that prevail beyond it. As if fighter-brothers whose mysterious animosity has somehow brought them to battle are saved by their father. . . .

In the final moment of the Hagler-Hearns fight, the dazed Hearns—on his feet but clearly not fully conscious, gamely prepared to take Hagler's next assault—was saved by the referee from what might well have been serious injury, if not death, considering the ferocity of Hagler's fighting and the personal anger he seems to have brought to it that night. This eight-minute fight, generally believed to be one of the great fights in boxing history, ends with Hearns in the referee's protective embrace—an image that is haunting, in itself profoundly mysterious, as if an indefinable human drama had been spontaneously created for us, brilliantly improvised, performed one time and one time only, yet permanently ingrained upon our consciousness.

Years ago in the early 1950s, when my father first took me to a Golden Gloves boxing tournament in Buffalo, I asked him why the boys wanted to fight one another, why they were willing to get hurt. My father said, "Boxers don't feel pain quite the way we do."

Gene Tunney's single defeat in an eleven-year career was to a flamboyant and dangerous fighter named Harry Greb ("The Human Windmill"), who seems to have been, judging from boxing literature, the dirtiest fighter in history. Low blows, butting, fouls, holding and hitting, using his laces on an opponent's eyes—Greb was famous for his lack of interest in the rules. He was world middleweight champion for three years but a presence in the boxing world for a long time. After the first of his several fights with Greb, the twenty-four-year-old Tunney had to spend a week in bed, he was so badly hurt; he'd lost two quarts of blood during the fifteen-round fight. But as Tunney said years afterward: "Greb gave me a terrible whipping. He broke my nose, maybe with a butt. He cut my eyes and ears, perhaps with his laces. . . . My jaw was swollen from the right temple down the cheek, along under the chin and part way up the other side. The referee, the ring itself, was full of blood. . . . But it was in that first fight, in which I lost my American light-heavyweight title, that I knew I had found a way to beat Harry eventually. I was fortunate, really. If boxing in those days had been afflicted with the commission doctors we have today—who are always poking their noses into the ring and examining superficial wounds—the first fight with Greb would have been stopped before I learned how to beat him. It's possible, even probable, that if this had happened I would never have been heard of again."

Tommy Loughran, the light-heavyweight champion from 1927 to 1929, was a master boxer greatly admired by other boxers. He approached boxing literally as a science—as Tunney did—studying his opponents' styles and mapping out ring strategy for each fight. He rigged up mirrors in his basement so that he could see himself as he worked out—for, as Loughran realized, no boxer ever sees himself quite as he appears to his opponent. But the secret of Loughran's career was that he had a right hand that broke so easily he could use it only once in each fight: It had to be the knockout punch or nothing. "I'd get one shot, then the agony of the thing would hurt me if the guy got up. Anybody I ever hit with a left hook, I knocked flat on his face, but I would never take a chance for fear if my left hand goes, I'm done for."

Both Tunney and Loughran, it is instructive to note, retired from boxing before they were forced to retire. Tunney was a highly successful businessman and Loughran a successful sugar broker on the Wall Street commodities market—just to suggest that boxers are not invariably illiterate, stupid, or punch-drunk.

One of the perhaps not entirely acknowledged reasons for the attraction of serious writers to boxing (from Swift, Pope, Johnson to Hazlitt, Lord Byron, Hemingway, and our own Norman Mailer, George Plimpton, Wilfrid Sheed, Daniel Halpern et al.) is the sport's systematic cultivation of pain in the interests of a project, a life-goal: the willed transposing of the sensation called "pain" (whether physical or psychological) into its opposite. If this is masochism—and I doubt that it is, or that it is simply—it is also intelligence, cunning, strategy. It is the active welcoming of that which most living beings try to avoid and to flee. It is the active subsuming of the present moment in terms of the future. Pain now but control (and therefore pleasure) later.

Still, it is the rigorous training period leading up to the public appearance that demands the most discipline. In this, too, the writer senses some kinship, however oblique and one-sided, with the professional boxer. The brief public spectacle of the boxing match (which could last as little as sixty seconds), like the publication of the writer's book, is but the final, visible stage in a long, arduous, fanatic, and sometimes quixotic, subordination of the self. It was Rocky Marciano who seems to have trained with the most monastic devotion, secluding himself from his wife and family for as long as three months before a fight. Quite apart from the grueling physical training of this period and the constant preoccupation with diet and weight, Marciano concentrated on only the upcoming fight, the opening bell, his opponent. Every minute of the boxer's life was planned for one purpose. In the training camp the name of the opponent was never mentioned and Marciano's associates were careful about conversation in his presence: They talked very little about boxing.

In the final month, Marciano would not write a letter. The last ten days before a fight he saw no mail, took no telephone calls, met no new acquaintances. The week before the fight he would not shake hands with anyone. Or go for a ride in a car. No new foods! No envisioning the morning after the fight! All that was not *the fight* was taboo: when Marciano worked out punching the bag he saw his opponent before him, when he jogged early in the morning he saw his opponent close beside him. What could be a more powerful image of discipline—madness?—than this absolute subordination of the self, this celibacy of the fighter-in-training? Instead of focusing his energies and fantasies upon Woman, the boxer focuses them upon the Opponent.

No sport is more physical, more direct, than boxing. No sport appears more powerfully homoerotic: the confrontation in the ring— the disrobing—the sweaty, heated combat that is part dance, courtship, coupling—the frequent urgent pursuit by one boxer of the other in the fight's natural and violent movement toward the "knockout." Surely boxing derives much of its appeal from this mimicry of a species of erotic love in which one man overcomes the other in an exhibition of superior strength.

Most fights, however fought, lead to an embrace between the boxers after the final bell—a gesture of mutual respect and apparent affection that appears to the onlooker to be more than perfunctory. Rocky Graziano, often derided for being a slugger rather than a "classic" boxer, sometimes kissed his opponents out of gratitude for the fight. Does the boxing match, one almost wonders, lead irresistibly to this moment: the public embrace of two men who otherwise, in public or in private, could not approach each other with such passion. Are men privileged to embrace with love only after having fought? A woman is struck by the tenderness men will express for boxers who have been hurt, even if it is only by way of commentary on photographs: the startling picture of Ray (Boom Boom) Mancini after his second losing fight with Livingstone Bramble, for instance, when Mancini's face was hideously battered (photographs in *Sports Illustrated* and elsewhere were gory, near-pornographic); the much-reprinted photograph of the defeated Thomas Hearns being carried to his corner in the arms of an enormous black man in formal attire— the "Hit Man" from Detroit now helpless, only semiconscious, looking precisely like a black Christ taken from the cross. These are powerful, haunting, unsettling images, cruelly beautiful, very much bound up with the primitive appeal of the sport.

Yet to suggest that men might love one another directly without

the violent ritual of combat is to misread man's greatest passion—
for war, not peace. Love, if there is to be love, comes second.

Boxing is, after all, about lying. It is about cultivating a double
personality. As José Torres, the ex-light-heavyweight champion who
is now the New York State Boxing Commissioner, says: "We fighters
understand lies. What's a feint? What's a left hook off the jab? What's
an opening? What's thinking one thing and doing another . . . ?"

There is nothing fundamentally playful about boxing, nothing
that seems to belong to daylight, to pleasure. At its moments of
greatest intensity it seems to contain so complete and so powerful
an image of life—life's beauty, vulnerability, despair, incalculable and
often reckless courage—that boxing *is* life, and hardly a mere game.
During a superior boxing match we are deeply moved by the body's
communion with itself by way of another's flesh. The body's dialogue
with its shadow-self—or Death. Baseball, football, basketball—these
quintessentially American pastimes are recognizably sports because
they involve play: They are games. One *plays* football; one doesn't
play boxing.

Observing team sports, teams of adult men, one sees how men
are children in the most felicitous sense of the word. But boxing in
its elemental ferocity cannot be assimilated into childhood—though
very young men box, even professionally, and numerous world champions began boxing when they were hardly more than children.
Spectators at public games derive much of their pleasure from reliving
the communal emotions of childhood, but spectators at boxing
matches relive the murderous infancy of the race. Hence the notorious cruelty of boxing crowds and the excitement when a man begins
to bleed. ("When I see blood," says Marvin Hagler, "I become a bull."
He means his own.)

The boxing ring comes to seem an altar of sorts, one of those
legendary magical spaces where the laws of a nation are suspended:
Inside the ropes, during an officially regulated three-minute round,
a man may be killed at his opponent's hands but he cannot be legally
murdered. Boxing inhabits a sacred space predating civilization; or,
to use D. H. Lawrence's phrase, before God was love. If it suggests a
savage ceremony or a rite of atonement, it also suggests the futility
of such rites. For what atonement is the fight waged, if it must
shortly be waged again . . . ?

All this is to speak of the paradox of boxing—its obsessive appeal
for many who find in it not only a spectacle involving sensational
feats of physical skill but an emotional experience impossible to

convey in words; an art form, as I have suggested, with no natural analogue in the arts. And of course this accounts, too, for the extreme revulsion it arouses in many people. ("Brutal," "disgusting," "barbaric," "inhuman," "a terrible, terrible sport"—typical comments on the subject.)

In December 1984, the American Medical Association passed a resolution calling for the abolition of boxing on the principle that it is the only sport in which the *objective* is to cause injury. This is not surprising. Humanitarians have always wanted to reform boxing—or abolish it altogether. The 1896 heavyweight title match between Ruby Robert Fitzsimmons and Peter Maher was outlawed in many parts of the United States, so canny promoters staged it across the Mexican border four hundred miles from El Paso. (Some three hundred people made the arduous journey to see what must have been one of the most disappointing bouts in boxing history—Fitzsimmons knocked out his opponent in a mere ninety-five seconds.)

During the prime of Jack Dempsey's career in the 1920s, boxing was illegal in many states, like alcohol, and like alcohol, seems to have aroused a hysterical public enthusiasm. Photographs of jammed outdoor arenas taken in the 1920s with boxing rings like postage-sized altars at their centers, the boxers themselves scarcely visible, testify to the extraordinary emotional appeal boxing had at that time, even as reform movements were lobbying against it. When Jack Johnson won the heavyweight title in 1908 (he had to pursue the white champion Tommy Burns all the way to Australia to confront him), the special "danger" of boxing was also that it might expose and humiliate white men in the ring. After Johnson's victory over the "White Hope" contender Jim Jeffries, there were race riots and lynchings throughout the United States; even films of some of Johnson's fights were outlawed in many states. And because boxing has become a sport in which black and Hispanic men have lately excelled, it is particularly vulnerable to attack by white middle-class reformers, who seem uninterested in lobbying against equally dangerous but "establishment" sports like football, auto racing, and thoroughbred horse racing.

There is something peculiarly American in the fact that, while boxing is our most controversial sport, it is also the sport that pays its top athletes the most money. In spite of the controversy, boxing has never been healthier financially. The three highest paid athletes in the world in both 1983 and 1984 were boxers; a boxer with a long career like heavyweight champion Larry Holmes—forty-eight fights in thirteen years as a professional—can expect to earn somewhere beyond $50 million. (Holmes said that after retirement what he would miss most about boxing is his million-dollar checks.) Dempsey, who said that a man fights for one thing only—money—made somewhere beyond $3,500,000 in the ring in his long and varied career. Now $1.5 million is a fairly common figure for a single fight. Thomas Hearns made at least $7 million in his fight with Hagler while Hagler made at least $7.5 million. For the first of his highly publicized matches with Roberto Duran in 1980—which he lost on a decision—the popular black welterweight champion Sugar Ray Leonard received a staggering $10 million to Duran's $1.3 million. And none of these figures takes into account various subsidiary earnings (from television commercials, for instance) which in Leonard's case are probably as high as his income was from boxing.

Money has drawn any number of retired boxers back into the ring, very often with tragic results. The most notorious example is perhaps Joe Louis, who, owing huge sums in back taxes, continued boxing well beyond the point at which he could perform capably. After a career of seventeen years he was stopped by Rocky Marciano—who was said to have felt as upset by his victory as Louis by the defeat. (Louis then went on to a degrading second career as a professional wrestler. This, too, ended abruptly when 300-pound Rocky Lee stepped on the forty-two-year-old Louis's chest and damaged his heart.) Ezzard Charles, Jersey Joe Walcott, Joe Frazier, Muhammad Ali—each continued fighting when he was no longer in condition to defend himself against young heavyweight boxers on the way up. Of all heavyweight champions, only Rocky Marciano, to whom fame and money were not of paramount significance, was prudent enough to retire before he was defeated. In any case, the prodigious sums of money a few boxers earn do not account for the sums the public is willing to pay them.

Though boxing has long been popular in many countries and under many forms of government, its popularity in the United States since the days of John L. Sullivan has a good deal to do with what is felt as the spirit of the individual—his "physical" spirit—in conflict with the constrictions of the state. The rise of boxing in the 1920s in particular might well be seen as a consequence of the diminution of the individual vis-à-vis society; the gradual attrition of personal freedom, will, and strength—whether "masculine" or otherwise. In the Eastern bloc of nations, totalitarianism is a function of the state;

in the Western bloc it has come to seem a function of technology, or history—"fate." The individual exists in his physical supremacy, but does the individual matter?

In the magical space of the boxing ring so disquieting a question has no claim. There, as in no other public arena, the individual as a unique physical being asserts himself; there, for a dramatic if fleeting period of time, the great world with its moral and political complexities, its terrifying impersonality, simply ceases to exist. Men fighting one another with only their fists and their cunning are all contemporaries, all brothers, belonging to no historical time. "He can run, but he can't hide"—so said Joe Louis before his famous fight with young Billy Conn in 1941. In the brightly lighted ring, man is *in extremis,* performing an atavistic rite or agon for the mysterious solace of those who can participate only vicariously in such drama: the drama of life in the flesh. Boxing has become America's tragic theater.

ROLAND BARTHES

The World of Wrestling

Roland Barthes (1915–1980) was a French philosopher and critic who argued that language is a system of signs that reflects social and temporal constraints. In *Writing Degree Zero* (1953), he speculated upon the knowledge necessary for a reader to understand complex cultural systems in language. The following selection is from *Mythologies* (1957), an analysis of French culture. *The System of Fashion* (1967) explains how clothing is used as a symbolic code, and *Empire of Signs* (1970) explores the symbolism of such things as food, writing, and pinball games in Japan. *The Rustle of Language* was published posthumously in 1986.

The grandiloquent truth of gestures on life's great occasions.

Baudelaire

The virtue of all-in wrestling is that it is the spectacle of excess. Here we find a grandiloquence which must have been that of ancient

---

Translated by Annette Lavers.

theatres. And in fact wrestling is an open-air spectacle, for what makes the circus or the arena what they are is not the sky (a romantic value suited rather to fashionable occasions), it is the drenching and vertical quality of the flood of light. Even hidden in the most squalid Parisian halls, wrestling partakes of the nature of the great solar spectacles, Greek drama and bullfights: in both, a light without shadow generates an emotion without reserve.

There are people who think that wrestling is an ignoble sport. Wrestling is not a sport, it is a spectacle, and it is no more ignoble to attend a wrestled performance of Suffering than a performance of the sorrows of Arnolphe or Andromaque.[1] Of course, there exists a false wrestling, in which the participants unnecessarily go to great lengths to make a show of a fair fight; this is of no interest. True wrestling, wrongly called amateur wrestling, is performed in second-rate halls, where the public spontaneously attunes itself to the spectacular nature of the contest, like the audience at a suburban cinema. Then these same people wax indignant because wrestling is a stage-managed sport (which ought, by the way, to mitigate its ignominy). The public is completely uninterested in knowing whether the contest is rigged or not, and rightly so; it abandons itself to the primary virtue of the spectacle, which is to abolish all motives and all consequences: what matters is not what it thinks but what it sees.

This public knows very well the distinction between wrestling and boxing; it knows that boxing is a Jansenist[2] sport, based on a demonstration of excellence. One can bet on the outcome of a boxing-match: with wrestling, it would make no sense. A boxing-match is a story which is constructed before the eyes of the spectator; in wrestling, on the contrary, it is each moment which is intelligible, not the passage of time. The spectator is not interested in the rise and fall of fortunes; he expects the transient image of certain passions. Wrestling therefore demands an immediate reading of the juxtaposed meanings, so that there is no need to connect them. The logical conclusion of the contest does not interest the wrestling-fan, while on the contrary a boxing-match always implies a science of the future. In other words, wrestling is a sum of spectacles, of which no single

---

[1] Characters from *L'École des Femmes* (1662) by Molière and *Andromaque* (1667) by Racine. (ED.)

[2] a member of the controversial movement called Jansenism, based on the writings of the Dutch Roman Catholic theologian Cornelis Jansen (1585–1638), stressing predestination and extreme forms of aceticism (ED.)

one is a function: each moment imposes the total knowledge of a passion which rises erect and alone, without ever extending to the crowning moment of a result.

Thus the function of the wrestler is not to win; it is to go exactly through the motions which are expected of him. It is said that judo contains a hidden symbolic aspect; even in the midst of efficiency, its gestures are measured, precise but restricted, drawn accurately but by a stroke without volume. Wrestling, on the contrary, offers excessive gestures, exploited to the limit of their meaning. In judo, a man who is down is hardly down at all, he rolls over, he draws back, he eludes defeat, or, if the latter is obvious, he immediately disappears; in wrestling, a man who is down is exaggeratedly so, and completely fills the eyes of the spectators with the intolerable spectacle of his powerlessness.

This function of grandiloquence is indeed the same as that of ancient theatre, whose principle, language and props (masks and buskins) concurred in the exaggeratedly visible explanation of a Necessity. The gesture of the vanquished wrestler signifying to the world a defeat which, far from disguising, he emphasizes and holds like a pause in music, corresponds to the mask of antiquity meant to signify the tragic mode of the spectacle. In wrestling, as on the stage in antiquity, one is not ashamed of one's suffering, one knows how to cry, one has a liking for tears.

Each sign in wrestling is therefore endowed with an absolute clarity, since one must always understand everything on the spot. As soon as the adversaries are in the ring, the public is overwhelmed with the obviousness of the roles. As in the theatre, each physical type expresses to excess the part which has been assigned to the contestant. Thauvin, a fifty-year-old with an obese and sagging body, whose type of asexual hideousness always inspires feminine nicknames, displays in his flesh the characters of baseness, for his part is to represent what, in the classical concept of the *salaud,* the 'bastard' (the key-concept of any wrestling-match), appears as organically repugnant. The nausea voluntarily provoked by Thauvin shows therefore a very extended use of signs: not only is ugliness used here in order to signify baseness, but in addition ugliness is wholly gathered into a particularly repulsive quality of matter: the pallid collapse of dead flesh (the public calls Thauvin *la barbaque,* 'stinking meat'), so that the passionate condemnation of the crowd no longer stems from its judgment, but instead from the very depth of its humours. It will thereafter let itself be frenetically embroiled in an idea of Thauvin which will conform entirely with this physical origin: his actions will perfectly correspond to the essential viscosity of his personage.

It is therefore in the body of the wrestler that we find the first key to the contest. I know from the start that all of Thauvin's actions, his treacheries, cruelties and acts of cowardice, will not fail to measure up to the first image of ignobility he gave me; I can trust him to carry out intelligently and to the last detail all the gestures of a kind of amorphous baseness, and thus fill to the brim the image of the most repugnant bastard there is: the bastard-octopus. Wrestlers therefore have a physique as peremptory as those of the characters of the *Commedia dell'Arte,* who display in advance, in their costumes and attitudes, the future contents of their parts: just as Pantaloon can never be anything but a ridiculous cuckold, Harlequin an astute servant and the Doctor a stupid pedant, in the same way Thauvin will never be anything but an ignoble traitor, Reinières (a tall blond fellow with a limp body and unkempt hair) the moving image of passivity, Mazaud (short and arrogant like a cock) that of grotesque conceit, and Orsano (an effeminate teddy-boy first seen in a blue-and-pink dressing-gown) that, doubly humorous, of a vindictive *salope,* or bitch (for I do not think that the public of the Elysée-Montmartre, like Littré,[3] believes the word *salope* to be a masculine).

The physique of the wrestlers therefore constitutes a basic sign, which like a seed contains the whole fight. But this seed proliferates, for it is at every turn during the fight, in each new situation, that the body of the wrestler casts to the public the magical entertainment of a temperament which finds its natural expression in a gesture. The different strata of meaning throw light on each other, and form the most intelligible of spectacles. Wrestling is like a diacritic writing: above the fundamental meaning of his body, the wrestler arranges comments which are episodic but always opportune, and constantly help the reading of the fight by means of gestures, attitudes and mimicry which make the intention utterly obvious. Sometimes the wrestler triumphs with a repulsive sneer while kneeling on the good sportsman; sometimes he gives the crowd a conceited smile which forebodes an early revenge; sometimes, pinned to the ground, he hits the floor ostentatiously to make evident to all the intolerable nature of his situation; and sometimes he erects a complicated set of signs

---

[3] Marimilien Paul Émile Littre (1801–1881), a French author and positivist philosopher, was best known for compiling a dictionary of the French language. Montmartre is a district in Paris known for its bohemian community and night life. (ED.)

meant to make the public understand that he legitimately personifies the ever-entertaining image of the grumbler, endlessly confabulating about his displeasure.

We are therefore dealing with a real Human Comedy, where the most socially-inspired nuances of passion (conceit, rightfulness, refined cruelty, a sense of 'paying one's debts') always felicitously find the clearest sign which can receive them, express them and triumphantly carry them to the confines of the hall. It is obvious that at such a pitch, it no longer matters whether the passion is genuine or not. What the public wants is the image of passion, not passion itself. There is no more a problem of truth in wrestling than in the theatre. In both, what is expected is the intelligible representation of moral situations which are usually private. This emptying out of interiority to the benefit of its exterior signs, this exhaustion of the content by the form, is the very principle of triumphant classical art. Wrestling is an immediate pantomime, infinitely more efficient than the dramatic pantomime, for the wrestler's gesture needs no anecdote, no decor, in short no transference in order to appear true.

Each moment in wrestling is therefore like an algebra which instantaneously unveils the relationship between a cause and its represented effect. Wrestling fans certainly experience a kind of intellectual pleasure in *seeing* the moral mechanism function so perfectly. Some wrestlers, who are great comedians, entertain as much as a Molière character, because they succeed in imposing an immediate reading of their inner nature: Armand Mazaud, a wrestler of an arrogant and ridiculous character (as one says that Harpagon[4] is a character), always delights the audience by the mathematical rigour of his transcriptions, carrying the form of his gestures to the furthest reaches of their meaning, and giving to his manner of fighting the kind of vehemence and precision found in a great scholastic disputation, in which what is at stake is at once the triumph of pride and the formal concern with truth.

What is thus displayed for the public is the great spectacle of Suffering, Defeat, and Justice. Wrestling presents man's suffering with all the amplification of tragic masks. The wrestler who suffers in a hold which is reputedly cruel (an arm-lock, a twisted leg) offers an excessive portrayal of Suffering; like a primitive Pietà, he exhibits for all to see his face, exaggeratedly contorted by an intolerable affliction.

---

[4] a character in Moliere's *The Miser* (ED.)

It is obvious, of course, that in wrestling reserve would be out of place, since it is opposed to the voluntary ostentation of the spectacle, to this Exhibition of Suffering which is the very aim of the fight. This is why all the actions which produce suffering are particularly spectacular, like the gesture of a conjuror who holds out his cards clearly to the public. Suffering which appeared without intelligible cause would not be understood; a concealed action that was actually cruel would transgress the unwritten rules of wrestling and would have no more sociological efficacy than a mad or parasitic gesture. On the contrary suffering appears as inflicted with emphasis and conviction, for everyone must not only see that the man suffers, but also and above all understand why he suffers. What wrestlers call a hold, that is, any figure which allows one to immobilize the adversary indefinitely and to have him at one's mercy, has precisely the function of preparing in a conventional, therefore intelligible, fashion the spectacle of suffering, of methodically establishing the conditions of suffering. The inertia of the vanquished allows the (temporary) victor to settle in his cruelty and to convey to the public this terrifying slowness of the torturer who is certain about the outcome of his actions; to grind the face of one's powerless adversary or to scrape his spine with one's fist with a deep and regular movement, or at least to produce the superficial appearance of such gestures: wrestling is the only sport which gives such an externalized image of torture. But here again, only the image is involved in the game, and the spectator does not wish for the actual suffering of the contestant; he only enjoys the perfection of an iconography. It is not true that wrestling is a sadistic spectacle: it is only an intelligible spectacle.

There is another figure, more spectacular still than a hold; it is the forearm smash, this loud slap of the forearm, this embryonic punch with which one clouts the chest of one's adversary, and which is accompanied by a dull noise and the exaggerated sagging of a vanquished body. In the forearm smash, catastrophe is brought to the point of maximum obviousness, so much so that ultimately the gesture appears as no more than a symbol; this is going too far, this is transgressing the moral rules of wrestling, where all signs must be excessively clear, but must not let the intention of clarity be seen. The public then shouts 'He's laying it on!', not because it regrets the absence of real suffering, but because it condemns artifice: as in the theatre, one fails to put the part across as much by an excess of sincerity as by an excess of formalism.

We have already seen to what extent wrestlers exploit the re-sources of a given physical style, developed and put to use in order to unfold before the eyes of the public a total image of Defeat. The flaccidity of tall white bodies which collapse with one blow or crash into the ropes with arms flailing, the inertia of massive wrestlers rebounding pitiably off all the elastic surfaces of the ring, nothing can signify more clearly and more passionately the exemplary abasement of the vanquished. Deprived of all resilience, the wrestler's flesh is no longer anything but an unspeakable heap spread out on the floor, where it solicits relentless reviling and jubilation. There is here a paroxysm of meaning in the style of antiquity, which can only recall the heavily underlined intentions in Roman triumphs. At other times, there is another ancient posture which appears in the coupling of the wrestlers, that of the suppliant who, at the mercy of his opponent, on bended knees, his arms raised above his head, is slowly brought down by the vertical pressure of the victor. In wrestling, unlike judo, Defeat is not a conventional sign, abandoned as soon as it is understood; it is not an outcome, but quite the contrary, it is a duration, a display, it takes up the ancient myths of public Suffering and Humiliation: the cross and the pillory. It is as if the wrestler is crucified in broad daylight and in the sight of all. I have heard it said of a wrestler stretched on the ground: 'He is dead, little Jesus, there, on the cross,' and these ironic words revealed the hidden roots of a spectacle which enacts the exact gestures of the most ancient purifications.

But what wrestling is above all meant to portray is a purely moral concept: that of justice. The idea of 'paying' is essential to wrestling, and the crowd's 'Give it to him' means above all else 'Make him pay'. This is therefore, needless to say, an immanent justice. The baser the action of the 'bastard', the more delighted the public is by the blow which he justly receives in return. If the villain—who is of course a coward—takes refuge behind the ropes, claiming unfairly to have a right to do so by a brazen mimicry, he is inexorably pursued there and caught, and the crowd is jubilant at seeing the rules broken for the sake of a deserved punishment. Wrestlers know very well how to play up to the capacity for indignation of the public by presenting the very limit of the concept of Justice, this outermost zone of confrontation where it is enough to infringe the rules a little more to open the gates of a world without restraints. For a wrestling-fan, nothing is finer than the revengeful fury of a betrayed fighter who throws himself vehemently not on a successful opponent but on the smarting image of foul play. Naturally, it is the pattern of Justice which matters here, much more than its content: wrestling is above all a quantitative sequence of compensations (an eye for an eye, a tooth for a tooth). This explains why sudden changes of circumstances have in the eyes of wrestling habitués a sort of moral beauty: they enjoy them as they would enjoy an inspired episode in a novel, and the greater the contrast between the success of a move and the reversal of fortune, the nearer the good luck of a contestant to his downfall, the more satisfying the dramatic mime is felt to be. Justice is therefore the embodiment of a possible transgression; it is from the fact that there is a Law that the spectacle of the passions which infringe it derives its value.

It is therefore easy to understand why out of five wrestling-matches, only about one is fair. One must realize, let it be repeated, that 'fairness' here is a role or a genre, as in the theatre: the rules do not at all constitute a real constraint; they are the conventional appearance of fairness. So that in actual fact a fair fight is nothing but an exaggeratedly polite one: the contestants confront each other with zeal, not rage; they can remain in control of their passions, they do not punish their beaten opponent relentlessly, they stop fighting as soon as they are ordered to do so, and congratulate each other at the end of a particularly arduous episode, during which, however, they have not ceased to be fair. One must of course understand here that all these polite actions are brought to the notice of the public by the most conventional gestures of fairness: shaking hands, raising the arms, ostensibly avoiding a fruitless hold which would detract from the perfection of the contest.

Conversely, foul play exists only in its excessive signs: administering a big kick to one's beaten opponent, taking refuge behind the ropes while ostensibly invoking a purely formal right, refusing to shake hands with one's opponent before or after the fight, taking advantage of the end of the round to rush treacherously at the adversary from behind, fouling him while the referee is not looking (a move which obviously only has any value or function because in fact half the audience can see it and get indignant about it). Since Evil is the natural climate of wrestling, a fair fight has chiefly the value of being an exception. It surprises the aficionado, who greets it when he sees it as an anachronism and a rather sentimental throwback to the sporting tradition ('Aren't they playing fair, those two'); he feels suddenly moved at the sight of the general kindness of the world, but would probably die of boredom and indifference if wrestlers did not quickly return to the orgy of evil which alone makes good wrestling.

Extrapolated, fair wrestling could lead only to boxing or judo, whereas true wrestling derives its originality from all the excesses which make it a spectacle and not a sport. The ending of a boxing-match or a judo-contest is abrupt, like the fullstop which closes a demonstration. The rhythm of wrestling is quite different, for its natural meaning is that of rhetorical amplification: the emotional magniloquence, the repeated paroxysms, the exasperation of the retorts can only find their natural outcome in the most baroque confusion. Some fights, among the most successful kind, are crowned by a final charivari,[5] a sort of unrestrained fantasia where the rules, the laws of the genre, the referee's censuring and the limits of the rings are abolished, swept away by a triumphant disorder which overflows into the hall and carries off pell-mell wrestlers, seconds, referee and spectators.

It has already been noted that in America wrestling represents a sort of mythological fight between Good and Evil (of a quasipolitical nature, the 'bad' wrestler always being supposed to be a Red). The process of creating heroes in French wrestling is very different, being based on ethics and not on politics. What the public is looking for here is the gradual construction of a highly moral image: that of the perfect 'bastard'. One comes to wrestling in order to attend the continuing adventures of a single major leading character, permanent and multiform like Punch or Scapino, inventive in unexpected figures and yet always faithful to his role. The 'bastard' is here revealed as a Molière character or a 'portrait' by La Bruyère,[6] that is to say as a classical entity, an essence, whose acts are only significant epiphenomena arranged in time. This stylized character does not belong to any particular nation or party, and whether the wrestler is called Kuzchenko (nicknamed Moustache after Stalin), Yerpazian, Gaspardi, Jo Vignola or Nollières, the aficionado does not attribute to him any country except 'fairness'—observing the rules.

What then is a 'bastard' for this audience composed in part, we are told, of people who are themselves outside the rules of society? Essentially someone unstable, who accepts the rules only when they are useful to him and transgresses the formal continuity of attitudes. He is unpredictable, therefore asocial. He takes refuge behind the law when he considers that it is in his favour, and breaks it when he finds it useful to do so. Sometimes he rejects the formal boundaries

---

[5] a noisy mock serenade (ED.)

[6] Jean de La Bruyère (1645–1696) was a French moralist and satirist best known for *The Characters of Theophrastus, Translated from the Greek, with the Characters and Mores of the Age* (1688). (ED.)

of the ring and goes on hitting an adversary legally protected by the ropes, sometimes he reestablishes these boundaries and claims the protection of what he did not respect a few minutes earlier. This inconsistency, far more than treachery or cruelty, sends the audience beside itself with rage: offended not in its morality but in its logic, it considers the contradiction of arguments as the basest of crimes. The forbidden move becomes dirty only when it destroys a quantitative equilibrium and disturbs the rigorous reckoning of compensations; what is condemned by the audience is not at all the transgression of insipid official rules, it is the lack of revenge, the absence of a punishment. So that there is nothing more exciting for a crowd than the grandiloquent kick given to a vanquished 'bastard'; the joy of punishing is at its climax when it is supported by a mathematical justification; contempt is then unrestrained. One is no longer dealing with a *salaud* but with a *salope*—the verbal gesture of the ultimate degradation.

Such a precise finality demands that wrestling should be exactly what the public expects of it. Wrestlers, who are very experienced, know perfectly how to direct the spontaneous episodes of the fight so as to make them conform to the image which the public has of the great legendary themes of its mythology. A wrestler can irritate or disgust, he never disappoints, for he always accomplishes completely, by a progressive solidification of signs, what the public expects of him. In wrestling, nothing exists except in the absolute, there is no symbol, no allusion, everything is presented exhaustively. Leaving nothing in the shade, each action discards all parasitic meanings and ceremonially offers to the public a pure and full signification, rounded like Nature. This grandiloquence is nothing but the popular and age-old image of the perfect intelligibility of reality. What is portrayed by wrestling is therefore an ideal understanding of things; it is the euphoria of men raised for a while above the constitutive ambiguity of everyday situations and placed before the panoramic view of a univocal Nature, in which signs at last correspond to causes, without obstacle, without evasion, without contradiction.

When the hero or the villain of the drama, the man who was seen a few minutes earlier possessed by moral rage, magnified into a sort of metaphysical sign, leaves the wrestling hall, impassive, anonymous, carrying a small suitcase and arm-in-arm with his wife, no one can doubt that wrestling holds that power of transmutation which is common to the Spectacle and to Religious Worship. In the ring, and even in the depths of their voluntary ignominy, wrestlers remain gods because they are, for a few moments, the key which

opens Nature, the pure gesture which separates Good from Evil, and
unveils the form of a Justice which is at last intelligible.

JOHAN HUIZINGA

The Nature and Significance of Play

Johan Huizinga (1872–1945) was a Dutch historian and educator.
His major work, *The Waning of the Middle Ages* (1924), is a classic
study of the forces which shaped the decline of the Middle Ages.
His other works include *In the Shadow of Tomorrow* (1936), and
Homo Ludens: A Study of the Play-Element in Culture (1949), from
which the following selection is taken.

In tackling the problem of play as a function of culture proper and
not as it appears in the life of the animal or the child, we begin
where biology and psychology leave off. In culture we find play as a
given magnitude existing before culture itself existed, accompanying
it and pervading it from the earliest beginnings right up to the phase
of civilization we are now living in. We find play present everywhere
as a well-defined quality of action which is different from "ordinary"
life. We can disregard the question of how far science has succeeded
in reducing this quality to quantitative factors. In our opinion it has
not. At all events it is precisely this quality, itself so characteristic of
the form of life we call "play", which matters. Play as a special form
of activity, as a "significant form", as a social function—that is our
subject. We shall not look for the natural impulses and habits conditioning play in general, but shall consider play in its manifold
concrete forms as itself a social construction. We shall try to take
play as the player himself takes it: in its primary significance. If we
find that play is based on the manipulation of certain images, on a
certain "imagination" of reality (i.e. its conversion into images), then
our main concern will be to grasp the value and significance of these
images and their "imagination". We shall observe their action in play
itself and thus try to understand play as a cultural factor in life.

The great archetypal activities of human society are all permeated with play from the start. Take language, for instance—that first and supreme instrument which man shapes in order to communicate, to teach, to command. Language allows him to distinguish, to establish, to state things; in short, to name them and by naming them to raise them into the domain of the spirit. In the making of speech and language the spirit is continually "sparking" between matter and mind, as it were, playing with this wondrous nominative faculty. Behind every abstract expression there lie the boldest of metaphors, and every metaphor is a play upon words. Thus in giving expression to life man creates a second, poetic world alongside the world of nature.

Or take myth. This, too, is a transformation or an "imagination" of the outer world, only here the process is more elaborate and ornate than is the case with individual words. In myth, primitive man seeks to account for the world of phenomena by grounding it in the Divine. In all the wild imaginings of mythology a fanciful spirit is playing on the border-line between jest and earnest. Or finally, let us take ritual. Primitive society performs its sacred rites, its sacrifices, consecrations and mysteries, all of which serve to guarantee the well-being of the world, in a spirit of pure play truly understood.

Now in myth and ritual the great instinctive forces of civilized life have their origin: law and order, commerce and profit, craft and art, poetry, wisdom and science. All are rooted in the primaeval soil of play.

The object of the present essay is to demonstrate that it is more than a rhetorical comparison to view culture *sub specie ludi*.[1] The thought is not at all new. There was a time when it was generally accepted, though in a limited sense quite different from the one intended here: in the 17th century, the age of world theatre. Drama, in a glittering succession of figures ranging from Shakespeare and Calderon to Racine, then dominated the literature of the West. It was the fashion to liken the world to a stage on which every man plays his part. Does this mean that the play-element in civilization was openly acknowledged? Not at all. On closer examination this fashionable comparison of life to a stage proves to be little more than an echo of the Neo-platonism[2] that was then in vogue, with a mark-

---

[1] in the aspect of play (ED.)

[2] an ancient philosophy developed by Plotinus in the third century, based on the later teachings of Plato (ED.)

edly moralistic accent. It was a variation on the ancient theme of the vanity of all things. The fact that play and culture are actually interwoven with one another was neither observed nor expressed, whereas for us the whole point is to show that genuine, pure play is one of the main bases of civilisation.

To our way of thinking, play is the direct opposite of seriousness. At first sight this opposition seems as irreducible to other categories as the play-concept itself. Examined more closely, however, the contrast between play and seriousness proves to be neither conclusive nor fixed. We can say: play is non-seriousness. But apart from the fact that this proposition tells us nothing about the positive qualities of play, it is extraordinarily easy to refute. As soon as we proceed from "play is non-seriousness" to "play is not serious", the contrast leaves us in the lurch—for some play can be very serious indeed. Moreover we can immediately name several other fundamental categories that likewise come under the heading "non-seriousness" yet have no correspondence whatever with "play". Laughter, for instance, is in a sense the opposite of seriousness without being absolutely bound up with play. Children's games, football, and chess are played in profound seriousness; the players have not the slightest inclination to laugh. It is worth noting that the purely physiological act of laughing is exclusive to man, whilst the significant function of play is common to both men and animals. The Aristotelian *animal ridens* characterizes man as distinct from the animal almost more absolutely than *homo sapiens*.[3]

What is true of laughter is true also of the comic. The comic comes under the category of non-seriousness and has certain affinities with laughter—it provokes to laughter. But its relation to play is subsidiary. In itself play is not comical either for player or public. The play of young animals or small children may sometimes be ludicrous, but the sight of grown dogs chasing one another hardly moves us to laughter. When we call a farce or a comedy "comic", it is not so much on account of the play-acting as such as on account of the situation or the thoughts expressed. The mimic and laughter-provoking art of the clown is comic as well as ludicrous, but it can scarcely be termed genuine play.

The category of the comic is closely connected with *folly* in the

---

[3] laughing being; thinking man (ED.)

highest and lowest sense of that word. Play, however, is not foolish. It lies outside the antithesis of wisdom and folly. The later Middle Ages tended to express the two cardinal moods of life—play and seriousness—somewhat imperfectly by opposing *folie* to *sense,* until Erasmus in his *Laus Stultitiae*[4] showed the inadequacy of the contrast.

All the terms in this loosely connected group of ideas—play, laughter, folly, wit, jest, joke, the comic, etc.—share the characteristic which we had to attribute to play, namely, that of resisting any attempt to reduce it to other terms. Their rationale and their mutual relationships must lie in a very deep layer of our mental being.

The more we try to mark off the form we call "play" from other forms apparently related to it, the more the absolute independence of the play-concept stands out. And the segregation of play from the domain of the great categorical antitheses does not stop there. Play lies outside the antithesis of wisdom and folly, and equally outside those of truth and falsehood, good and evil. Although it is a non-material activity it has no moral function. The valuations of vice and virtue do not apply here.

If, therefore, play cannot be directly referred to the categories of truth or goodness, can it be included perhaps in the realm of the aesthetic? Here our judgement wavers. For although the attribute of beauty does not attach to play as such, play nevertheless tends to assume marked elements of beauty. Mirth and grace adhere at the outset to the more primitive forms of play. In play the beauty of the human body in motion reaches its zenith. In its more developed forms it is saturated with rhythm and harmony, the noblest gifts of aesthetic perception known to man. Many and close are the links that connect play with beauty. All the same, we cannot say that beauty is inherent in play as such; so we must leave it at that: play is a function of the living, but is not susceptible of exact definition either logically, biologically, or aesthetically. The play-concept must always remain distinct from all the other forms of thought in which we express the structure of mental and social life. Hence we shall have to confine ourselves to describing the main characteristics of play.

Since our theme is the relation of play to culture we need not enter into all the possible forms of play but can restrict ourselves to its social manifestations. These we might call the higher forms of

---

[4] *In Praise of Folly* (1509), by Desiderius Erasmus (1466–1536), the Dutch humanist and scholar. (ED.)

play. They are generally much easier to describe than the more primitive play of infants and young animals, because they are more distinct and articulate in form and their features more various and conspicuous, whereas in interpreting primitive play we immediately come up against that irreducible quality of pure playfulness which is not, in our opinion, amenable to further analysis. We shall have to speak of contests and races, of performances and exhibitions, of dancing and music, pageants, masquerades and tournaments. Some of the characteristics we shall enumerate are proper to play in general, others to social play in particular.

First and foremost, then, all play is a voluntary activity. Play to order is no longer play: it could at best be but a forcible imitation of it. By this quality of freedom alone, play marks itself off from the course of the natural process. It is something added thereto and spread out over it like a flowering, an ornament, a garment. Obviously, freedom must be understood here in the wider sense that leaves untouched the philosophical problem of determinism. It may be objected that this freedom does not exist for the animal and the child; they *must* play because their instinct drives them to it and because it serves to develop their bodily faculties and their powers of selection. The term "instinct", however, introduces an unknown quantity, and to presuppose the utility of play from the start is to be guilty of a *petitio principii*.[5] Child and animal play because they enjoy playing, and therein precisely lies their freedom.

Be that as it may, for the adult and responsible human being play is a function which he could equally well leave alone. Play is superfluous. The need for it is only urgent to the extent that the enjoyment of it makes it a need. Play can be deferred or suspended at any time. It is never imposed by physical necessity or moral duty. It is never a task. It is done at leisure, during "free time". Only when play is a recognized cultural function—a rite, a ceremony—is it bound up with notions of obligation and duty.

Here, then, we have the first main characteristic of play: that it is free, is in fact freedom. A second characteristic is closely connected with this, namely, that play is not "ordinary" or "real" life. It is rather a stepping out of "real" life into a temporary sphere of activity with

[5] begging the question (ED.)

a disposition all of its own. Every child knows perfectly well that he is "only pretending", or that it was "only for fun". How deep-seated this awareness is in the child's soul is strikingly illustrated by the following story, told to me by the father of the boy in question. He found his four-year-old son sitting at the front of a row of chairs, playing "trains". As he hugged him the boy said: "Don't kiss the engine, Daddy, or the carriages won't think it's real". This "only pretending" quality of play betrays a consciousness of the inferiority of play compared with "seriousness", a feeling that seems to be something as primary as play itself. Nevertheless, as we have already pointed out, the consciousness of play being "only a pretend" does not by any means prevent it from proceeding with the utmost seriousness, with an absorption, a devotion that passes into rapture and, temporarily at least, completely abolishes that troublesome "only" feeling. Any game can at any time wholly run away with the players. The contrast between play and seriousness is always fluid. The inferiority of play is continually being offset by the corresponding superiority of its seriousness. Play turns to seriousness and seriousness to play. Play may rise to heights of beauty and sublimity that leave seriousness far beneath. Tricky questions such as these will come up for discussion when we start examining the relationship between play and ritual.

As regards its formal characteristics, all students lay stress on the *disinterestedness* of play. Not being "ordinary" life it stands outside the immediate satisfaction of wants and appetites, indeed it interrupts the appetitive process. It interpolates itself as a temporary activity satisfying in itself and ending there. Such at least is the way in which play presents itself to us in the first instance: as an intermezzo, and *interlude* in our daily lives. As a regularly recurring relaxation, however, it becomes the accompaniment, the complement, in fact an integral part of life in general. It adorns life, amplifies it and is to that extent a necessity both for the individual—as a life function— and for society by reason of the meaning it contains, its significance, its expressive value, its spiritual and social associations, in short, as a culture function. The expression of it satisfies all kinds of communal ideals. It thus has its place in a sphere superior to the strictly biological processes of nutrition, reproduction and self-preservation. This assertion is apparently contradicted by the fact that play, or rather sexual display, is predominant in animal life precisely at the mating-season. But would it be too absurd to assign a place *outside* the purely physiological, to the singing, cooing and strutting of birds just as we do to human play? In all its higher forms the latter at any rate always belongs to the sphere of festival and ritual—the sacred sphere.

Now, does the fact that play is a necessity, that it subserves culture, or indeed that it actually becomes culture, detract from its disinterested character? No, for the purposes it serves are external to immediate material interests or the individual satisfaction of biological needs. As a sacred activity play naturally contributes to the well-being of the group, but in quite another way and by other means than the acquisition of the necessities of life.

Play is distinct from "ordinary" life both as to locality and duration. This is the third main characteristic of play: its secludedness, its limitedness. It is "played out" within certain limits of time and place. It contains its own course and meaning.

Play begins, and then at a certain moment it is "over." It plays itself to an end. While it is in progress all is movement, change, alternation, succession, association, separation. But immediately connected with its limitation as to time there is a further curious feature of play: it at once assumes fixed form as a cultural phenomenon. Once played, it endures as a new-found creation of the mind, a treasure to be retained by the memory. It is transmitted, it becomes tradition. It can be repeated at any time, whether it be "child's play" or a game of chess, or at fixed intervals like a mystery. In this faculty of repetition lies one of the most essential qualities of play. It holds good not only of play as a whole but also of its inner structure. In nearly all the higher forms of play the elements of repetition and alternation (as in the *refrain*) are like the warp and woof of a fabric.

More striking even than the limitation as to time is the limitation as to space. All play moves and has its being within a play-ground marked off beforehand either materially or ideally, deliberately or as a matter of course. Just as there is no formal difference between play and ritual, so the "consecrated spot" cannot be formally distinguished from the play-ground. The arena, the card-table, the magic circle, the temple, the stage, the screen, the tennis court, the court of justice, etc., are all in form and function play-grounds, i.e. forbidden spots, isolated, hedged round, hallowed, within which special rules obtain. All are temporary worlds within the ordinary world, dedicated to the performance of an act apart.

Inside the play-ground an absolute and peculiar order reigns. Here we come across another, very positive feature of play: it creates order, *is* order. Into an imperfect world and into the confusion of life it brings a temporary, a limited perfection. Play demands order absolute and supreme. The least deviation from it "spoils the game", robs it of its character and makes it worthless. The profound affinity between play and order is perhaps the reason why play, as we noted in passing, seems to lie to such a large extent in the field of aesthetics. Play has a tendency to be beautiful. It may be that this aesthetic factor is identical with the impulse to create orderly form, which animates play in all its aspects. The words we use to denote the elements of play belong for the most part to aesthetics, terms with which we try to describe the effects of beauty: tension, poise, balance, contrast, variation, solution, resolution, etc. Play casts a spell over us; it is "enchanting", "captivating". It is invested with the noblest qualities we are capable of perceiving in things: rhythm and harmony.

The element of tension in play to which we have just referred plays a particularly important part. Tension means uncertainty, chanciness; a striving to decide the issue and so end it. The player wants something to "go", to "come off"; he wants to "succeed" by his own exertions. Baby reaching for a toy, pussy patting a bobbin, a little girl playing ball—all want to achieve something difficult, to succeed, to end a tension. Play is "tense", as we say. It is this element of tension and solution that governs all solitary games of skill and application such as puzzles, jig-saws, mosaic-making, patience, target-shooting, and the more play bears the character of competition the more fervent it will be. In gambling and athletics it is at its height. Though play as such is outside the range of good and bad, the element of tension imparts to it a certain ethical value in so far as it means a testing of the player's prowess: his courage, tenacity, resources and, last but not least, his spiritual powers—his "fairness"; because, despite his ardent desire to win, he must still stick to the rules of the game.

These rules in their turn are a very important factor in the play-concept. All play has its rules. They determine what "holds" in the temporary world circumscribed by play. The rules of a game are absolutely binding and allow no doubt. Paul Valéry[6] once in passing gave expression to a very cogent thought when he said: "No scepticism is possible where the rules of a game are concerned, for the principle underlying them is an unshakable truth. . . ." Indeed, as soon as the rules are transgressed the whole play-world collapses.

---

[6] Paul Valéry (1871–1945) was a French poet and critic and a member of the Symbolist movement. (ED.)

The game is over. The umpire's whistle breaks the spell and sets "real" life going again.

The player who trespasses against the rules or ignores them is a "spoil-sport". The spoil-sport is not the same as the false player, the cheat; for the latter pretends to be playing the game and, on the face of it, still acknowledges the magic circle. It is curious to note how much more lenient society is to the cheat than to the spoil-sport. This is because the spoil-sport shatters the play-world itself. By withdrawing from the game he reveals the relativity and fragility of the play-world in which he had temporarily shut himself with others. He robs play of its *illusion*—a pregnant word which means literally "in-play" (from *inlusio, illudere* or *inludere*). Therefore he must be cast out, for he threatens the existence of the play-community. The figure of the spoil-sport is most apparent in boys' games. The little community does not enquire whether the spoil-sport is guilty of defection because he dares not enter into the game or because he is not allowed to. Rather, it does not recognize "not being allowed" and calls it "not daring". For it, the problem of obedience and conscience is no more than fear of punishment. The spoil-sport breaks the magic world, therefore he is a coward and must be ejected. In the world of high seriousness, too, the cheat and the hypocrite have always had an easier time of it than the spoil-sports, here called apostates, heretics, innovators, prophets, conscientious objectors, etc. It sometimes happens, however, that the spoil-sports in their turn make a new community with rules of its own. The outlaw, the revolutionary, the cabbalist or member of a secret society, indeed heretics of all kinds are of a highly associative if not sociable disposition, and a certain element of play is prominent in all their doings.

A play-community generally tends to become permanent even after the game is over. Of course, not every game of marbles or every bridge-party leads to the founding of a club. But the feeling of being "apart together" in an exceptional situation, of sharing something important, of mutually withdrawing from the rest of the world and rejecting the usual norms, retains its magic beyond the duration of the individual game. The club pertains to play as the hat to the head. It would be rash to explain all the associations which the anthropologist calls "phratria"—e.g. clans, brotherhoods, etc.—simply as play-communities; nevertheless it has been shown again and again how difficult it is to draw the line between, on the one hand, permanent social groupings—particularly in archaic cultures with their extremely important, solemn, indeed sacred customs—and the sphere of play on the other.

The exceptional and special position of play is most tellingly illustrated by the fact that it loves to surround itself with an air of secrecy. Even in early childhood the charm of play is enhanced by making a "secret" out of it. This is for *us*, not for the "others". What the "others" do "outside" is no concern of ours at the moment. Inside the circle of the game the laws and customs of ordinary life no longer count. We are different and do things differently. This temporary abolition of the ordinary world is fully acknowledged in child-life, but it is no less evident in the great ceremonial games of savage societies. During the great feast of initiation when the youths are accepted into the male community, it is not the neophytes only that are exempt from the ordinary laws and regulations: there is a truce to all feuds in the tribe. All retaliatory acts and vendettas are suspended. This temporary suspension of normal social life on account of the sacred play-season has numerous traces in the more advanced civilizations as well. Everything that pertains to saturnalia and carnival customs belongs to it. Even with us a bygone age of robuster private habits than ours, more marked class-privileges and a more complaisant police recognized the orgies of young men of rank under the name of a "rag". The saturnalian licence of young men still survives, in fact, in the ragging at English universities, which the *Oxford English Dictionary* defines as "an extensive display of noisy and disorderly conduct carried out in defiance of authority and discipline".

The "differentness" and secrecy of play are most vividly expressed in "dressing up". Here the "extra-ordinary" nature of play reaches perfection. The disguised or masked individual "plays" another part, another being. He *is* another being. The terrors of childhood, open-hearted gaiety, mystic fantasy and sacred awe are all inextricably entangled in this strange business of masks and disguises.

Summing up the formal characteristics of play we might call it a free activity standing quite consciously outside "ordinary" life as being "not serious", but at the same time absorbing the player intensely and utterly. It is an activity connected with no material interest, and no profit can be gained by it. It proceeds within its own proper boundaries of time and space according to fixed rules and in an orderly manner. It promotes the formation of social groupings which tend to surround themselves with secrecy and to stress their difference from the common world by disguise or other means.

GEORGE SHEEHAN

Surf's Up! Head for the Waves

George Sheehan (1918–   ) is a physician who combines his medical expertise with his passion for fitness. He published *Encyclopedia of Athletic Medicine* (1972), *Dr. Sheehan on Running* (1975), and *Running and Being* (1978). He has been the medical editor of the magazine *Runner's World* since 1972 and has written a column for *Physician and Sports Medicine* magazine since 1974. Most recently he published *Personal Best* (1989), expanding on his philosophy of fitness. The following selection appeared in the *Asbury Park Press*.

This was no day to be at my desk. The surf was up. From my third-floor window at our beach house, I could see the waves building up at least a hundred yards from shore. The board surfers were performing their wizardry on combers, curling waves that looked 10 feet high. To the south, the younger fry on their boogie boards were catching rides that would provide conversation for the entire winter.

At seventysomething, bodysurfing is one thing I do as well as when I was a teen-ager. I have been a bodysurfer since I was a youngster. The best days I have spent at the beach have been those with a good surf, the wind from the west and the waves just right for riding.

There is an art to bodysurfing. It requires, however, very little talent. My swimming skills are marginal. I use them mostly to get out where the waves break. Then, with no more than two or three strong strokes at precisely the right time, I can catch any breaking wave.

Timing is the key. Some novices try to ride waves already broken and are engulfed in foam. Others start too late and miss entirely. There is a point in a wave when it is just about to break that offers the one and only opportunity for success.

When that happens, I am, for an instant, on the crest looking down from an incredible height at the flat expanse of water reaching to the shore. Then I feel the power of the wave twisting me forward. It takes me out into the clear, and like the figure on the prow of a ship, I ride it to the shore. At times the height is so alarming, I pull out rather than chance injury. And even when things go well there is that instant of fear. Will I be dashed to the bottom in this turbulence?

On the way out, I am conscious of the sea's overwhelming power. As I dive under one wave after another, I feel them crashing over me as if they were depth bombs. They toss me around under the surface, and I have to struggle to get my bearings and gain control. When I come up gasping for air, I am just in time for another huge breaker, which will submerge me once more.

Today, as on most days, I am almost alone in my sport. Body-surfing is a barely surviving sport at the beach. In my 50 years at the Shore, I have seen its adherents dwindle as younger generations took to their boards. It seems as if only the life guards, our family members and a handful of others have any proficiency or desire to take a cresting wave, glide down its break, head and shoulders out of the water, and ride it to the beach.

Nevertheless, there are times like today, when these huge waves are breaking almost beyond my ability to touch bottom. At that point, the riptide threatens to take me farther out.

JOHN CHEEVER

The Swimmer

John Cheever (1912–1982), born in Quincy, Massachusetts, published his first story, recounting his expulsion from school, when he was seventeen. Noted for his ability to depict the emptiness of suburban American life, he won a Pulitzer Prize for *The Stories of John Cheever* (1978), in which the following selection appears. His novels include *The Wapshot Scandal* (1964), *Bullet Park* (1969), *Falconer* (1977), and *Oh What a Paradise It Seems* (1982).

It was one of those midsummer Sundays when everyone sits around saying, "I *drank* too much last night." You might have heard it whispered by the parishioners leaving church, heard it from the lips of the priest himself, struggling with his cassock in the *vestiarium,* heard it from the golf links and the tennis courts, heard it from the wildlife preserve where the leader of the Audubon group was suffering from a terrible hangover. "I *drank* too much," said Donald Westerhazy. "We all *drank* too much," said Lucinda Merrill. "It must have been the wine," said Helen Westerhazy. "I *drank* too much of that claret."

This was at the edge of the Westerhazys' pool. The pool, fed by an artesian well with a high iron content, was a pale shade of green. It was a fine day. In the west there was a massive stand of cumulus cloud so like a city seen from a distance—from the bow of an approaching ship—that it might have had a name. Lisbon. Hackensack. The sun was hot. Neddy Merrill sat by the green water, one hand in it, one around a glass of gin. He was a slender man—he seemed to have the especial slenderness of youth—and while he was far from young he had slid down his banister that morning and given the bronze backside of Aphrodite on the hall table a smack, as he jogged toward the smell of coffee in his dining room. He might have been compared to a summer's day, particularly the last hours of one, and while he lacked a tennis racket or a sail bag the impression was definitely one of youth, sport, and clement weather. He had been swimming and now he was breathing deeply, stertorously as if he could gulp into his lungs the components of that moment, the heat of the sun, the intenseness of his pleasure. It all seemed to flow into his chest. His own house stood in Bullet Park, eight miles to the south, where his four beautiful daughters would have had their lunch and might be playing tennis. Then it occurred to him that by taking a dogleg to the southwest he could reach his home by water.

His life was not confining and the delight he took in this observation could not be explained by its suggestion of escape. He seemed to see, with a cartographer's eye, that string of swimming pools, that quasi-subterranean stream that curved across the county. He had made a discovery, a contribution to modern geography; he would name the stream Lucinda after his wife. He was not a practical joker nor was he a fool but he was determinedly original and had a vague and modest idea of himself as a legendary figure. The day was beautiful and it seemed to him that a long swim might enlarge and celebrate its beauty.

He took off a sweater that was hung over his shoulders and dove in. He had an inexplicable contempt for men who did not hurl themselves into pools. He swam a choppy crawl, breathing either with every stroke or every fourth stroke and counting somewhere well in the back of his mind the one-two one-two of a flutter kick. It was not a serviceable stroke for long distances but the domestication of swimming had saddled the sport with some customs and in his part of the world a crawl was customary. To be embraced and sustained by the light green water was less a pleasure, it seemed, than the resumption of a natural condition, and he would have liked to swim without trunks, but this was not possible, considering his project. He hoisted himself up on the far curb—he never used the ladder—and started across the lawn. When Lucinda asked where he was going he said he was going to swim home.

The only map and charts he had to go by were remembered or imaginary but these were clear enough. First there were the Grahams, the Hammers, the Lears, the Howlands, and the Crosscups. He would cross Ditmar Street to the Bunkers and come, after a short portage, to the Levys, the Welchers, and the public pool in Lancaster. Then there were the Hallorans, the Sachses, the Biswangers, Shirley Adams, the Gilmartins, and the Clydes. The day was lovely, and that he lived in a world so generously supplied with water seemed like a clemency, a beneficence. His heart was high and he ran across the grass. Making his way home by an uncommon route gave him the feeling that he was a pilgrim, an explorer, a man with a destiny, and he knew that he would find friends all along the way; friends would line the banks of the Lucinda River.

He went through a hedge that separated the Westerhazys' land from the Grahams', walked under some flowering apple trees, passed the shed that housed their pump and filter, and came out at the Grahams' pool. "Why, Neddy," Mrs. Graham said, "what a marvelous surprise. I've been trying to get you on the phone all morning. Here, let me get you a drink." He saw then, like an explorer, that the hospitable customs and traditions of the natives would have to be handled with diplomacy if he was ever going to reach his destination. He did not want to mystify or seem rude to the Grahams nor did he have the time to linger there. He swam the length of their pool and joined them in the sun and was rescued, a few minutes later, by the arrival of two carloads of friends from Connecticut. During the up-roarious reunions he was able to slip away. He went down by the front of the Grahams' house, stepped over a thorny hedge, and crossed a vacant lot to the Hammers'. Mrs. Hammer, looking up from her roses, saw him swim by although she wasn't quite sure who it was. The Lears heard him splashing past the open windows of their living room. The Howlands and the Crosscups were away. After leaving the Howlands' he crossed Ditmar Street and started for the Bunkers', where he could hear, even at the distance, the noise of a party.

The water refracted the sound of voices and laughter and seemed to suspend it in midair. The Bunkers' pool was on a rise and he

climbed some stairs to a terrace where twenty-five or thirty men and
women were drinking. The only person in the water was Rusty
Towers, who floated there on a rubber raft. Oh, how bonny and lush
were the banks of the Lucinda River! Prosperous men and women
gathered by the sapphire-colored waters while caterer's men in white
coats passed them cold gin. Overhead a red de Haviland trainer was
circling around and around and around in the sky with something
like the glee of a child in a swing. Ned felt a passing affection for
the scene, a tenderness for the gathering, as if it was something he
might touch. In the distance he heard thunder. As soon as Enid
Bunker saw him she began to scream: "Oh, look who's here! What
a marvelous surprise! When Lucinda said that you couldn't come I
thought I'd *die*." She made her way to him through the crowd, and
when they had finished kissing she led him to the bar, a progress
that was slowed by the fact that he stopped to kiss eight or ten other
women and shake the hands of as many men. A smiling bartender
he had seen at a hundred parties gave him a gin and tonic and he
stood by the bar for a moment, anxious not to get stuck in any
conversation that would delay his voyage. When he seemed about to
be surrounded he dove in and swam close to the side to avoid
colliding with Rusty's raft. At the far end of the pool he bypassed
the Tomlinsons with a broad smile and jogged up the garden path.
The gravel cut his feet but this was the only unpleasantness. The
party was confined to the pool, and as he went toward the house he
heard the brilliant, watery sound of voices fade, heard the noise of a
radio from the Bunkers' kitchen, where someone was listening to a
ball game. Sunday afternoon. He made his way through the parked
cars and down the grassy border of their driveway to Alewives Lane.
He did not want to be seen on the road in his bathing trunks but
there was no traffic and he made the short distance to the Levys'
driveway, marked with a PRIVATE PROPERTY sign and green tube for
The New York Times. All the doors and windows of the big house
were open but there were no signs of life; not even a dog barked. He
went around the side of the house to the pool and saw that the Levys
had only recently left. Glasses and bottles and dishes of nuts were
on a table at the deep end, where there was a bathhouse or gazebo,
hung with Japanese lanterns. After swimming the pool he got himself
a glass and poured a drink. It was his fourth or fifth drink and he
had swum nearly half the length of the Lucinda River. He felt tired,
clean, and pleased at that moment to be alone; pleased with everything.

It would storm. The stand of cumulus cloud—that city—had risen and darkened, and while he sat there he heard the percussiveness of thunder again. The de Haviland trainer was still circling overhead and it seemed to Ned that he could almost hear the pilot laugh with pleasure in the afternoon; but when there was another peal of thunder he took off for home. A train whistle blew and he wondered what time it had gotten to be. Four? Five? He thought of the provincial station at that hour, where a waiter, his tuxedo concealed by a raincoat, a dwarf with some flowers wrapped in newspaper, and a woman who had been crying would be waiting for the local. It was suddenly growing dark; it was that moment when the pin-headed birds seem to organize their song into some acute and knowledgeable recognition of the storm's approach. Then there was a fine noise of rushing water from the crown of an oak at his back, as if a spigot there had been turned. Then the noise of fountains came from the crowns of all the tall trees. Why did he love storms, what was the meaning of his excitement when the door sprang open and the rain wind fled rudely up the stairs, why had the simple task of shutting the windows of an old house seemed fitting and urgent, why did the first watery notes of a storm wind have for him the unmistakable sound of good news, cheer, glad tidings? Then there was an explosion, a smell of cordite, and rain lashed the Japanese lanterns that Mrs. Levy had bought in Kyoto the year before last, or was it the year before that?

He stayed in the Levys' gazebo until the storm had passed. The rain had cooled the air and he shivered. The force of the wind had stripped a maple of its red and yellow leaves and scattered them over the grass and the water. Since it was midsummer the tree must be blighted, and yet he felt a peculiar sadness at this sign of autumn. He braced his shoulders, emptied his glass, and started for the Welchers' pool. This meant crossing the Lindleys' riding ring and he was surprised to find it overgrown with grass and all the jumps dismantled. He wondered if the Lindleys had sold their horses or gone away for the summer and put them out to board. He seemed to remember having heard something about the Lindleys and their horses but the memory was unclear. On he went, barefoot through the wet grass, to the Welchers', where he found their pool was dry.

This breach in his chain of water disappointed him absurdly, and he felt like some explorer who seeks a torrential headwater and finds a dead stream. He was disappointed and mystified. It was common enough to go away for the summer but no one ever drained his pool. The Welchers had definitely gone away. The pool furniture was folded, stacked, and covered with a tarpaulin. The bathhouse was locked. All the windows of the house were shut, and when he went around to the driveway in front he saw a FOR SALE sign nailed to a tree. When had he last heard from the Welchers—when, that is, had he and Lucinda last regretted an invitation to dine with them? It seemed only a week or so ago. Was his memory failing or had he so disciplined it in the repression of unpleasant facts that he had damaged his sense of the truth? Then in the distance he heard the sound of a tennis game. This cheered him, cleared away all his apprehensions and let him regard the overcast sky and the cold air with indifference. This was the day that Neddy Merrill swam across the county. That was the day! He started off then for his most difficult portage.

Had you gone for a Sunday afternoon ride that day you might have seen him, close to naked, standing on the shoulders of Route 424, waiting for a chance to cross. You might have wondered if he was the victim of foul play, had his car broken down, or was he merely a fool. Standing barefoot in the deposits of the highway—beer cans, rags, and blowout patches—exposed to all kinds of ridicule, he seemed pitiful. He had known when he started that this was a part of his journey—it had been on his maps—but confronted with the lines of traffic, worming through the summery light, he found himself unprepared. He was laughed at, jeered at, a beer can was thrown at him, and he had no dignity or humor to bring to the situation. He could have gone back, back to the Westerhazys', where Lucinda would still be sitting in the sun. He had signed nothing, vowed nothing, pledged nothing, not even to himself. Why, believing as he did, that all human obduracy was susceptible to common sense, was he unable to turn back? Why was he determined to complete his journey even if it meant putting his life in danger? At what point had this prank, this joke, this piece of horseplay become serious? He could not go back, he could not even recall with any clearness the green water at the Westerhazys', the sense of inhaling the day's components, the friendly and relaxed voices saying that they had *drunk* too much. In the space of an hour, more or less, he had covered a distance that made his return impossible.

An old man, tooling down the highway at fifteen miles an hour, let him get to the middle of the road, where there was a grass divider. Here he was exposed to the ridicule of the northbound traffic, but after ten or fifteen minutes he was able to cross. From here he had only a short walk to the Recreation Center at the edge of the village of Lancaster, where there were some handball courts and a public pool.

The effect of the water on voices, the illusion of brilliance and suspense, was the same here as it had been at the Bunkers' but the sounds here were louder, harsher, and more shrill, and as soon as he entered the crowded enclosure he was confronted with regimentation. "ALL SWIMMERS MUST TAKE A SHOWER BEFORE USING THE POOL. ALL SWIMMERS MUST USE THE FOOTBATH. ALL SWIMMERS MUST WEAR THEIR IDENTIFICATION DISKS." He took a shower, washed his feet in a cloudy and bitter solution, and made his way to the edge of the water. It stank of chlorine and looked to him like a sink. A pair of lifeguards in a pair of towers blew police whistles at what seemed to be regular intervals and abused the swimmers through a public address system. Neddy remembered the sapphire water at the Bunkers' with longing and thought that he might contaminate himself—damage his own prosperousness and charm—by swimming in this murk, but he reminded himself that he was an explorer, a pilgrim, and that this was merely a stagnant bend in the Lucinda River. He dove, scowling with distaste, into the chlorine and had to swim with his head above water to avoid collisions, but even so he was bumped into, splashed, and jostled. When he got to the shallow end both lifeguards were shouting at him: "Hey, you, you without the identification disk, get outa the water." He did, but they had no way of pursuing him and he went through the reek of suntan oil and chlorine out through the hurricane fence and passed the handball courts. By crossing the road he entered the wooded part of the Halloran estate. The woods were not cleared and the footing was treacherous and difficult until he reached the lawn and the clipped beech hedge that encircled their pool.

The Hallorans were friends, an elderly couple of enormous wealth who seemed to bask in the suspicion that they might be Communists. They were zealous reformers but they were not Communists, and yet when they were accused, as they sometimes were, of subversion, it seemed to gratify and excite them. Their beech hedge was yellow and he guessed this had been blighted like the Levys' maple. He called hullo, hullo, to warn the Hallorans of his approach, to palliate his invasion of their privacy. The Hallorans, for reasons that had never been explained to him, did not wear bathing suits. No explanations were in order, really. Their nakedness was a detail in their uncompromising zeal for reform and he stepped politely out of his trunks before he went through the opening in the hedge.

Mrs. Halloran, a stout woman with white hair and a serene face,

was reading the *Times,* Mr. Halloran was taking beech leaves out of
the water with a scoop. They seemed not surprised or displeased to
see him. Their pool was perhaps the oldest in the county, a fieldstone
rectangle, fed by a brook. It had no filter or pump and its waters
were the opaque gold of the stream.

"I'm swimming across the county," Ned said.

"Why, I didn't know one could," exclaimed Mrs. Halloran.

"Well, I've made it from the Westerhazys'," Ned said. "That must
be about four miles."

He left his trunks at the deep end, walked to the shallow end,
and swam this stretch. As he was pulling himself out of the water
he heard Mrs. Halloran say, "We've been *terribly* sorry to hear about
all your misfortunes, Neddy."

"My misfortunes?" Ned asked. "I don't know what you mean."

"Why, we heard that you'd sold the house and that your poor
children . . ."

"I don't recall having sold the house," Ned said, "and the girls
are at home."

"Yes," Mrs. Halloran sighed. "Yes . . ." Her voice filled the air
with an unseasonable melancholy and Ned spoke briskly. "Thank
you for the swim."

"Well, have a nice trip," said Mrs. Halloran.

Beyond the hedge he pulled on his trunks and fastened them.
They were loose and he wondered if, during the space of an afternoon, he could have lost some weight. He was cold and he was tired
and the naked Hallorans and their dark water had depressed him.
The swim was too much for his strength but how could he have
guessed this, sliding down the banister that morning and sitting in
the Westerhazys' sun? His arms were lame. His legs felt rubbery and
ached at the joints. The worst of it was the cold in his bones and
the feeling that he might never be warm again. Leaves were falling
down around him and he smelled wood smoke on the wind. Who
would be burning wood at this time of year?

He needed a drink. Whiskey would warm him, pick him up, carry
him through the last of his journey, refresh his feeling that it was
original and valorous to swim across the county. Channel swimmers
took brandy. He needed a stimulant. He crossed the lawn in front of
the Hallorans' house and went down a little path to where they had
built a house for their only daughter, Helen, and her husband, Eric
Sachs. The Sachses' pool was small and he found Helen and her
husband there.

"Oh, *Neddy,*" Helen said. "Did you lunch at Mother's?"

"Not *really,*" Ned said. "I *did* stop to see your parents." This seemed to be explanation enough. "I'm terribly sorry to break in on you like this but I've taken a chill and I wonder if you'd give me a drink."

"Why, I'd *love* to," Helen said, "but there hasn't been anything in this house to drink since Eric's operation. That was three years ago."

Was he losing his memory, had his gift for concealing painful facts let him forget that he had sold his house, that his children were in trouble, and that his friend had been ill? His eyes slipped from Eric's face to his abdomen, where he saw three pale, sutured scars, two of them at least a foot long. Gone was his navel, and what, Neddy thought, would the roving hand, bed-checking one's gifts at 3 A.M., make of a belly with no navel, no link to birth, this breach in the succession?

"I'm sure you can get a drink at the Biswangers'," Helen said. "They're having an enormous do. You can hear it from here. Listen!"

She raised her head and from across the road, the lawns, the gardens, the woods, the fields, he heard again the brilliant noise of voices over water. "Well, I'll get wet," he said, still feeling that he had no freedom of choice about his means of travel. He dove into the Sachses' cold water and, gasping, close to drowning, made his way from one end of the pool to the other. "Lucinda and I want *terribly* to see you," he said over his shoulder, his face set toward the Biswangers'. "We're sorry it's been so long and we'll call you *very* soon."

He crossed some fields to the Biswangers' and the sounds of revelry there. They would be honored to give him a drink, they would be happy to give him a drink. The Biswangers invited him and Lucinda for dinner four times a year, six weeks in advance. They were always rebuffed and yet they continued to send out their invitations, unwilling to comprehend the rigid and undemocratic realities of their society. They were the sort of people who discussed the price of things at cocktails, exchanged market tips during dinner, and after dinner told dirty stories to mixed company. They did not belong to Neddy's set—they were not even on Lucinda's Christmas-card list. He went toward their pool with feelings of indifference, charity, and some unease, since it seemed to be getting dark and these were the longest days of the year. The party when he joined it was noisy and large. Grace Biswanger was the kind of hostess who asked the optometrist, the veterinarian, the real-estate dealer, and the dentist. No one was swimming and the twilight, reflected on the water of the pool, had a wintry gleam. There was a bar and he started for this. When Grace Biswanger saw him she came toward him, not affectionately as he had every right to expect, but bellicosely.

"Why, this party has everything," she said loudly, "including a gate crasher."

She could not deal him a social blow—there was no question about this and he did not flinch. "As a gate crasher," he asked politely, "do I rate a drink?"

"Suit yourself," she said. "You don't seem to pay much attention to invitations."

She turned her back on him and joined some guests, and he went to the bar and ordered a whiskey. The bartender served him but he served him rudely. His was a world in which the caterer's men kept the social score, and to be rebuffed by a part-time barkeep meant that he had suffered some loss of social esteem. Or perhaps the man was new and uninformed. Then he heard Grace at his back say: "They went for broke overnight—nothing but income—and he showed up drunk one Sunday and asked us to loan him five thousand dollars. . . ." She was always talking about money. It was worse than eating your peas off a knife. He dove into the pool, swam its length and went away.

The next pool on his list, the last but two, belonged to his old mistress, Shirley Adams. If he had suffered any injuries at the Biswangers' they would be cured here. Love—sexual roughhouse in fact—was the supreme elixir, the pain killer, the brightly colored pill that would put the spring back into his step, the joy of life in his heart. They had had an affair last week, last month, last year. He couldn't remember. It was he who had broken it off, his was the upper hand, and he stepped through the gate of the wall that surrounded her pool with nothing so considered as self-confidence. It seemed in a way to be his pool, as the lover, particularly the illicit lover, enjoys the possessions of his mistress with an authority unknown to holy matrimony. She was there, her hair the color of brass, but her figure, at the edge of the lighted, cerulean water, excited in him no profound memories. It had been, he thought, a lighthearted affair, although she had wept when he broke it off. She seemed confused to see him and he wondered if she was still wounded. Would she, God forbid, weep again?

"What do you want?" she asked.

"I'm swimming across the county."

"Good Christ. Will you ever grow up?"

"What's the matter?"

"If you've come here for money," she said, "I won't give you another cent."

"You could give me a drink."

"I could but I won't. I'm not alone."

"Well, I'm on my way."

He dove in and swam the pool, but when he tried to haul himself up onto the curb he found that the strength in his arms and shoulders had gone, and he paddled to the ladder and climbed out. Looking over his shoulders he saw, in the lighted bathhouse, a young man. Going out onto the dark lawn he smelled chrysanthemums or marigolds—some stubborn autumnal fragrance—on the night air, strong as gas. Looking overhead he saw that the stars had come out, but why should he seem to see Andromeda, Cepheus, and Cassiopeia? What had become of the constellations of midsummer? He began to cry.

It was probably the first time in his adult life that he had ever cried, certainly the first time in his life that he had ever felt so miserable, cold, tired, and bewildered. He could not understand the rudeness of the caterer's barkeep or the rudeness of a mistress who had come to him on her knees and showered his trousers with tears. He had swum too long, he had been immersed too long, and his nose and his throat were sore from the water. What he needed then was a drink, some company, and some clean, dry clothes, and while he could have cut directly across the road to his house he went on to the Gilmartins' pool. Here, for the first time in his life, he did not dive but went down the steps into the icy water and swam a hobbled sidestroke that he might have learned as a youth. He staggered with fatigue on his way to the Clydes' and paddled the length of their pool, stopping again and again with his hand on the curb to rest. He climbed up the ladder and wondered if he had the strength to get home. He had done what he wanted, he had swum the county, but he was so stupefied with exhaustion that his triumph seemed vague. Stooped, holding on to the gateposts for support, he turned up the driveway of his own house.

The place was dark. Was it so late that they had all gone to bed? Had Lucinda stayed at the Westerhazys' for supper? Had the girls joined her there or gone someplace else? Hadn't they agreed, as they usually did on Sundays, to regret all their invitations and stay at home? He tried the garage doors to see what cars were in but the doors were locked and rust came off the handles onto his hands. Going toward the house, he saw that the force of the thunderstorm had knocked one of the rain gutters loose. It hung down over the front door like an umbrella rib, but it could be fixed in the morning. The house was locked, and he thought that the stupid cook or the stupid maid must have locked the place up until he remembered that it had been some time since they had employed a maid or a cook. He shouted, pounded on the door, tried to force it with his shoulder, and then, looking in at the windows, saw that the place was empty.

JEFFREY SCHRANK

Sport and the American Dream

Jeffrey Schrank (1944–), an educator who writes about communications media, education, and psychology, also edits *Media Mix Newsletter*. "Sport and the American Dream" is from his book *Snap, Crackle, and Popular Taste: The Illusion of Free Choice in America* (1977). Other books include *Teaching Human Beings: 101 Subversive Activities for the Classroom* (1972) and *Feelings: Exploring Inner Space* (1973).

Sport is a ritual and acting out of a myth or series of myths. A sport that can be considered a national pastime can be expected to reflect national values and wishes. Sports that capture the national fancy are ritualistic enactments of the American Dream. Baseball is still called our national pastime but is rapidly being replaced by American football. That football should become our "national pastime" is understandable to those who can see sports as reflections of national character.

American football is passionately concerned with the gain and loss of land, of territory. The football field is measured and marked with all the care of a surveyor and the ball's progress noted to the nearest inch. Football is a precise game and its players are often trained like a military unit on a mission to gain territory for the mother country. The players are the popular heroes but the coaches and owners run the game, using the players to carry out their plans— there is comparatively little room for individual initiative. A score comes as the result of a strategic series of well-executed maneuvers and is bought on the installment plan, yard by yard.

The regulation and almost military precision of American football is a reflection of national psychology. Even the words we use to describe the game include throwing the bomb, marching downfield, game plan (which has become nearly a national phrase for any field, from selling toothpaste to covering up political scandals), guards, executions, blitz, zone, platoon, squad, drills, attack, drives, marching bands for entertainment, stars on helmets, lines that can be blasted through and even war paint. Much of the verbal similarity comes from the fact that war was originally the ultimate game played within the confines of certain rules agreed upon by both "teams."

Football, more than any other sport, is a game for spectators to watch superhuman, mythical heroes. Football is a sport that more people watch than play. The game requires too many people, too much space and is simply too dangerous for the weekend athlete. The size and speed of professional players and their uniforms make them into heroic figures capable of feats that invite admiration but not imitation. The football spectator is in awe of the armored monsters. The viewer of a gold match or even baseball or tennis dreams of going out the next day and doing likewise, but football is played only by the gods who can run the 100 yard dash in ten seconds, stand six feet three and weigh 260 pounds.

The demise of baseball as our national pastime reflects a change in national character. The change does not mean the disappearance of baseball, merely its relocation to a position as just another game rather than *the* game. Professor John Finlay of the University of Manitoba, writing in *Queen's Quarterlay,* compares baseball to an acting out of the robber baron stage of capitalism, whereas football more clearly reflects a more mature capitalism into which we are now moving. Hence, the rise in popularity of football and apparent decline in baseball. He notes that Japan, still in the early stages of capitalism, has taken avidly to baseball but not to football. It is not a question of Japanese physique serving as a determinant since rugby has a large Asian following. He predicts that when their capitalism moves into a higher stage, the Japanese will move on to football as have Americans.

Baseball is a game of a quieter age when less action was needed to hold interest, when going to the park was enjoyable (baseball is still played in ball parks while football is played in stadiums), when aggression was subservient to finesse. Baseball players did not need exposure as college players to succeed as football players do; they play a relatively calm game almost daily instead of a bruising gladiatorial contest weekly. Baseball has room for unique and colorful characters, while football stresses the more anonymous but effective team member. Baseball is a game in which any team can win at any given contest and there are no favorites; only football has real "up-sets." Football's careful concern with time adds a tension to the game that is lacking in the more leisurely world of baseball.

Football has replaced baseball as the favorite American spectator sport largely because of television. A comparison between a telecast of a football game on one channel and a baseball game on another could reveal baseball as a game with people standing around seemingly with little to do but watch two men play catch. Football would appear as twenty-two men engaged in almost constant, frenzied action. To watch baseball requires identification with the home team: to watch football requires only a need for action or a week of few thrills and the need for a touch of vicarious excitement.

Baseball is a pastoral game, timeless and highly ritualized: its appeal is to nostalgia and so might enjoy periods of revitalization in comparison to football. But for now, the myth of football suits the nation better.

According to a 1974 Harris survey, baseball has already been statistically dethroned. In a sports survey a cross section of nearly fourteen hundred fans was asked, "Which of these sports do you follow?"

The decision to play or "follow" a certain sport is also the decision to live a certain myth. The team violence of football, the craftiness of basketball, the mechanistic precision of bowling, the auto racer's devotion to machinery are all subworlds within the universe of sport.

Golf, for example, is a unique subworld, one of the few left as a sport (unlike hunting which does not involve scoring or teams) in which the game is played between man and nature. The winner of a match is one who has beaten the opponent, but the game itself is a person versus the environment. To understand the appeal of golf it is again necessary to consider the game as a ritual reenactment of an appealing myth.

Golf, perhaps more than any other sport, has to be played to be appreciated. Millions who never played football can enjoy the game on TV, but only a dedicated participant can sit through two hours of televised golf. Golf is growing in participation but still has the stigma of an upper-class game. Eighty percent of the nation's golfers must play on 20 percent of the nation's courses that are open to the public. The ratio of public to private facilities hurts public participation in the game but mirrors the inequities of society and provides a convenient status symbol for those who can afford club membership. Its TV audience is not the largest of any sport but it is the most well heeled.

Golf is a reenactment of the pioneer spirit. It is man versus a hostile environment in search of an oasis. The goal is a series of lush "greens," each protected by natural hazards such as water, sand and unmanageably long grass. The hazards are no threat to physical life but they are to the achievement of success. Golf is a journey game with a constantly changing field. Golfers start the eighteen-hole journey, can rest at a halfway point and then resume until they return to near the point of origination.

The winner of the match is one who has fallen victim to the fewest hazards and overcome the terrain. Many golf courses have Indian names as if to remind the golfer of the frontier ethos. A local course called Indian Lakes invites golfers to use either one of two courses—the Iroquois trail or the Sioux trail.

Golf, like baseball, is a pastoral sport—with a high degree of tensions and drama but relatively little action. It is a game in which players are constantly in awe of the magic flight of the golf ball. To hit any kind of ball 100 or 200 or more yards with accuracy or to hit a small target from 150 yards is an amazing feat to be appreciated only by those who have at least tried the game. Golf is very likely the most difficult game to master, yet one in which the average player occasionally hits a shot as good as the best of any professional. It is this dream of magic results that keeps the golfer on course.

EDWARD ABBEY

Blood Sport

Edward Abbey (1927–1989) was an essayist, novelist, and natural historian whose books include *Desert Solitaire* (1968), *Cactus Country* (1973), *The Monkey Wrench Gang* (1975), *Slumgullion Stew: An Edward Abbey Reader* (1984), *The Fool's Progress* (1988), and *One Life at a Time Please* (1988), from which the following selection is taken.

What can I say about hunting that hasn't been said before? Hunting is one of the hardest things even to think about. Such a storm of conflicting emotions!

I was born, bred, and raised on a farm in the Allegheny Mountains

of Pennsylvania. A little sidehill farm in hardscrabble country, a land
of marginal general farms, of submarginal specialized farms—our
specialty was finding enough to eat without the shame of going on
"The Relief," as we called it during the Great Depression of the
1930s. We lived in the hills, surrounded by scrubby third-growth
forests, little coal-mining towns down in the valleys, and sulfur-
colored creeks meandering among the corn patches. Few people
could make a living from farming alone: my father, for example,
supplemented what little we produced on the farm by occasional
work in the mines, by driving a school bus, by a one-man logging
business, by peddling subscriptions to a farmer's magazine, and by
attending every private and public shooting match within fifty miles
of home—he was an expert small-bore rifleman and a member, for
several years running, of the Pennsylvania state rifle team; he still
has a sashful of medals to show for those years. He almost always
brought back from the matches a couple of chickens, sometimes a
turkey, once a yearling pig.

None of this was quite enough, all together, to keep a family of
seven in meat, all the time, through the frozen Appalachian winters.
So he hunted. We all hunted. All of our neighbors hunted. Nearly
every boy I knew had his own rifle, and maybe a shotgun too, by
the time he was twelve years old. As I did myself.

What did we hunt? Cottontail rabbit, first and foremost; we'd kill
them, clean them, skin them, cut them up; my mother deep-fried
them in bread crumbs and cooked and canned the surplus in Mason
jars, as she did tomatoes, stringbeans, succotash, pork sausage,
peaches, pears, sweet corn, everything else that would keep. We had
no deep-freeze; in fact, we had no electricity until the Rural Electri-
fication Administration reached our neck of the woods in 1940.

So rabbit was almost a staple of our diet; fencerow chicken, we
called it, as good and familiar to us as henyard chicken. My father
seldom bothered with squirrel, but my brothers and I potted a few
with our little Sears Roebuck single-shot .22s, out among the great
ancient white oaks and red oaks that were still standing in our
woodlot. Squirrel meat can be good, but not so good as rabbit, and
a squirrel is much harder to kill: we missed about ten for every one
we hit.

There were no wild ducks or other waterfowl in the hills; our
only gamebird was the ringneck pheasant, rising with a thrilling rush
from the corn stubble. My father bagged a few of those with his old
taped-together double-barrel shotgun. Not many. He didn't like to
hunt with a shotgun. Wasteful, he thought, and the shells were too

expensive, and besides, he disliked chewing on lead pellets. The shotgun was primarily a weapon (though never needed) for home defense. Most of the time he shot rabbits with his target rifle, a massive magazine-loaded .22 with a peep sight. Shot them sitting.

Was that legal? Probably. I don't remember. But he had a good eye. And he was a hunter—not a sportsman. He hunted for a purpose: to put meat on the table.

We kept a couple of beagle hounds on the place, but their job was to lie under the front porch and bark at strangers. Only when our Uncle Jack came out from town, with his sleek gleaming 16-gauge pumpgun (as we called it), and the red bandana and hunting license pinned to the back of his hunting coat, only then would our old man load his own shotgun and turn loose the dogs for some sport hunting through the fields and along the edge of the woods. What my father really liked about those occasions was not the shooting but the talk, the wild stories—Uncle Jack was a great storyteller.

And then there were the deer. The woods of Pennsylvania swarmed with deer, though not so many then as now, when many small farms, abandoned, have gone back to brush, thicket, trees. There were even a few black bear still wandering the woods, rarely seen. But deer was the principal game.

My father usually bought a license for deer, when he could afford it, but only because the penalty for getting caught with an untagged deer would have been a small financial catastrophe. In any case, with or without a license, he always killed his deer on the evening before opening day, while those red-coated fellows from the towns and cities were busy setting up their elaborate camps along the back roads, stirring the deer into movement. Our father was not a stickler for strict legality, and he believed, as most country men did, that fear tainted the meat and therefore it was better to get your deer before the chase, the gunnery—The Terror—began. We liked our venison poached. (As a result I find that after these many years I retain more admiration and respect for the honest serious poacher than I do or ever could for the so-called "gentleman hunter.")

My old man practiced what we called "still hunting." On the day before opening, about noon, when the deer were bedded down for their midday siesta, he'd go out with his gun, his cornfodder-tan canvas coat with its many big pockets, and his coal miner's oval-shaped lunch bucket full of hot coffee and sandwiches and Mother's stewed-raisin cookies, and he'd pick a familiar spot along one of the half-dozen game paths in our neighborhood, settle down in the brush with his back to a comfortable tree, and wait. And keep on waiting, sometimes into the long autumn twilight, until at last the first somewhat nervous, always uneasy deer appeared. Doe or buck, he always shot whatever came first. You can't eat antlers, he pointed out.

Usually he shot his deer with a "punkin ball" from the battered, dangerous, taped-up shotgun. But at least once, as I recall, he dropped a doe with his target rifle, like a rabbit. Drilled her right between the eyes with a neat little .22-caliber long-rifle bullet. Those deer slugs for the shotgun were expensive.

Then he'd drag the deer into the brush, out of sight, and wait some more, to see if anyone had noticed the shot. When nothing happened, he hung the deer to the nearest tree limb, dressed it out, ate the liver for supper. If it was a legal kill he would wait through the night, tag it, and take it home by wheel first thing in the morning. If not, he slung the carcass over his shoulders and toted it home through the woods and over the hills in the dark. He was a strong, large, and resolute sort of man then, back in the thirties and early forties, with a wife and five children to feed. Nowadays, getting on a bit—he was born in 1901—he is still oversize, for an old man, but not so strong physically. Nor so resolute. He works only four or five hours a day, alone, out in the woods, cutting down trees, and then quits. He gave up deer hunting thirty years ago.

Why? "Well," he explains, "we don't need the meat any more."

Now that was how my brothers and I learned about hunting. My brothers still like to go out for deer now and then, but it's road hunting, with good companions, not "still hunting." I wonder if anybody hunts in that fashion these days. I did a lot of deer hunting in New Mexico from 1947 through the 1950s, during my student years and later, when I was living on seasonal jobs with the Park Service and Forest Service, often married, trying to write books. As my father had taught me, I usually went out on the day before opening. Much safer then, for one thing, before those orange-vested hordes were turned loose over the landscape, shooting at everything that moves.

Gradually, from year to year, my interest in hunting, as a sport, waned away to nothing. I began to realize that what I liked best about hunting was the companionship of a few good old trusted male buddies in the out-of-doors. Anything, any excuse, to get out into the hills, away from the crowds, to live, if only for a few days, beyond the wall. That was the point of hunting.

So why lug a ten-pound gun along? I began leaving my rifle in the truck. Then I left it at home. The last time I looked down the bore of that old piece there was a spider living there.

"We don't need the meat any more," says my old man. And I say, Let the mountain lions have those deer; they need the meat more than I do. Let the Indians have it, or hungry college students, or unpublished writers, or anyone else trying to get by on welfare, food stamps, and hope. When the money began arriving from New York by airmail, those checks with my name on them, like manna from heaven, I gave up hunting deer. I had no need. Every time you eat a cow, I tell myself, you are saving the life of an elk, or two mule deer, or about two dozen javelina. Let those wild creatures live. Let being be, said Martin Heidegger.[1] Of course, they're going to perish anyway. I know, whether by lion or wolf or starvation or disease—but so are we. We are all going to perish, and most of us miserably, by war or in a hospital, unless we are very lucky. Or very resolute. I am aware of that fact and of our fate, and furthermore, I have no objections to it, none whatsoever. I fear pain, suffering, the likely humiliations of old age (unless I am lucky or resolute), but I do not fear death. Death is simply and obviously a part of the process; the old, sooner or later, have got to get out of the way and make room for the young.

The subject remains: death. Blood sport. The instinct to hunt. The desire to kill. Henry David Thoreau, notorious nature lover, was also a hunter and fisherman, on occasion. And among the many things that Thoreau wrote on the matter was this, from *Walden*:

> There is a period in the history of the individual, as of the race, when the hunters are the "best men," as the Algonquins called them. We cannot but pity the boy who has never fired a gun; he is no more humane, while his education has been sadly neglected.

But he adds:

> No humane being, past the thoughtless age of boyhood, will wantonly murder any creature which holds its life by the same tenure he does. The hare in its extremity cries like a child. I warn you, mothers, that my sympathies do not make the usual *philanthropic* distinctions.

And concludes:

> But I see that if I were to live in a wilderness, I should become . . . a fisher and hunter in earnest.

---

[1] Martin Heidegger (1889–1976) was a German philosopher, considered one of the founders of Existentialism. (ED.)

In earnest. There lies the key to the ethical issue. Earnestness. Purpose. That sly sophist Ortega y Gasset[2] wrote, somewhere, that "one kills in order to have hunted." Not good enough. Thoreau would say, one kills in order to eat. The killing is justified by the need and must be done in a spirit of respect, reverence, gratitude. Otherwise hunting sinks to the level of mere fun, "harvesting animals," *divertissement,* sadism, or sport. *Sport!*

Where did the ugly term "harvesting" come from? To speak of "harvesting" other living creatures, whether deer or elk or birds or cottontail rabbits, as if they were no more than a crop, exposes the meanest, cruelest, most narrow and homocentric of possible human attitudes toward the life that surrounds us. The word reveals the pervasive influence of utilitarian economics in the modern mindset; and of all the sciences, economics is the most crude and obtuse as well as dismal. Such doctrine insults and violates both humanity and life; and humanity will be, already is, the victim of it.

Now I have railed against the sportsman hunter long enough. I wished only to explain why first my father and then I have given up hunting, for the time being. When times get hard again, as they surely will, when my family and kin need meat on the table, I shall not hesitate to take that old carbine down from the wall and ramrod that spider out of the barrel and wander back once more into the hills.

"Paw," says my little brother, as the old man loads the shotgun, "let me shoot the deer this time."

"You shut up," I say.

Our father smiles. "Quiet," he whispers, "both of you. Maybe next year." He peers down the dim path in the woods, into the gathering evening. "Be real still now. They're a-comin'. And Ned—" He squeezes my shoulder. "You hold that light on 'em good and steady this time."

"Yes, sir," I whisper back. "Sure will, Paw."

---

[2] José Ortega y Gasset (1883–1955) was a Spanish essayist and philosopher and author of the controversial *The Revolt of the Masses* (1929). (ED.)

IRWIN SHAW

The Eighty-Yard Run

Irwin Shaw (1913–1984) was a prolific writer whose short stories
appeared in the *New Yorker, Collier's* and *Esquire.* He began his
career writing scripts for radio shows like *Dick Tracy* in the 1930s.
His novel *Rich Man, Poor Man* (1971) and its sequel *Beggarman,
Thief* (1977) formed the basis for a television mini-series in the
seventies. His last two novels were *Bread upon the Waters* (1981)
and *Acceptable Losses* (1982).

The pass was high and wide and he jumped for it, feeling it slap
flatly against his hands, as he shook his hips to throw off the halfback
who was diving at him. The center floated by, his hands desperately
brushing Darling's knee as Darling picked his feet up high and
delicately ran over a blocker and an opposing linesman in a jumble
on the ground near the scrimmage line. He had ten yards in the clear
and picked up speed, breathing easily, feeling his thigh pads rising
and falling against his legs, listening to the sound of cleats behind
him, pulling away from them, watching the other backs heading him
off toward the sideline, the whole picture, the men closing in on
him, the blockers fighting for position, the ground he had to cross,
all suddenly clear in his head, for the first time in his life not a
meaningless confusion of men, sounds, speed. He smiled a little to
himself as he ran, holding the ball lightly in front of him with his
two hands, his knees pumping high, his hips twisting in the almost-
girlish run of a back in a broken field. The first halfback came to
him and he fed him his leg, then swung at the last moment, took
the shock of the man's shoulder without breaking stride, ran right
through him, his cleats biting securely into the turf. There was only
the safety man now, coming warily at him, his arms crooked, hands
spread. Darling tucked the ball in, spurted at him, driving hard,
hurling himself along, his legs pounding, knees high, all two hundred
pounds bunched into controlled attack. He was sure he was going
to get past the safety man. Without thought, his arms and legs
working beautifully together, he headed right for the safety man,
stiff-armed him, feeling blood spurt instantaneously from the man's
nose onto his hand, seeing his face go awry, head turned, mouth
pulled to one side. He pivoted away, keeping the arm locked, drop-

ping the safety man as he ran easily toward the goal line, with the drumming of cleats diminishing behind him.

How long ago? It was autumn then and the ground was getting hard because the nights were cold and leaves from the maples around the stadium blew across the practice fields in gusts of wind and the girls were beginning to put polo coats over their sweaters when they came to watch practice in the afternoons . . . Fifteen years. Darling walked slowly over the same ground in the spring twilight, in his neat shoes, a man of thirty-five dressed in a double-breasted suit, ten pounds heavier in the fifteen years, but not fat, with the years between 1925 and 1940 showing in his face.

The coach was smiling quietly to himself and the assistant coaches were looking at each other with pleasure the way they always did when one of the second stringers suddenly did something fine, bringing credit to them, making their $2,000 a year a tiny bit more secure.

Darling trotted back, smiling, breathing deeply but easily, feeling wonderful, not tired, though this was the tail end of practice and he'd run eighty yards. The sweat poured off his face and soaked his jersey and he liked the feeling, the warm moistness lubricating his skin like oil. Off in a corner of the field some players were punting and the smack of leather against the ball came pleasantly through the afternoon air. The freshmen were running signals on the next field and the quarterback's sharp voice, the pound of eleven pairs of cleats, the "Dig, now, *dig!*" of the coaches, the laughter of the players all somehow made him feel happy as he trotted back to midfield, listening to the applause and shouts of the students along the sidelines, knowing that after that run the coach would have to start him Saturday against Illinois.

Fifteen years, Darling thought, remembering the shower after the workout, the hot water steaming off his skin and the deep soapsuds and all the young voices singing with the water streaming down and towels going and managers running in and out and the sharp sweet smell of oil of wintergreen and everybody clapping him on the back as he dressed and Packard, the captain, who took being captain very seriously, coming over to him and shaking his hand and saying, "Darling, you're going to go places in the next two years."

The assistant manager fussed over him, wiping a cut on his leg with alcohol and iodine, the little sting making him realize suddenly how fresh and whole and solid his body felt. The manager slapped a piece of adhesive tape over the cut and Darling noticed the sharp clean white of the tape against the ruddiness of the skin, fresh from the shower.

He dressed slowly, the softness of his shirt and the soft warmth of his wool socks and his flannel trousers a reward against his skin after the harsh pressure of the shoulder harness and thigh and hip pads. He drank three glasses of cold water, the liquid reaching down coldly inside of him, soothing the harsh dry places in his throat and belly left by the sweat and running and shouting of practice.

Fifteen years.

The sun had gone down and the sky was green behind the stadium and he laughed quietly to himself as he looked at the stadium, rearing above the trees, and knew that on Saturday when the 70,000 voices roared as the team came running out onto the field, part of that enormous salute would be for him. He walked slowly, listening to the gravel crunch satisfactorily under his shoes in the still twilight, feeling his clothes swing lightly against his skin, breathing the thin evening air, feeling the wind move softly in his damp hair, wonderfully cool behind his ears and at the nape of his neck.

Louise was waiting for him at the road, in her car. The top was down and he noticed all over again, as he always did when he saw her, how pretty she was, the rough blonde hair and the large, inquiring eyes and the bright mouth, smiling now.

She threw the door open. "Were you good today?" she asked.

"Pretty good," he said. He climbed in, sank luxuriously into the soft leather, stretched his legs far out. He smiled, thinking of the eighty yards. "Pretty damn good."

She looked at him seriously for a moment, then scrambled around, like a little girl, kneeling on the seat next to him, grabbed him, her hands along his ears, and kissed him as he sprawled, head back, on the seat cushion. She let go of him, but kept her head close to his, over his. Darling reached up slowly and rubbed the back of his hand against her cheek, lit softly by a street lamp a hundred feet away. They looked at each other, smiling.

Louise drove down to the lake and they sat there silently, watching the moon rise behind the hills on the other side. Finally he reached over, pulled her gently to him, kissed her. Her lips grew soft, her body sank into his, tears formed slowly in her eyes. He knew, for the first time, that he could do whatever he wanted with her.

"Tonight," he said. "I'll call for you at seven-thirty. Can you get out?"

She looked at him. She was smiling, but the tears were still full in her eyes. "All right," she said "I'll get out. How about you? Won't the coach raise hell?"

Darling grinned. "I got the coach in the palm of my hand," he
said. "Can you wait till seven-thirty?"

She grinned back at him. "No," she said.

They kissed and she started the car and they went back to town
for dinner. He sang on the way home.

Christian Darling, thirty-five years old, sat on the frail spring grass,
greener now than it ever would be again on the practice field, looked
thoughtfully up at the stadium, a deserted ruin in the twilight. He
had started on the first team that Saturday and every Saturday after
that for the next two years, but it had never been as satisfactory as
it should have been. He never had broken away, the longest run he'd
ever made was thirty-five yards, and that in a game that was already
won, and then that kid had come up from the third team, Diederich,
a blank-faced German kid from Wisconsin, who ran like a bull,
ripping lines to pieces Saturday after Saturday, plowing through,
never getting hurt, never changing his expression, scoring more
points, gaining more ground than all the rest of the team put together,
making everybody's All-American, carrying the ball three times out
of four, keeping everybody else out of the headlines. Darling was a
good blocker and he spent his Saturday afternoons working on the
big Swedes and Polacks who played tackle and end for Michigan,
Illinois, Purdue, hurling into huge pile-ups, bobbing his head wildly
to elude the great raw hands swinging like meat-cleavers at him as
he went charging in to open up holes for Diederich coming through
like a locomotive behind him. Still, it wasn't so bad. Everybody liked
him and he did his job and he was pointed out on the campus and
boys always felt important when they introduced their girls to him
at their proms, and Louise loved him and watched him faithfully in
the games, even in the mud, when your own mother wouldn't know
you, and drove him around in her car keeping the top down because
she was proud of him and wanted to show everybody that she was
Christian Darling's girl. She bought him crazy presents because her
father was rich, watches, pipes, humidors, an icebox for beer for his
room, curtains, wallets, a fifty-dollar dictionary.

"You'll spend every cent your old man owns," Darling protested
once when she showed up at his room with seven different packages
in her arms and tossed them onto the couch.

"Kiss me," Louise said, "and shut up."

"Do you want to break your poor old man?"

"I don't mind. I want to buy you presents."

"Why?"

"It makes me feel good. Kiss me. I don't know why. Did you know that you're an important figure?"

"Yes," Darling said gravely.

"When I was waiting for you at the library yesterday two girls saw you coming and one of them said to the other, 'That's Christian Darling. He's an important figure.' "

"You're a liar."

"I'm in love with an important figure."

"Still, why the hell did you have to give me a forty-pound dictionary?"

"I wanted to make sure," Louise said, "that you had a token of my esteem. I want to smother you in tokens of my esteem."

Fifteen years ago.

They'd married when they got out of college. There'd been other women for him, but all casual and secret, more for curiosity's sake, and vanity, women who'd thrown themselves at him and flattered him, a pretty mother at a summer camp for boys, an old girl from his home town who'd suddenly blossomed into a coquette, a friend of Louise's who had dogged him grimly for six months and had taken advantage of the two weeks when Louise went home when her mother died. Perhaps Louise had known, but she'd kept quiet, loving him completely, filling his rooms with presents, religiously watching him battling with the big Swedes and Polacks on the line of scrimmage on Saturday afternoons, making plans for marrying him and living with him in New York and going with him there to the nightclubs, the theatres, the good restaurants, being proud of him in advance, tall, white-teethed, smiling, large, yet moving lightly, with an athlete's grace, dressed in evening clothes, approvingly eyed by magnificently dressed and famous women in theatre lobbies, with Louise adoringly at his side.

Her father, who manufactured inks, set up a New York office for Darling to manage and presented him with three hundred accounts and they lived on Beekman Place with a view of the river with fifteen thousand dollars a year between them, because everybody was buying everything in those days, including ink. They saw all the shows and went to all the speakeasies and spent their fifteen thousand dollars a year and in the afternoons Louise went to the art galleries and the matinees of the more serious plays that Darling didn't like to sit through and Darling slept with a girl who danced in the chorus of *Rosalie* and with the wife of a man who owned three copper mines. Darling played squash three times a week and remained as solid as a stone barn and Louise never took her eyes off him when they were in the same room together, watching him with a secret, miser's smile, with a trick of coming over to him in the middle of a crowded room and saying gravely, in a low voice, "You're the handsomest man I've ever seen in my whole life. Want a drink?"

Nineteen twenty-nine came to Darling and to his wife and father-in-law, the maker of inks, just as it came to everyone else. The father-in-law waited until 1933 and then blew his brains out and when Darling went to Chicago to see what the books of the firm looked like he found out all that was left were debts and three or four gallons of unbought ink.

"Please, Christian," Louise said, sitting in their neat Beekman Place apartment, with a view of the river and prints of paintings by Dufy and Braque and Picasso[1] on the wall, "please, why do you want to start drinking at two o'clock in the afternoon?"

"I have nothing else to do," Darling said, putting down his glass, emptied of its fourth drink. "Please pass the whiskey."

Louise filled his glass. "Come take a walk with me," she said. "We'll walk along the river."

"I don't want to walk along the river," Darling said, squinting intensely at the prints of paintings by Dufy, Braque and Picasso.

"We'll walk along Fifth Avenue."

"I don't want to walk along Fifth Avenue."

"Maybe," Louise said gently, "you'd like to come with me to some art galleries. There's an exhibition by a man named Klee[2]—"

"I don't want to go to any art galleries. I want to sit here and drink Scotch whiskey," Darling said. "Who the hell hung those goddam pictures up on the wall?"

"I did," Louise said.

"I hate them."

"I'll take them down," Louise said.

"Leave them there. It gives me something to do in the afternoon. I can hate them." Darling took a long swallow. "Is that the way people paint these days?"

---

[1] *Raoul Duffy* (1877–1953) was a French painter and designer whose work was characterized by a bold, colorful, expressionist style, identified with fauvism. *Georges Braque* (1882–1963) was a French painter who was involved in developing fauvism, and later, with Picasso, a pioneer in the cubist movement. *Pablo Picasso* (1881–1973) was a Spanish painter and sculptor whose cubist style greatly influenced modern art. (ED.)

[2] Paul Klee (1879–1940) was a Swiss abstract painter and art theorist. (ED.)

"Yes, Christian. Please don't drink any more."

"Do you like painting like that?"

"Yes, dear."

"Really?"

"Really."

Darling looked carefully at the prints once more. "Little Louise Tucker. The middle-western beauty. I like pictures with horses in them. Why should you like pictures like that?"

"I just happen to have gone to a lot of galleries in the last few years . . ."

"Is that what you do in the afternoon?"

"That's what I do in the afternoon," Louise said.

"I drink in the afternoon."

Louise kissed him lightly on the top of his head as he sat there squinting at the pictures on the wall, the glass of whiskey held firmly in his hand. She put on her coat and went out without saying another word. When she came back in the early evening, she had a job on a woman's fashion magazine.

They moved downtown and Louise went out to work every morning and Darling sat home and drank and Louise paid the bills as they came up. She made believe she was going to quit work as soon as Darling found a job, even though she was taking over more responsibility day by day at the magazine, interviewing authors, picking painters for the illustrations and covers, getting actresses to pose for pictures, going out for drinks with the right people, making a thousand new friends whom she loyally introduced to Darling.

"I don't like your hat," Darling said, once, when she came in in the evening and kissed him, her breath rich with Martinis.

"What's the matter with my hat, Baby?" she asked, running her fingers through his hair. "Everybody says it's very smart."

"It's too damned smart," he said. "It's not for you. It's for a rich, sophisticated woman of thirty-five with admirers."

Louise laughed. "I'm practicing to be a rich, sophisticated woman of thirty-five with admirers," she said. He stared soberly at her. "Now, don't look so grim, Baby. It's still the same simple little wife under the hat." She took the hat off, threw it into a corner, sat on his lap. "See? Homebody Number One."

"Your breath could run a train," Darling said, not wanting to be mean, but talking out of boredom, and sudden shock at seeing his wife curiously a stranger in a new hat, with a new expression in her eyes under the little brim, secret, confident, knowing.

Louise tucked her head under his chin so he couldn't smell her breath. "I had to take an author out for cocktails," she said. "He's a boy from the Ozark mountains and he drinks like a fish. He's a Communist."

"What the hell is a Communist from the Ozarks doing writing for a woman's fashion magazine?"

Louise chuckled. "The magazine business is getting all mixed up these days. The publishers want to have a foot in every camp. And anyway, you can't find an author under seventy these days who isn't a Communist."

"I don't think I like you to associate with all those people, Louise," Darling said. "Drinking with them."

"He's a very nice, gentle boy," Louise said. "He reads Ernest Dobson."

"Who's Ernest Dobson?"

Louise patted his arm, stood up, fixed her hair. "He's an English poet."

Darling felt that somehow he had disappointed her. "Am I supposed to know who Ernest Dobson is?"

"No dear, I'd better go in and take a bath."

After she had gone, Darling went over to the corner where the hat was lying and picked it up. It was nothing, a scrap of straw, a red flower, a veil, meaningless on his big hand, but on his wife's head a signal of something . . . big city, smart and knowing women drinking and dining with men other than their husbands, conversation about things a normal man wouldn't know much about, Frenchmen who painted as though they used their elbows instead of brushes, composers who wrote whole symphonies without a single melody in them, writers who knew all about politics and women who knew all about writers, the movement of the proletariat, Marx, somehow mixed up with five-dollar dinners and the best looking women in America and fairies who made them laugh and half-sentences immediately understood and secretly hilarious and wives who called their husbands "Baby." He put the hat down, a scrap of straw and a red flower, and a little veil. He drank some whiskey straight and went into the bathroom where his wife was lying deep in her bath, singing to herself and smiling from time to time like a little girl, paddling the water gently with her hands, sending up a slight spicy fragrance from the bath-salts she used.

He stood over her, looking down at her. She smiled up at him, her eyes half closed, her body pink and shimmering in the warm, scented water. All over again, with all the old suddenness, he was hit deep inside him with the knowledge of how beautiful she was, how much he needed her.

"I came in here," he said, "to tell you I wish you wouldn't call me 'Baby.' "

She looked up at him from the bath, her eyes quickly full of sorrow, half-understanding what he meant. He knelt and put his arms around her, his sleeves plunged heedless in the water, his shirt and jacket soaking wet as he clutched her wordlessly, holding her crazily tight, crushing her breath from her, kissing her desperately, searchingly, regretfully.

He got jobs after that, selling real estate and automobiles, but somehow, although he had a desk with his name on a wooden wedge on it, and he went to the office religiously at nine each morning, he never managed to sell anything and he never made any money.

Louise was made assistant editor and the house was always full of strange men and women who talked fast and got angry on abstract subjects like mural painting, novelists, labor unions. Negro short-story writers drank Louise's liquor, and a lot of Jews, and big solemn men with scarred faces and knotted hands who talked slowly but clearly about picket lines and battles with guns and leadpipe at mine-shaft-heads and in front of factory gates. And Louise moved among them all, confidently, knowing what they were talking about, with opinions that they listened to and argued about just as though she were a man. She knew everybody, condescended to no one, devoured books that Darling had never heard of, walked along the streets of the city, excited, at home, soaking in all the million tides of New York without fear, with constant wonder.

Her friends liked Darling and sometimes he found a man who wanted to get off in the corner and talk about the new boy who played fullback for Princeton, and the decline of the double wing-back, or even the state of the stock market, but for the most part he sat on the edge of things, solid and quiet in the high storm of words. "The dialectics of the situation . . . the theatre has been given over to expert jugglers . . . Picasso? What man has a right to paint old bones and collect ten thousand dollars for them? . . . I stand firmly behind Trotsky[3] . . . Poe was the last American critic. When he died

---

[3] Leon Trotsky (1879–1940) was a Russian marxist and leader in the Bolshevik seizure of power in 1917, and in the founding of the USSR. After the death of Lenin, he lost

they put lilies on the grave of American criticism. I don't say this because they panned my last book, but . . ."

Once in a while he caught Louise looking soberly and consideringly at him through the cigarette smoke and the noise and he avoided her eyes and found an excuse to get up and go into the kitchen for more ice or to open another bottle.

"Come on," Cathal Flaherty was saying, standing at the door with a girl, "you've got to come down and see this. It's down on Fourteenth Street, in the old Civic Repertory, and you can only see it on Sunday nights and I guarantee you'll come out of the theatre singing." Flaherty was a big young Irishman with a broken nose who was the lawyer for a longshoreman's union, and he had been hanging around the house for six months on and off, roaring and shutting everybody else up when he got in an argument. "It's a new play, *Waiting for Lefty,* it's about taxi-drivers."

"Odets,"[4] the girl with Flaherty said. "It's by a guy named Odets."

"I never heard of him," Darling said.

"He's a new one," the girl said.

"It's like watching a bombardment," Flaherty said. "I saw it last Sunday night. You've got to see it."

"Come on, Baby," Louise said to Darling, excitement in her eyes already. "We've been sitting in the Sunday *Times* all day, this'll be a great change."

"I see enough taxi-drivers every day," Darling said, not because he meant that, but because he didn't like to be around Flaherty, who said things that made Louise laugh a lot and whose judgment she accepted on almost every subject. "Let's go to the movies."

"You've never seen anything like this before," Flaherty said. "He wrote this play with a baseball bat."

"Come on," Louise coaxed, "I bet it's wonderful."

"He has long hair," the girl with Flaherty said. "Odets. I met him at a party. He's an actor. He didn't say a goddam thing all night."

"I don't feel like going down to Fourteenth Street," Darling said, wishing Flaherty and his girl would get out. "It's gloomy."

power to Stalin and was eventually exiled, where he continued to advocate his theory of revolution and pure communism. (ED.)

[4] Clifford Odets (1906–1963) was a Philadelphia-born dramatist of the 1930s. He became a screenwriter and director in Hollywood in the late 1930s. His works include *Waiting for Lefty* (1935), *The Big Knife* (1949), and *The Country Girl* (1950).

"Oh, hell!" Louise said loudly. She looked coolly at Darling, as though she'd just been introduced to him and was making up her mind about him, and not very favorably. He saw her looking at him, knowing there was something new and dangerous in her face and he wanted to say something, but Flaherty was there and his damned girl, and anyway, he didn't know what to say.

"I'm going," Louise said, getting her coat. "I don't think Fourteenth Street is gloomy."

"I'm telling you," Flaherty was saying, helping her on with her coat, "it's the Battle of Gettysburg, in Brooklynese."

"Nobody could get a word out of him," Flaherty's girl was saying as they went through the door. "He just sat there all night."

The door closed. Louise hadn't said good-night to him. Darling walked around the room four times, then sprawled out on the sofa, on top of the Sunday *Times*. He lay there for five minutes looking at the ceiling, thinking of Flaherty walking down the street talking in that booming voice, between the girls, holding their arms.

Louise had looked wonderful. She'd washed her hair in the afternoon and it had been very soft and light and clung close to her head as she stood there angrily putting her coat on. Louise was getting prettier every year, partly because she knew by now how pretty she was, and made the most of it.

"Nuts," Darling said, standing up. "Oh, nuts."

He put on his coat and went down to the nearest bar and had five drinks off by himself in a corner before his money ran out.

The years since then had been foggy and downhill. Louise had been nice to him, and in a way, loving and kind, and they'd fought only once, when he said he was going to vote for Landon.[5] ("Oh, Christ," she'd said, "doesn't *anything* happen inside your head? Don't you read the papers? The penniless Republican!") She'd been sorry later and apologized for hurting him, but apologized as she might to a child. He'd tried hard, had gone grimly to the art galleries, the concert halls, the bookshops, trying to gain on the trail of his wife, but it was no use. He was bored, and none of what he saw or heard or dutifully read made much sense to him and finally he gave it up. He had thought, many nights as he ate dinner alone, knowing Louise would come home late and drop silently into bed without explana-

---

[5] Alfred Landon (1887–1987) was governor of Kansas and an unsuccessful Republican candidate for the presidency in 1936. (ED.)

tion, of getting a divorce, but he knew the loneliness, the hopeless-ness, of not seeing her again would be too much to take. So he was good, completely devoted, ready at all times to go anyplace with her, do anything she wanted. He even got a small job, in a broker's office and paid his own way, bought his own liquor.

Then he'd been offered the job of going from college to college as a tailor's representative. "We want a man," Mr. Rosenberg had said, "who as soon as you look at him, you say 'There's a university man.'" Rosenberg had looked approvingly at Darling's broad shoul-ders and well-kept waist, at his carefully brushed hair and his honest, wrinkleless face. "Frankly, Mr. Darling, I am willing to make you a proposition. I have inquired about you, you are favorably known on your old campus, I understand you were in the backfield with Alfred Diederich."

Darling nodded. "Whatever happened to him?"

"He is walking around in a cast for seven years now. An iron brace. He played professional football and they broke his neck for him."

Darling smiled. That, at least, had turned out well.

"Our suits are an easy product to sell, Mr. Darling," Rosenberg said. "We have a handsome, custom-made garment. What has Brooks Brothers got that we haven't got? A name. No more."

"I can make fifty, sixty dollars a week," Darling said to Louise that night. "And expenses. I can save some money and then come back to New York and really get started here."

"Yes, Baby," Louise said.

"As it is," Darling said carefully, "I can make it back here once a month, and holidays and the summer. We can see each other often."

"Yes, Baby." He looked at her face, lovelier now at thirty-five than it had ever been before, but fogged over now as it had been for five years with a kind of patient, kindly, remote boredom.

"What do you say?" he asked. "Should I take it?" Deep within him he hoped fiercely, longingly for her to say, "No, Baby, you stay right here," but she said, as he knew she'd say, "I think you'd better take it."

He nodded. He had to get up and stand with his back to her, looking out the window, because there were things plain on his face that she had never seen in the fifteen years she'd known him. "Fifty dollars is a lot of money," he said. "I never thought I'd ever see fifty dollars again." He laughed. Louise laughed, too.

Christian Darling sat on the frail green grass of the practice field. The shadow of the stadium had reached out and covered him. In the distance the lights of the university shone a little mistily in the light haze of evening. Fifteen years. Flaherty even now was calling for his wife, buying her a drink, filling whatever bar they were in with that voice of his and that easy laugh. Darling half-closed his eyes, almost saw the boy fifteen years ago reach for the pass, slip the halfback, go skittering lightly down the field, his knees high and fast and graceful, smiling to himself because he knew he was going to get past the safety man. That was the high point, Darling thought, fifteen years ago, on an autumn afternoon, twenty years old and far from death, with the air coming easily into his lungs, and a deep feeling inside him that he could do anything, knock over anybody, outrun whatever had to be outrun. And the shower after and the three glasses of water and the cool night air on his damp head and Louise sitting hatless in the open car with a smile and the first kiss she ever really meant. The high point, an eighty-yard run in the practice, and a girl's kiss and everything after that a decline. Darling laughed. He had practiced the wrong thing, perhaps. He hadn't practiced for 1929 and New York City and a girl who would turn into a woman. Somewhere, he thought, there must have been a point where she moved up to me, was even with me for a moment, when I could have held her hand, if I'd known, held tight, gone with her. Well, he'd never known. Here he was on a playing field that was fifteen years away and his wife was in another city having dinner with another and better man, speaking with him a different, new language, a language nobody had ever taught him.

Darling stood up, smiled a little, because if he didn't smile he knew the tears would come. He looked around him. This was the spot. O'Connor's pass had come sliding out just to here . . . the high point. Darling put up his hands, felt all over again the flat slap of the ball. He shook his hips to throw off the halfback, cut back inside the center, picked his knees high as he ran gracefully over two men jumbled on the ground at the line of scrimmage, ran easily, gaining speed, for ten yards, holding the ball lightly in his two hands, swung away from the halfback diving at him, ran, swinging his hips in the almost-girlish manner of a back in a broken field, tore into the safety man, his shoes drumming heavily on the turf, stiff-armed, elbow locked, pivoted, raced lightly and exultantly for the goal line.

It was only after he had sped over the goal line and slowed to a trot that he saw the boy and girl sitting together on the turf, looking at him wonderingly.

He stopped short, dropping his arms. "I . . ." he said, gasping a little though his condition was fine and the run hadn't winded him, "I . . . Once I played here."

The boy and the girl said nothing. Darling laughed embarrassedly, looked hard at them sitting there, close to each other, shrugged, turned and went toward his hotel, the sweat breaking out on his face and running down into his collar.

T E N

War

It is well that war is so terrible—we would grow too fond of it.

Gen. Robert E. Lee

There is many a boy here today who looks on war as all glory, but
boys, it is all hell.

Gen. William T. Sherman

War is often a defining experience or event, not just for the
individual soldiers who fight it but for the nations that wage it. The
changes wrought by war are profound for those who fight, whether
or not they are injured. The friends and families of those who fight
are also affected, as are the people in whose countries the war takes
place. The fate of nations and the course of history are deeply affected
by war. Yet when war comes, even if it is sudden and unexpected,
nations and their people plunge into the conflict with little thought
other than winning.

A vast amount of literature has been produced about war. Most
of the selections in this section present the experience as recorded
by those who have fought in a war. In addition, two of the selections
touch on how the very nature of war has changed with the development of atomic weapons.

Two selections in this section have the same event, the Battle of
Agincourt, as their subject: the excerpt from William Shakespeare's
play *Henry V,* and historian John Keegan's account of the battle. You
might want to compare and contrast the two accounts. Shakespeare,
of course, offers the dramatic, patriotic account of a noble battle,
hard-fought but ending in deserved triumph for the English forces.
The king and his noblemen courageously defeat the French enemy.
Such is war as waged in literature.

Keegan, however, offers a different picture of the same battle.
With the sharp eye of the historian, he reconstructs the battle using
the stories of participants and other eyewitnesses. While his account
lacks any direct emotion or fervor, the objective nature of his narrative heightens the horror of the battle itself. Note in particular his
discussion of King Henry's decision to order the killing of the French
prisoners. The battle as described by Keegan lacks the glory of Shakespeare's account.

Frank A. Haskell and Paul Fussell give the soldier's view of war,
Haskell describing Pickett's famous charge at the battle of Gettysburg
during the American Civil War, and Fussell describing the traumatic

942

experience of battle in the Second World War. While both men tell of the confusion, death, and fear of battle, both also write with a detached point of view. They have survived and now give us their accounts from a distance. Haskell wrote his account a few weeks after the battle (he was killed in battle less than a year later); although there is a certain sense of immediacy, his account also reflects a kind of aloofness, as if he were observing the battle while simultaneously fighting in it. It is almost as if he cannot quite bring himself to recreate the full terror of the battle.

Paul Fussell's essay was written many years after World War II was over. He has the perspective of history, as well as the benefit of many years of thinking about his experiences. Yet for him the war remains a very real and immediate experience, not to be forgotten, and certainly not to be glorified.

But war has changed since Haskell and even Fussell fought. With the development of atomic weapons the very meaning of the word *war* has changed. What does it mean to wage war with atomic weapons? Can any nation "win" an atomic war? John Toland describes what it meant to one city to have just one atomic bomb dropped on it, while Jonathan Schell speculates about what could happen if a modern atomic bomb were dropped on New York City. Both accounts, the historical and the fictional, present terrifying pictures of a kind of war that has no winners.

While war has been an accepted means of resolving disputes between nations for as long as there has been recorded history, there have also been those who argue against war. Both Virginia Woolf and Olive Schreiner present powerful arguments against war, especially war as an instrument of state policy. Neither writer is an impractical idealist out of touch with political realities; rather, both are aware of a world that considers war a sometimes necessary if regrettable means of resolving problems. You will discover that in many ways these writers are in agreement with such writers as Paul Fussell and Tim O'Brien. You may also discover that the selections in this section will prompt you to question your *own* ideas and assumptions about war.

WILLIAM SHAKESPEARE

Henry V (Battle Scenes, Act IV)

William Shakespeare (1564–1616), English playwright and poet, is considered by many to be the greatest writer of all time. Noted for his compassion and insight into human nature as well as his formidable skill with language, his work is consistently read and produced to this day. His plays are usually divided into three categories: tragedies, including *Hamlet* and *Macbeth;* comedies, including *A Midsummer Night's Dream* and *The Taming of the Shrew;* and histories, including *Richard III* and *Henry V,* from which the following selection is excerpted.

[SCENE III. *The English camp.*]

Enter GLOUCESTER, BEDFORD, EXETER, ERPINGHAM, *with all his host:* SALISBURY *and* WESTMORELAND
Glou. Where is the King?
Bed. The King himself is rode to view their battle.
West. Of fighting men they have full threescore thousand.
Exe. There's five to one; besides, they all are fresh.
Sal. God's arm strike with us! 'tis a fearful odds.
God be wi' you, princes all; I'll to my charge.   6
If we no more meet till we meet in heaven,
Then, joyfully, my noble Lord of Bedford,
My dear Lord Gloucester, and my good Lord Exeter,
And my kind kinsman, warriors all, adieu!   10
    Bed. Farewell, good Salisbury, and good luck go with thee!
    Exe. Farewell, kind lord; fight valiantly to-day!
And yet I do thee wrong to mind thee of it,
For thou art fram'd of the firm truth of valour.

                                                [*Exit Salisbury.*]
    Bed. He is as full of valour as of kindness,   15
Princely in both.

Enter the KING.
    West. O that we now had here
But one ten thousand of those men in England
That do no work to-day!
    K. Hen. What's he that wishes so?
My cousin Westmoreland? No, my fair cousin.

If we are mark'd to die, we are enow   20
To do our country loss; and if to live,
The fewer men, the greater share of honour.
God's will! I pray thee, wish not one man more.
By Jove, I am not covetous for gold,
Nor care I who doth feed upon my cost;   25
It yearns me not if men my garments wear;
Such outward things dwell not in my desires;
But if it be a sin to covet honour
I am the most offending soul alive.
No, 'faith, my coz, wish not a man from England.   30
God's peace! I would not lose so great an honour
As one man more, methinks, would share from me
For the best hope I have. O, do not wish one more!
Rather proclaim it, Westmoreland, through my host,
That he which hath no stomach to this fight,   35
Let him depart. His passport shall be made,
And crowns for convoy put into his purse.
We would not die in that man's company
That fears his fellowship to die with us.
This day is call'd the feast of Crispian.   40
He that outlives this day and comes safe home
Will stand a tip-toe when this day is named,
And rouse him at the name of Crispian.
He that shall [live] this day, and [see] old age,
Will yearly on the vigil feast his neighbours,   45
And say, "To-morrow is Saint Crispian."
Then will he strip his sleeve and show his scars,
[And say, "These wounds I had on Crispin's day."]
Old men forget; yet all shall be forgot,
But he'll remember with advantages   50
What feats he did that day. Then shall our names,
Familiar in his mouth as household words,
Harry the King, Bedford, and Exeter,
Warwick and Talbot, Salisbury and Gloucester,
Be in their flowing cups freshly rememb'red.   55
This story shall the good man teach his son;
And Crispin Crispian shall ne'er go by,
From this day to the ending of the world,
But we in it shall be remembered,
We few, we happy few, we band of brothers.   60
For he to-day that sheds his blood with me

Shall be my brother; be he ne'er so vile,
This day shall gentle his condition;
And gentlemen in England now a-bed   64
Shall think themselves accurs'd they were not here,
And hold their manhoods cheap whiles any speaks
That fought with us upon Saint Crispin's day.

Re-enter SALISBURY.
    Sal. My sovereign lord, bestow yourself with speed.
The French are bravely in their battles set,
And will with all expedience charge on us.   70
    K. Hen. All things are ready, if our minds be so.
    West. Perish the man whose mind is backward now!
    K. Hen. Thou dost not wish more help from England, coz?
    West. God's will! my liege, would you and I alone,
Without more help, could fight this royal battle!   75
    K. Hen. Why, now thou has unwish'd five thousand men,
Which likes me better than to wish us one.
You know your places. God be with you all!

Tucket. Enter MONTJOY.
    Mont. Once more I come to know of thee, King Harry,
If for thy ransom thou wilt now compound,   80
Before thy most assured overthrow;
For certainly thou art so near the gulf,
Thou needs must be englutted. Besides, in mercy,
The Constable desires thee thou wilt mind
Thy followers of repentance; that their souls   85
May make a peaceful and a sweet retire
From off these fields, where, wretches, their poor bodies
Must lie and fester.
    K. Hen. Who hath sent thee now?
    Mont. The Constable of France.
    K. Hen. I pray thee, bear my former answer back: 90
Bid them achieve me and then sell my bones.
Good God! why should they mock poor fellows thus?
The man that once did sell the lion's skin
While the beast liv'd, was kill'd with hunting him.
A many of our bodies shall no doubt   95
Find native graves, upon the which, I trust,
Shall witness live in brass of this day's work;
And those that leave their valiant bones in France,
Dying like men, though buried in your dunghills,

They shall be fam'd; for there the sun shall greet them,   100
And draw their honours reeking up to heaven;
Leaving their earthly parts to choke your clime,
The smell whereof shall breed a plague in France.
Mark then abounding valour in our English,
That being dead, like to the bullet's grazing,   105
Break out into a second course of mischief,
Killing in relapse of mortality.
Let me speak proudly: tell the Constable
We are but warriors for the working-day.
Our gayness and our gilt are all besmirch'd   110
With rainy marching in the painful field;
There's not a piece of feather in our host—
Good argument, I hope, we will not fly—
And time hath worn us into slovenry;
But, by the mass, our hearts are in the trim;   115
And my poor soldiers tell me, yet ere night
They'll be in fresher robes, or they will pluck
The gay new coats o'er the French soldiers' heads
And turn them out of service. If they do this—
As, if God please, they shall,—my ransom then   120
Will soon be levied. Herald, save thou thy labour.
Come thou no more for ransom, gentle herald.
They shall have none, I swear, but these my joints;
Which if they have as I will leave 'em them,
Shall yield them little, tell the Constable.   125
    Mont. I shall, King Harry. And so fare thee well;
Thou never shalt hear herald any more.
                                                   [Exit]

    K. Hen. I fear thou will once more come again for ransom.

Enter YORK.
    York. My lord, most humbly on my knee I beg
The leading of the vaward,   130
    K. Hen. Take it, brave York. Now, soldiers, march away;
And how thou pleasest, God, dispose the day!
                                               [Exeunt.]

[SCENE V. *Another part of the field.*]

Enter CONSTABLE, ORLEANS, BOURBON, DAUPHIN, *and* RAMBURES.
    Con. O diable!
    Orl. O seigneur! le jour est perdu, tout est perdu!
    Dau. Mort de ma vie! all is confounded, all!

Reproach and everlasting shame
Sits mocking in our plumes. *O méchante fortune!*   5
Do not run away.

                                        [*A short alarum.*]

   Con. Why, all our ranks are broke.
   Dau. O perdurable shame! let's stab ourselves.
Be these the wretches that we play'd at dice for?
   Orl. Is this the king we sent to for his ransom?
   Bour. Shame and eternal shame, nothing but shame!   10
Let's die in [honour]! Once more back again!
And he that will not follow Bourbon now,
Let him go hence, and with his cap in hand
Like a base pandar hold the chamber door
Whilst [by a] slave, no gentler than my dog,   15
His fairest daughter is contaminated.
   Con. Disorder, that hath spoil'd us, friend us now!
Let us on heaps go offer up our lives.
   Orl. We are enow yet living in the field
To smother up the English in our throngs   20
If any order might be thought upon.
   Bour. The devil take order now! I'll to the throng.
Let life be short, else shame will be too long.

                                        [*Exeunt.*]

[SCENE VI. *Another part of the field.*]

Alarum. Enter KING HENRY *and his train, with prisoners.*
   K. Hen. Well have we done, thrice valiant countrymen.
But all's not done; yet keep the French the field.
   Exe. The Duke of York commends him to your Majesty.
   K. Hen. Lives he, good uncle? Thrice within this hour
I saw him down; thrice up again, and fighting.   5
From helmet to the spur all blood he was.
   Exe. In which array, brave soldier, doth he lie,
Larding the plain; and by his bloody side,
Yoke-fellow to his honour-owing wounds,
The noble Earl of Suffolk also lies.   10
Suffolk first died; and York, all haggled over,
Comes to him where in gore he lay insteeped,
And takes him by the beard; kisses the gashes
That bloodily did yawn upon his face.
He cries aloud, "Tarry, my cousin Suffolk!   15
My soul shall thine keep company to heaven;
Tarry, sweet soul, for mine, then fly abreast,

As in this glorious and well-foughten field
We kept together in our chivalry!"
Upon these words I came and cheer'd him up.   20
He smil'd me in the face, raught me his hand,
And, with a feeble gripe, says, "Dear my lord,
Commend my service to my sovereign."
So he did turn and over Suffolk's neck
He threw his wounded arm and kiss'd his lips;   25
And so espous'd to death, with blood he seal'd
A testament of noble-ending love.
The pretty and sweet manner of it forc'd
Those waters from me which I would have stopp'd;
But I had not so much of man in me,   30
And all my mother came into mine eyes
And gave me up to tears.
   K. Hen. I blame you not;
For, hearing this, I must perforce compound
With mistful eyes, or they will issue too.

                                               [Alarum.]
But, hark! what new alarum is this same?   35
The French have reinforc'd their scatter'd men.
Then every soldier kill his prisoners:
Give the word through.

                                               [Exeunt.]

[SCENE VII. *Another part of the field.*]

Enter FLUELLEN *and* GOWER.

   Flu. Kill the poys and the luggage! 'Tis expressly against the law of arms. 'Tis as arrant a piece of knavery, mark you now, as can be offer't; in your conscience, now, is it not?   3

   Gow. 'Tis certain there's not a boy left alive; and the cowardly rascals that ran from the battle ha' done this slaughter. Besides, they have burned and carried away all that was in the King's tent; wherefore the King, most worthily, hath caus'd every soldier to cut his prisoner's throat. O, 'tis a gallant king!   8

   Flu. Ay, he was porn at Monmouth, Captain Gower. What call you the town's name where Alexander the Pig was born!

   Gow. Alexander the Great.   11

   Flu. Why, I pray you, is not pig great? The pig, or the great, or the mighty, or the huge, or the magnanimous, are all one reckonings, save the phrase is a little variations.   14

   Gow. I think Alexander the Great was born in Macedon. His father was called Philip of Macedon, as I take it.

Flu. I think it is in Macedon where Alexander is porn. I tell you,
captain, if you look in the maps of the 'orld, I warrant you   18
sall find, in the comparisons between Macedon and Monmouth, that
the situations, look you, is both alike. There is a river in Macedon;
and there is also moreover a river at Monmouth. It is call'd Wye at
Monmouth; but it is out of my prains what is the name of the other
river; but 'tis all one, 'tis alike as my fingers is to my fingers,   23
and there is salmons in both. If you mark Alexander's life well, Harry
of Monmouth's life is come after it indifferent well; for there is figures
in all things. Alexander, God knows, and you know, in his   26
rages, and his furies, and his wraths, and his cholers, and his moods,
and his displeasures, and his indignations, and also being a little
intoxicates in his prains, did, in his ales and his angers, look you,
kill his best friend, Cleitus.   30
Gow. Our King is not like him in that. He never kill'd any of his
friends.
Flu. It is not well done, mark you now, to take the tales out of
my mouth, ere it is made and finished. I speak but in the   34
figures and comparisons of it. As Alexander kill'd his friend Cleitus,
being in his ales and his cups; so also Harry Monmouth, being in his
right wits and his good judgements, turn'd away the fat   37
knight with the great belly doublet. He was full of jests, and gipes,
and knaveries, and mocks; I have forgot his name.
Gow. Sir John Falstaff.   40
Flu. That is he. I'll tell you there is good men porn at
Monmouth.
Gow. Here comes his Majesty.

Alarum. Enter KING HENRY *and [forces;* WARWICK, GLOUCESTER, EX-
ETER,] *with prisoners. Flourish.*
K. Hen. I was not angry since I came to France
Until this instant. Take a trumpet, herald;   45
Ride thou unto the horsemen on yond hill.
If they will fight with us, bid them come down,
Or void the field; they do offend our sight.
If they'll do neither, we will come to them
And make them skirr away, as swift as stones   50
Enforced from the old Assyrian slings.
Besides, we'll cut the throats of those we have,
And not a man of them that we shall take
Shall taste our mercy. Go and tell them so.

Enter MONTJOY.

Exe. Here comes the herald of the French, my liege.   55
Glou. His eyes are humbler than they us'd to be.
K. Hen. How now! what means this, herald?
Know'st thou not that I have fin'd these bones of mine for ransom?
Com'st thou again for ransom?
    Mont. No, great King;   60
I come to thee for charitable license,
That we may wander o'er this bloody field
To book our dead, and then to bury them;
To sort our nobles from our common men.
For many of our princes—woe the while!—   65
Lie drown'd and soak'd in mercenary blood;
So do our vulgar drench their peasant limbs
In blood of princes; and their wounded steeds
Fret fetlock deep in gore, and with wild rage
Yerk out their armed heels at their dead masters,   70
Killing them twice. O, give us leave, great King,
To view the field in safety, and dispose
Of their dead bodies!
    K. Hen. I tell thee truly, herald,
I know not if the day be ours or no;   75
For yet a many of your horsemen peer
And gallop o'er the field.
    Mont. The day is yours.
    K. Hen. Praised be God, and not our strength, for it!
What is this castle call'd that stands hard by?   80
    Mont. They call it Agincourt.
    K. Hen. Then call we this the field of Agincourt,
Fought on the day of Crispin Crispianus.
    Flu. Your grandfather of famous memory, an't please your Majesty, and your great-uncle Edward the Plack Prince of Wales, as I have read in the chronicles, fought a most prave pattle here in France.
    K. Hen. They did, Fluellen.   87
    Flu. Your Majesty says very true. If your Majesties is rememb'red of it, the Welshmen did good service in the garden where leeks did grow, wearing leeks in their Monmouth caps; which, your Majesty know, to this hour is an honourable badge of the service; and I do believe your Majesty takes no scorn to wear the leek upon Saint Tavy's day.
    K. Hen. I wear it for a memorable honour;
For I am Welsh, you know, good countryman.   95
    Flu. All the water in Wye cannot wash your Majesty's Welsh

plood out of your pody, I can tell you that. God pless it and preserve
it, as long as it pleases His grace, and His majesty too!

    K. Hen. Thanks, good my countryman.   99

    Flu. By Jeshu, I am your Majesty's countryman, I care not who
know it. I will confess it to all the 'orld. I need not to be ashamed
of your Majesty, praised be God, so long as your Majesty is an honest
man.   103

    K. Hen. God keep me so!

[SCENE VIII. *Before King Henry's pavilion.*]

Enter [*an* English] HERALD.

    K. Hen. Now, herald, are the dead numb'red?

    Her. Here is the number of the slaught'red French.

    K. Hen. What prisoners of good sort are taken, uncle?   80

    Exe. Charles Duke of Orleans, nephew to the King;
John Duke of Bourbon, and Lord Bouciqualt:
Of other lords and barons, knights and squires,
Full fifteen hundred, besides common men.

    K. Hen. This note doth tell me of ten thousand French   85
That in the field lie slain; of princes, in this number,
And nobles bearing banners, there lie dead
One hundred twenty-six; added to these,
Of knights, esquires, and gallant gentlemen,
Eight thousand and four hundred; of the which,   90
Five hundred were but yesterday dubb'd knights;
So that, in these ten thousand they have lost,
There are but sixteen hundred mercenaries;
The rest are princes, barons, lords, knights, squires,
And gentlemen of blood and quality.   95
The names of those their nobles that lie dead:
Charles Delabreth, High Constable of France;
Jacques of Chatillon, Admiral of France;
The master of the cross-bows, Lord Rambures;
Great Master of France, the brave Sir Guichard Dauphin,   100
John Duke of Alençon, Anthony Duke of Brabant,
The brother to the Duke of Burgundy,
And Edward Duke of Bar; of lusty earls,
Grandpré and Roussi, Fauconberg and Foix,
Beaumont and Marle, Vaudemont and Lestrale.   105
Here was a royal fellowship of death!
Where is the number of our English dead?
                              [*Herald shows him another paper.*]

Edward the Duke of York, the Earl of Suffolk,
Sir Richard Ketly, Davy Gam, esquire:
None else of name; and of all other men   110
But five and twenty.—O God, thy arm was here;
And not to us, but to thy arm alone,
Ascribe we all! When, without stratagem,
But in plain shock and even play of battle,
Was ever known so great and little loss   115
On one part and on the other? Take it, God,
For it is none but thine!
    Exe. 'Tis wonderful!
    K. Hen. Come, go we in procession to the village;
And be it death proclaimed through our host
To boast of this or take that praise from God   120
Which is His only.
    Flu. Is it not lawful, an please your Majesty, to tell how many is
kill'd?
    K. Hen. Yes, captain, but with this acknowledgement,
That God fought for us.   125
    Flu. Yes, my conscience, He did us great good.
    K. Hen. Do we all holy rites.
Let there be sung *Non nobis* and *Te Deum.*
The dead with charity enclos'd in clay,
And then to Calais; and to England then,   130
Where ne'er from France arriv'd more happy men.

                                       [*Exeunt.*]

JOHN KEEGAN

Agincourt, October 25th, 1415

John Keegan (1934–   ) is a British journalist and military historian. He has been the deputy head of the Department of War Studies at the Royal Military Academy, Sandhurst, and is the editor of *The Times Atlas of the Second World War* (1989). Other books in-

clude *The Face of Battle* (1976), from which the following selection
is taken, *Six Armies in Normandy* (1982), *Zones of Conflict: An Atlas of Future Wars* (1986), *The Mask of Command* (1987), and *The
Second World War* (1990).

Agincourt is one of the most instantly and vividly visualized of all
epic passages in English history, and one of the most satisfactory to
contemplate. It is a victory of the weak over the strong, of the
common soldier over the mounted knight, of resolution over bom-
bast, of the desperate, cornered and far from home, over the pro-
prietorial and cocksure. Visually it is a pre-Raphaelite, perhaps better
a Medici Gallery print battle—a composition of strong verticals and
horizontals and a conflict of rich dark reds and Lincoln greens against
fishscale greys and arctic blues. It is a school outing to the Old Vic,
Shakespeare is fun, *son-et-lumière,* blank verse, Laurence Olivier in
armour battle; it is an episode to quicken the interest of any school-
boy ever bored by a history lesson, a set-piece demonstration of
English moral superiority and a cherished ingredient of a fading
national myth. It is also a story of slaughter-yard behaviour and of
outright atrocity.

THE BATTLE

Let us, to begin with, and however artificially, break the battle
down into a sequence of separate events. It opened, as we know,
with the armies forming up in the light of early morning: whether
that meant just after first light, or at the rather later hour of dawn
itself—about 6.40 a.m.—is a point of detail over which we cannot
expect the chroniclers to meet Staff College standards of precision.
Nor do they. They are even more imprecise about numbers, particularly as they concern the French. For though there is agreement,
supported by other evidence, that Henry's army had dwindled to
about five or six thousand archers and a thousand men-at-arms, the
French are variously counted between 10,000 and 200,000. Colonel
Burne convincingly reconciles the differences to produce a figure of
25,000, a very large proportion of which represented armoured men-
at-arms. Of these, about a thousand brought their horses to the
battlefield; the rest were to fight on foot.
    The two armies initially formed up at a distance of some thousand
yards from each other; at either end of a long, open and almost flat
expanse of ploughland, bordered on each side by woodland. The
width of the field, which had recently been sown with winter wheat,

was about twelve hundred yards at the French end. The woods converged slightly on the English and, at the point where the armies were eventually to meet, stood about nine hundred to a thousand yards apart. (These measurements suppose—as seems reasonable, field boundaries remaining remarkably stable over centuries—that the outlines of the woods have not much changed.)

The English men-at-arms, most of whom were on foot, took station in three blocks, under the command of the Duke of York, to the right, the King, in the centre, and Lord Camoys, on the left. The archers were disposed between them and also on the flanks; the whole line was about four or five deep. The archer flanks may have been thrown a little forward, and the archers of the two inner groups may have adopted a wedge-like formation. This would have made it appear as if the men-at-arms were deployed a little to their rear. Opposite them, the French were drawn up in three lines, of which the third was mounted, as were two groups, each about five hundred strong, on the flanks. The two forward lines, with a filling of cross-bowmen between and some ineffectual cannon on the flanks were each, perhaps, eight thousand strong, and so ranked some eight deep. On both sides, the leaders of the various contingents—nobles, bannerets and knights—displayed armorial banners, under which they and their men would fight, and among the French there was a great deal of tiresome struggling, during the period of deployment, to get these banners into the leading rank.

Deployed, the armies were ready for the battle, which, as we have seen, resolved itself into twelve main episodes: a period of waiting; an English advance; an English arrow strike; a French cavalry charge; a French infantry advance; a mêlée between the French and English men-at-arms; an intervention in the mêlée by the English archers; the flight of the French survivors from the scene of the mêlée; a second period of waiting, during which the French third line threatened, and a small party delivered, another charge; a French raid on the baggage park; a massacre of the French prisoners; finally, mutual departure from the battlefield. What was each of these episodes like, and what impetus did it give to the course of events?

The period of waiting—three or four hours long, and so lasting probably from about seven to eleven o'clock—must have been very trying. Two chroniclers mention that the soldiers in the front ranks sat down and ate and drank and that there was a good deal of shouting, chaffing and noisy reconciliation of old quarrels among the French. But that was after they had settled, by pushing and shoving, who was to stand in the forward rank; not a real argument, one may surmise, but a process which put the grander and the braver in front of the more humble and timid. There is no mention of the English imitating them, but given their very real predicament, and their much thinner line of battle, they can have felt little need to dispute the place of honour among themselves. It is also improbable that they did much eating or drinking, for the army had been short of food for nine days and the archers are said to have been subsisting on nuts and berries on the last marches. Waiting, certainly for the English, must then have been a cold, miserable and squalid business. It had been raining, the ground was recently ploughed, air temperature was probably in the forties or low fifties Fahrenheit and many in the army were suffering from diarrhoea. Since none would presumably have been allowed to leave the ranks while the army was deployed for action, sufferers would have had to relieve themselves where they stood. For any afflicted man-at-arms wearing mail leggings laced to his plate armour, even that may not have been possible.

The King's order to advance, which he gave after the veterans had endorsed his guess that the French would not be drawn, may therefore have been generally and genuinely welcome. Movement at least meant an opportunity to generate body heat, of which the metal-clad men-at-arms would have dissipated an unnatural amount during the morning. Not, however, when the moment came, that they would have moved forward very fast. An advance in line, particularly by men unequally equipped and burdened, has to be taken slowly if order is to be preserved. The manœuvre, moreover, was a change of position, not a charge, and the King and his subordinate leaders would presumably have recognized the additional danger of losing cohesion in the face of the enemy who, if alert, would seize on the eventuality as an opportune moment to launch an attack. Several chroniclers indeed mention that on the King's orders a knight, Sir Thomas Erpingham, inspected the archers before they marched off in order to 'check their dressing', as a modern drill sergeant would put it, and to ensure that they had their bows strung. The much smaller groups of men-at-arms would have moved as did the banners of their lords, which in turn would have followed the King's.

The army had about seven hundred yards of rain-soaked plough-land to cover. At a slow walk (no medieval army marched in step, and no modern army would have done so over such ground—the 'cadenced pace' followed from the hardening and smoothing of the surface of roads), with halts to correct dressing, it would have reached its new position in ten minutes or so, though one may guess that the pace slackened a good deal as they drew nearer the French army and the leaders made mental reckoning of the range. 'Extreme bowshot', which is the distance at which Henry presumably planned to take ground, is traditionally calculated at three hundred yards. That is a tremendous carry for a bow, however, and two hundred and fifty yards would be a more realistic judgment of the distance at which he finally halted his line from the French. If, however, his archer flanks were thrown a little forward, his centre would have been further away; and if, as one chronicler suggests, he had infiltrated parties of bowmen into the woods, the gap between the two armies might have been greater still. Something between two hundred and fifty and three hundred yards is a reasonable bracket therefore.

The archers were now in position to open fire (an inappropriate expression, belonging to the gunpowder age, which was barely beginning). Each man disposed his arrows as convenient. He would have had a sheaf, perhaps two, of twenty-four arrows and probably struck them point down into the ground by his feet. The men in the front two ranks would have a clear view of the enemy, those behind only sporadic glimpses: there must therefore have been some sort of ranging order passed by word of mouth. For the archers' task at this opening moment of the battle was to provoke the French into attacking, and it was therefore essential that their arrows should 'group' as closely as possible on the target. To translate their purpose into modern artillery language, they had to achieve a very narrow 100° zone (i.e. that belt of territory into which *all* missiles fell) and a Time on Target effect (i.e. all their missiles had to arrive simultaneously).

To speculate about their feelings at this moment is otiose. They were experienced soldiers in a desperate spot; and their fire, moreover, was to be 'indirect', in that their arrows would not depart straight into the enemy's faces but at a fairly steeply angled trajectory. They need have had no sense of initiating an act of killing, therefore; it was probably their technical and professional sense which was most actively engaged in an activity which was still preliminary to any 'real' fighting that might come.

They must have received at least two orders: the first to draw their bows, the second to loose their strings. How the orders were synchronized between different groups of archers is an unanswerable question, but when the shout went up or the banner down, four clouds of arrows would have streaked out of the English line to reach a height of a hundred feet before turning in flight to plunge at a steeper angle on and among the French men-at-arms opposite. These arrows cannot, however, given their terminal velocity and angle of impact, have done a great deal of harm, at least to the men-at-arms. For armour, by the early fifteenth century, was composed almost completely of steel sheet, in place of the iron mail which had been worn on the body until fifty years before but now only covered the awkward points of movement around the shoulder and groin. It was deliberately designed, moreover, to offer a glancing surface, and the contemporary helmet, a wide-brimmed 'bascinet', was particularly adapted to deflect blows away from the head and the shoulders. We can suppose that the armour served its purpose effectively in this, the opening moment of Agincourt. But one should not dismiss the moral effect of the arrow strike. The singing of the arrows would not have moved ahead of their flight, but the sound of their impact must have been extraordinarily cacophonous, a weird clanking and banging on the bowed heads and backs of the French men-at-arms. If any of the horses in the flanking squadrons were hit, they were likely to have been hurt, however, even at this extreme range, for they were armoured only on their faces and chests, and the chisel-pointed head of the clothyard arrow would have penetrated the padded cloth hangings which covered the rest of their bodies. Animal cries of pain and fear would have risen above the metallic clatter.

We can also imagine oaths and shouted threats from the French. For the arrow strike achieved its object. How quickly, the chroniclers do not tell us; but as a trained archer could loose a shaft every ten seconds we can guess that it took at most a few minutes to trigger the French attack. The French, as we know, were certain of victory. What they had been waiting for was a tactical pretext: either that of the Englishmen showing them their backs or, on the contrary, cocking a snook. One or two volleys would have been insult enough. On the arrival of the first arrows the two large squadrons of horse on either flank mounted—or had they mounted when the English line advanced?—walked their horses clear of the line and broke into a charge.

A charge at what? The two chroniclers who are specific about this point make it clear that the two groups of cavalry, each five or six hundred strong, of which that on the left hand was led by Clignet de Brébant and Guillaume de Saveuse, made the English archer flanks their target. Their aim, doubtless, was to clear these, the largest blocks of the enemy which immediately threatened them, off the field, leaving the numerically much inferior centre of English men-at-arms, with the smaller groups of their attendant archers, to be overwhelmed by the French infantry. It was nevertheless a strange and dangerous decision, unless, that is, we work on the supposition that the archers had planted their stakes among their own ranks, so concealing that array of obstacles from the French. We may then visualize the French bearing down on the archers in ignorance of the hedgehog their ranks concealed; and of the English giving ground just before the moment of impact, to reveal it.

For 'the moment of impact' otherwise begs an important, indeed a vital question. It is not difficult to picture the beginning of the charge: the horsemen booting their mounts to form line, probably two or three rows deep, so that, riding knee to knee, they would have presented a front of two or three hundred lances, more or less equalling in width the line of the archers opposite, say three hundred yards. We can imagine them setting off, sitting (really standing) 'long' in their high-backed, padded saddles, legs straight and thrust forward, toes down in the heavy stirrups, lance under right arm, left free to manage the reins (wearing plate armour obviated the need to carry a shield); and we can see them in motion, riding at a pace which took them across all but the last fifty of the two or three hundred yards they had to cover in forty seconds or so and then spurring their horses to ride down on the archers at the best speed they could manage—twelve or fifteen miles an hour.

So far so good. The distance between horses and archers narrows. The archers, who have delivered three or four volleys at the bowed heads and shoulders of their attackers, get off one more flight. More horses—some have already gone down or broken back with screams of pain—stumble and fall, tripping their neighbours, but the mass drive on and . . . and what? It is at this moment that we have to make a judgment about the difference between what happens in a battle and what happens in a violent accident. A horse, in the normal course of events, will not gallop at an obstacle it cannot jump or see a way through, and it cannot jump or see a way through a solid line of men. Even less will it go at the sort of obviously dangerous obstacle which the archers' stakes presented. Equally, a man will not stand in the path of a running horse: he will run himself, or seek shelter, and only if exceptionally strong-nerved and knowing in its ways, stand his ground. Nevertheless, accidents happen. Men, miscalculating or slow-footed, and horses, confused or maddened, do collide, with results almost exclusively unpleasant for the man. We cannot therefore say, however unnatural and exceptional we recognize collisions between man and horse to be, that nothing of that nature occurred between the archers and the French cavalry at Agincourt. For the archers were trained to 'receive cavalry', the horses trained to charge home, while it was the principal function of the *riders* to insist on the horses doing that against which their nature rebelled. Moreover, two of the eye-witness chroniclers, St Remy and the Priest of the Cottonian MS, are adamant that some of the French cavalry did get in among the archers.

The two opposed 'weapon principles' which military theorists recognize had, in short, both failed: the 'missile' principle, personified by the archers, had failed to stop or drive off the cavalry; they, embodying the 'shock' principle, had failed to crush the infantry— or, more particularly, to make them run away, for the 'shock' which cavalry seek to inflict is really moral, not physical in character. It was the stakes which must have effected the compromise. The French, coming on fast, and in great numbers over a short distance, had escaped the deaths and falls which should have toppled their charge over on itself; the English, emboldened by the physical security the hedgehog of stakes lent their formation, had given ground only a little before the onset; the horses had then found themselves on top of the stakes too late to refuse the obstacle; and a short, violent and noisy collision had resulted.

Some of the men-at-arms' horses 'ran out' round the flanks of the archers and into the woods. Those in the rear ranks turned their horses, or were turned by them, and rode back. But three at least, including Guillaume de Saveuse, had their horses impaled on the stakes, thumped to the ground and were killed where they lay, either by mallet blows or by stabs between their armour-joints. The charge, momentarily terrifying for the English, from many of whom French men-at-arms, twice their height from the ground, and moving at ten or fifteen miles an hour on steel-shod and grotesquely caparisoned war-horses, had stopped only a few feet distant, had been a disaster for the enemy. And as they rode off, the archers, with all the violent anger that comes with release from sudden danger, bent their bows and sent fresh flights of arrows after them, bringing down more horses and maddening others into uncontrolled flight.

But the results of the rout went beyond the demoralization of the survivors. For, as their horses galloped back, they met the first division of dismounted men-at-arms marching out to attack the English centre. Perhaps eight thousand strong, and filling the space between the woods eight or ten deep, they could not easily or quickly open their ranks to let the fugitives through. Of what happened in consequence we can get a clear idea, curiously, from a cinema news-reel of the Grosvenor Square demonstration against the Vietnam war in 1968. There, a frightened police horse, fleeing the demonstrators, charged a line of constables on foot. Those directly in its path, barging sideways and backwards to open a gap and seizing their neighbours, set up a curious and violent ripple which ran along the ranks on each side, reaching policemen some good distance away who, tightly packed, clutched at each other for support, and stumbled clumsily backwards and then forwards to keep their balance. The sensations of that ripple are known to anyone who has been a member of a dense, mobile and boisterous crowd and it was certainly what was felt, to a sudden and exaggerated degree, by the French men-at-arms in the face of that involuntary cavalry charge. As in that which had just failed against the archers, many of the horses would have shied off at the moment of impact. But those that barged in, an occurrence to which the chroniclers testify, broke up the rhythm of the advance and knocked some men to the ground, an unpleasant experience when the soil is wet and trampled and one is wearing sixty or seventy pounds of sheet metal on the body.

This interruption in an advance which should have brought the French first division to within weapon's length of the English in three or four minutes at most gave Henry's men-at-arms ample time to brace themselves for the encounter. It also gave the archers, both those in the large groups on the wings and the two smaller groups in the central wedges, the chance to prolong their volleying of arrows into the French ranks. The range was progressively shortened by the advance, and the arrows, coming in on a flat trajectory in sheets of five thousand at ten-second intervals, must have begun to cause casualties among the French foot. For though they bowed their heads and hunched their shoulders, presenting a continuous front of de-flecting surface (bascinet top, breastplate, 'taces'—the overlapping bands across the stomach and genitals—and leg-pieces) to the storm, some of the arrows must have found the weak spots in the visor and at the shoulders and, as the range dropped right down, might even have penetrated armour itself. The 'bodkin-point' was designed to do so, and its terminal velocity, sufficient to drive it through an inch of oak from a short distance, could also, at the right angle of impact, make a hole in sheet steel.

The archers failed nevertheless to halt the French advance. But they succeeded in channelling it—or helping to channel it—on to a narrower front of attack.

THE KILLING OF THE PRISONERS

Indeed, soon after midday, the English men were 'in possession of the field'—by which soldiers would understand that they were able to move freely over the ground earlier occupied by the French, of whom only dead, wounded and fugitives were now to be seen. Fugitives too slow-footed to reach hiding in the woods, or sanctuary among the cavalry of the still uncommitted third division, were chased and tackled by bounty-hunters; others, greedy for ransom, were sorting through the recumbent bodies and pulling 'down the heaps . . . to separate the living from the dead, proposing to keep the living as slaves, to be ransomed'. At the back of the battlefield the most valuable prisoners were massed together under guard. They were still wearing their armour but had surrendered their right gauntlets to their captors, as a token of submission (and subsequent reidentification), and taken off their helmets, without which they could not fight.

Henry could not allow each captor individually to sequester his prisoners because of the need to keep the army together as long as the French third division threatened a charge. So while small parties, acting both on their own behalf and that of others still in the ranks, reaped the rewards of the fight, the main bodies of men-at-arms and archers stood their ground—now about two or three hundred yards forward of the line on which they had received the French charge. Henry's caution was justified. Soon after midday, the Duke of Brabant, arriving late, half-equipped, and with a tiny following, charged into these ranks. He was overpowered and led to the rear. But this gallant intervention inspired at least two French noblemen in the third division, the Counts of Masle and Fauquemberghes, to marshal some six hundred of their followers for a concerted charge. They could clearly be seen massing, two or three hundred yards from the English line, and their intentions were obvious. At about the same time, moreover, shouting from the rear informed the English of a raid by the enemy on the baggage park, which had been left almost unguarded.

It was these events which precipitated Henry's notorious order to kill the prisoners. As it turned out, the charge was not delivered and the raid was later revealed to have been a mere rampage by the local peasantry, under the Lord of Agincourt. The signs were enough, however, to convince Henry that his victory, in which he can scarcely have yet believed, was about to be snatched from him. For if the French third division attacked the English where they stood, the archers without arrows or stakes, the men-at-arms weary after a morning of hacking and banging in full armour, all of them hungry, cold and depressed by the reaction from the intense fears and elations of combat, they might easily have been swept from the field. They could certainly not have withstood the simultaneous assault on their rear, to which, with so many inadequately guarded French prisoners standing about behind them on ground littered with discarded weapons, they were likely also to have been subjected. In these circumstances, his order is comprehensible.

Comprehensible in harsh tactical logic; in ethical, human and practical terms much more difficult to understand. Henry, a Christian king, was also an experienced soldier and versed in the elaborate code of international law governing relations between a prisoner and his captor. Its most important provision was that which guaranteed the prisoner his life—the only return, after all, for which he would enter into anything so costly and humiliating as a ransom bargain. And while his treachery broke that immunity, the mere suspicion, even if well-founded, that he was about to commit treason could not justify his killing. At a more fundamental level, moreover, the prisoner's life was guaranteed by the ~~Christian~~ commandment against murder, however much more loosely that commandment was interpreted in the fifteenth century. If Henry could give the order and, as he did, subsequently escape the reproval of his peers, of the Church and of the chroniclers, we must presume it was because the battlefield itself was still regarded as a sort of moral no-man's land and the hour of battle as a legal *dies non.*

His subordinates nevertheless refused to obey. Was this because they felt a more tender conscience? The notion is usually dismissed by medieval specialists, who insist that, at best, the captors objected to the King's interference in what was a personal relationship, the prisoners being not the King's or the army's but the vassals of those who had accepted their surrender; that, at worst, they refused to forgo the prospect of so much ransom money (there being almost no way for a man of the times to make a quick fortune except on the battlefield). But it is significant that the King eventually got his order obeyed only by detailing two hundred *archers,* under the command of an esquire, to carry out the task. This may suggest that, among the captors, the men-at-arms at any rate felt something more than a financially motivated reluctance. There is, after all, an important difference between fighting with lethal weapons, even if it ends in killing, and mere butchery, and we may expect it to have been all the stronger when the act of fighting was as glorified as it was in the Middle Ages. To meet a similarly equipped opponent was the occasion for which the armoured soldier trained perhaps every day of his life from the onset of manhood. To meet and beat him was a triumph, the highest form which self-expression could take in the medieval nobleman's way of life. The events of the late morning at Agincourt, when men had leapt and grunted and hacked at each other's bodies, behaving in a way which seems grotesque and horrifying to us, was for them, therefore, a sort of apotheosis, giving point to their existence, and perhaps assuring them of commemoration after death (since most chroniclers were principally concerned to celebrate individual feats of arms). But there was certainly no honour to be won in killing one's social equal after he had surrendered and been disarmed. On the contrary, there was a considerable risk of incurring dishonour, which may alone have been strong enough to deter the men-at-arms from obeying Henry's order.

Archers stood outside the chivalric system; nor is there much to the idea that they personified the yeoman virtues. The bowmen of Henry's army were not only tough professional soldiers. There is also evidence that many had enlisted in the first place to avoid punishment for civil acts of violence, including murder. The chroniclers also make clear that, in the heat of combat, and during the more leisurely taking of prisoners after the rout of the French second division, there had been a good deal of killing, principally by the archers, of those too poor or too badly hurt to be worth keeping captive. The question of how more or less reluctant they were to carry out the King's command need not therefore delay us.

But the mechanics of the execution do demand a pause. Between one and two thousand prisoners accompanied Henry to England after the battle, of whom most must have been captured before he issued his order to kill. The chroniclers record that the killers spared the most valuable prisoners and were called off as soon as Henry assured himself that the French third division was not going to attack after all. We may take it therefore that the two hundred archers whom he detailed were heavily outnumbered by their victims, probably by about ten to one. The reason for wanting them killed, however, was that they were liable to re-arm themselves from the jetsam of battle if it were renewed. Why did they not do so when they saw themselves threatened with death, for the announcement of the King's order 'by trumpet' and the refusal of their captors to carry it out can have left them in no doubt of the fate he planned for them? And how were the archers able to offer them a match? It may have been that they were roughly pinioned (some contemporary pictures of battle show prisoners being led away with their hands bound); but in that case they offered no proper—or a very much reduced—menace to the army's rear, which in turn diminishes the justification for Henry's order. And even if they were tied, their actual killing is an operation difficult to depict for oneself. The act of surrender is notably accompanied by the onset of lassitude and self-reproach. Is it realistic to imagine, however, these proud and warlike men passively awaiting the arrival of a gang of their social inferiors to do them to death—standing like cattle in groups of ten for a single archer to break their skulls with an axe?

It does seem very improbable, and all the more because what we know of twentieth-century mass-killing suggests that it is very difficult for small numbers of executioners, even when armed with machine-guns, to kill people much more defenceless than armoured knights quickly and in large numbers. What seems altogether more likely, therefore, is that Henry's order, rather than bring about the prisoners' massacre, was intended by its threat to terrorize them into abject inactivity. We may imagine something much less clinical than a *Sonderkommando*[1] at work: the captors loudly announcing their refusal to obey the proclamation and perhaps assuring their prisoners that they would see them come to no harm; argument and even scuffling between them and members of the execution squad; and then a noisy and bloody cattle-drive to the rear, the archers harrying round the flanks of the crowd of armoured Frenchmen as they stumbled away from the scene of fighting and its dangerous debris to a spot nearer the baggage park, whence they could offer no serious threat at all. Some would have been killed in the process, and quite deliberately, but we need not reckon their number in thousands, perhaps not even in hundreds.

The killing, moreover, had a definite term, for Henry ordered it to end when he saw the French third division abandon their attack formation and begin to leave the battlefield. The time was about three o'clock in the afternoon, leaving some two hours more of daylight. The English began at once to spread out over the field looking for prisoners and spoil in places not yet visited. The King made a circuit

---

[1] an inmate in a Nazi concentration camp forced to dispose of the bodies of fellow prisoners who had been killed (ED.)

and, on turning back for his quarters at Maisoncelles, summoned to him the French and English heralds.

THE WOUNDED

The heralds had watched the battle in a group together and, though the French army had left, the French heralds had not yet followed them. For the heralds belonged not to the armies but to the international corporation of experts who regulated civilized warfare. Henry was anxious to hear the verdict on the day's fighting and to fix a name for the battle, so that its outcome and the army's exploits could be readily identified when chroniclers came to record it. Montjoie, the principal French herald, confirmed that the English were the victors and provided Henry with the name of the nearest castle—Agincourt—to serve as eponym.

That decision ended the battle as a military and historical episode. The English drove their prisoners and carried their own wounded back to Maisoncelles for the night, where the twenty surgeons of the army set to work. English casualties had been few: the Duke of York, who was pulled from under a heap of corpses, dead either from suffocation or a heart-attack, and the Earl of Suffolk were the only notable fatalities. The wounded numbered only some hundreds. What were their prospects? In the main, probably quite good. The English had not undergone an arrow attack, so most of the wounds would have been lacerations rather than penetrations, clean even if deep cuts which, if bound up and left, would heal quickly. There would also have been some fractures; depressed fractures of the skull could not be treated—the secret of trepanning awaited rediscovery—but breaks of the arm and lower leg could have been successfully set and splinted. The French wounded enjoyed a much graver prognosis. Many would have suffered penetrating wounds, either from arrows or from thrusts through the weak spots of their armour. Those which had pierced the intestines, emptying its contents into the abdomen, were fatal: peritonitis was inevitable. Penetrations of the chest cavity, which had probably carried in fragments of dirty clothing, were almost as certain to lead to sepsis. Many of the French would have suffered depressed fractures of the skull, and there would have been broken backs caused by falls from horses in armour at speed. Almost all of these injuries we may regard as fatal, the contemporary surgeons being unable to treat them. Many of the French, of course, had not been collected from the battlefield and, if they did not bleed to death, would have succumbed to the combined effects of exposure and shock during the night, when temperatures might have descended into the middle-30s Fahrenheit. It was, therefore, not arbitrary brutality when, in crossing the battlefield next morning, the English killed those whom they found alive. They were almost certain to have died, in any case, when their bodies would have gone to join those which the local peasants, under the supervision of the Bishop of Arras, dug into pits on the site. They are said to have buried about six thousand altogether.

THE WILL TO COMBAT

What sustained men in a combat like Agincourt, when the penalty of defeat, or of one's own lack of skill or nimbleness was so final and unpleasant? Some factors, either general to battle—as will appear—or more or less particular to this one are relatively easy to isolate. Of the general factors, drink is the most obvious to mention. The English, who were on short rations, presumably had less to drink than the French, but there was drinking in the ranks on both sides during the period of waiting and it is quite probable that many soldiers in both armies went into the mêlée less than sober, if not indeed fighting drunk. For the English, the presence of the King would also have provided what present-day soldiers called a 'moral factor' of great importance. The personal bond between leader and follower lies at the root of all explanations of what does and does not happen in battle: and that bond is always strongest in martial societies, of which fifteenth-century England is one type and the warrior states of India, which the British harnessed so successfully to their imperial purpose, are another. The nature of the bond is more complex, and certainly more materialistic than modern ethologists would like to have us believe. But its importance must not be underestimated. And though the late-medieval soldier's immediate loyalty lay towards his captain, the presence on the field of his own and his captain's anointed king, visible to all and ostentatiously risking his life in the heart of the mêlée, must have greatly strengthened his resolve.

Serving to strengthen it further was the endorsement of religion. The morality of killing is not something with which the professional soldier is usually thought to trouble himself, but the Christian knight, whether we mean by that the ideal type as seen by the chroniclers or some at least of the historical figures of whom we have knowledge, was nevertheless exercised by it. What constituted unlawful killing in time of war was well-defined, and carried penalties under civil, military and religious law. Lawful killing, on the other hand, was an act which religious precept specifically endorsed, within the circumscription of the just war; and however dimly or marginally religious doctrine impinged on the consciousness of the simple soldier or more unthinking knight, the religious preparations which all in the English army underwent before Agincourt must be counted among the most important factors affecting its mood. Henry himself heard Mass three times in succession before the battle, and took Communion, as presumably did most of his followers; there was a small army of priests in the expedition. The soldiers ritually entreated blessing before entering the ranks, going down on their knees, making the sign of the cross and taking earth into their mouths as a symbolic gesture of the death and burial they were thereby accepting.

Drink and prayer must be seen, however, as last-minute and short-term reinforcements of the medieval soldier's (though, as we shall see, not only his) will to combat. Far more important, and, given the disparity of their stations, more important still for the common soldier than the man-at-arms, was the prospect of enrichment. Medieval warfare, like all warfare, was about many things, but medieval battle, at the personal level, was about only three: victory first, of course, because the personal consequences of defeat could be so disagreeable; personal distinction in single combat—something of which the man-at-arms would think a great deal more than the bowman; but, ultimately and most important, ransom and loot. Agincourt was untypical of medieval battle in yielding, and then snatching back from the victors the bonanza of wealth that it did; but it is the gold-strike and gold-fever character of medieval battle which we should keep foremost in mind when seeking to understand it.

We should balance it, at the same time, against two other factors. The first of these is the pressure of compulsion. The role which physical coercion or force of unavoidable circumstance plays in bringing men into, and often through, the ordeal of battle is one which almost all military historians consistently underplay, or ignore. Yet we can clearly see that the force of unavoidable circumstances was among the most powerful of the drives to combat at work on the field of Agincourt. The English had sought by every means to avoid battle throughout their long march from Harfleur and, though accepting it on October 25th as a necessary alternative to capitulation and perhaps life-long captivity, were finally driven to attack by the pains of hunger and cold. The French had also hoped to avoid bringing their confrontation with the English to a fight; and we may convincingly surmise that many of those who went down under the swords or mallet-blows of the English had been drawn into the battle with all the free-will of a man who finds himself going the wrong way on a moving-staircase.

The second factor confounds the former just examined. It concerns the commonplace character of violence in medieval life. What went on at Agincourt appals and horrifies the modern imagination which, vicariously accustomed though it is to the idea of violence, rarely encounters it in actuality and is outraged when it does. The sense of outrage was no doubt as keenly felt by the individual victim of violence five hundred years ago. But the victim of assault, in a world where the rights of lordship were imposed and the quarrels of neighbours settled by sword or knife as a matter of course, was likely to have been a good deal less surprised by it when it occurred. As the language of English law, which we owe to the Middle Ages, reveals, through its references to 'putting in fear', 'making an affray' and 'keeping the Queen's peace', the medieval world was one in which the distinction between private, civil and foreign war, though recognized, could only be irregularly enforced. Thus battle, though an extreme on the spectrum of experience, was not something unimaginable, something wholly beyond the peace-loving individual's ken. It offered the soldier risk in a particularly concentrated form; but it was a treatment to which his upbringing and experience would already have partially inured him.

FRANK A. HASKELL

The Battle of Gettysburg: A Participant's View

Frank A. Haskell (1828–1864) was born in Vermont, graduated from Dartmouth College, and was a Union officer during the Civil War. He wrote the following account of the Battle of Gettysburg a few weeks after it took place, during the summer of 1863. Haskell's account of the battle was originally privately printed in pam-

phlet form, and it became a standard reference work for students
of warfare. It was not published for the general public until 1958.

There was a pause between the acts, with the curtain down, soon to
rise upon the great final act, and catastrophe of Gettysburg. We have
passed by the left of the Second Division, coming from the First;
when we crossed the crest the enemy was not in sight, and all was
still—we walked slowly along in the rear of the troops, by the ridge
cut off now from a view of the enemy in his position, and were
returning to the spot where we had left our horses. General Gibbon
had just said that he inclined to the belief that the enemy was falling
back, and that the cannonade was only one of his noisy modes of
covering the movement. I said that I thought that fifteen minutes
would show that, by all his bowling, the Rebel did not mean retreat.
We were near our horses when we noticed Brigadier General Hunt,
Chief of Artillery of the Army, near Woodruff's Battery, swiftly moving about on horseback, and apparently in a rapid manner giving
some orders about the guns. Thought we, what could this mean? In
a moment afterwards we met Captain Wessels and the orderlies who
had our horses; they were on foot leading the horses. Captain Wessels
was pale, and he said, excited: "General, they say the enemy's infantry
is advancing." We sprang into our saddles, a score of bounds brought
us upon the all-seeing crest. To say that men grew pale and held
their breath at what we and they there saw, would not be true. Might
not six thousand men be brave and without shade of fear, and yet,
before a hostile eighteen thousand, armed, and not five minutes'
march away, turn ashy white?

None on that crest now need be told that *the enemy is advancing.*
Every eye could see his legions, an overwhelming resistless tide of
an ocean of armed men sweeping upon us! Regiment after regiment
and brigade after brigade move from the woods and rapidly take
their places in the lines forming the assault. Pickett's proud division,
with some additional troops, hold their right; Pettigrew's (Worth's)
their left. The first line at short interval is followed by a second, and
that a third succeeds; and columns between support the lines. More
than half a mile their front extends; more than a thousand yards the
dull gray masses deploy, man touching man, rank pressing rank, and
line supporting line. The red flags wave, their horsemen gallop up
and down; the arms of eighteen thousand men, barrel and bayonet,
gleam in the sun, a sloping forest of flashing steel. Right on they
move, as with one soul, in perfect order, without impediment of

ditch, or wall or stream, over ridge and slope, through orchard and meadow, and cornfield, magnificent, grim, irresistible.

All was orderly and still upon our crest; no noise and no confusion. The men had little need of commands, for the survivors of a dozen battles knew well enough what this array in front portended, and, already in their places, they would be prepared to act when the right time should come. The click of the locks as each man raised the hammer to feel with his fingers that the cap was on the nipple; the sharp jar as a musket touched a stone upon the wall when thrust in aiming over it, and the clicking of the iron axles as the guns were rolled up by hand a little further to the front, were quite all the sounds that could be heard. Cap-boxes were slid around to the front of the body; cartridge boxes opened, officers opened their pistol-holsters. Such preparations, little more was needed. The trefoil flags, colors of the brigades and divisions moved to their places in rear; but along the lines in front the grand old ensign that first waved in battle at Saratoga in 1777, and which these people coming would rob of half its stars, stood up, and the west wind kissed it as the sergeants sloped its lance towards the enemy. I believe that not one above whom it then waved but blessed his God that he was loyal to it, and whose heart did not swell with pride towards it, as the emblem of the Republic before that treason's flaunting rag in front.

General Gibbon rode down the lines, cool and calm, and in an unimpassioned voice he said to the men, "Do not hurry, men, and fire too fast, let them come up close before you fire, and then aim low and steadily." The coolness of their General was reflected in the faces of his men. Five minutes has elapsed since first the enemy have emerged from the woods—no great space of time surely, if measured by the usual standard by which men estimate duration—but it was long enough for us to note and weigh some of the elements of mighty moment that surrounded us; the disparity of numbers between the assailants' and the assailed; that few as were our numbers we could not be supported or reinforced until support would not be needed or would be too late; that upon the ability of the two trefoil divisions to hold the crest and repel the assault depended not only their own safety or destruction, but also the honor of the Army of the Potomac and defeat or victory at Gettysburg. Should these advancing men pierce our line and become the entering wedge, driven home, that would sever our army asunder, what hope would there be afterwards, and where the blood-earned fruits of yesterday? It was long enough for the Rebel storm to drift across more than half the space that had at first separated us. None, or all, of these considerations either depressed or elevated us. They might have done the former, had we been timid; the latter had we been confident and vain. But, we were there waiting, and ready to do our duty—that done, results could not dishonor us.

Our skirmishers open a spattering fire along the front, and, fighting, retire upon the main line—the first drops, the heralds of the storm, sounding on our windows. Then the thunders of our guns, first Arnold's then Cushing's and Woodruff's and the rest, shake and reverberate again through the air, and their sounding shells smite the enemy. The General said I had better go and tell General Meade of this advance. To gallop to General Meade's headquarters, to learn there that he had changed them to another part of the field, to dispatch to him by the Signal Corps in General Gibbon's name the message, "The enemy is advancing his infantry in force upon my front," and to be again upon the crest, were but the work of a minute. All our available guns are now active, and from the fire of shells, as the range grows shorter and shorter, they change to shrapnel, and from shrapnel to canister; but in spite of shells, and shrapnel and canister, without wavering or halt, the hardy lines of the enemy continue to move on. The Rebel guns make no reply to ours, and no charging shout rings out to-day, as is the Rebel wont; but the courage of these silent men amid our shots seems not to need the stimulus of other noise. The enemy's right flank sweeps near Stannard's bushy crest, and his concealed Vermonters rake it with a well-delivered fire of musketry. The gray lines do not halt or reply, but withdrawing a little from that extreme, they still move on.

And so across all that broad open ground they have come, nearer and nearer, nearly half the way, with our guns bellowing in their faces, until now a hundred yards, no more, divide our ready left from their advancing right. The eager men there are impatient to begin. Let them. First, Harrow's breastworks flame; then Hall's; then Webb's. As if our bullets were the fire coals that touched off their muskets, the enemy in front halts, and his countless level barrels blaze back upon us. The Second Division is struggling in battle. The rattling storm soon spreads to the right, and the blue trefoils are vieing with the white. All along each hostile front, a thousand yards, with narrowest space between, the volleys blaze and roll; as thick the sound as when a summer hail-storm pelts the city roofs; as thick the fire as when the incessant lightning fringes a summer cloud. When the Rebel infantry had opened fire our batteries soon became silent, and this without their fault, for they were foul by long previous use. They were the targets of the concentrated Rebel bullets, and some of them had expended all their canister. But they were not silent before Rorty was killed, Woodruff had fallen mortally wounded, and Cushing, firing almost his last canister, had dropped dead among his guns shot through the head by a bullet. The conflict is left to the infantry alone.

Unable to find my general when I had returned to the crest after transmitting his message to General Meade, and while riding in the search having witnessed the development of the fight, from the first fire upon the left by the main lines until all of the two divisions were furiously engaged, I gave up hunting as useless—I was convinced General Gibbon could not be on the field; I left him mounted; I could easily have found him now had he so remained—but now, save myself, there was not a mounted officer near the engaged lines—and was riding towards the right of the Second Division, with purpose to stop there, as the most eligible position to watch the further progress of the battle, there to be ready to take part according to my own notions whenever and wherever occasion was presented. The conflict was tremendous, but I had seen no wavering in all our line.

Wondering how long the Rebel ranks, deep though they were, could stand our sheltered volleys, I had come near my destination, when—great heaven! were my senses mad? The larger portion of Webb's brigade—my God, it was true—there by the group of trees and the angles of the wall, was breaking from the cover of their works, and, without orders or reason, with no hand lifted to check them, was falling back, a fear-stricken flock of confusion! The fate of Gettysburg hung upon a spider's single thread! A great magnificent passion came on me at the instant, not one that overpowers and confounds, but one that blanches the face and sublimes every sense and faculty. My sword, that had always hung idle by my side, the sign of rank only in every battle, I drew, bright and gleaming, the symbol of command. Was that not a fit occasion, and these fugitives the men on whom to try the temper of the Solinzen steel? All rules and proprieties were forgotten; all considerations of person, and danger and safety despised; for, as I met the tide of these rabbits, the damned red flags of the rebellion began to thicken and flaunt along the wall they had just deserted, and one was already wavering over one of the guns of the dead Cushing. I ordered these men to "halt," and "face about" and "fire," and they heard my voice and gathered my meaning, and obeyed my commands. On some unpatriotic backs of those not quick of comprehension, the flat of my sabre fell not lightly, and at its touch their love of country returned, and, with a look at me as if I were the destroying angel, as I might have become theirs, they again faced the enemy. General Webb soon came to my assistance. He was on foot, but he was active, and did all that one could do to repair the breach, or to avert its calamity. The men that had fallen back, facing the enemy, soon regained confidence in themselves, and became steady.

This portion of the wall was lost to us, and the enemy had gained the cover of the reverse side, where he now stormed with fire. But Webb's men, with their bodies in part protected by the abruptness of the crest, now sent back in the enemies' faces as fierce a storm. Some scores of venturesome Rebels, that in their first push at the wall had dared to cross at the further angle, and those that had desecrated Cushing's guns were promptly shot down, and speedy death met him who should raise his body to cross it again. At this point little could be seen of the enemy, by reason of his cover and the smoke, except the flash of his muskets and his waving flags. These red flags were accumulating at the wall every moment, and they maddened us as the same color does the bull. Webb's men are falling fast, and he is among them to direct and to encourage; but, however well they may now do, with that walled enemy in front, with more than a dozen flags to Webb's three, it soon becomes apparent that in not many minutes they will be overpowered, or that there will be none alive for the enemy to overpower. Webb has but three regiments, all small, the 69th, 71st and 72d Pennsylvania—the 106th Pennsylvania, except two companies, is not here to-day—and he must have speedy assistance, or this crest will be lost.

Oh, where is Gibbon? where is Hancock?—some general—anybody with the power and the will to support that wasting, melting line? No general came, and no succor! I thought of Hays upon the right, but from the smoke and war along his front, it was evident that he had enough upon his hands, if he stayed the in-rolling tide of the Rebels there. Doubleday upon the left was too far off and too slow, and on another occasion I had begged him to send his idle regiments to support another line battling with thrice its numbers, and this "Old Sumpter Hero" had declined. At a last resort I resolved to see if Hall and Harrow could not send some of their commands to reinforce Webb. I galloped to the left in the execution of my purpose, and as I attained the rear of Hall's line, from the nature of the ground and the position of the enemy it was easy to discover the reason and the manner of this gathering of Rebel flags in front of Webb. The enemy, emboldened by his success in gaining our line by the group of trees and the angle of the wall, was concentrating all his right against and was further pressing that point. There was the stress of his assault; there would he drive his fiery wedge to split our line.

In front of Harrows' and Hall's Brigades he had been able to advance no nearer than when he first halted to deliver fire, and these commands had not yielded an inch. To effect the concentration before Webb, the enemy would march the regiment on his extreme right of each of his lines by the left flank to the rear of the troops, still halted and facing to the front, and so continuing to draw in his right, when they were all massed in the position desired, he would again face them to the front, and advance to the storming. This was the way he made the wall before Webb's line blaze red with his battle flags, and such was the purpose there of his thick-crowding battalions.

Not a moment must be lost. Colonel Hall I found just in rear of his line, sword in hand, cool, vigilant, noting all that passed and directing the battle of his brigade. The fire was constantly diminishing now in his front, in the manner and by the movement of the enemy that I have mentioned, drifting to the right. "How is it going?" Colonel Hall asked me, as I rode up. "Well, but Webb is hotly pressed and must have support, or he will be overpowered. Can you assist him?" "Yes." "You cannot be too quick." "I will move my brigade at once." "Good." He gave the order, and in briefest time I saw five friendly colors hurrying to the aid of the imperilled three; and each color represented true, battle-tried men, that had not turned back from Rebel fire that day nor yesterday, though their ranks were sadly thinned. To Webb's brigade, pressed back as it had been from the wall, the distance was not great from Hall's right. The regiments marched by the right flank. Col. Hall superintended the movement in person. Col. Devereux coolly commanded the 19th Massachusetts. His major, Rice, had already been wounded and carried off. Lieut. Col. Macy, of the 20th Mass., had just had his left hand shot off, and so Capt. Abbott gallantly led over this fine regiment. The 42d New York followed their excellent Colonel Mallon. Lieut. Col. Steele, 7th Mich., had just been killed, and his regiment, and the handful of the 59th N. Y., followed their colors. The movement, as it did, attracting the enemy's fire, and executed in haste, as it must be, was difficult; but in reasonable time, and in order that is serviceable, if not regular, Hall's men are fighting gallantly side by side with Webb's before the all important point. I did not stop to see all this movement of Hall's, but from him I went at once further to the left, to the 1st brigade. Gen. Harrow I did not see, but his fighting men would answer my purpose as well. The 19th Me., the 15th Mass., the 32d N. Y. and

the shattered old thunderbolt, the 1st Minn.—poor Farrell was dying
then upon the ground where he had fallen,—all men that I could
find I took over to the right at the *double quick.*

As we were moving to, and near the other brigade of the division,
from my position on horseback I could see that the enemy's right,
under Hall's fire, was beginning to stagger and to break. "See," I said
to the men, "See the *chivalry!* See the gray-backs run!" The men
saw, and as they swept to their places by the side of Hall and opened
fire, they roared, and this in a manner that said more plainly than
words—for the deaf could have seen it in their faces, and the blind
could have heard it in their voices—*the crest is safe!*

The whole Division concentrated, and changes of position, and
new phases, as well on our part as on that of the enemy, having as
indicated occurred, for the purpose of showing the exact present
posture of affairs, some further description is necessary. Before the
2d Division the enemy is massed, the main bulk of his force covered
by the ground that slopes to his rear, with his front at the stone wall.
Between his front and us extends the very apex of the crest. All there
are left of the White Trefoil Division—yesterday morning there were
three thousand eight hundred, this morning there were less than
three thousand—at this moment there are somewhat over two thousand;—twelve regiments in three brigades are below or behind the
crest, in such a position that by the exposure of the head and upper
part of the body above the crest they can deliver their fire in the
enemy's faces along the top of the wall. By reason of the disorgani-
zation incidental in Webb's brigade to his men's having broken and
fallen back, as mentioned, in the two other brigades to their rapid
and difficult change of position under fire, and in all the division in
part to severe and continuous battle, formation of companies and
regiments in regular ranks is lost; but commands, companies, regiments and brigades are blended and intermixed—an irregular extended mass—men enough, if in order, to form a line of four or five
ranks along the whole front of the division. The twelve flags of the
regiments wave defiantly at intervals along the front; at the stone
wall, at unequal distances from ours of forty, fifty or sixty yards,
stream nearly double this number of the battle flags of the enemy.
These changes accomplished on either side, and the concentration
complete, although no cessation or abatement in the general din of
conflict since the commencement had at any time been appreciable,
now it was as if a new battle, deadlier, stormier than before, had
sprung from the body of the old—a young Phoenix of combat, whose

eyes stream lightning, shaking his arrowy wings over the yet glowing ashes of his progenitor.

The jostling, swaying lines on either side boil, and roar, and dash their flamy spray, two hostile billows of a fiery ocean. Thick flashes stream from the wall, thick volleys answer from the crest. No threats or expostulation now, only example and encouragement. All depths of passion are stirred, and all combatives fire, down to their deep foundations. Individuality is drowned in a sea of clamor, and timid men, breathing the breath of the multitude, are brave. The frequent dead and wounded lie where they stagger and fall—there is no humanity for them now, and none can be spared to care for them. The men do not cheer or shout; they growl, and over that uneasy sea, heard with the roar of musketry, sweeps the muttered thunder of a storm of growls. Webb, Hall, Devereux, Mallon, Abbot among the men where all are heroes, are doing deeds of note. Now the loyal wave rolls up as if it would over-leap its barrier, the crest. Pistols flash with the muskets. My "Forward to the wall" is answered by the Rebel countercommand, "Steady, men!" and the wave swings back. Again it surges, and again it sinks. These men of Pennsylvania, on the soil of their homesteads, the first and only to flee the wall, must be the first to storm it.

"Major—, *lead* your men over the crest, they will follow." "By the tactics I understand my place is in rear of the men." "Your pardon, sir; I see *your* place is in rear of the men. I thought you were fit to lead." "Capt. Sapler, come on with your men." "Let me first stop this fire in the rear, or we shall be hit by our own men." "Never mind the fire in the rear; let us take care of this in front first." "Sergeant, forward with your color. Let the Rebels see it close to their eyes once before they die." The color sergeant of the 72d Pa., grasping the stump of the severed lance in both his hands, waved the flag above his head and rushed towards the wall. "Will you see your color storm the wall alone?" One man only starts to follow. Almost half way to the wall, down go color bearer and color to the ground—the gallant sergeant is dead. The line springs—the crest of the solid ground with a great roar heaves forward its maddened load, men, arms, smoke, fire, a fighting mass. It rolls to the wall—flash meets flash, the wall is crossed—a moment ensues of thrusts, yells, blows, shots, and undistinguishable conflict, followed by a shout universal that makes the welkin ring again, and the last and bloodiest fight of the great battle of Gettysburg is ended and won.

Many things cannot be described by pen or pencil—such a fight is one. Some hints and incidents may be given, but a description or picture never. From what is told the imagination may for itself construct the scene; otherwise he who never saw can have no adequate idea of what such a battle is.

When the vortex of battle passion had subsided, hopes, fears, rage, joy, of which the maddest and the noisiest was the last, and we were calm enough to look about us, we saw that, as with us, the fight with the Third Division was ended, and that in that division was a repetition of the scenes immediately about us. In that moment the judgment almost refused to credit the senses. Are these abject wretches about us, whom our men are now disarming and driving together in flocks, the jaunty men of Pickett's Division, whose steady lines and flashing arms but a few moments since came sweeping up the slope to destroy us? Are these red cloths that our men toss about in derision the "fiery Southern crosses," thrice ardent, the battle flags of the rebellion that waved defiance at the wall? We know, but so sudden has been the transition, we yet can scarce believe.

Just as the fight was over, and the first outburst of victory had a little subsided, when all in front of the crest was noise and confusion—prisoners being collected, small parties in pursuit of them far down into the fields, flags waving, officers giving quick, sharp commands to their men—I stood apart for a few moments upon the crest, by that group of trees which ought to be historic forever, a spectator of the thrilling scene around. Some few musket shots were still heard in the Third Division; and the enemy's guns, almost silent since the advance of his infantry until the moment of his defeat, were dropping a few sullen shells among friend and foe upon the crest. Rebellion fosters such humanity. Near me, saddest sight of the many of such a field and not in keeping with all this noise, were mingled alone the thick dead of Maine and Minnesota, and Michigan and Massachusetts, and the Empire and Keystone States, who, not yet cold, with the blood still oozing from their death-wounds, had given their lives to the country upon that stormy field.

So mingled upon that crest let their honored graves be. Look with me about us. These dead have been avenged already. Where the long lines of the enemy's thousands so proudly advanced, see how thick the silent men of gray are scattered. It is not an hour since these legions were sweeping along so grandly; now sixteen hundred of that fiery mass are strewn among the trampled grass, dead as the clods they load; more than seven thousand, probably eight thousand, are wounded, some there with the dead, in our hands, some fugitive far towards the woods, among them Generals Pettigrew, Garnett,

Kemper, and Armistead, the last three mortally, and the last one in our hands. "Tell General Hancock," he said to Lieutenant Mitchell, Hancock's aid-de-camp, to whom he handed his watch, "that I know I did my country a great wrong when I took up arms against her, for which I am sorry, but for which I cannot live to atone." Four thousand, not wounded, are prisoners of war. More in number of the captured than the captors. Our men are still "gathering them in." Some hold up their hands or a handkerchief in sign of submission; some have hugged the ground to escape our bullets and so are taken, few made resistance after the first moment of our crossing the wall; some yield submissively with good grace, some with grim, dogged aspect, showing that but for the other alternative they could not submit to this. Colonels, and all less grades of officers, in the usual proportion are among them, and all are being stripped of their arms. Such of them as escaped wounds and capture are fleeing routed and panic stricken, and disappearing in the woods. Small arms, more thousands than we can count, are in our hands, scattered over the field. And these defiant battle-flags, some inscribed with "First Manassas," the numerous battles of the Peninsula, "Second Manassas," "South Mountain," "Sharpsburg" (our Antietam), "Fredericksburg," "Chancellorsville," and many more names, our men have, and are showing about, *over thirty of them.*

Such was really the closing scene of the grand drama of Gettysburg.

VIRGINIA WOOLF

The Society of Outsiders and the Prevention of War

Virginia Woolf (1882–1941) was born in England into a social class in which women were rarely encouraged to work or to think. Yet she became one of our most influential novelists and writers, known especially for her innovative narrative technique. Among her novels are *Mrs. Dalloway* (1925), *To the Lighthouse* (1927), and *The Waves* (1931). Woolf's essay collections include *A Room of One's Own* (1929), *The Common Reader* (1938), and *Three Guineas* (1938) from which the following selection is taken.

War, as the result of impersonal forces, is you will agree beyond the grasp of the untrained mind. But war as the result of human nature is another thing. Had you not believed that human nature, the reasons, the emotions of the ordinary man and woman, lead to war, you would not have written asking for our help. You must have argued, men and women, here and now, are able to exert their wills; they are not pawns and puppets dancing on a string held by invisible hands. They can act, and think for themselves. Perhaps even they can influence other people's thoughts and actions. Some such reasoning must have led you to apply to us; and with justification. For happily there is one branch of education which comes under the heading "unpaid-for education"—that understanding of human beings and their motives which, if the word is rid of its scientific associations, might be called psychology. Marriage, the one great profession open to our class since the dawn of time until the year 1919;[1] marriage, the art of choosing the human being with whom to live life successfully, should have taught us some skill in that. But here again another difficulty confronts us. For though many instincts are held more or less in common by both sexes, to fight has always been the man's habit, not the woman's. Law and practice have developed that difference, whether innate or accidental. Scarcely a human being in the course of history has fallen to a woman's rifle; the vast majority of birds and beasts have been killed by you, not by us; it is difficult to judge what we do not share.

How then are we to understand your problem, and if we cannot, how can we answer your question, how to prevent war? The answer based upon our experience and our psychology—Why fight?—is not an answer of any value. Obviously there is for you some glory, some necessity, some satisfaction in fighting which we have never felt or enjoyed. Complete understanding could only be achieved by blood transfusion and memory transfusion—a miracle still beyond the reach of science. But we who live now have a substitute for blood transfusion and memory transfusion which must serve at a pinch. There is that marvellous, perpetually renewed, and as yet largely untapped aid to the understanding of human motives which is provided in our age by biography and autobiography. Also there is the daily paper, history in the raw. There is thus no longer any reason to be confined

[1] The Sex Disqualification Act of 1919 opened all public offices and professions to women. (ED.)

to the minute span of actual experience which is still, for us, so narrow, so circumscribed. We can supplement it by looking at the picture of the lives of others. It is of course only a picture at present, but as such it must serve. It is to biography then that we will turn first, quickly and briefly, in order to attempt to understand what war means to you. Let us extract a few sentences from a biography.

First, this from a soldier's life:

> "I have had the happiest possible life, and have always been working for war, and have now got into the biggest in the prime of life for a soldier. . . . Thank God, we are off in an hour. Such a magnificent regiment! Such men, such horses! Within ten days I hope Francis and I will be riding side by side straight at the Germans."[2]

To which the biographer adds:

> "From the first hour he had been supremely happy, for he had found his true calling."

To that let us add this from an airman's life:

> "We talked of the League of Nations and the prospects of peace and disarmament. On this subject he was not so much militarist as martial. The difficulty to which he could find no answer was that if permanent peace were ever achieved, and armies and navies ceased to exist, there would be no outlet for the manly qualities which fighting developed, and that human physique and human character would deteriorate."[3]

Here, immediately, are three reasons which lead your sex to fight; war is a profession; a source of happiness and excitement; and it is also an outlet for manly qualities, without which men would deteriorate. But that these feelings and opinions are by no means universally held by your sex is proved by the following extract from another biography, the life of a poet who was killed in the European war: Wilfred Owen.

> "Already I have comprehended a light which never will filter into the dogma of any national church: namely, that one of Christ's essential commands was: Passivity at any price! Suffer dishonour and disgrace, but never resort to arms. Be bullied, be outraged, be killed; but do not kill. . . . Thus you see how pure Christianity will not fit in with pure patriotism."

---

[2] *Francis and Riversdale Grenfell,* by John Buchan, pp. 189, 205.

[3] *Antony (Viscount Knebworth),* by the Earl of Lytton, p. 355.

And among some notes for poems that he did not live to write are these:

> "The unnaturalness of weapons. . . . Inhumanity of war. . . . The insupportability of war. . . . Horrible beastliness of war. . . . Foolishness of war."[4]

From these quotations it is obvious that the same sex holds very different opinions about the same thing. But also it is obvious, from today's newspaper, that however many dissentients there are, the great majority of your sex are today in favour of war. The Scarborough Conference of educated men, the Bournemouth Conference of working men are both agreed that to spend £300,000,000 annually upon arms is a necessity. They are of opinion that Wilfred Owen was wrong; that it is better to kill than to be killed. Yet since biography shows that differences of opinion are many, it is plain that there must be some one reason which prevails in order to bring about this overpowering unanimity. Shall we call it, for the sake of brevity, "patriotism"? What then, we must ask next, is this "patriotism" which leads you to go to war? Let the Lord Chief Justice of England interpret it for us:

> "Englishmen are proud of England. For those who have been trained in English schools and universities, and who have done the work of their lives in England, there are few loves stronger than the love we have for our country. When we consider other nations, when we judge the merits of the policy of this country or of that, it is the standard of our own country that we apply. . . . Liberty has made her abode in England. England is the home of democratic institutions. . . . It is true that in our midst there are many enemies of liberty—some of them, perhaps, in rather unexpected quarters. But we are standing firm. It has been said that an Englishman's Home is his Castle. The home of Liberty is in England. And it is a castle indeed—a castle that will be defended to the last. . . . Yes, we are greatly blessed, we Englishmen."[5]

That is a fair general statement of what patriotism means to an educated man and what duties it imposes upon him. But the educated man's sister—what does "patriotism" mean to her? Has she the same reasons for being proud of England, for loving England, for defending England? Has she been "greatly blessed" in England? History and

---

[4] *The Poems of Wilfred Owen,* edited by Edmund Blunden, pp. 25, 41.

[5] Lord Heward, proposing the toast of "England" at the banquet of the Society of St. George at Cardiff.

biography when questioned would seem to show that her position in the home of freedom has been different from her brother's; and psychology would seem to hint that history is not without its effect upon mind and body. Therefore her interpretation of the word "patriotism" may well differ from his. And that difference may make it extremely difficult for her to understand his definition of patriotism and the duties it imposes. If then our answer to your question, "How in your opinion are we to prevent war?" depends upon understanding the reasons, the emotions, the loyalties which lead men to go to war, this letter had better be torn across and thrown into the waste-paper basket. For it seems plain that we cannot understand each other because of these differences. It seems plain that we think differently according as we are born differently; there is a Grenfell point of view; a Knebworth point of view; a Wilfred Owen point of view; a Lord Chief Justice's point of view and the point of view of an educated man's daughter.

The educated man's daughter has now at her disposal an influence which is different from any influence that she has possessed before. It is not the influence which the great lady, the Siren,[6] possesses; nor is it the influence which the educated man's daughter possessed when she had no vote; nor is it the influence which she possessed when she had a vote but was debarred from the right to earn her living. It differs, because it is an influence from which the charm element has been removed; it is an influence from which the money element has been removed. She need no longer use her charm to procure money from her father or brother. Since it is beyond the power of her family to punish her financially she can express her own opinions. In place of the admirations and antipathies which were often unconsciously dictated by the need of money she can declare her genuine likes and dislikes. In short, she need not acquiesce; she can criticize. At last she is in possession of an influence that is disinterested.

Such in rough and rapid outlines is the nature of our new weapon, the influence which the educated man's daughter can exert now that she is able to earn her own living. The question that has next to be discussed, therefore, is how can she use this new weapon to help you prevent war? And it is immediately plain that if there is no difference between men who can earn their livings in the professions

---

[6] A part-human mythic Greek temptress or a woman who is beautiful and seductive. (ED.)

and women who earn their livings, then this letter can end; for if
our point of view is the same as yours then we must add our sixpence to your guinea;[7] follow your methods and repeat your words.
But, whether fortunately or unfortunately, that is not true. The two
classes still differ enormously. And to prove this, we need not have
recourse to the dangerous and uncertain theories of psychologists
and biologists; we can appeal to facts. Take the fact of education.
Your class has been educated at public schools and universities for
five or six hundred years, ours for sixty. Take the fact of property.
Your class possesses in its own right and not through marriage
practically all the capital, all the land, all the valuables, and all the
patronage in England. Our class possesses in its own right and not
through marriage practically none of the capital, none of the land,
none of the valuables, and none of the patronage in England. That
such differences make for very considerable differences in mind and
body, no psychologist or biologist would deny. It would seem to
follow then as an indisputable fact that "we"—meaning by "we" a
whole made up of body, brain, and spirit, influenced by memory and
tradition—must still differ in some essential respects from "you,"
whose body, brain, and spirit have been so differently trained and
are so differently influenced by memory and tradition. Though we
see the same world, we see it through different eyes. Any help we
can give you must be different from that you can give yourselves,
and perhaps the value of that help may lie in the fact of that difference. Therefore before we agree to sign your manifesto or join your
society, it might be well to discover where the difference lies, because
then we may discover where the help lies also. Let us then by way
of a very elementary beginning lay before you a photograph—a
crudely coloured photograph—of your world as it appears to us who
see it from the threshold of the private house; through the shadow
of the veil that St. Paul still lays upon our eyes; from the bridge
which connects the private house with the world of public life.

Your world, then, the world of professional, of public life, seen
from this angle undoubtedly looks queer. At first sight it is enormously impressive. Within quite a small space are crowded together
St. Paul's, the Bank of England, the Mansion House, the massive if
funereal battlements of the Law Courts; and on the other side, Westminster Abbey and the Houses of Parliament.[8] There, we say to

---

[7] A guinea equalled 252 pence. (ED.)

[8] These buildings represent the power of the British Church and state: St. Paul's

ourselves, pausing, in this moment of transition on the bridge, our fathers and brothers have spent their lives. All these hundreds of years they have been mounting those steps, passing in and out of those doors, ascending those pulpits, preaching, moneymaking, administering justice. It is from this world that the private house (somewhere, roughly speaking, in the West End) has derived its creeds, its laws, it clothes and carpets, its beef and mutton. And then, as is now permissible, cautiously pushing aside the swing doors of one of these temples, we enter on tiptoe and survey the scene in greater detail. The first sensation of colossal size, of majestic masonry is broken up into myriad points of amazement mixed with interrogation. Your clothes in the first place make us gape with astonishment. How many, how splendid, how extremely ornate they are—the clothes worn by the educated man in his public capacity! Now you dress in violet; a jewelled crucifix swings on your breast; now your shoulders are covered with lace; now furred with ermine; now slung with many linked chains set with precious stones. Now you wear wigs on your heads; rows of graduated curls descend to your necks. Now your hats are boat-shaped, or cocked; now they mount in cones of black fur; now they are made of brass and scuttle-shaped; now plumes of red, now of blue hair surmount them. Sometimes gowns cover your legs; sometimes gaiters. Tabards embroidered with lions and unicorns swing from your shoulders; metal objects cut in star shapes or in circles glitter and twinkle upon your breasts. Ribbons of all colours—blue, purple, crimson—cross from shoulder to shoulder. After the comparative simplicity of your dress at home, the splendour of your public attire is dazzling.

But far stranger are two other facts that gradually reveal themselves when our eyes have recovered from their first amazement. Not only are whole bodies of men dressed alike summer and winter—a strange characteristic to a sex which changes its clothes according to the season, and for reasons of private taste and comfort—but every button, rosette, and stripe seems to have some symbolical meaning. Some have the right to wear plain buttons only; others rosettes; some may wear a single stripe; others three, four, or five. And each curl or stripe is sewn on at precisely the right distance apart—it may be one inch for one man, one inch and a quarter for another. Rules

Cathedral is the center of the Church of England; Westminster Abbey is the site where all English Rulers are crowned and where many members of royalty, political leaders, and eminent writers are buried; and the Houses of Parliament contain the two legislative bodies of the British government. (ED.)

again regulate the gold wire on the shoulders, the braid on the trousers, the cockades on the hats—but no single pair of eyes can observe all these distinctions, let alone account for them accurately.

Even stranger, however, than the symbolic splendour of your clothes are the ceremonies that take place when you wear them. Here you kneel; there you bow; here you advance in procession behind a man carrying a silver poker; here you mount a carved chair; here you appear to do homage to a piece of painted wood; here you abase yourselves before tables covered with richly worked tapestry. And whatever these ceremonies may mean, you perform them always together, always in step, always in the uniform proper to the man and the occasion.

Apart from the ceremonies, such decorative apparel appears to us at first sight strange in the extreme. For dress, as we use it, is comparatively simple. Besides the prime function of covering the body, it has two other offices—that it creates beauty for the eye, and that it attracts the admiration of your sex. Since marriage until the year 1919—less than twenty years ago—was the only profession open to us, the enormous importance of dress to a woman can hardly be exaggerated. It was to her what clients are to you—dress was her chief, perhaps her only, method of becoming Lord Chancellor.[9] But your dress in its immense elaboration has obviously another function. It not only covers nakedness, gratifies vanity, and creates pleasure for the eye, but it serves to advertise the social, professional, or intellectual standing of the wearer. If you will excuse the humble illustration, your dress fulfils the same function as the tickets in a grocer's shop. But, here, instead of saying, "This is margarine; this pure butter; this is the finest butter in the market," it says, "This man is a clever man—he is Master of Arts; this man is a very clever man—he is Doctor of Letters; this man is a most clever man—he is a Member of the Order of Merit." It is this function—the advertisement function—of your dress that seems to us most singular. In the opinion of St. Paul, such advertisement, at any rate for our sex, was unbecoming and immodest; until a very few years ago we were denied the use of it. And still the tradition, or belief, lingers among us that to express worth of any kind, whether intellectual or moral, by wearing pieces of metal, or ribbon, coloured hoods or gowns, is a barbarity which deserves the ridicule which we bestow upon the rites

[9] President of the House of Lords, one of the two governing bodies comprising the British Parliament (ED.)

of savages. A woman who advertised her motherhood by a tuft of horsehair on the left shoulder would scarcely, you will agree, be a venerable object.

But what light does our difference here throw upon the problem before us? What connection is there between the sartorial splendours of the educated man and the photograph of ruined houses and dead bodies? Obviously the connection between dress and war is not far to seek; your finest clothes are those that you wear as soldiers. Since the red and the gold, the brass and the feathers are discarded upon active service, it is plain that their expensive and not, one might suppose, hygienic splendour is invented partly in order to impress the beholder with the majesty of the military office, partly in order through their vanity to induce young men to become soldiers. Here, then, our influence and our difference might have some effect; we, who are forbidden to wear such clothes ourselves, can express the opinion that the wearer is not to us a pleasing or an impressive spectacle. He is on the contrary a ridiculous, a barbarous, a displeasing spectacle. But as the daughters of educated men we can use our influence more effectively in another direction, upon our own class— the class of educated men. For there, in courts and universities, we find the same love of dress. There, too, are velvet and silk, fur and ermine. We can say that for educated men to emphasize their superiority over other people, either in birth or intellect, by dressing differently, or by adding titles before, or letters after their names are acts that rouse competition and jealousy—emotions which, as we need scarcely draw upon biography to prove, nor ask psychology to show, have their share in encouraging a disposition towards war. If we then express the opinion that such distinctions make those who possess them ridiculous and learning contemptible, we should do something, indirectly, to discourage the feelings that lead to war. Happily we can now do more than express an opinion; we can refuse all such distinctions and all such uniforms for ourselves. This would be a slight but definite contribution to the problem before us—how to prevent war; and one that a different training and a different tradition puts more easily within our reach than within yours.

That request then for a guinea answered, and the cheque signed, only one further request of yours remains to be considered—it is that we should fill up a form and become members of your society. On the face of it that seems a simple request, easily granted. For what can be simpler than to join the society to which this guinea has just been contributed? On the face of it, how easy, how simple;

but in the depths, how difficult, how complicated. . . . What possible
doubts, what possible hesitations can those dots stand for? What
reason or what emotion can make us hesitate to become members of
a society whose aims we approve, to whose funds we have contributed? It may be neither reason nor emotion, but something more
profound and fundamental than either. It may be difference. Different
we are, as facts have proved, both in sex and in education. And it is
from that difference, as we have already said, that our help can come,
if help we can, to protect liberty, to prevent war. But if we sign this
form which implies a promise to become active members of your
society, it would seem that we must lose that difference and therefore
sacrifice that help. To explain why this is so is not easy, even though
the gift of a guinea has made it possible (so we have boasted) to
speak freely without fear or flattery. Let us then keep the form
unsigned on the table before us while we discuss, so far as we are
able, the reasons and the emotions which make us hesitate to sign
it. For those reasons and emotions have their origin deep in the
darkness of ancestral memory; they have grown together in some
confusion; it is very difficult to untwist them in the light.

To begin with an elementary distinction: a society is a conglomeration of people joined together for certain aims; while you, who
write in your own person with your own hand are single. You the
individual are a man whom we have reason to respect; a man of the
brotherhood, to which, as biography proves, many brothers have
belonged. Thus Anne Clough,[10] describing her brother, says: "Arthur
is my best friend and adviser. . . . Arthur is the comfort and joy of
my life; it is for him, and from him, that I am incited to seek after
all that is lovely and of good report." To which William Wordsworth,[11] speaking of his sister but answering the other as if one
nightingale called to another in the forests of the past, replies:

> "The Blessing of my later years
> Was with me when a Boy:
> She gave me eyes, she gave me ears;
> And humble cares, and delicate fears;
> A heart, the fountain of sweet tears;
> And love, and thought, and joy."[12]

---

[10] Anne Clough (1820–1892) was an English educator and feminist who founded
Newnham College, the first residential college for women at Cambridge University.
(ED.)

[11] William Wordsworth (1770–1850) was an English Romantic poet. (ED.)

Such was, such perhaps still is, the relationship of many brothers and sisters in private, as individuals. They respect each other and help each other and have aims in common. Why then, if such can be their private relationship, as biography and poetry prove, should their public relationship, as law and history prove, be so very different? And here, since you are a lawyer, with a lawyer's memory, it is not necessary to remind you of certain decrees of English law from its first records to the year 1919 by way of proving that the public, the society relationship of brother and sister has been very different from the private. The very word "society" sets tolling in memory the dismal bells of a harsh music; shall not, shall not, shall not. You shall not learn; you shall not earn; you shall not own; you shall not—such was the society relationship of brother to sister for many centuries. And though it is possible, and to the optimistic credible, that in time a new society may ring a carillon of splendid harmony, and your letter heralds it, that day is far distant. Inevitably we ask ourselves, is there not something in the conglomeration of people into societies that releases what is most selfish and violent, least rational and humane in the individuals themselves? Inevitably we look upon society, so kind to you, so harsh to us, as an ill-fitting form that distorts the truth; deforms the mind; fetters the will. Inevitably we look upon societies as conspiracies that sink the private brother, whom many of us have reason to respect, and inflate in his stead a monstrous male, loud of voice, hard of fist, childishly intent upon scoring the floor of the earth with chalk marks, within whose mystic boundaries human beings are penned, rigidly, separately, artificially; where, daubed red and gold, decorated like a savage with feathers he goes through mystic rites and enjoys the dubious pleasures of power and dominion while we, "his" women, are locked in the private house without share in the many societies of which his society is composed. For such reasons compact as they are of many memories and emotions—for who shall analyse the complexity of a mind that holds so deep a reservoir of time past within it?—it seems both wrong for us rationally and impossible for us emotionally to fill up your form and join your society. For by so doing we should merge our identity in yours; follow and repeat and score still deeper the old worn ruts in which society, like a gramophone whose needle has stuck, is grinding out with intolerable unanimity "Three hundred

[12] *Memoir of Anne J. Clough,* by B. A. Clough, pp. 38, 67. "The Sparrow's Nest," by William Wordsworth.

millions spent upon arms." We should not give effect to a view which our own experience of "society" should have helped us to envisage. Thus, Sir, while we respect you as a private person and prove it by giving you a guinea to spend as you choose, we believe that we can help you most effectively by refusing to join your society; by working for our common ends—justice and equality and liberty for all men and women—outside your society, not within.

But this, you will say, if it means anything, can only mean that you, the daughters of educated men, who have promised us your positive help, refuse to join our society in order that you may make another of your own. And what sort of society do you propose to found outside ours, but in co-operation with it, so that we may both work together for our common ends? That is a question which you have every right to ask, and which we must try to answer in order to justify our refusal to sign the form you send. Let us then draw rapidly in outline the kind of society which the daughters of educated men might found and join outside your society but in co-operation with its ends. In the first place, this new society, you will be relieved to learn, would have no honorary treasurer, for it would need no funds. It would have no office, no committee, no secretary; it would call no meeting; it would hold no conferences. If name it must have, it could be called the Outsiders' Society. That is not a resonant name, but it has the advantage that it squares with facts—the facts of history, of law, of biography; even, it may be, with the still hidden facts of our still unknown psychology. It would consist of educated men's daughters working in their own class—how indeed can they work in any other?—and by their own methods for liberty, equality, and peace. Their first duty, to which they would bind themselves not by oath, for oaths and ceremonies have no part in a society which must be anonymous and elastic before everything, would be not to fight with arms. This is easy for them to observe, for in fact, as the papers inform us, "the Army Council have no intention of opening recruiting for any women's corps."[13] The country ensures it. Next they would refuse in the event of war to make munitions or nurse the wounded. Since in the last war both these activities were mainly discharged by

---

[13] "It was stated yesterday at the War Office that the Army Council have no intention of opening recruiting for any women's corps" (*The Times*, October 22nd, 1937). This marks a prime distinction between the sexes. Pacifism is enforced upon women. Men are still allowed liberty of choice.

the daughters of working men, the pressure upon them here too would be slight, though probably disagreeable. On the other hand the next duty to which they would pledge themselves is one of considerable difficulty, and calls not only for courage and initiative, but for the special knowledge of the educated man's daughter. It is, briefly, not to incite their brothers to fight, or to dissuade them, but to maintain an attitude of complete indifference. But the attitude expressed by the word "indifference" is so complex and of such importance that it needs even here further definition. Indifference in the first place must be given a firm footing upon fact. As it is a fact that she cannot understand what instinct compels him, what glory, what interest, what manly satisfaction fighting provides for him— "without war there would be no outlet for the manly qualities which fighting develops"—as fighting thus is a sex characteristic which she cannot share, the counterpart some claim of the maternal instinct which he cannot share, so is it an instinct which she cannot judge. The outsider therefore must leave him free to deal with this instinct by himself, because liberty of opinion must be respected, especially when it is based upon an instinct which is as foreign to her as centuries of tradition and education can make it. This is a fundamental and instinctive distinction upon which indifference may be based. But the outsider will make it her duty not merely to base her indifference upon instinct, but upon reason. When he says, as history proves that he has said, and may say again, "I'm fighting to protect our country" and thus seeks to rouse her patriotic emotion, she will ask herself, "What does 'our country' mean to me an outsider?" To decide this she will analyse the meaning of patriotism in her own case. She will inform herself of the position of her sex and her class in the past. She will inform herself of the amount of land, wealth, and property in the possession of her own sex and class in the present—how much of "England" in fact belongs to her. From the same sources she will inform herself of the legal protection which the law has given her in the past and now gives her. And if he adds that he is fighting to protect her body, she will reflect upon the degree of physical protection that she now enjoys when the words "Air Raid Precaution" are written on blank walls. And if he says that he is fighting to protect England from foreign rule, she will reflect that for her there are no "foreigners," since by law she becomes a foreigner if she marries a foreigner. And she will do her best to make this a fact, not by forced fraternity, but by human sympathy. All these facts will convince her reason (to put it in a nutshell) that her sex and class has very little to thank England for in the past; not much to thank England for in the present; while the security of her person in the future is highly dubious. But probably she will have imbibed, even from the governess, some romantic notion that Englishmen, those fathers and grandfathers whom she sees marching in the picture of history, are "superior" to the men of other countries. This she will consider it her duty to check by comparing French historians with English; German with French; the testimony of the ruled—the Indians or the Irish, say—with the claims made by their rulers. Still some "patriotic" emotion, some ingrained belief in the intellectual superiority of her own country over other countries may remain. Then she will compare English painting with French painting; English music with German music; English literature with Greek literature, for translations abound. When all these comparisons have been faithfully made by the use of reason, the outsider will find herself in possession of very good reasons for her indifference. She will find that she has no good reason to ask her brother to fight on her behalf to protect "our" country. " 'Our country,' " she will say, "throughout the greater part of its history has treated me as a slave; it has denied me education or any share in its possessions. 'Our' country still ceases to be mine if I marry a foreigner. 'Our' country denies me the means of protecting myself, forces me to pay others a very large sum annually to protect me, and is so little able, even so, to protect me that Air Raid precautions are written on the wall. Therefore if you insist upon fighting to protect me, or 'our' country, let it be understood, soberly and rationally between us, that you are fighting to gratify a sex instinct which I cannot share; to procure benefits which I have not shared and probably will not share; but not to gratify my instincts, or to protect myself or my country. For," the outsider will say, "in fact, as a woman, I have no country. As a woman I want no country. As a woman my country is the whole world." And if, when reason has said its say, still some obstinate emotion remains, some love of England dropped into a child's ears by the cawing of rooks in an elm tree, by the splash of waves on a beach, or by English voices murmuring nursery rhymes, this drop of pure, if irrational, emotion she will make serve her to give to England first what she desires of peace and freedom for the whole world.

Such then will be the nature of her "indifference" and from this indifference certain actions must follow. She will bind herself to take no share in patriotic demonstrations; to assent to no form of national self-praise; to make no part of any claque or audience that encourages war; to absent herself from military displays, tournaments, tattoos, prize-givings, and all such ceremonies as encourage the desire to impose "our" civilization of "our" dominion upon other people. The psychology of private life, moreover, warrants the belief that this use of indifference by the daughters of educated men would help materially to prevent war. For psychology would seem to show that it is far harder for human beings to take action when other people are indifferent and allow them complete freedom of action, than when their actions are made the centre of excited emotion. The small boy struts and trumpets outside the window: implore him to stop; he goes on; say nothing; he stops. That the daughters of educated men then should give their brothers neither the white feather of cowardice nor the red feather of courage, but no feather at all; that they should shut the bright eyes that rain influence, or let those eyes look elsewhere when war is discussed—that is the duty to which outsiders will train themselves in peace before the threat of death inevitably makes reason powerless.

The outsiders then would bind themselves not only to earn their own livings, but to earn them so expertly that their refusal to earn them would be a matter of concern to the work master. They would bind themselves to obtain full knowledge of professional practices, and to reveal any instance of tyranny or abuse in their professions. And they would bind themselves not to continue to make money in any profession, but to cease all competition and to practise their profession experimentally, in the interests of research and for love of the work itself, when they had earned enough to live upon. Also they would bind themselves to remain outside any profession hostile to freedom, such as the making or the improvement of the weapons of war. And they would bind themselves to refuse to take office or honour from any society which, while professing to respect liberty, restricts it, like the universities of Oxford and Cambridge. And they would consider it their duty to investigate the claims of all public societies to which, like the Church and the universities, they are forced to contribute as taxpayers as carefully and fearlessly as they would investigate the claims of private societies to which they contribute voluntarily. They would make it their business to scrutinize the endowments of the schools and universities and the objects upon which that money is spent. As with the educational, so with the religious profession. By reading the New Testament in the first place and next those divines and historians whose works are all easily accessible to the daughters of educated men, they would make it their business to have some knowledge of the Christian religion and its history. Further they would inform themselves of the practice of that religion by attending Church services, by analysing the spiritual and intellectual value of sermons; by criticizing the opinions of men whose profession is religion as freely as they would criticize the opinions of any other body of men. Thus they would be creative in their activities, not merely critical. By criticizing education they would help to create a civilized society which protects culture and intellectual liberty. By criticizing religion they would attempt to free the religious spirit from its present servitude and would help, if need be, to create a new religion based, it might well be, upon the New Testament, but, it might well be, very different from the religion now erected upon that basis. And in all this, and in much more than we have time to particularize, they would be helped, you will agree, by their position as outsiders, that freedom from unreal loyalties, that freedom from interested motives which are at present assured them by the State.

It would be easy to define in greater number and more exactly the duties of those who belong to the Society of Outsiders, but not profitable. Elasticity is essential; and some degree of secrecy, as will be shown later, is at present even more essential. But the description thus loosely and imperfectly given is enough to show you, Sir, that the Society of Outsiders has the same ends as your society—freedom, equality, peace; but that it seeks to achieve them by the means that a different sex, a different tradition, a different education, and the different values which result from those differences have placed within our reach. Broadly speaking, the main distinction between us who are outside society and you who are inside society must be that whereas you will make use of the means provided by your position— leagues, conferences, campaigns, great names, and all such public measures as your wealth and political influence place within your reach—we, remaining outside, will experiment not with public means in public but with private means in private.

PAUL FUSSELL

The Real War 1939–1945

Paul Fussell (1924–   ) is a professor of English who established
himself as a popularizer of modern history with *The Great War and
Modern Memory* (1975), which won the National Book Award.
Other books include *Class: a Guide through the American Status
System* (1983), *Thank God for the Atom Bomb and Other Essays*
(1988), *Wartime: Understanding and Behavior in the Second World
War* (1989), and *Bad* (1991). The following selection first appeared
in the *Atlantic*.

What was it about the Second World War that moved the troops to
constant verbal subversion and contempt? What was it that made
the Americans, especially, so fertile with insult and cynicism, calling
women Marines BAMS (broad-assed Marines) and devising SNAFU,
with its offspring TARFU ("Things are really fucked up"), FUBAR
("Fucked up beyond all recognition"), and the perhaps less satisfying
FUBB ("Fucked up beyond belief")? It was not just the danger and
fear, the boredom and uncertainty and loneliness and deprivation. It
was the conviction that optimistic publicity and euphemism had
rendered their experience so falsely that it would never be readily
communicable. They knew that in its representation to the laity,
what was happening to them was systematically sanitized and Norman Rockwellized, not to mention Disneyfied. They knew that despite the advertising and publicity, where it counted their arms and
equipment were worse than the Germans'. They knew that their
automatic rifles (First World War vintage) were slower and clumsier,
and they knew that the Germans had a much better light machine
gun. They knew, despite official assertions to the contrary, that the
Germans had real smokeless powder for their small arms and that
they did not. They knew that their own tanks, both American and
British, were ridiculously underarmed and underarmored, so that
they would inevitably be destroyed in an open encounter with an
equal number of German panzers. They knew that the anti-tank
mines supplied to them became unstable in subfreezing weather, and
that truckloads of them blew up in the winter of 1944–1945. And
they knew that the single greatest weapon of the war, the atomic
bomb excepted, was the German 88-mm flat-trajectory gun, which

brought down thousands of bombers and tens of thousands of soldiers. The Allies had nothing as good, despite the fact that one of them had designated itself the world's greatest industrial power. The troops' disillusion and their ironic response, in song and satire and sullen contempt, came from knowing that the home front then could (and very likely historiography later would) be aware of none of these things.

The Great War brought forth the stark, depressing *Journey's End;* the Second, as John Ellis notes in *The Sharp End,* the tuneful *South Pacific.* The real war was tragic and ironic beyond the power of any literary or philosophic analysis to suggest, but in unbombed America especially, the meaning of the war seemed inaccessible. Thus, as experience, the suffering was wasted. The same tricks of publicity and advertising might have succeeded in sweetening the actualities of Vietnam if television and a vigorous, uncensored, moral journalism hadn't been brought to bear. Because the Second World War was fought against palpable evil, and thus was a sort of moral triumph, we have been reluctant to probe very deeply into its murderous requirements. America has not yet understood what the war was like and thus has been unable to use such understanding to reinterpret and redefine the national reality and to arrive at something like public maturity.

"MEMBERS MISSING"

In the popular and genteel iconography of war during the bourgeois age, all the way from eighteenth- and nineteenth-century history paintings to twentieth-century photographs, the bodies of the dead are intact, if inert—sometimes bloody and sprawled in awkward positions, but, except for the absence of life, plausible and acceptable simulacra of the people they once were. But there is a contrary and much more "realistic" convention represented in, say, the Bayeaux tapestry,[1] whose ornamental border displays numerous severed heads and limbs. That convention is honored likewise in the Renaissance awareness of what happens to the body in battle. In Shakespeare's *Henry V* the soldier Michael Williams assumes the traditional understanding when he observes,

> But if the cause be not good, the King himself hath a heavy reckoning to make, when all those legs and arms and heads chopped off in a battle

[1] an embroidery 230 feet long recording the Norman conquest of England led by William the Conqueror (ED.)

shall join together at the latter day, and cry all, 'We died at such a place'—some swearing, some crying for a surgeon, some upon their wives left poor behind them, some upon the debts they owe, some upon their children rawly left.

And Goya's eighty etchings known as *The Disasters of War,* depicting events during the Peninsular War, feature plentiful dismembered and beheaded cadavers. One of the best-known of Goya's images is that of a naked body, its right arm severed, impaled on a tree.

But these examples date from well before the modern age of publicity and euphemism. The peruser (*reader* would be the wrong word) of the picture collection *Life Goes to War* (1977), a volume so popular and widely distributed as to constitute virtually a definitive and official anthology of Second World War photographs, will find even in its starkest images no depiction of bodies dismembered. There are three separated heads shown, but all, significantly, are Asian— one the head of a Chinese soldier hacked off by the Japanese at Nanking; one a Japanese soldier's badly burnt head (complete with helmet), mounted as a trophy on an American tank at Guadalcanal; and one a former Japanese head, now a skull sent home as a souvenir to a girlfriend by her navy beau in the Pacific. No American dismemberings were registered, even in the photographs of Tarawa and Iwo Jima. American bodies (decently clothed) are occasionally in evidence, but they are notably intact. The same is true in other popular collections of photographs, like *Collier's Photographic History of World War II,* Ronald Heiferman's *World War II,* A.J.P. Taylor's *History of World War II,* and Charles Herridge's *Pictorial History of World War II.* In these, no matter how severely wounded, Allied soldiers are never shown suffering what in the Vietnam War was termed traumatic amputation: everyone has all his limbs, his hands and feet and digits, not to mention an expression of courage and cheer. And recalling Shakespeare and Goya, it would be a mistake to assume that dismembering was more common when warfare was largely a matter of cutting weapons, like swords and sabers. Their results are nothing compared with the work of bombs, machine guns, pieces of shell, and high explosives in general. The difference between the two traditions of representation is not a difference in military technique. It is a difference in sensibility, especially in the ability of a pap-fed public to face unpleasant facts, like the actualities apparent at the site of a major airplane accident.

What annoyed the troops and augmented their sardonic, contemptuous attitude toward those who viewed them from afar was in large part this public innocence about the bizarre damage suffered by the human body in modern war. The troops could not contemplate without anger the lack of public knowledge of the Graves Registration form used by the U.S. Army Quartermaster Corps, with its space for indicating "Members Missing." You would expect frontline soldiers to be struck and hurt by bullets and shell fragments, but such is the popular insulation from the facts that you would not expect them to be hurt, sometimes killed, by being struck by parts of their friends' bodies violently detached. If you asked a wounded soldier or Marine what hit him, you'd hardly be ready for the answer "My buddy's head," or his sergeant's heel or his hand, or a Japanese leg, complete with shoe and puttees, or the West Point ring on his captain's severed hand. What drove the troops to fury was the complacent, unimaginative innocence of their home fronts and rear echelons about such an experience as the following, repeated in essence tens of thousands of times. Captain Peter Royle, a British artillery forward observer, was moving up a hill in a night attack in North Africa. "I was following about twenty paces behind," he wrote in a memoir,

> when there was a blinding flash a few yards in front of me. I had no idea what it was and fell flat on my face. I found out soon enough: a number of the infantry were carrying mines strapped to the small of their backs, and either a rifle or machine gun bullet had struck one, which had exploded, blowing the man into three pieces—two legs and head and chest. His inside was strewn on the hillside and I crawled into it in the darkness.

In war, as in air accidents, insides are much more visible than it is normally well to imagine. And there's an indication of what can be found on the ground after an air crash in one soldier's memories of the morning after an artillery exchange in North Africa. Neil Mc-Callum and his friend "S." came upon the body of a man who had been lying on his back when a shell, landing at his feet, had eviscerated him:

> "Good God," said S., shocked, "here's one of his fingers." S. stubbed with his toe at the ground some feet from the corpse. There is more horror in a severed digit than in a man dying: it savors of mutilation. "Christ," went on S. in a very low voice, "look, it's not his *finger*."

In the face of such horror, the distinction between friend and enemy vanishes, and the violent dismemberment of any human being becomes traumatic. After the disastrous Canadian raid at Dieppe, German soldiers observed: "The dead on the beach—I've never seen

such obscenities before." "There were pieces of human beings litter-
ing the beach. There were headless bodies, there were legs, there
were arms." There were even shoes "with feet in them." The soldiers
on one side know what the soldiers on the other side understand
about dismemberment and evisceration, even if that knowledge is
hardly shared by the civilians behind them. Hence the practice among
German U-boats of carrying plenty of animal intestines to shoot to
the surface to deceive those imagining that their depth charges have
done the job. Some U-boats, it was said, carried (in cold storage)
severed legs and arms to add verisimilitude. But among the thousands
of published photographs of sailors and submariners being rescued
after torpedoings and sinkings, there was no evidence of severed
limbs, intestines, or floating parts.

If American stay-at-homes could be almost entirely protected
from an awareness of the looks and smells of the real war, the British,
at least those living in bombed areas, could not. But even then, as
one Briton noted in 1941, "we shall never know half of the history . . .
of these times." What prompted that observation was this incident:
"The other night not half a mile from me a middle-aged woman [in
the civilian defense] went out with an ambulance. In a smashed
house she saw something she thought was a mop. It was no mop
but a man's head." So unwilling is the imagination to dwell on
genuine—as opposed to fictional or theatrical—horrors that, indeed,
"we shall never know half of the history . . . of these times." At home
under the bombs in April, 1941, Frances Faviell was suddenly aware
that the whole house was coming down on top of her, and she
worried about "Anne," who was in bed on the top floor.

> With great difficulty I raised my head and shook it free of heavy, choking,
> dusty stuff. An arm had fallen round my neck—a warm, living arm, and
> for one moment I thought that Richard had entered in the darkness and
> was holding me, but when very cautiously I raised my hand to it, I found
> that it was a woman's bare arm with two rings on the third finger and
> it stopped short in a sticky mess.

You can't take much of that sort of thing without going mad, as
General Sir John Hackett understood when he saw that the wild
destruction of enemy human beings had in it less of satisfaction than
of distress. Injured and on the German side of the line at Arnhem,
he was being taken to the German medical installation. Along the
road he saw "half a body, just naked buttocks and the legs joined on
and no more of it than that." For those who might have canted that
the only good German is a dead German, Hackett has a message:

"There was no comfort here. It was like being in a strange and terrible nightmare from which you longed to wake and could not."

THE DEMOCRACY OF FEAR

In the great war Wilfred Owen was driven very near to madness by having to remain for some time next to the scattered body pieces of one of his friends. He had numerous counterparts in the Second World War. At the botched assault on Tarawa Atoll, one coxswain at the helm of a landing vessel went quite mad, perhaps at the shock of steering through all the severed heads and limbs near the shore. One Marine battalion commander, badly wounded, climbed above the rising tide onto a pile of American bodies. Next afternoon he was found there, mad. But madness did not require the spectacle of bodies just like yours messily torn apart. Fear continued over long periods would do the job, as on the merchant and Royal Navy vessels on the Murmansk run, where "grown men went steadily and fixedly insane before each other's eyes," as Tristan Jones testified in *Heart of Oak*. Madness was likewise familiar in submarines, especially during depth-bomb attacks. One U.S. submariner reported that during the first months of the Pacific war such an attack sent three men "stark raving mad": they had to be handcuffed and tied to their bunks. Starvation and thirst among prisoners of the Japanese, and also among downed fliers adrift on rafts, drove many insane, and in addition to drinking their urine they tried to relieve their thirst by biting their comrades' jugular veins and sucking the blood. In one sense, of course, the whole war was mad, and every participant insane from the start, but in a strictly literal sense the result of the years of the bombing of Berlin and its final destruction by the Russian army was, for much of the population, actual madness. Just after the surrender, according to Douglas Botting, in *From the Ruins of the Reich,* some 50,000 orphans could be found living in holes like animals, "some of them one-eyed or one-legged veterans of seven or so, many so deranged by the bombing and the Russian attack that they screamed at the sight of any uniform, even a Salvation Army one."

Although in the Great War madness among the troops was commonly imputed to the effects of concussion ("shell shock"), in the Second it was more frankly attributed to fear, and in contrast to the expectations of heroic behavior which set the tone of the earlier war, the fact of fear was now squarely to be faced. The result was a whole new literature of fear, implying that terror openly confessed argued no moral disgrace, although failure to control visible symptoms is reprehensible. The official wartime attitude toward the subject was often expressed by quoting Marshal Ney: "The one who says he never knew fear is a compound liar." As the 1943 U.S. *Officer's Guide* goes on to instruct its anxious tyros,

> Physical courage is little more than the ability to control the physical fear which all normal men have, and cowardice does not consist in being afraid but in giving away to fear. What, then, keeps the soldier from giving away to fear? The answer is simply—his desire to retain the good opinion of his friends and associates . . . his pride smothers his fear.

The whole trick for the officer is to seem what you would be, and the formula for dealing with fear is ultimately rhetorical and theatrical: regardless of your actual feelings, you must simulate a carriage that will affect your audience as fearless, in the hope that you will be imitated, or at least not be the agent of spreading panic. Advice proffered to enlisted men admitted as frankly that fear was a normal "problem" and suggested ways of controlling it. Some of these are indicated in a wartime publication of the U.S. National Research Council, *Psychology for the Fighting Man.* Even if it is undeniable that in combat everyone will be "scared—terrified," there are some antidotes: keeping extra busy with tasks involving details, and engaging in roll calls and countings-off, to emphasize the proximity of buddies, both as support and as audience. And there is a "command" solution to the fear problem which has been popular among military theorists at least since the Civil War: when under shelling and mortar fire and scared stiff, the infantry should alleviate the problem by moving—never back but forward. This will enable trained personnel to take care of the wounded and will bring troops close enough to the enemy to make him stop the shelling. That it will also bring them close enough to put them within range of rifles and machine guns and hand grenades is what the theorists know but don't mention. The troops know it, which is why they like to move *back.* This upper- or remote-echelon hope that fear can be turned, by argument and reasoning, into something with the appearance of courage illustrates the overlap between the implausible persuasions of advertising and those of modern military motivators.

There was a lot of language devoted to such rationalizing of the irrational. A little booklet issued to infantry replacements joining the Fifth Army in Italy contained tips to ease the entry of innocents into combat: Don't believe all the horror stories circulating in the outfit you're joining. Don't carry too much stuff. Don't excrete in your foxhole—if you can't get out, put some dirt on a shovel, go on that, and throw the load out. Keep your rifle clean and ready. Don't tape down the handles of your grenades for fear of their flying off accidentally—it takes too long to get the tape off. Learn to dig in fast when shelling starts. Watch the ground for evidence of mines and booby traps. On the move, keep contact but don't bunch up. And use common sense in your fight against fear:

> Don't be too scared. Everybody is afraid, but you can learn to control your fear. And, as non-coms point out, "you have a good chance of getting through if you don't lose your head. Being too scared is harmful to you." Remember that a lot of noise you hear is ours, and not dangerous. It may surprise you that on the whole, many more are pulled out for sickness or accident than become battle casualties.

(After that bit of persuasion, the presence of first-aid sections on "If You Get Hit" and "If a Buddy Gets Hit" seems a bit awkward.)

This open, practical confrontation of a subject usually unmentioned has its counterpart in the higher reaches of the wartime literature of fear. The theme of Alan Rook's poem "Dunkirk Pier," enunciated in the opening stanza, is one hardly utterable during earlier wars:

> Deeply across the waves of our darkness fear
> like the silent octopus feeling, groping, clear
> as a star's reflection, nervous and cold as a bird,
> tells us that pain, tells us that death is near.

William Collins's "Ode to Fear," published in 1746, when the average citizen had his wars fought by others whom he never met, is a remote allegorical and allusive performance lamenting the want of powerful emotion in contemporary poetry. C. Day Lewis's "Ode to Fear" of 1943 is not literary but literal, frank, down-to-earth, appropriately disgusting.

> Now fear has come again
> To live with us
> In poisoned intimacy like pus. . . .

And fear is exhibited very accurately in its physical and psychological symptoms:

> The bones, the stalwart spine,
> The legs like bastions,
> The nerves, the heart's natural combustions,
> The head that hives our active thoughts—all pine,
> Are quenched or paralyzed

When Fear puts unexpected questions
And makes the heroic body freeze like a beast
   surprised.

The new frankness with which fear would be acknowledged in this modernist, secular, psychologically self-conscious wartime was registered in W. H. Auden's "September 1, 1939," in which the speaker, "uncertain and afraid," observes the "waves of anger and fear" washing over the face of the earth. And the new frankness became the virtual subject and center of *The Age of Anxiety,* which Auden wrote from 1944 to 1946.

Civilian bombing enjoined a new frankness on many Britons. "Perfect fear casteth out love" was Cyril Connolly's travesty of I John 4:18,[2] as if he were thoroughly acquainted with the experience of elbowing his dearest aside at the shelter entrance.

If the anonymous questionnaire, that indispensable mechanism of the social sciences, had been widely used during the Great War, more perhaps could be known or safely conjectured about the actualities of terror on the Western Front. Questionnaires were employed during the Second World War, and American soldiers were asked about the precise physical signs of their fear. The soldiers testified that they were well acquainted with such impediments to stability as (in order of frequency) "Violent pounding of the heart, sinking feeling in the stomach, shaking or trembling all over, feeling sick at the stomach, cold sweat, feeling weak or faint."

More than a quarter of the soldiers in one division admitted that they'd been so scared they'd vomited, and almost a quarter said that at terrifying moments they'd lost control of their bowels. Ten percent had urinated in their pants. As John Ellis observes of these data,

> Stereotypes of "manliness" and "guts" can readily accommodate the fact that a man's stomach or heart might betray his nervousness, but they make less allowance for his shitting his pants or wetting himself.

And furthermore, "If over one-fifth of the men in one division actually admitted that they had fouled themselves, it is a fair assumption that many more actually did so." One of the commonest fears, indeed, is that of wetting oneself and betraying one's fear for all to see by the most childish symptom. The fear of this fear augments as the rank rises: for a colonel to wet his pants under shellfire is much worse than for a PFC. The U.S. Marine Eugene B. Sledge confessed that

---

[2] "In love there is no room for fear, but perfect love drives out fear, because fear implies punishment, and whoever is afraid has not come to perfection in love." (ED.)

just before he landed at Peleliu, "I felt nauseated and feared that my bladder would surely empty itself and reveal me to be the coward I was."

If perfect fear casteth out love, perfect shame can cast out even agony. During the Normandy invasion a group of American soldiers came upon a paratroop sergeant caught by his chute in a tree. He had broken his leg, and fouled himself as well. He was so ashamed that he begged the soldiers not to come near him, despite his need to be cut down and taken care of. "We just cut off his pants," reported one of the soldiers who found him, "and gently washed him all over, so he wouldn't be humiliated at his next stop."

Men more experienced than that paratrooper had learned to be comfortable with the new frankness. A soldier unused to combat heard his sergeant utter an obscenity when their unit was hit by German 88 fire:

> I asked him if he was hit and he sort of smiled and said no, he had just pissed his pants. He always pissed them, he said, just when things started and then he was okay. He wasn't making any apologies either, and then I realized something wasn't quite right with me either. There was something warm down there and it seemed to be running down my leg. . . .
>
> I told the sarge, I said, "Sarge, I've pissed too," or something like that, and he grinned and said, "Welcome to the war."

Other public signs of fear are almost equally common, if even more "comic." One's mouth grows dry and black, and a strange squeaking or quacking comes out, joined sometimes with a stammer. It is very hard for a field-grade officer to keep his dignity when that happens.

For the ground troops, artillery and mortar fire were the most terrifying, partly because their noise was so deafening and unignorable, and partly because the damage they caused the body—sometimes total disappearance or atomization into tiny red bits—was worse than most damage by bullets. To be killed by bullets seemed "so clean and surgical" to Sledge. "But shells would not only tear and rip the body, they tortured one's mind almost beyond the brink of sanity." An occasional reaction to the terror of shelling was audible "confession." One American infantryman cringing under artillery fire in the Ardennes suddenly blurted out to his buddies, "In London I fucked prostitutes and then robbed them of their money." The shelling over, the soldier never mentioned this utterance again, nor did his friends, everyone understanding its stimulus and its meaning.

But for the infantry there was something to be feared almost as much as shelling: the German *Schü* mine, scattered freely just under the surface of the ground, which blew your foot entirely off if you stepped on it. For years after the war ex-soldiers seized up when confronted by patches of grass and felt safe only when walking on asphalt or concrete. Fear among the troops was probably greatest in the staging areas just before D-Day: that was the largest assembly of Allied troops yet unblooded and combat-virgin. "Don't think they weren't afraid," one American woman who worked with the Red Cross says in Studs Terkel's *"The Good War."* "Just before they went across to France, belts and ties were removed from some of these young men. They were very, very young."

WHAT UNCONDITIONAL SURRENDER MEANT

For those who fought, the war had other features unknown to those who looked on or got the war mediated through journalism. One such feature was the rate at which it destroyed human beings— friendly as well as enemy. Training for infantry fighting, few American soldiers were tough-minded enough to accept the full, awful implications of the term "replacement" in the designation of their Replacement Training Centers. (The proposed euphemism "reinforcement" never caught on.) What was going to happen to the soldiers they were being trained to replace? Why should so many "replacements"—hundreds of thousands of them, actually—be required? The answers came soon enough in the European theater, in Italy, France, and finally Germany. In six weeks of fighting in Normandy, the 90th Infantry Division had to replace 150 percent of its officers and more than 100 percent of its men. If a division was engaged for more than three months, the probability was that every one of its second lieutenants, all 132 of them, would be killed or wounded. For those being prepared as replacements at officer candidate schools, it was not mentally healthy to dwell on the oddity of the schools' turning out hundreds of new junior officers weekly after the army had reached its full wartime strength. Only experience would make the need clear. The commanding officer of the 6th King's Own Scottish Borderers, which finally arrived in Hamburg in 1945 after fighting all the way from Normandy, found an average of five original men remaining (out of around 200) in each rifle company. "I was appalled," he said. "I had no idea it was going to be like that."

And it was not just wounds and death that depopulated the rifle companies. In the South Pacific it was malaria, dengue, blackwater fever, and dysentery; in Europe, dysentery, pneumonia, and trench foot. What disease did to the troops in the Pacific has never been widely known. The ingestion of Atabrine, the wartime substitute for quinine as a malaria preventive, has caused ears to ring for a lifetime, and decades afterward thousands still undergo their regular malaria attacks, freezing and burning and shaking all over. In Burma, British and American troops suffered so regularly from dysentery that they cut large holes in the seats of their trousers to simplify things. But worse was the mental attrition suffered by combat troops, who learned from experience the inevitability of their ultimate mental breakdown, ranging from the milder forms of treatable psychoneurosis to outright violent insanity.

In war it is not just the weak soldiers, or the sensitive ones, or the highly imaginative or cowardly ones, who will break down. All will break down if in combat long enough. "Long enough" is now defined by physicians and psychiatrists as between 200 and 240 days. For every frontline soldier in the Second World War, according to John Ellis, there was the "slowly dawning and dreadful realisation that there was no way out, that . . . it was only a matter of time before they got killed or maimed or broke down completely." As one British officer put it, "You go in, you come out, you go in again and you keep doing it until they break you or you are dead." This "slowly dawning and dreadful realisation" usually occurs as a result of two stages of rationalization and one of accurate perception:

1. It *can't* happen to me. I am too clever / agile / well-trained / good-looking / beloved / tightly laced / etc. This persuasion gradually erodes into

2. It *can* happen to me, and I'd better be more careful. I can avoid the danger by keeping extra alert at all times / watching more prudently the way I take cover or dig in or expose my position by firing my weapon / etc. This conviction attenuates in turn to the perception that death and injury are matters more of bad luck than lack of skill, making inevitable the third stage of awareness:

3. It *is going to* happen to me, and only my not being there is going to prevent it.

Because of the words *unconditional surrender,* it became clear in this war that no sort of lucky armistice or surprise political negotiation was going to give the long-term frontline man his pardon. "It soon became apparent," John Ellis writes, "that every yard of ground would have to be torn from the enemy and only killing as many men as possible would enable one to do this. Combat was reduced to its absolute essentials, kill or be killed." It was this that made this second Western Front war unique: it could end only when the line (or the Soviet line) arrived in Berlin. In the Second World War the American military learned something very "modern"—modern because dramatically "psychological," utilitarian, unchivalric, and unheroic: it learned that men will inevitably go mad in battle and that no appeal to patriotism, manliness, or loyalty to the group will ultimately matter. Thus in latter wars things were arranged differently. In Korea and Vietnam it was understood that a man fulfilled his combat obligation and bought his reprieve if he served a fixed term, 365 days—and not days in combat but days in the theater of war. The infantry was now treated somewhat like the air corps had been in the Second War: performance of a stated number of missions guaranteed escape.

"DISORGANIZED INSANITY"

If most civilians didn't know about these things, most soldiers didn't know about them either, because only a relatively small number did any fighting that brought them into mortal contact with the enemy. For the rest, engaged in supply, transportation, and administrative functions, the war constituted a period of undesired and uncomfortable foreign travel under unaccustomed physical and social conditions, like enforced obedience, bad food, and an absence of baths. In 1943 the United States Army grew by 2 million men, but only about 365,000 of those went to combat units, and an even smaller number ended up in the rifle companies. The bizarre size and weight of the administrative tail dragged across Europe by the American forces is implied by statistics: from 1941 to 1945 the number of men whose job was fighting increased by only 100,000. If by the end there were 11 million men in the American army, only 2 million were in the ninety combat divisions, and of those, fewer than 700,000 were in the infantry. Regardless of the persisting fiction, those men know by experience the truth enunciated by John Ellis that

> World War II was not a war of movement, except on the rare occasions when the enemy was in retreat; it was a bloody slogging match in which mobility was only occasionally of real significance. Indeed, . . . the internal combustion engine was not a major consideration in the ground war.

The relative few who actually fought know that the war was not a matter of rational calculation. They know madness when they see it. They can draw the right conclusions from the fact that in order to invade the Continent the Allies killed 12,000 innocent French and Belgian civilians who happened to live in the wrong part of town— that is, too near the railway tracks, the bombers' target. The few who fought are able to respond appropriately—without surprise—to such a fact as this: in the Netherlands alone, more than 7,000 planes tore into the ground or the water, afflicted by bullets, flak, exhaustion of fuel or crew, "pilot error," discouragement, or suicidal intent. In a 1986 article in *Smithsonian* magazine about archaeological excavation in Dutch fields and drained marshes, Les Daly emphasized the multitudinousness, the mad repetitiveness of these 7,000 crashes, reminding readers that "the total fighter and bomber combat force of the U.S. Air Force today amounts to about 3,400 airplanes. To put it another way, the crash of 7,000 aircraft would mean that every square mile of the entire state of New Jersey would have shaken to the impact of a downed plane."

In the same way, the few who fought have little trouble understanding other outcroppings of the irrational element, in events like Hiroshima and Nagasaki, or for that matter the bombing of Hamburg or Darmstadt or Tokyo or Dresden. The destruction of Dresden *et al.* was about as rational as the German shooting of hostages to "punish" an area, or the American belief that an effective way into Germany was to plunge through the Hürtgen Forest, or the British and Canadian belief, two years earlier, that a great raid on Dieppe would be worthwhile. Revenge is not a rational motive, but it was the main motive in the American destruction of the Japanese empire.

Those who fought know this, just as they know that it is as likely for the man next to you to be shot through the eye, ear, testicles, or brain as through the shoulder (the way the cinema does it). A shell is as likely to blow his whole face off as to lodge a fragment in some mentionable and unvital tissue. Those who fought saw the bodies of thousands of self-destroyed Japanese men, women, and infants drifting off Saipan—sheer madness, but not essentially different from what Eisenhower described in *Crusade in Europe,* where, though not intending to make our flesh creep or to descend to nasty details, he couldn't help reporting honestly on the carnage in the Falaise Pocket. He wrote, "It was literally possible to walk for hundreds of yards at a time, stepping on nothing but dead and decaying flesh"—formerly German soldiers, who could have lived by surrendering but who chose, madly, not to.

How is it that these data are commonplaces only to the small number who had some direct experience of them? One reason is the normal human talent for looking on the bright side, for not receiving information likely to cause distress or to occasion a major overhaul of normal ethical, political, or psychological assumptions. But the more important reason is that the news correspondents, radio broad-casters, and film people who perceived these horrors kept quiet about them on behalf of the war effort, and so the large wartime audience never knew these things. As John Steinbeck finally confessed in 1958, "We were all part of the War Effort. We went along with it, and not only that, we abetted it. . . . I don't mean that the correspondents were liars. . . . It is in the things not mentioned that the untruth lies." By not mentioning a lot of things, a correspondent could give the audience at home the impression that there were no cowards in the service, no thieves or rapists or looters, no cruel or stupid com-manders. It is true, Steinbeck was aware, that most military opera-tions are examples of "disorganized insanity," but the morale of the home front could not be jeopardized by an eyewitness's saying so. And even if a correspondent wanted to deliver the noisome truth, patriotism would join censorship in stopping his mouth. As Steinbeck noted in *Once There Was a War,* "The foolish reporter who broke the rules would not be printed at home and in addition would be put out of the theater by the command."

TIM O'BRIEN

The Things They Carried

Tim O'Brien (1946–) was born in Minnesota, served as a foot soldier in Vietnam from 1967–1970, and worked as a national af-fairs reporter for the *Washington Post.* The Vietnam War is the focus of O'Brien's writing; his novel *Going after Cacciato* (1978) received a National Book Award. Other books include *If I Die in a Combat Zone* (1973), *Northern Lights* (1974), and *The Things They Carried* (1990). The following selection first appeared in *Esquire.*

First Lieutenant Jimmy Cross carried letters from a girl named Mar-tha, a junior at Mount Sebastian College in New Jersey. They were not love letters, but Lieutenant Cross was hoping, so he kept them folded in plastic at the bottom of his rucksack. In the late afternoon, after a day's march, he would dig his foxhole, wash his hands under a canteen, unwrap the letters, hold them with the tips of his fingers, and spend the last hour of light pretending. He would imagine romantic camping trips into the White Mountains in New Hampshire. He would sometimes taste the envelope flaps, knowing her tongue had been there. More than anything, he wanted Martha to love him as he loved her, but the letters were mostly chatty, elusive on the matter of love. She was a virgin, he was almost sure. She was an English major at Mount Sebastian, and she wrote beautifully about her professors and roommates and midterm exams, about her respect for Chaucer and her great affection for Virginia Woolf. She often quoted lines of poetry; she never mentioned the war, except to say, Jimmy, take care of yourself. The letters weighed ten ounces. They were signed "Love, Martha," but Lieutenant Cross understood that "Love" was only a way of signing and did not mean what he sometimes pretended it meant. At dusk, he would carefully return the letters to his rucksack. Slowly, a bit distracted, he would get up and move among his men, checking the perimeter, then at full dark he would return to his hole and watch the night and wonder if Martha was a virgin.

The things they carried were largely determined by necessity. Among the necessities or near necessities were P-38 can openers, pocket knives, heat tabs, wrist watches, dog tags, mosquito repellent, chewing gum, candy, cigarettes, salt tablets, packets of Kool-Aid, lighters, matches, sewing kits, Military Payment Certificates, C rations, and two or three canteens of water. Together, these items weighed between fifteen and twenty pounds, depending upon a man's habits or rate of metabolism. Henry Dobbins, who was a big man, carried extra rations; he was especially fond of canned peaches in heavy syrup over pound cake. Dave Jensen, who practiced field hygiene, carried a toothbrush, dental floss, and several hotel-size bars of soap he'd stolen on R&R in Sydney, Australia. Ted Lavender, who was scared, carried tranquilizers until he was shot in the head outside the village of Than Khe in mid-April. By necessity, and because it was SOP, they all carried steel helmets that weighed five pounds including the liner and camouflage cover. They carried the standard fatigue jackets and trousers. Very few carried underwear. On their feet they carried jungle boots—2.1 pounds—and Dave Jensen carried three pairs of socks and a can of Dr. Scholl's foot powder as a precaution against trench foot. Until he was shot, Ted Lavender carried six or seven ounces of premium dope, which for him was a necessity. Mitchell Sanders, the RTO, carried condoms. Norman

Bowker carried a diary. Rat Kiley carried comic books. Kiowa, a devout Baptist, carried an illustrated New Testament that had been presented to him by his father, who taught Sunday school in Oklahoma City, Oklahoma. As a hedge against bad times, however, Kiowa also carried his grandmother's distrust of the white man, his grandfather's old hunting hatchet. Necessity dictated. Because the land was mined and booby-trapped, it was SOP for each man to carry a steel-centered, nylon-covered flak jacket, which weighed 6.7 pounds, but which on hot days seemed much heavier. Because you could die so quickly, each man carried at least one large compress bandage, usually in the helmet band for easy access. Because the nights were cold, and because the monsoons were wet, each carried a green plastic poncho that could be used as a raincoat or ground sheet or makeshift tent. With its quilted liner, the poncho weighed almost two pounds, but it was worth every ounce. In April, for instance, when Ted Lavender was shot, they used his poncho to wrap him up, then to carry him across the paddy, then to lift him into the chopper that took him away.

They were called legs or grunts.

To carry something was to "hump" it, as when Lieutenant Jimmy Cross humped his love for Martha up the hills and through the swamps. In its intransitive form, "to hump" meant "to walk," or "to march," but it implied burdens far beyond the intransitive.

Almost everyone humped photographs. In his wallet, Lieutenant Cross carried two photographs of Martha. The first was a Kodachrome snapshot signed "Love," though he knew better. She stood against a brick wall. Her eyes were gray and neutral, her lips slightly open as she stared straight-on at the camera. At night, sometimes, Lieutenant Cross wondered who had taken the picture, because he knew she had boyfriends, because he loved her so much, and because he could see the shadow of the picture taker spreading out against the brick wall. The second photograph had been clipped from the 1968 Mount Sebastian yearbook. It was an action shot—women's volleyball—and Martha was bent horizontal to the floor, reaching, the palms of her hands in sharp focus, the tongue taut, the expression frank and competitive. There was no visible sweat. She wore white gym shorts. Her legs, he thought, were almost certainly the legs of a virgin, dry and without hair, the left knee cocked and carrying her entire weight, which was just over one hundred pounds. Lieutenant Cross remembered touching that left knee. A dark theater, he remembered, and the movie was *Bonnie and Clyde,* and Martha wore a tweed skirt, and during the final scene, when he touched her knee, she turned and looked at him in a sad, sober way that made him pull his hand back, but he would always remember the feel of the tweed skirt and the knee beneath it and the sound of the gunfire that killed Bonnie and Clyde, how embarrassing it was, how slow and oppressive. He remembered kissing her good night at the dorm door. Right then, he thought, he should've done something brave. He should've carried her up the stairs to her room and tied her to the bed and touched that left knee all night long. He should've risked it. Whenever he looked at the photographs, he thought of new things he should've done.

What they carried was partly a function of rank, partly of field specialty.

As a first lieutenant and platoon leader, Jimmy Cross carried a compass, maps, code books, binoculars, and a .45-caliber pistol that weighed 2.9 pounds fully loaded. He carried a strobe light and the responsibility for the lives of his men.

As an RTO, Mitchell Sanders carried the PRC-25 radio, a killer, twenty-six pounds with its battery.

As a medic, Rat Kiley carried a canvas satchel filled with morphine and plasma and malaria tablets and surgical tape and comic books and all the things a medic must carry, including M&M's for especially bad wounds, for a total weight of nearly twenty pounds.

As a big man, therefore a machine gunner, Henry Dobbins carried the M-60, which weighed twenty-three pounds unloaded, but which was almost always loaded. In addition, Dobbins carried between ten and fifteen pounds of ammunition draped in belts across his chest and shoulders.

As PFCs or Spec 4s, most of them were common grunts and carried the standard M-16 gas-operated assault rifle. The weapon weighed 7.5 pounds unloaded, 8.2 pounds with its full twenty-round magazine. Depending on numerous factors, such as topography and psychology, the riflemen carried anywhere from twelve to twenty magazines, usually in cloth bandoliers, adding on another 8.4 pounds at minimum, fourteen pounds at maximum. When it was available, they also carried M-16 maintenance gear—rods and steel brushes and swabs and tubes of LSA oil—all of which weighed about a pound. Among the grunts, some carried the M-79 grenade launcher, 5.9 pounds unloaded, a reasonably light weapon except for the ammunition, which was heavy. A single round weighed ten ounces. The typical load was twenty-five rounds. But Ted Lavender, who was scared, carried thirty-four rounds when he was shot and killed outside Than Khe, and he went down under an exceptional burden, more than twenty pounds of ammunition, plus the flak jacket and helmet and rations and water and toilet paper and tranquilizers and all the rest, plus the unweighed fear. He was dead weight. There was no twitching or flopping. Kiowa, who saw it happen, said it was like watching a rock fall, or a big sandbag or something—just boom, then down—not like the movies where the dead guy rolls around and does fancy spins and goes ass over teakettle—not like that, Kiowa said, the poor bastard just flat-fuck fell. Boom. Down. Nothing else. It was a bright morning in mid-April. Lieutenant Cross felt the pain. He blamed himself. They stripped off Lavender's canteens and ammo, all the heavy things, and Rat Kiley said the obvious, the guy's dead, and Mitchell Sanders used his radio to report one U.S. KIA and to request a chopper. Then they wrapped Lavender in his poncho. They carried him out to a dry paddy, established security, and sat smoking the dead man's dope until the chopper came. Lieutenant Cross kept to himself. He pictured Martha's smooth young face, thinking he loved her more than anything, more than his men, and now Ted Lavender was dead because he loved her so much and could not stop thinking about her. When the dust-off arrived, they carried Lavender aboard. Afterward they burned Than Khe. They marched until dusk, then dug their holes, and that night Kiowa kept explaining how you had to be there, how fast it was, how the poor guy just dropped like so much concrete. Boom-down, he said. Like cement.

In addition to the three standard weapons—the M-60, M-16, and M-79—they carried whatever presented itself, or whatever seemed appropriate as a means of killing or staying alive. They carried catch-as-catch-can. At various times, in various situations, they carried M-14s and CAR-15s and Swedish Ks and grease guns and captured AK-47s and Chi-Coms and RPGs and Simonov carbines and black-market Uzis and .38-caliber Smith & Wesson handguns and 66 mm LAWs and shotguns and silencers and blackjacks and bayonets and C-4 plastic explosives. Lee Strunk carried a slingshot; a weapon of last resort, he called it. Mitchell Sanders carried brass knuckles. Kiowa carried his grandfather's feathered hatchet. Every third or fourth man carried a Claymore antipersonnel mine—3.5 pounds with its firing device. They all carried fragmentation grenades—fourteen ounces each. They all carried at least one M-18 colored smoke grenade—twenty-four ounces. Some carried CS or tear-gas grenades. Some carried white-phosphorous grenades. They carried all they could bear, and then some, including a silent awe for the terrible power of the things they carried.

In the first week of April, before Lavender died, Lieutenant Jimmy Cross received a good-luck charm from Martha. It was a simple pebble, an ounce at most. Smooth to the touch, it was a milky-white color with flecks of orange and violet, oval-shaped, like a miniature egg. In the accompanying letter, Martha wrote that she had found the pebble on the Jersey shoreline, precisely where the land touched water at high tide, where things came together but also separated. It was this separate-but-together quality, she wrote, that had inspired her to pick up the pebble and to carry it in her breast pocket for several days, where it seemed weightless, and then to send it through the mail, by air, as a token of her truest feelings for him. Lieutenant Cross found this romantic. But he wondered what her truest feelings were, exactly, and what she meant by separate-but-together. He wondered how the tides and waves had come into play on that afternoon along the Jersey shoreline when Martha saw the pebble and bent down to rescue it from geology. He imagined bare feet. Martha was a poet, with the poet's sensibilities, and her feet would be brown and bare, the toenails unpainted, the eyes chilly and somber like the ocean in March, and though it was painful, he wondered who had been with her that afternoon. He imagined a pair of shadows moving along the strip of sand where things came together but also separated. It was phantom jealousy, he knew, but he couldn't help himself. He loved her so much. On the march, through the hot days of early April, he carried the pebble in his mouth, turning it with his tongue, tasting sea salts and moisture. His mind wandered. He had difficulty keeping his attention on the war. On occasion he would yell at his men to spread out the column, to keep their eyes open, but then he would slip away into daydreams, just pretending, walking barefoot along the Jersey shore, with Martha, carrying nothing. He would feel himself rising. Sun and waves and gentle winds, all love and lightness.

What they carried varied by mission.

When a mission took them to the mountains, they carried mosquito netting, machetes, canvas tarps, and extra bug juice.

If a mission seemed especially hazardous, or if it involved a place they knew to be bad, they carried everything they could. In certain heavily mined AOs, where the land was dense with Toe Poppers and Bouncing Betties, they took turns humping a twenty-eight-pound mine detector. With its headphones and big sensing plate, the equipment was a stress on the lower back and shoulders, awkward to handle, often useless because of the shrapnel in the earth, but they carried it anyway, partly for safety, partly for the illusion of safety.

On ambush, or other night missions, they carried peculiar little odds and ends. Kiowa always took along his New Testament and a pair of moccasins for silence. Dave Jensen carried night-sight vitamins high in carotin. Lee Strunk carried his slingshot; ammo, he claimed, would never be a problem. Rat Kiley carried brandy and M&M's. Until he was shot, Ted Lavender carried the starlight scope, which weighed 6.3 pounds with its aluminum carrying case. Henry Dobbins carried his girlfriend's pantyhose wrapped around his neck as a comforter. They all carried ghosts. When dark came, they would move out single file across the meadows and paddies to their ambush coordinates, where they would quietly set up the Claymores and lie down and spend the night waiting.

Other missions were more complicated and required special equipment. In mid-April, it was their mission to search out and destroy the elaborate tunnel complexes in the Than Khe area south of Chu Lai. To blow the tunnels, they carried one-pound blocks of pentrite high explosives, four blocks to a man, sixty-eight pounds in all. They carried wiring, detonators, and battery-powered clackers. Dave Jensen carried earplugs. Most often, before blowing the tunnels, they were ordered by higher command to search them, which was considered bad news, but by and large they just shrugged and carried out orders. Because he was a big man, Henry Dobbins was excused from tunnel duty. The others would draw numbers. Before Lavender died there were seventeen men in the platoon, and whoever drew the number seventeen would strip off his gear and crawl in head first with a flashlight and Lieutenant Cross's .45-caliber pistol. The rest of them would fan out as security. They would sit down or kneel, not facing the hole, listening to the ground beneath them, imagining cobwebs and ghosts, whatever was down there—the tunnel walls squeezing in—how the flashlight seemed impossibly heavy in the hand and how it was tunnel vision in the very strictest sense, compression in all ways, even time, and how you had to wiggle in—ass and elbows—a swallowed-up feeling—and how you found yourself worrying about odd things—will your flashlight go dead? Do rats carry rabies? If you screamed, how far would the sound carry? Would your buddies hear it? Would they have the courage to drag you out? In some respects, though not many, the waiting was worse than the tunnel itself. Imagination was a killer.

On April 16, when Lee Strunk drew the number seventeen, he laughed and muttered something and went down quickly. The morning was hot and very still. Not good, Kiowa said. He looked at the tunnel opening, then out across a dry paddy toward the village of Than Khe. Nothing moved. No clouds or birds or people. As they waited, the men smoked and drank Kool-Aid, not talking much, feeling sympathy for Lee Strunk but also feeling the luck of the draw. You win some, you lose some, said Mitchell Sanders, and sometimes you settle for a rain check. It was a tired line and no one laughed.

Henry Dobbins ate a tropical chocolate bar. Ted Lavender popped a tranquilizer and went off to pee.

After five minutes, Lieutenant Jimmy Cross moved to the tunnel, leaned down, and examined the darkness. Trouble, he thought—a cave-in maybe. And then suddenly, without willing it, he was thinking about Martha. The stresses and fractures, the quick collapse, the two of them buried alive under all that weight. Dense, crushing love. Kneeling, watching the hole, he tried to concentrate on Lee Strunk and the war, all the dangers, but his love was too much for him, he felt paralyzed, he wanted to sleep inside her lungs and breathe her blood and be smothered. He wanted her to be a virgin and not a virgin, all at once. He wanted to know her. Intimate secrets—why poetry? Why so sad? Why that grayness in her eyes? Why so alone? Not lonely, just alone—riding her bike across campus or sitting off by herself in the cafeteria. Even dancing, she danced alone—and it was the aloneness that filled him with love. He remembered telling her that one evening. How she nodded and looked away. And how, later, when he kissed her, she received the kiss without returning it, her eyes wide open, not afraid, not a virgin's eyes, just flat and uninvolved.

Lieutenant Cross gazed at the tunnel. But he was not there. He was buried with Martha under the white sand at the Jersey shore. They were pressed together, and the pebble in his mouth was her tongue. He was smiling. Vaguely, he was aware of how quiet the day was, the sullen paddies, yet he could not bring himself to worry about matters of security. He was beyond that. He was just a kid at war, in love. He was twenty-two years old. He couldn't help it.

A few moments later Lee Strunk crawled out of the tunnel. He came up grinning, filthy but alive. Lieutenant Cross nodded and closed his eyes while the others clapped Strunk on the back and made jokes about rising from the dead.

Worms, Rat Kiley said. Right out of the grave. Fuckin' zombie.

The men laughed. They all felt great relief.

Spook City, said Mitchell Sanders.

Lee Strunk made a funny ghost sound, a kind of moaning, yet very happy, and right then, when Strunk made that high happy moaning sound, when he went *Ahhooooo,* right then Ted Lavender was shot in the head on his way back from peeing. He lay with his mouth open. The teeth were broken. There was a swollen black bruise under his left eye. The cheekbone was gone. Oh shit, Rat Kiley said, the guy's dead. The guy's dead, he kept saying, which seemed profound—the guy's dead. I mean really.

The things they carried were determined to some extent by super-stition. Lieutenant Cross carried his good-luck pebble. Dave Jensen carried a rabbit's foot. Norman Bowker, otherwise a very gentle person, carried a thumb that had been presented to him as a gift by Mitchell Sanders. The thumb was dark brown, rubbery to the touch, and weighed four ounces at most. It had been cut from a VC corpse, a boy of fifteen or sixteen. They'd found him at the bottom of an irrigation ditch, badly burned, flies in his mouth and eyes. The boy wore black shorts and sandals. At the time of his death he had been carrying a pouch of rice, a rifle, and three magazines of ammunition.

You want my opinion, Mitchell Sanders said, there's a definite moral here.

He put his hand on the dead boy's wrist. He was quiet for a time, as if counting a pulse, then he patted the stomach, almost affection-ately, and used Kiowa's hunting hatchet to remove the thumb.

Henry Dobbins asked what the moral was.

Moral?

You know. *Moral.*

Sanders wrapped the thumb in toilet paper and handed it across to Norman Bowker. There was no blood. Smiling, he kicked the boy's head, watched the flies scatter, and said, It's like with that old TV show—Paladin. Have gun, will travel.

Henry Dobbins thought about it.

Yeah, well, he finally said. I don't see no moral.

There it *is,* man.

Fuck off.

They carried USO stationery and pencils and pens. They carried Sterno, safety pins, trip flares, signal flares, spools of wire, razor blades, chewing tobacco, liberated joss sticks and statuettes of the smiling Buddha, candles, grease pencils, *The Stars and Stripes,* fin-gernail clippers, Psy Ops leaflets, bush hats, bolos, and much more.

Twice a week, when the resupply choppers came in, they carried hot chow in green Mermite cans and large canvas bags filled with iced beer and soda pop. They carried plastic water containers, each with a two-gallon capacity. Mitchell Sanders carried a set of starched tiger fatigues for special occasions. Henry Dobbins carried Black Flag insecticide. Dave Jensen carried empty sandbags that could be filled at night for added protection. Lee Strunk carried tanning lotion. Some things they carried in common. Taking turns, they carried the big PRC-77 scrambler radio, which weighed thirty pounds with its battery. They shared the weight of memory. They took up what others could no longer bear. Often, they carried each other, the wounded or weak. They carried infections. They carried chess sets, basketballs, Vietnamese-English dictionaries, insignia of rank, Bronze Stars and Purple Hearts, plastic cards imprinted with the Code of Conduct. They carried diseases, among them malaria and dysentery. They carried lice and ringworm and leeches and paddy algae and various rots and molds. They carried the land itself—Vietnam, the place, the soil—a powdery orange-red dust that covered their boots and fatigues and faces. They carried the sky. The whole atmosphere, they carried it, the humidity, the monsoons, the stink of fungus and decay, all of it, they carried gravity. They moved like mules. By daylight they took sniper fire, at night they were mortared, but it was not battle, it was just the endless march, village to village, without purpose, nothing won or lost. They marched for the sake of the march. They plodded along slowly, dumbly, leaning forward against the heat, unthinking, all blood and bone, simple grunts, soldiering with their legs, toiling up the hills and down into the paddies and across the rivers and up again and down, just humping, one step and then the next and then another, but no volition, no will, because it was automatic, it was anatomy, and the war was entirely a matter of posture and carriage, the hump was everything, a kind of inertia, a kind of emptiness, a dullness of desire and intellect and conscience and hope and human sensibility. Their principles were in their feet. Their calculations were biological. They had no sense of strategy or mission. They searched the villages without knowing what to look for, not caring, kicking over jars of rice, frisking children and old men, blowing tunnels, sometimes setting fires and sometimes not, then forming up and moving on to the next village, then other villages, where it would always be the same. They carried their own lives. The pressures were enormous. In the heat of early afternoon, they would remove their helmets and flak jackets, walking bare, which was dangerous but which helped ease the strain.

They would often discard things along the route of march. Purely for comfort, they would throw away rations, blow their Claymores and grenades, no matter, because by nightfall the resupply choppers would arrive with more of the same, then a day or two later still more, fresh watermelons and crates of ammunition and sunglasses and woolen sweaters—the resources were stunning—sparklers for the Fourth of July, colored eggs for Easter. It was the great American war chest—the fruits of science, the smokestacks, the canneries, the arsenals at Hartford, the Minnesota forests, the machine shops, the vast fields of corn and wheat—they carried like freight trains; they carried it on their backs and shoulders—and for all the ambiguities of Vietnam, all the mysteries and unknowns, there was at least the single abiding certainty that they would never be at a loss for things to carry.

After the chopper took Lavender away, Lieutenant Jimmy Cross led his men into the village of Than Khe. They burned everything. They shot chickens and dogs, they trashed the village well, they called in artillery and watched the wreckage, then they marched for several hours through the hot afternoon, and then at dusk, while Kiowa explained how Lavender died, Lieutenant Cross found himself trembling.

He tried not to cry. With his entrenching tool, which weighed five pounds, he began digging a hole in the earth.

He felt shame. He hated himself. He had loved Martha more than his men, and as a consequence Lavender was now dead, and this was something he would have to carry like a stone in his stomach for the rest of the war.

All he could do was dig. He used his entrenching tool like an ax, slashing, feeling both love and hate, and then later, when it was full dark, he sat at the bottom of his foxhole and wept. It went on for a long while. In part, he was grieving for Ted Lavender, but mostly it was for Martha, and for himself, because she belonged to another world, which was not quite real, and because she was a junior at Mount Sebastian College in New Jersey, a poet and a virgin and uninvolved, and because he realized she did not love him and never would.

Like cement, Kiowa whispered in the dark. I swear to God—boom-down. Not a word.

I've heard this, said Norman Bowker.

A pisser, you know? Still zipping himself up. Zapped while zipping.

All right, fine. That's enough.

Yeah, but you had to see it, the guy just—

I *heard,* man. Cement. So why not shut the fuck *up?*

Kiowa shook his head sadly and glanced over at the hole where Lieutenant Jimmy Cross sat watching the night. The air was thick and wet. A warm, dense fog had settled over the paddies and there was the stillness that precedes rain.

After a time Kiowa sighed.

One thing for sure, he said. The Lieutenant's in some deep hurt. I mean that crying jag—the way he was carrying on—it wasn't fake or anything, it was real heavy-duty hurt. The man cares.

Sure, Norman Bowker said.

Say what you want, the man does care.

We all got problems.

Not Lavender.

No, I guess not. Bowker said. Do me a favor, though.

Shut up?

That's a smart Indian. Shut up.

Shrugging, Kiowa pulled off his boots. He wanted to say more, just to lighten up his sleep, but instead he opened his New Testament and arranged it beneath his head as a pillow. The fog made things seem hollow and unattached. He tried not to think about Ted Lavender, but then he was thinking how fast it was, no drama, down and dead, and how it was hard to feel anything except surprise. It seemed un-Christian. He wished he could find some great sadness, or even anger, but the emotion wasn't there and he couldn't make it happen. Mostly he felt pleased to be alive. He liked the smell of the New Testament under his cheek, the leather and ink and paper and glue, whatever the chemicals were. He liked hearing the sounds of night. Even his fatigue, it felt fine, the stiff muscles and the prickly awareness of his own body, a floating feeling. He enjoyed not being dead. Lying there, Kiowa admired Lieutenant Jimmy Cross's capacity for grief. He wanted to share the man's pain, he wanted to care as Jimmy Cross cared. And yet when he closed his eyes, all he could think was Boom-down, and all he could feel was the pleasure of having his boots off and the fog curling in around him and the damp soil and the Bible smells and the plush comfort of night.

After a moment Norman Bowker sat up in the dark.

What the hell, he said. You want to talk, *talk.* Tell it to me.

Forget it.

No, man, go on. One thing I hate, it's a silent Indian.

For the most part they carried themselves with poise, a kind of dignity. Now and then, however, there were times of panic, when they squealed or wanted to squeal but couldn't, when they twitched and made moaning sounds and covered their heads and said Dear Jesus and flopped around on the earth and fired their weapons blindly and cringed and sobbed and begged for the noise to stop and went wild and made stupid promises to themselves and to God and to their mothers and fathers, hoping not to die. In different ways, it happened to all of them. Afterward, when the firing ended, they would blink and peek up. They would touch their bodies, feeling shame, then quickly hiding it. They would force themselves to stand. As if in slow motion, frame by frame, the world would take on the old logic—absolute silence, then the wind, then sunlight, then voices. It was the burden of being alive. Awkwardly, the men would reassemble themselves, first in private, then in groups, becoming soldiers again. They would repair the leaks in their eyes. They would check for casualties, call in dust-offs, light cigarettes, try to smile, clear their throats and spit and begin cleaning their weapons. After a time someone would shake his head and say, No lie, I almost shit my pants, and someone else would laugh, which meant it was bad, yes, but the guy had obviously not shit his pants, it wasn't that bad, and in any case nobody would ever do such a thing and then go ahead and talk about it. They would squint into the dense, oppressive sunlight. For a few moments, perhaps, they would fall silent, lighting a joint and tracking its passage from man to man, inhaling, holding in the humiliation. Scary stuff, one of them might say. But then someone else would grin or flick his eyebrows and say, Roger-dodger, almost cut me a new asshole, *almost.*

There were numerous such poses. Some carried themselves with a sort of wistful resignation, others with pride or stiff soldierly discipline or good humor or macho zeal. They were afraid of dying but they were even more afraid to show it.

They found jokes to tell.

They used a hard vocabulary to contain the terrible softness. *Greased,* they'd say. *Offed, lit up, zapped while zipping.* It wasn't cruelty, just stage presence. They were actors and the war came at them in 3-D. When someone died, it wasn't quite dying, because in a curious way it seemed scripted, and because they had their lines mostly memorized, irony mixed with tragedy, and because they called it by other names, as if to encyst and destroy the reality of death itself. They kicked corpses. They cut off thumbs. They talked grunt lingo. They told stories about Ted Lavender's supply of tranquilizers, how the poor guy didn't feel a thing, how incredibly tranquil he was.

There's a moral here, said Mitchell Sanders.

They were waiting for Lavender's chopper, smoking the dead man's dope.

The moral's pretty obvious, Sanders said, and winked. Stay away from drugs. No joke, they'll ruin your day every time.

Cute, said Henry Dobbins.

Mind-blower, get it? Talk about wiggy—nothing left, just blood and brains.

They made themselves laugh.

There it is, they'd say, over and over, as if the repetition itself were an act of poise, a balance between crazy and almost crazy, knowing without going. There it is, which meant be cool, let it ride, because oh yeah, man, you can't change what can't be changed, there it is, there it absolutely and positively and fucking well *is*.

They were tough.

They carried all the emotional baggage of men who might die. Grief, terror, love, longing—these were intangibles, but the intangibles had their own mass and specific gravity, they had tangible weight. They carried shameful memories. They carried the common secret of cowardice barely restrained, the instinct to run or freeze or hide, and in many respects this was the heaviest burden of all, for it could never be put down, it required perfect balance and perfect posture. They carried their reputations. They carried the soldier's greatest fear, which was the fear of blushing. Men killed, and died, because they were embarrassed not to. It was what had brought them to the war in the first place, nothing positive, no dreams of glory or honor, just to avoid the blush of dishonor. They died so as not to die of embarrassment. They crawled into tunnels and walked point and advanced under fire. Each morning, despite the unknowns, they made their legs move. They endured. They kept humping. They did not submit to the obvious alternative, which was simply to close the eyes and fall. So easy, really. Go limp and tumble to the ground and let the muscles unwind and not speak and not budge until your buddies picked you up and lifted you into the chopper that would roar and dip its nose and carry you off to the world. A mere matter of falling, yet no one ever fell. It was not courage, exactly; the object was not valor. Rather, they were too frightened to be cowards.

By and large they carried these things inside, maintaining the masks of composure. They sneered at sick call. They spoke bitterly about guys who had found release by shooting off their own toes or fingers. Pussies, they'd say. Candyasses. It was fierce, mocking talk, with only a trace of envy or awe, but even so, the image played itself out behind their eyes.

They imagined the muzzle against flesh. They imagined the quick, sweet pain, then the evacuation to Japan, then a hospital with warm beds and cute geisha nurses.

They dreamed of freedom birds.

At night, on guard, staring into the dark, they were carried away by jumbo jets. They felt the rush of takeoff. *Gone!* they yelled. And then velocity, wings and engines, a smiling stewardess—but it was more than a plane, it was a real bird, a big sleek silver bird with feathers and talons and high screeching. They were flying. The weights fell off, there was nothing to bear. They laughed and held on tight, feeling the cold slap of wind and altitude, soaring, thinking *It's over, I'm gone!*—they were naked, they were light and free—it was all lightness, bright and fast and buoyant, light as light, a helium buzz in the brain, a giddy bubbling in the lungs as they were taken up over the clouds and the war, beyond duty, beyond gravity and mortification and global entanglements—*Sin loi!* they yelled, *I'm sorry, motherfuckers, but I'm out of it, I'm goofed, I'm on a space cruise, I'm gone!*—and it was a restful, disencumbered sensation, just riding the light waves, sailing that big silver freedom bird over the mountains and oceans, over America, over the farms and great sleeping cities and cemeteries and highways and the golden arches of Mc-Donald's. It was flight, a kind of fleeing, a kind of falling, falling higher and higher, spinning off the edge of the earth and beyond the sun and through the vast, silent vacuum where there were no burdens and where everything weighed exactly nothing. *Gone!* they screamed, *I'm sorry but I'm gone!* And so at night, not quite dreaming, they gave themselves over to lightness, they were carried, they were purely borne.

On the morning after Ted Lavender died, First Lieutenant Jimmy Cross crouched at the bottom of his foxhole and burned Martha's letters. Then he burned the two photographs. There was a steady rain falling, which made it difficult, but he used heat tabs and Sterno to build a small fire, screening it with his body, holding the photographs over the tight blue flame with the tips of his fingers.

He realized it was only a gesture. Stupid, he thought. Sentimental, too, but mostly just stupid.

Lavender was dead. You couldn't burn the blame.

Besides, the letters were in his head. And even now, without photographs, Lieutenant Cross could see Martha playing volleyball in her white gym shorts and yellow T-shirt. He could see her moving in the rain.

When the fire died out, Lieutenant Cross pulled his poncho over his shoulders and ate breakfast from a can.

There was no great mystery, he decided.

In those burned letters Martha had never mentioned the war, except to say, Jimmy, take care of yourself. She wasn't involved. She signed the letters "Love," but it wasn't love, and all the fine lines and technicalities did not matter.

The morning came up wet and blurry. Everything seemed part of everything else, the fog and Martha and the deepening rain.

It was a war, after all.

Half smiling, Lieutenant Jimmy Cross took out his maps. He shook his head hard, as if to clear it, then bent forward and began planning the day's march. In ten minutes, or maybe twenty, he would rouse the men and they would pack up and head west, where the maps showed the country to be green and inviting. They would do what they had always done. The rain might add some weight, but otherwise it would be one more day layered upon all the other days.

He was realistic about it. There was that new hardness in his stomach.

No more fantasies, he told himself.

Henceforth, when he thought about Martha, it would be only to think that she belonged elsewhere. He would shut down the daydreams. This was not Mount Sebastian, it was another world, where there were no pretty poems or midterm exams, a place where men died because of carelessness and gross stupidity. Kiowa was right. Boom-down, and you were dead, never partly dead.

Briefly, in the rain, Lieutenant Cross saw Martha's gray eyes gazing back at him.

He understood.

It was very sad, he thought. The things men carried inside. The things men did or felt they had to do.

He almost nodded at her, but didn't.

Instead he went back to his maps. He was now determined to perform his duties firmly and without negligence. It wouldn't help Lavender, he knew that, but from this point on he would comport himself as a soldier. He would dispose of his good-luck pebble. Swallow it, maybe, or use Lee Strunk's slingshot, or just drop it along the trail. On the march he would impose strict field discipline. He would be careful to send out flank security, to prevent straggling or bunching up, to keep his troops moving at the proper pace and at the proper interval. He would insist on clean weapons. He would confiscate the remainder of Lavender's dope. Later in the day, perhaps, he would call the men together and speak to them plainly. He would accept the blame for what had happened to Ted Lavender. He would be a man about it. He would look them in the eyes, keeping his chin level, and he would issue the new SOPs in a calm, impersonal tone of voice, an officer's voice, leaving no room for argument or discussion. Commencing immediately, he'd tell them, they would no longer abandon equipment along the route of march. They would police up their acts. They would get their shit together, and keep it together, and maintain it neatly and in good working order.

He would not tolerate laxity. He would show strength, distancing himself.

Among the men there would be grumbling, of course, and maybe worse, because their days would seem longer and their loads heavier, but Lieutenant Cross reminded himself that his obligation was not to be loved but to lead. He would dispense with love; it was not now a factor. And if anyone quarreled or complained, he would simply tighten his lips and arrange his shoulders in the correct command posture. He might give a curt little nod. Or he might not. He might just shrug and say Carry on, and they would saddle up and form into a column and move out toward the villages west of Than Khe.

SEYMOUR HERSH

My Lai 4

Seymour Hersh (1937–   ) is an investigative reporter who uncovered the secret bombing of Cambodia under the Nixon Administration and the C.I.A.'s domestic spying operations. He won a Pulitzer Prize in 1970 for *My Lai 4: A Report on the Massacre and Its Aftermath*, from which the following selection is taken. In 1972 he published *Cover-up: The Army's Secret Investigation of the Massacre of My Lai 4* and his more recent works include *The Price of Power: Kissinger in the Nixon White House* (1983), *The Target Is Destroyed: What Really Happened to Flight 007 and What America Knew about It* (1986) and *The Samson Option* (1991).

It was sunny and already hot when the first helicopter started its noisy flight to My Lai 4. The time was 7:22 A.M.; it was logged by a tape recorder at brigade headquarters. A brief artillery barrage had already begun; the My Lai 4 area was being "prepped" in anticipation of that day's search-and-destroy mission. A few heavily armed helicopters were firing thousands of small-caliber bullets into the area by the time Calley and his men landed in a soggy rice paddy 150 meters west of the hamlet. It was harvest season; the green fields were thick with growth.

The first platoon's mission was to secure the landing zone and make sure no enemy troops were left to fire at the second wave of helicopters—by then already airborne from LZ Dotti. As the flight of helicopters hovered over the landing area, the door gunners began spraying protective fire to keep the enemy—if he were there—busy. One of the helicopter's pilots had reported that the LZ was "hot," that is, Viet Cong were waiting below. The first platoon came out firing. But after a moment some men noticed that there was no return fire. "I didn't hear any bullets going past me," recalled Charles Hall, a machine gunner that day. "If you want to consider an area hot, you got to be fired on."

The platoon quickly formed a perimeter and secured the landing zone. Sergeant Cowen spotted an old man. Sledge was a few yards to Cowen's right: "We came to a well and there was a VC. We thought it was a VC. He was standing and waving his arms. Cowen fell back and said, 'Shoot the so-and-so.' I fired once, and then my [rifle] magazine fell out." Paul Meadlo noted that "the gook was standing up shaking and waving his arms and then he was shot." Allen Boyce saw it a little differently: "Some guy was in a rice field, doing something to a rice plant. He looked up and he got it. That was the most confused operation I ever went on. Just everything was screwed up."

Brigade headquarters, sure that there would be a major battle, sent along two men from the Army's 31st Public Information Detachment to record the event for history. Jay Roberts of Arlington, Virginia, a reporter, and photographer Ronald L. Haeberle of Cleveland, Ohio, arrived with the second wave of helicopters and immediately attached themselves to the third platoon, which was bringing up the rear.

The hamlet itself had a population of about 700 people, living either in flimsy thatch-covered huts—"hootches," as the GIs called them—or in solidly made red-brick homes, many with small porches in front. There was an east-west footpath just south of the main cluster of homes; a few yards further south was a loose surface road that marked a hamlet boundary. A deep drainage ditch and then a rice paddy marked the eastern boundary. To the south of My Lai 4 was a large center, or plaza area—clearly the main spot for mass meetings. The foliage was dense: there were high bamboo trees, hedges and plant life everywhere. Medina couldn't see thirty feet into the hamlet from the landing zone.

The first two platoons of Charlie Company, still unfired upon, entered the hamlet. Behind them, still in the rice paddy, were the third platoon and Captain Medina's command post. Calley and some of his men walked into the plaza area in the southern part of the hamlet. None of the people was running away; they knew that U. S. soldiers would assume that anyone running was a Viet Cong and would shoot to kill. There was no immediate sense of panic. The time was about 8 A.M. Grzesik and his fire team were a few meters north of Calley; they couldn't see each other because of the dense vegetation. Grzesik and his men began their usual job of pulling people from their homes, interrogating them, and searching for Viet Cong. The villagers were gathered up, and Grzesik sent Meadlo, who was in his unit, to take them to Calley for further questioning. Grzesik didn't see Meadlo again for more than an hour.

Some of Calley's men thought it was breakfast time as they walked in; a few families were gathered in front of their homes cooking rice over a small fire. Without a direct order, the first platoon also began rounding up the villagers. There still was no sniper fire, no sign of a large enemy unit. Sledge remembered thinking that "if there were VC around, they had plenty of time to leave before we came in. We didn't tiptoe in there."

The killings began without warning. Harry Stanley told the C.I.D.[1] that one young member of Calley's platoon took a civilian into custody and then "pushed the man up to where we were standing and then stabbed the man in the back with his bayonet . . . The man fell to the ground and was gasping for breath." The GI then "killed him with another bayonet thrust or by shooting him with a rifle . . . There was so many people killed that day it is hard for me to recall

---

[1] Central Intelligence Division of the Department of Defense (ED.)

exactly how some of the people died." The youth next "turned to where some soldiers were holding another forty- or fifty-year-old man in custody." He "picked this man up and threw him down a well. Then [he] pulled the pin from a M26 grenade and threw it in after the man." Moments later Stanley saw "some old women and some little children—fifteen or twenty of them—in a group around a temple where some incense was burning. They were kneeling and crying and praying, and various soldiers . . . walked by and executed these women and children by shooting them in the head with their rifles. The soldiers killed all fifteen or twenty of them . . ."

There were few physical protests from the people; about eighty of them were taken quietly from their homes and herded together in the plaza area. A few hollered out, "No VC. No VC." But that was hardly unexpected. Calley left Meadlo, Boyce and a few others with the responsibility of guarding the group. "You know what I want you to do with them," he told Meadlo. Ten minutes later—about 8:15 A.M.—he returned and asked, "Haven't you got rid of them yet? I want them dead." Radioman Sledge, who was trailing Calley, heard the officer tell Meadlo to "waste them." Meadlo followed orders: "We stood about ten to fifteen feet away from them and then he [Calley] started shooting them. Then he told me to start shooting them. I started to shoot them. So we went ahead and killed them. I used more than a whole clip—used four or five clips." There are seventeen M16 bullets in each clip. Boyce slipped away, to the northern side of the hamlet, glad he hadn't been asked to shoot. Women were huddled against their children, vainly trying to save them. Some continued to chant, "No VC." Others simply said, "No. No. No."

By this time, there was shooting everywhere. Dennis I. Conti, a GI from Providence, Rhode Island, later explained to C.I.D. investigators what he thought had happened: "We were all psyched up, and as a result, when we got there the shooting started, almost as a chain reaction. The majority of us had expected to meet VC combat troops, but this did not turn out to be so. First we saw a few men running . . . and the next thing I knew we were shooting at everything. Everybody was just firing. After they got in the village, I guess you could say that the men were out of control."

Brooks and his men in the second platoon to the north had begun to systematically ransack the hamlet and slaughter the people, kill the livestock and destroy the crops. Men poured rifle and machine-gun fire into huts without knowing—or seemingly caring—who was inside.

Roy Wood, one of Calley's men who was working next to Brooks' platoon, stormed into a hut, saw an elderly man hiding inside along with his wife and two young daughters: "I hit him with my rifle and pushed him out." A GI from Brooks' platoon, standing by with an M79 grenade launcher, asked to borrow his gun. Wood refused, and the soldier asked another platoon mate. He got the weapon, said, "Don't let none of them live," and shot the Vietnamese in the head. "These mothers are crazy," Wood remembered thinking. "Stand right in front of us and blow a man's brains out." Later he vomited when he saw more of the dead residents of My Lai 4.

The second platoon went into My Lai 4 with guns blazing. Gary Crossley said that some GIs, after seeing nothing but women and children in the hamlet, hesitated: "We phoned Medina and told him what the circumstances were, and he said just keep going. It wasn't anything we wanted to do. You can only kill so many women and children. The fact was that you can't go through and wipe out all of South Vietnam."

Carter testified that soon after the third platoon moved in, a woman was sighted. Somebody knocked her down, and then, Carter said, "Medina shot her with his M16 rifle. I was fifty or sixty feet away and saw this. There was no reason to shoot this girl." The men continued on, making sure no one was escaping. "We came to where the soldiers had collected fifteen or more Vietnamese men, women and children in a group. Medina said, 'Kill every one. Leave no one standing.'" A machine gunner began firing into the group. Moments later one of Medina's radio operators slowly "passed among them and finished them off." Medina did not personally shoot any of them, according to Carter, but moments later the captain "stopped a seventeen- or eighteen-year-old man with a water buffalo. Medina told the boy to make a run for it," Carter told the C.I.D. "He tried to get him to run but the boy wouldn't run, so Medina shot him with his M16 rifle and killed him."

Roberts and Haeberle also moved in just behind the third platoon. Haeberle watched a group of ten to fifteen GIs methodically pump bullets into a cow until it keeled over. A woman then poked her head out from behind some brush; she may have been hiding in a bunker. The GIs turned their fire from the cow to the woman. "They just kept shooting at her. You could see the bones flying in the air chip by chip." No one had attempted to question her; GIs inside the hamlet also were asking no questions. Before moving on, the photographer took a picture of the dead woman. Haeberle took many more pictures that day; he saw about thirty GIs kill at least a hundred Vietnamese civilians.

When the two correspondents entered My Lai 4, they saw dead animals, dead people, burning huts and houses. A few GIs were going through victims' clothing, looking for piasters. Another GI was chasing a duck with a knife; others stood around watching a GI slaughter a cow with a bayonet.

Haeberle noticed a man and two small children walking toward a group of GIs: "They just kept walking toward us . . . you could hear the little girl saying, 'No, no . . .' All of a sudden the GIs opened up and cut them down." Later he watched a machine gunner suddenly open fire on a group of civilians—women, children and babies—who had been collected in a big circle: "They were trying to run. I don't know how many got out." He saw a GI with an M16 rifle fire at two young boys walking along a road. The older of the two—about seven or eight years old—fell over the first to protect him. The GI kept on firing until both were dead.

As Haeberle and Roberts walked further into the hamlet, Medina came up to them. Eighty-five Viet Cong had been killed in action thus far, the captain told them, and twenty suspects had been captured. Roberts carefully jotted down the captain's statistics in his notepad.

Now it was nearly nine o'clock and all of Charlie Company was in My Lai 4. Most families were being shot inside their homes, or just outside the doorways. Those who had tried to flee were crammed by GIs into the many bunkers built throughout the hamlet for protection—once the bunkers became filled, hand grenades were lobbed in. Everything became a target. Gary Garfolo borrowed someone's M79 grenade launcher and fired it point-blank at a water buffalo: "I hit that sucker right in the head; went down like a shot. You don't get to shoot water buffalo with an M79 every day." Others fired the weapon into the bunkers full of people.

Carter recalled that some GIs were shouting and yelling during the massacre: "The boys enjoyed it. When someone laughs and jokes about what they're doing, they have to be enjoying it." A GI said, "Hey, I got me another one." Another said, "Chalk up one for me." Even Captain Medina was having a good time, Carter thought: "You can tell when someone enjoys their work." Few members of Charlie

Company protested that day. For the most part, those who didn't like what was going on kept their thoughts to themselves.

Herbert Carter also remembered seeing Medina inside the hamlet well after the third platoon began its advance: "I saw all those dead people laying there. Medina came right behind me." At one point in the morning one of the members of Medina's CP joined in the shooting. "A woman came out of a hut with a baby in her arms and she was crying," Carter told the C.I.D. "She was crying because her little boy had been in front of their hut and . . . someone had killed the child by shooting it." When the mother came into view, one of Medina's men "shot her with an M16 and she fell. When she fell, she dropped the baby." The GI next "opened up on the baby with his M16." The infant was also killed. Carter also saw an officer grab a woman by the hair and shoot her with a .45-caliber pistol: "He held her by the hair for a minute and then let go and she fell to the ground. Some enlisted man standing there said, 'Well, she'll be in the big rice paddy in the sky.' "

In the midst of the carnage, Michael Bernhardt got his first good look at My Lai 4. Bernhardt had been delayed when Medina asked him to check out a suspicious wood box at the landing zone. After discovering that it wasn't a booby trap, Bernhardt hurried to catch up with his mates in the third platoon. He went into the hamlet, where he saw Charlie Company "doing strange things. One: they were setting fire to the hootches and huts and waiting for people to come out and then shooting them. Two: they were going into the hootches and shooting them up. Three: they were gathering people in groups and shooting them. The whole thing was so deliberate. It was point-blank murder and I was standing there watching it. It's kind of made me wonder if I could trust people any more."

Those Vietnamese who were not killed on the spot were being shepherded by the first platoon to a large drainage ditch at the eastern end of the hamlet. After Grzesik left, Meadlo and a few others gathered seven or eight villagers in one hut and were preparing to toss in a hand grenade when an order came to take them to the ditch. There he found Calley, along with a dozen other first platoon members, and perhaps seventy-five Vietnamese, mostly women, old men and children.

Calley then turned his attention back to the crowd of Vietnamese and issued an order: "Push all those people in the ditch." Three or four GIs complied. Calley struck a woman with a rifle as he pushed

her down. Stanley remembered that some of the civilians "kept trying
to get out. Some made it to the top . . ." Calley began the shooting
and ordered Meadlo to join in. Meadlo told about it later: "So we
pushed our seven to eight people in with the big bunch of them.
And so I began shooting them all. So did Mitchell, Calley . . . I guess
I shot maybe twenty-five or twenty people in the ditch . . . men,
women and children. And babies." Some of the GIs switched from
automatic fire to single-shot to conserve ammunition. Herbert Carter
watched the mothers "grabbing their kids and the kids grabbing their
mothers. I didn't know what to do."

William C. Lloyd of Tampa, Florida, told the C.I.D. that some grenades were also thrown into the ditch. Dennis Conti noticed that "a
lot of women had thrown themselves on top of the children to protect
them, and the children were alive at first. Then the children who
were old enough to walk got up and Calley began to shoot the
children."

One further incident stood out in many GI's minds: seconds after
the shooting stopped, a bloodied but unhurt two-year-old boy miraculously crawled out of the ditch, crying. He began running toward
the hamlet. Someone hollered, "There's a kid." There was a long
pause. Then Calley ran back, grabbed the child, threw him back in
the ditch and shot him.

In other parts of My Lai 4, GIs were taking a break, or loafing. Others
were systematically burning those remaining houses and huts and
destroying food. Some villagers—still alive—were able to leave their
hiding places and walk away. Charles West recalled that one member
of his squad who simply wasn't able to slaughter a group of children
asked for and received permission from an officer to let them go.

By now it was nearly 10:30 A.M. and most of the company began
drifting aimlessly toward the plaza and the command post a few
yards to the south. Their work was largely over; a good part of the
hamlet was in flames. The villagers "were laying around like ants,"
William Wyatt remembered. "It was just like somebody had poisoned
the water and everybody took a drink and started falling out."

Herb Carter and Harry Stanley had shed their gear and were
taking a short break at the CP. Near them was a young Vietnamese
boy, crying, with a bullet wound in his stomach. Stanley watched
one of Captain Medina's three radio operators walk along a trail
toward them; he was without his radio gear. As Stanley told the

C.I.D., the radio operator went up to Carter and said, "Let me see your pistol." Carter gave it to him. The radio operator "then stepped within two feet of the boy and shot him in the neck with a pistol. Blood gushed from the child's neck. He then tried to walk off, but he could only take two or three steps. Then he fell onto the ground. He lay there and took four or five deep breaths and then he stopped breathing." The radio operator turned to Stanley and said, "Did you see how I shot that son of a bitch?" Stanley told him, "I don't see how anyone could just kill a kid."

Other children were also last-minute targets. After the scene with the women and children, West noticed a small boy, about seven years old, staring dazedly beside a footpath. He had been shot in the leg. "He was just standing there staring; I don't think he was crying. Somebody asked, 'What do we do with him?'" At this point West remembered there had been an order from Captain Medina to stop the shooting. "I just shrugged my shoulders," West recalled, "and said, 'I don't know,' and just kept walking." Seconds later he heard some shots, turned around and saw the boy no longer standing on the trail.

Some GIs, however, didn't hesitate to use their bayonets. Nineteen-year-old Nguyen Thi Ngoc Tuyet watched a baby trying to open her slain mother's blouse to nurse. A soldier shot the infant while it was struggling with the blouse, and then slashed it with his bayonet. Tuyet also said she saw another baby hacked to death by GIs wielding their bayonets.

In the early afternoon the men of Charlie Company mopped up to make sure all the houses and goods in My Lai 4 were destroyed. Medina ordered the underground tunnels in the hamlet blown up; most of them already had been blocked. Within another hour My Lai 4 was no more: its red-brick buildings demolished by explosives, its huts burned to the ground, its people dead or dying.

Michael Bernhardt later summarized the day: "We met no resistance and I only saw three captured weapons. We had no casualties. It was just like any other Vietnamese village—old papa-sans, women and kids. As a matter of fact, I don't remember seeing one military-age male in the entire place, dead or alive. The only prisoner I saw was in his fifties."

When Army investigators reached the barren area in November, 1969, in connection with the My Lai probe in the United States, they found mass graves at three sites, as well as a ditch full of bodies. It was estimated that between 450 and 500 people—most of them women, children and old men—had been slain and buried there.

JOHN TOLAND

Hiroshima

John Toland (1912–   ) is an American historian and novelist who won a Pulitzer Prize for *The Rising Sun: History of Japan 1936–1945* (1970), from which the following selection is taken. Other books include *The Dillinger Days* (1966), *Adolf Hitler* (1976), and the novel *Gods of War* (1985).

Hiroshima was serene and so was the sky above it as the people continued on their daily routine. Those who noticed the three parachutes imagined that the plane had been hit and that the crew was bailing out or that more propaganda leaflets had been jettisoned. One man, remembering how the last leaflets had shimmered down in the sun, thought, The Americans have brought us some more beautiful things.

Several hundred yards north of Aioi Bridge (Ferebee's target), Private Shigeru Shimoyama, a recent draftee, looked up and idly peered through his thick glasses at one of the drifting chutes. He was standing outside his barracks, a huge wooden structure once a warehouse. He had been in Hiroshima four days and was already "bored to death." He wished he were back in Tokyo making school notebooks. All at once a pinkish light burst in the sky like a cosmic flash bulb.

Clocks all over Hiroshima were fixed forever at 8:15.

The bomb exploded 660 yards from the ground into a fireball almost 110 yards in diameter. Those directly below heard nothing, nor could they later agree what color the *pika* (lightning) flash was— blue, pink, reddish, dark-brown, yellow or purple.

The heat emanating from the fireball lasted a fraction of a second but was so intense (almost 300,000 degrees Centigrade) that it melted the surface of granite within a thousand yards of the hypocenter, or ground zero—directly under the burst. Roof tiles softened and changed in color from black to olive or brown. All over the center of the city numerous silhouettes were imprinted on walls. On Yorozuyo Bridge ten people left permanent outlines of themselves on the railing and the tar-paved surface.

Moments later came an unearthly concussion that obliterated all but a few solid, earthquake-proof buildings within two miles. Ferebee had been almost on target, little more than 300 yards off the intended drop point.

Private Shimoyama was 550 yards north of ground zero. He was not directly exposed to the *pika* flash or his life would have been puffed out, but the blast hurled him into the vast barnlike warehouse, driving him into the collapsing roof beam where five long nails in his back held him suspended several feet off the ground. His glasses were still intact.

Five hundred yards farther north Captain Hideo Sematoo, a company commander, had just cantered up to his office and was removing his riding boots. The building fell on top of him and ignited. He thought of the seven years he had fought in Manchuria, China, Singapore, Malaya and New Guinea. How miserable to be burned to death rather than die in battle! *"Tenno Heika banzai!"* he shouted. As the flames reached for him, the wreckage above him was pulled away and he wrenched himself free. Nauseated, he looked at an eerie yellow sky. The ground was flat as far as he could see. Everything was gone—towering Hiroshima Castle and 2nd General Army headquarters. Instinctively he stumbled and crawled toward the main branch of the Ota River. There, crowded along the banks, were hundreds of dazed patients and nurses from the Army Hospital. Their hair was burned off, their skin charred a dark brown. He felt chilly.

A thousand yards on the other side of the hypocenter, Mrs. Yasuko Nukushina was trapped in the ruins of the family *sake* store. Her first thought was of her four-year-old daughter, Ikuko, who was playing outside somewhere. Unaccountably, she heard Ikuko's voice beside her: "I'm afraid, Mama." She told the child they were buried and would die there. Her own words made her claw desperately at the wreckage. She was a slight woman, four feet six inches tall, but in her frenzy she broke free into the yard. All around was devastation. She somehow felt responsible; "her" bomb had also destroyed the neighborhood. People drifted by expressionless and silent like sleepwalkers in tattered, smoldering clothing. It was a parade of wraiths, an evocation of a Buddhist hell. She watched mesmerized until someone touched her. Grasping Ikuko's hand, she joined the procession.

In her confusion she had the illusion that vast numbers of planes were roaring over the city, dropping bomb after bomb without cessation.

Fourteen hundred yards east of ground zero at the presbytery of the only Catholic church in the city, Father Superior Hugo Lassalle, a German, had heard a plane overhead. He went to the window. The empty sky glared yellow—and the ceiling dropped. Cut and bleeding, Father Lassalle found his way to the street. It was dark. The entire city was covered by a blanket of dust. With another German priest he began searching through the rubble for residents of the mission.

Half a dozen blocks south, fifteen-year-old Michiko Yamaoka had just left home for work at the telephone office. She remembered "a magnesium flash," then a faraway voice calling "Michiko!" Her mother. "I'm here," she answered but didn't know where that was. She couldn't see—she must be blind! She heard her mother shout, "My daughter is buried under there!" Another voice, a man's, advised the mother to escape the flames sweeping down the street. Michiko begged her mother to save herself and heard running steps diminish to silence. She was going to die. Then came a shaft of light as concrete blocks were pushed aside by soldiers. Her mother was bleeding profusely, one arm skewered by a piece of wood. She ordered Michiko to escape. She herself was staying to rescue two relatives under the ruins of their house.

Michiko moved through a nightmare world—past charred bodies—a crying baby sealed behind the twisted iron bars of a collapsed reinforced-concrete building. She saw someone she knew and called out.

"Who are you?" the other girl asked.

"Michiko."

The friend stared at her. "Your nose and eyebrows are gone!"

Michiko felt her face. It was so swollen that her nose seemed to have disappeared.

In the same area, 350 young girls from the Girls Commercial School had been working in an empty lot, clearing an evacuated area. They wore blue *mompei* and jackets but no hats or fire hoods, and those who turned, curious, toward the *pika*—almost 300 of them—were instantly doomed. Twelve-year-old Miyoko Matsubara's instinct was to bury her face in her arms. She regained consciousness in unimaginable desolation—no people, no buildings—only limitless rubble. Where were her *mompei*? All she had around her waist was a white cloth belt and it was on fire. (Everyone wearing dark clothing who was exposed to the *pika* suffered primary thermal burns but the cruel flash reflected harmlessly off white material.) She started to beat out the flames with her right hand but to her horror she saw strips of skin, her skin, dangling from it.

Mrs. Tomita had given birth to a baby girl that morning. Together with her husband, Torao, she was admiring their newborn daughter, Hiroko, when an intense light filled the window. Mrs. Tomita remembered a whooshing noise before losing consciousness. She came to on the floor. Her husband was gone. The baby in her little red dress was lying on top of the sewing machine—alive but unnaturally silent. Mrs. Tomita wrapped diapers tightly around her distended stomach—the midwife had told her to move as little as possible—and walked out into the street with the baby. Torao was hysterically digging in the ruins for their other two children. He found the elder daughter still alive, but her brother was hopelessly buried somewhere under the mass. There was a shout that more planes were on the way and the family sought shelter in a ditch trickling with foul water.

Less than a mile south of ground zero the main building of Hiroshima University stood intact amid the devastation. The hands of its huge clock, which faced the campus, had stopped at 8:15. But the bomb, which had stilled so many other clocks and watches at that time, had nothing to do with it; several days previously it had stopped prophetically at that catastrophic moment.

Two student nurses, who were ill in bed at a wooden dormitory of the Red Cross Hospital across the street, neither saw nor heard the bomb. Their first sensation was that their lungs were collapsing. Kyoko Sato crawled out of the caved-in building into a maelstrom of dust. A muffled call, "Sato-*san!*" led her to her friend, whom she pried loose from the debris. Together they tried to cross the highway to report to the hospital but couldn't penetrate the solid stream of silent humanity moving away from the city, half naked and bleeding but without hysteria, not even tears. The unreality of it was terrifying.

Dr. Fumio Shigeto, head of internal medicine at the hospital, never reached his office that morning. On his way to work, he was waiting for a trolley at the end of a long line which bent around the corner of the Hiroshima railway station, 2,000 yards east of the hypocenter. The flash seemed to turn a group of girls ahead of him white, almost invisible. An incendiary bomb! As he dropped to the sidewalk, covering eyes and ears, a heavy slate slammed into his back. Whirls of smoke blotted out the sun. In the darkness he groped blindly to reach shelter before the next wave of attackers came on. Fearing poison gas, he covered his mouth with a handkerchief.

A breeze from the east gradually cleared the area as though it were dawn, revealing an incredible scene: the buildings in front of the station were collapsed, flattened; half-naked and smoldering bodies covered the ground. Of the people at the trolley stop he alone, the last one in line, was unhurt, protected by the corner of the station building. Dr. Shigeto started for the hospital but was stopped by an impenetrable wall of advancing flames. He turned and ran for open space—toward an Army drill ground behind the station. He saw scores of survivors milling around, crying hysterically, and to ease the pain of their burns they extended their arms from which dangled long curls of skin.

A nurse approached him; he must be a doctor because he carried a black bag and had a trim little mustache. She begged him to help another doctor and his wife lying on the ground. His first thought was: What if this mob of desperate people discovers I am a physician? He couldn't help them all. "Please treat my wife first," said the injured doctor, who was bleeding profusely. Shigeto gave the woman a camphor shot for shock, followed by another injection to stop the bleeding. He rearranged the bandages the nurse had applied and then turned to the other wounded, treating them until he ran out of medicine and supplies. There was nothing else he could do. He fled toward the hills.

Two and a half miles south of the hypocenter, former news photographer Gonichi Kimura was working outside a stable for the Army when he saw a strong flash to his left and simultaneously felt a searing blast of heat. At first he thought the Hiroshima Gas Company's tank had exploded, but since he soon discovered that it was still standing, he felt intuitively that some special bomb must have been dropped and decided to take pictures as soon as he could get to his camera, which was stored in the warehouse nearby. By the time he had crawled through the wreckage of the stable, the narrow white column of smoke from the bomb had changed to pink and the top started to swell, making it look like a mushroom, and it kept growing massively.

At the warehouse Kimura found all the windows shattered from the blast, and there was so much broken glass on the floor where his camera was kept that he could not even step inside, but he managed to stretch in and pull the drawer open. The trees outside the warehouse were in the way, so he returned to the stable to take his first pictures of the atomic cloud—"indeed, a gruesome sight"—which was now covering most of the sky. Fires which had broken out in the western part of the city were spreading rapidly, and he finished his roll of film from the roof of a factory. Kimura escaped the bomb without injury, but he never saw his wife again—he had left her at home after breakfast that morning.

Those near the hypocenter never heard the explosion of the bomb. With distance, the noise grew perceptible, then shattering. From three miles it sounded like the rumbling of unworldly thunder; at four miles it was a distant moan which grew into a jarring boom. Near the port of Kure, twelve miles to the southeast, Tadahiko Kitayama thought a nearby ammunition dump had detonated, and several miles offshore, salvagers attempting to raise the four-man submarine *Koryu*, which was stuck in the bottom mud, heard a deafening "thunderbolt" clap. Moments later they noticed a B-29 coming from the direction of Hiroshima.

For a quarter of an hour the atmosphere above Hiroshima was churned by cosmic forces. Then huge drops of rain began to plummet down. The rising cloud column had carried moisture sufficiently high for water vapor to condense, and stained by radioactive dust, fall in large drops. The "black rain," weird and almost supernatural, horrified the survivors. Was it some kind of poisonous oil that would stick to the skin and slowly kill them? It pelted down on the half-naked people, leaving gray streaks on their bodies, releasing in many of them a sense of awareness of the unimaginable disaster that had been visited on Hiroshima. Mrs. Tomita tried to protect her two-hour-old baby, but little Hiroko was soaked by the fallout. She still had not uttered a sound since the blast.

The deadly rain, which had changed into a foggy, yellowish drizzle, spread to the northwest. Almost none fell on the area to the east where the fires were more intense, and Dr. Yoshimasa Matsuzaka, a skin specialist and head of the city's civil defense, was trying to bring some order out of chaos. Ignoring his own wounds, he put on his civil defense uniform which his wife had rescued from the wreckage of his office, and leaning on his son, marched toward the East District police station holding high a Rising Sun flag on a long stick. The sight of the determined little procession extending first-aid treatment—Mrs. Matsuzaka and three nurses brought up the rear—calmed the people. The group set up a first-aid station in front of the police headquarters—it was 1,200 yards from the hypocenter—and long lines of injured and burned began to form outside the shell of the station house.

From his destroyed home less than half a mile away the police chief, Shiroku Tanabe, was desperately trying to get to the station. But he was impeded by thousands of refugees (they looked "as if they had crawled out of a pool of blood") streaming away from ground zero. By the time Tanabe reached the station house, it had caught fire. He took command and organized a bucket brigade to a nearby "fire pool." Though half the building was ablaze, Dr. Matsuzaka and his indomitable first-aid team continued to treat the injured and to urge them to seek refuge outside the city.

All over town, charcoal braziers full of hot coals (housewives had been preparing breakfast) ignited the tinderbox rubble. These thousands of small fires were whipped into fury by a cyclonic wind that was sucked in toward the hypocenter with such force that large trees were uprooted. Blasts of flame—they could have come from monster blowtorches—erratically ripped off corrugated roofs as if they were cardboard, blasted houses apart and twisted metal bridges. Telephone poles ignited explosively.

Near the site of Hiroshima Castle four men staggered through the burning streets with a massive portrait of the Emperor; they had rescued it from the inferno of the 2nd General Army communications center and were trying to get it safely out of the city. At the sight of the picture, lines of apathetic refugees broke into cries of "The Emperor's portrait!" The burned and bleeding saluted or bowed low. Those unable to get to their feet clasped hands in prayer. As the picture was trundled through Asano Sentei Park to a waiting boat moored on the river, towering pine trees flamed into torches. Wounded soldiers on the banks, waiting to be rescued, struggled to attention and saluted as the boat headed upstream for safety through a shower of flaming debris.

Their commander, General Fujii, was incinerated in the first minutes at his quarters near the castle but Private Shigeru Shimoyama, who was closer to ground zero, was still alive even after being impaled on the spikes of a roof beam. He painfully pulled himself free from the spikes, and using his head as a battering ram, relentlessly slammed at the roof, blinded by streams of blood, until he broke through. Thick stifling clouds of dust swirled about him, but he could tell that some irresistible force had swept across the city like the hand of a vengeful giant. At the river he watched scores of wounded making the long frantic leap from its banks. What did they think they were doing? The surface of the water was covered with carmine scum. From blood? Shimoyama kept telling himself to remain calm. He was no stranger to disaster; he had almost been killed in the earthquake of '23, the Doolittle raid and the Tokyo fire bombing of April 13. He started up the river against the wind; it would help keep the fires behind him.

Directly in his path was a cavalry horse standing alone. It was pink; the blast had seared off its skin. It looked at him pleadingly and followed with a few faltering steps. The pitiful sight fascinated Shimoyama, and he had to force himself to press on (he would dream about the pink horse for years afterward). Half a dozen other soldiers were also purposefully following the bank north, but it was as if each man was solitary, preoccupied with his own survival. Civilians, some almost naked, tried to keep up with them, but as the dull rumble of flames behind grew louder, the soldiers quickened their pace, leaving the others far behind.

Several miles upstream Shimoyama forded the river where the water only came up to his neck. As he proceeded into the suburbs where the havoc of the bomb had not reached, he was obsessed by one thought—that it was an atomic bomb. He must get home and see his daughter before he died of the effects. In 1943 a brother-in-law of his had informed him that the Japanese were working on one and for the past few days, oddly, there had been so much talk in his barracks about such a bomb that if a man lost his temper someone would say, "He's like an atomic bomb." He passed scores of high school girls, horribly burned, sprawling on either side of the road. Long strips of skin hung in ribbons from their faces, arms and legs. They reached out in supplication for water. But what could he do? Farther up the road, villagers were laying sliced cucumbers on the burns of other survivors and carrying those most seriously hurt to first-aid stations in vegetable carts.

In the dying light of dusk the fires began to subside and from a distance Hiroshima looked peaceful, like the gigantic encampment of a quiescent army on the plain. And high overhead, stars appeared startlingly bright against the darkening sky. The flow out of the city had been reversed as the first trickle of help entered from the outside.

Dr. Shigeto of the Red Cross Hospital, who had fled the holocaust, was back. Going from one first-aid station to another, he was told that water was harmful for those suffering burns. On the contrary, he announced, it flushed the poison from burns out of the system. He had signs put up: YOU MAY GIVE WATER. DR. SHIGETO, VICE DIRECTOR, RED CROSS HOSPITAL.

As he penetrated deeper into the ravaged city, he found his way blocked by smoldering rubble. Although there seemed to be no passable road, he saw to his astonishment a large charcoal-burning truck come rumbling, out of the smoke, its cab crowded with men. He recognized the driver, a *sake* manufacturer from his suburb. He had braved the inferno to carry emergency food and *sake* to his customers, but found their stores burned down. Shigeto started past the truck. "There's not a living soul in there!" the driver called out. "Not an animal. What use is a doctor?" Shigeto was forcibly lifted into the truck.

The doctor had to borrow a bicycle to cover the last mile home. He came unexpectedly upon a woman, a baby on her back, wandering on the dark road. When she saw him she began to weep hysterically. It was his wife, and in his memory, she had already placed a burning candle on the family Buddhist shrine.

Outside the city, first-aid stations were powerless to help the hundreds dying every hour. Seven-year-old Shizuko Iura was close to death but no one had heard her cry or complain. She continually asked for water, which her mother gave her against the advice of attendants. Why not ease her dying? "Father [he was a sailor on some Pacific island] is far away from home in a dangerous place," Shizuko said as if she saw him in a vision. "Please stay alive, Mother. If both of us die, he will be very lonely." She mentioned the names of all her friends and relatives. When she came to her grandparents she added, "They were good to me." She cried "Papa, Papa!" and died.

That day perhaps 100,000 human beings perished in Hiroshima, and an equal number were dying from burns, injuries and a disease of the atomic age, radiation poisoning.

JONATHAN SCHELL

The Bomb Drops on New York

Jonathan Schell (1943–), born in New York City, is a journalist and contributing editor to the *New Yorker*. Schell's books *The Village of Ben Suc* (1967) and *The Military Half* (1968) vividly depict the violence of the Vietnam War. In *The Fate of the Earth* (1982), from which the following essay is taken, Schell warns of the threat of nuclear war. His most recent book is *Observing the Nixon Years* (1989).

One way to begin to grasp the destructive power of present-day nuclear weapons is to describe the consequences of the detonation

of a one-megaton bomb, which possesses eighty times the explosive
power of the Hiroshima bomb, on a large city, such as New York.
Burst some eighty-five hundred feet above the Empire State Building,
a one-megaton bomb would gut or flatten almost every building
between Battery Park and 125th Street, or within a radius of four
and four-tenths miles, or in an area of sixty-one square miles, and
would heavily damage buildings between the northern tip of Staten
Island and the George Washington Bridge, or within a radius of
about eight miles, or in an area of about two hundred square miles.
A conventional explosive delivers a swift shock, like a slap, to whatever it hits, but the blast wave of a sizable nuclear weapon endures
for several seconds and "can surround and destroy whole buildings"
(Glasstone).[1] People, of course, would be picked up and hurled away
from the blast along with the rest of the debris. Within the sixty-one
square miles, the walls, roofs, and floors of any buildings that had
not been flattened would be collapsed, and the people and furniture
inside would be swept down onto the street. (Technically, this zone
would be hit by various overpressures of at least five pounds per
square inch. Overpressure is defined as the pressure in excess of
normal atmospheric pressure.) As far away as ten miles from ground
zero, pieces of glass and other sharp objects would be hurled about
by the blast wave at lethal velocities. In Hiroshima, where buildings
were low and, outside the center of the city, were often constructed
of light materials, injuries from falling buildings were often minor.
But in New York, where the buildings are tall and are constructed
of heavy materials, the physical collapse of the city would certainly
kill millions of people. The streets of New York are narrow ravines
running between the high walls of the city's buildings. In a nuclear
attack, the walls would fall and the ravines would fill up. The people
in the buildings would fall to the street with the debris of the
buildings, and the people in the street would be crushed by this
avalanche of people and buildings. At a distance of two miles or so
from ground zero, winds would reach four hundred miles an hour,
and another two miles away they would reach a hundred and eighty
miles an hour. Meanwhile, the fireball would be growing, until it
was more than a mile wide, and rocketing upward, to a height of
over six miles. For ten seconds, it would broil the city below. Anyone
caught in the open within nine miles of ground zero would receive

---

[1] Quote from Samuel Glasstone, editor with Philip Dolan of *Effects of Nuclear Weapons.*
(ED.)

third-degree burns and would probably be killed; closer to the explosion, people would be charred and killed instantly. From Greenwich Village up to Central Park, the heat would be great enough to melt metal and glass. Readily inflammable materials, such as newspapers and dry leaves, would ignite in all five boroughs (though in only a small part of Staten Island) and west to the Passaic River, in New Jersey, within a radius of about nine and a half miles from ground zero, thereby creating an area of more than two hundred and eighty square miles in which mass fires were likely to break out.

If it were possible (as it would not be) for someone to stand at Fifth Avenue and Seventy-second Street (about two miles from ground zero) without being instantly killed, he would see the following sequence of events. A dazzling white light from the fireball would illumine the scene, continuing for perhaps thirty seconds. Simultaneously, searing heat would ignite everything flammable and start to melt windows, cars, buses, lampposts, and everything else made of metal or glass. People in the street would immediately catch fire, and would shortly be reduced to heavily charred corpses. About five seconds after the light appeared, the blast wave would strike, laden with the debris of a now nonexistent midtown. Some buildings might be crushed, as though a giant fist had squeezed them on all sides, and others might be picked up off their foundations and whirled uptown with the other debris. On the far side of Central Park, the West Side skyline would fall from south to north. The four-hundred-mile-an-hour wind would blow from south to north, die down after a few seconds, and then blow in the reverse direction with diminished intensity. While these things were happening, the fireball would be burning in the sky for the ten seconds of the thermal pulse. Soon huge, thick clouds of dust and smoke would envelop the scene, and as the mushroom cloud rushed overhead (it would have a diameter of about twelve miles) the light from the sun would be blotted out, and day would turn to night. Within minutes, fires, ignited both by the thermal pulse and by broken gas mains, tanks of gas and oil, and the like, would begin to spread in the darkness, and a strong, steady wind would begin to blow in the direction of the blast. As at Hiroshima, a whirlwind might be produced, which would sweep through the ruins, and radioactive rain, generated under the meteorological conditions created by the blast, might fall. Before long, the individual fires would coalesce into a mass fire, which, depending largely on the winds, would become either a conflagration or a firestorm. In a conflagration, prevailing winds spread a wall of fire as far as there is any combustible material to sustain it; in a firestorm, a vertical updraft caused by the fire itself sucks the surrounding air in toward a central point, and the fires therefore converge in a single fire of extreme heat. A mass fire of either kind renders shelters useless by burning up all the oxygen in the air and creating toxic gases, so that anyone inside the shelters is asphyxiated, and also by heating the ground to such high temperatures that the shelters turn, in effect, into ovens, cremating the people inside them. In Dresden, several days after the firestorm raised there by Allied conventional bombing, the interiors of some bomb shelters were still so hot that when they were opened the inrushing air caused the contents to burst into flame. Only those who had fled their shelters when the bombing started had any chance of surviving. (It is difficult to predict in a particular situation which form the fires will take. In actual experience, Hiroshima suffered a firestorm and Nagasaki suffered a conflagration.)

In this vast theatre of physical effects, all the scenes of agony and death that took place at Hiroshima would again take place, but now involving millions of people rather than hundreds of thousands. Like the people of Hiroshima, the people of New York would be burned, battered, crushed, and irradiated in every conceivable way. The city and its people would be mingled in a smoldering heap. And then, as the fires started, the survivors (most of whom would be on the periphery of the explosion) would be driven to abandon to the flames those family members and other people who were unable to flee, or else to die with them. Before long, while the ruins burned, the processions of injured, mute people would begin their slow progress out of the outskirts of the devastated zone. However, this time a much smaller proportion of the population than at Hiroshima would have a chance of escaping. In general, as the size of the area of devastation increases, the possibilities for escape decrease. When the devastated area is relatively small, as it was at Hiroshima, people who are not incapacitated will have a good chance of escaping to safety before the fires coalesce into a mass fire. But when the devastated area is great, as it would be after the detonation of a megaton bomb, and fires are springing up at a distance of nine and a half miles from ground zero, and when what used to be the streets are piled high with burning rubble, and the day (if the attack occurs in the daytime) has grown impenetrably dark, there is little chance that anyone who is not on the very edge of the devastated area will be able to make his way to safety. In New York, most people would die wherever the blast found them, or not very far from there.

If instead of being burst in the air the bomb were burst on or near the ground in the vicinity of the Empire State Building, the overpressure would be very much greater near the center of the blast area but the range hit by a minimum of five pounds per square inch of overpressure would be less. The range of the thermal pulse would be about the same as that of the air burst. The fireball would be almost two miles across, and would engulf midtown Manhattan from Greenwich Village nearly to Central Park. Very little is known about what would happen to a city that was inside a fireball, but one would expect a good deal of what was there to be first pulverized and then melted or vaporized. Any human beings in the area would be reduced to smoke and ashes; they would simply disappear. A crater roughly three blocks in diameter and two hundred feet deep would open up. In addition, heavy radioactive fallout would be created as dust and debris from the city rose with the mushroom cloud and then fell back to the ground. Fallout would begin to drop almost immediately, contaminating the ground beneath the cloud with levels of radiation many times lethal doses, and quickly killing anyone who might have survived the blast wave and the thermal pulse and might now be attempting an escape; it is difficult to believe that there would be appreciable survival of the people of the city after a megaton ground burst. And for the next twenty-four hours or so more fallout would descend downwind from the blast, in a plume whose direction and length would depend on the speed and the direction of the wind that happened to be blowing at the time of the attack. If the wind was blowing at fifteen miles an hour, fallout of lethal intensity would descend in a plume about a hundred and fifty miles long and as much as fifteen miles wide. Fallout that was sublethal but could still cause serious illness would extend another hundred and fifty miles downwind. Exposure to radioactivity in human beings is measured in units called rems—an acronym for "roentgen equivalent in man." The roentgen is a standard measurement of gamma- and X-ray radiation, and the expression "equivalent in man" indicates that an adjustment has been made to take into account the differences in the degree of biological damage that is caused by radiation of different types. Many of the kinds of harm done to human beings by radiation—for example, the incidence of cancer and of genetic damage—depend on the dose accumulated over many years; but radiation sickness, capable of causing death, results from an "acute" dose, received in a period of anything from a few seconds to several days. Because almost ninety per cent of the so-called "infinite-time dose" of radiation from fallout—that is, the dose from a given quantity of fallout that one would receive if one lived for many thousands of years—is emitted in the first week, the one-week accumulated dose is often used as a convenient measure for calculating the immediate harm from fallout. Doses in the thousands of rems, which could be expected throughout the city, would attack the central nervous system and would bring about death within a few hours. Doses of around a thousand rems, which would be delivered some tens of miles downwind from the blast, would kill within two weeks everyone who was exposed to them. Doses of around five hundred rems, which would be delivered as far as a hundred and fifty miles downwind (given a wind speed of fifteen miles per hour), would kill half of all exposed able-bodied young adults. At this level of exposure, radiation sickness proceeds in the three stages observed at Hiroshima. The plume of lethal fallout could descend, depending on the direction of the wind, on other parts of New York State and parts of New Jersey, Pennsylvania, Delaware, Maryland, Connecticut, Massachusetts, Rhode Island, Vermont, and New Hampshire, killing additional millions of people. The circumstances in heavily contaminated areas, in which millions of people were all declining together, over a period of weeks, toward painful deaths, are ones that, like so many of the consequences of nuclear explosions, have never been experienced.

A description of the effects of a one-megaton bomb on New York City gives some notion of the meaning in human terms of a megaton of nuclear explosive power, but a weapon that is more likely to be used against New York is the twenty-megaton bomb, which has one thousand six hundred times the yield of the Hiroshima bomb. The Soviet Union is estimated to have at least a hundred and thirteen twenty-megaton bombs in its nuclear arsenal, carried by Bear intercontinental bombers. In addition, some of the Soviet SS-18 missiles are capable of carrying bombs of this size, although the actual yields are not known. Since the explosive power of the twenty-megaton bombs greatly exceeds the amount necessary to destroy most military targets, it is reasonable to suppose that they are meant for use against large cities. If a twenty-megaton bomb were airburst over the Empire State Building at an altitude of thirty thousand feet, the zone gutted or flattened by the blast wave would have a radius of twelve miles and an area of more than four hundred and fifty square miles, reaching from the middle of Staten Island to the northern edge of the Bronx, the eastern edge of Queens, and well into New Jersey, and the zone of heavy damage from the blast wave (the zone hit by a minimum of two pounds of overpressure per square inch) would have a radius of twenty-one and a half miles, or an area of one thousand four hundred and fifty square miles, reaching to the southernmost tip of Staten Island, north as far as southern Rockland County, east into Nassau County, and west to Morris County, New Jersey. The fireball would be about four and a half miles in diameter and would radiate the thermal pulse for some twenty seconds. People caught in the open twenty-three miles away from ground zero, in Long Island, New Jersey, and southern New York State, would be burned to death. People hundreds of miles away who looked at the burst would be temporarily blinded and would risk permanent eye injury. (After the test of a fifteen-megaton bomb on Bikini Atoll, in the South Pacific, in March of 1954, small animals were found to have suffered retinal burns at a distance of three hundred and forty-five miles.) The mushroom cloud would be seventy miles in diameter. New York City and its suburbs would be transformed into a lifeless, flat, scorched desert in a few seconds.

If a twenty-megaton bomb were ground-burst on the Empire State Building, the range of severe blast damage would, as with the one-megaton ground blast, be reduced, but the fireball, which would be almost six miles in diameter, would cover Manhattan from Wall Street to northern Central Park and also parts of New Jersey, Brooklyn, and Queens, and everyone within it would be instantly killed, with most of them physically disappearing. Fallout would again be generated, this time covering thousands of square miles with lethal intensities of radiation. A fair portion of New York City and its incinerated population, now radioactive dust, would have risen into the mushroom cloud and would now be descending on the surrounding territory. On one of the few occasions when local fallout was generated by a test explosion in the multi-megaton range, the fifteen-megaton bomb tested on Bikini Atoll, which was exploded seven feet above the surface of a coral reef, "caused substantial contamination over an area of more than seven thousand square miles," according to Glasstone. If, as seems likely, a twenty-megaton bomb ground-burst on New York would produce at least a comparable amount of fallout, and if the wind carried the fallout onto populated areas, then this one bomb would probably doom upward of twenty million people, or almost ten per cent of the population of the United States.

OLIVE SCHREINER

Woman and War

Olive Schreiner (1855–1920) was a South African author, social
activist, and outspoken feminist who supported the causes of persecuted Jews and striking trade-union workers, and protested the
racist policies of her native country. She gained notoriety with *The
Story of a South African Farm* in 1883. The following selection is
from her book *Woman and Labour* (1911).

It may be said, 'Granting fully that you are right, that, as woman's
old fields of labour slip from her, she must grasp the new, or must
become wholly dependent on her sexual function alone, all the other
elements of human nature in her becoming atrophied and arrested
through lack of exercise: and, granting that her evolution being
arrested, the evolution of the whole race will be also arrested in her
person: granting all this to the full, and allowing that the bulk of
human labour tends to become more and more intellectual and less
and less purely mechanical, as perfected machinery takes the place
of crude human exertion; and that therefore if woman is to be saved
from degeneration and parasitism, and the body of humanity from
arrest, she must receive a training which will cultivate all the intellectual and all the physical faculties with which she is endowed, and
be allowed freely to employ them; nevertheless, would it not be
possible, and perhaps be well, that a dividing line of some kind
should be drawn between the occupations of men and of women?
Would it not, for example, be possible that woman should retain
agriculture, textile manufacture, trade, domestic management, the
education of youth, and medicine, in addition to child-bearing, as
her exclusive fields of toil; while to the male should be left the study
of abstract science, law, and war, and statecraft; as of old, man took
war and the chase, and woman absorbed the further labours of life?
Why should there not be again a fair and even division in the field
of social labour?'
    Superficially, this suggestion appears rational, having at least this
to recommend it—that it appears to harmonize with the course of
human evolution in the past; but closely examined, it will, we think,
be found to have no practical or scientific basis, and to be out of
harmony with the conditions of modern life. In ancient and primitive
societies, the mere larger size and muscular strength of man, and

woman's incessant physical activity in child-bearing and suckling and
rearing the young, made almost inevitable a certain sexual division
of labour in almost all countries, save perhaps in ancient Egypt.[1]
Woman naturally took the heavy agricultural and domestic labours,
which were yet more consistent with the continual dependence of
infant life on her own, than those of man in war and the chase. There
was nothing artificial in such a division; it threw the heaviest burden
of the most wearying and unexciting forms of social labour on
woman, but under it both sexes laboured in a manner essential to
the existence of society, and each transmitted to the other, through
inheritance, the fruit of its slowly expanding and always exerted
powers; and the race progressed.

Individual women might sometimes, and even often, become the
warrior chief of a tribe; the King of Ashantee might train his terrible
regiment of females; and men might now and again plant and weave
for their children: but in the main, and in most societies, the division
of labour was just, natural, beneficial; and it was inevitable that such
a division should take place. Were today a band of civilized men,
women, and infants thrown down absolutely naked and defenceless
in some desert, and cut off hopelessly from all external civilized life,
undoubtedly very much of the old division of labour would, at least
for a time, reassert itself; men would look about for stones and sticks
with which to make weapons to repel wild beasts and enemies, and
would go a-hunting meat and fighting savage enemies and tend the
beasts when tamed:[2] women would suckle their children, cook the
meat men brought, build shelters, look for roots and if possible
cultivate them; there certainly would be no parasite in the society;
the woman who refused to labour for her offspring, and the man
who refused to hunt or defend society, would not be supported by
their fellows, would soon be extinguished by want. As wild beasts
were extinguished and others tamed and the materials for war improved, fewer men would be needed for hunting and war; then they
would remain at home and aid in building and planting; many women
would retire into the house to perfect domestic toil and handicrafts,
and on a small scale the common ancient evolution of society would

---

[1] 'The division of labour between the sexes in ancient Egypt and other exceptional
countries, is a matter of much interest, which can not here be entered on.' (Olive
Schreiner's note.)

[2] 'The young captured animals would probably be tamed and reared by the women.'
(Olive Schreiner's note.)

practically repeat itself. But for the present, we see no such natural and spontaneous division of labour based on natural sexual distinctions in the new fields of intellectual or delicately skilled manual labour, which are taking the place of the old.

It is possible, though at present there is nothing to give indication of such a fact, and it seems highly improbable, that, in some subtle manner now incomprehensible, there might tend to be a subtle correlation between that condition of the brain and nervous system which accompanies ability in the direction of certain modern forms of mental, social labour, and the particular form of reproductive function possessed by an individual. It may be that, inexplicable as it seems, there may ultimately be found to be some connection between that condition of the brain and nervous system which fits the individual for the study of the higher mathematics, let us say, and the nature of their sex attributes. The mere fact that, of the handful of women who, up to the present, have received training and been allowed to devote themselves to abstract study, several have excelled in the higher mathematics, proves of necessity no pre-eminent tendency on the part of the female sex in the direction of mathematics, as compared to labour in the fields of statesmanship, administration, or law; as into these fields there has been practically no admittance for women. It is sometimes stated, that as several women of genius in modern times have sought to find expression for their creative powers in the art of fiction, there must be some inherent connection in the human brain between the ovarian sex function and the art of fiction. The fact is, that modern fiction being merely a description of human life in any of its phases, and being the only art that can be exercised without special training or special appliances, and produced in the moments stolen from the multifarious, brain-destroying occupations which fill the average woman's life, they have been driven to find this outlet for their powers as the only one presenting itself. How far otherwise might have been the directions in which their genius would naturally have expressed itself can be known only partially even to the women themselves; what the world has lost by that compulsory expression of genius, in a form which may not have been its most natural form of expression, or only one of its forms, no one can ever know. Even in the little third-rate novelist whose works cumber the ground, we see often a pathetic figure, when we recognize that beneath that failure in a complex and difficult art, may lie buried a sound legislator, an able architect, an original scientific investigator, or a good judge. Scientifically speaking, it is as unproven that there is any organic relation between the brain of the female and the production of art in the form of fiction, as that there is an organic relation between the hand of a woman and a typewriting machine. Both the creative writer and the typist, in their respective spheres, are merely finding outlets for their powers in the direction of least resistance. The tendency of women at the present day to undertake certain forms of labour, proves only that in the crabbed, walled-in, and bound conditions surrounding woman at the present day, these are the lines along which action is most possible to her.

It may possibly be that in future ages, when the male and female forms have been placed in like intellectual conditions, with like stimuli, like training, and like rewards, that some aptitudes may be found running parallel with the line of sex function when humanity is viewed as a whole. It may possibly be that, when the historian of the future looks back over the history of the intellectually freed and active sexes for countless generations, that a decided preference of the female intellect for mathematics, engineering, or statecraft may be made clear; and that a like marked inclination in the male to excel in acting, music, or astronomy may by careful and large comparison be shown. But, for the present, we have no adequate scientific data from which to draw any conclusion, and any attempt to divide the occupations in which male and female intellects and wills should be employed, must be to attempt a purely artificial and arbitrary division: a division not more rational and scientific than an attempt to determine by the colour of his eyes and the shape and strength of his legs, whether a lad should be an astronomer or an engraver. Those physical differences among mankind which divide races and nations—not merely those differences, enormously greater as they are generally, than any physical differences between male and female of the same race, which divide the Jew and the Swede, the Japanese and the Englishman, but even those subtle physical differences which divide closely allied races such as the English and German—often appear to be allied with certain subtle differences in intellectual aptitudes. Yet even with regard to these differences, it is almost impossible to determine scientifically in how far they are the result of national traditions, environment, and education, and in how far the result of real differences in organic conformation.[3]

---

[3] 'In thinking of physical sex differences, the civilised man of modern times has always to guard himself against being unconsciously misled by the very exaggerated external sex differences which our unnatural method of sex clothing and dressing the hair

No study of the mere physical differences between individuals of different races would have enabled us to arrive at any knowledge of their mental aptitude; nor does the fact that certain individuals of a given human variety have certain aptitudes form a rational ground for compelling all individuals of that variety to undertake a certain form of labour.

No analysis, however subtle, of the physical conformation of the Jew could have suggested *a priori,* and still less could have proved, apart from ages of practical experience, that, running parallel with any physical characteristics which may distinguish him from his fellows, was an innate and unique intellectual gift in the direction of religion. The fact that, during three thousand years, from Moses to Isaiah, through Jesus and Paul, on to Spinoza,[4] the Jewish race has produced men who have given half the world its religious faith and impetus, proves that, somewhere and somehow, whether connected organically with that physical organization that marks the Jew, or as the result of his traditions and training, there does go this gift in the matter of religion. Yet, on the other hand, we find millions of Jews who are totally and markedly deficient in it, and to base any practical legislation for the individual even on this proven intellectual aptitude of the race as a whole would be manifestly as ridiculous as abortive. Yet more markedly, with the German—no consideration of his physical peculiarities, though it proceeded to the subtlest analysis of nerve, bone, and muscle, could in the present stage of our knowledge

produces. The unclothed and natural human male and female bodies are not more divided from each other than those of the lion and lioness. Our remote Saxon ancestors, with their great, almost naked, white bodies and flowing hair worn long by both sexes, were but little distinguished from each other; while among their modern descendants the short hair, darkly clothed, manifestly two-legged male differs from the usually long-haired, color bedizened, much beskirted female. Were the structural differences between male and female really one-half as marked as the artificial visual differences, they would be greater than those dividing, not merely any species of man from another, but as great as those which divide orders in the animal world. Only a mind exceedingly alert and analytical can fail ultimately to be misled by habitual visual misrepresentation. There is not, probably, one man or woman in twenty thousand who is not powerfully influenced in modern life in their conception of the differences, physical and intellectual, dividing the human male and female, by the grotesque exaggerations of modern attire and artificial manners.' (Olive Schreiner's note.)

[4] Benedict de Spinoza (1632–77), Jewish Rationalist philosopher; elaborated theory of 'monism', or all being reducible to a single category, such as, in Spinoza's case, 'pantheism' (everything is part of god). (Note by Carol Barash, editor of *An Olive Schreiner Reader.*)

have proved to us what generations of experience appear to have proved, that, with that organization which constitutes the German, goes an unique aptitude for music. There is always the possibility of mistaking the result of training and external circumstance for inherent tendency, but when we consider the passion for music which the German has shown, and when we consider that the greatest musicians the world has seen, from Bach, Beethoven, and Mozart to Wagner,[5] have been of that race, it appears highly probable that such a correlation between the German organization and the intellectual gift of music does exist. Similar intellectual peculiarities seem to be connoted by the external differences which mark off other races from each other. Nevertheless, were persons of all these nationalities gathered in one colony, any attempt to legislate for their restriction to certain forms of intellectual labour on the ground of their apparently proved national aptitudes or disabilities, would be regarded as insane. To insist that all Jews, and none but Jews, should lead and instruct in religious matters; that all Englishmen, and none but Englishmen, should engage in trade; that each German should make his living by music, and none but a German allowed to practise it, would drive to despair the unfortunate individual Englishman, whose most marked deficiency might be in the direction of finance and bartering trade power; the Jew, whose religious instincts might be entirely rudimentary; or the German, who could not distinguish one note from another; and the society as a whole would be an irremediable loser, in one of the heaviest of all forms of social loss—the loss of the full use of the highest capacities of all its members.

It may be that with sexes as with races, the subtlest physical differences between them may have their fine mental correlatives; but no abstract consideration of the human body in relation to its functions of sex can, in the present state of our knowledge, show us what intellectual capacities tend to vary with sexual structure, and nothing in the present or past condition of male and female give us more than the very faintest possible indication of the relation of their intellectual aptitudes and their sexual functions. And even were it proved by centuries of experiment that with the possession of the uterine function of sex tends to go exceptional intellectual capacity in the direction of mathematics rather than natural history, or an

---

[5] Famous European composers: Johann Sebastian Bach (1685–1750); Ludwig van Beethoven (1770–1827); Wolfgang Amadeus Mozart (1756–91); Richard Wagner (1813–83). (Note by Carol Barash, editor of *An Olive Schreiner Reader*.)

inclination for statecraft rather than for mechanical invention; were it proved that, generally speaking and as a whole, out of twenty thousand women devoting themselves to law and twenty thousand to medicine, they tended to achieve relatively more in the field of law than of medicine, there would yet be no possible healthy or rational ground for restricting the activities of the individual female to that line in which the average female appeared rather more frequently to excel.[6]

That even one individual in a society should be debarred from undertaking that form of social toil for which it is most fitted, makes an unnecessary deficit in the general social assets. That one male Froebel[7] should be prohibited or hampered in his labour as an educator of infancy, on the ground that infantile instruction was the field of the female; that one female with gifts in the direction of state administration, should be compelled to instruct an infants' school, perhaps without the slightest gift for so doing, is a running to waste of social life-blood.

Free trade in labour and equality of training, intellectual or physical, is essential if the organic aptitudes of a sex or class are to be determined. And our demand to-day is that natural conditions inexorably, but beneficently, may determine the labours of each individual, and not artificial restrictions.

As there is no need to legislate that Hindus, being generally supposed to have a natural incapacity for field sports, shall not betake themselves to them—for, if they have no capacity, they will fail; and, as in spite of the Hindus' supposed general incapacity for sport, it is possible for an individual Hindu to become the noted batsman of his age; so, also, there is no need to legislate that woman should be restricted in her choice of fields of labour; for the organic incapacity of the individual, if it exists, will legislate far more powerfully than any artificial, legal, or social obstruction can do; and it may be that the one individual in ten thousand who selects a field not generally

[6] 'Minds not keenly analytical are always apt to mistake mere correlation of appearance with causative sequence. We have heard it gravely asserted that between potatoes, pigs, mud cabins and Irishmen there was an organic connection: but we who have lived in Colonies, know that within two generations the pure-bred descendant of the mud cabiner becomes often the successful politician, wealthy financier or great judge; and shows no more predilection for potatoes, pigs, and mud cabins than men of any other race.' (Olive Schreiner's note.)

[7] Friedrich Froebel (1782–1852) was the German founder of the kindergarten system, and author of many books on teaching including *The Education of Man* (1826). (ED.)

sought by his fellows will enrich humanity by the result of an especial genius. Allowing all to start from one point in the world of intellectual culture and labour, with our ancient Mother Nature sitting as umpire, distributing the prizes and scratching from the lists the incompetent, is all we demand, but we demand it determinedly. Throw the puppy into the water; if it swims, well; if it sinks, well; but do not tie a rope round its throat and weight it with a brick, and then assert its incapacity to keep afloat.

For the present our cry is, '*We take all labour for our province!*'

From the judge's seat to the legislator's chair; from the statesman's closet to the merchant's office; from the chemist's laboratory to the astronomer's tower, there is no post or form of toil for which it is not our intention to attempt to fit ourselves; and there is no closed door we do not intend to force open; and there is no fruit in the garden of knowledge it is not our determination to eat. Acting in us, and through us, nature we know will mercilessly expose to us our deficiencies in the field of human toil, and reveal to us our powers. *And, for to-day, we take all labour for our province!*

But, it may then be said: 'What of war, that struggle of the human creature to attain its ends by physical force and at the price of the life of others: will you take part in that also?' We reply: Yes; more particularly in that field we intend to play our part. We have always borne part of the weight of war, and the major part. It is not merely that in primitive times we suffered from the destruction of the fields we tilled and the houses we built; or that in later times as domestic labourers and producers, though unwaged, we, in taxes and material loss and additional labour, paid as much as our males towards the cost of war; nor is it that in a comparatively insignificant manner, as nurses of the wounded in modern times, or now and again as warrior chieftainesses and leaders in primitive and other societies, we have borne our part; nor is it even because the spirit of resolution in its women, and their willingness to endure, has in all ages again and again largely determined the fate of a race that goes to war, that we demand our controlling right where war is concerned. Our relation to war is far more intimate, personal, and indissoluble than this. Men have made boomerangs, bows, swords, or guns with which to destroy one another; we have made the men who destroyed and were destroyed! We have in all ages produced, at an enormous cost, the primal munition of war, without which no other would exist. There is no battlefield on earth, nor ever has been, howsoever covered with slain, which it has not cost the women of the race more in actual bloodshed and anguish to supply, than it has cost the men who lie there. *We pay the first cost on all human life.*

In supplying the men for the carnage of a battlefield, women have not merely lost actually more blood, and gone through a more acute anguish and weariness, in the long months of bearing and in the final agony of child-birth, than has been experienced by the men who cover it; but, in the long months and years of rearing that follow, the women of the race go through a long, patiently endured strain which no knapsacked soldier on his longest march has ever more than equalled; while, even in the matter of death, in all civilized societies, the probability that the average woman will die in child-birth is immeasurably greater than the probability that the average male will die in battle.

There is, perhaps, no woman, whether she have borne children, or be merely potentially a child-bearer, who could look down upon a battlefield covered with slain, but the thought would rise in her, 'So many mothers' sons! So many bodies brought into the world to lie there! So many months of weariness and pain while bones and muscles were shaped within; so many hours of anguish and struggle that breath might be; so many baby mouths drawing life at woman's breasts;—all this, that men might lay with glazed eyeballs, and swollen bodies, and fixed, blue, unclosed mouths, and great limbs tossed—this, that an acre of ground might be manured with human flesh, that next year's grass or poppies or karoo bushes may spring up greener and redder, where they have lain, or that the sand of a plain may have a glint of white bones!' And we cry, 'Without an inexorable cause, this should not be!' No woman who is a woman says of a human body, 'It is nothing!'

On that day, when the woman takes her place beside the man in the governance and arrangement of external affairs of her race will also be that day that heralds the death of war as a means of arranging human differences. No tinsel of trumpets and flags will ultimately seduce women into the insanity of recklessly destroying life, or gild the wilful taking of life with any other name than that of murder, whether it be the slaughter of the million or of one by one. And this will be, not because with the sexual function of maternity necessarily goes in the human creature a deeper moral insight, or a loftier type of social instinct than that which accompanies the paternal. Men have in all ages led as nobly as women in many paths of heroic virtue, and toward the higher social sympathies; in certain ages, being freer and more widely cultured, they have led further and better. The fact that woman has no inherent all-round moral superiority over her male companion, or naturally on all points any higher social instinct, is perhaps most clearly exemplified by one curious very small fact: the two terms signifying intimate human relationships which in almost all human languages bear the most sinister and antisocial significance are both terms which have as their root the term 'mother', and denote feminine relationships—the words 'mother-in-law' and 'step-mother.'

In general humanity, in the sense of social solidarity, and in magnanimity, the male has continually proved himself at least the equal of the female.

Nor will women shrink from war because they lack courage. Earth's women of every generation have faced suffering and death with an equanimity that no soldier on a battlefield has ever surpassed and few have equalled; and where war has been to preserve life, or land, or freedom, unparasitized and labouring women have in all ages known how to bear an active part, and die.

Nor will woman's influence militate against war because in the future woman will not be able physically to bear her part in it. The smaller size of her muscle, which would severely have disadvantaged her when war was conducted with a battle-axe or sword and hand to hand, would now little or at all affect her. If intent on training for war, she might acquire the skill for guiding a Maxim or shooting down a foe with a Lee-Metford[8] at four thousand yards as ably as any male; and undoubtedly, it has not been only the peasant girl of France, who has carried latent and hid within her person the gifts that make the supreme general. If our European nations should continue in their present semi-civilized condition, which makes war possible, for a few generations longer, it is highly probably that as financiers, as managers of the commissariat department, as inspectors of provisions and clothing for the army, women will play a very leading part; and that the nation which is the first to employ its women so may be placed at a vast advantage over its fellows in time of war. It is not because of woman's cowardice, incapacity, nor, above all, because of her general superior virtue, that she will end war when her voice is fully, finally, and clearly heard in the governance of states—it is because, on this one point, and on this point almost alone, the knowledge of woman, simply as woman, is superior to

[8] sleek, accurate, nineteenth-century rifle with .45 calibre bullets (Note by Carol Barash, editor of *An Olive Schreiner Reader*.)

that of man; she knows the history of human flesh; she knows its cost; he does not.[9]

In a besieged city, it might well happen that men in the streets might seize upon statues and marble carvings from public buildings and galleries and hurl them in to stop the breaches made in their ramparts by the enemy, unconsideringly and merely because they came first to hand, not valuing them more than had they been paving-stones. But one man could not do this—the sculptor! He, who, though there might be no work of his own chisel among them, yet knew what each of these works of art had cost, knew by experience the long years of struggle and study and the infinitude of toil which had gone to the shaping of even one limb, to the carving of even one perfected outline, *he* could never so use them without thought or care. Instinctively, he would seek to throw in household goods, even gold and silver, all the city held, before he sacrificed its works of art!

Men's bodies are our woman's works of art. Given to us power of control, we will never carelessly throw them in to fill up the gaps in human relationships made by international ambitions and greeds. The thought would never come to us as woman, 'Cast in men's bodies; settle the thing so!' Arbitration and compensation would as naturally occur to her as cheaper and simpler methods of bridging the gaps in national relationships, as to the sculptor it would occur to throw in anything rather than statuary, though he might be driven to that at last!

This is one of those phases of human life, not very numerous, but very important, towards which the man as man, and the woman as woman, on the mere ground of their different sexual function with regard to reproduction, stand, and must stand, at a somewhat differing angle. The physical creation of human life, which, in as far as the male is concerned, consists in a few moments of physical pleasure; to the female must always signify months of pressure and physical endurance, crowned with danger to life. To the male, the giving of life is a laugh; to the female, blood, anguish, and sometimes death. Here we touch one of the few yet important differences between man and woman as such.

---

[9] 'It is noteworthy that even Catherine of Russia, a ruler and statesman of a virile and uncompromising type, and not usually troubled with moral scruples, yet refused with indignation the offer of Frederick of Prussia to pay her heavily for a small number of Russian recruits in an age when the hiring out of soldiers was common among the sovereigns of Europe.' (Olive Schreiner's note.)

The twenty thousand men prematurely slain on a field of battle, mean, to the women of their race, twenty thousand human creatures to be borne within them for months, given birth to in anguish, fed from their breasts and reared with toil, if the numbers of the tribe and the strength of the nation are to be maintained. In nations continually at war, incessant and unbroken child-bearing is by war imposed on all women if the state is to survive; and whenever war occurs, if numbers are to be maintained, there must be an increased child-bearing and rearing. This throws upon woman as woman a war tax, compared with which all that the male expends in military preparations is comparatively light.

The relations of the female towards the production of human life influences undoubtedly even her relation towards animal and all life. 'It is a fine day, let us go out and kill something!' cries the typical male of certain races, instinctively. 'There is a living thing, it will die if it is not cared for,' says the average woman, almost equally instinctively. It is true, that the woman will sacrifice as mercilessly, as cruelly, the life of a hated rival or an enemy, as any male; *but she always knows what she is doing, and the value of the life she takes!* There is no lighthearted, careless enjoyment in the sacrifice of life to the normal woman; her instinct, instructed by practical experience, steps in to prevent it. She always knows what life costs; and that it is more easy to destroy than create it.

It is also true, that, from the loftiest standpoint, the condemnation of war which has arisen in the advancing human spirit, is in no sense related to any particular form of sex function. The man and the woman alike, who with Isaiah on the hills of Palestine, or the Indian Buddha under his bo-tree,[10] have seen the essential unity of all sentient life; and who therefore see in war but a symptom of that crude discoordination of life on earth, not yet at one with itself, which affects humanity in these early stages of its growth: and who are compelled to regard as the ultimate goal of the race, though yet perhaps far distant across the ridges of innumerable coming ages, that harmony between all forms of conscious life, metaphorically prefigured by the ancient Hebrew, when he cried, 'The wolf shall dwell with the lamb; and the leopard shall lie down with the kid;

---

[10] Schreiner here conflates 'prophets' of two very different religious traditions; points up her tendency to generalise around these religious symbols and figures rather than reflecting real similarities or differences between them. (Note by Carol Barash, editor of *An Olive Schreiner Reader*.)

and the calf and the young lion and the fatling together and a little child shall lead them!'[11]—to that individual, whether man or woman, who has reached this standpoint, there is no need for enlightenment from the instincts of the child-bearers of society as such; their condemnation of war, rising not so much from the fact that it is a wasteful destruction of human flesh, as that it is an indication of the non-existence of that co-ordination, the harmony which is summed up in the cry, 'My little children, love one another.'

But for the vast bulk of humanity, probably for generations to come, the instinctive antagonism of the human child-bearer to reckless destruction of that which she has at so much cost produced, will be necessary to educate the race to any clear conception of the bestiality and insanity of war.

War will pass when intellectual culture and activity have made possible to the female an equal share in the control and governance of modern national life; it will probably not pass away much sooner; its extinction will not be delayed much longer.

It is especially in the domain of war that we, the bearers of men's bodies, who supply its most valuable munition, who, not amid the clamour and ardour of battle, but singly, and alone, with a three-in-the-morning courage, shed our blood and face death that the battle-field may have its food, a food more precious to us than our heart's blood; it is we especially, who in the domain of war, have our word to say, a word no man can say for us. It is our intention to enter into the domain of war and to labour there till in the course of generations we have extinguished it.

If to-day we claim all labour for our province, yet more especially do we claim those fields in which the difference in the reproductive function between man and woman may place male and female at a slightly different angle with regard to certain phases of human life.

---

[11] Isaiah 11:6. (Note by Carol Barash, editor of *An Olive Schreiner Reader.*)

THUCYDIDES

The Funeral Oration of Pericles

Thucydides (c. 460–400 B.C.), a general in the Athenian army,
wrote *The History of the Peloponnesian Wars,* considered one of the
first modern histories. Notable for its accuracy and powerful
speeches, it reported the conflict between Athens and Sparta from
431–411 B.C.

'Many of those who have spoken here in the past have praised the
institution of this speech at the close of our ceremony. It seemed to
them a mark of honour to our soldiers who have fallen in war that
a speech should be made over them. I do not agree. These men have
shown themselves valiant in action, and it would be enough, I think,
for their glories to be proclaimed in action, as you have just seen it
done at this funeral organized by the state. Our belief in the courage
and manliness of so many should not be hazarded on the goodness
or badness of one man's speech. Then it is not easy to speak with a
proper sense of balance, when a man's listeners find it difficult to
believe in the truth of what one is saying. The man who knows the
facts and loves the dead may well think that an oration tells less than
what he knows and what he would like to hear: others who do not
know so much may feel envy for the dead, and think the orator over-
praises them, when he speaks of exploits that are beyond their own
capacities. Praise of other people is tolerable only up to a certain
point, the point where one still believes that one could do oneself
some of the things one is hearing about. Once you get beyond this
point, you will find people becoming jealous and incredulous. However, the fact is that this institution was set up and approved by our
forefathers, and it is my duty to follow the tradition and do my best
to meet the wishes and the expectations of every one of you.

'I shall begin by speaking about our ancestors, since it is only
right and proper on such an occasion to pay them the honour of
recalling what they did. In this land of ours there have always been
the same people living from generation to generation up till now,
and they, by their courage and their virtues, have handed it on to

Translated by Max Warner.

us, a free country. They certainly deserve our praise. Even more so do our fathers deserve it. For to the inheritance they had received they added all the empire we have now, and it was not without blood and toil that they handed it down to us of the present generation. And when we ourselves, assembled here today, who are mostly in the prime of life, have, in most directions, added to the power of our empire and have organized our State in such a way that it is perfectly well able to look after itself both in peace and in war.

'I have no wish to make a long speech on subjects familiar to you all: so I shall say nothing about the warlike deeds by which we acquired our power or the battles in which we or our fathers gallantly resisted our enemies, Greek or foreign. What I want to do is, in the first place, to discuss the spirit in which we faced our trials and also our constitution and the way of life which has made us great. After that I shall speak in praise of the dead, believing that this kind of speech is not inappropriate to the present occasion, and that this whole assembly, of citizens and foreigners, may listen to it with advantage.

'Let me say that our system of government does not copy the institutions of our neighbours. It is more the case of our being a model to others, than of our imitating anyone else. Our constitution is called a democracy because power is in the hands not of a minority but of the whole people. When it is a question of settling private disputes, everyone is equal before the law; when it is a question of putting one person before another in positions of public responsibility, what counts is not membership of a particular class, but the actual ability which the man possesses. No one, so long as he has it in him to be of service to the state, is kept in political obscurity because of poverty. And, just as our political life is free and open, so is our day-to-day life in our relations with each other. We do not get into a state with our next-door neighbour if he enjoys himself in his own way, nor do we give him the kind of black looks which, though they do no real harm, still do hurt people's feelings. We are free and tolerant in our private lives; but in public affairs we keep to the law. This is because it commands our deep respect.

'We give our obedience to those whom we put in positions of authority, and we obey the laws themselves, especially those which are for the protection of the oppressed, and those unwritten laws which it is an acknowledged shame to break.

'And here is another point. When our work is over, we are in a position to enjoy all kinds of recreation for our spirits. There are various kinds of contests and sacrifices regularly throughout the year;

in our own homes we find a beauty and a good taste which delight us every day and which drive away our cares. Then the greatness of our city brings it about that all the good things from all over the world flow in to us, so that to us it seems just as natural to enjoy foreign goods as our own local products.

'Then there is a great difference between us and our opponents, in our attitude towards military security. Here are some examples: Our city is open to the world, and we have no periodical deportations in order to prevent people observing or finding out secrets which might be of military advantage to the enemy. This is because we rely, not on secret weapons, but on our own real courage and loyalty. There is a difference, too, in our educational systems. The Spartans, from their earliest boyhood, are submitted to the most laborious training in courage; we pass our lives without all these restrictions, and yet are just as ready to face the same dangers as they are. Here is proof of this: When the Spartans invade our land, they do not come by themselves, but bring all their allies with them; whereas we, when we launch an attack abroad, do the job by ourselves, and, though fighting on foreign soil, do not often fail to defeat opponents who are fighting for their own hearths and homes. As a matter of fact none of our enemies has ever yet been confronted with our total strength, because we have to divide our attention between our navy and the many missions on which our troops are sent on land. Yet, if our enemies engage a detachment of our forces and defeat it, they give themselves credit for having thrown back our entire army; or, if they lose, they claim that they were beaten by us in full strength. There are certain advantages, I think, in our way of meeting danger voluntarily, with an easy mind, instead of with a laborious training, with natural rather than with state-induced courage. We do not have to spend our time practising to meet sufferings which are still in the future; and when they are actually upon us we show ourselves just as brave as these others who are always in strict training. This is one point in which, I think, our city deserves to be admired. There are also others:

'Our love of what is beautiful does not lead to extravagance; our love of the things of the mind does not make us soft. We regard wealth as something to be properly used, rather than as something to boast about. As for poverty, no one need be ashamed to admit it: the real shame is in not taking practical measures to escape from it. Here each individual is interested not only in his own affairs but in the affairs of the state as well: even those who are mostly occupied with their own business are extremely well-informed on general politics—this is a peculiarity of ours: we do not say that a man who takes no interest in politics is a man who minds his own business; we say that he has no business here at all. We Athenians, in our own persons, take our decisions on policy or submit them to proper discussions: for we do not think that there is an incompatibility between words and deeds; the worst thing is to rush into action before the consequences have been properly debated. And this is another point where we differ from other people. We are capable at the same time of taking risks and of estimating them beforehand. Others are brave out of ignorance; and, when they stop to think, they begin to fear. But the man who can most truly be accounted brave is he who best knows the meaning of what is sweet in life and of what is terrible, and then goes out undeterred to meet what is to come.

'Again, in questions of general good feeling there is a great contrast between us and most other people. We make friends by doing good to others, not by receiving good from them. This makes our friendship all the more reliable, since we want to keep alive the gratitude of those who are in our debt by showing continued goodwill to them: whereas the feelings of one who owes us something lack the same enthusiasm, since he knows that, when he repays our kindness, it will be more like paying back a debt than giving something spontaneously. We are unique in this. When we do kindnesses to others, we do not do them out of any calculations of profit or loss: we do them without afterthought, relying on our free liberality. Taking everything together then, I declare that our city is an education to Greece, and I declare that in my opinion each single one of our citizens, in all the manifold aspects of life, is able to show himself the rightful lord and owner of his own person, and do this, moreover, with exceptional grace and exceptional versatility. And to show that this is no empty boasting for the present occasion, but real tangible fact, you have only to consider the power which our city possesses and which has been won by those very qualities which I have mentioned. Athens, alone of the states we know, comes to her testing time in a greatness that surpasses what was imagined of her. In her case, and in her case alone, no invading enemy is ashamed at being defeated, and no subject can complain of being governed by people unfit for their responsibilities. Mighty indeed are the marks and monuments of our empire which we have left. Future ages will wonder at us, as the present age wonders at us now. We do not need the praises of a Homer, or of anyone else whose words may delight us for the moment, but whose estimation of facts will fall short of what is really true. For our adventurous spirit has forced an entry into every sea and into every land; and everywhere we have left behind us everlasting memorials of good done to our friends or suffering inflicted on our enemies.

'This, then, is the kind of city for which these men, who could not bear the thought of losing her, nobly fought and nobly died. It is only natural that every one of us who survive them should be willing to undergo hardships in her service. And it was for this reason that I have spoken at such length about our city, because I wanted to make it clear that for us there is more at stake than there is for others who lack our advantages; also I wanted my words of praise for the dead to be set in the bright light of evidence. And now the most important of these words has been spoken. I have sung the praises of our city; but it was the courage and gallantry of these men, and of people like them, which made her splendid. Nor would you find it true in the case of many of the Greeks, as it is true of them, that no words can do more than justice to their deeds.

'To me it seems that the consummation which has overtaken these men shows us the meaning of manliness in its first revelation and in its final proof. Some of them, no doubt, had their faults; but what we ought to remember first is their gallant conduct against the enemy in defence of their native land. They have blotted out evil with good, and done more service to the commonwealth than they ever did harm in their private lives. No one of these men weakened because he wanted to go on enjoying his wealth: no one put off the awful day in the hope that he might live to escape his poverty and grow rich. More to be desired than such things, they chose to check the enemy's pride. This, to them, was a risk most glorious, and they accepted it, willing to strike down the enemy and relinquish everything else. As for success or failure, they left that in the doubtful hands of Hope, and when the reality of battle was before their faces, they put their trust in their own selves. In the fighting, they thought it more honourable to stand their ground and suffer death than to give in and save their lives. So they fled from the reproaches of men, abiding with life and limb the brunt of battle; and, in a small moment of time, the climax of their lives, a culmination of glory, not of fear, were swept away from us.

'So and such they were, these men—worthy of their city. We who remain behind may hope to be spared their fate, but must resolve to keep the same daring spirit against the foe. It is not simply a question of estimating the advantages in theory. I could tell you a long story (and you know it as well as I do) about what is to be gained by beating the enemy back. What I would prefer is that you should fix your eyes every day on the greatness of Athens as she really is, and should fall in love with her. When you realize her greatness, then reflect that what made her great was men with a spirit of adventure, men who knew their duty, men who were ashamed to fall below a certain standard. If they ever failed in an enterprise, they made up their minds that at any rate the city should not find their courage lacking to her, and they gave to her the best contribution that they could. They gave her their lives, to her and to all of us, and for their own selves they won praises that never grow old, the most splendid of sepulchres—not the sepulchre in which their bodies are laid, but where their glory remains eternal in men's minds, always there on the right occasion to stir others to speech or to action. For famous men have the whole earth as their memorial: it is not only the inscriptions on their graves in their own country that mark them out; no, in foreign lands also, not in any visible form but in people's hearts, their memory abides and grows. It is for you to try to be like them. Make up your minds that happiness depends on being free, and freedom depends on being courageous. Let there be no relaxation in the face of the perils of the war. The people who have most excuse for despising death are not the wretched and unfortunate, who have no hope of doing well for themselves, but those who run the risk of a complete reversal in their lives, and who would feel the difference most intensely, if things went wrong for them. Any intelligent man would find a humiliation caused by his own slackness more painful to bear than death, when death comes to him unperceived, in battle, and in the confidence of his patriotism.

'For these reasons I shall not commiserate with those parents of the dead, who are present here. Instead I shall try to comfort them. They are well aware that they have grown up in a world where there are many changes and chances. But this is good fortune—for men to end their lives with honour, as these have done, and for you honourably to lament them: their life was set to a measure where death and happiness went hand in hand. I know that it is difficult to convince you of this. When you see other people happy you will often be reminded of what used to make you happy too. One does not feel sad at not having some good thing which is outside one's experience: real grief is felt at the loss of something which one is used to. All the same, those of you who are of the right age must bear up and take comfort in the thought of having more children. In your own homes these new children will prevent you from brooding over those who are no more, and they will be a help to the city, too, both in filling the empty places, and in assuring her security. For it is impossible for a man to put forward fair and honest views about our affairs if he has not, like everyone else, children whose lives may be at stake. As for those of you who are now too old to have children, I would ask you to count as gain the greater part of your life, in which you have been happy, and remember that what remains is not long, and let your hearts be lifted up at the thought of the fair fame of the dead. One's sense of honour is the only thing that does not grow old, and the last pleasure, when one is worn out with age, is not, as the poet said, making money, but having the respect of one's fellow men.

'As for those of you here who are sons or brothers of the dead, I can see a hard struggle in front of you. Everyone always speaks well of the dead, and, even if you rise to the greatest heights of heroism, it will be a hard thing for you to get the reputation of having come near, let alone equalled, their standard. When one is alive, one is always liable to the jealousy of one's competitors, but when one is out of the way, the honour one receives is sincere and unchallenged.

'Perhaps I should say a word or two on the duties of women to those among you who are now widowed. I can say all I have to say in a short word of advice. Your great glory is not to be inferior to what God has made you, and the greatest glory of a woman is to be least talked about by men, whether they are praising you or criticizing you. I have now, as the law demanded, said what I had to say. For the time being our offerings to the dead have been made, and for the future their children will be supported at the public expense by the city, until they come of age. This is the crown and prize which she offers, both to the dead and to their children, for the ordeals which they have faced. Where the rewards of valour are the greatest, there you will find also the best and bravest spirits among the people. And now, when you have mourned for your dear ones, you must depart.'

E L E V E N

Science, Technology, and Society

The whole of science is nothing more than a refinement of everyday thinking.

Albert Einstein

The essays in this section deal essentially with one topic, for science, technology, and society are all bound together. Whether we like it or not, our society and our future depend on science and technology. This is not to say that all our problems will be solved by science and technology. Pollution, the depletion of natural resources, the massive challenge of disposing of all the garbage produced in the world each day, and a host of other serious and life-threatening problems probably do not have purely scientific or technological solutions. We will have to look elsewhere for help with these problems.

Yet there is no doubt that who we are as a culture and as a society has been determined to a great extent by the growth of science and the remarkable developments of technology. So accustomed are we to technological developments that we have come to expect them. While the invention of television was once considered a wonder of science, the development of the home computer is now taken almost as a matter of course. Cellular telephones, videotape recorders, microwave ovens, compact disc players, and hundreds of other technological developments are accepted as the natural course of events. Little thought is given to how such technology affects not just our personal lives but our collective life as a society and a culture. (As a way of illustrating the rapid advances of technology, you might quickly write a list of all the technological developments you can think of that have occurred in your lifetime, and then compare your list with the lists prepared by your classmates.)

The pace of discovery, development, and application in science and technology has accelerated so markedly that new products now flow not just from the research laboratories and factories of our own country but from the laboratories and factories of countries around the world. Science and technology have in an unexpected way brought many countries of the world closer together. The economies of the United States, Japan, Germany, Great Britain, Taiwan, Singapore, China, Thailand, Korea, and other countries are intimately bound together through the development, manufacturing, and sale of new products produced by science and technology. Such technological and economic dependence will surely alter political alliances,

1070

affecting the relations between both traditionally friendly and traditionally unfriendly nations.

The influence of science and technology on our society and our lives is more profound than we might think possible. As Lewis Mumford notes in his essay, technology has affected and will continue to affect us in ways in which we are unaware. So simple an invention as the mechanical clock forever changed society, altering its very basis and structure. No one anticipated these changes, and few people noticed them as they were happening. What changes will occur in society because of the development of personal computers, fax machines, and genetic engineering?

Today time itself is under investigation. Where the medieval world was concerned with measuring the passage of time and developed the clock to achieve this feat, physicists are now concerned with the very nature of time itself, and the relation of time to the structure of the universe. For the physicist, time does not flow in one direction but in at least two directions. Going even further, science today does not speak of time but of *times*. As Stephen Hawking points out in his essay on the nature of time, we must always distinguish which time we are discussing.

Science deals with the complexity of the simple, as Stephen Jay Gould and Paul Gruchow discuss in their essays. Science also deals with the simplicity of the complex, as Lewis Thomas relates in his essay. The term *science* itself is a broad one, encompassing a vast array of knowledge and information. As you read the essays in this section, keep notes on the distinctions between the terms *science* and *technology*. Based on these essays, how might you define each term? With what issues and problems are the practitioners of each field concerned?

We live in a time of paradox, when science and technology are recognized as both necessary and threatening. Will science and technology solve some of the major problems we face, or will they complicate those problems instead? Or is the issue even as simple as those two alternatives? As you read these essays, construct your own alternatives, your own possibilities.

THOMAS HENRY HUXLEY

The Method of Scientific Investigation

Thomas Henry Huxley (1825–1895) was an English biologist and professor who popularized science for a lay audience. His books include *Man's Place in Nature* (1863), in which he defended Darwin's evolutionary theory, and *Collected Essays* (1893).

The method of scientific investigation is nothing but the expression of the necessary mode of working of the human mind. It is simply the mode at which all phenomena are reasoned about, rendered precise and exact. There is no more difference, but there is just the same kind of difference, between the mental operations of a man of science and those of an ordinary person, as there is between the operations and methods of a baker or of a butcher weighing out his goods in common scales and the operation of a chemist in performing a difficult and complex analysis by means of his balance and finely graduated weights. It is not that the action of the scales in the one case and the balance in the other differ in the principles of their construction or manner of working; but the beam of one is set on an infinitely finer axis than the other, and of course turns by the addition of a much smaller weight.

You will understand this better, perhaps, if I give you some familiar example. You have all heard it repeated, I dare say, that men of science work by means of induction and deduction, and that by the help of these operations, they, in a sort of sense, wring from Nature certain other things, which are called natural laws and causes, and that out of these, by some cunning skill of their own, they build up hypotheses and theories. And it is imagined by many that the operations of the common mind can be by no means compared with these processes, and that they have to be acquired by a sort of special apprenticeship to the craft. To hear all these large words, you would think that the mind of a man of science must be constituted differently from that of his fellow men; but if you will not be frightened by terms, you will discover that you are quite wrong, and that all these terrible apparatus are being used by yourselves every day and every hour of your lives.

There is a well-known incident in one of Molière's plays, where the author makes the hero express unbounded delight on being told that he has been talking prose during the whole of his life. In the same way, I trust that you will take comfort, and be delighted with yourselves, on the discovery that you have been acting on the principles of inductive and deductive philosophy during the same period. Probably there is not one here who has not in the course of the day had occasion to set in motion a complex train of reasoning, of the very same kind, though differing of course in degree, as that which a scientific man goes through in tracing the causes of natural phenomena.

A very trivial circumstance will serve to exemplify this. Suppose you go into a fruiterer's shop, wanting an apple—you take one up, and, on biting, you find it is sour; you look at it, and see that it is hard, and green. You take up another one and that too is hard, green, and sour. The shop man offers you a third; but, before biting it, you examine it, and find that it is hard and green, and you immediately say that you will not have it, as it must be sour, like those that you have already tried.

Nothing can be more simple than that, you think; but if you will take the trouble to analyze and trace out into its logical elements what has been done by the mind, you will be greatly surprised. In the first place, you have performed the operation of induction. You found, that, in two experiences, hardness and greenness in apples went together with sourness. It was so in the first case, and it was confirmed by the second. True, it is a very small basis, but still it is enough to make an induction from; you generalize the facts, and you expect to find sourness in apples where you get hardness and greenness. You found upon that a general law, that all hard and green apples are sour; and that, so far as it goes, is a perfect induction. Well, having got your natural law in this way, when you are offered another apple which you find is hard and green, you say, "All hard and green apples are sour; this apple is hard and green, therefore this apple is sour." That train of reasoning is what logicians call a syllogism and has all its various parts and terms—its major premise, its minor premise, and its conclusion. And, by the help of further reasoning, which, if drawn out, would have to be exhibited in two or three other syllogisms, you arrive at your final determination: "I will not have that apple." So that, you see, you have, in the first place, established a law by induction, and upon that you have founded a deduction and reasoned out the special conclusion of the particular case. Well now, suppose, having got your law, that at some time afterwards, you are discussing the qualities of apples with a friend; you will say to him, "It is a very curious thing—but I find that all hard and green apples are sour!" Your friend says to you, "But how do you know that?" You at once reply, "Oh, because I have tried them over and over again and have always found them to be so." Well, if we were talking science instead of common sense, we should call that an experimental verification. And, if still opposed, you go further and say, "I have heard from the people in Somersetshire and Devonshire, where a large number of apples are grown, that they have observed the same thing. It is also found to be the case in Normandy, and in North America. In short, I find it to be the universal experience of mankind wherever attention has been directed to the subject." Whereupon your friend, unless he is a very unreasonable man, agrees with you and is convinced that you are quite right in the conclusion you have drawn. He believes, although perhaps he does not know he believes it, that the more extensive verifications are—that the more frequently experiments have been made and results of the same kind arrived at—that the more varied the conditions under which the same results are attained, the more certain is the ultimate conclusion, and he disputes the question no further. He sees that the experiment has been tried under all sorts of conditions, as to time, place, and people, with the same result; and he says with you, therefore, that the law you have laid down must be a good one, and he must believe it.

In science we do the same thing; the philosopher exercises precisely the same faculties, though in a much more delicate manner. In scientific inquiry it becomes a matter of duty to expose a supposed law to every possible kind of verification and to take care, moreover, that this is done intentionally and not left to a mere accident, as in the case of the apples. And in science, as in common life, our confidence in a law is in exact proportion to the absence of variation in the result of our experimental verifications. For instance, if you let go your grasp of an article you may have in your hand, it will immediately fall to the ground. That is a very common verification of one of the best established laws of nature—that of gravitation. The method by which men of science established the existence of that law is exactly the same as that by which we have established the trivial proposition about the sourness of hard and green apples. But we believe it in such an extensive, thorough, and unhesitating manner because the universal experience of mankind verifies it, and we can verify it ourselves at any time; and

that is the strongest possible foundation on which any natural law
can rest.

STEPHEN JAY GOULD

Nasty Little Facts

Stephen Jay Gould (1941–   ) is an evolutionary paleontologist
who teaches biology, geology, and history of science at Harvard
University. Gould writes monthly essays for *Natural History Magazine,* in which the following selection originally appeared. He has
published numerous collections of essays, including *The Panda's
Thumb: More Reflections in Natural History* (1980) and *The Flamin-
go's Smile: More Reflections in Natural History* (1985). Other books
include *Ontogeny and Phylogeny* (1977) and *The Mismeasure of Man*
(1981).

As a devotee of Grade B detective films, from Charlie Chan (in all
his incarnations) to the *Thin Man,* I have, perforce, spent an undue
amount of time passively engaged in conversations about fingerprints.
Since these discussions are interminable, one might suspect that they
have also been eternal in the annals of criminology.

In fact, Scotland Yard officially introduced fingerprints as a tool
for identifying criminals in 1901 (replacing the older Bertillon system, based on complex series of body measurements and the accompanying assumption, not always vindicated, that no two people will
be alike in so many ways). The chief architect and promoter of the
new system was Francis Galton, England's most eccentric scientific
genius.

In his autobiography, Galton tells a story of Herbert Spencer's
visit to his fingerprint lab. Galton took Spencer's prints and "spoke
of the failure to discover the origin of these patterns, and how the
fingers of unborn children had been dissected to ascertain their
earliest stages." Spencer, quick to offer certain opinions about almost
anything, told Galton that he had been working the wrong way
round.

> Spencer remarked . . . that I ought to consider the purpose the ridges
> had to fulfil, and to work backwards. Here, he said, it was obvious that

the delicate mouths of the sudorific glands required the protection given to them by the ridges on either side of them, and therefrom he elaborated a consistent and ingenious hypothesis at great length. I replied that his arguments were beautiful and deserved to be true, but it happened that the mouths of the ducts did not run in the valleys between the crests, but along the crests of the ridges themselves.

Galton then ends his anecdote by giving the original source for one of the top ten among scientific quotes. Spencer, dining with T. H. Huxley one night at the Athenaeum, stated that he had once written a tragedy. Huxley replied that he knew all about it. Spencer rebutted Huxley, arguing that he had never mentioned it to anyone. But Huxley insisted that he knew anyway and identified Spencer's debacle—"a beautiful theory, killed by a nasty, ugly little fact."

Some theories may be subject to such instant, brutal, and unambiguous rejection. I stated last month, for example, that no left-coiling periwinkle had ever been found among millions of snails examined. If I happen to find one during my walk on Nopsca Beach tomorrow morning, a century of well-nurtured negative evidence will collapse in an instant.

This Huxleyan vision of clean refutation buttresses one of our worst stereotypes about science. We tend to view science as a truth-seeking machine, driven by two forces that winnow error: the new discovery and the crucial experiment—prime generators of those nasty, ugly little facts. Science does, of course, seek truth; it even succeeds reasonably often, so far as we can tell. But science, like all of life, is filled with rich and complex ambiguity. The path to truth is rarely straight, marked by a gate of entry that sorts applicants by such relatively simple criteria as age and height. (When I was a kid, you could get into Yankee Stadium for half price if your head didn't reach a line prominently drawn on the entrance gate about four and a half feet above the ground. You could scrunch down, but they checked. One nasty, ugly day, I started to pay full price, and that was that.)

Little facts rarely undo big theories all by themselves—the myth of David and Goliath notwithstanding. They can refute little, highly specific theories, like my conjecture about lefty periwinkles, but they rarely slay grand and comprehensive views of nature. No single, pristine fact taught us that the earth revolves around the sun or that evolution produced the similarities among organisms. Overarching theories are much bigger than single facts, just as the army of Grenada really didn't have much chance against the combined forces of the

United States (though you'd think from the consequent appeals to patriotism that some gigantic and improbable victory had been won).

Instead, little facts are assimilated into large theories. They may reside there uncomfortably, bothering the honorable proponents. Large numbers of little facts may eventually combine with other social and intellectual forces to topple a grand theory. The history of ideas is a play of complex human passions interacting with an external reality only slightly less intricate. We debase the richness of both nature and our own minds if we view the great pageant of our intellectual history as a compendium of new information leading from primal superstition to final exactitude. We know that the sun is hub to our little corner of the universe, and that ties of genealogy connect all living things on our planet, because these theories assemble and explain so much otherwise disparate and unrelated information—not because Galileo trained his telescope on the moons of Jupiter or because Darwin took a ride on a Galápagos tortoise.

This essay tells the story of a pristine, unexpected little fact that should have mattered, but didn't particularly. It was widely reported, discussed, and personally studied by the greatest naturalists of Europe, and then assimilated into each of several contradictory systems. Fifty years later, in 1865, a second discovery resolved the paradox generated by the first fact—and should have won, by Huxley's principle, a big and important victory for Darwin and evolution. It was welcomed, to be sure, but largely ignored. One foot soldier could not decide a battle waged on so many fronts.

Trigonia is a distinctive clam, thick shelled and triangular in shape. It flourished with dinosaurs during the Mesozoic era and then became extinct in the same debacle that wiped out the ruling reptiles—one of the five greatest mass dyings in our geologic record. No trigonian had ever been found in the overlying Cenozoic strata—the entire age of mammals (about sixty million years, as we now know). *Trigonia* had therefore become a valued "guide fossil"; when you found one, you knew you had rocks of the earth's middle age. Everyone (who was anybody) understood this.

Then, the nasty, ugly little—and quite undeniable—fact. In 1802, P. Péron, a French naturalist, found the shell of a living trigonian washed up on the beaches of southern Australia. Twenty-five years later, and following several failures, J. Quoy and J. Gaimard, naturalists aboard the *Astrolabe*, finally found a live trigonian. They had dredged for several days with definite purpose, but without success. Becalmed one night in Bass Strait and with little else to do, they tried again and brought up their single prize, a molluscan life soon snuffed and preserved in the (perhaps welcome) medium of the collector's trade—a bottle of alcohol. Quoy and Gaimard treasured their booty and wrote later:

> We were so anxious to bring back this shell with its animal that when we were, for three days, stranded on the reefs of Tonga-Tabu, it was the only object that we took from our collection. Doesn't this recall the ardent shell collector who, during seven years' war, carried constantly in his pocket an extraordinary *Phasianella,* which he had bought for twenty-five louis?

A simple story. A fact and a puzzle. *Trigonia* had not disappeared in the great Cretaceous debacle, for it was hanging tough in Australia. But no fossil trigonians had been found in all the strata in between— throughout the long and well-recorded history of the age of mammals (now called the Cenozoic era). Where were they? Had they ever existed? Could such a distinctive animal die and be reborn (or re-created) later? The "Cenozoic gap" became as puzzling and portentous as the one later associated with Mr. Nixon and Ms. Woods.

Trigonia occupies a specially interesting place in the history of biology because its unexpected fact and consequent puzzle arose and prevailed at such an important time—at the dawn and through the greatest conceptual transition ever experienced by the profession: from creationist to evolutionary views of life. It also (or rather therefore) attracted the attention and commentary of most leaders in nineteenth-century natural history. J. B. Lamarck, most famous of pre-Darwinian evolutionists, formally described the first living trigonian. Darwin himself thought and commented about *Trigonia* for thirty years. Louis Agassiz, most able and cogent of Darwin's opponents, wrote the major technical monograph of his generation on the genus *Trigonia.*

The lesson of the living *Trigonia* can be distilled in a sentence: Everyone made the best of it, incorporating favorable aspects of this new fact into his system and either ignoring or explaining away the difficulties. *Trigonia* became an illustration for everyone, not a crucial test of rival theories. Evolutionists celebrated the differences in form and distribution between ancient and modern trigonians—and ignored the Cenozoic gap. Creationists highlighted the gap and made light of the differences.

Today, we remember Lamarck best as the author of a rejected evolutionary theory based on the inheritance of acquired characters (quite an unfair designation since so-called Lamarckian inheritance represents a minor part of Lamarck's own system—this, however, is another story, for another time). But his day-to-day work in post-revolutionary France involved the description of living and fossil invertebrates in his role as curator at the *Muséum d'Histoire Naturelle* in Paris. He therefore received Péron's precious shell for formal description, and he named it *Trigonia margaritacea* in 1804 (*margarita* is a Latin pearl, and the interior of a trigonian shell shines with a beautiful pearly luster). But since 1804 lay squarely between Lamarck's initial (1802) and definitive (1809) statement of his evolutionary theory, he also used his short paper on *Trigonia* to sharpen and defend his developing transmutationist views.

Most fossil trigonians are ornamented with concentric ridges at their anterior ends (enclosing the mouth and digestive apparatus) and radial ribs on the rear flank. A single strong rib usually separates these two areas. But all modern trigonians cover their shells entirely with radial ribs (although the embryonic shell still bears traces of the ancestral concentrics). Lamarck seized upon these differences to claim that changing environments had pressed their influence upon the shell. The shell had then altered in response and the animal within passed the favorable change to future generations by "Lamarckian" inheritance.

> They have undergone changes under the influence of circumstances that act upon them and that have themselves changed; so that fossil remains . . . of the greatest antiquity may display several differences from animals of the same type living now but nevertheless derived from them.

(But Lamarck had only demonstrated that the fossils looked different from the moderns. Any theory could account for this basic datum in the absence of further information—evolution by use and disuse, by natural selection, or even re-creation by God for that matter.)

Lamarck then proceeded to extract more from modern trigonians to buttress other pet themes. He was, for example, a partisan at the wrong end of a great debate resolved a decade later to his disadvantage by Cuvier—does extinction occur in nature? Human rapacity, Lamarck believed, might exterminate some conspicuous beasts, but the ways of nature do not include termination without descent (Lamarck, as a transmutationist, obviously accepted the pseudoextinction that occurs when one form evolves into another). Lamarck gave the old arguments against extinction a novel twist by embedding his justification within his newfangled evolutionary views. How can extinction occur if all organisms respond creatively to changing environments and pass their favorable responses to future generations in the form of altered inheritance?

Yet Lamarck's conviction was sorely challenged by burgeoning data in his own field of marine invertebrate paleontology. So many kinds of fossils are confined to rocks of early periods. Where are their descendants today? Lamarck offered the only plausible argument in a world with few remaining terrae incognitae—they live still in the unexplored depths of the sea. Since Lamarck reveals his own discomfort with such an ad hoc solution in the form of a defense too often and too zealously repeated—recall Shakespeare's "the lady doth protest too much, methinks"—we may take as genuine his delight in *Trigonia* as a real case for a generalization devoutly to be wished: "Small species, especially those that dwell in the depths of the sea, have the means to escape man; truly among these we do not find any that are really extinct." Lamarck then ends his paper by predicting that a large suite of creatures apparently extinct will soon be found at oceanic depths. We are still waiting.

Since Lamarck's argument centers upon an explanation for why creatures still living yield no evidence of their continued vitality, we should not be surprised that the Cenozoic gap inspired no commentary at all. We must assume that trigonians spent the entire Cenozoic safe in the bosom of Neptune, full fathom five hundred or more, and unrecorded in a fossil archive of shallow-water sediments.

Charles Darwin, leading evolutionist of the next generation, selected yet another aspect of living trigonians—their geographic distribution—to bolster a different theme dear to his view of life. Darwin's creationist opponents, as we shall see, rendered the history of life as a series of static faunas and floras separated by episodes of sudden extirpation and renewal. To confute this catastrophist credo, and to advance his own distinctive and uncompromisingly gradualist view of nature, Darwin argued that the extinction of a group should be as smooth and extended as its origin. A group should peter out, dwindle slowly, decrease steadily in numbers and geographic range—not die in full vigor during an environmental crisis. What better evidence than a family once spread throughout the world in stunning diversity but now confined to one small region and one single species. In his private essay of 1844, precursor to the *Origin of Species* (1859), Darwin wrote: "We have reason to believe that . . . the numbers of the species decrease till finally the group becomes extinct—the *Trigonia* was extinct much sooner in Europe, but now lives in the seas of Australia."

(We now regard this claim for extinction of large groups as gradual dwindling in the face of competition from more successful forms—the central theme of chapter 10 in the *Origin of Species*—as among the least successful of Darwin's major arguments. Darwin may have feared that mass extinction supported the creationist view of debacle followed by divine reconstitution. But mass extinction may also clear the way for subsequent, vigorous periods of *evolution*. Again, as so often, Darwin's commitment to gradualism restricted his options for legitimate evolutionary hypotheses.)

Darwin followed Lamarck in dismissing the Cenozoic gap as an artifact of our imperfect fossil record (I can, indeed, imagine no other option for an evolutionist committed to genealogical connection). But Darwin was explicit where Lamarck had been silent. Darwin also tried to accentuate the positive by arguing that the rarity of such long gaps strongly implied their artificial status. He wrote in the *Origin of Species*:

> A group does not reappear after it has once disappeared; or its existence, as long as it lasts, is continuous. I am aware that there are some apparent exceptions to this rule, but the exceptions are surprisingly few, so few that . . . the rule strictly accords with my theory.

Creationists, meanwhile, looked at *Trigonia* from the other side. They treasured the Cenozoic gap and found nearly everything else puzzling. The major creationist thinkers tended to agree that life's history had been episodic—a series of stages separated by sudden, worldwide paroxysms that removed the old and set a stage for the new. But they divided into two camps on the issue of progress. Did each new episode improve upon the last; was God, in other words, learning by doing? Or had life maintained a fairly consistent complexity throughout its episodic history? Progressionists and non-progressionists found different messages in *Trigonia*.

James Parkinson, England's leading progressionist (though he switched allegiances later on), chose *Trigonia* as a premier example in his *Organic Remains of a Former World* (1811). He read the Cenozoic gap literally, extracting from it the congenial message that life's history features a series of creations not connected by ties of genealogy and physical continuity.

But *Trigonia* also presented a special problem for Parkinson. He argued that each successive episode of creation had been marked "with increasing excellence in its objects," thus matching in all ways but one the Mosaic progression from chaos to Adam as described in Genesis. "So close indeed is this agreement, that the Mosaic account is thereby confirmed in every respect except as to the age of the world" (a problem then resolved by an allegorical interpretation of God's six creative "days"). Now a *Trigonia,* as some folks say about roses, is a *Trigonia* (subtleties evident to the professional eye aside). Why should a modern shell with radial ribs alone be better than a fossil representative with radials and concentrics? Why are the modern versions superior, as Parkinson's theory of progressive creation required? Parkinson was evidently troubled. In the summary statement to his three-volume work, he devoted more space to *Trigonia* than to any other genus. He clutched at the one available straw, but clearly without conviction. At least the modern trigonians are different. *"Raffiniert ist der Herrgott"* (Subtle is the Lord), as Einstein said later. We don't know why, but different must be better:

> This shell, although really of this genus, is of a different species from any shell, which has been found in a fossil state. So that none of the species of shells of this genus, which are known in a fossil state, have, in fact, been found in any stratum above the hard chalk [the Cretaceous, or last period of dinosaurs], or in our present seas.

Louis Agassiz, most able of all creationists, followed Parkinson's personal route in reverse. He began as an advocate of progress in each successive creation and ended by defending the earliest of God's creatures as fully up to snuff (largely because he despised Darwinism with such passion and felt that any admission of progress would bolster the evolutionary cause). For him, therefore, the apparent lack of improvement in modern trigonians posed no problem, while the Cenozoic gap brought nothing but pleasure and confirmation. In the major pre-Darwinian work on these clams, his *Mémoire sur les trigonies* (1840), Agassiz argued explicitly that a Cenozoic gap, if conclusively affirmed, would effectively disprove evolution (quite a cogent claim, by the way):

> The absence of *Trigonia* in Tertiary [Cenozoic] strata is a very important fact for discussions of the origin and relationships of species of different epochs; for if it could one day be shown that *Trigonia* never existed throughout the entire duration of Tertiary time, it would no longer be possible to maintain the principle that species of a genus living in successive geological epochs are derived from each other.

But Agassiz well understood the discomforting uncertainty of negative evidence. Find one nasty, ugly little Cenozoic trigonian tomorrow, and the entire argument collapses. So Agassiz decided to cover his rear and disclaim: No Cenozoic trigonian is dandy; but future discovery of a Cenozoic trigonian would prove nothing. God may, after all, ordain temporal continuity among a group of related, created forms.

Although his passage is an exercise in special pleading, it also contains one of the most succinct and eloquent defenses ever written for the Platonic version of creationism.

> Although I now invoke this fact [the Cenozoic gap] to support my conviction that the different species of a genus are not variants of a single type . . . the discovery of a Tertiary trigonian would still not demonstrate, to my eyes, that the relationship among species of a genus is one of direct descent and successive transformation of original types. . . . I certainly do not deny that natural relationships exist among different species of a genus; on the contrary, I am convinced that species are related to each other by bonds of a higher nature than those of simple direct procreation, bonds that may be compared to the order of a system of ideas whose elements, developed at different times, form in their union an organic whole—although the elements of each time period also appear, within their limits, to be finished products.

In summary, as Darwin's revolution dawned in 1859, the supposedly pure and simple little fact of modern trigonians stood neither as arbiter nor slayer of theories but as touted support for all major conflicting and contradictory views of life—for evolution by Lamarckian and Darwinian agencies, and for creationism in both progressionist and directionless versions. How can something so important be so undecisive? Unless Huxley's heroic vision of raw empiricism triumphant rarely describes the history of ideas or even the progress of science. Percepts do not create and drive concepts; but concepts are not intractable and immune to perceptual nudges either. Thought and observation form a wonderfully complex web of interpenetration and mutual influence—and the interaction often seems to get us somewhere useful.

The *Trigonia* story has a natural ending that should be conventional and happy, but isn't quite. The resolution is not hard to guess, since Darwin's vision has prevailed. The elusive Cenozoic trigonian was found in Australian rocks—at just the right time, in 1865, when nascent evolutionism needed all the help it could get.

H. M. Jenkins, a minor figure in British geology, explicitly defended Darwin in describing the first Cenozoic trigonians. He interpreted the happy closure of the Cenozoic gap as a clear vindication of Darwin's characteristic attitude toward the fossil record and as direct support for evolution. Darwin viewed the fossil record as riddled with imperfections—"a history of the world imperfectly kept . . .

of this history we possess the last volume alone. . . . Of this volume, only here and there a short chapter has been preserved; and of each page, only here and there a few lines" (*Origin of Species*, 1859). Gaps, as the old saying goes, represent absence of evidence, not evidence of absence. Jenkins wrote, linking the newly discovered Cenozoic trigonian to this fundamental Darwinian prediction:

> Every paleontologist believes that, when a genus of animals is represented by species occurring in strata of widely different ages, it must have been perpetuated by some one or more species during the whole of the intervening period. . . . The only rational meaning that has ever been attached to this presumed general law . . . is that the perpetuation of the genus . . . has been due to "descent with modification." *Trigonia subundulata* [the formal name for the Cenozoic trigonian] is one of the links hitherto wanting; first, in explanation of the existence of the genus *Trigonia* in the Australian seas of the present day; and secondly, as showing that the great gap which before existed in its life-history was . . . simply a consequence of the imperfection of our knowledge of the geological record.

Finally, a personal confession in closing. This essay has been an exercise in self-indulgence and expiation. I put together the trigonian story at the very beginning of my professional career (when I was just barely big enough to pay full price at the stadium). I published a rather poor account in a technical journal in 1968 (frankly, it stunk).

I got part of the story right. I did recognize that everyone managed to slot the living trigonian into his system and that simple, single facts did not (at least in this case) undo general theories. But I got the end all wrong because the traditional, Huxleyan view still beguiled me. I told the happy ending because I read Jenkin's quote and took it at face value—as an evolutionary prediction fulfilled and an empirical vindication provided. I forgot (or hadn't yet learned) a cardinal rule of scholarly detection: Don't only weigh what you have; ask why you don't see what you ought to find. Negative evidence is important—especially when the record is sufficiently complete to indicate that an absence may be genuine.

I now read the Cenozoic discovery quite differently, because I have confronted what should have happened but didn't. If Darwin's vindication required a set of new, clean, pristine, unexpected facts, then why didn't the Cenozoic trigonian inspire a wave of rejoicing? Darwin had predicted it; Agassiz had invested much hope in its nonexistence.

Sure, Jenkins said the right things in his article; I quoted them and regarded my task as complete. But the key to the story lies elsewhere—in the nonevents. Jenkins wrote a two and a half page note in a minor journal. No one else seemed to notice. Darwin never commented, though the *Origin of Species* still had several editions to run. *Trigonia* did not become a textbook example of evolution triumphant. Most curiously, Jenkins did not find the Cenozoic trigonian. It was unearthed by Frederick McCoy, an eminent leader of Australian science, the founder and head of the Museum of Natural History and Geology in Melbourne. He must have known what he had and what it meant. But he didn't even bother to publish his description. I should have taken my clue from the opening lines of Jenkins's paper, but I passed them by:

> The very interesting discovery of a species of *Trigonia* in the Tertiary deposits of Australia has in England remained entirely in the background, and I have been several times surprised at finding students of Tertiary paleontology, generally *au courant* with the progress of their special branch of science, unacquainted with the circumstance. Its importance, in a theoretical point of view, is beyond all question, hence the deep interest always exhibited by those to whom I have spoken on the subject.

I had, in short, succumbed to the view I was questioning. I had recognized that the original discovery of the living trigonian upended no theory, but I had let the Cenozoic fossil act as a Huxleyan nasty fact because Jenkins had so presented it. But when we consider what the Cenozoic trigonian did *not* provoke, we obtain a more general and consistent account of the entire affair. The living trigonian changed no theory, because it could fit (however uncomfortably) with all major views of life. The Cenozoic trigonian did not prove evolution either, because Agassiz's position of retreat was defensible (however embarrassing) and because evolution was too big a revolution to rely critically on any one datum. *Trigonia* didn't hurt, but a multitude of fish were frying, and one extra clam, however clean and pretty, didn't bring the meal to perfection (I shall anticipate a suitable recipe next month, Mr. Sokolov).

Sherlock Holmes once solved a case because the dog didn't bark, but would have sounded off had it been a dog. Nonevents matter, not only the new and nasty facts. Which reminds me: I must have looked at a thousand periwinkles this morning. Still no lefties. Maybe someday.

PAUL GRUCHOW

Bones

Paul Gruchow (1947–   ) was a newspaper and magazine editor for
twenty years before turning to writing essays. He currently teaches
writing at Saint Olaf College and is the author of the essay collections *Journal of a Prairie Year* (1985) and *The Necessity of Empty
Places* (1988). The following selection first appeared in *Minnesota
Monthly.*

I have always had an eye for bones. As a child, I collected them, and
labeled them, and arranged them from biggest to littlest on a shelf
in the hayloft of our barn. On rainy summer afternoons and snowy
winter days, I retired to my museum and played with the bones—
turning them over in my hands, examining them in the dim light
that seeped through the cracks in the walls of the barn, running my
fingers over worn incisors, feeling the bald smoothness of skull bones,
admiring the way femurs balanced in my hands, listening to the wind
in the cupolas and to the cooing pigeons, hearing the music of
raindrops or ice crystals pattering against the shingles. The bones
spoke to me on those dank afternoons, but I was a long time in
deciphering what they said.

Even from the beginning, I declined to collect some bones. There
was a sinkhole at the bottom of our pasture. A cow had mired and
died there years before I chanced upon the place. Its flesh had long
since rotted away, devoured by billions of microbes. Nothing remained but a few tufts of its brown hair, some scraps of leathery
hide, and its bones. The bones, already bleached, had begun to gray
with age. They lay half buried in the muck, contorted still in the last
paroxysm of life. The cow's skull had separated from the vertebrae
of its neck; it rested upwind from the rest of the skeleton, facing
north into the bitter winds.

I encountered it one cold November afternoon when the leaves
had fallen from the willows and the sedges had turned russet and
gold. A pheasant bolted from the meadow grasses underfoot, startling
me, and when I looked up I was staring into the cow's vacant eye
sockets. They seemed to be staring back at me.

My first impulse was to collect the bones of the mired cow. But
I resisted it. Something in those bones—some integrity—restrained

me, commanded my reverence. Everything else I had collected had appeared at random: a skull here, a rib cage there—leavings scattered by scavengers, by wind and water and frost. To pick up such a bone is to join the forces of dispersal at restless work in the world, to become part of its natural history. But the bones of the cow, for whatever reasons, had remained intact, held in the continuing entrapment of the sinkhole. The site harbored something more than a death. It seemed to me that the cow was entombed there, and my passion for bones did not extend to the robbery of graves.

I was only a boy, but I knew something of graves. I knew the scent of gladiolus and strong perfume in the parlor, where the embalmed body of my grandfather had been propped for viewing before the ritual of the grave, and I'd felt the strong, icy wind blowing across the open prairie cemetery on the brown day when his bones were buried, and I'd heard the cold clank of the pebble in the first shovelful of earth hurled upon his burnished bronze casket. I remembered, even then, nothing of my living grandfather, but the memory of his bones lingers still. And I knew the smell of urine and rubber in the sickroom of my grandmother—the same parlor that had held my dead grandfather. She had been laid out there to die in a rented hospital bed, insensible after a stroke. We watched as she shriveled up day by day into a sack of sharp-edged bones.

And I had dug my share of graves. One of them was for the cottontail rabbit I'd raised in a chicken-wire cage in the back yard. I'd found it abandoned as an infant and had tended it all summer, feeding it with an eyedropper until it could be weaned. I'd brought it fresh tidbits from the garden: young cabbages and carrots and leaves of lettuce—treating it as the younger brother I did not have.

"You have got to let that thing go," my father had been saying. "The sooner the better. It can't stay the winter in that pen. It won't survive."

"Yes," I said. "I'll do it. Tomorrow."

One admonishment led to another, one tomorrow to the next. There were many distractions, and I didn't want to relinquish the rabbit.

One morning late in September, I went out to greet it, barefoot and still in my pajamas, and I found it quivering in the corner of its box, bleeding thickly from several savage gashes, inflicted by some predator that had improbably spared it. I wept over it and treated its wounds, but it did not survive the school day. That evening, I buried it—my heart heavier for the conviction, no doubt vain, that it might have escaped had it not been penned. At that age, I still had faith in a benign and brotherly nature, and I felt personally betrayed when it answered me in the language of violence and death.

On another day, a hot one in July, I learned to speak the same language myself. I had a cat, for whom I had vowed responsibility; she had produced a litter of kittens. I had been told, emphatically, that I could not keep those kittens—and as desperately as I tried, I could find no one to adopt them. None of the farming folks I knew needed or wanted another cat. So one awful day, in a terrible heat, I took them into an abandoned henhouse and did what needed to be done. One by one I picked up the lovely, mewing kittens and held them at the bottom of a bucket of water. When they stopped struggling, I carried them into the grove to the place where the rabbit's bones rested, and made ten tiny graves for them, and buried them like pieces of my own flesh. I hated my own flesh then, hated the ruthless efficiency with which it could be made to do such dirty work, and would as soon have buried myself. But another part of me yearned to live as violently as those kittens did when they were suffocating in a water pail in the close heat of a July afternoon.

There were many kinds of bones in those days: the leg bone our big tomcat chewed off—his own—when it was snapped in a trap, and withered, and rotted; the bones of the family goats, caught in a fire I had carelessly set and stinking like old tire burning; the neck bones of chickens crunching under the blows of my ax on butchering days; the carcasses of the rodents I trapped, skinned, and offered to my dog, Mitsy, as a sacrifice of love; the bones of the ground squirrels I drowned in their holes and sold to the county government for a bounty of ten cents a head; the bones I carried home from my wanderings in fields and meadows. My life in those days had more to do with bones than it does now. I live a more genteel life these days, and a life a lot further from nature.

The bones often told stories of cruelty—many of them cruelties of my own creation. What was I to make of this? The obvious thing, I suppose: that life is sometimes cruel. That is a fact more to be respected than explained—like the fact that when you press your tongue to a pump handle in the wintertime, it bonds to the metal and you cannot pry it loose without tearing away some skin. I couldn't explain cruelty, and I didn't try. When my father insisted that my sister wear skirts to the schoolbus stop half a mile away in vicious midwinter because he had religious scruples against females in trousers, and when she froze her legs and whimpered all the way to school from the sting and itch of the thawing, I thought him cruel and stupid and pious to a horrible fault, but still I loved him, and so, in her own way, did she. It was a mystery, but when was life or love ever not a mystery?

I vowed at a fairly early age to give up voluntary cruelties. I stopped keeping wild pets. I quit hunting and trapping for sport. I practiced a boyish asceticism, finding myself irregularly but powerfully attracted to the most extravagant habits of the third- and fourth-century desert eremites.[1] One saint, whose name I've forgotten, particularly enchanted me. I'd read that he once spent forty days and forty nights sitting motionless in a swamp, enduring impassively whatever abuses came his way, in penance for having swatted a mosquito—one of God's creatures. I did not dare to hope for such saintliness, but I did, for a time, passionately admire it.

Still, I remained cruel. In the winter, feeling neither gratitude nor regret, I ate the sheep that had pulled me around the yard in a cart all summer. I fished for northerns in the rapids above the dam on the river—not for food, but for the fun of it. I particularly enjoyed beheading grasshoppers, and spent many pleasant hours doing so in the grain wagons at harvest time. It was a crooked world, running along an ambiguous path overgrown with many obstructions, and I could not see the straight way through it.

I suffer over this with my own children. My daughter is sometimes sensitive beyond reason. Once, as we were sitting around a campfire, I absentmindedly crushed a cricket that had crawled near the flame. My daughter burst into tears. I did not know what she was crying about, which made everything much worse. I begged her to explain what was wrong.

"You murdered it!" she finally said, between her sobs.

"Murdered it! Murdered what?" I said.

She stopped crying, looked at me coldly. "I suppose you really don't know," she said.

I looked blank.

"The cricket!" she said. "The poor helpless cricket! Why did you have to go and do that? It wasn't hurting anything, was it?"

"No," I had to admit, "it wasn't." At the same time, I was impatient and unrepenting. My God, I thought, I have raised an eremite. I wanted to say: "Be reasonable." And: "You know, there are greater tragedies in life than the wanton death of a cricket." But I kept silent,

---

[1] hermits (ED.)

out of confusion and embarrassment, and because I did not want to endorse wantonness, however trivial. In some moral sense, I suspected, she was right. That is one of the troubles with morality: its indifference to distinctions of degree; its impracticality.

My son, on the other hand, sees nature as many children do: as something to pillage, to plunder, to maim, to shoot, to catch. So far as he is concerned, every wild creature is meant to be carried home on a stringer or carted home in a box or a glass bottle.

We fished one night for bullheads—a sport in which I indulge him, though I find it contemptible: for the ease with which bullheads can be caught; for the execrable waters they inhabit; for their slimy skins, which seem to get slimier as the summer wears on; for the greedy way they swallow hooks; for the grotesque belches they emit when you squeeze their air bladders, as you must if you wish to avoid their painful barbs while unhooking them. I am suspicious of all hierarchies, but there is no doubt in my mind that any one bass or trout or walleye is infinitely more desirable than any dumpster full of bullheads.

We caught a mess of bullheads that day—and because the two of us were on an indulgent father-and-son outing, I promised to cook them for breakfast. We stashed the fish in the minnow bucket, watched the fire burn down and the heavens come alive, and went to bed. An hour or two later, I was awakened by the clatter of dishes in the opened camping box. Peering out into the moonlit night, I saw a raccoon sitting next to the box on the picnic table, picking marshmallows daintily out of a bag and eating them one at a time, very noisily and with much smacking of lips.

A raccoon is an exceedingly handsome and beguiling creature. I rather regretted getting up out of habit and shooing it away. I stashed the marshmallows in the car and went back to bed. Fifteen minutes later, the raccoon was back. This time it took hold of the minnow bucket, dragged it a little way off, tipped it on its side, inserted one paw through the trap door to hold it open, fished a bullhead out of the bucket, and ate it, smacking its lips even more loudly, obviously having a wonderful time. And so it went—bullhead after bullhead after bullhead. It was clear from the aplomb with which the raccoon executed this banquet that he was a grizzled veteran of the minnow-bucket circuit.

I made no attempt to stop him. The raccoon's gain was all the more mine. In my mind, I substituted pancakes for bullheads at breakfast—and fell contentedly, even joyfully, to sleep. In the morning, I put on a sad face and announced the tragedy to my son. I expected him to be heartbroken. He wasn't—not in the least. He immediately saw the germ of a grand new opportunity.

"I know what!" he said. "Let's go catch some more bullheads, and then we can use them for bait to catch that old raccoon!"

"But why would you want to do that?" I said, and then, looking into his face and seeing the futility in such a question, I lied. "We'll see," I said, knowing that I was seeming to acquiesce in a scheme that I had no intention of carrying forward.

I want to find, for myself, some middle ground between my daughter's naïve reverence for nature and my son's view of nature as a sport. Once, I think, I found it, but as my life grew more complicated, I lost it. I am thinking of that brief time when, as a country boy, I lived in the out-of-doors essentially as one might occupy a living room. I didn't make distinctions then that I routinely make now, because those distinctions—between inside and outside, between wild and domestic, between house and home—did not, for practical purposes, exist.

As a child in Chippewa County, Minnesota, I was never confined to any space so constricted as a house. Our family had a house, of course—a succession of houses: first a cement-block basement house; then a balloon-frame shack; finally an honest, full-fledged farmhouse with rooms and staircases and a real basement and rag rugs on the linoleum floors. But none of those houses fully contained the place in which I lived. Partly this was a matter of definition: in the country, one lives not in a house but on a farm, and one thinks of the space one occupies as including everything within the farm's fence lines. But for me, something else was at work. In our little country church, I heard often the promise of heaven. I visualized it not as cloudy and ethereal but as a concrete place, according to the words of Jesus: "In my father's house are many mansions." I thought of my own home as a smaller version of heaven—as a house of many mansions. There was the wooden frame house with the green mansard roof where I slept and ate and joined the life of the family. But it was only one of many mansions in which I lived contemporaneously.

I lived in the hayloft, where I stored my collection of bones. When it was too stormy to be outside, I was likely to spend the day there, swinging on the ropes and standing in the crow's nest at the peak of the gables, where I could see out across the river valley through a little round window. I kept company with the pigeons, read books, napped in a bed of hay, teased spiders out of their chambers, daydreamed.

And I lived in the limbs of an enormous black walnut tree at the far end of the pasture, in the company of squirrels and pale little tree frogs. It was always shady there, and even in the stillest and hottest weather, a fresh breeze always seemed to be blowing around it. Its limbs were broad enough to lie down upon, and I often did just that, listening to the lazy music of summer afternoons: the buzzing of flies, the droning of bumblebees, the singing of birds. Near the black walnut tree were the hollow of a pioneer's sod hut and a sweetwater spring that ran all winter long; hundreds of times I imagined that the sod house was mine in the making, that the spring had drawn me there, and that I would live forever in the shadow of the wide arms of the walnut tree.

And I lived along the shores of the pasture pond, where the pussy willows swelled in the springtime; where blackbirds wheezed and wheedled in the cattails; where muskrats swam in the musty, warm waters of summer, green with algae and duckweed. I lived among the arrowroots and jewelweeds, among the strawberries hiding in the cordgrass, in the company of minks and weasels and fat skunks. Water striders and boatmen and pill bugs squatted in my front yard, righthanded pond snails and leopard frogs in my back yard, dragon-flies and damselflies in the fetid air overhead. I passed many happy hours in the upper reaches of a black willow tree, monitoring the progress of life in the fecund chambers of my pond mansion.

And I lived by the blue light of the moon along country lanes so quiet I could hear the traffic in the town, miles away, visible only as a burst of mysterious light on the distant horizon. Fireflies flashed in the ditches, and the long leaves of the corn sighed in the evening breezes. Here and there a dog barked in a farmyard. The sound of dogs barking in the night, echoing across the vast, empty countryside, was the surfacing sound of the wilderness in them. I could hear in their voices the ancient cries of gray wolves, echoing from the days when great herds of bison roamed the plains and the moonlight danced in the endless waves of grass. I could feel, then, the wilderness in my *own* bones.

And I lived in a woodpile, in a plum thicket, in the striped shade of a sweltering August cornfield where whirlwinds raced, showering dust like rain. I lived in a prairie meadow, among overgrazed river bluffs, on a granite island in a widening of the river, along a grassy fenceline where a lone green ash grew.

I lived along the banks of the river—where beaver built their dams; where mud turtles sunned on half-submerged logs; where bullheads and northern pike, saugers and buffalo fish swam the murky waters; where white-tailed deer came down to drink; where the tracks of mink mingled in the shoreline mud with the remains of the clams that raccoons had fished from the shallows. But mainly I dwelled along the river under the spell of its mysterious waters, running into the Minnesota River, and then into the Mississippi, and then down the central nervous cord of the continent, over the plains of Iowa, through the hills of Missouri and Arkansas, across the bayous of Louisiana, and into the Gulf of Mexico.

In my house were many mansions.

When I sat on the overhanging limb of the willow tree and dangled my bare feet into the brown waters of the Chippewa River and felt the slow, steady tug of its unfailing current against my toes, I connected myself to the great body of the continent. I was linked not merely with a small river in western Minnesota, but swept up into the gigantic stream of life. I lived then in the piney waters of the North Woods, in the thundering waters of St. Anthony Falls, in the icy rush of mountain streams, in the stagnant backwaters of Southern marshes, in the oceanic brine. I shared my mansion with little bullheads, yes, but also with ancient paddlefishes and cutthroat trout and sharks and catfishes as big as logs. I lived then among bald eagles and alligators and panthers. I lived where it always snows and where it never snows, high in the mountains and at the edge of the sea.

As a high school biology student, I once traced the cardiovascular system of a domestic cat whose blood vessels had been injected with a rubbery substance—blue for the veins, red for the arteries. Beginning at the heart, I traced the vessels up into its skull and down into its toes and out along its tail, following them as they branched into smaller and smaller streams. It was an ecstatic experience; I carried my half-excavated specimen home on the bus in a clear plastic bag, unable to bear the suspense of waiting until the next day's class to discover where all the vessels ran. No one would sit next to me. Everyone else on the bus found the smell of the preservative nauseating, the sight of the opened carcass disgusting, my enthusiasm for the project weird, sick. But I was too excited to mind. Here, in the body of the cat, lay a map of the world as I perceived it from my vantage point along the Chippewa River. I might be one red corpuscle swimming in the slenderest of the tail arteries, but I was an undeniable part of something big and alive, a constituent particle of the whole animal. I had seen the universe in a two-dollar laboratory specimen.

Now I live in a single house of eight rooms, from which I venture forth into nature as a tourist. Most mornings, I walk from my house around a shallow prairie lake to the two-room office in which I spend my days pacing, writing, reading, and staring out of the second-story windows into the canopy of a black walnut tree. It buds. It leaves. It flowers. It bears nuts. The yellow-green nuts turn brown and fall; the green leaves turn yellow and flutter to earth. In the winter I watch frozen pieces of the tree break off in the wind and scatter to the earth. In the spring, the tree buds again. Some would call this a cycle—the eternal cycle of nature—and find comfort in it. I don't. The tree is a little less young each spring, and so am I. Our time is running out. For the tree, as for me, the path is linear, not cyclical—and the end of the line is death. The best that can be said, in the meantime, is that neither of us has moved.

The skies beyond the tree change. One day dawns clear; the next, cloudy. Some days rain patters against the window glass. Some mornings the branches of the walnut are white with rime frost; others, with new snow. The wind blows, or doesn't. In the heated and air conditioned solitude of my study, it is all the same.

One summer afternoon a couple of years ago, the sky suddenly turned as black as ink. The streetlights switched on. A stillness fell, so deafening that it intruded even into my already silent rooms. Rain began to pour in torrents, as it does in a tropical forest, but the downpour was swept and swirled by violent winds that howled in the corners of the building. As suddenly as the rain came, so came the hail, thundering down upon the rooftop and smashing against the windows. One by one, the panes of glass shattered as I cowered in the middle of the outer room, paralyzed with awe and fear. Then, as suddenly as it had arrived, the storm cloud passed. The branches of the walnut tree hung in tatters, and icy water puddled on the windowsills where the rain had been driven through the cracks in the glass. In the streets, mist had already begun to rise from the hail drifts dissipating in the blazing heat of the sun. Ten million dollars' damage in ten minutes in one small prairie town. I thought of an outburst of John Berryman's I'd witnessed on another summer day. Suddenly, while walking to the auditorium's center stage to deliver a lecture on James Joyce, he had smashed a chair into the orchestra pit and bellowed incoherently against janitors. "It was good for them," he later wrote of us, his bewildered students. "A Zen touch: action in the midst of thought."

But most days are not graced with such drama. They come to a close, and I walk home—noticing, perhaps, whether it is hot or cold, windy or calm; passing through a landscape so familiar that I have ceased to see it; ready to take up residence for the night in the only house I now know: a gray one of eight rooms, a tight fortress against the world beyond its windows. I take the telephone off the hook, throw the junk mail unopened into the wastebasket, and sit in my brown chair, in the yellow light of a lamp, listening to piano music arranged on a compact disc in the order that someone else has determined would please me. There are rooms in the house that I seldom visit, and, so far as I am concerned, there are no other houses anywhere else in the wide world.

When I want to visit the world in which I once lived, I consult my maps, arrange my schedule, embark on an expedition to the local stores for perishable supplies, pack the car, and set out from my house—fearful sometimes, but full of new energy too, as a tourist always is at the beginning of a journey. And when I arrive, and set out on foot into some untamed place, I come sooner or later to a bone or a shell, and often I pick it up and carry it home with me. I keep my souvenirs here in my office with me and on the mantel of the fireplace in my house: the tooth of a bison washed out of the mud of a Nebraska streambed; the carapace of a horseshoe crab picked up in a Florida mangrove swamp; a bowlful of fossil shark teeth collected on a Gulf Coast beach; the shell of a land snail found in the sandy soil of an arroyo in the Baja desert; the jaw bone of a cow from the Great Basin of Wyoming; the antler of a white-tailed deer, shed in the North Woods; the skull of a mule deer attacked by coyotes on Montana's Front Range. Every bone reminds me of many others that I left uncollected somewhere when I was out hunting for lost mansions. Like the prophet, I have walked in a valley full of bones.

But the remarkable thing, in fact, is that one finds so few bones. Millions of creatures die every day. Where are their remains? Where have they all gone? And as for the creatures dying but not yet dead— where are they? You can walk for a thousand miles and never once see a creature dying. Death is nothing if not discreet.

The bones, every one, are miracles—the alms nature offers to life. We do not easily accept miracles; they seem to fall beyond the boundaries of cause and effect. But a miracle is nothing more than a story that begins after the cause and ends before the effect. It is the mysterious void at the heart of the story: the space between the particles of an atom that makes the substance of things possible. The miracle of a bone is that it is a moment frozen. A bone is the evidence of a life—a life unique, unprecedented, and never to be repeated, which, though it has vanished, nevertheless endures in the bone: a faint white glimmering, in some offhand place, of life everlasting.

LEWIS THOMAS

The Music of This Sphere

Lewis Thomas (1913–   ) is an American physician who writes about medicine and science for a general audience. A former president of Sloan–Kettering Cancer Center, his books include *The Medusa and the Snail* (1979), *Late Night Thoughts on Listening to Mahler's Ninth Symphony* (1983), and *The Lives of a Cell* (1974), from which the following selection is taken.

It is one of our problems that as we become crowded together, the sounds we make to each other, in our increasingly complex communication systems, become more random-sounding, accidental or incidental, and we have trouble selecting meaningful signals out of the noise. One reason is, of course, that we do not seem able to restrict our communication to information-bearing, relevant signals. Given any new technology for transmitting information, we seem bound to use it for great quantities of small talk. We are only saved by music from being overwhelmed by nonsense.

It is a marginal comfort to know that the relatively new science of bioacoustics must deal with similar problems in the sounds made by other animals to each other. No matter what sound-making device is placed at their disposal, creatures in general do a great deal of gabbling, and it requires long patience and observation to edit out the parts lacking syntax and sense. Light social conversation, designed to keep the party going, prevails. Nature abhors a long silence.

Somewhere, underlying all the other signals, is a continual music. Termites make percussive sounds to each other by beating their heads against the floor in the dark, resonating corridors of their nests. The sound has been described as resembling, to the human ear, sand falling on paper, but spectrographic analysis of sound records has recently revealed a high degree of organization in the drumming; the beats occur in regular, rhythmic phrases, differing in duration, like notes for a tympani section.

From time to time, certain termites make a convulsive movement of their mandibles to produce a loud, high-pitched clicking sound, audible ten meters off. So much effort goes into this one note that it must have urgent meaning, at least to the sender. He cannot make it without such a wrench that he is flung one or two centimeters into the air by the recoil.

There is obvious hazard in trying to assign a particular meaning to this special kind of sound, and problems like this exist throughout the field of bioacoustics. One can imagine a woolly-minded Visitor from Outer Space, interested in human beings, discerning on his spectrograph the click of that golf ball on the surface of the moon, and trying to account for it as a call of warning (unlikely), a signal of mating (out of the question), or an announcement of territory (could be).

Bats are obliged to make sounds almost ceaselessly, to sense, by sonar, all the objects in their surroundings. They can spot with accuracy, on the wing, small insects, and they will home onto things they like with infallibility and speed. With such a system for the equivalent of glancing around, they must live in a world of ultrasonic batsound, most of it with an industrial, machinery sound. Still, they communicate with each other as well, by clicks and high-pitched greetings. Moreover, they have been heard to produce, while hanging at rest upside down in the depths of woods, strange, solitary, and lovely bell-like notes.

Almost anything that an animal can employ to make a sound is put to use. Drumming, created by beating the feet, is used by prairie hens, rabbits, and mice; the head is banged by woodpeckers and certain other birds; the males of deathwatch beetles make a rapid ticking sound by percussion of a protuberance on the abdomen against the ground; a faint but audible ticking is made by the tiny beetle *Lepinotus inquilinus,* which is less than two millimeters in length. Fish make sounds by clicking their teeth, blowing air, and drumming with special muscles against tuned inflated air bladders. Solid structures are set to vibrating by toothed bows in crustaceans and insects. The proboscis of the death's-head hawk moth is used as a kind of reed instrument, blown through to make high-pitched, reedy notes.

Gorillas beat their chests for certain kinds of discourse. Animals with loose skeletons rattle them, or, like rattlesnakes, get sounds from externally placed structures. Turtles, alligators, crocodiles, and even snakes make various more or less vocal sounds. Leeches have been heard to tap rhythmically on leaves, engaging the attention of other leeches, which tap back, in synchrony. Even earthworms make sounds, faint staccato notes in regular clusters. Toads sing to each other, and their friends sing back in antiphony.

Birdsong has been so much analyzed for its content of business communication that there seems little time left for music, but it is there. Behind the glossaries of warning calls, alarms, mating messages, pronouncements of territory, calls for recruitment, and demands for dispersal, there is redundant, elegant sound that is unaccountable as part of the working day. The thrush in my backyard sings down his nose in meditative, liquid runs of melody, over and over again, and I have the strongest impression that he does this for his own pleasure. Some of the time he seems to be practicing, like a virtuoso in his apartment. He starts a run, reaches a midpoint in the second bar where there should be a set of complex harmonics, stops, and goes back to begin over, dissatisfied. Sometimes he changes his notation so conspicuously that he seems to be improvising sets of variations. It is a meditative, questioning kind of music, and I cannot believe that he is simply saying, "thrush here."

The robin sings flexible songs, containing a variety of motifs that he rearranges to his liking; the notes in each motif constitute the syntax, and the possibilities of variation produce a considerable repertoire. The meadow lark, with three hundred notes to work with, arranges these in phrases of three to six notes and elaborates fifty types of song. The nightingale has twenty-four basic songs, but gains wild variety by varying the internal arrangement of phrases and the length of pauses. The chaffinch listens to other chaffinches, and incorporates into his memory snatches of their songs.

The need to make music, and to listen to it, is universally expressed by human beings. I cannot imagine, even in our most primitive times, the emergence of talented painters to make cave paintings without there having been, near at hand, equally creative people making song. It is, like speech, a dominant aspect of human biology.

The individual parts played by other instrumentalists—crickets or earthworms, for instance—may not have the sound of music by themselves, but we hear them out of context. If we could listen to them all at once, fully orchestrated, in their immense ensemble, we might become aware of the counterpoint, the balance of tones and timbres and harmonics, the sonorities. The recorded songs of the humpback whale, filled with tensions and resolutions, ambiguities and allusions, incomplete, can be listened to as a *part* of music, like an isolated section of an orchestra. If we had better hearing, and could discern the descants of sea birds, the rhythmic tympani of schools of mollusks, or even the distant harmonics of midges hanging over meadows in the sun, the combined sound might lift us off our feet.

There are, of course, other ways to account for the songs of whales. They might be simple, down-to-earth statements about navigation, or sources of krill, or limits of territory. But the proof is not in, and until it is shown that these long, convoluted, insistent melodies, repeated by different singers with ornamentations of their own, are the means of sending through several hundred miles of undersea such ordinary information as "whale here," I shall believe otherwise. Now and again, in the intervals between songs, the whales have been seen to breach, leaping clear out of the sea and landing on their backs, awash in the turbulence of their beating flippers. Perhaps they are pleased by the way the piece went, or perhaps it is celebration at hearing one's own song returning after circumnavigation; whatever, it has the look of jubilation.

I suppose that my extraterrestrial Visitor might puzzle over my records in much the same way, on first listening. The 14th Quartet might, for him, be a communication announcing, "Beethoven here," answered, after passage through an undersea of time and submerged currents of human thought, by another long signal a century later, "Bartók[1] here."

If, as I believe, the urge to make a kind of music is as much a characteristic of biology as our other fundamental functions, there ought to be an explanation for it. Having none at hand, I am free to make one up. The rhythmic sounds might be the recapitulation of something else—an earliest memory, a score for the transformation of inanimate, random matter in chaos into the improbable, ordered dance of living forms. Morowitz has presented the case, in thermodynamic terms, for the hypothesis that a steady flow of energy from the inexhaustible source of the sun to the unfillable sink of outer space, by way of the earth, is mathematically destined to cause the organization of matter into an increasingly ordered state. The resulting balancing act involves a ceaseless clustering of bonded atoms into molecules of higher and higher complexity, and the emergence of cycles for the storage and release of energy. In a nonequilibrium steady state, which is postulated, the solar energy would not just flow to the earth and radiate away; it is thermodynamically inevitable

---

[1] Bela Bartók (1881–1945), was a Hungarian composer. (ED.)

that it must rearrange matter into symmetry, away from probability, against entropy, lifting it, so to speak, into a constantly changing condition of rearrangement and molecular ornamentation. In such a system, the outcome is a chancy kind of order, always on the verge of descending into chaos, held taut against probability by the unremitting, constant surge of energy from the sun.

If there were to be sounds to represent this process, they would have the arrangement of the Brandenburg Concertos[2] for my ear, but I am open to wonder whether the same events are recalled by the rhythms of insects, the long, pulsing runs of birdsong, the descants of whales, the modulated vibrations of a million locusts in migration, the tympani of gorilla breasts, termite heads, drumfish bladders. A "grand canonical ensemble" is, oddly enough, the proper term for a quantitative model system in thermodynamics, borrowed from music by way of mathematics. Borrowed back again, provided with notation, it would do for what I have in mind.

STEPHEN HAWKING

The Arrow of Time

> Stephen Hawking (1942–   ) is a British theoretical physicist. In 1979 he was appointed Lucasian Professor of Mathematics at Cambridge University, a post previously held by Isaac Newton. Among his publications are *Superspace and Supergravity* (1981), edited with M. Rocek, and *A Brief History of Time: From the Big Bang to Black Holes* (1988), from which the following selection is taken.

In previous chapters we have seen how our views of the nature of time have changed over the years. Up to the beginning of this century people believed in an absolute time. That is, each event could be labeled by a number called "time" in a unique way, and all good clocks would agree on the time interval between two events. However, the discovery that the speed of light appeared the same to every

---

[2] Six compositions by Johan Sebastian Bach (1685–1750) written in 1721 for different and unusual combinations of instruments. (ED.)

observer, no matter how he was moving, led to the theory of relativity—and in that one had to abandon the idea that there was a unique absolute time. Instead, each observer would have his own measure of time as recorded by a clock that he carried: clocks carried by different observers would not necessarily agree. Thus time became a more personal concept, relative to the observer who measured it.

When one tried to unify gravity with quantum mechanics, one had to introduce the idea of "imaginary" time. Imaginary time is indistinguishable from directions in space. If one can go north, one can turn around and head south; equally, if one can go forward in imaginary time, one ought to be able to turn round and go backward. This means that there can be no important difference between the forward and backward directions of imaginary time. On the other hand, when one looks at "real" time, there's a very big difference between the forward and backward directions, as we all know. Where does this difference between the past and the future come from? Why do we remember the past but not the future?

The laws of science do not distinguish between the past and the future. More precisely, as explained earlier, the laws of science are unchanged under the combination of operations (or symmetries) known as C, P, and T. (C means changing particles for antiparticles. P means taking the mirror image, so left and right are interchanged. And T means reversing the direction of motion of all particles: in effect, running the motion backward.) The laws of science that govern the behavior of matter under all normal situations are unchanged under the combination of the two operations C and P on their own. In other words, life would be just the same for the inhabitants of another planet who were both mirror images of us and who were made of antimatter, rather than matter.

If the laws of science are unchanged by the combination of operations C and P, and also by the combination C, P, and T, they must also be unchanged under the operation T alone. Yet there is a big difference between the forward and backward directions of real time in ordinary life. Imagine a cup of water falling off a table and breaking into pieces on the floor. If you take a film of this, you can easily tell whether it is being run forward or backward. If you run it backward you will see the pieces suddenly gather themselves together off the floor and jump back to form a whole cup on the table. You can tell that the film is being run backward because this kind of behavior is never observed in ordinary life. If it were, crockery manufacturers would go out of business.

The explanation that is usually given as to why we don't see broken cups gathering themselves together off the floor and jumping back onto the table is that it is forbidden by the second law of thermodynamics. This says that in any closed system disorder, or entropy, always increases with time. In other words, it is a form of Murphy's law: Things always tend to go wrong! An intact cup on the table is a state of high order, but a broken cup on the floor is a disordered state. One can go readily from the cup on the table in the past to the broken cup on the floor in the future, but not the other way round.

The increase of disorder or entropy with time is one example of what is called an arrow of time, something that distinguishes the past from the future, giving a direction to time. There are at least three different arrows of time. First, there is the thermodynamic arrow of time, the direction of time in which disorder or entropy increases. Then, there is the psychological arrow of time. This is the direction in which we feel time passes, the direction in which we remember the past but not the future. Finally, there is the cosmological arrow of time. This is the direction of time in which the universe is expanding rather than contracting.

In this chapter I shall argue that the no boundary condition for the universe, together with the weak anthropic principle, can explain why all three arrows point in the same direction—and moreover, why a well-defined arrow of time should exist at all. I shall argue that the psychological arrow is determined by the thermodynamic arrow, and that these two arrows necessarily always point in the same direction. If one assumes the no boundary condition for the universe, we shall see that there must be well-defined thermodynamic and cosmological arrows of time, but they will not point in the same direction for the whole history of the universe. However, I shall argue that it is only when they do point in the same direction that conditions are suitable for the development of intelligent beings who can ask the question: Why does disorder increase in the same direction of time as that in which the universe expands?

I shall discuss first the thermodynamic arrow of time. The second law of thermodynamics results from the fact that there are always many more disordered states than there are ordered ones. For example, consider the pieces of jigsaw in a box. There is one, and only one, arrangement in which the pieces make a complete picture. On the other hand, there are a very large number of arrangements in which the pieces are disordered and don't make a picture.

Suppose a system starts out in one of the small number of ordered states. As time goes by, the system will evolve according to the laws

of science and its state will change. At a later time, it is more probable that the system will be in a disordered state than in an ordered one because there are more disordered states. Thus disorder will tend to increase with time if the system obeys an initial condition of high order.

Suppose the pieces of the jigsaw start off in a box in the ordered arrangement in which they form a picture. If you shake the box, the pieces will take up another arrangement. This will probably be a disordered arrangement in which the pieces don't form a proper picture, simply because there are so many more disordered arrangements. Some groups of pieces may still form parts of the picture, but the more you shake the box, the more likely it is that these groups will get broken up and the pieces will be in a completely jumbled state in which they don't form any sort of picture. So the disorder of the pieces will probably increase with time if the pieces obey the initial condition that they start off in a condition of high order.

Suppose, however, that God decided that the universe should finish up in a state of high order but that it didn't matter what state it started in. At early times the universe would probably be in a disordered state. This would mean that disorder would *decrease* with time. You would see broken cups gathering themselves together and jumping back onto the table. However, any human beings who were observing the cups would be living in a universe in which disorder decreased with time. I shall argue that such beings would have a psychological arrow of time that was backward. That is, they would remember events in the future, and not remember events in their past. When the cup was broken, they would remember it being on the table, but when it was on the table, they would not remember it being on the floor.

It is rather difficult to talk about human memory because we don't know how the brain works in detail. We do, however, know all about how computer memories work. I shall therefore discuss the psychological arrow of time for computers. I think it is reasonable to assume that the arrow for computers is the same as that for humans. If it were not, one could make a killing on the stock exchange by having a computer that would remember tomorrow's prices!

A computer memory is basically a device containing elements that can exist in either of two states. A simple example is an abacus. In its simplest form, this consists of a number of wires; on each wire is a bead that can be put in one of two positions. Before an item is recorded in a computer's memory, the memory is in a disordered state, with equal probabilities for the two possible states. (The abacus beads are scattered randomly on the wires of the abacus.) After the memory interacts with the system to be remembered, it will definitely be in one state or the other, according to the state of the system. (Each abacus bead will be at either the left or the right of the abacus wire.) So the memory has passed from a disordered state to an ordered one. However, in order to make sure that the memory is in the right state, it is necessary to use a certain amount of energy (to move the bead or to power the computer, for example). This energy is dissipated as heat, and increases the amount of disorder in the universe. One can show that this increase in disorder is always greater than the increase in the order of the memory itself. Thus the heat expelled by the computer's cooling fan means that when a computer records an item in memory, the total amount of disorder in the universe still goes up. The direction of time in which a computer remembers the past is the same as that in which disorder increases.

Our subjective sense of the direction of time, the psychological arrow of time, is therefore determined within our brain by the thermodynamic arrow of time. Just as a computer, we must remember things in the order in which entropy increases. This makes the second law of thermodynamics almost trivial. Disorder increases with time because we measure time in the direction in which disorder increases. You can't have a safer bet than that!

Buy why should the thermodynamic arrow of time exist at all? Or, in other words, why should the universe be in a state of high order at one end of time, the end that we call the past? Why is it not in a state of complete disorder at all times? After all, this might seem more probable. And why is the direction of time in which disorder increases the same as that in which the universe expands?

In the classical theory of general relativity one cannot predict how the universe would have begun because all the known laws of science would have broken down at the big bang singularity. The universe could have started out in a very smooth and ordered state. This would have led to well-defined thermodynamic and cosmological arrows of time, as we observe. But it could equally well have started out in a very lumpy and disordered state. In that case, the universe would already be in a state of complete disorder, so disorder could not increase with time. It would either stay constant, in which case there would be no well-defined thermodynamic arrow of time, or it would decrease, in which case the thermodynamic arrow of time would point in the opposite direction to the cosmological arrow. Neither of these possibilities agrees with what we observe. However, as we have seen, classical general relativity predicts its own downfall. When the curvature of spacetime becomes large, quantum gravitational effects will become important and the classical theory will cease to be a good description of the universe. One has to use a quantum theory of gravity to understand how the universe began.

In a quantum theory of gravity, as we saw in the last chapter, in order to specify the state of the universe one would still have to say how the possible histories of the universe would behave at the boundary of space-time in the past. One could avoid this difficulty of having to describe what we do not and cannot know only if the histories satisfy the no boundary condition: they are finite in extent but have no boundaries, edges, or singularities. In that case, the beginning of time would be a regular, smooth point of space-time and the universe would have begun its expansion in a very smooth and ordered state. It could not have been completely uniform, because that would violate the uncertainty principle of quantum theory. There had to be small fluctuations in the density and velocities of particles. The no boundary condition, however, implied that these fluctuations were as small as they could be, consistent with the uncertainty principle.

The universe would have started off with a period of exponential or "inflationary" expansion in which it would have increased its size by a very large factor. During this expansion, the density fluctuations would have remained small at first, but later would have started to grow. Regions in which the density was slightly higher than average would have had their expansion slowed down by the gravitational attraction of the extra mass. Eventually, such regions would stop expanding and collapse to form galaxies, stars, and beings like us. The universe would have started in a smooth and ordered state, and would become lumpy and disordered as time went on. This would explain the existence of the thermodynamic arrow of time.

But what would happen if and when the universe stopped expanding and began to contract? Would the thermodynamic arrow reverse and disorder begin to decrease with time? This would lead to all sorts of science-fictionlike possibilities for people who survived from the expanding to the contracting phase. Would they see broken cups gathering themselves together off the floor and jumping back onto the table? Would they be able to remember tomorrow's prices and make a fortune on the stock market? It might seem a bit academic to worry about what would happen when the universe collapses again, as it will not start to contract for at least another ten thousand million years. But there is a quicker way to find out what will happen: jump into a black hole. The collapse of a star to form a black hole is rather like the later stages of the collapse of the whole universe. So if disorder were to decrease in the contracting phase of the universe, one might also expect it to decrease inside a black hole. So perhaps an astronaut who fell into a black hole would be able to make money at roulette by remembering where the ball went before he placed his bet. (Unfortunately, however, he would not have long to play before he was turned to spaghetti. Nor would he be able to let us know about the reversal of the thermodynamic arrow, or even bank his winnings, because he would be trapped behind the event horizon of the black hole.)

At first, I believed that disorder would decrease when the universe recollapsed. This was because I thought that the universe had to return to a smooth and ordered state when it became small again. This would mean that the contracting phase would be like the time reverse of the expanding phase. People in the contracting phase would live their lives backward: they would die before they were born and get younger as the universe contracted.

This idea is attractive because it would mean a nice symmetry between the expanding and contracting phases. However, one cannot adopt it on its own, independent of other ideas about the universe. The question is: Is it implied by the no boundary condition, or is it inconsistent with that condition? As I said, I thought at first that the no boundary condition did indeed imply that disorder would decrease in the contracting phase. I was misled partly by the analogy with the surface of the earth. If one took the beginning of the universe to correspond to the North Pole, then the end of the universe should be similar to the beginning, just as the South Pole is similar to the North. However, the North and South Poles correspond to the beginning and end of the universe in imaginary time. The beginning and end in real time can be very different from each other. I was also misled by work I had done on a simple model of the universe in which the collapsing phase looked like the time reverse of the expanding phase. However, a colleague of mine, Don Page, of Penn State University, pointed out that the no boundary condition did not require the contracting phase necessarily to be the time reverse of the expanding phase. Further, one of my students, Raymond Laflamme, found that in a slightly more complicated model, the collapse of the universe was very different from the expansion. I realized that I had made a mistake: the no boundary condition implied that disorder would in fact continue to increase during the contraction. The thermodynamic and psychological arrows of time would not reverse when the universe begins to recontract or inside black holes.

What should you do when you find you have made a mistake

like that? Some people never admit that they are wrong and continue to find new, and often mutually inconsistent, arguments to support their case—as Eddington did in opposing black hole theory. Others claim to have never really supported the incorrect view in the first place or, if they did, it was only to show that it was inconsistent. It seems to me much better and less confusing if you admit in print that you were wrong. A good example of this was Einstein, who called the cosmological constant, which he introduced when he was trying to make a static model of the universe, the biggest mistake of his life.

To return to the arrow of time, there remains the question: Why do we observe that the thermodynamic and cosmological arrows point in the same direction? Or in other words, why does disorder increase in the same direction of time as that in which the universe expands? If one believes that the universe will expand and then contract again, as the no boundary proposal seems to imply, this becomes a question of why we should be in the expanding phase rather than the contracting phase.

One can answer this on the basis of the weak anthropic principle. Conditions in the contracting phase would not be suitable for the existence of intelligent beings who could ask the question: Why is disorder increasing in the same direction of time as that in which the universe is expanding? The inflation in the early stages of the universe, which the no boundary proposal predicts, means that the universe must be expanding at very close to the critical rate at which it would just avoid recollapse, and so will not recollapse for a very long time. By then all the stars will have burned out and the protons and neutrons in them will probably have decayed into light particles and radiation. The universe would be in a state of almost complete disorder. There would be no strong thermodynamic arrow of time. Disorder couldn't increase much because the universe would be in a state of almost complete disorder already. However, a strong thermodynamic arrow is necessary for intelligent life to operate. In order to survive, human beings have to consume food, which is an ordered form of energy, and convert it into heat, which is a disordered form of energy. Thus intelligent life could not exist in the contracting phase of the universe. This is the explanation of why we observe that the thermodynamic and cosmological arrows of time point in the same direction. It is not that the expansion of the universe causes disorder to increase. Rather, it is that the no boundary condition causes disorder to increase and the conditions to be suitable for intelligent life only in the expanding phase.

To summarize, the laws of science do not distinguish between the forward and backward directions of time. However, there are at least three arrows of time that do distinguish the past from the future. They are the thermodynamic arrow, the direction of time in which disorder increases; the psychological arrow, the direction of time in which we remember the past and not the future; and the cosmological arrow, the direction of time in which the universe expands rather than contracts. I have shown that the psychological arrow is essentially the same as the thermodynamic arrow, so that the two would always point in the same direction. The no boundary proposal for the universe predicts the existence of a well-defined thermodynamic arrow of time because the universe must start off in a smooth and ordered state. And the reason we observe this thermodynamic arrow to agree with the cosmological arrow is that intelligent beings can exist only in the expanding phase. The contracting phase will be unsuitable because it has no strong thermodynamic arrow of time.

The progress of the human race in understanding the universe has established a small corner of order in an increasingly disordered universe. If you remember every word in this book, your memory will have recorded about two million pieces of information: the order in your brain will have increased by about two million units. However, while you have been reading the book, you will have converted at least a thousand calories of ordered energy, in the form of food, into disordered energy, in the form of heat that you lose to the air around you by convection and sweat. This will increase the disorder of the universe by about twenty million million million million units—or about ten million million million times the increase in order in your brain—and that's if you remember *everything* in this book.

C. P. S N O W

The Moral Un-Neutrality of Science

C. P. Snow (1905–1980) was an English physicist, government official, essayist, novelist, and playwright. His *Strangers and Brothers*
(1940–1970) is a series of eleven novels which address moral issues involving the use power and the conflict between private conscience and public life. The following selection appears in his book
Public Affairs (1971), a collection of lectures.

Scientists are the most important occupational group in the world
today. At this moment, what they do is of passionate concern to the
whole of human society. At this moment, the scientists have little
influence on the world effect of what they do. Yet, potentially, they
can have great influence. The rest of the world is frightened both of
what they do—that is, of the intellectual discoveries of science—and
of its effect. The rest of the world, transferring its fears, is frightened
of the scientists themselves and tends to think of them as radically
different from other men.

As an ex-scientist, if I may call myself so, I know that is nonsense.
I have even tried to express in fiction some kinds of scientific temperament and scientific experience. I know well enough that scientists are very much like other men. After all, we are all human, even
if some of us don't give that appearance. I think I would be prepared
to risk a generalization. The scientists I have known (and because of
my official life I have known as many as anyone in the world) have
been in certain respects just perceptibly more morally admirable than
most other groups of intelligent men.

That is a sweeping statement, and I mean it only in a statistical
sense. But I think there is just a little in it. The moral qualities I
admire in scientists are quite simple ones, but I am very suspicious
of attempts to oversubtilize moral qualities. It is nearly always a sign,
not of true sophistication, but of a specific kind of triviality. So I
admire in scientists very simple virtues—like courage, truth-telling,
kindness—in which, judged by the low standards which the rest of
us manage to achieve, the scientists are not deficient. I think on the
whole the scientists make slightly better husbands and fathers than
most of us, and I admire them for it. I don't know the figures, and I
should be curious to have them sorted out, but I am prepared to bet

that the proportion of divorces among scientists is slightly but significantly less than that among other groups of similar education and income. I do not apologize for considering that a good thing.

A close friend of mine is a very distinguished scientist. He is also one of the few scientists I know who has lived what we used to call a Bohemian life. When we were both younger, he thought he would undertake historical research to see how many great scientists had been as fond of women as he was. I think he would have felt mildly supported if he could have found a precedent. I remember his reporting to me that his researchers hadn't had any luck. The really great scientists seemed to vary from a few neutral characters to a large number who were depressingly "normal." The only gleam of comfort was to be found in the life of Jerome Cardan; and Cardan wasn't anything like enough to outweigh all the others.

So scientists are not much different from other men. They are certainly no worse than other men. But they do differ from other men in one thing. That is the point I started with. Whether they like it or not, what they do is of critical importance for the human race. Intellectually, it has transformed the climate of our time. Socially, it will decide whether we live or die, and how we live or die. It holds decisive powers for good and evil. That is the situation in which the scientists find themselves. They may not have asked for it, or may only have asked for it in part, but they cannot escape it. They think, many of the most sensitive of them, that they don't deserve to have this weight of responsibility heaved upon them. All they want to do is to get on with their work. I sympathize. But the scientists can't escape the responsibility—any more than they, or the rest of us, can escape the gravity of the moment in which we stand.

DOCTRINE OF ETHICAL NEUTRALITY

There is of course one way to contract out. It has been a favorite way for intellectual persons caught in the midst of water too rough for them.

It consists of the invention of categories—or, if you like, of the division of moral labor. That is, the scientists who want to contract out say, we produce the tools. We stop there. It is for you—the rest of the world, the politicians—to say how the tools are used. The tools may be used for purposes which most of us would regard as bad. If so, we are sorry. But as scientists, that is no concern of ours.

This is the doctrine of the ethical neutrality of science. I can't accept it for an instant. I don't believe any scientist of serious feeling can accept it. It is hard, some think, to find the precise statements which will prove it wrong. Yet we nearly all feel untuitively that the invention of comfortable categories is a moral trap. It is one of the easier methods of letting the conscience rust. It is exactly what the early 19th century economists, such as Ricardo,[1] did in the face of the facts of the first industrial revolution. We wonder now how men, intelligent men, can have been so morally blind. We realize how the exposure of that moral blindness gave Marxism its apocalyptic force. We are now, in the middle of the scientific or second industrial revolution, in something like the same position as Ricardo. Are we going to let our consciences rust? Can we ignore that intimation we nearly all have, that scientists have a unique responsibility? Can we believe it, that science is morally neutral?

To me—it would be dishonest to pretend otherwise—there is only one answer to those questions. Yet I have been brought up in the presence of the same intellectual categories as most western scientists. It would also be dishonest to pretend that I find it easy to construct a rationale which expresses what I now believe. The best I can hope for is to fire a few sighting shots. Perhaps someone who sees more clearly than I can will come along and make a real job of it.

THE BEAUTY OF SCIENCE

Let me begin with a remark which seems some way off the point. Anyone who has ever worked in any science knows how much esthetic joy he has obtained. That is, in the actual *activity* of science, in the process of making a discovery, however humble it is, one can't help feeling an awareness of beauty. The subjective experience, the esthetic satisfaction, seems exactly the same as the satisfaction one gets from writing a poem or a novel, or composing a piece of music. I don't think anyone has succeeded in distinguishing between them. The literature of scientific discovery is full of this esthetic joy. The very best communication of it that I know comes in G. H. Hardy's book, *A Mathematician's Apology*. Graham Greene once said he

---

[1] David Ricardo (1772–1823) was a British economist whose theory of wages argued that it was futile to attempt to improve workers' incomes as they tended to stabilize at the subsistence level. (ED.)

thought that, along with Henry James's prefaces, this was the best account of the artistic experience ever written. But one meets the same thing throughout the history of science. Bolyai's great yell of triumph when he saw he could construct a self-consistent, non-Euclidean geometry; Rutherford's revelation to his colleagues that he knew what the atom was like; Darwin's slow, patient, timorous certainty that at last he had got there—all these are voices, different voices, of esthetic ecstasy.

That is not the end of it. The result of the activity of science, the actual finished piece of scientific work, has an esthetic value in itself. The judgments passed on it by other scientists will more often than not be expressed in esthetic terms: "That's beautiful!" or "That really is very pretty!" (as the understating English tend to say). The esthetics of scientific constructs, like the esthetics of works of art, are variegated. We think some of the great syntheses, like Newton's, beautiful because of their classical simplicity, but we see a different kind of beauty in the relativistic extension of the wave equation or the interpretation of the structure of deoxyribonucleic acid, perhaps because of the touch of unexpectedness. Scientists know their kinds of beauty when they see them. They are suspicious, and scientific history shows they have always been right to have been so, when a subject is in an "ugly" state. For example, most physicists feel in their bones that the present bizarre assembly of nuclear particles, as grotesque as a stamp collection, can't possibly be, in the long run, the last word.

We should not restrict the esthetic values to what we call "pure" science. Applied science has its beauties, which are, in my view, identical in nature. The magnetron has been a marvelously useful device, but it was a beautiful device, not exactly apart from its utility but because it did, with such supreme economy, precisely what it was designed to do. Right down in the field of development, the esthetic experience is as real to engineers. When they forget it, when they begin to design heavy-power equipment about twice as heavy as it needs to be, engineers are the first to know that they are lacking virtue.

There is no doubt, then, about the esthetic content of science, both in the activity and the result. But esthetics has no connection with morals, say the categorizers. I don't want to waste time on peripheral issues—but are you quite sure of that? Or is it possible that these categories are inventions to make us evade the human and social conditions in which we now exist? But let us move straight on to something else, which is right in the grain of the activity of science and which is at the same time quintessentially moral. I mean, the desire to find the truth.

THE SEARCH FOR TRUTH

By truth, I don't intend anything complicated, once again. I am using the word as a scientist uses it. We all know that the philosophical examination of the concept of empirical truth gets us into some curious complexities, but most scientists really don't care. They know that the truth, as they use the word and as the rest of us use it in the language of common speech, is what makes science work. That is good enough for them. On it rests the whole great edifice of modern science. They have a sneaking sympathy for Rutherford, who, when asked to examine the philosophical bases of science, was inclined to reply, as he did to the metaphysician Samuel Alexander: "Well, what have you been talking all your life, Alexander? Just hot air! Nothing but hot air!"

Anyway, truth in their own straightforward sense is what the scientists are trying to find. They want to find what is there. Without that desire, there is no science. It is the driving force of the whole activity. It compels the scientist to have an overriding respect for truth, every stretch of the way. That is, if you're going to find what is there, you mustn't deceive yourself or anyone else. You mustn't lie to yourself. At the crudest level, you mustn't fake your experiments.

Curiously enough, scientists do try to behave like that. A short time ago, I wrote a novel in which the story hinged on a case of scientific fraud. But I made one of my characters, who was himself a very good scientist, say that, considering the opportunities and temptations, it is astonishing how few such cases there are. We have all heard of perhaps half a dozen open and notorious ones, which are on the record for anyone to read—ranging from the "discovery" of the L radiation to the singular episode of the Piltdown man.

We have all, if we have lived any time in the scientific world, heard private talk of something like another dozen cases which for various reasons are not yet public property. In some cases, we know the motives for the cheating—sometimes, but not always, sheer personal advantage, such as getting money or a job. But not always. A special kind of vanity has led more than one man into scientific faking. At a lower level of research, there are presumably some more cases. There must have been occasional Ph.D. students who scraped by with the help of a bit of fraud.

But the total number of all these men is vanishingly small by the side of the total number of scientists. Incidentally, the effect on science of such frauds is also vanishingly small. Science is a self-correcting system. That is, no fraud (or honest mistake) is going to stay undetected for long. There is no need for an extrinsic scientific criticism, because criticism is inherent in the process itself. So that all that a fraud can do is waste the time of the scientists who have to clear it up.

The remarkable thing is not the handful of scientists who deviate from the search for truth but the overwhelming numbers who keep to it. That is a demonstration, absolutely clear for anyone to see, of moral behavior on a very large scale.

We take it for granted. Yet it is very important. It differentiates science in its widest sense (which includes scholarship) from all other intellectual activities. There is a built-in moral component right in the core of the scientific activity itself. The desire to find the truth is itself a moral impulse, or at least contains a moral impulse. The way in which a scientist tries to find the truth imposes on him a constant moral discipline. We say a scientific conclusion—such as the contradiction of parity by Lee and Yang—is "true" in the limited sense of scientific truth, just as we say that it is "beautiful" according to the criteria of scientific esthetics. We also know that to reach this conclusion took a set of actions which would have been useless without the moral nature. That is, all through the marvelous experiments of Wu and her colleagues, there was the constant moral exercise of seeking and telling the truth. To scientists, who are brought up in this climate, this seems as natural as breathing. Yet it is a wonderful thing. Even if the scientific activity contained only this one moral component, that alone would be enough to let us say that it was morally un-neutral.

But is this the only moral component? All scientists would agree about the beauty and the truth. In the western world, they wouldn't agree on much more. Some will feel with me in what I am going to say. Some will not. That doesn't affect me much, except that I am worried by the growth of an attitude I think very dangerous, a kind of technological conformity disguised as cynicism. I shall say a little more about that later. As for disagreement, G. H. Hardy used to comment that a serious man ought not to waste his time stating a majority opinion—there are plenty of others to do that. That was the voice of classical scientific nonconformity. I wish that we heard it more often.

SCIENCE IN THE TWENTIES

Let me cite some grounds for hope. Any of us who were working in science before 1933 can remember what the atmosphere was like. It is a terrible bore when aging men in their fifties speak about the charms of their youth. Yet I am going to irritate you—just as Talleyrand irritated his juniors—by saying that unless one was on the scene before 1933, one hasn't known the sweetness of the scientific life. The scientific world of the twenties was as near to being a full-fledged international community as we are likely to get. Don't think I'm saying that the men involved were superhuman or free from the ordinary frailties. That wouldn't come well from me, who have spent a fraction of my writing life pointing out that scientists are, first and foremost, men. But the atmosphere of the twenties in science was filled with an air of benevolence and magnanimity which transcended the people who lived in it.

Anyone who ever spent a week in Cambridge or Göttingen or Copenhagen felt it all round him. Rutherford had very human faults, but he was a great man with abounding human generosity. For him the world of science was a world that lived on a plane above the nation-state, and lived there with joy. That was at least as true of those two other great men, Niels Bohr and Franck, and some of that spirit rubbed off on to the pupils round them. The same was true of the Roman school of physics.

The personal links within this international world were very close. It is worth remembering that Peter Kapitza, who was a loyal Soviet citizen, honored my country by working in Rutherford's laboratory for many years. He became a fellow of the Royal Society, a fellow of Trinity College, Cambridge, and the founder and kingpin of the best physics club Cambridge has known. He never gave up his Soviet citizenship and is now director of the Institute of Physical Problems in Moscow. Through him a generation of English scientists came to have personal knowledge of their Russian colleagues. These exchanges were then, and have remained, more valuable than all the diplomatic exchanges ever invented.

The Kapitza phenomenon couldn't take place now. I hope to live to see the day when a young Kapitza can once more work for 16 years in Berkeley or Cambridge and then go back to an eminent place in his own country. When that can happen, we are all right. But after the idyllic years of world science, we passed into a tempest of history, and, by an unfortunate coincidence, we passed into a technological tempest too.

The discovery of atomic fission broke up the world of international physics. "This has killed a beautiful subject," said Mark Oliphant, the father figure of Australian physics, in 1945, after the bombs had dropped. In intellectual terms, he has not turned out to be right. In spiritual and moral terms, I sometimes think he has.

A good deal of the international community of science remains in other fields—in great areas of biology, for example. Many biologists are feeling the identical liberation, the identical joy at taking part in a magnanimous enterprise, that physicists felt in the twenties. It is more than likely that the moral and intellectual leadership of science will pass to biologists, and it is among them that we shall find the Rutherfords, Bohrs, and Francks of the next generation.

THE PHYSICIST, A MILITARY RESOURCE

Physicists have had a bitter task. With the discovery of fission, and with some technical breakthroughs in electronics, physicists became, almost overnight, the most important military resource a nation-state could call on. A large number of physicists became soldiers not in uniform. So they have remained, in the advanced societies, ever since.

It is very difficult to see what else they could have done. All this began in the Hitler war. Most scientists thought then that Nazism was as near absolute evil as a human society can manage. I myself thought so. I still think so, without qualification. That being so, Nazism had to be fought, and since the Nazis might make fission bombs—which we thought possible until 1944, and which was a continual nightmare if one was remotely in the know—well, then, we had to make them too. Unless one was an unlimited pacifist, there was nothing else to do. And unlimited pacifism is a position which most of us cannot sustain.

Therefore I respect, and to a large extent share, the moral attitudes of those scientists who devoted themselves to making the bomb. But the trouble is, when you get onto any kind of moral escalator, to know whether you're ever going to be able to get off. When scientists became soldiers they gave up something, so imperceptibly that they didn't realize it, of the full scientific life. Not intellectually. I see no evidence that scientific work on weapons of maximum destruction has been different from other scientific work. But there is a moral difference.

It may be—scientists who are better men than I am often take this attitude, and I have tried to represent it faithfully in one of my books—that this is a moral price which, in certain circumstances, has to be paid. Nevertheless, it is no good pretending that there is not a moral price. Soldiers have to obey. That is the foundation of their morality. It is not the foundation of the scientific morality. Scientists have to question and if necessary rebel. I don't want to be misunderstood. I am no anarchist. I am not suggesting that loyalty is not a prime virtue. I am not saying that all rebellion is good. But I am saying that loyalty can easily turn into conformity, and that conformity can often be a cloak for the timid and self-seeking. So can obedience, carried to the limit. When you think of the long and gloomy history of man, you will find that far more, and far more hideous, crimes have been committed in the name of obedience than have ever been committed in the name of rebellion. If you doubt that, read William Shirer's *Rise and Fall of the Third Reich*. The German officer corps were brought up in the most rigorous code of obedience. To them, no more honorable and God-fearing body of men could conceivably exist. Yet in the name of obedience, they were party to, and assisted in, the most wicked large-scale actions in the history of the world.

Scientists must not go that way. Yet the duty to question is not much of a support when you are living in the middle of an organized society. I speak with feeling here. I was an official for 20 years. I went into official life at the beginning of the war, for the reasons that prompted my scientific friends to begin to make weapons. I stayed in that life until a year ago, for the same reason that made my scientific friends turn into civilian soldiers. The official's life in England is not quite so disciplined as a soldier's, but it is very nearly so. I think I know the virtues, which are very great, of the men who live that disciplined life. I also know what for me was the moral trap. I, too, had got onto an escalator. I can put the result in a sentence: I was coming to hide behind the institution; I was losing the power to say no.

A SPUR TO MORAL ACTION

Only a very bold man, when he is a member of an organized society, can keep the power to say no. I tell you that, not being a very bold man, or one who finds it congenial to stand alone, away from his colleagues. We can't expect many scientists to do it. Is there any tougher ground for them to stand on? I suggest to you that there is. I believe that there is a spring of moral action in the scientific activity which is at least as strong as the search for truth. The name of this spring is *knowledge*. Scientists *know* certain things in a fashion more immediate and more certain than those who don't comprehend what science is. Unless we are abnormally weak or abnormally wicked men, this knowledge is bound to shape our actions. Most of us are timid, but to an extent, knowledge gives us guts. Perhaps it can give us guts strong enough for the jobs in hand.

I had better take the most obvious example. All physical scientists *know* that it is relatively easy to make plutonium. We know this, not as a journalistic fact at second hand, but as a fact in our own experience. We can work out the number of scientific and engineering personnel needed for a nation-state to equip itself with fission and fusion bombs. We *know* that, for a dozen or more states, it will only take perhaps six years, perhaps less. Even the best informed of us always exaggerate these periods.

This we know, with the certainty of—what shall I call it?— engineering truth. We also—most of us—are familiar with statistics and the nature of odds. We know, with the certainty of statistical truth, that if enough of these weapons are made, by enough different states, some of them are going to blow up, through accident, or folly, or madness—the motives don't matter. What does matter is the nature of the statistical fact.

All this we *know*. We know it in a more direct sense than any politician because it comes from our direct experience. It is part of our minds. Are we going to let it happen?

All this we *know*. It throws upon scientists a direct and personal responsibility. It is not enough to say that scientists have a responsibility as citizens. They have a much greater one than that, and one different in kind. For scientists have a moral imperative to say what they know. It is going to make them unpopular in their own nation-states. It may do worse than make them unpopular. That doesn't matter. Or at least, it does matter to you and me, but it must not count in the face of the risks.

ALTERNATIVES

For we genuinely know the risks. We are faced with an either-or, and we haven't much time. The *either* is acceptance of a restriction of nuclear armaments. This is going to begin, just as a token, with an agreement on the stopping of nuclear tests. The United States is not going to get the 99.9-percent "security" that it has been asking for. This is unobtainable, though there are other bargains that the United States could probably secure. I am not going to conceal from you that this course involves certain risks. They are quite obvious, and no honest man is going to blink them. That is the *either*. The *or* is not a risk but a certainty. It is this. There is no agreement on tests. The nuclear arms race between the United States and U.S.S.R. not only continues but accelerates. Other countries join in. Within, at the most, six years, China and several other states have a stock of nuclear bombs. Within, at the most, ten years, some of those bombs are going off. I am saying this as responsibly as I can. *That* is the certainty. On the one side, therefore, we have a finite risk. On the other side we have a certainty of disaster. Between a risk and a certainty, a sane man does not hesitate.

It is the plain duty of scientists to explain this either-or. It is a duty which seems to me to come from the moral nature of the scientific activity itself.

The same duty, though in a much more pleasant form, arises with respect to the benevolent powers of science. For scientists know, and again with the certainty of scientific knowledge, that we possess every scientific fact we need to transform the physical life of half the world. And transform it within the span of people now living. I mean, we have all the resources to help half the world live as long as we do and eat enough. All that is missing is the will. We *know* that. Just as we know that you in the United States, and to a slightly lesser extent we in the United Kingdom, have been almost unimaginably lucky. We are sitting like people in a smart and cozy restaurant and we are eating comfortably, looking out of the window into the streets. Down on the pavement are people who are looking up at us, people who by chance have different colored skins from ours, and are rather hungry. Do you wonder that they don't like us all that much? Do you wonder that we sometimes feel ashamed of ourselves, as we look out through that plate glass?

Well, it is within our power to get started on that problem. We are morally impelled to. We all know that, if the human species does solve that one, there will be consequences which are themselves problems. For instance, the population of the world will become embarrassingly large. But that is another challenge. There are going to be challenges to our intelligence and to our moral nature as long as man remains man. After all, a challenge is not, as the word is coming to be used, an excuse for slinking off and doing nothing. A challenge is something to be picked up.

For all these reasons, I believe the world community of scientists has a final responsibility upon it—a greater responsibility than is pressing on any other body of men. I do not pretend to know how they will bear this responsibility. These may be famous last words, but I have an inextinguishable hope. For, as I have said, there is no doubt that the scientific activity is both beautiful and truthful. I cannot prove it, but I believe that, simply because scientists cannot escape their own knowledge, they also won't be able to avoid showing themselves disposed to good.

CAPTAIN X

Mr. Spock

Captain X (1922–   ) is the pseudonym for Rodney Stich, who with Reynolds Dodson wrote an exposé about the effects of airline deregulation entitled *Unfriendly Skies: Revelations of a Deregulated Airline Pilot* (1989). The following selection is taken from this book. A greatly revised version of Stich's *The Real Unfriendly Skies: A Saga of Corruption,* 3rd edition (1990), has recently been published.

It should have been routine.

We were bringing a 727 into Saginaw, Michigan.[1] The weather was clear, and we had already begun our descent. I could see the airport spread out below me in a little geometric spill among the snowbanks.

In one of those boardroom maneuvers that's become endemic in our industry, my company had recently merged with a smaller airline. This had given us some new and, to me, unfamiliar routes. I had never been to Saginaw. I had spent the past several years flying DC-9s and 10s along the southern tier, and although I knew about 200 U.S. airports like the palm of my hand, this particular field was not among them.

On coming aboard I had introduced myself to the crew members.

---

[1] Not the true location. Where necessary, airports and locales have been changed to protect the author and his airline.

My copilot and my flight engineer were both new to me. They were employees of the now-absorbed smaller airline. My flight engineer looked eager. Like all flight engineers, he undoubtedly hoped someday to move into the copilot's seat, and from there into the captain's seat where I was sitting. My copilot was a man of about my age. I was forty-two.

Saginaw was the second leg of our trip. The flight had originated in Miami, and, following the custom of our industry, I had turned the controls over to the copilot after the first leg. During our preflight checkout I had asked him how long he had been driving the Seven-Two.

"Eight years," he said as he busied himself with the hundreds of minute details that go into every preflight checklist.

Eight years, I said to myself. That's pretty good.

While I was qualified to fly the 727, I was not as comfortable on it as I might have been. My experience on it had been mostly of a training nature, and I was glad to have a man at my side who had been living with the plane on such an intimate basis.

"And you know Saginaw," I said.

"Been flying there since the day I joined the company," came the succinct and perhaps slightly smug reply.

Terrific, Superterrific.

Through Flight Control, we had learned that the airport was undergoing renovation. The longer of her two runways—about 6,800 feet—had been temporarily shortened. It was now about 5,500 feet, which was well within the requirements of a 727, but considerably short of the 7,000 or so feet that would be considered average.

Her second runway—Runway 18—was about 5,000 feet.

Now 5,000 feet on a 727 is cutting it pretty close. Technically the plane can land in shorter runway space, but unless you've been making your home in that cockpit for quite a while you really don't want to go around testing a plane's minimum landing requirements.

As we neared our destination, air traffic control was reporting a twenty-five-knot headwind on Runway 18. This was significant. A strong headwind would greatly reduce ground speed, slowing the plane to a velocity acceptable to the shorter runway space.

"How do you plan to take her in?" I asked. (As captain, I'm the copilot's chief and mentor. From gate to gate, no matter who is actually handling the controls, everything that happens is the captain's responsibility.)

"Runway 18," he said. "I'll bring her in at a forty flap."

As you might imagine, a plane's flap setting is crucial to the

landing procedure. The farther the flaps are down, the lower the
nose is tilted. It's what we call the *deck angle*. The usual flap setting—
the one I had been performing day in and day out along the southern
tier—is thirty degrees. By choosing a forty-degree setting, my copilot
was indicating that he was planning to alter our deck angle, augment
the amount of "drag" (resistance of air as it flows across the wings),
and take advantage of the headwind to lessen our velocity. These
factors would enable us to land the plane at a relatively slow 120
knots and come to a stop well within the 5,000-foot limit.

"Good decision," I said.

As a passenger, you've probably applauded when the pilot brings
the plane in on one of those smooth-as-glass, I-hardly-even-felt-
us-touch-the-ground grease jobs. From where you sit, there's no
greater testimony to your pilot's skill than that he didn't ruffle your
in-flight reading matter. That's great. But what you don't know is
that sometimes those ultra-smooth landings can kill you. If the
weather is bad . . . if there's just a little too much ice out there on
the tarmac . . . if the runway is too slick, or too short, or too sloped,
or too *anything*, sometimes the *right* decision is to bring that plane
down, cut your forward momentum to a crawl, and *slam* the wheels
onto the pavement. That way you'll get full braking power and
diminish the risk of skidding or hydroplaning.

That's the *right* decision.

Which is not to say it's the greatest crowd-pleaser.

In this case, it took me about half a second to conclude that my
copilot was making an absolutely 100 percent *right* decision, and
once again I congratulated myself on having the good fortune to
draw Mr. Spock as my first officer.

So there I sat, ignorant and blissful, my arms folded across my
chest, my Coke and my peanuts at my side, 152 equally ignorant
and blissful passengers in the cabin behind me, and none of us having
the faintest idea we had about ninety-seven seconds to live.

One of the great thrills of flying is that you're constantly getting
to experience what other men spend their entire lives clawing and
scratching to achieve—namely, that awe-inspiring, ego-swelling phenomenon called "The View from the Fortieth Floor." I never tire of
it. The landscape is constantly changing. As I crisscross the country,
I marvel at what most other people get to see only a relatively few
times in their lives. I wouldn't trade offices with Donald Trump on
a bet.

But when you're coming in for that delicate operation called the
landing, "The View from the Fortieth Floor" takes on a special

significance. You're not sitting in an office with your feet up on the desk, you're sitting at the tip of a very fast and very powerful falling arrow. Your decisions are crucial. You're scanning your instrument panel. You're making numerous small adjustments in your ailerons and your elevators. You're watching to see that your wings are level, your airspeed's steady, your landing gear's down, your altitude's proper. And while you're doing all that, and while you're looking at your engine pressure and your compass headings and your rate of descent and your altitude gauges, you're also looking through your windshield and you're comparing what you're seeing on the ground with what you've seen a thousand times before in a thousand other similar landings. It's all very fast, and very instinctive. Only when the airport is new to you; when the terrain is just a little different from any you've ever seen before; when it's a plane you're not quite comfortable with, and it's coming in on a configuration that is almost never used except in the most unusual circumstances, sometimes then your instincts don't work right. You sit there and you stare and you realize that all your exhaustive training has not prepared you for the unique and somewhat confusing sensations you're actually experiencing. And when that happens, all you can do is marvel at what a weird and unsettling feeling this is, and you look for support in your copilot's competence.

As I sat there, I couldn't help thinking. Now isn't this strange? As many times as I've looked at runways through these windshields . . . as many hours as I've spent training on a Seven-Two and lifting her off and setting her down and going through God-knows-how-many exercises and emergency training procedures with her, isn't it strange how, when you come in at this steep angle toward a runway you've never seen before, you have the optical illusion you're about to crash?

I rolled a peanut over on my tongue.

The ground rose closer.

And isn't it strange, I thought, the way it looks like you may not even clear those trees down there, but even if you do clear those trees you're certainly going to hit those lights, and aren't you lucky that Mr. Spock here knows so much more than you do, and that the lump rising in your throat, which seems to be getting larger with every passing moment, is apparently not rising in his much more knowledgeable one.

In twenty years of service, I've listened to more than my share of dead men's chatter on voice recorders. I've sat through more than my share of postcrash conferences and listened to more than my share of ghostly conversations coming from those charred and battered "black boxes." And I know that the last word a pilot often utters before his plane disappears in a fiery ball of flame is *shit.* That may not be a very noble way to depart this planet, but that's the way we usually exit.

I can't swear that that particular Anglo-Saxonism was the one that escaped my lips at that moment, but if it wasn't, it wasn't for lack of thinking it.

Snapping forward, I grabbed the yoke with one hand and pushed the throttle forward with the other. We were a good hundred yards short of the runway, and we were doomed to crash.

Looking back on it now, I realize how silly it was. I realize how foolish I was to have placed so much confidence in a man I didn't know and whose only collateral was his self-assured arrogance. The group dynamics of cockpit crew members are pivotal to the success or failure of every flight, and it is just this kind of misunderstanding that can snuff out lives in a fraction of a second. But I didn't have the luxury of thinking about all that at that moment. There was the ground, here came the airplane, and all I could do was to act reflexively.

"*Power . . . full power!*" I cried.

I knew that my only chance, if I had a chance, was to bring the nose up, push the throttles to the limit, and hope like hell we would clear those approach lights. Straining forward against my shoulder harness, I slammed the throttles against the firewall.

The plane leaped forward.

I won't even venture to guess what the passengers must have thought at that moment. Even through the closed cockpit door I could hear the first of what would be many crashes as dirty food trays, coffeepots, and various pieces of overhead baggage shifted violently in their compartments. Within microseconds the airspeed indicator shot from 122 to 143 knots. The plane bolted, flared—then hit the pavement.

Later inspection would show that our main gear had cleared the end of the runway by less than thirty inches. A pilot is trained to land a plane within the first thousand feet of runway space. Landing it within the first thirty inches of runway space is cutting it just a little closer than the company that owns the airplane might wish.

But that wasn't the bad part. The bad part—the part that would bring my heart almost literally into my throat and make me wonder how my mother's little boy had ever come to be in this predicament— was that we were now hurtling down a dwarf-sized runway at a speed approximating a Grand Prix race car's!

As any pilot will tell you, when you have executed a landing as sloppy and screwed-up as this one, there is only one right thing to do. The right thing to do is keep the throttle shoved forward, lift the plane back off the ground, and execute what's called a "go-around." It's an inelegant and rather embarrassing maneuver, but it's the one the experts consider most prudent.

And the experts are right.

Unfortunately, that is not the procedure my reflexes chose to perform. The procedure my reflexes chose was to cut the throttle, reverse the engine thrust, raise the spoilers (those are the big noisy flaps on the tops of the wings), and apply the brakes. In other words, in the split-second's confusion caused by the poorly planned landing, my instincts overrode my training—and I decided to *stop the goddamn airplane!*

If you think the crashes in the cabin were bad before, you should have heard the outlandish noises coming from that quarter now. Everything that was not nailed down in the galley flew against the forward bulkhead. Along the aisle, the overhead compartments began springing open, *pop, pop, pop,* showering overcoats, garment bags, pillows, blankets, you name it, onto the hapless heads of the people below them. All the oxygen masks came down. These masks are held in place by barometric latches which release during pressure changes. The reactionary force of our landing had pulled the pins, and now there were a hundred-and-some-odd oxygen masks and hoses dangling before the bewildered and panic-stricken eyes of our whiplashed passengers.

Still the plane roared on.

I sat clench-jawed at the controls. I could see the end of the runway rising up before me. The plane was skipping and skidding along the pavement, its tires alternately grabbing and sliding as we heaved and rattled across the asphalt. My feet were pressed as hard as they would go against the brake pedals. In another few seconds the plane would nose-dive off the far end of the runway, slide along the ground on its belly, and end up in the same fiery inferno we had so narrowly averted at the runway's near end.

God have mercy on us all.

The fact that that didn't happen is, to me, still a bit of a miracle. Somehow the combined forces of brakes and spoilers and Lady Luck managed to slow our momentum, and the plane, after no small amount of protest, shuddered to a halt. We were sitting with our nose practically overhanging the end of the runway, but we were breathing.

The next few minutes are unclear. Somehow I managed to get the plane turned around and taxied toward the gate. Somehow I managed to get the switches off and the knobs turned and the levers pulled and the engines shut down. Somehow the ground crew managed to get the stairs rolled over to the passenger door, the cabin crew managed to get the passenger door open, and those poor scared passengers managed to crawl out of the Valley of Death and into the lap of sweet terra firma. (*"Thanks for flying with us, and we do hope you'll choose us again the next time you travel!"*)

The three of us in the cockpit sat there white-faced. For the next couple of minutes you could hear a pin drop. Finally—softly, and as offhandedly as possible—I suggested that the flight engineer might want to go out and get a cup of coffee.

"Roger!" said the flight engineer, and you've never seen a man exit a cockpit door as fast as that one did.

This left just me and Mr. Spock.

"I will try to put this as kindly and succinctly as I can," I said. "Just what the bloody fuck did you think you were doing back there? Just what the bloody fuck did you, in your eight distinguished years of flying Seven-Twos, mean by coming in on such an erroneous and obviously half-assed approach angle? Didn't you see we were about to crash? Didn't you in your infinite wisdom see that that was completely the wrong sight picture we were getting through the windshield, and that we were all about two seconds away from becoming crispy critters on this North Woods landscape?"

Mr. Spock squirmed uncomfortably.

I won't belabor this poor fellow's humiliation. Suffice it to say that it was as sincere as it was deserved. Suffice it also to say that when the dust had settled, not to mention my pulse rate, I learned that everything he had told me during our preflight checkout was true. He *had* been flying 727s for eight years. He *had* been coming into the Saginaw airport since the day he joined his company. As a *flight engineer!* This was only his third trip as a copilot! He had never actually *landed* a plane at Saginaw, and he had never made a forty-flap landing in his life!

In the years since, I've had a lot of time to think about that incident. I've awakened in the middle of the night, and I can still see the end of that runway racing toward me like some ghostly image from Christmas Future. And it never ceases to impress me that, had we crashed, the report issued by the National Transportation Safety Board would have attributed the carnage to "pilot error." About seven out of ten airline accidents in this country are labeled that way, and this, most assuredly, would have been one of them.

But as someone once wrote, "Most pilot errors are not really pilot errors so much as booby traps that the pilot has fallen into." Indeed, "pilot error" is itself an error. That pilots are human and make mistakes is self-evident; but there are reasons for those mistakes, and those are the factors which must be examined.

Let's take another look at that incident, and this time let's see it for what it really was:

Factor 1: Both my copilot and my flight engineer were new to me.

This in and of itself is not unusual. The airline I work for has more than 5,000 assorted pilots, copilots, and flight engineers. It is not unlikely that I am going to have many strangers share my flight deck as we sail about the world from this city to that.

What is worth noting is that, before deregulation, I could usually assume that my associates were competent. Since we worked for the same company, we had probably been hired with the same criteria in mind; we had gone through the same academic and practical exercises; and we were subject to the same corporate objectives and operations guidelines.

We were a *team.*

Since deregulation, there have been dozens of mergers involving hundreds of air routes and many thousands of disconsolate employees. This means that on a significant number of flights part of the crew will have been trained on one airline, part on another. Many of today's crew members come from small airlines who have neither the money nor the equipment to give them the sophisticated jet training they need. The result can be disastrous.

This was shown on a snowy afternoon in November 1987. That was the day a Continental DC-9 tipped a wing on takeoff from Denver's Stapleton Airport and flipped over, strewing bodies, glass, and twisted debris along a thousand feet of windswept runway. Twenty-eight of the eighty-two people on board were killed. Subsequent investigation showed that the captain had spent a mere thirty-three hours in the airplane's captain's seat. His first officer, who was at the controls at the time, had been hired a couple of months earlier from a small commuter airline in Texas. He had flown a DC-9 on only one previous scheduled flight, and he had never taken off in snow. This may not have been the most *immediate* cause of this accident (accidents are almost always the result of a series of errors, misjudgments, flukes, and coincidences), but the unfortunate pairing of these two men was undoubtedly a factor that helped to precipitate it.

In my case, the only information I had about my copilot was that he had been "flying" a 727 for a considerable length of time. It never occurred to me to question his definition of "flying." Nor did I doubt his meaning when he said that he had been landing planes in Saginaw since the day he joined the company. In retrospect, I can see how the misunderstanding arose. I can assure you that I have been much more careful in my questioning of copilots since that incident, but at the time that it happened it had just never occurred to me, and the fact that it didn't almost cost us all dearly.

Factor 2: I, as captain, didn't know the airport.

Before deregulation, when a crew took off in an airplane, there was at least a pretty good chance that the place they were going was familiar to one or more of the crew members. Because the industry was so controlled, air routes were fairly static. A pilot for, say, Piedmont knew the Southern and Mid-Atlantic areas like the back of his hand. He didn't have to wake up one morning and start worrying about thunderstorms in Dallas/Fort Worth or the Chinook winds that whip the Rockies.

Today it's different. Our schedules are so rushed, the economics of flying are so tight, the distances we travel are so great, that we often find ourselves caroming this way and that like so many billiard balls around a pool table. To take but one example: In the twelve-month period that included Texas Air's now famous merger binge (that's the period when Continental was merged with Eastern, Frontier, People Express, and New York Air), that one company alone added 177 new cities to its route structure. At the same time it shuffled some 61,000 employees, including approximately 8,000 pilots and copilots. You can imagine the chaos. While many of the pilots may have known many of the airports they now had to serve, it was not unusual for a pilot from one airline to be teamed with a copilot from another, and the two of them sent off to some hell-and-gone airport neither one of them had ever seen before.

That's a formula for disaster.

Pilots don't like to admit that this is a problem. Every pilot likes to think that, as a professional, he can handle any new circumstance as it arises. But I can tell you from personal experience: not knowing an airport, or not knowing a geographical or meteorological area through which you have to fly in order to reach that airport, is one more factor that can lead to misjudgment.

Factor 3: The copilot and I were about the same age.

In commercial aviation, flight crews advance in one way and one way only: seniority. When you are hired, your name goes on at the bottom of a list. From that moment on your career will consist of climbing that list one number at a time. You will climb it first as a flight engineer, then as a first officer, and finally as a captain. That's the way it has always been, and that's the way it will probably always be.

Unfortunately, the seniority track at one airline may be quite different from the seniority track at another. If your airline is financially unhealthy—if it is poorly managed, or if it is caught between the price-slashing big guys and the aggressive commuters—your chances for advancement are nil. I know many highly capable men— men who have just as much commercial flight time as I do, and probably a great deal more military flight time—who, even after fifteen or twenty years, are still flying as flight engineers or copilots. It's not their fault, it's just the luck of the draw. Those who in their youth were fortunate enough to link up with a well-managed company with growth potential have made out okay. Those who weren't—too bad.

Looking back on it, I'm convinced that this "unevenness" of seniority contributed to our near-disaster in Saginaw. I had been with my airline thirteen years. My airline was healthy, and I had long been a captain. My copilot had been with his airline twelve years, and he had barely made it past flight engineer. What could be more natural than his not wanting to admit—to me, of all people—that he had never actually landed in Saginaw.

It's been said that a pilot's ego is exceeded only by the size of his wristwatch. In this case, my copilot's ego (ably abetted by my own complacency) almost killed us.

Of course deregulation isn't the only thing that keeps things jumping in the airplane business nowadays. Flying one of today's new jets—an MD-80, say, or a 767—verges on something out of "Star Trek." Since my brush with fate in Michigan, I've flown 727s, 737s and 747s, and now I fly the near-state-of-the-art 767s almost exclusively. I'm one of a fairly select number of pilots who's qualified to do so. And my experiences on these planes—my run-ins with passengers, my relations with stewardesses, my tangles with weather and crazies and security problems—are probably enough to fill a book.

In fact, they *are* enough to fill a book.

The question is, Where to begin?

Well, there's an old saying in our industry: When an air traveler dies, it makes no difference whether he's going to heaven or hell. Either way (come on, you know this) . . . either way, he has to change in Atlanta.

DANIEL J. BOORSTIN

Technology and Democracy

Daniel J. Boorstin (1914–   ) is an American historian who won a Pulitzer Prize in 1974 for *The Americans: The Democratic Experience*. He served as Librarian of Congress from 1975–1987 and is a contributing editor to *U.S. News and World Report*. Other books include *Democracy and Its Discontents* (1974), from which the following selection is taken, *The Discoverers* (1983), and *Hidden History* (1987).

One of the most interesting and characteristic features of democracy is, of course, the difficulty of defining it. And this difficulty has been compounded in the United States, where we have been giving new meanings to almost everything. It is, therefore, especially easy for anyone to say that democracy in America has failed.

"Democracy," according to political scientists, usually describes a form of government by the people, either directly or through their elected representatives. But I prefer to describe a democratic society as one which is governed by a spirit of equality and dominated by the desire to equalize, to give everything to everybody. In the United States the characteristic wealth and skills and know-how and optimism of our country have dominated this quest.

My first and overshadowing proposition is that our problems arise not so much from our failures as from our successes. Of course no success is complete; only death is final. But we have probably come closer to attaining our professed objectives than any other society of comparable size and extent, and it is from this that our peculiarly American problems arise.

The use of technology to democratize our daily life has given a quite new shape to our hopes. In this final chapter I will explore some of the consequences of democracy, not for government but for experience. What are the consequences for everybody every day of

this effort to democratize life in America? And especially the consequences of our fantastic success in industry and technology and in
invention?

There have been at least four of these consequences. I begin with
what I call *attenuation,* which means the thinning out or the flattening
of experience. We might call this the democratizing of experience.
It might otherwise be described as the decline of poignancy. One of
the consequences of our success in technology, of our wealth, of our
energy and our imagination, has been the removal of distinctions,
not just between people but between everything and everything else,
between every place and every other place, between every time and
every other time. For example, television removes the distinction
between being here and being there. And the same kind of process,
of thinning out, of removing distinctions, has appeared in one area
after another of our lives.

For instance, in the seasons. One of the great unheralded achievements of American civilization was the rise of transportation and
refrigeration, the development of techniques of canning and preserving meat, vegetables, and fruits in such a way that it became possible
to enjoy strawberries in winter, to enjoy fresh meat at seasons when
the meat was not slaughtered, to thin out the difference between the
diet of winter and the diet of summer. There are many unsung heroic
stories in this effort.

One of them, for example, was the saga of Gustavus Swift in
Chicago. In order to make fresh meat available at a relatively low
price to people all over the country, it was necessary to be able to
transport it from the West, where the cattle were raised, to the
Eastern markets and the cities where population was concentrated.
Gustavus Swift found the railroad companies unwilling to manufacture refrigerator cars. They were afraid that, if refrigeration was
developed, the cattle would be butchered in the West and then
transported in a more concentrated form than when the cattle had
to be carried live. The obvious consequence, they believed, would be
to reduce the amount of freight. So they refused to develop the
refrigerator car. Gustavus Swift went ahead and developed it, only
to find that he had more cars than he had use for. The price of fresh
meat went down in the Eastern cities, and Gustavus Swift had refrigerator cars on his hands. He then sent agents to the South and
to other parts of the country, and tried to encourage people to raise
produce which had to be carried in refrigerator cars. One of the
consequences of this was the development of certain strains of fruits

and vegetables, especially of fruit, which would travel well. And Georgia became famous for the peaches which were grown partly as a result of Swift's efforts to encourage people to raise something that he could carry in his refrigerator cars.

There were other elements in this story which we may easily forget—for example, how central heating and air conditioning have affected our attitude toward the seasons, toward one time of year or another. Nowadays visitors from abroad note that wherever they are in our country, it is not unusual to find that in winter it is often too warm indoors, and in summer, often too cool.

But the development of central heating during the latter part of the nineteenth century had other, less obvious consequences. For example, as people built high-rise apartments in the cities they found it impossible to have a fireplace in every room. You could not construct a high building with hundreds of apartments and have enough room for all the chimneys. So central heating was developed and this became a characteristic of city life. As central heating was developed it was necessary to have a place to put the machinery, and the machinery went in the cellar. But formerly people, even in the cities, had used their cellars to store fruit and vegetables over the winter. When the basement was heated by a furnace, of course it was no longer possible to store potatoes or other vegetables or fruit there. This increased the market for fresh fruits and vegetables that were brought in from truck farms just outside the cities or by refrigerator cars from greater distances. And this was another way of accelerating the tendency toward equalizing the seasons and equalizing the diet of people all over the country.

Also important in attenuating experience was the development of what I would call homogenized space, especially the development of vertical space as a place to live in. There is a great deal less difference between living on the thirty-fifth floor and living on the fortieth floor of an apartment building than there is between living in a house in the middle of a block and living on the corner. The view is pretty much the same as you go up in the air. Vertical space is much more homogenized, and as we live in vertical space more and more, we live in places where "where we are" makes much less difference than it used to.

An important element in this which has been a product of American technology is, of course, glass. We forget that the innovations in the production of glass resulting in large sheets which you could look through was an achievement largely of American technology in the nineteenth century. Of course, one by-product was the development of the technology of bottling, which is related to some of the levelings-out of the seasons which I mentioned before in relation to food. But we forget that when we admire those old leaded-glass windows which we see in medieval or early modern buildings, what we are admiring is the inability of people to produce plate glass.

When a large plate of glass became technologically possible, this affected daily life in the United States. It affected merchandising, for example, because the "show window" became possible in which you could, with a relatively unobstructed view, display garments and other large objects in a way to make them appealing to people who passed by. But glass was also important in producing one of the main characteristics of modern American architecture—an architecture in which there is relatively less difference between the indoors and the outdoors than elsewhere. And that is one of the great functions of glass in modern architecture.

Along with the attenuation of places and time comes the attenuation of occasions and events. One of the more neglected aspects of modern technology is what I have called the rise of "repeatable experience." It used to be thought that one of the characteristics of life, one of the things that distinguished being alive from being dead, was the uniqueness of the individual moment. Something happened which could never happen again. If you missed it then, you were out of luck. But the growth of popular photography, which we can trace from about 1888 when Kodak #1 went on the market, began to allow everybody to make his own experience repeatable. If you had not seen this baby when he was so cute, you could still see him that way right now if you were so unlucky as to be in the living room with the parents who wanted to show you. Kodak #1 was a great achievement and was the beginning of our taking for granted that there was such a thing as a repeatable experience.

The phonograph, of course, beginning about 1877, created new opportunities to repeat audible experience. If you want to hear the voice of Franklin Delano Roosevelt now, you can hear him on a record. At the opening of the Woodrow Wilson Center for International Scholars at the Smithsonian Institution in 1971, part of the dedicating ceremony was the playing of a record with the voice of Woodrow Wilson. It was not a very warm voice, but it was identifiable and distinctive. The growth of the phonograph, then, has accustomed us to the fact that experience is not a one-time thing.

When we watch the Winter Olympics in our living room and see the ski jumper in the seventy-meter jump who makes a mistake or who performs very well, we can see the same performance just a minute later with all the failures and successes pointed out. Is instant replay the last stage in the technology of repeatable experience?

In the attenuating of events there is another element which I call the "pseudo-event." As more and more of the events which have public notice are planned in advance, as the accounts of them are made available before they happen, then it becomes the responsibility of the event to live up to its reputation. In this way the spontaneity of experience, the unpredictableness of experience, dissolves and disappears. The difference between the present and the future becomes less and less.

Another aspect of this is what I have called the "neutralization of risks," a result of the rise of insurance. For insurance, too, is a way of reducing the difference between the future and the present. You reduce risks by assuring yourself that if your house burns down, at least you will have the money so you can rebuild it. In this sense, insurance, and especially casualty insurance, provides a way of thinning out the difference between present and future, removing the suspense and the risk of experience.

What have been the everyday consequences of the democratizing of property for our experience of property? In his classic defense of property in his essay *On Civil Government* (1690), John Locke argued that because property is the product of the mixing of a person's labor with an object, no government has the right to take it without his consent. This simplistic conception of property has dominated a great deal of political and economic thinking. It was prominent in the thinking of the authors of the Declaration of Independence and of the Founding Fathers of the Constitution. It was based on a simpler society where there was something poignant and characteristic about the experience of ownership. Owning meant the right to exclude people. You had the pleasure of possession.

But what has happened to property in our society? Of course, the most important new form of property in modern American life is corporate property: shares of stock in a corporation. And the diffusion of the ownership of shares is one of the most prominent features of American life. There are companies like AT&T, for example, which have as many as a million stockholders. What does it mean to be a stockholder? You are a lucky person. You own property and you have some shares. So what? One doesn't need to be rich or even middle-class in this country to own shares of stock. But very few of my friends who own shares of stock know precisely what it means or what their legal powers are as stockholders. They are solicited to send in their proxies—by somebody who has a special interest in getting them to vote for something or other. They feel very little pleasure of control; they don't have the sense of wreaking themselves on any object. Yet this—a share of stock—is the characteristic and most important form of property in modern times. This property, too, is attenuated.

Other developments in American life concerning property have had a similar effect. For example, installment and credit buying. This phenomenon first grew in connection with the wide marketing of the sewing machine and then in relation to the cash register, but its efflorescence has come with the automobile. When it became necessary to sell millions of automobiles—and necessary in order to keep the machinery of our society going to sell them to people who could not afford to lay out the full cost of an automobile—it was necessary to find ways of financing their purchases. Installment and credit buying was developed. One of the results was that people became increasingly puzzled over whether they did or did not (and if so in what sense) own their automobile. Of course, it is not uncommon for people to divest themselves of their physical control of an object like an automobile or a color television set before they have really acquired full ownership—and then to enter on another ambiguous venture of part ownership.

Another aspect of this is the rise of franchising: the development of what I would call the "semi-independent businessman." In the United States today, between 35 percent and 50 percent of all retail merchandising is done through franchised outlets. Well, of course, we all know what a franchised outlet is: a typical example would be a McDonald's hamburger stand or any other outlet in which the person who is in control of the shop has been authorized to use a nationally advertised name like Midas Mufflers or Colonel Sanders' Kentucky Fried Chicken. He is then instructed in the conduct of his business. He must meet certain standards in order to be allowed to continue to advertise as a Holiday Inn or Howard Johnson or whatever. And he is in the business "for himself." Now, what does that mean? If you go into a franchised outlet and you find the hamburger unsatisfactory, what can you do? Whom would you complain to? The man who runs the shop has received his instructions and his materials from the people who have franchised him. It is not his fault. And, of course, it's not the fault of the people at the center who franchised him, because the shop is probably badly run by the franchisee.

This phenomenon grew out of the needs of the automobile because in order to sell Fords or any other makes, it was necessary to have an outlet which would take continuous responsibility for stocking parts. Then the purchaser could replace that part at the outlet where he had purchased the car. After automobile franchising came the franchising of filling stations. People wanted some assurance about the quality of the fuel they put in their cars; they were given this by the identification of what they purchased with some nationally advertised brand in which they had confidence.

Now, perhaps the most important example of attenuation, of the decline of poignancy in our experience in relation to property, is so obvious and so universal that it has hardly been discussed. That is packaging. Until relatively recently if you went into a store to buy coffee, you would have to bring a container to the grocery store, and the grocer would ladle out the coffee to you.

Packaging began to develop in this country after the Civil War. In a sense it was a by-product of the Civil War because the necessities of the war (especially the need to package flour) produced certain innovations which were important. And later there were decisive, although what seems to us rather trivial, innovations. For example, the invention of the folding box was important. Until there was a way to make boxes which could be transported and stored compactly, it was impossible or impractical to use them for industrial purposes. The folding box and certain improvements in the paper bag, such as the paper bag that had a square bottom so that it could stand up, and on the side of which you could print an advertisement—these were American inventions.

If we will risk seeming pompous or pedantic, we can say that the most important consequences of packaging have been epistemological. They have had to do with the nature of knowledge and they have especially had the effect of confusing us about what knowledge is, and what's real, about what's form and what's substance. When you think about a Winston cigarette, you don't think about the tobacco inside the cigarette. You think about the package. And in one area after another of American life, the form and the content become confused, and the form becomes that which dominates our consciousness. One area perhaps in which this has ceased to be true, happily or otherwise, is the area which I have always thought of as an aspect of packaging—namely, clothing. In the United States we have developed ready-made clothing, too, in such a way as to obscure the differences of social class and even of sex.

All around us we see attenuation—as our technology has succeeded, as we have tried to make everything available to everybody.

The very techniques we use in preparing our food, in transporting our food, in controlling the climate and temperature of the rooms we live in, the shapes of the buildings in which we do business and reside, the ways we look at past experience—in all these ways our experience becomes attenuated. As we democratize experience, the poignancy of the moment, of the season, of the control of the object, of the spontaneous event, declines.

Now to a second consequence of the success of our technology for our daily experience. This is what I would call the *decline of congregation*. Or it might be called a new segregation. This is the consequence of increasingly organized and centralized sources of anything and everything. Example: Rebecca at the well.[1] When I wrote an article for the issue of *Life* magazine which was intended to celebrate the twenty-fifth anniversary of the introduction of television in this country, I entitled the article at first "Rebecca at the TV Set." But my friends at *Life* said, "Rebecca who?" Deferring to their greater, wider knowledge of American life and of the literariness of the American people, instead we called it simply "The New Segregation."

When Rebecca lived in her village and needed to get water for the household, she went to the well. At the well she met the other women of the village; she heard the gossip; she met her fiancé there, as a matter of fact. And then what happened? With the progress of democracy and technology, running water was introduced; and Rebecca stayed in the kitchenette of her eighth-floor apartment. She turned the faucet on and got the water out of the faucet; she didn't have to go to the well any more. She had only the telephone to help her collect gossip and she would have to find other ways to meet her fiancé. This is a parable of the problem of centralizing sources of everything.

The growth of centralized plumbing was itself, of course, a necessary by-product of the development of the skyscraper and the concentration of population in high buildings. You had to have effective sanitary facilities. But we forget other features of this development. Even those of us who have never made much use of the old "privy" know that the privy characteristically had more than one hole in it. Why was this? The plural facility was not peculiar simply to the privy; it was also found in the sanitary arrangements of many

---

[1] In the Bible, the wife of Isaac and mother of Jacob and Esau. (ED.)

older buildings, including some of the grandest remaining medieval structures. The development of centralized plumbing led to privatizing; "privy" was the wrong word for the old facility. The privatizing of the bodily functions made them less sociable. People engaged in them in private.

The most dramatic example today of the privatizing of experience by centralizing a facility is, of course, television. We could start with the newspaper, for that matter. The town crier communicated the news to people in their presence. If you wanted to hear it you had to be there, or talk to somebody else who was there when he brought the news. But as the newspaper developed, with inexpensive printing, the messages were brought to you and you could look at them privately as you sat by yourself at breakfast. Television is perhaps one of the most extreme examples of the decline of congregation. Until the development of television, if you wanted to see a play you had to go out to a theater; if you wanted to hear a concert you had to go to a concert hall. These performances were relatively rare. They were special events. But with the coming of television, everybody acquired his private theater. Rebecca had her theater in her kitchen. She no longer needed to go out for entertainment.

The centralized source, the centralizing of the source, then, led to the isolating of the consumer. Of course, much was gained by this. But one of the prices paid was the decline of congregation— congregation being the drawing together of people where they could enjoy and react to and respond to the reactions and feelings of their fellows.

There is a third consequence of our technological success in democratic America, which I would call the new determinism, or *the rising sense of momentum*. Technology has had a deep and pervasive effect on our attitude toward history, and especially on the citizen's attitude toward his control over the future. In the seventeenth century the Puritans spoke about Providence; that was their characteristic way of describing the kind of control that God exercised over futurity. In the nineteenth century, when people became more scientifically minded, they still retained some notion of divine foresight in the form of the concept of destiny or mission or purpose. But in our time in this country we have developed a different kind of approach toward futurity; and this is what I would call the sense of momentum.

Momentum in physics is the product of a body's mass and its linear velocity. Increasing scale and speed of operation increase the momentum. One of the characteristics of our technology and especially of our most spectacular successes has been to increase this sense of momentum. I will mention three obvious examples. It happens that each of these developments came, too, as a result of overwhelming international pressure. When such pressures added to the forces at work inside the nation, in each case they produced a phenomenon of great mass and velocity which became very difficult to stop.

The first example is, of course, atomic research. The large-scale concerted efforts in this country to build an atomic bomb began and were accelerated at the time of World War II because of rumors that the Nazis were about to succeed in nuclear fission. When this information became available, national resources were massed and organized in an unprecedented fashion; futurity was scheduled and groups were set to work in all parts of the continent exploring different possible ways of finding the right form of uranium or of some other element. And the search for the first atomic chain reaction, which was accomplished at my University of Chicago, went on.

One of the more touching human aspects of this story is the account, now well chronicled by several historians, of the frantic efforts of the atomic scientists, the people who had been most instrumental in getting this process started (Albert Einstein, Leo Szilard, and James Franck, among others), when they saw that the atomic bomb was about to become possible, to persuade the President of the United States either not to use the bomb or to use it only in a demonstration in the uninhabited mid-Pacific. Such a use, they urged, would so impress the enemy with the horrors of the bomb that he would surrender, eliminating the need for us to use the bomb against a live target. They pursued this purpose—trying to put the brakes on military use of the bomb—with a desperation that even exceeded the energy they had shown in developing the bomb. But, of course, they had no success.

They could develop the bomb, but they couldn't stop it. Why? There were many reasons, including President Truman's reasonable belief that use of the bomb could in the long run save hundreds of thousands of Japanese and American lives that would have been lost in an invasion, and also would shorten the war. But surely one reason was that there had already been too much investment in the bomb. Billions of dollars had gone into the making of it. People were organized all over the country in various ways. It was impossible to stop.

Another example of this kind of momentum is the phenomenon of space exploration. I happen to be an enthusiast for space exploration, so by describing this momentum I do not mean to suggest that I think the space enterprise itself has not been a good thing. Nevertheless, as a historian I am increasingly impressed by the pervasive phenomenon of momentum in our time. Billions of dollars have been spent in developing the machinery for going off to the moon or going then to Mars or elsewhere. The mass of the operation has been enormous. The velocity of it is enormous, and it becomes virtually impossible to stop. The recent problem with the SST is a good example. For when any enterprise in our society has reached a certain scale, the consequences in unemployment and in dislocation of the economy are such that it becomes every year more difficult to cease doing what we are already doing.

A third example, more in the area of institutions, is foreign aid: the international pressures to give foreign aid to one country or another. We have an enormous mass of wealth being invested, a great velocity with lots of people going off all over the world and performing this operation of giving aid, and it becomes almost impossible to stop it. The other countries resent the decline of aid and consider it a hostile act, even though they might not have felt that way if we hadn't started the aid in the first place. Foreign aid is, I think, the most characteristic innovation in foreign policy in this century.

Each of these three enterprises illustrates the attitude of the American citizen in the later twentieth century toward his control over experience. Increasingly, the citizen comes to feel that events are moving, and moving so fast with such velocity and in such mass that he has very little control. The sense of momentum itself becomes possible only because of our success in achieving these large purposes which no other democratic society, no other society before us, had even imagined.

Now, what does this bring us to? Before I come to my fourth and concluding point on the ways in which the successes of democracy have affected our experience, I would like briefly to recall some of the remedies that have been suggested for the ills of democracy and the problems of democracy in the past. Al Smith[2] once said, "All the ills of democracy can be cured by more democracy." I must confess, though I admire Al Smith for some of his enterprises, the Empire

[2] Alfred Smith (1873–1944) served as governor of New York four times, instituting many reforms, and campaigned unsuccessfully for the presidency in 1928. (ED.)

State Building for example, I think he was on the wrong track here. In fact, I would take an almost contrary position. Even at the risk of seeming flip, I might sum up the democratic paradoxes that I have been describing: "Getting there is *all* the fun."

Is there a law of democratic impoverishment? Is it possible that while *democratizing* enriches experience, *democracy* dilutes experience?

Example: photography. Before the invention of photography, it was a remarkable experience to see an exact likeness of the Sphinx or of Notre Dame or of some exotic animal or to see a portrait of an ancestor. Then, as photography was publicized in the 1880's and thoroughly popularized in this century, it opened up a fantastic new range of experience for everybody. Suddenly people were able to see things they had never been able to see before. And then what happened? Everyone had a camera, or two or three cameras; and everywhere he went he took pictures and when he came home he had to find a victim, somebody to show the pictures to. And this became more and more difficult.

While photography was being introduced, it was life-enriching and vista-opening; but once it was achieved, once everybody had a camera, the people were looking in their cameras instead of looking at the sight they had gone to see. It had an attenuating effect. A picture came to mean less and less, simply because people saw pictures everywhere. And the experience of being there also somehow meant less because the main thing people saw everywhere was the inside of their viewfinders, and their concern over their lens cap and finding the proper exposure made it hard for them to notice what was going on around them at the moment.

Another example is, of course, the phonograph. Has the phonograph—in its universal late-twentieth-century uses—necessarily made people more appreciative of music? In the 1920's when I was raised in Tulsa, Oklahoma, I had never heard an opera, nor had I really heard any classical music properly performed by an orchestra. But in our living room we had a wind-up Victrola, and I heard Galli-Curci singing arias from *Rigoletto,* and I heard Caruso, and I heard some symphonies, and it was fantastic. And then hi-fi came and everybody had a phonograph, a hi-fi machine or a little transistor radio which you could carry with you and hear music any time.

Today when I walk into the elevator in an office building, it is not impossible that I will hear Beethoven or Verdi. Sitting in the airplane I hear Mozart coming out of the public-address system.

Wherever we go we hear music whether we want to hear it or not, whether we are in the mood for it or not. It becomes an everywhere, all-the-time thing. The experience is attenuated.

And one of the most serious consequences of all this, finally, is the attenuation of community itself. What holds people together? What has held people together in the past? For the most part it has been their sense of humanity, their pleasure in the presence of one another, their feeling for another person's expression, the sound of a voice, the look on his or her face. But the kind of community I describe increasingly becomes attenuated. People are trying to enjoy the community all by themselves.

We are led to certain desperate quests in American life. These, the by-products of our success, are clues to the vitality and energy of our country, to the quest for novelty to keep life interesting and vistas open, to the quest for community and the quest for autonomy. Can we inoculate ourselves against these perils of our technological success? Samuel Butler[3] once said, "If I die prematurely, at any rate I shall be saved from being bored by my own success." Our problem, too, is partly that.

And now a fourth characteristic of the relation of technology to democracy in our time: *the belief in solutions.* One of the most dangerous popular fallacies—nourished by American history and by some of our most eloquent and voluble patriots—is the notion that democracy is attainable. There is a subtle difference between American democratic society and many earlier societies in the extent to which their ideals could be attained. The objectives of other societies have for the most part been definable and attainable. Aristocracy and monarchy do present attainable ideals. Even totalitarianism presents objectives which can be attained in the sense in which the objectives of democracy never can be.

This nation has been a place of renewal, of new beginnings for nations and for man. Vagueness has been a national resource: the vagueness of the continent, the mystery of our resources, the vagueness of our social classes, the misty miasma of our hopes.

Our society has been most distinctively a way of reaching for rather than of finding. American democracy, properly speaking, has been a process and not a product, a quest and not a discovery. But a great danger which has been nourished by our success in technol-

---

[3] Samuel Butler (1835–1902) was an English author on a variety of subjects, his literary fame derived from his satires of English society. (ED.)

ogy has been the belief in solutions. For technological problems there *are* solutions. It is possible to set yourself the task of developing an economic and workable internal-combustion engine, a prefabricated house, or a way of reaching the moon. Technological problems are capable of solutions.

We are inclined, then, using the technological problem as our prototype, to believe that somehow democracy itself is a solution, a dissolving of the human condition. But we should have learned, and even the history of technology—especially the history of technology in our democratic society—should have taught us otherwise.

In human history in the long run there are no solutions, only problems. This is what I have suggested in my description of "self-liquidating" ideals. And the examples are all around us—in our effort to create a pluralistic society by assimilating and Americanizing people, in our effort to give everybody an uncrowded wilderness vacation, in our effort to find an exciting new model each year.

Every seeming solution is a new problem. When you democratize the speedy automobile and give everybody an automobile, the result is a traffic jam; and this is the sense in which the "solution" of technological problems present us with obstacles to the fulfillment of what is human in our society. When we think about American democratic society, then, we must learn not to think about a condition, but about a process; not about democracy, but about the quest for democracy, which we might call "democratizing."

The most distinctive feature of our system is not a system, but a quest, not a neat arrangement of men and institutions, but a flux. What other society has ever committed itself to so tantalizing, so fulfilling, so frustrating a community enterprise?

To prepare ourselves for this view of American democracy there are two sides to our personal need. One is on the side of prudence and wisdom; the other on the side of poetry and imagination.

On the side of prudence, there is a need for a sense of history. Only by realizing the boundaries that we have been given can we discover how to reach beyond them. Only so can we have the wisdom not to mistake passing fads for great movements, not to mistake the fanaticisms of a few for the deep beliefs of the many, not to mistake fashion for revolution. This wisdom is necessary if we are to secure sensibly the benefits of a free society for those who have for whatever reason been deprived of its benefits. We were not born yesterday, nor was the nation. And between the day before yesterday and yesterday, crucial events have happened. We can discover these and come to terms with them only through history. As Pascal[4] said, "It is only by knowing our condition that we can transcend it." Our technology brings us the omnipresent present. It dulls our sense of history, and if we are not careful it can destroy it.

We in the U.S.A. are always living in an age of transition. Yet we have tended to believe that our present is always the climax of history, even though American history shows that the climax is always in the future. By keeping suspense alive, we can prepare ourselves for the shocks of change.

And finally, on the side of poetry and imagination, how do we keep alive the spirit of adventure, what I would call the exploring spirit? This should be the easiest because it is the most traditional of our achievements and efforts. We must remember that we live in a new world. We must keep alive the exploring spirit. We must not sacrifice the infinite promise of the unknown, of man's unfulfilled possibilities in the universe's untouched mysteries, for the cozy satisfactions of predictable, statistical benefits. Space exploration is a symbol.

Recently I had the pleasure of talking with Thor Heyerdahl,[5] the *Kon Tiki* man, whose latest venture was the Ra expedition, in which he explored the possibilities of men having come from Egypt or elsewhere in the Mediterranean to this continent long ago in boats made of reeds. He and his crew, to test their hypothesis, actually crossed the Atlantic in a reed boat. And as I talked to Thor Heyerdahl about the Ra expedition, I said that it must have been a terrible feeling of risk when you suddenly left the sight of land and got out into the open sea. It seemed to me that the fear and perils of the open sea would be the greatest. Thor Heyerdahl said not at all: the great dangers, the dangers of shoals and rocks, existed along the shore. The wonderful sense of relief, he observed, came when he went out on the ocean where there was openness all around, although also high waves and strong currents. The promise of American de-

---

[4] Blaise Pascal (1623–1662) was a French scientist and religious philosopher and author of *Pensées* (1670). (ED.)

[5] Thor Heyerdahl (1914–   ) is a Norwegian explorer and anthropologist who sailed a raft from Peru to the Polynesian Islands in an attempt to prove that early Americans could have settled the islands as recounted in his book *Kon Tiki* (1950). He later sailed a papyrus boat across the Atlantic to prove that ancient Egyptians could have sailed to the American continent, reported in *The Ra Expeditions* (1971). (ED.)

mocracy, I suggest, depends on our ability to stay at sea, to work
together in community while we all reach to the open horizon.

LEWIS MUMFORD

The Monastery and the Clock

Lewis Mumford (1895–1990) was an American sociologist, writer,
and critic, whose major interests were architecture and urban planning. *The Culture of Cities* (1938), *The Conduct of Life* (1951), and
The City in History (1961), which won a National Book Award, all
reveal his interest in the relationship between human need and
urban planning. The following selection is from *Technics and Civilization* (1934).

> . . . One is not straining the facts when one suggests that the monaster-
> ies . . . helped to give human enterprise the regular collective beat and
> rhythm of the machine; for the clock is not merely a means of keeping
> track of the hours, but of synchronizing the actions of men.

Where did the machine first take form in modern civilization? There
was plainly more than one point of origin. Our mechanical civilization represents the convergence of numerous habits, ideas, and modes
of living, as well as technical instruments; and some of these were,
in the beginning, directly opposed to the civilization they helped to
create. But the first manifestation of the new order took place in the
general picture of the world: during the first seven centuries of the
machine's existence the categories of time and space underwent an
extraordinary change, and no aspect of life was left untouched by
this transformation. The application of quantitative methods of
thought to the study of nature had its first manifestation in the regular
measurement of time; and the new mechanical conception of time
arose in part out of the routine of the monastery. Alfred Whitehead[1]
has emphasized the importance of the scholastic belief in a universe

---

[1] Alfred Whitehead (1861–1947) was an English mathematician and philosopher and
author of *Process and Reality* (1929) whose work in science and in metaphysics was
closely interrelated. (ED.)

ordered by God as one of the foundations of modern physics: but behind that belief was the presence of order in the institutions of the Church itself.

The technics of the ancient world were still carried on from Constantinople and Baghdad to Sicily and Cordova: hence the early lead taken by Salerno in the scientific and medical advances of the Middle Age. It was, however, in the monasteries of the West that the desire for order and power, other than that expressed in the military domination of weaker men, first manifested itself after the long uncertainty and bloody confusion that attended the breakdown of the Roman Empire. Within the walls of the monastery was sanctuary: under the rule of the order surprise and doubt and caprice and irregularity were put at bay. Opposed to the erratic fluctuations and pulsations of the worldly life was the iron discipline of the rule. Benedict added a seventh period to the devotions of the day, and in the seventh century, by a bull of Pope Sabinianus, it was decreed that the bells of the monastery be rung seven times in the twenty-four hours. These punctuation marks in the day were known as the canonical hours, and some means of keeping count of them and ensuring their regular repetition became necessary.

According to a now discredited legend, the first modern mechanical clock, worked by falling weights, was invented by the monk named Gerbert who afterwards became Pope Sylvester II, near the close of the tenth century. This clock was probably only a water clock, one of those bequests of the ancient world either left over directly from the days of the Romans, like the water-wheel itself, or coming back again into the West through the Arabs. But the legend, as so often happens, is accurate in its implications if not in its facts. The monastery was the seat of a regular life, and an instrument for striking the hours at intervals or for reminding the bell-ringer that it was time to strike the bells, was an almost inevitable product of this life. If the mechanical clock did not appear until the cities of the thirteenth century demanded an orderly routine, the habit of order itself and the earnest regulation of time-sequences had become almost second nature in the monastery. Coulton agrees with Sombart in looking upon the Benedictines, the great working order, as perhaps the original founders of modern capitalism: their rule certainly took the curse off work and their vigorous engineering enterprises may even have robbed warfare of some of its glamor. So one is not straining the facts when one suggests that the monasteries—at one time there were 40,000 under the Benedictine rule—helped to give human enterprise the regular collective beat and rhythm of the machine; for the clock is not merely a means of keeping track of the hours, but of synchronizing the actions of men.

Was it by reason of the collective Christian desire to provide for the welfare of souls in eternity by regular prayers and devotions that time keeping and the habits of temporal order took hold of men's minds: habits that capitalist civilization presently turned to good account? One must perhaps accept the irony of this paradox. At all events, by the thirteenth century there are definite records of mechanical clocks, and by 1370 a well-designed "modern" clock had been built by Heinrich von Wyck at Paris. Meanwhile, bell towers had come into existence, and the new clocks, if they did not have, till the fourteenth century, a dial and a hand that translated the movement of time into a movement through space, at all events struck the hours. The clouds that could paralyze the sundial, the freezing that could stop the water clock on a winter night, were no longer obstacles to time-keeping: summer or winter, day or night, one was aware of the measured clank of the clock. The instrument presently spread outside the monastery; and the regular striking of the bells brought a new regularity into the life of the workman and the merchant. The bells of the clock tower almost defined urban existence. Time-keeping passed into time-serving and time-accounting and time-rationing. As this took place, Eternity ceased gradually to serve as the measure and focus of human actions.

The clock, not the steam-engine, is the key machine of the modern industrial age. For every phase of its development the clock is both the outstanding fact and the typical symbol of the machine: even today no other machine is so ubiquitous. Here, at the very beginning of modern technics, appeared prophetically the accurate automatic machine which, only after centuries of further effort, was also to prove the final consummation of this technics in every department of industrial activity. There had been power-machines, such as the water-mill, before the clock; and there had also been various kinds of automata, to awaken the wonder of the populace in the temple, or to please the idle fancy of some Moslem caliph: machines one finds illustrated in Hero and Al-Jazari. But here was a new kind of power-machine, in which the source of power and the transmission were of such a nature as to ensure the even flow of energy throughout the works and to make possible regular production and a standardized product. In its relationship to determinable quantities of energy, to standardization, to automatic action, and finally to its own special product, accurate timing, the clock has been the foremost machine in modern technics; and at each period it has remained in the lead:

it marks a perfection toward which other machines aspire. The clock, moreover, served as a model for many other kinds of mechanical works, and the analysis of motion that accompanied the perfection of the clock, with the various types of gearing and transmission that were elaborated, contributed to the success of quite different kinds of machine. Smiths could have hammered thousands of suits of armor or thousands of iron cannon, wheelwrights could have shaped thousands of great water-wheels or crude gears, without inventing any of the special types of movement developed in clockwork, and without any of the accuracy of measurement and fineness of articulation that finally produced the accurate eighteenth-century chronometer.

The clock, moreover, is a piece of power-machinery whose "product" is seconds and minutes: by its essential nature it dissociated time from human events and helped to create the belief in an independent world of mathematically measurable sequences: the special world of science. There is relatively little foundation for this belief in common human experience: throughout the year the days are of uneven duration, and not merely does the relation between day and night steadily change, but a slight journey from East to West alters astronomical time by a certain number of minutes. In terms of the human organism itself, mechanical time is even more foreign: while human life has regularities of its own, the beat of the pulse, the breathing of the lungs, these change from hour to hour with mood and action, and in the longer span of days, time is measured not by the calendar but by the events that occupy it. The shepherd measures from the time the ewes lambed; the farmer measures back to the day of sowing or forward to the harvest: if growth has its own duration and regularities, behind it are not simply matter and motion but the facts of development: in short, history. And while mechanical time is strung out in a succession of mathematically isolated instants, organic time—what Bergson[2] calls duration—is cumulative in its effects. Though mechanical time can, in a sense, be speeded up or run backward, like the hands of a clock or the images of a moving picture, organic time moves in only one direction—through the cycle of birth, growth, development, decay, and death—and the past that is already dead remains present in the future that has still to be born.

Around 1345, according to Thorndike, the division of hours into

---

[2] Henri Bergson (1859–1941) was a French philosopher and author of *Time and Free Will* (1889) in which he presents his belief that time is a duration of life experience which is in a constant flow, not a series of measured moments. (ED.)

sixty minutes and of minutes into sixty seconds became common: it was this abstract framework of divided time that became more and more the point of reference for both action and thought, and in the effort to arrive at accuracy in this department, the astronomical exploration of the sky focused attention further upon the regular implacable movements of the heavenly bodies through space. Early in the sixteenth century a young Nuremberg mechanic, Peter Henlein, is supposed to have created "many-wheeled watches out of small bits of iron" and by the end of the century the small domestic clock had been introduced in England and Holland. As with the motor car and the airplane, the richer classes first took over the new mechanism and popularized it: partly because they alone could afford it, partly because the new bourgeoisie were the first to discover that, as Franklin later put it, "time is money." To become "as regular as clockwork" was the bourgeois ideal, and to own a watch was for long a definite symbol of success. The increasing tempo of civilization led to a demand for greater power: and in turn power quickened the tempo.

Now, the orderly punctual life that first took shape in the monasteries is not native to mankind, although by now Western peoples are so thoroughly regimented by the clock that it is "second nature" and they look upon its observance as a fact of nature. Many Eastern civilizations have flourished on a loose basis in time: the Hindus have in fact been so indifferent to time that they lack even an authentic chronology of the years. Only yesterday, in the midst of the industrializations of Soviet Russia, did a society come into existence to further the carrying of watches there and to propagandize the benefits of punctuality. The popularization of time-keeping, which followed the production of the cheap standardized watch, first in Geneva, then in America around the middle of the last century, was essential to a well-articulated system of transportation and production.

To keep time was once a peculiar attribute of music: it gave industrial value to the workshop song or the tattoo or the chantey of the sailors tugging at a rope. But the effect of the mechanical clock is more pervasive and strict: it presides over the day from the hour of rising to the hour of rest. When one thinks of the day as an abstract span of time, one does not go to bed with the chickens on a winter's night: one invents wicks, chimneys, lamps, gaslights, electric lamps, so as to use all the hours belonging to the day. When one thinks of time, not as a sequence of experiences, but as a collection of hours, minutes, and seconds, the habits of adding time and saving time come into existence. Time took on the character of an enclosed space: it could be divided, it could be filled up, it could even be expanded by the invention of labor-saving instruments.

Abstract time became the new medium of existence. Organic functions themselves were regulated by it: one ate, not upon feeling hungry, but when prompted by the clock: one slept, not when one was tired, but when the clock sanctioned it. A generalized time-consciousness accompanied the wider use of clocks: dissociating time from organic sequences, it became easier for the men of the Renaissance to indulge the fantasy of reviving the classic past or of reliving the splendors of antique Roman civilization: the cult of history, appearing first in daily ritual, finally abstracted itself as a special discipline. In the seventeenth century journalism and periodic literature made their appearance: even in dress, following the lead of Venice as fashion-center, people altered styles every year rather than every generation.

The gain in mechanical efficiency through co-ordination and through the closer articulation of the day's events cannot be over-estimated: while this increase cannot be measured in mere horse-power, one has only to imagine its absence today to foresee the speedy disruption and eventual collapse of our entire society. The modern industrial régime could do without coal and iron and steam more easily than it could do without the clock.

JOHN F. AVEDON

Tibetan Medicine

John F. Avedon (1952–) was born in New York City and has written for *Geo, Rolling Stone,* and the *New York Times Magazine.* His books include *In Exile from the Land of Snows* (1979), from which the following selection is taken, *An Interview with the Dalai Lama* (1980), and *Tibet Today* (1988). His most recent work is *Wings for the Mad Flight: In Pursuit of Understanding the Brain* (1989).

Dr. Yeshi Dhonden pressed the three middle fingers of his right hand gently along the inside of William Schneider's left wrist, bowed his head and listened. The fifty-two-year-old patient smiled, perplexed.

The physician before him wore neither a white coat nor a name tag. He asked no questions and carried no charts or instruments. Dressed in maroon robes, head shaved, a turquoise-studded charm box bulging beneath his orange shirt, Dr. Dhonden remained motionless, deep in concentration. A minute later, he took the patient's right arm and briefly pressed the radial artery as if to confirm his findings. Ushering Mr. Schneider into an adjacent room, the doctor gestured for him to undress, whereupon he pressed selected points along his spine. With each touch, Mr. Schneider cried out in pain. Dr. Dhonden nodded sympathetically and told him to get dressed.

In his guest suite at the University of Virginia, Dr. Yeshi Dhonden offered his diagnosis of William Schneider, a man he knew nothing of and had met only minutes before. "Many years ago you lifted a heavy object," he said, speaking through an interpreter. "At that time you damaged a channel in the vicinity of your right kidney, blocking the normal flow of wind through your back. The wind has accumulated outside the channel, there is bone deterioration and the disease has become quite severe." Mr. Schneider was stunned. For three years, he confirmed, he had suffered from acute arthritis along the neck and lower back. The illness had caused incapacitating pain, and he had been forced to give up his job. But he was even more astonished at Dr. Dhonden's ability to reconstruct his past. "In 1946," he recalled, "I injured my back lifting a milk can out of a cooler. I was in bed a week, and as soon as I got up I reinjured it and was bed-ridden again. That must have been the start of the whole problem."

It was a diagnosis that Western physicians could arrive at simply by using an X ray, but Dr. Yeshi Dhonden, the Dalai Lama's[1] personal physician, sent by him in the winter of 1980 to introduce Tibetan medicine to the West, enthralled American doctors and patients alike with his unique skills. "It's quite conceivable that in our attempt to be scientific, some of our powers of observation have atrophied," said Dr. Gerald Goldstein, a professor at the University of Virginia's Medical Oncology Department, who worked closely with the Tibetan physician during his stay. "Dr. Dhonden, on the other hand, is totally attuned to everything that is going on. He uses all of his senses as his medical instrument. Our patients have been very impressed." Dr.

---

[1] Tenzin Gyatso (1935–) is the fourteenth Dalai Lama, supreme leader of Tibetan Buddhists. He has lived in exile since 1959 following an unsuccessful Tibetan uprising against the Chinese occupation of Tibet, which took place in 1950. (ED.)

Richard Selzer, assistant professor of surgery at Yale University, met Yeshi Dhonden in 1974 on his first visit to the United States. "I went to observe Dr. Dhonden with some healthy skepticism," he recounted. "I was surprised and elated by what I found. It was as if he was a human electrocardiogram machine interpreting the component parts of the pulse. We have nothing like it in the West. It's a dimension of medicine that we have not yet realized." "Western scientific documentation of Tibetan claims is nonexistent," observed Dr. Herbert Benson, leader of a team of Harvard researchers that visited the Tibetan Medical Center in 1981. "It would be nice, though, to discover the worth of what they have developed over thousands of years. If their claims are only partly true they would be worthy of investigation. Therefore, can we really afford to ignore this?"

To test the efficacy of Tibetan drugs by laboratory standards, Yeshi Dhonden agreed, while in Virginia, to engage in an experiment with cancerous mice. On the basis of a visual examination alone, he prescribed a general Tibetan cancer drug, comprised of over sixty ingredients, for nine tumor-implanted mice in a lab in the University of Virginia's vivarium. Six mice refused the medicine and died within thirty-five days. Three mice accepted it and survived up to fifty-three days. A second experiment involving sixteen animals confirmed the findings, producing the most successful results since work with the particular tumor involved began in 1967. Of even greater interest, though, was the fact that Dr. Dhonden had no knowledge of the nature of the cancer he was dealing with. "There are literally hundreds of kinds of tumors," commented Dr. Donald Baker, the researcher in charge of the experiment. "How often has Dr. Dhonden encountered a KHT anaplastic sarcoma growing in a highly inbred strain of $_3$CH/HEJ female mice? It would be utterly unreasonable to ask him to decide what would be the best treatment. If he had been familiar with these conditions he might well have effected a complete cure." "There is no question that this is a very fertile area for cancer quacks," added Dr. Goldstein. "In the end, though, things either work or they don't work. Dr. Dhonden has things that work."

Sitting cross-legged over a cup of butter tea in his Virginia apartment, Dr. Dhonden offered a brief description of cancer in Tibetan terms. "I've treated perhaps one thousand cancer patients of which sixty to seventy percent have been cured," he maintained. "Our medical texts specify fifty-four types of tumors which appear at eighteen places in the body in one of three forms. We consider cancer to be a disease of the blood. It begins with pollutants in the environment. These, in turn, affect seven types of sentient beings in the body, two of which are most susceptible. They are extremely minute, but if you could see them, they would be round, red and flat. They can travel through the bloodstream in an instant, are formed with the embryo in the womb and normally function to maintain strength. In general the Buddha[2] predicted that eighteen diseases would become prevalent in our time due to two causes, low moral conduct and pollution. Cancer is one of the eighteen."

Based on the results of his first experiment those physicians working with Yeshi Dhonden hoped to initiate a broader study of Tibetan medicine in the West. Dr. Dhonden, too, was eager to undertake an in-depth exchange of medical lore. "If Western medicine can come to understand the Tibetan view of the human organism," he commented toward the close of his stay in Virginia, "I feel it will be of inestimable value. Our medicine has many cures for diseases which Western doctors currently don't understand or have incorrectly identified. We successfully treat diabetes, various forms of coronary disease, arthritis, hepatitis, Parkinson's disease, cancers, ulcers and the common cold. We have difficulty treating epilepsy and paralysis. But because the Tibetan system is scientific, Western physicians, as scientists, will see what is of value and what is not." To illuminate an ancient science hidden behind the Himalayas for over two thousand years, Yeshi Dhonden described his own life and training as a Tibetan doctor.

Dr. Dhonden was born in 1929 into a wealthy family of farmers living in the small village of Namro, south of the Tsangpo River, one day's ride from Lhasa.[3] Much of the land surrounding Namro belonged to the Dhonden family and their relatives. Five thousand sheep, yaks and horses and many fields of *chingko* or mountain barley were owned by Yeshi Dhonden's aunt and uncle, who, not having a male child, assumed he would grow up to run the estate. Dr. Dhonden's parents, however, felt differently. As their only child, they decided that Yeshi Dhonden should devote his life to the Dharma.[4] Accordingly, at the age of six, their son left his home and traveled a

---

[2] the title given to Siddartha Gautama (c. 563–c. 483 B.C.), who founded Buddhism in the sixth and fifth centuries B.C. (ED.)

[3] capital of Tibet and center of Tibetan Buddhism before the 1950 Chinese occupation (ED.)

[4] religious and moral teachings of Buddhism (ED.)

short way up the mountain behind Namro, to be accepted as a novice monk in the local monastery of Shedrup Ling. "I remember it all," recollected Dr. Dhonden. "Becoming a monk, entering into the comfort of the group, living with my teacher. I had a strong wish to learn quickly and my mind was very clear. I could memorize four of our long pages in a single day." Yeshi Dhonden's facility for memorization earned him a high position among his peers, on the basis of which he was selected at the age of eleven to represent Shedrup Ling at Mendzekhang, the larger of Lhasa's two state-run medical colleges. Like all monasteries, district headquarters and military camps, Shedrup Ling was required by the government to send medical students to Lhasa. Upon the completion of their training, they would then return to practice in their region. But while the monastery's superiors were not averse to receiving the government salary paid to them for their students' attendance, the four hundred monks were less than enthusiastic at the prospect of medical studies. "Everyone in the monastery was afraid that he would be selected," recalled Dr. Dhonden, laughing. "No one wanted to become a doctor. You have to spend at least eleven years in classes and there is a tremendous amount of memorization. But because I liked to memorize, when my parents told me that I had been chosen, I was eager to go."

The medical system Yeshi Dhonden was to study had begun as one of the ten branches of learning originally pursued by all Mahayana Buddhist monks. It flourished for over a thousand years in the great monastic universities of northern India, from whence it was taken to Tibet by two Indian pandits[5] in the first century B.C. Thereafter, it was the province for almost seven hundred years of a single family of physicians attendant on the Royal Tibetan Court. With the introduction of over a hundred Buddhist medical texts in the sixth century, however, it grew into a widespread practice and was ultimately acclaimed by a conference of physicians from nine nations convened in Tibet, as the preeminent medical science of its time. Subsequently, Tibet's first medical college, called Melung or "Country of Medicine," was built in the eighth century by King Trisong Detsen in Kongpo, south of Lhasa. Melung inspired the founding of scores of medical schools, most contained in *dratsangs* or colleges appended to the country's larger monasteries. In the mid-seventeenth century, the Fifth Dalai Lama built Tibet's second medical college, called

[5] wise or learned man (ED.)

Chokpori, atop Iron Hill, just across from the Potala. There, doctors from all across Tibet and Mongolia were trained to practice a composite of the various schools of medicine that had developed over the years. The need for more physicians in modern times resulted in the Thirteenth Dalai Lama's construction of Tibet's most recent central medical college, Mendzekhang or "Medicine House," in 1916.

Mendzekhang lay on the west side of Lhasa, next to the Tibetan government's newly built post and telegraph office. It was centered on a flagstone courtyard, with dormitories for students, both lay and monk, occupying two long wings, at the head of which, facing the main gate, stood the classrooms, assembly hall and the Master's quarters. Outside, the college walls were lined with display beds of frequently used medicinal plants. Inside, life at Mendzekhang followed a spartan schedule. At four each morning a bell sounded in the main temple at the head of the courtyard. Yeshi Dhonden had a few minutes to wash and roll up his bedding before hurrying to his classroom to begin memorizing by the soft light of butter lamps. As the mind was believed to be most fresh on waking, the first three hours before sunrise were given over to the memorization of the 1,140 pages of the four medical tantras, the root texts, preached by the Buddha, which, together with hundreds of commentaries and pharmacological catalogues, were the basis of Tibetan medicine. At seven o'clock instructors quizzed their students on the morning's work, after which they would return to their rooms for the day's first bowl of tea. A second bell then rang, and the whole college gathered to pray in long seated rows running the length of the pillared assembly hall, its walls hung with *thankas* illustrating herbs, anatomy, embryonic development and surgical instruments. On the way back to his room, Yeshi Dhonden would pass patients lined up for treatment beneath the apartments of Kenrab Norbu, the Master of Mendzekhang. Under their instructors' observation, senior students examined the sick while other professors, along with all the doctors of Chokpori, fanned out into the city on morning house calls, visiting those too ill to come to the colleges. As always in Tibet, medical treatment was free, only the medicines themselves having to be paid for.

Although Yeshi Dhonden's day was spent mainly in memorization, he often looked in on Mendzekhang's chief pharmacist and his staff. Two doors east of the front gate, they carried out the first step in the preparation of medicines, pounding into a fine powder the various roots, stems, leaves and branches as well as the numerous gems, minerals and animal products used in the 2,000 drugs routinely made by the college. The demands of their work were so great that Mendzekhang was covered with the raw materials of the trade. Hundreds of pungent medicinal plants, collected on expeditions into the mountains, were laid out to dry throughout the school's hallways, classrooms and rooftops. Subsequently they were administered either in powder form or as shiny black and brown pills.

Following an early dinner at five o'clock, the student body once again assembled, this time to practice debate. Seated by class in the courtyard, the college would, on the Master's signal, break into a cacophony of shouts, claps and loud retorts as attackers queried their respondents on the correct interpretation of the tantras' description of the causes, conditions and treatments of various illnesses. Often debates became so heated that when the five-hour session had concluded, individual pairs, a small group of entranced onlookers seated around them, their *sens* or outer robes wrapped tightly against the chill, continued debating far into the night.

After two years and four months, Yeshi Dhonden completed memorizing the medical tantras. He then recited for a full day before his teacher, declining to divide his first test over a period of time, as was customary. Promoted, despite his youth, to be senior student among the five in his room, he went on to take his official examination. The mornings of four days were set aside. His parents came from Namro to attend, while his home monastery, Shedrup Ling, offered a tea service at each session. Yeshi Dhonden, aged thirteen and a half, then appeared in the Assembly Hall before the Master of Mendzekhang, the faculty and the entire student body and after prostrating three times to the images of the Medicine Buddha and Tibet's most famous doctor, Yuthok Yonten Gonpo, on the main altar, recited verbatim the one hundred fifty-six chapters of the four tantras—in and out of sequence—as he was requested. Only minor mistakes were accepted—a lapse of any kind being considered grounds for failure. On the afternoon of the fourth day Yeshi Dhonden was informed that he had passed in good standing. Rewarded with a white scarf and a set of brocade book covers, he was admitted into the college to commence his formal education.

After graduating, Dr. Dhonden served as Kenrab Norbu's special assistant for three years. In the evenings he continued to debate with Mendzekhang's senior students and faculty members. Once a month he went to the Lingkhor, Lhasa's Holy Walk, to treat the hundreds of poor pilgrims and beggars who rarely came on their own for help. In conjunction with this, he paid special attention to cultivating the eleven vows of the physicians' code which attempted to instill an altruistic motive as the basis of a doctor's practice. As Yeshi Dhonden commented, concerning his own application of the ancient code, "I am just an ordinary person afflicted by desire, hatred and ignorance. But through contemplating the suffering I see in my work, I have tried to increase my compassion. As doctors we are expected to put kindness before all else." Out of his own curiosity, Dr. Dhonden also went, two hours a day, to the British Legation, to acquaint himself with Western medicine. Finally, in 1951, Kenrab Norbu sent Yeshi Dhonden's diploma to the office of the Cabinet, where it was officially confirmed. The Kashag then dispatched letters to district officials in Lhoka, as well as the government transport center, from which Yeshi Dhonden received free passage home. Thirteen years after his education began, Dr. Dhonden left Lhasa, looking forward to taking up practice on his own.

He didn't have long to wait. An epidemic had broken out along the Bhutanese border, imported—along with chocolate, batteries, silks and the beloved fedora hats—by traders returning from India. In Tibet's high, germ-scarce environment, those who contracted the disease—a form of intestinal influenza—died quickly. Scores of doctors had already flocked to the area.

Traveling to a monastery called Sungroling Gonpa, Dr. Dhonden joined three physicians who had been attempting, unsuccessfully, to check the epidemic. Nine of the monastery's 300 monks had already died, as well as many of the inhabitants of the village below its walls. Arriving just before nightfall, Dr. Dhonden was shown to a private room, where, after his regular evening meditation session, he went to sleep, expecting to see his first patients in the morning. During the night, however, he experienced an unusual dream, one which, though seemingly inexplicable by Western standards, demonstrated the close relationship of religion to science in Tibetan medicine. "In the night I dreamt that a naked woman came before me, a *khadroma*," said Dr. Dhonden, referring to a spiritual being believed, in a manner similar to that of an angel, to aid practitioners in meditation. "In her right hand she held a tantric drum; in her left hand she held a skull. She carried a bag of medicine under her left arm. A white tin cup with a red design and a slight crack on its rim, filled with urine, appeared before her. Then the woman asked me, 'After examining this urine can you tell me the disease of the patient? What is your diagnosis?' In the dream I looked at the urine and replied, 'This is today's epidemic, one of sixty-five types of the eighteen new diseases predicted in the tantras for this era.' 'What is its cause?' she asked. I responded that it was due, as the tantras state, to environmental pollution and that it was a hot disease. 'You said that externally it is a fever, but are you sure that internally it's not cold?' she said. At that time, because my memory was fresh from constant study, I recalled that the thirteenth and fourteenth chapters of the third Tantra address the topic of cold and hot diseases together. I answered her in debate form, quoting the text as proof, stating that there was no hidden cold fever, but that the ailment was hot both inside and out. We debated back and forth for some time and finally she said, 'What treatment will you give?' I replied, 'Because the bacteria causing the disease have mixed the blood and bile, medicine should be given to separate them.' Then she asked what the patient's behavior and diet should be—two aspects of treatment that always accompany medicine. I answered and she said, 'Tell me again. How will you cut the tail of this disease?' Once more we debated vigorously and then she laughed and suddenly disappeared. There was complete silence and I woke up."

In a short while, as the day began, Dr. Dhonden was brought tea. Afterwards he was asked to visit his first patient, a twenty-three-year-old monk, infected by the illness, languishing in his room. "I went to see the young man," continued Dr. Dhonden. "It was a very serious case. The room he lay in stank. Diarrhea mixed with blood was pouring from him onto the bed and he was semi-comatose; he couldn't talk. I asked for his urine specimen and it was brought to me in a tin cup. All of a sudden I remembered my dream. It was the exact cup, even with the crack on the rim. 'Oh, I have already examined this before,' I thought. I was amazed. Then the whole dream came back. I recalled the debate and the treatment and immediately I prepared the correct medicines. The man recovered and after that, the epidemic in the village was completely stopped. Now when I look back on it," Dr. Dhonden said, "I feel that whoever came to me in the form of a *khadroma* that night was actually administering my true final examination."

As Dr. Dhonden's reputation spread, he spent the remainder of the 1950s traveling from one district to another. "Each day I rode from village to village, returning periodically to Lhasa to obtain medicines," he recounted. "I was able to cure three quarters of my patients. And because I gave penicillin injections for skin disease— a great novelty among Tibetans—my reputation continued to increase. I never had a free day." A group of young relations began to study with him, but before long the uprising against the nine-year-old Chinese occupation broke out in Lhasa and the Dalai Lama fled.

"I saw His Holiness when his party came through my area," recalled
Dr. Dhonden. "Those who weren't following him had joined the
guerrillas to put up a last fight for our freedom. My students all had
family members whom they couldn't leave. My own mother's legs
were too poor for her to walk out and my father had said that he
was too old to cross the high passes into Bhutan. As a monk, I
wouldn't fight. So I felt that I had no other choice but to leave. I
borrowed a horse, said farewell and set off."

Though Namro was only a few days from the border, the presence
of Chinese troops forced Dr. Dhonden to hide for over a month
before finally, in the company of eighty other refugees, he descended
a steep snow-covered slope, trekked through a valley and crossed a
glacial stream into the forests of Bhutan. With only a few texts,
instruments and medicines in his possession, he then walked across
Bhutan begging day to day. "After I was forced to flee my homeland,
I was overwhelmed by a deep sense of renunciation," reflected Dr.
Dhonden. "I saw life as essenceless, without real stability. I only
wanted to practice religion." Arriving at Buxa, Yeshi Dhonden requested permission to remain with the monks there while the rest
of his group was transferred to road work. The Tibetan government
official in charge replied, "You have the right to practice religion and
you are also young and fit to work on the roads. However, if the
Kashag asks me, 'Has any doctor come out of Tibet?' and I've sent
you elsewhere, what will I say? Therefore, you studied medicine at
the government's expense, and now the time has come for you to
help us."

Dr. Dhonden was sent to Dalhousie, where 3,000 refugees, including the elite monks of Lhasa's two Tantric colleges, Gyudto and
Gyudme, were camped in squalid conditions. Tuberculosis, hepatitis
and amoebic dysentery were rampant. Preparing what medicines he
could from the few herbs available in Indian stores, he set up a clinic
and went to work. "One day a sweeper in my clinic was bitten by a
poisonous snake," he related. "Just as I was applying a Tibetan
tourniquet, an Indian doctor arrived. He examined the bite and
declared that unless his leg was amputated immediately the man
would die in half an hour. I told him this was unnecessary; I had
already given the man Tibetan medicine effective for poison. The
doctor turned to the sweeper and said, 'You will die within minutes
unless I operate, but the Tibetan'—indicating me—'thinks otherwise.'
He asked him whose diagnosis he wished to accept. The sweeper had
seen my work and so he replied mine. The doctor then compelled

me to sign a paper releasing him from all responsibility in the case. There were many aspects to my treatment, but after ten days the sweeper could move about and in a month he was completely cured."

Despite the man's recovery, the episode proved to be the start of a serious conflict. Once a week Indian doctors came to inspect the refugees, in the course of which they dropped by Dr. Dhonden's clinic to demand that, as he was not certified in India, he discontinue practice. "During one of their visits I was examining a patient with skin disease," continued Dr. Dhonden. "The physicians saw this woman and together announced that she had chicken pox. They claimed that unless she was isolated an epidemic would sweep over all the refugees. I said bluntly that they were wrong. It was a minor heat disorder and no more. They departed, leaving medicine for her to take. I forbade her to. In a short while they came back and tried to remove her to an isolated house in the forest. I refused to let her go. They asked if I was willing to have an outbreak of chicken pox on my hands and I replied, 'The Tibetans are my own people. How could I ever harm them?' I then demanded that now *they* sign a paper, just as I had been made to, certifying that indeed this woman had chicken pox. They stalled and within a few days the woman was cured." Despite this minor victory, more battles ensued, until, in mid-1960, Yeshi Dhonden was unexpectedly summoned to Dharamsala. Word had reached the government-in-exile that a Mendzekhang-trained physician had escaped. Apprised of his existence, the Dalai Lama had called for Dr. Dhonden personally.

"I arrived in Dharamsala just before sunset," Dr. Dhonden remembered. "The hills were covered with tents. People were living in very poor conditions. They had refused to leave His Holiness and were going wherever he went." Directed to the kitchen area of the Secretariat compound at Mortimer Hall, Yeshi Dhonden sat and waited. He was finishing his tea when the Dalai Lama arrived. "Suddenly I heard His Holiness in the other room. 'Where is the doctor?' he said. I stood up, folding my hands in prayer, praying for his long life. I had a very strong mind of faith. But when he entered the room I began to weep. I had never wept upon meeting someone before. I must have been thinking of Tibet . . ."

The Dalai Lama questioned Dr. Dhonden on his escape and then requested him to treat those camped around Dharamsala. Working out of the Nursery at Conium House, Dr. Dhonden began seeing patients under the observation of Tibetan government officials. Having met with their approval, he was summoned to the Dalai Lama once more, this time in the capacity of examining physician. After curing the Dalai Lama of a skin disorder, he was asked to see Kyabjé Ling Rinpoché, the Dalai Lama's senior tutor and head of the Gelugpa sect, who was bedridden in a hospital in Calcutta suffering from a severe case of pericarditis, an inflammation and swelling around the heart. In little over a year Ling Rinpoché was cured and Dr. Dhonden was officially appointed to be the Dalai Lama's personal physician, a post normally filled by up to four doctors in Tibet. His enthusiasm for his practice now fully recovered, he set about the monumental task of preserving Tibetan medicine in exile.

Only two other doctors had escaped from Tibet, neither of whom could assist Dr. Dhonden in Dharamsala. Alone, he began to train ten students in the rudiments of his science, their progress hampered by an almost total lack of funds. Yeshi Dhonden could do little until, one day in 1963, his many run-ins with Indian doctors yielded an ironically positive result.

Responding to repeated complaints from local physicians that the Tibetan was "stealing" their patients, a senior minister in the Indian Health Department arrived in Dharamsala to investigate. For a week he watched Dr. Dhonden diagnose patients by their pulse and urine, after which he carefully asked each individual his ailment. At one point, five officers from the nearby army cantonment came in to refill prescriptions. "When the minister saw them he exploded in a rage," recalled Dr. Dhonden. " 'We give you the best health care in India and now you've come here to eat shit from a Tibetan!' he yelled." The officers replied that in many cases they had been ill for fifteen years or more. Where Western medicine had failed, Tibetan medicine had succeeded. "Unlike other doctors," they said, "we don't have to tell Dr. Dhonden what's wrong. He tells us." The day before he departed for New Delhi, the minister came to Yeshi Dhonden's office. "You are doing very good work here," he said. "There is only one problem. You don't have enough students. I'm going to give you thirty thousand rupees a year and a twenty-bed hospital." In this manner, the Tibetan Medical Center was formally organized.

Dr. Dhonden assumed the roles of director and pharmacologist as well as chief examining physician. In 1965 he was joined by a second physician, who assisted in teaching the now seven-year curriculum, leading expeditions into the mountains behind Dharamsala to collect herbs and manufacturing 165 principal drugs. With 15 students graduating to join the 150 or so doctors practicing Tibetan medicine outside of Tibet and plans underway for a research wing, a museum and nine outpatient clinics in the settlements, Dr. Dhonden resigned from the Center in 1969. Opening a private practice in

McLeod Ganj, he continued to see the Dalai Lama, taking his pulse each day just after sunrise, until in 1978 another physician was appointed to assist him. Dr. Dhonden was then freed to introduce Tibetan medicine to the West.

"The information required before Tibetan medicines could be approved for use in the United States would take an army of lab technicians years to develop," commented Dr. Gerald Goldstein, speculating on the future of an exchange between Tibetan and Western doctors as Yeshi Dhonden's visit in Virginia drew to an end. "Each ingredient must be individually identified, purified from its crude state and then thoroughly tested. Who is going to pay for it?" "Research today is a cost-benefit situation," concurred Dr. Donald Baker. "How is a drug company going to collect all of these medicines in northern India and still make a profit at it?" "The impetus for the work, though, is clear," added Dr. Goldstein. "Over one third of our pharmacopoeia comes from plants and microorganisms, specifically some of our oldest and most effective cancer drugs. These are just the sort of materials Tibetans have acquired experience with over centuries of use. Personally, I think the drug companies are missing a bet. Some of these medicines are definitely going to be active."

In the East, the bet has not been missed. Whereas Peking destroyed every institution of the old Tibet soon after 1959, it preserved and later expanded Mendzekhang. Now called the Hospital of Tibetan Medicine, Mendzekhang's 127-member staff treats 700 to 800 patients a day. Though the doctors have been forced to curtail their unique knowledge of the mind's relation to the body (considered, as a basic component of Buddhist teachings, anathema), volumes of color photographs cataloguing medicinal plants have been compiled, while many of the most valuable herbs indigenous to the Himalayas have begun to be cultivated on high-altitude farms. Concurrently, Tibetan drugs are in widespread use throughout mainland China though they are referred to as Chinese in origin and not Tibetan.

"Tibetan and Western medicine begin from completely opposite standpoints," said Dr. Dhonden, summing up his view of the two sciences after visiting the United States. "To start with, a Western scientist looks through a microscope to examine the cause of a disease in terms of its molecular particles. Only then does he take into account the particular patient. Tibetan doctors begin with the patient. We consider his disposition in terms of wind, bile and phlegm. And then we approach the disease. The difference, I feel, makes for weakness and strength in both. We lack many of the symptomatic treatments modern physicians possess. On the other hand, it would be useful for Western doctors to understand the Tibetan presentation of the humors, their balance and imbalance in the human body. Without this, their medical system remains incomplete. It cannot establish a clear view of the correct causes and conditions governing all disease. If young Western doctors would come and train with us for a period of years—as well as relating their own system's analysis of disease—then, I feel, a true exchange could occur. So each of us it seems," he concluded, judiciously, "has something of value to learn from the other."

T W E L V E

The Idea of Progress

All progress has resulted from people who took unpopular positions.
Adlai Stevenson

If you are of typical college-student age, or even a little older, one of your chief long-range concerns may be whether or not you will be able to live as materially satisfying a life as your parents have lived. There are some exceptions to this generalization, of course. If you and your parents are immigrants from a less affluent country, or if your family has in your lifetime transcended some of the major barriers of poverty or racism, then you are indeed likely to be better off than your parents were. But many people under thirty feel that they may not be so fortunate.

The essays and stories in this section suggest that the idea of progress, which has stood at the heart of the Western world view for much of the nineteenth and twentieth centuries, is up for reevaluation. As the title of E. B. White's essay, "Progress and Change," suggests, not all historical *change* does in fact constitute *progress*. List for yourself the changes in our society that you have seen in your own lifetime. How many of those changes have actually proven to be sources of real progress? Or, if you think it may be too early to tell, make a similar list for your parents' or grandparents' generation.

You might start with synthetic packaging, at first thought to be a wonderful, time-saving advance, but now an ecological problem. Or you might consider television, which was seen, upon its introduction, as a wonderful transformation of communication. That it certainly is, but there are grave questions about its impact upon the skills and behavior of American young people and its role in the American political process, for example.

What about "progress" in personal behavior? What are you free to do that your parents or grandparents were not free to do? What are the likely social consequences of this "progress"? In the course of this exercise, you will need to define carefully what you mean by the term *progress*.

Turning from progress in daily life to the idea of progress as a governing force in the understanding of history, Francis Fukuyama's "The End of History?" and Samuel P. Huntington's "The Errors of Endism" constitute a dialogue about the path history is likely to travel in the coming century. Fukuyama believes that history, in a metaphorical sense, has come to an "end," and that all of the great

1166

material issues of civilization have essentially resolved themselves. His essay was published at about the same time as the collapse of Communism in Eastern Europe and was hailed as one of the great intellectual touchstones of the second half of this century. More recent conflicts, such as those in the Middle East, however, may prove him wrong. On the other hand, those conflicts may prove to be tangents to the great issues that come to define the future. What is your reaction to Fukuyama's thesis?

You may want to construct an argument for or against the positions espoused by Paul Johnson in his essay, "Experimenting with Half Mankind." Johnson is explicitly arguing against the repression of freedom and democracy in China under the Communist party. His implicit point is that utopian social planning always leads to the repression of human freedom. Do you share that point of view, or do you think differently?

This section concludes with pictures of various alternatives for humanity. The one drawn by Tadeusz Borowski in "This Way for the Gas, Ladies and Gentlemen" may seem too horrible to be possible. Yet it is an accurate account of how one set of human beings treated another set of human beings *in this very century*. We pray that such things may never happen again, but we know, from past experience, that the possibility exists. What measures, if any, can be taken to prevent a recurrence of the Holocaust?

Not all the monsters that could put an end to progress are human ones. In the sixties and seventies, there was a general sense that humanity was on its way to wiping out disease, or at least the mass spread of disease. Then came AIDS. We now know that plagues like the one Barbara Tuchman describes in her essay, " 'This Is the End of the World': The Black Death," can return. It may be that we must abandon the idea of progress altogether and return to the simple things that comfort us, as E. B. White does in "Once More to the Lake." Or it may be that William Faulkner is right when he tells us that ultimately a spirit of human cooperation and steadfastness will "prevail."

E. B. WHITE

Progress and Change

E. B. White (1899–1985) was an American journalist, editor, and
essayist who worked as a staff writer for the *New Yorker* magazine
for sixty years. Among his essay collections are *One Man's Meat*
(1939), from which the following essay is taken, and *Essays of
E. B. White* (1941). His three children's books, *Stuart Little* (1945),
Charlotte's Web (1952), and *The Trumpet of the Swan* (1970) have
earned him enduring praise. He is also known for *Elements of Style*
(1959), the preeminent style manual which he contributed to and
revised, written by William Strunk, Jr.

My friends in the city tell me that the Sixth Avenue El is coming
down, but that's a hard thing for anyone to believe who once lived
in its fleeting and audible shadow. The El was the most distinguished
and outstanding vein on the town's neck, a varicosity tempting to
the modern surgeon. One wonders whether New York can survive
this sort of beauty operation, performed in the name of civic splendor
and rapid transit.

A resident of the city grew accustomed to the heavenly railroad
which swung implausibly in air; cutting off his sun by day, wandering
in and out of his bedchamber by night. The presence of the structure
and the passing of the trains were by all odds the most pervasive of
New York's influences. Here was a sound which, if it ever got in the
conch of your ear, was ineradicable—forever singing, like the sea. It
punctuated the morning with brisk tidings of repetitious adventure,
and it accompanied the night with sad but reassuring sounds of life-
going-on—the sort of threnody which cricket and katydid render for
suburban people sitting on screened porches, the sort of lullaby
which the whippoorwill sends up to the Kentucky farm wife on a
summer evening.

I spent a lot of time, once, doing nothing in the vicinity of Sixth
Avenue. Naturally I know something of the El's fitful charm. It was,
among other things, the sort of railroad you would occasionally ride
just for the hell of it, a higher existence into which you would escape
unconsciously and without destination. Let's say you had just
emerged from the Child's on the west side of Sixth Avenue between
14th and 15th Streets, where you had had a bowl of vegetable soup

and a stack of wheat cakes. The syrup still was a cloying taste on your tongue. You intended to go back to the apartment and iron a paragraph, or wash a sock. But miraculously, at the corner of 14th, there rose suddenly in front of you a flight of stairs all wrapt in celestial light, with treads of shining steel, and risers richly carved with the names of the great, and a canopy overhead where danced the dust in the shafts of golden sunshine. As in a trance, you mounted steadily to the pavilion above, where there was an iron stove and a man's hand visible through a mousehole. And the first thing you knew you were in South Ferry, with another of life's inestimable journeys behind you—and before you the dull, throbbing necessity of getting uptown again.

For a number of years I went to work every morning on the uptown trains of the Sixth Avenue El. I had it soft, because my journey wasn't at the rush hour and I often had the platform of the car to myself. It was a good way to get where you wanted to go, looking down on life at just the right speed, and peeking in people's windows, where the sketchy pantomime of potted plant and half-buttoned undershirt and dusty loft provided a curtain raiser to the day. The railroad was tolerant and allowed its passengers to loll outdoors if they wished; and on mornings when the air was heady that was the place to be—with the sudden whiff of the candy factory telling you that your ride was half over, and the quick eastward glance through 24th Street to check your time with the clock in the Metropolitan Tower, visible for the tenth part of a second.

The El always seemed to me to possess exactly the right degree of substantiality: it seemed reasonably strong and able to carry its load, and competent with that easy slovenly competence of an old drudge; yet it was perceptibly a creature of the clouds, the whole structure vibrating ever so slightly following the final grasping success of the applied brake. The El had giddy spells, too—days when a local train would shake off its patient, plodding manner and soar away in a flight of sheer whimsy, skipping stations in a drunken fashion and scaring the pants off everybody. To go roaring past a scheduled stop, hell bent for 53rd Street and the plunge into space, was an experience which befell every El rider more than once. On this line a man didn't have to be a locomotophobe to suffer from visions of a motorman's lifeless form slumped over an open throttle. And if the suspense got too great and you walked nervously to the front of the train the little window in the booth gave only the most tantalizing view of the driver—three inert fingers of a gloved hand, or a *Daily News* wedged in some vital cranny.

One thing I always admired about the El was the way it tormented its inexperienced customers. Veterans like myself, approaching a station stop, knew to a fraction of an inch how close it was advisable to stand to the little iron gates on the open type cars. But visitors to town had no such information. When the train halted and the guard, pulling his two levers, allowed the gates to swing in and take the unwary full in the stomach, there was always a dim pleasure in it for the rest of us. Life has little enough in the way of reward; these small moments of superiority are not to be despised.

The El turned the Avenue into an arcade. That, in a way, was its chief contribution. It made Sixth Avenue as distinct from Fifth as Fifth is from Jones Street. Its pillars, straddling the car tracks in the long channel of the night, provided the late cruising taxicab with the supreme challenge, and afforded the homing pedestrian, his wine too much with him, forest sanctuary and the friendly accommodation of a tree.

Of course I have read about the great days of the El, when it was the railroad of the élite and when financial giants rode elegantly home from Wall Street in its nicely appointed coaches. But I'm just as glad I didn't meet the El until after it had lost its money. Its lazy crescendos, breaking into one's dreams, will always stick in the mind—and the soiled hands of the guards on the bellcords, and the brusque, husky-throated bells that had long ago lost their voices, cuing each other along the whole length of the train. Yes, at this distance, it's hard to realize that the Sixth Avenue El is just a problem in demolition. I can't for the life of me imagine what New York will have to offer in its place. It will have to be something a good deal racier, a good deal more open and aboveboard, than a new subway line.

I suppose a man can't ask railroads to stand still. For twenty or thirty years the railroads of America stood about as still as was consistent with swift transportation. The gas mantles were removed and electric lights installed, but outside of that the cars remained pretty much the same. It's only in the past couple of years that the railroads, fretting over the competition from busses and planes, have set about transforming their interiors into cocktail lounges, ballrooms, and modern apartments.

In my isolated position here in the country, I have plenty of time to study Pullman trends—which are readily accessible in fullpage color ads in the popular magazines. I note that the Pullman Company, although emphasizing the high safety factor implicit in Pullman travel, is advertising a new type of accommodation called, somewhat ominously, "S.O.S." This is the Single Occupancy Section. It is for the dollar-wise and the travel-wise, the ads point out. From the illustration, the single occupancy section appears to have a dead body in it, hooded in a sheet, bound and gagged. There is also a live occupant—a girl in a pink dressing gown, apparently in the best of spirits. More careful examination of the photograph reveals that the dead body is nothing more nor less than the bed itself, which has reared up on its hind end and been lashed to the bulkhead, while the occupant (who is single, of course) stands erect and goes through the motions of dressing in comfort.

I feel that the Pullman Company, in introducing the note of *comfort* into its adventurous calling, is perhaps slipping outside the particular field in which it has made such an enviable reputation. This being able to stand erect in an ordinary single berth and dress in something like ease—isn't it likely to destroy the special flavor of Pullman travel? I don't take a night journey on a railroad for the sake of duplicating the experiences and conveniences of my own home: when I travel I like to get into some new kind of difficulty, not just the same old trouble I put up with around the house.

Travelers, I will admit, differ temperamentally, differ in their wants and needs; but for me the Pullman Company will never improve on its classic design of upper and lower berth. In my eyes it is a perfect thing, perfect in conception and execution, this small green hole in the dark moving night, this soft warren in a hard world. In it I have always found the peace of spirit which accompanies grotesque bodily situations, peace and a wonderful sense of participation in cosmic rhythms and designs. I have experienced these even on cold nights when I all but died from exposure, under blankets of virgin gossamer.

In a Pullman berth, a man can truly be alone with himself. (The nearest approach to this condition is to be found in a hotel bedroom, but a hotel room can be mighty depressing sometimes, it stands so still.) Now if a modern Pullman proposes to provide headroom for everyone it will have to answer for whatever modification this may cause in human character. The old act of drawing one's pants on and off while in a horizontal position did much to keep Man in a mood of decent humility. It gave him a picture of himself at a moment of wild comic contortion. To tuck in the tails of a shirt while supine demanded a certain persistence, a certain virtuosity, wholly healthful and character-building.

The new single occupancy section, besides changing all this and permitting a man to stand erect as though he had no ape in his family background, has another rather alarming feature. The bed not only is capable of being cocked up by the occupant, to resemble a cadaver, but it can be hoisted by a separate control from the aisle by the dark, notional hand of the porter as he glides Puckishly through the car. It does not sound conducive to calm.

In resenting progress and change, a man lays himself open to censure. I suppose the explanation of anyone's defending anything as rudimentary and cramped as a Pullman berth is that such things are associated with an earlier period in one's life and that this period in retrospect seems a happy one. People who favor progress and improvements are apt to be people who have had a tough enough time without any extra inconvenience. Reactionaries who pout at innovations are apt to be well-heeled sentimentalists who had the breaks. Yet for all that, there is always a subtle danger in life's refinements, a dim degeneracy in progress. I have just been refining the room in which I sit, yet I sometimes doubt that a writer should refine or improve his workroom by so much as a dictionary: one thing leads to another and the first thing you know he has a stuffed chair and is fast asleep in it. Half a man's life is devoted to what he calls improvements, yet the original had some quality which is lost in the process. There was a fine natural spring of water on this place when I bought it. Our drinking water had to be lugged in a pail, from a wet glade of alder and tamarack. I visited the spring often in those first years and had friends there—a frog, a woodcock, and an eel which had churned its way all the way up through the pasture creek to enjoy the luxury of pure water. In the normal course of development, the spring was rocked up, fitted with a concrete curb, a copper pipe, and an electric pump. I have visited it only once or twice since. This year my only gesture was the purely perfunctory one of sending a sample to the state bureau of health for analysis. I felt cheap, as though I were smelling an old friend's breath.

Another phase of life here which has lost something through refinement is the game of croquet. We used to have an old croquet set whose wooden balls, having been chewed by dogs, were no rounder than eggs. Paint had faded, wickets were askew. The course had been laid out haphazardly and eagerly by a child, and we all used to go out there on summer nights and play goodnaturedly, with the dogs romping on the lawn in the beautiful light, and the mosquitoes sniping at us, and everyone in good spirits, racing after balls and making split shots for the sheer love of battle. Last spring we decided the croquet set was beyond use, and invested in a rather fancy new one with hoops set in small wooden sockets, and mallets with rubber faces. The course is now exactly seventy-two feet long and we lined the wickets up with a string; but the little boy is less fond of it now, for we make him keep still while we are shooting. A dog isn't even allowed to cast his shadow across the line of play. There are frequent quarrels of a minor nature, and it seems to me we return from the field of honor tense and out of sorts.

FRANCIS FUKUYAMA

The End of History?

Francis Fukuyama (1952–   ) is a former United States State De- partment Planner who caused a furor with "Have We Reached the End of History?" (1989). In this article Fukuyama argued that Western democracy has become the final, and best, form of gov- ernment in history and, given the collapse of communism, is not likely to be overtaken by any other form of social organization. His other works include *U.S.–Soviet Interactions in the Third World* (1985), *The Soviet Union and the Third World* (1987) (with Andrzej Korbonski), and *Gorbachev and the New Soviet Agenda in the Third World* (1989). The following selection first appeared in *The National Interest* and formed the basis for *The End of History and the Last Man* (1992).

In watching the flow of events over the past decade or so, it is hard to avoid the feeling that something very fundamental has happened in world history. The past year has seen a flood of articles commem- orating the end of the Cold War, and the fact that "peace" seems to be breaking out in many regions of the world. Most of these analyses lack any larger conceptual framework for distinguishing between what is essential and what is contingent or accidental in world history, and are predictably superficial. If Mr. Gorbachev were ousted from the Kremlin or a new Ayatollah proclaimed the millennium from a desolate Middle Eastern capital, these same commentators would scramble to announce the rebirth of a new era of conflict.

And yet, all of these people sense dimly that there is some larger process at work, a process that gives coherence and order to the daily headlines. The twentieth century saw the developed world descend into a paroxysm of ideological violence, as liberalism contended first with the remnants of absolutism, then bolshevism and fascism, and finally an updated Marxism that threatened to lead to the ultimate apocalypse of nuclear war. But the century that began full of self-confidence in the ultimate triumph of Western liberal democracy seems at its close to be returning full circle to where it started: not to an "end of ideology" or a convergence between capitalism and socialism, as earlier predicted, but to an unabashed victory of economic and political liberalism.

The triumph of the West, of the Western *idea*, is evident first of all in the total exhaustion of viable systematic alternatives to Western liberalism. In the past decade, there have been unmistakable changes in the intellectual climate of the world's two largest communist countries, and the beginnings of significant reform movements in both. But this phenomenon extends beyond high politics and it can be seen also in the ineluctable spread of consumerist Western culture in such diverse contexts as the peasant's markets and color television sets now omnipresent throughout China, the cooperative restaurants and clothing stores opened in the past year in Moscow, the Beethoven piped into Japanese department stores, and the rock music enjoyed alike in Prague, Rangoon, and Tehran.

What we may be witnessing is not just the end of the Cold War, or the passing of a particular period of postwar history, but the end of history as such; that is, the end point of mankind's ideological evolution and the universalization of Western liberal democracy as the final form of human government. This is not to say that there will no longer be events to fill the pages of *Foreign Affairs*'s yearly summaries of international relations, for the victory of liberalism has occurred primarily in the realm of ideas or consciousness and is as yet incomplete in the real or material world. But there are powerful reasons for believing that it is the ideal that will govern the material world *in the long run*. To understand how this is so, we must first consider some theoretical issues concerning the nature of historical change.

The notion of the end of history is not an original one. Its best known propagator was Karl Marx, who believed that the direction of historical development was a purposeful one determined by the interplay of material forces, and would come to an end only with the achieve-

ment of a communist utopia that would finally resolve all prior contradictions. But the concept of history as a dialectical process with a beginning, a middle, and an end was borrowed by Marx from his great German predecessor, Georg Wilhelm Friedrich Hegel.[1]

For better or worse, much of Hegel's historicism has become part of our contemporary intellectual baggage. The notion that mankind has progressed through a series of primitive stages of consciousness on his path to the present, and that these stages corresponded to concrete forms of social organization, such as tribal, slave-owning, theocratic, and finally democratic-egalitarian societies, has become inseparable from the modern understanding of man. Hegel was the first philosopher to speak the language of modern social science, insofar as man for him was the product of his concrete historical and social environment and not, as earlier natural right theorists would have it, a collection of more or less fixed "natural" attributes. The mastery and transformation of man's natural environment through the application of science and technology was originally not a Marxist concept, but a Hegelian one. Unlike later historicists whose historical relativism degenerated into relativism *tout court,* however, Hegel believed that history culminated in an absolute moment—a moment in which a final, rational form of society and state became victorious.

It is Hegel's misfortune to be known now primarily as Marx's precursor, and it is our misfortune that few of us are familiar with Hegel's work from direct study, but only as it has been filtered through the distorting lens of Marxism.

Max Weber[2] begins his famous book, *The Protestant Ethic and the Spirit of Capitalism,* by noting the different economic performance of Protestant and Catholic communities throughout Europe and America, summed up in the proverb that Protestants eat well while Catholics sleep well. Weber notes that according to any economic theory that posited man as a rational profit-maximizer, raising the piece-work rate should increase labor productivity. But in fact, in many traditional peasant communities, raising the piece-work rate actually

---

[1] *Karl Marx* (1818–1883) was a German social philosopher and founder of democratic socialism and revolutionary communism. He wrote *Das Kapital* (1867–94) and, with Friedrich Engels, the *Communist Manifesto* (1848). *Georg Hegel* (1770–1831) was a German philosopher known for the Hegelian dialectic, his theory of a process of change and progress that unfolds throughout history. (ED.)

[2] Max Weber (1864–1920) was a German sociologist and economist who studied the impact of religious and ideological beliefs, rather than economic factors, on the development of societies. (ED.)

had the opposite effect of *lowering* labor productivity: at the higher rate, a peasant accustomed to earning two and one-half marks per day found he could earn the same amount by working less, and did so because he valued leisure more than income. The choices of leisure over income, or of the militaristic life of the Spartan hoplite over the wealth of the Athenian trader, or even the ascetic life of the early capitalist entrepreneur over that of a traditional leisured aristocrat, cannot possibly be explained by the impersonal working of material forces, but come preeminently out of the sphere of consciousness— what we have labeled here broadly as ideology. And indeed, a central theme of Weber's work was to prove that, contrary to Marx, the material mode of production, far from being the "base," was itself a "superstructure" with roots in religion and culture, and that to understand the emergence of modern capitalism and the profit motive one had to study their antecedents in the realm of the spirit.

As we look around the contemporary world, the poverty of materialist theories of economic development is all too apparent. The *Wall Street Journal* school of deterministic materialism habitually points to the stunning economic success of Asia in the past few decades as evidence of the viability of free market economics, with the implication that all societies would see similar development were they simply to allow their populations to pursue their material self-interest freely. Surely free markets and stable political systems are a necessary precondition to capitalist economic growth. But just as surely the cultural heritage of those Far Eastern societies, the ethic of work and saving and family, a religious heritage that does not, like Islam, place restrictions on certain forms of economic behavior, and other deeply ingrained moral qualities, are equally important in explaining their economic performance.[3] And yet the intellectual weight of materialism is such that not a single respectable contemporary theory of economic development addresses consciousness and culture seriously as the matrix within which economic behavior is formed.

Failure to understand that the roots of economic behavior lie in the realm of consciousness and culture leads to the common mistake of

---

[3] One need look no further than the recent performance of Vietnamese immigrants in the U.S. school system when compared to their black or Hispanic classmates to realize that culture and consciousness are absolutely crucial to explain not only economic behavior but virtually every other important aspect of life as well.

attributing material causes to phenomena that are essentially ideal in nature. For example, it is commonplace in the West to interpret the reform movements first in China and most recently in the Soviet Union as the victory of the material over the ideal—that is, a recognition that ideological incentives could not replace material ones in stimulating a highly productive modern economy, and that if one wanted to prosper one had to appeal to baser forms of self-interest. But the deep defects of socialist economies were evident thirty or forty years ago to anyone who chose to look. Why was it that these countries moved away from central planning only in the 1980s? The answer must be found in the consciousness of the elites and leaders ruling them, who decided to opt for the "Protestant" life of wealth and risk over the "Catholic" path of poverty and security.[4] That change was in no way made inevitable by the material conditions in which either country found itself on the eve of the reform, but instead came about as the result of the victory of one idea over another.[5]

Have we in fact reached the end of history? Are there, in other words, any fundamental "contradictions" in human life that cannot be resolved in the context of modern liberalism, that would be resolvable by an alternative political-economic structure? If we accept the idealist premises laid out above, we must seek an answer to this question in the realm of ideology and consciousness. Our task is not to answer exhaustively the challenges to liberalism promoted by every crackpot messiah around the world, but only those that are embodied in important social or political forces and movements, and which are therefore part of world history. For our purposes, it matters very little what strange thoughts occur to people in Albania or Burkina Faso, for we are interested in what one could in some sense call the common ideological heritage of mankind.

In the past century, there have been two major challenges to

---

[4] I understand that a full explanation of the origins of the reform movements in China and Russia is a good deal more complicated than this simple formula would suggest. The Soviet reform, for example, was motivated in good measure by Moscow's sense of *insecurity* in the technological-military realm. Nonetheless, neither country on the eve of its reforms was in such a state of *material* crisis that one could have predicted the surprising reform paths ultimately taken.

[5] It is still not clear whether the Soviet peoples are as "Protestant" as Gorbachev and will follow him down that path.

liberalism, those of fascism and of communism. The former[6] saw the
political weakness, materialism, anomie, and lack of community of
the West as fundamental contradictions in liberal societies that could
only be resolved by a strong state that forged a new "people" on the
basis of national exclusiveness. Fascism was destroyed as a living
ideology by World War II. This was a defeat, of course, on a very
material level, but it amounted to a defeat of the idea as well. What
destroyed fascism as an idea was not universal moral revulsion against
it, since plenty of people were willing to endorse the idea as long as
it seemed the wave of the future, but its lack of success. After the
war, it seemed to most people that German Fascism as well as its
other European and Asian variants were bound to self-destruct. There
was no material reason why new fascist movements could not have
sprung up again after the war in other locales, but for the fact that
expansionist ultranationalism, with its promise of unending conflict
leading to disastrous military defeat, had completely lost its appeal.
The ruins of the Reich chancellory as well as the atomic bombs
dropped on Hiroshima and Nagasaki killed this ideology on the level
of consciousness as well as materially, and all of the proto-fascist
movements spawned by the German and Japanese examples like the
Peronist movement in Argentina or Subhas Chandra Bose's Indian
National Army withered after the war.

The ideological challenge mounted by the other great alternative
to liberalism, communism, was far more serious. Marx, speaking
Hegel's language, asserted that liberal society contained a fundamental contradiction that could not be resolved within its context, that
between capital and labor, and this contradiction has constituted the
chief accusation against liberalism ever since. But surely, the class
issue has actually been successfully resolved in the West; the egalitarianism of modern America represents the essential achievement of
the classless society envisioned by Marx. This is not to say that there
are not rich people and poor people in the United States, or that the

---

[6] I am not using the term "fascism" here in its most precise sense, fully aware of the
frequent misuse of this term to denounce anyone to the right of the user. "Fascism"
here denotes any organized ultra-nationalist movement with universalistic pretensions—not universalistic with regard to its nationalism, of course, since the latter is
exclusive by definition, but with regard to the movement's belief in its right to rule
other people. Hence Imperial Japan would qualify as fascist while former strongman
Stoessner's Paraguay or Pinochet's Chile would not. Obviously fascist ideologies cannot
be universalistic in the sense of Marxism or liberalism, but the structure of the doctrine
can be transferred from country to country.

gap between them has not grown in recent years. But the root causes of economic inequality do not have to do with the underlying legal and social structure of our society, which remains fundamentally egalitarian and moderately redistributionist, so much as with the cultural and social characteristics of the groups that make it up, which are in turn the historical legacy of premodern conditions. Thus black poverty in the United States is not the inherent product of liberalism, but is rather the "legacy of slavery and racism" which persisted long after the formal abolition of slavery.

The first Asian alternative to liberalism to be decisively defeated was the fascist one represented by Imperial Japan. Japanese fascism (like its German version) was defeated by the force of American arms in the Pacific war, and liberal democracy was imposed on Japan by a victorious United States. Western capitalism and political liberalism when transplanted to Japan were adapted and transformed by the Japanese in such a way as to be scarcely recognizable.[7] Many Americans are now aware that Japanese industrial organization is very different from that prevailing in the United States or Europe, and it is questionable what relationship the factional maneuvering that takes place with the governing Liberal Democratic Party bears to democracy. Nonetheless, the very fact that the essential elements of economic and political liberalism have been so successfully grafted onto uniquely Japanese traditions and institutions guarantees their survival in the long run. More important is the contribution that Japan has made in turn to world history by following in the footsteps of the United States to create a truly universal consumer culture that has become both a symbol and an underpinning of the universal homogenous state. V. S. Naipaul travelling in Khomeini's Iran shortly after the revolution noted the omnipresent signs advertising the products of Sony, Hitachi, and JVC, whose appeal remained virtually irresistible and gave the lie to the regime's pretensions of restoring a state based on the rule of the *Shariah*. Desire for access to the consumer culture, created in large measure by Japan, has played a crucial role in fostering the spread of economic liberalism throughout Asia, and hence in promoting political liberalism as well.

---

[7] I use the example of Japan with some caution, since Kojève late in his life came to conclude that Japan, with its culture based on purely formal arts, proved that the universal homogenous state was not victorious and that history had perhaps not ended. See the long note at the end of the second edition of *Introduction à la Lecture de Hegel*, 462–3.

If we admit for the moment that the fascist and communist challenges to liberalism are dead, are there any other ideological competitors left? Or put another way, are there contradictions in liberal society beyond that of class that are not resolvable? Two possibilities suggest themselves, those of religion and nationalism.

The rise of religious fundamentalism in recent years within the Christian, Jewish, and Muslim traditions has been widely noted. One is inclined to say that the revival of religion in some way attests to a broad unhappiness with the impersonality and spiritual vacuity of liberal consumerist societies. Yet while the emptiness at the core of liberalism is most certainly a defect in the ideology—indeed, a flaw that one does not need the perspective of religion to recognize[8]—it is not at all clear that it is remediable through politics. Modern liberalism itself was historically a consequence of the weakness of religiously-based societies which, failing to agree on the nature of the good life, could not provide even the minimal preconditions of peace and stability. In the contemporary world only Islam has offered a theocratic state as a political alternative to both liberalism and communism. But the doctrine has little appeal for non-Muslims, and it is hard to believe that the movement will take on any universal significance. Other less organized religious impulses have been successfully satisfied within the sphere of personal life that is permitted in liberal societies.

The other major "contradiction" potentially unresolvable by liberalism is the one posed by nationalism and other forms of racial and ethnic consciousness. It is certainly true that a very large degree of conflict since the Battle of Jena has had its roots in nationalism. Two cataclysmic world wars in this century have been spawned by the nationalism of the developed world in various guises, and if those passions have been muted to a certain extent in postwar Europe, they are still extremely powerful in the Third World. Nationalism has been a threat to liberalism historically in Germany, and continues to be one in isolated parts of "post-historical" Europe like Northern Ireland.

But it is not clear that nationalism represents an irreconcilable contradiction in the heart of liberalism. In the first place, nationalism

[8] I am thinking particularly of Rousseau and the Western philosophical tradition that flows from him that was highly critical of Lockean or Hobbesian liberalism, though one could criticize liberalism from the standpoint of classical political philosophy as well.

is not one single phenomenon but several, ranging from mild cultural nostalgia to the highly organized and elaborately articulated doctrine of National Socialism.[9] Only systematic nationalisms of the latter sort can qualify as a formal ideology on the level of liberalism or communism. The vast majority of the world's nationalist movements do not have a political program beyond the negative desire of independence *from* some other group or people, and do not offer anything like a comprehensive agenda for socio-economic organization. As such, they are compatible with doctrines and ideologies that do offer such agendas. While they may constitute a source of conflict for liberal societies, this conflict does not arise from liberalism itself so much as from the fact that the liberalism in question is incomplete. Certainly a great deal of the world's ethnic and nationalist tension can be explained in terms of peoples who are forced to live in unrepresentative political systems that they have not chosen.

While it is impossible to rule out the sudden appearance of new ideologies or previously unrecognized contradictions in liberal societies, then, the present world seems to confirm that the fundamental principles of socio-political organization have not advanced terribly far since 1806. Many of the wars and revolutions fought since that time have been undertaken in the name of ideologies which claimed to be more advanced than liberalism, but whose pretensions were ultimately unmasked by history. In the meantime, they have helped to spread the universal homogenous state to the point where it could have a significant effect on the overall character of international relations.

The passing of Marxism-Leninism first from China and then from the Soviet Union will mean its death as a living ideology of world historical significance. For while there may be some isolated true believers left in places like Managua, Pyongyang, or Cambridge, Massachusetts, the fact that there is not a single large state in which it is a going concern undermines completely its pretensions to being in the vanguard of human history. And the death of this ideology means the growing "Common Marketization"[10] of international re-

---

[9] the policies of the German Nazi party of Adolf Hitler which advocated anti-Semitism, anti-Communism, the supremacy of the Aryan race, and the annihilation of Germany's enemies (ED.)

[10] The Common Market is an economic organization designed to economically unify the European nations which are members by eliminating trade barriers and developing common price levels. (ED.)

lations, and the diminution of the likelihood of large-scale conflict between states.

This does not by any means imply the end of international conflict *per se*. For the world at that point would be divided between a part that was historical and a part that was post-historical. Conflict between states still in history, and between those states and those at the end of history, would still be possible. There would still be a high and perhaps rising level of ethnic and nationalist violence, since those are impulses incompletely played out, even in parts of the post-historical world. Palestinians and Kurds, Sikhs and Tamils, Irish Catholics and Walloons, Armenians and Azeris, will continue to have their unresolved grievances. This implies that terrorism and wars of national liberation will continue to be an important item on the international agenda. But large-scale conflict must involve large states still caught in the grip of history, and they are what appear to be passing from the scene.

The end of history will be a very sad time. The struggle for recognition, the willingness to risk one's life for a purely abstract goal, the worldwide ideological struggle that called forth daring, courage, imagination, and idealism, will be replaced by economic calculation, the endless solving of technical problems, environmental concerns, and the satisfaction of sophisticated consumer demands. In the post-historical period there will be neither art nor philosophy, just the perpetual caretaking of the museum of human history. I can feel in myself, and see in others around me, a powerful nostalgia for the time when history existed. Such nostalgia, in fact, will continue to fuel competition and conflict even in the post-historical world for some time to come. Even though I recognize its inevitability, I have the most ambivalent feelings for the civilization that has been created in Europe since 1945, with its north Atlantic and Asian offshoots. Perhaps this very prospect of centuries of boredom at the end of history will serve to get history started once again.

SAMUEL P. HUNTINGTON

The Errors of Endism

Samuel P. Huntington (1927–   ) is a professor of political science
at Harvard and the director of Harvard University's Center of International Affairs. He is the author of *Political Order in Changing
Societies* (1968) and *American Politics: The Promise of Disharmony*
(1981), and co-editor of *Reorganizing America's Defense* (1985).
The following selection first appeared in *The National Interest.*

For a second year serious discussion of international affairs has been
dominated by a major theoretical and academic issue. In 1988 the
issue was American decline. The theory of declinism, articulated by
many thinkers, but most notably by Paul Kennedy, became the focus
of extended and intense debate. Was the United States following in
the path of Great Britain and declining as a great power? To what
extent was its economic base being undermined by spending too
much on defense and/or too much on consumption?

The theory of declinism has been displaced by the theory of
endism. Its central element is that bad things are coming to an end.[1]
Endism manifests itself in at least three ways. At its most specific
level, endism hails the end of the Cold War. In the spring of 1989
the *New York Times* and the International Institute for Strategic
Studies, George Kennan and George Bush, all set forth this proposition in one form or another. The end of the Cold War became the
Foreign Policy Establishment's Established Truth.

At a second level, endism manifested itself in the more academic
and more general proposition that wars among nation states, or at
least among some types of nation states, were coming to an end.
Many scholars pointed to the historical absence of wars between
democratic countries and saw the multiplication of democratic regimes since 1974 as evidence that the probability of war was declining. In a related but somewhat different version of this proposition,

---

[1] Some have raised the question as to what extent endist writers are really serious in
their arguments. The time and intellectual effort they have devoted to elaborating
those arguments suggest that they are, and I will assume this to be the case. The
arguments also deserve to be taken seriously because of their widespread popularity.

Michael Doyle argued that wars were impossible between liberal states. In a still more sweeping formulation, John Mueller contended that the advance of civilization was making war obsolescent and that it would disappear the same way that slavery and duelling had disappeared in advanced societies.[2] Wars still might occur among backward Third World countries, but among developed countries, communist or capitalist, war was unthinkable.

The third and most extreme formulation of endism was advanced by Francis Fukuyama in a brilliant essay called "The End of History?" in the Summer issue of this journal. Fukuyama celebrates not just the end of the Cold War or the end of wars among developed nation states, but instead "the end of history as such." This results from the "unabashed victory of economic and political liberalism" and the "exhaustion of viable systematic alternatives." Like Mueller, Fukuyama concedes that wars may occur among Third World states still caught up in the historical process. But for the developed countries, the Soviet Union, and China, history is at an end.

Endism—the intellectual fad of 1989—contrasts rather dramatically with declinism—the intellectual fad of 1988. Declinism is conditionally pessimistic. It is rooted in the study of history and draws on the parallels between the United States in the late twentieth century, Britain in the late nineteenth century, and France, Spain, and other powers in earlier centuries. Its proponents and its critics debate the relevance of these parallels and argue over detailed, historical data concerning economic growth, productivity, defense spending, savings, and investment.[3] Endism, on the other hand, is oriented to the future rather than the past and is unabashedly optimistic. In its most developed form, as with Fukuyama, it is rooted

---

[2] Michael W. Doyle, "Kant, Liberal Legacies, and Foreign Affairs," *Philosophy and Public Affairs,* vol. 12 (Summer, Fall 1983), pp. 205–235, 323–353, and "Liberalism and World Politics," *American Political Science Review,* vol. 80 (December 1986), pp. 1151–1169; John Mueller, *Retreat from Doomsday: The Obsolescence of Major War* (New York: Basic Books, 1989). Also see Dean V. Babst, "A Force for Peace," *Industrial Research,* vol. 14 (April 1972), pp. 55–58; R. J. Rummel, "Libertarianism and International Violence," *Journal of Conflict Resolution,* vol. 27 (March 1983), pp. 27–71; Ze'ev Maoz and Nasrin Abdolali, "Regime Types and International Conflict, 1816–1976," *Journal of Conflict Resolution,* vol. 33 (March 1989), pp. 3–35; Bruce Russett, "The Politics of an Alternative Security System: Toward a More Democratic and Therefore More Peaceful World," in Burns Weston, ed., *Alternatives to Nuclear Deterrence* (Boulder: Westview Press, forthcoming 1989).

[3] For a careful analysis of the evidence and arguments on this issue, see Joseph S. Nye, Jr.'s forthcoming book, *American Power: Past and Future* (New York: Basic Books).

in philosophical speculation rather than historical analysis. It is based not so much on evidence from history as on assumptions about history. In its extreme form, declinism is historically deterministic: nations naturally, and perhaps inevitably, evolve through phases of rise, expansion, and decline. They are caught in the inexorable grip of history. In the extreme form of endism, in contrast, nations escape from history.

The message of declinism for Americans is "We're losing"; the message of endism is "We've won!" Despite or perhaps even because of its deterministic strand, declinism performs a useful historical function. It provides a warning and a goad to action in order to head off and reverse the decline that it says is taking place. It serves that purpose now as it did in its earlier manifestations in the 1950s, 1960s, and 1970s. Endism, in contrast, provides not a warning of danger but an illusion of well-being. It invites not corrective action but relaxed complacency. The consequences of its thesis being in error, hence, are far more dangerous and subversive than those that would result if the declinist thesis should be wrong.

THE END OF THE COLD WAR

"The Cold War is over" was the prevailing cry in the spring of 1989. What does this mean? It typically referred to two related developments: the changes usually referred to as glasnost and perestroika in the Soviet Union and the improvements that were occurring in Soviet-American relations. "The cold war," as the *New York Times* put it, "of poisonous Soviet-American feelings, of domestic political hysteria, of events enlarged and distorted by East-West confrontation, of almost perpetual diplomatic deadlock is over."[4] Several questions can be raised about this proposition.

First, is it really true? The easing in Soviet-American relations in the late 1950s was followed by the Berlin and Cuban crises; detente in the early 1970s was followed by Angola and Afghanistan. How do we know that the current relaxation is not simply another swing of the cycle? One answer is that the changes occurring within the Soviet Union are far more fundamental than those that have occurred in the past, and this is certainly the case. The opening up of political debate, limited but real competition in elections, the formation of political groups outside the Party, the virtual abandonment, indeed,

---

[4] "The Cold War Is Over," *New York Times*, April 2, 1989, p. E30.

of the idea of a monolithic party, the assertion of power by the Supreme Soviet—all these will, if continued, lead to a drastically different Soviet political system. The price of attempting to reverse them increases daily, but it would be rash to conclude that they are as yet irreversible, and the costs of reversing them could decline in the future.

On the international level, the Soviets have cooperated in resolving regional conflicts in the Persian Gulf, southern Africa, and Indochina. They have promised to reduce their overall military forces and their deployments in Eastern Europe. As yet, however, no perceptible changes have taken place in Soviet force structure, Soviet deployments, or Soviet output of military equipment. Even if these do occur, the competition between the United States and the Soviet Union for influence and power in world affairs will still go on. It has been continuing as President Bush and President Gorbachev attempt to woo Eastern and Western European publics. Europe, it is well to remember, is where the Cold War started. It is the overwhelmingly preeminent stake in the Cold War, and Gorbachev's public relations can be as much a threat to American interests in Europe as were Brezhnev's tanks (which, for the moment at any rate, Gorbachev also has).

Let us, however, concede that in some meaningful and not transitory sense the Cold War is over and that a real change has occurred in Soviet-American relations. How do the proponents of this thesis see the post-Cold War world? The "we-they world" that has existed, the editors of the New York Times assure us, is giving way "to the more traditional struggles of great powers." In a similar vein, George Kennan alleges that the Soviet Union "should now be regarded essentially as another great power, like other great powers." Its interests may differ from ours but these differences can be "adjusted by the normal means of compromise and accommodation."[5]

Russia was, however, just "another great power" for several centuries before it became a communist state. As a great power, Russia frequently deployed its armies into Europe and repeatedly crushed popular uprisings in central Europe. Soviet troops bloodily suppressed the Hungarian Revolution in 1956 and trampled the embryonic Czech democracy in 1968. Russian troops bloodily suppressed the Hungarian revolution of 1848–49 and violently put down upris-

---

[5] "Just Another Great Power," New York Times, April 9, 1989, p. E25.

ings in Poland in 1831 and again in 1863–64. Soviet forces occupied Berlin in 1945; Russian troops occupied and burnt Berlin in 1760. In pursuit of Russia's interests as a great power, Russian troops appeared many places where as yet Soviet troops have not. In 1799 Russian troops occupied Milan and Turin and fought a battle on the outskirts of Zurich. The same year, they occupied the Ionian islands off Greece and stayed there until 1807. These excursions preceded Napoleon's invasion of Russia. As a great power, Russia regularly participated in the partitions of Poland. In 1914 Nicholas II directly ruled more of Europe (including most of Poland) than Gorbachev does today.

The past record of Russia as a "normal" great power, therefore, is not reassuring for either the liberty of Eastern Europe or the security of Western Europe. Some suggest that the liberalizing and democratizing trends in the Soviet Union will prevent that country from bludgeoning other countries in the manner of the tsars. One cannot assume, Fukuyama argues, that "the evolution of human consciousness has stood still" and that "the Soviets will return to foreign policy views a century out of date in the rest of Europe." Fukuyama is right: one cannot assume that the Soviets will revert to the bad old ways of the past. One also cannot assume that they will not. Gorbachev may be able to discard communism but he cannot discard geography and the geopolitical imperatives that have shaped Russian and Soviet behavior for centuries. And, as any Latin American will quickly point out, even a truly democratic superpower is capable of intervening militarily in the affairs of its smaller neighbors.

The era of the Cold War, John Lewis Gaddis reminds us, has also been the era of the Long Peace, the longest period in history without hot war between major powers. Does the end of the Cold War mean the end of the Long Peace? Two central elements of both have been bipolarity and nuclear weapons: they have in considerable measure defined both the Soviet-American rivalry and its limits. The end of the Cold War will mean a loosening of bipolarity even if it does not mean, as some declinists predict, a world of five or more roughly equal major powers. The delegitimation of nuclear weapons and the increasing constraints on their deployment and potential use would increase the probability of conventional war.

Active American involvement in world affairs has been substantially limited to two world wars and one prolonged and ideologically-driven cold war. In the absence of the Kaiser, Hitler, Stalin, and Brezhnev, the American inclination may well be to relax and to

assume that peace, goodwill, and international cooperation will prevail: that if the Cold War is over, American relations with the Soviet
Union will be similar to its relations with Canada, France, or Japan.
Americans tend to see competition and conflict as normal and even
desirable features of their domestic economy and politics and yet
perversely assume them to be abnormal and undesirable in relations
among states. In fact, however, the history of the relations among
great powers, when it has not been the history of hot wars, has
usually been the history of cold wars.

The end of the Cold War does not mean the end of political,
ideological, diplomatic, economic, technological, or even military
rivalry among nations. It does not mean the end of the struggle for
power and influence. It very probably does mean increased instability,
unpredictability, and violence in international affairs. It could mean
the end of the Long Peace.

In his book, *Retreat from Doomsday,* John Mueller argues for the
growing obsolescence of war on more general grounds. He sees the
Long Peace since 1945 not as the result of bipolarity or nuclear
weapons but rather as the result of a learning experience that wars
do not pay and that there are few conflicts of interest among countries
where it would be reasonable for either side to resort to war to
achieve its goals. World War II was an aberration from the twentieth-
century trend away from war due largely to the idiosyncratic and
irrational personality of Hitler. As countries become more developed
and civilized, they will become more peaceful. Denmark is the future
model for individual countries, U.S.-Canadian relations the future
model for relations between countries.

Mueller makes much of the argument that war will become "obsolete, subrationally unthinkable," and unacceptable in civilized society in the way slavery and duelling have become. Why, however,
are those social practices the appropriate parallels to war? Why not
murder? Murder has been unacceptable in civilized societies for
millennia, and yet it seems unlikely that the murder rate in twentieth-
century New York is less than it was in fifth-century Athens. While
major wars between developed countries have not occurred since
World War II, interstate and intrastate violence has been widespread
with the casualties numbering in the tens of millions.

Mueller himself substantially qualifies his case. He agrees that
wars will continue among less developed countries. He also concedes
that irrational leaders on the Hitler model could involve their countries in future wars. Economic considerations motivate strongly

against war, he says, but economic prosperity "is not always an overriding goal even now." Territorial issues exist even in the developed world that "could lead to wars of expansion or territorial readjustment." The Cold War is being resolved peacefully, "but there is no firm guarantee that this trend will continue."

A more general problem may also exist with the end-of-war or even a decline-in-war thesis. As Michimi Muranushi of Yale has pointed out, peace can be self-limiting rather than cumulative. If relations between two countries become more peaceful, this may, in some circumstances, increase the probability that either or both of those countries will go to war with a third country. The Hitler-Stalin pact paves the way for the attacks on Poland; normalization of U.S.-China relations precipitates China's war with Vietnam. If the Soviet threat disappears, so also does an inhibitor of Greek-Turkish war.

In addition, if more countries become like Denmark, forswearing war and committing themselves to material comfort, that in itself may produce a situation which other countries will wish to exploit. History is full of examples of leaner, meaner societies overrunning richer, less martial ones.

THE END OF HISTORY

"The end of history" is a sweeping, dramatic, and provocative phrase. What does Fukuyama mean by it? The heart of Fukuyama's argument is an alleged change in political consciousness throughout the principal societies in the world and the emergence of a pervasive consensus on liberal-democratic principles. It posits the triumph of one ideology and the consequent end of ideology and ideological conflict as significant factors in human existence. His choice of language suggests, however, that he may have something more sweeping in mind than simply the obsolescence of war highlighted by Mueller or the end of ideology predicted by Daniel Bell twenty-five years ago.

Insofar as it is focused on war, Fukuyama's argument suffers all the weaknesses that Mueller's does. He admits that "conflict between states still in history, and between those states and those at the end of history, would still be possible." At the same time he includes China and the Soviet Union among those states that are out of history. Current Soviet leaders, he says, have arrived at the "end-of-history view" and "assimilated the consciousness of the universal homogenous state that is post-Hitler Europe"; yet he also admits that the Soviet Union could turn to Slavophile Russian chauvinism and thus remain stuck in history.

Fukuyama ridicules the idea that Germany and France might fight each other again. That is a valid but irrelevant point. A hundred years ago one could have validly made the point that Pennsylvania and Virginia would not fight each other again. That did not prevent the United States, of which each was a part, from engaging in world wars in the subsequent century. One trend in history is the amalgamation of smaller units into larger ones. The probability of war between the smaller units declines but the probability of war between the larger amalgamated units does not necessarily change. A united European community may end the possibility of Franco-German war; it does not end the possibility of war between that community and other political units.

With respect to China, Fukuyama argues that "Chinese competitiveness and expansionism on the world scene have virtually disappeared" and, he implies strongly, will not reappear. A more persuasive argument, however, could be made for exactly the opposite proposition that Chinese expansionism has yet to appear on the world scene. Britain and France, Germany and Japan, the United States and the Soviet Union, all became expansionist and imperialist powers in the course of industrialization. China is just beginning seriously to develop its industrial strength. Maybe China will be different from all the other major powers and not attempt to expand its influence and control as it industrializes. But how can one be confident that it will pursue this deviant course? And if it follows the more familiar pattern, a billion Chinese engaged in imperial expansion are likely to impose a lot of history on the rest of the world.

Fukuyama quite appropriately emphasizes the role of consciousness, ideas, and ideology in motivating and shaping the actions of men and nations. He is also right in pointing to the virtual end of the appeal of communism as an ideology. Ideologically, communism has been "the grand failure" that Brzezinski labels it. It is erroneous, however, to jump from the decline of communism to the global triumph of liberalism and the disappearance of ideology as a force in world affairs.

First, revivals are possible. A set of ideas or an ideology may fade from the scene in one generation only to reappear with renewed strength a generation or two later. From the 1940s to the 1960s, dominant currents in economic thinking were Keynesianism,[6] welfare

---

[6] economic policies, based on the theories of the English economist John Keynes

statism, social democracy, and planning. It was hard to find much support for classical economic liberalism. By the late 1970s, however, the latter had staged an amazing comeback: economists and economic institutions were devoted to The Plan in the 1950s; they have been devoted to The Market in the 1980s. Somewhat similarly, social scientists in the decades immediately after World War II argued that religion, ethnic consciousness, and nationalism would all be done in by economic development and modernization. But in the 1980s these have been the dominant bases of political action in most societies. The revival of religion is now a global phenomenon. Communism may be down for the moment, but it is rash to assume that it is out for all time.

Second, the universal acceptance of liberal democracy does not preclude conflicts within liberalism. The history of ideology is the history of schism. Struggles between those who profess different versions of a common ideology are often more intense and vicious than struggles between those espousing entirely different ideologies. To a believer the heretic is worse than the nonbeliever. An ideological consensus on Christianity existed in Europe in 1500 but that did not prevent Protestants and Catholics from slaughtering each other for the next century and a half. Socialists and communists, Trotskyites and Leninists, Shi'ites and Sunnis have treated each other in similar fashion.

Third, the triumph of one ideology does not preclude the emergence of new ideologies. Nations and societies presumably will continue to evolve. New challenges to human well-being will emerge, and people will develop new concepts, theories, and ideologies as to how those challenges should be met. Unless all social, economic, and political distinctions disappear, people will also develop belief systems that legitimate what they have and justify their getting more. Among its other functions, for instance, communism historically legitimized the power of intellectuals and bureaucrats. If it is gone for good, it seems highly likely that intellectuals and bureaucrats will develop new sets of ideas to rationalize their claims to power and wealth.

Fourth, has liberal democracy really triumphed? Fukuyama admits that it has not won out in the Third World. To what extent, however, has it really been accepted in the Soviet Union and China?

(1883–1946), advocating increased government spending and market intervention to stimulate business activity and promote employment (ED.)

Between them these societies encompass well over one-quarter of the world's population. If any one trend is operative in the world today it is for societies to turn back toward their traditional cultures, values, and patterns of behavior. This trend is manifest in the revival of traditional identities and characters of Eastern European countries, escaping from the deadly uniformity of Soviet-imposed communism, and also in the increasing differentiation among the republics within the Soviet Union itself. Russia and China do not lack elements of liberalism and democracy in their histories. These are, however, minor chords, and their subordinate importance is underlined by the contemporary problems facing economic liberalism in the Soviet Union and political democracy in communist China.

More generally, Fukuyama's thesis itself reflects not the disappearance of Marxism but its pervasiveness. His image of the end of history is straight from Marx. Fukuyama speaks of the "universal homogeneous state," in which "all prior contradictions are resolved and all human needs are satisfied." What is this but the Marxist image of a society without class conflict or other contradictions organized on the basis of from each according to his abilities and to each according to his needs? The struggles of history, Fukuyama says, "will be replaced by economic calculation, the endless solving of technical problems, environmental concerns, and the satisfaction of sophisticated consumer demands." Engels said it even more succinctly: "The government of persons is replaced by the administration of things and the direction of the process of production." Fukuyama says liberalism is the end of history. Marx says communism "is the solution to the riddle of history." They are basically saying the same thing and, most importantly, they are thinking the same way. Marxist ideology is alive and well in Fukuyama's arguments to refute it.

TWO FALLACIES

The Soviet Union is increasingly preoccupied with its own problems and a significant political loosening has occurred in that country. The ideological intensity of the early Cold War has virtually disappeared, and the probability of hot war between the two superpowers is as low as it has ever been. War is even more unlikely between any of the advanced industrialized democracies. On these points, endist propositions are accurate. The more extensive formulations of the endist argument, however, suffer from two basic fallacies.

First, endism overemphasizes the predictability of history and the permanence of the moment. Current trends may or may not continue into the future. Past experience certainly suggests that they are unlikely to do so. The record of past predictions by social scientists is not a happy one. Fifteen years ago, just as the democratic wave was beginning, political analysts were elaborating fundamental reasons why authoritarianism had to prevail in the Third World. Ten years ago foreign policy journals were filled with warnings of the rise of Soviet military power and political influence throughout the world. Five years ago what analyst of the Soviet Union predicted the extent of the political changes that have occurred in that country? Given the limitations of human foresight, endist predictions of the end of war and ideological conflict deserve a heavy dose of skepticism. Indeed, in the benign atmosphere of the moment, it is sobering to speculate on the possible future horrors that social analysts are now failing to predict.

Second, endism tends to ignore the weakness and irrationality of human nature. Endist arguments often assume that because it would be rational for human beings to focus on their economic well-being, they will act in that way, and therefore they will not engage in wars that do not meet the tests of cost-benefit analysis or in ideological conflicts that are much ado about nothing. Human beings are at times rational, generous, creative, and wise, but they are also often stupid, selfish, cruel, and sinful. The struggle that is history began with the eating of the forbidden fruit and is rooted in human nature. In history there may be total defeats, but there are no final solutions. So long as human beings exist, there is no exit from the traumas of history.

To hope for the benign end of history is human. To expect it to happen is unrealistic. To plan on it happening is disastrous.

PAUL JOHNSON

Experimenting with Half Mankind

Paul Johnson (1928–   ) is a British historian and writer. His works include *A History of Christianity* (1976), *Modern Times: The World from the Twenties to the Eighties* (1983), from which this selection is taken, *A History of the English People* (1985), *A History*

of the Jews (1987), and *The Birth of the Modern World Society
1815–1830* (1991).

In the summer of 1966, the official Peking press reported that on 16
July Mao Tse-tung, the Chairman of the Chinese Communist Party,
then in his seventieth year, had organized and led a mass swim in
the Yangtze. Somewhat fuzzy photographs were published of what
appeared to be his large round head bobbing in the water. Reports
said he had swum nearly ten miles in just over sixty minutes and he
was described as 'radiant with vigour and in buoyant spirits'.[1] This
was merely one of the prodigies which appeared to have taken place
in China in the quarter-century between Mao's accession to power
and his death in 1976. It was widely believed China was steadily
overcoming the economic problems facing large, backward and heavily populated countries, and was doing so within the framework of
an enthusiastic national consensus.

Visitors returned fervent admirers of Mao's brand of Communism.
China, one of them wrote, was 'a kind of benign monarchy ruled by
an emperor-priest who had won the complete devotion of his subjects'. Its people, another predicted, would be 'the incarnation of the
new civilization of the world'. Simone de Beauvoir[2] testified: 'life in
China today is exceptionally pleasant'. The country had become, said
another witness, 'almost as painstakingly careful about human lives
as New Zealand'. David Rockefeller praised 'the sense of national
harmony' and argued that Mao's revolution[3] had succeeded 'not only
in producing more efficient and dedicated administration, but also
in fostering high morale and community of purpose'. Another American visitor found the changes 'miraculous. . . . The Maoist revolution
is on the whole the best thing that happened to the Chinese people
in centuries.' What attracted most admiration was the improvement
in moral tone. 'Of the many communes I visited,' Felix Greene
reported, 'all except one denied any knowledge of any children born
out of wedlock.' 'Law and order', another American visitor found,
'. . . are maintained more by the prevailing high moral code than by

---

[1] Jack Chen, *Inside the Cultural Revolution* (London 1976), 219–20.

[2] Simone de Beauvoir (1908–1986) was a French novelist, essayist, and feminist,
whose works include *The Second Sex* (1949). (ED.)

[3] Communist revolution in China led by Mao Tse-tung (1893–1976) who became the
first chairman of the People's Republic of China in 1949 (ED.)

any threat of police action.' Yet another insisted that government tax collectors had become 'incorruptible' and that intellectuals were anxious to prove their lack of 'contempt for peasants' by 'lugging buckets of manure in their free time'.[4]

These testimonies recalled the uncritical praise lavished by visitors on Stalin and his regime during the horrors of collectivization and the great purges. When taxed on this point, admiring visitors replied that the lessons of Soviet mistakes had been learnt, largely through the extraordinary genius of Mao. He was, Jan Myrdal wrote, 'third in line with Marx and Lenin' and had solved the problem of how 'the revolution can be prevented from degenerating'. He 'combined', wrote an American political scientist, 'qualities which rarely coexist in one being in such intensity'. Han Suyin argued that, unlike Stalin, Mao 'is extremely patient, and believes in debate and re-education', and had 'an ever-present concern with the practical application of democracy'. When a problem arose, an American sinologist reported, Mao 'invariably' responded 'in a uniquely creative and profoundly ethical way'. Felix Greene believed that the hunger for power had been eliminated and that there was 'no evidence of that jockeying for power or of the personal rivalry that we have so often seen in the Kremlin'. Mao was not merely a soldier, a leader, a poet, philosopher, teacher, thinker and charismatic: he was also a kind of saint. What struck Hewlett Johnson most about him was 'something no picture has ever caught, an inexpressible look of kindness and sympathy, an obvious preoccupation with the needs of others . . . these formed the deep content of his thoughts.'[5]

Needless to say, these travellers' tales, as in Stalin's Russia, bore little or no relation to the truth, which was more interesting and infinitely more depressing. And Mao's public image, too, was as remote from the reality as Stalin's. Mao was not a saint. There was nothing of the scholar or the mandarin about him. He was a big, coarse, brutal, earthy and ruthless peasant, a *kulak*[6] indeed; an educated version of his father. Khrushchev, not unjustly, compared him to 'a bear, swaying from side to side as he moved, calmly and slowly'.[7]

---

[4] Paul Hollander, *Political Pilgrims: Travels of Western Intellectuals to the Soviet Union, China and Cuba 1928–1978* (Oxford 1981), chapter 7, 'The Pilgrimage to China', 278ff.

[5] Ibid., 326–30.

[6] a Russian farmer considered excessively wealthy by the Communists (ED.)

[7] Strobe Talbot (ed.), *Khrushchev Remembers: The Last Testament* (London 1974), 249.

Talking to the Politburo in 1956, Mao warned: 'We must not blindly follow the Soviet Union. . . . Every fart has some kind of smell, and we cannot say that all Soviet farts smell sweet.'[8] Three years later, admitting the failure of the 'Great Leap', he told the same group: 'Comrades, you must all analyse your own responsibility. If you have to shit, shit! If you have to fart, fart! You will feel much better for it.'[9] Again, in 1974, reviewing the shortcomings of the Cultural Revolution[10] he philosophized: 'The need to shit after eating does not mean that eating is a waste of time.'[11] A Belgian Communist described him, during the great Red Guards rally in Heavenly Peace Square on 18 August 1966, retiring from time to time to take off his vest and wipe his chest and armpits, remarking, 'It's unhealthy to let sweat dry on your body.'[12]

Beneath this coarse exterior, however, there beat a strong—indeed a wild—romantic heart. It is probably true, as Stalin insisted in 1949, that Mao was not really a Marxist at all: 'He doesn't understand the most elementary Marxist truths.'[13] While he used the Marxist formulations, and indeed considered himself a great Marxist thinker, much superior to Stalin's contemptible successors, he never in practice attempted to apply objective Marxist analysis. He did not believe in 'objective situations' at all. It was all in the mind: he might be described as a geopolitical Emile Coué[14] who believed in 'mind over matter'. On the basis of 'the tremendous energy of the masses', he argued, 'it is possible to accomplish any task whatever'.[15] 'There is only unproductive thought,' he said, 'no unproductive regions. There

[8] John Gittings, The World and China, 1922–1975 (London 1974), 236.

[9] Bill Brugger, China: Liberation and Transformation 1942–1962 (New Jersey 1981), 212.

[10] a campaign, begun by Mao Tse-tung and lasting from 1966 to 1969, to purge China of those who opposed or criticized strict Communist ideology (ED.)

[11] Ross Terrill, Mao: a Biography (New York 1980), 383.

[12] Quoted in Han Suyin, Wind in the Tower: Mao Tse-Tung and the Chinese Revolution 1945–1975 (London 1976), 291.

[13] Talbot (ed.), op. cit., 249.

[14] Emile Coué (1857–1926) was a French pharmacist and psychotherapist who instituted an autosuggestive method of psychotherapy in which the patient repeats the formula: "Every day, and in every way, I am becoming better and better." (ED.)

[15] Stuart Schram, Mao Tse-tung (London 1966), 253–4.

are only poor methods of cultivating the land, no such thing as poor land.'[16] This contempt for objective reality explains his willingness to accept the prospect of nuclear war, and his conviction that China would win it. 'The East wind prevails over the West wind,' he said in 1957. 'If imperialism insists on fighting a war, we will have no alternative but to make up our minds and fight to the finish before going ahead with our construction.'[17] The same year, in Moscow, he shocked his Communist colleagues by the same argument: 'We may lose more than 300 million people. So what? War is war. The years will pass and we'll get to work producing more babies than ever before' (according to Khrushchev, he 'used an indecent expression').[18] He later took a similar view of war with Russia: 'Even if it goes on for ever, the sky won't fall, trees will grow, women will give birth and fishes will swim.'[19] He seems to have believed all his life that the true dynamic of history was not so much the maturation of classes (that might be the outward expression) as heroic determination. He saw himself as the Nietzschean superman[20] made flesh.

In his artistic longings, in his romanticism and in his belief that will is the key not only to power but to accomplishment, Mao was an oriental Hitler. Though the cult of Mao bore a superficial resemblance to Stalinism, it actually had a far more creative and central role in the Maoist state. Like Hitler, Mao loved politics as theatre. The *décor* of his regime was far more striking and original than Stalin's lacklustre imitations of Nazi pomp. He drew on and transformed the majesty of the imperial era. The crowds were trained to greet him with the ritual chant 'Boundless life to Chairman Mao'. Like the emperors, he ploughed a symbolic annual furrow, used the Imperial City for his residence and gave calligraphic instructions for monuments.[21] But to this he added a sun-culture of his own, reflected in his hymn 'The East is Red', which he imposed on China as a second national anthem:

---

[16] Ibid., 295.

[17] Ibid., 291.

[18] Talbot (ed.), op. cit., 255.

[19] Terrill, op. cit., 53.

[20] a superhuman leader in the German philosopher Friedrich Nietzsche's (1844–1900) theory of a new society based on heroic morality and the "will to power" (ED.)

[21] Roger Garside, *Coming Alive: China after Mao* (London 1981), 45.

From the Red East rises the sun:
There appears in China a Mao Tse-tung.

His round, sun-like face appeared on huge posters; and, like the sun, he appeared at dawn to inspect a million Red Guards in the summer of 1966.

These occasions, of which there were eight within a few weeks, allowing the sun to shine on over 11 million people, strongly resembled the Nuremberg rallies. The Red Guards rhythmically chanted Maoist slogans, while Lin Piao (rather like Goebbels)[22] called out the litanies: 'Beat down the capitalist roaders in power! Beat down the reactionary bourgeois authorities! Sweep away all wicked devils and evil spirits! Do away with the Four Old Things: old thought, old culture, old customs, old habits. The Thought of Mao Tse-tung must rule and transform the spirit, until the power of the spirit transforms matter!' (18 August 1966).[23] Mao's thought was 'the sun of our heart, the root of our life, the source of our strength', 'his thought is a compass and spiritual food', it was 'like a massive cudgel swung by a golden monkey', a 'brilliant beam of light' exposing 'monsters and goblins', a series of 'magic mirrors to detect demons', and he himself was 'the source of all wisdom'. The Revolution and its achievements were (in a manner of speaking) a gigantic thought-form of Mao's, since 'all our victories are victories of the Thought of Mao Tse-tung'.[24]

The *Little Red Book* played a similar role to *Mein Kampf* and, like Hitler, Mao used military drill, massed bands and *son et lumiére* to produce illusion and hysteria. For his 1966 rallies, 1,000-piece bands played 'The East is Red', and a film of the ninth National Congress of the CCP in 1969 showed delegates, holding the *Little Red Book* aloft, jigging up and down in frenzy, tears rolling down their cheeks, yelping and baying like animals, in the Great Hall of the People.[25] The virulently abusive language Mao and his henchmen used to evoke violent and intolerant activism was very reminiscent of Hitler's anti-Semitism.

[22] *Lin Piao*, a compatriot of Mao Tse-tung, was China's defense minister and Mao's selected successor until he was killed in 1971 after an abortive assassination attempt on Mao. *Paul Joseph Goebbels* (1897–1945) was the German propaganda minister under Adolf Hitler. (ED.)

[23] Ibid., 46–7.

[24] Robert Jay Lifton, *Revolutionary Immortality* (London 1969), 72–3.

[25] Garside, op. cit., 50.

The most important respect in which Mao recalled Hitler was in his imminent eschatology.[26] Mao was, above all, a violently impatient man. He lacked the unhurried stoicism with which Stalin remorselessly pursued his objectives and his hatreds. Mao, like Hitler, wanted to speed up history. He thought his successors would prove poltroons and faint-hearts and that unless things were done in his own lifetime, they would not be done at all. He always heard time's winged chariot at his back, and his impetuosity found expression in his complementary and insatiable love of drama. In a sense, Mao never made the transition from revolution to administration. He lacked Stalin's bureaucratic appetite. For him, history was a cosmic play, a succession of spectacular episodes, in which he was actor, impresario and spectator. No sooner had the curtain come crashing down on one scene— 'the Long March', say, or 'the Fall of the KMT'[27]—than he clamoured for it to rise again and the action to recommence, faster and more furious than before.

Hence Mao's reign was a lurid melodrama, sometimes degenerating into farce but always, in the deepest sense, a tragedy: for what he caused to be enacted was not theatre but a gigantic series of experiments on hundreds of millions of real, living, suffering people. The first drama after the defeat of the KMT seems to have occurred towards the end of 1950. Initially, the land reform introduced in the south under the law of 1949 was not radical. A speech of Lin Piao's as late as 14 June 1950 applied the brakes. The benevolent term 'prosperous middle peasant' replaced 'rich peasant' and new categories of 'enlightened gentry' and 'small landlords' were coined to keep efficient farmers in business.[28] Then the coming of the Korean War gave Mao the pretext for his first post-war cataclysm. In 1951 and still more in 1952–3, the land reform was continually accelerated and conducted with great savagery. There was 'the Three-Antis campaign', quickly followed by 'the Five-Antis campaign'. On 21 February 1951 new 'Regulations regarding the punishment of counter-revolu-

[26] a branch of theology that deals with the ultimate events of humankind and the world (ED.)

[27] On the *Long March* from 1934 to 1935, the Communist army, led by Mao Tse-tung, fled from Chiang Kai-shek's Nationalist forces to the northern province of Shaanxi. *Kuomintang* (KMT), the Nationalist party of China, was organized in 1912. After being defeated by the Communists in 1949, the KMT, under Chiang Kai-shek, fled to Taiwan. (ED.)

[28] Brugger, op. cit., 44–55.

tionaries' provided death and life-sentences for a wide range of
'crimes'. All major towns held mass rallies at which social 'enemies'
were publicly denounced and sentenced. Over a few months, nearly
30,000 such meetings were held in Peking alone, attended by 3
million people. The papers published long lists of names every day
of executed 'counter-revolutionaries'. In October 1951 it was stated
that 800,000 cases had been dealt with in the first six months of the
year (Chou En-lai[29] later said that 16.8 per cent had received death-
sentences, which would mean 135,000 executions, or 22,500 a
month, a high rate even by Stalin's worst standards). The total number of killed during this first post-war drama of Mao's may have been
as high as 15 million, though a figure of 1 to 3 million is more
likely.[30]

This gigantic piece of social engineering was also accompanied
by Mao's first shot at mental engineering, or brainwashing, which he
termed 'thought reform'. It was designed to replace traditional family
piety with filial piety to the state as the central moral value of the
nation and to elevate Mao into a substitute father-figure.[31] Mao
defined 'thought reform' (23 October 1951) as a vital precondition
for 'the thoroughgoing democratic transformation and the progressive
industrialization of our country'. He set up a nationwide 'Movement
for the study of Mao Tse-tung's Thoughts'; those who rejected them
were branded as 'Westerners' and 'reformed' in prison, often shackled
for varying periods with heavy, painful irons.[32] The drama, however,
embraced not only the victims of the 'land reform' and those who
criticized the way it was done. Many of the total of eight 'Antis' were
directed at merchants, industrial managers and bureaucrats: the campaign in fact embraced virtually the whole nation.

Like all Mao's successive dramas, it fizzled out as he lost interest
or confidence in its results, or as the disastrous consequences became
apparent in lower agricultural productivity and famine. But by 1955
Mao's impatience was rising again. In a speech of 31 July 1955 he

[29] Chou En-lai (1898–1976) was premier of the People's Republic of China from 1949
until his death in 1976. (ED.)

[30] Schram, op. cit., 267, footnote; see Jacques Guillermaz, La Chine Populaire (3rd ed.,
Paris 1964).

[31] Robert Jay Lifton, Thought Reform and the Psychology of Totalism: A Study of
Brainwashing in China (New York 1961), chapter 19.

[32] Schram, op. cit., 271 footnote.

suddenly announced a speed-up in the rate of collectivization of farms and the abrupt nationalization of all commerce and industry still in private hands. He called 1955 'the year of decision in the struggle between socialism and capitalism'.[33] This campaign, too, was to change mentalities: the 'poor peasants' would acquire 'control' and then 'strengthen unity' with the 'middle peasants', even the 'upper-middle peasants', against the 'infiltration' of 'counter-revolutionaries', 'rascals' and 'devils'. Disappointed by the response, Mao produced with equal suddenness his 'Let a hundred flowers bloom' policy in 1956, to persuade a variety of voices to speak out. As he put it, 'Correct ideas, if pampered in hot-houses without exposure to the elements or immunization against disease, will not win against wrong ones.' Khrushchev took the view that the whole 'hundred flowers' episode was a mere 'provocation'. Mao merely 'pretended to be opening wide the floodgates of democracy' to 'goad people into expressing their innermost thoughts', so he could 'destroy those whose thinking he considered harmful'.[34] At all events the campaign was brutally reversed without warning. 'Rightist elements' were sent to work-camps; professors who had briefly 'bloomed' found themselves cleaning lavatories; and in 1957 the tentative protections of 'socialist legality' were withdrawn.[35]

These confused events, or abortive mini-dramas, should be seen against the background of Mao's increasing dissatisfaction with the policies of Stalin's successors in Moscow. He had disliked and disagreed with Stalin: his reaction to Stalin's death was to instigate the suicide or murder of Kao Kang, the Stalinist agent and head of the State Planning Committee, in February 1954. But he objected strongly to 'deStalinization' as an attempt to blame collective mistakes on the character of a single man. He thought Khrushchev's 'secret session speech' repudiating Stalinism of 1956 a hypocrisy. The others, Khrushchev included, had been up to their necks in Stalin's crimes. How did Khrushchev, he demanded, see his role 'when he beats his breast, pounds the table and shouts abuse at the top of his voice'? Was he a 'murderer' and a 'bandit' himself? Or merely a 'fool' and

[33] Ibid., 277.

[34] Talbot (ed.), op. cit., 272.

[35] Jerome A. Cohen, 'The Criminal Process in the People's Republic of China: An Introduction', *Harvard Law Review*, January 1966.

an 'idiot'?[36] Mao was clearly afraid that the Moscow campaign against 'the cult of personality' might be used against himself. More fundamentally, however, he felt that the sheer intellectual poverty of the new Moscow leadership strengthened his claim, now Stalin was dead, to the pontifical primacy of the bloc. He determined to astound the comrades, east and west, by the sheer audacity of his next move, and in September–October 1957 announced the new drama of the Great Leap Forward,[37] which was launched with tremendous publicity the following spring.

The Great Leap was perhaps the purest expression of Mao's chronic impatience, his belief in mind over matter, his confidence that, granted the will, the age of miracles was not over. He wanted to move to Communism in one bound, even to the stage when the state would 'wither away'. He projected his itch to telescope history onto the peasants: they were 'poor and blank', and this was 'a good thing—poor people want change, want to do things, want revolution. A clean sheet of paper has no blotches and so the newest and most beautiful words can be written on it.'[38] As a piece of social engineering, the Leap was reckless and impulsive even by Mao's standards. He justified it by arguing that Stalin had walked 'only on one leg'— that is, he created industrial and agricultural areas, each separate and monoped. China would begin 'walking on two legs', moving directly to self-reliant communes (modelled historically on the Paris Commune of 1870), each with its own industrial, agricultural and service sectors and its own defence militia: 'unity of work and arms'.[39]

The scale and speed of this experimental theatre was almost beyond belief. In January–February 1958, then after a brief pause to sort out the confusion, between August and December, about 700 million people (90 per cent of the population) had their economic, political and administrative life completely transformed. In Henan Province, for instance, 5,376 agricultural collectives were knocked into 208 large 'people's communes' with an average of 8,000 households in each. These units were expected to be virtually self-supporting and, in particular, to produce their own steel. It was a case, as Khrushchev put it, of Mao 'acting like a lunatic on a throne and

[36] Editorials, *Peking Review*, 6, 13, 20 September 1963.

[37] a radical program, begun in 1958, to transform China's economy (ED.)

[38] Quoted Schram, op. cit., 253.

[39] Brugger, op. cit., 174ff.

turning his country upside down'. He said that Chou En-lai came to Moscow and admitted that the Chinese steel industry was in a mess as a result. A.F. Zasyadki, deputy-chairman of the State Planning Commission, was sent out to investigate. He reported to Khrushchev that the Soviet-trained steel engineers were now being forced to work in agriculture and the steel industry was 'a shambles'. The steel mill he visited was 'in the charge of an old man'. All Russia's equipment, money and effort was being wasted.[40] Khrushchev seems to have concluded that Mao was another Stalin and worse; a madman who would wreck his country and blow up the world if he had the means. The Great Leap therefore led directly to the end of Russia's technical assistance programme (including nuclear weapons) in 1959 and to the open admission of the Sino–Soviet breach the following year at the Romanian Party Congress, when Khrushchev denounced the Chinese leadership as 'madmen', 'pure nationalists' who wanted to unleash a nuclear war.

In China itself the Great Leap movement came to a juddering halt on 23 July 1959, Mao ringing down the curtain with an abrupt 'The chaos caused was on a grand scale, and I take responsibility'.[41] But the consequences of the drama had their own irresistible momentum. Nineteen-fifty-nine was a year of natural disasters, and combining with the unnatural disaster of the Great Leap produced a man-made famine on the scale of Stalin's catastrophe in the early 1930s, which lasted till 1962.[42] To this day outsiders do not know exactly what happened to Chinese agriculture during these terrible years. The steel industry was wrecked and had to be rebuilt virtually from its foundations. Agriculture was yet again reorganized by a return to co-operatives and a fall in the size of commune units to 2,000 households. But the crops and livestock lost were lost for good. People just starved. How many millions died from the Leap is a matter of conjecture: figures are not available.

The Great Leap disaster seems to have exhausted a large portion of the political capital Mao had banked with his colleagues during the successful revolutionary war. He never held the supreme and solitary power of a Hitler and a Stalin, both because of the intractable

[40] Talbot (ed.), op. cit., 272–8.

[41] Brugger, op. cit., 212.

[42] K. Walker, *Planning in Chinese Agriculture: Socialization and the Private Sector 1956–62* (London 1965), 444–5.

nature of China's problems, her lack of centralization and modern communications, and because he never possessed a terror apparatus on the same scale as the KGB or the Gestapo-SS. The party was more regionalized than in Russia; in particular, there was a profound polarity between the conservatism of Peking and the radicalism of Shanghai. After the curtain came down on the drama of 1959, Mao eschewed histrionics for a while; he seems to have been 'resting'. From this point dated the beginning of 'the two-line struggle', with 'revisionists' temporarily on top. They never again allowed Mao to touch the productive process directly, either in agriculture or in heavy industry. Instead he brooded on culture and education. He had always disliked mandarinism[43] and the cultural establishment. In a sense, he hated 'civilization' as much as Hitler did. In China it represented not the international Jewish conspiracy but the dead hand, the insufferable, insupportable weight of a 4,000-year past. In this respect his revolution appeared to have changed nothing—and it was because of this cultural failure, he reasoned, that the Great Leap had proved impractical.

By 13 February 1964 Mao was making ominous noises: 'The present method of education ruins talent and ruins youth. I do not approve of reading so many books. The method of examination is a method of dealing with the enemy. It is most harmful and should be stopped.'[44] Nine months later he betrayed unmistakable signs of impatience and a hankering for a new drama: 'We cannot follow the old paths of technical development of every country in the world, and crawl step by step behind the others. We must smash conventions . . . when we talk of a Great Leap Forward, we mean just this.'[45] Thus the Leap was transmuted from a physical to a mental one: by the beginning of 1965 Mao's interest in brainwashing had revived and was to be the dominant feature of his next and greatest drama.

By this point China was effectively run by a triumvirate: Mao himself, the head of state Liu Shao-chi, in charge of the Party and in particular of the Peking apparatus, and the army head, Lin Piao. Mao chose to open the new play indirectly, by pushing onto centre-stage his film-actress wife, Chiang Ching. She was well cast for the star

---

[43] system of mandarins, public officials of high rank in imperial China (ED.)

[44] Bill Brugger, *China: Radicalism and Revisionism 1962–1972* (New Jersey 1981), 36.

[45] Ibid., 47.

role in what was soon termed the 'Cultural Revolution'. It was characteristic of Mao's romanticism that he always had a soft spot for actresses. He had had an affair, for instance, with the famous Lily Wu. His then wife, Ho Tzu-chen, found out, brought an action and got a divorce at a special Central Committee court, which then banished both women.[46] In 1939 Mao married Chiang Ching, who had acted in Shanghai in the 1930s under the stage name of Lan Ping. According to her account, she went into the profession at the age of thirteen, became a party member at nineteen, and was twenty-three when Mao sought her out in Yenan, by offering her a free ticket to a lecture he was giving at the Marxist-Leninist institute.[47] But other versions make her older and say she was married three if not four times in 1930s Shanghai, had numerous affairs in the film world and acquired many hatreds and enmities.

Chiang Ching kept, or was kept, very much in the background for the first twenty years of her marriage. There is a deep-rooted suspicion of the scheming political wife in China, what might be called the 'Dowager Empress syndrome'. In the early 1960s it was considered remarkable that Wang Kwang-mei, the wife of the head of state, Liu, should dress fashionably, wear pearls and even dance (she had been born in the USA) while accompanying her husband abroad, and this may have excited Chiang's jealousy. She herself became the centre of a group of disgruntled pseudo-intellectuals, failed writers and minor actors and film-directors, mainly from Shanghai, who wanted to take over the arts and radicalize them. There was a certain party mandate for their 'line'. In 1950, following the Zhdanov cultural purges in Soviet Russia, an 'opera reform bureau' was set up in China, drawing its inspiration from a theatre group founded at the Red Army Academy in 1931 and the so-called 'Chinese Blue Blouse Regiment' which used impromptu theatre to project ideology from mobile stages. In 1952 the Peking People's Art Theatre was set up to produce 'modern' didactic drama.[48] But little came of this. Well into the 1960s, Chinese classics remained dominant and many independent theatres flourished, performing Ibsen, O'Neill, Shaw, Chekhov and using the Stanislavsky method.[49]

---

[46] Roxane Witke, *Comrade Chiang Ching* (London 1977), 162.

[47] Ibid., 154; Chiang Ching confided at great length in Witke.

[48] Colin Mackerras, *The Chinese Theatre in Modern Times* (Amherst, Mass., 1975).

[49] Witke, op. cit., 383.

Chiang's own group, the League of Left-Wing Dramatists, found it difficult to get their works performed and was even suspected of Trotskyism.[50] She seems to have brought to the Chinese scene, already envenomed by the bitter sectarian factionalism inherent in Marxist-Leninist politics, the spirit of the theatrical vendetta.

She got her breakthrough in June–July 1964 when the frustrated Mao allowed her to put on the Festival of Peking Opera on Contemporary Themes in the Great Hall of the People. This consisted of thirty-seven new operas (thirty-three on the Revolution, four on earlier revolts), performed by twenty-eight proletarian companies from nineteen provinces. Even more surprisingly, Mao allowed her to deliver a speech, the first by a woman since he took power. She said there were 3,000 professional theatrical companies in China, including ninety supposed to be dealing with 'modern' drama. Nevertheless, the Chinese stage was dominated by old themes, heroes and heroines, 'by emperors, princes, generals, ministers, scholars and beauties, and on top of these, ghosts and monsters'. There were 'well over 600 million workers, peasants and soldiers in our country' as opposed to 'only a handful of landlords, rich peasants, counter-revolutionaries, bad elements, Rightists and bourgeois'. Why should the theatre serve these few and not the 600 million? She recommended for universal performance certain 'model operas', such as *Raid on the White Tiger Regiment* and *Taking Tiger Mountain by Strategy*.[51] None of this went down well in Peking, the repository and guardian of Chinese culture. Its mayor and party boss, the ultramandarin Peng Chen, called her operas 'still at the stage of wearing trousers with a slit-seat and thumb-sucking'. Everyone disliked her burgeoning habit of phoning her opponents and critics in order to 'struggle with them'. When she asked Peng to give her an opera troupe 'to reform on my own' and showed him a new revolutionary opera with which she proposed to reform it, he flatly refused, snatched the score from her hands and challenged her 'to take up a strong position if she pleased'.[52]

Her strong position was to persuade Mao to leave Peking and

[50] Ibid., 158–9. [*Trotskyism* is the Communist idology of Leon Trotsky (1879–1940) advocating worldwide revolution. (ED.)]

[51] Ibid., 309–10.

[52] Ibid., 312–14.

spend most of 1965 in Shanghai. There a number of themes came together in his head: hatred of Soviet Russia and its leadership, and of the new class of bourgeois bureaucrats who had frustrated his Great Leap, the longing of an elderly hero to appeal to the young again, his contempt for formal education, his loathing for the people who flourished by virtue of mandarinism, his jealousy of Liu. Liu's book, *How to be a Good Communist,* sold fifteen million copies between 1962–6, as many as Mao's books at that time. Official editorials urged the comrades to study Liu on a par with .Mao. The two men had quarrelled violently over the reasons for the failure of the Leap.[53] Thus to the suppressed ambitions of a failed actress were added the grievances of an injured author. Mao gave up reading the Peking *People's Daily,* turning instead to the forces paper, *Liberation Army Daily.* He was gearing up for another dramatic explosion. He observed grimly to André Malraux: 'I am alone with the masses—waiting.' To the sycophantic French ambassador, who told him youth was with him, Mao retorted: 'The things you saw represented only one side of the situation—you didn't see the other side.' He told a group of Albanians that the new privileged élite in Russia had sprung first from literary and artistic circles and the same was happening in China: 'Why are there so many literary and artistic associations in Peking? They have nothing to do . . . army performances are the best, local troupes rank second and those from Peking are the worst.' Official culture groups, he said to a group of planners, were 'just transplants from the Soviet Union . . . all ruled by foreigners and dead men'. Peking's Academy of Sciences was 'fairyland', stuffed with 'antiquarians' who 'read unreadable journals'.[54] He would rely on the earthly, peasant army. He broke its chief of staff, Luo Rui-qing, for alleged pro-Soviet activities. He built up its head, Lin Piao, against Liu and his Peking 'clique'. The shape of things to come was his permission to Chiang Ching to convene in Shanghai a 'Forum on Work in Literature and Art in the Armed Forces'. Before it took place, a nervous Lin held a briefing of senior officers:

> She is very sharp politically on questions of literature and art. . . . She has many opinions which are valuable. You should pay good attention to them and see that they are applied ideologically and organiza-

[53] Terrill, op. cit., 305 footnote.

[54] Ibid., 304–9.

tionally. From now on, all the army's documents concerning literature and art should be sent to her.[55]

Having lined up the army behind himself, Mao went over to the attack. The actual detonator to what soon became known as the 'Cultural Revolution' was personal pique—Mao's reaction to a play, *Hai Jui Dismissed from Office,* actually written in 1961 by Wu Han, Deputy-Mayor of Peking, and another official mandarin.[56] It was about an upright Ming-dynasty official who disagreed with the Emperor's land policy and was unjustly punished for being frank. When Mao finally saw it he could not but regard it as a clear attack on himself, plainly inspired by Liu and all the more galling in that the agricultural disasters for which he was thus publicly blamed had undeniably occurred. His attack was launched with a review of the play in the Shanghai daily, *Literary Currents,* 10 November 1965. Back in Peking near the end of the year, he saw the Soviet premier, Alexei Kosygin, and sneeringly asked him if Soviet Russia would come to China's help if America attacked her over the Vietnam War: Kosygin had no answer. But Mao admitted to him frankly that he was at loggerheads with his colleagues. Indeed he made little attempt to conceal the coming explosion. Back in Shanghai early in the new year, he snarled at Teng Hsiao-ping and other senior colleagues (who had travelled down from Peking) in front of an amazed delegation of Japanese Communists, addressing them as 'You weak-kneed people in Peking' for being 'soft on Russia'. The Japanese 'cringed in amazement'.[57]

From that point on, the Cultural Revolution gathered momentum. Mao (as he later put it) 'gave the nod'. In February 1966 Lin, now Chiang Ching's firm if apprehensive ally, appointed her 'Cultural Adviser' to the entire army forces. The obnoxious mandarin Mayor of Peking was dismissed and moved, along with Liu, into the shadows, though the two men, Teng and others were not arrested until the next year. On 20 March Mao, the old wizard, decided to conjure the brutal force of unlettered youth out of the earth. 'We need determined people who are young, have little education, a firm atti-

---

[55] Witke, op. cit., 318.

[56] For the long-term origins of the Cultural Revolution, see Roderick MacFarquhar, *The Origins of the Cultural Revolution, 1 Contradictions among the People 1956–7* (London 1974).

[57] *China Quarterly,* 45.

tude and the political experience to take over the work', he said. 'When we started to make revolution, we were mere twenty-three-year-old boys, while the rulers of that time . . . were old and experienced. They had more learning—but we had more truth'.[58] On 16 May, Chiang Ching, now the leading spirit in a group of activists, mainly from Shanghai, whom Mao had officially designated as in charge of the Cultural Revolution, issued her first circular. It attacked 'scholar-tyrants' who had 'abstruse' language to silence the class struggle and keep politics out of academia, using the fallacy 'everyone is equal before the truth'. Its sixth point was an open invitation to vandalism: 'Chairman Mao often says that there is no construction without destruction. Destruction means criticism and repudiation— it means revolution.' The *People's Daily* and other Peking papers refused to print it. Two days later Lin Piao made a remarkable speech about power to the Politburo, analysing the history of *coups d'état*. Echoing Goebbels, he argued that force and propaganda were irresistible in conjunction: 'Seizure of political power depends upon gunbarrels and inkwells.' And what was power for? 'Political power is an instrument by which one class oppresses another. It is exactly the same with revolution and with counter-revolution. As I see it, *political power is the power to oppress others.*'[59] That was frank enough; and, coming from the man who was supposed to be in charge of the nation's stability, it might well make the men round the table tremble. Even worse news was that the man in charge of the secret police, Kang Sheng, had thrown in his lot with the cultural revolutionaries. That meant there would be no restraint on the new 'gun-barrels and inkwells', which in the second half of May rapidly made their appearance, in the shape of Red Guards and wall-posters.

Scholastic violence and political change had long been linked in China. The student revolt in Peking had detonated the 4th May Movement in 1919 and the 9th December Movement in 1935. There had been a similar upsurge during the 'hundred flowers', eventually put down (by Teng and Liu, among others, eagerly reacting to Mao's 'nod') with the sacking of 100,000 teachers in 1957–8.[60] But this was something on an altogether different scale. With a population of 800

---

[58] Terrill, *Mao,* 315.

[59] Witke, op. cit., 320, 356ff.

[60] Naranarayan Das, *China's Hundred Weeds: A Study of the Anti-Rightist Campaign in China 1957–1958* (Calcutta 1979); Garside, op. cit., 69.

million, China now had 90 million children in primary schools, 10 million in middle schools and 600,000 in university.[61] The first Red Guards appeared on 29 May. They were from the middle school, aged about twelve to fourteen, wearing red cotton armbands with the characters 'Hung Wei Ping' (Red Guards) on them in yellow. Their first act was to attack Tsinghua University.[62] Soon they were joined by children from younger and older age-groups, by students and, most important, by members of the CCP Youth Leagues who, with Mao's encouragement, revolted against their official leadership and took to the streets in gangs. During the early summer, the entire educational system in China came to a standstill, as dons and teachers fled in terror (when they were lucky enough to escape capture and 're-education') and juvenile lynch-law took over.

There was later some misunderstanding of the Cultural Revolution in the West. It was represented as a revolt of intellectuals. In fact it was quite the reverse. It was a revolution of illiterates and semi-literates against intellectuals, the 'spectacle-wearers' as they were called. It was xenophobic, aimed at those who 'think the moon is rounder abroad'. The Red Guards had a great deal in common with Roehm's Brownshirts, and the entire movement with Hitler's campaign against 'cosmopolitan civilization'. It was the greatest witch-hunt in history, which made the Zhdanov purges in post-war Russia seem almost trivial. Nevertheless, it is significant that this great upsurge of vandalism attracted a certain type of radical academic, who was to become depressingly familiar in Europe and North America over the next few years. At Peking, the first 'big-character poster', addressed to and attacking the university authorities, was put up by a woman philosophy don, Nieh Yuan-tzu, who was to become the Madame Defarge of the campus horrors. It read: 'Why are you so afraid of the big-character posters? This is a life and death struggle to counter the Black Gang!' Within a week, 10,000 students had put up 100,000 posters, 'as big as doors', often with characters four feet high.[63] The phrases were reiterated: 'You absolutely won't get away with this . . . our patience is exhausted.' The first violence began at the same time. The rampaging street-gangs seized girls with long

[61] Chen, op. cit., 388.

[62] Ibid., 226.

[63] Ibid., 211.

braided hair and cut it short; boys with foreign-style stove-pipe pants had them ripped off. Hairdressers were told not to give 'duck-tail' cuts, restaurants to simplify menus, shops to stop selling cosmetics, dresses with slit skirts, sunglasses, fur-coats and other finery. Neon signs were smashed. There were huge street bonfires of forbidden goods, which included (as an exhibition of 'confiscations' showed) bolts of silk and brocade, gold and silver bars, chess-sets, ancient trunks and chests, playing-cards, mah-jong sets, gowns, frock-coats, top-hats, jazz records and a vast range of works of art. The Red Guards shut down teashops, coffee-houses, independent private theatres and all private restaurants, they put itinerant musicians, acrobats and strolling actors out of business, and they forbade weddings and funerals, holding hands and kite-flying. In Peking the ancient walls were pulled down, Bei Hai Park and the National Gallery of Fine Arts closed. Libraries were ransacked and shut, books burnt. Even when libraries remained open, few dared to visit them. Ten years later, Teng said that of the eight hundred technicians of the Research Institute for Non-ferrous Metals, for example, only four had the courage to use the library during the Cultural Revolution; he said that any of the 150,000 technical cadres of the Academy of Sciences who visited their laboratories during this dark time were denounced as 'white specialists'.[64]

There was no authority to prevent these activities. When shopkeepers and other injured parties sought police protection, they were reminded of 'The Decision of the Central Committee of the Chinese Communist Party Concerning the Great Proletarian Cultural Revolution' (1 August 1966), which read: 'The only method is for the masses to liberate themselves . . . trust the masses, rely on them and respect their initiative. . . . Don't be afraid of disturbances. . . . Let the masses educate themselves . . . no measures should be taken against students at universities, colleges, middle and primary schools . . .'[65] In fact party leaders who sought to curb the Red Guards were paraded through the streets wearing dunces' caps and placards. Every single school superintendent seems to have been dismissed.

As the movement got under way, violence became common, then

[64] Garside, op. cit., 70, 91; Witke, op. cit., 379; Terrill, op. cit., 315; Chen, op. cit., 226ff.

[65] Chen, op. cit., 221–4.

universal. Red Guard leaders seem to have come from the lowest social strata.[66] Some of them were mere street-thieves and hooligans, sporting thick leather belts with brass buckles. Their posters urged 'Boil him in oil', 'Smash his dog's head' and so on. Men and women classified as 'ghosts and monsters', 'bad elements' and 'counter-revolutionaries' had their heads shaved. Snippets of 'political debates' were later reported: 'Of course he is a capitalist. He has a sofa and two matching armchairs.'[67] Hundreds of thousands of private homes were broken into and ransacked for such reasons. But Red Guards raided government offices too, and forced officials to give them their archives on pain of being denounced as 'tools of the revisionists'. The Foreign Ministry was taken over by a gang led by Yao Teng-shan, a former petty official. He recalled every ambassador except one, stripped them of rank and assigned them to minor tasks. His notes to foreign powers, written in the style of Red Guard posters, were politely returned with the request that future communications be signed by Premier Chou. But Chou himself, normally the still centre of Chinese life through all Mao's dramas, seems to have been in danger at one stage. While it is true that, at the very top level, the Red Guards were not allowed to kill anyone, many died in gaol.[68] Liu himself was left to die (1973) in his own excrement, naked on the freezing floor of his concrete cell.[69] But at a lower level the loss of life was catastrophic. The *Agence France Presse,* in the most widely respected figure, estimated (3 February 1979) that the Red Guards had murdered about 400,000 people.

Meanwhile Chiang Ching had been ruling the world of culture and addressing mass meetings at which she denounced capitalism (which she said destroyed art), jazz, rock and roll, striptease, Impressionism, Symbolism, abstract art, Fauvism, Modernism—'in a word, decadence and obscenity, to poison and corrupt the minds of the people'. Her platform oratory was modelled on that of the secret police boss, Kang Sheng, with whom she often appeared. 'Do you want to study the Communiqué and the Sixteen-Point Directive?' 'Yes.' 'Do you want to study them again and again?' 'Yes.' 'Do you

[66] Anita Chan, *et al.,* 'Students and Class Warfare: The Social Roots of the Red Guard Conflict in Guangzhon (Conton)', *China Quarterly,* 83, September 1980.

[67] Chen, op. cit., 228–31.

[68] jail (ED.)

[69] See Simon Leys in *The Times Literary Supplement,* 6 March 1981, 259–60.

want to learn them thoroughly?' 'Yes.' 'Do you want to understand them?' 'Yes.' 'Do you want to apply them?' 'Yes.' 'Do you want to use them to carry out the Cultural Revolution in your school?' 'Yes, Yes, Yes!'[70] During the second half of 1966, virtually every main cultural organization in China was brought under her army organization. All her old scores against the theatre and film world, some dating from the 1930s, were worked off. Leading directors, playwrights, poets, actors and composers were accused of 'fawning on foreigners', praising 'secondary foreign devils', 'ridiculing the Boxers' (now seen as cultural heroes), and portraying ordinary Chinese as 'prostitutes, opium smokers, jugglers and women with bound feet', thus breeding a 'national inferiority complex'. The Red Guards were ordered by her to 'dig up the roots of the Black Line', 'rip off the masks', destroy films, songs and plays of the 'national defence line' and 'drag out' members of the 'Black Gang'.

On 12 December 1966 many 'public enemies', the ex-mayor of Peking and leading cultural mandarins—including, it seems, every film and theatre director who had ever crossed Chiang Ching—were marched to the Workers' Stadium in front of 10,000 people, with heavy wooden placards round their necks.[71] One of the worst aspects of the Cultural Revolution was the treatment of wives, who were often more brutally humiliated than their husbands. On 10 April 1967, for instance, Liu's wife was dragged in front of 300,000 people on the campus of Tsinghua University, dressed in a tight evening gown, with stiletto-heel shoes, an English straw hat and necklace of ping-pong balls decorated with skulls, while the mob bayed, 'Down with ox-devils and snake-gods!'[72]

Chiang Ching's squads took over radio and TV stations, newspapers and magazines; they seized cameras and films, ransacked studios for evidence, confiscated all existing films and issued them re-edited, and impounded scripts, prompt-copies and musical scores. Painters no longer dared to sign work with their own name but instead used the slogan 'Ten Thousand Years to Chairman Mao'.[73] 'With hammer in hand', said Chiang Ching, 'I set out to attack all

[70] Witke, op. cit., 324–5.

[71] Witke, op. cit., 328.

[72] William Hinton, *Hundred Days War: The Cultural Revolution at Tsinghua University* (New York 1972), 101–4.

[73] Terrill, op. cit., 319.

the old conventions.' She attended rehearsals of the Central Philharmonic Orchestra and interrupted them, goading the conductor Li Te-
lun into a furious shriek 'You're attacking me with a big hammer!'
She made composers write works which were then tried out on 'the
masses' and altered to take account of their reaction. She claimed
she had to 'hit them with a hammer' to make them obey and eliminate
'foreign influences'.[74] Some of her followers took her imagery literally,
and one Western-trained concert pianist had his hands smashed.
Hammers, fists, thumping and smashing were the emblems of revolutionary art. Taking over the ballet, Chiang Ching banned 'orchid
fingers' and upturned palms, favouring instead clenched fists and
violent movements to show 'hatred of landlord class' and 'determination to seek revenge.'[75]

Having banned virtually all forms of artistic expression in 1966,
Chiang Ching strove desperately to fill the void. But not much was
produced: two orchestral works, the Yellow River piano concerto and
the Shachiaping symphony, four operas and two ballets, all eight
classified as *yang-pan hsi* or 'model repertory', on the analogy of
model farms. There was a sculpture series called The Rent-Collectors'
Courtyard and a few paintings, of which the best known was a
portrait of Mao wearing a blue gown, investigating mining conditions
in the early 1920s, which was 'composed' by a collective of Peking
students and actually painted by the son of a 'poor peasant'. Few
films were made because (she later claimed), there was 'sabotage';
her actors, actresses and directors were given 'bad dormitories', no
hot meals and power was cut off from her stages and film-sets.[76]

After the heady days of 1966, when Mao did his swim and the
cult of his personality reached its apogee, China began to lurch into
civil war. On 5 February 1967, Mao's protégés in Shanghai set up a
'commune', an indication he was still hankering after the Great Leap
policy. It was based upon the dockers, especially the militant 2,500
of the Fifth Loading and Unloading District, who in a single day (in
June 1966) had written and put up 10,000 big-character posters. Of
this district, 532 workers resisted. They had posters written against
them and were made to wear tall dunces' hats and carry opprobrious
posters with mysterious slogans such as 'Four-Family Village' and

[74] Witke, op. cit., 388–90.

[75] Ibid., 435.

[76] Ibid., 391–2, 402.

'Anti-Party Clique'; they also had their houses ransacked and were sentenced to 'symbolic' death sentences, which might easily become real ones.[77] The Shanghai commune was supposed to detonate others across the country. But the workers did not rise. Indeed they often resisted Red Guard invasions of their factories. Even in Shanghai the city authorities fought back with their own Scarlet Guards. Each side had enormous banks of loud-speakers, whose slogans battled it out deafeningly from dawn to dusk: 'The February seizure of power is illegal', 'The February seizure of power is admirable'. There were kidnappings, torture and gang-warfare, using bicycle chains and knuckle-dusters, 'troops' being rushed from one part of the city to another.

At the universities, private armies were formed. The 'Chingkan-shang regiment' of Tsinghua University, an 'élite group' of the Far Left, fought pitched battles against 'ghosts and monsters' using bamboo spears and hand-made armoured cars and cannon. Other units included the Five-One-Six, the New Peita commune, the Geological Institute's 'East is Red' commune, and the 'Sky' faction of the Aeronautical Institute. These were imitated in the factories and the non-university towns, and a kind of feudal anarchy began to develop, as China lurched back into organized gang-warfare and war-lordism. In July 1967 there was a 'mutiny', as it was called, in Wuhan, actually a large-scale battle between a Red Guard workers' force and a conservative group known as the Million Heroes. The local army commander backed the Heroes. Chou En-lai was sent down to restore peace. He was lucky to escape with his life and two of his companions were arrested and tortured. As a result, Chiang Ching produced the slogan 'Offend by reason and defend by force', and quantities of arms were issued to Red Guard groups.[78]

The violence seems to have reached a climax in the late summer of 1967. At that point Mao, as usual, became both alarmed at what he had done and bored with the incessant wrangling. He seems to have told Chiang Ching to call it all off. In September she announced that violence must be verbal only; machine-guns were to be used

[77] Parris Chang, 'Shanghai and Chinese Politics before and after the Cultural Revolution' in Christopher Howe (ed.), *Shanghai* (Cambridge 1981).

[78] Philip Bridgham, 'Mao's Cultural Revolution in 1967' in Richard Baum and Louis Bennett (eds), *China in Ferment* (Yale 1971), 134–5; Thomas Robinson, 'Chou En-lai and the Cultural Revolution in China' in Baum and Bennett (eds), *The Cultural Revolution in China* (Berkeley 1971), 239–50.

only when 'absolutely necessary'. Those who disobeyed were accused of 'mountain-strongholdism'. Attacks on the British Embassy and its staff were the work of 'ultra-Leftists instigated by the May Sixteenth clique'.[79] Mao also took a hand. 'The situation developed so rapidly as to surprise me,' he told the Central Committee. 'I cannot blame you if you have complaints against me.' He was annoyed that the Foreign Minister, Chen Yi, had lost twenty-seven pounds during a Red Guard grilling, adding, 'I cannot show him to foreign visitors in this condition.' He told the 'young firebrands' and 'little devils' to go back to school. He broke the Shanghai commune. 'China is now like a country divided into eight hundred princely states,' he complained.[80]

In the autumn of 1967 Mao withdrew official support for the Cultural Revolution, at any rate in its active Red Guard form, and used the People's Liberation Army (PLA) to restore order and take over from groups he now denounced as 'incompetent' and 'politically immature'. He justified this use of force by remarking, 'Soldiers are just workers and peasants wearing uniforms.' Fighting continued in some places in 1968, but in diminishing volume. In the summer, at his home in South-and-Central Lakes, he had a curious 'dawn dialogue' with Red Guard leaders: 'I have never made any tape recordings before, but I am doing it today. Otherwise you will interpret what I say today in the way you wish after you go home. . . . Too many people were arrested, because I nodded my head.' Police Minister: 'I am the one to blame for excessive arrests.' Mao: 'Don't try to free me from my mistakes or cover up for me.' Chen Boda (left-wing theorist): 'Follow the Chairman's teaching closely.' Mao (snappish): 'Don't talk to me about teachings.' Later he threatened that if Red Guards fought the army, killed people, 'destroyed means of transportation' or 'lit fires', they would be 'annihilated'. But he was unwilling to drop his anarchism entirely: 'Let the students fight for another ten years. The earth will revolve as usual. Heaven is not going to fall.' All the same, the five chief Red Guard leaders were soon at work on pig-farms deep in the country-side.[81] The drama was over.

The years which followed the collapse of the Cultural Revolution, when the bill for it was being paid by the economy and ordinary

---

[79] Witke, op. cit., 349; Edward Rice, *Mao's Way* (Berkeley 1972), 376–8.

[80] *Far Eastern Economic Review*, 2 October 1969; Terrill, op. cit., 321–8.

[81] Terrill, op. cit., 328–30.

Chinese, were grim. Someone had to take the blame. On 12 September 1971, a Trident aircraft crashed 250 miles beyond the Chinese border in the Mongolian People's Republic. It contained the bodies of the PLA commander, Lin Piao, and his second wife, Yeh Chun. Everyone on board was dead and some of the corpses were riddled with bullets. According to Peking, Lin had been fleeing after the discovery of a plot of his to murder Mao. 'Captured documents', in which Mao was referred to by the code-name 'B-52', were produced, proving that Lin had sought to kill Mao in a traffic-accident, poison his food, use the air force to bomb his house, and blow up his train. He had written: 'B-52 is a paranoid and a sadist . . . the greatest dictator and tyrant in China's history. . . . Those who are his greatest friends today will be his prisoners tomorrow. . . . Even his own son has been driven mad by him.' The plot was allegedly betrayed to Chou En-lai by Lin's daughter by an earlier marriage, 'Little Bean', who hated her stepmother.[82] A more plausible version had it that Lin had been killed some time before by his colleagues, at a meeting in the Great Hall of the People—a real-life revolutionary drama this time. The next year a major plot was 'exposed' within the army, and a score of senior officers tried to escape to Hong Kong. A great many books and documents in which Lin had had a hand were recalled, together with his 'epitaphs' and portraits. Eleven famous photos of Mao, with Lin on them, were withdrawn. The episode, about which the truth remains obscure, closed with a note in the Chinese press, 20 February 1974, revealing that 'Little Bean' had been shot to death near Canton, a strip of red cloth pinned to the body reading 'Treason and heinous crime'.[83]

By this time the Mao era was drawing to its close. Chou was already suffering from cancer, Mao himself from Parkinson's Disease. His last phase was marked by acrimony, consciousness of failure and confusion. He quarrelled with Chiang Ching and by 1973 they had ceased to live together. She had to submit in writing requests to see him, stating her reasons. A note from him to her dated 21 March 1974 read: 'It is better not to see each other. You have not carried out what I have been telling you for many years. What is the good of seeing each other any more? You have books by Marx and Lenin and you have my books. You stubbornly refuse to study them'. He

---

[82] Chen, op. cit., 344ff.; Terrill, op. cit., 345ff.

[83] Terrill, op. cit., 369; Witke, op. cit., 365.

told her her 'demands' had injured his health. 'I am already eighty years old. Even so you bother me by saying various things. Why don't you have sympathy? I envy Chou En-lai and his wife.' What must have frightened her as much was the reappearance of her enemy Teng, back from the dead and thereafter known as 'Lazarus';[84] he told journalists he had been at 'reform school' in Jiangsi Province. In 1975 Mao produced his final slogan, 'Three Mores and one Less': 'Chou should rest more, Teng should work more, Wang should study more and Chiang Ching should talk less.' He appended a maxim: 'The ears are made so as to remain open but the mouth may shut.'[85]

Sometimes, in his last period, Mao was perky: 'People say that China loves peace. That's boasting. In fact the Chinese love struggle. I do for one.' He kept his hatred of formal education: 'The more books one reads, the stupider one becomes.' On the other hand, just before his death he received a report on the education system from the head of Qinghua University, who had been purged by Chiang Ching, then rehabilitated. Mao told him to speak only for three minutes. He was told, grimly: 'Thirty seconds will be enough. College students study textbooks of secondary schools, and *their* academic level is that of primary schools.' Mao (sadly): 'If this situation goes on, not only will the Party fail, but the nation itself will perish.'[86] His mind wandered between religious and secular belief. 'My body is riddled with diseases. I have an appointment with God.' On another occasion he asked colleagues: 'Are there not some of you who thought I would go to see Marx sooner?' 'None.' 'I don't believe it.'[87] His last saying was enigmatic: 'The people do not support the reversals of verdicts.'

The watershed year of 1976 opened an era of opaque confusion. Chou died early in April. This discreet mandarin, much respected abroad, who kept himself curiously detached from the failures and murderous squalor of the regime, seems to have been the only member of it to have aroused genuine popular feelings in China. When, on 5 April, the authorities removed wreaths placed in his memory in Peking's main square, 100,000 people rioted. Teng was immediately blamed for this disturbance and disgraced for the second time.

[84] the brother of Mary and Martha whom Jesus raised from the dead (ED.)

[85] Terrill, op. cit., 387–90; Witke, op. cit., 475–6.

[86] Terrill, op. cit., 402 footnote.

[87] Ibid., 381, 420.

Mao died on 9 September. During the last months of his life there was intense faction-fighting around his bedside. As soon as he was dead, Chiang Ching claimed a reconciliation had taken place. She produced a bit of paper which she claimed was a poem Mao had written to her *in extremis:* 'You have been wronged,' it said. 'I have tried to reach the peak of revolution but I was not successful. But you could reach the top.'[88]

However, another bit of paper was waved by Hua Kuo-Feng, who had succeeded Chou as premier. Hua was then fifty-five, a relative newcomer, having been on the Central Committee only since 1969 and Minister of Public Security since the previous year. He was almost a 'helicopter', a term more usually applied to Chiang Ching's fast-rising protégé Wang Hung-wen, now the party boss of Shanghai. Mao liked Hua partly because he was a peasant from his favourite province, Hunan, chiefly because he was cunningly sycophantic. On 30 April the old tyrant had scratched out for Hua six characters: 'With you in charge I have no worries.' Hua's bit of paper was undoubtedly authentic. In any case he had more impressive credentials: control of the top security unit in Peking, Number 8341, which protected Mao himself and which Hua had inherited from the old security boss Kang Sheng, who had died in December 1975.

The showdown came on 6 October, a month after Mao's death, at a Politburo meeting held in the home of his old comrade Yeh Chien-ying, the Defence Minister and effective second man of the regime. Chiang Ching was present with Wang and two other leading Shanghai cronies. She brandished her paper and demanded the chairmanship for herself, with her 'brains', the Shanghai journalist Chang Chun-chiao, as premier, and Wang as head of the National People's Congress. But the 'Gang of Four', as henceforth they were known, lost the 'argument', and were taken straight from the meeting to prison. In Shanghai, their stronghold, their followers planned to arm 30,000 leftist militia-members, but the local party leadership and the garrison commander were removed before anything decisive could be done. Hua had the security services and Chiang Ching had made herself much hated in the army.[89] She may have had a following in Shanghai but in Peking the mob loathed her and called her 'the Empress', a term of abuse since Boxer days; the 5 April riot had been

---

[88] Quoted in Ross Terrill, *The Future of China after Mao* (London 1978), 121.

[89] Ibid., 115–17.

directed against her and her friends. It was unfortunate for her, too, that 1976 was a year of appalling natural disasters, which the Chinese associate with a change in the dynasty. In April the largest meteor ever recorded fell on Kirin Province. In July and August three earthquakes hit north China, destroying parts of Peking and the whole of the nearby industrial centre of Tangshan, killing about 665,000 people (775,000 more were injured)—the second-worst earthquake disaster in China's history.

It was a simple matter to blame such things, and genuine manmade catastrophes—economic failure, the collapse of the education system, the destruction of art treasures and China's cultural life—upon the malign influence of 'the Empress' and her gang. Soon posters were up: 'Cut Chiang Ching into Ten Thousand Pieces', 'Deep-fry the Gang of Four in Oil'. For her trial in 1980–1, the eventual indictment ran to forty-eight pages. All four were accused of an astonishing variety of crimes, and each separately of specific acts of wickedness, vanity and extravagance—the last to emphasize that their puritanical reign of terror had been hypocritical. Chang had even been 'a spy in the pay of Chiang Kai-shek'. Wang was accused of philandering, importing expensive stereophonic equipment and, only four days before his arrest, having no less than 114 photographs taken of himself. Yao Wen-yuan, the fourth member of the gang, had spent $500 on a sumptuous banquet to celebrate Chou's death. Chiang Ching herself had drunk saffron water, dined off golden carp, kept an entire truckload of pornographic films, including the notorious *Sound of Music,* which she watched every night, ridden a horse then changed into a limousine, taken out library books on empresses, said that 'Even under Communism there can still be an Empress', closed a Canton shipyard because the noise disturbed her, prohibited planes landing so she could get to sleep, called the Empress-Dowager 'a legalist', had diverted traffic, ordered the leaves in Canton to be dusted before she arrived, said 'it is better to have socialist trains which run late than revisionist trains which run on time', hastened Mao's death by shifting him from one bed to another, played poker while he lay dying and said, 'The man must abdicate and let the woman take over.' She and the others were 'bad eggs' who 'worshipped things foreign, fawned on foreigners and maintained illicit foreign relations' and had 'engaged in flagrant capitulationism and national betrayal'. They were 'the evil lords of literature and the theatre'.[90] Chiang Ching remained defiant throughout her

---

[90] Witke, op. cit., 472ff.; Terrill, *China after Mao,* 121–3.

seven-week trial, which ended early in 1981, even extracting further drama from the proceedings at one point by suddenly stripping naked.[91] She was found guilty on all charges and condemned to death, sentence being provisionally suspended for two years.

By this time Hua himself was in the shadows, elbowed aside by Teng, old Lazarus himself, who had re-emerged into public life in 1977 and from the end of 1978 was clearly in charge. He was a rough, hard man from Szechuan, with something of Mao's own coarse brutality but without a suspicion of romanticism or any interest in politics as an art-form. Teng had been the most consistent opponent of Mao's political dramas, though he had sometimes been obliged to play bit-parts in them. He had spoken out grittily and often against the excesses of the Cultural Revolution. Now that it was disavowed and punished, his emergence at the top was logical and perhaps inevitable. He despised people for whom politics was the only thing in life that mattered, especially the hard Left: 'They sit on the lavatory and can't even manage to shit.' 'One should not talk of class struggle every day. In real life, not everything is class struggle.' He had nothing but contempt for proletarian art. 'You just see a bunch of people running to and fro on the stage. Not a trace of art. . . . Foreigners clap them only out of courtesy.' Having heard the Vienna Philharmonic Orchestra, he said, 'This is what I call food for the spirit.' Chinese operas 'nowadays', he added, were nothing more than 'gong-and-drum shows'. 'You go to a theatre and you find yourself on a battlefield.' Teng had no particular animosities: 'Let bygones be bygones. Those dismissed from office should be reinstated.' He said he wanted an end to the 'shouting and yelling'. The country must get back to work again. 'Most college students now carry nothing but one brush for all posters. They can't do anything else.' 'Scientists today are not given time for research. How can they create or invent things?' Not least, the army was demoralized, as in Chiang Kai-shek's day, and liable to revert to war-lordism. It had become 'thick-skinned, disunited, arrogant, lazy and soft'.[92]

Teng, in short was an old-fashioned, reactionary disciplinarian, now in his late seventies, who believed in law and order and hard work. He promptly sent the army into Vietnam, partly to punish the Vietnamese pro-Soviet leadership for persecuting its Chinese minority, but mainly to teach the PLA that life was a serious business:

[91] *Daily Telegraph,* 9 January 1981, quoting *Zheng Ming* magazine.

[92] Garside, op. cit., 67ff.

undisciplined units were put in the van and suffered appalling casualties. That done, he set about clearing up some of the mess Mao's long reign had left behind in the economy. It was now admitted publicly that the Mao era had been characterized, not by the puritanical austerity of which it had boasted, but by appalling corruption in high places.[93] The Peking *People's Daily* apologized to readers for 'all the lies and distortions' it had carried and, more remarkably, warned them against 'the false, boastful and untrue reports' which it 'still often prints'.[94]

In 1978–9 decisions were taken to move away from a Stalinist–Maoist stress on heavy industry and towards an economic structure more suited to a semi-developed country. The percentage of GNP invested was to fall from the unsustainable 38 per cent of 1978 to about 25 per cent by the mid-1980s. Profit-motives and bonuses were to be introduced; the law was to be reformed with emphasis on civil rights; democratic means were to be devised to check bureaucratic abuse; above all, market forces were to be allowed to exert their beneficent force.[95] The party was to cease to be the all-powerful force in national life. Its membership, 39 million in 1982, had apparently doubled in size during the Cultural Revolution, and Teng warned that many of these people had not been properly 'educated' and were 'below standard'. In a report issued in spring 1981, he claimed that many party members 'loved flattery', were 'complacent and fuzzy-minded', had stopped 'caring about the hardships of the masses', were 'covered in the dust of bureaucracy' and were 'arrogant, conservative, lazy, interested only in pleasure and imbued with an ideology of privilege.'[96] The 'new realism' coincided with more natural disasters, including a drought which dominated agriculture in 1980 and 1981 and forced a proud regime to beg the West for help. As the 1980s opened, therefore, China ceased to be the miraculous new superpower and finally rang down the curtain on the make-believe world of Maoist romanticism, which had ended in horrific melodrama. Instead it entered the real world of slow, painful and pragmatic progress.

---

[93] Ibid., 73ff.

[94] Leys, op. cit.

[95] Michael Oksenberg 'China Policy for the 1980s', *Foreign Affairs,* 59 (Winter 1980–1), 304–22.

[96] *Guardian,* 5 February 1982.

TADEUSZ BOROWSKI

This Way for the Gas, Ladies and Gentlemen

Tadeusz Borowski (1922–1951), a Polish short story writer and poet, published three collections of verse based on his experience of internment in a Nazi concentration camp during World War II. *This Way for the Gas, Ladies and Gentlemen and Other Stories* (1967), from which the following selection is taken, is his fictionalized account of the brutalization of prisoners in Auschwitz. Borowski committed suicide at the age of 29.

All of us walk around naked. The delousing is finally over, and our striped suits are back from the tanks of Cyclone B solution, an efficient killer of lice in clothing and of men in gas chambers. Only the inmates in the blocks cut off from ours by the "Spanish goats"[1] still have nothing to wear. But all the same, all of us walk around naked: the heat is unbearable. The camp has been sealed off tight. Not a single prisoner, not one solitary louse, can sneak through the gate. The labour Kommandos have stopped working. All day, thousands of naked men shuffle up and down the roads, cluster around the squares, or lie against the walls and on top of the roofs. We have been sleeping on plain boards, since our mattresses and blankets are still being disinfected. From the rear blockhouses we have a view of the F.K.L.—*Frauen Konzentration Lager,*[2] there too the delousing is in full swing. Twenty-eight thousand women have been stripped naked and driven out of the barracks. Now they swarm around the large yard between the blockhouses.

The heat rises, the hours are endless. We are without even our usual diversion: the wide roads leading to the crematoria are empty. For several days now, no new transports have come in. Part of "Canada"[3] has been liquidated and detailed to a labour Kommando—

Translated by Barbara Vedder.

[1] Crossed beams surrounded with barbed wire. (ED.)

[2] Women's concentration camp. (ED.)

[3] A designation of the well-being of members of the labour gang, or Kommando, who unloaded incoming transports of prisoners. (ED.)

one of the very toughest—at Harmenz. For there exists in the camp a special brand of justice based on envy: when the rich and mighty fall, their friends see to it that they fall to the very bottom. And Canada, our Canada, which smells not of maple forests but of French perfume, has amassed great fortunes in diamonds and currency from all over Europe.

Several of us sit on the top bunk, our legs dangling over the edge. We slice the neat loaves of crisp, crunchy bread. It is a bit coarse to the taste, the kind that stays fresh for days. Sent all the way from Warsaw—only a week ago my mother held this white loaf in her hands . . . dear Lord, dear Lord . . .

We unwrap the bacon, the onion, we open a can of evaporated milk. Henri, the fat Frenchman, dreams aloud of the French wine brought by the transports from Strasbourg, Paris, Marseille . . . Sweat streams down his body.

"Listen, *mon ami*,[4] next time we go up on the loading ramp, I'll bring you real champagne. You haven't tried it before, eh?"

"No. But you'll never be able to smuggle it through the gate, so stop teasing. Why not try and 'organize' some shoes for me instead— you know, the perforated kind, with a double sole, and what about that shirt you promised me long ago?"

"*Patience, patience.* When the new transports come, I'll bring all you want. We'll be going on the ramp again!"

"And what if there aren't any more 'cremo' transports?" I say spitefully. "Can't you see how much easier life is becoming around here: no limit on packages, no more beatings? You even write letters home . . . One hears all kind of talk, and, dammit, they'll run out of people!"

"Stop talking nonsense." Henri's serious fat face moves rhythmically, his mouth is full of sardines. We have been friends for a long time, but I do not even know his last name. "Stop talking nonsense," he repeats, swallowing with effort. "They can't run out of people, or we'll starve to death in this blasted camp. All of us live on what they bring."

"All? We have our packages . . ."

"Sure, you and your friend, and ten other friends of yours. Some of you Poles get packages. But what about us, and the Jews, and the Russkis? And what if we had no food, no 'organization' from the

---

[4] My friend (ED.)

transports, do you think you'd be eating those packages of yours in peace? We wouldn't let you!"

"You would, you'd starve to death like the Greeks. Around here, whoever has grub, has power."

"Anyway, you have enough, we have enough, so why argue?"

Right, why argue? They have enough, I have enough, we eat together and we sleep on the same bunks. Henri slices the bread, he makes a tomato salad. It tastes good with the commissary mustard.

Below us, naked sweat-drenched men crowd the narrow barracks aisles or lie packed in eights and tens in the lower bunks. Their nude, withered bodies stink of sweat and excrement; their cheeks are hollow. Directly beneath me, in the bottom bunk, lies a rabbi. He has covered his head with a piece of rag torn off a blanket and reads from a Hebrew prayer book (there is no shortage of this type of literature at the camp), wailing loudly, monotonously.

"Can't somebody shut him up? He's been raving as if he'd caught God himself by the feet."

"I don't feel like moving. Let him rave. They'll take him to the oven that much sooner."

"Religion is the opium of the people," Henri, who is a Communist and a *rentier*,[5] says sententiously. "If they didn't believe in God and eternal life, they'd have smashed the crematoria long ago."

"Why haven't you done it then?"

The question is rhetorical; the Frenchman ignores it.

"Idiot," he says simply, and stuffs a tomato in his mouth.

Just as we finish our snack, there is a sudden commotion at the door. The Muslims scurry in fright to the safety of their bunks, a messenger runs into the Block Elder's shack. The Elder, his face solemn, steps out at once.

"Canada! *Antreten.*[6] But fast! There's a transport coming!"

"Great God!" yells Henri, jumping off the bunk. He swallows the rest of his tomato, snatches his coat, screams *"Raus"*[7] at the men below, and in a flash is at the door. We can hear a scramble in the other bunks. Canada is leaving for the ramp.

"Henri, the shoes!" I call after him.

---

[5] name for a prisoner who had been physically and spiritually destroyed (ED.)

[6] Get going (ED.)

[7] Get out (ED.)

"Keine Angst!"[8] he shouts back, already outside.

I proceed to put away the food. I tie a piece of rope around the suitcase where the onions and the tomatoes from my father's garden in Warsaw mingle with Portuguese sardines, bacon from Lublin (that's from my brother), and authentic sweetmeats from Salonica. I tie it all up, pull on my trousers, and slide off the bunk.

"Platz!"[9] I yell, pushing my way through the Greeks. They step aside. At the door I bump into Henri.

"Was ist los?"[10]

"Want to come with us on the ramp?"

"Sure, why not?"

"Come along then, grab your coat! We're short a few men. I've already told the Kapo," and he shoves me out of the barracks door.

We line up. Someone has marked down our numbers, someone up ahead yells, "March, march," and now we are running towards the gate, accompanied by the shouts of a multilingual throng that is already being pushed back to the barracks. Not everybody is lucky enough to be going on the ramp . . . We have almost reached the gate. *Links, zwei, drei, vier! Mützen ab!*[11] Erect, arms stretched stiffly along our hips, we march past the gate briskly, smartly, almost gracefully. A sleepy S.S. man with a large pad in his hand checks us off, waving us ahead in groups of five.

"Hundert!" he calls after we have all passed.

"Stimmt!"[12] comes a hoarse answer from out front.

We march fast, almost at a run. There are guards all around, young men with automatics. We pass camp II B, then some deserted barracks and a clump of unfamiliar green—apple and pear trees. We cross the circle of watchtowers and, running, burst on to the highway. We have arrived. Just a few more yards. There, surrounded by trees, is the ramp.

A cheerful little station, very much like any other provincial railway stop: a small square framed by tall chestnuts and paved with yellow gravel. Not far off, beside the road, squats a tiny wooden

[8] Don't worry (ED.)

[9] Place! (ED.)

[10] What's the matter? (ED.)

[11] Left, two, three, four! Hats off! (ED.)

[12] One hundred! . . . OK! (ED.)

shed, uglier and more flimsy than the ugliest and flimsiest railway shack; farther along lie stacks of old rails, heaps of wooden beams, barracks parts, bricks, paving stones. This is where they load freight for Birkenau: supplies for the construction of the camp, and people for the gas chambers. Trucks drive around, load up lumber, cement, people—a regular daily routine.

And now the guards are being posted along the rails, across the beams, in the green shade of the Silesian chestnuts, to form a tight circle around the ramp. They wipe the sweat from their faces and sip out of their canteens. It is unbearably hot; the sun stands motionless at its zenith.

"Fall out!"

We sit down in the narrow streaks of shade along the stacked rails. The hungry Greeks (several of them managed to come along, God only knows how) rummage underneath the rails. One of them finds some pieces of mildewed bread, another a few half-rotten sardines. They eat.

"*Schweinedreck,*"[13] spits a young, tall guard with corn-coloured hair and dreamy blue eyes. "For God's sake, any minute you'll have so much food to stuff down your guts, you'll bust!" He adjusts his gun, wipes his face with a handkerchief.

"Hey you, fatso!" His boot lightly touches Henri's shoulder. "*Pass mal auf,*[14] want a drink!"

"Sure, but I haven't got any marks," replies the Frenchman with a professional air.

"*Schade,* too bad."

"Come, come, Herr Posten, isn't my word good enough any more? Haven't we done business before? How much?"

"One hundred. *Gemacht?*"

"*Gemacht.*"[15]

We drink the water, lukewarm and tasteless. It will be paid for by the people who have not yet arrived.

"Now you be careful," says Henri, turning to me. He tosses away the empty bottle. It strikes the rails and bursts into tiny fragments. "Don't take any money, they might be checking. Anyway, who the hell needs money? You've got enough to eat. Don't take suits, either,

---

[13] Filthy pigs (ED.)

[14] Pay attention (ED.)

[15] Done? . . . Done (ED.)

or they'll think you're planning to escape. Just get a shirt, silk only, with a collar. And a vest. And if you find something to drink, don't bother calling me. I know how to shift for myself, but you watch your step or they'll let you have it."

"Do they beat you up here?"

"Naturally. You've got to have eyes in your ass. *Arschaugen.*"[16]

Around us sit the Greeks, their jaws working greedily, like huge human insects. They munch on stale lumps of bread. They are restless, wondering what will happen next. The sight of the large beams and the stacks of rails has them worried. They dislike carrying heavy loads.

"*Was wir arbeiten?*"[17] they ask.

"*Niks. Transport kommen, alles Krematorium, compris?*"[18]

"*Alles verstehen,*"[19] they answer in crematorium Esperanto. All is well—they will not have to move the heavy rails or carry the beams.

In the meantime, the ramp has become increasingly alive with activity, increasingly noisy. The crews are being divided into those who will open and unload the arriving cattle cars and those who will be posted by the wooden steps. They receive instructions on how to proceed most efficiently. Motorcycles drive up, delivering S.S. officers, bemedalled, glittering with brass, beefy men with highly polished boots and shiny, brutal faces. Some have brought their briefcases, others hold thin, flexible whips. This gives them an air of military readiness and agility. They walk in and out of the commissary—for the miserable little shack by the road serves as their commissary, where in the summertime they drink mineral water, *Studentenquelle,* and where in winter they can warm up with a glass of hot wine. They greet each other in the state-approved way, raising an arm Roman fashion, then shake hands cordially, exchange warm smiles, discuss mail from home, their children, their families. Some stroll majestically on the ramp. The silver squares on their collars glitter, the gravel crunches under their boots, their bamboo whips snap impatiently.

We lie against the rails in the narrow streaks of shade, breathe unevenly, occasionally exchange a few words in our various tongues,

---

[16] Ass eyes (ED.)

[17] What will we be working on? (ED.)

[18] Nothing. Transport coming, all Crematorium, understand? (ED.)

[19] We understand (ED.)

and gaze listlessly at the majestic men in green uniforms, at the green trees, and at the church steeple of a distant village.

"The transport is coming," somebody says. We spring to our feet, all eyes turn in one direction. Around the bend, one after another, the cattle cars begin rolling in. The train backs into the station, a conductor leans out, waves his hand, blows a whistle. The locomotive whistles back with a shrieking noise, puffs, the train rolls slowly alongside the ramp. In the tiny barred windows appear pale, wilted, exhausted human faces, terror-stricken women with tangled hair, unshaven men. They gaze at the station in silence. And then, suddenly, there is a stir inside the cars and a pounding against the wooden boards.

"Water! Air!"—weary, desperate cries.

Heads push through the windows, mouths gasp frantically for air. They draw a few breaths, then disappear; others come in their place, then also disappear. The cries and moans grow louder.

A man in a green uniform covered with more glitter than any of the others jerks his head impatiently, his lips twist in annoyance. He inhales deeply, then with a rapid gesture throws his cigarette away and signals to the guard. The guard removes the automatic from his shoulder, aims, sends a series of shots along the train. All is quiet now. Meanwhile, the trucks have arrived, steps are being drawn up, and the Canada men stand ready at their posts by the train doors. The S.S. officer with the briefcase raises his hand.

"Whoever takes gold, or anything at all besides food, will be shot for stealing Reich property. Understand? *Verstanden?*"

"*Jawohl!*"[20] we answer eagerly.

"*Also los!* Begin!"

The bolts crack, the doors fall open. A wave of fresh air rushes inside the train. People . . . inhumanly crammed, buried under incredible heaps of luggage, suitcases, trunks, packages, crates, bundles of every description (everything that had been their past and was to start their future). Monstrously squeezed together, they have fainted from heat, suffocated, crushed one another. Now they push towards the opened doors, breathing like fish cast out on the sand.

"Attention! Out, and take your luggage with you! Take out everything. Pile all your stuff near the exits. Yes, your coats too. It is summer. March to the left. Understand?"

---

[20] Yes, indeed! (ED.)

"Sir, what's going to happen to us?" They jump from the train on to the gravel, anxious, worn-out.

"Where are you people from?"

"Sosnowiec-Będzin. Sir, what's going to happen to us?" They repeat the question stubbornly, gazing into our tired eyes.

"I don't know. I don't understand Polish."

It is the camp law: people going to their death must be deceived to the very end. This is the only permissible form of charity. The heat is tremendous. The sun hangs directly over our heads, the white, hot sky quivers, the air vibrates, an occasional breeze feels like a sizzling blast from a furnace. Our lips are parched, the mouth fills with the salty taste of blood, the body is weak and heavy from lying in the sun. Water!

A huge, multicoloured wave of people loaded down with luggage pours from the train like a blind, mad river trying to find a new bed. But before they have a chance to recover, before they can draw a breath of fresh air and look at the sky, bundles are snatched from their hands, coats ripped off their backs, their purses and umbrellas taken away.

"But please, sir, it's for the sun, I cannot . . ."

"Verboten!"[21] one of us barks through clenched teeth. There is an S.S. man standing behind your back, calm, efficient, watchful.

"Meine Herrschaften,[22] this way, ladies and gentlemen, try not to throw your things around, please. Show some goodwill," he says courteously, his restless hands playing with the slender whip.

"Of course, of course," they answer as they pass, and now they walk alongside the train somewhat more cheerfully. A woman reaches down quickly to pick up her handbag. The whip flies, the woman screams, stumbles, and falls under the feet of the surging crowd. Behind her, a child cries in a thin little voice *"Mamele!"*—a very small girl with tangled black curls.

The heaps grow. Suitcases, bundles, blankets, coats, handbags that open as they fall, spilling coins, gold, watches; mountains of bread pile up at the exits, heaps of marmalade, jams, masses of meat, sausages; sugar spills on the gravel. Trucks, loaded with people, start up with a deafening roar and drive off amidst the wailing and scream-ing of the women separated from their children, and the stupefied

---

[21] Forbidden! (ED.)

[22] Distinguished ladies and gentlemen (ED.)

silence of the men left behind. They are the ones who had been ordered to step to the right—the healthy and the young who will go to the camp. In the end, they too will not escape death, but first they must work.

Trucks leave and return, without interruption, as on a monstrous conveyor belt. A Red Cross van drives back and forth, back and forth, incessantly: it transports the gas that will kill these people. The enormous cross on the hood, red as blood, seems to dissolve in the sun.

The Canada men at the trucks cannot stop for a single moment, even to catch their breath. They shove the people up the steps, pack them in tightly, sixty per truck, more or less. Near by stands a young, cleanshaven "gentleman," an S.S. officer with a notebook in his hand. For each departing truck he enters a mark; sixteen gone means one thousand people, more or less. The gentleman is calm, precise. No truck can leave without a signal from him, or a mark in his notebook: *Ordnung muss sein.*[23] The marks swell into thousands, the thousands into whole transports, which afterwards we shall simply call "from Salonica," "from Strasbourg," "from Rotterdam." This one will be called "Sosnowiec-Będzin." The new prisoners from Sosnowiec-Będzin will receive serial numbers 131-2—thousand, of course, though afterwards we shall simply say 131-2, for short.

The transports swell into weeks, months, years. When the war is over, they will count up the marks in their notebooks—all four and a half million of them. The bloodiest battle of the war, the greatest victory of the strong, united Germany. *Ein Reich, ein Volk, ein Führer*[24]—and four crematoria.

The train has been emptied. A thin, pock-marked S.S. man peers inside, shakes his head in disgust, and motions to our group, pointing his finger at the door.

"*Rein.* Clean it up!"

We climb inside. In the corners amid human excrement and abandoned wrist-watches lie squashed, trampled infants, naked little monsters with enormous heads and bloated bellies. We carry them out like chickens, holding several in each hand.

"Don't take them to the trucks, pass them on to the women," says the S.S. man, lighting a cigarette. His cigarette lighter is not working properly, he examines it carefully.

[23] There must be order (ED.)

[24] One Empire, one People, one Leader (ED.)

"Take them, for God's sake!" I explode as the women run from me in horror, covering their eyes.

The name of God sounds strangely pointless, since the women and the infants will go on the trucks, every one of them, without exception. We all know what this means, and we look at each other with hate and horror.

"What, you don't want to take them?" asks the pock-marked S.S. man with a note of surprise and reproach in his voice, and reaches for his revolver.

"You mustn't shoot, I'll carry them." A tall, grey-haired woman takes the little corpses out of my hands and for an instant gazes straight into my eyes.

"My poor boy," she whispers and smiles at me. Then she walks away, staggering along the path. I lean against the side of the train. I am terribly tired. Someone pulls at my sleeve.

"*Ev avant,* to the rails, come on!"

I look up, but the face swims before my eyes, dissolves, huge and transparent, melts into the motionless trees and the sea of people . . . I blink rapidly: Henri.

"Listen, Henri, are we good people?"

"That's stupid. Why do you ask?"

"You see, my friend, you see, I don't know why, but I am furious, simply furious with these people—furious because I must be here because of them. I feel no pity. I am not sorry they're going to the gas chamber. Damn them all! I could throw myself at them, beat them with my fists. It must be pathological, I just can't understand . . ."

"Ah, on the contrary, it is natural, predictable, calculated. The ramp exhausts you, you rebel—and the easiest way to relieve your hate is to turn against someone weaker. Why, I'd even call it healthy. It's simply logic, *compris?*" He props himself up comfortably against the heap of rails. "Look at the Greeks, they know how to make the best of it! They stuff their bellies with anything they find. One of them has just devoured a full jar of marmalade."

"Pigs! Tomorrow half of them will die of the shits."

"Pigs? You've been hungry."

"Pigs!" I repeat furiously. I close my eyes. The air is filled with ghastly cries, the earth trembles beneath me, I can feel sticky moisture on my eyelids. My throat is completely dry.

The morbid procession streams on and on—trucks growl like mad dogs. I shut my eyes tight, but I can still see corpses dragged from the train, trampled infants, cripples piled on top of the dead,

wave after wave . . . freight cars roll in, the heaps of clothing,
suitcases, and bundles grow, people climb out, look at the sun, take
a few breaths, beg for water, get into the trucks, drive away. And
again freight cars roll in, again people . . . The scenes become
confused in my mind—I am not sure if all of this is actually happening, or if I am dreaming. There is a humming inside my head; I
feel that I must vomit.

Henri tugs at my arm.

"Don't sleep, we're off to load up the loot."

All the people are gone. In the distance, the last few trucks roll
along the road in clouds of dust, the train has left, several S.S. officers
promenade up and down the ramp. The silver glitters on their collars.
Their boots shine, their red, beefy faces shine. Among them there is
a woman—only now I realize she has been here all along—withered,
flat-chested, bony, her thin, colourless hair pulled back and tied in
a "Nordic" knot; her hands are in the pockets of her wide skirt. With
a rat-like, resolute smile glued on her thin lips she sniffs around the
corners of the ramp. She detests feminine beauty with the hatred of
a woman who is herself repulsive, and knows it. Yes, I have seen her
many times before and I know her well: she is the commandant of
the F.K.L. She has come to look over the new crop of women, for
some of them, instead of going on the trucks, will go on foot—to
the concentration camp. There our boys, the barbers from Zauna,
will shave their heads and will have a good laugh at their "outside
world" modesty.

We proceed to load the loot. We lift huge trunks, heave them on
to the trucks. There they are arranged in stacks, packed tightly.
Occasionally somebody slashes one open with a knife, for pleasure
or in search of vodka and perfume. One of the crates falls open; suits,
shirts, books drop out on the ground . . . I pick up a small, heavy
package. I unwrap it—gold, about two handfuls, bracelets, rings,
brooches, diamonds . . .

"Gib hier,"[25] an S.S. man says calmly, holding up his briefcase
already full of gold and colourful foreign currency. He locks the case,
hands it to an officer, takes another, an empty one, and stands by
the next truck, waiting. The gold will go to the Reich.

It is hot, terribly hot. Our throats are dry, each word hurts.
Anything for a sip of water! Faster, faster, so that it is over, so that

---

[25] Give it here (ED.)

we may rest. At last we are done, all the trucks have gone. Now we swiftly clean up the remaining dirt: there must be "no trace left of the *Schweinerei*."[26] But just as the last truck disappears behind the trees and we walk, finally, to rest in the shade, a shrill whistle sounds around the bend. Slowly, terribly slowly, a train rolls in, the engine whistles back with a deafening shriek. Again weary, pale faces at the windows, flat as though cut out of paper, with huge, feverishly burning eyes. Already trucks are pulling up, already the composed gentleman with the notebook is at his post, and the S.S. men emerge from the commissary carrying briefcases for the gold and money. We unseal the train doors.

It is impossible to control oneself any longer. Brutally we tear suitcases from their hands, impatiently pull off their coats. Go on, go on, vanish! They go, they vanish. Men, women, children. Some of them know.

Here is a woman—she walks quickly, but tries to appear calm. A small child with a pink cherub's face runs after her and, unable to keep up, stretches out his little arms and cries: "Mama! Mama!"

"Pick up your child, woman!"

"It's not mine, sir, not mine!" she shouts hysterically and runs on, covering her face with her hands. She wants to hide, she wants to reach those who will not ride the trucks, those who will go on foot, those who will stay alive. She is young, healthy, good-looking, she wants to live.

But the child runs after her, wailing loudly: "Mama, mama, don't leave me!"

"It's not mine, not mine, no!"

Andrei, a sailor from Sevastopol, grabs hold of her. His eyes are glassy from vodka and the heat. With one powerful blow he knocks her off her feet, then, as she falls, takes her by the hair and pulls her up again. His face twitches with rage.

"Ah, you bloody Jewess! So you're running from your own child! I'll show you, you whore!" His huge hand chokes her, he lifts her in the air and heaves her on to the truck like a heavy sack of grain.

"Here! And take this with you, bitch!" and he throws the child at her feet.

"*Gut gemacht,* good work. That's the way to deal with degenerate mothers," says the S.S. man standing at the foot of the truck. "*Gut, gut, Russki.*"

---

[26] Obscenity (ED.)

"Shut your mouth," growls Andrei through clenched teeth, and walks away. From under a pile of rags he pulls out a canteen, unscrews the cork, takes a few deep swallows, passes it to me. The strong vodka burns the throat. My head swims, my legs are shaky, again I feel like throwing up.

And suddenly, above the teeming crowd pushing forward like a river driven by an unseen power, a girl appears. She descends lightly from the train, hops on to the gravel, looks around inquiringly, as if somewhat surprised. Her soft, blonde hair has fallen on her shoulders in a torrent, she throws it back impatiently. With a natural gesture she runs her hands down her blouse, casually straightens her skirt. She stands like this for an instant, gazing at the crowd, then turns and with a gliding look examines our faces, as though searching for someone. Unknowingly, I continue to stare at her, until our eyes meet.

"Listen, tell me, where are they taking us?"

I look at her without saying a word. Here, standing before me, is a girl, a girl with enchanting blonde hair, with beautiful breasts, wearing a little cotton blouse, a girl with a wise, mature look in her eyes. Here she stands, gazing straight into my face, waiting. And over there is the gas chamber: communal death, disgusting and ugly. And over in the other direction is the concentration camp: the shaved head, the heavy Soviet trousers in sweltering heat, the sickening, stale odour of dirty, damp female bodies, the animal hunger, the inhuman labour, and later the same gas chamber, only an even more hideous, more terrible death . . .

Why did she bring it? I think to myself, noticing a lovely gold watch on her delicate wrist. They'll take it away from her anyway.

"Listen, tell me," she repeats.

I remain silent. Her lips tighten.

"I know," she says with a shade of proud contempt in her voice, tossing her head. She walks off resolutely in the direction of the trucks. Someone tries to stop her; she boldly pushes him aside and runs up the steps. In the distance I can only catch a glimpse of her blonde hair flying in the breeze.

I go back inside the train; I carry out dead infants; I unload luggage. I touch corpses, but I cannot overcome the mounting, uncontrollable terror. I try to escape from the corpses, but they are everywhere: lined up on the gravel, on the cement edge of the ramp, inside the cattle cars. Babies, hideous naked women, men twisted by convulsions. I run off as far as I can go, but immediately a whip slashes across my back. Out of the corner of my eye I see an S.S.

man, swearing profusely. I stagger forward and run, lose myself in the Canada group. Now, at last, I can once more rest against the stack of rails. The sun has leaned low over the horizon and illuminates the ramp with a reddish glow; the shadows of the trees have become elongated, ghostlike. In the silence that settles over nature at this time of day, the human cries seem to rise all the way to the sky.

Only from this distance does one have a full view of the inferno on the teeming ramp. I see a pair of human beings who have fallen to the ground locked in a last desperate embrace. The man has dug his fingers into the woman's flesh and has caught her clothing with his teeth. She screams hysterically, swears, cries, until at last a large boot comes down over her throat and she is silent. They are pulled apart and dragged like cattle to the truck. I see four Canada men lugging a corpse, a huge, swollen female corpse. Cursing, dripping wet from the strain, they kick out of their way some stray children who have been running all over the ramp, howling like dogs. The men pick them up by the collars, heads, arms and toss them inside the trucks, on top of the heaps. The four men have trouble lifting the fat corpse on to the car, they call others for help, and all together they hoist up the mound of meat. Big, swollen, puffed-up corpses are being collected from all over the ramp; on top of them are piled the invalids, the smothered, the sick, the unconscious. The heap seethes, howls, groans. The driver starts the motor, the truck begins rolling.

"Halt! Halt!" an S.S. man yells after them. "Stop, damn you!"

They are dragging to the truck an old man wearing tails and a band around his arm. His head knocks against the gravel and pavement; he moans and wails in an uninterrupted monotone: *"Ich will mit dem Herrn Kommandanten sprechen*—I wish to speak with the commandant . . ." With senile stubbornness he keeps repeating those words all the way. Thrown on the truck, trampled by others, choked, he still wails: *"Ich will mit dem* . . ."

"Look here, old man!" a young S.S. man calls, laughing jovially. "In half an hour you'll be talking with the top commandant! Only don't forget to greet him with a *Heil Hitler!*"

Several other men are carrying a small girl with only one leg. They hold her by the arms and the one leg. Tears are running down her face and she whispers faintly: "Sir, it hurts, it hurts . . ." They throw her on the truck on top of the corpses. She will burn alive along with them.

The evening has come, cool and clear. The stars are out. We lie against the rails. It is incredibly quiet. Anaemic bulbs hang from the top of the high lamp-posts; beyond the circle of light stretches an impenetrable darkness. Just one step, and a man could vanish for ever. But the guards are watching, their automatics ready.

"Did you get the shoes?" asks Henri.

"No."

"Why?"

"My God, man, I am finished, absolutely finished!"

"So soon? After only two transports? Just look at me, I . . . since Christmas, at least a million people have passed through my hands. The worst of all are the transports from around Paris—one is always bumping into friends."

"And what do you say to them?"

"That first they will have a bath, and later we'll meet at the camp. What would you say?"

I do not answer. We drink coffee with vodka; somebody opens a tin of cocoa and mixes it with sugar. We scoop it up by the handful, the cocoa sticks to the lips. Again coffee, again vodka.

"Henri, what are we waiting for?"

"There'll be another transport."

"I'm not going to unload it! I can't take any more."

"So, it's got you down? Canada is nice, eh?" Henri grins indulgently and disappears into the darkness. In a moment he is back again.

"All right. Just sit here quietly and don't let an S.S. man see you. I'll try to find you your shoes."

"Just leave me alone. Never mind the shoes." I want to sleep. It is very late.

Another whistle, another transport. Freight cars emerge out of the darkness, pass under the lamp-posts, and again vanish in the night. The ramp is small, but the circle of lights is smaller. The unloading will have to be done gradually. Somewhere the trucks are growling. They back up against the steps, black, ghostlike, their searchlights flash across the trees. *Wasser! Luft!* The same all over again, like a late showing of the same film: a volley of shots, the train falls silent. Only this time a little girl pushes herself halfway through the small window and, losing her balance, falls out on to the gravel. Stunned, she lies still for a moment, then stands up and begins walking around in a circle, faster and faster, waving her rigid arms in the air, breathing loudly and spasmodically, whining in a faint voice. Her mind has given way in the inferno inside the train. The whining is hard on the nerves: an S.S. man approaches calmly, his heavy boot strikes between her shoulders. She falls. Holding her down with his foot, he draws his revolver, fires once, then again. She remains face down, kicking the gravel with her feet, until she stiffens. They proceed to unseal the train.

I am back on the ramp, standing by the doors. A warm, sickening smell gushes from inside. The mountain of people filling the car almost halfway up to the ceiling is motionless, horribly tangled, but still steaming.

"Ausladen!"[27] comes the command. An S.S. man steps out from the darkness. Across his chest hangs a portable searchlight. He throws a stream of light inside.

"Why are you standing about like sheep? Start unloading!" His whip flies and falls across our backs. I seize a corpse by the hand; the fingers close tightly around mine. I pull back with a shriek and stagger away. My heart pounds, jumps up to my throat. I can no longer control the nausea. Hunched under the train I begin to vomit. Then, like a drunk, I weave over to the stack of rails.

I lie against the cool, kind metal and dream about returning to the camp, about my bunk, on which there is no mattress, about sleep among comrades who are not going to the gas tonight. Suddenly I see the camp as a haven of peace. It is true, others may be dying, but one is somehow still alive, one has enough food, enough strength to work . . .

The lights on the ramp flicker with a spectral glow, the wave of people—feverish, agitated, stupefied people—flows on and on, endlessly. They think that now they will have to face a new life in the camp, and they prepare themselves emotionally for the hard struggle ahead. They do not know that in just a few moments they will die, that the gold, money, and diamonds which they have so prudently hidden in their clothing and on their bodies are now useless to them. Experienced professionals will probe into every recess of their flesh, will pull the gold from under the tongue and the diamonds from the uterus and the colon. They will rip out gold teeth. In tightly sealed crates they will ship them to Berlin.

The S.S. men's black figures move about, dignified, businesslike. The gentleman with the notebook puts down his final marks, rounds out the figures: fifteen thousand.

Many, very many, trucks have been driven to the crematoria today.

[27] Unload! (ED.)

It is almost over. The dead are being cleared off the ramp and piled into the last truck. The Canada men, weighed down under a load of bread, marmalade, and sugar, and smelling of perfume and fresh linen, line up to go. For several days the entire camp will live off this transport. For several days the entire camp will talk about "Sosnowiec-Będzin." "Sosnowiec-Będzin" was a good, rich transport.

The stars are already beginning to pale as we walk back to the camp. The sky grows translucent and opens high above our heads— it is getting light.

Great columns of smoke rise from the crematoria and merge up above into a huge black river which very slowly floats across the sky over Birkenau and disappears beyond the forests in the direction of Trzebinia. The "Sosnowiec-Będzin" transport is already burning.

We pass a heavily armed S.S. detachment on its way to change guard. The men march briskly, in step, shoulder to shoulder, one mass, one will.

"*Und morgen die ganze, Welt . . .*"[28] they sing at the top of their lungs.

"*Rechts ran!* To the right march!" snaps a command from up front. We move out of their way.

C. S. LEWIS

The Abolition of Man

C. S. Lewis (1898–1963) was an English theologian, novelist, literary scholar, and critic. He is popularly known for both children's novels (*The Chronicles of Narnia,* 1950–56) and science fiction. Of his scholarly works, *The Allegory of Love* (1936), stands as one of the major texts on medieval poetry. Other works include *The Problem of Pain* (1940), *The Abolition of Man* (1943), from which the following selection is taken, and *The Four Loves* (1960).

"Man's conquest of Nature" is an expression often used to describe the progress of applied science. "Man has Nature whacked" said

[28] And tomorrow the whole world . . . (ED.)

someone to a friend of mine not long ago. In their context the words had a certain tragic beauty, for the speaker was dying of tuberculosis. "No matter," he said, "I know I'm one of the casualties. Of course there are casualties on the winning as well as on the losing side. But that doesn't alter the fact that it is winning." I have chosen this story as my point of departure in order to make it clear that I do not wish to disparage all that is really beneficial in the process described as "Man's conquest," much less all the real devotion and self-sacrifice that has gone to make it possible. But having done so I must proceed to analyse this conception a little more closely. In what sense is Man the possessor of increasing power over Nature?

Let us consider three typical examples: the aeroplane, the wireless, and the contraceptive. In a civilized community, in peace-time, anyone who can pay for them may use these things. But it cannot strictly be said that when he does so he is exercising his own proper or individual power over Nature. If I pay you to carry me, I am not therefore myself a strong man. Any or all of the three things I have mentioned can be withheld from some men by other men—by those who sell, or those who allow the sale, or those who own the sources of production, or those who make the goods. What we call Man's power is, in reality, a power possessed by some men which they may, or may not, allow other men to profit by. Again, as regards the powers manifested in the aeroplane or the wireless, Man is as much the patient or subject as the possessor, since he is the target both for bombs and for propaganda. And as regards contraceptives, there is a paradoxical, negative sense in which all possible future generations are the patients or subjects of a power wielded by those already alive. By contraception simply, they are denied existence; by contraception used as a means of selective breeding, they are, without their concurring voice, made to be what one generation, for its own reasons, may choose to prefer. From this point of view, what we call Man's power over Nature turns out to be a power exercised by some men over other men with Nature as its instrument.

It is, of course, a commonplace to complain that men have hitherto used badly, and against their fellows, the powers that science has given them. But that is not the point I am trying to make. I am not speaking of particular corruptions and abuses which an increase of moral virtue would cure: I am considering what the thing called "Man's power over Nature" must always and essentially be. No doubt, the picture could be modified by public ownership of raw materials and factories and public control of scientific research. But unless we have a world state this will still mean the power of one nation over others. And even within the world state or the nation it will mean (in principle) the power of majorities over minorities, and (in the concrete) of a government over the people. And all long-term exercises of power, especially in breeding, must mean the power of earlier generations over later ones.

The latter point is not always sufficiently emphasized, because those who write on social matters have not yet learned to imitate the physicists by always including Time among the dimensions. In order to understand fully what Man's power over Nature, and therefore the power of some men over other men, really means, we must picture the race extended in time from the date of its emergence to that of its extinction. Each generation exercises power over its successors: and each, in so far as it modifies the environment bequeathed to it and rebels against tradition, resists and limits the power of its predecessors. This modifies the picture which is sometimes painted of a progressive emancipation from tradition and a progressive control of natural processes resulting in a continual increase of human power. In reality, of course, if any one age really attains, by eugenics and scientific education, the power to make its descendants what it pleases, all men who live after it are the patients of that power. They are weaker, not stronger: for though we may have put wonderful machines in their hands we have pre-ordained how they are to use them. And if, as is almost certain, the age which had thus attained maximum power over posterity were also the age most emancipated from tradition, it would be engaged in reducing the power of its predecessors almost as drastically as that of its successors. And we must also remember that, quite apart from this, the later a generation comes—the nearer it lives to that date at which the species becomes extinct—the less power it will have in the forward direction, because its subjects will be so few. There is therefore no question of a power vested in the race as a whole steadily growing as long as the race survives. The last men, far from being the heirs of power, will be of all men most subject to the dead hand of the great planners and conditioners and will themselves exercise least power upon the future. The real picture is that of one dominant age—let us suppose the hundredth century A.D.—which resists all previous ages most successfully and dominates all subsequent ages most irresistibly, and thus is the real master of the human species. But even within this master generation (itself an infinitesimal minority of the species) the power will be exercised by a minority smaller still. Man's conquest of Nature, if the dreams of some scientific planners are realized, means the rule of a few hundreds of men over billions upon billions

of men. There neither is nor can be any simple increase of power on
Man's side. Each new power won *by* man is a power *over* man as
well. Each advance leaves him weaker as well as stronger. In every
victory, besides being the general who triumphs, he is also the prisoner who follows the triumphal car.

I am not yet considering whether the total result of such ambivalent victories is a good thing or a bad. I am only making clear
what Man's conquest of Nature really means and especially that final
stage in the conquest, which, perhaps, is not far off. The final stage
is come when Man by eugenics, by pre-natal conditioning, and by
an education and propaganda based on a perfect applied psychology,
has obtained full control over himself. *Human* nature will be the last
part of Nature to surrender to Man. The battle will then be won. We
shall have "taken the thread of life out of the hand of Clotho"[1] and
be henceforth free to make our species whatever we wish it to be.
The battle will indeed be won. But who, precisely, will have won it?

For the power of Man to make himself what he pleases means,
as we have seen, the power of some men to make other men what
they please. In all ages, no doubt, nurture and instruction have, in
some sense, attempted to exercise this power. But the situation to
which we must look forward will be novel in two respects. In the
first place, the power will be enormously increased. Hitherto the
plans of educationalists have achieved very little of what they attempted and indeed, when we read them—how Plato would have
every infant "a bastard nursed in a bureau," and Elyot would have
the boy see no men before the age of seven and, after that, no women,[2]
and how Locke wants children to have leaky shoes and no turn for
poetry[3]—we may well thank the beneficent obstinacy of real mothers,
real nurses, and (above all) real children for preserving the human
race in such sanity as it still possesses. But the man-moulders of the

---

[1] In Greek mythology, Clotho, one of the Fates, spun the thread of destiny. (ED.)

[2] *The Boke Named the Governour,* I. iv: 'Al men except physitions only shulde be
excluded and kepte out of the norisery.' I. vi: 'After that a childe is come to seuen
yeres of age . . . the most sure counsaile is to withdrawe him from all company of
women.'

[3] *Some Thoughts concerning Education,* § 7: 'I will also advise his *Feet to be wash'd*
every Day in cold Water, and to have his Shoes so thin that they might leak and *let
in Water,* whenever he comes near it.' § 174: 'If he have a poetick vein, 'tis to me the
strangest thing in the World that the Father should desire or suffer it to be cherished
or improved. Methinks the Parents should labour to have it stifled and suppressed as
much as may be.' Yet Locke is one of our most sensible writers on education.

new age will be armed with the powers of an omnicompetent state and an irresistible scientific technique: we shall get at last a race of conditioners who really can cut out all posterity in what shape they please. The second difference is even more important. In the older systems both the kind of man the teachers wished to produce and their motives for producing him were prescribed by the *Tao*[4]—a norm to which the teachers themselves were subject and from which they claimed no liberty to depart. They did not cut men to some pattern they had chosen. They handed on what they had received: they initiated the young neophyte into the mystery of humanity which overarched him and them alike. It was but old birds teaching young birds to fly. This will be changed. Values are now mere natural phenomena. Judgements of value are to be produced in the pupil as part of the conditioning. Whatever *Tao* there is will be the product, not the motive, of education. The conditioners have been emancipated from all that. It is one more part of Nature which they have conquered. The ultimate springs of human action are no longer, for them, something given. They have surrendered—like electricity: it is the function of the Conditioners to control, not to obey them. They know how to *produce* conscience and decide what kind of conscience they will produce. They themselves are outside, above. For we are assuming the last stage of Man's struggle with Nature. The final victory has been won. Human nature has been conquered—and, of course, has conquered, in whatever sense those words may now bear.

The Conditioners, then, are to choose what kind of artificial *Tao* they will, for their own good reasons, produce in the Human race. They are the motivators, the creators of motives. But how are they going to be motivated themselves? For a time, perhaps, by survivals, within their own minds, of the old "natural" *Tao*. Thus at first they may look upon themselves as servants and guardians of humanity and conceive that they have a "duty" to do it "good." But it is only by confusion that they can remain in this state. They recognize the concept of duty as the result of certain processes which they can now control. Their victory has consisted precisely in emerging from the state in which they were acted upon by those processes to the state in which they use them as tools. One of the things they now have to decide is whether they will, or will not, so condition the rest of us that we can go on having the old idea of duty and the old

---

[4] Chinese term, meaning "the Way," for the principle that orders the universe (ED.)

reactions to it. How can duty help them to decide that? Duty itself is up for trial: it cannot also be the judge. And "good" fares no better. They know quite well how to produce a dozen different conceptions of good in us. The question is which, if any, they should produce. No conception of good can help them to decide. It is absurd to fix on one of the things they are comparing and make it the standard of comparison.

To some it will appear that I am inventing a factitious difficulty for my Conditioners. Other, more simple-minded, critics may ask "Why should you suppose they will be such bad men?" But I am not supposing them to be bad men. They are, rather, not men (in the old sense) at all. They are, if you like, men who have sacrificed their own share in traditional humanity in order to devote themselves to the task of deciding what "Humanity" shall henceforth mean. "Good" and "bad," applied to them, are words without content: for it is from them that the content of these words is henceforward to be derived. Nor is their difficulty factitious. We might suppose that it was possible to say "After all, most of us want more or less the same things— food and drink and sexual intercourse, amusement, art, science, and the longest possible life for individuals and for the species. Let them simply say, This is what we happen to like, and go on to condition men in the way most likely to produce it. Where's the trouble?" But this will not answer. In the first place, it is false that we all really like the same things. But even if we did, what motive is to impel the Conditioners to scorn delights and live laborious days in order that we, and posterity, may have what we like? Their duty? But that is only the *Tao,* which they may decide to impose on us, but which cannot be valid for them. If they accept it, then they are no longer the makers of conscience but still its subjects, and their final conquest over Nature has not really happened. The preservation of the species? But why should the species be preserved? One of the questions before them is whether this feeling for posterity (they know well how it is produced) shall be continued or not. However far they go back, or down, they can find no ground to stand on. Every motive they try to act on becomes at once a *petitio.*[5] It is not that they are bad men. They are not men at all. Stepping outside the *Tao,* they have stepped into the void. Nor are their subjects necessarily unhappy men. They are not men at all: they are artefacts. Man's final conquest has proved to be the abolition of Man.

---

[5] *Petitio principii:* circular argument (ED.)

Yet the Conditioners will act. When I said just now that all motives fail them, I should have said all motives except one. All motives that claim any validity other than that of their felt emotional weight at a given moment have failed them. Everything except the *sic volo, sic jubeo*[6] has been explained away. But what never claimed objectivity cannot be destroyed by subjectivism. The impulse to scratch when I itch or to pull to pieces when I am inquisitive is immune from the solvent which is fatal to my justice, or honour, or care for posterity. When all that says "it is good" has been debunked, what says "I want" remains. It cannot be exploded or "seen through" because it never had any pretensions. The Conditioners, therefore, must come to be motivated simply by their own pleasure. I am not here speaking of the corrupting influence of power nor expressing the fear that under it our Conditioners will degenerate. The very words *corrupt* and *degenerate* imply a doctrine of value and are therefore meaningless in this context. My point is that those who stand outside all judgements of value cannot have any ground for preferring one of their own impulses to another except the emotional strength of that impulse. We may legitimately hope that among the impulses which arise in minds thus emptied of all "rational" or "spiritual" motives, some will be benevolent. I am very doubtful myself whether the benevolent impulses, stripped of that preference and encouragement which the *Tao* teaches us to give them and left to their merely natural strength and frequency as psychological events, will have much influence. I am very doubtful whether history shows us one example of a man who, having stepped outside traditional morality and attained power, has used that power benevolently. I am inclined to think that the Conditioners will hate the conditioned. Though regarding as an illusion the artificial conscience which they produce in us their subjects, they will yet perceive that it creates in us an illusion of meaning for our lives which compares favourably with the futility of their own: and they will envy us as eunuchs envy men. But I do not insist on this, for it is mere conjecture. What is not conjecture is that our hope even of a "conditioned" happiness rests on what is ordinarily called "chance"—the chance that benevolent impulses may on the whole predominate in our Conditioners. For without the judgement "Benevolence is good"—that is, without re-entering the *Tao*—they can have no ground for promoting or

---

[6] This I want, this I command (ED.)

stabilizing their benevolent impulses rather than any others. By the logic of their position they must just take their impulses as they come, from chance. And Chance here means Nature. It is from heredity, digestion, the weather, and the association of ideas, that the motives of the Conditioners will spring. Their extreme rationalism, by "seeing through" all "rational" motives, leaves them creatures of wholly irrational behaviour. If you will not obey the *Tao,* or else commit suicide, obedience to impulse (and therefore, in the long run, to mere "nature") is the only course left open.

At the moment, then, of Man's victory over Nature, we find the whole human race subjected to some individual men, and those individuals subjected to that in themselves which is purely "natural"—to their irrational impulses. Nature, untrammelled by values, rules the Conditioners and, through them, all humanity. Man's conquest of Nature turns out, in the moment of its consummation, to be Nature's conquest of Man. Every victory we seemed to win has led us, step by step, to this conclusion. All Nature's apparent reverses have been but tactical withdrawals. We thought we were beating her back when she was luring us on. What looked to us like hands held up in surrender was really the opening of arms to enfold us for ever. If the fully planned and conditioned world (with its *Tao* a mere product of the planning) comes into existence, Nature will be troubled no more by the restive species that rose in revolt against her so many millions of years ago, will be vexed no longer by its chatter of truth and mercy and beauty and happiness. *Ferum victorem cepit:*[7] and if the eugenics are efficient enough there will be no second revolt, but all snug beneath the Conditioners, and the Conditioners beneath her, till the moon falls or the sun grows cold.

My point may be clearer to some if it is put in a different form. Nature is a word of varying meanings, which can best be understood if we consider its various opposites. The Natural is the opposite of the Artificial, the Civil, the Human, the Spiritual, and the Supernatural. The Artificial does not now concern us. If we take the rest of the list of opposites, however, I think we can get a rough idea of what men have meant by Nature and what it is they oppose to her. Nature seems to be the spatial and temporal, as distinct from what is less fully so or not so at all. She seems to be the world of quantity, as against the world of quality: of objects as against consciousness:

---

[7] Nature captures the victor (ED.)

of the bound, as against the wholly or partially autonomous: of that which knows no values as against that which both has and perceives value: of efficient causes (or, in some modern systems, of no causality at all) as against final causes. Now I take it that when we understand a thing analytically and then dominate and use it for our own convenience we reduce it to the level of "Nature" in the sense that we suspend our judgements of value about it, ignore its final cause (if any), and treat it in terms of quantity. This repression of elements in what would otherwise be our total reaction to it is sometimes very noticeable and even painful: something has to be overcome before we can cut up a dead man or a live animal in a dissecting room. These objects *resist* the movement of the mind whereby we thrust them into the world of mere Nature. But in other instances too, a similar price is exacted for our analytical knowledge and manipulative power, even if we have ceased to count it. We do not look at trees either as Dryads or as beautiful objects while we cut them into beams: the first man who did so may have felt the price keenly, and the bleeding trees in Virgil and Spenser may be far-off echoes of that primeval sense of impiety. The stars lost their divinity as astronomy developed, and the Dying God has no place in chemical agriculture. To many, no doubt, this process is simply the gradual discovery that the real world is different from what we expected, and the old opposition to Galileo or to "bodysnatchers" is simply obscurantism. But that is not the whole story. It is not the greatest of modern scientists who feel most sure that the object, stripped of its qualitative properties and reduced to mere quantity, is wholly real. Little scientists, and little unscientific followers of science, may think so. The great minds know very well that the object, so treated, is an artificial abstraction, that something of its reality has been lost.

From this point of view the conquest of Nature appears in a new light. We reduce things to mere Nature *in order that* we may "conquer" them. We are always conquering Nature, because "Nature" is the name for what we have, to some extent, conquered. The price of conquest is to treat a thing as mere Nature. Every conquest over Nature increases her domain. The stars do not become Nature till we can weigh and measure them: the soul does not become Nature till we can psycho-analyse her. The wresting of powers *from* Nature is also the surrendering of things *to* Nature. As long as this process stops short of the final stage we may well hold that the gain outweighs the loss. But as soon as we take the final step of reducing our own species to the level of mere Nature, the whole process is stultified, for this time the being who stood to gain and the being who has been sacrificed are one and the same. This is one of the many instances where to carry a principle to what seems its logical conclusion produces absurdity. It is like the famous Irishman who found that a certain kind of stove reduced his fuel bill by half and thence concluded that two stoves of the same kind would enable him to warm his house with no fuel at all. It is the magician's bargain: give up our soul, get power in return. But once our souls, that is, our selves, have been given up, the power thus conferred will not belong to us. We shall in fact be the slaves and puppets of that to which we have given our souls. It is in Man's power to treat himself as a mere "natural object" and his own judgements of value as raw material for scientific manipulation to alter at will. The objection to his doing so does not lie in the fact that his point of view (like one's first day in a dissecting room) is painful and shocking till we grow used to it. The pain and the shock are at most a warning and a symptom. The real objection is that if man chooses to treat himself as raw material, raw material he will be: not raw material to be manipulated, as he fondly imagined, by himself, but by mere appetite, that is, mere Nature, in the person of his dehumanized Conditioners.

We have been trying, like Lear[8], to have it both ways: to lay down our human prerogative and yet at the same time to retain it. It is impossible. Either we are rational spirit obliged for ever to obey the absolute values of the *Tao,* or else we are mere nature to be kneaded and cut into new shapes for the pleasures of masters who must, by hypothesis, have no motive but their own "natural" impulses. Only the *Tao* provides a common human law of action which can overarch rulers and ruled alike. A dogmatic belief in objective value is necessary to the very idea of a rule which is not tyranny or an obedience which is not slavery.

I am not here thinking solely, perhaps not even chiefly, of those who are our public enemies at the moment. The process which, if not checked, will abolish Man, goes on apace among Communists and Democrats no less than among Fascists. The methods may (at first) differ in brutality. But many a mild-eyed scientist in pincenez, many a popular dramatist, many an amateur philosopher in our midst, means in the long run just the same as the Nazi rulers of Germany. Traditional values are to be "debunked" and mankind to be cut out into some fresh shape at the will (which must, by hy-

---

[8] In Shakespeare's *King Lear,* the aging Lear relinquishes his authority to his daughters but is not prepared for his subsequent dependency and helplessness. (ED.)

pothesis, be an arbitrary will) of some few lucky people in one lucky generation which has learned how to do it. The belief that we can invent "ideologies" at pleasure, and the consequent treatment of mankind as mere υλη, specimens, preparations, begins to affect our very language. Once we killed bad men: now we liquidate unsocial elements. Virtue has become *integration* and diligence *dynamism,* and boys likely to be worthy of a commission are "potential officer material." Most wonderful of all, the virtues of thrift and temperance, and even of ordinary intelligence, are *sales-resistance.*

The true significance of what is going on has been concealed by the use of the abstraction Man. Not that the word Man is necessarily a pure abstraction. In the *Tao* itself, as long as we remain within it, we find the concrete reality in which to participate is to be truly human: the real common will and common reason of humanity, alive, and growing like a tree, and branching out, as the situation varies, into ever new beauties and dignities of application. While we speak from within the *Tao* we can speak of Man having power over himself in a sense truly analogous to an individual's self-control. But the moment we step outside and regard the *Tao* as a mere subjective product, this possibility has disappeared. What is now common to all men is a mere abstract universal, an H.C.F.[9], and Man's conquest of himself means simply the rule of the Conditioners over the conditioned human material, the world of post-humanity which, some knowingly and some unknowingly, nearly all men in all nations are at present labouring to produce.

Nothing I can say will prevent some people from describing this lecture as an attack on science. I deny the charge, of course: and real Natural Philosophers (there are some now alive) will perceive that in defending value I defend *inter alia*[10] the value of knowledge, which must die like every other when its roots in the *Tao* are cut. But I can go further than that. I even suggest that from Science herself the cure might come. I have described as a "magician's bargain" that process whereby man surrenders object after object, and finally himself, to Nature in return for power. And I meant what I said. The fact that the scientist has succeeded where the magician failed has put such a wide contrast between them in popular thought that the real story of the birth of Science is misunderstood. You will even

[9] Highest Common Factor (ED.)

[10] among other things (ED.)

find people who write about the sixteenth century as if Magic were a medieval survival and Science the new thing that came to sweep it away. Those who have studied the period know better. There was very little magic in the Middle Ages: the sixteenth and seventeenth centuries are the high noon of magic. The serious magical endeavour and the serious scientific endeavour are twins: one was sickly and died, the other strong and throve. But they were twins. They were born of the same impulse. I allow that some (certainly not all) of the early scientists were actuated by a pure love of knowledge. But if we consider the temper of that age as a whole we can discern the impulse of which I speak. There is something which unites magic and applied science while separating both from the "wisdom" of earlier ages. For the wise men of old the cardinal problem had been how to conform the soul to reality, and the solution had been knowledge, self-discipline, and virtue. For magic and applied science alike the problem is how to subdue reality to the wishes of men: the solution is a technique; and both, in the practice of this technique, are ready to do things hitherto regarded as disgusting and impious—such as digging up and mutilating the dead. If we compare the chief trumpeter of the new era (Bacon)[11] with Marlowe's Faustus, the similarity is striking. You will read in some critics that Faustus has a thirst for knowledge. In reality, he hardly mentions it. It is not truth he wants from his devils, but gold and guns and girls. "All things that move between the quiet poles shall be at his command" and "a sound magician is a mighty god." In the same spirit Bacon condemns those who value knowledge as an end in itself: this, for him, is to use as a mistress for pleasure what ought to be a spouse for fruit. The true object is to extend Man's power to the performance of all things possible. He rejects magic because it does not work, but his goal is that of the magician. In Paracelsus[12] the characters of magician and scientist are combined. No doubt those who really founded modern science were usually those whose love of truth exceeded their love of power; in every mixed movement the efficacy comes from the good elements not from the bad. But the presence of the bad elements is not irrelevant to the direction the efficacy takes. It might be going too far to say that the modern scientific movement was tainted from

[11] Francis Bacon (1561–1626) was an English philosopher, essayist, and statesman. (ED.)

[12] Paracelsus (1493?–1541) was a Swiss physician and alchemist whose dictum was, "Magic is a great wisdom—Reason is a great open folly." (ED.)

its birth: but I think it would be true to say that it was born in an unhealthy neighbourhood and at an inauspicious hour. Its triumphs may have been too rapid and purchased at too high a price: reconsideration, and something like repentance, may be required.

Is it, then, possible to imagine a new Natural Philosophy, continually conscious that the "natural object" produced by analysis and abstraction is not reality but only a view, and always correcting the abstraction? I hardly know what I am asking for. I hear rumours that Goethe's approach to nature deserves fuller consideration—that even Dr. Steiner[13] may have seen something that orthodox researchers have missed. The regenerate science which I have in mind would not do even to minerals and vegetables what modern science threatens to do to man himself. When it explained it would not explain away. When it spoke of the parts it would remember the whole. While studying the *It* it would not lose what Martin Buber calls the *Thou*-situation. The analogy between the *Tao* of Man and the instincts of an animal species would mean for it new light cast on the unknown thing, Instinct, by the only known reality of conscience and not a reduction of conscience to the category of Instinct. Its followers would not be free with the words *only* and *merely*. In a word, it would conquer Nature without being at the same time conquered by her and buy knowledge at a lower cost than that of life.

Perhaps I am asking impossibilities. Perhaps, in the nature of things, analytical understanding must always be a basilisk which kills what it sees and only sees by killing. But if the scientists themselves cannot arrest this process before it reaches the common Reason and kills that too, then someone else must arrest it. What I most fear is the reply that I am "only one more" obscurantist, that this barrier, like all previous barriers set up against the advance of science, can be safely passed. Such a reply springs from the fatal serialism of the modern imagination—the image of infinite unilinear progression which so haunts our minds. Because we have to use numbers so much we tend to think of every process as if it must be like the numeral series, where every step, to all eternity, is the same kind of step as the one before. I implore you to remember the Irishman and his two stoves. There are progressions in which the last step is *sui*

---

[13] *Johann Wolfgang von Goethe* (1749–1832) was a German poet, dramatist, novelist, and scientist. *Rudolf Steiner* (1861–1925) was a German occultist and social philosopher and an admirer of Goethe's. Both stressed the importance of human spiritual nature in addition to objective scientific knowledge. (ED.)

generis—incommensurable with the others—and in which to go the whole way is to undo all the labour of your previous journey. To reduce the *Tao* to a mere natural product is a step of that kind. Up to that point, the kind of explanation which explains things away may give us something, though at a heavy cost. But you cannot go on "explaining away" for ever: you will find that you have explained explanation itself away. You cannot go on "seeing through" things for ever. The whole point of seeing through something is to see something through it. It is good that the window should be transparent, because the street or garden beyond it is opaque. How if you saw through the garden too? It is no use trying to "see through" first principles. If you see through everything, then everything is transparent. But a wholly transparent world is an invisible world. To "see through" all things is the same as not to see.

BARBARA TUCHMAN

"This Is the End of the World": The Black Death

> Barbara Tuchman (1912–1989), an American historian and biographer, received Pulitzer prizes for two of her books: *The Guns of August* (1962), an account of the beginnings of World War I, and *Stilwell and the American Experience in China* (1971). Her later works include *A Distant Mirror: The Calamitous Fourteenth Century* (1978), from which the following selection is taken, *Practicing History* (1981), and *The March of Folly: From Troy to Vietnam* (1948).

In October 1347, two months after the fall of Calais, Genoese trading ships put into the harbor of Messina in Sicily with dead and dying men at the oars. The ships had come from the Black Sea port of Caffa (now Feodosiya) in the Crimea, where the Genoese maintained a trading post. The diseased sailors showed strange black swellings about the size of an egg or an apple in the armpits and groin. The swellings oozed blood and pus and were followed by spreading boils and black blotches on the skin from internal bleeding. The sick suffered severe pain and died quickly within five days of the first symptoms. As the disease spread, other symptoms of continuous fever and spitting of blood appeared instead of the swellings or buboes. These victims coughed and sweated heavily and died even more quickly, within three days or less, sometimes in 24 hours. In both types everything that issued from the body—breath, sweat, blood from the buboes and lungs, bloody urine, and blood-blackened excrement—smelled foul. Depression and despair accompanied the physical symptoms, and before the end "death is seen seated on the face."[1]

The disease was bubonic plague, present in two forms: one that infected the bloodstream, causing the buboes and internal bleeding, and was spread by contact; and a second, more virulent pneumonic type that infected the lungs and was spread by respiratory infection. The presence of both at once caused the high mortality and speed of contagion. So lethal was the disease that cases were known of persons going to bed well and dying before they woke, of doctors catching the illness at a bedside and dying before the patient. So rapidly did it spread from one to another that to a French physician, Simon de Covino, it seemed as if one sick person "could infect the whole world."[2] The malignity of the pestilence appeared more terrible because its victims knew no prevention and no remedy.

The physical suffering of the disease and its aspects of evil mystery were expressed in a strange Welsh lament which saw "death coming into our midst like black smoke, a plague which cuts off the young, a rootless phantom which has no mercy for fair countenance. Woe is me of the shilling in the armpit! It is seething, terrible . . . a head that gives pain and causes a loud cry . . . a painful angry knob . . . Great is its seething like a burning cinder . . . a grievous thing of ashy color." Its eruption is ugly like the "seeds of black peas, broken fragments of brittle sea-coal . . . the early ornaments of black death, cinders of the peelings of the cockle weed, a mixed multitude, a black plague like half-pence, like berries. . . ."[3]

Rumors of a terrible plague supposedly arising in China and spreading through Tartary (Central Asia) to India and Persia, Mes-

[1] Anna M. Campbell, *The Black Death and Men of Learning* (New York: Columbia University Press, 1931), 80.

[2] Francis Aidan Gasquet, Abbot, *The Black Death of 1348 and 1349,* 2nd ed. (London, 1908), 41.

[3] Philip Ziegler, *The Black Death* (New York, 1969), 190.

opotamia, Syria, Egypt, and all of Asia Minor had reached Europe in 1346. They told of a death toll so devastating that all of India was said to be depopulated, whole territories covered by dead bodies, other areas with no one left alive. As added up by Pope Clement VI at Avignon, the total of reported dead reached 23,840,000. In the absence of a concept of contagion, no serious alarm was felt in Europe until the trading ships brought their black burden of pestilence into Messina while other infected ships from the Levant carried it to Genoa and Venice.

By January 1348 it penetrated France via Marseille, and North Africa via Tunis. Shipborne along coasts and navigable rivers, it spread westward from Marseille through the ports of Languedoc to Spain and northward up the Rhône to Avignon, where it arrived in March. It reached Narbonne, Montpellier, Carcassonne, and Toulouse between February and May, and at the same time in Italy spread to Rome and Florence and their hinterlands. Between June and August it reached Bordeaux, Lyon, and Paris, spread to Burgundy and Normandy, and crossed the Channel from Normandy into southern England. From Italy during the same summer it crossed the Alps into Switzerland and reached eastward to Hungary.

In a given area the plague accomplished its kill within four to six months and then faded, except in the larger cities, where, rooting into the close-quartered population, it abated during the winter, only to reappear in spring and rage for another six months.

In 1349 it resumed in Paris, spread to Picardy, Flanders, and the Low Countries, and from England to Scotland and Ireland as well as to Norway, where a ghost ship with a cargo of wool and a dead crew drifted offshore until it ran aground near Bergen. From there the plague passed into Sweden, Denmark, Prussia, Iceland, and as far as Greenland. Leaving a strange pocket of immunity in Bohemia, and Russia unattacked until 1351, it had passed from most of Europe by mid-1350. Although the mortality rate was erratic, ranging from one fifth in some places to nine tenths or almost total elimination in others, the overall estimate of modern demographers has settled— for the area extending from India to Iceland—around the same figure expressed in Froissart's casual words: "a third of the world died." His estimate, the common one at the time, was not an inspired guess but a borrowing of St. John's figure for mortality from plague in Revelation, the favorite guide to human affairs of the Middle Ages.

A third of Europe would have meant about 20 million deaths. No one knows in truth how many died. Contemporary reports were an awed impression, not an accurate count. In crowded Avignon, it was said, 400 died daily; 7,000 houses emptied by death were shut up; a single graveyard received 11,000 corpses in six weeks; half the city's inhabitants reportedly died, including 9 cardinals or one third of the total, and 70 lesser prelates. Watching the endlessly passing death carts, chroniclers let normal exaggeration take wings and put the Avignon death toll at 62,000 and even at 120,000, although the city's total population was probably less than 50,000.

When graveyards filled up, bodies at Avignon were thrown into the Rhône until mass burial pits were dug for dumping the corpses. In London in such pits corpses piled up in layers until they overflowed. Everywhere reports speak of the sick dying too fast for the living to bury. Corpses were dragged out of homes and left in front of doorways. Morning light revealed new piles of bodies. In Florence the dead were gathered up by the Compagnia della Misericordia—founded in 1244 to care for the sick—whose members wore red robes and hoods masking the face except for the eyes. When their efforts failed, the dead lay putrid in the streets for days at a time. When no coffins were to be had, the bodies were laid on boards, two or three at once, to be carried to graveyards or common pits. Families dumped their own relatives into the pits, or buried them so hastily and thinly "that dogs dragged them forth and devoured their bodies."[4]

Amid accumulating death and fear of contagion, people died without last rites and were buried without prayers, a prospect that terrified the last hours of the stricken. A bishop in England gave permission to laymen to make confession to each other as was done by the Apostles, "or if no man is present then even to a woman," and if no priest could be found to administer extreme unction, "then faith must suffice."[5] Clement VI found it necessary to grant remissions of sin to all who died of the plague because so many were unattended by priests. "And no bells tolled," wrote a chronicler of Siena, "and nobody wept no matter what his loss because almost everyone expected death. . . . And people said and believed, 'This is the end of the world.' "[6]

---

[4] Ziegler, *The Black Death,* 58.

[5] Ziegler, *The Black Death,* 125.

[6] Ferdinand Schevill, *Siena: The History of a Medieval Commune* (New York, 1909), 211.

In Paris, where the plague lasted through 1349, the reported death rate was 800 a day, in Pisa 500, in Vienna 500 to 600. The total dead in Paris numbered 50,000 or half the population. Florence, weakened by the famine of 1347, lost three to four fifths of its citizens, Venice two thirds, Hamburg and Bremen, though smaller in size, about the same proportion. Cities, as centers of transportation, were more likely to be affected than villages, although once a village was infected, its death rate was equally high. At Givry, a prosperous village in Burgundy of 1,200 to 1,500 people, the parish register records 615 deaths in the space of fourteen weeks, compared to an average of thirty deaths a year in the previous decade.[7] In three villages of Cambridgeshire, manorial records show a death rate of 47 percent, 57 percent, and in one case 70 percent.[8] When the last survivors, too few to carry on, moved away, a deserted village sank back into the wilderness and disappeared from the map altogether, leaving only a grass-covered ghostly outline to show where mortals once had lived.

In enclosed places such as monasteries and prisons, the infection of one person usually meant that of all, as happened in the Franciscan convents of Carcassonne and Marseille, where every inmate without exception died. Of the 140 Dominicans at Montpellier only seven survived. Petrarch's brother Gherardo, member of a Carthusian monastery, buried the prior and 34 fellow monks one by one, sometimes three a day, until he was left alone with his dog and fled to look for a place that would take him in.[9] Watching every comrade die, men in such places could not but wonder whether the strange peril that filled the air had not been sent to exterminate the human race. In Kilkenny, Ireland, Brother John Clyn of the Friars Minor, another monk left alone among dead men, kept a record of what had happened lest "things which should be remembered perish with time and vanish from the memory of those who come after us." Sensing "the whole world, as it were, placed within the grasp of the Evil One," and waiting for death to visit him too, he wrote, "I leave

---

[7] Yves Renouard, "La Peste noirs de 1348–50," Rev. de Paris, (March, 1959), 111.

[8] John Saltmarsh, "Plague and Economic Decline in England in the Later Middle Ages," Cambridge Historical Journal, vol. VII, no. 1, 1941.

[9] Morris Bishop, Petrarch and His World (Bloomington: Indiana University Press, 1963), 273.

parchment to continue this work, if perchance any man survive and any of the race of Adam escape this pestilence and carry on the work which I have begun."[10] Brother John, as noted by another hand, died of the pestilence, but he foiled oblivion.

The largest cities of Europe, with populations of about 100,000, were Paris and Florence, Venice and Genoa. At the next level, with more than 50,000, were Ghent and Bruges in Flanders, Milan, Bologna, Rome, Naples, and Palermo, and Cologne. London hovered below 50,000, the only city in England except York with more than 10,000. At the level of 20,000 to 50,000 were Bordeaux, Toulouse, Montpellier, Marseille, and Lyon in France, Barcelona, Seville, and Toledo in Spain, Siena, Pisa, and other secondary cities in Italy, and the Hanseatic trading cities of the Empire. The plague raged through them all, killing anywhere from one third to two thirds of their inhabitants. Italy, with a total population of 10 to 11 million, probably suffered the heaviest toll. Following the Florentine bankruptcies, the crop failures and workers' riots of 1346–47, the revolt of Cola di Rienzi that plunged Rome into anarchy, the plague came as the peak of successive calamities. As if the world were indeed in the grasp of the Evil One, its first appearance on the European mainland in January 1348 coincided with a fearsome earthquake that carved a path of wreckage from Naples up to Venice. Houses collapsed, church towers toppled, villages were crushed, and the destruction reached as far as Germany and Greece. Emotional response, dulled by horrors, underwent a kind of atrophy epitomized by the chronicler who wrote, "And in these days was burying without sorrowe and wedding without friendschippe."[11]

In Siena, where more than half the inhabitants died of the plague, work was abandoned on the great cathedral, planned to be the largest in the world, and never resumed, owing to loss of workers and master masons and "the melancholy and grief" of the survivors. The cathedral's truncated transept still stands in permanent witness to the sweep of death's scythe. Agnolo di Tura, a chronicler of Siena, recorded the fear of contagion that froze every other instinct. "Father abandoned child, wife husband, one brother another," he wrote, "for this plague seemed to strike through the breath and sight. And so

---

[10] Ziegler, *The Black Death,* 195.

[11] George Deaux, *The Black Death,* 1347, (London, 1969), 143.

they died. And no one could be found to bury the dead for money or friendship. . . . And I, Angolo di Tura, called the Fat, buried my five children with my own hands, and so did many others likewise."[12]

There were many to echo his account of inhumanity and few to balance it, for the plague was not the kind of calamity that inspired mutual help. Its loathsomeness and deadliness did not herd people together in mutual distress, but only prompted their desire to escape each other. "Magistrates and notaries refused to come and make the wills of the dying," reported a Franciscan friar of Piazza in Sicily; what was worse, "even the priests did not come to hear their confessions."[13] A clerk of the Archbishop of Canterbury reported the same of English priests who "turned away from the care of their benefices from fear of death."[14] Cases of parents deserting children and children their parents were reported across Europe from Scotland to Russia.[15] The calamity chilled the hearts of men, wrote Boccaccio in his famous account of the plague in Florence that serves as introduction to the *Decameron*. "One man shunned another . . . kinsfolk held aloof, brother was forsaken by brother, oftentimes husband by wife; nay, what is more, and scarcely to be believed, fathers and mothers were found to abandon their own children to their fate, untended, unvisited as if they had been strangers." Exaggeration and literary pessimism were common in the 14th century, but the Pope's physician, Guy de Chauliac, was a sober, careful observer who reported the same phenomenon: "A father did not visit his son, nor the son his father. Charity was dead."[16]

Yet not entirely. In Paris, according to the chronicler Jean de Venette, the nuns of the Hotel Dieu or municipal hospital, "having no fear of death, tended the sick with all sweetness and humility." New nuns repeatedly took the places of those who died, until the majority "many times renewed by death now rest in peace with Christ as we may piously believe."[17]

---

[12] Ziegler, *The Black Death*, 58.

[13] Deaux, *The Black Death*, 49.

[14] Ziegler, *The Black Death*, 261.

[15] J. F. C. Hecker, *The Epidemics of the Middle Ages* (London, 1844), 30.

[16] Gasquet, *The Black Death of 1348 and 1349*, 50–51.

[17] Jean Birdsall, trans., and Richard A. Newhall, ed., *Chronicle of Jean de Venette* (New York: Columbia University Press, 1853), 49.

When the plague entered northern France in July 1348, it settled first in Normandy and, checked by winter, gave Picardy a deceptive interim until the next summer. Either in mourning or warning, black flags were flown from church towers of the worst-stricken villages of Normandy. "And in that time," wrote a monk of the abbey of Fourcarment, "the mortality was so great among the people of Normandy that those of Picardy mocked them." The same unneighborly reaction was reported of the Scots, separated by a winter's immunity from the English. Delighted to hear of the disease that was scourging the "southrons," they gathered forces for an invasion, "laughing at their enemies." Before they could move, the savage mortality fell upon them too, scattering some in death and the rest in panic to spread the infection as they fled.[18]

In Picardy in the summer of 1349 the pestilence penetrated the castle of Coucy to kill Enguerrand's mother, Catherine, and her new husband. Whether her nine-year-old son escaped by chance or was perhaps living elsewhere with one of his guardians is unrecorded.[19] In nearby Amiens, tannery workers, responding quickly to losses in the labor force, combined to bargain for higher wages.[20] In another place villagers were seen dancing to drums and trumpets, and on being asked the reason, answered that, seeing their neighbors die day by day while their village remained immune, they believed that they could keep the plague from entering "by the jollity that is in us. That is why we dance."[21] Further north in Tournai on the border of Flanders, Gilles li Muisis, Abbot of St. Martin's, kept one of the epidemic's most vivid accounts. The passing bells rang all day and all night, he recorded, because sextons were anxious to obtain their fees while they could. Filled with the sound of mourning, the city became oppressed by fear, so that the authorities forbade the tolling of bells and the wearing of black and restricted funeral services to two mourners. The silencing of funeral bells and of criers' announcements of deaths was ordained by most cities. Siena imposed a fine on the wearing of mourning clothes by all except widows.

Flight was the chief recourse of those who could afford it or

---

[18] Gasquet, *The Black Death of 1348 and 1349*, 53, and Ziegler, *The Black Death,* 198.

[19] *L'Art de vérifier les dates des faits historiques,* par un Religieux de la Congregation de St.-Maur, vol. XII (Paris, 1818), 237.

[20] Gasquet, *The Black Death of 1348 and 1349,* 57.

[21] Paulin Paris, ed., *Grandes Croniques de France,* vol. VI (Paris, 1838), 486–87.

arrange it. The rich fled to their country places like Boccaccio's young patricians of Florence, who settled in a pastoral palace "removed on every side from the roads" with "wells of cool water and vaults of rare wines." The urban poor died in their burrows, "and only the stench of their bodies informed neighbors of their deaths." That the poor were more heavily afflicted than the rich was clearly remarked at the time, in the north as in the south. A Scottish chronicler, John of Fordun, stated flatly that the pest "attacked especially the meaner sort and common people—seldom the magnates."[22] Simon de Covino of Montpellier made the same observation. He ascribed it to the misery and want and hard lives that made the poor more susceptible, which was half the truth.[23] Close contact and lack of sanitation was the unrecognized other half. It was noticed too that the young died in greater proportion than the old; Simon de Covino compared the disappearance of youth to the withering of flowers in the fields.[24]

In the countryside peasants dropped dead on the roads, in the fields, in their houses. Survivors in growing helplessness fell into apathy, leaving ripe wheat uncut and livestock untended. Oxen and asses, sheep and goats, pigs and chickens ran wild and they too, according to local reports, succumbed to the pest. English sheep, bearers of the precious wool, died throughout the country. The chronicler Henry Knighton, canon of Leicester Abbey, reported 5,000 dead in one field alone, "their bodies so corrupted by the plague that neither beast nor bird would touch them," and spreading an appalling stench.[25] In the Austrian Alps wolves came down to prey upon sheep and then, "as if alarmed by some invisible warning, turned and fled back into the wilderness." In remote Dalmatia bolder wolves descended upon a plague-stricken city and attacked human survivors.[26] For want of herdsmen, cattle strayed from place to place and died in hedgerows and ditches. Dogs and cats fell like the rest.[27]

The dearth of labor held a fearful prospect because the 14th

[22] Ziegler, *The Black Death,* 199.

[23] Gasquet, *The Black Death of 1348 and 1349,* 42.

[24] Raymond Cazelles, "La Peste de 1348–49 en Langue d'oil: épidémie proletarienne et enfantine," *Bull philologique et historique* (1962), 293–305.

[25] Ziegler, *The Black Death,* 175.

[26] Ziegler, *The Black Death,* 84, 111.

[27] Gasquet, *The Black Death of 1348 and 1349,* 44, 61.

century lived close to the annual harvest both for food and for next year's seed. "So few servants and laborers were left," wrote Knighton, "that no one knew where to turn for help." The sense of a vanishing future created a kind of dementia of despair. A Bavarian chronicler of Neuberg on the Danube recorded that "Men and women . . . wandered around as if mad" and let their cattle stray "because no one had any inclination to concern themselves about the future."[28] Fields went uncultivated, spring seed unsown. Second growth with nature's awful energy crept back over cleared land, dikes crumbled, salt water reinvaded and soured the lowlands. With so few hands remaining to restore the work of centuries, people felt, in Walsingham's words, that "the world could never again regain its former prosperity."[29]

Though the death rate was higher among the anonymous poor, the known and the great died too. King Alfonso XI of Castile was the only reigning monarch killed by the pest, but his neighbor King Pedro of Aragon lost his wife, Queen Leonora, his daughter Marie, and a niece in the space of six months. John Cantacuzene, Emperor of Byzantium, lost his son. In France the lame Queen Jeanne and her daughter-in-law Bonne de Luxemburg, wife of the Dauphin, both died in 1349 in the same phase that took the life of Enguerrand's mother. Jeanne, Queen of Navarre, daughter of Louis X, was another victim. Edward III's second daughter, Joanna, who was on her way to marry Pedro, the heir of Castile, died in Bordeaux. Women appear to have been more vulnerable than men, perhaps because, being more housebound, they were more exposed to fleas. Boccaccio's mistress Fiammetta, illegitimate daughter of the King of Naples, died, as did Laura, the beloved—whether real or fictional—of Petrarch. Reaching out to us in the future, Petrarch cried, "Oh happy posterity who will not experience such abysmal woe and will look upon our testimony as a fable."[30]

In Florence Giovanni Villani, the great historian of his time, died at 68 in the midst of an unfinished sentence: ". . . *e dure questo pistolenza fino a* . . . (in the midst of this pestilence there came to an

---

[28] Ziegler, *The Black Death,* 84.

[29] Henri Denifle, *La Dësolation des églises, monastères et hopitaux en France pendant la guerre de cent ans,* vol. I (Paris, 1899), 273.

[30] Ziegler, *The Black Death,* 45.

end . . .)."[31] Siena's master painters, the brothers Ambrogio and Pietro Lorenzetti, whose names never appear after 1348, presumably perished in the plague, as did Andrea Pisano, architect and sculptor of Florence. William of Ockham and the English mystic Richard Rolle of Hampole both disappear from mention after 1349. Francisco Datini, merchant of Prato, lost both his parents and two siblings. Curious sweeps of mortality afflicted certain bodies of merchants in London. All eight wardens of the Company of Cutters, all six wardens of the Hatters, and four wardens of the Goldsmiths died before July 1350. Sir John Pulteney, master draper and four times Mayor of London, was a victim, likewise Sir John Montgomery, Governor of Calais.

Among the clergy and doctors the mortality was naturally high because of the nature of their professions. Out of 24 physicians in Venice, 20 were said to have lost their lives in the plague, although, according to another account, some were believed to have fled or to have shut themselves up in their houses. At Montpellier, site of the leading medieval medical school, the physician Simon de Covino reported that, despite the great number of doctors, "hardly one of them escaped."[32] In Avignon, Guy de Chauliac confessed that he performed his medical visits only because he dared not stay away for fear of infamy, but "I was in continual fear."[33] He claimed to have contracted the disease but to have cured himself by his own treatment; if so, he was one of the few who recovered.

Clerical mortality varied with rank. Although the one-third toll of cardinals reflects the same proportion as the whole, this was probably due to their concentration in Avignon. In England, in strange and almost sinister procession, the Archbishop of Canterbury, John Stratford, died in August 1348, his appointed successor died in May 1349, and the next appointee three months later, all three within a year. Despite such weird vagaries, prelates in general managed to sustain a higher survival rate than the lesser clergy. Among bishops the deaths have been estimated at about one in twenty. The loss of priests, even if many avoided their fearful duty of attending the dying, was about the same as among the population as a whole.

---

[31] Frederick Snell, *The Fourteenth Century* (Edinburgh, 1899), 334.

[32] Campbell, *The Black Death and Men of Learning,* 98, 31.

[33] James Westfall Thompson, *Economic and Social History of Europe in the Later Middle Ages* (New York, 1931), 379.

Government officials, whose loss contributed to the general chaos, found, on the whole, no special shelter. In Siena four of the nine members of the governing oligarchy died, in France one third of the royal notaries, in Bristol 15 out of the 52 members of the Town Council or almost one third. Tax-collecting obviously suffered, with the result that Philip VI was unable to collect more than a fraction of the subsidy granted him by the Estates in the winter of 1347–48.

Lawlessness and debauchery accompanied the plague as they had during the great plague of Athens of 430 B.C., when according to Thucydides, men grew bold in the indulgence of pleasure: "For seeing how the rich died in a moment and those who had nothing immediately inherited their property, they reflected that life and riches were alike transitory and they resolved to enjoy themselves while they could."[34] Human behavior is timeless. When St. John had his vision of plague in Revelation, he knew from some experience or race memory that those who survived "repented not of the work of their hands. . . . Neither repented they of their murders, nor of their sorceries, nor of their fornication, nor of their thefts."

E. B. WHITE

Once More to the Lake

E. B. White (1899–1985) was an American journalist, editor, and essayist who worked as a staff writer for the *New Yorker* magazine for sixty years. Among his essays collections are *One Man's Meat* (1939) and *Essays of E. B. White* (1941), from which the following essay is taken. His three children's books, *Stuart Little* (1945), *Charlotte's Web* (1952), and *The Trumpet of the Swan* (1970) have earned him enduring praise. He is also known for *Elements of Style* (1959), the preeminent style manual which he contributed to and revised, written by William Strunk, Jr.

[34] Raymond Crawfurd, *Plague and Pestilence in Literature and Art* (Oxford, 1914), 30–31.

AUGUST 1941

One summer, along about 1904, my father rented a camp on a lake in Maine and took us all there for the month of August. We all got ringworm from some kittens and had to rub Pond's Extract on our arms and legs night and morning, and my father rolled over in a canoe with all his clothes on; but outside of that the vacation was a success and from then on none of us ever thought there was any place in the world like that lake in Maine. We returned summer after summer—always on August 1 for one month. I have since become a salt-water man, but sometimes in summer there are days when the restlessness of the tides and the fearful cold of the sea water and the incessant wind that blows across the afternoon and into the evening make me wish for the placidity of a lake in the woods. A few weeks ago this feeling got so strong I bought myself a couple of bass hooks and a spinner and returned to the lake where we used to go, for a week's fishing and to revisit old haunts.

I took along my son, who had never had any fresh water up his nose and who had seen lily pads only from train windows. On the journey over to the lake I began to wonder what it would be like. I wondered how time would have marred this unique, this holy spot— the coves and streams, the hills that the sun set behind, the camps and the paths behind the camps. I was sure that the tarred road would have found it out, and I wondered in what other ways it would be desolated. It is strange how much you can remember about places like that once you allow your mind to return into the grooves that lead back. You remember one thing, and that suddenly reminds you of another thing. I guess I remembered clearest of all the early mornings, when the lake was cool and motionless, remembered how the bedroom smelled of the lumber it was made of and of the wet woods whose scent entered through the screen. The partitions in the camp were thin and did not extend clear to the top of the rooms, and as I was always the first up I would dress softly so as not to wake the others, and sneak out into the sweet outdoors and start out in the canoe, keeping close along the shore in the long shadows of the pines. I remembered being very careful never to rub my paddle against the gunwale for fear of disturbing the stillness of the cathedral.

The lake had never been what you would call a wild lake. There were cottages sprinkled around the shores, and it was in farming country although the shores of the lake were quite heavily wooded. Some of the cottages were owned by nearby farmers, and you would live at the shore and eat your meals at the farmhouse. That's what our family did. But although it wasn't wild, it was a fairly large and undisturbed lake and there were places in it that, to a child at least, seemed infinitely remote and primeval.

I was right about the tar: it led to within half a mile of the shore. But when I got back there, with my boy, and we settled into a camp near a farmhouse and into the kind of summertime I had known, I could tell that it was going to be pretty much the same as it had been before—I knew it, lying in bed the first morning smelling the bedroom and hearing the boy sneak quietly out and go off along the shore in a boat. I began to sustain the illusion that he was I, and therefore, by simple transposition, that I was my father. This sensation persisted, kept cropping up all the time we were there. It was not an entirely new feeling, but in this setting it grew much stronger. I seemed to be living a dual existence. I would be in the middle of some simple act, I would be picking up a bait box or laying down a table fork, or I would be saying something and suddenly it would be not I but my father who was saying the words or making the gesture. It gave me a creepy sensation.

We went fishing the first morning. I felt the same damp moss covering the worms in the bait can, and saw the dragonfly alight on the tip of my rod as it hovered a few inches from the surface of the water. It was the arrival of this fly that convinced me beyond any doubt that everything was as it always had been, that the years were a mirage and that there had been no years. The small waves were the same, chucking the rowboat under the chin as we fished at anchor, and the boat was the same boat, the same color green and the ribs broken in the same places, and under the floorboards the same fresh water leavings and débris—the dead hellgrammite, the wisps of moss, the rusty discarded fishhook, the dried blood from yesterday's catch. We stared silently at the tips of our rods, at the dragonflies that came and went. I lowered the tip of mine into the water, tentatively, pensively dislodging the fly, which darted two feet away, poised, darted two feet back, and came to rest again a little farther up the rod. There had been no years between the ducking of this dragonfly and the other one—the one that was part of memory. I looked at the boy, who was silently watching his fly, and it was my hands that held his rod, my eyes watching. I felt dizzy and didn't know which rod I was at the end of.

We caught two bass, hauling them in briskly as though they were mackerel, pulling them over the side of the boat in a businesslike manner without any landing net, and stunning them with a blow on the back of the head. When we got back for a swim before lunch, the lake was exactly where we had left it, the same number of inches from the dock, and there was only the merest suggestion of a breeze. This seemed an utterly enchanted sea, this lake you could leave to its own devices for a few hours and come back to, and find that it had not stirred, this constant and trustworthy body of water. In the shallows, the dark, water-soaked sticks and twigs, smooth and old, were undulating in clusters on the bottom against the clean ribbed sand, and the track of the mussel was plain. A school of minnows swam by, each minnow with its small individual shadow, doubling the attendance, so clear and sharp in the sunlight. Some of the other campers were in swimming, along the shore, one of them with a cake of soap, and the water felt thin and clear and unsubstantial. Over the years there had been this person with the cake of soap, this cultist, and here he was. There had been no years.

Up to the farmhouse to dinner through the teeming dusty field, the road under our sneakers was only a two-track road. The middle track was missing, the one with the marks of the hooves and the splotches of dried, flaky manure. There had always been three tracks to choose from in choosing which track to walk in; now the choice was narrowed down to two. For a moment I missed terribly the middle alternative. But the way led past the tennis court, and something about the way it lay there in the sun reassured me; the tape had loosened along the backline, the alleys were green with plantains and other weeds, and the net (installed in June and removed in September) sagged in the dry noon, and the whole place steamed with midday heat and hunger and emptiness. There was a choice of pie for dessert, and one was blueberry and one was apple, and the waitresses were the same country girls, there having been no passage of time, only the illusion of it as in a dropped curtain—the waitresses were still fifteen; their hair had been washed, that was the only difference—they had been to the movies and seen the pretty girls with the clean hair.

Summertime, oh, summertime, pattern of life indelible with fade-proof lake, the wood unshatterable, the pasture with the sweetfern and the juniper forever and ever, summer without end; this was the background, and the life along the shore was the design, the cottages with their innocent and tranquil design, their tiny docks with the flagpole and the American flag floating against the white clouds in the blue sky, the little paths over the roots of the trees leading from camp to camp and the paths leading back to the outhouses and the can of lime for sprinkling, and at the souvenir counters at the store the miniature birchbark canoes and the postcards that showed things looking a little better than they looked. This was the American family at play, escaping the city heat, wondering whether the newcomers in the camp at the head of the cove were "common" or "nice," wondering whether it was true that the people who drove up for Sunday dinner at the farmhouse were turned away because there wasn't enough chicken.

It seemed to me, as I kept remembering all this, that those times and those summers had been infinitely precious and worth saving. There had been jollity and peace and goodness. The arriving (at the beginning of August) had been so big a business in itself, at the railway station the farm wagon drawn up, the first smell of the pine-laden air, the first glimpse of the smiling farmer, and the great importance of the trunks and your father's enormous authority in such matters, and the feel of the wagon under you for the long ten-mile haul, and at the top of the last long hill catching the first view of the lake after eleven months of not seeing this cherished body of water. The shouts and cries of the other campers when they saw you, and the trunks to be unpacked, to give up their rich burden. (Arriving was less exciting nowadays, when you sneaked up in your car and parked it under a tree near the camp and took out the bags and in five minutes it was all over, no fuss, no loud wonderful fuss about trunks.)

Peace and goodness and jollity. The only thing that was wrong now, really, was the sound of the place, an unfamiliar nervous sound of the outboard motors. This was the note that jarred, the one thing that would sometimes break the illusion and set the years moving. In those other summertimes all motors were inboard; and when they were at a little distance, the noise they made was a sedative, an ingredient of summer sleep. They were one-cylinder and two-cylinder engines, and some were make-and-break and some were jump-spark, but they all made a sleepy sound across the lake. The one-lungers throbbed and fluttered, and the twin-cylinder ones purred and purred, and that was a quiet sound, too. But now the campers all had outboards. In the daytime, in the hot mornings, these motors made a petulant, irritable sound; at night in the still evening when the afterglow lit the water, they whined about one's ears like mosquitoes. My boy loved our rented outboard, and his great desire was to achieve single-handed mastery over it, and authority, and he soon learned the trick of choking it a little (but not too much), and the adjustment of the needle valve. Watching him I would remember the things you could do with the old one-cylinder engine with the heavy flywheel, how you could have it eating out of your hand if you got really close to it spiritually. Motorboats in those days didn't have clutches, and you would make a landing by shutting off the motor at the proper time and coasting in with a dead rudder. But there was a way of reversing them, if you learned the trick, by cutting the switch and putting it on again exactly on the final dying revolution of the flywheel, so that it would kick back against compression and begin reversing. Approaching a dock in a strong following breeze, it was difficult to slow up sufficiently by the ordinary coasting method, and if a boy felt he had complete mastery over his motor, he was tempted to keep it running beyond its time and then reverse it a few feet from the dock. It took a cool nerve, because if you threw the switch a twentieth of a second too soon you would catch the flywheel when it still had speed enough to go up past center, and the boat would leap ahead, charging bull-fashion at the dock.

We had a good week at the camp. The bass were biting well and the sun shone endlessly, day after day. We would be tired at night and lie down in the accumulated heat of the little bedrooms after the long hot day and the breeze would stir almost imperceptibly outside and the smell of the swamp drift in through the rusty screens. Sleep would come easily and in the morning the red squirrel would be on the roof, tapping out his gay routine. I kept remembering everything, lying in bed in the mornings—the small steamboat that had a long rounded stern like the lip of a Ubangi, and how quietly she ran on the moonlight sails, when the older boys played their mandolins and the girls sang and we ate doughnuts dipped in sugar, and how sweet the music was on the water in the shining night, and what it had felt like to think about girls then. After breakfast we would go up to the store and the things were in the same place—the minnows in a bottle, the plugs and spinners disarranged and pawed over by the youngsters from the boys' camp, the Fig Newtons and the Beeman's gum. Outside, the road was tarred and cars stood in front of the store. Inside, all was just as it had always been, except there was more Coca-Cola and not so much Moxie and root beer and birch beer and sarsaparilla. We would walk out with the bottle of pop apiece and sometimes the pop would backfire up our noses and hurt. We explored the streams, quietly, where the turtles slid off the sunny logs and dug their way into the soft bottom; and we lay on the town wharf and fed worms to the tame bass. Everywhere we went I had trouble making out which was I, the one walking at my side, the one walking in my pants.

One afternoon while we were at that lake a thunderstorm came up. It was like the revival of an old melodrama that I had seen long ago with childish awe. The second-act climax of the drama of the electrical disturbance over a lake in America had not changed in any important respect. This was the big scene, still the big scene. The whole thing was so familiar, the first feeling of oppression and heat and a general air around camp of not wanting to go very far away. In midafternoon (it was all the same) a curious darkening of the sky, and a lull in everything that had made life tick; and then the way the boats suddenly swung the other way at their moorings with the coming of a breeze out of the new quarter, and the premonitory rumble. Then the kettle drum, then the snare, then the bass drum and cymbals, then crackling light against the dark, and the gods grinning and licking their chops in the hills. Afterward the calm, the rain steadily rustling in the calm lake, the return of light and hope and spirits, and the campers running out in joy and relief to go swimming in the rain, their bright cries perpetuating the deathless joke about how they were getting simply drenched, and the children screaming with delight at the new sensation of bathing in the rain, and the joke about getting drenched linking the generations in a strong indestructible chain. And the comedian who waded in carrying an umbrella.

When the others went swimming my son said he was going in, too. He pulled his dripping trunks from the line where they had hung all through the shower and wrung them out. Languidly, and with no thought of going in, I watched him, his hard little body, skinny and bare, saw him wince slightly as he pulled up around his vitals the small, soggy, icy garment. As he buckled the swollen belt, suddenly my groin felt the chill of death.

WILLIAM FAULKNER

Nobel Prize Acceptance Speech

William Faulkner (1897–1962) was born in New Albany, Mississippi, and spent most of his life in nearby Oxford, after which he modelled the mythical Yoknapatawpha County in which most of his novels are set. Generally considered one of the greatest American fiction writers, Faulkner won the Nobel Prize for literature in

1949. The following selection is his acceptance speech. His novels include *The Sound and the Fury* (1929), *As I Lay Dying* (1930), *Sanctuary* (1931), *Light in August* (1932), and *Intruder in the Dust* (1948).

I feel that this award was not made to me as a man, but to my work—a life's work in the agony and sweat of the human spirit, not for glory and least of all for profit, but to create out of the materials of the human spirit something which did not exist before. So this award is only mine in trust. It will not be difficult to find a dedication for the money part of it commensurate with the purpose and significance of its origin. But I would like to do the same with the acclaim too, by using this moment as a pinnacle from which I might be listened to by the young men and women already dedicated to the same anguish and travail, among whom is already that one who will some day stand here where I am standing.

Our tragedy today is a general and universal physical fear so long sustained by now that we can even bear it. There are no longer problems of the spirit. There is only the question: When will I be blown up? Because of this, the young man or woman writing today has forgotten the problems of the human heart in conflict with itself which alone can make good writing because only that is worth writing about, worth the agony and the sweat.

He must learn them again. He must teach himself that the basest of all things is to be afraid; and, teaching himself that, forget it forever, leaving no room in his workshop for anything but the old verities and truths of the heart, the old universal truths lacking which any story is ephemeral and doomed—love and honor and pity and pride and compassion and sacrifice. Until he does so, he labors under a curse. He writes not of love but of lust, of defeats in which nobody loses anything of value, of victories without hope and, worst of all, without pity or compassion. His griefs grieve on no universal bones, leaving no scars. He writes not of the heart but of the glands.

Until he relearns these things, he will write as though he stood among and watched the end of man. I decline to accept the end of man. It is easy enough to say that man is immortal simply because he will endure: that when the last ding-dong of doom has clanged and faded from the last worthless rock hanging tideless in the last red and dying evening, that even then there will still be one more sound: that of his puny inexhaustible voice, still talking. I refuse to accept this. I believe that man will not merely endure: he will prevail.

He is immortal, not because he alone among creatures has an inexhaustible voice, but because he has a soul, a spirit capable of compassion and sacrifice and endurance. The poet's, the writer's, duty is to write about these things. It is his privilege to help man endure by lifting his heart, by reminding him of the courage and honor and hope and pride and compassion and pity and sacrifice which have been the glory of his past. The poet's voice need not merely be the record of man, it can be one of the props, the pillars to help him endure and prevail.

KURT VONNEGUT, JR.

Harrison Bergeron

Kurt Vonnegut, Jr. (1922–   ), a novelist, short story writer, dramatist, and essayist, was born in Indianapolis, Indiana. His best known novel, *Slaughterhouse Five, or the Children's Crusade* (1969), recounts some of his own experiences as a prisoner of war in the firebombed city of Dresden during World War II. Other works include the novels *Player Piano* (1952), *Cat's Cradle* (1963), *Breakfast of Champions* (1973), and *Galapagos* (1985); the play *Happy Birthday, Wanda June* (1970), and the story collection *Welcome to the Monkey House* (1968), from which the following selection is taken.

The year was 2081, and everybody was finally equal. They weren't only equal before God and the law. They were equal every which way. Nobody was smarter than anybody else. Nobody was better looking than anybody else. Nobody was stronger or quicker than anybody else. All this equality was due to the 211th, 212th, and 213th Amendments to the Constitution, and to the unceasing vigilance of agents of the United States Handicapper General.

Some things about living still weren't quite right, though. April, for instance, still drove people crazy by not being springtime. And it was in the clammy month that the H-G men took George and Hazel Bergeron's fourteen-year-old son, Harrison, away.

It was tragic, all right, but George and Hazel couldn't think about it very hard. Hazel had a perfectly average intelligence, which meant she couldn't think about anything except in short bursts. And George, while his intelligence was way above normal, had a little mental handicap radio in his ear. He was required by law to wear it at all times. It was tuned to a government transmitter. Every twenty seconds or so, the transmitter would send out some sharp noise to keep people like George from taking unfair advantage of their brains.

George and Hazel were watching television. There were tears on Hazel's cheeks, but she'd forgotten for the moment what they were about.

On the television screen were ballerinas.

A buzzer sounded in George's head. His thoughts fled in panic, like bandits from a burglar alarm.

"That was a real pretty dance, that dance they just did," said Hazel.

"Huh?" said George.

"That dance—it was nice," said Hazel.

"Yup," said George. He tried to think a little about the ballerinas. They weren't really very good—no better than anybody else would have been, anyway. They were burdened with sashweights and bags of birdshot, and their faces were masked, so that no one, seeing a free and graceful gesture or a pretty face, would feel like something the cat drug in. George was toying with the vague notion that maybe dancers shouldn't be handicapped. But he didn't get very far with it before another noise in his ear radio scattered his thoughts.

George winced. So did two of the eight ballerinas.

Hazel saw him wince. Having no mental handicap herself, she had to ask George what the latest sound had been.

"Sounded like somebody hitting a milk bottle with a ball peen hammer," said George.

"I'd think it would be real interesting, hearing all the different sounds," said Hazel, a little envious. "All the things they think up."

"Um," said George.

"Only, if I was Handicapper General, you know what I would do?" said Hazel. Hazel, as a matter of fact, bore a strong resemblance to the Handicapper General, a woman named Diana Moon Glampers. "If I was Diana Moon Glampers," said Hazel, "I'd have chimes on Sunday—just chimes. Kind of in honor of religion."

"I could think, if it was just chimes," said George.

"Well—maybe make 'em real loud," said Hazel. "I think I'd make a good Handicapper General."

"Good as anybody else," said George.

"Who knows better'n I do what normal is?" said Hazel.

"Right," said George. He began to think glimmeringly about his abnormal son who was now in jail, about Harrison, but a twenty-one-gun salute in his head stopped that.

"Boy!" said Hazel, "that was a doozy, wasn't it?"

It was such a doozy that George was white and trembling, and tears stood on the rims of his red eyes. Two of the eight ballerinas had collapsed to the studio floor, were holding their temples.

"All of a sudden you look so tired," said Hazel. "Why don't you stretch out on the sofa, so's you can rest your handicap bag on the pillows, honeybunch." She was referring to the forty-seven pounds of birdshot in a canvas bag, which was padlocked around George's neck. "Go on and rest the bag for a little while," she said. "I don't care if you're not equal to me for a while."

George weighed the bag with his hands. "I don't mind it," he said. "I don't notice it any more. It's just a part of me."

"You been so tired lately—kind of wore out," said Hazel. "If there was just some way we could make a little hole in the bottom of the bag, and just take out a few of them lead balls. Just a few."

"Two years in prison and two thousand dollars fine for every ball I took out," said George. "I don't call that a bargain."

"If you could just take a few out when you came home from work," said Hazel. "I mean—you don't compete with anybody around hear. You just set around."

"If I tried to get away with it," said George, "then other people'd get away with it—and pretty soon we'd be right back to the dark ages again, with everybody competing against everybody else. You wouldn't like that, would you?"

"I'd hate it," said Hazel.

"There you are," said George. "The minute people start cheating on laws, what do you think happens to society?"

If Hazel hadn't been able to come up with an answer to this question, George couldn't have supplied one. A siren was going off in his head.

"Reckon it'd fall all apart," said Hazel.

"What would?" said George blankly.

"Society," said Hazel uncertainly. "Wasn't that what you just said?"

"Who knows?" said George.

The television program was suddenly interrupted for a news bulletin. It wasn't clear at first as to what the bulletin was about, since the announcer, like all announcers, had a serious speech impediment. For about half a minute, and in a state of high excitement, the announcer tried to say, "Ladies and gentlemen—"

He finally gave up, handed the bulletin to a ballerina to read.

"That's all right—" Hazel said of the announcer, "he tried. That's the big thing. He tried to do the best he could with what God gave him. He should get a nice raise for trying so hard."

"Ladies and gentlemen—" said the ballerina, reading the bulletin. She must have been extraordinarily beautiful, because the mask she wore was hideous. And it was easy to see that she was the strongest and most graceful of all the dancers, for her handicap bags were as big as those worn by two-hundred-pound men.

And she had to apologize at once for her voice, which was a very unfair voice for a woman to use. Her voice was a warm, luminous, timeless melody. "Excuse me—" she said, and she began again, making her voice absolutely uncompetitive.

"Harrison Bergeron, age fourteen," she said in a grackle squawk, "has just escaped from jail, where he was held on suspicion of plotting to overthrow the government. He is a genius and an athlete, is under-handicapped, and should be regarded as extremely dangerous."

A police photograph of Harrison Bergeron was flashed on the screen upside down, then sideways, upside down again, then right side up. The picture showed the full length of Harrison against a background calibrated in feet and inches. He was exactly seven feet tall.

The rest of Harrison's appearance was Halloween and hardware. Nobody had ever borne heavier handicaps. He had outgrown hindrances faster than the H-G men could think them up. Instead of a little ear radio for a mental handicap, he wore a tremendous pair of earphones, and spectacles with thick wavy lenses. The spectacles were intended to make him not only half blind, but to give him whanging headaches besides.

Scrap metal was hung all over him. Ordinarily, there was a certain symmetry, a military neatness to the handicaps issued to strong people, but Harrison looked like a walking junkyard. In the race of life, Harrison carried three hundred pounds.

And to offset his good looks, the H-G men required that he wear at all times a red rubber ball for a nose, keep his eyebrows shaved off, and cover his even white teeth with black caps at snaggle-tooth random.

"If you see this boy," said the ballerina, "do not—I repeat, do not—try to reason with him."

There was the shriek of a door being torn from its hinges.

Screams and barking cries of consternation came from the television set. The photograph of Harrison Bergeron on the screen jumped again and again, as though dancing to the tune of an earthquake.

George Bergeron correctly identified the earthquake, and well he might have—for many was the time his own home had danced to the same crashing tune. "My God—" said George, "that must be Harrison!"

The realization was blasted from his mind instantly by the sound of an automobile collision in his head.

When George could open his eyes again, the photograph of Harrison was gone. A living, breathing Harrison filled the screen.

Clanking, clownish, and huge, Harrison stood in the center of the studio. The knob of the uprooted studio door was still in his hand. Ballerinas, technicians, musicians, and announcers cowered on their knees before him, expecting to die.

"I am the Emperor!" cried Harrison. "Do you hear? I am the Emperor! Everybody must do what I say at once!" He stamped his foot and the studio shook.

"Even as I stand here—" he bellowed, "cripple, hobbled, sickened—I am a greater ruler than any man who ever lived! Now watch me become what I *can* become!"

Harrison tore the straps of his handicap harness like wet tissue paper, tore straps guaranteed to support five thousand pounds.

Harrison's scrap-iron handicaps crashed to the floor.

Harrison thrust his thumbs under the bars of the padlock that secured his head harness. The bar snapped like celery. Harrison smashed his headphones and spectacles against the wall.

He flung away his rubber-ball nose, revealed a man that would have awed Thor, the god of thunder.

"I shall now select my Empress!" he said, looking down on the cowering people. "Let the first woman who dares rise to her feet claim her mate and her throne!"

A moment passed, and then a ballerina arose, swaying like a willow.

Harrison plucked the metal handicap from her ear, snapped off her physical handicaps with marvelous delicacy. Last of all, he removed her mask.

She was blindingly beautiful.

"Now—" said Harrison, taking her hand, "shall we show the people the meaning of the word dance? Music!" he commanded.

The musicians scrambled back into their chairs, and Harrison stripped them of their handicaps, too. "Play your best," he told them, "and I'll make you barons and dukes and earls."

The music began. It was normal at first—cheap, silly, false. But Harrison snatched two musicians from their chairs, waved them like batons as he sang the music as he wanted it played. He slammed them back into their chairs.

The music began again and was much improved.

Harrison and his Empress merely listened to the music for a while—listened gravely, as though synchronizing their heartbeats with it.

They shifted their weights to their toes.

Harrison placed his big hands on the girl's tiny waist, letting her sense the weightlessness that would soon be hers.

And then, in an explosion of joy and grace, into the air they sprang!

Not only were the laws of the land abandoned, but the law of gravity and the laws of motion as well.

They reeled, whirled, swiveled, flounced, capered, gamboled, and spun.

They leaped like deer on the moon.

The studio ceiling was thirty feet high, but each leap brought the dancers nearer to it.

It became their obvious intention to kiss the ceiling.

They kissed it.

And then, neutralizing gravity with love and pure will, they remained suspended in air inches below the ceiling, and they kissed each other for a long, long time.

It was then that Diana Moon Glampers, the Handicapper General, came into the studio with a double-barreled ten-gauge shotgun. She fired twice, and the Emperor and the Empress were dead before they hit the floor.

Diana Moon Glampers loaded the gun again. She aimed it at the musicians and told them they had ten seconds to get their handicaps back on.

It was then that the Bergerons' television tube burned out.

Hazel turned to comment about the blackout to George. But George had gone out into the kitchen for a can of beer.

George came back in with the beer, paused while a handicap signal shook him up. And then he sat down again. "You been crying?" he said to Hazel.

"Yup," she said.

"What about?" he said.

"I forgot," she said. "Something real sad on television."

"What was it?" he said.

"It's all kind of mixed up in my mind," said Hazel.

"Forget sad things," said George.

"I always do," said Hazel.

"That's my girl," said George. He winced. There was the sound of a rivetting gun in his head.

"Gee—I could tell that one was a doozy," said Hazel.

"You can say that again," said George.

"Gee—" said Hazel, "I could tell that one was a doozy."

Acknowledgments (continued from page iv)

John F. Avedon, "Tibetian Medicine: The Science of Healing." From *In Exile from the Land of Snows* by John F. Avedon. Copyright © 1979, 1984 by John F. Avedon. Reprinted by permission of Alfred A. Knopf, Inc.

Russell Baker, "Big Brother Really Is Watching." From *The New York Times*, March 6, 1969. Copyright © 1969 by The New York Times Company. Reprinted by permission.

James Baldwin, "Why I Left America." Copyright © 1970 Hollingsworth Group, Inc. Originally appeared in *Essence* Magazine. Reprinted by arrangement with the James Baldwin Estate.

Donald Barthelme, "The Author." Originally appeared in *The New Yorker*, June 15, 1987. Reprinted by permission.

Roland Barthes, "The World of Wrestling." From *Mythologies* by Roland Barthes. Translation copyriight © 1972 by Jonathan Cape Ltd. Reprinted by permission of Hill and Wang, a division of Farrar, Straus and Giroux, Inc.

Walter Benjamin, "Unpacking My Library." From *Illuminations* by Walter Benjamin, copyright © 1955 by Suhrkamp Verlag, Frankfurt a.M., English translation copyright © 1968 by Harcourt Brace Jovanovich, Inc., reprinted by permission of Harcourt Brace Jovanovich, Inc.

Bernard Berenson, "Value." From *Aesthetics and History in the Visual Arts* by Bernard Berenson. Copyright © 1948 by Pantheon Books, Inc. Reprinted by permission of Pantheon Books, a division of Random House, Inc.

Joseph H. Berke, "So Will I Turn Her Virtue Into Pitch." From *The Tyranny of Malice* by Joseph H. Berke. Copyright © 1988 by Joseph H. Berke. Reprinted by permission of Summit Books, a division of Simon & Schuster, Inc.

Allan Bloom, "Western Civ." From *Giants and Dwarfs* by Allan Bloom. Copyright © 1990 by Allan Bloom. Reprinted by permission of Simon & Schuster, Inc.

Sissela Bok, "White Lies." From *Lying: Moral Choice in Public and Private Life* by Sissela Bok. Copyright © 1978 by Sissela Bok. Reprinted by permission of Pantheon Books, a division of Random House, Inc.

Daniel J. Boorstin, "Technology and Democracy." By Daniel J. Boorstin, author of *The Americans* and *The Discoverers*, copyright © 1974 by Daniel J. Boorstin, from *Democracy and its Discontents*.

Alan Booth, "Buddha and the Floating Bridge of Heaven." From *The Roads to Sata: A 2,000 Mile Walk through Japan* by Alan Booth. Copyright © 1985 by Alan Booth. Reproduced by permission of Penguin Books Ltd.

Tadeusz Borowski, "This Way for the Gas, Ladies and Gentlemen." From *This Way for the Gas, Ladies and Gentlemen* by Tadeusz Borowski, translated by Barbara Vedder. Translation copyright © 1967 by Penguin Books Ltd. Original text copyright © 1959 by Maria Borowski. Used by permission of Viking Penguin, a division of Penguin Books USA, Inc.

Elizabeth Bowen, "The Demon Lover." From *The Collected Stories of Elizabeth Bowen* by Elizabeth Bowen. Copyright 1946 and renewed 1974 by Elizabeth Bowen. Reprinted by permission of Alfred A. Knopf, Inc.

Harry Brent, "'Bullets Hurt, Corpses Stink': George Orwell and the Language of Warfare." From *Beyond 1984: Doublespeak in a Post-Orwellian Age*, edited by William Lutz. Copyright 1989 by the National Council of Teachers of English. Reprinted with permission.

John Cheever, "The Swimmer." From *The Stories of John Cheever* by John Cheever. Copyright © 1964 by John Cheever. Reprinted by permission of Alfred A. Knopf, Inc.

Michelle Cliff, "A Journey into Speech." From *The Land of Look Behind*. Copyright © 1985 by Michelle Cliff. Reprinted by permission of Firebrand Books, Ithaca, NY.

Nicholas Coleridge, "The Emperor's New Clothes." From *The Fashion Conspiracy* by Nicholas Coleridge. Copyright © 1989 by Nicholas Coleridge. Reprinted by permission of HarperCollins Publishers Inc.

Frank Conroy, "Think about It." From *Harper's* Magazine, November 1988. Copyright © 1988 by *Harper's* Magazine. All rights reserved. Reprinted from the November issue by special permission.

Aaron Copland, "How We Listen to Music." From *What to Listen for in Music* by Aaron Copland. Copyright © Estate of Aaron Copland 1957, 1985. Reprinted by permission.

Vincent Crapanzano, "Growing Up White in South Africa." From *Waiting: The Whites of South Africa* by Vincent Crapanzano. Copyright © 1985 by Vincent Crapanzano. Reprinted by permission of Random House, Inc.

Alfred W. Crosby, Jr., "Conquistador y Pestilencia." From *Hispanic American Historical Review*, v. 47:3, pp. 321–327. Copyright © 1967, Duke University Press, Durham, NC. Reprinted by permission of the publisher.

David Dabydeen, "On Not Being Milton: Nigger Talk in England Today." From Christopher Ricks and Leonard Michaels eds., *The State of the Language*, 1990 edition. Copyright © 1989 The Regents of the University of California. Reprinted by permission of University of California Press.

Arthur Danto, "The Canon and the Wisdom of the East." From *Harper's* Magazine, May 1990. Copyright © 1990 by *Harper's* Magazine. All rights reserved. Reprinted from the May issue by special permission.

Jared Diamond, "The Accidental Conqueror." From *Discover*, December 1989. Jared Diamond/© 1989 Discover Publications.

Andre Dubus, "The Curse." From *Selected Stories of Andre Dubus* by Andre Dubus. Copyright © 1975, 1977, 1980, 1983, 1984, 1986, 1988 by Andre Dubus. Reprinted by permission of David R. Godine, Publisher.

William Faulkner, "Nobel Prize Acceptance Speech." From *Essays, Speeches and Public Letters* by William Faulkner. Copyright © 1965 by Random House, Inc. Reprinted by permission of Random House, Inc.

Frances FitzGerald, "Rewriting American History." From *America Revised: History Schoolbooks in the Twentieth Century* by Frances FitzGerald. Copyright © 1979 by Frances FitzGerald. First appeared in *The New Yorker*. By permission of Little, Brown and Company.

Milton Friedman, "The Social Responsibility of Business Is to Increase Its Profits." From *The New York Times*, September 13, 1970. Copyright © 1970 by The New York Times Company. Reprinted by permission.

Francis Fukuyama, "The End of History?" Reprinted with permission of The Free Press, a Division of Macmillan, Inc. From *The End of History and the Last Man* by Francis Fukuyama. Copyright © 1992 by Francis Fukuyama.

Paul Fussell, "The Real War 1939–1945." Abridged from *Wartime: Understanding and Behavior in the Second World War* by Paul Fussell. Copyright © 1989 by Oxford University Press, Inc. Reprinted by permission.

Helen Louise Gardner, "Art in Everyday Life." From *Understanding the Arts* by Helen
    Gardner. Copyright 1932 by Harcourt Brace Jovanovich, Inc. and renewed 1960
    by Louise Gardner. Reprinted by permission of the publisher.
Henry Louis Gates, Jr., "Talking Black." From Christopher Ricks and Leonard Mi-
    chaels, eds., *The State of the Language*, 1990 edition. Copyright © 1989 The Regents
    of the University of California. Reprinted by permission of University of California
    Press.
Denise Gess, "Underground." Copyright © 1989 Denise Gess. Reprinted by permission
    of the author.
Ellen Gilchrist, "Revenge." From *In the Land of Dreamy Dreams* by Ellen Gilchrist.
    Copyright © 1981 by Ellen Gilchrist. By permission of Little, Brown and Company.
Stephen Jay Gould, "Nasty Little Facts." From *Natural History*, Vol. 94, No. 2, 1985.
    With permission from *Natural History*, February 1985; Copyright the American
    Museum of Natural History, 1985.
Paul Gruchow, "Bones." Copyright © 1988 by Paul Gruchow. Originally appeared in
    Minnesota Monthly in 1988. Reprinted by permission of the author.
Edith Hamilton, "The Way of the East and the West in Art." Reprinted from *The
    Greek Way* by Edith Hamilton, by permission of W. W. Norton & Company, Inc.
    Copyright © 1930, 1943 by W. W. Norton & Company, Inc. Copyright renewed
    1958 by W. W. Norton & Company, Inc.
Frank A. Haskell, "The Battle of Gettysburg: A Participant's View." From *The Battle
    of Gettysburg* by Bruce Catton. Copyright © renewed 1985, 1986 by William B.
    Catton. Reprinted by permission of Houghton Mifflin Company. All rights reserved.
Stephen Hawking, "The Arrow of Time." From *A Brief History of Time* by Stephen W.
    Hawking. Copyright © 1988 by Stephen W. Hawking. Used by permission of
    Bantam Books, a division of Bantam Doubleday Dell Publishing Group, Inc.
Bessie Head, "Looking for a Rain God." © The Bessie Head Estate, from *The Collector
    of Treasures*, Heinemann Educational Books, African Writers Series, London 1977.
    Permission granted by John Johnson Ltd., London and Heinemann Publishers Ltd.
Werner Heisenberg, "Language and Reality in Modern Physics." From *Physics and
    Philosophy* by Werner Heisenberg. Copyright © 1958 by Werner Heisenberg.
    Reprinted by permission of HarperCollins Publishers Inc.
Seymour Hersh, "My Lai 4." From *My Lai 4* by Seymour Hersh. Copyright © 1970
    by Seymour Hersh. All rights reserved.
Eric Hoffer, "The True Believer." From *The True Believer* by Eric Hoffer. Copyright
    1951 by Eric Hoffer; copyright © renewed 1979 by Eric Hoffer. Reprinted by
    permission of HarperCollins Publishers Inc.
Johan Huizinga, "The Nature and Significance of Play." From *Homo Ludens* by Johan
    Huizinga. Copyright © 1955 by Beacon Press. Reprinted by permission of Beacon
    Press.
Samuel P. Huntington, "The Errors of Endism." Reprinted with permission. © *The
    National Interest*, Fall 1989, no. 17, Washington, D.C.
Pico Iyer, "Video Night in Kathmandu: Love Match." From *Video Night in Kathmandu*
    by Pico Iyer. Copyright © 1988 by Pico Iyer. Reprinted by permission of Alfred
    A. Knopf, Inc.
Ian Jack, "Unsteady People." From *Granta*, No. 28, Autumn 1989. Copyright © 1989
    by Ian Jack. Reprinted by permission of *Granta*.
Paul Johnson, "Experimenting with Half Mankind." Excerpt from *Modern Times* by

Paul Johnson. Copyright © 1983 by Paul Johnson. Reprinted with permission of HarperCollins Publishers Inc.

Gayl Jones, "The Roundhouse." From *White Rat: Short Stories* by Gayl Jones. Copyright © 1971, 1973, 1975, 1977 by Gayl Jones. Reprinted by permission of Random House, Inc.

Carl Jung, "The Concept of the Collective Unconscious." From *The Collected Works of C. G. Jung*, translated by R. F. C. Hull, Bollingen Series XX, Vol. 9i. *The Archetypes and the Collective Unconscious*. Copyright © 1959, 1969 by Princeton University Press. Reprinted by permission.

Ryszard Kapuściński, "The Snow in Ghana." From *The Soccer War* by Ryszard Kapuściński. Copyright © 1991 by Ryszard Kapuściński. Reprinted by permission of Alfred A. Knopf, Inc.

Wycliffe Kato, "An Escape from Kampala." From *Granta*, No. 22, Autumn 1987. Copyright © 1987 by Wycliffe Kato. Reprinted by permission of *Granta*.

John Keegan, "Agincourt, October 25th, 1415." From *The Face of Battle* by John Keegan. Copyright © 1976 by John Keegan. Used by permission of Viking Penguin, a division of Penguin Books USA Inc.

Martin Luther King, Jr., "Letter from Birmingham Jail." from *Why We Can't Wait* by Martin Luther King, Jr. Copyright © 1963, 1964 by Martin Luther King, Jr.; copyright © renewed 1991 by Coretta Scott King. Reprinted by permission of HarperCollins Publishers Inc.

Maxine Hong Kingston, "No Name Woman." From *The Woman Warrior* by Maxine Hong Kingston. Copyright © 1975, 1976 by Maxine Hong Kingston. Reprinted by permission of Alfred A. Knopf, Inc.

Arthur Koestler, "Cultural Snobbery." From *The Anchor Review*, No. 1 by Melvin J. Lasky. Copyright © 1955 by Doubleday, a division of Bantam Doubleday Dell Publishing Group, Inc. Used by permission of Doubleday, a division of Bantam Doubleday Dell Publishing Group, Inc.

Jonathan Kozol, "The Homeless." From *Rachel and Her Children: Homeless Families in America* by Jonathan Kozol. Copyright © 1988 by Jonathan Kozol. Reprinted by permission of Crown Publishers, Inc.

Milan Kundera, "The Golden Apple of Eternal Desire." From *Laughable Loves* by Milan Kundera, S. Rappaport, translator. Copyright © 1974 by Alfred A. Knopf, Inc. Reprinted by permission of the publisher.

Ursula K. Le Guin, "Imaginary Countries." Copyright © 1973 by Ursula K. Le Guin; first appeared in *The Harvard Advocate*; reprinted by permission of the author and the author's agent, Virginia Kidd.

C. S. Lewis, "The Abolition of Man." From C. S. Lewis, *The Abolition of Man*, copyright © C. S. Lewis 1943, 1946, 1978. Published by HarperCollins Publishers Ltd.

R. W. Livingstone, "The Rainbow Bridge." From *The Rainbow Bridge and other Essays on Education*, copyright © 1959. Published by Clark Irwin & Company Ltd. Reprinted by permission.

Lu Xun, "The Fair of the Five Fierce Gods." Copyright © Oxford University Press 1973. Reprinted from *Silent China: Selected Writings of Lu Xun*, edited and translated by Gladys Yang (1973) by permission of Oxford University Press.

William Lutz, "Doublespeak." From *Doublespeak* by William Lutz. Copyright © 1980 by William Lutz. Reprinted by permission of HarperCollins Publishers Inc.

Nancy Mairs, "On Being a Cripple." By permission, Nancy Mairs, "On Being a Cripple,"

George Orwell, "Politics and the English Language." From *Shooting an Elephant and Other Essays* by George Orwell, copyright 1946 by Sonia Brownell and renewed 1974 by Sonia Orwell, reprinted by permission of Harcourt Brace Jovanovich, Inc., and the Estate of Sonia Brownell Orwell and Martin Secker & Warburg Ltd.

Cynthia Ozick, "On Excellence." From "The Seam of the Snail" in *Metaphor & Memory* by Cynthia Ozick. Copyright © 1989 by Cynthia Ozick. Reprinted by permission of Alfred A. Knopf, Inc.

Grace Paley, "Mother." From *Later the Same Day* by Grace Paley. Copyright © 1985 by Grace Paley. Reprinted by permission of Farrar, Straus and Giroux, Inc.

Diane Ravitch, "Multiculturalism." Reprinted from *The American Scholar*, Volume 59, Number 3, Summer 1990. Copyright © 1990 by Diane Ravitch. Reprinted by permission.

Phyllis Rose, "Mothers and Fathers." Published as "Of Shared Memories" in *Never Say Goodbye* by Phyllis Rose. Copyright © 1991 by Phyllis Rose. Used by permission of Doubleday, a division of Bantam Doubleday Dell Publishing Group, Inc.

Mark Salzman, "Unsuitable Reading." From *Iron and Silk* by Mark Salzman. Copyright © 1986 by Mark Salzman. Reprinted by permission of Random House, Inc.

Dorothy L. Sayers, "Are Women Human?" From *Unpopular Opinions* by Dorothy L. Sayers, published by Gollancz. Copyright 1947 by Dorothy Sayers. Used by permission of David Higham Associates Ltd.

Jonathan Schell, "The Bomb Drops on New York." From *The Fate of the Earth* by Jonathan Schell. Copyright © 1982 by Jonathan Schell. Originally appeared in *The New Yorker*. Reprinted by permission of Alfred A. Knopf, Inc.

Jeffrey Schrank, "Sport and the American Dream." From *Snap, Crackle, and Popular Taste: The Illusion of Free Choice in America* by Jeffrey Schrank. Copyright © 1977 by Jeffrey Schrank. Used by permission of Delacorte Press, a division of Bantam Doubleday Dell Publishing Group, Inc.

Roger Scruton, "Ideologically Speaking." From Christopher Ricks and Leonard Michaels, eds., *The State of the Language*, 1990 Edition. Copyright © 1989 The Regents of the University of California. Reprinted by permission of University of California Press.

Scott Seligman, "Some Basic Cultural Differences." Reprinted by permission of Warner Books/New York. From *Dealing with the Chinese*. Copyright © 1989 by Scott D. Seligman.

Irwin Shaw, "The Eighty-Yard Run." From *Five Decades* by Irwin Shaw. Copyright © 1978 by Irwin Shaw. Used by permission of Dell Books, a division of Bantam Doubleday Dell Publishing Group, Inc.

George Sheehan, "Surf's Up! Head for the Waves." Copyright © 1990 by George Sheehan, M.D. Reprinted by permission of George Sheehan, M.D., medical editor and columnist, *Runner's World* Magazine.

Randy Shilts, "AIDS." From *And the Band Played on* by Randy Shilts. Copyright © 1987 by Randy Shilts. Reprinted with permission from St. Martin's Press, Inc., New York, NY.

C. P. Snow, "The Moral Un-Neutrality of Science." From *Public Affairs* by C. P. Snow. Copyright © 1971 by C. P. Snow. Reproduced by permission of Curtis Brown Ltd, London.

Shelby Steele, "On Being Black and Middle Class." Reprinted from *Commentary*, January 1988, by permission; all rights reserved.

Virginia Woolf, "Professions for Women." From *The Death of the Moth and Other Essays* by Virginia Woolf, copyright 1942 by Harcourt Brace Jovanovich, Inc. and renewed 1970 by Marjorie T. Parsons, Executrix, reprinted by permission of Harcourt Brace Jovanovich, Inc. and The Hogarth Press.

Virginia Woolf, "The Society of Outsiders and the Prevention of War." From *Three Guineas* by Virginia Woolf, copyright 1938 by Harcourt Brace Jovanovich, Inc. and renewed 1966 by Leonard Woolf, reprinted by permission of Harcourt Brace Jovanovich, Inc. and The Hogarth Press.

Captain X, "Mr Spock." From *Unfriendly Skies* by Captain X and Reynolds Dodson. Copyright © 1989 by Captain X and Reynolds Dodson. Used by permission of Doubleday, a division of Bantam Doubleday Dell Publishing Group, Inc.

Xiao Hong, "A Tale of Hulan River." From *Field of Life and Death: Tales of Hulan River*, by Xiao Hong, translated by Howard Goldblatt. Reprinted by permission of Indiana University Press.

INDEX